MEANING
AND
EXISTENCE

MEANING
AND
EXISTENCE

INTRODUCTORY READINGS
IN PHILOSOPHY

Edited by

William T. Blackstone
The University of Georgia

HOLT, RINEHART AND WINSTON, INC.
New York   Chicago   San Francisco
Atlanta   Dallas   Montreal   Toronto

To my children, Lisa Brooks and Jeffrey Thomas

Cover collage by Jerome Seckler

Preface

Two objectives were considered in preparing this text. First, the choice of selections brings together in a single volume important readings, both classical and contemporary, on a set of philosophical problems of which any student or generally educated person should be aware. An understanding of these problems is essential in the practical and theoretical life of every human being.

Second, although there are a number of excellent introductory philosophy texts now in existence, this volume makes available materials that are generally not found in other texts, and it deals with philosophical problems of great contemporary relevance, frequently not treated in other volumes. Chapter Four, "The Problem of Political Norms," for example, deals with the aims and purposes of political society, with the notions of justice, rights, freedom, and democracy, and with the issue of civil disobedience. These questions, so much the concern of students today, have been ignored in other texts.

There are, of course, a variety of ways of introducing students to philosophy, and for reasons of space this book had to forego treatment of a number of problems in aesthetics, philosophy of mind, philosophy of science, and philosophy of history. Leaving these issues for more advanced work, it begins with problems of direct concern and interest to the student—the existence of God, the basis for moral norms and one's moral life, the justification of political norms, the question of freedom and responsibility, the nature of man, and the issue of immortality. These are questions that continually bear on the experience and lives of us all, and systematic philosophical reflection has a natural birthplace in these issues. The latter part of the book deals with more abstruse and abstract questions—the nature of truth and knowledge, induction, language, and metaphysics.

The introduction to each chapter has been carefully designed; it provides *not* summaries of the selections but a general overview of the philosophical problem treated in the chapter. The goal is to assist the student in understanding both the problem-area and the way in which the selections in the chapter are related to the problem and to each other. The introductions were also designed to provide certain distinctions and conceptual tools that will help the student as he reads the various selections. The glossary of common philosophical terms at the beginning of the book will help the student overcome terminological difficulties that attend the initial study of any academic discipline. The bibliographies at the end of each chapter introduction will assist in directing the beginning student to additional treatments of the problem discussed in the chapter and in preparing research or term papers.

Care was exercised in each chapter to make sure that a wide variety of positions on each philosophical problem was represented. Exposure to these different, and frequently opposing, views should encourage students themselves to participate in the philosophical debate.

There is an abundance of readings in this book, far more than can be covered in a one-quarter or one-semester course. This was done deliberately, to provide maximum flexibility and variety for instructors who use the text. Furthermore, concerning the order of the readings in the book, a number of possibilities are open that are different from the one presented, depending upon the interests and purposes of the individual instructor.

In editing this book I have profited greatly from the criticism and advice of several anonymous readers selected by the publishers, Holt, Rinehart and Winston, Inc.; of my colleagues at the University of Georgia, Professors Bowman Clarke, Leroy Cebik, Walter O'Briant, John Granrose, Robert Burton, Lyle Angene, James Harris, Waltraut Stein, Scott Kleiner, Robert Heslep, George Newsome, Richard Severens, William Power, Robert Ayers, Anthony Nemetz, and Frank Harrison; and of Professor Ralf Munster of Georgia State University. I am grateful to Herbert J. Addison for his gentle encouragement and prodding, to Miss Jane Mayo for expert editorial assistance, to Mrs. Julia Harris and Tensey Whitmire for secretarial assistance, and to Don Daniels for multiple efforts. My wife, Jean, who not only typed much of the manuscript but, with infinite patience, held the household together, deserves a special acknowledgement of gratitude.

William T. Blackstone

Athens, Georgia
January 1971

Contents

CHAPTER FIVE
THE PROBLEM OF FREE WILL, DETERMINISM, AND RESPONSIBILITY   445

CHAPTER SIX
THE PROBLEM OF THE NATURE OF MAN: MIND-BODY AND IMMORTALITY   509

GLOSSARY

OF COMMON PHILOSOPHICAL TERMS

AGNOSTICISM   The doctrine that knowledge about God is not possible. Sometimes confused with *atheism.*

A POSTERIORI   Reasoning or knowledge which is derived from experience. Generally opposed to *a priori.*

A PRIORI   Prior to experience. Known without reference to experience.

ARCHETYPE   The model or form of which other things are viewed as copies. Platonic Ideas are frequently cited as examples.

ATHEISM   The doctrine which denies the existence of God.

AUTHORITARIANISM   The doctrine that authority of some type is the most valid source of knowledge. For example, the Bible or the Church.

AXIOLOGY   The theory or study of value of all kinds.

BEHAVIORISM   The psychological theory which insists that all knowledge of man must be based on an objective observation of his behavior.

BEING   Used to refer to the category of reality or whatever is. Sometimes used in contrast to "becoming" or change.

CARTESIAN   Refers to the philosophy of René Descartes (1596–1650).

CATEGORY   A basic mode or type of being or existence, or (in Kant) a fundamental form of understanding.

COGNITION   The act of perceiving or knowing. Generally contrasted with other modes of consciousness such as *conation* and *affection.*

COHERENCE THEORY OF TRUTH   The view that "truth" constitutes a coherent, integrated system and that the truth of any given statement is determined by its coherence with other accepted truths.

CONCEPT   The general idea of a class of objects. Generally distinguished from *percept* or *sensation.*

CONFIRMATION   The process of establishing the probable truth of a proposition by reference to evidence.

CONTINGENT   That which can be equally well conceived as not existing. Generally contrasted with *necessary*.

CONTRADICTION   A false proposition which can be shown to be false by an examination of the symbols and the logic of one's language.

CORRESPONDENCE THEORY OF TRUTH   The theory that the truth of a proposition is determined by its correspondence to facts. Sometimes called the *semantic* theory of truth.

COSMOLOGICAL ARGUMENT   An effort to prove the existence of God by using the principal of causality. The argument that the existence of the universe requires a cause and that this cause is God.

COSMOLOGY   That part of philosophy which studies both the origin and the constitution of the universe. Generally contrasted with *ontology*, an effort to discover the nature of Being.

DEDUCTION   The process of reasoning in which conclusions are drawn from accepted premises. Sometimes defined as reasoning from the general to the particular. Contrasted with *induction*.

DEISM   The doctrine that God created the universe but left it unattended. For the deist, God is not a being to whom one can properly pray; nor is He a moral being or the source of goodness.

DETERMINISM   The thesis that every event in the world is totally conditioned by its cause or sequence of causes. Causal principle, this doctrine holds, applies to all phenomena.

DIALECTIC   A dialogue in which the meaning and truth of concepts and beliefs are subjected to critical examination. Frequently associated with Socrates' method of buttonholing persons and drawing out the implications and presuppositions of their statements.

DUALISM   Any theory which reduces a field to two irreducible ultimates. For example, reality seen as "mind" and "matter."

ECLECTICISM   The bringing together of different philosophical doctrines into one theory.

EGOISM   In the area of ethics, a theory which states that the good is one's own pleasure or well being.

EMPIRICISM   A doctrine which maintains that the source of all knowledge is experience. Also, that human knowledge is limited to the possible scope of human experience.

EPICURIANISM   A way of life or ethic taught by Epicurus (342–270 B.C.) which advocates a moderate and enlightened kind of Hedonism.

EPIPHENOMENALISM   The doctrine that the mind is simply a by-product or effect of the brain and that all mental activity is simply physical change.

EPISTEMOLOGY   That area of philosophy which is concerned with the nature, sources, and limitations of knowledge. Sometimes simply called the "theory of knowledge."

ESSENCE   The essential or necessary nature of a thing, in contrast to its accidental or nonessential qualities.

EXISTENTIALISM   The philosophical theory which states that existence is prior to essence. Man is viewed as having no fixed nature but as free and creative.

FATALISM   The doctrine that all events are determined by nonhuman causes.

HEDONISM   In ethics, the view that pleasure is the only intrinsic good. In psychology, the view that all of man's actions are motivated by desire for pleasure and to avoid pain.

HEDONISTIC CALCULUS   A theory or device formulated by Jeremy Bentham to calculate pleasure as opposed to pain. A method for evaluating the rightness of an action.

HUMANISM   In philosophy, this frequently indicates a naturalist or non-theistic philosophy. Emphasis upon man, his growth and development, as opposed to God and the supernatural.

IDEALISM   A philosophical theory which reduces all existence to mind. Also used more generally to refer to any theory formulated on the basis of an ideal.

IDEOLOGY   Generally refers to a set of social or political ideals.

INDETERMINISM   The thesis that man has free choice and is not determined.

INDUCTION   Inference from observation of particular instances to general conclusions. Inductive inference is generally seen as yielding "probable" knowledge.

INTERACTIONISM   A view of the mind-body relation in which mind and body are viewed as distinct substances which interrelate. Generally associated with the philosopher Descartes.

MATERIALISM   The philosophical doctrine which maintains that the entire universe, including life and mind, can be explained in terms of matter in motion.

METAPHYSICS   The study of being as such. The study of ultimate reality. Generally contrasted with the study of a particular part of nature as in a given science.

METHODOLOGY   The study of the basic principles of inquiry, frequently involving issues concerning logic, classification, and basic assumptions. Sometimes used loosely to mean the means whereby the activity in any given field is carried on.

MYSTICISM   The view that fundamental truth about reality cannot be had by sense experience or reason but only through a kind of intuitive experience.

NATURALISM   The thesis that both man and the universe can be explained in purely natural terms without the need for any appeal to the supernatural.

NIHILISM   A philosophical theory which denies the value of human life and activity.

NORMATIVE   That which relates to any norm or standard of evaluation.

PANTHEISM   The doctrine that the universe and God are identical.

PHENOMENALISM   The view that reality and our knowledge of reality are limited to phenomena or appearances.

PHENOMENOLOGY   A view generally identified with the philosophy of E. Husserl. Described as the science of the subjective and its intended objects.

PLURALISM   Generally used to mean a view that reality is comprised of several independent or ultimate substances.

POSITIVISM   A theory which limits all knowledge to the scientifically verifiable. In the past it treated all metaphysical claims as meaningless. In recent years proponents of this view no longer insist upon conclusive verification.

PRAGMATISM   A philosophical view normally associated with Peirce, James, Dewey, Schiller, and Mead, which emphasizes that meaning and truth depend upon consequences or results.

RATIONALISM   The epistemological doctrine that truth and knowledge are to be tested not by sensory methods, but by deduction and "reason." Generally opposed to *empiricism*.

RELATIVISM   The thesis that absolute final truth is impossible and that truth is relative to time, place and group.

SCEPTICISM   The doctrine that certain or absolute knowledge cannot be attained by human beings. Sometimes limited to only parts of human experience. Generally distinguished from *cynicism*.

SOLIPSISM   An extreme form of subjectivism which holds that the mind can know only its own experiences. In metaphysics, the doctrine that one's self or mind and its perceptions are all that exist.

SUBSTANCE   That which constitutes the essential nature of a thing and makes it what it is. That which underlies the properties or modifications of a thing, but which itself is not a property or modification.

SUMMUM BONUM   The highest good. The ultimate goal of human conduct.

TELEOLOGICAL ARGUMENT   One of the "proofs" for the existence of God which holds that the existence of order and design in nature constitutes evidence that there is a creative God.

TELEOLOGY   The doctrine of final causes. It holds that certain ends and purposes govern the universe. Generally opposed to "machanism."

THEISM   The doctrine that a God exists. Opposed to *atheism*. Generally conceives of God as infinite, personal, immanent, and transcendant.

THEODICY   A theory or effort to justify the goodness of God in the face of the existence of evil in the world.

TRANSCENDENT   Generally used to refer to that which lies beyond human experience and knowledge. In theology, it designates the doctrine that God is outside of nature. Used by Kant (transcendental) to refer to the *a priori* categories of mind.

UTILITARIANISM   The ethical doctrine which holds that the fundamental norm of human conduct should be "the greatest good for the greatest number." Generally identified with Jeremy Bentham and John Stuart Mill.

VALIDITY   In logic, a valid proposition is one which necessarily follows from accepted premises. An argument is called "valid" under these circumstances.

VERIFIABILITY   The possibility of a statement being in principle established as true or false. Sometimes identified with *confirmability*. Generally identified with the philosophical movement known as "logical empiricism," in which verifiability is the criterion of empirical meaningfulness.

VERIFICATION   The process of determining the truth or falsity of a statement.

WELTANSCHAUUNG   Generally used to designate any systematic world view.

Chapter One

WHAT IS PHILOSOPHY?

Philosophy is not easy to define. It has no subject matter in the sense that a specialized discipline such as chemistry or geology does, for there is no restricted set of phenomena or objects with which philosophy is concerned. Philosophy is concerned with nearly everything, and this lack of limitations distinguishes it from the specialized sciences. The questions it asks and the explanations it seeks are of such general or universal scope that they cannot be resolved or answered merely by the methods of the sciences. This is so in part because the sciences operate upon assumptions that are themselves problematic for philosophy.

These remarks require considerable qualification and clarification. The term "philosophy" comes from the Greek *philein* ("to love") and *sophia* ("wisdom"); and for the Greeks philosophy, as love of wisdom, embraced the effort to know in general and to live the good life. At this stage of man's history (400 B.C.), philosophy and science were one; there was no highly developed scientific method nor were there any specified scientific disciplines. Philosophy was all embracing; and it was not until the techniques of observation, measurement, and testing were developed and applied to certain areas that specific sciences—physics, biology, geology, and so on—came into being. They broke off from philosophy, one might say, just as today when specialized techniques of observation, measurement, and testing are being developed, we find other specialized disciplines breaking off from scientific parents (microbiology, biochemistry, and so on).

Such specialization will undoubtedly continue. Does this mean that at

1

some time in the future philosophy as a discipline will be useless? Will it become unnecessary and cease to exist when every kind of data and all human experience are some day covered by some science? Are we not moving in this direction with the development of psychology, sociology and anthropology as specific sciences? Even questions and theories about the nature of man and of mind seem to be subsumed under a specific science. Will nothing be left for philosophy? It does not seem likely, for philosophy also has always been concerned with issues which cannot in principle be resolved by the empirical, scientific method. Indeed, there are some who say that issues which cannot in principle be resolved scientifically are meaningless issues. But this view itself seems to be a philosophical rather than a scientific thesis. Further, there seems to be no sound basis for this claim, because human beings continue to be puzzled and ask questions about problems that cannot be resolved by science—problems that seem to lie outside the purview of any specific science.

Let me cite some examples. When a scientist uses the scientific method, he operates on the assumption that the future will resemble the past and that one is justified in drawing inferences about events yet unobserved on the basis of present and past observed events. This rule of inference is part of the very definition of his method. Thus the psychologist draws inferences about how human beings will behave in the future on the basis of past behavior; the geologist predicts future volcanic activity on the basis of past observation; and so on for all of the sciences. But philosophy treats as a problem this key theoretical assumption of the sciences. It asks: Are we justified in drawing inferences about future unobserved events on the basis of previously observed ones? The scientist cannot use his own method to justify this belief because that belief is part of his method. Hence it would be presupposed in any attempt scientifically to justify it.

Or one might ask: Can human beings freely choose among different courses of action or are all of their actions determined causally? Although psychologists adopt different positions on this issue, they do not, as psychologists, confront it. Rather they seek to explain human behavior by looking for regularities and laws. This determinism–free will issue is related to yet another philosophical problem which falls outside the scope of any particular science: If the actions of human beings are causally determined, can human beings be held morally responsible for their actions?

Other problems outside the scope of particular sciences and generally classified as philosophical are: What is knowledge? What is truth? What is justice? What is moral goodness or morally right action? Do men have natural rights? What is the basis of political obligation? Is mind substantially different from body? Is there a God? Did the universe have a beginning? What is the best form of government? These questions involve concepts with which philosophy has traditionally been concerned: justice, time, mind, knowledge, truth, natural rights, obligation, God, and so on. All these concepts are important in the theoretical and practical life of man. Philosophers from Socrates to Sartre have tried to analyze and clarify them and to answer fundamental questions about them.

Philosophy, then, includes the analysis and clarification of concepts and beliefs which cover the full range of human existence and which are fundamental and important to all aspects of man's life—scientific, political, ethical, theological, and artistic. But philosophy is more than *mere* analysis and clarification (even though some philosophers argue that this is the only proper function of philosophy). Philosophers have frequently been concerned with very practical issues. They have not *always* engaged in the analysis and clarification of ideas and beliefs merely for their own sake. They have been puzzled by certain terms and by claims in which these terms were used; and they have been concerned with the misuse of such terms— with false claims, as it were—and the impact of these claims on man and society. In Plato's *Republic,* Socrates' argument with Thrasymachus that justice does not mean "that which is in the interest of the stronger" was not a purely academic exercise. Nor were Marx and Engels being purely theoretical and academic in pressing their materialist conception of history—the view that the division of society into classes and the ultimate causes of all social change and revolution are the result of changes in the modes of production and exchange of economic goods. Analysis and clarification has invariably taken place in the effort to obtain philosophical knowledge—in the effort to obtain the truth about man, society, and the world—and frequently in the effort to change the world.

Classical philosophers, as a result of their quest for wisdom, adopted certain positions or theories (many of which conflicted with one another) concerning man, society, and the world. Some philosophers accepted determinism, some indeterminism. Some adopted materialism as an account of reality, others accepted idealism. Some adopted subjectivism in ethics, others objectivism. Some were atheists, others theists. Some were democrats, others totalitarians. In each case, the ideal philosophical procedure (though not always carried out) was an impartial analysis and weighing of all the available evidence relative to a particular issue.

Some philosophers accepted and expounded certain views about man and the world without critically assessing and weighing all the available evidence or all sides of an issue. Like the rest of us, they tended to favor one view over another, theism or atheism, for example—and they sometimes ignored or brushed aside contrary evidence. When they let personal preferences operate, they were not fully carrying out the philosophical task. For philosophy requires more than merely expounding views about man, society, and the world. Philosophical positions must be held critically, with an examination and evaluation of all relevant evidence. Of course, there may always be data of which the philosopher is unaware or data which are unavailable at the time, and these data may, when discovered, falsify certain philosophical views. This happens in science too, of course. A philosopher may also not understand the full implications of a given theory (the implications, for example, of determinism for one's moral or political philosophy) and be led into inconsistencies as a result. It is not always possible to foresee the implications of a concept or theory in one area of human experience for concepts and theories in other areas. Thus the philosopher must always be willing to alter his theories and his views in the light of new data and newly understood implications.

Such critical assessment is not a simple task, and it cannot, as already indicated, be done simply in the manner and with the method of the scientist. Empirical, scientifically acquired data are relevant to the rational assessment of many philosophical issues, and the philosopher fails if he does not include them in his assessment. Suppose that the justification of capital punishment is being debated. Suppose further that data collected by the social scientist show that the practice of capital punishment does not act as a deterrent to crime. Plainly, those who argue in favor of capital punishment on the grounds that it does deter crime must alter their views or be guilty of irrationality.

But evidence is not always scientific in nature, and the evaluation of reasons for and against a given philosophical theory may include evidence or reasons not covered by any science. Many of the concepts and questions of philosophy cut across a number of the sciences, and some involve facets of our everyday lives not treated in the sciences at all. Questions involving values—What is the *good* life? What *ought* I to do? Is democracy better than totalitarianism? Is Picasso's *Guernica* a better painting than the *Mona Lisa*?—and questions about the existence of God appear not to be open to purely scientific resolution. The effort to arrive at a reasoned view of man and the world involves weighing evidence and examining the uses and implications of concepts and theories of an interdisciplinary character. It requires an overview not possible within any science alone.

We have noticed that certain philosophical questions appear not to be open to purely scientific resolution. But the claim that they are not so open itself involves a philosophical theory, a theory about the nature of these issues. Such a thesis is what is often called a "second-order" thesis, one that centers around the foundations of knowledge in a certain area or the basis for statements and knowledge claims of a certain *kind.* Thus, in the area of ethical theory, philosophers have not only proposed fundamental moral norms for the guidance of human conduct (for example: Act so as to maximize the happiness of all human beings) but have also theorized about the nature and status of moral claims and norms and of moral discourse in general. Some argue that moral claims are subjective in nature, which means that such claims refer only to the feelings or attitudes of the one making the claim. Others argue that moral claims are objective and refer to unique moral properties or standards that exist independently of the speaker. Neither of these views is a moral claim itself but a theory (epistemological) about moral claims.

Philosophy, then, includes not only theories about man, the world, and how man ought to live—morally, politically, religiously, and so on—but also second-order, epistemological theories about types of human discourse and alleged knowledge claims. Some philosophers restrict their activities entirely to second-order theory and indeed define philosophy in this way. But plainly, both classical and contemporary philosophy includes theses about man and the world as well as reflections on the nature, presuppositions, and knowledge status of these theses.

Similar things can be said about political theory and theology. For instance, some political theorists hold to the doctrine of natural, inalienable rights and try to define explicitly the content of these rights or the kinds of treatment to which the holder is entitled. But they also reflect on the nature of these claims and offer epistemological and metaphysical theories about the existence of rights. Also, in theology and the philosophy of religion, philosophers frequently subscribe both to theological doctrines and to second-order theories about how theological claims are verified or justified as knowledge claims. For example, one may believe in God and appeal to revelation as grounds for this belief. Or one may be a theist, reject the appeal to revelation, and appeal to the order and apparent design in nature as grounds for one's belief. Or one may reject theological claims as meaningless on the grounds that they are not verifiable in principle.

Philosophy, then, involves (1) views or theories about man, society, and reality. And when it endeavors to arrive at rational theories, it necessarily includes (2) assessments of whatever empirical data are made available by the sciences or common experience. Furthermore, it includes (3) reflective, conceptual analyses of the nature and status of knowledge claims and discourse of many kinds. Both the selections on the nature of philosophy in this chapter and the selections in subsequent chapters dealing with traditional philosophical problems reflect this view of philosophy.

It goes without saying that one should not ordinarily expect to solve philosophic problems in a semester or two. Indeed, it may take a lifetime or longer. But everyone must confront these problems, for the activities of living require the adoption of attitudes and positions on these issues. One can simply accept uncritically or rationalize the answers offered by one's parents, church, or culture. Or one can analyze and reflect on these issues in the manner of the philosopher, letting reason and evidence be one's guide. It may be impossible to obtain completely certain answers. We may have to live our lives with tentative answers and a willingness to alter our opinions and attitudes in the light of new information. But surely only a critical, reflective approach to these questions is consistent with the dignity of man as a rational being. It is hoped that this volume will facilitate this critical approach.

SELECTED BIBLIOGRAPHY

Ayer, A. J. *Language, Truth and Logic.* London, 1936.

Blanshard, Brand. *Reason and Analysis.* La Salle, Ill., 1962.

Burtt, E. A. *In Search of Philosophic Understanding.* New York, 1965.

Dewey, John. *Reconstruction in Philosophy.* New York, 1920.

Ducasse, Curt J. *Philosophy as a Science.* New York, 1941.

Grene, Marjorie. *An Introduction to Existentialism.* Chicago, 1948.

Heidegger, Martin. *What is Philosophy?.* New York, 1958.

James, William. *Some Problems of Philosophy,* New York, 1911.

1 Philosophy as the Quest for the Meaning of Life*

A. K. ROGERS

A. K. Rogers (1868–1936) taught philosophy at Butler University in Missouri and at Yale University. He is the author of *English and American Philosophy Since 1800, A Theory of Ethics, Ethics and Moral Tolerance, A Student's History of Philosophy,* and *A Brief Introduction to Modern Philosophy.*

No man who is able to learn from experience at all, can live very long in the world without finding himself continually passing judgment, in one way or another, on the meaning and the value of life. At the very least there will be some things which it will seem to him to be worth the while to do, and other things, again, which will fail to interest him, and which by implication therefore he will condemn; but besides such fragmentary and instinctive judgments, he also, if he reflects at all, can hardly help but ask himself at times whether life has not some meaning as a whole, which would serve to throw light on the scattered and chaotic fragments of his everyday experience, and bring them into some degree of unity. Now philosophy, apart from technicalities of definition, is nothing but an attempt, in a reasoned and comprehensive way, to answer this question, What is the meaning of life? Every one, therefore, in so far as he adopts a certain general attitude towards the problems that meet him, looks at them from a certain point of view, and does not simply let himself drift from one experience to another without any purpose or unity to connect them, is taking the standpoint of philosophy. Such an attitude we call his philosophy of life, and if he is more or less clearly conscious of what this attitude is, and is able to express it in a unified and consistent way, we say in a popular sense that he is a philosopher. Technical philosophy differs from this only in the fact that it tries to do thoroughly, and in full consciousness of itself, what in popular thinking we do in a loose and unsystematic fashion. Instead of picking out those factors in life which appeal to us more personally and directly, it tries to set individual prejudices and limitations aside, and to include, as impartially as it can, all the elements which experience presents. It is true that in doing this it frequently gets far

* From the Introduction to *A Brief Introduction to Modern Philosophy* (New York: The Macmillan Company, 1899).

enough from what seem to be living interests; but back of all technical discussions, there is still the underlying conviction that by this path, and this alone, can we get at the vital and essential meaning of the world, or else we have no longer philosophy, but mere pedantry and hair-splitting. It is natural, then, that we should find the definitions which men have given of philosophy at different times are not by any means the same. They are not the same because, under different circumstances, men's interests are directed to different points, now to the importance of conduct, now to the nature of the external world, now to the existence of supersensible realities. But to say that their interest lies at one point or another, is only to say in other words that here they find the value of life; this is the test that can always be applied, the real motive, if not the apparent one. So we can speak of the philosophy of any pursuit whatever in which men can engage, or of any subject which can occupy them, of science, of history, of the technical arts. Between science and the philosophy of science, history and the philosophy of history, there is indeed no hard and fast separation; but what in the one case we are specially concerned with is the positive nature and the laws of a certain group of facts, which have been selected out from the rest of the world to be studied by themselves, while in the other we restore that connection with the whole which for the time being we had set aside, and try to look at our facts in the light of the meaning which they have for life in its entirety.

Even when it is stated in this preliminary way, the definition which has been given of philosophy will be seen to have a bearing on the disputes which have been common about the value of the study, and the very unequal estimation in which it has been held. There are many people to whom the pursuit of philosophy has seemed to be, at best, of very doubtful utility. Sometimes it is one who, like Matthew Arnold, is so impressed with the concrete values of art and conduct that the world of the philosopher seems to him abstract and barren in comparison. More often it is the man of science, who feels that he has got hold of reality so immediately and palpably in the world of matter, and of reality which is so far-reaching in its significance, that he has no interest left to give the supersensuous and very doubtful world which he understands that philosophy is trying to construct by merely thinking about it. Now the answer to be made the scientist is this, that he is not getting along without philosophy, as he supposes, but only is adopting one particular kind of philosophy, whose implications, however, he does not try to understand. And he can hardly hold that this refusal to examine into the presuppositions of his thinking is, in opposition to the metaphysician's course, a highly meritorious thing, without stultifying his whole scientific procedure. He may, indeed, as a scientist, merely devote himself to the discovery of facts; but unless he is prepared to say that the bare objective fact is everything, and its meaning, its value for us, is nothing (which is very like a contradiction in terms), he cannot avoid encroaching on the philosopher's field. In reality he always does bring with him his own interpretation of the facts of science, and they differentiate the way in which he looks at the world from the way in which other men look at it; the only question is as to whether this should be conscious and thoroughgoing, or whether it should be unconscious, and unaware of the possible difficulties that may be involved. In any case the mere facts of the objective world, as objective, cannot exhaust the problems which arise, and arise necessarily, for this external world would not exist, for us, if it did not have a value as coming within our conscious life, and so it forms but a part of experience, not the whole. Whatever it may be in itself, for human interest at least the objective fact or law as such cannot possibly be a final and sufficient goal. Even the man who thinks that it is so, must have some reason why the search for objective truth appeals to him; its simple existence in itself does not explain why he should want to know it. It may of course be that, in the end, one might be driven to admit that no vital relation to human life could be discovered; in that case science at once would cease to be pursued. But answerable or not, at least it cannot be said that when the problems go beyond mere scientific matter of fact they cease to have any *interest* for us; knowing the chemical composition of water will not satisfy us in face of the larger question, What is this world of which our lives form a part? what is its meaning and destiny? And it is through philosophy, not through science, that this latter question must receive an answer, if it is answered at all.

Nevertheless there is some justification for this contemptuous attitude which science is apt to adopt towards philosophy, and which grows out of the true feeling that any value which is really worth our consideration must attach to the actual world in which we live, not to some far-away abstract world, which only can be got at by the occasional philosopher, and through the colorless medium of thought. What we are after is the meaning of life as we live it, and if we come out at the end with something that finds no place for the concrete values with which we are familiar, then certainly a large factor in the problem has without any justification been juggled out of sight. So that we have to insist, in the second place, that the data which the philosopher uses are not something which, by a pure act of intellectual creation, he spins out of his own head, but the same facts with which science, and history, and everyday living, deal. In this sense, therefore, the philosopher is dependent on the scientist; he cannot go his own way and construct his world *a priori*, but he must continually be falling back upon the concrete knowledge which science represents. So, also, philosophy does not "give us God, freedom, immortality," if by this we mean that it somehow puts us in possession of values which we had not before suspected. Religion, morality, the social life, all come before philosophy, and are presupposed by it; and philosophy, in turn, in so far as it is only a bare recognition of truths, and not a vital appreciation of them, in so far as it stops with itself as mere knowing, and does not hand back the material which it has been elaborating intellectually, to the immediate experience in which this originated, is forgetting its place as the handmaid of life, and so is rendering itself barren and formal. All that philosophy can do is to take the actual values which come to us in experience, work out their implications and their mutual relationships, and, it may be, get at some unitary point of view, from which each element can be looked at, and have full justice done it. But by this very process it will be making a positive addition to the value of experience itself, not by creating truths which are entirely new, but by clearing up and throwing new light upon the meaning which already has been present in our lives, and so making it more real to us.

And this will also serve to indicate the answer to a very common complaint against philosophy, in which it is set over against feeling, as something quite opposed. It is common to hear people say, After all, it is feeling truth, not reasoning about it, which is the important thing; and philosophy, by translating everything over into the cold and impersonal medium of thought, and by introducing all sorts of doubts and limitations, is a foe to that immediate enjoyment of truth which alone is worth the having. Whether this is true or not depends entirely on what we mean by it. If we mean by feeling unintelligent, blind feeling, just the mere confused sense of satisfaction, it is not true at all. But this is not what we mean when we speak of feeling as it is aroused by poetry or art: that is equivalent rather to insight, intelligent appreciation. It is, therefore, not something which is opposed to reason, but its highest, most immediate exercise. But here again we shall be doing an injustice if we oppose immediacy too sharply to the more laborious and reflective work of thought. It is not philosophy which comes in to spoil the fineness of the enjoyment we get in immediate feeling, but it is the fact that feeling breaks down, and will no longer satisfy us, that compels us to betake ourselves to thought. Feelings are sure to clash, and then they possess no criterion within themselves which shall say whether this feeling or that one is the truer; merely as feeling they cannot tell us whether they are valid objectively, or whether we are only deluding ourselves with subjective emotions. To compare their values, and to bring them to the test of their consonancy with the whole of life, thought is needed; but that does not mean that we pass from immediate experience to something higher, thought; it means that, through thought, we get from an immediacy which is limited and partial, to one which is truer, richer, and more inclusive.

2 Philosophy as Analysis and Synthesis*

C. I. LEWIS

C. I. Lewis (1883–1964) made important contributions to logic and is well known for his books *Mind and The World Order* and *An Analysis of Knowledge and Valuation*. He taught principally at the University of California and Harvard.

It is—I take it—a distinguishing character of philosophy that it is everybody's business. The man who is his own lawyer or physician, will be poorly served; but everyone both can and must be his own philosopher. He must be, because philosophy deals with ends, not means. It includes the questions, What is good? What is right? What is valid? Since finally the responsibility for his own life must rest squarely upon the shoulders of each, no one can delegate the business of answering such questions to another. Concerning the means whereby the valid ends of life may be attained, we seek expert advice. The natural sciences and the techniques to which they give rise, though they may serve some other interests also, are primarily directed to the discovery of such means. But the question of the ultimately valuable ends which shall be served, remains at once the most personal, and the most general of all questions.

And everyone *can* be his own philosopher, because in philosophy we investigate what we already know. It is not the business of philosophy, as it is of the natural sciences, to add to the sum total of phenomena with which men are acquainted. Philosophy is concerned with what is already familiar. To know in the sense of familiarity and to comprehend in clear ideas are, of course, quite different matters. Action precedes reflection and even precision of behavior commonly outruns precision of thought—fortunately for us. If it were not for this, naïve common-sense and philosophy would coincide, and there would be no problem. Just this business of bringing to clear consciousness and expressing coherently the principles which are implicitly intended in our dealing with the familiar, is the distinctively philosophic enterprise.

For instance, everybody knows the difference between right and wrong; if we had no moral sense, philosophy would not give us one. But who can

* From *Mind and the World* by Clarence Irving Lewis, Dover Publications, Inc., New York, 1956. Reprinted through permission of the publisher.

state, with complete satisfaction to himself, the adequate and consistent grounds of moral judgment? Likewise, everyone knows the distinction of cogent reasoning from fallacy. The study of logic appeals to no criterion not already present in the learner's mind. That logical error is, in the last analysis some sort of inadvertence, is an indispensable assumption of the study. Even if it should be in some part an unwarranted assumption, we could not escape it, for the very business of learning through reflection or discussion presumes our logical sense as a trustworthy guide.

That the knowledge sought in ethics and in logic is, thus, something already implicit in our commerce with the familiar, has usually been recognized. But that the same is true in metaphysics, has not been equally clear. Metaphysics studies the nature of reality in general. Reality is presumably independent of any principles of ours, in a sense in which the right and the valid may not be. At least initial presumption to the contrary might be hopelessly prejudicial. Moreover, reality forever runs beyond the restricted field of familiar experience. What hope that cosmic riddles can be solved by self-interrogation! The secret which we seek may be in some field which is not yet adequately explored or even opened to investigation. Or it may be forever beyond the reach of human senses.

But it is not the business of philosophy to go adventuring beyond space and time. And so far as a true knowledge of the nature of reality depends on determining questions of phenomenal fact which are not yet settled, the philosopher has no special insight which enables him to pose as a prophet. We can do nothing but wait upon the progress of the special sciences. Or if speculate we must, at least such speculation is in no special sense the philosopher's affair. It is true that metaphysics has always been the dumping ground for problems which are only partly philosophic. Questions of the nature of life and mind, for example, are of this mixed sort. In part such issues wait upon further data from the sciences, from biology and physical-chemistry and psychology; in part they are truly philosophic, since they turn upon questions of the fundamental criteria of classification and principles of interpretation. No amassing of scientific data can determine these.

If, for example, the extreme behaviorists in psychology deny the existence of consciousness on the ground that analysis of the "mental" must always be eventually in terms of bodily behavior, then it is the business of philosophy to correct their error, because it consists simply in a fallacy of logical analysis. The analysis of any immediately presented X must always interpret this X in terms of its constant relations to other things—to Y and Z. Such end-terms of analysis—the Y and Z—will not in general be temporal or spatial constituents of X, but may be anything which bears a constant correlation with it. It is as if one should deny the existence of colors because, for purposes of exact investigation, the colors must be defined as frequencies of vibratory motion. In general terms, if such analysis concludes by stating "X is a certain kind of Y–Z complex, hence X does not exist as a distinct reality," the error lies in overlooking a general characteristic of logical analysis—that it does not discover the "substance" or cosmic constituents of the phenomenon whose nature is analyzed but only the constant context of experience in which it will be found.

So far, then, as the divergence of psychological theories, from behaviorism which interprets mind in terms of physical behavior to theories of the subconscious which assimilate much of physiological activity to mind, represents no dispute about experimental fact but only disparity of definition and methodological criteria, psychology and metaphysics have a common ground. The delineation of the fundamental concepts "mind" and "mental" is a truly philosophic enterprise. A similar thing might be discovered in the case of other sciences.

Newly discovered scientific data might make such problems of fundamental concepts and classification easier—or more difficult—but of itself it cannot solve them because, in the nature of the case, they are antecedent to the investigation. Such concepts are not simply dictated by the findings of the laboratory, or by any sort of sense-experience. Their origin is social and historical and represents some enduring human interest. It is the human mind itself which brings them to experience, though the mind does not invent them in a vacuum or cut them from whole cloth. The tendency to forget that initial concepts are never merely dictated by empirical findings is precisely what accounts for the absurd prejudice—now happily obsolescent—that science is "just the report of facts." And this likewise helps to explain the common failure to distinguish between those cosmological speculations which are not philosophic at all, because they are merely guesses at what future observation or experiment may reveal, from the legitimate and necessary philosophic question of a coherent set of fundamental categories, such as "life" and "mind" and "matter," in terms of which experience may consistently and helpfully be interpreted.

It would, of course, be captious to reserve this problem of initial concepts to philosophers, even though we should remember that, since everybody is to be his own philosopher, this merely means reserving them as *general* problems. The expert in the scientific field will have his special competence with respect to them; but they are not his exclusive property, because they are to be resolved as much by criticism and reflection as by empirical investigation. Conversely, it would be pedantic if we should forbid the philosophic student to speculate concerning undetermined scientific fact. It is even questionable to deny the caption "metaphysics" to those cosmological and ontological problems which have this partly speculative and partly critical or reflective character. Historically their title to the name is fairly good. All I wish to point out is that there is a real distinction here between the speculative and the reflective elements; that this distinction coincides with a difference in the method by which resolution of the problem is to be sought; and that it is only the reflective element in such "metaphysical" problems which coincides in its nature and in the method of its solution with the problems of ethics and logic.

With this explanation, I hope I shall cause no confusion if I say that it is only so far as they are thus critical and reflective that the problems of ontology and cosmology are truly philosophic; and that metaphysics as a philosophic discipline is concerned with the nature of the real only so far as that problem is amenable to the reflective method and does not trench upon the field where only scientific investigation can achieve success. There are such reflective problems within any special science, and these may be said to constitute the philosophy of that science. There are also those problems of initial principle and criteria which are common to all the sciences and to the general business of life. These last are the problems of philosophy proper.

However, I should not like to appear to defend the notion that such analysis is a simple matter or that it requires only to express in precise terms the principles of common-sense. As has often enough been emphasized, common-sense is itself a naïve metaphysics and one which frequently breaks down on examination. Just as naïve morality may become confused before the dialectical attack, so common-sense categories of reality fail in crucial cases to meet the tests of consistency and accord with intelligent practice. It is true in metaphysics, as it is in ethics and in logic, that while valid principles must be supposed somehow implicit in the ordinary intercourse of mind with reality, they are not present in the sense of being fatally adhered to. If they were, the philosophic enterprise would have no practical value. Self-consciousness may be an end in itself, but if it did not have eventual influence upon human action it would be a luxury which humanity could not afford. That we coincide in our logical sense, does not make logic a work of supererogation. No more does coincidence in our ultimate sense of reality and in our categories render metaphysical discussion nugatory. Just as the study of logic may conduce to cogency of thought, and ethics contribute to greater clarity and consistency in moral judgment, so too the elucidation of metaphysical problems may contribute to the precision and adequacy of our interpretation of the real; it may even serve, on occasion, to work improvement in the concepts of the special sciences. Philosophy cannot be merely a verbally more precise rendering of common-sense, nor a direct generalization from actual practice. Though it rises from what is implicit in experience, its procedure must be critical, not descriptive. So far as it is to be of use, it must assume the function of sharpening and correcting an interpretation which has already entered into the fabric of that experience which is its datum. Logical principles aim to replace the uncritical moral sense, ethics, our naïve morality, and metaphysics, our unreflective ontological judgments. Such an enterprise is no simple matter of formulating the obvious.

The reflective method must, of course, be dialectical—in the Socratic-Platonic, not the Hegelian, sense. It accords with the Socratic presumption that the truth which is sought is already implicit in the mind which seeks it, and needs only to be elicited and brought to clear expression. It accords, further, in the recognition that it is definitions or "essences" which are the philosophic goal. And it likewise recognizes that the hope of agreement between minds, to be reached by philosophic discussion, must rest upon the presumption that this accord somehow exists already.

Historically, however, the dialectical method has been overlaid with all sorts of addenda, and perverted by extraneous assumptions which are fallacious. So that I should choose the name "reflective" as less liable to unwarranted interpretation. It does not follow from the dialectical method that the basis of the accord between minds represents some universal pattern of human reason, apart from the world of sense in which we live; nor that the mind has access to some realm of transcendent concepts which it recovers, of its own powers, at the instigation of experience; nor that agreement of minds presumes initial principles which are self-evident. It does not even follow that the agreement which we seek is already implicitly complete in all respects. To all such notions there is an alternative, to account for this agreement between minds, which is simple and even obvious. The coincidence of our fundamental criteria and principles is the combined result of the similarity of human animals, and of their primal interests, and the similarities of the experience with which they have to deal. More explicitly, it represents one result of the interplay between these two; the coincidence of human modes of behavior, particularly when the interests which such behavior serves involve coöperation.

It may be pointed out also that if we recognize critical reflection or dialectic as the only method which holds promise in philosophy, we do not thereby commit ourselves to the assumption that coherence or internal consistency is the only test, or a sufficient test, of philosophic truth. In philosophy, as elsewhere, consistency is only a negative test of truth; it is possible, however unlikely, to be consistently in error. Consistency would be a sufficient test only if we should suppose that there is nothing external to our logic which we must be true to. The reflective method does not take it for granted that all fact follows, Hegelian-fashion, from the logical structure of thought itself. As has been suggested, it does not even presuppose that what is a priori and of the mind—our categorial attitude of interpretation—is completely independent of the general character of experience.

It is of the essence of the dialectical or reflective method that we should recognize that proof, in philosophy, can be nothing more at bottom than persuasion. It makes no difference what the manner of presentation should be, whether deductive from initial assumptions, or inductive from example, or merely following the order dictated by clarity of exposition. If it be deductive, then the initial assumptions cannot coerce the mind. There are no propositions which are self-evident in isolation. So far as the deductive presentation hopes to convince of what was not previously believed, it must either seek out initial agreements from which it may proceed, or—as is more frequently the case—the deductively first propositions must be rendered significant and acceptable by exhibiting the cogency and general consonance with experience of their consequences. If the method be inductive from example, then the principles to be proved are implicit in the assumption that cited examples are veridical and typical and genuinely fall under the category to be investigated. There can be no Archimedean point for the philosopher. Proof, he can offer only in the sense of so connecting his theses as to exhibit their mutual support, and only through appeal to other minds to reflect upon their experience and their own attitudes and perceive that he correctly portrays them. If there be those minds which find no alternatives save certainty, apart from all appeal to prior fact, or skepticism, then to skepticism they are self-condemned. And much good may it do them! As philosophers, we have something we must be faithful to, even if that something be ourselves. If we are perverse, it is possible that our philosophy will consist of lies.

3 Philosophy and Science[*]

HENRY SIDGWICK

Henry Sidgwick (1838–1900), educated at Cambridge University where he also taught, is well known for his work in ethics, especially his *Methods of Ethics*.

I regard 'Philosophy' then—if the term is used without qualification—as the study which 'takes all knowledge for its province.' To such a study the human mind would be palpably incompetent if it attempted to deal with all the facts: it therefore selects the most important. Thus if we conceive the sciences as sets of connected knowledge, and imagine them as rising from the particular to the general, we may consider these sets in their turn as connected by Philosophy at the higher end. Philosophy, therefore, deals not with the whole matter of any science, but with the most important of its special notions, its fundamental principles, its distinctive method, its main conclusions. Philosophy examines these with the view of co-ordinating them with the fundamental notions and principles, methods and conclusions of other sciences. It may be called in this sense 'scientia scientiarum.'

The important distinction is that the Sciences concentrate attention on particular parts or aspects while it is, in contrast, the essential characteristic of Philosophy that it aims at putting together the parts of knowledge thus attained into a systematic whole; so that all methods of attaining truth may be grasped as parts of one method; and all the conclusions attained may be presented, so far as possible, as harmonious and consistent.

Perhaps some devotee of a special science may ask, "Is it worth while to do this till we have gone further in our knowledge of the parts?"

To this there is more than one answer. The most important answer I will give more fully later. Here I will say that in fact we cannot help doing it somehow. We grow up with ideas of the whole, which are continually modified as our knowledge extends: and no student of any special science ever acquiesces in having no idea of the relation of his part of knowledge to the rest. He may avoid philosophy in the sense of avoiding the attempt to make his conception of the universe as clear, precise, and systematic as possible, but that only means that he will be content with a vague, obscure, and altogether inadequate conception.

[*] From Henry Sidgwick, *Philosophy, Its Scope and Relations: An Introductory Course of Lectures* (London: Macmillan and Co., Ltd., 1902).

17

In fact, when a writer speaks of another's arguments as 'unphilosophical,' he often seems to mean no more than that he profoundly disagrees with him. It would, however, be a pity to allow the word to be used in this sense: and perhaps the different schools would agree that there is an instructed and an uninstructed way of reasoning on behalf of what each school regards as sound conclusions; the characteristic of an instructed way of reasoning being that it shows an adequate knowledge of the arguments used on the other side, some apprehension of their force, and that it endeavours either to meet or to avoid those arguments. Philosophical knowledge in this sense—on points on which experts are disagreed—would be knowledge of the confusions of thought to which the human intellect is liable when it begins to speculate on the questions of Philosophy, knowledge of how to state these questions so as to avoid to some extent confusions of thought, and knowledge of considerations that have some force, though not necessarily decisive force, for or against conclusions on disputed questions of Philosophy. And if Philosophy is regarded as a subject of academic teaching and study, this, I conceive, is the kind of knowledge which the teacher ought mainly to seek to convey, on subjects of controversy.

But it is evident that this acquaintance with arguments is not the kind of knowledge at which Philosophy *aims*, although it may be all the knowledge for which a consensus of experts can be claimed at present. So long as this is so, the notion of philosophy being a *pursuit* rather than a system of knowledge will maintain itself, as it has maintained itself throughout two thousand years in which dogmatic systems have succeeded each other. This lack of a 'consensus of experts' as to the method and main conclusions of Philosophy, is, I fear, strong evidence that study of it is still—after so many centuries—in a rudimentary condition as compared with the more special studies of the branches of systematised knowledge that we call Sciences. As philosophers we aim at knowledge of the whole, and therefore at knowledge of the underlying reality.

The complete unification at which Philosophy aims must enable us to view every portion of knowledge—and every object known—as a part of a coherent whole, and in comprehending the relation of diverse parts of a whole to the whole, and to each other, systematic difference—difference essentially belonging to the nature of the whole—is as important a feature as resemblance.

The knowledge at which the sciences aim, and which they claim to have partially attained, is knowledge of what exists or has existed or will exist.

On the other hand, the aim of Philosophy, in dealing with the same beliefs, is to arrange them in such orders as may make manifest the important permanent relations among them,—*e.g.* the relations of the simple to the complex, of the more general to the less general, of the fundamental principles of any science to their applications or the deductions founded on them.

In connexion with this I may observe that in my view Philosophy—so far as it does not construct its system, or aim at constructing it completely *a priori*—uses primarily what I may call the Dialectical Method, *i.e.* the method of reflection on the thought which we all share, by the aid of the symbolism which we all share, language.

4 The Value of Philosophy[*]

BERTRAND RUSSELL

Bertrand Russell (1872–1969) was perhaps the most influential and controversial philosopher of the twentieth century. He taught and lectured at universities around the world and wrote on nearly every philosophical topic. Perhaps his most famous philosophical work is *Principia Mathematica* (with Alfred North Whitehead), a study of the foundations of mathematics.

Having now come to the end of our brief and very incomplete review of the problems of philosophy, it will be well to consider, in conclusion, what is the value of philosophy and why it ought to be studied. It is the more necessary to consider this question, in view of the fact that many men, under the influence of science or of practical affairs, are inclined to doubt whether philosophy is anything better than innocent but useless trifling, hair-splitting distinctions, and controversies on matters concerning which knowledge is impossible.

This view of philosophy appears to result, partly from a wrong conception of the ends of life, partly from a wrong conception of the kind of goods which philosophy strives to achieve. Physical science, through the medium of inventions, is useful to innumerable people who are wholly ignorant of it; thus the study of physical science is to be recommended, not only, or primarily, because of the effect on the student, but rather because of the effect on mankind in general. Thus utility does not belong to philosophy. If the study of philosophy has any value at all for others than students of philosophy, it must be only indirectly, through its effects upon the lives of those who study it. It is in these effects, therefore, if anywhere, that the value of philosophy must be primarily sought.

But further, if we are not to fail in our endeavour to determine the value of philosophy, we must first free our minds from the prejudices of what are wrongly called 'practical' men. The 'practical' man, as this word is often used, is one who recognizes only material needs, who realizes that men must have food for the body, but is oblivious of the necessity of providing food for the mind. If all men were well off, if poverty and disease had been reduced to their lowest possible point, there would still remain much to be

* From Bertrand Russell, *The Problems of Philosophy*, 1912, by permission of the Clarendon Press, Oxford.

done to produce a valuable society; and even in the existing world the goods of the mind are at least as important as the goods of the body. It is exclusively among the goods of the mind that the value of philosophy is to be found; and only those who are not indifferent to these goods can be persuaded that the study of philosophy is not a waste of time.

Philosophy, like all other studies, aims primarily at knowledge. The knowledge it aims at is the kind of knowledge which gives unity and system to the body of the sciences, and the kind which results from a critical examination of the grounds of our convictions, prejudices, and beliefs. But it cannot be maintained that philosophy has had any very great measure of success in its attempts to provide definite answers to its questions. If you ask a mathematician, a mineralogist, a historian, or any other man of learning, what definite body of truths has been ascertained by his science, his answer will last as long as you are willing to listen. But if you put the same question to a philosopher, he will, if he is candid, have to confess that his study has not achieved positive results such as have been achieved by other sciences. It is true that this is partly accounted for by the fact that, as soon as definite knowledge concerning any subject becomes possible, this subject ceases to be called philosophy, and becomes a separate science. The whole study of the heavens, which now belongs to astronomy, was once included in philosophy; Newton's great work was called 'the mathematical principles of natural philosophy.' Similarly, the study of the human mind, which was a part of philosophy, has now been separated from philosophy and has become the science of psychology. Thus, to a great extent, the uncertainty of philosophy is more apparent than real: those questions which are already capable of definite answers are placed in the sciences, while those only to which, at present, no definite answer can be given, remain to form the residue which is called philosophy.

This is, however, only a part of the truth concerning the uncertainty of philosophy. There are many questions—and among them those that are of the profoundest interest to our spiritual life—which, so far as we can see, must remain insoluble to the human intellect unless its powers become of quite a different order from what they are now. Has the universe any unity of plan or purpose, or is it a fortuitous concourse of atoms? Is consciousness a permanent part of the universe, giving hope of indefinite growth in wisdom, or is it a transitory accident on a small planet on which life must ultimately become impossible? Are good and evil of importance to the universe or only to man? Such questions are asked by philosophy, and variously answered by various philosophers. But it would seem that, whether answers be otherwise discoverable or not, the answers suggested by philosophy are none of them demonstrably true. Yet, however slight may be the hope of discovering an answer, it is part of the business of philosophy to continue the consideration of such questions, to make us aware of their importance, to examine all the approaches to them, and to keep alive that speculative interest in the universe which is apt to be killed by confining ourselves to definitely ascertainable knowledge.

Many philosophers, it is true, have held that philosophy could establish the truth of certain answers to such fundamental questions. They have supposed that what is of most importance in religious beliefs could be proved by strict demonstration to be true. In order to judge of such attempts, it is necessary to take a survey of human knowledge, and to form an opinion as to its methods and its limitations. On such a subject it would be unwise to pronounce dogmatically; but if the investigations of our previous chapters have not led us astray, we shall be compelled to renounce the hope of finding philosophical proofs of religious beliefs. We cannot, therefore, include as part of the value of philosophy any definite set of answers to such questions. Hence, once more, the value of philosophy must not depend upon any supposed body of definitely ascertainable knowledge to be acquired by those who study it.

The value of philosophy is, in fact, to be sought largely in its very uncertainty. The man who has no tincture of philosophy goes through life imprisoned in the prejudices derived from common sense, from the habitual beliefs of his age or his nation, and from convictions which have grown up in his mind without the co-operation or consent of his deliberate reason. To such a man the world tends to become definite, finite, obvious; common objects rouse no questions, and unfamiliar possibilities are contemptuously rejected. As soon as we begin to philosophize, on the contrary, we find, as we saw in our opening chapters, that even the most everyday things lead to problems to which only very incomplete answers can be given. Philosophy, though unable to tell us with certainty what is the true answer to the doubts which it raises, is able to suggest many possibilities which enlarge our thoughts and free them from the tyranny of custom. Thus, while diminishing our feeling of certainty as to what things are, it greatly increases our knowledge as to what they may be; it removes the somewhat arrogant dogmatism of those who have never travelled into the region of liberating doubt, and it keeps alive our sense of wonder by showing familiar things in an unfamiliar aspect.

5 Philosophy as Dialectic*

PLATO

Plato (427–347 B.C.) was a student of Socrates and later founded the Academy, the first "university" in Europe. He has had incalculable influence on Western thought. His best known works are the *Apology, Crito, Meno, Protagoras, Gorgias, Phaedo, Symposium, Republic, Theatetus, Sophist, Parmenides, Phaedrus, Laws, Politicus,* and *Timaeus.*

EUTHYPHRO*

PERSONS OF THE DIALOGUE

Socrates   Euthyphro

SCENE:—*The Porch of the King Archon*

Euthyphro. Why have you left the Lyceum, Socrates? and what are you doing in the Porch of the King Archon? Surely you cannot be concerned in a suit before the King, like myself?

Socrates. Not in a suit, Euthyphro; impeachment is the word which the Athenians use.

Euth. What! I suppose that some one has been prosecuting you, for I cannot believe that you are the prosecutor of another.

Soc. Certainly not.

Euth. Then some one else has been prosecuting you?

Soc. Yes.

Euth. And who is he?

Soc. A young man who is little known, Euthyphro; and I hardly know him: his name is Meletus, and he is of the deme of Pitthis. Perhaps you may remember his appearance; he has a beak, and long straight hair, and a beard which is ill grown.

Euth. No, I do not remember him, Socrates. But what is the charge which he brings against you?

Soc. What is the charge? Well, a very serious charge, which shows a good deal of character in the young man, and for which he is certainly not to be despised. He says he knows how the youth are corrupted and who are their

* From *The Dialogues of Plato,* trans. B. Jowett (New York: The Macmillan Company, 1892).

corruptors. I fancy that he must be a wise man, and seeing that I am the reverse of a wise man, he has found me out, and is going to accuse me of corrupting his young friends. And of this our mother the state is to be the judge. Of all our political men he is the only one who seems to me to begin in the right way, with the cultivation of virtue in youth; like a good husband-man, he makes the young shoots his first care, and clears away us who are the destroyers of them. This is only the first step; he will afterwards attend to the elder branches; and if he goes on as he has begun, he will be a very great public benefactor.

Euth. I hope that he may; but I rather fear, Socrates, that the opposite will turn out to be the truth. My opinion is that in attacking you he is simply aiming a blow at the foundation of the state. But in what way does he say that you corrupt the young?

Soc. He brings a wonderful accusation against me, which at first hearing excites surprise: he says that I am a poet or maker of gods, and that I invent new gods and deny the existence of old ones; this is the ground of his indictment.

Euth. I understand, Socrates; he means to attack you about the familiar sign which occasionally, as you say, comes to you. He thinks that you are a neologian, and he is going to have you up before the court for this. He knows that such a charge is readily received by the world, as I myself know too well; for when I speak in the assembly about divine things, and foretell the future to them, they laugh at me and think me a madman. Yet every word that I say is true. But they are jealous of us all; and we must be brave and go at them.

Soc. Their laughter, friend Euthyphro, is not a matter of much consequence. For a man may be thought wise; but the Athenians, I suspect, do not much trouble themselves about him until he begins to impart his wisdom to others; and then for some reason or other, perhaps, as you say, from jealousy, they are angry.

Euth. I am never likely to try their temper in this way.

Soc. I dare say not, for you are reserved in your behaviour, and seldom impart your wisdom. But I have a benevolent habit of pouring out myself to everybody, and would even pay for a listener, and I am afraid that the Athenians may think me too talkative. Now if, as I was saying, they would only laugh at me, as you say that they laugh at you, the time might pass gaily enough in the court; but perhaps they may be in earnest, and then what the end will be you soothsayers only can predict.

Euth. I dare say that the affair will end in nothing, Socrates, and that you will win your cause; and I think that I shall win my own.

Soc. And what is your suit, Euthyphro? are you the pursuer or the defendant?

Euth. I am the pursuer.

Soc. Of whom?

Euth. You will think me mad when I tell you.

Soc. Why, has the fugitive wings?

Euth. Nay, he is not very volatile at his time of life.

Soc. Who is he?

Euth. My father.

Soc. Your father! my good man?

Euth. Yes.

Soc. And of what is he accused?

Euth. Of murder, Socrates.

Soc. By the powers, Euthyphro! how little does the common herd know of the nature of right and truth. A man must be an extraordinary man, and have made great strides in wisdom, before he could have seen his way to bring such an action.

Euth. Indeed, Socrates, he must.

Soc. I suppose that the man whom your father murdered was one of your relatives—clearly he was; for if he had been a stranger you would never have thought of prosecuting him.

Euth. I am amused, Socrates, at your making a distinction between one who is a relation and one who is not a relation; for surely the pollution is the same in either case, if you knowingly associate with the murderer when you ought to clear yourself and him by proceeding against him. The real question is whether the murdered man has been justly slain. If justly, then your duty is to let the matter alone; but if unjustly, then even if the mur- derer lives under the same roof with you and eats at the same table, proceed against him. Now the man who is dead was a poor dependant of mine who worked for us as a field labourer on our farm in Naxos, and one day in a fit of drunken passion he got into a quarrel with one of our domestic servants and slew him. My father bound him hand and foot and threw him into a ditch, and then sent to Athens to ask of a diviner what he should do with him. Meanwhile he never attended to him and took no care about him, for he regarded him as a murderer; and thought that no great harm would be done even if he did die. Now this was just what happened. For such was the effect of cold and hunger and chains upon him, that before the messenger returned from the diviner, he was dead. And my father and family are angry with me for taking the part of the murderer and prosecuting my father. They say that he did not kill him, and that if he did, the dead man was but a murderer, and I ought not to take any notice, for that a son is impious who prosecutes a father. Which shows, Socrates, how little they know what the gods think about piety and impiety.

Soc. Good heavens, Euthyphro! and is your knowledge of religion and of things pious and impious so very exact, that, supposing the circumstances to be as you state them, you are not afraid lest you too may be doing an impious thing in bringing an action against your father?

Euth. The best of Euthyphro, and that which distinguishes him, Socrates, from other men, is his exact knowledge of all such matters. What should I be good for without it?

Soc. Rare friend! I think that I cannot do better than be your disciple. Then before the trial with Meletus comes on I shall challenge him, and say that I have always had a great interest in religious questions, and now, as he charges me with rash imaginations and innovations in religion, I have become your disciple. You, Meletus, as I shall say to him, acknowledge Euthyphro to be a great theologian, and sound in his opinions; and if you approve of him you ought to approve of me, and not have me into court; but if you disapprove, you should begin by indicting him who is my teacher, and who will be the ruin, not of the young, but of the old; that is to say, of myself whom he instructs, and of his old father whom he admonishes and chastises. And if Meletus refuses to listen to me, but will go on, and will not shift the indictment from me to you, I cannot do better than repeat this challenge in the court.

Euth. Yes, indeed, Socrates; and if he attempts to indict me I am mistaken if I do not find a flaw in him; the court shall have a great deal more to say to him than to me.

Soc. And I, my dear friend, knowing this, am desirous of becoming your disciple. For I observe that no one appears to notice you—not even this Meletus; but his sharp eyes have found me out at once, and he has indicted me for impiety. And therefore, I adjure you to tell me the nature of piety and impiety, which you said that you knew so well, and of murder, and of other offences against the gods. What are they? Is not piety in every action always the same? and impiety, again—is it not always the opposite of piety, and also the same with itself, having, as impiety, one notion which includes whatever is impious?

Euth. To be sure, Socrates.

Soc. And what is piety, and what is impiety?

Euth. Piety is doing as I am doing; that is to say, prosecuting any one who is guilty of murder, sacrilege, or of any similar crime—whether he be your father or mother, or whoever he may be—that makes no difference; and not to prosecute them is impiety. And please to consider, Socrates, what a notable proof I will give you of the truth of my words, a proof which I have already given to others:—of the principle, I mean, that the impious, whoever he may be, ought not to go unpunished. For do not men regard Zeus as the best and most righteous of the gods?—and yet they admit that he bound his father (Cronos) because he wickedly devoured his sons, and that he too had punished his own father (Uranus) for a similar reason, in a nameless manner. And yet when I proceed against my father, they are angry with me. So inconsistent are they in their way of talking when the gods are concerned, and when I am concerned.

Soc. May not this be the reason, Euthyphro, why I am charged with impiety—that I cannot away with these stories about the gods? and therefore I suppose that people think me wrong. But, as you who are well informed about them approve of them, I cannot do better than assent to your superior wisdom. What else can I say, confessing as I do, that I know nothing about them? Tell me, for the love of Zeus, whether you really believe that they are true.

Euth. Yes, Socrates; and things more wonderful still, of which the world is in ignorance.

Soc. And do you really believe that the gods fought with one another, and had dire quarrels, battles, and the like, as the poets say, and as you may see represented in the works of great artists? The temples are full of them; and notably the robe of Athene, which is carried up to the Acropolis at the great Panathenaea, is embroidered with them. Are all these tales of the gods true, Euthyphro?

Euth. Yes, Socrates; and, as I was saying, I can tell you, if you would like to hear them, many other things about the gods which would quite amaze you.

Soc. I dare say; and you shall tell me them at some other time when I have leisure. But just at present I would rather hear from you a more precise answer, which you have not as yet given, my friend, to the question, What is 'piety'? When asked, you only replied, Doing as you do, charging your father with murder.

Euth. And what I said was true, Socrates.

Soc. No doubt, Euthyphro; but you would admit that there are many other pious acts?

Euth. There are.

Soc. Remember that I did not ask you to give me two or three examples of piety, but to explain the general idea which makes all pious things to be pious. Do you not recollect that there was one idea which made the impious impious, and the pious pious?

Euth. I remember.

Soc. Tell me what is the nature of this idea, and then I shall have a standard to which I may look, and by which I may measure actions, whether yours or those of any one else, and then I shall be able to say that such and such an action is pious, such another impious.

Euth. I will tell you, if you like.

Soc. I should very much like.

Euth. Piety, then, is that which is dear to the gods, and impiety is that which is not dear to them.

Soc. Very good, Euthyphro; you have now given me the sort of answer which I wanted. But whether what you say is true or not I cannot as yet tell, although I make no doubt that you will prove the truth of your words.

Euth. Of course.

Soc. Come, then, and let us examine what we are saying. That thing or person which is dear to the gods is pious, and that thing or person which is hateful to the gods is impious, these two being the extreme opposites of one another. Was not that said?

Euth. It was.

Soc. And well said?

Euth. Yes, Socrates, I thought so; it was certainly said.

Soc. And further, Euthyphro, the gods were admitted to have enmities and hatreds and differences?

Euth. Yes, that was also said.

Soc. And what sort of difference creates enmity and anger? Suppose for example that you and I, my good friend, differ about a number; do differences of this sort make us enemies and set us at variance with one another? Do we not go at once to arithmetic, and put an end to them by a sum?

Euth. True.

Soc. Or suppose that we differ about magnitudes, do we not quickly end the differences by measuring?

Euth. Very true.

Soc. And we end a controversy about heavy and light by resorting to a weighing machine?

Euth. To be sure.

Soc. But what differences are there which cannot be thus decided, and which therefore make us angry and set us at enmity with one another? I dare say the answer does not occur to you at the moment, and therefore I will suggest that these enmities arise when the matters of difference are the just and unjust, good and evil, honourable and dishonourable. Are not these the points about which men differ, and about which when we are unable satisfactorily to decide our differences, you and I and all of us quarrel, when we do quarrel[1]?

Euth. Yes, Socrates, the nature of the differences about which we quarrel is such as you describe.

Soc. And the quarrels of the gods, noble Euthyphro, when they occur, are of a like nature?

Euth. Certainly they are.

Soc. They have differences of opinion, as you say, about good and evil, just and unjust, honourable and dishonourable: there would have been no quarrels among them, if there had been no such differences—would there now?

Euth. You are quite right.

Soc. Does not every man love that which he deems noble and just and good, and hate the opposite of them?

Euth. Very true.

Soc. But, as you say, people regard the same things, some as just and others as unjust,—about these they dispute; and so there arise wars and fightings among them.

Euth. Very true.

Soc. Then the same things are hated by the gods and loved by the gods, and are both hateful and dear to them?

---

[1] Cp. I Alcib. III foll.

Euth. True.

Soc. And upon this view the same things, Euthyphro, will be pious and also impious?

Euth. So I should suppose.

Soc. Then, my friend, I remark with surprise that you have not answered the question which I asked. For I certainly did not ask you to tell me what action is both pious and impious: but now it would seem that what is loved by the gods is also hated by them. And therefore, Euthyphro, in thus chastising your father you may very likely be doing what is agreeable to Zeus but disagreeable to Cronos or Uranus, and what is acceptable to Hephaestus but unacceptable to Herè, and there may be other gods who have similar differences of opinion.

Euth. But I believe, Socrates, that all the gods would be agreed as to the propriety of punishing a murderer: there would be no difference of opinion about that.

Soc. Well, but speaking of men, Euthyphro, did you ever hear any one arguing that a murderer or any sort of evil-doer ought to be let off?

Euth. I should rather say that these are the questions which they are always arguing, especially in courts of law: they commit all sorts of crimes, and there is nothing which they will not do or say in their own defence.

Soc. But do they admit their guilt, Euthyphro, and yet say that they ought not to be punished?

Euth. No; they do not.

Soc. Then there are some things which they do not venture to say and do: for they do not venture to argue that the guilty are to be unpunished, but they deny their guilt, do they not?

Euth. Yes.

Soc. Then they do not argue that the evil-doer should not be punished, but they argue about the fact of who the evil-doer is, and what he did and when?

Euth. True.

Soc. And the gods are in the same case, if as you assert they quarrel about just and unjust, and some of them say while others deny that injustice is done among them. For surely neither God nor man will ever venture to say that the doer of injustice is not to be punished?

Euth. That is true, Socrates, in the main.

Soc. But they join issue about the particulars—gods and men alike; and, if they dispute at all, they dispute about some act which is called in question, and which by some is affirmed to be just, by others to be unjust. Is not that true?

Euth. Quite true.

Soc. Well then, my dear friend Euthyphro, do tell me, for my better instruction and information, what proof have you that in the opinion of all the gods a servant who is guilty of murder, and is put in chains by the master of the dead man, and dies because he is put in chains before he who bound him can learn from the interpreters of the gods what he ought to do with him, dies unjustly; and that on behalf of such an one a son ought to proceed against his father and accuse him of murder. How would you show that all the gods absolutely agree in approving of his act? Prove to me that they do, and I will applaud your wisdom as long as I live.

Euth. It will be a difficult task; but I could make the matter very clear indeed to you.

Soc. I understand; you mean to say that I am not so quick of apprehension as the judges: for to them you will be sure to prove that the act is unjust, and hateful to the gods.

Euth. Yes indeed, Socrates; at least if they will listen to me.

Soc. But they will be sure to listen if they find that you are a good speaker. There was a notion that came into my mind while you were speaking; I said to myself: 'Well, and what if Euthyphro does prove to me that all the gods regarded the death of the serf as unjust, how do I know anything more of the nature of piety and impiety? for granting that this action may be hateful to the gods, still piety and impiety are not adequately defined by these distinctions, for that which is hateful to the gods has been shown to be also pleasing and dear to them.' And therefore, Euthyphro, I do not ask you to prove this; I will suppose, if you like, that all the gods condemn and abominate such an action. But I will amend the definition so far as to say that what all the gods hate is impious, and what they love pious or holy; and what some of them love and others hate is both or neither. Shall this be our definition of piety and impiety?

Euth. Why not, Socrates?

Soc. Why not! certainly, as far as I am concerned, Euthyphro, there is no reason why not. But whether this admission will greatly assist you in the task of instructing me as you promised, is a matter for you to consider.

Euth. Yes, I should say that what all the gods love is pious and holy, and the opposite which they all hate, impious.

Soc. Ought we to enquire into the truth of this, Euthyphro, or simply to accept the mere statement on our own authority and that of others? What do you say?

Euth. We should enquire; and I believe that the statement will stand the test of enquiry.

Soc. We shall know better, my good friend, in a little while. The point which I should first wish to understand is whether the pious or holy is beloved by the gods because it is holy, or holy because it is beloved of the gods.

Euth. I do not understand your meaning, Socrates.

Soc. I will endeavour to explain: we speak of carrying and we speak of being carried, of leading and being led, seeing and being seen. You know that in all such cases there is a difference, and you know also in what the difference lies?

Euth. I think that I understand.

Soc. And is not that which is beloved distinct from that which loves?

Euth. Certainly.

Soc. Well; and now tell me, is that which is carried in this state of carrying because it is carried, or for some other reason?

Euth. No; that is the reason.

Soc. And the same is true of what is led and of what is seen?

Euth. True.

Soc. And a thing is not seen because it is visible, but conversely, visible because it is seen; nor is a thing led because it is in the state of being led, or carried because it is in the state of being carried, but the converse of this. And now I think, Euthyphro, that my meaning will be intelligible; and my meaning is, that any state of action or passion implies previous action or passion. It does not become because it is becoming, but it is in a state of becoming because it becomes; neither does it suffer because it is in a state of suffering, but it is in a state of suffering because it suffers. Do you not agree?

Euth. Yes.

Soc. Is not that which is loved in some state either of becoming or suffering?

Euth. Yes.

Soc. And the same holds as in the previous instances; the state of being loved follows the act of being loved, and not the act the state.

Euth. Certainly.

Soc. And what do you say of piety, Euthyphro: is not piety, according to your definition, loved by all the gods?

Euth. Yes.

Soc. Because it is pious or holy, or for some other reason?

Euth. No, that is the reason.

Soc. It is loved because it is holy, not holy because it is loved?

Euth. Yes.

Soc. And that which is dear to the gods is loved by them, and is in a state to be loved of them because it is loved of them?

Euth. Certainly.

Soc. Then that which is dear to the gods, Euthyphro, is not holy, nor is that which is holy loved of God, as you affirm; but they are two different things.

Euth. How do you mean, Socrates?

Soc. I mean to say that the holy has been acknowledged by us to be loved of God because it is holy, not to be holy because it is loved.

Euth. Yes.

Soc. But that which is dear to the gods is dear to them because it is loved by them, not loved by them because it is dear to them.

Euth. True.

Soc. But, friend Euthyphro, if that which is holy is the same with that which is dear to God, and is loved because it is holy, then that which is dear to God would have been loved as being dear to God; but if that which is dear to God is dear to him because loved by him, then that which is holy would have been holy because loved by him. But now you see that the reverse is the case, and that they are quite different from one another. For one (θεοφιλὲς) is of a kind to be loved because it is loved, and the other (ὅσιον) is loved because it is of a kind to be loved. Thus you appear to me, Euthyphro, when I ask you what is the essence of holiness, to offer an atttribute only, and not the essence—the attribute of being loved by all the gods. But you still refuse to explain to me the nature of holiness. And therefore, if you please, I will ask you not to hide your treasure, but to tell me once more what holiness or piety really is, whether dear to the gods or not (for that is a matter about which we will not quarrel); and what is impiety?

Euth. I really do not know, Socrates, how to express what I mean. For somehow or other our arguments, on whatever ground we rest them, seem to turn round and walk away from us.

Soc. Your words, Euthyphro, are like the handiwork of my ancestor Daedalus; and if I were the sayer or propounder of them, you might say that my arguments walk away and will not remain fixed where they are placed because I am a descendant of his. But now, since these notions are your own, you must find some other gibe, for they certainly, as you yourself allow, show an inclination to be on the move.

Euth. Nay, Socrates, I shall still say that you are the Daedalus who sets arguments in motion; not I, certainly, but you make them move or go round, for they would never have stirred, as far as I am concerned.

Soc. Then I must be a greater than Daedalus: for whereas he only made his own inventions to move, I move those of other people as well. And the beauty of it is, that I would rather not. For I would give the wisdom of Daedalus, and the wealth of Tantalus, to be able to detain them and keep them fixed. But enough of this. As I perceive that you are lazy, I will myself endeavor to show you how you might instruct me in the nature of piety; and I hope that you will not grudge your labour. Tell me, then,—Is not that which is pious necessarily just?

Euth. Yes.

Soc. And is, then, all which is just pious? or, is that which is pious all just, but that which is just, only in part and not all, pious?

Euth. I do not understand you, Socrates.

Soc. And yet I know that you are as much wiser than I am, as you are younger. But, as I was saying, revered friend, the abundance of your wisdom makes you lazy. Please to exert yourself, for there is no real difficulty in understanding me. What I mean I may explain by an illustration of what I do not mean. The poet (Stasinus) sings—

'Of Zeus, the author and creator of all these things,
You will not tell: for where there is fear there is also reverence.'

Now I disagree with this poet. Shall I tell you in what respect?

Euth. By all means.

Soc. I should not say that where there is fear there is also reverence; for I am sure that many persons fear poverty and disease, and the like evils, but I do not perceive that they reverence the objects of their fear.

Euth. Very true.

Soc. But where reverence is, there is fear; for he who has a feeling of reverence and shame about the commission of any action, fears and is afraid of an ill reputation.

Euth. No doubt.

Soc. Then we are wrong in saying that where there is fear there is also reverence; and we should say, where there is reverence there is also fear. But there is not always reverence where there is fear; for fear is a more extended notion, and reverence is a part of fear, just as the odd is a part of number, and number is a more extended notion than the odd. I suppose that you follow me now?

Euth. Quite well.

Soc. That was the sort of question which I meant to raise when I asked whether the just is always the pious, or the pious always the just; and whether there may not be justice where there is not piety; for justice is the more extended notion of which piety is only a part. Do you dissent?

Euth. No, I think that you are quite right.

Soc. Then, if piety is a part of justice, I suppose that we should enquire what part? If you had pursued the enquiry in the previous cases; for instance, if you had asked me what is an even number, and what part of number the even is, I should have had no difficulty in replying, a number which represents a figure having two equal sides. Do you not agree?

Euth. Yes, I quite agree.

Soc. In like manner, I want you to tell me what part of justice is piety or holiness, that I may be able to tell Meletus not to do me injustice, or indict me for impiety, as I am now adequately instructed by you in the nature of piety or holiness, and their opposites.

Euth. Piety or holiness, Socrates, appears to me to be that part of justice which attends to the gods, as there is the other part of justice which attends to men.

Soc. That is good, Euthyphro; yet still there is a little point about which I should like to have further information, What is the meaning of 'attention'? For attention can hardly be used in the same sense when applied to the gods as when applied to other things. For instance, horses are said to require attention, and not every person is able to attend to them, but only a person skilled in horsemanship. Is it not so?

Euth. Certainly.

Soc. I should suppose that the art of horsemanship is the art of attending to horses?

Euth. Yes.

Soc. Nor is every one qualified to attend to dogs, but only the huntsman?

Euth. True.

Soc. And I should also conceive that the art of the huntsman is the art of attending to dogs?

Euth. Yes.

Soc. As the art of the oxherd is the art of attending to oxen?

Euth. Very true.

Soc. In like manner holiness or piety is the art of attending to the gods? —that would be your meaning, Euthyphro?

Euth. Yes.

Soc. And is not attention always designed for the good or benefit of that to which the attention is given? As in the case of horses, you may observe that when attended to by the horseman's art they are benefited and improved, are they not?

Euth. True.

Soc. As the dogs are benefited by the huntsman's art, and the oxen by the art of the oxherd, and all other things are tended or attended for their good and not for their hurt?

Euth. Certainly, not for their hurt.

Soc. But for their good?

Euth. Of course.

Soc. And does piety or holiness, which has been defined to be the art of attending to the gods, benefit, or improve them? Would you say that when you do a holy act you make any of the gods better?

Euth. No, no; that was certainly not what I meant.

Soc. And I, Euthyphro, never supposed that you did. I asked you the question about the nature of the attention, because I thought that you did not.

Euth. You do me justice, Socrates; that is not the sort of attention which I mean.

Soc. Good: but I must still ask what is this attention to the gods which is called piety?

Euth. It is such, Socrates, as servants show to their masters.

Soc. I understand—a sort of ministration to the gods.

Euth. Exactly.

Soc. Medicine is also a sort of ministration or service, having in view the attainment of some object—would you not say of health?

Euth. I should.

Soc. Again, there is an art which ministers to the ship-builder with a view to the attainment of some result?

Euth. Yes, Socrates, with a view to the building of a ship.

Soc. As there is an art which ministers to the housebuilder with a view to the building of a house?

Euth. Yes.

Soc. And now tell me, my good friend, about the art which ministers to the gods: what work does that help to accomplish? For you must surely know if, as you say, you are of all men living the one who is best instructed in religion.

Euth. And I speak the truth, Socrates.

Soc. Tell me then, oh tell me—what is that fair work which the gods do by the help of our ministrations?

Euth. Many and fair, Socrates, are the works which they do.

Soc. Why, my friend, and so are those of a general. But the chief of them is easily told. Would you not say that victory in war is the chief of them?

Euth. Certainly.

Soc. Many and fair, too, are the works of the husbandman, if I am not mistaken; but his chief work is the production of food from the earth?

Euth. Exactly.

Soc. And of the many and fair things done by the gods, which is the chief or principal one?

Euth. I have told you already, Socrates, that to learn all these things accurately will be very tiresome. Let me simply say that piety or holiness is learning how to please the gods in word and deed, by prayers and sacrifices. Such piety is the salvation of families and states, just as the impious, which is unpleasing to the gods, is their ruin and destruction.

Soc. I think that you could have answered in much fewer words the chief question which I asked, Euthyphro, if you had chosen. But I see plainly that you are not disposed to instruct me—clearly not: else why, when we reached the point, did you turn aside? Had you only answered me I should have truly learned of you by this time the nature of piety. Now, as the asker of a question is necessarily dependent on the answerer, whither he leads I must follow; and can only ask again, what is the pious, and what is piety? Do you mean that they are a sort of science of praying and sacrificing?

Euth. Yes, I do.

Soc. And sacrificing is giving to the gods, and prayer is asking of the gods?

Euth. Yes, Socrates.

Soc. Upon this view, then, piety is a science of asking and giving?

Euth. You understand me capitally, Socrates.

Soc. Yes, my friend; the reason is that I am a votary of your science, and give my mind to it, and therefore nothing which you say will be thrown away upon me. Please then to tell me, what is the nature of this service to the gods? Do you mean that we prefer requests and give gifts to them?

Euth. Yes, I do.

Soc. Is not the right way of asking to ask of them what we want?

Euth. Certainly.

Soc. And the right way of giving is to give to them in return what they want of us. There would be no meaning in an art which gives to any one that which he does not want.

Euth. Very true, Socrates.

Soc. Then piety, Euthyphro, is an art which gods and men have of doing business with one another?

Euth. That is an expression which you may use, if you like.

Soc. But I have no particular liking for anything but the truth. I wish, however, that you would tell me what benefit accrues to the gods from our gifts. There is no doubt about what they give to us; for there is no good thing which they do not give; but how we can give any good thing to them in return is far from being equally clear. If they give everything and we give nothing, that must be an affair of business in which we have very greatly the advantage of them.

Euth. And do you imagine, Socrates, that any benefit accrues to the gods from our gifts?

Soc. But if not, Euthyphro, what is the meaning of gifts which are conferred by us upon the gods?

Euth. What else, but tributes of honour; and, as I was just now saying, what pleases them?

Soc. Piety, then, is pleasing to the gods, but not beneficial or dear to them?

Euth. I should say that nothing could be dearer.

Soc. Then once more the assertion is repeated that piety is dear to the gods?

Euth. Certainly.

Soc. And when you say this, can you wonder at your words not standing firm, but walking away? Will you accuse me of being the Daedalus who makes them walk away, not perceiving that there is another and far greater artist than Daedalus who makes them go round in a circle, and he is yourself; for the argument, as you will perceive, comes round to the same point. Were we not saying that the holy or pious was not the same with that which is loved of the gods? Have you forgotten?

Euth. I quite remember.

Soc. And are you not saying that what is loved of the gods is holy; and is not this the same as what is dear to them—do you see?

Euth. True.

Soc. Then either we were wrong in our former assertion; or, if we were right then, we are wrong now.

Euth. One of the two must be true.

Soc. Then we must begin again and ask, What is piety? That is an enquiry which I shall never be weary of pursuing as far as in me lies; and I entreat you not to scorn me, but to apply your mind to the utmost, and tell me the truth. For, if any man knows, you are he; and therefore I must detain you, like Proteus, until you tell. If you had not certainly known the nature of piety and impiety, I am confident that you would never, on behalf of a serf, have charged your aged father with murder. You would not have run such a risk of doing wrong in the sight of the gods, and you would have had too much respect for the opinions of men. I am sure, therefore, that you know the nature of piety and impiety. Speak out then, my dear Euthyphro, and do not hide your knowledge.

Euth. Another time, Socrates; for I am in a hurry, and must go now.

Soc. Alas! my companion, and will you leave me in despair? I was hoping that you would instruct me in the nature of piety and impiety; and then I might have cleared myself of Meletus and his indictment. I would have told him that I had been enlightened by Euthyphro, and had given up rash innovations and speculations, in which I indulged only through ignorance, and that now I am about to lead a better life.

Chapter Two

THE PROBLEM
OF THE EXISTENCE OF GOD

It was stated in Chapter One that philosophy involves the effort to analyze and clarify key concepts and rationality to assess beliefs, statements, or theories in which these concepts are used. Religious ideas and beliefs surely constitute some of the most important and controversial of all. They are perhaps the most puzzling. They arouse great passion among men, and, indeed, wars have been fought over them. This is not surprising, given the central role that religion plays in the lives of men.

The role that a belief plays in the life of a man may be a central criterion in identifying that belief as religious or not (although one need not fight a war over it in order for it to play a central role). But defining "religion" is not a simple task, for there are so many different beliefs and practices to which the term seems applicable. This problem of definition, in fact, constitutes one of the problems of the philosophy of religion.

Erich Fromm defines religion as "any system of thought and action shared by a group which gives the individual a frame of orientation and an object of devotion."[1] William Kennick goes further, stating that "an attitude's being religious seems to be a function of its proportion or what we might call its 'weight'. If it assumes a vital, and above all, *pervasive* role in the life of a man or of a society, conditioning, determining, and focusing all or most other attitudes and reactions—those which have as their objects the natural world, cultural institutions, and other men and

[1] Erich Fromm, *Psychoanalysis and Religion* (New Haven: Yale University Press, 1950), p. 21.

other societies and even, or perhaps especially, those attitudes which a man takes toward himself—then we may properly call such an attitude or group of attitudes 'religious'."[2] Accordingly, if religious beliefs are defined as those which play an all-pervasive role in one's life and provide an object (or objects) of devotion, there is no wonder that men feel very strongly about them. But if the above suggested definitions are accepted, then religion would include many different beliefs that we normally distinguish from religious ones, for example, the tenets of Marxism, Nazism, and democracy. These beliefs certainly play all-pervasive roles in the lives of men and even provide objects of devotion. One recent theologian, Paul Tillich, would support this broad definition, for he speaks of God as any object of "ultimate concern." Others would find the definition so broad as to be meaningless or useless.

The fact is that there are many uses or meanings of the terms God and religion, some narrow, some broad. A narrow definition has the disadvantage of arbitrarily ruling out as religious any beliefs except those of a specified group. One finds such definitions not only among lay people but also among scholars in religion. For example, Albert C. Knudson, in arguing that the phrase "Godless religion" is self-contradictory, states that "to give up the belief . . . in divine providence is to turn over to the enemy the innermost citadel of religious faith."[3] Knudson would apparently restrict the term religion to a certain form of theism. For the most part this accurately characterizes religion in the West but not religion as a worldwide phenomenon. Historically at least we have used the term religion to characterize some systems of beliefs and practices in which the notion of a personal God or of divine providence was *not* a part.

Although the broad definition of religion or God avoids this narrow provincialism (it does not rule out the Buddhist or Taoist as being religious), it has the disadvantage of permitting most any belief to count as religious and hence makes it diffcult for one to delineate the subject matter of religion. As indicated, the problem of defining religion itself is a philosophical problem;[4] but since a form of theism, that is, a belief in an omniscient, perfectly good creator of the world, is basic to our Western religious tradition, the selections in this chapter reflect that standpoint.

PHILOSOPHY OF RELIGION AS SUBSTANTIVE BELIEF

Most of us have inherited as a part of our culture a set of religious beliefs. To some individuals, these beliefs pose no special problems. Such people accept the beliefs and live the greater part of their lives without subjecting their beliefs to critical scrutiny. Other individuals find great difficulty in

[2] William Kennick, "The Language of Religion," *The Philosophical Review*, vol. 65 (1956), p. 68.
[3] Albert C. Knudson, *Basic Issues in Christian Thought* (Nashville, Tenn.: Abingdon-Cokesbury Press, 1950), p. 28.
[4] See Chapter 5, "Defining Religious Beliefs," in my book *The Problem of Religious Knowledge* (Englewood Cliffs, N.J.: Prentice-Hall, Inc., 1963).

continuing to accept religious beliefs, at least in the form in which they were taught the beliefs. Is there a God? What is his nature? Is Christ the son of God? Do miracles occur? Do men have souls? Are they immortal? Is there a heaven and a hell? These are some of the questions raised by believer and disbeliever alike, as they seek explanations of their experience and the world in which they live and as they examine their religious heritage. Some respond by denying the existence of God, the occurrence of miracles, the divinity of Christ, the immortality of the soul, and so on. They are generally called religious "skeptics" or "atheists". Others accept certain traditional beliefs but maintain that we do not have adequate evidence either to affirm or to deny these beliefs. They suggest that we simply keep an open mind on such matters. These persons are generally known as religious "agnostics." "Theists" on the other hand, maintain that an affirmative answer to the question of God's existence (as well as to some but not necessarily all the other beliefs) is justified.

PHILOSOPHY OF RELIGION AS ANALYTIC AND CONCEPTUAL

However, believer and disbeliever frequently disagree not merely on the truth of some substantive religious belief but also on what constitutes evidence for or against a belief. The latter disagreement is at a quite different philosophical level, and indeed the basic differences between religious believers and disbelievers are frequently rooted in disagreement over what is taken to be evidence or good grounds for belief. The issue is a matter of one's theory of knowledge or epistemology. Some religious skeptics approach the question of the existence of God entirely from the scientific point of view. The meaning of proof or evidence they define in terms of the canons of reasoning of the scientific method; and not finding proof or evidence of God's existence in the scientific sense, they either deny that God exists or they advocate agnosticism. On the other hand, many religious believers maintain that although God's existence can not be scientifically verified, there is evidence and proof of a nonscientific sort of his existence. Some theists appeal to religious authority, a tradition, or a revealed scripture like the Bible as proof. The authority is seen as one that reveals God's existence and nature. The believer accepts on faith doctrines as revealed through this authority. He implicitly trusts this authority and accepts it as a type of proof. Other theists (see the discussion by James in this chapter) maintain that they have a *direct* revelatory experience of God, which is known as mysticism without an intervening authority such as Scripture. Still others (such as Aquinas and Hume in this chapter) maintain that God's existence can be proven empirically by reference to the existence of design and order in the natural world or to other data. They thus maintain that we can at least have probable proof of his existence. Some maintain that we can prove God's existence without reference to experience at all, simply by analysis and working out the implications of the concept of God itself. (See the selection by Saint Anselm.)

These are fundamentally different senses of proof or evidence. Although religious disagreement is often rooted in the acceptance of such different epistemological appeals, this is not always the case. A believer and a disbeliever may both accept the canons of proof of science and yet disagree on the existence and interpretation of empirical data. But disagreement is frequently traceable to different implicit or explicit theories of knowledge or different accounts of what it means to know something or to prove a belief, or to what constitutes good reasons for holding a belief.

It is at this level that many of the classical and contemporary disputes in philosophy of religion take place. Thus, although St. Thomas Aquinas and John Locke agree that God's existence can be proved by reason, they disagree on the relative importance of reason as opposed to faith and revelation. St. Thomas considers faith a province that cannot be contradicted by reason, whereas Locke insists that faith must always be judged by reason. William James argues (in this chapter) that belief in God can be neither proved nor disproved and must be accepted on pragmatic grounds. Less "risk" is involved if one is a religious believer. Freud, on the other hand, offers a psychoanalytic explanation of belief in God—that it is man's projection of a father image on the world in an effort to gain security. He suggests *not* that this renders belief in God false but that it casts serious doubts on such beliefs, for, in his view, a psychoanalytic explanation of these beliefs renders elaborate theological explanation unnecessary. Similarly, Feuerbach (in this chapter) speaks of belief in God as a human "projection." Kierkegaard argues (see his selection in this chapter) that religious questions, at least for the Christian, must be resolved or settled on a subjective level, that "it is subjectivity that Christianity is concerned with and it is only in subjectivity that its truth exists, if it exists at all; objectively Christianity has absolutely no existence."[5]

More recently, logical positivists have argued that some key religious beliefs are simply meaningless. Basing their thesis on the verifiability principle (which states that a statement is factually meaningful only if it can, in principle, be tested by experience or empirical data), they argue that religious beliefs assert nothing whatsoever. They *cannot* be true or false. Not only the theist but also the atheist and agnostic are mistaken and conceptually confused, for the denial that God exists or the position that we have not enough evidence to decide one way or another presupposes that the statement "God exists" asserts something. But if no empirical evidence can possibly verify or falsify this purported claim, the positivist argues, it is factually meaningless. It may express one's feelings or one's emotions but it *says* nothing. Obviously this kind of scepticism cuts deeper than that represented by either the atheist or the agnostic. It is represented in this chapter by the selection from Antony Flew.

Responses to the position of the logical positivist have gone in several directions. Some philosophers, while apparently accepting the verificationist test of whether a sentence constitutes a factual claim, argue that the positivist's position ignores the possibility of empirical data available after death and that although we cannot verify or falsify religious beliefs in this life, we may be able to in the next life, *if there is one*. (See the selection by

[5] Sören Kierkegaard, *Concluding Unscientific Postscript*, trans. and ed. David Swenson and Walter Lowrie (Princeton: Princeton University Press, 1944), pp. 220–221.

John Hick.) Still others argue that the verificationist test is inadequate as a test of meaning and truth in religion (indeed in science also). They maintain that religion, as a unique area of human experience, must be understood on its own grounds. External and extraneous tests cannot be imposed upon it. In other words, one conceptually errs if one assimilates the logic of religious discourse to the logic of scientific discourse or some other mode of discourse.

These viewpoints are not themselves religious beliefs but beliefs about religious beliefs. They are analyses of certain concepts or terms and of statements or theories in which the concepts are used. They presume to inform us about the meaning and status of a claim (or of certain kinds of claims) and of the kind of evidence and avenue of verification or justification appropriate to it.

Philosophy of religion, then, involves issues on at least three levels: (1) Substantive beliefs, such as the existence of God and his nature, the validity of miracles, immortality, divine moral law, heaven and hell, and souls; (2) theories of the meaning of religious concepts and theories of how religious beliefs may be justified; (3) empirical issues about the existence of certain facts, such as whether Jesus Christ was literally resurrected from the dead, whether life can be created in a test tube, and the like. These are, in principle, empirically determinable questions, on which some religious or theological arguments turn. Concern with questions on levels 2 and 3 is primarily for the sake of solving questions at level 1.

Substantially different answers to theological questions or questions in philosophy of religion on all three levels have been given in the history of thought. A full appreciation of these alternative answers can be achieved only by an analysis and understanding of the beliefs and concepts involved (for example, God, soul, man, heaven, hell, love, divine law, creation, time, revelation, religious experience, mediator, reason, faith). One must also be sensitive to the cultural and scientific contexts or heritage within which religious or theological claims are made and the amount and kind of information available at a given time. One cannot fully appreciate the religious beliefs or systems of great theologians (St. Thomas or Paul Tillich, for example) or of ordinary religious believers without knowledge of this heritage and context. Nor can one rationally judge those beliefs without also assessing the arguments used or presupposed by the religious thinker (which include empirical, metaphysical, and epistemological beliefs).

Issues in philosophy of religion, then, are complex and not easy to resolve, for even the manner and method of resolution is itself one of the issues to be resolved. Disagreements and disputes can occur at any one or on all of the three levels depicted, and the latter is not unusual.

Does this mean that we should despair of the very attempt to philosophize about religious beliefs? The philosopher must answer to this question. A final resolution of the problems in philosophy of religion may perhaps never be attained, for there are always new empirical data and new ways of conceiving of man and his world. But as rational human beings we must meet the challenge of new data and concepts. Indeed, this is the task of each new generation.

SELECTED BIBLIOGRAPHY

Alston, W. P. (ed.). *Religious Belief and Philosophical Thought.* New York, 1963.

Bertocci, Peter. *An Introduction to the Philosophy of Religion.* New York, 1951.

Blackstone, W. T. *The Problem of Religious Knowledge.* New York, 1963.

Braithwaite, R. B. *An Empiricist's View of the Nature of Religious Belief.* Cambridge, 1955.

Clarke, B. L. *Language and Natural Theology.* The Hague, 1965.

Ferré, Frederick. *Language, Logic and God.* London, 1959.

Flew, Antony, and MacIntyre, Alasdair (eds.). *New Essays in Philosophical Theology.* London, 1955.

Hartshorne, Charles, and W. L. Reese. (eds.). *Philosophers Speak of God.* Chicago, 1953.

Hartshorne, Charles. *The Logic of Perfection.* La Salle, Ill., 1962.

Hick, John. *Faith and Knowledge.* Ithaca, N.Y., 1957.

———. *Philosophy of Religion.* Englewood Cliffs, N.J., 1957.

———. *The Existence of God.* New York, 1964.

Hook, Sidney (ed.). *Religious Experience and Truth.* New York, 1961.

Maritian, Jacques. *Approaches to God.* New York, 1954.

Martin, C. B. *Religious Belief.* Ithaca, N.Y., 1959.

Matson, W. I. *The Existence of God.* Ithaca, N.Y., 1965.

Mitchell, Basil (ed.). *Faith and Logic.* London, 1957.

Paton, H. J. *The Modern Predicament.* New York, 1962.

Pike, N. (ed.). *God and Evil.* Englewood Cliffs, N.J., 1964.

Plantinga, Alvin (ed.). *The Ontological Argument.* New York, 1965.

Russell, Bertrand. *Religion and Science.* London, 1935.

Smart, N. *Philosophers and Religious Truth.* Naperville, Ill., 1964.

Smith, Houston. *The Religions of Man.* New York, 1958.

Smith, John (ed.). *Philosophy of Religion.* New York, 1965.

Taylor, A. E. *Does God Exist?* New York, 1947.

ARGUMENTS FOR THE EXISTENCE OF GOD

6 *The Ontological Argument for God's Existence*[*]

ST. ANSELM

St. Anselm of Canterbury (1033–1109), a member of the Benedictine Order, is best known for his ontological argument for the existence of God. His basic writings are the *Monologium, Proslogium,* and *Cur Deus Homo.*

PREFACE

Some time ago, at the urgent request of some of my brethren, I published a brief work,[1] as an example of meditation on the grounds of faith. I wrote it in the role of one who seeks, by silent reasoning with himself, to learn what he does not know. But when I reflected on this little book, and saw that it was put together as a long chain of arguments, I began to ask myself whether *one* argument might possibly be found, resting on no other argument for its proof, but sufficient in itself to prove that God truly exists and that he is the supreme good, needing nothing outside himself, but needful for the being and well-being of all things. I often turned my earnest attention to this problem, and at times I believed that I could put my finger on what I was looking for, but at other times it completely escaped my mind's eye, until finally, in despair, I decided to give up searching for something that seemed impossible to find. But when I tried to put the whole question out of my mind,

[*] From *A Scholastic Miscellany,* edited and translated by Eugene R. Fairweather, Vol. X, Library of Christian Classics. Published simultaneously in Great Britain and the United States of America by S.C.M. Press, Ltd., London, and The Westminster Press, Philadelphia. First published in 1956. Used by permission.
[1] The *Monologion,* probably Anselm's first work, was written at Bec in the second half of 1076 (cf. Landgraf, *Einführung,* 53). Text in Schmitt, I, 7–87.

so as to avoid crowding out other matters, with which I might make some progress, by this useless preoccupation, then, despite my unwillingness and resistance, it began to force itself on me more persistently than ever. Then, one day, when I was worn out by my vigorous resistance to the obsession, the solution I had ceased to hope for presented itself to me, in the very turmoil of my thoughts, so that I enthusiastically embraced the idea which, in my disquiet, I had spurned.

I thought that the proof I was so glad to find would please some readers if it were written down. Consequently, I have written the little work that follows, dealing with this and one or two other matters, in the role of one who strives to raise his mind to the contemplation of God and seeks to understand what he believes. Neither this essay nor the other one I have already mentioned really seemed to me to deserve to be called a book or to bear an author's name; at the same time, I felt that they could not be published without some title that might encourage anyone into whose hands they fell to read them, and so I gave each of them a title. The first I called *An Example of Meditation on the Grounds of Faith*, and the second *Faith Seeking Understanding*.

But when both of them had been copied under these titles by a number of people, I was urged by many people—and especially by Hugh, the reverend archbishop of Lyons, apostolic legate in Gaul, who ordered this with apostolic authority—to attach my name to them. In order to do this more fittingly, I have named the first *Monologion* (or *Soliloquy*), and the second *Proslogion* (or *Address*).

CHAPTER II

God Truly Is

And so, O Lord, since thou givest understanding to faith, give me to understand—as far as thou knowest it to be good for me—that thou dost exist, as we believe, and that thou art what we believe thee to be. Now we believe that thou art a being than which none greater can be thought. Or can it be that there is no such being, since "the fool hath said in his heart, 'There is no God' "? But when this same fool hears what I am saying—"A being than which none greater can be thought"—he understands what he hears, and what he understands is in his understanding, even if he does not understand that it exists. For it is one thing for an object to be in the understanding, and another thing to understand that it exists. When a painter considers beforehand what he is going to paint, he has it in his understanding, but he does not suppose that what he has not yet painted already exists. But when he has painted it, he both has it in his understanding and understands that what he has now produced exists. Even the fool, then, must be convinced that a being than which none greater can be thought exists at least in his understanding, since when he hears this he understands it, and whatever is understood is in the understanding. But clearly that than which a greater cannot be thought cannot exist in the understanding alone. For if it is actually in the understanding alone, it can be thought of as existing also in reality, and this is greater. Therefore, if that than which a greater cannot be thought is in the understanding alone, this same thing than which a greater cannot be thought is that than which a greater can be thought. But obviously this is impossible. Without doubt, therefore, there exists, both in the understanding and in reality, something than which a greater cannot be thought.

CHAPTER III

God Cannot Be Thought of as Nonexistent

And certainly it exists so truly that it cannot be thought of as nonexistent. For something can be thought of as existing, which cannot be thought of as not existing, and this is greater than that which *can* be thought of as not existing. Thus, if that than which a greater cannot be thought can be thought of as not existing, this very thing than which a greater cannot be thought is *not* that than which a greater cannot be thought. But this is contradictory. So, then, there truly is a being than which a greater cannot be thought—so truly that it cannot even be thought of as not existing.

And *thou* art this being, O Lord our God. Thou so truly art, then, O Lord my God, that thou canst not even be thought of as not existing. And this is right. For if some mind could think of something better than thou, the creature would rise above the Creator and judge its Creator; but this is altogether absurd. And indeed, whatever is, except thyself alone, can be thought of as not existing. Thou alone, therefore, of all beings, hast being in the truest and highest sense, since no other being so truly exists, and thus every other being has less being. Why, then, has "the fool said in his heart, 'There is no God,' " when it is so obvious to the rational mind that, of all beings, thou dost exist supremely? Why indeed, unless it is that he is a stupid fool?

CHAPTER IV

How the Fool Has Said in His Heart What Cannot Be Thought

But how did he manage to say in his heart what he could not think? Or how is it that he was unable to think what he said in his heart? After all, to say in one's heart and to think are the same thing. Now if it is true—or, rather, since it is true—that he thought it, because he said it in his heart, but did not say it in his heart, since he could not think it, it is clear that something can be said in one's heart or thought in more than one way. For we think of a thing, in one sense, when we think of the word that signifies it, and in another sense, when we understand the very thing itself. Thus, in the first sense God can be thought of as nonexistent, but in the second sense this is quite impossible. For no one who understands what God is can think that God does not exist, even though he says these words in his heart— perhaps without any meaning, perhaps with some quite extraneous meaning. For God is that than which a greater cannot be thought, and whoever understands this rightly must understand that he exists in such a way that he cannot be nonexistent even in thought. He, therefore, who understands that God thus exists cannot think of him as nonexistent.

Thanks be to thee, good Lord, thanks be to thee, because I now understand by thy light what I formerly believed by thy gift, so that even if I were to refuse to believe in thy existence, I could not fail to understand its truth.

AN EXCERPT FROM THE AUTHOR'S REPLY TO THE CRITICISMS OF GAUNILO

3. But, you say, suppose that someone imagined an island in the ocean, surpassing all lands in its fertility. Because of the difficulty, or rather the impossibility, of finding something that does not exist, it might well be called "Lost Island." By reasoning like yours, he might then say that we cannot doubt that it truly exists in reality, because anyone can easily conceive it from a verbal description.[2] I state confidently that if anyone discovers something for me, other than that "than which a greater cannot be thought," existing either in reality or in thought alone, to which the logic of my argument can be applied, I shall find his lost island and give it to him, never to be lost again. But it now seems obvious that this being than which a greater cannot be thought cannot be thought of as nonexistent, because it exists by such a sure reason of truth. For otherwise it would not exist at all. In short, if anyone says that he thinks it does not exist, I say that when he thinks this, he either thinks of something than which a greater cannot be thought or he does not think. If he does not think, he does not think of what he is not thinking of as nonexistent. But if he does think, then he thinks of something which cannot be thought of as nonexistent. For if it could be thought of as nonexistent, it could be thought of as having a beginning and an end. But this is impossible. Therefore, if anyone thinks of it, he thinks of something that cannot even be thought of as nonexistent. But he who thinks of this does not think that it does not exist; if he did, he would think what cannot be thought. Therefore, that than which a greater cannot be thought cannot be thought of as nonexistent.

[2] Cf. Gaunilo, *Pro insipiente*, 6 (Schmitt, I, 128).

4. You say, moreover, that when it is said that the highest reality cannot be *thought of* as nonexistent, it would perhaps be better to say that it cannot be *understood* as nonexistent, or even as possibly nonexistent.[3] But it is more correct to say, as I said, that it cannot be thought. For if I had said that the reality itself cannot be understood not to exist, perhaps you yourself, who say that according to the very definition of the term what is false cannot be understood,[4] would object that nothing that is can be understood as non-existent. For it is false to say that what exists does not exist. Therefore it would not be peculiar to God to be unable to be understood as nonexistent.[5] But if some one of the things that most certainly are can be understood as nonexistent, other certain things can similarly be understood as nonexistent. But this objection cannot be applied to "thinking," if it is rightly considered. For although none of the things that exist can be understood not to exist, still they can all be thought of as nonexistent, except that which most fully is. For all those things—and only those—which have a beginning or end or are composed of parts can be thought of as nonexistent, along with anything that does not exist as a whole anywhere or at any time (as I have already said).[6] But the only being that cannot be thought of as nonexistent is that in which no thought finds beginning or end or composition of parts, but which any thought finds as a whole, always and everywhere.

You must realize, then, that you can think of yourself as nonexistent, even while you know most certainly that you exist. I am surprised that you said you did not know this.[7] For we think of many things as nonexistent when we know that they exist, and of many things as existent when we know that they do not exist—all this not by a real judgment, but by imagining that what we think is so. And indeed, we can think of something as nonexistent, even while we know that it exists, because we are able at the same time to think the one and know the other. And yet we cannot think of it as nonexistent, while we know that it exists, because we cannot think of something as at once existent and nonexistent. Therefore, if anyone distinguishes these two senses of the statement in this way, he will understand that nothing, as long as it is known to exist, can be thought of as nonexistent, and that whatever exists, except that than which a greater cannot be thought, can be thought of as nonexistent, even when it is known to exist. So, then, it is peculiar to God to be unable to be thought of as nonexistent, and nevertheless many things, as long as they exist, cannot be thought of as nonexistent. I think that the way in which it can still be said that God is thought of as non-existent is stated adequately in the little book itself.[8]

[3] *Ibid.*, 7 (I, 129).
[4] *Ibid.*
[5] *Ibid.*
[6] *Responsio*, 1 (I, 131 f.).
[7] Gaunilo, *loc. cit.*
[8] Cf. *Proslogion*, Chapter IV.

7 Five Proofs of God's Existence*

ST. THOMAS AQUINAS

St. Thomas Aquinas (1226–1274) was the founder of a philosophical tradition now known as Thomism, which is the official philosophy of the Roman Catholic Church. His basic works are *Summa Theologica* and *Summa Contra Gentiles* where he systematically develops a kind of Christianized Aristotelianism.

THE EXISTENCE OF GOD CAN BE PROVED IN FIVE WAYS

The first and more manifest way is the argument from motion. It is certain, and evident to our senses, that in the world some things are in motion. Now whatever is moved is moved by another, for nothing can be moved except it is in potentiality to that towards which it is moved; whereas a thing moves inasmuch as it is in act. For motion is nothing else than the reduction of something from potentiality to actuality. But nothing can be reduced from potentiality to actuality, except by something in a state of actuality. Thus that which is actually hot, as fire, makes wood, which is potentially hot, to be actually hot, and thereby moves and changes it. Now it is not possible that the same thing should be at once in actuality and potentiality in the same respect, but only in different respects. For what is actually hot cannot simultaneously be potentially hot; but it is simultaneously potentially cold. It is therefore impossible that in the same respect and in the same way a thing should be both mover and moved, *i.e.*, that it should move itself. Therefore, whatever is moved must be moved by another. If that by which it is moved be itself moved, then this also must needs be moved by another, and that by another again. But this cannot go on to infinity, because then there would be no first mover, and, consequently, no other mover seeing that subsequent movers move only inasmuch as they are moved by the first mover; as the staff moves only because it is moved by the hand. Therefore it is necessary to arrive at a first mover, moved by no other; and this everyone understands to be God.

The second way is from the nature of efficient cause. In the world of sen-

---

* From *Basic Writings of St. Thomas Aquinas*, ed. Anton C. Pegis (New York: Random House, Inc., 1945). Reprinted by permission of the publisher.

sible things we find there is an order of efficient causes. There is no case known (neither is it, indeed, possible) in which a thing is found to be the efficient cause of itself; for so it would be prior to itself, which is impossible. Now in efficient causes it is not possible to go on to infinity, because in all efficient causes following in order, the first is the cause of the intermediate cause, and the intermediate is the cause of the ultimate cause, whether the intermediate cause be several, or one only. Now to take away the cause is to take away the effect. Therefore, if there be no first cause among efficient causes, there will be no ultimate, nor any intermediate, cause. But if in efficient causes it is possible to go on to infinity, there will be no first efficient cause, neither will there be an ultimate effect, nor any intermediate efficient causes; all of which is plainly false. Therefore it is necessary to admit a first efficient cause, to which everyone gives the name of God.

The third way is taken from possibility and necessity, and runs thus. We find in nature things that are possible to be and not to be, since they are found to be generated, and to be corrupted, and consequently, it is possible for them to be and not to be. But it is impossible for these always to exist, for that which can not-be at some time is not. Therefore, if everything can not-be, then at one time there was nothing in existence. Now if this were true, even now there would be nothing in existence, because that which does not exist begins to exist only through something already existing. Therefore, if at one time nothing was in existence, it would have been impossible for anything to have begun to exist; and thus even now nothing would be in existence— which is absurd. Therefore, not all beings are merely possible, but there must exist something the existence of which is necessary. But every necessary thing either has its necessity caused by another, or not. Now it is impossible to go on to infinity in necessary things which have their necessity caused by an- other, as has been already proved in regard to efficient causes. Therefore we cannot but admit the existence of some being having of itself its own neces- sity, and not receiving it from another, but rather causing in others their necessity. This all men speak of as God.

The fourth way is taken from the gradation to be found in things. Among beings there are some more and some less good, true, noble, and the like. But *more* and *less* are predicated of different things according as they re- semble in their different ways something which is the maximum, as a thing is said to be hotter according as it more nearly resembles that which is hottest; so that there is something which is truest, something best, something noblest, and, consequently, something which is most being, for those things that are greatest in truth are greatest in being, as it is written in *Metaph.* ii. Now the maximum in any genus is the cause of all in that genus, as fire, which is the maximum of heat, is the cause of all hot things, as is said in the same book. Therefore there must also be something which is to all beings the cause of their being, goodness, and every other perfection; and this we call God.

The fifth way is taken from the governance of the world. We see that

8 The Pragmatic Argument for the Existence of God (The Will to Believe)*

WILLIAM JAMES

William James (1842–1910) was influential both as a psychologist and philosopher. Author of numerous articles, some of his important books include *Pragmatism: A New Name for Some Old Ways of Thinking*, *Principles of Psychology*, and *Varieties of Religious Experience*. He is known as a leading American exponent of pragmatism.

In the recently published Life by Leslie Stephen of his brother, Fitz-James, there is an account of a school to which the latter went when he was a boy. The teacher, a certain Mr. Guest, used to converse with his pupils in this wise: "Gurney, what is the difference between justification and sanctification? —Stephen, prove the omnipotence of God!" etc. In the midst of our Harvard freethinking and indifference we are prone to imagine that here at your good old orthodox College conversation continues to be somewhat upon this order; and to show you that we at Harvard have not lost all interest in these vital subjects, I have brought with me to-night something like a sermon on justification by faith to read to you,—I mean an essay in justification *of* faith, a defence of our right to adopt a believing attitude in religious matters, in spite of the fact that our merely logical intellect may not have been coerced. 'The Will to Believe,' accordingly, is the title of my paper.

I have long defended to my own students the lawfulness of voluntarily adopted faith; but as soon as they have got well imbued with the logical spirit, they have as a rule refused to admit my contention to be lawful philosophically, even though in point of fact they were personally all the time chock-full of some faith or other themselves. I am all the while, however, so profoundly convinced that my own position is correct, that your invitation has seemed to me a good occasion to make my statements more clear. Perhaps your minds will be more open than those with which I have hitherto had to deal. I will be as little technical as I can, though I must begin by setting up some technical distinctions that will help us in the end.

* An Address to the Philosophical Clubs of Yale and Brown Universities. Published in the *New World*, June, 1896.

Let us give the name of *hypothesis* to anything that may be proposed to our belief; and just as the electricians speak of live and dead wires, let us speak of any hypothesis as either *live* or *dead*. A live hypothesis is one which appeals as a real possibility to him to whom it is proposed. If I ask you to believe in the Mahdi, the notion makes no electric connection with your nature,—it refuses to scintillate with any credibility at all. As an hypothesis it is completely dead. To an Arab, however (even if he be not one of the Mahdi's followers), the hypothesis is among the mind's possibilities: it is alive. This shows that deadness and liveness in an hypothesis are not intrinsic properties, but relations to the individual thinker. They are measured by his willingness to act. The maximum of liveness in an hypothesis means willingness to act irrevocably. Practically, that means belief; but there is some believing tendency wherever there is willingness to act at all.

Next, let us call the decision between two hypotheses an *option*. Options may be of several kinds. They may be—1, *living* or *dead*; 2, *forced or avoidable*; 3, *momentous* or *trivial*; and for our purposes we may call an option a *genuine* option when it is of the forced, living, and momentous kind.

1. A living option is one in which both hypotheses are live ones. If I say to you: "Be a theosophist or be a Mohammedan," it is probably a dead option, because for you neither hypothesis is likely to be alive. But if I say: "Be an agnostic or be a Christian," it is otherwise: trained as you are, each hypothesis makes some appeal, however small, to your belief.

2. Next, if I say to you: "Choose between going out with your umbrella or without it," I do not offer you a genuine option, for it is not forced. You can easily avoid it by not going out at all. Similarly, if I say, "Either love me or hate me," "Either call my theory true or call it false," your option is avoidable. You may remain indifferent to me, neither loving nor hating, and you may decline to offer any judgment as to my theory. But if I say, "Either accept this truth or go without it," I put on you a forced option, for there is no standing place outside of the alternative. Every dilemma based on a complete logical disjunction, with no possibility of not choosing, is an option of this forced kind.

3. Finally, if I were Dr. Nansen and proposed to you to join my North Pole expedition, your option would be momentous; for this would probably be your only similar opportunity, and your choice now would either exclude you from the North Pole sort of immortality altogether or put at least the chance of it into your hands. He who refuses to embrace a unique opportunity loses the prize as surely as if he tried and failed. *Per contra*, the option is trivial when the opportunity is not unique, when the stake is insignificant, or when the decision is reversible if it later prove unwise. Such trivial options abound in the scientific life. A chemist finds an hypothesis live enough to spend a year in its verification: he believes in it to that extent. But if his experiments prove inconclusive either way, he is quit for his loss of time, no vital harm being done.

The thesis I defend is, briefly stated, this: *Our passional nature not only lawfully may, but must, decide an option between propositions, whenever it is a genuine option that cannot by its nature be decided on intellectual grounds; for to say, under such circumstances, "Do not decide, but leave the question open," is itself a passional decision,—just like deciding yes or no,— and is attended with the same risk of losing the truth.* The thesis thus abstractly expressed will, I trust, soon become quite clear.

One more point, small but important, and our preliminaries are done. There are two ways of looking at our duty in the matter of opinion,—ways entirely different, and yet ways about whose difference the theory of knowledge seems hitherto to have shown very little concern. *We must know the truth;* and *we must avoid error,*—these are our first and great commandments as would-be knowers; but they are not two ways of stating an identical commandment, they are two separable laws. Although it may indeed happen that when we believe the truth A, we escape as an incidental consequence from believing the falsehood B, it hardly ever happens that by merely disbelieving B we necessarily believe A. We may in escaping B fall into believing other falsehoods, C or D, just as bad as B; or we may escape B by not believing anything at all, not even A.

Believe truth! Shun error!—these, we see, are two materially different laws; and by choosing between them we may end by coloring differently our whole intellectual life. We may regard the chase for truth as paramount, and the avoidance of error as secondary; or we may, on the other hand, treat the avoidance of error as more imperative, and let truth take its chance. Clifford, in the instructive passage which I have quoted, exhorts us to the latter course. Believe nothing, he tells us, keep your mind in suspense forever, rather than by closing it on insufficient evidence incur the awful risk of believing lies. You, on the other hand, may think that the risk of being in error is a very small matter when compared with the blessings of real knowledge, and be ready to be duped many times in your investigation rather than postpone indefinitely the chance of guessing true. I myself find it impossible to go with Clifford. We must remember that these feelings of our duty about either truth or error are in any case only expressions of our passional life. Biologically considered, our minds are as ready to grind out falsehood as veracity, and he who says, "Better go without belief forever than believe a lie!" merely shows his own preponderant private horror of becoming a dupe. He may be critical of many of his desires and fears, but this fear he slavishly obeys. He cannot imagine any one questioning its binding force. For my own part, I have also a horror of being duped; but I can believe that worse things than being duped may happen to a man in this world: so Clifford's exhortation has to my ears a thoroughly fantastic sound. It is like a general informing his soldiers that it is better to keep out of battle forever than to risk a single wound. Not so are victories either over enemies or over nature gained. Our errors are surely not such awfully solemn things. In a world where we are so certain to incur them in spite of all our caution, a certain lightness of heart seems healthier than this excessive nervousness on their behalf. At any rate, it seems the fittest thing for the empiricist philosopher.

And now, after all this introduction, let us go straight at our question. I have said, and now repeat it, that not only as a matter of fact do we find our passional nature influencing us in our opinions, but that there are some options between opinions in which this influence must be regarded both as an inevitable and as a lawful determinant of our choice.

I fear hear that some of you my hearers will begin to scent danger, and lend an inhospitable ear. Two first steps of passion you have indeed had to admit as necessary,—we must think so as to avoid dupery, and we must think so as to gain truth; but the surest path to those ideal consummations, you will probably consider, is from now onwards to take no further passional step.

Well, of course, I agree as far as the facts will allow. Wherever the option between losing truth and gaining it is not momentous, we can throw the chance of *gaining truth* away, and at any rate save ourselves from any chance of *believing falsehood*, by not making up our minds at all till objective evidence has come. In scientific questions, this is almost always the case; and even in human affairs in general, the need of acting is seldom so urgent that a false belief to act on is better than no belief at all. Law courts, indeed, have to decide on the best evidence attainable for the moment, because a judge's duty is to make law as well as to ascertain it, and (as a learned judge once said to me) few cases are worth spending much time over: the great thing is to have them decided on *any* acceptable principle, and got out of the way. But in our dealings with objective nature we obviously are recorders, not makers, of the truth; and decisions for the mere sake of deciding promptly and getting on to the next business would be wholly out of place. Throughout the breadth of physical nature facts are what they are quite independently of us, and seldom is there any such hurry about them that the risks of being duped by believing a premature theory need be faced. The questions here are always trivial options, the hypotheses are hardly living (at any rate not living for us spectators), the choice between believing truth or falsehood is seldom forced. The attitude of sceptical balance is therefore the absolutely wise one if we would escape mistakes. What difference, indeed, does it make to most of us whether we have or have not a theory of the Röntgen rays, whether we believe or not in mind-stuff, or have a conviction about the causality of conscious states? It makes no difference. Such options are not forced on us. On every account it is better not to make them, but still keep weighing reasons *pro et contra* with an indifferent hand.

I speak, of course, here of the purely judging mind. For purposes of discovery such indifference is to be less highly recommended, and science would be far less advanced than she is if the passionate desires of individuals to get their own faiths confirmed had been kept out of the game. See for example the sagacity which Spencer and Weismann now display. On the other hand, if you want an absolute duffer in an investigation, you must, after all, take the man who has no interest whatever in its results: he is the warranted incapable, the positive fool. The most useful investigator, because the most sensitive observer, is always he whose eager interest in one side of the question is balanced by an equally keen nervousness lest he become deceived. Science has organized this nervousness into a regular *technique*, her so-called method of verification; and she has fallen so deeply in love with the method that one may even say she has ceased to care for truth by itself at all. It is only truth as technically verified that interests her. The truth of truths might come in merely affirmative form, and she would decline to touch it. Such truth as that, she might repeat with Clifford, would be stolen in defiance of her duty to mankind. Human passions, however, are stronger than technical rules. "Le cœur a ses raisons," as Pascal says, "que la raison ne connaît pas"; and however indifferent to all but the bare rules of the game the umpire, the abstract intellect, may be, the concrete players who furnish him the materials to judge of are usually, each one of them, in love with some pet 'live hypothesis' of his own. Let us agree, however, that wherever there is no forced option, the dispassionately judicial intellect with no pet hypothesis, saving us, as it does, from dupery at any rate, ought to be our ideal.

The question next arises: Are there not somewhere forced options in our speculative questions, and can we (as men who may be interested at least as much in positively gaining truth as in merely escaping dupery) always wait with impunity till the coercive evidence shall have arrived? It seems *a priori* improbable that the truth should be so nicely adjusted to our needs and powers as that. In the great boardinghouse of nature, the cakes and the butter and the syrup seldom come out so even and leave the plates so clean. Indeed, we should view them with scientific suspicion if they did.

Moral questions immediately present themselves as questions whose solution cannot wait for sensible proof. A moral question is a question not of what sensibly exists, but of what is good, or would be good if it did exist. Science can tell us what exists; but to compare the *worths*, both of what exists and of what does not exist, we must consult not science, but what Pascal calls our heart. Science herself consults her heart when she lays it down that the infinite ascertainment of fact and correction of false belief are the supreme goods for man. Challenge the statement, and science can only repeat it oracularly, or else prove it by showing that such ascertainment and correction bring man all sorts of other goods which man's heart in turn declares. The question of having moral beliefs at all or not having them is decided by our will. Are our moral preferences true or false, or are they only odd biological phenomena, making things good or bad for *us*, but in themselves indifferent? How can your pure intellect decide? If your heart does not *want* a world of moral reality, your head will assuredly never make you believe in one. Mephistophelian scepticism, indeed, will satisfy the head's play-instincts much

better than any rigorous idealism can. Some men (even at the student age)
are so naturally cool-hearted that the moralistic hypothesis never has for them
any pungent life, and in their supercilious presence the hot young moralist
always feels strangely ill at ease. The appearance of knowingness is on their
side, of *naïveté* and gullibility on his. Yet, in the inarticulate heart of him,
he clings to it that he is not a dupe, and that there is a realm in which (as
Emerson says) all their wit and intellectual superiority is no better than the
cunning of a fox. Moral scepticism can no more be refuted or proved by logic
than intellectual scepticism can. When we stick to it that there *is* truth
(be it of either kind), we do so with our whole nature, and resolve to stand
or fall by the results. The sceptic with his whole nature adopts the doubting
attitude; but which of us is the wiser, Omniscience only knows.

Turn now from these wide questions of good to a certain class of questions
of fact, questions concerning personal relations, states of mind between one
man and another. *Do you like me or not?*—for example. Whether you do or
not depends, in countless instances, on whether I meet you half-way, am willing to assume that you must like me, and show you trust and expectation.
The previous faith on my part in your liking's existence is in such cases what
makes your liking come. But if I stand aloof, and refuse to budge an inch
until I have objective evidence, until you shall have done something apt, as
the absolutists say, *ad extorquendum assensum meum*, ten to one your liking
never comes. How many women's hearts are vanquished by the mere sanguine
insistence of some man that they *must* love him! he will not consent to the
hypothesis that they cannot. The desire for a certain kind of truth here brings
about that special truth's existence; and so it is in innumerable cases of other
sorts. Who gains promotions, boons, appointments, but the man in whose
life they are seen to play the part of live hypotheses, who discounts them,
sacrifices other things for their sake before they have come, and takes risks
for them in advance? His faith acts on the powers above him as a claim, and
creates its own verification.

A social organism of any sort whatever, large or small, is what it is because
each member proceeds to his own duty with a trust that the other members
will simultaneously do theirs. Wherever a desired result is achieved by the
co-operation of many independent persons, its existence as a fact is a pure
consequence of the precursive faith in one another of those immediately concerned. A government, an army, a commercial system, a ship, a college, an
athletic team, all exist on this condition, without which not only is nothing
achieved, but nothing is even attempted. A whole train of passengers (individually brave enough) will be looted by a few highwaymen, simply because
the latter can count on one another, while each passenger fears that if he
makes a movement of resistance, he will be shot before any one else backs
him up. If we believed that the whole car-full would rise at once with us,
we should each severally rise, and train-robbing would never even be attempted. There are, then, cases where a fact cannot come at all unless a

preliminary faith exists in its coming. *And where faith in a fact can help create the fact,* that would be an insane logic which should say that faith running ahead of scientific evidence is the 'lowest kind of immorality' into which a thinking being can fall. Yet such is the logic by which our scientific absolutists pretend to regulate our lives! In truths dependent on our personal action, then, faith based on desire is certainly a lawful and possibly an indispensable thing.

But now, it will be said, these are all childish human cases, and have nothing to do with great cosmical matters, like the question of religious faith. Let us then pass on to that. Religions differ so much in their accidents that in discussing the religious question we must make it very generic and broad. What then do we now mean by the religious hypothesis? Science says things are; morality says some things are better than other things; and religion says essentially two things.

First, she says that the best things are the more eternal things, the overlapping things, the things in the universe that throw the last stone, so to speak, and say the final word. "Perfection is eternal,"—this phrase of Charles Secrétan seems a good way of putting this first affirmation of religion, an affirmation which obviously cannot yet be verified scientifically at all.

The second affirmation of religion is that we are better off even now if we believe her first affirmation to be true.

Now, let us consider what the logical elements of this situation are *in case the religious hypothesis in both its branches be really true.* (Of course, we must admit that possibility at the outset. If we are to discuss the question at all, it must involve a living option. If for any of you religion be a hypothesis that cannot, by any living possibility be true, then you need go no farther. I speak to the 'saving remnant' alone.) So proceeding, we see, first, that religion offers itself as a *momentous* option. We are supposed to gain, even now, by our belief, and to lose by our non-belief, a certain vital good. Secondly, religion is a *forced* option, so far as that good goes. We cannot escape the issue by remaining sceptical and waiting for more light, because, although we do avoid error in that way *if religion be untrue,* we lose the good, *if it be true,* just as certainly as if we positively chose to disbelieve. It is as if a man should hesitate indefinitely to ask a certain woman to marry him because he was not perfectly sure that she would prove an angel after he brought her home. Would he not cut himself off from that particular angel-possibility as decisively as if he went and married some one else? Scepticism, then, is not avoidance of option; it is option of a certain particular kind of risk. *Better risk loss of truth than chance of error,*—that is your faith-vetoer's exact position. He is actively playing his stake as much as the believer is; he is backing the field against the religious hypothesis, just as the believer is backing the religious hypothesis against the field. To preach scepticism to us as a duty until 'sufficient evidence' for religion be found, is tantamount therefore to telling us, when in presence of the religious hypothesis, that to yield to our fear of its being error is wiser and better than to yield to our hope that it may be true. It is not intellect against all passions, then; it is only intellect with one passion laying down its law. And by what, forsooth, is the supreme wisdom of this passion warranted? Dupery for dupery, what proof is there that dupery through hope is so much worse than dupery through fear? I, for one, can see no proof; and I simply refuse obedience to the scientist's command to imitate his kind of option, in a case where my own stake is important enough to give me the right to choose my own form of risk. If religion be true and the evidence for it be still insufficient, I do not wish, by putting your extinguisher upon my nature (which feels to me as if it had after all some business in this matter), to forfeit my sole chance in life of getting upon the winning side,—that chance depending, of course, on my willingness to run the risk of acting as if my passional need of taking the world religiously might be prophetic and right.

All this is on the supposition that it really may be prophetic and right, and that, even to us who are discussing the matter, religion is a live hypothesis which may be true. Now, to most of us religion comes in a still further way that makes a veto on our active faith even more illogical. The more perfect and more eternal aspect of the universe is represented in our religions as having personal form. The universe is no longer a mere *It* to us, but a *Thou*, if we are religious; and any relation that may be possible from person to person might be possible here. For instance, although in one sense we are passive portions of the universe, in another we show a curious autonomy, as if we were small active centres on our own account. We feel, too, as if the appeal of religion to us were made to our own active good-will, as if evidence might be forever withheld from us unless we met the hypothesis halfway. To take a trivial illustration: just as a man who in a company of gentlemen made no advances, asked a warrant for every concession, and believed no one's word without proof, would cut himself off by such churlishness from all the social rewards that a more trusting spirit would earn,—so here, one who should shut himself up in snarling logicality and try to make the gods extort his recognition willy-nilly, or not get it at all, might cut himself off forever from his only opportunity of making the gods' acquaintance. This feeling, forced on us we know not whence, that by obstinately believing that there are gods (although not to do so would be so easy both for our logic and our life) we are doing the universe the deepest service we can, seems part of the living essence of the religious hypothesis. If the hypothesis *were* true in all its parts, including this one, then pure intellectualism, with its veto on our making willing advances, would be an absurdity; and some participation of our sympathetic nature would be logically required. I, therefore, for one, cannot see my way to accepting the agnostic rules for truth-seeking, or wilfully agree to keep my willing nature out of the game. I cannot do so for this plain reason, that *a rule of thinking which would absolutely prevent me from acknowledging certain kinds of truth if those kinds of truth were really there, would be an irrational rule*. That for me is the long and short of the formal logic of the situation, no matter what the kinds of truth might materially be.

I confess I do not see how this logic can be escaped. But sad experience makes me fear that some of you may still shrink from radically saying with me, *in abstracto*, that we have the right to believe at our own risk any hypothesis that is live enough to tempt our will. I suspect, however, that if this is so, it is because you have got away from the abstract logical point of view altogether, and are thinking (perhaps without realizing it) of some particular religious hypothesis which for you is dead. The freedom to 'believe what we will' you apply to the case of some patent superstition; and the faith you think of is the faith defined by the schoolboy when he said, "Faith is when you believe something that you know ain't true." I can only repeat that this is misapprehension. *In concreto*, the freedom to believe can only cover living options which the intellect of the individual cannot by itself resolve; and living options never seem absurdities to him who has them to consider. When I look at the religious question as it really puts itself to concrete men, and when I think of all the possibilities which both practically and theoretically it involves, then this command that we shall put a stopper on our heart, instincts, and courage, and *wait*—acting of course meanwhile more or less as if religion were *not* true[47]—till doomsday, or till such time as our intellect and senses working together may have raked in evidence enough,—this command, I say, seems to me the queerest idol ever manufactured in the philosophic cave. Were we scholastic absolutists, there might be more excuse. If we had an infallible intellect with its objective certitudes, we might feel ourselves disloyal to such a perfect organ of knowledge in not trusting to it exclusively, in not waiting for its releasing word. But if we are empiricists, if we believe that no bell in us tolls to let us know for certain when truth is in our grasp, then it seems a piece of idle fantasticality to preach so solemnly our duty of waiting for the bell. Indeed we *may* wait if we will,—I hope you do not think that I am denying that,—but if we do so, we do so at our peril as much as if we believed. In either case we *act*, taking our life in our hands. No one of us ought to issue vetoes to the other, nor should we bandy words of abuse. We ought, on the contrary, delicately and profoundly to respect one another's mental freedom: then only shall we bring about the intellectual republic; then only shall we have that spirit of inner tolerance without which all our outer tolerance is soulless, and which is empiricism's glory; then only shall we live and let live, speculative as well as in practical things.

I began by a reference to Fitz-James Stephen; let me end by a quotation from him. "What do you think of yourself? What do you think of the world? . . . These are questions with which all must deal as it seems good to them. They are riddles of the Sphinx, and in some way or other we must deal with them. . . . In all important transactions of life we have to take a leap in the dark. . . . If we decide to leave the riddles unanswered, that is a choice; if we waver in our answer, that, too, is a choice: but whatever choice we make, we make it at our peril. If a man chooses to turn his back altogether on God and the future, no one can prevent him; no one can show beyond reasonable doubt that he is mistaken. If a man thinks otherwise and acts as he thinks, I do not see that any one can prove that *he* is mistaken. Each must act as he thinks best; and if he is wrong, so much the worse for him. We stand on a mountain pass in the midst of whirling snow and blinding mist, through which we get glimpses now and then of paths which may be deceptive. If we stand still we shall be frozen to death. If we take the wrong road we shall be dashed to pieces. We do not certainly know whether there is any right one. What must we do? 'Be strong and of a good courage.' Act for the best, hope for the best, and take what comes. . . . If death ends all, we cannot meet death better."

9 Religion as Subjective Truth[*]

SÖREN KIERKEGAARD

Sören Kierkegaard (1813–1855) is generally recognized as one of the founders of the philosophy of existentialism. In his philosophical-theological works, *Either-Or, Concluding Unscientific Postscript,* and *Philosophical Fragments,* he rejected abstract speculation as an adequate basis for a Christian philosophy.

Whoever therefore attempts to demonstrate the existence of God (except in the sense of clarifying the concept, and without the *reservatio finalis* noted above, that the existence emerges from the demonstration by a leap) proves in lieu thereof something else, something which at times perhaps does not need a proof, and in any case needs none better; for the fool says in his heart that there is no God, but whoever says in his heart or to men: Wait just a little and I will prove it—what a rare man of wisdom is he! If in the moment of beginning his proof it is not absolutely undetermined whether God exists or not, he does not prove it; and if it is thus undetermined in the beginning he will never come to begin, partly from fear of failure, since God perhaps does not exist, and partly because he has nothing with which to begin.—A project of this kind would scarcely have been undertaken by the ancients. Socrates at least, who is credited with having put forth the physico-teleological proof for God's existence, did not go about it in any such manner. He always presupposes God's existence, and under this presupposition seeks to interpenetrate nature with the idea of purpose. Had he been asked why he pursued this method, he would doubtless have explained that he lacked the courage to venture out upon so perilous a voyage of discovery without having made sure of God's existence behind him. At the word of God he casts his net as if to catch the idea of purpose; for nature herself finds many means of frightening the inquirer, and distracts him by many a digression.

* From *Philosophical Fragments,* by Sören Kierkegaard, originally translated by David F. Swenson, translation revised by Howard V. Hong (Copyright © 1936, 1962 by Princeton University Press), pp. 34 and 35. And from *Concluding Unscientific Postscript,* by Sören Kierkegaard, transl. by David F. Swenson and Walter Lowrie, for the American Scandinavian Foundation (Copyright 1941 by Princeton University Press; Princeton Paperback 1968), pp. 177–189. Reprinted by permission of the Princeton University Press and The American Scandinavian Foundation.

SUBJECTIVITY

Truth Is Subjectivity

In an attempt to make clear the difference of way that exists between an objective and a subjective reflection, I shall now proceed to show how a subjective reflection makes its way inwardly in inwardness. Inwardness in an existing subject culminates in passion; corresponding to passion in the subject the truth becomes a paradox; and the fact that the truth becomes a paradox is rooted precisely in its having a relationship to an existing subject. Thus the one corresponds to the other. By forgetting that one is an existing subject, passion goes by the board and the truth is no longer a paradox; the knowing subject becomes a fantastic entity rather than a human being, and the truth becomes a fantastic object for the knowledge of this fantastic entity.

When the question of truth is raised in an objective manner, reflection is directed objectively to the truth, as an object to which the knower is related. Reflection is not focussed upon the relationship, however, but upon the question of whether it is the truth to which the knower is related. If only the object to which he is related is the truth, the subject is accounted to be in the truth. When the question of the truth is raised subjectively, reflection is directed subjectively to the nature of the individual's relationship; if only the mode of this relationship is in the truth, the individual is in the truth even if he should happen to be thus related to what is not true.[1] Let us take as an example the knowledge of God. Objectively, reflection is directed to the problem of whether this object is the true God; subjectively, reflection is directed to the question whether the individual is related to a something *in such a manner* that his relationship is in truth a God-relationship. On which side is the truth now to be found? Ah, may we not here resort to a mediation, and say: It is on neither side, but in the mediation of both? Excellently well said, provided we might have it explained how an existing individual manages to be in a state of mediation. For to be in a state of mediation is to be finished, while to exist is to become. Nor can an existing individual be in two places at the same time—he cannot be an identity of subject and object. When he is nearest to being in two places at the same time he is in passion; but passion is momentary, and passion is also the highest expression of subjectivity.

The existing individual who chooses to pursue the objective way enters upon the entire approximation-process by which it is proposed to bring God to light objectively. But this is in all eternity impossible, because God is a subject, and therefore exists only for subjectivity in inwardness. The existing individual who chooses the subjective way apprehends instantly the entire dialectical difficulty involved in having to use some time, perhaps a long time,

---

[1] The reader will observe that the question here is about essential truth, or about the truth which is essentially related to existence, and that it is precisely for the sake of clarifying it as inwardness or as subjectivity that this contrast is drawn.

in finding God objectively; and he feels this dialectical difficulty in all its painfulness, because every moment is wasted in which he does not have God.[2] That very instant he has God, not by virtue of any objective deliberation, but by virtue of the infinite passion of inwardness. The objective inquirer, on the other hand, is not embarrassed by such dialectical difficulties as are involved in devoting an entire period of investigation to finding God—since it is possible that the inquirer may die tomorrow; and if he lives he can scarcely regard God as something to be taken along if convenient, since God is precisely that which one takes *a tout prix*, which in the understanding of passion constitutes the true inward relationship to God.

It is at this point, so difficult dialectically, that the way swings off for everyone who knows what it means to think, and to think existentially; which is something very different from sitting at a desk and writing about what one has never done, something very different from writing *de omnibus dubitandum* and at the same time being as credulous existentially as the most sensuous of men. Here is where the way swings off, and the change is marked by the fact that while objective knowledge rambles comfortably on by way of the long road of approximation without being impelled by the urge of passion, subjective knowledge counts every delay a deadly peril, and the decision so infinitely important and so instantly pressing that it is as if the opportunity had already passed.

Now when the problem is to reckon up on which side there is most truth, whether on the side of one who seeks the true God objectively, and pursues the approximate truth of the God-idea; or on the side of one who, driven by the infinite passion of his need of God, feels an infinite concern for his own relationship to God in truth (and to be at one and the same time on both sides equally, is as we have noted not possible for an existing individual, but is merely the happy delusion of an imaginary I-am-I): the answer cannot be in doubt for anyone who has not been demoralized with the aid of science. If one who lives in the midst of Christendom goes up to the house of God, the house of the true God, with the true conception of God in his knowledge, and prays, but prays in a false spirit; and one who lives in an idolatrous community prays with the entire passion of the infinite, although his eyes rest upon the image of an idol: where is there most truth? The one prays in truth to God though he worships an idol; the other prays falsely to the true God, and hence worships in fact an idol.

When one man investigates objectively the problem of immortality, and another embraces an uncertainty with the passion of the infinite: where is

---

[2] In this manner God certainly becomes a postulate, but not in the otiose manner in which this word is commonly understood. It becomes clear rather that the only way in which an existing individual comes into relation with God, is when the dialectical contradiction brings his passion to the point of despair, and helps him to embrace God with the "category of despair" (faith). Then the postulate is so far from being arbitrary that it is precisely a life-necessity. It is then not so much that God is a postulate, as that the existing individual's postulation of God is a necessity.

there most truth, and who has the greater certainty? The one has entered upon a never-ending approximation, for the certainty of immortality lies precisely in the subjectivity of the individual; the other is immortal, and fights for his immortality by struggling with the uncertainty. Let us consider Socrates.[7] Nowadays everyone dabbles in a few proofs; some have several such proofs, others fewer. But Socrates! He puts the question objectively in a problematic manner: *if* there is an immortality. He must therefore be accounted a doubter in comparison with one of our modern thinkers with the three proofs? By no means. On this "if" he risks his entire life, he has the courage to meet death, and he has with the passion of the infinite so determined the pattern of his life that it must be found acceptable—*if* there is an immortality. Is any better proof capable of being given for the immortality of the soul? But those who have the three proofs do not at all determine their lives in conformity therewith; if there is an immortality it must feel disgust over their manner of life: can any better refutation be given of the three proofs? The bit of uncertainty that Socrates had, helped him because he himself contributed the passion of the infinite; the three proofs that the others have do not profit them at all, because they are dead to spirit and enthusiasm, and their three proofs, in lieu of proving anything else, prove just this. A young girl may enjoy all the sweetness of love on the basis of what is merely a weak hope that she is beloved, because she rests everything on this weak hope; but many a wedded matron more than once subjected to the strongest expressions of love, has in so far indeed had proofs, but strangely enough has not enjoyed *quod erat demonstrandum*. The Socratic ignorance, which Socrates held fast with the entire passion of his inwardness, was thus an expression for the principle that the eternal truth is related to an existing individual, and that this truth must therefore be a paradox for him as long as he exists; and yet it is possible that there was more truth in the Socratic ignorance as it was in him, than in the entire objective truth of the System, which flirts with what the times demand and accommodates itself to *Privatdocents*.

The objective accent falls on WHAT is said, the subjective accent on HOW it is said. This distinction holds even in the aesthetic realm, and receives definite expression in the principle that what is in itself true may in the mouth of such and such a person become untrue. In these times this distinction is particularly worthy of notice, for if we wish to express in a single sentence the difference between ancient times and our own, we should doubtless have to say: "In ancient times only an individual here and there knew the truth; now all know it, except that the inwardness of its appropriation stands in an inverse relationship to the extent of its dissemination."[3]

---

[3] *Stages on Life's Way*, Note on p. 426. Though ordinarily not wishing an expression of opinion on the part of reviewers, I might at this point almost desire it, provided such opinions, so far from flattering me, amounted to an assertion of the daring truth that what I say is something that everybody knows, even every child, and that the

Aesthetically the contradiction that truth becomes untruth in this or that person's mouth, is best construed comically: In the ethico-religious sphere, accent is again on the "how." But this is not to be understood as referring to demeanor, expression, or the like; rather it refers to the relationship sustained by the existing individual, in his own existence, to the content of his utterance. Objectively the interest is focused merely on the thought-content, subjectively on the inwardness. At its maximum this inward "how" is the passion of the infinite, and the passion of the infinite is the truth. But the passion of the infinite is precisely subjectivity, and thus subjectivity becomes the truth. Objectively there is no infinite decisiveness, and hence it is objectively in order to annul the difference between good and evil, together with the principle of contradiction, and therewith also the infinite difference between the true and the false. Only in subjectivity is there decisiveness, to seek objectivity is to be in error. It is the passion of the infinite that is the decisive factor and not its content, for its content is precisely itself. In this manner subjectivity and the subjective "how" constitute the truth.

But the "how" which is thus subjectively accentuated precisely because the subject is an existing individual, is also subject to a dialectic with respect to time. In the passionate moment of decision, where the road swings away from objective knowledge, it seems as if the infinite decision were thereby realized. But in the same moment the existing individual finds himself in the temporal order, and the subjective "how" is transformed into a striving, a striving which receives indeed its impulse and a repeated renewal from the decisive passion of the infinite, but is nevertheless a striving.

When subjectivity is the truth, the conceptual determination of the truth must include an expression for the antithesis to objectivity, a memento of the fork in the road where the way swings off; this expression will at the same time serve as an indication of the tension of the subjective inwardness. Here is such a definition of truth: *An objective uncertainty held fast in an appropriation-process of the most passionate inwardness is the truth*, the highest truth attainable for an *existing* individual. At the point where the way swings off (and where this is cannot be specified objectively, since it is a matter of subjectivity), there objective knowledge is placed in abeyance. Thus the subject merely has, objectively, the uncertainty; but it is this which precisely increases the tension of that infinite passion which constitutes his

---

cultured know infinitely much better. If it only stands fast that everyone knows it, my standpoint is in order, and I shall doubtless make shift to manage with the unity of the comic and the tragic. If there were anyone who did not know it I might perhaps be in danger of being dislodged from my position of equilibrium by the thought that I might be in a position to communicate to someone the needful preliminary knowledge. It is just this which engages my interest so much, this that the cultured are accustomed to say: that everyone knows what the highest is. This was not the case in paganism, nor in Judaism, nor in the seventeen centuries of Christianity. Hail to the nineteenth century! Everyone knows it. What progress has been made since the time when only a few knew it. To make up for this, perhaps, we must assume that no one nowadays does it.

inwardness. The truth is precisely the venture which chooses an objective uncertainty with the passion of the infinite. I contemplate the order of nature in the hope of finding God, and I see omnipotence and wisdom; but I also see much else that disturbs my mind and excites anxiety. The sum of all this is an objective uncertainty. But it is for this very reason that the inwardness becomes as intense as it is, for it embraces this objective uncertainty with the entire passion of the infinite. In the case of a mathematical proposition the objectivity is given, but for this reason the truth of such a proposition is also an indifferent truth.

But the above definition of truth is an equivalent expression for faith. Without risk there is no faith. Faith is precisely the contradiction between the infinite passion of the individual's inwardness and the objective uncertainty. If I am capable of grasping God objectively, I do not believe, but precisely because I cannot do this I must believe. If I wish to preserve myself in faith I must constantly be intent upon holding fast the objective uncertainty, so as to remain out upon the deep, over seventy thousand fathoms of water, still preserving my faith.

In the principle that subjectivity, inwardness, is the truth, there is comprehended the Socratic wisdom, whose everlasting merit it was to have become aware of the essential significance of existence, of the fact that the knower is an existing individual. For this reason Socrates was in the truth by virtue of his ignorance, in the highest sense in which this was possible within paganism. To attain to an understanding of this, to comprehend that the misfortune of speculative philosophy is again and again to have forgotten that the knower is an existing individual, is in our objective age difficult enough. "But to have made an advance upon Socrates without even having understood what he understood, is at any rate not "Socratic." Compare the "Moral" of the *Fragments*.

Let us now start from this point, and as was attempted in the *Fragments*, seek a determination of thought which will really carry us further. I have nothing here to do with the question of whether this proposed thought-determination is true or not, since I am merely experimenting; but it must at any rate be clearly manifest that the Socratic thought is understood within the new proposal, so that at least I do not come out behind Socrates.

When subjectivity, inwardness, is the truth, the truth becomes objectively a paradox; and the fact that the truth is objectively a paradox shows in its turn that subjectivity is the truth. For the objective situation is repellent; and the expression for the objective repulsion constitutes the tension and the measure of the corresponding inwardness. The paradoxical character of the truth is its objective uncertainty; this uncertainty is an expression for the passionate inwardness, and this passion is precisely the truth. So far the Socratic principle. The eternal and essential truth, the truth which has an essential relationship to an existing individual because it pertains essentially to existence (all other knowledge being from the Socratic point of view accidental, its scope and degree a matter of indifference), is a paradox. But the eternal essential truth is by no means in itself a paradox; but it becomes paradoxical by virtue of its relationship to an existing individual. The Socratic ignorance gives expression to the objective uncertainty attaching to the truth, while his inwardness in existing is the truth. To anticipate here what will be developed later, let me make the following remark. The Socratic ignorance is an analogue to the category of the absurd, only that there is still less of objective certainty in the absurd, and in the repellent effect than the absurd exercises. It is certain only that it is absurd, and precisely on that account it incites to an infinitely greater tension in the corresponding inwardness. The Socratic inwardness in existing is an analogue to faith; only that the inwardness of faith, corresponding as it does, not to the repulsion of the Socratic ignorance, but to the repulsion exerted by the absurd, is infinitely more profound.

Socratically the eternal essential truth is by no means in its own nature paradoxical, but only in its relationship to an existing individual. This finds expression in another Socratic proposition, namely, that all knowledge is recollection. This proposition is not for Socrates a cue to the speculative enterprise, and hence he does not follow it up; essentially it becomes a Platonic principle. Here the way swings off; Socrates concentrates essentially upon accentuating existence, while Plato forgets this and loses himself in speculation. Socrates' infinite merit is to have been an *existing* thinker, not a speculative philosopher who forgets what it means to exist. For Socrates therefore the principle that all knowledge is recollection has at the moment of his leave-taking and as the constantly rejected possibility of engaging in speculation, the following two-fold significance: (1) that the knower is essentially *integer*, and that with respect to the knowledge of the eternal truth he is confronted with no other difficulty than the circumstance that he exists; which difficulty, however, is so essential and decisive for him that it means that existing, the process of transformation to inwardness in and by existing, is the truth; (2) that existence in time does not have any decisive significance, because the possibility of taking oneself back into eternity through recollection is always there, though this possibility is constantly nullified by utilizing the time, not for speculation, but for the transformation to inwardness in existing.[4]

---

[4] This will perhaps be the proper place to offer an explanation with respect to a difficulty in the plan of the *Fragments*, which had its ground in the fact that I did not wish at once to make the case as difficult dialectically as it is, because in our age terminologies and the like are turned so topsy-turvy that it is almost impossible to secure oneself against confusion. In order if possible clearly to exhibit the difference between the Socratic position (which was supposed to be the philosophical, the pagan-philosophical position) and the experimentally evoked thought-determination which really makes an advance beyond the Socratic, I carried the Socratic back to the principle that all knowledge is recollection.[9] This is, in a way, commonly assumed, and only one who with a specialized interest concerns himself with the Socratic, returning again and again to the sources, only for

The infinite merit of the Socratic position was precisely to accentuate the fact that the knower is an existing individual, and that the task of existing is his essential task. Making an advance upon Socrates by failing to understand this, is quite a mediocre achievement. This Socratic principle we must therefore bear in mind, and then inquire whether the formula may not be altered as really to make an advance beyond the Socratic position.

Subjectivity, inwardness, has been posited as the truth; can any expression for the truth be found which has a still higher degree of inwardness? Aye, there is such an expression, provided the principle that subjectivity or inwardness is the truth begins by positing the opposite principle: that subjectivity is untruth. Let us not at this point succumb to such haste as to fail in making the necessary distinctions. Speculative philosophy also says that subjectivity is untruth, but says it in order to stimulate a movement in precisely the opposite direction, namely, in the direction of the principle that objectivity is the truth. Speculative philosophy determines subjectivity negatively as tending toward objectivity. This second determination of ours, however, places a hindrance in its own way while proposing to begin, which has the effect of making the inwardness far more intensive. Socratically speaking, subjectivity is untruth if it refuses to understand that subjectivity is truth, but, for example, desires to become objective. Here, on the other hand, sub-

---

him would it be of importance on this point to distinguish between Socrates and Plato. The proposition does indeed belong to both, only that Socrates is always departing from it, in order to exist. By holding Socrates down to the proposition that all knowledge is recollection, he becomes a speculative philosopher instead of an existential thinker, for whom existence is the essential thing. The recollection-principle belongs to speculative philosophy, and recollection is immanence, and speculatively and eternally there is no paradox. But the difficulty is that no human being is speculative philosophy; the speculative philosopher himself is an existing individual, subject to the claims that existence makes upon him. There is no merit in forgetting this, but a great merit in holding it fast, and this is precisely what Socrates did. To accentuate existence, which also involves the qualification of inwardness, is the Socratic position; the Platonic tendency, on the other hand, is to pursue the lure of recollection and immanence This puts Socrates fundamentally in advance of speculative philosophy; he does not have a fantastic beginning, in which the speculative philosopher first disguises himself, and then goes on and on to speculate, forgetting the most important thing of all, which is to exist. But precisely because Socrates is thus in advance of speculation, he presents, when properly delineated, a certain analogous resemblance to that which the experiment described as in truth going beyond the Socratic. The truth as paradox in the Socratic sense becomes analogous to the paradox *sensu eminentiori*, the passion of inwardness in existing becomes an analogue to faith *sensu eminentiori*. That the difference is none the less infinite, that the characterization which the *Fragments* made of that which in truth goes beyond the Socratic remains unchanged, it will be easy to show; but by using at once apparently the same determinations, or at any rate the same words, about these two different things, I feared to cause a misunderstanding. Now I think there can be no objection to speaking of the paradoxical and of faith in reference to Socrates, since it is quite correct to do so when properly understood. Besides, the old Greeks also used the word πίστις, though not by any means in the sense of the experiment; and they used it in such a manner that, especially with reference to a work of Aristotle[10] where the term is employed, it would be possible to set forth some very enlightening considerations bearing upon its difference from faith *sensu eminentiori*.

jectivity in beginning upon the task of becoming the truth through a subjectifying process, is in the difficulty that it is already untruth. Thus, the labor of the task is thrust backward, backward, that is, in inwardness. So far is it from being the case that the way tends in the direction of objectivity, that the beginning merely lies still deeper in subjectivity.

But the subject cannot be untruth eternally, or eternally be presupposed as having been untruth; it must have been brought to this condition in time, or here become untruth in time. The Socratic paradox consisted in the fact that the eternal was related to an existing individual, but now existence has stamped itself upon the existing individual a second time. There has taken place so essential an alteration in him that he cannot now possibly take himself back into the eternal by way of recollection. To do this is to speculate; to be able to do this, but to reject the possibility by apprehending the task of life as a realization of inwardness in existing, is the Socratic position. But now the difficulty is that what followed Socrates on his way as a rejected possibility, has become an impossibility. If engaging in speculation was a dubious merit even from the point of view of the Socratic, it is now neither more nor less than confusion.

The paradox emerges when the eternal truth and existence are placed in juxtaposition with one another; each time the stamp of existence is brought to bear, the paradox becomes more clearly evident. Viewed Socratically the knower was simply an existing individual, but now the existing individual bears the stamp of having been essentially altered by existence.

Let us now call the untruth of the individual *Sin*. Viewed eternally he cannot be sin, nor can he be eternally presupposed as having been in sin. By coming into existence therefore (for the beginning was that subjectivity is untruth), he becomes a sinner. He is not born as a sinner in the sense that he is presupposed as being a sinner before he is born, but he is born in sin and as a sinner. This we might call *Original Sin*. But if existence has in this manner acquired a power over him, he is prevented from taking himself back into the eternal by way of recollection. If it was paradoxical to posit the eternal truth in relationship to an existing individual, it is now absolutely paradoxical to posit it in relationship to such an individual as we have here defined. But the more difficult it is made for him to take himself out of existence by way of recollection, the more profound is the inwardness that his existence may have in existence; and when it is made impossible for him, when he is held so fast in existence that the back door of recollection is forever closed to him, then his inwardness will be the most profound possible. But let us never forget that the Socratic merit was to stress the fact that the knower is an existing individual; for the more difficult the matter becomes, the greater the temptation to hasten along the easy road of speculation, away from fearful dangers and crucial decisions, to the winning of renown and honors and property, and so forth. If even Socrates understood the dubiety of taking himself speculatively out of existence back into the eternal, although no other difficulty confronted the existing individual except that he existed, and that existing was his essential task, now it is impossible. Forward he must, backward he cannot go.

Subjectivity is the truth. By virtue of the relationship subsisting between the eternal truth and the existing individual, the paradox came into being. Let us now go further, let us suppose that the eternal essential truth is itself a paradox. How does the paradox come into being? By putting the eternal essential truth into juxtaposition with existence. Hence when we posit such a conjunction within the truth itself, the truth becomes a paradox. The eternal truth has come into being in time: this is the paradox. If in accordance with the determinations just posited, the subject is prevented by sin from taking himself back into the eternal, now he need not trouble himself about this; for now the eternal essential truth is not behind him but in front of him, through its being in existence or having existed, so that if the individual does not existentially and in existence lay hold of the truth, he will never lay hold of it.

Existence can never be more sharply accentuated than by means of these determinations. The evasion by which speculative philosophy attempts to recollect itself out of existence has been made impossible. With reference to this, there is nothing for speculation to do except to arrive at an understanding of this impossibility; every speculative attempt which insists on being speculative shows *eo ipso* that it has not understood it. The individual may thrust all this away from him, and take refuge in speculation; but it is impossible first to accept it, and then to revoke it by means of speculation, since it is definitely calculated to prevent speculation.

When the eternal truth is related to an existing individual it becomes a paradox. The paradox repels in the inwardness of the existing individual, through the objective uncertainty and the corresponding Socratic ignorance. But since the paradox is not in the first instance itself paradoxical (but only in its relationship to the existing individual), it does not repel with a sufficient intensive inwardness. For without risk there is no faith, and the greater the risk the greater the faith; the more objective security the less inwardness (for inwardness is precisely subjectivity), and the less objective security the more profound the possible inwardness. When the paradox is paradoxical in itself, it repels the individual by virtue of its absurdity, and the corresponding passion of inwardness is faith. But subjectivity, inwardness, is the truth; for otherwise we have forgotten what the merit of the Socratic position is. But there can be no stronger expression for inwardness than when the retreat out of existence into the eternal by way of recollection is impossible; and when, with truth confronting the individual as a paradox, gripped in the anguish and pain of sin, facing the tremendous risk of the objective insecurity, the individual believes. But without risk no faith, not even the Socratic form of faith, much less the form of which we here speak.

When Socrates believed that there was a God, he held fast to the objective uncertainty with the whole passion of his inwardness, and it is precisely in this contradiction and in this risk, that faith is rooted. Now it is otherwise. Instead of the objective uncertainty, there is here a certainty, namely, that objectively it is absurd; and this absurdity, held fast in the passion of inwardness, is faith. The Socratic ignorance is as a witty jest in comparison with the earnestness of facing the absurd; and the Socratic existential inwardness is as Greek light-mindedness in comparison with the grave strenuosity of faith.

What now is the absurd? The absurd is—that the eternal truth has come into being in time, that God has come into being, has been born, has grown up, and so forth, precisely like any other individual human being, quite indistinguishable from other individuals. For every assumption of immediate recognizability is pre-Socratic paganism, and from the Jewish point of view, idolatry; and every determination of what really makes an advance beyond the Socratic must essentially bear the stamp of having a relationship to God's having come into being; for faith *sensu strictissimo*, as was developed in the *Fragments*, refers to becoming. When Socrates believed that there was a God, he saw very well that where the way swings off there is also an objective way of approximation, for example by the contemplation of nature and human history, and so forth. His merit was precisely to shun this way, where the quantitative siren song enchants the mind and deceives the existing individual.

In relation to the absurd, the objective approximation-process is like the comedy, *Misunderstanding upon Misunderstanding*, which is generally played by *Privatdocents* and speculative philosophers. The absurd is precisely by its objective repulsion the measure of the intensity of faith in inwardness. Suppose a man who wishes to acquire faith; let the comedy begin. He wishes to have faith, but he wishes also to safeguard himself by means of an objective inquiry and its approximation-process. What happens? With the help of the approximation-process the absurd becomes something different; it becomes probable, it becomes increasingly probable, it becomes extremely and emphatically probable. Now he is ready to believe it, and he ventures to claim for himself that he does not believe as shoemakers and tailors and simple folk believe, but only after long deliberation. Now he is ready to believe it; and lo, now it has become precisely impossible to believe it. Anything that is almost probable, or probable, or extremely and emphatically probable, is something he can almost know, or as good as know, or extremely and emphatically almost *know*—but it is impossible to *believe*. For the absurd is the object of faith, and the only object that can be believed.

10 The Argument from Mystical Experience[*]

WILLIAM JAMES

William James (1842–1910) was influential both as a psychologist and philosopher. Author of numerous articles, some of his important books include *Pragmatism: A New Name for Some Old Ways of Thinking*, *Principles of Psychology*, and *Varieties of Religious Experience*. He is known as a leading American exponent of pragmatism.

But now the hour has come when mysticism must be faced in good earnest, and those broken threads wound up together. One may say truly, I think, that personal religious experience has its root and centre in mystical states of consciousness; so for us, who in these lectures are treating personal experience as the exclusive subject of our study, such states of consciousness ought to form the vital chapter from which the other chapters get their light. Whether my treatment of mystical states will shed more light or darkness, I do not know, for my own constitution shuts me out from their enjoyment almost entirely, and I can speak of them only at second hand. But though forced to look upon the subject so externally, I will be as objective and receptive as I can; and I think I shall at least succeed in convincing you of the reality of the states in question, and of the paramount importance of their function.

First of all, then, I ask, What does the expression 'mystical states of consciousness' mean? How do we part off mystical states from other states?

The words 'mysticism' and 'mystical' are often used as terms of mere reproach, to throw at any opinion which we regard as vague and vast and sentimental, and without a base in either facts or logic. For some writers a 'mystic' is any person who believes in thought-transference, or spirit-return. Employed in this way the word has little value: there are too many less ambiguous synonyms. So, to keep it useful by restricting it, I will do what I did in the case of the word 'religion,' and simply propose to you four marks which, when an experience has them, may justify us in calling it mystical for the purpose of the present lectures. In this way we shall save verbal disputation, and the recriminations that generally go therewith.

* From William James, *Varieties of Religious Experience*, (London: Longmans, Green & Co., Ltd., 1903).

1. *Ineffability*.   The handiest of the marks by which I classify a state of mind as mystical is negative. The subject of it immediately says that it defies expression, that no adequate report of its contents can be given in words. It follows from this that its quality must be directly experienced; it cannot be imparted or transferred to others. In this peculiarity mystical states are more like states of feeling than like states of intellect. No one can make clear to another who has never had a certain feeling, in what the quality or worth of it consists. One must have musical ears to know the value of a symphony; one must have been in love one's self to understand a lover's state of mind. Lacking the heart or ear, we cannot interpret the musician or the lover justly, and are even likely to consider him weak-minded or absurd. The mystic finds that most of us accord to his experiences an equally incompetent treatment.

2. *Noetic quality*.   Although so similar to states of feeling, mystical states seem to those who experience them to be also states of knowledge. They are states of insight into depths of truth unplumbed by the discursive intellect. They are illuminations, revelations, full of significance and importance, all inarticulate though they remain; and as a rule they carry with them a curious sense of authority for after-time.

These two characters will entitle any state to be called mystical, in the sense in which I use the word. Two other qualities are less sharply marked, but are usually found. These are: —

3. *Transiency*.   Mystical states cannot be sustained for long. Except in rare instances, half an hour, or at most an hour or two, seems to be the limit beyond which they fade into the light of common day. Often, when faded, their quality can but imperfectly be reproduced in memory; but when they recur it is recognized; and from one recurrence to another it is susceptible of continuous development in what is felt as inner richness and importance.

4. *Passivity*.   Although the oncoming of mystical states may be facilitated by preliminary voluntary operations, as by fixing the attention, or going through certain bodily performances, or in other ways which manuals of mysticism prescribe; yet when the characteristic sort of consciousness once has set in, the mystic feels as if his own will were in abeyance, and indeed sometimes as if he were grasped and held by a superior power. This latter peculiarity connects mystical states with certain definite phenomena of secondary or alternative personality, such as prophetic speech, automatic writing, or the mediumistic trance. When these latter conditions are well pronounced, however, there may be no recollection whatever of the phenomenon, and it may have no significance for the subject's usual inner life, to which, as it were, it makes a mere interruption. Mystical states, strictly so called, are never merely interruptive. Some memory of their content always remains, and a profound sense of their importance. They modify the inner life of the subject between the times of their recurrence. Sharp divisions in this region are, however, difficult to make, and we find all sorts of gradations and mixtures.

These four characteristics are sufficient to mark out a group of states of consciousness peculiar enough to deserve a special name and to call for careful study. Let it then be called the mystical group.

Our next step should be to gain acquaintance with some typical examples. Professional mystics at the height of their development have often elaborately organized experiences and a philosophy based thereupon. But you remember what I said in my first lecture: phenomena are best understood when placed within their series, studied in their germ and in their over-ripe decay, and compared with their exaggerated and degenerated kindred. The range of mystical experience is very wide, much too wide for us to cover in the time at our disposal. Yet the method of serial study is so essential for interpretation that if we really wish to reach conclusions we must use it. I will begin, therefore, with phenomena which claim no special religious significance, and end with those of which the religious pretensions are extreme.

The simplest rudiment of mystical experience would seem to be that deepened sense of the significance of a maxim or formula which occasionally sweeps over one. "I've heard that said all my life," we exclaim, "but I never realized its full meaning until now." "When a fellow-monk," said Luther, "one day repeated the words of the Creed: 'I believe in the forgiveness of sins,' I saw the Scripture in an entirely new light; and straightway I felt as if I were born anew. It was as if I had found the door of paradise thrown wide open." This sense of deeper significance is not confined to rational propositions. Single words, and conjunctions of words, effects of light on land and sea, odors and musical sounds, all bring it when the mind is tuned aright. Most of us can remember the strangely moving power of passages in certain poems read when we were young, irrational doorways as they were through which the mystery of fact, the wildness and the pang of life, stole into our hearts and thrilled them. The words have now perhaps become mere polished surfaces for us; but lyric poetry and music are alive and significant only in proportion as they fetch these vague vistas of a life continuous with our own, beckoning and inviting, yet ever eluding our pursuit. We are alive or dead to the eternal inner message of the arts according as we have kept or lost this mystical susceptibility.

A more pronounced step forward on the mystical ladder is found in an extremely frequent phenomenon, that sudden feeling, namely, which sometimes sweeps over us, of having 'been here before,' as if at some indefinite past time, in just this place, with just these people, we were already saying just these things. As Tennyson writes:

> "Moreover, something is or seems,
> That touches me with mystic gleams,
> Like glimpses of forgotten dreams—

> "Of something felt, like something here;
> Of something done, I know not where;
> Such as no language may declare."

Somewhat deeper plunges into mystical consciousness are met with in yet other dreamy states. Such feelings as these which Charles Kingsley describes are surely far from being uncommon, especially in youth:—

"When I walk the fields, I am oppressed now and then with an innate feeling that everything I see has a meaning, if I could but understand it. And this feeling of being surrounded with truths which I cannot grasp amounts to indescribable awe sometimes. . . . Have you not felt that your real soul was imperceptible to your mental vision, except in a few hallowed moments?"

A much more extreme state of mystical consciousness is described by J. A. Symonds; and probably more persons than we suspect could give parallels to it from their own experience.

"Suddenly," writes Symonds, "at church, or in company, or when I was reading, and always, I think, when my muscles were at rest, I felt the approach of the mood. Irresistibly it took possession of my mind and will, lasted what seemed an eternity, and disappeared in a series of rapid sensations which resembled the awakening from anæsthetic influence. One reason why I disliked this kind of trance was that I could not describe it to myself. I cannot even now find words to render it intelligible. It consisted in a gradual but swiftly progressive obliteration of space, time, sensation, and the multitudinous factors of experience which seem to qualify what we are pleased to call our Self. In proportion as these conditions of ordinary consciousness were subtracted, the sense of an underlying or essential consciousness acquired intensity. At last nothing remained but a pure, absolute, abstract Self. The universe became without form and void of content. But Self persisted, formidable in its vivid keenness, feeling the most poignant doubt about reality, ready, as it seemed, to find existence break as breaks a bubble round about it. And what then? The apprehension of a coming dissolution, the grim conviction that this state was the last state of the conscious Self, the sense that I had followed the last thread of being to the verge of the abyss, and had arrived at demonstration of eternal Maya or illusion, stirred or seemed to stir me up again. The return to ordinary conditions of sentient existence began by my first recovering the power of touch, and then by the gradual though rapid influx of familiar impressions and diurnal interests. At last I felt myself once more a human being; and though the riddle of what is meant by life remained unsolved, I was thankful for this return from the abyss—this deliverance from so awful an initiation into the mysteries of skepticism.

"This trance recurred with diminishing frequency until I reached the age of twenty-eight. It served to impress upon my growing nature the phantasmal unreality of all the circumstances which contribute to a merely phenomenal consciousness. Often have I asked myself with anguish, on waking from that formless state of denuded, keenly sentient being, Which is the unreality?—the trance of fiery, vacant, apprehensive, skeptical Self from which I issue, or these surrounding phenomena and habits which veil that inner Self and build a self of flesh-and-blood conventionality? Again, are men the factors of some dream, the dream-like unsubstantiality of which they comprehend at such eventful moments? What would happen if the final stage of the trance were reached?"

In a recital like this there is certainly something suggestive of pathology. The next step into mystical states carries us into a realm that public opinion and ethical philosophy have long since branded as pathological, though private practice and certain lyric strains of poetry seem still to bear witness to its ideality. I refer to the consciousness produced by intoxicants and anæsthetics, especially by alcohol. The sway of alcohol over mankind is unquestionably due to its power to stimulate the mystical faculties of human nature, usually crushed to earth by the cold facts and dry criticisms of the sober hour. Sobriety diminishes, discriminates, and says no; drunkenness expands, unites, and says yes. It is in fact the great exciter of the *Yes* function in man. It brings its votary from the chill periphery of things to the radiant core. It makes him for the moment one with truth. Not through mere perversity do men run after it. To the poor and the unlettered it stands in the place of symphony concerts and of literature; and it is part of the deeper mystery and tragedy of life that whiffs and gleams of something that we immediately recognize as excellent should be vouchsafed to so many of us only in the fleeting earlier phases of what in its totality is so degrading a poisoning. The drunken consciousness is one bit of the mystic consciousness, and our total opinion of it must find its place in our opinion of that larger whole.

Nitrous oxide and ether, especially nitrous oxide, when sufficiently diluted with air, stimulate the mystical consciousness in an extraordinary degree. Depth beyond depth of truth seems revealed to the inhaler. This truth fades out, however, or escapes, at the moment of coming to; and if any words remain over in which it seemed to clothe itself, they prove to be the veriest nonsense. Nevertheless, the sense of a profound meaning having been there persists; and I know more than one person who is persuaded that in the nitrous oxide trance we have a genuine metaphysical revelation.

Some years ago I myself made some observations on this aspect of nitrous oxide intoxication, and reported them in print. One conclusion was forced upon my mind at that time, and my impression of its truth has ever since remained unshaken. It is that our normal waking consciousness, rational consciousness as we call it, is but one special type of consciousness, whilst all about it, parted from it by the filmiest of screens, there lie potential forms of consciousness entirely different. We may go through life without suspecting their existence; but apply the requisite stimulus, and at a touch they are there in all their completeness, definite types of mentality which probably somewhere have their field of application and adaptation. No account of the universe in its totality can be final which leaves these other forms of consciousness quite disregarded. How to regard them is the question,—for they are so discontinuous with ordinary consciousness. Yet they may determine attitudes though they cannot furnish formulas, and open a region though they fail to give a map. At any rate, they forbid a premature closing of our accounts with reality. Looking back on my own experiences, they all converge towards

a kind of insight to which I cannot help ascribing some metaphysical significance. The keynote of it is invariably a reconciliation. It is as if the opposites
of the world, whose contradictoriness and conflict make all our difficulties and
troubles, were melted into unity. Not only do they, as contrasted species,
belong to one and the same genus, but *one of the species,* the nobler and
better one, *is itself the genus, and so soaks up and absorbs its opposite into
itself.* This is a dark saying, I know, when thus expressed in terms of common
logic, but I cannot wholly escape from its authority. I feel as if it must mean
something, something like what the hegelian philosophy means, if one could
only lay hold of it more clearly. Those who have ears to hear, let them hear;
to me the living sense of its reality only comes in the artificial mystic state
of mind.

I just now spoke of friends who believe in the anæsthetic revelation. For
them too it is a monistic insight, in which the *other* in its various forms
appears absorbed into the One.

> "Into this pervading genius," writes one of them, "we pass, forgetting and
> forgotten, and thenceforth each is all, in God. There is no higher, no deeper,
> no other, than the life in which we are founded. 'The One remains, the many
> change and pass;' and each and every one of us *is* the One that remains. . . .
> This is the ultimatum. . . . As sure as being—whence is all our care—so sure
> is content, beyond duplexity, antithesis, or trouble, where I have triumphed
> in a solitude that God is not above."

Certain aspects of nature seem to have a peculiar power of awakening such
mystical moods. Most of the striking cases which I have collected have
occurred out of doors. Literature has commemorated this fact in many passages of great beauty—this extract, for example, from Amiel's Journal
Intime:—

> "Shall I ever again have any of those prodigious reveries which sometimes
> came to me in former days? One day, in youth, at sunrise, sitting in the ruins
> of the castle of Faucigny; and again in the mountains, under the noonday
> sun, above Lavey, lying at the foot of a tree and visited by three butterflies;
> once more at night upon the shingly shore of the Northern Ocean, my back
> upon the sand and my vision ranging through the milky way;—such grand and
> spacious, immortal, cosmogonic reveries, when one reaches to the stars, when
> one owns the infinite! Moments divine, ecstatic hours; in which our thought
> flies from world to world, pierces the great enigma, breathes with a respiration
> broad, tranquil, and deep as the respiration of the ocean, serene and limitless
> as the blue firmament; . . . instants of irresistible intuition in which one feels
> one's self great as the universe, and calm as a god. . . . What hours, what
> memories! The vestiges they leave behind are enough to fill us with belief and
> enthusiasm, as if they were visits of the Holy Ghost."

Here is a similar record from the memoirs of that interesting German
idealist, Malwida von Meysenbug:—

"I was alone upon the seashore as all these thoughts flowed over me, liberating and reconciling; and now again, as once before in distant days in the Alps of Dauphiné, I was impelled to kneel down, this time before the illimitable ocean, symbol of the Infinite. I felt that I prayed as I had never prayed before, and knew now what prayer really is: to return from the solitude of individuation into the consciousness of unity with all that is, to kneel down as one that passes away, and to rise up as one imperishable. Earth, heaven, and sea resounded as in one vast world-encircling harmony. It was as if the chorus of all the great who had ever lived were about me. I felt myself one with them, and it appeared as if I heard their greeting: 'Thou too belongest to the company of those who overcome.' "

MYSTICAL ELEMENT IN RELIGION

Even the least mystical of you must by this time be convinced of the existence of mystical moments as states of consciousness of an entirely specific quality, and of the deep impression which they make on those who have them.

We have now seen enough of this cosmic or mystic consciousness, as it comes sporadically. We must next pass to its methodical cultivation as an element of the religious life. Hindus, Buddhists, Mohammedans, and Christians all have cultivated it methodically.

In India, training in mystical insight has been known from time immemorial under the name of yoga. Yoga means the experimental union of the individual with the divine. It is based on persevering exercise; and the diet, posture, breathing, intellectual concentration, and moral discipline vary slightly in the different systems which teach it. The yogi, or disciple, who has by these means overcome the obscurations of his lower nature sufficiently, enters into the condition termed *samâdhi*, "and comes face to face with facts which no instinct or reason can ever know." He learns—

"That the mind itself has a higher state of existence, beyond reason, a superconscious state, and that when the mind gets to that higher state, then this knowledge beyond reasoning comes. . . . All the different steps in yoga are intended to bring us scientifically to the superconscious state or samâdhi. . . . Just as unconscious work is beneath consciousness, so there is another work which is above consciousness, and which, also, is not accompanied with the feeling of egoism. . . . There is no feeling of I, and yet the mind works, desireless, free from restlessness, objectless, bodiless. Then the Truth shines in its full effulgence, and we know ourselves—for Samâdhi lies potential in us all—for what we truly are, free, immortal, omnipotent, loosed from the finite, and its contrasts of good and evil altogether, and identical with the Atman or Universal Soul."

The Vedantists say that one may stumble into superconsciousness sporadically, without the previous discipline, but it is then impure. Their test of its purity, like our test of religion's value, is empirical: its fruits must be good for life. When a man comes out of Samâdhi, they assure us that he remains "enlightened, a sage, a prophet, a saint, his whole character changed, his life changed, illumined."

The Buddhists use the word 'samâdhi' as well as the Hindus; but 'dhyâna' is their special word for higher states of contemplation. There seem to be four stages recognized in dhyâna. The first stage comes through concentration of the mind upon one point. It excludes desire, but not discernment or judgment: it is still intellectual. In the second stage the intellectual functions drop off, and the satisfied sense of unity remains. In the third stage the satisfaction departs, and indifference begins, along with memory and self-consciousness. In the fourth stage the indifference, memory, and self-consciousness are perfected. [Just what 'memory' and 'self-consciousness' mean in this connection is doubtful. They cannot be the faculties familiar to us in the lower life.] Higher stages still of contemplation are mentioned —a region where there exists nothing, and where the mediator says: "There exists absolutely nothing," and stops. Then he reaches another region where he says: "There are neither ideas nor absence of ideas," and stops again. Then another region where, "having reached the end of both idea and perception, he stops finally." This would seem to be, not yet Nirvâna, but as close an approach to it as this life affords.

In the Christian church there have always been mystics. Although many of them have been viewed with suspicion, some have gained favor in the eyes of the authorities. The experiences of these have been treated as precedents, and a codified system of mystical theology has been based upon them, in which everything legitimate finds its place. The basis of the system is 'orison' or meditation, the methodical elevation of the soul towards God. Through the practice of orison the higher levels of mystical experience may be attained. It is odd that Protestantism, especially evangelical Protestantism, should seemingly have abandoned everything methodical in this line. Apart from what prayer may lead to, Protestant mystical experience appears to have been almost exclusively sporadic. It has been left to our mind-curers to reintroduce methodical meditation into our religious life.

The first thing to be aimed at in orison is the mind's detachment from outer sensations, for these interfere with its concentration upon ideal things. Such manuals as Saint Ignatius's Spiritual Exercises recommend the disciple to expel sensation by a graduated series of efforts to imagine holy scenes. The acme of this kind of discipline would be a semi-hallucinatory monoideism—an imaginary figure of Christ, for example, coming fully to occupy the mind. Sensorial images of this sort, whether literal or symbolic, play an enormous part in mysticism. But in certain cases imagery may fall away entirely, and in the very highest raptures it tends to do so. The state of consciousness becomes then insusceptible of any verbal description. Mystical teachers are unanimous as to this. Saint John of the Cross, for instance, one of the best of them, thus describes the condition called the 'union of love,' which, he says, is reached by 'dark contemplation.' In this the Deity compenetrates the soul, but in such a hidden way that the soul—

"finds no terms, no means, no comparison whereby to render the sublimity of the wisdom and the delicacy of the spiritual feeling with which she is filled. . . . We receive this mystical knowledge of God clothed in none of the kinds of images, in none of the sensible representations, which our mind makes use of in other circumstances. Accordingly in this knowledge, since the senses and the imagination are not employed, we get neither form nor impression, nor can we give any account or furnish any likeness, although the mysterious and sweet-tasting wisdom comes home so clearly to the inmost parts of our soul. Fancy a man seeing a certain kind of thing for the first time in his life. He can understand it, use and enjoy it, but he cannot apply a name to it, nor communicate any idea of it, even though all the while it be a mere thing of sense. How much greater will be his powerlessness when it goes beyond the senses! This is the peculiarity of the divine language. The more infused, intimate, spiritual, and supersensible it is, the more does it exceed the senses, both inner and outer, and impose silence upon them. . . . The soul then feels as if placed in a vast and profound solitude, to which no created thing has access, in an immense and boundless desert, desert the more delicious the more solitary it is. There, in this abyss of wisdom, the soul grows by what it drinks in from the well-springs of the comprehension of love, . . . and recognizes, however sublime and learned may be the terms we employ, how utterly vile, insignificant, and improper they are, when we seek to discourse of divine things by their means."

I cannot pretend to detail to you the sundry stages of the Christian mystical life. Our time would not suffice, for one thing; and moreover, I confess that the subdivisions and names which we find in the Catholic books seem to me to represent nothing objectively distinct. So many men, so many minds: I imagine that these experiences can be as infinitely varied as are the idiosyncrasies of individuals.

The cognitive aspects of them, their value in the way of revelation, is what we are directly concerned with, and it is easy to show by citation how strong an impression they leave of being revelations of new depths of truth. Saint Teresa is the expert of experts in describing such conditions, so I will turn immediately to what she says of one of the highest of them, the 'orison of union.'

"In the orison of union," says Saint Teresa, "the soul is fully awake as regards God, but wholly asleep as regards things of this world and in respect of herself. During the short time the union lasts, she is as it were deprived of every feeling, and even if she would, she could not think of any single thing. Thus she needs to employ no artifice in order to arrest the use of her understanding: it remains so stricken with inactivity that she neither knows what she loves, nor in what manner she loves, nor what she wills. In short, she is utterly dead to the things of the world and lives solely in God. . . . I do not even know whether in this state she has enough life left to breathe. It seems to me she has not; or at least that if she does breathe, she is unaware of it. Her intellect would fain understand something of what is going on within her, but it has so little force now that it can act in no way whatsoever. So a person who falls into a deep faint appears as if dead. . . .

"Thus does God, when he raises a soul to union with himself, suspend the natural action of all her faculties. She neither sees, hears, nor understands, so long as she is united with God. But this time is always short, and it seems even shorter than it is. God establishes himself in the interior of this soul in such a way, that when she returns to herself, it is wholly impossible for her to doubt that she has been in God, and God in her. This truth remains so strongly impressed on her that, even though many years should pass without the condition returning, she can neither forget the favor she received, nor doubt of its reality. If you, nevertheless, ask how it is possible that the soul can see and understand that she has been in God, since during the union she has neither sight nor understanding, I reply that she does not see it then, but that she sees it clearly later, after she has returned to herself, not by any vision, but by a certitude which abides with her and which God alone can give her. I knew a person who was ignorant of the truth that God's mode of being in everything must be either by presence, by power, or by essence, but who, after having received the grace of which I am speaking, believed this truth in the most unshakable manner. So much so that, having consulted a half-learned man who was as ignorant on this point as she had been before she was en-lightened, when he replied that God is in us only by 'grace,' she disbelieved his reply, so sure she was of the true answer; and when she came to ask wiser doctors, they confirmed her in her belief, which much consoled her. . . .

"But how, you will repeat, can one have such certainty in respect to what one does not see? This question, I am powerless to answer. These are secrets of God's omnipotence which it does not appertain to me to penetrate. All that I know is that I tell the truth; and I shall never believe that any soul who does not possess this certainty has ever been really united to God."

The deliciousness of some of these states seems to be beyond anything known in ordinary consciousness. It evidently involves organic sensibilities, for it is spoken of as something too extreme to be borne, and as verging on bodily pain. But it is too subtle and piercing a delight for ordinary words to denote. God's touches, the wounds of his spear, references to ebriety and to nuptial union have to figure in the phraseology by which it is shadowed forth. Intellect and senses both swoon away in these highest states of ecstasy. "If our understanding comprehends," says Saint Teresa, "it is in a mode which remains unknown to it, and it can understand nothing of what it com-prehends. For my own part, I do not believe that it does comprehend, because, as I said, it does not understand itself to do so. I confess that it is all a mystery in which I am lost." In the condition called *raptus* or ravish-ment by theologians, breathing and circulation are so depressed that it is a question among the doctors whether the soul be or be not temporarily dis-severed from the body. One must read Saint Teresa's descriptions and the very exact distinctions which she makes, to persuade one's self that one is dealing, not with imaginary experiences, but with phenomena which, however rare, follow perfectly definite psychological types.

To the medical mind these ecstasies signify nothing but suggested and imitated hypnoid states, on an intellectual basis of superstition, and a corporeal one of degeneration and hysteria. Undoubtedly these pathological conditions have existed in many and possibly in all the cases, but that fact tells us nothing about the value for knowledge of the consciousness which they induce. To pass a spiritual judgment upon these states, we must not content ourselves with superficial medical talk, but inquire into their fruits for life.

Their fruits appear to have been various. Stupefaction, for one thing, seems not to have been altogether absent as a result. You may remember the helplessness in the kitchen and schoolroom of poor Margaret Mary Alacoque. Many other ecstatics would have perished but for the care taken of them by admiring followers. The 'other-worldliness' encouraged by the mystical consciousness makes this over-abstraction from practical life peculiarly liable to befall mystics in whom the character is naturally passive and the intellect feeble; but in natively strong minds and characters we find quite opposite results. The great Spanish mystics, who carried the habit of ecstasy as far as it has often been carried, appear for the most part to have shown indomitable spirit and energy, and all the more so for the trances in which they indulged.

Saint Ignatius was a mystic, but his mysticism made him assuredly one of the most powerfully practical human engines that ever lived. Saint John of the Cross, writing of the intuitions and 'touches' by which God reaches the substance of the soul, tells us that—

> "They enrich it marvelously. A single one of them may be sufficient to abolish at a stroke certain imperfections of which the soul during its whole life had vainly tried to rid itself, and to leave it adorned with virtues and loaded with supernatural gifts. A single one of these intoxicating consolations may reward it for all the labors undergone in its life—even were they numberless. Invested with an invincible courage, filled with an impassioned desire to suffer for its God, the soul then is seized with a strange torment—that of not being allowed to suffer enough."

Mystical conditions may, therefore, render the soul more energetic in the lines which their inspiration favors. But this could be reckoned an advantage only in case the inspiration were a true one. If the inspiration were erroneous, the energy would be all the more mistaken and misbegotten. So we stand once more before that problem of truth which confronted us at the end of the lectures on saintliness. You will remember that we turned to mysticism precisely to get some light on truth. Do mystical states establish the truth of those theological affections in which the saintly life has its root?

In spite of their repudiation of articulate self-description, mystical states in general assert a pretty distinct theoretic drift. It is possible to give the outcome of the majority of them in terms that point in definite philosophical directions. One of these directions is optimism, and the other is monism. We pass into mystical states from out of ordinary consciousness as from a less into a more, as from a smallness into a vastness, and at the same time as from an unrest to a rest. We feel them as reconciling, unifying states. They appeal to the yes-function more than to the no-function in us. In them the unlimited absorbs the limits and peacefully closes the account. Their very denial of every adjective you may propose as applicable to the ultimate truth,—He, the Self, the Atman, is to be described by 'No! no!' only, say the Upanishads,—though it seems on the surface to be a no-function, is a denial made on behalf of a deeper yes. Whoso calls the Absolute anything in particular, or says that it is *this*, seems implicitly to shut it off from being *that* —it is as if he lessened it. So we deny the 'this,' negating the negation which it seems to us to imply, in the interests of the higher affirmative attitude by which we are possessed. The fountain-head of Christian mysticism is Dionysius the Areopagite. He describes the absolute truth by negatives exclusively.

> "The cause of all things is neither soul nor intellect; nor has it imagination, opinion, or reason, or intelligence; nor is it reason or intelligence; nor is it spoken or thought. It is neither number, nor order, nor magnitude, nor littleness, nor equality, nor inequality, nor similarity, nor dissimilarity. It neither stands, nor moves, nor rests. . . . It is neither essence, nor eternity, nor time. Even intellectual contact does not belong to it. It is neither science nor truth. It is not even royalty or wisdom; not one; not unity; not divinity or goodness; nor even spirit as we know it," etc., *ad libitum.*

But these qualifications are denied by Dionysius, not because the truth falls short of them, but because it so infinitely excels them. It is above them. To this dialectical use, by the intellect, of negation as a mode of passage towards a higher kind of affirmation, there is correlated the subtlest of moral counterparts in the sphere of the personal will. Since denial of the finite self and its wants, since asceticism of some sort, is found in religious experience to be the only doorway to the larger and more blessed life, this moral mystery intertwines and combines with the intellectual mystery in all mystical writings.

> "Love," continues Behmen, is Nothing, for "when thou art gone forth wholly from the Creature and from that which is visible, and art become Nothing to all that is Nature and Creature, then thou art in that eternal One, which is God himself, and then thou shalt feel within thee the highest virtue of Love. . . . The treasure of treasures for the soul is where she goeth out of the Somewhat into that Nothing out of which all things may be made. The soul here saith, *I have nothing,* for I am utterly stripped and naked; *I can do nothing,* for I have no manner of power, but am as water poured out; *I am nothing,* for

all that I am is no more than an image of Being, and only God is to me I AM; and so, sitting down in my own Nothingness, I give glory to the eternal Being, and *will nothing* of myself, that so God may will all in me, being unto me my God and all things."

In Paul's language, I live, yet not I, but Christ liveth in me. Only when I become as nothing can God enter in and no difference between his life and mine remain outstanding.

I have now sketched with extreme brevity and insufficiency, but as fairly as I am able in the time allowed, the general traits of the mystic range of consciousness. *It is on the whole pantheistic and optimistic, or at least the opposite of pessimistic. It is anti-naturalistic, and harmonizes best with twice-bornness and so-called other-worldly states of mind.*

IS MYSTICAL EXPERIENCE A WARRANT FOR TRUTH?

My next task is to inquire whether we can invoke it as authoritative. Does it furnish any *warrant for the truth* of the twice-bornness and supernaturality and pantheism which it favors? I must give my answer to this question as concisely as I can.

In brief my answer is this,—and I will divide it into three parts:—

(1) Mystical states, when well developed, usually are, and have the right to be, absolutely authoritative over the individuals to whom they come.

(2) No authority emanates from them which should make it a duty for those who stand outside of them to accept their revelations uncritically.

(3) They break down the authority of the non-mystical or rationalistic consciousness, based upon the understanding and the senses alone. They show it to be only one kind of consciousness. They open out the possibility of other orders of truth, in which, so far as anything in us vitally responds to them, we may freely continue to have faith.

I will take up these points one by one.

1

As a matter of psychological fact, mystical states of a well-pronounced and emphatic sort *are* usually authoritative over those who have them. They have been 'there,' and know. It is vain for rationalism to grumble about this. If the mystical truth that comes to a man proves to be a force that he can live by, what mandate have we of the majority to order him to live in another way? We can throw him into a prison or a madhouse, but we cannot change his mind—we commonly attach it only the more stubbornly to its beliefs. It mocks our utmost efforts, as a matter of fact, and in point of logic it absolutely escapes our jurisdiction. Our own more 'rational' beliefs are based on evidence exactly similar in nature to that which mystics quote for theirs. Our senses, namely, have assured us of certain states of fact; but mystical experiences are as direct perceptions of fact for those who have them as any sensations ever were for us. The records show that even though the five senses be in abeyance in them, they are absolutely sensational in their epistemological quality, if I may be pardoned the barbarous expression,— that is, they are face to face presentations of what seems immediately to exist.

The mystic is, in short, *invulnerable*, and must be left, whether we relish it or not, in undisturbed enjoyment of his creed. Faith, says Tolstoy, is that by which men live. And faith-state and mystic state are practically convertible terms.

2

But I now proceed to add that mystics have no right to claim that we ought to accept the deliverance of their peculiar experiences, if we are ourselves outsiders and feel no private call thereto. The utmost they can ever ask of us in this life is to admit that they establish a presumption. They form a consensus and have an unequivocal outcome; and it would be odd, mystics might say, if such a unanimous type of experience should prove to be altogether wrong. At bottom, however, this would only be an appeal to numbers, like the appeal of rationalism the other way; and the appeal to numbers has no logical force. If we acknowledge it, it is for 'suggestive,' not for logical reasons: we follow the majority because to do so suits our life.

But even this presumption from the unanimity of mystics is far from being strong. In characterizing mystic states as pantheistic, optimistic, etc., I am afraid I over-simplified the truth. I did so for expository reasons, and to keep the closer to the classic mystical tradition. The classic religious mysticism, it now must be confessed, is only a 'privileged case.' It is an *extract*, kept true to type by the selection of the fittest specimens and their preservation in 'schools.' It is carved out from a much larger mass; and if we take the larger mass as seriously as religious mysticism has historically taken itself, we find that the supposed unanimity largely disappears. To begin with, even religious mysticism itself, the kind that accumulates traditions and makes schools, is much less unanimous than I have allowed. It has been both ascetic and antinomianly self-indulgent within the Christian church. It is dualistic in Sankhya, and monistic in Vedanta philosophy. I called it pantheistic; but the great Spanish mystics are anything but pantheists. They are with few exceptions non-metaphysical minds, for whom 'the category of personality' is absolute. The 'union' of man with God is for them much more like an occasional miracle than like an original identity. How different again, apart from the happiness common to all, is the mysticism of Walt Whitman, Edward Carpenter, Richard Jeffries, and other naturalistic pantheists, from the more distinctively Christian sort. The fact is that the mystical feeling of enlargement, union, and emancipation has no specific intellectual content whatever of its own. It is capable of forming matrimonial alliances with material furnished by the most diverse philosophies and theologies, provided only they can find a place in their framework for its peculiar emotional mood. We have no right, therefore, to invoke its prestige as distinctively in favor of any special belief, such as that in absolute idealism, or in the absolute monistic identity, or in the absolute goodness, of the world. It is only relatively in favor of all these things—it passes out of common human consciousness in the direction in which they lie.

So much for religious mysticism proper. But more remains to be told, for religious mysticism is only one half of mysticism. The other half has no accumulated traditions except those which the text-books on insanity supply. Open any one of these, and you will find abundant cases in which 'mystical ideas' are cited as characteristic symptoms of enfeebled or deluded states of mind. In delusional insanity, paranoia, as they sometimes call it, we may have a *diabolical* mysticism, a sort of religious mysticism turned upside down. The same sense of ineffable importance in the smallest events, the same texts and words coming with new meanings, the same voices and visions and leadings and missions, the same controlling by extraneous powers; only this time the emotion is pessimistic: instead of consolations we have desolations; the meanings are dreadful; and the powers are enemies to life. It is evident that from the point of view of their psychological mechanism, the classic mysticism and these lower mysticisms spring from the same mental level, from that great subliminal or transmarginal region of which science is beginning to admit the existence, but of which so little is really known. That region contains every kind of matter: 'seraph and snake' abide there side by side. To come from thence is no infallible credential. What comes must be sifted and tested, and run the gauntlet of confrontation with the total context of experience, just like what comes from the outer world of sense. Its value must be ascertained by empirical methods, so long as we are not mystics ourselves.

Once more, then, I repeat that non-mystics are under no obligation to acknowledge in mystical states a superior authority conferred on them by their intrinsic nature.

3

Yet, I repeat once more, the existence of mystical states absolutely overthrows the pretension of non-mystical states to be the sole and ultimate dictators of what we may believe. As a rule, mystical states merely add a supersensuous meaning to the ordinary outward data of consciousness. They are excitements like the emotions of love or ambition, gifts to our spirit by means of which facts already objectively before us fall into a new expressiveness and make a new connection with our active life. They do not contradict these facts as such, or deny anything that our senses have immediately seized. It is the rationalistic critic rather who plays the part of denier in the controversy, and his denials have no strength, for there never can be a state of facts to which new meaning may not truthfully be added, provided the mind ascend to a more enveloping point of view. It must always remain an open question whether mystical states may not possibly be such superior points of view, windows through which the mind looks out upon a more extensive and inclusive world. The difference of the views seen from the different mystical windows need not prevent us from entertaining this supposition. The wider world would in that case prove to have a mixed constitution like that of this world, that is all. It would have its celestial and its infernal regions, its tempting and its saving moments, its valid experiences and its counterfeit ones, just as our world has them; but it would be a wider world all the same. We should have to use its experiences by selecting and subordinating and substituting just as is our custom in this ordinary naturalistic world; we should be liable to error just as we are now; yet the counting in of that wider world of meanings, and the serious dealing with it, might, in spite of all the perplexity, be indispensable stages in our approach to the final fullness of the truth.

AGNOSTICISM AND ATHEISM

11 Critique of the First-Cause and Design Arguments for the Existence of God[*]

DAVID HUME

David Hume (1711–1776) has had a tremendous influence on the developments of modern philosophy. Along with John Locke and Bishop Berkeley, he began the philosophical tradition known as empiricism. His principal philosophical works are A *Treatise of Human Nature, Inquiry Concerning the Human Understanding,* and *Dialogues Concerning Natural Religion.*

THE FIRST-CAUSE ARGUMENT

The argument, replied DEMEA, which I would insist on is the common one. Whatever exists must have a cause or reason of its existence; it being absolutely impossible for any thing to produce itself, or be the cause of its own existence. In mounting up, therefore, from effects to causes, we must either go on in tracing an infinite succession, without any ultimate cause at all, or must at last have recourse to some ultimate cause, that is *necessarily* existent: Now that the first supposition is absurd may be thus proved. In the infinite chain or succession of causes and effects, each single effect is determined to exist by the power and efficacy of that cause which immediately preceded; but the whole eternal chain or succession, taken together, is not determined or caused by any thing: And yet it is evident that it requires a cause or reason, as much as any particular object, which begins to exist in time. The question is still reasonable, why this particular succession of causes existed from eternity, and not any other succession, or no succession at all. If there be no

* From David Hume, *Dialogues Concerning Natural Religion,* first published in 1779.

necessarily existent Being, any supposition, which can be formed, is equally possible; nor is there any more absurdity in nothing's having existed from eternity, than there is in that succession of causes, which constitutes the universe. What was it, then, which determined something to exist rather than nothing, and bestowed being on a particular possibility, exclusive of the rest? *External causes*, there are supposed to be none. *Chance* is a word without a meaning. Was it *nothing*? But that can never produce any thing. We must, therefore, have recourse to a necessarily existent Being, who carries the REASON of his existence in himself; and who cannot be supposed not to exist without an express contradiction. There is consequently such a Being, that is, there is a Deity.

I shall not leave it to PHILO, said CLEANTHES (though I know that the starting objections is his chief delight), to point out the weakness of this metaphysical reasoning. It seems to me so obviously ill-grounded, and at the same time of so little consequence to the cause of true piety and religion, that I shall myself venture to show the fallacy of it.

I shall begin with observing, that there is evident absurdity in pretending to demonstrate a matter of fact, or to prove it by any arguments *a priori*. Nothing is demonstrable, unless the contrary implies a contradiction. Nothing, that is distinctly conceivable, implies a contradiction. Whatever we conceive as existent, we can also conceive as non-existent. There is no Being, therefore, whose non-existence implies a contradiction. Consequently there is no Being, whose existence is demonstrable. I propose this argument as entirely decisive, and am willing to rest the whole controversy upon it.

It is pretended that the Deity is a necessarily existent Being; and this necessity of his existence is attempted to be explained by asserting, that, if we knew his whole essence or nature, we should perceive it to be as impossible for him not to exist as for twice two not to be four. But it is evident, that this can never happen, while our faculties remain the same as at present. It will still be possible for us, at any time, to conceive the non-existence of what we formerly conceived to exist; nor can the mind ever lie under a necessity of supposing any object to remain always in being; in the same manner as we lie under a necessity of always conceiving twice two to be four. The words, therefore, *necessary existence*, have no meaning; or, which is the same thing, none that is consistent.

But farther; why may not the material universe be the necessarily existent Being, according to this pretended explication of necessity? We dare not affirm that we know all the qualities of matter; and for aught we can determine, it may contain some qualities, which, were they known, would make its non-existence appear as great a contradiction as that twice two is five. I find only one argument employed to prove, that the material world is not the necessarily existent Being; and this argument is derived from the contingency both of the matter and the form of the world. "Any particle of matter," it is said, "may be *conceived* to be annihilated; and any form may be *conceived* to be altered. Such an annihilation or alteration, therefore, is not impossible." But it seems a great partiality not to perceive, that the same argument extends equally to the Deity, so far as we have any conception of him; and that the mind can at least imagine him to be non-existent, or his attributes to be altered. It must be some unknown, inconceivable qualities, which can make his non-existence appear impossible, or his attribute unalterable: And no reason can be assigned, why these qualities may not belong to matter. As they are altogether unknown and inconceivable, they can never be proved incompatible with it.

Add to this, that in tracing an eternal succession of objects, it seems absurd to inquire for a general cause or first Author. How can any thing, that exists from eternity, have a cause, since that relation implies a priority in time and a beginning of existence?

In such a chain too, or succession of objects, each part is caused by that which preceded it, and causes that which succeeds it. Where then is the difficulty? But the WHOLE, you say, wants a cause. I answer, that the uniting of these parts into a whole, like the uniting of several distinct counties into one kingdom, or several distinct members into one body, is performed merely by an arbitrary act of the mind, and has no influence on the nature of things. Did I show you the particular causes of each individual in a collection of twenty particles of matter, I should think it very unreasonable, should you afterwards ask me, what was the cause of the whole twenty. This is sufficiently explained in explaining the cause of the parts.

Though the reasonings, which you have urged, CLEANTHES, may well excuse me, said PHILO, from starting any farther difficulties; yet I cannot forbear insisting still upon another topic. It is observed by arithmeticians, that the products of 9 compose always either 9 or some lesser product of 9; if you add together all the characters, of which any of the former products is composed. Thus, of 18, 27, 36, which are products of 9, you make 9 by adding 1 to 8, 2 to 7, 3 to 6. Thus 369 is a product also of 9; and if you add 3, 6, and 9, you make 18, a lesser product of 9. To a superficial observer, so wonderful a regularity may be admired as the effect either of chance or design; but a skilful algebraist immediately concludes it to be the work of necessity, and demonstrates, that it must for ever result from the nature of these numbers. Is it not probable, I ask, that the whole œconomy of the universe is conducted by a like necessity, though no human algebra can furnish a key which solves the difficulty? And instead of admiring the order of natural beings, may it not happen, that, could we penetrate into the intimate nature of bodies, we should clearly see why it was absolutely impossible, they could ever admit of any other disposition? So dangerous is it to introduce this idea of necessity into the present question! And so naturally does it afford an inference directly opposite to the religious hypothesis!

THE DESIGN ARGUMENT

Not to lose any time in circumlocutions, said CLEANTHES, addressing himself to DEMEA, much less in replying to the pious declamations of PHILO; I shall briefly explain how I conceive this matter. Look round the world: Contemplate the whole and every part of it: You will find it to be nothing but one great machine, subdivided into an infinite number of lesser machines, which again admit of subdivisions, to a degree beyond what human senses and faculties can trace and explain. All these various machines, and even their most minute parts, are adjusted to each other with an accuracy, which ravishes into admiration all men, who have ever contemplated them. The curious adapting of means to ends, throughout all nature, resembles exactly, though it much exceeds, the productions of human contrivance; of human design, thought, wisdom, and intelligence. Since therefore the effects resemble each other, we are led to infer, by all the rules of analogy, that the causes also resemble; and that the Author of nature is somewhat similar to the mind of man; though possessed of much larger faculties, proportioned to the grandeur of the work, which he has executed. By this argument *a posteriori*, and by this argument alone, we do prove at once the existence of a Deity, and his similarity to human mind and intelligence.

I shall be so free, CLEANTHES, said DEMEA, as to tell you, that from the beginning, I could not approve of your conclusion concerning the similarity of the Deity to men; still less can I approve of the mediums, by which you endeavour to establish it. What! No demonstration of the being of a God! No abstract arguments! No proofs *a priori*! Are these, which have hitherto been so much insisted on by philosophers, all fallacy, all sophism? Can we reach no farther in this subject than experience and probability? I will not say, that this is betraying the cause of a Deity: But surely, by this affected candour, you give advantage to atheists, which they never could obtain, by the mere dint of argument and reasoning.

What I chiefly scruple in this subject, said PHILO, is not so much, that all religious arguments are by CLEANTHES reduced to experience, as that they appear not to be even the most certain and irrefragable of that inferior kind. That a stone will fall, that fire will burn, that the earth has solidity, we have observed a thousand and a thousand times; and when any new instance of this nature is presented, we draw without hesitation the accustomed inference. The exact similarity of the cases gives us a perfect assurance of a similar event; and a stronger evidence is never desired nor sought after. But wherever you depart, in the least, from the similarity of the cases, you diminish proportionably the evidence; and may at last bring it to a very weak *analogy*, which is confessedly liable to error and uncertainty. After having experienced the circulation of the blood in human creatures, we make no doubt that it takes place in Titius and Mævius: But from its circulation in frogs and fishes, it is only a presumption, though a strong one, from analogy, that it takes place in men and other animals. The analogical reasoning is much weaker, when we infer the circulation of the sap in vegetables from our experience that the blood circulates in animals; and those, who hastily followed that imperfect analogy, are found, by more accurate experiments, to have been mistaken.

If we see a house, CLEANTHES, we conclude, with the greatest certainty, that it had an architect or builder; because this is precisely that species of effect, which we have experienced to proceed from that species of cause. But surely you will not affirm, that the universe bears such a resemblance to a house, that we can with the same certainty infer a similar cause, or that the analogy is here entire and perfect. The dissimilitude is so striking, that the utmost you can here pretend to is a guess, a conjecture, a presumption concerning a similar cause; and how that pretension will be received in the world, I leave you to consider.

It would surely be very ill received, replied CLEANTHES; and I should be deservedly blamed and detested, did I allow that the proofs of a Deity amounted to no more than a guess or conjecture. But is the whole adjustment of means to ends in a house and in the universe so slight a resemblance? The œconomy of final causes? The order, proportion, and arrangement of every part? Steps of a stair are plainly contrived, that human legs may use them in mounting; and this inference is certain and infallible. Human legs are also contrived for walking and mounting; and this inference, I allow, is not altogether so certain, because of the dissimilarity which you remark; but does it, therefore, deserve the name only of presumption or conjecture?

Good God! cried DEMEA, interrupting him, where are we? Zealous defenders of religion allow, that the proofs of a Deity fall short of perfect evidence! And you, PHILO, on whose assistance I depended, in proving the adorable mysteriousness of the divine nature, do you assent to all these extravagant opinions of CLEANTHES? For what other name can I give them? Or why spare my censure, when such principles are advanced, supported by such an authority, before so young a man as PAMPHILUS?

You seem not to apprehend, replied PHILO, that I argue with CLEANTHES in his own way; and by showing him the dangerous consequences of his tenets, hope at last to reduce him to our opinion. But what sticks most with you, I observe, is the representation which CLEANTHES has made of the argument *a posteriori*; and finding that that argument is likely to escape your hold and vanish into air, you think it so disguised that you can scarcely believe it to be set in its true light. Now, however much I may dissent, in other respects, from the dangerous principles of CLEANTHES, I must allow, that he has fairly represented that argument; and I shall endeavour so to state the matter to you, that you will entertain no farther scruples with regard to it.

Were a man to abstract from every thing which he knows or has seen, he would be altogether incapable, merely from his own ideas, to determine what kind of scene the universe must be, or to give the preference to one state or situation of things above another. For as nothing, which he clearly conceives, could be esteemed impossible or implying a contradiction, every chimera of his fancy would be upon an equal footing; nor could he assign any just reason, why he adheres to one idea or system, and rejects the others, which are equally possible.

Again; after he opens his eyes, and contemplates the world, as it really is, it would be impossible for him, at first, to assign the cause of any one event; much less, of the whole of things or of the universe. He might set his fancy a rambling; and she might bring him in an infinite variety of reports and representations. These would all be possible; but being all equally possible, he would never, of himself, give a satisfactory account for his preferring one of them to the rest. Experience alone can point out to him the true cause of any phenomenon.

Now according to this method of reasoning, DEMEA, it follows (and is, indeed, tacitly allowed by CLEANTHES himself) that order, arrangement, or the adjustment of final causes is not, of itself, any proof of design; but only so far as it has been experienced to proceed from that principle. For aught we can know *a priori*, matter may contain the source or spring of order originally, within itself, as well as mind does; and there is no more difficulty in conceiving, that the several elements, from an internal unknown cause, may fall into the most exquisite arrangement, than to conceive that their ideas, in the great, universal mind, from a like internal, unknown cause, fall into that arrangement. The equal possibility of both these suppositions is allowed. By experience we find (according to CLEANTHES), that there is a difference between them. Throw several pieces of steel together, without shape or form; they will never arrange themselves so as to compose a watch: Stone, and mortar, and wood, without an architect, never erect a house. But the ideas in a human mind, we see, by an unknown, inexplicable œconomy, arrange themselves so as to form the plan of a watch or house. Experience, therefore, proves, that there is an original principle of order in mind, not in matter. From similar effects we infer similar causes. The adjustment of means to ends is alike in the universe, as in a machine of human contrivance. The causes, therefore, must be resembling.

I was from the beginning scandalised, I must own, with this resemblance, which is asserted, between the Deity and human creatures; and must conceive it to imply such a degradation of the supreme Being as no sound theist could endure. With your assistance, therefore, DEMEA, I shall endeavour to defend what you justly call the adorable mysteriousness of the divine nature, and shall refute this reasoning of CLEANTHES; provided he allows, that I have made a fair representation of it.

When CLEANTHES had assented, PHILO, after a short pause, proceeded in the following manner.

That all inferences, CLEANTHES, concerning fact, are founded on experience, and that all experimental reasonings are founded on the supposition, that similar causes prove similar effects, and similar effects similar causes; I shall not, at present, much dispute with you. But observe, I entreat you, with what extreme caution all just reasoners proceed in the transferring of experiments to similar cases. Unless the cases be exactly similar, they repose no perfect confidence in applying their past observation to any particular phenomenon. Every alteration of circumstances occasions a doubt concerning the event; and it requires new experiments to prove certainly, that the new circumstances are of no moment or importance. A change in bulk, situation, arrangement, age, disposition of the air, or surrounding bodies; any of these particulars may be attended with the most unexpected consequences: And unless the objects be quite familiar to us, it is the highest temerity to expect with assurance, after any of these changes, an event similar to that which before fell under our observation. The slow and deliberate steps of philosophers, here, if any where, are distinguished from the precipitate march of the vulgar, who, hurried on by the smallest similitude, are incapable of all discernment or consideration.

But can you think, CLEANTHES, that your usual phlegm and philosophy have been preserved in so wide a step as you have taken, when you compared to the universe houses, ships, furniture, machines; and from their similarity in some circumstances inferred a similarity in their causes? Thought, design, intelligence, such as we discover in men and other animals, is no more than one of the springs and principles of the universe, as well as heat or cold, attraction or repulsion, and a hundred others, which fall under daily observation. It is an active cause, by which some particular parts of nature, we find, produce alterations on other parts. But can a conclusion, with any propriety, be transferred from parts to the whole? Does not the great disproportion bar all comparison and inference? From observing the growth of a hair, can we learn any thing concerning the generation of a man? Would the manner of a leaf's blowing, even though perfectly known, afford us any instruction concerning the vegetation of a tree?

But allowing that we were to take the *operations* of one part of nature upon another for the foundation of our judgment concerning the *origin* of the whole (which never can be admitted) yet why select so minute, so weak, so bounded a principle as the reason and design of animals is found to be upon this planet? What peculiar privilege has this little agitation of the rain which we call thought, that we must thus make it the model of the whole universe? Our partiality in our own favour does indeed present it on all occasions: But sound philosophy ought carefully to guard against so natural an illusion.

So far from admitting, continued PHILO, that the operations of a part can afford us any just conclusion concerning the origin of the whole, I will not allow any one part to form a rule for another part, if the latter be very remote from the former. Is there any reasonable ground to conclude, that the inhabitants of other planets possess thought, intelligence, reason, or any thing similar to these faculties in men? When nature has so extremely diversified her manner of operation in this small globe; can we imagine, that she incessantly copies herself throughout so immense a universe? And if thought, as we may well suppose, be confined merely to this narrow corner, and has even there so limited a sphere of action; with what propriety can we assign it for the original cause of all things? The narrow views of a peasant, who makes his domestic œconomy the rule for the government of kingdoms, is in comparison a pardonable sophism.

But were we ever so much assured, that a thought and reason, resembling the human, were to be found throughout the whole universe, and were its activity elsewhere vastly greater and more commanding than it appears in this globe: Yet I cannot see, why the operations of a world, constituted, arranged, adjusted, can with any propriety be extended to a world, which is in its embryo-state, and is advancing towards that constitution and arrangement. By observation, we know somewhat of the œconomy, action, and nourishment of a finished animal; but we must transfer with great caution that observation to the growth of a fœtus in the womb, and still more, to the formation of an animalcule in the loins of its male parent. Nature, we find, even from our limited experience, possesses an infinite number of springs and principles, which incessantly discover themselves on every change of her position and situation. And what new and unknown principles would actuate her in so new and unknown a situation as that of the formation of a universe, we cannot, without the utmost temerity, pretend to determine.

A very small part of this great system, during a very short time, is very imperfectly discovered to us: And do we thence pronounce decisively concerning the origin of the whole?

Admirable conclusion! Stone, wood, brick, iron, brass have not, at this time, in this minute globe of earth, an order or arrangement without human art and contrivance: Therefore the universe could not originally attain its order and arrangement, without something similar to human art. But is a part of nature a rule for another part very wide of the former? Is it a rule for the whole? Is a very small part a rule for the universe? Is nature in one situation, a certain rule for nature in another situation, vastly different from the former?

And can you blame me, CLEANTHES, if I here imitate the prudent reserve of SIMONIDES, who, according to the noted story, being asked by HIERO, *What God was?* desired a day to think of it, and then two days more; and after that manner continually prolonged the term, without ever bringing in his definition or description? Could you even blame me, if I had answered at first, *that I did not know*, and was sensible that this subject lay vastly beyond the reach of my faculties? You might cry out sceptic and raillier as much as you pleased: But having found, in so many other subjects, much more familiar, the imperfections and even contradictions of human reason, I never should expect any success from its feeble conjectures, in a subject, so sublime, and so remote from the sphere of our observation. When two *species* of objects have always been observed to be conjoined together, I can *infer*, by custom, the existence of one whenever I *see* the existence of the other: And this I call an argument from experience. But how this argument can have place, where the objects, as in the present case, are single, individual, without parallel, or specific resemblance, may be difficult to explain. And will any man tell me with a serious countenance, that an orderly universe must arise from some thought and art, like the human; because we have experience of it? To ascertain this reasoning, it were requisite, that we had experience of the origin of worlds; and it is not sufficient surely, that we have seen ships and cities arise from human art and contrivance. . . .

But because I know you are not much swayed by names and authorities, I shall endeavour to show you, a little more distinctly, the inconveniences of that anthropomorphism, which you have embraced; and shall prove, that there is no ground to suppose a plan of the world to be formed in the divine mind, consisting of distinct ideas, differently arranged; in the same manner as an architect forms in his head the plan of a house which he intends to execute.

It is not easy, I own, to see what is gained by this supposition, whether we judge of the matter by *reason* or by *experience*. We are still obliged to mount higher, in order to find the cause of this cause, which you had assigned as satisfactory and conclusive.

If *reason* (I mean abstract reason, derived from enquiries *a priori*) be not alike mute with regard to all questions concerning cause and effect; this sentence at least it will venture to pronounce, That a mental world or universe of ideas requires a cause as much as does a material world or universe of objects; and if similar in its arrangement must require a similar cause. For what is there in this subject, which should occasion a different conclusion or inference? In an abstract view, they are entirely alike; and no difficulty attends the one supposition, which is not common to both of them.

Again, when we will needs force *experience* to pronounce some sentence, even on these subjects, which lie beyond her sphere; neither can she perceive any material difference in this particular, between these two kinds of worlds, but finds them to be governed by similar principles, and to depend upon an equal variety of causes in their operations. We have specimens in miniature of both of them. Our own mind resembles the one: A vegetable or animal body the other. Let experience, therefore, judge from these samples. Nothing seems more delicate with regard to its causes than thought; and as these causes never operate in two persons after the same manner, so we never find two persons, who think exactly alike. Nor indeed does the same person think exactly alike at any two different periods of time. A difference of age, of the disposition of his body, of weather, of food, of company, of books, of passions; any of these particulars or others more minute, are sufficient to alter the curious machinery of thought, and communicate to it very different movements and operations. As far as we can judge, vegetables and animal bodies are not more delicate in their motions, nor depend upon a greater variety or more curious adjustment of springs and principles.

How therefore shall we satisfy ourselves concerning the cause of that Being, whom you suppose the Author of nature, or, according to your system of anthropomorphism, the ideal world, into which you trace the material? Have we not the same reason to trace that ideal world into another ideal world, or new intelligent principle? But if we stop, and go no farther; why go so far? Why not stop at the material world? How can we satisfy ourselves without going on *in infinitum*? And after all, what satisfaction is there in that infinite progression? Let us remember the story of the INDIAN philosopher and his elephant. It was never more applicable than to the present subject. If the material world rests upon a similar ideal world, this ideal world must rest upon some other; and so on, without end. It were better, therefore, never to look beyond the present material world. By supposing it to contain the principle of its order within itself, we really assert it to be God; and the sooner we arrive at that divine Being so much the better. When you go one step beyond the mundane system you only excite an inquisitive humour, which it is impossible ever to satisfy.

To say, that the different ideas, which compose the reason of the supreme Being, fall into order, of themselves, and by their own nature, is really to talk without any precise meaning. If it has a meaning, I would fain know, why it is not as good sense to say, that the parts of the material world fall into order, of themselves, and by their own nature? Can the one opinion be intelligible, while the other is not so?

We have, indeed, experience of ideas, which fall into order, of themselves, and without any *known* cause: But, I am sure, we have a much larger experience of matter, which does the same; as in all instances of generation and vegetation, where the accurate analysis of the cause exceeds all human comprehension. We have also experience of particular systems of thought and of matter, which have no order; of the first, in madness, of the second, in corruption. Why then should we think, that order is more essential to one than the other? And if it requires a cause in both, what do we gain by your system, in tracing the universe of objects into a similar universe of ideas? The first step, which we make, leads us on for ever. It were, therefore, wise in us, to limit all our enquiries to the present world, without looking farther. No satisfaction can ever be attained by these speculations, which so far exceed the narrow bounds of human understanding.

In like manner, when it is asked, what cause produces order in the ideas of the supreme Being, can any other reason be assigned by you, anthropomorphites, than that it is a *rational* faculty, and that such is the nature of the Deity? But why a similar answer will not be equally satisfactory in accounting for the order of the world, without having recourse to any such intelligent Creator as you insist on, may be difficult to determine. It is only to say, that *such* is the nature of material objects, and that they are all originally possessed of a *faculty* of order and proportion. These are only more learned and elaborate ways of confessing our ignorance; nor has the one hypothesis any real advantage above the other, except in its greater conformity to vulgar prejudices.

You have displayed this argument with great emphasis, replied CLEANTHES: You seem not sensible, how easy it is to answer it. Even in common life, if I assign a cause for any event; is it any objection, PHILO, that I cannot assign the cause of that cause, and answer every new question, which may incessantly be started? And what philosophers could possibly submit to so rigid a rule? philosophers, who confess ultimate causes to be totally unknown, and are sensible, that the most refined principles, into which they trace the phenomena, are still to them as inexplicable as these phenomena themselves are to the vulgar. The order and arrangement of nature, the curious adjustment of final causes, the plain use and intention of every part and organ; all these bespeak in the clearest language an intelligent cause or Author. The heavens and the earth join in the same testimony: The whole chorus of nature raises one hymn to the praises of its Creator: You alone, or almost alone, disturb this general harmony. You start abstruse doubts, cavils, and objections: You ask me, what is the cause of this cause? I know not; I care not; that concerns not me. I have found a Deity; and here I stop my enquiry. Let those go farther, who are wiser or more enterprising.

I pretend to be neither, replied PHILO: And for that very reason, I should never perhaps have attempted to go so far; especially when I am sensible, that I must at last be contented to sit down with the same answer, which, without farther trouble, might have satisfied me from the beginning.

But to show you still more inconveniences, continued PHILO, in your anthropomorphism; please to take a new survey of your principles. *Like effects prove like causes.* This is the experimental argument; and this, you say too, is the sole theological argument. Now it is certain, that the liker the effects are, which are seen, and the liker the causes, which are inferred, the stronger is the argument. Every departure on either side diminishes the probability, and renders the experiment less conclusive. You cannot doubt of this principle: Neither ought you to reject its consequences.

Now, CLEANTHES, said PHILO, with an air of alacrity and triumph, mark the consequences. *First*, By this method of reasoning, you renounce all claim to infinity in any of the attributes of the Deity. For as the cause ought only to be proportioned to the effect, and the effect, so far as it falls under our cognisance, is not infinite; what pretensions have we, upon your suppositions, to ascribe that attribute to the divine Being? You will still insist, that, by removing him so much from all similarity to human creatures, we give into the most arbitrary hypothesis, and at the same time weaken all proofs of his existence.

Secondly, You have no reason, on your theory, for ascribing perfection to the Deity, even in his finite capacity; or for supposing him free from every error, mistake, or incoherence in his undertakings. There are many inexplicable difficulties in the works of nature, which, if we allow a perfect Author to be proved *a priori*, are easily solved, and become only seeming difficulties, from the narrow capacity of man, who cannot trace infinite relations. But according to your method of reasoning, these difficulties become all real; and perhaps will be insisted on, as new instances of likeness to human art and contrivance. At least, you must acknowledge, that it is impossible for us to tell, from our limited views, whether this system contains any great faults, or deserves any considerable praise, if compared to other possible, and even real systems. Could a peasant, if the ÆNEID were read to him, pronounce that poem to be absolutely faultless, or even assign to it its proper rank among the productions of human wit; he, who had never seen any other production?

But were this world ever so perfect a production, it must still remain uncertain, whether all the excellencies of the work can justly be ascribed to the workman. If we survey a ship, what an exalted idea must we form of the ingenuity of the carpenter, who framed so complicated, useful, and beautiful a machine? And what surprise must we entertain, when we find him a stupid mechanic, who imitated others, and copied an art, which, through a long succession of ages, after multiplied trials, mistakes, corrections, deliberations, and controversies, had been gradually improving? Many worlds might have been botched and bungled, throughout an eternity, ere this system was struck out: Much labour lost: Many fruitless trials made: And a slow, but continued improvement carried on during infinite ages in the art of world-making. In such subjects, who can determine, where the truth; nay, who can conjecture where the probability, lies; amidst a great number of hypotheses which may be proposed, and a still greater number which may be imagined?

And what shadow of an argument, continued PHILO, can you produce, from your hypothesis, to prove the unity of the Deity? A great number of men join in building a house or ship, in rearing a city, in framing a commonwealth: Why may not several Deities combine in contriving and framing a world? This is only so much greater similarity to human affairs. By sharing the work among several, we may so much farther limit the attributes of each, and get rid of that extensive power and knowledge, which must be supposed in one Deity, and which, according to you, can only serve to weaken the proof of his existence. And if such foolish, such vicious creatures as man can yet often unite in framing and executing one plan; how much more those Deities or Dæmons, whom we may suppose several degrees more perfect?

It must be a slight fabric, indeed, said DEMEA, which can be erected on so tottering a foundation. While we are uncertain, whether there is one Deity or many; whether the Deity or Deities, to whom we owe our existence, be perfect or imperfect, subordinate or supreme, dead or alive; what trust or confidence can we repose in them? What devotion or worship address to them? What veneration or obedience pay them? To all the purposes of life, the theory of religion becomes altogether useless: And even with regard to speculative consequences, its uncertainty, according to you, must render it totally precarious and unsatisfactory.

To render it still more unsatisfactory, said PHILO, there occurs to me another hypothesis, which must acquire an air of probability from the method of reasoning so much insisted on by CLEANTHES. That like effects arise from like causes: This principle he supposes the foundation of all religion. But there is another principle of the same kind, no less certain, and derived from the same source of experience; that where several known circumstances are *observed* to be similar, the unknown will also be *found* similar. Thus, if we see the limbs of a human body, we conclude, that it is also attended with a human head, though hid from us. Thus, if we see, through a chink in a wall, a small part of the sun, we conclude, that, were the wall removed, we should see the whole body. In short, this method of reasoning is so obvious and familiar, that no scruple can ever be made with regard to its solidity.

Now if we survey the universe, so far as it falls under our knowledge, it bears a great resemblance to an animal or organized body, and seems actuated with a like principle of life and motion. A continual circulation of matter in it produces no disorder: A continual waste in every part is incessantly repaired: The closest sympathy is perceived throughout the entire system: And each part or member, in performing its proper offices, operates both to its own preservation and to that of the whole. The world, therefore, I infer, is an animal, and the Deity is the SOUL of the world, actuating it, and actuated by it.

You have too much learning, CLEANTHES, to be at all surprised at this opinion, which, you know, was maintained by almost all the theists of antiquity, and chiefly prevails in their discourses and reasonings. For though sometimes the ancient philosophers reason from final causes, as if they thought the world the workmanship of God; yet it appears rather their favourite notion to consider it as his body, whose organization renders it subservient to him. And it must be confessed, that as the universe resembles more a human body than it does the works of human art and contrivance; if our limited analogy could ever, with any propriety, be extended to the whole of nature, the inference seems juster in favour of the ancient than the modern theory.

There are many other advantages too, in the former theory, which recommended it to the ancient theologians. Nothing more repugnant to all their notions, because nothing more repugnant to common experience, than mind without body; a mere spiritual substance, which fell not under their senses nor comprehension, and of which they had not observed one single instance throughout all nature. Mind and body they knew, because they felt both: An order, arrangement, organization, or internal machinery in both they likewise knew, after the same manner: And it could not but seem reasonable to transfer this experience to the universe, and to suppose the divine mind and body to be also coeval, and to have, both of them, order and arrangement naturally inherent in them, and inseparable from them.

Here therefore is a new species of anthropomorphism, CLEANTHES, on which you may deliberate; and a theory which seems not liable to any considerable difficulties. You are too much superior surely to *systematical prejudices*, to find any more difficulty in supposing an animal body to be, originally, of itself, or from unknown causes, possessed of order and organization, than in supposing a similar order to belong to mind. But the *vulgar prejudice*, that body and mind ought always to accompany each other, ought not, one should think, to be entirely neglected; since it is founded on *vulgar experience*, the only guide which you profess to follow in all these theological inquiries. And if you assert, that our limited experience is an unequal standard, by which to judge of the unlimited extent of nature; you entirely abandon your own hypothesis, and must thenceforward adopt our mysticism, as you call it, and admit of the absolute incomprehensibility of the divine nature.

This theory, I own, replied CLEANTHES, has never before occurred to me, though a pretty natural one; and I cannot readily, upon so short an examination and reflection, deliver any opinion with regard to it. You are very scrupulous, indeed, said PHILO; were I to examine any system of yours, I should not have acted with half that caution and reserve, in starting objections and difficulties to it. However, if any thing occur to you, you will oblige us by proposing it.

Why then, replied CLEANTHES, it seems to me that, though the world does, in many circumstances, resemble an animal body; yet is the analogy also effective in many circumstances, the most material: No organs of sense; no seat of thought or reason; no one precise origin of motion and action. In short, it seems to bear a stronger resemblance to a vegetable than to an animal; and your inference would be so far inconclusive in favour of the soul of the world.

But here, continued PHILO, in examining the ancient system of the soul of the world, there strikes me, all on a sudden, a new idea, which, if just, must go near to subvert all your reasoning, and destroy even your first inferences, on which you repose such confidence. If the universe bears a greater likeness to animal bodies and to vegetables, than to the works of human art, it is more probable that its cause resembles the cause of the former than that of the latter, and its origin ought rather to be ascribed to generation or vegetation than to reason or design. Your conclusion, even according to your own principles, is therefore lame and defective.

Pray open up this argument a little farther, said DEMEA. For I do not rightly apprehend it, in that concise manner in which you have expressed it.

Our friend, CLEANTHES, replied PHILO, as you have heard, asserts, that since no question of fact can be proved otherwise than by experience, the existence of a Deity admits not of proof from any other medium. The world, says he, resembles the works of human contrivance: Therefore its cause must also resemble that of the other. Here we may remark, that the operation of one very small part of nature, to wit man, upon another very small part, to wit that inanimate matter lying within his reach, is the rule by which CLEANTHES judges of the origin of the whole; and he measures objects, so widely disproportioned, by the same individual standard. But to waive all objections drawn from this topic; I affirm, that there are other parts of the universe (besides the machines of human invention) which bear still a greater resemblance to the fabric of the world, and which therefore afford a better conjecture concerning the universal origin of this system. These parts are animals and vegetables. The world plainly resembles more an animal or a vegetable, than it does a watch or a knitting-loom. Its cause, therefore, it is more probable, resembles the cause of the former. The cause of the former is generation or vegetation. The cause, therefore, of the world, we may infer to be some thing similar or analogous to generation or vegetation.

But how is it conceivable, said DEMEA, that the world can arise from any thing similar to vegetation or generation?

In reality, DEMEA, it may reasonably be expected, that the larger the views are which we take of things, the better will they conduct us in our conclusions concerning such extraordinary and such magnificent subjects. In this little corner of the world alone, there are four principles, *reason, instinct, generation, vegetation,* which are similar to each other, and are the causes of similar effects. What a number of other principles may we naturally suppose in the immense extent and variety of the universe, could we travel from planet to planet and from system to system, in order to examine each part of this mighty fabric? Any one of these four principles above mentioned (and a hundred others which lie open to our conjecture) may afford us a theory, by which to judge of the origin of the world; and it is a palpable and egregious partiality, to confine our view entirely to that principle, by which our own minds operate. Were this principle more intelligible on that account, such a partiality might be somewhat excusable: But reason, in its internal fabric and structure, is really as little known to us as instinct or vegetation; and perhaps even that vague, undeterminate word, nature, to which the vulgar refer every thing, is not at the bottom more inexplicable. The effects of these principles are all known to us from experience: But the principles themselves, and their manner of operation, are totally unknown: Nor is it less intelligible, or less conformable to experience to say, that the world arose by vegetation from a seed shed by another world, than to say that it arose from a divine reason or contrivance, according to the sense in which CLEANTHES understands it.

But methinks, said DEMEA, if the world had a vegetative quality, and could sow the seeds of new worlds into the infinite chaos, this power would be still an additional argument for design in its Author. For whence could arise so wonderful a faculty but from design? Or how can order spring from any thing, which perceives not that order which it bestows?

You need only look around you, replied PHILO, to satisfy yourself with regard to this question. A tree bestows order and organization on that tree which springs from it, without knowing the order: an animal, in the same manner, on its offspring: a bird, on its nest: And instances of this kind are even more frequent in the world, than those of order, which arise from reason and contrivance. To say that all this order in animals and vegetables proceeds ultimately from design is begging the question; nor can that great point be ascertained otherwise than by proving *a priori*, both that order is, from its nature, inseparably attached to thought, and that it can never, of itself, or from original unknown principles, belong to matter.

But farther, DEMEA; this objection, which you urge, can never be made use of by CLEANTHES, without renouncing a defence which he has already made against one of my objections. When I enquired concerning the cause of that supreme reason and intelligence, into which he resolves every thing; he told me, that the impossibility of satisfying such enquiries could never be admitted as an objection in any species of philosophy. *We must stop somewhere*, says he; *nor is it ever within the reach of human capacity to explain ultimate causes, or show the last connections of any objects. It is sufficient, if the steps, so far as we go, are supported by experience and observation.* Now that vegetation and generation, as well as reason, are experienced to be principles of order in nature, is undeniable. If I rest my system of cosmogony on the former, preferably to the latter, it is at my choice. The matter seems entirely arbitrary. And when CLEANTHES asks me what is the cause of my great vegetative or generative faculty, I am equally entitled to ask him the cause of his great reasoning principle. These questions we have agreed to forbear on both sides; and it is chiefly his interest on the present occasion to stick to this agreement. Judging by our limited and imperfect experience, generation has some privileges above reason: For we see every day the latter arise from the former, never the former from the latter.

Compare, I beseech you, the consequences on both sides. The world, say I, resembles an animal, therefore it is an animal, therefore it arose from generation. The steps, I confess, are wide; yet there is some small appearance of analogy in each step. The world, says CLEANTHES, resembles a machine, therefore it is a machine, therefore it arose from design. The steps are here equally wide, and the analogy less striking. And if he pretends to carry on *my* hypothesis a step farther, and to infer design or reason from the great principle of generation, on which I insist; I may, with better authority, use the same freedom to push farther *his* hypothesis, and infer a divine generation or theogony from his principle of reason. I have at least some faint shadow of experience, which is the utmost that can ever be attained in the present subject. Reason, in innumerable instances, is observed to arise from the principle of generation, and never to arise from any other principle.

The BRAHMINS assert, that the world arose from an infinite spider, who spun this whole complicated mass from his bowels, and annihilates afterwards the whole or any part of it, by absorbing it again, and resolving it into his own essence. Here is a species of cosmogony, which appears to us ridiculous; because a spider is a little contemptible animal, whose operations we are never likely to take for a model of the whole universe. But still here is a new species of analogy, even in our globe. And were there a planet wholly inhabited by spiders (which is very possible), this inference would there appear as natural and irrefragable as that which in our planet ascribes the origin of all things to design and intelligence, as explained by CLEANTHES. Why an orderly system may not be spun from the belly as well as from the brain, it will be difficult for him to give a satisfactory reason.

I must confess, PHILO, replied CLEANTHES, that of all men living, the task which you have undertaken, of raising doubts and objections, suits you best, and seems, in a manner, natural and unavoidable to you. So great is your fertility of invention, that I am not ashamed to acknowledge myself unable, in a sudden, to solve regularly such out-of-the-way difficulties as you incessantly start upon me: Though I clearly see, in general, their fallacy and error. And I question not, but you are yourself, at present, in the same case, and have not the solution so ready as the objection; while you must be sensible, that common sense and reason is entirely against you, and that such whimsies, as you have delivered, may puzzle, but never can convince us.

What you ascribe to the fertility of my invention, replied PHILO, is entirely owing to the nature of the subject. In subjects, adapted to the narrow compass of human reason, there is commonly but one determination, which carries probability or conviction with it; and to a man of sound judgment, all other suppositions, but that one, appear entirely absurd and chimerical. But in such questions as the present, a hundred contradictory views may preserve a kind of imperfect analogy; and invention has here full scope to exert itself. Without any great effort of thought, I believe that I could, in an instant, propose other systems of cosmogony, which would have some faint appearance of truth; though it is a thousand, a million to one, if either yours or any one of mine be the true system.

For instance; what if I should revive the old EPICUREAN hypothesis? This is commonly, and I believe, justly, esteemed the most absurd system, that has yet been proposed; yet, I know not, whether, with a few alterations, it might not be brought to bear a faint appearance of probability. Instead of supposing matter infinite, as EPICURUS did; let us suppose it finite. A finite number of particles is only susceptible of finite transpositions: And it must happen, in an eternal duration, that every possible order or position must be tried an infinite number of times. This world, therefore, with all its events, even the most minute, has before been produced and destroyed, and will again be produced and destroyed, without any bounds and limitations. No one, who has a conception of the powers of infinite, in comparison of finite, will ever scruple this determination.

But this supposes, said DEMEA, that matter can acquire motion, without any voluntary agent or first mover.

And where is the difficulty, replied PHILO, of that supposition? Every event, before experience, is equally difficult and incomprehensible; and every event, after experience, is equally easy and intelligible. Motion, in many instances, from gravity, from elasticity, from electricity, begins in matter, without any known voluntary agent; and to suppose always, in these cases, an unknown voluntary agent, is mere hypothesis; and hypothesis attended with no advantages. The beginning of motion in matter itself is as conceivable *a priori* as its communication from mind and intelligence.

Besides, why may not motion have been propagated by impulse through all eternity, and the same stock of it, or nearly the same, be still upheld in the universe? As much as is lost by the composition of motion, as much is gained by its resolution. And whatever the causes are, the fact is certain, that matter is, and always has been in continual agitation, as far as human experience or tradition reaches. There is not probably, at present, in the whole universe, one particle of matter at absolute rest.

And this very consideration too, continued PHILO, which we have stumbled on in the course of the argument, suggests a new hypothesis of cosmogony, that is not absolutely absurd and improbable. Is there a system, an order, an œconomy of things, by which matter can preserve that perpetual agitation, which seems essential to it, and yet maintain a constancy in the forms, which it produces? There certainly is such an œconomy: For this is actually the case with the present world. The continual motion of matter, therefore, in less than infinite transpositions, must produce this œconomy or order; and by its very nature, that order, when once established, supports itself, for many ages, if not to eternity. But wherever matter is so poised, arranged, and adjusted as to continue in perpetual motion, and yet preserve a constancy in the forms, its situation must, of necessity, have all the same appearance of art and contrivance which we observe at present. All the parts of each form must have a relation to each other, and to the whole: And the whole itself must have a relation to the other parts of the universe; to the element, in which the form subsists; to the materials, with which it repairs its waste and decay; and to every other form, which is hostile or friendly. A defect in any of these particulars destroys the form; and the matter, of which it is composed, is again set loose, and is thrown into irregular motions and fermentations, till it unite itself to some other regular form. If no such form be prepared to receive it, and if there be a great quantity of this corrupted matter in the universe, the universe itself is entirely disordered; whether it be the feeble embryo of a world in its first beginnings, that is thus destroyed, or the rotten carcass of one, languishing in old age and infirmity. In either case, a chaos ensues; till finite, though innumerable revolutions produce at last some forms, whose parts and organs are so adjusted as to support the forms amidst a continued succession of matter.

Suppose (for we shall endeavour to vary the expression), that matter were thrown into any position, by a blind, unguided force; it is evident that this first position must in all probability be the most confused and most disorderly imaginable, without any resemblance to those works of human contrivance, which, along with a symmetry of parts, discover an adjustment of means to ends and a tendency to self-preservation. If the actuating force cease after this operation, matter must remain for ever in disorder, and continue an immense chaos, without any proportion or activity. But suppose, that the actuating force, whatever it be, still continues in matter, this first position will immediately give place to a second, which will likewise in all probability be as disorderly as the first, and so on, through many successions of changes and revolutions. No particular order or position ever continues a moment unaltered. The original force, still remaining in activity, gives a perpetual restlessness to matter. Every possible situation is produced, and instantly destroyed. If a glimpse or dawn of order appears for a moment, it is instantly hurried away, and confounded, by that never-ceasing force, which actuates every part of matter.

Thus the universe goes on for many ages in a continued succession of chaos and disorder. But is it not possible that it may settle at last, so as not to lose its motion and active force (for that we have supposed inherent in it), yet so as to preserve an uniformity of appearance, amidst the continual motion and fluctuation of its parts? This we find to be the case with the universe at present. Every individual is perpetually changing, and every part of every individual, and yet the whole remains, in appearance, the same. May we not hope for such a position, or rather be assured of it, from the eternal revolutions of unguided matter, and may not this account for all the appearing wisdom and contrivance which is in the universe? Let us contemplate the subject a little, and we shall find, that this adjustment, if attained by matter, of a seeming stability in the forms, with a real and perpetual revolution or motion of parts, affords a plausible, if not a true solution of the difficulty.

It is in vain, therefore, to insist upon the uses of the parts in animals or vegetables, and their curious adjustment to each other. I would fain know how an animal could subsist, unless its parts were so adjusted? Do we not find, that it immediately perishes whenever this adjustment ceases, and that its matter corrupting tries some new form? It happens, indeed, that the parts of the world are so well adjusted, that some regular form immediately lays claim to this corrupted matter: And if it were not so, could the world subsist? Must it not dissolve as well as the animal, and pass through new positions and situations; till in a great, but finite succession, it fall at last into the present or some such order?

It is well, replied CLEANTHES, you told us, that this hypothesis was suggested on a sudden, in the course of the argument. Had you had leisure to examine it, you would soon have perceived the insuperable objections, to which it is exposed. No form, you say, can subsist, unless it possess those powers and organs, requisite for its subsistence: Some new order or œconomy must be tried, and so on, without intermission; till at last some order, which can support and maintain itself, is fallen upon. But according to this hypothesis, whence arise the many conveniences and advantages which men and all animals possess? Two eyes, two ears, are not absolutely necessary for the subsistence of the species. Human race might have been propagated and preserved, without horses, dogs, cows, sheep, and those innumerable fruits and products which serve to our satisfaction and enjoyment. If no camels had been created for the use of man in the sandy deserts of AFRICA and ARABIA, would the world have been dissolved? If no loadstone had been framed to give that wonderful and useful direction to the needle, would human society and the human kind have been immediately extinguished? Though the maxims of nature be in general very frugal, yet instances of this kind are far from being rare; and any one of them is a sufficient proof of design, and of a benevolent design, which gave rise to the order and arrangement of the universe.

At least, you may safely infer, said PHILO, that the foregoing hypothesis is so far incomplete and imperfect; which I shall not scruple to allow. But can we ever reasonably expect greater success in any attempts of this nature? Or can we ever hope to erect a system of cosmogony, that will be liable to no exceptions, and will contain no circumstance repugnant to our limited and imperfect experience of the analogy of nature? Your theory itself cannot surely pretend to any such advantage; even though you have run into *anthropomorphism*, the better to preserve a conformity to common experience. Let us once more put it to trial. In all instances which we have ever seen, ideas are copied from real objects, and are ectypal, not archetypal, to express myself in learned terms: You reverse this order, and give thought the precedence. In all instances which we have ever seen, thought has no influence upon matter, except where that matter is so conjoined with it, as to have an equal reciprocal influence upon it. No animal can move immediately any thing but the members of its own body; and indeed, the equality of action and re-action seems to be an universal law of nature: But your theory implies a contradiction to this experience. These instances, with many more, which it were easy to collect (particularly the supposition of a mind or system of thought that is eternal, or in other words, an animal ingenerable and immortal, these instances, I say, may teach, all of us, sobriety in condemning each other, and let us see, that as no system of this kind ought ever to be received from a slight analogy, so neither ought any to be rejected on account of a small incongruity. For that is an inconvenience from which we can justly pronounce no one to be exempted.

All religious systems, it is confessed, are subject to great and insuperable difficulties. Each disputant triumphs in his turn; while he carries on an offensive war, and exposes the absurdities, barbarities, and pernicious tenets of his antagonist. But all of them, on the whole, prepare a complete triumph for the sceptic; who tells them, that no system ought ever to be embraced with regard to such subjects: For this plain reason, that no absurdity ought ever to be assented to with regard to any subject. A total suspense of judgment is here our only reasonable resource. And if every attack, as is commonly observed, and no defence, among theologians, is successful; how complete must be his victory, who remains always, with all mankind, on the offensive, and has himself no fixed station or abiding city, which he is ever, on any occasion, obliged to defend?

12 An Agnostic's Attitude Toward the Existence of God*

THOMAS HUXLEY

Thomas Huxley (1825–1895) was a prominent British biologist and philosopher. He served as assistant surgeon on the H.M.S. Rattlesnake, examining marine organisms. His published results brought election to fellowship in the Royal Society. He supported Darwin's theory of evolution, argued for agnosticism in religion, and advocated an extension of education in science. His principal works are *Man's Place in Nature*, *Collected Essays*, *Scientific Memoirs*, and *Science and Christian Tradition*.

The people who call themselves "Agnostics" have been charged with doing so because they have not the courage to declare themselves "Infidels." It has been insinuated that they have adopted a new name in order to escape the unpleasantness which attaches to their proper denomination. To this wholly erroneous imputation, I have replied by showing that the term "Agnostic" did, as a matter of fact, arise in a manner which negatives it; and my statement has not been, and cannot be, refuted. Moreover, speaking for myself, and without impugning the right of any other person to use the term in another sense, I further say that Agnosticism is not properly described as a "negative" creed, nor indeed as a creed of any kind, except in so far as it expresses absolute faith in the validity of a principle, which is as much ethical as intellectual. This principle may be stated in various ways, but they all amount to this: that it is wrong for a man to say that he is certain of the objective truth of any proposition unless he can produce evidence which logically justifies that certainty. This is what Agnosticism asserts; and, in my opinion, it is all that is essential to Agnosticism. That which Agnostics deny and repudiate, as immoral, is the contrary doctrine, that there are propositions which men ought to believe, without logically satisfactory evidence; and that reprobation ought to attach to the profession of disbelief in such inadequately supported propositions. The justification of the Agnostic principle lies in the success which follows upon its application, whether in the field of natural, or in that of civil, history; and in the fact that, so far as these topics are concerned, no sane man thinks of denying its validity.

* From Thomas Huxley, *Science and Christian Tradition* (New York: D. Appleton & Company, Inc., 1896).

Still speaking for myself, I add, that though Agnosticism is not, and cannot be, a creed, except in so far as its general principle is concerned; yet that the application of that principle results in the denial of, or the suspension of judgment concerning, a number of propositions respecting which our contemporary ecclesiastical "gnostics" profess entire certainty. And, in so far as these ecclesiastical persons can be justified in their old-established custom (which many nowadays think more honoured in the breach than the observance) of using opprobrious names to those who differ from them, I fully admit their right to call me and those who think with me "Infidels"; all I have ventured to urge is that they must not expect us to speak of ourselves by that title.

The extent of the region of the uncertain, the number of the problems the investigation of which ends in a verdict of not proven, will vary according to the knowledge and the intellectual habits of the individual Agnostic. I do not very much care to speak of anything as "unknowable." What I am sure about is that there are many topics about which I know nothing; and which, so far as I can see, are out of reach of my faculties. But whether these things are knowable by any one else is exactly one of those matters which is beyond my knowledge, though I may have a tolerably strong opinion as to the probabilities of the case. Relatively to myself, I am quite sure that the region of uncertainty—the nebulous country in which words play the part of realities—is far more extensive than I could wish. Materialism and Idealism; Theism and Atheism; the doctrine of the soul and its mortality or immortality—appear in the history of philosophy like the shades of Scandinavian heroes, eternally slaying one another and eternally coming to life again in a metaphysical "Nifelheim." It is getting on for twenty-five centuries, at least, since mankind began seriously to give their minds to these topics. Generation after generation, philosophy has been doomed to roll the stone uphill; and, just as all the world swore it was at the top, down it has rolled to the bottom again. All this is written in innumerable books; and he who will toil through them will discover that the stone is just where it was when the work began. Hume saw this; Kant saw it; since their time, more and more eyes have been cleansed of the films which prevented them from seeing it; until now the weight and number of those who refuse to be the prey of verbal mystifications has begun to tell in practical life.

It was inevitable that a conflict should arise between Agnosticism and Theology; or rather, I ought to say, between Agnosticism and Ecclesiasticism. For Theology, the science, is one thing; and Ecclesiasticism, the championship of a foregone conclusion as to the truth of a particular form of Theology, is another. With scientific Theology, Agnosticism has no quarrel. On the contrary, the Agnostic, knowing too well the influence of prejudice and idiosyncrasy, even on those who desire most earnestly to be impartial, can wish for nothing more urgently than that the scientific theologian should not only be at perfect liberty to thresh out the matter in his own fashion; but that he should, if he can, find flaws in the Agnostic position; and, even if demonstration is not to be had, that he should put, in their full force, the grounds of the conclusions he thinks probable. The scientific theologian admits the Agnostic principle, however widely his results may differ from those reached by the majority of Agnostics.

But, as between Agnosticism and Ecclesiasticism, or, as our neighbours across the Channel call it, Clericalism, there can be neither peace nor truce. The Cleric asserts that it is morally wrong not to believe certain propositions, whatever the results of a strict scientific investigation of the evidence of these propositions. He tells us "that religious error is, in itself, of an immoral nature." He declares that he has prejudged certain conclusions, and looks upon those who show cause for arrest of judgment as emissaries of Satan. It necessarily follows that, for him, the attainment of faith, not the ascertainment of truth, is the highest aim of mental life. And, on careful analysis of the nature of his faith, it will too often be found to be, not the mystic process of unity with the Divine, understood by the religious enthusiast; but that which the candid simplicity of a Sunday scholar once defined it to be. "Faith," said this unconscious plagiarist of Tertullian, "is the power of saying you believe things which are incredible."

Now I, and many other Agnostics, believe that faith, in this sense, is an abomination; and though we do not indulge in the luxury of self-righteousness so far as to call those who are not of our way of thinking hard names, we do feel that the disagreement between ourselves and those who hold this doctrine is even more moral than intellectual. It is desirable there should be an end of any mistakes on this topic. If our clerical opponents were clearly aware of the real state of the case, there would be an end of the curious delusion, which often appears between the lines of their writings, that those whom they are so fond of calling "Infidels" are people who not only ought to be, but in their hearts are, ashamed of themselves. It would be discourteous to do more than hint the antipodal opposition of this pleasant dream of theirs to facts.

The clerics and their lay allies commonly tell us, that if we refuse to admit that there is good ground for expressing definite convictions about certain topics, the bonds of human society will dissolve and mankind lapse into savagery. There are several answers to this assertion. One is that the bonds of human society were formed without the aid of their theology; and, in the opinion of not a few competent judges, have been weakened rather than strengthened by a good deal of it. Greek science, Greek art, the ethics of old Israel, the social organisation of old Rome, contrived to come into being, without the help of any one who believed in a single distinctive article of the simplest of the Christian creeds. The science, the art, the jurisprudence, the chief political and social theories, of the modern world have grown out of those of Greece and Rome—not by favour of, but in the teeth of, the fundamental teachings of early Christianity, to which science, art, and any serious occupation with the things of this world, were alike despicable.

Again, all that is best in the ethics of the modern world, in so far as it has not grown out of Greek thought, or Barbarian manhood, is the direct development of the ethics of old Israel. There is no code of legislation, ancient or modern, at once so just and so merciful, so tender to the weak and poor, as the Jewish law; and, if the Gospels are to be trusted, Jesus of Nazareth himself declared that he taught nothing but that which lay implicitly, or explicitly, in the religious and ethical system of his people.

> And the scribe said unto him, Of a truth, Teacher, thou hast well said that he is one; and there is none other but he and to love him with all the heart, and with all the understanding, and with all the strength, and to love his neighbour as himself, is much more than all whole burnt offerings and sacrifices. (Mark xii. 32, 33.)

Here is the briefest of summaries of the teaching of the prophets of Israel of the eighth century; does the Teacher, whose doctrine is thus set forth in his presence, repudiate the exposition? Nay; we are told, on the contrary, that Jesus saw that he "answered discreetly," and replied, "Thou art not far from the kingdom of God."

So that I think that even if the creeds, from the so-called "Apostles'" to the so-called "Athanasian," were swept into oblivion; and even if the human race should arrive at the conclusion that, whether a bishop washes a cup or leaves it unwashed, is not a matter of the least consequence, it will get on very well. The causes which have led to the development of morality in mankind, which have guided or impelled us all the way from the savage to the civilised state, will not cease to operate because a number of ecclesiastical hypotheses turn out to be baseless. And, even if the absurd notion that morality is more the child of speculation than of practical necessity and inherited instinct, had any foundation; if all the world is going to thieve, murder, and otherwise misconduct itself as soon as it discovers that certain portions of ancient history are mythical; what is the relevance of such arguments to any one who holds by the Agnostic principle?

The writers of the Gospels and of the Acts take it for granted, as a matter of common knowledge; and it is easy to gather from these sources a series of propositions, which only need arrangement to form a complete system.

In this system, Man is considered to be a duality formed of a spiritual element, the soul; and a corporeal element, the body. And this duality is repeated in the Universe, which consists of a corporeal world embraced and interpenetrated by a spiritual world. The former consists of the earth, as its principal and central constituent, with the subsidiary sun, planets, and stars. Above the earth is the air, and below is the watery abyss. Whether the heaven, which is conceived to be above the air, and the hell in, or below, the subterranean deeps, are to be taken as corporeal or incorporeal is not clear. However this may be, the heaven and the air, the earth and the abyss, are peopled by innumerable beings analogous in nature to the spiritual element in man, and these spirits are of two kinds, good and bad. The chief of the good spirits, infinitely superior to all the others, and their creator, as well as the creator of the corporeal world and of the bad spirits, is God. His residence is heaven, where he is surrounded by the ordered hosts of good spirits; his angels, or messengers, and the executors of his will throughout the universe.

On the other hand, the chief of the bad spirits is Satan, *the* devil *par excellence*. He and his company of demons are free to roam through all parts of the universe, except the heaven. These bad spirits are far superior to man in power and subtlety; and their whole energies are devoted to bringing physical and moral evils upon him, and to thwarting, so far as their power goes, the benevolent intentions of the Supreme Being. In fact, the souls and bodies of men form both the theatre and the prize of an incessant warfare between the good and the evil spirits—the powers of light and the powers of darkness. By leading Eve astray, Satan brought sin and death upon mankind. As the gods of the heathen, the demons are the founders and maintainers of idolatry; as the "powers of the air" they afflict mankind with pestilence and famine; as "unclean spirits" they cause disease of mind and body.

The significance of the appearance of Jesus, in the capacity of the Messiah, or Christ, is the reversal of the satanic work by putting an end to both sin and death. He announces that the kingdom of God is at hand, when the "Prince of this world" shall be finally "cast out" (John xii. 31) from the cosmos, as Jesus, during his earthly career, cast him out from individuals. Then will Satan and all his devilry, along with the wicked whom they have seduced to their destruction, be hurled into the abyss of unquenchable fire—there to endure continual torture, without a hope of winning pardon from the merciful God, their Father; or of moving the glorified Messiah to one more act of pitiful intercession; or even of interrupting, by a momentary sympathy with their wretchedness, the harmonious psalmody of their brother angels and men, eternally lapped in bliss unspeakable.

The straitest Protestant, who refuses to admit the existence of any source of Divine truth, except the Bible, will not deny that every point of the pneumatological theory here set forth has ample scriptural warranty. The Gospels, the Acts, the Epistles, and the Apocalypse assert the existence of the devil, of his demons and of Hell, as plainly as they do that of God and his angels and Heaven. It is plain that the Messianic and the Satanic conceptions of the writers of these books are the obverse and the reverse of the same intellectual coinage. If we turn from Scripture to the traditions of the Fathers and the confessions of the Churches, it will appear that, in this one particular, at any rate, time has brought about no important deviation from primitive belief. From Justin onwards, it may often be a fair question whether God, or the devil, occupies a larger share of the attention of the Fathers. It is the devil who instigates the Roman authorities to persecute; the gods and goddesses of paganism are devils, and idolatry itself is an invention of Satan; if a saint falls away from grace, it is by the seduction of the demon;

if heresy arises, the devil has suggested it; and some of the Fathers go so far as to challenge the pagans to a sort of exorcising match, by way of testing the truth of Christianity. Mediæval Christianity is at one with patristic, on this head. The masses, the clergy, the theologians, and the philosophers alike, live and move and have their being in a world full of demons, in which sorcery and possession are everyday occurrences. Nor did the Reformation make any difference. Whatever else Luther assailed, he left the traditional demonology untouched; nor could any one have entertained a more hearty and uncompromising belief in the devil, than he and, at a later period, the Calvinistic fanatics of New England did. Finally, in these last years of the nineteenth century, the demonological hypotheses of the first century are, explicitly or implicitly, held and occasionally acted upon by the immense majority of Christians of all confessions.

Only here and there has the progress of scientific thought, outside the ecclesiastical world, so far affected Christians, that they and their teachers fight shy of the demonology of their creed. They are fain to conceal their real disbelief in one half of Christian doctrine by judicious silence about it; or by flight to those refuges for the logically destitute, accommodation or allegory. But the faithful who fly to allegory in order to escape absurdity resemble nothing so much as the sheep in the fable who—to save their lives —jumped into the pit. The allegory pit is too commodious, is ready to swallow up so much more than one wants to put into it. If the story of the temptation is an allegory; if the early recognition of Jesus as the Son of God by the demons is an allegory; if the plain declaration of the writer of the first Epistle of John (iii. 8), "To this end was the Son of God manifested, that He might destroy the works of the devil," is allegorical, then the Pauline version of the Fall may be allegorical, and still more the words of consecration of the Eucharist, or the promise of the second coming; in fact, there is not a dogma of ecclesiastical Christianity the scriptural basis of which may not be whittled away by a similar process.

Agnosticism (*me judice*) says: There is no good evidence of the existence of a demoniac spiritual world, and much reason for doubting it.

Hereupon the ecclesiastic may observe: Your doubt means that you disbelieve Jesus; therefore you are an "Infidel" instead of an "Agnostic." To which the agnostic may reply: No; for two reasons: first, because your evidence that Jesus said what you say he said is worth very little; and secondly, because a man may be an agnostic, in the sense of admitting he has no positive knowledge, and yet consider that he has more or less probable ground for accepting any given hypothesis about the spiritual world. Just as a man may frankly declare that he has no means of knowing whether the planets generally are inhabited or not, and yet may think one of the two possible hypotheses more likely than the other, so he may admit that he has no means of knowing anything about the spiritual world, and yet may think one or other of the current views on the subject, to some extent, probable.

When I reached intellectual maturity and began to ask myself whether I was an atheist, a theist, or a pantheist; a materialist or an idealist; a Christian or a freethinker; I found that the more I learned and reflected, the less ready was the answer; until, at last, I came to the conclusion that I had neither art nor part with any of these denominations, except the last. The one thing in which most of these good people were agreed was the one thing in which I differed from them. They were quite sure they had attained a certain "gnosis,"—had, more or less successfully, solved the problem of existence; while I was quite sure I had not, and had a pretty strong conviction that the problem was insoluble.

This was my situation when I had the good fortune to find a place among the members of that remarkable confraternity of antagonists, long since deceased, but of green and pious memory, the Metaphysical Society. Every variety of philosophical and theological opinion was represented there, and expressed itself with entire openness; most of my colleages were -ists of one sort or another; and, however kind and friendly they might be, I, the man without a rag of a label to cover himself with, could not fail to have some of the uneasy feelings which must have beset the historical fox when, after leaving the trap in which his tail remained, he presented himself to his normally elongated companions. So I took thought, and invented what I conceived to be the appropriate title of "agnostic." It came into my head as suggestively antithetic to the "gnostic" of Church history, who professed to know so much about the very things of which I was ignorant; and I took the earliest opportunity of parading it at our Society, to show that I, too, had a tail, like the other foxes. To my great satisfaction, the term took; and when the *Spectator* had stood godfather to it, any suspicion in the minds of respectable people, that a knowledge of its parentage might have awakened was, of course, completely lulled.

That is the history of the origin of the terms "agnostic" and "agnosticism"; I verily believe that the great good which has been effected in the world by Christianity has been largely counteracted by the pestilent doctrine on which all the Churches have insisted, that honest disbelief in their more or less astonishing creeds is a moral offence, indeed a sin of the deepest dye, deserving and involving the same future retribution as murder and robbery. If we could only see, in one view, the torrents of hypocrisy and cruelty, the lies, the slaughter, the violations of every obligation of humanity, which have flowed from this source along the course of the history of Christian nations, our worst imaginations of Hell would pale beside the vision.

I am very well aware, as I suppose most thoughtful people are in these times, that the process of breaking away from old beliefs is extremely unpleasant; and I am much disposed to think that the encouragement, the consolation, and the peace afforded to earnest believers in even the worst forms of Christianity are of great practical advantage to them. What deductions must be made from this gain on the score of the harm done to the citizen by the ascetic other-worldliness of logical Christianity; to the ruler, by the hatred, malice, and all uncharitableness of sectarian bigotry; to the legislator, by the spirit of exclusiveness and domination of those that count themselves pillars of orthodoxy; to the philosopher, by the restraints on the freedom of learning and teaching which every Church exercises, when it is strong enough; to the conscientious soul, by the introspective hunting after sins of the mint and cummin type, the fear of theological error, and the overpowering terror of possible damnation, which have accompanied the Churches like their shadow, I need not now consider; but they are assuredly not small. If agnostics lose heavily on the one side, they gain a good deal on the other. People who talk about the comforts of belief appear to forget its discomforts; they ignore the fact that the Christianity of the Churches is something more than faith in the ideal personality of Jesus, which they create for themselves, *plus* so much as can be carried into practice, without disorganising civil society, of the maxims of the Sermon on the Mount. Trip in morals or in doctrine (especially in doctrine), without due repentance or retractation, or fail to get properly baptized before you die, and a *plébiscite* of the Christians of Europe, if they were true to their creeds, would affirm your everlasting damnation by an immense majority.

Agnosticism, in fact, is not a creed, but a method, the essence of which lies in the rigorous application of a single principle. That principle is of great antiquity; it is as old as Socrates; as old as the writer who said, "Try all things, hold fast by that which is good;" it is the foundation of the Reformation, which simply illustrated the axiom that every man should be able to give a reason for the faith that is in him; it is the great principle of Descartes; it is the fundamental axiom of modern science. Positively the principle may be expressed: In matters of the intellect, follow your reason as far as it will take you, without regard to any other consideration. And negatively: In matters of the intellect do not pretend that conclusions are certain which are not demonstrated or demonstrable. That I take to be the agnostic faith, which if a man keep whole and undefiled, he shall not be ashamed to look the universe in the face, whatever the future may have in store for him.

How far Jesus positively sanctioned all these indrainings of circumjacent Paganism into Judaism; how far any one has a right to declare, that the refusal to accept one or other of these doctrines, as ascertained verities, comes to the same thing as contradicting Jesus, it appears to me not easy to say. But it is hardly less difficult to conceive that he could have distinctly nega- tived any of them; and, more especially, that demonology which has been accepted by the Christian Churches, in every age and under all their mutual antagonisms. But, I repeat my conviction that, whether Jesus sanctioned the demonology of his time and nation or not, it is doomed. The future of Chris- tianity, as a dogmatic system and apart from the old Israelitish ethics which it has appropriated and developed, lies in the answer which mankind will eventually give to the question, whether they are prepared to believe such

13 God as a Projection[*]

LUDWIG FEUERBACH

Ludwig Feuerbach (1804–1872) studied philosophy under Hegel at the University of Berlin and taught at Erlanger. He was dismissed from his position when he published a book critical of Christianity. He stated that one of his aims was to change "the friends of God into friends of man and believers into thinkers." *The Essence of Christianity* and *The Philosophy of the Future* are his best-known books.

I have only found the key to the cipher of the Christian religion, only extricated its true meaning from the web of contradictions and delusions called theology;—but in doing so I have certainly committed a sacrilege. If therefore my work is negative, irreligious, atheistic, let it be remembered that atheism—at least in the sense of this work—is the secret of religion itself; that religion itself, not indeed on the surface, but fundamentally, not in intention or according to its own supposition, but in its heart, in its essence, believes in nothing else than the truth and divinity of human nature. . . .

Religion is the dream of the human mind. But even in dreams we do not find ourselves in emptiness or in heaven, but on earth, in the realm of reality; we only see real things in the entrancing splendour of imagination and caprice, instead of in the simple daylight of reality and necessity. Hence I do nothing more to religion—and to speculative philosophy and theology also—than to open its eyes, or rather to turn its gaze from the internal towards the external, i.e., I change the object as it is in the imagination into the object as it is in reality.

In the perceptions of the senses consciousness of the object is distinguishable from consciousness of self; but in religion, consciousness of the object and self-consciousness coincide. The object of the senses is out of man, the religious object is within him, and therefore as little forsakes him as his self-consciousness or his conscience; it is the intimate, the closest object. "God," says Augustine, for example, "is nearer, more related to us, and therefore more easily known by us, than sensible, corporeal things" (*De Genesi ad litteram*, 1. v. c. 16). The object of the senses is in itself indifferent—independent of the disposition or of the judgment; but the object of religion is a selected object; the most excellent, the first, the supreme being; it essentially

* From Ludwig Feuerbach, *The Essence of Christianity*, trans. George Eliot (Marian Evans) (New York: C. Blanchard, 1855; and New York: Harper & Row Publishers, Incorporated, 1957).

presupposes a critical judgment, a discrimination between the divine and the non-divine, between that which is worthy of adoration and that which is not worthy. And here may be applied, without any limitation, the proposition: the object of any subject is nothing else than the subject's own nature taken objectively. Such as are a man's thoughts and dispositions, such is his God; so much worth as a man has, so much and no more has his God. Consciousness of God is self-consciousness, knowledge of God is self-knowledge. By his God thou knowest the man, and by the man, his God; the two are identical. Whatever is God to a man, that is his heart and soul; and conversely, God is the manifested inward nature, the expressed self of a man,—religion the solemn unveiling of a man's hidden treasures, the revelation of his intimate thoughts, the open confession of his love secrets.

But when religion—consciousness of God—is designated as the self-consciousness of man, this is not to be understood as affirming that the religious man is directly aware of this identity; for, on the contrary, ignorance of it is fundamental to the peculiar nature of religion. To preclude this misconception, it is better to say, religion is man's earliest and also indirect form of self-knowledge. Hence, religion everywhere precedes philosophy, as in the history of the race, so also in that of the individual. Man first of all sees his nature as if *out of* himself, before he finds it in himself. His own nature is in the first instance contemplated by him as that of another being. Religion is the childlike condition of humanity; but the child sees his nature—man— out of himself; in childhood a man is an object to himself, under the form of another man. Hence the historical progress of religion consists in this; that what by an earlier religion was regarded as objective, is now recognized as subjective; that is, what was formerly contemplated and worshipped as God is now perceived to be something *human*. What was at first religion becomes at a later period idolatry; man is seen to have adored his own nature. Man has given objectivity to himself, but has not recognized the object as his own nature: a later religion takes this forward step; every advance in religion is therefore a deeper self-knowledge. But every particular religion, while it pronounces its predecessors idolatrous, excepts itself—and necessarily so, otherwise it would no longer be religion—from the fate, the common nature of all religions: it imputes only to other religions what is the fault, if fault it be, of religion in general. Because it has a different object, a different tenor, because it has transcended the ideas of preceding religions, it erroneously supposes itself exalted above the necessary eternal laws which constitute the essence of religion—it fancies its objects, its ideas, to be super-human. But the essence of religion, thus hidden from the religious, is evident to the thinker, by whom religion is viewed objectively, which it cannot be by its votaries. And it is our task to show that the antithesis of divine and human is altogether illusory, that it is nothing else than the antithesis between the human nature in general and the human individual; that, consequently, the object and contents of the Christian religion are altogether human.

Religion, at least the Christian, is the relation of man to himself, or more correctly to his own nature (i.e., his subjective nature); but a relation to it, viewed as a nature apart from his own. The divine being is nothing else than the human being, or, rather, the human nature purified, freed from the limits of the individual man, made objective—i.e., contemplated and revered as another, a distinct being. All the attributes of the divine nature are, therefore, attributes of the human nature.

In relation to the attributes, the predicates of the Divine Being, this is admitted without hesitation, but by no means in relation to the subject of these predicates. The negation of the subject is held to be irreligion, nay, atheism; though not so the negation of the predicates. But that which has no predicates or qualities, has no effect upon me; that which has no effect upon me has no existence for me. To deny all the qualities of a being is equivalent to denying the being himself. A being without qualities is one which cannot become an object to the mind, and such a being is virtually non-existent. Where man deprives God of all qualities, God is no longer anything more to him than a negative being. To the truly religious man, God is not a being without qualities, because to him he is a positive, real being.

The denial of determinate, positive predicates concerning the divine nature is nothing else than a denial of religion, with, however, an appearance of religion in its favor, so that it is not recognized as a denial; it is simply a subtle, disguised atheism. The alleged religious horror of limiting God by positive predicates is only the irreligious wish to know nothing more of God, to banish God from the mind.

There is, however, a still milder way of denying the divine predicates than the direct one just described. It is admitted that the predicates of the divine nature are finite, and more particularly, human qualities, but their rejection is rejected; they are even taken under protection, because it is necessary to man to have a definite conception of God, and since he is man he can form no other than a human conception of him. In relation to God, it is said, these predicates are certainly without any objective validity; but to me, if he is to exist for me, he cannot appear otherwise than as he does appear to me, namely, as a being with attributes analogous to the human. But this distinction between what God is in himself, and what he is for me destroys the peace of religion, and is besides in itself an unfounded and untenable distinction. I cannot know whether God is something else in himself or for himself than he is for me; for I can make the distinction between the object as it is in itself, and the object as it is for me, only where an object can really appear otherwise to me.

Scepticism is the arch-enemy of religion; but the distinction between object and conception—between God as he is in himself, and God as he is for me—is a sceptical distinction, and therefore an irreligious one. . . .

Wherever, therefore, this idea, that the religious predicates are only anthropomorphisms, has taken possession of a man, there has doubt, has unbelief, obtained the mastery of faith. And it is only the inconsequence of faint-heartedness and intellectual imbecility which does not proceed from this idea to the formal negation of the predicates, and from thence to the negation of the subject to which they relate. If thou doubtest the objective truth of the predicates, thou must also doubt the objective truth of the subject whose predicates they are. If thy predicates are anthropomorphisms, the subject of them is an anthropomorphism, too. If love, goodness, personality, etc., are human attributes, so also is the subject which thou presupposest, the exist-ence of God, the belief that there is a God, an anthropomorphism—a pre-supposition purely human.

Thou believest in love as a divine attribute because thou thyself lovest; thou believest that God is a wise, benevolent being because thou knowest nothing better in thyself than benevolence and wisdom; and thou believest that God exists, that therefore he is a subject—whatever exists is a subject, whether it be defined as substance, person, essence, or otherwise—because thou thyself existed, art thyself a subject. Thou knowest no higher human good than to love, than to be good and wise; and even so thou knowest no higher happiness than to exist, to be a subject; for the consciousness of all reality, of all bliss, is for thee bound up in the consciousness of being a sub-ject, of existing. God is an existence, a subject to thee, for the same reason that he is to thee a wise, a blessed, a personal being. The distinction between the divine predicates and the divine subject is only this, that to thee the subject, the existence, does not appear an anthropomorphism, because the conception of it is necessarily involved in thy own existence as a subject, whereas the predicates do appear anthropomorphisms, because their necessity —the necessity that God should be conscious, wise, good, etc.,—is not an immediate necessity, identical with the being of man, but is evolved by his self-consciousness, by the activity of his thought. I am a subject, I exist, whether I be wise or unwise, good or bad. To exist is to man the first datum; it constitutes the very idea of the subject; it is presupposed by the predicates. Hence man relinquishes the predicates, but the existence of God is to him a settled, irrefragable, absolutely certain, objective truth. But, nevertheless, this distinction is merely an apparent one. The necessity of the subject lies only in the necessity of the predicate. Thou art a subject only in so far as thou art a human subject; the certainty and reality of thy existence lie only in the certainty and reality of thy human attributes. What the subject is lies only in the predicate; the predicate is the *truth* of the subject—the sub-ject only the personified, existing predicate, the predicate conceived as existing. . . .

Thus what theology and philosophy have held to be God, the Absolute, the Infinite, is not God; but that which they have held not to be God is God: namely, the attribute, the quality, whatever has reality. Hence he alone is the true atheist to whom the predicates of the Divine Being,—for example, love, wisdom, justice,—are nothing; not he to whom merely the subject of these predicates is nothing. And in no wise is the negation of the subject necessarily also a negation of the predicates considered in themselves. These have an intrinsic, independent reality; they force their recognition upon man by their very nature; they are self-evident truths to him; they prove, they attest themselves. It does not follow that goodness, justice, wisdom, are chimeras because the existence of God is a chimera, nor truths because this is a truth. The idea of God is dependent on the idea of justice, of benevolence; a God who is not benevolent, not just, not wise, is no God; but the converse does not hold. The fact is not that a quality is divine because God has it, but that God has it because it is in itself divine; because without it God would be a defective being. Justice, wisdom, in general every quality which constitutes the divinity of God, is determined and known by itself independently, but the idea of God is determined by the qualities which have thus been previously judged to be worthy of the divine nature. . . .

Now, when it is shown that what the subject is lies entirely in the attributes of the subject; that is, that the predicate is the true subject; it is also proved that if the divine predicates are attributes of the human nature, the subject of those predicates is also of the human nature. But the divine predicates are partly general, partly personal. The general predicates are the metaphysical, but these serve only as external points of support to religion; they are not the characteristic definitions of religion. It is the personal predicates alone which constitute the essence of religion—in which the Divine Being is the object of religion. Such are, for example, that God is a Person, that he is the moral Lawgiver, the Father of mankind, the Holy One, the Just, the Good, the Merciful. It is, however, at once, clear, or it will at least be clear in the sequel, with regard to these and other definitions, that, especially as applied to a personality, they are purely human definitions, and that consequently man in religion—in his relation to God—is in relation to his own nature; for to the religious sentiment these predicates are not mere conceptions, mere images, which man forms of God, to be distinguished from that which God is in himself, but truths, facts, realities. . . .

We have shown that the substance and object of religion is altogether human; we have shown that divine wisdom is human wisdom; that the secret of theology is anthropology; that the absolute mind is the so-called finite subjective mind. But religion is not conscious that its elements are human; on the contrary, it places itself in opposition to the human, or at least it does not admit that its elements are human. The necessary turning-point of history is therefore the open confession, that the consciousness of God is nothing else than the consciousness of the species; that man can and should raise himself only above the limits of his individuality, and not above the laws, the positive essential conditions of his species; that there is no other essence which man can think, dream of, imagine, feel, believe in, wish for, love and adore as the *absolute*, than the essence of human nature itself. . . .

14 Is the Existence of God Compatible with the Existence of Evil?*

DAVID HUME

David Hume (1711–1776) has had a tremendous influence on the development of modern philosophy. Along with John Locke and Bishop Berkeley, he began the philosophical tradition known as empiricism. His principal philosophical works are A *Treatise of Human Nature, Inquiry Concerning the Human Understanding,* and *Dialogues Concerning Natural Religion.*

And it is possible, CLEANTHES, said PHILO, that after all these reflections, and infinitely more, which might be suggested, you can still persevere in your anthropomorphism, and assert the moral attributes of the Deity, his justice, benevolence, mercy, and rectitude, to be of the same nature with these virtues in human creatures? His power we allow infinite: Whatever he wills is executed: But neither man nor any other animal are happy: Therefore he does not will their happiness. His wisdom is infinite: He is never mistaken in choosing the means to any end: But the course of nature tends not to human or animal felicity: Therefore it is not established for that purpose. Through the whole compass of human knowledge, there are no inferences more certain and infallible than these. In what respect, then, do his benevolence and mercy resemble the benevolence and mercy of men?

EPICURUS's old questions are yet unanswered. Is he willing to prevent evil, but not able? then is he impotent. Is he able, but not willing? then is he malevolent. Is he both able and willing? whence then is evil?

You ascribe, CLEANTHES (and I believe justly) a purpose and intention to nature. But what, I beseech you, is the object of that curious artifice and machinery, which she has displayed in all animals? The preservation alone of individuals and propagation of the species. It seems enough for her purpose, if such a rank be barely upheld in the universe, without any care or concern for the happiness of the members that compose it. No resource for this purpose: No machinery, in order merely to give pleasure or ease: No fund of pure joy and contentment: No indulgence without some want or

* From David Hume, *Dialogues Concerning Natural Religion,* first published in 1779.

necessity accompanying it. At least, the few phenomena of this nature are overbalanced by opposite phenomena of still greater importance.

Our sense of music, harmony, and indeed beauty of all kinds, gives satisfaction, without being absolutely necessary to the preservation and propagation of the species. But what racking pains, on the other hand, arise from gouts, gravels, megrims, tooth-aches, rheumatisms; where the injury to the animal-machinery is either small or incurable? Mirth, laughter, play, frolic, seem gratuitous satisfactions, which have no farther tendency: Spleen, melancholy, discontent, superstition, are pains of the same nature. How then does the divine benevolence display itself, in the sense of you anthropomorphites? None but we mystics, as you were pleased to call us, can account for this strange mixture of phenomena, by deriving it from attributes, infinitely perfect, but incomprehensible.

And have you at last, said CLEANTHES smiling, betrayed your intentions, PHILO? Your long agreement with DEMEA did indeed a little surprise me; but I find you were all the while erecting a concealed battery against me. And I must confess, that you have now fallen upon a subject worthy of your noble spirit of opposition and controversy. If you can make out the present point, and prove mankind to be unhappy or corrupted, there is an end at once of all religion. For to what purpose establish the natural attributes of the Deity, while the moral are still doubtful and uncertain?

You take umbrage very easily, replied DEMEA, at opinions the most innocent, and the most generally received even amongst the religious and devout themselves: And nothing can be more surprising than to find a topic like this, concerning the wickedness and misery of man, charged with no less than atheism and profaneness. Have not all pious divines and preachers, who have indulged their rhetoric on so fertile a subject; have they not easily, I say, given a solution of any difficulties which may attend it? This world is but a point in comparison of the universe: This life but a moment in comparison of eternity. The present evil phenomena, therefore, are rectified in other regions, and in some future period of existence. And the eyes of men, being then opened to larger views of things, see the whole connection of general laws, and trace, with adoration, the benevolence and rectitude of the Deity, through all the mazes and intricacies of his providence.

No! replied CLEANTHES, No! These arbitrary suppositions can never be admitted, contrary to matter of fact, visible and uncontroverted. Whence can any cause be known but from its known effects? Whence can any hypothesis be proved but from the apparent phenomena? To establish one hypothesis upon another is building entirely in the air; and the utmost we ever attain, by these conjectures and fictions, is to ascertain the bare possibility of our opinion; but never can we, upon such terms, establish its reality.

The only method of supporting divine benevolence (and it is what I willingly embrace) is to deny absolutely the misery and wickedness of man. Your representations are exaggerated: Your melancholy views mostly fictitious: Your inferences contrary to fact and experience. Health is more common than sickness: Pleasure than pain: Happiness than misery. And for one vexation which we meet with, we attain, upon computation, a hundred enjoyments.

Admitting your position, replied PHILO, which yet is extremely doubtful, you must, at the same time, allow, that, if pain be less frequent than pleasure, it is infinitely more violent and durable. One hour of it is often able to outweigh a day, a week, a month of our common insipid enjoyments: And how many days, weeks, and months are passed by several in the most acute torments? Pleasure, scarcely in one instance, is ever able to reach ecstasy and rapture: And in no one instance can it continue for any time at its highest pitch and altitude. The spirits evaporate; the nerves relax; the fabric is disordered; and the enjoyment quickly degenerates into fatigue and uneasiness. But pain often, Good God, how often! rises to torture and agony; and the longer it continues, it becomes still more genuine agony and torture. Patience is exhausted; courage languishes; melancholy seizes us; and nothing terminates our misery but the removal of its cause, or another event, which is the sole cure of all evil, but which, from our natural folly, we regard with still greater horror and consternation.

But not to insist upon these topics, continued PHILO, though most obvious, certain, and important; I must use the freedom to admonish you, CLEANTHES, that you have put this controversy upon a most dangerous issue, and are unawares introducing a total scepticism into the most essential articles of natural and revealed theology. What! no method of fixing a just foundation for religion, unless we allow the happiness of human life, and maintain a continued existence even in this world, with all our present pains, infirmities, vexations, and follies, to be eligible and desirable! But this is contrary to every one's feeling and experience: It is contrary to an authority so established as nothing can subvert: No decisive proofs can ever be produced against this authority; nor is it possible for you to compute, estimate, and compare all the pains and all the pleasures in the lives of all men and of all animals: And thus by your resting the whole system of religion on a point, which, from its very nature, must for ever be uncertain, you tacitly confess, that that system is equally uncertain.

But allowing you, what never will be believed; at least, what you never possibly can prove, that animal, or at least, human happiness, in this life, exceeds its misery; you have yet done nothing: For this is not, by any means, what we expect from infinite power, infinite wisdom, and infinite goodness. Why is there any misery at all in the world? Not by chance surely. From some cause then. Is it from the intention of the Deity? But he is perfectly benevolent. Is it contrary to his intention? But he is almighty. Nothing can shake the solidity of this reasoning, so short, so clear, so decisive; except we assert, that these subjects exceed all human capacity, and that our common measures of truth and falsehood are not applicable to them; a topic, which

I have all along insisted on, but which you have, from the beginning, rejected with scorn and indignation.

But I will be contented to retire still from this intrenchment: For I deny that you can ever force me in it: I will allow, that pain or misery in man is *compatible* with infinite power and goodness in the Deity, even in your sense of these attributes: What are you advanced by all these concessions? A mere possible compatibility is not sufficient. You must *prove* these pure, unmixed, and uncontrollable attributes from the present mixed and confused phenomena, and from these alone. A hopeful undertaking! Were the phenomena ever so pure and unmixed, yet being finite, they would be insufficient for that purpose. How much more, were they are also so jarring and discordant?

Here, CLEANTHES, I find myself at ease in my argument. Here I triumph. Formerly, when we argued concerning the natural attributes of intelligence and design, I needed all my sceptical and metaphysical subtilty to elude your grasp. In many views of the universe, and of its parts, particularly the latter, the beauty and fitness of final causes strike us with such irresistible force, that all objections appear (what I believe they really are) mere cavils and sophisms; nor can we then imagine how it was ever possible for us to repose any weight on them. But there is no view of human life, or of the condition of mankind, from which, without the greatest violence, we can infer the moral attributes, or learn that infinite benevolence, conjoined with infinite power and infinite wisdom, which we must discover by the eyes of faith alone. It is your turn now to tug the labouring oar, and to support your philosophical subtilties against the dictates of plain reason and experience.

I scruple not to allow, said CLEANTHES, that I have been apt to suspect the frequent repetition of the word, *infinite*, which we meet with in all theological writers, to savour more of panegyric than of philosophy, and that any purposes of reasoning, and even of religion, would be better served, were we to rest contented with more accurate and more moderate expressions. The terms, *admirable, excellent, superlatively great, wise,* and *holy*; these sufficiently fill the imaginations of men; and any thing beyond, besides that it leads into absurdities, has no influence on the affections or sentiments. Thus, in the present subject, if we abandon all human analogy, as seems your intention, DEMEA, I am afraid we abandon all religion, and retain no conception of the great object of our adoration. If we preserve human analogy, we must for ever find it impossible to reconcile any mixture of evil in the universe with infinite attributes; much less, can we ever prove the latter from the former. But supposing the Author of nature to be finitely perfect, though far exceeding mankind; a satisfactory account may then be given of natural and moral evil, and every untoward phenomenon be explained and adjusted. A less evil may then be chosen, in order to avoid a greater: Inconveniences be submitted to, in order to reach a desirable end: And in a word, benevolence, regulated by wisdom, and limited by necessity, may produce just such a world as the present. You, PHILO, who are so prompt at starting views, and reflections, and analogies; I would gladly hear, at length, without interruption, your opinion of this new theory; and if it deserve our attention, we may afterwards, at more leisure, reduce it into form.

My sentiments, replied PHILO, are not worth being made a mystery of; and therefore, without any ceremony, I shall deliver what occurs to me with regard to the present subject. It must, I think, be allowed, that, if a very limited intelligence, whom we shall suppose utterly unacquainted with the universe, were assured, that it were the production of a very good, wise, and powerful Being, however finite, he would, from his conjectures, form *beforehand* a different notion of it from what we find it to be by experience; nor would he ever imagine, merely from these attributes of the cause, of which he is informed, that the effect could be so full of vice and misery and disorder, as it appears in this life. Supposing now, that this person were brought into the world, still assured, that it was the workmanship of such a sublime and benevolent Being; he might, perhaps, be surprised at the disappointment; but would never retract his former belief, if founded on any very solid argument; since such a limited intelligence must be sensible of his own blindness and ignorance, and must allow, that there may be many solutions of those phenomena, which will for ever escape his comprehension. But supposing, which is the real case with regard to man, that this creature is not antecedently convinced of a supreme intelligence, benevolent, and powerful, but is left to gather such a belief from the appearances of things; this entirely alters the case, nor will he ever find any reason for such a conclusion. He may be fully convinced of the narrow limits of his understanding; but this will not help him in forming an inference concerning the goodness of superior powers, since he must form that inference from what he knows, not from what he is ignorant of. The more you exaggerate his weakness and ignorance, the more diffident you render him, and give him the greater suspicion, that such subjects are beyond the reach of his faculties. You are obliged, therefore, to reason with him merely from the known phenomena, and to drop every arbitrary supposition or conjecture.

Did I show you a house or palace, where there was not one apartment convenient or agreeable; where the windows, doors, fires, passages, stairs, and the whole œconomy of the building were the source of noise, confusion, fatigue, darkness, and the extremes of heat and cold; you would certainly blame the contrivance, without any farther examination. The architect would in vain display his subtilty, and prove to you, that if this door or that window were altered, greater ills would ensue. What he says, may be strictly true: The alteration of one particular, while the other parts of the building remain, may only augment the inconveniences. But still you would assert in general, that, if the architect had had skill and good intentions, he might have formed such a plan of the whole, and might have adjusted the parts in such a manner, as would have remedied all or most of these inconveniences. His ignorance, or even your own ignorance of such a plan, will never convince you of the impossibility of it. If you find many inconveniences and deformities in the building, you will always, without entering into any detail, condemn the architect.

In short, I repeat the question: Is the world considered in general, and as it appears to us in this life, different from what a man or such a limited being would, *beforehand*, expect from a very powerful, wise, and benevolent Deity? It must be strange prejudice to assert the contrary. And from thence I conclude, that, however consistent the world may be, allowing certain suppositions and conjectures, with the idea of such a Deity, it can never afford us an inference concerning his existence. The consistence is not absolutely denied, only the inference. Conjectures, especially where infinity is excluded from the divine attributes, may, perhaps, be sufficient to prove a consistence; but can never be foundations for any inference.

There seem to be *four* circumstances, on which depend all, or the greatest part of the ills, that molest sensible creatures; and it is not impossible but all these circumstances may be necessary and unavoidable. We know so little beyond common life, or even of common life, that, with regard to the œconomy of a universe, there is no conjecture, however wild, which may not be just; nor any one, however plausible, which may not be erroneous. All that belongs to human understanding, in this deep ignorance and obscurity, is to be sceptical, or at least cautious; and not to admit of any hypothesis, whatever; much less, of any which is supported by no appearance of probability. Now this I assert to be the case with regard to all the causes of evil, and the circumstances on which it depends. None of them appear to human reason, in the least degree, necessary or unavoidable; nor can we suppose them such, without the utmost licence of imagination.

The *first* circumstance which introduces evil, is that contrivance or œconomy of the animal creation, by which pains, as well as pleasures, are employed to excite all creatures to action, and make them vigilant in the great work of self-preservation. Now pleasure alone, in its various degrees, seems to human understanding sufficient for this purpose. All animals might be constantly in a state of enjoyment; but when urged by any of the necessities of nature, such as thirst, hunger, weariness; instead of pain, they might feel a diminution of pleasure, by which they might be prompted to seek that object, which is necessary to their subsistence. Men pursue pleasure as eagerly as they avoid pain; at least, might have been so constituted. It seems, therefore, plainly possible to carry on the business of life without any pain. Why then is any animal ever rendered susceptible of such a sensation? If animals can be free from it an hour, they might enjoy a perpetual exemption from it; and it required as particular a contrivance of their organs to produce that feeling, as to endow them with sight, hearing, or any of the senses. Shall we conjecture, that such a contrivance was necessary, without any appearance of reason? And shall we build on that conjecture as on the most certain truth?

But a capacity of pain would not alone produce pain, were it not for the *second* circumstance, viz. the conducting of the world by general laws; and this seems nowise necessary to a very perfect Being. It is true; if every thing were conducted by particular volitions, the course of nature would be perpetually broken, and no man could employ his reason in the conduct of life. But might not other particular volitions remedy this inconvenience? In short, might not the Deity exterminate all ill, wherever it were to be found; and produce all good, without any preparation or long progress of causes and effects?

Besides, we must consider, that, according to the present œconomy of the world, the course of nature, though supposed exactly regular, yet to us appears not so, and many events are uncertain, and many disappoint our expectations. Health and sickness, calm and tempest, with an infinite number of other accidents, whose causes are unknown and variable, have a great influence both on the fortunes of particular persons and on the prosperity of public societies: And indeed all human life, in a manner, depends on such accidents. A Being, therefore, who knows the secret springs of the universe, might easily, by particular volitions, turn all these accidents to the good of mankind, and render the whole world happy, without discovering himself in any operation. A fleet, whose purposes were salutary to society, might always meet with a fair wind: Good princes enjoy sound health and long life: Persons born to power and authority, be framed with good tempers and virtuous dispositions. A few such events as these, regularly and wisely conducted, would change the face of the world; and yet would no more seem to disturb the course of nature or confound human conduct, than the present œconomy of things, where the causes are secret, and variable, and compounded. Some small touches, given to CALIGULA's brain in his infancy, might have converted him into a TRAJAN: One wave, a little higher than the rest, by burying CÆSAR and his fortune in the bottom of the ocean, might have restored liberty to a considerable part of mankind. There may, for aught we know, be good reasons, why providence interposes not in this manner; but they are unknown to us: And though the mere supposition, that such reasons exist, may be sufficient to *save* the conclusion concerning the divine attributes, yet surely it can never be sufficient to *establish* that conclusion.

If every thing in the universe be conducted by general laws, and if animals be rendered susceptible of pain, it scarcely seems possible but some ill must arise in the various shocks of matter, and the various concurrence and opposition of general laws: But this ill would be very rare, were it not for the *third* circumstances, which I proposed to mention, viz. the great frugality with which all powers and faculties are distributed to every particular being. So well adjusted are the organs and capacities of all animals, and so well fittted to their preservation, that, as far as history or tradition reaches, there appears not to be any single species which has yet been extinguished in the universe. Every animal has the requisite endowments; but these endowments are bestowed with so scrupulous an œconomy, that any considerable diminution must entirely destroy the creature. Wherever one power is increased, there is a proportional abatement in the others. Animals, which excel in swiftness, are commonly defective in force. Those, which possess both, are either imperfect in some of their senses, or are oppressed with the most craving wants. The human species, whose chief excellency is reason and sagacity, is of all others the most necessitous, and the most deficient in bodily advantages; without clothes, without arms, without food, without lodging, without any convenience of life, except what they owe to their own skill and industry. In short, nature seems to have formed an exact calculation of the necessities of her creatures; and like a *rigid master*, has afforded them little more powers or endowments, than what are strictly sufficient to supply those necessities. An *indulgent parent* would have bestowed a large stock, in order to guard against accidents, and secure the happiness and welfare of the creature, in the most unfortunate concurrence of circumstances. Every course of life would not have been so surrounded with precipices, that the least departure from the true path, by mistake or necessity, must involve us in misery and ruin. Some reserve, some fund would have been provided to ensure happiness; nor would the powers and the necessities have been adjusted with so rigid an œconomy. The Author of nature is inconceivably powerful: His force is supposed great, if not altogether inexhaustible: Nor is there any reason, as far as we can judge, to make him observe this strict frugality in his dealings with his creatures. It would have been better, were his power extremely limited, to have created fewer animals, and to have endowed these with more faculties for their happiness and preservation. A builder is never esteemed prudent, who undertakes a plan, beyond what his stock will enable him to finish.

In order to cure most of the ills of human life, I require not that man should have the wings of the eagle, the swiftness of the stag, the force of the ox, the arms of the lion, the scales of the crocodile or rhinoceros; much less do I demand the sagacity of an angel or cherubim. I am contented to take an increase in one single power of faculty of his soul. Let him be endowed with a greater propensity to industry and labour; a more vigorous spring and activity of mind; a more constant bent to business and application. Let the whole species possess naturally an equal diligence with that which many individuals are able to attain by habit and reflection; and the most beneficial consequences, without any allay of ill, is the immediate and necessary result of this endowment. Almost all the moral, as well as natural evils of human life arise from idleness; and were our species, by the original constitution of their frame, exempt from this vice or infirmity, the perfect cultivation of land, the improvement of arts and manufactures, the exact execution of every office and duty, immediately follow; and men at once may fully reach that state of society, which is so imperfectly attained by the best-regulated government. But as industry is a power, and the most valuable of any, nature seems determined, suitably to her usual maxims, to bestow it on men with a very sparing hand; and rather to punish him severely for his deficiency in it, than to reward him for his attainments. She has so contrived his frame, that nothing but the most violent necessity can oblige him to labour; and she employs all his other wants to overcome, at least in part, the want of diligence, and to endow him with some share of a faculty, of which she has thought fit naturally to bereave him. Here our demands may be allowed very humble, and therefore the more reasonable. If we required the endowments of superior penetration and judgment, of a more delicate taste of beauty, of a nicer sensibility to benevolence and friendship; we might be told, that we impiously pretend to break the order of nature, that we want to exalt ourselves into a higher rank of being, that the presents which we require, not being suitable to our state and condition, would only be pernicious to us. But it is hard; I dare to repeat it, it is hard, that being placed in a world so full of wants and necessities; where almost every being and element is either our foe or refuses us their assistance; we should also have our own temper to struggle with, and should be deprived of that faculty which can alone fence against these multiplied evils.

The *fourth* circumstance, whence arises the misery and ill of the universe, is the inaccurate workmanship of all the springs and principles of the great machine of nature. It must be acknowledged, that there are few parts of the universe, which seem not to serve some purpose, and whose removal would not produce a visible defect and disorder in the whole. The parts hang all together; nor can one be touched without affecting the rest, in a greater or less degree. But at the same time, it must be observed, that none of these parts or principles, however useful, are so accurately adjusted, as to keep precisely within those bounds in which their utility consists; but they are, all of them, apt, on every occasion, to run into the one extreme or the other. One would imagine, that this grand production has not received the last hand of the maker; so little finished is every part, and so coarse are the strokes, with which it is executed. Thus, the winds are requisite to convey the vapours along the surface of the globe, and to assist men in navigation: But how oft, rising up to tempests and hurricanes, do they become pernicious? Rains are necessary to nourish all the plants and animals of the earth: But how often are they defective? how often excessive? Heat is requisite to all life and vegetation; but is not always found in the due proportion. On the mixture and secretion of the humours and juices of the body depend the health and prosperity of the animal: But the parts perform not regularly their proper function. What more useful than all the passions of the mind, ambition, vanity, love, anger? But how oft do they break their bounds, and cause the greatest convulsions in society? There is nothing so advantageous in the universe, but what frequently becomes pernicious, by its excess or defect; nor has nature guarded, with the requisite accuracy, against all disorder or confusion. The irregularity is never, perhaps, so great as to destroy any species; but is often sufficient to involve the individuals in ruin and misery.

On the concurrence, then, of these *four* circumstances does all or the greatest part of natural evil depend. Were all living creatures incapable of pain, or were the world administered by particular volitions, evil never could have found access into the universe: And were animals endowed with a large stock of powers and faculties, beyond what strict necessity requires; or were the several springs and principles of the universe so accurately framed as to preserve always the just temperament and medium; there must have been very little ill in comparison of what we feel at present. What then shall we pronounce on this occasion? Shall we say, that these circumstances are not necessary, and that they might easily have been altered in the contrivance of the universe? This decision seems too presumptuous for creatures so blind and ignorant. Let us be more modest in our conclusions. Let us allow, that, if the goodness of the Deity (I mean a goodness like the human) could be established on any tolerable reasons *a priori*, these phenomena, however untoward, would not be sufficient to subvert that principle; but might easily, in some unknown manner, be reconcilable to it. But let us still assert, that as this goodness is not antecedently established, but must be inferred from the phenomena, there can be no grounds for such an inference, while there are so many ills in the universe, and while these ills might so easily have been remedied, as far as human understanding can be allowed to judge on such a subject. I am sceptic enough to allow, that the bad appearances, notwithstanding all my reasonings, may be compatible with such attributes as you suppose: But surely they can never prove these attributes. Such a conclusion cannot result from scepticism; but must arise from the phenomena, and from our confidence in the reasonings which we deduce from these phenomena.

Look round this universe. What an immense profusion of beings, animated and organized, sensible and active! You admire this prodigious variety and fecundity. But inspect a little more narrowly these living existences, the only beings worth regarding. How hostile and destructive to each other! How insufficient all of them for their own happiness! How contemptible or odious to the spectator! The whole presents nothing but the idea of a blind nature, impregnated by a great vivifying principle, and pouring forth from her lap, without discernment or parental care, her maimed and abortive children.

Here the MANICHÆAN system occurs as a proper hypothesis to solve the difficulty: And no doubt, in some respects, it is very specious, and has more probability than the common hypothesis, by giving a plausible account of the strange mixture of good and ill which appears in life. But if we consider, on the other hand, the perfect uniformity and agreement of the parts of the universe, we shall not discover in it any marks of the combat of a malevolent with a benevolent Being. There is indeed an opposition of pains and pleasures in the feelings of sensible creatures: But are not all the operations of nature carried on by an opposition of principles, of hot and cold, moist and dry, light and heavy? The true conclusion is, that the original source of all things is entirely indifferent to all these principles, and has no more regard to good above ill than to heat above cold, or to drought above moisture, or to light above heavy.

There may *four* hypotheses be framed concerning the first causes of the universe: *that* they are endowed with perfect goodness, *that* they have perfect malice, *that* they are opposite and have both goodness and malice, *that* they have neither goodness nor malice. Mixed phenomena can never prove the two former unmixed principles. And the uniformity and steadiness of general laws seem to oppose the third. The fourth, therefore, seems by far the most probable.

What I have said concerning natural evil will apply to moral, with little or no variation; and we have no more reason to infer, that the rectitude of the supreme Being resembles human rectitude than that his benevolence resembles the human. Nay, it will be thought, that we have still greater cause to exclude from him moral sentiments, such as we feel them; since moral evil, in the opinion of many, is much more predominant above moral good than natural evil above natural good.

But even though this should not be allowed, and though the virtue, which is in mankind, should be acknowledged much superior to the vice; yet so long as there is any vice at all in the universe, it will very much puzzle you anthropomorphites, how to account for it. You must assign a cause for it, without having recourse to the first cause. But as every effect must have a cause, and that cause another; you must either carry on the progression *in infinitum*, or rest on that original principle, who is the ultimate cause of all things.

RELIGIOUS LANGUAGE
AND VERIFICATION

15 Religious Symbols and Our Knowledge of God*

PAUL TILLICH

Paul Tillich (1886–1965) was an influential theologian and philosopher, well known for his reformulation of Christian doctrine. A native of Germany, he lived in the United States a major portion of his life, teaching at Union Theological Seminary in New York, Harvard, and the University of Chicago. His basic works are *The Courage to Be*, *Dynamics of Faith*, and *Systematic Theology*.

The fact that there is so much discussion about the meaning of symbols going on in this country as well as in Europe is a symptom of something deeper. I believe it is a symptom of two things, something negative and something positive. It is a symptom of the fact that we are in a confusion of language in theology and philosophy and related subjects which has hardly been surpassed in any time in history. Words do not communicate to us anymore what they originally did and what they were invented to communicate. This has something to do with the fact that our present culture has no clearing house such as medieval scholasticism was, and Protestant scholasticism in the 17th century at least tried to be, and philosophers like Kant tried to renew. We have no such clearing house and this is the one point in which I am in sympathy with the present day so-called logical positivists or symbolic logicians or logicians generally. They at least try to produce a clearing house. My only criticism is that this clearing house is a very small room, perhaps only a corner of a house, and not a real house. It excludes

* From Paul Tillich, "Religious Symbols and Our Knowledge of God," *The Christian Scholar*, vol. 38, no. 3 (1955). Reprinted by permission of the National Council of The Churches of Christ in the U.S.A.

most of life. But it could become useful if it increased in reach and acceptance of realities beyond the mere logical calculus. The second point which I want to make is that we are in a process in which a very important thing is being rediscovered: namely, that there are levels of reality of great difference, and that these different levels demand different approaches and different languages: that not everything in reality can be grasped by the language which is most adequate for mathematical sciences; the insight into this situation is the most positive side of the fact that the problem of symbols is taken seriously again.

I

I want to proceed in my own presentation with the intention of clearing concepts as far as I am able. And in order to do this I want to make five steps, the first of which is the discussion of "symbols and signs." Symbols are similar to signs in one decisive respect: both symbols and signs point beyond themselves to something else. The typical sign, for instance the red light of the corner of the street, does not point to itself but it points to the necessity of cars stopping. And every symbol points beyond itself to a reality for which it stands. In this, symbols and signs have an essential identity—they point beyond themselves. And this is the reason that the confusion of language with which I started this lecture has also conquered the discussion about symbols for centuries and has produced confusion between signs and symbols. The first step in any clearing up of the meaning of symbols is to distinguish it from the meaning of signs.

The difference which I see as a fundamental difference between them is that signs do not participate in any way in the reality and power of that to which they point. Symbols, although they are not the same as that which they symbolize, participate in its meaning and power. The difference between symbol and sign is the participation in the symbolized reality which characterizes the symbols, and the non-participation in the "pointed-to" reality which characterizes a sign. For example, letters of the alphabet as they are written, an "A" or an "R" do not participate in the sound to which they point; on the other hand, the flag participates in the power of the king or the nation for which it stands and which it symbolizes. There has, therefore, been a fight since the days of William Tell as to how to behave in the presence of the flag. This would be meaningless if the flag did not participate as a symbol in the power of that which it symbolizes. The whole monarchic idea is itself entirely ununderstandable, if you do not understand that the king always is both: on the one hand, a symbol of the power of the group of which he is the king and on the other hand, he who exercised partly (never fully, of course) this power.

But something has happened which is very dangerous for all our attempts to find a clearing house of the concepts of symbols and signs. I have experienced this in three seminars which I have had in Columbia University with my philosophical colleagues there. The mathematician has usurped the term "symbol" for mathematical "sign," and this makes a disentanglement of the confusion almost impossible. The only thing we can do is to distinguish different groups, signs which are called symbols, and genuine symbols. The mathematical signs are signs which are wrongly called symbols. Let me again say something about language. Language is a very good example of the difference between signs and symbols. Words in a language are signs for a meaning which they express. The word "desk" is a sign which points to something quite different—namely, the thing on which my paper is lying here and at which I am looking and which hides me partly from you. This has nothing to do with the word "desk," with these four letters. But there are words in every language which are more than this, and in the moment in which they get connotations which go beyond something to which they point as signs, then they can become symbols; and this is a very important distinction for every speaker. He can speak almost completely in signs, reducing the meaning of his words almost to mathematical signs, and this is the absolute ideal of the logical positivist. The other pole of this is the liturgical or the poetic language where words have a power through centuries, or more than centuries. They have connotations in situations in which they appear so that they cannot be replaced. They have become not only signs pointing to a meaning which is defined, but also symbols standing for a reality in the power of which they participate.

II

Now I come to my second consideration dealing with the functions of symbols. The first function is implied in what I have already said—namely, the representative function. The symbol represents something which is not itself, for which it stands and in the power and meaning of which it participates. This is a basic function of every symbol, and therefore, if that word had not been used in so many other ways, one could perhaps even translate "symbolic" as "representative," but for some reason that is not possible. If the symbols stand for something which they are not, then the question is, "Why do we not have that for which they stand directly? Why do we need symbols at all?" And now I come to something which is perhaps the main function of the symbol—namely, the opening up of levels of reality which otherwise are hidden and cannot be grasped in any other way.

Every symbol opens up a level of reality for which non-symbolic speaking is inadequate. Let me interpret this or explain this in terms of artistic symbols. I resisted for many years the temptation to call works of art symbolic for the simple reason that there is a special artistic style which we call symbolistic and which produces only bad works of art. For this reason I disliked the idea of saying that works of art are symbolic. But in the meantime, the more I tried to enter into the meaning of symbols, the more I was convinced that it was a function of art to open up levels of reality; in poetry, in visual art, and in music, levels of reality are opened up which can be opened up in no other way. Now if this is the function of art, then certainly artistic creations have symbolic character. You can take that which a landscape of Rubens, for instance, mediates to you. You can not have this experience in any other way than through this painting made by Rubens. This landscape has some heroic character; it has character of balance, of colors, of weights, of values, and so on. All this is very external. What this mediates to you cannot be expressed in any other way than through the painting itself. The same is true also in the relationship of poetry and philosophy. The temptation may often be to confuse the issue by bringing too many philosophical concepts into a poem. Now this is really the problem; one cannot do this. If one uses philosophical language or scientific language, it does not mediate the same thing which is mediated in the use of really poetic language without a mixture of any other language. This example may show what I mean by the phrase "opening up of levels of reality." But in order to do this, something else must be opened up—namely, levels of the soul, levels of our interior reality. And they must correspond to the levels in exterior reality which are opened up by a symbol. So every symbol is two-edged. It opens up reality and it opens up the soul. Here I could give the same example—namely, the artistic experience. There are people who are not opened up by music, or who are not opened up by poetry, or more of them (mostly in Protestant America) who are not opened up at all by visual arts. The "opening up" is a two-sided function—namely, reality in deeper levels and the human soul in special levels.

If this is the function of symbols then it is obvious that symbols cannot be replaced by other symbols. Every symbol has a special function which is just *it* and cannot be replaced by more or less adequate symbols. This is different from signs, for signs can always be replaced. If one finds that a green light is not so expedient as perhaps a blue light (this is not true, but could be true), then we simply put on a blue light, and nothing is changed. But a symbolic word (such as the word "God") cannot be replaced. No symbol can be replaced when used in its special function. So one asks rightly, "How do symbols arise, and how do they come to an end?" As different from signs, symbols are born and die. Signs are consciously invented and removed. This is a fundamental difference. "Out of which womb are symbols born?" I would say out of the womb which is usually called today the "group unconscious" or "collective unconscious," or whatever you want to call it—out of a group which acknowledges, in this thing, this word, this flag, or whatever it may be, its own being. It is not invented intentionally; and even if somebody would try to invent a symbol, as sometimes happens, then it becomes a symbol only if the unconscious of a group says "yes" to it. It means that something is opened up by it in the sense which I have just described. Now this implies further that in the moment in which this inner situation of the human group to a symbol has ceased to exist, then the symbol dies. The symbol does not "say" anything any more. In this way, all of the polytheistic gods have died; the situation in which they were born, has changed or does not exist any more, and so the symbols died. But these are events which cannot be described in terms of intention and invention.

III

Now I come to my third consideration—namely, the nature of religious symbols. Religious symbols do exactly the same thing as all symbols do— namely, they open up a level of reality, which otherwise is not opened at all, which is hidden. I would call this the depth dimension of reality itself, the dimension of reality which is the ground of every other dimension and every other depth, and which therefore, is not one level beside the others but is the fundamental level, the level below all other levels, the level of being itself, or the ultimate power of being. Religious symbols open up the experience of the dimension of this depth in the human soul. If a religious symbol has ceased to have this function, then it dies. And if new symbols are born, they are born out of a changed relationship to the ultimate ground of being, i.e., to the Holy.

The dimension of ultimate reality is the dimension of the Holy. And so we can also say, religious symbols are symbols of the Holy. As such they participate in the holiness of the holy according to our basic definition of a symbol. But participation is not identity: they are not themselves *the* Holy. The wholly transcendent transcends every symbol of the Holy. Religious symbols are taken from the infinity of material which the experienced reality gives us. Everything in time and space has become at some time in the history of religion a symbol for the Holy. And this is naturally so, because everything that is in the world we encounter rests on the ultimate ground of being. This is the key to the otherwise extremely confusing history of religion. Those of you who have looked into this seeming chaos of the history of religion in all periods of history from the earliest primitives to the latest developments in California, will be extremely confused about the chaotic character of this development. But the key which makes order out of this chaos is comparatively simple. And the key is that everything in reality can impress itself as a symbol for a special relationship of the human mind to its own ultimate ground and meaning. So in order to open up the seemingly closed door to this chaos of religious symbols, one simply has to ask, "Which is the relationship to the ultimate which is symbolized in these symbols?" And then they cease to be meaningless; and they become, on the contrary, the most revealing creations of the human mind, the most genuine ones, the most powerful ones, those who control the human consciousness, and perhaps even more the unconsciousness, and have therefore this tremendous tenacity which is characteristic of all religious symbols in the history of religion.

Religion, as everything in life, stands under the law of ambiguity, "ambiguity" meaning that it is creative and destructive at the same time. Religion has its holiness and its unholiness, and the reason for this is obvious from what I have said about religious symbolism. Religious symbols point symbolically to that which transcends all of them. But since, as symbols, they participate in that to which they point, they always have the tendency (in the human mind, of course) to replace that to which they are supposed to point, and to become ultimate in themselves. And in the moment in which they do this, they become idols. All idolatry is nothing else than the absolutizing of symbols of the Holy, and making them identical with the Holy itself. In this way, for instance, holy persons can become god. Ritual acts can take on unconditional validity, although they are only expressions of a special situation. In all sacramental activities of religion, in all holy objects, holy books, holy doctrines, holy rites, you find this danger which I like to call demonization. They become demonic in the moment in which they become elevated to the unconditional and ultimate character of the Holy itself.

IV

Now I come to my fourth consideration—namely the levels of religious symbols. I distinguish two fundamental levels in all religious symbols: the transcendent level, the level which goes *beyond* the empirical reality we encounter, and the immanent level, the level which we find *within* the encounter with reality. Let us first look at the first level, the transcendent level. The basic symbol on the transcendent level would be God himself. But we cannot simply say that God is a symbol. We must always say two things about him: we must say that there is a non-symbolic element in our image of God —namely that he is ultimate reality, being itself, ground of being, power of being; and the other, that he is the highest being in which everything that we have does exist in the most perfect way. If we say this we have in our mind the image of a highest being, a being with the characteristics of highest perfection. That means we have a symbol for that which is not symbolic in the idea of God—namely "Being Itself." It is important, and I think more than important, to distinguish these two elements in the idea of God. Thus all of these discussions going on about God being a person or not a person, God being similar to other beings or not similar, these discussions which have a great impact on the destruction of the religious experience through false interpretations of it, could be overcome if we would say, "Certainly the awareness of something unconditional is in itself what it is, is not symbolic." We can call it *"Being Itself,"* esse qua esse, esse ipsum, as the scholastics did. But in our relationship to this ultimate we symbolize and must symbolize. We could not be in communication with God if he were only "ultimate being." But in our relationship to him we encounter him with the highest of what we ourselves are, *person*. And so in the symbolic form of speaking about him, we have both that which transcends infinitely our experience of ourselves as persons, and that which is so adequate to our being persons that we can say, "Thou" to God, and can pray to him. And these two elements must be preserved. If we preserve only the element of the unconditional, then no relationship to God is possible. If we preserve only the element of the ego-thou relationship, as it is called today, we lose the element of the divine—namely, the unconditional which transcends subject and object and all other polarities. This is the first point on the transcendent level.

The second is the qualities, the attributes of God, whatever you say about him: that he is love, that he is mercy, that he is power, that he is omniscient, that he is omnipresent, that he is almighty and all this. These attributes of God are taken from experienced qualities we have ourselves. They cannot be applied to God in the literal sense. If this is done, it leads to an infinite amount of absurdities. This again is one of the reasons for the destruction of religion through wrong communicative interpretation of it. And again the symbolic character of these qualities must be maintained consistently. Otherwise, every speaking about the divine becomes absurd.

A third element on the transcendent level is the acts of God. For instance, when we say, "He has created the world," "He has sent his son," "He will fulfill the world." In all these temporal, causal, and other expressions we speak symbolically of God. And I would like here to give an example in which the four main categories of our finitude are combined in *one* small sentence: "*God has sent his son.*" Here we have in the word "has" temporality. But God is beyond *our* temporality, though not beyond every temporality. Here is space; "sending somebody" means moving him from one place to another place. This certainly is speaking symbolically, although spatiality is in God as an element in his creative ground. We say that he "has sent," that meant that he has caused something. In this way God is subject to the category of causality. And when we speak of him and his Son, we have two different substances and apply the category of substance to him. Now all this, if taken literally, is absurd. If it is taken symbolically, it is a profound expression, the ultimate Christian expression, of the relationship between God and man in the Christian experience. But to distinguish these two kinds of speech, the non-symbolic and the symbolic, in such a point is so important that if we are not able to make understandable to our contemporaries that we speak symbolically when we use such language, they will rightly turn away from us, as from people who live still in absurdities and superstitions.

Now consider the immanent level, the level of the appearances of the divine in time and space. Here we have first of all the incarnations of the divine, different beings in time and space, divine beings transmuted into animals or men or any kinds of other beings as they appear in time and space. This is often forgotten by those within Christianity who like to use in every second theological proposition the word, "incarnation." They forget that this is not an especially Christian characteristic, because incarnation is something which happens in paganism all the time. The divine beings always incarnate in different forms. That is very easy in paganism. This is not the real distinction between Christianity and other religions. Let me say something here, about the relationships of the transcendent to the immanent level just in connection with the incarnation idea. Historically, one must say that preceding both of them was the situation in which the transcendent and immanent were not distinguished. In the Indonesian doctrine of "Mana," that divine mystical power which permeates all reality, we have some divine presence which is both immanent in everything as a hidden power, and at the same time transcendent, something which can be grasped only through very difficult ritual activities known to the priest. Out of this identity of the immanent and the transcendent the gods of the great mythologies have developed in Greece and in the Semitic nations and in India. There we find incarnations as the immanent element of the divine. The more transcendent the gods become, the more incarnations of personal or sacramental character are needed in order to overcome the remoteness of the divine which develops with the strengthening of the transcendent element.

And from this follows the second element in the immanent religious symbolism namely, the sacramental. The sacramental is nothing else than some reality becoming the bearer of the Holy in a special way and under special circumstances. In this sense, the Lord's Supper, or better the materials in the Lord's Supper, are symbolic. Now you will ask perhaps, "only symbolic?" That sounds as if there were something more than symbolic namely, "literal." But the literal is not more but less than symbolic. If we speak of those dimensions of reality which we cannot approach in any other way than by symbols, then symbols are not used in terms of "only" but in terms of that which is necessary, of that which we *must* apply. Sometimes, because of nothing more than the confusion of signs with symbols, the phrase "only a symbol" means "only a sign." And then the question is justified. "Only a sign?" "No." The sacrament is not only a sign. And in the famous discussion between Luther and Zwingli, in Marburg in 1529, it was just this point on which the discussion was held. Luther wanted to maintain the genuinely symbolic character of the elements, but Zwingli said that the sacramental materials, bread and wine, are "only symbolic." Thus Zwingli meant that they are only signs pointing to a story of the past. Even in that period there was semantic confusion. And let us not be misled by this. In the real sense of symbol, the sacramental materials are symbols. But if the symbol is used as *only* symbol (i.e., only signs), then of course the sacramental materials are more than this.

Then there is the third element on the immanent level. Many things, like special parts of the church building, like the candles, like the water at the entrance of the Roman Church, like the cross in all churches, especially Protestant churches, were originally only signs, but in use became symbols. I call them sign-symbols, signs which have become symbols.

V

And now I come to my last consideration—namely, the truth of religious symbols. Here I must distinguish a negative, a positive, and an absolute statement. First the negative statement. Symbols are independent of any empirical criticism. You cannot kill a symbol by criticism in terms of natural sciences or in terms of historical research. As I said, symbols can only die if the situation in which they have been created has passed. Symbols are not on a level on which empirical criticism can dismiss them. I will give you two examples, both connected with Mary, the mother of Jesus, as Holy Virgin. Here you have first of all a symbol which has died in Protestanism by the changed situation of the relation to God. The special, direct, immediate relationship to God, makes any mediating power impossible. Another reason which has made this symbol disappear is the negation of the ascetic element which is implied in the glorification of virginity. And as long as the Protestant religious situation lasts it cannot be reestablished. It has not died because Protestant scholars have said, "Now there is no empirical reason for saying all this about the Holy Virgin." There certainly is not, but this the Roman Church also knows. But the Roman Church sticks to it on the basis of its tremendous symbolic power which step by step brings her nearer to Trinity itself, especially in the development of the last decade. If this should ever be completed as is now discussed in groups of the Roman Church, Mary would become co-Saviour with Jesus. Then, whether this is admitted or not, she is actually taken into the divinity itself. Another example is the story of the virginal birth of Jesus. This is from the point of view of historical research a most obviously legendary story, unknown to Paul and to John. It is a late creation, trying to make understandable the full possession of the divine Spirit of Jesus of Nazareth. But again its legendary character is not the reason why this symbol will die or has died in many groups of people, in even quite conservative groups within the Protestant churches. The reason is different. The reason is that it is theologically quasi-heretical. It takes away one of the fundamental doctrines of Chalcedon, viz., the classical Christian doctrine that the full humanity of Jesus must be maintained beside his whole divinity. A human being who has no human father has no full humanity. This story, then has to be criticized on inner-symbolic grounds, but not on historical grounds. This is the negative statement about the truth of religious symbols. Their truth is their adequacy to the religious situation in which they are created, and their inadequacy to another situation is their untruth. In the last sentence both the positive and the negative statement about symbols are contained. Only a few words about the absolute statement about the truth of religious symbols. I said that religion is ambiguous and that every religious symbol may became idolatrous, may be demonized, may elevate itself to ultimate validity although nothing is ultimate but the ultimate itself; no religious doctrine and no religious ritual may be. I believe that if Christianity claims to have a truth superior to any other truth in its symbolism, then it is the symbol of the cross in which this is expressed, the cross of the Christ. He who himself embodies the fullness of the divine's presence sacrifices himself in order not to became an idol, another god beside God, a god into whom the disciples wanted to make him. And therefore the decisive story is the story in which he accepts the title "Christ" when Peter offers it to him. He accepts it under the one condition that he has to go to Jerusalem to suffer and to die; that means to deny the idolatrous tendency even with respect to himself. This is at the same time the criterion of all other symbols, and it is the criterion to which every Christian church should subject itself.

16 *Theology and Falsification**

ANTONY FLEW

Antony Flew (1923–   ) is professor of philosophy at the University of Keele, Staffordshire, England. He is coeditor (with Alasdair Mac-Intyre) of *New Essays in Philosophical Theology*, editor of *Logic and Language* (first and second series), *Hume's Philosophy of Belief*, and *God and Philosophy*.

Let us begin with a parable. It is a parable developed from a tale told by John Wisdom in his haunting and revelatory article 'Gods.'[1] Once upon a time two explorers came upon a clearing in the jungle. In the clearing were growing many flowers and many weeds. One explorer says, 'Some gardener must tend this plot.' The other disagrees, 'There is no gardener.' So they pitch their tents and set a watch. No gardener is ever seen. 'But perhaps he is an invisible gardener.' So they set up a barbed-wire fence. They electrify it. They patrol with bloodhounds. (For they remember how H. G. Wells's *The Invisible Man* could be both smelt and touched though he could not be seen.) But no shrieks ever suggest that some intruder has received a shock. No movements of the wire ever betray an invisible climber. The bloodhounds never give cry. Yet still the Believer is not convinced. 'But there is a gardener, invisible, intangible, insensible to electric shocks, a gardener who has no scent and makes no sound, a gardener who comes secretly to look after the garden which he loves.' At last the Sceptic despairs, 'But what remains of your original assertion? Just how does what you call an invisible, intangible, eternally elusive gardener differ from an imaginary gardener or even from no gardener at all?'

In this parable we can see how what starts as an assertion, that something exists or that there is some analogy between certain complexes of phenomena, may be reduced step by step to an altogether different status, to an expression perhaps of a 'picture preference.'[2] The Sceptic says there is no gardener. The Believer says there is a gardener (but invisible, etc.). One man talks about sexual behaviour. Another man prefers to talk of Aphrodite (but knows

* From *New Essays in Philosophical Theology*, ed. Antony Flew and Alasdair Mac-Intyre (London: SCM Press, Ltd., 1955; New York: Macmillan, 1953). Reprinted by permission of SCM Press and The Macmillan Company.
[1] *P.A.S.*, 1944–5, reprinted as Ch. X of *Logic and Language*, Vol I (Blackwell, 1951), and in his *Philosophy and Psychoanalysis* (Blackwell, 1953).
[2] Cf. J. Wisdom, 'Other Minds', *Mind*, 1940; reprinted in his *Other Minds* (Blackwell, 1952).

that there is not really a superhuman person additional to, and somehow responsible for, all sexual phenomena).[3] The process of qualification may be checked at any point before the original assertion is completely withdrawn and something of that first assertion will remain (Tautology). Mr. Wells's invisible man could not, admittedly, be seen, but in all other respects he was a man like the rest of us. But though the process of qualification may be, and of course usually is, checked in time, it is not always judiciously so halted. Someone may dissipate his assertion completely without noticing that he has done so. A fine brash hypothesis may thus be killed by inches, the death by a thousand qualifications.

And in this, it seems to me, lies the peculiar danger, the endemic evil, of theological utterance. Take such utterances as 'God has a plan,' 'God created the world,' 'God loves us as a father loves his children.' They look at first sight very much like assertions, vast cosmological assertions. Of course, this is no sure sign that they either are, or are intended to be, assertions. But let us confine ourselves to the cases where those who utter such sentences intend them to express assertions. (Merely remarking parenthetically that those who intend or interpret such utterances as crypto-commands, expressions of wishes, disguised ejaculations, concealed ethics, or as anything else but assertions, are unlikely to succeed in making them either properly orthodox or practically effective.)

Now to assert that such and such is the case is necessarily equivalent to denying that such and such is not the case.[4] Suppose then that we are in doubt as to what someone who gives vent to an utterance is asserting, or suppose that, more radically, we are sceptical as to whether he is really asserting anything at all, one way of trying to understand (or perhaps it will be to expose) his utterance is to attempt to find what he would regard as counting against, or as being incompatible with, its truth. For if the utterance is indeed an assertion, it will necessarily be equivalent to a denial of the negation of that assertion. And anything which would count against the assertion, or which would induce the speaker to withdraw it and to admit that it had been mistaken, must be part of (or the whole of) the meaning of the negation of that assertion. And to know the meaning of the negation of an assertion, is as near as makes no matter, to know the meaning of that assertion.[5] And if there is nothing which a putative assertion denies then there is nothing which it asserts either: and so it is not really an assertion. When

---

[3] Cf. Lucretius, *De Rerum Natura*, II, 655–60,

> Hic siquis mare Neptunum Cereremque vocare
> Constituet fruges et Bacchi nomine abuti
> Mavolat quam laticis proprium proferre vocamen
> Concedamus ut hic terrarum dictitet orbem
> Esse deum matrem dum vera re tamen ipse
> Religione animum turpi contingere parcat.

[4] For those who prefer symbolism: $p \equiv \sim \sim p$.
[5] For by simply negating $\sim p$ we get $p: \sim \sim p \equiv p$.

the Sceptic in the parable asked the Believer, 'Just how does what you call an invisible, intangible, eternally elusive gardener differ from an imaginary gardener or even from no gardener at all?' he was suggesting that the Believer's earlier statement had been so eroded by qualification that it was no longer an assertion at all.

Now it often seems to people who are not religious as if there was no conceivable event or series of events the occurrence of which would be admitted by sophisticated religious people to be a sufficient reason for conceding 'There wasn't a God after all' or 'God does not really love us then.' Someone tells us that God loves us as a father loves his children. We are reassured. But then we see a child dying of inoperable cancer of the throat. His earthly father is driven frantic in his efforts to help, but his Heavenly Father reveals no obvious sign of concern. Some qualification is made—God's love is 'not a merely human love' or it is 'an inscrutable love,' perhaps—and we realize that such sufferings are quite compatible with the truth of the assertion that 'God loves us as a father (but, of course, . . .)'. We are reassured again. But then perhaps we ask: what is this assurance of God's (appropriately qualified) love worth, what is this apparent guarantee really a guarantee against? Just what would have to happen not merely (morally and wrongly) to tempt but also (logically and rightly) to entitle us to say 'God does not love us' or even 'God does not exist'? I therefore put to the succeeding symposiasts the simple central questions, 'What would have to occur or to have occurred to constitute for you a disproof of the love of, or of the existence of, God?'

17 Theology and Verification*

JOHN HICK

John Hick is well known for his contributions to the philosophy of religion. Formerly Professor of Christian Philosophy at Princeton Theological Seminary, he is now Lecturer in the Philosophy of Religion at Cambridge University. His books include *Faith and Knowledge*, *Philosophy of Religion*, and *Evil and the God of Love*.

To ask "Is the existence of God verifiable?" is to pose a question which is too imprecise to be capable of being answered.[1] There are many different concepts of God, and it may be that statements employing some of them are open to verification or falsification while statements employing others of them are not. Again, the notion of verifying is itself by no means perfectly clear and fixed; and it may be that on some views of the nature of verification the existence of God is verifiable, whereas on other views it is not.

Instead of seeking to compile a list of the various different concepts of God and the various possible senses of "verify," I wish to argue with regard to one particular concept of deity, namely the Christian concept, that divine existence is in principle verifiable; and as the first stage of this argument I must indicate what I mean by "verifiable."

I

The central core of the concept of verification, I suggest, is the removal of ignorance or uncertainty concerning the truth of some proposition. That p is verified (whether p embodies a theory, hypothesis, prediction, or straightforward assertion) means that something happens which makes it clear that p is true. A question is settled so that there is no longer room for rational doubt concerning it. The way in which grounds for rational doubt are ex-

---

* From *Theology Today*, vol. 17 (1960). Reprinted with permission of *Theology Today*.
[1] In this paper I assume that an indicative sentence expresses a factual assertion if and only if the state in which the universe would be if the putative assertion could correctly be said to be true differs in some experienceable way from the state in which the universe would be if the putative assertion could correctly be said to be false, all aspects of the universe other than that referred to in the putative assertion being the same in either case. This criterion acknowledges the important core of truth in the logical positivist verification principle. "Experienceable" in the above formulation means, in the case of alleged subjective or private facts (*e.g.*, pains, dreams, after-images, etc.), "experienceable by the subject in question" and, in the case of alleged objective or public facts, "capable in principle of being experienced by anyone." My contention is going to be that "God exists" asserts a matter of objective fact.

cluded varies, of course, with the subject matter. But the general feature common to all cases of verification is the ascertaining of truth by the removal of grounds for rational doubt. Where such grounds are removed, we rightly speak of verification having taken place.

To characterize verification in this way is to raise the question whether the notion of verification is purely logical or is both logical and psychological. Is the statement that p is verified simply the statement that a certain state of affairs exists (or has existed), or is it the statement also that someone is aware that this state of affairs exists (or has existed) and notes that its existence establishes the truth of p? A geologist predicts that the earth's surface will be covered with ice in 15 million years time. Suppose that in 15 million years time the earth's surface *is* covered with ice, but that in the meantime the human race has perished, so that no one is left to observe the event or to draw any conclusion concerning the accuracy of the geologist's prediction. Do we now wish to say that his prediction has been verified, or shall we deny that it has been verified, on the ground that there is no one left to do the verifying?

The range of "verify" and its cognates is sufficiently wide to permit us to speak in either way. But the only sort of verification of theological propositions which is likely to interest us is one in which human beings participate. We may therefore, for our present purpose, treat verification as a logico-psychological rather than as a purely logical concept. I suggest, then, that "verify" be construed as a verb which has its primary uses in the active voice: I verify, you verify, we verify, they verify, or have verified. The impersonal passive, it is verified, now becomes logically secondary. To say that p has been verified is to say that (at least) someone has verified it, often with the implication that his or their report to this effect is generally accepted. But it is impossible, on this usage, for p to have been verified without someone having verified it. "Verification" is thus primarily the name for an event which takes place in human consciousness.[2] It refers to an experience, the experience of ascertaining that a given proposition or set of propositions is true. To this extent verification is a psychological notion. But of course it is also a logical notion. For needless to say, not *any* experience is rightly called an experience of verifying p. Both logical and psychological conditions must be fulfilled in order for verification to have taken place. In this respect, "verify" is like "know." Knowing is an experience which someone has or undergoes, or perhaps a dispositional state in which someone is, and it cannot take place without someone having or undergoing it or being in it; but not by any means every experience which people have, or every dispositional state in which they are, is rightly called knowing.

---

[2] This suggestion is closely related to Carnap's insistence that, in contrast to "true," "confirmed" is time-dependent. To say that a statement is confirmed, or verified, is to say that it has been confirmed at a particular time—and, I would add, by a particular person. See Rudolf Carnap, "Truth and Confirmation," Feigl and Sellars, *Readings in Philosophical Analysis*, 1949, pp. 119 f.

With regard to this logico-psychological concept of verification, such questions as the following arise. When A, but nobody else, has ascertained that p is true, can p be said to have been verified; or is it required that others also have undergone the same ascertainment? How public, in other words, must verification be? Is it necessary that p could in principle be verified by anyone, without restriction, even though perhaps only A has in fact verified it? If so, what is meant here by "in principle"; does it signify, for example, that p must be verifiable by anyone who performs a certain operation; and does it imply that to do this is within everyone's power?

These questions cannot, I believe, be given any general answer applicable to all instances of the exclusion of rational doubt. The answers must be derived in each case from an investigation of the particular subject matter. It will be the object of subsequent sections of this article to undertake such an investigation concerning the Christian concept of God.

Verification is often construed as the verification of a prediction. However, verification, as the exclusion of grounds for rational doubt, does not necessarily consist in the proving correct of a prediction; a verifying experience does not always need to have been predicted in order to have the effect of excluding rational doubt. But when we are interested in the verifiability of propositions as the criterion for their having factual meaning, the notion of prediction becomes central. If a proposition contains or entails predictions which can be verified or falsified, its character as an assertion (though not of course its character as a true assertion) is thereby guaranteed.

Such predictions may be and often are conditional. For example, statements about the features of the dark side of the moon are rendered meaningful by the conditional predictions which they entail to the effect that if an observer comes to be in such a position in space, he will make such-and-such observations. It would in fact be more accurate to say that the prediction is always conditional, but that sometimes the conditions are so obvious and so likely to be fulfilled in any case that they require no special mention, while sometimes they require for their fulfillment some unusual expedition or operation. A prediction, for example, that the sun will rise within twenty-four hours is intended unconditionally, at least as concerns conditions to be fulfilled by the observer; he is not required by the terms of the prediction to perform any special operation. Even in this case, however, there is an implied negative condition that he shall not put himself in a situation (such as immuring himself in the depths of a coal mine) from which a sunrise would not be perceptible. Other predictions, however, are explicitly conditional. In these cases it is true for any particular individual that in order to verify the statement in question he must go through some specified course of action. The prediction is to the effect that if you conduct such an experiment you will obtain such a result; for example, if you go into the next room you will have such-and-such visual experiences, and if you then touch the table which you see you will have such-and-such tactual experiences, and so on. The content of the "if" clause is of course always determined by the particular subject matter. The logic of "table" determines what you must do to verify statements about tables; the logic of "molecule" determines what you must do to verify statements about molecules; and the logic of "God" determines what you must do to verify statements about God.

In those cases in which the individual who is to verify a proposition must himself first perform some operation, it clearly cannot follow from the circumstances that the proposition is true that everybody has in fact verified it, or that everybody will at some future time verify it. For whether or not any particular person performs the requisite operation is a contingent matter.

II

What is the relation between verification and falsification? We are all familiar today with the phrase, "theology and falsification." A. G. N. Flew and others,[3] taking their cue from John Wisdom,[4] have raised instead of the question, "What possible experiences would verify 'God exists'?" the matching question, "What possible experiences would falsify 'God exists'? What conceivable state of affairs would be incompatible with the existence of God?" In posing the question in this way it was apparently assumed that verification and falsification are symmetrically related, and that the latter is apt to be the more accessible of the two.

In the most common cases, certainly, verification and falsification are symmetrically related. The logically simplest case of verification is provided by the crucial instance. Here it is integral to a given hypothesis that if, in specified circumstances, A occurs, the hypothesis is thereby shown to be true, whereas if B occurs the hypothesis is thereby shown to be false. Verification and falsification are also symmetrically related in the testing of such a proposition as "There is a table in the next room." The verifying experiences in this case are experiences of seeing and touching, predictions of which are entailed by the proposition in question, under the proviso that one goes into the next room; and the absence of such experiences in those circumstances serves to falsify the proposition.

But it would be rash to assume, on this basis, that verification and falsification must always be related in this symmetrical fashion. They do not necessarily stand to one another as do the two sides of a coin, so that once the coin is spun it must fall on one side or the other. There are cases in which verification and falsification each correspond to a side on a different coin, so that one can fail to verify without this failure constituting falsification.

Consider, for example, the proposition that "there are three successive sevens in the decimal determination of π." So far as the value of π has been

[3] A. G. N. Flew, editor, *New Essays in Philosophical Theology*, 1955, Chapter VI.
[4] "Gods," *Proceedings of the Aristotelian Society*, 1944–45. Reprinted in A. G. N. Flew, editor, *Logic and Language*, First Series, 1951, and in John Wisdom, *Philosophy and Psycho-Analysis*, 1953.

worked out, it does not contain a series of three sevens, but it will always be true that such a series may occur at a point not yet reached in anyone's calculations. Accordingly, the propostion may one day be verified, if it is true, but can never be falsified, if it is false.

The hypothesis of continued conscious existence after bodily death provides an instance of a different kind of such asymmetry, and one which has a direct bearing upon the theistic problem. This hypothesis has built into it a prediction that one will after the date of one's bodily death have conscious experiences, including the experience of remembering that death. This is a prediction which will be verified in one's own experience if it is true, but which cannot be falsified if it is false. That is to say, it can be false, but *that* it is false can never be a fact which anyone has experientially verified. But this circumstance does not undermine the meaningfulness of the hypothesis, since it is also such that if it be true, it will be known to be true.

It is important to remember that we do not speak of verifying logically necessary truths, but only propositions concerning matters of fact. Accordingly verification is not to be identified with the concept of logical certification or proof. The exclusion of rational doubt concerning some matter of fact is not equivalent to the exclusion of the logical possibility of error or illusion. For truths concerning fact are not logically necessary. Their contrary is never self-contradictory. But at the same time the bare logical possibility of error does not constitute ground for rational doubt as to the veracity of our experience. If it did, no empirical proposition could ever be verified, and indeed the notion of empirical verification would be without use and therefore without sense. What we rightly seek, when we desire the verification of a factual proposition, is not a demonstration of the logical impossibility of the proposition being false (for this would be a self-contradictory demand), but such weight of evidence as suffices, in the type of case in question, to exclude rational doubt.

III

These features of the concept of verification—that verification consists in the exclusion of grounds for rational doubt concerning the truth of some proposition; that this means its exclusion from particular minds; that the nature of the experience which serves to exclude grounds for rational doubt depends upon the particular subject matter; that verification is often related to predictions and that such predictions are often conditional; that verification and falsification may be asymmetrically related; and finally, that the verification of a factual proposition is not equivalent to logical certification —are all relevant to the verification of the central religious claim, "God exists." I wish now to apply these discriminations to the notion of eschatological verification, which has been briefly employed by Ian Crombie in his contribution to *New Essays in Philosophical Theology*,[5] and by myself in

[5] *Op. cit.*, p. 126.

Faith and Knowledge.[6] This suggestion has on each occasion been greeted with disapproval by both philosophers and theologians. I am, however, still of the opinion that the notion of eschatological verification is sound; and further, that no viable alternative to it has been offered to establish the factual character of theism.

The strength of the notion of eschatological verification is that it is not an *ad hoc* invention but is based upon an actually operative religious concept of God. In the language of Christian faith, the word "God" stands at the center of a system of terms, such as Spirit, grace, Logos, incarnation, Kingdom of God, and many more; and the distinctly Christian conception of God can only be fully grasped in its connection with these related terms.[7] It belongs to a complex of notions which together constitute a picture of the universe in which we live, of man's place therein, of a comprehensive divine purpose interacting with human purposes, and of the general nature of the eventual fulfillment of that divine purpose. This Christian picture of the universe, entailing as it does certain distinctive expectations concerning the future, is a very different picture from any that can be accepted by one who does not believe that the God of the New Testament exists. Further, these differences are such as to show themselves in human experience. The possibility of experiential confirmation is thus built into the Christian concept of God; and the notion of eschatological verification seeks to relate this fact to the logical problem of meaning.

Let me first give a general indication of this suggestion, by repeating a parable which I have related elsewhere,[8] and then try to make it more precise and eligible for discussion. Here, first, is the parable.

Two men are travelling together along a road. One of them believes that it leads to a Celestial City, the other that it leads nowhere; but since this is the only road there is, both must travel it. Neither has been this way before, and therefore neither is able to say what they will find around each next corner. During their journey they meet both with moments of refreshment and delight, and with moments of hardship and danger. All the time one of them thinks of his journey as a pilgrimage to the Celestial City and interprets the pleasant parts as encouragements and the obstacles as trials of his purpose and lessons in endurance, prepared by the king of that city and designed to make of him a worthy citizen of the place when at last he arrives there. The other, however, believes none of this and sees their journey as an unavoidable and aimless ramble. Since he has no choice in the matter, he enjoys the good and endures the bad. But for him there is no Celestial City to be reached, no all-encompassing purpose ordaining their journey;

---

[6] Cornell University Press, 1957, pp. 150–62.

[7] Its clear recognition of this fact, with regard not only to Christianity but to any religion, is one of the valuable features of Ninian Smart's *Reasons and Faiths* (1958). He remarks, for example, that "the claim that God exists can only be understood by reference to many, if not all, other propositions in the doctrinal scheme from which it is extrapolated" (p. 12).

[8] *Faith and Knowledge*, pp. 150 f.

only the road itself and the luck of the road in good weather and in bad.

During the course of the journey the issue between them is not an experimental one. They do not entertain different expectations about the coming details of the road, but only about its ultimate destination. And yet when they do turn the last corner it will be apparent that one of them has been right all the time and the other wrong. Thus although the issue between them has not been experimental, it has nevertheless from the start been a real issue. They have not merely felt differently about the road; for one was feeling appropriately and the other inappropriately in relation to the actual state of affairs. Their opposed interpretations of the road constituted genuinely rival assertions, though assertions whose assertion-status has the peculiar characteristic of being guaranteed retrospectively by a future crux.

This parable has of course (like all parables) strict limitations. It is designed to make only one point: that Christian doctrine postulates an ultimate unambiguous state of existence *in patria* as well as our present ambiguous existence *in via*. There is a state of having arrived as well as a state of journeying, an eternal heavenly life as well as an earthly pilgrimage. The alleged future experience of this state cannot, of course, be appealed to as evidence for theism as a present interpretation of our experience; but it does suffice to render the choice between theism and atheism a real and not a merely empty or verbal choice. And although this does not affect the logic of the situation, it should be added that the alternative interpretations are more than theoretical, for they render different practical plans and policies appropriate now.

The universe as envisaged by the theist, then, differs as a totality from the universe as envisaged by the atheist. This difference does not, however, from our present standpoint within the universe, involve a difference in the objective content of each or even any of its passing moments. The theist and the atheist do not (or need not) expect different events to occur in the successive details of the temporal process. They do not (or need not) entertain divergent expectations of the course of history viewed from within. But the theist does and the atheist does not expect that when history is completed it will be seen to have led to a particular end-state and to have fulfilled a specific purpose, namely that of creating "children of God."

The idea of an eschatological verification of theism can make sense, however, only if the logically prior idea of continued personal existence after death is intelligible. A desultory debate on this topic has been going on for several years in some of the philosophical periodicals. C. I. Lewis has contended that the hypothesis of immortality "is an hypothesis about our own future experience. And our understanding of what would verify it has no lack of clarity."[9] And Morris Schlick agreed, adding, "We must conclude

---

[9] "Experience and Meaning," *Philosophical Review*, 1934, reprinted in Feigl and Sellars, *Readings in Philosophical Analysis*, 1949, p. 142.

that immortality, in the sense defined [i.e. 'survival after death,' rather than 'never-ending life'], should not be regarded as a 'metaphysical problem,' but is an empirical hypothesis, because it possesses logical verifiability. It could be verified by following the prescription: 'Wait until you die!' "[10] However, others have challenged this conclusion, either on the ground that the phrase "surviving death" is self-contradictory in ordinary language or, more substantially, on the ground that the traditional distinction between soul and body cannot be sustained.[11] I should like to address myself to this latter view. The only self of which we know, it is said, is the empirical self, the walking, talking, acting, sleeping individual who lives, it may be, for some sixty to eighty years and then dies. Mental events and mental characteristics are analyzed into the modes of behavior and behavioral dispositions of this empirical self. The human being is described as an organism capable of acting in the "high-level" ways which we characterize as intelligent, thought, humorous, calculating, and the like. The concept of mind or soul is thus not the concept of a "ghost in the machine" (to use Gilbert Ryle's loaded phrase[12]), but of the more flexible and sophisticated ways in which human beings behave and have it in them to behave. On this view there is no room for the notion of soul in distinction from body; and if there is no soul in distinction from body, there can be no question of the soul surviving the death of the body. Against this philosophical background the specifically Christian (and also Jewish) belief in the resurrection of the flesh, or body, in contrast to the Hellenic notion of the survival of a disembodied soul, might be expected to have attracted more attention than it has. For it is consonant with the conception of man as an indissoluble psycho-physical unity, and yet it also offers the possibility of an empirical meaning for the idea of "life after death."

Paul is the chief Biblical expositor of the idea of the resurrection of the body.[13] His view, as I understand it, is this. When someone has died he is, apart from any special divine action, extinct. A human being is by nature mortal and subject to annihilation by death. But in fact God, by an act of sovereign power, either sometimes or always resurrects or (better) reconstitutes or recreates him—not, however, as the identical physical organism that he was before death, but as a *soma pneumatikon*, ("spiritual body") embodying the dispositional characteristics and memory traces of the deceased physical organism, and inhabiting an environment with which the *soma pneumatikon* is continuous as the *ante-mortem* body was continuous with our present world. In discussing this notion we may well abandon the word "spiritual," as lacking today any precise established usage, and speak of

---

[10] "Meaning and Verification," *Philosophical Review*, 1936, reprinted in Feigl and Sellars, *op. cit.*, p. 160.

[11] E.g. A. G. N. Flew, "Death," *New Essays in Philosophical Theology*; "Can a Man Witness his own Funeral?" *Hibbert Journal*, 1956.

[12] *The Concept of Mind*, 1949, which contains an important exposition of the interpretation of "mental" qualities as characteristics of behavior.

[13] I Cor. 15.

"resurrection bodies" and of "the resurrection world." The principal questions to be asked concern the relation between the physical world and the resurrection world, and the criteria of personal identity which are operating when it is alleged that a certain inhabitant of the resurrection world is the same person as an individual who once inhabited this world. The first of these questions turns out on investigation to be the more difficult of the two, and I shall take the easier one first.

Let me sketch a very odd possibility (concerning which, however, I wish to emphasize not so much its oddness as its possibility!), and then see how far it can be stretched in the direction of the notion of the resurrection body. In the process of stretching it will become even more odd than it was before; but my aim will be to show that, however odd, it remains within the bounds of the logically possible. This progression will be presented in three pictures, arranged in a self-explanatory order.

First picture: Suppose that at some learned gathering in this country one of the company were suddenly and inexplicably to disappear, and that at the same moment an exact replica of him were suddenly and inexplicably to appear at some comparable meeting in Australia. The person who appears in Australia is exactly similar, as to both bodily and mental characteristics, with the person who disappears in America. There is continuity of memory, complete similarity of bodily features, including even fingerprints, hair and eye coloration and stomach contents, and also of beliefs, habits, and mental propensities. In fact there is everything that would lead us to identify the one who appeared with the one who disappeared, except continuity of occupancy of space. We may suppose, for example, that a deputation of the colleagues of the man who disappeared fly to Australia to interview the replica of him which is reported there, and find that he is in all respects but one exactly as though he had travelled from say, Princeton to Melbourne, by conventional means. The only difference is that he describes how, as he was sitting listening to Dr. Z reading a paper, on blinking his eyes he suddenly found himself sitting in a different room listening to a different paper by an Australian scholar. He asks his colleagues how the meeting had gone after he ceased to be there, and what they had made of his disappearance, and so on. He clearly thinks of himself as the one who was present with them at their meeting in the United States. I suggest that faced with all these circumstances his colleagues would soon, if not immediately, find themselves thinking of him and treating him as the individual who had so inexplicably disappeared from their midst. We should be extending our normal use of "same person" in a way which the postulated facts would both demand and justify if we said that the one who appears in Australia is the same person as the one who disappears in America. The factors inclining us to identify them would far outweigh the factors disinclining us to do this. We should have no reasonable alternative but to extend our usage of "the same person" to cover the strange new case.

Second picture: Now let us suppose that the event in America is not a sudden and inexplicable disappearance, and indeed not a disappearance at all, but a sudden death. Only, at the moment when the individual dies, a replica of him as he was at the moment before his death, complete with memory up to that instant, appears in Australia. Even with the corpse on our hands, it would still, I suggest, be an extension of "same person" required and warranted by the postulated facts, to say that the same person who died has been miraculously recreated in Australia. The case would be considerably odder than in the previous picture, because of the existence of the corpse in America contemporaneously with the existence of the living person in Australia. But I submit that, although the oddness of this circumstance may be stated as strongly as you please, and can indeed hardly be overstated, yet it does not exceed the bounds of the logically possible. Once again we must imagine some of the deceased's colleagues going to Australia to interview the person who has suddenly appeared there. He would perfectly remember them and their meeting, be interested in what had happened, and be as amazed and dumbfounded about it as anyone else; and he would perhaps be worried about the possible legal complications if he should return to America to claim his property; and so on. Once again, I believe, they would soon find themselves thinking of him and treating him as the same person as the dead Princetonian. Once again the factors inclining us to say that the one who died and the one who appeared are the same person would outweigh the factors inclining us to say that they are different people. Once again we should have to extend our usage of "the same person" to cover this new case.

Third picture: My third supposal is that the replica, complete with memory, etc. appears, not in Australia, but as a resurrection replica in a different world altogether, a resurrection world inhabited by resurrected persons. This world occupies its own space, distinct from the space with which we are now familiar. That is to say, an object in the resurrection world is not situated at any distance or in any direction from an object in our present world, although each object in either world is spatially related to each other object in the same world.

Mr. X, then, dies. A Mr. X replica, complete with the set of memory traces which Mr. X had at the last moment before his death, comes into existence. It is composed of other material than physical matter, and is located in a resurrection world which does not stand in any spatial relationship with the physical world. Let us leave out of consideration St. Paul's hint that the resurrection body may be as unlike the physical body as is a full grain of wheat from the wheat seed, and consider the simpler picture in which the resurrection body has the same shape as the physical body.[14]

In these circumstances, how does Mr. X know that he has been resurrected or recreated? He remembers dying; or rather he remembers being on what he took to be his death-bed, and becoming progressively weaker until,

[14] As would seem to be assumed, for example, by Irenaeus (*Adversus Haereses*, Bk. II Ch. 34, Sec. 1).

presumably, he lost consciousness. But how does he know that (to put it Irishly) his "dying" proved fatal; and that he did not, after losing consciousness, begin to recover strength, and has now simply waked up?

The picture is readily enough elaborated to answer this question. Mr. X meets and recognizes a number of relatives and friends and historical personages whom he knows to have died; and from the fact of their presence, and also from their testimony that he has only just now appeared in their world, he is convinced that he has died. Evidences of this kind could mount up to the point at which they are quite as strong as the evidence which, in pictures one and two, convince the individual in question that he has been miraculously translated to Australia. Resurrected persons would be individually no more in doubt about their own identity than we are now, and would be able to identify one another in the same kinds of ways, and with a like degree of assurance, as we do now.

If it be granted that resurrected persons might be able to arrive at a rationally founded conviction that their existence is *post-mortem*, how could they know that the world in which they find themselves is in a different space from that in which their physical bodies were? How could such a one know that he is not in a like situation with the person in picture number two, who dies in America and appears as a full-bodied replica in Australia, leaving his corpse in the U. S. A.—except that now the replica is situated, not in Australia, but on a planet of some other star?

It is of course conceivable that the space of the resurrection world should have properties which are manifestly incompatible with its being a region of physical space. But on the other hand, it is not of the essence of the notion of a resurrection world that its space should have properties different from those of physical space. And supposing it not to have different properties, it is not evident that a resurrected individual could learn from any direct observations that he was not on a planet of some sun which is at so great a distance from our own sun that the stellar scenery visible from it is quite unlike that which we can now see. The grounds that a resurrected person would have for believing that he is in a different space from physical space (supposing there to be no discernible difference in spatial properties) would be the same as the grounds that any of us may have now for believing this concerning resurrected individuals. These grounds are indirect and consist in all those considerations (*e.g.*, Luke 16:26) which lead most of those who consider the question to reject as absurd the possibility of, for example, radio communication or rocket travel between earth and heaven.

V

In the present context my only concern is to claim that this doctrine of the divine creation of bodies, composed of a material other than that of physical matter, which bodies are endowed with sufficient correspondence of characteristics with our present bodies, and sufficient continuity of memory with our present consciousness, for us to speak of the same person being raised up again to life in a new environment, is not self-contradictory. If, then, it cannot be ruled out *ab initio* as meaningless, we may go on to consider whether and how it is related to the possible verification of Christian theism.

So far I have argued that a survival prediction such as is contained in the *corpus* of Christian belief is in principle subject to future verification. But this does not take the argument by any means as far as it must go if it is to succeed. For survival, simply as such, would not serve to verify theism. It would not necessarily be a state of affairs which is manifestly incompatible with the non-existence of God. It might be taken just as a surprising natural fact. The atheist, in his resurrection body, and able to remember his life on earth, might say that the universe has turned out to be more complex, and perhaps more to be approved of, than he had realized. But the mere fact of survival, with a new body in a new environment, would not demonstrate to him that there is a God. It is fully compatible with the notion of survival that the life to come be, so far as the theistic problem is concerned, essentially a continuation of the present life, and religiously no less ambiguous. And in this event, survival after bodily death would not in the least constitute a final verification of theistic faith.

I shall not spend time in trying to draw a picture of a resurrection existence which would merely prolong the religious ambiguity of our present life. The important question, for our purpose, is not whether one can conceive of after-life experiences which would *not* verify theism (and in point of fact one can fairly easily conceive them), but whether one can conceive of after-life experiences which *would* serve to verify theism.

I think that we can. In trying to do so I shall not appeal to the traditional doctrine, which figures especially in Catholic and mystical theology, of the Beatific Vision of God. The difficulty presented by this doctrine is not so much that of deciding whether there are grounds for believing it, as of deciding what it means. I shall not, however, elaborate this difficulty, but pass directly to the investigation of a different and, as it seems to me, more intelligible possibility. This is the possibility not of a direct vision of God, whatever that might mean, but of a *situation* which points unambiguously to the existence of a loving God. This would be a situation which, so far as its religious significance is concerned, contrasts in a certain important respect with our present situation. Our present situation is one which in some ways seems to confirm and in other ways to contradict the truth of theism. Some events around us suggest the presence of an unseen benevolent intelligence and others suggest that no such intelligence is at work. Our situation is religiously ambiguous. But in order for us to be aware of this fact we must already have some idea, however vague, of what it would be for our situation to be not ambiguous, but on the contrary wholly evidential of God. I therefore want to try to make clearer this presupposed concept of a religiously unambiguous situation.

There are, I suggest, two possible developments of our experience such that, if they occurred in conjunction with one another (whether in this life or in another life to come), they would assure us beyond rational doubt of the reality of God, as conceived in the Christian faith. These are, *first*, an experience of the fulfillment of God's purpose for ourselves, as this has been disclosed in the Christian revelation; in conjunction, *second*, with an experience of communion with God as he has revealed himself in the person of Christ.

The divine purpose for human life, as this is depicted in the New Testament documents, is the bringing of the human person, in society with his fellows, to enjoy a certain valuable quality of personal life, the content of which is given in the character of Christ—which quality of life (*i.e.*, life in relationship with God, described in the Fourth Gospel as eternal life) is said to be the proper destiny of human nature and the source of man's final self-fulfillment and happiness. The verification situation with regard to such a fulfillment is asymmetrical. On the one hand, so long as the divine purpose remains unfulfilled, we cannot know that it never will be fulfilled in the future; hence no final falsification is possible of the claim that this fulfillment will occur—unless, of course, the prediction contains a specific time clause which, in Christian teaching, it does not. But on the other hand, if and when the divine purpose *is* fulfilled in our own experience, we must be able to recognize and rejoice in that fulfillment. For the fulfillment would not be for us the promised fulfillment without our own conscious participation in it.

It is important to note that one can say this much without being cognizant in advance of the concrete form which such fulfillment will take. The before-and-after situation is analogous to that of a small child looking forward to adult life and then, having grown to adulthood, looking back upon childhood. The child possesses and can use correctly in various contexts the concept of "being grown-up," although he does not know, concretely, what it is like to be grown-up. But when he reaches adulthood he is nevertheless able to know that he has reached it; he is able to recognize the experience of living a grown-up life even though he did not know in advance just what to expect. For his understanding of adult maturity grows as he himself matures. Something similar may be supposed to happen in the case of the fulfillment of the divine purpose for human life. That fulfillment may be as far removed from our present condition as is mature adulthood from the mind of a little child; nevertheless, we possess already a comparatively vague notion of this final fulfillment, and as we move towards it our concept will itself become more adequate; and if and when we finally reach that fulfillment, the problem of recognizing it will have disappeared in the process.

The other feature that must, I suggest, be present in a state of affairs that would verify theism, is that the fulfillment of God's purpose be apprehended *as* the fulfillment of God's purpose and not simply as a natural state of affairs. To this end it must be accompanied by an experience of communion with God as he has made himself known to men in Christ.

The specifically Christian clause, "as he has made himself known to men in Christ," is essential, for it provides a solution to the problem of recognition in the awareness of God. Several writers have pointed out the logical difficulty involved in any claim to have encountered God.[15] How could one know that it was *God* whom one had encountered? God is described in Christian theology in terms of various absolute qualities, such as omnipotence, omnipresence, perfect goodness, infinite love, etc., which cannot as such be observed by us, as can their finite analogues, limited power, local presence, finite goodness, and human love. One can recognize that a being whom one "encounters" has a given finite degree of power, but how does one recognize that he has *un*limited power? How does one observe that an encountered being is *omni*present? How does one perceive that his goodness and love, which one can perhaps see to exceed any human goodness and love, are actually infinite? Such qualities cannot be given in human experience. One might claim, then, to have encountered a Being whom one presumes, or trusts, or hopes to be God; but one cannot claim to have encountered a Being whom one recognized to be the infinite, almighty, eternal Creator.

This difficulty is met in Christianity by the doctrine of the Incarnation—although this was not among the considerations which led to the formulation of that doctrine. The idea of incarnation provides answers to the two related questions: "How do we know that God has certain absolute qualities which, by their very nature, transcend human experience?" and "How can there be an eschatological verification of theism which is based upon a recognition of the presence of God in his Kingdom?"

In Christianity God is known as "the God and Father of our Lord Jesus Christ."[16] God is the Being about whom Jesus taught; the Being in relation to whom Jesus lived, and into a relationship with whom he brought his disciples; the Being whose *agape* toward men was seen on earth in the life of Jesus. In short, God is the transcendent Creator who has revealed himself in Christ. Now Jesus' teaching about the Father is a part of that self-disclosure, and it is from this teaching (together with that of the prophets who preceded him) that the Christian knowledge of God's transcendent being is derived. Only God himself knows his own infinite nature; and our human belief about that nature is based upon his self-revelation to men in Christ. As Karl Barth expresses it, "Jesus Christ is the knowability of God."[17] Our beliefs about God's infinite being are not capable of observational verification, being beyond the scope of human experience, but they are susceptible of indirect verification by the removal of rational doubt concerning the authority of Christ. An experience of the reign of the Son in the Kingdom of the Father would confirm that authority, and therewith, indirectly, the

[15] For example, H. W. Hepburn, *Christianity and Paradox*, 1958, pp. 56 f.
[16] II Cor. 11:31.
[17] *Church Dogmatics*, Vol. II, Pt. I, p. 150.

validity of Jesus' teaching concerning the character of God in his infinite transcendent nature.

The further question as to how an eschatological experience of the King-dom of God could be known to be such has already been answered by impli-cation. It is God's union with man in Christ that makes possible man's recognition of the fulfillment of God's purpose for man as being indeed the fulfillment of *God's* purpose for him. The presence of Christ in his Kingdom marks this as being beyond doubt the Kingdom of the God and Father of the Lord Jesus Christ.

It is true that even the experience of the realization of the promised Kingdom of God, with Christ reigning as Lord of the New Aeon, would not constitute a logical certification of his claims nor, accordingly, of the reality of God. But this will not seem remarkable to any philosopher in the em-piricist tradition, who knows that it is only a confusion to demand that a factual proposition be an analytic truth. A set of expectations based upon faith in the historic Jesus as the incarnation of God, and in his teaching as being divinely authoritative, could be so fully confirmed in *post-mortem* experience as to leave no grounds for rational doubt as to the validity of that faith.

VI

There remains of course the problem (which falls to the New Testament scholar rather than to the philosopher) whether Christian tradition, and in particular the New Testament, provides a sufficiently authentic "picture" of the mind and character of Christ to make such recognition possible. I can-not here attempt to enter into the vast field of Biblical criticism, and shall confine myself to the logical point, which only emphasizes the importance of the historical question, that a verification of theism made possible by the Incarnation is dependent upon the Christian's having a genuine contact with the person of Christ, even though this is mediated through the life and tradi-tion of the Church.

One further point remains to be considered. When we ask the question, "*To whom* is theism verified?" one is initially inclined to assume that the answer must be, "To everyone." We are inclined to assume that, as in my parable of the journey, the believer must be confirmed in his belief, and the unbeliever converted from his unbelief. But this assumption is neither de-manded by the nature of verification or by any means unequivocably sup-ported by our Christian sources.

We have already noted that a verifiable prediction may be conditional. "There is a table in the next room" entails conditional predictions of the form: if someone goes into the next room he will see, etc. But no one is compelled to go into the next room. Now it may be that the predictions concerning human experience which are entailed by the proposition that God exists are conditional predictions and that no one is compelled to fulfill those conditions. Indeed we stress in much of our theology that the manner of the divine self-disclosure to men is such that our human status as free and responsible beings is respected, and an awareness of God never is forced upon us. It may then be a condition of *post-mortem* verification that we be already in some degree conscious of God by an uncompelled response to his modes of revelation in this world. It may be that such a voluntary consciousness of God is an essential element in the fulfillment of the divine purpose for human nature, so that the verification of theism which consists in an experience of the final fulfillment of that purpose can only be experienced by those who have already entered upon an awareness of God by the religious mode of apperception which we call faith.

If this be so, it has the consequence that only the theistic believer can find the vindication of his belief. This circumstance would not of course set any restriction upon who can become a believer, but it would involve that while theistic faith can be verified—found by one who holds it to be beyond rational doubt—yet it cannot be proved to the nonbeliever. Such an asymmetry would connect with that strain of New Testament teaching which speaks of a division of mankind even in the world to come.

Having noted this possibility I will only express my personal opinion that the logic of the New Testament as a whole, though admittedly not always its explicit content, leads to a belief in ultimate universal salvation. However, my concern here is not to seek to establish the religious facts, but rather to establish that there are such things as religious facts, and in particular that the existence or non-existence of the God of the New Testament is a matter of fact, and claims as such eventual experiential verification.

18 Linguistic Analysis and the Philosophy of Religion*

BOWMAN L. CLARKE

Bowman L. Clarke (1927–   ) is Professor of Philosophy at the University of Georgia. He is the author of a number of articles in the area of philosophy of religion and of *Language and Natural Theology*.

To the fifth edition of the *Socratic*, which was devoted to the subject "Contemporary Philosophy and the Christian Faith," the editor appended the following note:

> The Oxford University Socratic Club, to which these papers . . . have been read, is an open forum for the discussions between Christians and agnostics of topics relevant to the claim of the Christian Faith to be *true* in some ultimate sense. But nowdays we have to revert to an ancient problem and begin further back—not with truth but with language and meaning. So here we are concerned with "clarification" rather than with argument . . . philosophical developments . . . have not only outdated arguments for the existence of God with modern intellectuals, but have thrown doubt on whether sentences mentioning God can ever have any meaning.[1]

This note is significant for the topic of this paper for several reasons. For one thing it introduces one of the earliest public encounters between theology and what has come to be called analytical philosophy. Since these discussions, which were published in 1955, the problem of language and religion has become one of the more lively and interesting problems in philosophical analysis, both in England and America. Most of the articles which will be mentioned in this paper did, in fact, develop from these early discussions in the Socratic Club. This editorial note is also significant for the pointed way in which it states the problem with which this paper is concerned—that is, the impact which the "revolution in philosophy," as A. J. Ayer called it, is having on theology and the philosophy of religion. According to the editor, ". . . nowdays we have to revert to an ancient problem and being further back—not with truth but with language and meaning."

The historical background of this so-called revolution in philosophy is now

---

* Reprinted from *The Monist*, Volume 47, Number 3, 1963 with permission of The Open Court Publishing Co., La Salle, Illinois.
[1] *The Socratic*, V (Oxford: Basil Blackwell, 1952).

well-known. One root lies in England, and, as Ian T. Ramsey suggests,[2] goes back to the turn of the century and owes much to the influence of G. E. Moore and Bertrand Russell. The other lies in Vienna and the now famous Vienna Circle, which evolved in 1923 out of a seminar led by Moritz Schlick. But the man whose influence has been most formative in England and Vienna is Ludwig Wittgenstein. Behind the approach of the Vienna Circle to the problem of language and meaning lay his *Tractatus Logico-Philosophicus*.[3] Likewise the particular style which dominates most British analysis owes more to Wittgenstein's later writings and teaching than it does to either Moore or Russell. And there is no doubt that the unity of aim and method which lies behind this so-called revolution in philosophy, whether in England or on the continent, owes much to the thesis of both the *Tractatus* and his later writings—the thesis that the aim of philosophy is clarification and the method which philosophy uses for this purpose is the method of linguistic analysis.

No matter what one may think of this basic thesis of Wittgenstein, he cannot ignore the fact that it has changed the vocabulary and style of philosophy in the English speaking countries. I think it could be successfully argued that this revolution in philosophy is, in fact, little more than a change in style and vocabulary and that its aim and method are far closer to the aim and method of traditional philosophy than most would admit. But philosophy, too, has a right to its stylistic fads. It is not the purpose of this paper, however, to justify this basic thesis or to discuss the virtues or vices of this new style of philosophizing. And there are both. Its primary purpose is to raise two questions: First, if one accepts the thesis that the aim and method of philosophy is clarification through the analysis of language, what does this do to that questionable discipline which has traditionally been called the philosophy of religion. And secondly, how can such a conception of the philosophy of religion meet the challenge proposed by the editor of the *Socratic* in his closing sentence: ". . . philosophical developments . . . have not only outdated arguments for the existence of God with modern intellectuals, but have thrown doubt on whether sentences mentioning God can ever have any meaning."

If the aim of philosophy is taken to be clarification through the method of linguistic analysis, then it would seem that the aim and method of philosophy of religion would be the clarification of religious language through an analysis of the language used in a religious context—that is, language in so far as it is related to the religious act of worship.[4] This would include the language of systematic theology, myth, liturgy, sacred writings, prayers, etc.

[2] I. T. Ramsey, *Religious Language* (London: SCM Press, Ltd., 1957), p. 4.
[3] Ludwig Wittgenstein, *Tractatus Logico-Philosophicus* (London: Kegan Paul, 1922).
[4] A similar conception of the philosophy of religion has been suggested by Zuurdeeg and Ramsey. See Willem Zuurdeeg, *An Analytical Philosophy of Religion* (New York: Abingdon Press, 1958) and I. T. Ramsey, *op. cit.*

So interpreted, the philosophy of religion would be the bridge between the philosophic activity of clarifying and the religious activity of worship.

In an attempt to clarify what is involved in linguistic analysis, let me make a few remarks about the nature of language. Plato, in the *Cratylus* (388 C), was perhaps the first to recognize that language is an instrument, or tool, associated with a specific art—the art of communicating and distinguishing. As an instrument, or tool, it must have a structure adapted to its end—that of communicating and distinguishing. Aristotle, however, was the first to clearly express the fact that this structure was reflected in the rules which, either implicitly or explicitly, govern the use of the symbols in the language. To speak intelligibly, or meaningfully, is simply to use symbols according to a given set of rules. Aristotle was also perhaps the first to recognize that there are different structures and consequently different sets of rules within language. In *On Interpretation*, for example, he writes: "Every sentence has meaning, not as being the natural means by which a physical faculty is realized, but, as we have said, by convention." (17a) In other words, a sentence is meaningful, or intelligible, by virtue of the fact that there are certain rules, or conventions, which govern the symbols which compose the sentence. But he goes on to add: "Yet every sentence is not a proposition; only such are propositions as have in them either truth or falsity. Thus a prayer is a sentence, but is neither true nor false." (17a) And these other sentences, such as prayers, he tells us belong not to science, but to rhetoric or poetry. Thus Aristotle recognizes not only that language is meaningful by virtue of a structure which is reflected in the rules which govern the language, but that there are sub-structures in a language depending upon the end for which the sentences are to be used and the rules which govern this usage.

This idea that meaningfulness is related to the structure of language and the rules which govern its symbols, along with the recognition that there are different sub-languages, or linguistic structures, is one of the more mature insights of the entire analytic movement as it has moved away from the position that verifiability is the sole criterion of meaning. Wittgenstein, for example, in his later work, *Philosophical Investigations*, defines meaning in terms of use: ". . . the meaning of a word," he writes, "is its use in the language."[5] And he finds not one linguistic structure, as he did in the *Tractatus*, but "families of structures more or less related to one another."[6] The story of the criticisms of the original narrowness of the verification principle, its reformulations, and sometimes its outright rejection among the various members and disciples of the original Vienna Circle is likewise well known. Basil Mitchell has expressed this parallel change in British philosophy in this way: ". . . in place of the dogmatic *assertion* that those statements alone have

---

[5] Ludwig Wittgenstein, *Philosophical Investigations*, translated by G. E. M. Anscombe (Oxford: Basil Blackwell, 1953), p. 20e.
[6] *Ibid.*, p. 46e.

meaning which are empirically verifiable, they ask the *question*—of any class of statements—'what is the logic of statements of this kind?' That is to say, 'how are they to be verified, or tested, or justified? What is their use and function, what jobs do they do?' "[7]

To analyze a language simply means to determine its structure, or the rules which govern the symbols of the language. This includes the purposes for which the symbols are employed by the user, the way in which the symbols refer to or stand for something, the way in which the symbols themselves are related to each other, the rules, if there be any, which govern the truth and falsity of the sentences, etc. Now if the symbols which are used in religious language are meaningful, then they too must have a structure, or structures, which can be analyzed. And just as the analysis of the logical structure of a scientific theory clarifies the nature of the science, as well as the meaning of its symbols, so an analysis of religious language should clarify both the meaning of its symbols and the nature of religion. If, however, philosophy is to make an adequate analysis of religious language, it must not only guard against violating its own integrity, it must likewise guard against destroying the integrity of religious language by forcing upon it alien rules or criteria. The philosophy of religion, in other words, must be an honest attempt to clarify, to discover the rules which do in fact govern the symbols which are used in a religious context. Only in this way will it be a legitimate bridge between the philosophic activity of clarifying and the religious activity of worship. In order to make a little clearer which I mean by an adequate analysis which preserves both the integrity of philosophical analysis and the integrity of religious language, let me illustrate with three concrete cases which I take to be a violation of this integrity.

The first example is a case in which I think an alien rule, or criterion, has been imposed which violates the integrity of religious language. It is the position which R. M. Hare takes in *New Essays in Philosophical Theology.*[8] In a series of discussions entitled "Theology and Falsification," Antony Flew[9] proposes a criterion for the meaningfulness of assertive statements which might be called the criterion of falsification; that is, a statement which denies nothing, asserts nothing. According to this rule, if the statement 'God exists' asserts something, it must likewise deny something. We must know, in other words, what event or series of events would have to occur in order for us to conclude that the statement 'God exists' is false, otherwise the statement asserts nothing whatsoever. Hare[10] responds to this challenge by maintaining that both the statement 'God exists' and the statement 'God does not exist' are compatible with anything that happens. The difference between these

---

[7] *Faith and Logic,* ed. Basil Mitchell (London: George Allen and Unwin, Ltd., 1957), p. 5.
[8] *New Essays in Philosophical Theology,* eds. Antony Flew and Alasdair MacIntyre (New York: Macmillan Co., 1955). (Hereafter referred to as *New Essays.*)
[9] *Ibid.,* p. 98.
[10] *Ibid.,* pp. 99–103.

two statements is not a difference between what is *asserted* about the world, but a difference in what he calls a *blick* about the world which, so far as I can determine, simply means a difference in attitudes toward the world.

Although Flew's rule of meaningfulness is questionable on philosophic grounds and will be discussed below, it is Hare's position I wish to examine here, for I think it is questionable on religious grounds. Now Hare himself may use the statement 'God exists' to express his *blick*, or attitude, toward the world. Or he may suggest that we use the statement in this way. This is his privilege. But when the philosopher is analyzing religious language, he must concern himself primarily with how this statement is used in a religious context. No doubt a large part of religious language, and perhaps most of religious language, is used to express attitudes. "Though he slay me, yet will I trust him," for example, is an expression of a worshipful attitude of trust. "O Lord, our Lord, how excellent is thy name in all the earth" is an expression of a worshipful attitude of praise. But in both cases God is taken to be the object of trust and praise, not the attitude itself. When we are considering the statement 'God exists' I think we would have to agree with Mascall:

> It is . . . transparently clear to anyone whose judgment is not shackled by a predetermined dogma that, if two men respectively affirm and deny that God exists, they are in fact disagreeing about the nature of reality, and not merely expressing different emotions or aesthetic attitudes.[11]

It may well be that the statement 'God exists' is false or even meaningless, but as it is commonly used it is not, I think, intended to express a person's *blick* or attitude toward the world. And the analytic philosopher who imposes such an alien interpretation on religious statements, even in an effort to salvage them, is violating the integrity of religious language itself.

The second case I want to mention is an example of a position which I would call philosophically inadequate. It is the position of Thomas McPherson in his article, "Religion as the Inexpressible."[12] McPherson accepts the classical positivist's position that religious statements are nonsense, for, according to him, religion *is* the inexpressible. In order to explicate his position he attempts to bring together Rudolph Otto and Wittgenstein. Using Otto's conception of the numinous, McPherson points out that the numinous experience, which he takes to be "the distinctive thing in religion," is precisely that which "cannot be put into words."[13] This he relates to Wittgenstein's statement in the *Tractatus* that "the feeling of the world as a limited whole is the mystical feeling." (6.45) And this, according to Wittgenstein, cannot be said, it "shows itself; it is the mystical." (6.522)

---

[11] E. L. Mascall, *Existence and Analogy* (London: Longmans, Green and Co., 1949), p. 94.
[12] *New Essays*, pp. 131–143.
[13] *Ibid.*, p. 137.

It is not quite clear to me precisely what McPherson means by 'ineffable' here. If he means that religious statements are no more than a series of sounds obeying no rules whatever, then one could not distinguish religious language from the babblings of an idiot—it would be "full of sound and fury, signifying nothing." Obviously this is not what he means. It is clear, however, what Wittgenstein, and perhaps Otto, mean by 'ineffable.' Wittgenstein tells us that the ineffable is that which cannot be expressed in the form of propositions, namely the form itself.[14] And Otto, too, seems to be pointing to the limitations of propositions when he writes: "All language, is so far as it consists of words, purports to convey ideas or concepts—that is what language means—and the more clearly and unequivocally it does so, the better the language."[15] Now if McPherson, like Aristotle, is maintaining that much in religious language cannot be expressed in the form of propositions, then there is no doubt truth in this. But the point which I wish to make is that this still does not relieve the philosopher of religion of the obligation to seek the rules which do in fact govern the different symbols used in religious language.

The metaphor, 'God is a father,' for example, does not obey the rules governing propositions, but a metaphor does have a structure and a function of its own. Plato noticed that a metaphor has a structure; it has the structure of a proportion. To illustrate, this metaphor says that 'God is to a man as a father is to his child.' The paradox, "He that looseth his life for my sake shall find it," likewise does not obey the rules for propositions. If it did it would be a contradiction and necessarily false. This does not mean, however, that the paradox cannot have its own meaningful structure and function. The stories related in the Bible may not obey in all respects the rules which govern historical proposition, but they likewise have their own meaningful structure and function. St. Thomas, as well as Dante, recognized that the stories of the Bible have a literal meaning, and in this sense function somewhat as historical propositions, but that the things signified by their literal meaning, also, have a signification, and it is here that their religious meaning is to be found.

Now any philosophical approach to religious language which retreats into the "ineffable" or into "nonsense" and does not make an attempt to analyze such meaningful nonpropositional structures and their use in religion is simply philosophically inadequate.

The third case which I would consider as an inadequate approach to the problem of religious language is A. G. A. Rainer's[16] response to what has been called J. N. Findlay's ontological disproof of the existence of God.

---

[14] See particularly *Tractatus Logico-Philosophicus*, 4.112–4.115; 5.4711; 6.124; 6.13; and 6.54.

[15] Rudolph Otto, *Idea of the Holy*, translated by J. W. Harvey (London: Oxford University Press, 1926), p. 2.

[16] *New Essays*, pp. 67–71.

Findlay argues in *New Essays in Philosophical Theology* that the existence of God can only be conceived "in a religiously satisfactory manner, if we also conceive it as something inescapable and necessary, whether for thought or reality."[17] Since necessary propositions, according to him, are senseless, it follows that the proposition 'God exists' asserts nothing. I am not concerned here with the question of Findlay's disproof, which I shall consider below, but with Rainer's response. Rainer answers Findlay by saying that "our assertion of God's existence may be contingent, although God's existence is necessary."[18] He explains in this way: "The 'necessity' of assertions about God's nature and of the connection betwen his nature and his existence is relative to God's omniscience and not to human reason or experience."[19]

Rainer, unlike our second case, is not maintaining that there are no rules governing the statement 'God exists,' rather he is maintaining that we must consider it as obeying God's linguistic rules, not man's. From the point of view of God's omniscience, the statement is necessarily true, but from our point of view it is contingently true. The religious man, however, must, in some unknown way, look at the statement from God's point of view. I'm not at all sure what this means. Either God's rules, whatever they may be, are intelligible to us or they are not. If they are, then there is no problem; if they are not, then we cannot even discuss what it means for a statement to be necessary from God's point of view. One thing is certain, and that is that Rainer is in danger of placing himself in the position of A. N. Prior's Barthian. In his delightful little dialogue, "Can Religion be Discussed?," Prior has the Barthian say:

> Of course we can only talk nonsense when we try to talk about God—our language is the language of sinful men and is utterly unfitted for such use. But God, with whom all things are possible, comes to our rescue and takes up our words . . . and *makes* them carry his meaning and his message to men.[20]

Now if religious language, or a part of it, obeys God's rules and not man's, then apologetics is in trouble, unless the unbeliever knows God's rules. Or even more puzzling, how do two believers know they are confessing the same thing unless they can agree on God's rules? Not only does communication between believer and non-believer become questionable, but communication between two believers becomes questionable. Perhaps at this point we should heed St. Paul's advice concerning speaking in unknown tongues. To retreat into God's omniscience which is hidden from man or to resort to a miracle for the justification of the meaningfulness of religious language, not only makes a philosophical analysis of religious language impossible, it runs the risk of making religious language itself impossible. Such a position I would consider inadequate on both religious and philosophic grounds.

---

[17] *Ibid.*, p. 48.
[18] *Ibid.*, p. 68.
[19] *Ibid.*, p. 68.
[20] *Ibid.*, p. 9.

With this interpretation of the philosophy of religion in mind, I want to raise the second main question of this paper, "whether statements mentioning God," to use the words of the editor of the *Socratic*, "can ever have any meaning," not in order to give a yes or no answer, but to suggest how they might be meaningful. And for the purposes of this discussion, I want to focus our attention on the one proposition 'There is a God.' There are good reasons for this. For one thing, it narrows our problem. This proposition merely asserts that there is a being who is an adequate object of the religious attitude of worship. Since it is surely taken to assert something, then it must be taken as a proposition and as obeying the rules which govern the use of propositions. Thus in considering this proposition we need not consider any other linguistic structures which might be used in religious language. No matter what one may find in an analysis of the use of language in the human activity of worship, ultimately all religious language revolves around the meaningfulness of this proposition, since the act of religious worship itself is directed toward the being mentioned in this proposition. Findlay is quite right when he points out that "all attitudes presume characters in their objects, and are, in consequence, strengthened by the discovery that their objects have these characters, as they are weakened by the discovery that they really haven't got them."[21] Certainly the attitude of religious worship would be weakened by the discovery that the attitude itself has no object. If, therefore, this proposition is either false or meaningless according to the rules governing propositions, then religious language as a whole is seriously called into question. At this point, like it or not, the God of Abraham, Isaac, and Jacob does become the God of the philosophers.

In order to analyze 'There is a God' as a proposition, I want to consider Findlay's so-called "ontological disproof" of the existence of God. Findlay has done an excellent job of clarifying precisely what is involved in this proposition and in so doing has brought the issue to a very sharp focus. He begins by characterizing the religious attitude as one in which we tend "to abase ourselves before some object, to defer to it wholly, to devote ourselves to it with unquestioning enthusiasm, to bend the knee before it, whether literally or metaphorically."[22] This is simply to take the first great commandment as a characterization of the religious attitude: "Thou shalt love the Lord thy God with all thy heart, and with all thy soul, and with all thy mind, and with all thy strength." (Mark 12:30) Now Findlay raises this question: What would be an adequate object of this religious attitude? What kind of being could evoke or justify such an attitude? It cannot be, he argues, a being which merely *happens* to exist, nor one on which other objects merely *happen* to depend. It must be a thing upon whom everything that exists and everything that is of value ultimately depends. Thus, "not only must the existence of other things be unthinkable without him," he

---

[21] *Ibid.*, p. 50.
[22] *Ibid.*, p. 49.

writes, but "his own non-existence must be wholly unthinkable in any circumstances . . . There must, in short, be no conceivable alternative to an existence properly termed 'divine.' "[23] Another being, as he says, might deserve the veneration cannonically accorded to the saints, but not the worship we properly owe to God.

In a very subtle way, Findlay has brought together the essence of the ontological argument and the argument from contingency to give us an explication for the only adequate object of the religious attitude expressed in the first great commandment. In explicating the term 'God' in this way, he has also clarified the logical status of the proposition, 'There is a God.' Since "the existence of other things is unthinkable without him," then by the definition of God, the proposition 'There is a God' must be a necessary condition for any contingent proposition. This is the essence of the argument from contingency; that is, the existence of any contingent being is dependent upon the existence of God. The other phrase, "his own non-existence must be wholly unthinkable in any circumstances," gives the essence of the ontological argument; that is, the negation of the proposition 'There is a God' results in a contradiction. Thus Findlay concludes that if the word 'God' is used to refer to a being who is an adequate object of religious worship, then the proposition 'There is a God' cannot be verified or falsified by any contingent state of affairs whatsoever. It follows, then, that if the concept of God is not a self-contradiction, such as 'round square,' the proposition must be logically or necessarily true.[24]

But what, then, is Findlay's disproof. He writes: "Plainly (for all who share a contemporary outlook), . . . [these considerations] entail not only that there isn't a God, but that the Divine Existence is either senseless or impossible."[25] And what is this "contemporary outlook" which makes the proposition 'There is a God' senseless? It is the position that "necessity in propositions merely reflects our use of words, the arbitrary conventions of our language."[26] In other words, since the proposition must be logically true and cannot be falsified by any contingent state-of-affairs, it asserts nothing whatsoever; it is senseless. This, you will remember, was Flew's criterion for meaningfulness: "If there is nothing which a putative assertion denies, then there is nothing which it asserts either: and so it is not really an assertion."[27]

It is quite crucial to see what Findlay and Flew are maintaining here. They are not erroneously arguing as Hume, that no existential proposition can be necessary on the grounds that the negation of an existential proposition can

---

[23] *Ibid.*, p. 52.
[24] For a thorough discussion of the problem of contingency and the existence of God see Charles Hartshorne, "Ten Ontological or Modal Proofs for God's Existence," *The Logic of Perfection* (LaSalle: Open Court Publishing Co., 1962).
[25] *New Essays*, p. 54.
[26] *Ibid.*, p. 54.
[27] *Ibid.*, p. 98.

never produce a contradiction. Nor are they, like Kant, limiting the category of existence and non-existence *ex cathedra* to possible objects given through the sensibility, among which they do not find God listed. Their argument rests solely on what Findlay has called "a contemporary outlook" and is taken to involve only the logical rules of language. It is the position that logically true propositions assert nothing but "merely reflect our use of words, the arbitrary conventions of our language." Once we have denied that the proposition 'There is a God' is a contingent proposition, then this is the dilemma which Findlay and a large portion of the analytic movement has presented to religious language: Either the concept of God is self-contradictory or it isn't. If it is self-contradictory, then the proposition 'There is a God' is necessarily false and God's existence is impossible. If it is not self-contradictory, then the proposition 'There is a God' is logically true and asserts nothing at all. Either God's existence is impossible or senseless.

I think we must agree with Findlay that the only being that could be considered an adequate object of the religious attitude of worship is the being treated in the argument from contingency and the ontological argument. Also, I think we must agree with Findlay that in both arguments the proposition 'There is a God' must be taken to be logically or necessarily true. For if the existence of God cannot be a contingent fact, then the proposition which asserts his existence cannot be a contingent proposition. We must, therefore, examine closely this "contemporary outlook," as Findlay calls it, which declares that a logically true proposition is senseless and asserts nothing.

In the first place, this outlook is not as contemporary as it might appear. In fact, we can find a similar position expressed in Hobbes' Fourth Objection to Descartes' *Meditations*. In this objection Hobbes makes the following proposal to Descartes:

> . . . what shall we say, if reasoning chance to be nothing more than the uniting and stringing together of names or designations by the word is? It will be a consequence of this that reason gives us no conclusions about the nature of things, but only about the terms that designate them, whether, indeed, or not there is a convention (arbitrarily made about their meanings) according to which we join these names together.[28]

Here Hobbes is suggesting that logically true propositions give us no conclusions about the nature of things, and reason is nothing more than the uniting and stringing together of symbols by the word 'is.' In other words, the rules of logic govern only the way in which we manipulate our symbols and have nothing to do with what the symbols might stand for. If this is true, says Hobbes, then logically true propositions assert nothing about the nature of things, but "only about the terms . . . whether . . . or not there is

[28] *The Complete Works of Descartes*, translated by Elizabeth S. Haldane and G. R. T. Ross (Cambridge: Cambridge University Press, 1955), reprinted in Walter Kaufmann, *Philosophic Classics*, II (Englewood Cliffs, Prentice-Hall, Inc., 1961). p. 80.

a convention according to which we join these names together," or to use Findlay's words, "they merely reflect our use of words, the arbitrary conventions of our language."

In the second place, the phrases 'asserts nothing' and 'merely reflects our use of words, the arbitrary conventions of our language' are quite ambiguous. When the contemporary analysts, or Hobbes, tells us that a logically true proposition "asserts nothing" just what do they mean? If they mean that it does not assert a contingent state-of-affairs, then there is no quarrel. But if they mean that the symbols in a logically true proposition are uninterpreted, then they are wrong. Descartes, in his reply to Hobbes, seems to interpret him in this way. He writes:

> . . . in reasoning we unite not names but the things signified by names; and I marvel that the opposite can occur to anyone . . . For, if he admits that words signify anything, why will he not allow our reasonings to refer to this something that is signified, rather than to words alone?[29]

Descartes may have marveled that the opposite could occur to anyone, but it seems to have occurred to many. Yet I must say that I still share something of Descartes' amazement. For if the contingent proposition, 'a is red,' asserts something and the contingent proposition, 'a is not red,' asserts something, it certainly appears that the logically true proposition, 'It is not the case that a is red and a is not red,' asserts something. It seems to assert a state-of-affairs in which the state-of-affairs asserted by the first contingent proposition and the state-of-affairs asserted by the second contingent proposition are incompatible. If one maintains, as most would, that a contradiction, or a logically false proposition, asserts an impossible state-of-affairs—one that could not be actualized—and a logically indeterminate proposition asserts a contingent state-of-affairs—one that may or may not be actualized—, on what intelligible basis can he deny that a logically true proposition asserts a necessary state-of-affairs—one that could not be otherwise? Yet Hobbes, Findlay, Flew, and most contemporary analysts tell us that a logically true proposition "asserts nothing" whatsoever about any state-of-affairs; it "merely reflects our use of words, the arbitrary conventions of our language."

Here, again, the phrase, 'reflects our use of words, . . . the arbitrary conventions of our language,' is ambiguous. Do they mean that logically true propositions disclose to us something of the syntactical and semantical rules which govern our symbols, in the sense that we are able to learn something of the rules through an examination of these propositions? If so, there is no quarrel; but it should be pointed out that factually true, or contingent propositions, likewise reflect, in this sense, the rules of the language. If, however, they mean, as Hobbes seems to think, that logically true propositions do not assert (tell us) anything about "the nature of things, but only about the terms

[29] *Ibid.*, p. 81.

that designate them," then they are quite wrong. Logically true propositions in a language which describes the world assert nothing whatsoever about terms, words, rules, or conventions. Such propositions would be in a meta-language, not in the object language as logically true propositions are. "If 'if A then B' is true and 'A' is true, then 'B' is true" is a metalinguistic rule which tells us something about propositions, or, if you will, expresses a convention. On the other hand, 'If A then B and A, then B' is a logically true proposition in an object language and asserts nothing about propositions, rules, or conventions. In summary, it seems that when the analyst is telling us that logically true propositions "assert nothing," he is either saying that they do not assert a contingent fact, or they are uninterpreted. If he means the former, he has only said the obvious; if he means the latter, he is wrong. And when he tells us that they "reflect our use of words," he is either saying that they, like any proposition, "disclose" to us something of the rules of the language, or that they "assert" something about our rules. If he means the former, then, again, he has only stated the obvious; if he means the latter, again, he is quite wrong.

There is a clear and intelligible distinction which can be made between logically true propositions and factually true propositions, but it is not the fact that one "asserts nothing" and the other does not, nor is it the fact that one "reflects our use of words" and the other does not. They both assert something and they both reflect our rules. The difference lies in how we determine whether or not they are true. A logically true proposition can be determined to be true solely on the basis of the syntactical and semantical rules alone, whereas a factually true proposition cannot. One needs additional information about the contingent state of the world in order to verify it. This is due to the fact that a logically true proposition asserts a necessary state-of-affairs, one that could not be otherwise no matter what the contingent states-of-affairs might be, whereas a factually true proposition asserts a contingent state-of-affairs, one that could be otherwise. If these conclusions are justifiable, and I think they are, then the dilemma which contemporary linguistic analysis has presented to the philosophy of religion is not a real dilemma.

Findlay, along with Hartshorne,[30] has done a great service in clarifying the logical status of the proposition 'There is a God.' If the being mentioned in the proposition is a being who is an adequate object of the religious attitude of worship, then this proposition cannot be a contingent proposition. The traditional ontological argument was a way of saying this; that is, if the concept of God is adequate and not self-contradictory, then the proposition asserting his existence must be logically true. However, the problem remains: Can the conception of such a being be formulated? It seems to have been

---

[30] Charles Hartshorne, *op. cit.*

the burden of the various cosmological arguments to demonstrate that the concept of such a being can be formulated in the language which was used for a scientific description of the world. St. Thomas' Five Ways can be interpreted as an attempt to do precisely this. In his First Way, for example, he formulates in the language of Aristotelian physics, or metaphysics, the conception of an unmoved mover which fulfills the criterion. Likewise in each of the five ways St. Thomas formulates a concept, then adds a phrase similar to this: This all men call God. But Aristotle's language is no longer adequate for a scientific description of the world today. And it is the task of the philosophy of religion to attempt a similar task in our day. Only then will an adequate analysis of religious language be possible.

This, however, is only to pose the problem of the meaningfulness of statements mentioning God in its proper setting; it is not to solve it. In fact, the question of a language adequate for a scientific description of the world in our day is itself a significant problem and one which is yet to be solved. This is the metaphysical task of our day. Significant beginnings along this line have been suggested by Whitehead in *An Enquiry into the Principles of Natural Knowledge*,[31] *The Concept of Nature*,[32] and *Process and Reality*;[33] by Bertrand Russell in *The Analysis of Matter*[34] and *Human Knowledge, Its Scope and Limits*;[35] by Carnap in *Der logische Aufbau der Welt*[36] and *Introduction to Symbolic Logic and Its Applications*;[37] and by Nelson Goodman in *The Structure of Appearance*.[38] These beginnings need to be developed and evaluated and the possibilities of formulating the theological problem in such a language investigated. This would involve the formulation of the conception of a being which meets our criterion in such a language and demonstrating that the proposition asserting his existence follows from the rules of the language alone. Such a task is immense and not easy. It is perhaps far more difficult than most have realized. But with the tools which symbolic logic has developed since the last century and placed at our disposal, the task is not impossible. Whitehead's prediction in the closing paragraphs of his essay, "Analysis of Meaning," can become a reality. He writes:

[31] A. N. Whitehead, *An Enquiry into the Principles of Natural Knowledge* (Cambridge: Cambridge University Press, 1917).
[32] A. N. Whitehead, *The Concept of Nature* (Cambridge: Cambridge University Press, 1920).
[33] A. N. Whitehead, *Process and Reality* (Cambridge: Cambridge University Press, 1930). See particularly "Part IV."
[34] Bertrand Russell, *The Analysis of Matter* (London: George Allen and Unwin, Ltd., 1927).
[35] Bertrand Russell, *Human Knowledge, Its Scope and Limits* (New York: Simon and Schuster, 1948).
[36] Rudolph Carnap, *Der logische Aufbau der Welt* (Leipzig: F. Meiner, 1928).
[37] Rudolph Carnap, *Introduction to Symbolic Logic and Its Applications*, translated by William H. Meyer and John Wilkinson (New York: Dover Publications, Inc., 1958). See "Part II."
[38] Nelson Goodman, *The Structure of Appearance* (Cambridge: Harvard University Press, 1951).

We must end with my first love—Symbolic Logic. When in the distant future the subject has expanded, so as to examine patterns depending on connections other than those of space, number and quantity—when this expansion has occurred, I suggest that Symbolic Logic . . . will become the foundation of aesthetics. From this stage it will proceed to conquer ethics and theology. The circle will have made its full turn, and we shall be back to the logical attitude of the epoch of St. Thomas Aquinas.[39]

---

[39] A. N. Whitehead, *Science and Philosophy* (New York: The Wisdom Library, 1948), p. 140.

Chapter Three

THE PROBLEM
OF MORAL NORMS

THE NORMATIVE ASPECT OF MORAL PHILOSOPHY

All of us operate on the basis of standards of right and wrong conduct, standards acquired from our parents and our culture. In many cases these standards serve to answer our moral problems. But even with these standards, we are sometimes puzzled about what we ought to do. The moral rules of our culture themselves seem to conflict on occasion. They also sometimes support actions which one feels are immoral. Then, too, new conditions of life and human relationships develop. These create moral quandaries with which the old standards seem unable to cope. In such situations one may begin to question the adequacy of his inherited moral standards. This is the inception of moral philosophy, for moral philosophy or ethical theory is the endeavor to judge rationally existing ethical beliefs and practices and to provide a set of principles for human conduct. This is the normative aspect of moral philosophy. (We will see in a moment that there are other aspects.)

The basic normative questions which concern both the classical and contemporary ethical theorist are: (1) What is the *good* or the good life for man? (2) What is the *right* thing to do? These are distinct though related questions. Generally we must know what is to count as a good or desirable experience or objective before we can know or discover what is the right thing to do, for rules of right conduct are formulated as instruments to attain the good life. But an answer to the first does not provide an answer to the second. Nor does agreement on the first assure agreement on the second.

One of the traditional answers to the question of what is the good is that it is *pleasure* or the life of pleasure. This position is known as hedonism. It has a long history. It was held, for example, by one of the disputants in Plato's *Republic* in the fourth century B.C., by Jeremy Bentham in the seventeenth century (see selection in this chapter), and is still held by some contemporary moral philosophers.[1] But hedonism as an account of what is good-in-itself does not seem to provide a specific norm for right conduct. One can be a hedonist and, at the same time, an egoist, maintaining that a right act is that act which provides the greatest pleasure for oneself. Or one can be a hedonist and, at the same time, an altruist (a "utilitarian"), maintaining that a right act is one which provides the greatest pleasure, not only for oneself but for all human beings affected by the act. In such cases, the rightness of an act is determined by different standards, even though there is agreement on what constitutes goodness.

Many philosophers reject a narrow kind of hedonism as an adequate account of the good or the good life. Plato and Aristotle, while not ruling out pleasure as a component in the good life, argue that what distinguishes man from animals is his rational capacity; and they say that the life of reason and the acquisition of knowledge are intrinsically good. Any account of the good life or of right conduct that ignores such basic facts about the nature of man is at best incomplete and at worst simply false. One ingredient of human nature is physical, but a life of purely sensual pleasure ignores other essential aspects of man's nature. An ethic based on a single component, the sensual, is too narrow and is an inadequate guide for human behavior (although a carefully worked-out hedonism many avoid this error).

As noted above, the identification of an ethical theorist as a hedonist does not tell us which actions he supports as right actions, for one can be either an egoistic hedonist or a hedonistic utilitarian. Furthermore, even egoistic hedonists might disagree on which actual acts are right. Some might recommend seizing the pleasure of the moment; others might say that moderation in satisfying appetites produces desirable long-range pleasure. Epicurus, popularly but wrongly interpreted as a "wine, women, and song" theorist, argues for such moderation. Again, hedonists of the utilitarian type might also disagree on which actions are right, depending on their view regarding the consequences of a course of conduct for all human beings affected. Thus, two hedonistic utilitarians might disagree over whether a promise should be kept, one arguing that the best consequences for human beings lies in breaking it, the other, by keeping it. Disagreement here might turn on their respective appraisals of the facts in the case. Or such disagreement could be lodged in the type of utilitarianism held. Some utilitarians, who are known as "act-utilitarians," judge the consequences of an act by focusing on the act *alone* and asking: Will that act probably produce the best consequences for all concerned? Others, known as "rule-utilitarians," insist that we assess the consequences of the rule on which the act is based as well as the results of a particular act. They point out that the short-term good consequences of

---

[1] See Charles Baylis, *Ethics: Principles of Wise Choice* (New York: Holt, Rinehart and Winston, Inc., 1958), especially chaps. 8 and 12.

breaking a promise, for example, are more than offset by the long-term consequences of violating the rule of promise-keeping; for if public confidence
in the practice of promise-keeping is destroyed, a practice fundamental to
civilization itself is endangered. (What would happen to civilization if men
lost confidence in the practice of keeping promises, agreements, contracts,
and so on?)

Disagreements among utilitarian theorists, then, can be rooted either in
the form of their theory or in their interpretation of facts. It should also be
noted that one could be a utilitarian in ethics without also being a hedonist;
that is, one could accept the definition of right as "that act which produces
the greatest good of those affected" without accepting the definition of good
as "pleasure." G. E. Moore holds such a theory.[2]

So far we have talked only of those ethical theories—egoism and utilitarianism—which emphasize consequences of some kind as the ground for
moral obligation. These accounts of obligation have traditionally been classified as "teleological" (from the Greek word *telos* meaning "end"). There
are teleological theories which emphasize ends quite different from those of
the utilitarian. Friedrich Nietzsche (see selection in this chapter) denounces
concern for mere pleasure and recommends that our highest moral value be
the development of a species of men which he characterizes as supermen
(*Übermensch*), men who have strength of character, nobility, and the will to
power.

However, there is an entirely different account of the meaning of right or
moral obligation which *denies* that consequences, no matter how they are
conceived, are the only relevant considerations. Such theories are known as
"formalist" or "deontological." They are represented in this chapter by the
selections from Kant and Ross. Kant, in fact, denies that consequential considerations are relevant *at all* in determining the rightness of an act. We need
only ask whether the act is based on good will or whether the maxim or rule
on which the act is based is such that it can be willed to be a universal law.
Ross, on the other hand, does not deny the relevance of consequences but
insists that there are other considerations relevant to making a sound moral
judgment, considerations which on occasion justifiably override concern for
consequences.

Much of moral philosophy involves the effort to evaluate the adequacy of
some basic norm or set of norms for solving moral problems. Does the utilitarian ethic (or some form of it) provide adequately for the resolution of
problems of justice, problems centering around the proper or proportionate
distribution of goods and services? Many argue that the utilitarian does not
deal with this issue at all, and that his ethic, therefore, cannot handle a major
segment of moral problems. The same question might be asked of the Christian ethic: Is it adequate to resolve problems of justice? If the basic and
underlying principle of that ethic is *love*, love of God and of man, how does
this norm answer the question of the manner or criterion for the distribution
of goods and services in society? Or take Kant's formalistic ethic. If some
ethical problems involve the calculation and assessment of the consequences

[2] See G. E. Moore, *Principia Ethica* (New York: Cambridge University Press), 1903.

of an act or policy of action (as they surely do), can a purely formal ethical principle, which excludes any reference to consequences, solve such problems? And if ethical issues are interpersonal issues involving the weighing of the consequences of acts and the proper distribution of goods and services, then surely the ethical egoist's position, whose only rule is "What will this do for me?" is totally inadequate. (Some argue that egoism is not an ethic at all, since an ethic by definition requires rules designed to resolve conflicts between persons. This issue involves analysis beyond the purely normative, and we will turn to this type of question in a moment.) A more popular ethic, widely publicized by *Playboy* magazine and known as the "playboy ethic" purports to offer adequate and enlightened rules for the resolution of moral problems of sex. What are those rules? Are they adequate for the limited area of sex? Do they cover other areas of human experience as well?

Critical evaluation of such normative ethical theories requires an overview of ethics and a sensitivity to ethical problems. It requires the formulation of tests of adequacy for ethical principles themselves. This is a more general and abstract level of analysis and justification than that involved in solving a particular ethical problem *within* the rules of a given ethic. Such an overview also requires that one ask questions about ethical statements and principles that are epistemological in nature. This level of analysis has come to be known as "metaethics." Indeed, it is perhaps the dominant activity of the contemporary moral philosopher. Some go so far as to say that it should be his only activity, that the normative dimension of moral issues is not the philosopher's concern. It is obvious that this is not the position of the author of this volume. There is in fact a growing trend among philosophers to engage in normative argument on substantive moral issues, and this is surely in keeping with the classical view of the task of the moral philosopher. Both Plato and Aristotle, for example, although concerned with the epistemological and semantic functions of moral concepts and statements, were primarily concerned with the normative issue "What is the good life?" and "What is justice?" But let us turn briefly to the epistemological or metaethical level of moral philosophy. (Epistemology as a general area of philosophical concern will be discussed in detail in Chapter Seven.)

METAETHICS

The basic issues in metaethics are: (1) What are the linguistic functions of ethical concepts and statements? (2) Can such statements be verified or justified, and if so, in what sense? (3) What is the relationship between key ethical concepts—good, right, obligatory? Both classical and contemporary philosophers have attempted to answer these questions. Let us look briefly at some of their efforts.

Ruth Benedict, the anthropologist, argues that the meaning of right conduct is "accepted by one's culture" (see selection in this chapter). Her thesis is not a moral one but a thesis about morality. She argues that all moral standards simply reflect the mores of different cultures, that each of us is malleable and learns his moral code from his culture, and that there are many different cultures with many different moral codes. She infers from all this that no moral standard is universally valid. There is little doubt that the anthropological studies of Benedict and other social scientists have strongly influenced popular scepticism and relativism in ethics.

Benedict's position is known as "cultural relativism." There are other forms of relativism. Thrasymachus, one of the disputants in Plato's *Republic*, argues that right means "whatever is dictated by the powerful." When power changes, right conduct changes. An even more extreme form of ethical relativism states that right is "whatever is approved by the individual at a given time." Not only may that approval disagree with the standards of one's culture; it may also be supplanted by a change in the same individual's judgment or feeling a few minutes later. For the cultural relativist, it is possible for the individual to err in his moral evaluations by misunderstanding or misrepresenting the mores of his culture. But with extreme individualistic relativism, even that sort of moral mistake is impossible.

Those who deny relativism in its various forms and maintain that there are universally valid moral standards are known as "ethical objectivists." But just as there are different kinds of ethical relativism, there are different kinds of ethical objectivism. Thus, there are cultural objectivists who deny the Benedict thesis, maintaining that although there are differences among cultures, there are certain fundamental cross-cultural norms which are universal. This is argued by Kroeber and Kluckholm in this chapter. Other objectivists do not dispute the empirical findings of Benedict but deny that those findings substantiate relativism. They ask: Is not the existence of objective moral standards compatible with relative standards in cultures? Surely the answer here is yes; but the objectivist must do more than show the logical possibility of his thesis. He must provide reasons or grounds for believing it.

Historically, objectivists have offered widely different grounds for their views. Aristotle admits that right conduct varies somewhat from one man to another but grounded certain objective norms in a theory of human nature. Plato also argues for objectivism by appeal to human nature but combined this appeal with his famous theory of "forms," which states that concepts like justice refer to timeless, eternal truths. Kant grounds his objectivism on formal principles derived from man's "pure practical reason," not from empirical sources. Ross, a contemporary Neo-Kantian, appeals to a kind of intuitive, nonempirical source of moral knowledge. Mill and Bentham, classical utilitarians, deny that the principle of utility can be proven but hold out the utilitarian norm as an objective standard. St. Thomas, on the other hand, although holding that natural law or moral rules can be substantiated by reason, appeals ultimately to Scripture as revelatory of God's will as grounds for his objectivism.

Theses about the grounds of justification of moral norms are not themselves moral theses. Nor are they moral arguments. Rather they are epistemological (and metaphysical) theses. The theories discussed above fall *generally* into two main classes: (1) those which maintain that moral predicates or moral statements refer to natural properties verifiable by the methods of science (known as a "naturalist" metaethic), and (2) those which maintain that moral statements refer to nonnatural properties not open to sense observation and scientific test (known as "nonnaturalism"). More recent metaethical theories have rejected *both* naturalism and nonnaturalism. For example, A. J. Ayer argues that moral concepts and judgments do not refer to any kind of property (see the selection in this chapter). They simply *express* one's emotion. To say that act *x* is right is equivalent to shouting: Hurrah for *x*. Ayer's theory is known as the emotive theory of ethics, and it is one formulation of what is generally known as "noncognitivism," the view that ethical judgments do not *assert* anything and cannot be either true *or* false. Hence, there can be no such thing as moral knowledge. Other noncognitivists give somewhat different accounts of moral judgments. Some argue that they are disguised commands; others, that they are prescriptions for action.

Other moral philosophers have stressed the point that moral judgments perform a variety of linguistic tasks in different contexts and uses. These judgments are used to exhort, persuade, cajole, command, prescribe, describe, appraise, warn, and the like. And, reintroducing in somewhat different form the traditional subjectivist-objectivist controversy in ethics, some philosophers argue that the *very concept of morality* requires rules which are impartial and universal in scope. (This is also argued by some traditional theorists, including the eighteenth-century philosopher David Hume.) Rationality in ethics logically requires this kind of objectivity, that is, rules that are impartially and universally applied to all similar circumstances. Furthermore, they contend that knowledge is possible in ethics. (The argument here is not entirely unlike the ontological argument for God's existence, that is, the attempt to move from the concept of God to his existence.)

EMPIRICAL ISSUES IN ETHICS

Thus far we have distinguished two levels of moral philosophy: (1) normative ethics—the attempt to formulate, defend, and evaluate normative arguments and normative principles; and (2) metaethics—the endeavor to analyze the meaning and linguistic functions of ethical concepts and statements, the relationships between these concepts, and the type of justification possible in ethics. The distinction between 1 and 2 is itself not without its difficulties; and sometimes in practice it is hard to tell whether a given claim or argument by a philosopher is normative or metaethical. Nonetheless, the distinction is a useful one.

Another level of activity in which the philosopher sometimes engages is straightforwardly empirical. There are some people who doubt that the philosopher's task is the collection of data and the testing of empirical hypotheses. It seems more the task of the scientist. There is some point to this. Surely the scientist is better qualified for such work. But scientists themselves often reflect on methods and assumptions as well as conduct empirical research; and philosophers, especially before the development of science, have occasionally conducted empirical investigations along with their more traditional analytic and reflective activities. Given the development of the sciences and of new techniques and methods of empirical research, this is indeed infrequent today. But no matter who does the empirical research, it is plain that data from such research are essential for rational appraisal of beliefs and practices, which most certainly includes ethical beliefs and practices. Although something more than empirical data is required to justify a philosophical theory or thesis, the philosopher who does not stay abreast of new data and discoveries in the sciences does so, it may be argued, at the peril of his philosophical views.

For example, consider the question of capital punishment. Social scientists have accumulated considerable evidence that the practice of capital punishment does *not* serve as a deterrent to crime. If the practice of capital punishment is based on the assumption that it does deter crime (as it generally is), then the grounds for this course of action are severely undercut. Rational men must either give up the practice, show that the social scientist is wrong in his data, or find other grounds for approving the practice. Again, suppose it could be shown that the practice of contraception would, after a time, prevent the starvation and suffering of millions of persons. Would such information not be relevant to making a rational decision about the adoption of this practice?

We have stressed that at least three levels of activity or inquiry are essential in the formulation of an adequate moral philosophy or ethical theory—(1) the empirical, (2) the analytic or epistemological, and (3) the normative. If a fundamental concern of the moral philosopher is the formulation and rational appraisal of moral beliefs and practices, then simple empirical information will not do the trick. This information must be combined with basic moral norms before one can arrive at normative conclusions bearing on moral practice. Nor can pure analysis or the epistemology of moral concepts and statements provide such rational critique. Moral philosophy must also be normative if it is to perform its principal (and classical) function—providing rational norms or standards for moral practice and for the resolution of moral conflict. The empirical and epistemological components are essential, but in the last analysis, they are subsidiary to this primary task.

The selections from classical and contemporary philosophers in this chapter expose the student to these multiple facets of moral philosophy. But the student's task is not an easy one, for if he wants more than historical knowledge of who said what and when, if he wants to understand and appraise the positions of these philosophers, their arguments, and the kinds of justifications each offers for his theory, then he must understand and evaluate the various components of their theories. These components include a philosopher's position on empirical facts, his epistemology, his metaphysics (including, frequently, his theology), and his normative beliefs. Moreover, philosophers obviously do not have final and neatly packaged answers to the problems of moral philosophy.

In fact, it would seem that a characteristic of philosophical problems is that they do not lend themselves to once-for-all answers. Changing conditions of human existence, new empirical data, and alternative conceptual ways of viewing both man and the world seem to prevent us from attaining conclusive answers to the questions of moral philosophy. Each moral theorist represented in this chapter has made significant contributions, but the views of each are based on different conceptual and empirical perspectives which, although adequate in some respects, are inadequate in others. The student of moral philosophy must attempt to sort out these adequacies and inadequacies as he tries to answer the principal questions of moral philosophy.

SELECTED BIBLIOGRAPHY

Baier, Kurt. *The Moral Point of View.* New York, 1965.

Baylis, Charles. *Ethics: Principles of Wise Choice.* New York, 1958.

Brandt, Richard. *Ethical Theory.* Englewood Cliffs, N.J., 1961.

Broad, C. D. *Five Types of Ethical Theory.* New York, 1930.

Dewey, John. *Theory of Valuations.* Chicago, 1939.

Edel, Abraham. *Ethical Judgment.* New York, 1955.

Edwards, Paul. *The Logic of Moral Discourse.* New York, 1955.

Frankena, William K. *Ethics.* Englewood Cliffs, N.J., 1963.

Girvetz, Harry K. (ed.). *Contemporary Moral Issues.* Belmont, Calif., 1968.

Hare, R. M. *Freedom and Reason.* London, 1963.

————. *The Language of Morals.* Oxford, 1952.

Hill, T. E. *Contemporary Ethical Theories.* New York, 1951.

Hospers, John. *Human Conduct.* New York, 1961.

Kerner, George C. *The Revolution in Ethical Theory.* New York, 1966.

Melden, A. I. (ed.). *Essays in Moral Philosophy.* Seattle, Wash., 1958.

Moore, G. E. *Principia Ethica.* Cambridge, 1903.

Nowell-Smith, P. H. *Ethics.* Harmondsworth, England, 1954.

Perry, R. B. *Realms of Value.* Cambridge, 1954.

Rader, Melvin. *Ethics and the Human Community.* New York, 1964.

Raphael, D. D. *Moral Judgment.* London, 1955.

Rice, Phillip Blair. *On the Knowledge of Good and Evil.* New York, 1955.

Sellars, Wilfrid, and Hospers, John (eds.). *Readings in Ethical Theory.* New York, 1952.

Stevenson, Charles L. *Ethics and Language.* New Haven, Conn., 1944.

Stinger, Marcus George. *Generalization in Ethics.* New York, 1961.

Taylor, Paul. *Normative Discourse.* Englewood Cliffs, N.J., 1961.

Toulmin, Stephen E. *An Examination of the Place of Reason in Ethics.* Cambridge, 1950.

Warnock, Mary. *Ethics Since 1900.* London, 1960.

Wellman, Carl. *The Language of Ethics.* Cambridge, 1961.

19 Justice and Happiness[*]

PLATO

Plato (427–347 B.C.) was a student of Socrates and later founded the Academy, the first "university" in Europe. He has had incalculable influence on Western thought. His best-known works are the *Apology, Crito, Meno, Protagoras, Gorgias, Phaedo, Symposium, Republic, Theatetus, Sophist, Parmenides, Phaedrus, Laws, Politicus,* and *Timaeus.*

PART I (BOOK I)

Some Current Views of Justice

The main question to be answered in the *Republic* is: What does Justice mean, and how can it be realized in human society? The Greek word for 'just' has as many senses as the English 'right.' It can mean: observant of custom or of duty, righteous; fair, honest; legally right, lawful; what is due to or from a person, deserts, rights; what one ought to do. Thus it covers the whole field of the individual's conduct in so far as it affects others—all that they have a 'right' to expect from him or he has a right to expect from them, whatever is right as opposed to wrong. A proverbial saying declared that justice is the sum of all virtue.

The demand for a definition of Justice seems to imply that there is some conception in which all these applications of the word meet like lines converging to a common centre; or, in more concrete terms, that there is some principle whereby human life might be so organized that there would exist a just society composed of just men. The justice of the society would secure that each member of it should perform his duties and enjoy his rights. As a quality residing in each individual, justice would mean that his personal life—or as a Greek would say, his soul—was correspondingly ordered with respect to the rights and duties of each part of his nature.

A society so composed and organized would be ideal, in the sense that it would offer a standard of perfection by which all existing societies might be measured and appraised according to the degrees in which they fell short of it. Any proposed reform, moreover, might be judged by its tendency to bring us nearer to, or farther from, this goal. The *Republic* is the first systematic attempt ever made to describe this ideal, not as a baseless dream, but

* From *The Republic of Plato*, trans. F. M. Cornford (New York: Oxford University Press, 1945). Reprinted by permission.

as a possible framework within which man's nature, with its unalterable claims, might find well-being and happiness. Without some such goal in view, statecraft must be either blind and aimless or directed (as it commonly is) to false and worthless ends.

If a man of sceptical and inquiring mind were to ask, in any mixed company of intelligent people, for a definition of 'right' or 'justice,' the answers produced would be likely to be superficial and to cover only some part of the field. They might also reveal fundamental differences of conviction about what Socrates calls the most important of all questions: how we ought to live. In the first Part of the *Republic* Socrates opens up the whole range of inquiry by eliciting some typical views of the nature of justice and criticizing them as either inadequate or false. The criticism naturally reveals some glimpses of the principles which will guide the construction that is to follow.

CHAPTER I (1. 327–331 D)

Cephalus: Justice as Honesty in Word and Deed

The whole imaginary conversation is narrated by Socrates to an unspecified audience. The company who will take part in it assemble at the house of Cephalus, a retired manufacturer living at the Piraeus, the harbour town about five miles from Athens. It includes, besides Plato's elder brothers, Glaucon and Adeimantus, Cephalus' sons, Polemarchus, Lysias, well known as a writer of speeches, and Euthydemus; Trasymachus of Chalcedon, a noted teacher of rhetoric, who may have formulated the definition of justice as 'the interest of the stronger,' though hardly any evidence about his opinions exists outside the Republic; and a number of Socrates' young friends. The occasion is the festival of Bendis, a goddess whose cult had been imported from Thrace. Cephalus embodies the wisdom of a long life honourably spent in business. He is well to do, but values money as a means to that peace of mind which comes of honesty and the ability to render to gods and men their due. This is what he understands by 'right' conduct or justice.

Socrates. I walked down to the Piraeus yesterday with Glaucon, the son of Ariston, to make my prayers to the goddess. As this was the first celebration of her festival, I wished also to see how the ceremony would be conducted. The Thracians, I thought, made as fine a show in the procession as our own people, though they did well enough. The prayers and the spectacle were over, and we were leaving to go back to the city, when from some way off Polemarchus, the son of Cephalus, caught sight of us starting homewards and sent his slave running to ask us to wait for him. The boy caught my garment from behind and gave me the message.

I turned round and asked where his master was.

There, he answered; coming up behind. Please wait.

Very well, said Glaucon; we will.

A minute later Polemarchus joined us, with Glaucon's brother, Adeimantus, and Niceratus, the son of Nicias, and some others who must have been at the procession.

Socrates, said Polemarchus, I do believe you are starting back to town and leaving us.

You have guessed right, I answered.

Well, he said, you see what a large party we are?

I do.

Unless you are more than a match for us, then, you must stay here.

Isn't there another alternative? said I; we might convince you that you must let us go.

How will you convince us, if we refuse to listen?

We cannot, said Glaucon.

Well, we shall refuse; make up your minds to that.

Here Adeimantus interposed: Don't you even know that in the evening there is going to be a torch-race on horseback in honour of the goddess?

On horseback! I exclaimed; that is something new. How will they do it? Are the riders going to race with torches and hand them on to one another?

Just so, said Polemarchus. Besides, there will be a festival lasting all night, which will be worth seeing. We will go out after dinner and look on. We shall find plenty of young men there and we can have a talk. So please stay, and don't disappoint us.

It looks as if we had better stay, said Glaucon.

Well, said I, if you think so, we will.

Accordingly, we went home with Polemarchus; and there we found his brothers, Lysias and Euthydemus, as well as Thrasymachus of Chalcedon, Charmantides of Paeania, and Cleitophon, the son of Aristonymus. Polemarchus' father, Cephalus, was at home too. I had not seen him for some time, and it struck me that he had aged a good deal. He was sitting in a cushioned chair, wearing a garland, as he had just been conducting a sacrifice in the courtyard. There were some chairs standing round, and we sat down beside him.

As soon as he saw me, Cephalus greeted me. You don't often come down to the Piraeus to visit us, Socrates, he said. But you ought to. If I still had the strength to walk to town easily, you would not have to come here; we would come to you. But, as things are, you really ought to come here oftener. I find, I can assure you, that in proportion as bodily pleasures lose their savour, my appetite for the things of the mind grows keener and I enjoy discussing them more than ever. So you must not disappoint me. Treat us like old friends, and come here often to have a talk with these young men.

To tell the truth, Cephalus, I answered, I enjoy talking with very old people. They have gone before us on a road by which we too may have to travel, and I think we do well to learn from them what it is like, easy or difficult, rough or smooth. And now that you have reached an age when your foot, as the poets say, is on the threshold, I should like to hear what report you can give and whether you find it a painful time of life.

I will tell you by all means what it seems like to me, Socrates. Some of us old men often meet, true to the old saying that people of the same age like to be together. Most of our company are very sorry for themselves, looking back with regret to the pleasures of their young days, all the delights connected with love affairs and merry-making. They are vexed at being deprived of what seems to them so important; life was good in those days, they think, and now they have no life at all. Some complain that their families have no respect for their years, and make that a reason for harping on all the miseries old age has brought. But to my mind, Socrates, they are laying the blame on the wrong shoulders. If the fault were in old age, so far as that goes, I and all who have ever reached my time of life would have the same experience; but in point of fact, I have met many who felt quite differently. For instance, I remember someone asking Sophocles, the poet, whether he was still capable of enjoying a woman. 'Don't talk in that way,' he answered; 'I am only too glad to be free of all that; it is like escaping from bondage to a raging madman.' I thought that a good answer at the time, and I still think so; for certainly a great peace comes when age sets us free from passions of that sort. When they weaken and relax their hold, most certainly it means, as Sophocles said, a release from servitude to many forms of madness. All these troubles, Socrates, including the complaints about not being respected, have only one cause; and that is not old age, but a man's character. If you have a contented mind at peace with itself, age is no intolerable burden; without that, Socrates, age and youth will be equally painful.

I was charmed with these words and wanted him to go on talking; so I tried to draw him out. I fancy, Cephalus, said I, most people will not accept that account; they imagine that it is not character that makes your burden light, but your wealth. The rich, they say, have many consolations.

That is true, he replied; they do not believe me; and there is something in their suggestion, though not so much as they suppose. When a man from Seriphus[1] taunted Themistocles and told him that his fame was due not to himself but to his country, Themistocles made a good retort: 'Certainly, if I had been born a Seriphian, I should not be famous; but no more would you, if you had been born at Athens.' And so one might say to men who are not rich and feel old age burdensome: If it is true that a good man will not find it easy to bear old age and poverty combined, no more will riches ever make a bad man contented and cheerful.

And was your wealth, Cephalus, mostly inherited or have you made your own fortune?

[1] An insignificant island, among the Cyclades.

Made my fortune, Socrates? As a man of business I stand somewhere between my grandfather and my father. My grandfather, who was my namesake, inherited about as much property as I have now and more than doubled it; whereas my father Lysanias reduced it below its present level. I shall be content if I can leave these sons of mine not less than I inherited, and perhaps a little more.

I asked, said I, because you strike me as not caring overmuch about money; and that is generally so with men who have not made their own fortune. Those who have are twice as fond of their possessions as other people. They have the same affection for the money they have earned that poets have for their poems, or fathers for their children: they not merely find it useful, as we all do, but it means much to them as being of their own creation. That makes them disagreeable company; they have not a good word for anything but riches.

That is quite true.

It is indeed, I said; but one more question: what do you take to be the greatest advantage you have got from being wealthy?

One that perhaps not many people would take my word for. I can tell you, Socrates, that, when the prospect of dying is near at hand, a man begins to feel some alarm about things that never troubled him before. He may have laughed at those stories they tell of another world and of punishments there for wrongdoing in this life; but now the soul is tormented by a doubt whether they may not be true. Maybe from the weakness of old age, or perhaps because, now that he is nearer to what lies beyond, he begins to get some glimpse of it himself—at any rate he is beset with fear and misgiving; he begins thinking over the past: is there anyone he has wronged? If he finds that his life has been full of wrongdoing, he starts up from his sleep in terror like a child, and his life is haunted by dark forebodings; whereas, if his conscience is clear, that 'sweet Hope' that Pindar speaks of is always with him to tend his age. Indeed, Socrates, there is great charm in those lines describing the man who has led a life of righteousness:

> Hope is his sweet companion, she who guides
> Man's wandering purpose, warms his heart
> And nurses tenderly his age.

That is admirably expressed, admirably. Now in this, as I believe, lies the chief value of wealth, not for everyone, perhaps, but for the right-thinking man. It can do much to save us from going to that other world in fear of having cheated or deceived anyone even unintentionally or of being in debt to some god for sacrifice or to some man for money. Wealth has many other uses, of course; but, taking one with another, I should regard this as the best use that can be made of it by a man of sense.

You put your case admirably, Cephalus, said I. But take this matter of doing right: can we say that it really consists in nothing more nor less than telling the truth and paying back anything we may have received? Are not these very actions sometimes right and sometimes wrong? Suppose, for example, a friend who had lent us a weapon were to go mad and then ask for it back, surely anyone would say we ought not to return it. It would not be 'right' to do so; nor yet to tell the truth without reserve to a madman.

No, it would not.

Right conduct, then, cannot be defined as telling the truth and restoring anything we have been trusted with.

Yes, it can, Polemarchus broke in, at least if we are to believe Simonides.

Well, well, said Cephalus, I will bequeath the argument to you. It is time for me to attend to the sacrifice.

Your part, then, said Polemarchus, will fall to me as your heir.

By all means, said Cephalus with a smile; and with that he left us, to see to the sacrifice.

CHAPTER II (1. 331 E–336 A)

Polemarchus: Justice as Helping Friends and Harming Enemies

Criticism now begins. No doubt it is generally right or just to tell the truth and pay one's debts; but no list of external actions such as these can tell us what is meant by justice, the name of the quality they have in common. Also what is superficially the same action, e.g. repayment of a loan, may completely change its character when we take into account the antecedents and consequences which form its wider context.

Polemarchus can only meet this objection by citing a maxim borrowed from a famous poet. In Greece, where there was no sacred book like the Bible, the poets were regarded as inspired authorities on religion and morals; but Socrates, when he questioned them, found them unable to give any rational account of their teaching (Apology, 22 B). Polemarchus, too, has never thought out the implications of defining justice as 'giving every man his due.' What is it that is due, and to whom?

Socrates' first object is to bring home to Polemarchus the vagueness of his ideas by leading him on to an absurd conclusion. In approaching a very large and obscure question, the first step is to convince one who thinks he can answer it with a compact formula that he knows much less than he imagines and cannot even understand his own formula.

Plato often, as here, compares the practice of morality to the useful (not the fine) arts of crafts: medicine, navigation, shoemaking. He even speaks of an 'art of justice.' He adopted Socrates' belief that there should be an art of living, analogous to the craftsman's knowledge and consequent ability to achieve a purposed end. A builder, building a house, knows what he is setting out to do and how to do it; he can account for all his actions as contributing to his end. *This knowledge and ability constitute the craft embodied in the builder and his special excellence or 'virtue' (areté), qua builder. Similarly a man can live well only if he knows clearly what is the end of life, what things are of real value, and how they are to be attained. This knowledge is the moral virtue of man, qua man, and constitutes the art of living. If a man imagines that the end of life is to gain wealth or power, which are valueless in themselves, all his actions will be misdirected. This doctrine is fundamental in the* Republic. *It leads to the central thesis that society must be ruled by men who have learnt, by long and severe training, not only the true end of human life, but the meaning of goodness in all its forms.*

Then, said I, if you are to inherit this discussion, tell me, what is this saying of Simonides about right conduct which you approve?

That it is just to render every man his due. That seems to me a fair statement.

It is certainly hard to question the inspired wisdom of a poet like Simonides; but what this saying means you may know, Polemarchus, but I do not. Obviously it does not mean what we were speaking of just now—returning something we have been entrusted with to the owner even when he has gone out of his mind. And yet surely it is his due, if he asks for it back?

Yes.

But it is out of the question to give it back when he has gone mad?

True.

Simonides, then, must have meant something different from that when he said it was just to render a man his due.

Certainly he did; his idea was that, as between friends, what one owes to another is to do him good, not harm.

I see, said I; to repay money entrusted to one is not to render what is due, if the two parties are friends and the repayment proves harmful to the lender. That is what you say Simonides meant?

Yes, certainly.

And what about enemies? Are we to render whatever is their due to them?

Yes certainly, what really is due to them; which means, I suppose, what is appropriate to an enemy—some sort of injury.

It seems, then, that Simonides was using words with a hidden meaning, as poets will. He really meant to define justice as rendering to everyone what is appropriate to him; only he called that his 'due.'

Well, why not?

But look here, said I. Suppose we could question Simonides about the art of medicine—whether a physician can be described as rendering to some object what is due or appropriate to it; how do you think he would answer?

That the physician administers the appropriate diet or remedies to the body.

And the art of cookery—can that be described in the same way?

Yes; the cook gives the appropriate seasoning to his dishes.

Good. And the practice of justice?

If we are to follow those analogies, Socrates, justice would be rendering services or injuries to friends or enemies.

So Simonides means by justice doing good to friends and harm to enemies?

I think so.

And in matters of health who would be the most competent to treat friends and enemies in that way?

A physician.

And on a voyage, as regards the dangers of the sea?

A ship's captain.

In what sphere of action, then, will the just man be the most competent to do good or harm?

In war, I should imagine; when he is fighting on the side of his friends and against his enemies.

I see. But when we are well and staying on shore, the doctor and the ship's captain are of no use to us.

True.

Is it also true that the just man is useless when we are not at war?

I should not say that.

So justice has its uses in peace-time too?

Yes.

Like farming, which is useful for producing crops, or shoemaking, which is useful for providing us with shoes. Can you tell me for what purposes justice is useful or profitable in time of peace?

For matters of business, Socrates.

In a partnership, you mean?

Yes.

But if we are playing draughts, or laying bricks, or making music, will the just man be as good and helpful a partner as an expert draught-player, or a builder, or a musician?

No.

Then in what kind of partnership will he be more helpful?

Where money is involved, I suppose.

Except, perhaps, Polemarchus, when we are putting our money to some use. If we are buying or selling a horse, a judge of horses would be a better partner; or if we are dealing in ships, a shipwright or a sea-captain.

I suppose so.

Well, when will the just man be specially useful in handling our money?

When we want to deposit it for safe-keeping.

When the money is to lie idle, in fact?

Yes.

So justice begins to be useful only when our money is out of use?

Perhaps so.

And in the same way, I suppose, if a pruning-knife is to be used, or a shield, or a lyre, then a vine-dresser, or a soldier, or a musician will be of service; but justice is helpful only when these things are to be kept safe. In fact justice is never of any use in using things; it becomes useful when they are useless.

That seems to follow.

If that is so, my friend, justice can hardly be a thing of much value. And here is another point. In boxing or fighting of any sort skill in dealing blows goes with skill in keeping them off; and the same doctor that can keep us from disease would also be clever at producing it by stealth; or again, a general will be good at keeping his army safe, if he can also cheat the enemy and steal his plans and dispositions. So a man who is expert in keeping things will always make an expert thief.

Apparently.

The just man, then, being good at keeping money safe, will also be good at stealing it.

That seems to be the conclusion, at any rate.

So the just man turns out to be a kind of thief. You must have learnt that from Homer, who showed his predilection of Odysseus' grandfather Auto-lycus by remarking that he surpassed all men in cheating and perjury. Justice, according to you and Homer and Simonides, turns out to be a form of skill in cheating, provided it be to help a friend or harm an enemy. That was what you meant?

Good God, no, he protested; but I have forgotten now what I did mean. All the same, I do still believe that justice consists in helping one's friends and harming one's enemies.

[*The argument now becomes more serious. Polemarchus, though puz-*
zled, clings to the belief that it must be right to help friends and harm
enemies. This was a traditional maxim of Greek morality, never doubted till
Socrates denied it: no one had ever said that we ought to do good, or even
refrain from doing harm, to them that hate us. Socrates' denial rests on his
principle, later adopted by the Stoics, that the only thing that is good in
itself is the goodness, virtue, well-being of the human soul. The only way
really to injure a man is to make him a worse man. This cannot be the
function of justice.]

Which do you mean by a man's friends and enemies—those whom he believes to be good honest people and the reverse, or those who really are, though they may not seem so?

Naturally, his loves and hates depend on what he believes.

But don't people often mistake an honest man for a rogue, or a rogue for an honest man; in which case they regard good people as enemies and bad people as friends?

No doubt.

But all the same, it will then be right for them to help the rogue and to injure the good man?

Apparently.

And yet a good man is one who is not given to doing wrong.

True.

According to your account, then, it is right to ill-treat a man who does no wrong.

No, no, Socrates; that can't be sound doctrine.

It must be the wrongdoers, then, that it is right to injure, and the honest that are to be helped.

That sounds better.

Then, Polemarchus, the conclusion will be that for a bad judge of character it will often be right to injure his friends, when they really are rogues, and to help his enemies, when they really are honest men—the exact opposite of what we took Simonides to mean.

That certainly does follow, he said. We must shift our ground. Perhaps our definition of friend and enemy was wrong.

What definition, Polemarchus?

We said a friend was one whom we believe to be an honest man.

And how are we to define him now?

As one who really is honest as well as seeming so. If he merely seems so, he will be only a seeming friend. And the same will apply to enemies.

On this showing, then, it is the good people that will be our friends, the wicked our enemies.

Yes.

You would have us, in fact, add something to our original definition of justice: it will not mean merely doing good to friends and harm to enemies, but doing good to friends who are good, and harm to enemies who are wicked.

Yes, I think that is all right.

Can it really be a just man's business to harm any human being?

Certainly; it is right for him to harm bad men who are his enemies.

But does not harming a horse or a dog mean making it a worse horse or dog, so that each will be a less perfect creature in its own special way?

Yes.

Isn't that also true of human beings—that to harm them means making them worse men by the standard of human excellence?

Yes.

And is not justice a peculiarly human excellence?

Undoubtedly.

To harm a man, then, must mean making him less just.

I suppose so.

But a musician or a riding-master cannot be exercising his special skill, if he makes his pupils unmusical or bad riders.

No.

Whereas the just man is to exercise his justice by making men unjust? Or, in more general terms, the good are to make men bad by exercising their virtue? Can that be so?

No, it cannot.

It can no more be the function of goodness to do harm than of heat to cool or of drought to produce moisture. So if the just man is good, the business of harming people, whether friends or not, must belong to his opposite, the unjust.

I think that is perfectly true, Socrates.

So it was not a wise saying that justice is giving every man his due, if that means that harm is due from the just man to his enemies, as well as help to his friends. That is not true; because we have found that it is never right to harm anyone.

I agree.

Then you and I will make common cause against anyone who attributes that doctrine to Simonides or to any of the old canonical sages, like Bias or Pittacus.

Yes, he said, I am prepared to support you.

Do you know, I think that account of justice, as helping friends and harming enemies, must be due to some despot, so rich and powerful that he thought he could do as he liked—someone like Periander, or Perdiccas, or Xerxes, or Ismenias of Thebes.

That is extremely probable.

Very good, said I; and now that we have disposed of that definition of justice, can anyone suggest another?

CHAPTER III (1. 336 B–347 E)

Thrasymachus: Justice as the Interest of the Stronger

Socrates has opposed to the popular conception of justice one of his own deepest convictions. Polemarchus' ready acceptance of this provokes a violent protest from Thrasymachus, who represents the doctrine that might is right in an extreme form. He holds that justice or right is nothing but the name given by the men actually holding power in any state to any actions they enjoin by law upon their subjects; and that all their laws are framed to promote their own personal or class interests. 'Just' accordingly means what is for the interest of the stronger, ruling party. Right and wrong have no other meaning at all. This is not a theory of social contract: it is not suggested that the subject has ever made a bargain with the ruler, sacrificing some of his liberty to gain the benefits of a social order. The ruler imposes his 'rights' by sheer force. The perfect example of such a ruler is the despot (The Greek 'tyrant'), whose position Thrasymachus regards as supremely

*enviable. He is precisely the man who has the will and the power to 'do
good to himself and his friends and to harm his enemies.'*

*The discussion begins by clearing up the ambiguities of Thrasymachus'
formula. The word translated 'stronger' commonly means also 'superior' or
'better'; but 'better' has no moral sense for Thrasymachus, who does not
recognize the existence of morality. The superiority of the stronger lies in
the skill and determination which enable them to seize and hold power.
'Interest,' again, means the personal satisfaction and aggrandizement of the
ruling individuals.*

All this time Thrasymachus had been trying more than once to break in
upon our conversation; but his neighbours had restrained him, wishing to
hear the argument to the end. In the pause after my last words he could
keep quiet no longer; but gathering himself up like a wild beast he sprang
at us as if he would tear us in pieces. Polemarchus and I were frightened out
of our wits, when he burst out to the whole company:

What is the matter with you two, Socrates? Why do you go on in this
imbecile way, politely deferring to each other's nonsense? If you really want
to know what justice means, stop asking questions and scoring off the answers
you get. You know very well it is easier to ask questions than to answer them.
Answer yourself, and tell us what you think justice means. I won't have you
telling us it is the same as what is obligatory or useful or advantageous or
profitable or expedient; I want a clear and precise statement; I won't put up
with that sort of verbiage.

I was amazed by this onslaught and looked at him in terror. If I had not
seen this wolf before he saw me, I really believe I should have been struck
dumb[2] but fortunately I had looked at him earlier, when he was beginning
to get exasperated with our argument; so I was able to reply, though rather
tremulously:

Don't be hard on us, Thrasymachus. If Polemarchus and I have gone
astray in our search, you may be quite sure the mistake was not intentional.
If we had been looking for a piece of gold, we should never have deliberately
allowed politeness to spoil our chance of finding it; and now when we are
looking for justice, a thing much more precious than gold, you cannot imagine we should defer to each other in that foolish way and not do our best to
bring it to light. You must believe we are in earnest, my friend; but I am
afraid the task is beyond our powers, and we might expect a man of your
ability to pity us instead of being so severe.

Thrasymachus replied with a burst of sardonic laughter.

Good Lord, he said; Socrates at his old trick of shamming ignorance! I
knew it; I told the others you would refuse to commit yourself and do anything sooner than answer a question.

[2] A popular superstition, that if a wolf sees you first, you become dumb.

Yes, Thrasymachus, I replied; because you are clever enough to know that if you asked someone what are the factors of the number twelve, and at the same time warned him: 'Look here, you are not to tell me that 12 is twice 6, or 3 times 4, or 6 times 2, or 4 times 3; I won't put up with any such nonsense'—you must surely see that no one would answer a question put like that. He would say: 'What do you mean, Thrasymachus? Am I forbidden to give any of these answers, even if one happens to be right? Do you want me to give a wrong one?' What would you say to that?

Humph! said he. As if that were a fair analogy!

I don't see why it is not, said I; but in any case, do you suppose our barring a certain answer would prevent the man from giving it, if he thought it was the truth?

Do you mean that you are going to give me one of those answers I barred?

I should not be surprised, if it seemed to me true, on reflection.

And what if I give you another definition of justice, better than any of those? What penalty are you prepared to pay?[3]

The penalty deserved by ignorance, which must surely be to receive instruction from the wise. So I would suggest that as a suitable punishment.

I like your notion of a penalty! he said; but you must pay the costs as well.

I will, when I have any money.

That will be all right, said Glaucon; we will all subscribe for Socrates. So let us have your definition, Thrasymachus.

Oh yes, he said; so that Socrates may play the old game of questioning and refuting someone else, instead of giving an answer himself!

But really, I protested, what can you expect from a man who does not know the answer or profess to know it, and, besides that, has been forbidden by no mean authority to put forward any notions he may have? Surely the definition should naturally come from you, who say you do know the answer and can tell it us. Please do not disappoint us. I should take it as a kindness, and I hope you will not be chary of giving Glaucon and the rest of us the advantage of your instruction.

Glaucon and the others added their entreaties to mine. Thrasymachus was evidently longing to win credit, for he was sure he had an admirable answer ready, though he made a show of insisting that I should be the one to reply. In the end he gave way and exclaimed:

So this is what Socrates' wisdom comes to! He refuses to teach, and goes about learning from others without offering so much as thanks in return.

I do learn from others, Thrasymachus; that is quite true; but you are

---

[3] In certain lawsuits the defendant, if found guilty, was allowed to propose a penalty alternative to that demanded by the prosecution. The judges then decided which should be inflicted. The 'costs' here means the fee which the sophist, unlike Socrates, expected from his pupils.

wrong to call me ungrateful. I give in return all I can—praise; for I have no money. And how ready I am to applaud any idea that seems to me sound, you will see in a moment, when you have stated your own; for I am sure that will be sound.

Listen then, Thrasymachus began. What I say is that 'just' or 'right' means nothing but what is to the interest of the stronger party. Well, where is your applause? You don't mean to give it me.

I will, as soon as I understand, I said. I don't see yet what you mean by right being the interest of the stronger party. For instance, Polydamas, the athlete, is stronger than we are, and it is to his interest to eat beef for the sake of his muscles; but surely you don't mean that the same diet would be good for weaker men and therefore be right for us?

You are trying to be funny, Socrates. It's a low trick to take my words in the sense you think will be most damaging.

No, no, I protested; but you must explain.

Don't you know, then, that a state may be ruled by a despot, or a democracy, or an aristocracy?

Of course.

And that the ruling element is always the strongest?

Yes.

Well then, in every case the laws are made by the ruling party in its own interest; a democracy makes democratic laws, a despot autocratic ones, and so on. By making these laws they define as 'right' for their subjects whatever is for their own interest, and they call anyone who breaks them a 'wrongdoer' and punish him accordingly. That is what I mean: in all states alike 'right' has the same meaning, namely what is for the interest of the party established in power, and that is the strongest. So the sound conclusion is that what is 'right' is the same everywhere: the interest of the stronger party.

Now I see what you mean, said I; whether it is true or not, I must try to make out. When you define right in terms of interest, you are yourself giving one of those answers you forbade to me; though, to be sure, you add 'to the stronger party.'

An insignificant addition, perhaps!

Its importance is not clear yet; what is clear is that we must find out whether your definition is true. I agree myself that right is in a sense a matter of interest; but when you add 'to the stronger party,' I don't know about that. I must consider.

Go ahead, then.

I will. Tell me this. No doubt you also think it is right to obey the men in power?

I do.

Are they infallible in every type of state, or can they sometimes make a mistake?

Of course they can make a mistake.

In framing laws, then, they may do their work well or badly?

No doubt.

Well, that is to say, when the laws they make are to their own interest; badly, when they are not?

Yes.

But the subjects are to obey any law they lay down, and they will then be doing right?

Of course.

If so, by your account, it will be right to do what is not to the interest of the stronger party, as well as what is so.

What's that you are saying?

Just what you said, I believe; but let us look again. Haven't you admitted that the rulers, when they enjoin certain acts on their subjects, sometimes mistake their own best interests, and at the same time that it is right for the subjects to obey, whatever they may enjoin?

Yes, I suppose so.

Well, that amounts to admitting that it is right to do what is not to the interest of the rulers or the stronger party. They may unwittingly enjoin what is to their own disadvantage; and you say it is right for the others to do as they are told. In that case, their duty must be the opposite of what you said, because the weaker will have been ordered to do what is against the interest of the stronger. You with your intelligence must see how that follows.

Yes, Socrates, said Polemarchus, that is undeniable.

No doubt, Cleitophon broke in, if you are to be a witness on Socrates' side.

No witness is needed, replied Polemarchus; Thrasymachus himself admits that rulers sometimes ordain acts that are to their own disadvantage, and that it is the subjects' duty to do them.

That is because Thrasymachus said it was right to do what you are told by the men in power.

Yes, but he also said that what is to the interest of the stronger party is right; and, after making both these assertions, he admitted that the stronger sometimes command the weaker subjects to act against their interests. From all which it follows that what is in the stronger's interest is no more right than what is not.

No, said Cleitophon; he meant whatever the stronger *believes* to be in his own interest. That is what the subject must do, and what Thrasymachus meant to define as right.

That was not what he said, rejoined Polemarchus.

No matter, Polemarchus, said I; if Thrasymachus says so now, let us take him in that sense. Now, Thrasymachus, tell me, was that what you intended to say—that right means what the stronger thinks is to his interest, whether it really is so or not?

Most certainly not, he replied. Do you suppose I should speak of a man as 'stronger' or 'superior' at the very moment when he is making a mistake?

I did think you said as much when you admitted that rulers are not always infallible.

That is because you are a quibbler, Socrates. Would you say a man deserves to be called a physician at the moment when he makes a mistake in treating his patient and just in respect of that mistake; or a mathematician, when he does a sum wrong and just in so far as he gets a wrong result? Of course we do commonly speak of a physician or a mathematician or a scholar having made a mistake; but really none of these, I should say, is ever mistaken, in so far as he is worthy of the name we give him. So strictly speaking—and you are all for being precise—no one who practises a craft makes mistakes. A man is mistaken when his knowledge fails him; and at that moment he is no craftsman. And what is true of craftsmanship or any sort of skill is true of the ruler: he is never mistaken so long as he is acting as a ruler; though anyone might speak of a ruler making a mistake, just as he might of a physician. You must understand that I was talking in that loose way when I answered your question just now; but the precise statement is this. The ruler, in so far as he is acting as a ruler, makes no mistakes and consequently enjoins what is best for himself; and that is what the subject is to do. So, as I said at first, 'right' means doing what is to the interest of the stronger.

Very well, Thrasymachus, said I. So you think I am quibbling?

I am sure you are.

You believe my questions were maliciously designed to damage your position?

I know it. But you will gain nothing by that. You cannot outwit me by cunning, and you are not the man to crush me in the open.

Bless your soul, I answered, I should not think of trying. But, to prevent any more misunderstanding, when you speak of that ruler or stronger party whose interest the weaker ought to serve, please make it clear whether you are using the words in the ordinary way or in that strict sense you have just defined.

I mean a ruler in the strictest possible sense. Now quibble away and be as malicious as you can. I want no mercy. But you are no match for me.

Do you think me mad enough to beard a lion or try to outwit a Thrasymachus?

You did try just now, he retorted, but it wasn't a success.

[*Thrasymachus has already shifted his ground. At first 'the stronger' meant only the men ruling by superior force; but now their superiority must include the knowledge and ability needed to govern without making mistakes. This knowledge and ability constitute an art of government, comparable to other useful arts or crafts requiring special skill. The ruler in his capacity as ruler, or the craftsman* qua *craftsman, can also be spoken of as the craft personified, since a craft exists only in the man who embodies it, and we are considering the man only as the embodiment of this special capacity, neglecting all personal characteristics and any other capacities he may chance to have. When Socrates talks of the art or craft in this abstract way as having an interest of its own, he means the same thing as if he spoke of the interest of the craftsman* qua *craftsman. Granted that there is, as Thrasymachus suggested, an art of government exercised by a ruler who,* qua *ruler, is infallible and so in the full sense 'superior,' the question now is, what his interest should be, on the analogy of other crafts.]*

Enough of this, said I. Now tell me about the physician in that strict sense you spoke of: is it his business to earn money or to treat his patients? Remember, I mean your physician who is worthy of the name.

To treat his patients.

And what of the ship's captain in the true sense? Is he a mere seaman or the commander of the crew?

The commander.

Yes, we shall not speak of him as a seaman just because he is on board a ship. That is not the point. He is called captain because of his skill and authority over the crew.

Quite true.

And each of these people has some special interest?[4]

No doubt.

And the craft in question exists for the very purpose of discovering that interest and providing for it?

Yes.

Can it equally be said of any craft that it has an interest, other than its own greatest possible perfection?

What do you mean by that?

Here is an illustration. If you ask me whether it is sufficient for the human body just to be itself, with no need of help from without, I should say, Certainly not; it has weaknesses and defects, and its condition is not all that it might be. That is precisely why the art of medicine was invented: it was designed to help the body and provide for its interests. Would not that be true?

It would.

But now take the art of medicine itself. Has that any defects or weaknesses? Does any art stand in need of some further perfection, as the eye would be imperfect without the power of vision or the ear without hearing,

---

[4] All the persons mentioned have some interest. The craftsman *qua* craftsman has an interest in doing his work as well as possible, which is the same thing as serving the interest of the subjects on whom his craft is exercised; and the subjects have their interest, which the craftsman is there to promote.

so that in their case an art is required that will study their interests and provide for their carrying out those functions? Has the art itself any corresponding need of some further art to remedy its defects and look after its interests; and will that further art require yet another, and so on for ever? Or will every art look after its own interests? Or, finally, is it not true that no art needs to have its weaknesses remedied or its interests studied either by another art or by itself, because no art has in itself any weakness or fault, and the only interest it is required to serve is that of its subject-matter? In itself, an art is sound and flawless, so long as it is entirely true to its own nature as an art in the strictest sense—and it is the strict sense that I want you to keep in view. Is not that true?

So it appears.

Then, said I, the art of medicine does not study its own interest, but the needs of the body, just as a groom shows his skill by caring for horses, not for the art of grooming. And so every art seeks, not its own advantage— for it has no deficiencies—but the interest of the subject on which it is exercised.

It appears so.

But surely, Thrasymachus, every art has authority and superior power over its subject.

To this he agreed, though very reluctantly.

So far as arts are concerned, then, no art ever studies or enjoins the interest of the superior or stronger party, but always that of the weaker over which it has authority.

Thrasymachus assented to this at last, though he tried to put up a fight. I then went on:

So the physician, as such, studies only the patient's interest, not his own. For as we agreed, the business of the physician, in the strict sense, is not to make money for himself, but to exercise his power over the patient's body; and the ship's captain, again, considered strictly as no mere sailor, but in command of the crew, will study and enjoin the interest of his subordinates, not his own.

He agreed reluctantly.

And so with government of any kind: no ruler, in so far as he is acting as ruler, will study or enjoin what is for his own interest. All that he says and does will be said and done with a view to what is good and proper for the subject for whom he practises his art.

[*Thrasymachus can hardly challenge this last argument, based as it is on his own 'precise' distinction of the ruler acting in his special capacity with knowledge and ability like the craftsman's and impeccable. Accordingly he takes refuge in an appeal to facts. The ruler, from the Homeric king onwards, had been called the shepherd of the people. Thrasymachus truly remarks that these shepherds have commonly been less concerned with the good of their flock than with shearing and butchering them for their own profit and aggrandizement. This behaviour is called 'injustice' because it means getting more than one's fair share; but the entirely selfish autocrat who practises it on a grand scale is envied and admired; and Thrasymachus himself regards him as the happiest of men. Justice, fairness, honesty, he concludes, never pay; the life of injustice is always more profitable.*

Socrates leaves this more general proposition to be challenged in the next chapter. Here he is still concerned with the art of government. He takes up the analogy of the shepherd and applies once more Thrasymachus' own distinction of 'capacities.' The shepherd qua *shepherd cares for his flock; he receives wages in a different capacity,* qua *wage-earner. The fact that the rulers of mankind expect to be rewarded shows that the proper task of governing is commonly regarded as an irksome and unprofitable business.]*

At this point, when everyone could see that Thrasymachus' definition of justice had been turned inside out, instead of making any reply, he said:

Socrates, have you a nurse?

Why do you ask such a question as that? I said. Wouldn't it be better to answer mine?

Because she lets you go about sniffling like a child whose nose wants wiping. She hasn't even taught you to know a shepherd when you see one, or his sheep either.

What makes you say that?

Why, you imagine that a herdsman studies the interests of his flocks or cattle, tending and fattening them up with some other end in view than his master's profit or his own; and so you don't see that, in politics, the genuine ruler regards his subjects exactly like sheep, and thinks of nothing else, night and day, but the good he can get out of them for himself. You are so far out in your notions of right and wrong, justice and injustice, as not to know that 'right' actually means what is good for someone else, and to be 'just' means serving the interest of the stronger who rules, at the cost of the subject who obeys; whereas injustice is just the reverse, asserting its authority over those innocents who are called just, so that they minister solely to their master's advantage and happiness, and not in the least degree to their own. Innocent as you are yourself, Socrates, you must see that a just man always has the worst of it. Take a private business: when a partnership is wound up, you will never find that the more honest of two partners comes off with the larger share; and in their relations to the state, when there are taxes to be paid, the honest man will pay more than the other on the same amount of property; or if there is money to be distributed, the dishonest will get it all. When either of them hold some public office, even if the just man loses in no other way, his private affairs at any rate will suffer from neglect, while his principles will not allow him to help himself from the public funds; not to mention the offence he will give to his friends and relations by refusing to

sacrifice those principles to do them a good turn. Injustice has all the opposite advantages. I am speaking of the type I described just now, the man who
can get the better of other people on a large scale: you must fix your eye on
him, if you want to judge how much it is to one's own interest not to be just.
You can see that best in the most consummate form of injustice, which
rewards wrongdoing with supreme welfare and happiness and reduces its
victims, if they won't retaliate in kind, to misery. That form is despotism,
which uses force or fraud to plunder the goods of others, public or private,
sacred or profane, and to do it in a wholesale way. If you are caught committing any one of these crimes on a small scale, you are punished and disgraced; they call it sacrilege, kidnapping, burglary, theft and brigandage. But
if, besides taking their property, you turn all your countrymen into slaves,
you will hear no more of those ugly names; your countrymen themselves
will call you the happiest of men and bless your name, and so will everyone
who hears of such a complete triumph of injustice; for when people denounce
injustice, it is because they are afraid of suffering wrong, not of doing it. So
true is it, Socrates, that injustice, on a grand enough scale, is superior to
justice in strength and freedom and autocratic power; and 'right,' as I said
at first, means simply what serves the interest of the stronger party; 'wrong'
means what is for the interest and profit of oneself.

Having deluged our ears with this torrent of words, as the man at the
baths might empty a bucket over one's head, Thrasymachus meant to take
himself off; but the company obliged him to stay and defend his position.
I was specially urgent in my entreaties.

My good Thrasymachus, said I, do you propose to fling a doctrine like
that at our heads and then go away without explaining it properly or letting
us point out to you whether it is true or not? Is it so small a matter in your
eyes to determine the whole course of conduct which everyone of us must
follow to get the best out of life?

Don't I realize it is a serious matter? he retorted.

Apparently not, said I; or else you have no consideration for us, and do
not care whether we shall lead better or worse lives for being ignorant of this
truth you profess to know. Do take the trouble to let us into your secret; if
you treat us handsomely, you may be sure it will be a good investment; there
are so many of us to show our gratitude. I will make no secret of my own
conviction, which is that injustice is not more profitable than justice, even
when left free to work its will unchecked. No; let your unjust man have full
power to do wrong, whether by successful violence or by escaping detection;
all the same he will not convince me that he will gain more than he would by
being just. There may be others here who feel as I do, and set justice above
injustice. It is for you to convince us that we are not well advised.

How can I? he replied. If you are not convinced by what I have just
said, what more can I do for you? Do you want to be fed with my ideas
out of a spoon?

God forbid! I exclaimed; not that. But I do want you to stand by your own words; or, if you shift your ground, shift it openly and stop trying to hoodwink us as you are doing now. You see, Thrasymachus, to go back to your earlier argument, in speaking of the shepherd you did not think it necessary to keep to that strict sense you laid down when you defined the genuine physician. You represent him, in his character of shepherd, as feeding up his flock, not for their own sake but for the table or the market, as if he were out to make money as a caterer or a cattle-dealer, rather than a shepherd. Surely the sole concern of the shepherd's art is to do the best for the charges put under its care; its own best interest is sufficiently provided for, so long as it does not fall short of all that shepherding should imply. On that principle it followed, I thought, that any kind of authority, in the state or in private life, must, in its character of authority, consider solely what is best for those under its care. Now what is your opinion? Do you think that the men who govern states—I mean rulers in the strict sense—have no reluctance to hold office?

I don't think so, he replied; I know it.

Well, but haven't you noticed, Thrasymachus, that in other positions of authority no one is willing to act unless he is paid wages, which he demands on the assumption that all the benefit of his action will go to his charges? Tell me: Don't we always distinguish one form of skill from another by its power to effect some particular result? Do say what you really think, so that we may get on.

Yes, that is the distinction.

And also each brings us some benefit that is peculiar to it: medicine gives health, for example; the art of navigation, safety at sea; and so on.

Yes.

And wage-earning brings us wages; that is its distinctive product. Now, speaking with that precision which you proposed, you would not say that the art of navigation is the same as the art of medicine, merely on the ground that a ship's captain regained his health on a voyage, because the sea air was good for him. No more would you identify the practice of medicine with wage-earning because a man may keep his health while earning wages, or a physician attending a case may receive a fee.

No.

And, since we agreed that the benefit obtained by each form of skill is peculiar to it, any common benefit enjoyed alike by all these practitioners must come from some further practice common to them all?

It would seem so.

Yes, we must say that if they all earn wages, they get that benefit in so far as they are engaged in wage-earning as well as in practising their several arts.

He agreed reluctantly.

This benefit, then—the receipt of wages—does not come to a man from his special art. If we are to speak strictly, the physician, as such, produces health; the builder, a house; and then each, in his further capacity of wage-earner, gets his pay. Thus every art has its own function and benefits its proper subject. But suppose the practitioner is not paid; does he then get any benefit from his art?

Clearly not.

And is he doing no good to anyone either, when he works for nothing?

No, I suppose he does some good.

Well then, Thrasymachus, it is now clear that no form of skill or authority provides for its own benefit. As we were saying some time ago, it always studies and prescribes what is good for its subject—the interest of the weaker party, not of the stronger. And that, my friend, is why I said that no one is willing to be in a position of authority and undertake to set straight other men's troubles, without demanding to be paid; because, if he is to do his work well, he will never, in his capacity of ruler, do, or command others to do, what is best for himself, but only what is best for the subject. For that reason, if he is to consent, he must have his recompense, in the shape of money or honour, or of punishment in case of refusal.

What do you mean, Socrates? asked Glaucon. I recognize two of your three kinds of reward; but I don't understand what you mean by speaking of punishment as a recompense.

Then you don't understand the recompense required by the best type of men, or their motive for accepting authority when they do consent. You surely know that a passion for honours or for money is rightly regarded as something to be ashamed of.

Yes, I do.

For that reason, I said, good men are unwilling to rule, either for money's sake or for honour. They have no wish to be called mercenary for demanding to be paid, or thieves for making a secret profit out of their office; nor yet will honours tempt them, for they are not ambitious. So they must be forced to consent under threat of penalty; that may be why a readiness to accept power under no such constraint is thought discreditable. And the heaviest penalty for declining to rule is to be ruled by someone inferior to yourself. That is the fear, I believe, that makes decent people accept power; and when they do so, they face the prospect of authority with no idea that they are coming into the enjoyment of a comfortable berth; it is forced upon them because they can find no one better than themselves, or even as good, to be entrusted with power. If there could ever be a society of perfect men, there might well be as much competition to evade office as there now is to gain it; and it would then be clearly seen that the genuine ruler's nature is to seek only the advantage of the subject, with the consequence that any man of understanding would sooner have another to do the best for him than be at the pains to do the best for that other himself. On this point, then, I entirely disagree with Thrasymachus' doctrine that right means what is to the interest of the stronger.

CHAPTER IV (1. 347 E–354 C)

Thrasymachus: Is Injustice More Profitable than Justice?

Socrates now turns from the art of government to Thrasymachus' whole view of life: that injustice, unlimited self-seeking, pursued with enough force of character and skill to ensure success, brings welfare and happiness. This is what he ultimately means by the interest of the stronger.

Socrates and Thrasymachus have a common ground for argument in that both accept the notion of an art of living, comparable to the special crafts in which trained intelligence creates some product. The goodness, excellence, or virtue of a workman lies in his efficiency, the Greek areté, a word which, with the corresponding adjective agathos, 'good,' never lost its wide application to whatever does its work or fulfils its function well, as a good knife is one that cuts efficiently. The workman's efficiency involves trained intelligence or skill, an old sense of the word sophia, which also means wisdom. None of these words necessarily bears any moral sense; but they can be applied to the art of living. Here the product to be aimed at is assumed to be a man's own happiness and well-being. The efficiency which makes him good at attaining this end is called 'virtue'; the implied knowledge of the end and of the means to it is like the craftsman's skill and may be called 'wisdom.' But as it sounds in English almost a contradiction to say that to be unjust is to be virtuous or good and wise, the comparatively colourless phrase 'superior in character and intelligence' will be used instead.

Where Socrates and Thrasymachus differ is in their views of the nature of happiness or well-being. Thrasymachus thinks it consists in getting more than your fair share of what are commonly called the good things of life, pleasure, wealth, power. Thus virtue and wisdom mean to him efficiency and skill in achieving injustice.

However, I continued, we may return to that question later. Much more important is the position Thrasymachus is asserting now: that a life of injustice is to be preferred to a life of justice. Which side do you take, Glaucon? Where do you think the truth lies?

I should say that the just life is the better worth having.

You heard Thrasymachus' catalogue of all the good things in store for injustice?

I did, but I am not convinced.

Shall we try to convert him, then, supposing we can find some way to prove him wrong?

By all means.

We might answer Thrasymachus' case in a set speech of our own, drawing up a corresponding list of the advantages of justice; he would then have the right to reply, and we should make our final rejoinder; but after that we should have to count up and measure the advantages on each list, and we should need a jury to decide between us. Whereas, if we go on as before, each securing the agreement of the other side, we can combine the functions of advocate and judge. We will take whichever course you prefer.

I prefer the second, said Glaucon.

Come then, Thrasymachus, said I, let us start afresh with our questions. You say that injustice pays better than justice, when both are carried to the furthest point?

I do, he replied; and I have told you why.

And how would you describe them? I suppose you would call one of them an excellence and the other a defect?

Of course.

Justice an excellence, and injustice a defect?

Now is that likely, when I am telling you that injustice pays, and justice does not?

Then what do you say?

The opposite.

That justice is a defect?

No; rather the mark of a good-natured simpleton.

Injustice, then, implies being ill-natured?

No; I should call it good policy.

Do you think the unjust are positively superior in character and intelligence, Thrasymachus?

Yes, if they are the sort that can carry injustice to perfection and make themselves masters of whole cities and nations. Perhaps you think I was talking of pickpockets. There is profit even in that trade, if you can escape detection; but it doesn't come to much as compared with the gains I was describing.

I understand you now on that point, I replied. What astonished me was that you should class injustice with superior character and intelligence and justice with the reverse.

Well, I do, he rejoined.

That is a much more stubborn position, my friend; and it is not so easy to see how to assail it. If you would admit that injustice, however well it pays, is nevertheless, as some people think, a defect and a discreditable thing, then we could argue on generally accepted principles. But now that you have gone so far as to rank it with superior character and intelligence, obviously you will say it is an admirable thing as well as a source of strength, and has all the other qualities we have attributed to justice.

You read my thoughts like a book, he replied.

However, I went on, it is no good shirking; I must go through with the argument, so long as I can be sure you are really speaking your mind. I do believe you are not playing with us now, Thrasymachus, but stating the truth as you conceive it.

Why not refute the doctrine? he said. What does it matter to you whether I believe it or not?

It does not matter, I replied.

[*Socrates attacks separately three points in Thrasymachus' position:* (1) *that the unjust is superior to the just in character ('virtue') and intelligence;* (2) *that injustice is a source of strength;* (3) *that it brings happiness.*

(1) *The first argument* (349 B–350 C) *is omitted here, because only a very loose paraphrase could liberate the meaning from the stiff and archaic form of the original. Thrasymachus has upheld the superman who will try to outdo everyone else and go to any lengths in getting the better of his neighbors. Socrates attacks this ideal of unlimited self-assertion, relying once more on the admitted analogy between the art of living and other arts. The musician, tuning an instrument, knows that there is for each string a certain pitch which is absolutely right. He shows his excellence and mastery of the art by aiming at that 'limit' or 'measure' (as the Greeks would call it), and he would be satisfied if he could attain it. In doing so he would be outdoing or 'going one better than' less skilful musicians or the unmusical; but he would not be showing superior skill if he tried to outdo a musician who acknowledged the same measure and had actually attained it. Socrates holds that in moral conduct also there is a measure which is absolutely right, whether we recognize it or not. The just man, who does recognize it, shows a wisdom and virtue corresponding to the skill of the good musician. The unjust, who acknowledges no measure or limit, because there is no limit to getting more and more for yourself at others' expense and that is his object, is, by all analogy, exhibiting rather a lack of intelligence and character. As a man, and therefore a moral agent, he is no more 'wise and good' than an instrumentalist who should refuse to recognize such a thing as the right pitch. Jowett quotes: 'When workmen strive to do better than well, They do confound their skill in covetousness' (K. John iv. 2). Socrates concludes:*

'*It is evident, then, that it is the just man that is wise and good (superior in character and intelligence), the unjust that is ignorant and bad.*'

(2) *In the following passage Socrates has little difficulty in showing that unlimited self-assertion is not a source of strength in any association formed for a common purpose. 'Honour among thieves' is common sense, which Thrasymachus cannot challenge. Socrates infers that injustice will have the same effect within the individual soul, dividing a man against himself and destroying unity of purpose. The various desires and impulses in his nature will be in conflict, if each asserts an unlimited claim to satisfaction. This view of justice as a principle of internal order and unity will become clearer when the soul has been analysed into its principal elements.*]

Thrasymachus' assent was dragged out of him with a reluctance of which my account gives no idea. He was sweating at every pore, for the weather was hot; and I saw then what I had never seen before—Thrasymachus blushing. However, now that we have agreed that justice implies superior character and intelligence, injustice a deficiency in both respects, I went on:

Good; let us take that as settled. But we were also saying that injustice was a source of strength. Do you remember, Thrasymachus?

I do remember; only your last argument does not satisfy me, and I could say a good deal about that. But if I did, you would tell me I was haranguing you like a public meeting. So either let me speak my mind at length, or else, if you want to ask questions, ask them, and I will nod or shake my head, and say 'Hm?' as we do to encourage an old woman telling us a story.

No, please, said I; don't give your assent against your real opinion.

Anything to please you, he rejoined, since you won't let me have my say. What more do you want?

Nothing, I replied. If that is what you mean to do, I will go on with my questions.

Go on, then.

Well, to continue where we left off. I will repeat my question: What is the nature and quality of justice as compared with injustice? It was suggested, I believe, that injustice is the stronger and more effective of the two; but now we have seen that justice implies superior character and intelligence, it will not be hard to show that it will also be superior in power to injustice, which implies ignorance and stupidity; that must be obvious to anyone. However, I would rather look deeper into this matter than take it as settled off-hand. Would you agree that a state may be unjust and may try to enslave other states or to hold a number of others in subjection unjustly?

Of course it may, he said; above all if it is the best sort of state, which carries injustice to perfection.

I understand, said I; that was your view. But I am wondering whether a state can do without justice when it is asserting its superior power over another in that way.

Not if you are right, that justice implies intelligence; but if I am right, injustice will be needed.

I am delighted with your answer, Thrasymachus; this is much better than just nodding and shaking your head.

It is all to oblige you.

Thank you. Please add to your kindness by telling me whether any set of men—a state or an army or a band of robbers or thieves—who were acting together for some unjust purpose would be likely to succeed, if they were always trying to injure one another. Wouldn't they do better, if they did not?

Yes, they would.

Because, of course, such injuries must set them quarrelling and hating each other. Only fair treatment can make men friendly and of one mind.

Be it so, he said; I don't want to differ from you.

Thank you once more, I replied. But don't you agree that, if injustice has this effect of implanting hatred wherever it exists, it must make any set of people, whether freemen or slaves, split into factions, at feud with one another and incapable of any joint action?

Yes.

And so with any two individuals: injustice will set them at variance and make them enemies to each other as well as to everyone who is just.

It will.

And will it not keep its character and have the same effect, if it exists in a single person?

Let us suppose so.

The effect being, apparently, wherever it occurs—in a state or a family or an army or anywhere else—to make united action impossible because of factions and quarrels, and moreover to set whatever it resides in at enmity with itself as well as with any opponent and with all who are just.

Yes, certainly.

Then I suppose it will produce the same natural results in an individual. He will have a divided mind and be incapable of action, for lack of single-ness of purpose; and he will be at enmity with all who are just as well as with himself?

Yes.

And 'all who are just' surely includes the gods?

Let us suppose so.

The unjust man, then, will be a god-forsaken creature; the good-will of heaven will be for the just.

Enjoy your triumph, said Thrasymachus. You need not fear my contradict-ing you. I have no wish to give offense to the company.

[(3) *The final question is, whether justice (now admitted to be a virtue) or injustice brings happiness. The argument turns on the doctrine (adopted as fundamental in Aristotle's* Ethics) *that man, like any other living species, has a peculiar work or function or activity, in the satisfactory exercise of which his well-being or happiness will consist; and also a peculiar excellence or virtue, namely a state of his soul from which that satisfactory activity will result. Aristotle argues (Eth. Nic. i. 7) that, a thing's function being the work or activity of which it alone is capable, man's function will be an activity involving the use of reason, which man alone possesses. Man's virtue is 'the state of character which makes him a good man and makes him do his work well' (ibid. ii. 6). It is the quality which enables him to 'live well,' for living is the soul's function; and to live well is to be happy.*

'Here again,' writes Nettleship on the following passage, 'the argument is intensely abstract. We should be inclined to break in on it and say that virtue means something very different in morality from what it means in the case of seeing or hearing, and that by happiness we mean a great many other things besides what seems to be meant here by living well. All depends, in

this argument, on the strictness of the terms, upon assuming each of them to have a definite and distinct meaning. The virtues of a man and of a horse are very different, but what is the common element in them which makes us call them virtue? Can we call anything virtue which does not involve the doing well of the function, never mind what, of the agent that possesses the virtue? Is there any other sense in which we can call a thing good or bad, except that it does or does not do well that which it was made to do? Again, happiness in its largest sense, welfare, well-being, or doing well, is a very complex thing, and one cannot readily describe in detail all that goes to make it up; but does it not necessarily imply that the human soul, man's vital activity as a whole, is in its best state, or is performing well the function it is made to perform? If by virtue and by happiness we mean what it seems we do mean, this consequence follows: when men are agreed that a certain sort of conduct constitutes virtue, if they mean anything at all, they must mean that in that conduct man finds happiness. And if a man says that what he calls virtue has nothing to do with what he calls happiness or well-being, then either in calling the one virtue he does not really mean what he says, or in calling the other happiness he does not really mean what he says. This is substantially the position that Plato takes up in this section.' (Lectures on Plato's Republic, p. 43.)]

You will make my enjoyment complete, I replied, if you will answer my further questions in the same way. We have made out so far that just men are superior in character and intelligence and more effective in action. Indeed without justice men cannot act together at all; it is not strictly true to speak of such people as ever having effected any strong action in common. Had they been thoroughly unjust, they could not have kept their hands off one another; they must have had some justice in them, enough to keep them from injuring one another at the same time with their victims. This it was that enabled them to achieve what they did achieve: their injustice only partially incapacitated them for their career of wrongdoing; if perfect, it would have disabled them for any action whatsover. I can see that all this is true, as against your original position. But there is a further question which we postponed: Is the life of justice the better and happier life? What we have said already leaves no doubt in my mind; but we ought to consider more carefully, for this is no light matter: it is the question, what is the right way to live?

Go on, then.

I will, said I. Some things have a function;[5] a horse, for instance, is useful for certain kinds of work. Would you agree to define a thing's function in

---

[5] The word translated 'function' is the common word for 'work.' Hence the need for illustrations to confine it to the narrower sense of 'function,' here defined for the first time.

general as the work for which that thing is the only instrument or the best one?

I don't understand.

Take an example. We can see only with the eyes, hear only with the ears; and seeing and hearing might be called the functions of those organs.

Yes.

Or again, you might cut vine-shoots with a carving-knife or a chisel or many other tools, but with none so well as with a pruning-knife made for the purpose; and we may call that its function.

True.

Now, I expect, you see better what I meant by suggesting that a thing's function is the work that it alone can do, or can do better than anything else.

Yes, I will accept that definition.

Good, said I; and to take the same examples, the eye and the ear, which we said have each its particular function: have they not also a specific excellence or virtue? Is not that always the case with things that have some appointed work to do?

Yes.

Now consider: is the eye likely to do its work well, if you take away its peculiar virtue and substitute the corresponding defect?

Of course not, if you mean substituting blindness for the power of sight.

I mean whatever its virtue may be; I have not come to that yet. I am only asking, whether it is true of things with a function—eyes or ears or anything else—that there is always some specific virtue which enables them to work well; and if they are deprived of that virtue, they work badly.

I think that is true.

Then the next point is this. Has the soul a function that can be performed by nothing else? Take for example such actions as deliberating or taking charge and exercising control: is not the soul the only thing of which you can say that these are its proper and peculiar work?

That is so.

And again, living—is not that above all the function of the soul?

No doubt.

And we also speak of the soul as having a certain specific excellence or virtue?

Yes.

Then, Thrasymachus, if the soul is robbed of its peculiar virtue, it cannot possibly do its work well. It must exercise its power of controlling and taking charge well or ill according as it is itself in a good or a bad state.

That follows.

And did we not agree that the virtue of the soul is justice, and injustice its defect?

We did.

So it follows that just soul, or in other words a just man, will live well; the unjust will not.

Apparently, according to your argument.

But living well involves well-being and happiness.

Naturally.

Then only the just man is happy; injustice will involve unhappiness.

Be it so.

But you cannot say it pays better to be unhappy.

Of course not.

Injustice then, my dear Thrasymachus, can never pay better than justice.

Well, he replied, this is a feast-day, and you may take all this as your share of the entertainment.

For which I have to thank you, Thrasymachus; you have been so gentle with me since you recovered your temper. It is my own fault if the entertainment has not been satisfactory. I have been behaving like a greedy guest, snatching a taste of every new dish that comes round before he has properly enjoyed the last. We began by looking for a definition of justice; but before we had found one, I dropped that question and hurried on to ask whether or not it involved superior character and intelligence; and then, as soon as another idea cropped up, that injustice pays better, I could not refrain from pursuing that.

So now the whole conversation has left me completely in the dark; for so long as I do not know what justice is, I am hardly likely to know whether or not it is a virtue, or whether it makes a man happy or unhappy.

20 A Formalistic Ethic*

IMMANUEL KANT

Immanuel Kant (1726–1806) is one of the most influential philosophers in the history of thought. He formulated his rationalistic system of thought in his *Critique of Pure Reason* (1781). Other of his influential philosophical treatises include the *Prolegomena to All Future Metaphysics, The Critique of Practical Reason, The Foundations of the Metaphysics of Morals, Religion Within the Limits of Pure Reason*, and *The Critique of Judgment*.

Intending to publish hereafter a metaphysic of morals, I issue in the first instance these fundamental principles. Indeed there is properly no other foundation for it than the *critical examination of a pure practical reason*; just as that of metaphysics is the critical examination of the pure speculative reason. . . .

The present treatise is, however, nothing more than the investigation and establishment of *the supreme principle of morality*, and this alone constitutes a study complete in itself, and one which ought to be kept apart from every other moral investigation.

FIRST SECTION

Transition from the Common Rational Knowledge of Morality to the Philosophical

Nothing can possibly be conceived in the world, or even out of it, which can be called good, without qualification, except a Good Will. Intelligence, wit, judgment, and the other *talents* of the mind, however they may be named, or courage, resolution, perseverance, as qualities of temperament, are undoubtedly good and desirable in many respects; but these gifts of nature may also become extremely bad and mischievous if the will which is to make use of them, and which, therefore, constitutes what is called *character*, is not good. It is the same with the *gifts of fortune*. Power, riches, honour, even health, and the general well-being and contentment with one's condition which is called *happiness*, inspire pride, and often presumption, if there is

---

* From Immanuel Kant, *Fundamental Principles of the Metaphysics of Morals*, trans. T. K. Abbott (1889).

not a good will to correct the influence of these on the mind, and with this also to rectify the whole principle of acting, and adapt it to its end. The sight of a being who is not adorned with a single feature of a pure and good will, enjoying unbroken prosperity, can never give pleasure to an impartial rational spectator. Thus a good will appears to constitute the indispensable condition even of being worthy of happiness.

There are even some qualities which are of service to this good will itself, and may facilitate its action, yet which have no intrinsic unconditional value, but always presuppose a good will, and this qualifies the esteem that we justly have for them, and does not permit us to regard them as absolutely good. Moderation in the affections and passions, self-control, and calm deliberation are not only good in many respects, but even seem to constitute part of the intrinsic worth of the person; but they are far from deserving to be called good without qualification, although they have been so unconditionally praised by the ancients. For without the principles of a good will, they may become extremely bad; and the coolness of a villian not only makes him far more dangerous, but also directly makes him more abominable in our eyes than he would have been without it.

A good will is good not because of what it performs or effects, not by its aptness for the attainment of some proposed end, but simply by virtue of the volition, that is, it is good in itself, and considered by itself is to be esteemed much higher than all that can be brought about by it in favour of any inclination, nay, even of the sum-total of all inclinations. Even if it should happen that, owing to special disfavour of fortune, or the niggardly provision of a step-motherly nature, this will should wholly lack power to accomplish its purpose, if with its greatest efforts it should yet achieve nothing, and there should remain only the good will (not, to be sure, a mere wish, but the summoning of all means in our power), then, like a jewel, it would still shine by its own light, as a thing which has its whole value in itself. Its usefulness or fruitlessness can neither add to nor take away anything from this value. It would be, as it were, only the setting to enable us to handle it the more conveniently in common commerce, or to attract to it the attention of those who are not yet connoisseurs, but not to recommend it to true connoisseurs, or to determine is value.

We have then to develop the notion of a will which deserves to be highly esteemed for itself, and is good without a view to anything further, a notion which exists already in the sound natural understanding, requiring rather to be cleared up than to be taught, and which in estimating the value of our actions always takes the first place, and constitutes the condition of all the rest. In order to do this, we will take the notion of duty, which includes that of a good will, although implying certain subjective restrictions and hindrances. These, however, far from concealing it, or rendering it unrecognizable, rather bring it out by contrast, and make it shine forth so much the brighter.

SECOND SECTION

Transition from Popular Moral Philosophy to the Metaphysic of Morals

If we have hitherto drawn our notion of duty from the common use of our practical reason, it is by no means to be inferred that we have treated it as an empirical notion. On the contrary, if we attend to the experience of men's conduct, we meet frequent and, as we ourselves allow, just complaints that one cannot find a single certain example of the disposition to act from pure duty. Although many things are done in *conformity* with what *duty* pre-scribes, it is nevertheless always doubtful whether they are done strictly *from duty*, so as to have a moral worth. Hence there have at all times been philosophers who have altogether denied that this disposition actually exists at all in human actions, and have ascribed everything to a more or less refined self-love. Not that they have on that account questioned the soundness of the conception of morality; on the contrary, they spoke with sincere regret of the frailty and corruption of human nature, which though noble enough to take as its rule an idea so worthy of respect, is yet too weak to follow it, and employs reason, which ought to give it the law only for the purpose of providing for the interest of the inclinations, whether singly or at the best in the greatest possible harmony with one another.

But in order that in this study we may not merely advance by the natural steps from the common moral judgment (in this case very worthy of respect) to the philosophical, as has been already done, but also from a popular philosophy, which goes no further than it can reach by groping with the help of examples, to metaphysic (which does not allow itself to be checked by anything empirical, and as it must measure the whole extent of this kind of rational knowledge, goes as far as ideal conceptions, where even examples fail us), we must follow and clearly describe the practical faculty of reason, from the general rules of its determination to the point where the notion of duty springs from it.

Everything in nature works according to laws. Rational beings alone have the faculty of acting according *to the conception* of laws, that is according to principles, *i.e.* have a *will*. Since the deduction of actions from principles requires *reason*, the will is nothing but practical reason. If reason infallibly determines the will, then the actions of such a being which are recognized as objectively necessary are subjectively necessary also, *i.e.* the will is a faculty to choose *that only* which reason independent on inclination recognizes as practically necessary, *i.e.* as good. But if reason of itself does not sufficiently determine the will, if the latter is subject also to subjective conditions (par-ticular impulses) which do not always coincide with the objective condi-tions; in a word, if the will does not *in itself* completely accord with reason (which is actually the case with men), then the actions which objectively are recognized as necessary are subjectively contingent, and the determination of such a will according to objective laws is *obligation*, that is to say, the relation of the objective laws to a will that is not thoroughly good is conceived as the determination of the will of a rational being by principles of reason, but which the will from its nature does not of necessity follow.

The conception of an objective principle, in so far as it is obligatory for a will, is called a command (of reason), and the formula of the command is called an Imperative.

All imperatives are expressed by the word *ought* [or *shall*], and thereby indicate the relation of an objective law of reason to a will, which from its subjective constitution is not necessarily determined by it (an obligation). They say that something would be good to do or to forbear, but they say it to a will which does not always do a thing because it is conceived to be good to do it. That is practically *good*, however, which determines the will by means of the conceptions of reason, and consequently not from subjective causes, but objectively, that is on principles which are valid for every rational being as such. It is distinguished from the *pleasant*, as that which influences the will only by means of sensation from merely subjective causes, valid only for the sense of this or that one, and not as a principle of reason, which holds for every one.

A perfectly good will would therefore be equally subject to objective laws (viz. laws of good), but could not be conceived as *obliged* thereby to act lawfully, because of itself from its subjective constitution it can only be determined by the conception of good. Therefore no imperatives hold for the Divine will, or in general for a *holy* will; *ought* is here out of place, because the volition is already of itself necessarily in unison with the law. Therefore imperatives are only formulæ to express the relation of objective laws of all volition to the subjective imperfection of the will of this or that rational being, *e.g.* the human will.

Now all *imperatives* command either *hypothetically* or *categorically*. The former represent the practical necessity of a possible action as means to something else that is willed (or at least which one might possibly will). The categorical imperative would be that which represented an action as necessary of itself without reference to another end, *i.e.*, as objectively necessary.

Since every practical law represents a possible action as good, and on this account, for a subject who is practically determinable by reason, necessary, all imperatives are formulæ determining an action which is necessary according to the principle of a will good in some respects. If now the action is good only as a means *to something else*, then the imperative is *hypothetical*; if it is conceived as good *in itself* and consequently as being necessarily the principle of a will which of itself conforms to reason, then it is *categorical*.

Accordingly the hypothetical imperative only says that the action is good for some purpose, *possible* or *actual*. In the first case it is a Problematical, in the second an Assertorial practical principle. The categorical imperative which declares an action to be objectively necessary in itself without reference to any purpose, *i.e.* without any other end, is valid as an Apodictic (practical) principle.

Whatever is possible only by the power of some rational being may also be conceived as a possible purpose of some will; and therefore the principles of action as regards the means necessary to attain some possible purpose are in fact infinitely numerous. All sciences have a practical part, consisting of problems expressing that some end is possible for us, and of imperatives directing how it may be attained. These may, therefore, be called in general imperatives of Skill. Here there is no question whether the end is rational and good, but only what one must do in order to attain it. The precepts for the physician to make his patient thoroughly healthy, and for a poisoner to ensure certain death, are of equal value in this respect, that each serves to effect its purpose perfectly. Since in early youth it cannot be known what ends are likely to occur to us in the course of life, parents seek to have their children taught a *great many things*, and provide for their *skill* in the use of means for all sorts of arbitrary ends, of none of which can they determine whether it may not perhaps hereafter be an object to their pupil, but which it is at all events *possible* that he might aim at; and this anxiety is so great that they commonly neglect to form and correct their judgment on the value of the things which may be chosen as ends.

There is *one* end, however, which may be assumed to be actually such to all rational beings (so far as imperatives apply to them, viz. as dependent beings), and, therefore, one purpose which they not merely *may* have, but which we may with certainty assume that they all actually *have* by a natural necessity, and this is *happiness*. The hypothetical imperative which expresses the practical necessity of an action as means to the advancement of happiness is Assertorial. We are not to present it as necessary for an uncertain and merely possible purpose, but for a purpose which we may presuppose with certainty and *à priori* in every man, because it belongs to his being. Now skill in the choice of means to his own greatest well-being may be called *prudence*, in the narrowest sense. And thus the imperative which refers to the choice of means to one's own happiness, *i.e.* the precept of prudence, is still always *hypothetical*; the action is not commanded absolutely, but only as means to another purpose.

Finally, there is an imperative which commands a certain conduct immediately, without having as its condition any other purpose to be attained by it. This imperative is Categorical. It concerns not the matter of the action, or its intended result, but its form and the principle of which it is itself a result; and what is essentially good in it consists in the mental disposition, let the consequence be what it may. This imperative may be called that of Morality.

When I conceive a hypothetical imperative, in general I do not know beforehand what it will contain until I am given the condition. But when I conceive a categorical imperative, I know at once what it contains. For as the imperative contains besides the law only the necessity that the maxims shall conform to this law, while the law contains no conditions restricting it, there remains nothing but the general statement that the maxim of the action should conform to a universal law, and it is this conformity alone that the imperative properly represents as necessary.

There is therefore but one categorical imperative, namely, this: *Act only on that maxim whereby thou canst at the same time will that it should become a universal law.*

Now if all imperatives of duty can be deduced from this one imperative as from their principle, then, although it should remain undecided whether what is called duty is not merely a vain notion, yet at least we shall be able to show what we understand by it and what this notion means.

Since the universality of the law according to which effects are produced constitutes what is properly called *nature* in the most general sense (as to form), that is the existence of things so far as it is determined by general laws, the imperative of duty may be expressed thus: *Act as if the maxim of thy action were to become by thy will a universal law of nature.*

We will now enumerate a few duties, adopting the usual division of them into duties to ourselves and to others, and into perfect and imperfect duties.

1. A man reduced to despair by a series of misfortunes feels wearied of life, but is still so far in possession of his reason that he can ask himself whether it would not be contrary to his duty to himself to take his own life. Now he inquires whether the maxim of his action could become a universal law of nature. His maxim is: From self-love I adopt it as a principle to shorten my life when its longer duration is likely to bring more evil than satisfaction. It is asked then simply whether this principle founded on self-love can become a universal law of nature. Now we see at once that a system of nature of which it should be a law to destroy life by means of the very feeling whose special nature it is to impel to the improvement of life would contradict itself, and therefore could not exist as a system of nature; hence that maxim cannot possibly exist as a universal law of nature, and consequently would be wholly inconsistent with the supreme principle of all duty.

2. Another finds himself forced by necessity to borrow money. He knows that he will not be able to repay it, but sees also that nothing will be lent to him, unless he promises stoutly to repay it in a definite time. He desires to make this promise, but he has still so much conscience as to ask himself: Is it not unlawful and inconsistent with duty to get out of a difficulty in this way? Suppose, however, that he resolves to do so, then the maxim of his action would be expressed thus: When I think myself in want of money, I will borrow money and promise to repay it, although I know that I never can do so. Now this principle of self-love or of one's own advantage may perhaps be consistent with my whole future welfare; but the question now is,

Is it right? I change then the suggestion of self-love into a universal law, and state the question thus: How would it be if my maxim were a universal law? Then I see at once that it could never hold as a universal law of nature, but would necessarily contradict itself. For supposing it to be a universal law that everyone when he thinks himself in a difficulty should be able to promise whatever he pleases, with the purpose of not keeping his promise, the promise itself would become impossible, as well as the end that one might have in view in it, since no one would consider that anything was promised to him, but would ridicule all such statements as vain pretences.

3. A third finds in himself a talent which with the help of some culture might make him a useful man in many respects. But he finds himself in comfortable circumstances, and prefers to indulge in pleasure rather than to take pains in enlarging and improving his happy natural capacities. He asks, however, whether his maxim of neglect of his natural gifts, besides agreeing with his inclination to indulgence, agrees also with what is called duty. He sees then that a system of nature could indeed subsist with such a universal law although men (like the South Sea islanders) should let their talents rest, and resolve to devote their lives merely to idleness, amusement, and propagation of their species—in a word, to enjoyment; but he cannot possibly *will* that this should be a universal law of nature, or be implanted in us as such by a natural instinct. For, as a rational being, he necessarily wills that his faculties be developed, since they serve him, and have been given him, for all sorts of possible purposes.

4. A fourth, who is in prosperity, while he sees that others have to contend with great wretchedness and that he could help them, thinks: What concern is it of mine? Let everyone be as happy as Heaven pleases, or as he can make himself; I will take nothing from him nor even envy him, only I do not wish to contribute anything to his welfare or to his assistance in distress! Now no doubt if such a mode of thinking were a universal law, the human race might very well subsist, and doubtless even better than in a state in which everyone talks of sympathy and good-will, or even takes care occasionally to put it into practice, but, on the other side, also cheats when he can, betrays the rights of men, or otherwise violates them. But although it is possible that a universal law of nature might exist in accordance with that maxim, it is impossible to *will* that such a principle should have the universal validity of a law of nature. For a will which resolved this would contradict itself, inasmuch as many cases might occur in which one would have need of the love and sympathy of others, and in which, by such a law of nature, sprung from his own will, he would deprive himself of all hope of the aid he desires.

These are a few of the many actual duties, or at least what we regard as such, which obviously fall into two classes on the one principle that we have laid down. We must be *able to will* that a maxim of our action should be a universal law. This is the canon of the moral appreciation of the action generally. Some actions are of such a character that their maxim cannot without contradiction be even *conceived* as a universal law of nature, far from it being possible that we should *will* that it *should* be so. In others this intrinsic impossibility is not found, but still it is impossible to *will* that their maxim should be raised to the universality of a law of nature, since such a will would contradict itself. It is easily seen that the former violate strict or rigorous (inflexible) duty; the latter only laxer (meritorious) duty. Thus it has been completely shown by these examples how all duties depend as regards the nature of the obligation (not the object of the action) on the same principle.

If now we attend to ourselves on occasion of any transgression of duty, we shall find that we in fact do not will that our maxim should be a universal law, for that is impossible for us; on the contrary, we will that the opposite should remain a universal law, only we assume the liberty of making an *exception* in our own favour or (just for this time only) in favour of our inclination. Consequently if we considered all cases from one and the same point of view, namely, that of reason, we should find a contradiction in our own will, namely, that a certain principle should be objectively necessary as a universal law, and yet subjectively should not be universal, but admit of exceptions. As, however, we at one moment regard our action from the point of view of a will wholly conformed to reason, and then again look at the same action from the point of view of a will affected by inclination, there is not really any contradiction, but an antagonism of inclination to the precept of reason, whereby the universality of the principle is changed into a mere generality, so that the practical principle of reason shall meet the maxim half way. Now, although this cannot be justified in our own impartial judgment, yet it proves that we do really recognize the validity of the categorical imperative and (with all respect for it) only allow ourselves a few exceptions, which we think unimportant and forced from us.

We have thus established at least this much, that if duty is a conception which is to have any import and real legislative authority for our actions, it can only be expressed in categorical, and not at all in hypothetical imperatives. We have also, which is of great importance, exhibited clearly and definitely for every practical application the content of the categorical imperative, which must contain the principle of all duty if there is such a thing at all. We have not yet, however, advanced so far as to prove *à priori* that there actually is such an imperative, that there is a practical law which commands absolutely of itself, and without any other impulse, and that the following of this law is duty.

The question then is this: Is it a necessary law *for all rational beings* that they should always judge of their actions by maxims of which they can themselves will that they should serve as universal laws? If it is so, then it must be connected (altogether *à priori*) with the very conception of the will of a rational being generally. But in order to discover this connexion we must, however reluctantly, take a step into metaphysic, although into a domain of it which is distinct from speculative philosophy, namely, the metaphysic of morals.

The will is conceived as a faculty of determining oneself to action *in accordance with the conception of certain laws*. And such a faculty can be found only in rational beings. Now that which serves the will as the objective ground of its self-determination is the *end*, and if this is assigned by reason alone, it must hold for all rational beings. On the other hand, that which merely contains the ground of possibility of the action of which the effect is the end, this is called the *means*. The subjective ground of the desire is the *spring*, the objective ground of the volition is the *motive*; hence the distinction between subjective ends which rest on springs, and objective ends which depend on motives valid for every rational being. Practical principles are *formal* when they abstract from all subjective ends; they are *material* when they assume these, and therefore particular springs of action. The ends which a rational being proposes to himself at pleasure as *effects* of his actions (material ends) are all only relative, for it is only their relation to the particular desires of the subject that gives them their worth, which therefore cannot furnish principles universal and necessary for all rational beings and for every volition, that is to say practical laws. Hence all these relative ends can give rise only to hypothetical imperatives.

Supposing, however, that there were something *whose existence* has *in itself* an absolute worth, something which, being *an end in itself*, could be a source of definite laws, then in this and this alone would lie the source of a possible categorical imperative, *i.e.* a practical law.

Now I say: man and generally any rational being *exists* as an end in himself, *not merely as a means* to be arbitrarily used by this or that will, but in all his actions, whether they concern himself or other rational beings, must be always regarded at the same time as an end. All objects of the inclinations have only a conditional worth; for if the inclinations and the wants founded on them did not exist, then their object would be without value. But the inclinations themselves being sources of want are so far from having an absolute worth for which they should be desired, that, on the contrary, it must be the universal wish of every rational being to be wholly free from them. Thus the worth of any object which is *to be acquired* by our action is always conditional. Beings whose existence depends not on our will but on nature's, have nevertheless, if they are rational beings, only a relative value as means, and are therefore called *things*; rational beings, on the contrary, are called *persons*, because their very nature points them out as ends in themselves, that is as something which must not be used merely as means, and so far therefore restricts freedom of action (and is an object of respect). These, therefore, are not merely subjective ends whose existence has a worth *for us* as an effect of our action, but *objective ends*, that is things whose existence is an end in itself: an end moreover for which no other can be substituted, which they should subserve *merely* as means, for otherwise nothing whatever would possess *absolute worth*; but if all worth were conditioned and therefore contingent, then there would be no supreme practical principle of reason whatever.

If then there is a supreme practical principle or, in respect of the human will, a categorical imperative, it must be one which, being drawn from the conception of that which is necessarily an end for everyone because it is *an end in itself*, constitutes an *objective* principle of will, and can therefore serve as a universal practical law. The foundation of this principle is: *rational nature exists as an end in itself.* Man necessarily conceives his own existence as being so: so far then this is a *subjective* principle of human actions. But every other rational being regards its existence similarly, just on the same rational principle that holds for me: so that it is at the same time an objective principle, from which as a supreme practical law all laws of the will must be capable of being deduced. Accordingly the practical imperative will be as follows: *So act as to treat humanity, whether in thine own person or in that of any other, in every case as an end withal, never as means only.* We will now inquire whether this can be practically carried out.

To abide by the previous examples:

Firstly, under the head of necessary duty to oneself: He who contemplates suicide should ask himself whether his action can be consistent with the idea of humanity *as an end in itself*. If he destroys himself in order to escape from painful circumstances, he uses a person merely as *a mean* to maintain a tolerable condition up to the end of life. But a man is not a thing, that is to say, something which can be used merely as means, but must in all his actions be always considered as an end in himself. I cannot, therefore, dispose in any way of a man in my own person so as to mutilate him, to damage or kill him. (It belongs to ethics proper to define this principle more precisely, so as to avoid all misunderstanding, *e.g.* as to the amputation of the limbs in order to preserve myself; as to exposing my life to danger with a view to preserve it, &c. This questions is therefore omitted here.)

Secondly, as regards necessary duties, or those of strict obligation, towards others; he who is thinking of making a lying promise to others will see at once that he would be using another man *merely as a mean*, without the latter containing at the same time the end in himself. For he whom I propose by such a promise to use for my own purposes cannot possibly assent to my mode of acting towards him, and therefore cannot himself contain the end of this action. This violation of the principle of humanity in other men is more obvious if we take in examples of attacks on the freedom and property of others. For then it is clear that he who transgresses the rights of men intends to use the person of others merely as means, without considering that as rational beings they ought always to be esteemed also as ends, that is, as beings who must be capable of containing in themselves the end of the very same action.

Thirdly, as regards contingent (meritorious) duties to oneself; it is not enough that the action does not violate humanity in our own person as an end in itself, it must also *harmonize with* it. Now there are in humanity capacities of greater perfection which belong to the end that nature has in view in regard to humanity in ourselves as the subject: to neglect these might perhaps be consistent with the *maintenance* of humanity as an end in itself, but not with the *advancement* of this end.

Fourthly, as regards meritorious duties towards others: the natural end which all men have is their own happiness. Now humanity might indeed subsist, although no one should contribute anything to the happiness of others, provided he did not intentionally withdraw anything from it; but after all, this would only harmonize negatively, not positively, with *humanity as an end in itself*, if everyone does not also endeavour, as far as in him lies, to forward the ends of others. For the ends of any subject which is an end in himself, ought as far as possible to be *my* ends also, if that conception is to have its *full* effect with me.

21 A Utilitarian Ethic*

JEREMY BENTHAM

Jeremy Bentham (1740–1832) is generally viewed as the father of the utilitarian theory of ethics. Concerned with reform of both the penal and the civil law in England, Bentham wrote prolifically in the area of ethics and jurisprudence. His best known work is the *Introduction to the Principles of Morals and Legislation* (1789). He established the influential Westminster Review and assisted in founding University College, London.

CHAPTER I

Of the Principle of Utility

Nature has placed mankind under the governance of two sovereign masters, *pain* and *pleasure*. It is for them alone to point out what we ought to do, as well as to determine what we shall do. On the one hand the standard of right and wrong, on the other the chain of causes and effects, are fastened to their throne. They govern us in all we do, in all we say, in all we think: every effort we can make to throw off our subjection, will serve but to demonstrate and confirm it. In words a man may pretend to abjure their empire: but in reality he will remain subject to it all the while. The *principle of utility* recognises this subjection, and assumes it for the foundation of that system, the object of which is to rear the fabric of felicity by the hands of reason and of law. Systems which attempt to question it, deal in sounds instead of sense, in caprice instead of reason, in darkness instead of light.

But enough of metaphor and declamation: it is not by such means that moral science is to be improved.

II

The principle of utility is the foundation of the present work: it will be proper therefore at the outset to give an explicit and determinate account of what is meant by it. By the principle of utility is meant that principle which approves or disapproves of every action whatsoever, according to the tendency which it appears to have to augment or diminish the happiness of the party whose interest is in question: or, what is the same thing in other words, to

* From Jeremy Bentham, Introduction to the *Principles of Morals and Legislation*, first published in 1789.

promote or to oppose that happiness. I say of every action whatsoever; and therefore not only of every action of a private individual, but of every measure of government.

III

By utility is meant that property in any object, whereby it tends to produce benefit, advantage, pleasure, good, or happiness (all this in the present case comes to the same thing), or (what comes again to the same thing) to prevent the happening of mischief, pain, evil, or unhappiness to the party whose interest is considered: if that party be the community in general, then the happiness of the community: if a particular individual, then the happiness of that individual.

IV

The interest of the community is one of the most general expressions that can occur in the phraseology of morals: no wonder that the meaning of it is often lost. When it has a meaning, it is this. The community is a fictitious *body*, composed of the individual persons who are considered as constituting as it were its *members*. The interest of the community then is, what?—the sum of the interests of the several members who compose it.

V

It is in vain to talk of the interest of the community, without understanding what is the interest of the individual. A thing is said to promote the interest, or to be *for* the interest, of an individual, when it tends to add to the sum total of his pleasures: or, what comes to the same thing, to diminish the sum total of his pains.

VI

An action then may be said to be conformable to the principle of utility, or, for shortness sake, to utility (meaning with respect to the community at large), when the tendency it has to augment the happiness of the community is greater than any it has to diminish it.

VII

A measure of government (which is but a particular kind of action, performed by a particular person or persons) may be said to be conformable to or dictated by the principle of utility, when in like manner the tendency which it has to augment the happiness of the community is greater than any which it has to diminish it.

VIII

When an action, or in particular a measure of government, is supposed by a man to be conformable to the principle of utility, it may be convenient, for the purposes of discourse, to imagine a kind of law or dictate, called a law or dictate of utility: and to speak of the action in question, as being conformable to such law or dictate.

IX

A man may be said to be a partizan of the principle of utility, when the approbation or disapprobation he annexes to any action, or to any measure, is determined, by and proportioned to the tendency which he conceives it to have to augment or to diminish the happiness of the community: or in other words, to its conformity or unconformity to the laws or dictates of utility.

X

Of an action that is conformable to the principle of utility, one may always say either that it is one that ought to be done, or at least that it is not one that ought not to be done. One may say also, that it is right it should be done; at least that it is not wrong it should be done: that it is a right action; at least that it is not a wrong action. When thus interpreted, the words *ought*, and *right* and *wrong*, and others of that stamp, have a meaning: when otherwise, they have none.

XI

Has the rectitude of this principle been ever formally contested? It should seem that it had, by those who have not known what they have been meaning. Is it susceptible of any direct proof? It should seem not: for that which is used to prove every thing else, cannot itself be proved: a chain of proofs must have their commencement somewhere. To give such proof is as impossible as it is needless.

XII

Not that there is or ever has been that human creature breathing, however stupid or perverse, who has not on many, perhaps on most occasions of his life, deferred to it. By the natural constitution of the human frame, on most occasions of their lives men in general embrace this principle, without thinking of it: if not for the ordering of their own actions, yet for the trying of their own actions, as well as of those of other men. There have been, at the same time, not many, perhaps, even of the most intelligent, who have been disposed to embrace it purely and without reserve. There are even few who have not taken some occasion or other to quarrel with it, either on account of their not understanding always how to apply it, or on account of some prejudice or other which they were afraid to examine into, or could not bear to part with. For such is the stuff that man is made of: in principle and in practice, in a right track and in a wrong one, the rarest of all human qualities is consistency.

XIII

When a man attempts to combat the principle of utility, it is with reasons drawn, without his being aware of it, from that very principle itself. His arguments, if they prove any thing, prove not that the principle is *wrong*, but that, according to the applications he supposes to be made of it, it is *mis-applied*. Is it possible for a man to move the earth? Yes; but he must first find out another earth to stand upon.

XIV

To disprove the propriety of it by arguments is impossible; but, from the causes that have been mentioned, or from some confused or partial view of it, a man may happen to be disposed not to relish it. Where this is the case, if he thinks the settling of his opinions on such a subject worth the trouble, let him take the following steps, and at length, perhaps, he may come to reconcile himself to it.

1. Let him settle with himself, whether he would wish to discard this principle altogether; if so, let him consider what it is that all his reasonings (in matters of politics especially) can amount to?

2. If he would, let him settle with himself, whether he would judge and act without any principle, or whether there is any other he would judge and act by?

3. If there be, let him examine and satisfy himself whether the principle he thinks he has found is really any separate intelligible principle; or whether it be not a mere principle in words, a kind of phrase, which at bottom expresses neither more nor less than the mere averment of his own unfounded sentiments; that is, what in another person he might be apt to call caprice?

4. If he is inclined to think that his own approbation or disapprobation, annexed to the idea of an act, without any regard to its consequences, is a sufficient foundation for him to judge and act upon, let him ask himself whether his sentiment is to be a standard of right and wrong, with respect to every other man, or whether every man's sentiment has the same privilege of being a standard to itself?

5. In the first case, let him ask himself whether his principle is not despotical, and hostile to all the rest of human race?

6. In the second case, whether it is not anarchial, and whether at this rate there are not as many different standards of right and wrong as there are men? and whether even to the same man, the same thing, which is right to-day, may not (without the least change in its nature) be wrong to-morrow? and whether the same thing is not right and wrong in the same place at the same time? and in either case, whether all argument is not at an end? and whether, when two men have said, "I like this," and "I don't like it," they can (upon such a principle) have any thing more to say?

7. If he should have said to himself, No: for that the sentiment which

he proposes as a standard must be grounded on reflection, let him say on what particulars the reflection is to turn? If on particulars having relation to the utility of the act, then let him say whether this is not deserting his own principle, and borrowing assistance from that very one in opposition to which he sets it up: or if not on those particulars, on what other particulars?

8. If he should be for compounding the matter, and adopting his own principle in part, and the principle of utility in part, let him say how far he will adopt it?

9. When he has settled with himself where he will stop, then let him ask himself how he justifies to himself the adopting it so far? and why he will not adopt it any farther?

10. Admitting any other principle than the principle of utility to be a right principle, a principle that it is right for a man to pursue; admitting (what is not true) that the word *right* can have a meaning without reference to utility, let him say whether there is any such thing as a *motive* that a man can have to pursue the dictates of it: if there is, let him say what that motive is, and how it is to be distinguished from those which enforce the dictates of utility: if not, then lastly let him say what it is this other principle can be good for?

CHAPTER II

Of Principles Adverse to That of Utility

I

If the principle of utility be a right principle to be governed by, and that in all cases, it follows from what has been just observed, that whatever principle differs from it in any case must necessarily be a wrong one. To prove any other principle, therefore, to be a wrong one, there needs no more than just to show it to be what it is, a principle of which the dictates are in some point or other different from those of the principle of utility: to state it is to confute it.

II

A principle may be different from that of utility in two ways: 1. By being constantly opposed to it: this is the case with a principle which may be termed the principle of *asceticism*. 2. By being sometimes opposed to it, and sometimes not, as it may happen: this is the case with another, which may be termed the principle of *sympathy* and *antipathy*.

III

By the principle of asceticism I mean that principle, which, like the principle of utility, approves or disapproves of any action, according to the tendency which it appears to have to augment or diminish the happiness of the party whose interest is in question; but in an inversive manner: approving of actions in as far as they tend to diminish his happiness; disapproving of them in as far as they tend to augment it.

IV

It is evident that any one who reprobates any the least particle of pleasure, as such, from whatever source derived, is *pro tanto* a partizan of the principle of asceticism. It is only upon that principle, and not from the principle of utility, that the most abominable pleasure which the vilest of malefactors ever reaped from his crime would be to be reprobated, if it stood alone. The case is, that it never does stand alone; but is necessarily followed by such a quantity of pain (or, what comes to the same thing, such a chance for a certain quantity of pain) that the pleasure in comparison of it, is as nothing; and this is the true and sole, but perfectly sufficient, reason for making it a ground for punishment.

V

There are two classes of men of very different complexions, by whom the principle of asceticism appears to have been embraced; the one a set of moralists, the other a set of religionists. Different accordingly have been the motives which appear to have recommended it to the notice of these different parties. Hope, that is, the prospect of pleasure, seems to have animated the former: hope, the aliment of philosophic pride: the hope of honour and reputation at the hands of men. Fear, that is, the prospect of pain, the latter: fear, the offspring of superstitious fancy: the fear of future punishment at the hands of a splenetic and revengeful Deity. I say in this case fear: for of the invisible future, fear is more powerful than hope. These circumstances characterize the two different parties among the partizans of the principle of asceticism: the parties and their motives different, the principle the same.

VI

The religious party, however, appear to have carried it farther than the philosophical: they have acted more consistently and less wisely. The philosophical party have scarcely gone farther than to reprobate pleasure: the religious party have frequently gone so far as to make it a matter of merit and of duty to court pain. The philosophical party have hardly gone farther than the making pain a matter of indifference. It is no evil, they have said: they have not said, it is a good. They have not so much as reprobated all pleasure in the lump. They have discarded only what they have called the gross; that is, such as are organical, or of which the origin is easily traced up to such as are organical: they have even cherished and magnified the refined. Yet this, however, not under the name of pleasure: to cleanse itself from the sordes of its impure original, it was necessary it should change its name: the honourable, the glorious, the reputable, the becoming, the *honestum*, the *decorum*, it was to be called: in short, anything but pleasure.

VII

From these two sources have flowed the doctrines from which the sentiments of the bulk of mankind have all along received a tincture of this principle; some from the philosophical, some from the religious, some from both. Men of education more frequently from the philosophical, as more suited to the elevation of their sentiments: the vulgar more frequently from the superstitious, as more suited to the narrowness of their intellect, undilated by knowledge: and to the abjectness of their condition, continually open to the attacks of fear. The tinctures, however, derived from the two sources, would naturally intermingle, insomuch that a man would not always know by which of them he was most influenced: and they would often serve to corroborate and enliven one another. It was this conformity that made a kind of alliance between parties of a complexion otherwise so dissimilar: and disposed them to unite upon various occasions against the common enemy, the partizan of the principle of utility, whom they joined in branding with the odious name of Epicurean.

VIII

The principle of asceticism, however, with whatever warmth it may have been embraced by its partizans as a rule of private conduct, seems not to have been carried to any considerable length, when applied to the business of government. In a few instances it has been carried a little way by the philosophical party: witness the Spartan regimen. Though then, perhaps, it may be considered as having been a measure of security: and an application, though a precipitate and perverse application, of the principle of utility. Scarcely in any instances, to any considerable length, by the religious: for the various monastic orders, and the societies of the Quakers, Dumplers, Moravians, and other religionists, have been free societies, whose regimen no man has been astricted to without the intervention of his own consent. Whatever merit a man may have thought there would be in making himself miserable, no such notion seems ever to have occurred to any of them, that it may be a merit, much less a duty, to make others miserable: although it should seem, that if a certain quantity of misery were a thing so desirable, it would not matter much whether it were brought by each man upon himself, or by one man upon another. It is true, that from the same source from whence, among the religionists, the attachment to the principle of asceticism took its rise, flowed other doctrines and practices, from which misery in abundance was produced in one man by the instrumentality of another: witness the holy wars, and the persecutions for religion. But the passion for producing misery in these cases proceeded upon some special ground: the exercise of it was confined to persons of particular descriptions: they were tormented, not as men, but as heretics and infidels. To have inflicted the same miseries on their fellow-believers and fellow-sectaries, would have been as blameable in the eyes even of these religionists, as in those of a partizan of the principle of utility. For a man to give himself a certain number of stripes was indeed meritorious: but to give the same number of stripes to another man, not consenting, would have been a sin. We read of saints, who for the good of their souls, and the mortification of their bodies, have voluntarily yielded themselves a prey to vermin: but though many persons of this class have wielded the reins of empire, we read of none who have set themselves to work, and made laws on purpose, with a view of stocking the body politic with the breed of highwaymen, housebreakers, or incendiaries. If at any time they have suffered the nation to be preyed upon by swarms of idle pensioners, or useless placemen, it has rather been from negligence and imbecility, than from any settled plan for oppressing and plundering of the people. If at any time they have sapped the sources of national wealth, by cramping commerce, and driving the inhabitants into emigration, it has been with other views, and in pursuit of other ends. If they have declaimed against the pursuit of pleasure, and the use of wealth, they have commonly stopped at declamation: they have not, like Lycurgus, made express ordinances for the purpose of banishing the precious metals. If they have established idleness by a law, it has been not because idleness, the mother of vice and misery, is itself a virtue, but because idleness (say they) is the road to holiness. If under the notion of fasting, they have joined in the plan of confining their subjects to a diet, thought by some to be of the most nourishing and prolific nature, it has been not for the sake of making them tributaries to the nations by whom that diet was to be supplied, but for the sake of manifesting their own power, and exercising the obedience of the people. If they have established, or suffered to be established, punishments for the breach of celibacy, they have done no more than comply with the petitions of those deluded rigorists, who, dupes to the ambitious and deep-laid policy of their rulers, first laid themselves under that idle obligation by a vow.

IX

The principle of asceticism seems originally to have been the reverie of certain hasty speculators, who having perceived, or fancied, that certain pleasures, when reaped in certain circumstances, have, at the long run, been attended with pains more than equivalent to them, took occasion to quarrel with every thing that offered itself under the name of pleasure. Having then got thus far, and having forgot the point which they set out from, they pushed on, and went so much further as to think it meritorious to fall in love with pain. Even this, we see, is at bottom but the principle of utility misapplied.

X

The principle of utility is capable of being consistently pursued; and it is but tautology to say, that the more consistently it is pursued, the better it must ever be for human-kind. The principle of asceticism never was, nor ever can be, consistently pursued by any living creature. Let but one tenth part of the inhabitants of this earth pursue it consistently, and in a day's time they will have turned it into a hell.

XI

Among principles adverse to that of utility, that which at this day seems to have most influence in matters of government, is what may be called the principle of sympathy and antipathy. By the principle of sympathy and antipathy, I mean that principle which approves or disapproves of certain actions, not on account of their tending to augment the happiness, nor yet on account of their tending to diminish the happiness of the party whose interest is in question, but merely because a man finds himself disposed to approve or disapprove of them: holding up that approbation or disapprobation as a sufficient reason for itself, and disclaiming the necessity of looking out for any extrinsic ground. Thus far in the general department of morals: and in the particular department of politics, measuring out the quantum (as well as determining the ground) of punishment, by the degree of the disapprobation.

XII

It is manifest, that this is rather a principle in name than in reality: it is not a positive principle of itself, so much as a term employed to signify the negation of all principle. What one expects to find in a principle is something that points out some external consideration, as a means of warranting and guiding the internal sentiments of approbation and disapprobation: this expectation is but ill fulfilled by a proposition, which does neither more nor less than hold up each of those sentiments as a ground and standard for itself.

XIII

In looking over the catalogue of human actions (says a partizan of this principle) in order to determine which of them are to be marked with the seal of disapprobation, you need but to take counsel of your own feelings: whatever you find in yourself a propensity to condemn, is wrong for that very reason. For the same reason it is also meet for punishment: in what proportion it is adverse to utility, or whether it be adverse to utility at all, is a matter that makes no difference. In that same *proportion* also is it meet for punishment: if you hate much, punish much: if you hate little, punish little: punish as you hate. If you hate not all all, punish not at all: the fine feelings of the soul are not to be overborne and tyrannized by the harsh and rugged dictates of political utility.

XIV

The various systems that have been formed concerning the standard of right and wrong, may all be reduced to the principle of sympathy and antipathy. One account may serve for all of them. They consist all of them in so many contrivances for avoiding the obligation of appealing to any external standard, and for prevailing upon the reader to accept of the author's sentiment or opinion as a reason, and that a sufficient one, for itself. The phrases different, but the principle the same.

XV

It is manifest, that the dictates of this principle will frequently coincide with those of utility, though perhaps without intending any such thing. Probably more frequently than not: and hence it is that the business of penal justice is carried on upon that tolerable sort of footing upon which we see it carried on in common at this day. For what more natural or more general ground of hatred to a practice can there be, than the mischievousness of such practice? What all men are exposed to suffer by, all men will be disposed to hate. It is far yet, however, from being a constant ground: for when a man suffers, it is not always that he knows what it is he suffers by. A man may suffer grievously, for instance, by a new tax, without being able to trace up the cause of his sufferings to the injustice of some neighbour, who has eluded the payment of an old one.

XVI

The principle of sympathy and antipathy is most apt to err on the side of severity. It is for applying punishment in many cases which deserve none: in many cases which deserve some, it is for applying more than they deserve. There is no incident imaginable, be it ever so trivial, and so remote from mischief, from which this princple may not extract a ground of punishment. Any difference in taste: any difference in opinion: upon one subject as well as upon another. No disagreement so trifling which perseverance and altercation will not render serious. Each becomes in the other's eyes an enemy, and, if laws permit, a criminal. This is one of the circumstances by which the human race is distinguished (not much indeed to its advantage) from the brute creation.

XVII

It is not, however, by any means unexampled for this principle to err on the side of lenity. A near and perceptible mischief moves antipathy. A remote and imperceptible mischief, though not less real, has no effect. Instances in proof of this will occur in numbers in the course of the work. It would be breaking in upon the order of it to give them here.

XVIII

It may be wondered, perhaps, that in all this while no mention has been made of the *theological* principle; meaning that principle which professes to recur for the standard of right and wrong to the will of God. But the case is, this is not in fact a distinct principle. It is never any thing more or less than one or other of the three before-mentioned principles presenting itself under another shape. The *will* of God here meant cannot be his revealed will, as contained in the sacred writings: for that is a system which nobody ever thinks of recurring to at this time of day, for the details of political administration: and even before it can be applied to the details of private conduct, it is universally allowed, by the most eminent divines of all persuasions, to stand in need of pretty ample interpretations: else to what use are the works of those divines? And for the guidance of these interpretations, it is also allowed, that some other standard must be assumed. The will then which is meant on this occasion, is that which may be called the *presumptive* will: that is to say, that which is presumed to be his will on account of the conformity of its dictates to those of some other principle. What then may be this other principle? it must be one or other of the three mentioned above: for there cannot, as we have seen, be any more. It is plain, therefore, that, setting revelation out of the question, no light can ever be thrown upon the standard of right and wrong, by any thing that can be said upon the question, what is God's will. We may be perfectly sure, indeed, that whatever is right is conformable to the will of God: but so far it is that from answering the purpose of showing us what is right, that it is necessary to know first whether a thing is right, in order to know from thence whether it be conformable to the will of God.[1]

---

[1] The principle of theology refers everything to God's pleasure. But what is God's pleasure? God does not, he confessedly does not now, either speak or write to us. How then are we to know what is his pleasure? By observing what is our own pleasure, and pronouncing it to be his. Accordingly, what is called the pleasure of God is and must necessarily be (revelation apart) neither more nor less than the good pleasure of the person, whoever he be, who is pronouncing what he believes, or pretends, to be God's pleasure. How know you it to be God's pleasure that such or such an act should be abstained from? whence come you even to suppose as much? "Because the engaging in it would, I imagine, be prejudicial upon the whole to the happiness of mankind;" says the partizan of the principle of utility: "Because the commission of it is attended with a gross and sensual, or at least with a trifling and transient satisfaction;" says the partizan of the principle of asceticism: "Because I detest the thoughts of it; and I cannot, neither ought I to be called upon to tell why;" says he who proceeds upon the principle of antipathy. In the words of one or other of these must that person necessarily answer (revelation apart) who professes to take for his standard the will of God.

XIX

There are two things which are very apt to be confounded, but which it imports us carefully to distinguish:—the motive or cause, which, by operating on the mind of an individual, is productive of any act . and the ground or reason which warrants a legislator, or other by-stander, in regarding that act with an eye of approbation. When the act happens, in the particular instance in question, to be productive of effects which we approve of, much more if we happen to observe that the same motive may frequently be productive, in other instances, of the like effects, we are apt to transfer our approbation to the motive itself, and to assume, as the just ground for the approbation we bestow on the act, the circumstance of its originating from that motive. It is in this way that the sentiment of antipathy has often been considered as a just ground of action. Antipathy, for instance, in such or such a case, is the cause of an action which is attended with good effects: but this does not make it a right ground of action in that case, any more than in any other. Still farther. Not only the effects are good, but the agent sees beforehand that they will be so. This may make the action indeed a perfectly right action: but it does not make antipathy a right ground of action. For the same sentiment of antipathy, if implicitly deferred to, may be, and very frequently is, productive of the very worst effects. Antipathy, therefore, can never be a right ground of action. No more, therefore, can resentment, which, as will be seen more particularly hereafter, is but a modification of antipathy. The only right ground of action, that can possibly subsist, is, after all, the consideration of utility, which, if it is a right principle of action, and of approbation, in any one case, is so in every other. Other principles in abundance, that is, other motives, may be the reasons why such and such an act *has* been done: that is, the reasons or causes of its being done: but it is this alone that can be the reason why it might or ought to have been done. Antipathy or resentment requires always to be regulated, to prevent its doing mischief; to be regulated by what? always by the principle of utility. The principle of utility neither requires nor admits of any other regulator than itself.

CHAPTER III

Of the Four Sanctions or Sources of Pain and Pleasure

I

It has been shown that the happiness of the individuals, of whom a community is composed, that is, their pleasures and their security, is the end and the sole end which the legislator ought to have in view: the sole standard, in conformity to which each individual ought, as far as depends upon the legislator, to be *made* to fashion his behaviour. But whether it be this or any thing else that is to be *done*, there is nothing by which a man can ultimately be *made* to do it, but either pain or pleasure. Having taken a general view of these two grand objects (*viz.* pleasure, and what comes to the same thing, immunity from pain) in the character of *final* causes; it will be necessary to take a view of pleasure and pain itself, in the character of *efficient* causes or means.

II

There are four distinguishable sources from which pleasure and pain are in use to flow: considered separately, they may be termed the *physical*, the *political*, the *moral*, and the *religious:* and inasmuch as the pleasures and pains belonging to each of them are capable of giving a binding force to any law or rule of conduct, they may all of them be termed *sanctions*.

III

If it be in the present life, and from the ordinary course of nature, not purposely modified by the interposition of the will of any human being, nor by any extraordinary interposition of any superior invisible being, that the pleasure or the pain takes place or is expected, it may be said to issue from, or to belong to, the *physical sanction*.

IV

If at the hands of a *particular* person or set of persons in the community, who under names correspondent to that of *judge*, are chosen for the particular purpose of dispensing it, according to the will of the sovereign or supreme ruling power in the state, it may be said to issue from the *political sanction*.

V

If at the hands of such *chance* persons in the community, as the party in question may happen in the course of his life to have concerns with, according to each man's spontaneous disposition, and not according to any settled or concerted rule, it may be said to issue from the *moral* or *popular sanction*.

VI

If from the immediate hand of a superor invisible being, either in the present life, or in a future, it may be said to issue from the *religious sanction*.

VII

Pleasures or pains which may be expected to issue from the *physical*, *political*, or *moral* sanctions, must all of them be expected to be experienced, if ever, in the *present* life: those which may be expected to issue from the *religious* sanction, may be expected to be experienced either in the *present* life or in a *future*.

VIII

Those which can be experienced in the present life, can of course be no others than such as human nature in the course of the present life is susceptible of: and from each of these sources may flow all the pleasures or pains of which, in the course of the present life, human nature is susceptible. With regard to these, then (with which alone we have in this place any concern), those of them which belong to any one of those sanctions, differ not ultimately in kind from those which belong to any one of the other three: the only difference there is among them lies in the circumstances that accompany their production. A suffering which befals a man in the natural and spontaneous course of things, shall be styled, for instance, a *calamity*; in which case, if it be supposed to befal him through any imprudence of his, it may be styled a punishment issuing from the physical sanction. Now this same suffering, if inflicted by the law, will be what is commonly called a *punishment*; if incurred for want of any friendly assistance, which the misconduct, or supposed misconduct, of the sufferer has occasioned to be withholden, a punishment issuing from the *moral* sanction; if through the immediate interposition of a particular providence, a punishment issuing from the religious sanction.

IX

A man's goods, or his person, are consumed by fire. If this happened to him by what is called an accident, it was a calamity: if by reason of his own imprudence (for instance, from his neglecting to put his candle out), it may be styled a punishment of the physical sanction: if it happened to him by the sentence of the political magistrate, a punishment belonging to the political sanction—that is, what is commonly called a punishment: if for want of any assistance which his *neighbour* withheld from him out of some dislike to his *moral* character, a punishment of the *moral* sanction: if by an immediate act of *God's* displeasure, manifested on account of some *sin* committed by him, or through any distraction of mind, occasioned by the dread of such displeasure, a punishment of the *religious* sanction.

X

As to such of the pleasures and pains belonging to the religious sanction, as regard a future life, of what kind these may be, we cannot know. These lie not open to our observation. During the present life they are matter only of expectation: and, whether that expectation be derived from natural or revealed religion, the particular kind of pleasure or pain, if it be different from all those which lie open to our observation, is what we can have no idea of. The best ideas we can obtain of such pains and pleasures are altogether unliquidated in point of quality. In what other respects our ideas of them *may* be liquidated, will be considered in another place.

XI

Of these four sanctions, the physical is altogether, we may observe, the ground-work of the political and the moral: so is it also of the religious, in as far as the latter bears relation to the present life. It is included in each of those other three. This may operate in any case (that is, any of the pains or pleasures belonging to it may operate) independently of *them:* none of *them* can operate but by means of this. In a word, the powers of nature may operate of themselves; but neither the magistrate, nor men at large, *can* operate, nor is God in the case in question *supposed* to operate, but through the powers of nature.

XII

For these four objects, which in their nature have so much in common, it seemed of use to find a common name. It seemed of use, in the first place, for the convenience of giving a name to certain pleasures and pains, for which a name equally characteristic could hardly otherwise have been found: in the second place, for the sake of holding up the efficacy of certain moral forces, the influence of which is apt not to be sufficiently attended to. Does the political sanction exert an influence over the conduct of mankind? The moral, the religious sanctions, do so too. In every inch of his career are the operations of the political magistrate liable to be aided or impeded by these two foreign powers: who, one or other of them, or both, are sure to be either his rivals or his allies. Does it happen to him to leave them out in his calculations? he will be sure almost to find himself mistaken in the result. Of all this we shall find abundant proofs in the sequel of this work. It behoves him, therefore, to have them continually before his eyes; and that under such a name as exhibits the relation they bear to his own purposes and designs.

CHAPTER IV

Value of a Lot of Pleasure or Pain, How to Be Measured

I

Pleasures then, and the avoidance of pains are the *ends* which the legislator has in view it behoves him therefore to understand their *value*. Pleasures and pains are the *instruments* he has to work with: it behoves him therefore to understand their force, which is again, in another point of view, their value.

II

To a person considered *by himself*, the value of a pleasure or pain considered *by itself*, will be greater or less, according to the four following circumstances:

1. Its *intensity*.
2. Its *duration*.
3. Its *certainty* or *uncertainty*.
4. Its *propinquity* or *remoteness*.

III

These are the circumstances which are to be considered in estimating a pleasure or a pain considered each of them by itself. But when the value of any pleasure or pain is considered for the purpose of estimating the tendency of any *act* by which it is produced, there are two other circumstances to be taken into the account; these are,

5. Its *fecundity*, or the chance it has of being followed by sensations of the *same* kind: that is, pleasures, if it be a pleasure: pains, if it be a pain.

6. Its *purity*, or the chance it has of *not* being followed by sensations of the *opposite* kind: that is, pains, if it be a pleasure: pleasures, if it be a pain.

These two last, however, are in strictness scarcely to be deemed properties of the pleasure or the pain itself; they are not, therefore, in strictness to be taken into the account of the value of that pleasure or that pain. They are in strictness to be deemed properties only of the act, or other event, by which such pleasure or pain has been produced; and accordingly are only to be taken into the account of the tendency of such act or such event.

IV

To a *number* of persons, with reference to each of whom the value of a pleasure or a pain is considered, it will be greater or less, according to seven circumstances: to wit, the six preceding ones; *viz.*

1. Its *intensity*.
2. Its *duration*.
3. Its *certainty* or *uncertainty*.
4. Its *propinquity* or *remoteness*.
5. Its *fecundity*.
6. Its *purity*.

And one other; to wit:

7. Its *extent*; that is, the number of persons to whom it *extends*; or (in other words) who are affected by it.

V

To take an exact account, then, of the general tendency of any act, by which the interests of a community are affected, proceed as follows. Begin with any one person of those whose interests seem most immediately to be affected by it: and take an account,

1. Of the value of each distinguishable *pleasure* which appears to be produced by it in the *first* instance.

2. Of the value of each *pain* which appears to be produced by it in the *first* instance.

3. Of the value of each pleasure which appears to be produced by it *after* the first. This constitutes the *fecundity* of the first *pleasure* and the *impurity* of the first *pain*.

4. Of the value of each *pain* which appears to be produced by it after the first. This constitutes the *fecundity* of the first *pain*, and the *impurity* of the first pleasure.

5. Sum up all the values of all the *pleasures* on the one side, and those of all the pains on the other. The balance, if it be on the side of pleasure, will give the *good* tendency of the act upon the whole, with respect to the interests of that *individual* person; if on the side of pain, the *bad* tendency of it upon the whole.

6. Take an account of the *number* of persons whose interests appear to be concerned; and repeat the above process with respect to each. *Sum up* the numbers expressive of the degrees of *good* tendency, which the act has, with respect to each individual, in regard to whom the tendency of it is *good* upon the whole: do this again with respect to each individual, in regard to whom the tendency of it is *good* upon the whole: do this again with respect to each individual, in regard to whom the tendency of it is *bad* upon the whole. Take the *balance*; which, if on the side of *pleasure*, will give the general *good tendency* of the act, with respect to the total number or community of individuals concerned; if on the side of pain, the general *evil tendency*, with respect to the same community.

VI

It is not to be expected that this process should be strictly pursued previously to every moral judgment, or to every legislative or judicial operation. It may, however, be always kept in view: and as near as the process actually pursued on these occasions approaches to it, so near will such process approach to the character of an exact one.

CHAPTER X

Of Motives

No Motives Either Constantly Good or Constantly Bad

IX

In all this chain of motives, the principal or original link seems to be the last internal motive in prospect; it is to this that all the other motives in prospect owe their materiality: and the immediately acting motive its existence. This motive in prospect, we see, is always some pleasure, or some pain: some pleasure, which the act in question is expected to be a means of continuing or producing: some pain which it is expected to be a means of discontinuing or preventing. A motive is substantially nothing more than pleasure or pain, operating in a certain manner.

X
Now, pleasure is in *itself* a good; nay, even setting aside immunity from pain, the only good: pain is in itself an evil; and, indeed, without exception, the only evil; or else the words good and evil have no meaning. And this is alike true of every sort of pain, and of every sort of pleasure. It follows, therefore, immediately and incontestibly, that *there is no such thing as any sort of motive that is in itself a bad one.*[2]

XI
It is common, however, to speak of actions as proceeding from *good* or *bad* motives: in which case the motives meant are such as are internal. The expression is far from being an accurate one; and as it is apt to occur in the consideration of almost every kind of offence, it will be requisite to settle the precise meaning of it, and observe how far it quadrates with the truth of things.

XII
With respect to goodness and badness, as it is with every thing else that is not itself either pain or pleasure, so is it with motives. If they are good or bad, it is only on account of their effects: good, on account of their tendency to produce pleasure, or avert pain: bad, on account of their tendency to produce pain or avert pleasure. . . .

---

[2] Let a man's motive be ill-will; call it even malice, envy, cruelty; it is still a kind of pleasure that is his motive: the pleasure he takes at the thought of the pain which he sees, or expects to see, his adversary undergo.

22 Can We Reconcile Egoistic Hedonism and Utilitarianism?[*]

HENRY SIDGWICK

Henry Sidgwick (1838–1900), educated at Cambridge University where he also taught, is well known for his work in ethics, especially his *Methods of Ethics.*

It would be contrary to Common Sense to deny that the distinction between any one individual and any other is real and fundamental, and that consequently "I" am concerned with the quality of my existence as an individual in a sense, fundamentally important, in which I am not concerned with the quality of the existence of other individuals: and this being so, I do not see how it can be proved that this distinction is not to be taken as fundamental in determining the ultimate end of rational action for an individual. And it may be observed that most Utilitarians, however anxious they have been to convince men of the reasonableness of aiming at happiness generally, have not commonly sought to attain this result by any logical transition from the Egoistic to the Universalistic principle. They have relied almost entirely on the Sanctions of Utilitarian rules; that is, on the pleasures gained or pains avoided by the individual conforming to them. Indeed, if an Egoist remains impervious to what we have called Proof, the only way of rationally inducing him to aim at the happiness of all, is to show him that his own greatest happiness can be best attained by so doing. And further, even if a man admits the self-evidence of the principle of Rational Benevolence, he may still hold that his own happiness is an end which it is irrational for him to sacrifice to any other; and that therefore a harmony between the maxim of Prudence and the maxim of Rational Benevolence must be somehow demonstrated, if morality is to be made completely rational. This latter view, indeed (as I have before said), appears to me, on the whole, the view of Common Sense: and it is that which I myself hold. It thus becomes needful to examine how far and in what way the required demonstration can be affected.

While in any tolerable state of society the performance of duties towards others and the exercise of social virtues seem *generally* likely to coincide with the attainment of the greatest possible happiness in the long run for

---

[*] From Henry Sidgwick, *The Methods of Ethics* (London: 1893).

the virtuous agent, still the *universality* and *completeness* of this coincidence are at least incapable of empirical proof: and that, indeed, the more carefully we analyse and estimate the different sanctions—Legal, Social, and Conscientious—considered as operating under the actual conditions of human life, the more difficult it seems to believe that they can be always adequate to produce this coincidence. The natural effect of this argument upon a convinced Utilitarian is merely to make him anxious to alter the actual conditions of human life: and it would certainly be a most valuable contribution to the actual happiness of mankind, if we could so improve the adjustment of the machine of Law in any society, and so stimulate and direct the common awards of praise and blame, and so develop and train the moral sense of the members of the community, as to render it clearly prudent for every individual to promote as much as possible the general good. However, we are not now considering what a consistent Utilitarian will try to effect for the future, but what a consistent Egoist is to do in the present. And it must be admitted that, as things are, whatever difference exists between Utilitarian morality and that of Common Sense is of such a kind as to render the coincidence with Egoism still more improbable in the case of the former. For we have seen that Utilitarianism is more rigid than Common Sense in exacting the sacrifice of the agent's private interests where they are incompatible with the greatest happiness of the greatest number: and of course in so far as the Utilitarian's principles bring him into conflict with any of the commonly accepted rules of morality, the whole force of the Social Sanction operates to deter him from what he conceives to be his duty.

There are, however, writers of the Utilitarian school who seem to maintain or imply, that by due contemplation of the paramount importance of Sympathy as an element of human happiness we shall be led to see the coincidence of the good of each with the good of all. In opposing this view, I am as far as possible from any wish to depreciate the value of sympathy as a source of happiness even to human beings as at present constituted. Indeed I am of opinion that its pleasures and pains really constitute a great part of that internal reward of social virtue, and punishment of social misconduct. . . .

But besides admitting the actual importance of sympathetic pleasures to the majority of mankind, I should go further and maintain that, on empirical grounds alone, enlightened self-interest would direct most men to foster and develop their sympathetic susceptibilities to a greater extent than is now commonly attained. The effectiveness of Butler's famous argument against the vulgar antithesis between Self-love and Benevolence is undeniable: and it seems scarcely extravagant to say that, amid all the profuse waste of the means of happiness which men commit, there is no imprudence more flagrant than that of Selfishness in the ordinary sense of the term,—that excessive concentration of attention on the individual's own happiness which renders it impossible for him to feel any strong interest in the pleasures and pains of others. The perpetual prominence of self that hence results tends to deprive all enjoyments of their keenness and zest, and produce rapid satiety and *ennui*: the selfish man misses the sense of elevation and enlargement given by wide interests; he misses the more secure and serene satisfaction that attends continually on activities directed towards ends more stable in prospect than an individual's happiness can be; he misses the peculiar rich sweetness, depending upon a sort of complex reverberation of sympathy, which is always found in services rendered to those whom we love and who are grateful. He is made to feel in a thousand various ways, according to the degree of refinement which his nature has attained, the discord between the rhythms of his own life and of that larger life of which his own is but an insignificant fraction.

But allowing all this, it yet seems to me as certain as any conclusion arrived at by hedonistic comparison can be, that the utmost development of sympathy, intensive and extensive, which is now possible to any but a very few exceptional persons, would not cause a perfect coincidence between Utilitarian duty and self-interest.

Suppose a man finds that a regard for the general good—Utilitarian Duty —demands from him a sacrifice, or extreme risk, of life. There are perhaps one or two human beings so dear to him that the remainder of a life saved by sacrificing their happiness to his own would be worthless to him from an egoistic point of view. But it is doubtful whether many men, "sitting down in a cool hour" to make the estimate, would affirm even this: and of course that particular portion of the general happiness, for which one is called upon to sacrifice one's own, may easily be the happiness of persons not especially dear to one. But again, from this normal limitation of our keenest and strongest sympathy to a very small circle of human beings, it results that the very development of sympathy may operate to increase the weight thrown into the scale against Utilitarian duty. There are very few persons, however strongly and widely sympathetic, who are so constituted as to feel for the pleasures and pains of mankind generally a degree of sympathy at all commensurate with their concern for wife or children, or lover, or intimate friend: and if any training of the affections is at present possible which would materially alter this proportion in the general distribution of our sympathy, it scarcely seems that such a training is to be recommended as on the whole felicific. And thus when Utilitarian Duty calls on us to sacrifice not only our own pleasures but the happiness of those we love to the general good, the very sanction on which Utilitarianism most relies must act powerfully in opposition to its precepts.

It seems, then, that we must conclude, from the arguments that the inseparable connexion between Utilitarian Duty and the greatest happiness of the individual who conforms to it cannot be satisfactorily demonstrated on empirical grounds. Hence another section of the Utilitarian school has preferred to throw the weight of Duty on the Religious Sanction: and this procedure has been partly adopted by some of those who have chiefly dwelt on sympathy as a motive. From this point of view the Utilitarian Code is conceived as the Law of God, who is to be regarded as having commanded men to promote the general happiness, and as having announced an intention of rewarding those who obey His commands and punishing the disobedient.

Or, again, we may argue thus. If—as all theologians agree—we are to conceive God as acting for some end, we must conceive that end to be Universal Good, and, if Utilitarians are right, Universal Happiness: and we cannot suppose that in a world morally governed it can be prudent for any man to act in conscious opposition to what we believe to be the Divine Design. Hence if in any case after calculating the consequences of two alternatives of conduct we choose that which seems likely to be less conducive to Happiness generally, we shall be acting in a manner for which we cannot but expect to suffer.

If, then, we may assume the existence of such a Being, as God, by the *consensus* of theologians, is conceived to be, it seems that Utilitarians may legitimately infer the existence of Divine sanctions to the code of social duty as constructed on a Utilitarian basis; and such sanctions would, of course, suffice to make it always every one's interest to promote universal happiness to the best of his knowledge. It is, however, desirable, before we conclude, to examine carefully the validity of this assumption, in so far as it is supported on ethical grounds alone. For by the result of such an examination will be determined, as we now see, the very important question whether ethical science can be constructed on an independent basis; or whether it is forced to borrow a fundamental and indispensable premiss from Theology or some similar source. In order fairly to perform this examination, let us reflect upon the clearest and most certain of our moral intuitions. I find that I undoubtedly seem to perceive, as clearly and certainly as I see any axiom in Arithmetic or Geometry, that it is 'right' and 'reasonable' for me to treat others as I should think that I myself ought to be treated under similar conditions, and to do what I believe to be ultimately conducive to universal Good or Happiness. But I cannot find inseparably connected with this conviction, and similarly attainable by mere reflective intuition, any cognition that there actually is a Supreme Being who will adequately reward me for obeying these rules of duty, or punish me for violating them. Or,—omitting the strictly theological element of the proposition,—I may say that I do not find in my moral consciousness any intuition, claiming to be clear and certain, that the performance of duty will be adequately rewarded and its violation punished. I feel indeed a desire, apparently inseparable from the moral sentiments, that this result may be realised not only in my own case but universally; but the mere existence of the desire would not go far to establish the probability of its fulfilment, considering the large proportion of human desires that experience shows to be doomed to disappointment. I also judge that in a certain sense this result *ought* to be realised: in this judgment, however, 'ought' is not used in a strictly ethical meaning; it only expresses the vital need that our Practical Reason feels of proving or postulating this connexion of Virtue and self-interest, if it is to be made consistent with itself. For the negation of the connexion must force us to admit an ultimate and fundamental contradiction in our apparent intuitions of what is Reasonable in conduct; and from this admission it would seem to follow that the apparently intuitive operation of the Practical Reason, manifested in these contradictory judgments, is after all illusory.

I do not mean that if we gave up the hope of attaining a practical solution of this fundamental contradiction, through any legitimately obtained conclusion or postulate as to the moral order of the world, it would become reasonable for us to abandon morality altogether: but it would seem necessary to abandon the idea of rationalising it completely. We should doubtless still, not only from self-interest, but also through sympathy and sentiments protective of social wellbeing, imparted by education and sustained by communication with other men, feel a desire for the general observance of rules conducive to general happiness; and practical reason would still impel us decisively to the performance of duty in the more ordinary cases in which what is recognised as duty is in harmony with self-interest properly understood. But in the rarer cases of a recognised conflict between self-interest and duty, practical reason, being divided against itself, would cease to be a motive on either side; the conflict would have to be decided by the comparative preponderance of one or other of two groups of non-rational impulses.

If then the reconciliation of duty and self-interest is to be regarded as a hypothesis logically necessary to avoid a fundamental contradiction in one chief department of our thought, it remains to ask how far this necessity constitutes a sufficient reason for accepting this hypothesis. This, however, is a profoundly difficult and controverted question, the discussion of which belongs rather to a treatise on General Philosophy than to a work on the Methods of Ethics: as it could not be satisfactorily answered, without a general examination of the criteria of true and false beliefs. Those who hold that the edifice of physical science is really constructed of conclusions logically inferred from self-evident premises, may reasonably demand that any practical judgments claiming philosophic certainty should be based on an equally firm foundation. If on the other hand we find that in our supposed knowledge of the world of nature propositions are commonly taken to be universally true, which yet seem to rest on no other grounds than that we have a strong disposition to accept them, and that they are indispensable to the systematic coherence of our beliefs,—it will be more difficult to reject a similarly supported assumption in ethics, without opening the door to universal scepticism.

23 What Makes Right Acts Right? —A Synthesis of Formalism and Utilitarianism*

W. D. ROSS

W. D. Ross (1877–   ) taught at Oriel College, Oxford, and was later elected provost of Oriel, a post which he held for nearly two decades. He is well known for his translations of Aristotle—*Metaphysics* (1908) and the *Ethics* (1925)—but he is perhaps most famous for his contributions to the field of moral philosophy through his two books *The Right and the Good* and *Foundations of Ethics.*

The real point at issue between hedonism and utilitarianism on the one hand and their opponents on the other is not whether 'right' means 'productive of so and so'; for it cannot with any plausibility be maintained that it does. The point at issue is that to which we now pass, viz. whether there is any general character which makes right acts right, and if so, what it is. Among the main historical attempts to state a single characteristic of all right actions which is the foundation of their rightness are those made by egoism and utilitarianism. But I do not propose to discuss these, not because the subject is unimportant, but because it has been dealt with so often and so well already, and because there has come to be so much agreement among moral philosophers that neither of these theories is satisfactory. A much more attractive theory has been put forward by Professor Moore: that what makes actions right is that they are productive of more *good* than could have been produced by any other action open to the agent.

This theory is in fact the culmination of all the attempts to base rightness on productivity of some sort of result. The first form this attempt takes is the attempt to base rightness on conduciveness to the advantage or pleasure of the agent. This theory comes to grief over the fact, which stares us in the face, that a great part of duty consists in an observance of the rights and a furtherance of the interests of others, whatever the cost to ourselves may be. Plato and others may be right in holding that a regard for the rights of others never in the long run involves a loss of happiness for the agent, that

* From W. D. Ross, *The Right and the Good*, 1930, by permission of the Clarendon Press, Oxford.

'the just life profits a man'. But this, even if true, is irrelevant to the right-ness of the act. As soon as a man does an action *because* he thinks he will promote his own interests thereby, he is acting not from a sense of its right-ness but from self-interest.

To the egoistic theory hedonistic utilitarianism supplies a much-needed amendment. It points out correctly that the fact that a certain pleasure will be enjoyed by the agent is no reason why he *ought* to bring it into being rather than an equal or greater pleasure to be enjoyed by another, though, human nature being what it is, it makes it not unlikely that he *will* try to bring it into being. But hedonistic utilitarianism in its turn needs a correc-tion. On reflection it seems clear that pleasure is not the only thing in life that we think good in itself, that for instance we think the possession of a good character, or an intelligent understanding of the world, as good or better. A great advance is made by the substitution of 'productive of the greatest good' for 'productive of the greatest pleasure'.

Not only is this theory more attractive than hedonistic utilitarianism, but its logical relation to that theory is such that the latter could not be true unless *it* were true, while it might be true though hedonistic utilitarianism were not. It is in fact one of the logical bases of hedonistic utilitarianism. For the view that what produces the maximum pleasure is right has for its bases the views (1) that what produces the maximum good is right, and (2) that pleasure is the only thing good in itself. If they were not assuming that what produces the maximum *good* is right, the utilitarians' attempt to show that pleasure is the only thing good in itself, which is in fact the point they take most pains to establish, would have been quite irrelevant to their attempt to prove that only what produces the maximum *pleasure* is right. If, therefore, it can be shown that productivity of the maximum good is not what makes all right actions right, we shall *a fortiori* have refuted hedonis-tic utilitarianism.

When a plain man fulfils a promise because he thinks he ought to do so, it seems clear that he does so with no thought of its total consequences, still less with any opinion that these are likely to be the best possible. He thinks in fact much more of the past than of the future. What makes him think it right to act in a certain way is the fact that he has promised to do so—that and, usually, nothing more. That his act will produce the best possible con-sequences is not his reason for calling it right. What lends colour to the theory we are examining, then, is not the actions (which form probably a great majority of our actions) in which some such reflection as 'I have prom-ised' is the only reason we give ourselves for thinking a certain action right, but the exceptional cases in which the consequences of fulfilling a promise (for instance) would be so disastrous to others that we judge it right not to do so. It must of course be admitted that such cases exist. If I have prom-ised to meet a friend at a particular time for some trivial purpose, I should certainly think myself justified in breaking my engagement if by doing so I could prevent a serious accident or bring relief to the victims of one. And the supporters of the view we are examining hold that my thinking so is due to my thinking that I shall bring more good into existence by the one action than by the other. A different account may, however, be given of the matter, an account which will, I believe, show itself to be the true one. It may be said that besides the duty of fulfilling promises I have and recognize a duty of relieving distress, and that when I think it right to do the latter at the cost of not doing the former, it is not because I think I shall produce more good thereby but because I think it the duty which is in the circumstances more of a duty. This account surely corresponds much more closely with what we really think in such a situation. If, so far as I can see, I could bring equal amounts of good into being by fulfilling my promise and by helping some one to whom I had made no promise, I should not hesitate to regard the former as my duty. Yet on the view that what is right is right because it is productive of the most good I should not so regard it.

There are two theories, each in its way simple, that offer a solution of such cases of conscience. One is the view of Kant, that there are certain duties of perfect obligation, such as those of fulfilling promises, of paying debts, of telling the truth, which admit of no exception whatever in favour of duties of imperfect obligation, such as that of relieving distress. The other is the view of, for instance, Professor Moore and Dr. Rashdall, that there is only the duty of producing good, and that all 'conflicts of duties' should be resolved by asking 'by which action will most good be produced?' But it is more important that our theory fit the facts than that it be simple, and the account we have given above corresponds (it seems to me) better than either of the simpler theories with what we really think, viz. that normally promise-keeping, for example, should come before benevolence, but that when and only when the good to be produced by the benevolent act is very great and the promise comparatively trivial, the act of benevolence becomes our duty.

In fact the theory of 'ideal utilitarianism', if I may for brevity refer so to the theory of Professor Moore, seems to simplify unduly our relations to our fellows. It says, in effect, that the only morally significant relation in which my neighbours stand to me is that of being possible beneficiaries by my action.[1] They do stand in this relation to me, and this relation is morally significant. But they may also stand to me in the relation of promisee to promiser, of creditor to debtor, of wife to husband, of child to parent, of friend to friend, of fellow countryman to fellow countryman, and the like; and each of these relations is the foundation of a *prima facie* duty, which is more or less incumbent on me according to the circumstances of the case. When I am in a situation, as perhaps I always am, in which more than one of these *prima facie* duties is incumbent on me, what I have to do is to study

[1] Some will think it, apart from other considerations, a sufficient refutation of this view to point out that I also stand in that relation to myself, so that for this view the distinction of oneself from others is morally insignificant.

the situation as fully as I can until I form the considered opinion (it is never more) that in the circumstances one of them is more incumbent than any other; then I am bound to think that to do this *prima facie* duty is my duty *sans phrase* in the situation.

I suggest '*prima facie* duty' or 'conditional duty' as a brief way of referring to the characteristic (quite distinct from that of being a duty proper) which an act has, in virtue of being of a certain kind (e.g. the keeping of a promise), of being an act which would be a duty proper if it were not at the same time of another kind which is morally significant. Whether an act is a duty proper or actual duty depends on *all* the morally significant kinds it is an instance of. . . .

There is nothing arbitrary about these *prima facie* duties. Each rests on a definite circumstance which cannot seriously be held to be without moral significance. Of *prima facie* duties I suggest, without claiming completeness or finality for it, the following division.[2]

(1) Some duties rest on previous acts of my own. These duties seem to include two kinds, (*a*) those resting on a promise or what may fairly be called an implicit promise, such as the implicit undertaking not to tell lies which seems to be implied in the act of entering into conversation (at any rate by civilized men), or of writing books that purport to be history and not fiction. These may be called the duties of fidelity. (*b*) Those resting on a previous wrongful act. These may be called the duties of reparation. (2) Some rest on previous acts of other men, i.e. services done by them to me. These may be loosely described as the duties of gratitude. (3) Some rest on the fact or possibility of a distribution of pleasure or happiness (or of the means thereto) which is not in accordance with the merit of the persons concerned; in such cases there arises a duty to upset or prevent such a distribution. These are the duties of justice. (4) Some rest on the mere fact that there are other beings in the world whose condition we can make better in respect of virtue, or of intelligence, or of pleasure. These are the duties of beneficence. (5) Some rest on the fact that we can improve our own condition in respect of virtue or of intelligence. These are the duties of self-improvement. (6) I think that we should distinguish from (4) the duties that may be summed up under the title of 'not injuring others'. No doubt

---

[2] I should make it plain at this stage that I am assuming the correctness of some of our main convictions as to *prima facie* duties, or, more strictly, am claiming that we *know* them to be true. To me it seems as self-evident as anything could be, that to make a promise, for instance, is to create a moral claim on us in someone else. Many readers will perhaps say that they do *not* know this to be true. If so, I certainly cannot prove it to them; I can only ask them to reflect again, in the hope that they will ultimately agree that they also know it to be true. The main moral convictions of the plain man seem to me to be, not opinions which it is for philosophy to prove or disprove, but knowledge from the start; and in my own case I seem to find little difficulty in distinguishing these essential convictions from other moral convictions which I also have, which are merely fallible opinions based on an imperfect study of the working for good or evil of certain institutions or types of action.

to injure others is incidentally to fail to do them good; but it seems to me clear that non-maleficence is apprehended as a duty distinct from that of beneficence, and as a duty of a more stringent character. It will be noticed that this alone among the types of duty has been stated in a negative way. An attempt might no doubt be made to state this duty, like the others, in a positive way. It might be said that it is really the duty to prevent ourselves from acting either from an inclination to harm others or from an inclination to seek our own pleasure, in doing which we should incidentally harm them. But on reflection it seems clear that the primary duty here is the duty not to harm others, this being a duty whether or not we have an inclination that if followed would lead to our harming them; and that when we have such an inclination the primary duty not to harm others gives rise to a consequential duty to resist the inclination. The recognition of this duty of non-maleficence is the first step on the way to the recognition of the duty of beneficence; and that accounts for the prominence of the commands 'thou shalt not kill', 'thou shalt not commit adultery', 'thou shalt not steal', 'thou shalt not bear false witness', in so early a code as the Decalogue. But even when we have come to recognize the duty of beneficence, it appears to me that the duty of non-maleficence is recognized as a distinct one, and as *prima facie* more binding. We should not in general consider it justifiable to kill one person in order to keep another alive, or to steal from one in order to give alms to another.

The essential defect of the 'ideal utilitarian' theory is that it ignores, or at least does not do full justice to, the highly personal character of duty. If the only duty is to produce the maximum of good, the question who is to have the good—whether it is myself, or my benefactor, or a person to whom I have made a promise to confer that good on him, or a mere fellow man to whom I stand in no such special relation—should make no difference to my having a duty to produce that good. But we are all in fact sure that it makes a vast difference. . . .

If the objection be made, that this catalogue of the main types of duty is an unsystematic one resting on no logical principle, it may be replied, first, that it makes no claim to being ultimate. It is a *prima facie* classification of the duties which reflection on our moral convictions seems actually to reveal. And if these convictions are, as I would claim that they are, of the nature of knowledge, and if I have not misstated them, the list will be a list of authentic conditional duties, correct as far as it goes though not necessarily complete. The list of *goods* put forward by the rival theory is reached by exactly the same method—the only sound one in the circumstances—viz. that of direct reflection on what we really think. Loyalty to the facts is worth more than a symmetrical architectonic or a hastily reached simplicity. If further reflection discovers a perfect logical basis for this or for a better classification, so much the better. . . .

Or again, the sense of a general obligation to bring about (so far as we can) a just apportionment of happiness to merit is often greatly reinforced by the fact that many of the existing injustices are due to a social and economic system which we have, not indeed created, but taken part in and assented to; the duty of justice is then reinforced by the duty of reparation.

It is necessary to say something by way of clearing up the relation between *prima facie* duties and the actual or absolute duty to do one particular act in particular circumstances. If, as almost all moralists except Kant are agreed, and as most plain men think, it is sometimes right to tell a lie or to break a promise, it must be maintained that there is a difference between *prima facie* duty and actual or absolute duty. When we think ourselves justified in breaking, and indeed morally obliged to break, a promise in order to relieve some one's distress, we do not for a moment cease to recognize a *prima facie* duty to keep our promise, and this leads us to feel, not indeed shame or repentance, but certainly compunction, for behaving as we do; we recognize, further, that it is our duty to make up somehow to the promisee for the breaking of the promise. We have to distinguish from the characteristic of being our duty that of tending to be our duty. Any act that we do contains various elements in virtue of which it falls under various categories. In virtue of being the breaking of a promise, for instance, it tends to be wrong; in virtue of being an instance of relieving distress it tends to be right. Tendency to be one's duty may be called a parti-resultant attribute, i.e. one which belongs to an act in virtue of some one component in its nature. *Being* one's duty is a toti-resultant attribute, one which belongs to an act in virtue of its whole nature and of nothing less than this. This distinction between parti-resultant and toti-resultant attributes is one which we shall meet in another context also.

The general principles of duty are obviously not self-evident from the beginning of our lives. How do they come to be so? The answer is, that they come to be self-evident to us just as mathematical axioms do. We find by experience that this couple of matches and that couple make four matches, that this couple of balls on a wire and that couple make four balls; and by reflection on these and similar discoveries we come to see that it is of the nature of two and two to make four. In a precisely similar way, we see the *prima facie* rightness of an act which would be the fulfilment of a particular promise, and of another which would be the fulfilment of another promise, and when we have reached sufficient maturity to think in general terms, we apprehend *prima facie* rightness to belong to the nature of any fulfilment of promise. What comes first in time is the apprehension of the self-evident *prima facie* rightness of an individual act of a particular type. From this we come by reflection to apprehend the self-evident general principle of *prima facie* duty. From this, too, perhaps along with the apprehension of the self-evident *prima facie* rightness of the same act in virtue of its having another characteristic as well, and perhaps in spite of the apprehension of its *prima facie* wrongness in virtue of its having some third characteristic, we come to believe something not self-evident at all, but an object of probable opinion, viz. that this particular act is (not *prima facie* but) actually right. . . .

Supposing it to be agreed, as I think on reflection it must, that no one *means* by 'right' just 'productive of the best possible consequences', or 'optimific', the attributes 'right' and 'optimific' might stand in either of two kinds of relation to each other. (1) They might be so related that we could apprehend *a priori*, either immediately or deductively, that any act that is optimific is right and any act that is right is optimific, as we can apprehend that any triangle that is equilateral is equiangular and *vice versa*. Professor Moore's view is, I think, that the coextensiveness of 'right' and 'optimific' is apprehended immediately. He rejects the possibility of any proof of it. Or (2) the two attributes might be such that the question whether they are invariably connected had to be answered by means of an inductive inquiry. Now at first sight it might seem as if the constant connexion of the two attributes could be immediately apprehended. It might seem absurd to suggest that it could be right for any one to do an act which would produce consequences less good than those which would be produced by some other act in his power. Yet a little thought will convince us that this is not absurd. The type of case in which it is easiest to see that this is so is, perhaps, that in which one has made a promise. In such a case we all think that *prima facie* it is our duty to fulfil the promise irrespective of the precise goodness of the total consequences. And though we do not think it is necessarily our actual or absolute duty to do so, we are far from thinking that any, even the slightest, gain in the value of the total consequences will necessarily justify us in doing something else instead. Suppose, to simplify the case by abstraction, that the fulfilment of a promise to A would produce 1,000 units of good[3] for him, but that by doing some other act I could produce 1,001 units of good for B, to whom I have made no promise, the other consequences of the two acts being of equal value; should we really think it self-evident that it was our duty to do the second act and not the first? I think not. We should, I fancy, hold that only a much greater disparity of value between the total consequences would justify us in failing to discharge our *prima facie* duty to A. After all, a promise is a promise, and is not to be treated so lightly as the theory we are examining would imply What, exactly, a promise is, is not so easy to determine, but we are surely agreed that it constitutes a serious moral limitation to our freedom of action. To produce the 1,001 units of good for B rather than fulfil our promise to A would be to take, not perhaps our duty as philanthropists too seriously, but certainly our duty as makers of promises too lightly.

I conclude that the attributes 'right' and 'optimific' are not identical, and

---

[3] I am assuming that good is objectively quantitative . . . , but not that we can accurately assign an exact quantitative measure to it. Since it is of a definite amount, we can make the *supposition* that its amount is so-and-so, though we cannot with any confidence *assert* that it is.

that we do not know either by intuition, by deduction, or by induction that they coincide in their application, still less that the latter is the foundation of the former. It must be added, however, that if we are ever under no special obligation such as that of fidelity to a promisee or of gratitude to a benefactor, we ought to do what will produce most good; and that even when we are under a special obligation the tendency of acts to promote general good is one of the main factors in determining whether they are right.

In what has preceded, a good deal of use has been made of 'what we really think' about moral questions; a certain theory has been rejected because it does not agree with what we really think. It might be said that this is in principle wrong; that we should not be content to expound what our present moral consciousness tells us but should aim at a criticism of our existing moral consciousness in the light of theory. Now I do not doubt that the moral consciousness of men has in detail undergone a good deal of modification as regards the things we think right, at the hands of moral theory. But if we are told, for instance, that we should give up our view that there is a special obligatoriness attaching to the keeping of promises because it is self-evident that the only duty is to produce as much good as possible, we have to ask ourselves whether we really, when we reflect, *are* convinced that this is self-evident, and whether we really *can* get rid of our view that promise-keeping has a bindingness independent of productiveness of maximum good. In my own experience I find that I cannot, in spite of a very genuine attempt to do so; and I venture to think that most people will find the same, and that just because they cannot lose the sense of special obligation, they cannot accept as self-evident, or even as true, the theory which would require them to do so. In fact it seems, on reflection, self-evident that a promise, simply as such, is something that *prima facie* ought to be kept, and it does *not*, on reflection, seem self-evident that production of maximum good is the only thing that makes an act obligatory. And to ask us to give up at the bidding of a theory our actual apprehension of what is right and what is wrong seems like asking people to repudiate their actual experience of beauty, at the bidding of a theory which says 'only that which satisfies such and such conditions can be beautiful'. If what I have called our actual apprehension is (as I would maintain that it is) truly an apprehension, i.e. an instance of knowledge, the request is nothing less than absurd.

I would maintain, in fact, that what we are apt to describe as 'what we think' about moral questions contains a considerable amount that we do not think but know, and that this forms the standard by reference to which the truth of any moral theory has to be tested, instead of having itself to be tested by reference to any theory. I hope that I have in what precedes indicated what in my view these elements of knowledge are that are involved in our ordinary moral consciousness.

It would be a mistake to found a natural science on 'what we really think', i.e. on what reasonably thoughtful and well-educated people think about the subjects of the science before they have studied them scientifically. For such opinions are interpretations, and often misinterpretations, of sense-experience; and the man of science must appeal from these to sense-experience itself, which furnishes his real data. In ethics no such appeal is possible. We have no more direct way of access to the facts about rightness and goodness and about what things are right or good, than by thinking about them; the moral convictions of thoughtful and well-educated people are the data of ethics just as sense-perceptions are the data of a natural science. Just as some of the latter have to be rejected as illusory, so have some of the former; but as the latter are rejected only when they are in conflict with other more accurate sense-perceptions, the former are rejected only when they are in conflict with other convictions which stand better the test of reflection. The existing body of moral convictions of the best people is the cumulative product of the moral reflection of many generations, which has developed an extremely delicate power of appreciation of moral distinctions; and this the theorist cannot afford to treat with anything other than the greatest respect. The verdicts of the moral consciousness of the best people are the foundation on which he must build; though he must first compare them with one another and eliminate any contradictions they may contain.

24 The Ethic of the Superman[*]

FRIEDRICH NIETZSCHE

Friedrich Nietzsche (1844–1900) was professor of philology at Basel. Nietzsche authored many books, including *The Will to Power, Beyond Good and Evil, The Antichrist, Thus Spake Zarathustra,* and *The Geneology of Morals.* A severe critic of existing morality and culture, Nietzsche advocated a "transvaluation of all values," a rejection of Christian morality, and the development of what he calls a "master-morality."

Every elevation of the type "man," has hitherto been the work of an aristocratic society—and so will it always be—a society believing in a long scale of gradations of rank and differences of worth among human beings, and requiring slavery in some form or other. Without the *pathos of distance,* such as grows out of the incarnated difference of classes, out of the constant outlooking and downlooking of the ruling caste on subordinates and instruments, and out of their equally constant practice of obeying and commanding, of keeping down and keeping at a distance—that other more mysterious pathos could never have arisen, the longing for an ever new widening of distance within the soul itself, the formation of ever higher, rarer, further, more extended, more comprehensive states, in short, just the elevation of the type "man," the continued "self-surmounting of man," to use a moral formula in a supermoral sense. To be sure, one must not resign oneself to any humanitarian illusions about the history of the origin of an aristocratic society (that is to say, of the preliminary condition for the elevation of the type "man"): the truth is hard. Let us acknowledge unprejudicedly how every higher civilisation hitherto has *originated!* Men with a still natural nature, barbarians in every terrible sense of the word, men of prey, still in possession of unbroken strength of will and desire for power, threw themselves upon weaker, more moral, more peaceful races (perhaps trading or cattle-rearing communities), or upon old mellow civilisations in which the final vital force was flickering out in brilliant fireworks of wit and depravity. At the commencement, the noble caste was always the barbarian caste: their superiority did not consist first of all in their physical, but in their psychical power—they were more *complete* men (which at every point also implies the same as "more complete beasts").

* From Friedrich Nietzsche, *Beyond Good and Evil,* trans. Helen Zimmern (New York: Macmillan, 1970).

258

Corruption—as the indication that anarchy threatens to break out among the instincts, and that the foundation of the emotions, called "life," is convulsed—is something radically different according to the organisation in which it manifests itself. When, for instance, an aristocracy like that of France at the beginning of the Revolution, flung away its privileges with sublime disgust and sacrificed itself to an excess of its moral sentiments, it was corruption:—it was really only the closing act of the corruption which had existed for centuries, by virtue of which that aristocracy had abdicated step by step its lordly prerogatives and lowered itself to a *function* of royalty (in the end even to its decoration and parade-dress). The essential thing, however, in a good and healthy aristocracy is that it should *not* regard itself as a function either of the kingship or the commonwealth, but as the *significance* and highest justification thereof—that it should therefore accept with a good conscience the sacrifice of a legion of individuals, who, *for its sake*, must be suppressed and reduced to imperfect men, to slaves and instruments. Its fundamental belief must be precisely that society is *not* allowed to exist for its own sake, but only as a foundation and scaffolding, by means of which a select class of beings may be able to elevate themselves to their higher duties, and in general to a higher *existence*: like those sun-seeking climbing plants in Java—they are called *Sipo Matador*,—which encircle an oak so long and so often with their arms, until at last, high above it, but supported by it, they can unfold their tops in the open light, and exhibit their happiness.

259

To refrain mutually from injury, from violence, from exploitation, and put one's will on a par with that of others: this may result in a certain rough sense in good conduct among individuals when the necessary conditions are given (namely, the actual similarity of the individuals in amount of force and degree of worth, and their co-relation within one organisation). As soon, however, as one wished to take this principle more generally, and if possible even as *the fundamental principle of society*, it would immediately disclose what it really is—namely, a Will to the *denial* of life, a principle of dissolution and decay. Here one must think profoundly to the very basis and resist all sentimental weakness: life itself is *essentially* appropriation, injury, conquest of the strange and weak, suppression, severity, obtrusion of peculiar forms, incorporation, and at the least, putting it mildest, exploitation;—but why should one for ever use precisely these words on which for ages a disparaging purpose has been stamped? Even the organisation within which, as was previously supposed, the individuals treat each other as equal—it takes place in every healthy aristocracy—must itself, if it be a living and not a dying organisation, do all that towards other bodies, which the individuals within it refrain from doing to each other: it will have to be the incarnated Will to Power, it will endeavour to grow, to gain ground, attract to itself and acquire ascendency—not owing to any morality or immorality, but because it *lives*, and because life *is* precisely Will to Power. On no point, however, is the ordinary consciousness of Europeans more unwilling to be corrected than on this matter; people now rave everywhere, even under the guise of science, about coming conditions of society in which "the exploiting character" is to be absent:—that sounds to my ears as if they promised to invent a mode of life which should refrain from all organic functions. "Exploitation" does not belong to a depraved, or imperfect and primitive society: it belongs to the *nature* of the living being as a primary organic function; it is a consequence of the intrinsic Will to Power, which is precisely the Will to Life.—Granting that as a theory this is a novelty—as a reality it is the *fundamental fact* of all history: let us be so far honest towards ourselves!

260

In a tour through the many finer and coarser moralities which have hitherto prevailed or still prevail on the earth, I found certain traits recurring regularly together, and connected with one another, until finally two primary types revealed themselves to me, and a radical distinction was brought to light. There is *master-morality* and *slave-morality*;—I would at once add, however, that in all higher and mixed civilisations, there are also attempts at the reconciliation of the two moralities; but one finds still oftener the confusion and mutual misunderstanding of them, indeed, sometimes their close juxtaposition—even in the same man, within one soul. The distinctions of moral values have either originated in a ruling caste, pleasantly conscious of being different from the ruled—or among the ruled class, the slaves and dependents of all sorts. In the first case, when it is the rulers who determine the conception "good," it is the exalted, proud disposition which is regarded as the distinguishing feature, and that which determines the order of rank. The noble type of man separates from himself the beings in whom the opposite of this exalted, proud disposition displays itself: he despises them. Let it at once be noted that in this first kind of morality the antithesis "good" and "bad" means practically the same as "noble" and "despicable"; the antithesis "good" and "*evil*" is of a different origin. The cowardly, the timid, the insignificant, and those thinking merely of narrow utility are despised; moreover, also, the distrustful, with their constrained glances, the self-abasing, the dog-like kind of men who let themselves be abused, the mendicant flatterers, and above all the liars:—it is a fundamental belief of all aristocrats that the common people are untruthful. "We truthful ones"—the nobility in ancient Greece called themselves. It is obvious that everywhere the designations of moral value were at first applied to *men*, and were only derivatively and at a later period applied to *actions*; it is a gross mistake, there-fore, when historians of morals start with questions like, "Why have sympathetic actions been praised?" The noble type of man regards *himself* as a determiner of values; he does not require to be approved of; he passes the judgment: "What is injurious to me is injurious in itself"; he knows that it is he himself only who confers honour on things; he is a *creator of values.* He honours whatever he recognises in himself: such morality is self-glorification. In the foreground there is the feeling of plenitude, of power, which seeks to overflow, the happiness of high tension, the consciousness of a wealth which would fain give and bestow:—the noble man also helps the unfortunate, but not—or scarcely—out of pity, but rather from an impulse generated by the superabundance of power. The noble man honours in himself the powerful one, him also who has power over himself, who knows how to speak and how to keep silence, who takes pleasure in subjecting himself to severity and hardness, and has reverence for all that is severe and hard. "Wotan placed a hard heart in my breast," says an old Scandinavian Saga: it is thus rightly expressed from the soul of a proud Viking. Such a type of man is even proud of *not* being made for sympathy; the hero of the Saga therefore adds warningly: "He who has not a hard heart when young, will never have one." The noble and brave who think thus are the furthest removed from the morality which sees precisely in sympathy, or in acting for the good of others, or in *désintéressement,* the characteristic of the moral; faith in oneself, pride in oneself, a radical enmity and irony towards "selflessness," belong as definitely to noble morality, as do a careless scorn and precaution in presence of sympathy and the "warm heart."—It is the powerful who *know* how to honour, it is their art, their domain for invention. The profound reverence for age and for tradition—all law rests on this double reverence,—the belief and prejudice in favour of ancestors and unfavourable to newcomers, is typical in the morality of the powerful; and if, reversely, men of "modern ideas" believe almost instinctively in "progress" and the "future," and are more and more lacking in respect for old age, the ignoble origin of these "ideas" has complacently betrayed itself thereby. A morality of the ruling class, however, is more especially foreign and irritating to present-day taste in the sternness of its principle that one has duties only to one's equals; that one may act towards beings of a lower rank, towards all that is foreign, just as seems good to one, or "as the heart desires," and in any case "beyond good and evil": it is here that sympathy and similar sentiments can have a place. The ability and obligation to exercise prolonged gratitude and prolonged revenge—both only within the circle of equals,— artfulness in retaliation, *raffinement* of the idea in friendship, a certain necessity to have enemies (as outlets for the emotions of envy, quarrelsomeness, arrogance—in fact, in order to be a good *friend*): all these are typical characteristics of the noble morality, which, as has been pointed out, is not the morality of "modern ideas," and is therefore at present difficult to realise, and also to unearth and disclose.—It is otherwise with the second type of morality, *slave-morality.* Supposing that the abused, the oppressed,

the suffering, the unemancipated, the weary, and those uncertain of themselves, should moralise, what will be the common element in their moral
estimates? Probably a pessimistic suspicion with regard to the entire situation
of man will find expression, perhaps a condemnation of man, together with
his situation. The slave has an unfavourable eye for the virtues of the powerful; he has a scepticism and distrust, a *refinement* of distrust of everything
"good" that is there honoured—he would fain persuade himself that the very
happiness there is not genuine. On the other hand, *those* qualities which
serve to alleviate the existence of sufferers are brought into prominence and
flooded with light; it is here that sympathy, the kind, helping hand, the warm
heart, patience, diligence, humility, and friendliness attain to honour; for
here these are the most useful qualities, and almost the only means of supporting the burden of existence. Slave-morality is essentially the morality of
utility. Here is the seat of the origin of the famous antithesis "good" and
"*evil*":—power and dangerousness are assumed to reside in the evil, a certain
dreadfulness, subtlety, and strength, which do not admit of being despised.
According to slave-morality, therefore, the "evil" man arouses fear; according
to master-morality, it is precisely the "good" man who arouses fear and seeks
to arouse it, while the bad man is regarded as the despicable being. The
contrast attains its maximum when, in accordance with the logical consequences of slave-morality, a shade of depreciation—it may be slight and well-
intentioned—at last attaches itself even to the "good" man of this morality;
because, according to the servile mode of thought, the good man must in any
case be the *safe* man: he is good-natured, easily deceived, perhaps a little
stupid, *un bonhomme*. Everywhere that slave-morality gains the ascendency,
language shows a tendency to approximate the significations of the words
"good" and "stupid."

264

It cannot be effaced from a man's soul what his ancestors have preferably
and most constantly done: whether they were perhaps diligent economisers
attached to a desk and a cash-box, modest and citizen-like in their desires,
modest also in their virtues; or whether they were accustomed to commanding from morning till night, fond of rude pleasures and probably of still
ruder duties and responsibilities; or whether, finally, at one time or another,
they have sacrificed old privileges of birth and possession, in order to live
wholly for their faith—for their "God,"—as men of an inexorable and sensitive
conscience, which blushes at every compromise. It is quite impossible for a
man *not* to have the qualities and predilections of his parents and ancestors
in his constitution, whatever appearances may suggest to the contrary. This
is the problem of race. Granted that one knows something of the parents, it
is admissible to draw a conclusion about the child: any kind of offensive
incontinence, any kind of sordid envy, or of clumsy self-vaunting—the three
things which together have constituted the genuine plebeian type in all

times—such must pass over to the child, as surely as bad blood; and with the help of the best education and culture one will only succeed in *deceiving* with regard to such heredity.—And what else does education and culture try to do nowadays! In our very democratic, or rather, very plebeian age, "education" and "culture" *must* be essentially the art of deceiving—deceiving with regard to origin, with regard to the inherited plebeianism in body and soul. An educator who nowadays preached truthfulness above everything else, and called out constantly to his pupils: "Be true! Be natural! Show yourselves as you are!"—even such a virtuous and sincere ass would learn in a short time to have recourse to the *furca* of Horace, *naturam expellere*: with what results? "Plebeianism" *usque recurret.*[1]

265

At the risk of displeasing innocent ears, I submit that egoism belongs to the essence of a noble soul, I mean the unalterable belief that to a being such as "we," other beings must naturally be in subjection, and have to sacrifice themselves. The noble soul accepts the fact of his egoism without question, and also without consciousness of harshness, constraint, or arbitrariness therein, but rather as something that may have its basis in the primary law of things:—if he sought a designation for it he would say: "It is justice itself." He acknowledges under certain circumstances, which made him hesitate at first, that there are other equally privileged ones; as soon as he has settled this question of rank, he moves among those equals and equally privileged ones with the same assurance, as regards modesty and delicate respect, which he enjoys in intercourse with himself—in accordance with an innate heavenly mechanism which all the stars understand. It is an *additional* instance of his egoism, this artfulness and self-limitation in intercourse with his equals—every star is a similar egoist; he honours *himself* in them, and in the rights which he concedes to them, he has no doubt that the exchange of honours and rights, as the *essence* of all intercourse, belongs also to the natural condition of things. The noble soul gives as he takes, prompted by the passionate and sensitive instinct of requital, which is at the root of his nature. The notion of "favour" has, *inter pares*, neither significance nor good repute; there may be a sublime way of letting gifts as it were light upon one from above, and of drinking them thirstily like dew-drops; but for those arts and displays the noble soul has no aptitude. His egoism hinders him here: in general, he looks "aloft" unwillingly—he looks either *forward* horizontally and deliberately, or downwards—*he knows that he is on a height.*

---

[1] Horace's "Epistles," I. x. 24.

25 Cultural Relativism*

RUTH BENEDICT

Ruth Benedict (1887–1948) was a famous anthropologist who taught at Columbia University. She is the author of *Patterns of Culture; Race: Science and Politics;* and *The Chrysanthemum and the Sword: Patterns of Japanese Culture.*

Modern social anthropology has become more and more a study of the varieties and common elements of cultural environment and the consequences of these in human behavior. For such a study of diverse social orders primitive peoples fortunately provide a laboratory not yet entirely vitiated by the spread of a standardized worldwide civilization. Dyaks and Hopis, Fijians and Yakuts are significant for psychological and sociological study because only among these simpler peoples has there been sufficient isolation to give opportunity for the development of localized social forms. In the higher cultures the standardization of custom and belief over a couple of continents has given a false sense of the inevitability of the particular forms that have gained currency, and we need to turn to a wider survey in order to check the conclusions we hastily base upon this near-universality of familiar customs. Most of the simpler cultures did not gain the wide currency of the one which, out of our experience, we identify with human nature, but this was for various historical reasons, and certainly not for any that gives us as its carriers a monopoly of social good or of social sanity. Modern civilization, from this point of view, becomes not a necessary pinnacle of human achievement but one entry in a long series of possible adjustments.

These adjustments, whether they are in mannerisms like the ways of showing anger, or joy, or grief in any society, or in major human drives like those of sex, prove to be far more variable than experience in any one culture would suggest. In certain fields, such as that of religion or of formal marriage arrangements, these wide limits of variability are well known and can be fairly described. In others it is not yet possible to give a generalized account, but that does not absolve us of the task of indicating the significance of the work that has been done and of the problems that have arisen.

One of these problems relates to the customary modern normal-abnormal

* From "Anthropology and the Abnormal," by Ruth Benedict, which appeared in *The Journal of General Psychology*, 1934, 10, 59–82. Reprinted by permission of *The Journal Press*.

categories and our conclusions regarding them. In how far are such categories culturally determined, or in how far can we with assurance regard them as absolute? In how far can we regard inability to function socially as diagnostic of abnormality, or in how far is it necessary to regard this as a function of the culture?

As a matter of fact, one of the most striking facts that emerge from a study of widely varying cultures is the ease with which our abnormals function in other cultures. It does not matter what kind of "abnormality" we choose for illustration, those which indicate extreme instability, or those which are more in the nature of character traits like sadism or delusions of grandeur or of persecution, there are well-described cultures in which these abnormals function at ease and with honor, and apparently without danger or difficulty to the society.

The most notorious of these is trance and catalepsy. Even a very mild mystic is aberrant in our culture. But most peoples have regarded even extreme psychic manifestations not only as normal and desirable, but even as characteristic of highly valued and gifted individuals. This was true even in our own cultural background in that period when Catholicism made the ecstatic experience the mark of sainthood. It is hard for us, born and brought up in a culture that makes no use of the experience, to realize how important a rôle it may play and how many individuals are capable of it, once it has been given an honorable place in any society.

Cataleptic and trance phenomena are, of course, only one illustration of the fact that those whom we regard as abnormals may function adequately in other cultures. Many of our culturally discarded traits are selected for elaboration in different societies. Homosexuality is an excellent example, for in this case our attention is not constantly diverted, as in the consideration of trance, to the interruption of routine activity which it implies. Homosexuality poses the problem very simply. A tendency toward this trait in our culture exposes an individual to all the conflicts to which all aberrants are always exposed, and we tend to identify the consequences of this conflict with homesexuality. But these consequences are obviously local and cultural. Homosexuals in many societies are not incompetent, but they may be such if the culture asks adjustments of them that would strain any man's vitality. Wherever homosexuality has been given an honorable place in any society, those to whom it is congenial have filled adequately the honorable rôles society assigns to them. Plato's *Republic* is, of course, the most convincing statement of such a reading of homosexuality. It is presented as one of the major means to the good life, and it was generally so regarded in Greece at that time.

The cultural attitude toward homosexuals has not always been on such a high ethical plane, but it has been very varied. Among many American Indian tribes there exists the institution of the berdache, as the French called them. These men-women were men who at puberty or thereafter took the dress and the occupations of women. Sometimes they married other men and lived with them. Sometimes they were men with no inversion, persons of weak sexual endowment who chose this rôle to avoid the jeers of the women. The berdaches were never regarded as of first-rate supernatural power, as similar men-women were in Siberia, but rather as leaders in women's occupations, good healers in certain diseases, or, among certain tribes, as the genial organizers of social affairs. In any case, they were socially placed. They were not left exposed to the conflicts that visit the deviant who is excluded from participation in the recognized patterns of his society.

The most spectacular illustrations of the extent to which normality may be culturally defined are those cultures where an abnormality of our culture is the cornerstone of their social structure. It is not possible to do justice to these possibilities in a short discussion. A recent study of an island of north-west Melanesia by Fortune describes a society built upon traits which we regard as beyond the border of paranoia. In this tribe the exogamic groups look upon each other as prime manipulators of black magic, so that one marries always into an enemy group which remains for life one's deadly and unappeasable foes. They look upon a good garden crop as a confession of theft, for everyone is engaged in making magic to induce into his garden the productiveness of his neighbors'; therefore no secrecy in the island is so rigidly insisted upon as the secrecy of a man's harvesting of his yams. Their polite phrase at the acceptance of a gift is, "And if you now poison me, how shall I repay you this present?" Their preoccupation with poisoning is constant; no woman ever leaves her cooking pot for a moment untended. Even the great affinal economic exchanges that are characteristic of this Melanesian culture area are quite altered in Dobu since they are incompatible with this fear and distrust that pervades the culture. They go farther and people the whole world outside their own quarters with such malignant spirits that all-night feasts and ceremonials simply do not occur here. They have even rigorous religiously enforced customs that forbid the sharing of seed even in one family group. Anyone else's food is deadly poison to you, so that communality of stores is out of the question. For some months before harvest the whole society is on the verge of starvation, but if one falls to the temptation and eats up one's seed yams, one is an outcast and a beachcomber for life. There is no coming back. It involves, as a matter of course, divorce and the breaking of all social ties.

Now in this society where no one may work with another and no one may share with another, Fortune describes the individual who was regarded by all his fellows as crazy. He was not one of those who periodically ran amok and, beside himself and frothing at the mouth, fell with a knife upon anyone he could reach. Such behavior they did not regard as putting anyone outside the pale. They did not even put the individuals who were known to be liable to these attacks under any kind of control. They merely fled when they saw the attack coming on and kept out of the way. "He would be all right tomorrow." But there was one man of sunny, kindly disposition who liked work and liked to be helpful. The compulsion was too strong for him to repress it in favor of the opposite tendencies of his culture. Men and women never spoke of him without laughing; he was silly and simple and definitely crazy. Nevertheless, to the ethnologist used to a culture that has, in Christianity, made his type the model of all virtue, he seemed a pleasant fellow.

An even more extreme example, because it is of a culture that has built itself upon a more complex abnormality, is that of the North Pacific Coast of North America. The civilization of the Kwakiutl, at the time when it was first recorded in the last decades of the nineteenth century, was one of the most vigorous in North America. It was built up on an ample economic supply of goods, the fish which furnished their food staple being practically inexhaustible and obtainable with comparatively small labor, and the wood which furnished the material for their houses, their furnishings, and their arts being, with however much labor, always procurable. They lived in coastal villages that compared favorably in size with those of any other American Indians and they kept up constant communication by means of sea-going dug-out canoes.

It was one of the most vigorous and zestful of the aboriginal cultures of North America, with complex crafts and ceremonials, and elaborate and striking arts. It certainly had none of the earmarks of a sick civilization. The tribes of the Northwest Coast had wealth, and exactly in our terms. That is, they had not only a surplus of economic goods, but they made a game of the manipulation of wealth. It was by no means a mere direct transcription of economic needs and the filling of those needs. It involved the idea of capital, of interest, and of conspicuous waste. It was a game with all the binding rules of a game, and a person entered it as a child. His father distributed wealth for him, according to his ability, at a small feast or potlatch, and each gift the receiver was obliged to accept and to return after a short interval with interest that ran to about 100 per cent a year. By the time the child was grown, therefore, he was well launched, a larger potlatch had been given for him on various occasions of exploit or initiation, and he had wealth either out at usury or in his own possession. Nothing in the civilization could be enjoyed without validating it by the distribution of this wealth. Everything that was valued, names and songs as well as material objects, were passed down in family lines, but they were always publicly assumed with accompanying sufficient distributions of property. It was the game of validating and exercising all the privileges one could accumulate from one's various forbears, or by gift, or by marriage, that made the chief interest of the culture. Everyone in his degree took part in it, but many, of course, mainly as spectators. In its highest form it was played out between rival chiefs representing not only themselves and their family lines but their communities, and the object of the contest was to glorify oneself and to humiliate one's opponent. On this level of greatness the property involved was no longer represented by blankets, so many thousand of them to a pot-latch, but by higher units of value. These higher units were like our bank notes. They were incised copper tablets, each of them named, and having a value that depended upon their illustrious history. This was as high as ten thousand blankets, and to possess one of them, still more to enhance its value at a great potlatch, was one of the greatest glories within the compass of the chiefs of the Northwest Coast.

The details of this manipulation of wealth are in many ways a parody on our own economic araangements, but it is with the motivations that were recognized in this contest that we are concerned in this discussion. The drives were those which in our own culture we should call megalomaniac. There was an uncensored self-glorification and ridicule of the opponent that it is hard to equal in other cultures outside of the monologues of the abnormal. . . .

All of existence was seen in terms of insult. Not only derogatory acts performed by a neighbor or an enemy, but all untoward events, like a cut when one's axe slipped, or a ducking when one's canoe overturned, were insults. All alike threatened first and foremost one's ego security, and the first thought one was allowed was how to get even, how to wipe out the insult.

In their behavior at great bereavements this set of the culture comes out most strongly. Among the Kwakiutl it did not matter whether a relative had died in bed of disease, or by the hand of an enemy, in either case death was an affront to be wiped out by the death of another person. The fact that one had been caused to mourn was proof that one had been put upon. A chief's sister and her daughter had gone up to Victoria, and either because they drank bad whiskey or because their boat capsized they never came back. The chief called together his warriors. "Now I ask you, tribes, who shall wail? Shall I do it or shall another?" The spokesman answered, of course, "Not you, Chief. Let some other of the tribes." Immediately they set up the war pole to announce their intention of wiping out the injury, and gath-ered a war party. They set out, and found seven men and two children asleep and killed them. "Then they felt good when they arrived at Sebaa in the evening."

The point which is of interest to us is that in our society those who on that occasion would feel good when they arrived at Sebaa that evening would be the definitely abnormal. There would be some, even in our society, but it is not a recognized and approved mood under the circumstances. On the Northwest Coast those are favored and fortunate to whom that mood under those circumstances is congenial, and those to whom it is repugnant are unlucky. This latter minority can register in their own culture only by doing violence to their congenial responses and acquiring others that are difficult for them. The person, for instance, who, like a Plains Indian whose wife has been taken from him, is too proud to fight, can deal with the Northwest Coast civilization only by ignoring its strongest bents. If he cannot achieve it, he is the deviant in that culture, their instance of abnormality.

This head-hunting that takes place on the Northwest Coast after a death is no matter of blood revenge or of organized vengeance. There is no effort to tie up the subsequent killing with any responsibility on the part of the victim for the death of the person who is being mourned. A chief whose son has died goes visiting wherever his fancy dictates, and he says to his host, "My prince has died today, and you go with him." Then he kills him. In this, according to their interpretation, he acts nobly because he has not been downed. He has thrust back in return. The whole procedure is meaningless without the fundamental paranoid reading of bereavement. Death, like all the other untoward accidents of existence, confounds man's pride and can only be handled in the category of insults.

Behavior honored upon the Northwest Coast is one which is recognized as abnormal in our civilization, and yet it is sufficiently close to the attitudes of our own culture to be intelligible to us and to have a definite vocabulary with which we may discuss it. The megalomaniac paranoid trend is a definite danger in our society. It is encouraged by some of our major preoccupations, and it confronts us with a choice of two possible attitudes. One is to brand it as abnormal and reprehensible, and is the attitude we have chosen in our civilization. The other is to make it an essential attribute of ideal man, and this is the solution in the culture of the Northwest Coast.

These illustrations, which it has been possible to indicate only in the briefest manner, force upon us the fact that normality is culturally defined. An adult shaped to the drives and standards of either of these cultures, if he were transported into our civilization, would fall into our categories of abnormality. He would be faced with the psychic dilemmas of the socially unavailable. In his own culture, however, he is the pillar of society, the end result of socially inculcated mores, and the problem of personal instability in his case simply does not arise.

No one civilization can possibly utilize in its mores the whole potential range of human behavior. Just as there are great numbers of possible phonetic articulations, and the possibility of language depends on a selection and standardization of a few of these in order that speech communication may be possible at all, so the possibility of organized behavior of every sort, from the fashions of local dress and houses to the dicta of a people's ethics and religion, depends upon a similar selection among the possible behavior traits. In the field of recognized economic obligations or sex tabus this selection is as nonrational and subconscious a process as it is in the field of phonetics. It is a process which goes on in the group for long periods of time and is historically conditioned by innumerable accidents of isolation or of contact of peoples. In any comprehensive study of psychology, the selection that different cultures have made in the course of history within the great circumference of potential behavior is of great significance.

Every society, beginning with some slight inclination in one direction or another, carries its preference farther and farther, integrating itself more and more completely upon its chosen basis, and discarding those types of behavior that are uncongenial. Most of those organizations of personality that seem to us most incontrovertibly abnormal have been used by different civilizations in the very foundations of their institutional life. Conversely the most valued traits of our normal individuals have been looked on in differently organized cultures as aberrant. Normality, in short, within a very wide range, is culturally defined. It is primarily a term for the socially elaborated segment of human behavior in any culture; and abnormality, a term for the segment that that particular civilization does not use. The very eyes with which we see the problem are conditioned by the long traditional habits of our own society.

It is a point that has been made more often in relation to ethics than in relation to psychiatry. We do not any longer make the mistake of deriving the morality of our own locality and decade directly from the inevitable constitution of human nature. We do not elevate it to the dignity of a first principle. We recognize that morality differs in every society, and is a convenient term for socially approved habits. Mankind has always preferred to say, "It is a morally good," rather than "It is habitual," and the fact of this preference is matter enough for a critical science of ethics. But historically the two phrases are synonymous.

The concept of the normal is properly a variant of the concept of the good. It is that which society has approved. A normal action is one which falls well within the limits of expected behavior for a particular society. Its variability among different peoples is essentially a function of the variability of the behavior patterns that different societies have created for themselves, and can never be wholly divorced from a consideration of culturally institutionalized types of behavior.

Each culture is a more or less elaborate working-out of the potentialities of the segment it has chosen. In so far as a civilization is well integrated and consistent within itself, it will tend to carry farther and farther, according to its nature, its initial impulse toward a particular type of action, and from the point of view of any other culture those elaborations will include more and more extreme and aberrant traits.

Each of these traits, in proportion as it reinforces the chosen behavior patterns of that culture, is for that culture normal. Those individuals to whom it is congenial either congenitally, or as the result of childhood sets, are accorded prestige in that culture, and are not visited with the social contempt or disapproval which their traits would call down upon them in a society that was differently organized. On the other hand, those individuals whose characteristics are not congenial to the selected type of human behavior in that community are the deviants, no matter how valued their personality traits may be in a contrasted civilization.

The Dobuan who is not easily susceptible to fear of treachery, who enjoys work and likes to be helpful, is their neurotic and regarded as silly. On the Northwest Coast the person who finds it difficult to read life in terms of an insult contest will be the person upon whom fall all the difficulties of the culturally unprovided for. The person who does not find it easy to humiliate a neighbor, nor to see humiliation in his own experience, who is genial and loving, may, of course, find some unstandardized way of achieving satisfactions in his society, but not in the major patterned responses that his culture requires of him. If he is born to play an important rôle in a family with many hereditary privileges, he can succeed only by doing violence to his whole personality. If he does not succeed, he has betrayed his culture; that is, he is abnormal.

I have spoken of individuals as having sets toward certain types of behavior, and of these sets as running sometimes counter to the types of behavior which are institutionalized in the culture to which they belong. From all that we know of contrasting cultures it seems clear that differences of temperament occur in every society. The matter has never been made the subject of investigation, but from the available material it would appear that these temperament types are very likely of universal recurrence. That is, there is an ascertainable range of human behavior that is found wherever a sufficiently large series of individuals is observed. But the proportion in which behavior types stand to one another in different societies is not universal. The vast majority of the individuals in any group are shaped to the fashion of that culture. In other words, most individuals are plastic to the moulding force of the society into which they are born. In a society that values trance, as in India, they will have supernormal experience. In a society that institutionalizes homosexuality, they will be homosexual. In a society that sets the gathering of possessions as the chief human objective, they will amass property. The deviants, whatever the type of behavior the culture has institutionalized, will remain few in number, and there seems no more difficulty in moulding the vast malleable majority to the "normality" of what we consider an aberrant trait, such as delusions of reference, than to the normality of such accepted behavior patterns as acquisitiveness. The small proportion of the number of the deviants in any culture is not a function of the sure instinct with which that society has built itself upon the fundamental sanities, but of the universal fact that, happily, the majority of mankind quite readily take any shape that is presented to them.

The relativity of normality is not an academic issue. In the first place, it suggests that the apparent weakness of the aberrant is most often and in great measure illusory. It springs not from the fact that he is lacking in necessary vigor, but that he is an individual upon whom that culture has put more than the usual strain. His inability to adapt himself to society is a reflection of the fact that that adaptation involves a conflict in him that it does not in the so-called normal.

The relativity of normality is important in what may some day come to be a true social engineering. Our picture of our own civilization is no longer in this generation in terms of a changeless and divinely derived set of categorical imperatives. We must face the problems our changed perspective has put upon us. In this matter of mental ailments, we must face the fact that even our normality is man-made, and is of our own seeking. Just as we have been handicapped in dealing with ethical problems so long as we held to an absolute definition of morality, so too in dealing with the problems of abnormality we are handicapped so long as we identify our local normalities with the universal sanities. I have taken illustrations from different cultures, because the conclusions are most inescapable from the contrasts as they are presented in unlike social groups. But the major problem is not a consequence of the variability of the normal from culture to culture, but its variability from era to era. This variability in time we cannot escape if we would, and it is not beyond the bounds of possibility that we may be able to face this inevitable change with full understanding and deal with it rationally. No society has yet achieved self-conscious and critical analysis of its own normalities and attempted rationally to deal with its own social process of creating new normalities within its next generation. But the fact that it is unachieved is not therefore proof of its impossibility. It is a faint indication of how momentous it could be in human society.

The problem of understanding abnormal human behavior in any absolute sense independent of cultural factors is still far in the future. The categories of borderline behavior which we derive from the study of the neuroses and psychoses of our civilization are categories of prevailing local types of instability. They give much information about the stresses and strains of Western civilization, but no final picture of inevitable human behavior. Any conclusions about such behavior must await the collection by trained observers of psychiatric data from other cultures. Since no adequate work of the kind has been done at the present time, it is impossible to say what core of definition of abnormality may be found valid from the comparative material. It is as it is in ethics: all our local conventions of moral behavior and of immoral are without absolute validity, and yet it is quite possible that a modicum of what is considered right and what wrong could be disentangled that is shared by the whole human race. When data are available in psychiatry, this minimum definition of abnormal human tendencies will be probably quite unlike our culturally conditioned, highly elaborated psychoses such as those that are described, for instance, under the terms of schizophrenia and manic-depressive.

26 Cultural Objectivism*

ALFRED KROEBER and CLYDE KLUCKHOHN

Alfred L. Kroeber (1876–1960) was a very influential American anthropologist who taught at the Universities of California and Chicago,
and Columbia, Harvard, and Yale. Founder of the American Anthropological Association, his book, *Anthropology* was the first general text
in the field. Author of hundreds of articles, his books include *Peruvian
Archeology in 1942; Configuration of Culture: Growth, Stimulus Diffusion; The Nature of Culture;* and *Style and Civilization.*

Clyde Kluckhohn (1905–   ) has taught anthropology at the University of New Mexico and Harvard. He is the author of *Beyond the Rainbow, The Navaho, Children of the People,* and *Mirror for Man.*

VALUES AND RELATIVITY

We know by experience that sincere comparison of cultures leads quickly to
recognition of their "relativity." What this means is that cultures are differently weighted in their values, hence are differently structured, and differ
both in part-functioning and in total-functioning; and that true understanding of cultures therefore involves recognition of their particular value systems. Comparisons of cultures must not be simplistic in terms of an arbitrary
or preconceived universal value system, but must be multiple, with each
culture first understood in terms of its own particular value system and
therefore its own idiosyncratic structure. After that, comparison can with
gradually increasing reliability reveal to what degree values, significances,
and qualities are common to the compared cultures, and to what degree
distinctive. In proportion as common structures and qualities are discovered,
the uniquenesses will mean more. And as the range of variability of differ-
entiations becomes better known, it will add to the significance of more
universal or common features—somewhat as knowledge of variability
deepens significance of a statistical mean.

In attaining the recognition of the so-called relativity of culture, we have
only begun to do what students of biology have achieved. The "natural
classification" of animals and plants, which underlies and supplements

* From Alfred Kroeber and Clyde Kluckhohn, *Culture: A Critical Review of Concepts
and Definitions,* Papers of The Peabody Museum, Vol. 47 (1952), No. 1. Reprinted
by permission.

evolutionary development, is basically relativistic. Biologists no longer group together plants by the simple but arbitrary factors of the number of their stamens and pistils, nor animals by the external property of living in sea, air, or land, but by degrees of resemblances in the totality of their structures. The relationship so established then proves usually also to correspond with the sequential developments of forms from one another. It is evident that the comparative study of cultures is aiming at something similar, a "natural history of culture"; and however imperfectly as yet, is beginning to attain it.

It will also be evident from this parallel why so much of culture investigation has been and remains historical in the sense in which we have defined that word. "A culture described in terms of its own structure" is in itself idiographic rather than nomothetic. And if a natural classification implicitly contains an evolutionary development—that is, a history—in the case of life, there is some presupposition that the same will more or less hold for culture. We should not let the customary difference in appelations disturb us. Just as we are in culture de facto trying to work out a natural classification and a developmental history without usually calling them that, we may fairly say that the results attained in historical biology rest upon recognition of the "relativity" of organic structures.

We have already dwelt on the difficulties and slow progress made in determining the causes of cultural phenomena. An added reason for this condition will now be apparent. That is the fact that the comparison of structural patterns is in its nature directed toward what is significant in form rather than what is efficient in mechanism. This is of course even more true for cultural material, in which values are so conspicuously important, than for biological phenomena. And yet there is no reason why causation should not also be determinable in culture data, even if against greater difficulties— much as physiology flourishes successfully alongside comparative and evolutionary biology.

It is evident that as cultures are relativistically compared, both unique and common values appear, or, to speak less in extremes, values of lesser and greater frequency. Here an intellectual hazard may be predicted: an inclination to favor the commoner values as more nearly universal and therefore more "normal" or otherwise superior. This procedure may be anticipated because of the security sense promoted by refuge into absolutes or even majorities. Some attempts to escape from relativism are therefore expectable. The hazard lies in a premature plumping upon the commoner and nearer values and the forcing of these into false absolutes—a process of intellectual short-circuiting. The longer the quest for new absolute values can be postponed and the longer the analytic comparison of relative values can be prosecuted, the closer shall we come to reemerging with at least near-absolutes. There will be talk in those days, as we are beginning to hear it already, that the principle of relativism is breaking down, that its own negativism is defeating it. There have been, admittedly, extravagances and unsound vulgarizations of cultural relativity. Actually, objective relativistic differences between cultures are not breaking down but being fortified. And relativism is not a negative principle except to those who feel that the whole world has lost its values when comparison makes their own private values lose their false absoluteness. Relativism may seem to turn the world fluid; but so did the concepts of evolution and of relativity in physics seem to turn the world fluid when they were new. Like them, cultural and value relativism is a potent instrument of progress in deeper understanding—and not only of the world but of man in the world.

On the other hand, the inescapable fact of cultural relativism does not justify the conclusion that cultures are in all respects utterly disparate monads and hence strictly noncomparable entities. If this were literally true, a comparative science of culture would be *ex hypothesi* impossible. It is, unfortunately the case that up to this point anthropology has not solved very satisfactorily the problem of describing cultures in such a way that objective comparison is possible. Most cultural monographs organize the data in terms of the categories of our own contemporary Western culture: economics, technology, social organization, and the like. Such an ordering, of course, tears many of the facts from their own actual context and loads the analysis. The implicit assumption is that our categories are "given" by nature—an assumption contradicted most emphatically by these very investigations of different cultures. A smaller number of studies have attempted to present the information consistently in terms of the category system and whole way of thought of the culture being described. This approach obviously excludes the immediate possibility of a complete set of common terms of reference for comparison. Such a system of comparable concepts and terms remains to be worked out, and will probably be established only gradually.

In principle, however, there is a generalized framework that underlies the more apparent and striking facts of cultural relativity. All cultures constitute so many somewhat distinct answers to essentially the same questions posed by human biology and by the generalities of the human situation. These are the considerations explored by Wissler under the heading of "the universal culture pattern" and by Murdock under the rubric of "the least common denominators of cultures." Every society's patterns for living must provide approved and sanctioned ways for dealing with such universal circumstances as the existence of two sexes; the helplessness of infants; the need for satisfaction of the elementary biological requirements such as food, warmth, and sex; the presence of individuals of different ages and of differing physical and other capacities. The basic similarities in human biology the world over are vastly more massive than the variations. Equally, there are certain necessities in social life for this kind of animal regardless of where that life is carried on or in what culture. Cooperation to obtain subsistence and for other ends requires a certain minimum of reciprocal behavior, of a standard system of communication, and indeed of mutually accepted values. The facts of human biology and of human group living supply, therefore, certain invariant points of reference from which cross-cultural comparison can start without begging questions that are themselves at issue. As Wissler pointed out, the broad outlines of the ground plan of all cultures is and has to be about the same because men always and everywhere are faced with certain unavoidable problems which arise out of the situation "given" by nature. Since most of the patterns of all cultures crystalize around the same foci, there are significant respects in which each culture is not wholly isolated, self-contained, disparate but rather related to and comparable with all other cultures.

Nor is the similarity between cultures, which in some ways transcends the fact of relativity, limited to the sheer forms of the universal culture pattern. There are at least some broad resemblances in content and specifically in value content. Considering the exhuberant variation of cultures in most respects, the circumstance that in some particulars almost identical values prevail throughout mankind is most arresting. No culture tolerates indiscriminate lying, stealing, or violence within the in-group. The essential universality of the incest taboo is well-known. No culture places a value upon suffering as an end in itself; as a means to the ends of the society (punishment, discipline, etc.), yes; as a means to the ends of the individual (purification, mystical exaltation, etc.), yes; but of and for itself, never. We know of no culture in either space or time, including the Soviet Russian, where the official idology denies an after-life, where the fact of death is not ceremonialized. Yet the more superficial conception of cultural relativity would suggest that at least one culture would have adopted the simple expedient of disposing of corpses in the same way most cultures do dispose of dead animals—i.e., just throwing the body out far enough from habitations so that the odor is not troubling. When one first looks rather carefully at the astonishing variety of cultural detail over the world one is tempted to conclude: human individuals have tried almost everything that is physically possible and nearly every individual habit has somewhere at some time been institutionalized in at least one culture. To a considerable degree this is a valid generalization—but not completely. In spite of loose talk (based upon an uncritical acceptance of an immature theory of cultural relativity) to the effect that the symptoms of mental disorder are completely relative to culture, the fact of the matter is that all cultures define as abnormal individuals who are permanently inaccessible to communication or who fail to maintain some degree of control over their impulse life. Social life is impossible without communication, without some measure of order: the behavior of any "normal" individual must be predictable—within a certain range—by his fellows and interpretable by them.

To look freshly at values of the order just discussed is very difficult because they are commonplaces. And yet it is precisely because they are commonplaces that they are interesting and important. Their vast theoretical significance rests in the fact that despite all the influences that predispose toward cultural variation (biological variation, difference in physical environments, and the processes of history) all of the very many different cultures known to us have converged upon these universals. It is perfectly true (and for certain types of enquiry important) that the value "thou shalt not kill thy fellow tribesman" is not concretely identical either in its cognitive or in its affective aspects for a Navaho, an Ashanti, and a Chukchee. Nevertheless the central conception is the same, and there is understanding between representatives of different cultures as to the general intent of the prohibition. A Navaho would be profoundly shocked if he were to discover that there were no sanctions against in-group murder among the Ashanti.

There is nothing supernatural or even mysterious about the existences of these universalities in culture content. Human life is—and has to be—a moral life (up to a point) because it is a social life. It may safely be presumed that human groups which failed to incorporate certain values into their nascent cultures or which abrogated these values from their older tradition dissolved as societies or perished without record. Similarly, the biological sameness of the human animal (needs and potentialities) has also contributed to convergences.

The fact that a value is a universal does not, of course, make it an absolute. It is possible that changed circumstances in the human situation may lead to the gradual disappearance of some of the present universals. However, the mere existence of universals after so many millennia of culture history and in such diverse environments suggests that they correspond to something extremely deep in man's nature and/or are necessary conditions to social life.

When one moves from the universals or virtual universals to values which merely are quite widespread, one would be on most shaky ground to infer "rightness" or "wrongness," "better" or "worse" from relative incidence. A value may have a very wide distribution in the world at a particular time just because of historical accidents such as the political and economic power of one nation at that time. Nations diffuse their culture into the areas their power reaches. Nevertheless this does not mean one must take all cultural values except universals as of necessarily equal validity. Slavery or cannibalism may have a place in certain cultures that is not evident to the ethnocentric Christian. Yet even if these culture patterns play an important part in the smooth functioning of these societies, they are still subject to a judgment which is alike moral and scientific. This judgment is not just a projection of values, local in time and space, that are associated with Western culture. Rather, it rests upon a *consensus gentium* and the best scientific evidence as to the nature of raw human nature—i.e., that human nature which all cultures mold and channel but never entirely remake. To say that certain aspects of Naziism were morally wrong—is not parochial arrogance. It is—or can be—an assertion based both upon cross-cultural evidence as to the universalities in human needs, potentialities, and fulfillments and upon natural science knowledge with which the basic assumptions of any philosophy must be congruent.

Any science must be adequate to explain both the similarities and the differences in the phenomena with which it deals. Recent anthropology has focussed its attention preponderantly upon the differences. They are there; they are very real and very important. Cultural relativism has been completely established and there must be no attempt to explain it away or to deprecate its importance because it is inconvenient, hard to take, hard to live with. Some values are almost purely cultural and draw their significance only from the matrix of that culture. Even the universal values have their special phrasings and emphases in accord with each distinct culture. And when a culture pattern, such as slavery, is derogated on the ground that it transgresses one of the more universal norms which in some sense and to some degree transcend cultural differences, one must still examine it not within a putatively absolutistic frame but in the light of cultural relativism.

At the same time one must never forget that cultural differences, real and important though they are, are still so many variations on themes supplied by raw human nature and by the limits and conditions of social life. In some ways culturally altered human nature is a comparatively superficial veneer. The common understandings between men of different cultures are very broad, very general, very easily obscured by language and many other observable symbols. True universals or near universals are apparently few in number. But they seem to be as deep-going as they are rare. Relativity exists only within a universal framework. Anthropology's facts attest that the phrase "a common humanity" is in no sense meaningless. This is also important.

Rapoport has recently argued that objective relativism can lead to the development of truly explicit and truly universal standards in science and in values:

> So it is incorrect to say that the scientific outlook is simply a by-product of a particular culture. It is rather the essence of a culture which has not yet been established—a *culture-studying* culture. Ironically, the anthropologists, who often are most emphatic in stating that no noncultural standards of evaluation exist, are among the most active builders of this new culture-studying culture, whose standards transcend those of the cultures which anthropologists study and thus give them an opportunity to emancipate themselves from the limitations of the local standards. The anthropologist can remain the anthropologist both in New Guinea and in Middletown, in spite of the fact that he may have been born in Middletown or in New Guinea.
>
> The moral attitudes contained in the scientific outlook have a different genesis from those contained in ordinary "unconscious" cultures. They are a result of a "freer choice," because they involve a deeper insight into the consequences of the choice.

In sum, cultures are distinct yet similar and comparable. As Steward has pointed out, the features that lend uniqueness are the secondary or variable ones. Two or more cultures can have a great deal of content—and even of patterning—in common and still there is distinctness; there are universals, but relativistic autonomy remains a valid principle. Both perspectives are true and important, and no false either-or antinomy must be posed between them. Once again there is a proper analogy between cultures and personalities. Each human being is unique in his concrete totality, and yet he resembles all other human beings in certain respects and some particular human beings a great deal. It is no more correct to limit each culture to its distinctive features and organization, abstracting out as "precultural" or as "conditions of culture" the likenesses that are universal, than to deny to each personality those aspects that derive from its cultural heritage and from participation in common humanity.

27 An Existentialist Ethic*

JEAN-PAUL SARTRE

Jean-Paul Sartre (1905–) is well known as a leading exponent of atheistic existentialism. Famous for his novels and plays, Sartre's philosophical books include *Existentialism* and *Being and Nothingness*.

What is meant by the term *existentialism?* Can it be that what really scares them in the doctrine I shall try to present here is that it leaves to man a possibility of choice? To answer this question, we must re-examine it on a strictly philosophical plane.

Most people who use the word would be rather embarrassed if they had to explain it, since, now that the word is all the rage, even the work of a musician or painter is being called existentialist. A gossip columnist in *Clartés* signs himself *The Existentialist,* so that by this time the word has been so stretched and has taken on so broad a meaning, that it no longer means anything at all. It seems that for want of an advance-guard doctrine analogous to surrealism, the kind of people who are eager for scandal and flurry turn to this philosophy which in other respects does not at all serve their purposes in this sphere.

Actually, it is the least scandalous, the most austere of doctrines. It is intended strictly for specialists and philosophers. Yet it can be defined easily. What complicates matters is that there are two kinds of existentialist; first, those who are Christian, among whom I would include Jaspers and Gabriel Marcel, both Catholic; and on the other hand the atheistic existentialists, among whom I class Heidegger, and then the French existentialists and myself. What they have in common is that they think that existence precedes essence, or, if you prefer, that subjectivity must be the starting point.

Just what does that mean? Let us consider some object that is manufactured, for example, a book or a paper-cutter: here is an object which has been made by an artisan whose inspiration came from a concept. He referred to the concept of what a paper-cutter is and likewise to a known method of production, which is part of the concept, something which is, by and large, a routine. Thus, the paper-cutter is at once an object produced in a certain way and, on the other hand, one having a specific use; and one can

* From Jean-Paul Sartre, *Existentialism*, trans. Bernard Frechtman, (New York: Philosophical Library, 1947). Reprinted by permission.

not postulate a man who produces a paper-cutter but does not know what it is used for. Therefore, let us say that, for the paper-cutter, essence—that is, the ensemble of both the production routines and the properties which enable it to be both produced and defined—precedes existence. Thus, the presence of the paper-cutter or book in front of me is determined. Therefore, we have here a technical view of the world whereby it can be said that production precedes existence.

When we conceive God as the Creator, He is generally thought of as a superior sort of artisan. Whatever doctrine we may be considering, whether one like that of Descartes or that of Leibnitz, we always grant that will more or less follows understanding or, at the very least, accompanies it, and that when God creates He knows exactly what He is creating. Thus, the concept of man in the mind of God is comparable to the concept of paper-cutter in the mind of the manufacturer, and, following certain techniques and a conception, God produces man, just as the artisan, following a definition and a technique, makes a paper-cutter. Thus, the individual man is the realization of a certain concept in the divine intelligence.

In the eighteenth century, the atheism of the *philosophes* discarded the idea of God, but not so much for the notion that essence precedes existence. To a certain extent, this idea is found everywhere; we find it in Diderot, in Voltaire, and even in Kant. Man has a human nature; this human nature, which is the concept of the human, is found in all men, which means that each man is a particular example of a universal concept, man. In Kant, the result of this universality is that the wild-man, the natural man, as well as the bourgeois, are circumscribed by the same definition and have the same basic qualities. Thus, here too the essence of man precedes the historical existence that we find in nature.

Atheistic existentialism, which I represent, is more coherent. It states that if God does not exist, there is at least one being in whom existence precedes essence, a being who exists before he can be defined by any concept, and that this being is man, or, as Heidegger says, human reality. What is meant here by saying that existence precedes essence? It means that, first of all, man exists, turns up, appears on the scene, and, only afterwards, defines himself. If man, as the existentialist conceives him, is indefinable, it is because at first he is nothing. Only afterward will he be something, and he himself will have made what he will be. Thus, there is no human nature, since there is no God to conceive it. Not only is man what he conceives himself to be, but he is also only what he wills himself to be after this thrust toward existence.

Man is nothing else but what he makes of himself. Such is the first principle of existentialism. It is also what is called subjectivity, the name we are labeled with when charges are brought against us. But what do we mean by this, if not that man has a greater dignity than a stone or table? For we mean that man first exists, that is, that man first of all is the being who hurls himself toward a future and who is conscious of imagining himself as being in the future. Man is at the start a plan which is aware of itself, rather than a patch of moss, a piece of garbage, or a cauliflower; nothing exists prior to this plan; there is nothing in heaven; man will be what he will have planned to be. Not what he will want to be. Because by the word "will" we generally mean a conscious decision, which is subsequent to what we have already made of ourselves. I may want to belong to a political party, write a book, get married; but all that is only a manifestation of an earlier, more spontaneous choice that is called "will." But if existence really does precede essence, man is responsible for what he is. Thus, existentialism's first move is to make every man aware of what he is and to make the full responsibility of his existence rest on him. And when we say that a man is responsible for himself, we do not only mean that he is responsible for this own individuality, but that he is responsible for all men.

The word subjectivism has two meanings, and our opponents play on the two. Subjectivism means, on the one hand, that an individual chooses and makes himself; and, on the other, that it is impossible for man to transcend human subjectivity. The second of these is the essential meaning of existentialism. When we say that man chooses his own self, we mean that every one of us does likewise; but we also mean by that that in making this choice he also chooses all men. In fact, in creating the man that we want to be, there is not a single one of our acts which does not at the same time create an image of man as we think he ought to be. To choose to be this or that is to affirm at the same time the value of what we choose, because we can never choose evil. We always choose the good, and nothing can be good for us without being good for all.

If, on the other hand, existence precedes essence, and if we grant that we exist and fashion our image at one and the same time, the image is valid for everybody and for our whole age. Thus, our responsibility is much greater than we might have supposed, because it involves all mankind. If I am a workingman and choose to join a Christian trade-union rather than be a communist, and if by being a member I want to show that the best thing for man is resignation, that the kingdom of man is not of this world, I am not only involving my own case—I want to be resigned for everyone. As a result, my action has involved all humanity. To take a more individual matter, if I want to marry, to have children; even if this marriage depends solely on my own circumstances or passion or wish, I am involving all humanity in monogamy and not merely myself. Therefore, I am responsible for myself and for everyone else. I am creating a certain image of man of my own choosing. In choosing myself, I choose man.

This helps us understand what the actual content is of such rather grandiloquent words as anguish, forlornness, despair. As you will see, it's all quite simple.

First, what is meant by anguish? The existentialists say at once that man is anguish. What that means is this: the man who involves himself and who realizes that he is not only the person he chooses to be, but also a lawmaker who is, at the same time, choosing all mankind as well as himself, can not help escape the feeling of his total and deep responsibility. Of course, there are many people who are not anxious; but we claim that they are hiding their anxiety, that they are fleeing from it. Certainly, many people believe that when they do something, they themselves are the only ones involved, and when someone says to them, "What if everyone acted that way?" they shrug their shoulders and answer, "Everyone doesn't act that way." But really, one should always ask himself, "What would happen if everybody looked at things that way?" There is no escaping this disturbing thought except by a kind of double-dealing. A man who lies and makes excuses for himself by saying "not everybody does that," is someone with an uneasy conscience, because the act of lying implies that a universal value is conferred upon the lie.

Anguish is evident even when it conceals itself. This is the anguish that Kierkegaard called the anguish of Abraham. You know the story: an angel has ordered Abraham to sacrifice his son; if it really were an angel who has come and said, "You are Abraham, you shall sacrifice your son," everything would be all right. But everyone might first wonder, "Is it really an angel, and am I really Abraham? What proof do I have?"

There was a madwoman who had hallucinations; someone used to speak to her on the telephone and give her orders. Her doctor asked her, "Who is it who talks to you?" She answered, "He says it's God." What proof did she really have that it was God? If an angel comes to me, what proof is there that it's an angel? And if I hear voices, what proof is there that they come from heaven and not from hell, or from the subconscious, or a pathological condition? What proves that they are addressed to me? What proof is there that I have been appointed to impose my choice and my conception of man on humanity? I'll never find any proof or sign to convince me of that. If a voice addresses me, it is always for me to decide that this is the angel's voice; if I consider that such an act is a good one, it is I who will choose to say that it is good rather than bad.

Now, I'm not being singled out as an Abraham, and yet at every moment I'm obliged to perform exemplary acts. For every man, everything happens as if all mankind had its eyes fixed on him and were guiding itself by what he does. And every man ought to say to himself, "Am I really the kind of man who has the right to act in such a way that humanity might guide itself by my actions?" And if he does not say that to himself, he is masking his anguish.

There is no question here of the kind of anguish which would lead to quietism, to inaction. It is a matter of a simple sort of anguish that anybody who has had responsibilities is familiar with. For example, when a military officer takes the responsibility for an attack and sends a certain number of men to death, he chooses to do so, and in the main he alone makes the choice. Doubtless, orders come from above, but they are too broad; he interprets them, and on this interpretation depend the lives of ten or fourteen or twenty men. In making a decision he can not help having a certain anguish. All leaders know this anguish. That doesn't keep them from acting; on the contrary, it is the very condition of their action. For it implies that they envisage a number of possibilities, and when they choose one, they realize that it has value only because it is chosen. We shall see that this kind of anguish, which is the kind that existentialism describes, is explained, in addition, by a direct responsibility to the other men whom it involves. It is not a curtain separating us from action, but is part of action itself.

When we speak of forlornness, a term Heidegger was fond of, we mean only that God does not exist and that we have to face all the consequences of this. The existentialist is strongly opposed to a certain kind of secular ethics which would like to abolish God with the least possible expense. About 1880, some French teachers tried to set up a secular ethics which went something like this: God is a useless and costly hypothesis; we are discarding it; but, meanwhile, in order for there to be an ethics, a society, a civilization, it is essential that certain values be taken seriously and that they be considered as having an *a priori* existence. It must be obligatory, *a priori*, to be honest, not to lie, not to beat your wife, to have children, etc., etc. So we're going to try a little device which will make it possible to show that values exist all the same, inscribed in a heaven of ideas, though otherwise God does not exist. In other words—and this, I believe, is the tendency of everything called reformism in France—nothing will be changed if God does not exist. We shall find ourselves with the same norms of honesty, progress, and humanism, and we shall have made of God an outdated hypothesis which will peacefully die off by itself.

The existentialist, on the contrary, thinks it very distressing that God does not exist, because all possibility of finding values in a heaven of ideas disappears along with Him; there can no longer be an *a priori* Good, since there is no infinite and perfect consciousness to think it. Nowhere is it written that the Good exists, that we must be honest, that we must not lie; because the fact is we are on a plane where there are only men. Dostoievsky said, "If God didn't exist, everything would be possible." That is the very starting point of existentialism. Indeed, everything is permissible if God does not exist, and as a result man is forlorn, because neither within him nor without does he find anything to cling to. He can't start making excuses for himself.

If existence really does precede essence, there is no explaining things away by reference to a fixed and given human nature. In other words, there is no determinism, man is free, man is freedom. On the other hand, if God does not exist, we find no values or commands to turn to which legitimize our conduct. So, in the bright realm of values, we have no excuse behind us, nor justification before us. We are alone, with no excuses.

That is the idea I shall try to convey when I say that man is condemned to be free. Condemned, because he did not create himself, yet, in other respects is free; because, once thrown into the world, he is responsible for everything he does. The existentialist does not believe in the power of passion. He will never agree that a sweeping passion is a ravaging torrent which fatally leads a man to certain acts and is therefore an excuse. He thinks that man is responsible for his passion.

The existentialist does not think that man is going to help himself by finding in the world some omen by which to orient himself. Because he thinks that man will interpret the omen to suit himself. Therefore, he thinks that man, with no support and no aid, is condemned every moment to invent man. Ponge, in a very fine article, has said, "Man is the future of man." That's exactly it. But if it is taken to mean that this future is recorded in heaven, that God sees it, then it is false, because it would really no longer be a future. If it is taken to mean that, whatever a man may be, there is a future to be forged, a virgin future before him, then this remark is sound. But then we are forlorn.

To give you an example which will enable you to understand forlorn-ness better, I shall cite the case of one of my students who came to see me under the following circumstances: his father was on bad terms with his mother, and, moreover, was inclined to be a collaborationist; his older brother had been killed in the German offensive of 1940, and the young man, with somewhat immature but generous feelings, wanted to avenge him. His mother lived alone with him, very much upset by the half-treason of her husband and the death of her older son; the boy was her only consolation.

The boy was faced with the choice of leaving for England and joining the Free French Forces—that is, leaving his mother behind—or remaining with his mother and helping her to carry on. He was fully aware that the woman lived only for him and that his going-off—and perhaps his death— would plunge her into despair. He was also aware that every act that he did for his mother's sake was a sure thing, in the sense that it was helping her to carry on, whereas every effort he made toward going off and fighting was an uncertain move which might run aground and prove completely useless; for example, on his way to England he might, while passing through Spain, be detained indefinitely in a Spanish camp; he might reach England or Algiers and be stuck in an office at a desk job. As a result, he was faced with two very different kinds of action: one, concrete, immediate, but concerning only one individual; the other concerned an incomparably vaster group, a national collectivity, but for that very reason was dubious, and might be interrupted en route. And, at the same time, he was wavering between two kinds of ethics. On the one hand, an ethics of sympathy, of personal devotion; on the other, a broader ethics, but one whose efficacy was more dubious. He had to choose between the two.

Who could help him choose? Christian doctrine? No. Christian doctrine says, "Be charitable, love your neighbor, take the more rugged path, etc., etc." But which is the more rugged path? Whom should he love as a brother? The fighting man or his mother? Which does the greater good, the vague act of fighting in a group, or the concrete one of helping a particular human being to go on living? Who can decide *a priori*? Nobody. No book of ethics can tell him. The Kantian ethics says, "Never treat any person as a means, but as an end." Very well, if I stay with my mother, I'll treat her as an end and not as a means; but by virtue of this very fact, I'm running the risk of treating the people around me who are fighting, as means; and, conversely, if I go to join those who are fighting, I'll be treating them as an end, and, by doing that, I run the risk of treating my mother as a means.

If values are vague, and if they are always too broad for the concrete and specific case that we are considering, the only thing left for us is to trust our instincts. That's what this young man tried to do; and when I saw him, he said, "In the end, feeling is what counts. I ought to choose whichever pushes me in one direction. If I feel that I love my mother enough to sacrifice everything else for her—my desire for vengeance, for action, for adventure—then I'll stay with her. If, on the contrary, I feel that my love for my mother isn't enough, I'll leave." . . .

Forlornness implies that we ourselves choose our being. Forlornness and anguish go together.

As for despair, the term has a very simple meaning. It means that we shall confine ourselves to reckoning only with what depends upon our will, or on the ensemble of probabilities which make our action possible. When we want something, we always have to reckon with probabilities. I may be counting on the arrival of a friend. The friend is coming by rail or street-car; this supposes that the train will arrive on schedule, or that the street-car will not jump the track. I am left in the realm of possibility; but possibilities are to be reckoned with only to the point where my action comports with the ensemble of these possibilities, and no further. The moment the possibilities I am considering are not rigorously involved by my action, I ought to disengage myself from them, because no God, no scheme, can adapt the world and its possibilities to my will. When Descartes said, "Conquer yourself rather than the world," he meant essentially the same thing.

The Marxists to whom I have spoken reply, "You can rely on the support of others in your action, which obviously has certain limits because you're not going to live forever. That means: rely on both what others are doing elsewhere to help you, in China, in Russia, and what they will do later on, after your death, to carry on the action and lead it to its fulfillment, which will be the revolution. You even *have* to rely upon that, otherwise you're immoral." I reply at once that I will always rely on fellow-fighters insofar as these comrades are involved with me in a common struggle, in the unity of a party or a group in which I can more or less make my weight felt; that is, one whose ranks I am in as a fighter and whose movements I am aware of at every moment. In such a situation, relying on the unity and will of the party is exactly like counting on the fact that the train will arrive on time or that the car won't jump the track. But, given that man is free and that there is no human nature for me to depend on, I can not count on men whom I do not know by relying on human goodness or man's concern for the good of society. I don't know what will become of the Russian revolution; I may make an example of it to the extent that at the present time it is apparent that the proletariat plays a part in Russia that it plays in no other nation. But I can't swear that this will inevitably lead to a triumph of the proletariat. I've got to limit myself to what I see.

Given that men are free and that tomorrow they will freely decide what man will be, I can not be sure that, after my death, fellow-fighters will carry on my work to bring it to its maximum perfection. Tomorrow, after my death, some men may decide to set up Fascism, and the others may be cowardly and muddled enough to let them do it. Fascism will then be the human reality, so much the worse for us.

Actually, things will be as man will have decided they are to be. Does that mean that I should abandon itself to quietism? No. First, I should involve myself; then, act on the old saw, "Nothing ventured, nothing gained." Nor does it mean that I shouldn't belong to a party, but rather that I shall have no illusions and shall do what I can. For example, suppose I ask myself, "Will socialization, as such, ever come about?" I know nothing about it. All I know is that I'm going to do everything in my power to bring it about. Beyond that, I can't count on anything. Quietism is the attitude of people who say, "Let others do what I can't do." The doctrine I am presenting is the very opposite of quietism, since it declares, "There is no reality except in action." Moreover, it goes further, since it adds, "Man is nothing else than his plan; he exists only to the extent that he fulfills himself; he is therefore nothing else than the ensemble of his acts, nothing else than his life."

According to this, we can understand why our doctrine horrifies certain people. Because often the only way they can bear their wretchedness is to think, "Circumstances have been against me. What I've been and done doesn't show my true worth. To be sure, I've had no great love, no great friendship, but that's because I haven't met a man or woman who was worthy. The books I've written haven't been very good because I haven't had the proper leisure. I haven't had children to devote myself to because I didn't find a man with whom I could have spent my life. So there remains within me, unused and quite viable, a host of propensities, inclinations, possibilities, that one wouldn't guess from the mere series of things I've done."

Now, for the existentialist there is really no love other than one which manifests itself in a person's being in love. There is no genius other than one which is expressed in works of art; the genius of Proust is the sum of that, there is nothing. Why say that Racine could have written another tragedy, when he didn't write it? A man is involved in life, leaves his impress on it, and outside of that there is nothing. To be sure, this may seem a harsh thought to someone whose life hasn't been a success. But, on the other hand, it prompts people to understand that reality alone is what counts, that dreams, expectations, and hopes warrant no more than to define a man as a disappointed dream, as miscarried hopes, as vain expectations. In other words, to define him negatively and not positively. However, when we say, "You are nothing else than your life," that does not imply that the artist will be judged solely on the basis of his works of art; a thousand other things will contribute toward summing him up. What we mean is that a man is nothing else than a series of undertakings, that he is the sum, the organization, the ensemble of the relationships which make up these undertakings. . . .

Besides, if it is impossible to find in every man some universal essence which would be human nature, yet there does exist a universal human condition. It's not by chance that today's thinkers speak more readily of man's condition than of his nature. By condition they mean, more or less definitely, the *a priori* limits which outline man's fundamental situation in the universe. Historical situations vary; a man may be born a slave in a pagan society or a feudal lord or a proletarian. What does not vary is the necessity for him to exist in the world, to be at work there, to be there in the midst of other people, and to be mortal there. The limits are neither subjective nor objective, or, rather, they have an objective and a subjective side. Objective because they are to be found everywhere and are recognizable everywhere; subjective because they are *lived* and are nothing if man does not live them, that is, freely determine his existence with reference to them. And though the configurations may differ, at least none of them are completely strange to me, because they all appear as attempts either to pass beyond these limits or recede from them or deny them or adapt to them. Consequently, every configuration, however individual it may be, has a universal value.

Every configuration, even the Chinese, the Indian, or the Negro, can be understood by a Westerner. "Can be understood" means that by virtue of a situation that he can imagine, a European of 1945 can, in like manner, push himself to his limits and reconstitute within himself the configuration of the Chinese, the Indian, or the African. Every configuration has universality in the sense that every configuration can be understood by every man. This does not at all mean that this configuration defines man forever, but that it can be met with again. There is always a way to understand the idiot, the child, the savage, the foreigner, provided one has the necessary information. . . .

If anybody thinks that he recognizes here Gide's theory of the arbitrary act, he fails to see the enormous difference between this doctrine and Gide's. Gide does not know what a situation is. He acts out of pure caprice. For us, on the contrary, man is in an organized situation in which he himself is involved. Through his choice, he involves all mankind, and he can not avoid making a choice: either he will remain chaste, or he will marry without having children, or he will marry and have children; anyhow, whatever he may do, it is impossible for him not to take full responsibility for the way he handles this problem. Doubtless, he chooses without referring to pre-established values, but it is unfair to accuse him of caprice. Instead, let us say that moral choice is to be compared to the making of a work of art. And before going any further, let it be said at once that we are not dealing here with an aesthetic ethics, because our opponents are so dishonest that they even accuse us of that. The example I've chosen is a comparison only.

Having said that, may I ask whether anyone has ever accused an artist who has painted a picture of not having drawn his inspiration from rules set up *a priori*? Has anyone ever asked, "What painting ought he to make?" It is clearly understood that there is no definite painting to be made, that the artist is engaged in the making of his painting, and that the painting to be made is precisely the painting he will have made. It is clearly understood that there are no *a priori* aesthetic values, but that there are values which appear subsequently in the coherence of the painting, in the correspondence between what the artist intended and the result. Nobody can tell what the painting of tomorrow will be like. Painting can be judged only after it has once been made. What connection does that have with ethics? We are in the same creative situation. We never say that a work of art is arbitrary. When we speak of a canvas of Picasso, we never say that it is arbitrary; we understand quite well that he was making himself what he is at the very time he was painting, that the ensemble of his work is embodied in his life.

The same holds on the ethical plane. What art and ethics have in common is that we have creation and invention in both cases. We can not decide *a priori* what there is to be done. I think that I pointed that out quite sufficiently when I mentioned the case of the student who came to see me, and who might have applied to all the ethical systems, Kantian or otherwise, without getting any sort of guidance. He was obliged to devise his law himself. Never let it be said by us that this man—who, taking affection, individual action, and kind-heartedness toward a specific person as his ethical first principle, chooses to remain with his mother, or who, preferring to make a sacrifice, chooses to go to England—has made an arbitrary choice. Man makes himself. He isn't ready made at the start. In choosing his ethics, he makes himself, and force of circumstances is such that he can not abstain from choosing one. We define man only in relationship to involvement. It is therefore absurd to charge us with arbitrariness of choice. . . .

28 Ethics without Religion*

KAI NIELSEN

Kai Nielsen is professor of philosophy and chairman of the department
of philosophy of New York University, Washington Square. He is the
author of many important articles in the areas of ethics, political philosophy, and philosophy of religion.

There certainly are fundamental difficulties and perhaps even elements of
incoherence in Christian ethics, but what can a secular moralist offer in its
stead? Religious morality—and Christian morality in particular—may have its
difficulties, but secular morality, religious apologists argue, has still greater
difficulties. It leads, they claim, to ethical scepticism, nihilism, or, at best, to
a pure conventionalism. Such apologists could point out that if we look at
morality with the cold eye of an anthropologist we will—assuming we are
clearheaded—find morality to be nothing more than the often conflicting
mores of the various tribes spread around the globe. If we eschew the kind
of insight that religion can give us, we will have no Archimedean point in
accordance with which we can decide how it is that we ought to live and
die. If we look at ethics from such a purely secular point of view, we will
discover that it is constituted by tribal conventions, conventions which we are
free to reject if we are sufficiently free from ethnocentrism. We can continue
to act in accordance with them or we can reject them and adopt a different
set of conventions; but whether we act in accordance with the old conventions or forge "new tablets," we are still acting in accordance with certain
conventions. Relative to them certain acts are right or wrong, reasonable or
unreasonable, but we cannot justify these fundamental moral conventions
themselves or the ways of life which they partially codify.

When these points are conceded, theologians are in a position to press
home a powerful apologetic point. When we become keenly aware, they
argue, of the true nature of such conventionalism and when we become
aware that there is no overarching purpose that men were destined to fulfill,
the myriad purposes, the aims and goals humans create for themselves, will
be seen not to be enough. When we realize that life does not have a meaning—that is, a significance—which is there to be found, but that we human
beings must by our deliberate decisions give it whatever meaning it has, we

* From Kai Nielsen's "Ethics Without Religion," *The Ohio University Review*, vol. 6
(1964). Reprinted by permission of Professor Nielsen and *The Ohio University Review*.

will (as Sartre so well understood) undergo estrangement and despair. We will drain our cup to its last bitter drop and feel our alienation to the full. Perhaps there are human purposes, purposes to be found *in* life, and we can and do have them even in a Godless world, but without God there can be no one overarching purpose, no one basic scheme of human existence, in virtue of which we could find a meaning for our grubby lives. It is this overall sense of meaning that man so ardently strives for, but it is not to be found in a purely secular worldview. You secularists, a new Pascal might argue, must realize, if you really want to be clear-headed, that no purely human purposes are ultimately worth striving for. What you humanists can give us by way of a scheme of human existence will always be a poor second-best and not what the human heart most ardently longs for.

The considerations for and against an ethics not rooted in a religion are complex and involuted; a fruitful discussion of them is difficult, for in considering the matter our passions, our anxieties, our (if you will) ultimate concerns are involved, and they tend to blur our vision, enfeeble our understanding, of what exactly is at stake. But we must not forget that what is at stake here is just what kind of ultimate commitments or obligations a man could have without evading any issue, without self-deception or without delusion. I shall be concerned to display and assess, to make plain but also to weigh, some of the most crucial considerations for and against a purely secular ethic. While I shall in an objective fashion try to make clear what the central issues are, I shall also give voice to my reflective convictions on this matter. I shall try to make evident my reasons for believing that we do not need God or any religious conception to support our moral convictions. I shall do this, as I think one should in philosophy, by making apparent the dialectic of the problem (by bringing to the fore the conflicting and evolving considerations for and against) and by arguing for what I take to be their proper resolution.

II

I am aware that Crisis Theologians would claim that I am being naive, but I do not see why purposes of purely human devising are not ultimately worth striving for. There is much that we humans prize and would continue to prize even in a Godless world. Many things would remain to give our lives meaning and point even after "the death of God."

Take a simple example. All of us *want* to be happy. But in certain bitter or sceptical moods we question what happiness is or we despairingly ask ourselves whether anyone can really be happy. Is this, however, a sober, sane view of the situation? I do not think that it is. Indeed we cannot adequately define "happiness" in the way that we can "bachelor," but neither can we in that way define "chair," "wind," "pain," and the vast majority of words in everyday discourse. For words like "bachelor," "triangle," or "father" we can specify a consistent set of properties that all the things and only the things denoted by these words have, but we cannot do this for "happiness," "chair," "pain," and the like. In fact, we cannot do it for the great majority of our words. Yet there is no great loss here. Modern philosophical analysis has taught us that such an essentially Platonic conception of definition is unrealistic and unnecessary. I may not be able to define "chair" in the way that I can define "bachelor," but I understand the meaning of "chair" perfectly well. In normal circumstances, at least, I know what to sit on when someone tells me to take a chair. I may not be able to define "pain," but I know what it is like to be in pain, and sometimes I can know when others are in pain. Similarly, though I cannot define "happiness" in the same way that I can define "bachelor," I know what it is like to be happy, and I sometimes can judge with considerable reliability whether others are happy or sad. "Happiness" is a slippery word, but it is not so slippery that we are justified in saying that nobody knows what happiness is.

A man could be said to have lived a happy life if he had found lasting sources of satisfaction in his life and if he had been able to find certain goals worthwhile and to achieve at least some of them. He could indeed have suffered some pain and anxiety, but his life must, for the most part, have been free from pain, estrangement, and despair, and must, on balance, have been a life which he has liked and found worthwhile. But surely we have no good grounds for saying that no one achieves such a balance or that no one is ever happy even for a time. We all have some idea of what would make us happy and of what would make us unhappy; many people, at least, can remain happy even after "the death of God." At any rate, we need not strike Pascalian attitudes, for even in a purely secular world there are permanent sources of human happiness for anyone to avail himself of.

What are they? What are these relatively permanent sources of human happiness that we all want or need? What is it which, if we have it, will give us the basis for a life that could properly be said to be happy? We all desire to be free from pain and want. Even masochists do not seek pain for its own sake; they endure pain because this is the only psychologically acceptable way of achieving something else (usually sexual satisfaction) that is so gratifying to them that they will put up with the pain to achieve it. We all want a life in which sometimes we can enjoy ourselves and in which we can attain our fair share of some of the simple pleasures that we all desire. They are not everything in life, but they are important, and our lives would be impoverished without them.

We also need security and emotional peace. We need and want a life in which we will not be constantly threatened with physical or emotional harassment. Again this is not the only thing worth seeking, but it is an essential ingredient in any adequate picture of the good life.

Human love and companionship are also central to a significant or happy life. We prize them, and a life which is without them is most surely an impoverished life, a life that no man, if he would take the matter to heart, would desire. But I would most emphatically assert that human love and companionship are quite possible in a Godless world, and the fact that life will some day inexorably come to an end and cut off love and companionship altogether enhances rather than diminishes their present value.

Furthermore, we all need some sort of creative employment or meaningful work to give our lives point, to save them from boredom, drudgery, and futility. A man who can find no way to use the talents he has or a man who can find no work which is meaningful to him will indeed be a miserable man. But again there is work—whether it be as a surgeon, a farmer, or a fisherman—that has a rationale even in a world without God. And poetry, music, and art retain their beauty and enrich our lives even in the complete absence of God or the gods.

We want and need art, music, and the dance. We find pleasure in travel and conversation and in a rich variety of experiences. The sources of human enjoyment are obviously too numerous to detail. But all of them are achievable in a Godless universe. If some can be ours, we can attain a reasonable measure of happiness. Only a Steppenwolfish personality beguiled by impossible expectations and warped by irrational guilts and fears can fail to find happiness in the realization of such ends. But to be free of impossible expectations people must clearly recognize that there is no "one big thing" or, for that matter, "small thing" which would make them permanently happy; almost anything permanently and exclusively pursued will lead to that nausea that Sartre has so forcefully brought to our attention. But we can, if we are not too sick and if our situation is not too precarious, find lasting sources of human happiness in a purely secular world.

It is not only happiness for ourselves that can give us something of value, but there is the need to do what we can to diminish the awful sum of human misery in the world. I have never understood those who say that they find contemporary life meaningless because they find nothing worthy of devoting their energies to. Throughout the world there is an immense amount of human suffering, suffering that can, through a variety of human efforts, be partially alleviated. Why can we not find a meaningful life in devoting ourselves, as did Doctor Rieux in Albert Camus's *The Plague*, to relieving somewhat the sum total of human suffering? Why cannot this give our lives point, and for that matter an overall rationale? It is childish to think that by human effort we will someday totally rid the world of suffering and hate, of deprivation and sadness. This is a permanent part of the human condition. But specific bits of human suffering can be alleviated. The plague is always potentially with us, but we can destroy the Nazis and we can fight for racial and social equality throughout the world. And as isolated people, as individuals in a mass society, we find people turning to us in dire need, in suffering and in emotional deprivation, and we can as individuals respond to those people and alleviate or at least acknowledge that suffering and deprivation. A man who says, "If God is dead, nothing matters," is a spoilt child who has never looked at his fellow men with compassion.

Yet, it might be objected, if we abandon a Judaeo-Christian *Weltan-schauung*, there can, in a secular world, be no "one big thing" to give our lives an overall rationale. We will not be able to see written in the stars the final significance of human effort. There will be no architectonic purpose to give our lives such a rationale. Like Tolstoy's Pierre in *War and Peace*, we desire *somehow* to gather the sorry scheme of things entire into one intelligible explanation so that we can finally crack the riddle of human destiny. We long to understand why it is that men suffer and die. If it is a factual answer that is wanted when such a question is asked, it is plain enough. Ask any physician. But clearly this is not what people who seek such answers are after. They want some *justification* for suffering; they want some way of showing that suffering is after all for a good purpose. It can, of course, be argued that suffering sometimes is a good thing, for it occasionally gives us insight and at times even brings about in the man who suffers a capacity to love and to be kind. But there is plainly an excessive amount of human suffering—the suffering of children in childrens' hospitals, the suffering of people devoured by cancer, and the sufferings of millions of Jews under the Nazis—for which there simply is no justification. Neither the religious man nor the secularist can explain, that is justify, such suffering and find some overall "scheme of life" in which it has some place, but only the religious man needs to do so. The secularist understands that suffering is not something to be justified but simply to be struggled against with courage and dignity. And in this fight, even the man who has been deprived of that which could give him some measure of happiness can still find or make for himself a meaningful human existence.

III

I have argued that purely human purposes—those goals that we set for ourselves, the intentions we form—are enough to give meaning to our lives. We desire happiness, and we can find, even in a purely secular world, abundant sources of it. Beyond this we can find a rationale for living in seeking to mitigate the awful burden of human suffering. Given these two considerations we have enough to make life meaningful. But it might be objected that I have put far too great stress on the value of human happiness. There are other considerations in life; there are other values that are intrinsically worthwhile. We desire self-consciousness and some sense of self-identity as well as happiness. And we do not desire them for the enjoyment and happiness that will come from them but for their own sakes.

I am inclined to agree that this is so; human happiness and the desire to avoid suffering are central but not the only facets of morality. To acknowledge this, however, only complicates the secular picture of morality: it gives us no reason to bring in theistic concepts. I admire human beings who are nonevasive and who have a sense of their own identity, and I regard an understanding of myself as something which is to be prized for its own sake. I do not need a deity to support this or give it value.

Philosophers, and some theologians as well, might challenge what I have said in a slightly different way. Even if we add consciousness as another intrinsic good, there is not the close connection between happiness and self-awareness on the one hand and virtue or moral good on the other that I have claimed there is. That men *do* seek happiness as an end is one thing; that they *ought* to seek it as an end is another. As G. E. Moore has in effect shown, we cannot derive "X is good" from "people desire X" or from "X makes people happy," for it is always *meaningful* to ask whether or not happiness is good and whether or not we ought to seek it for its own sake. It will be argued that I, like all secularists, have confused factual and moral issues. An "ought" cannot be derived from an "is"; we cannot deduce that something is good from a discovery that it will make people happy. My hypothetical critic could well go on to claim that we first must justify the fundamental claim that happiness is good. Do we really have any reason to believe that happiness is good? Is the secularist in any more of a position to justify his claim than is the religionist to justify his claim that whatever God wills is good?

I would first like to point out that I have not confused factual and moral issues. One of the basic reasons I have for rejecting either a natural-law ethics or an ethics of divine commands is that both systematically confuse factual and moral issues. We cannot deduce that people ought to do something from discovering that they do it or seek it; nor can we conclude from the proposition that a being exists whom people call "God" that we ought to do whatever that being commands. In both cases we unjustifiably pass from a factual premise to a moral conclusion. Moral statements are not factual statements about what people seek or avoid, or about what a Deity commands. But we do justify moral claims by an appeal to factual claims, and there is a close connection between what human beings desire on reflection and what they deem to be good. "X is good" does not mean "X makes for happiness," but in deciding that something is good, it is crucial to know what makes human beings happy. Both the Christian moralist and the secular moralist lay stress on human happiness. The Christian moralist—St. Augustine and Pascal are perfect examples—argues that only the Christian has a clear insight into what human happiness really is and that there is no genuine happiness without God. But we have no valid grounds for believing that only in God can we find happiness and that there are no stable sources of human happiness apart from God.

I cannot prove that happiness is good, but Christian and non-Christian alike take it in practice to be a very fundamental good. I can, in sum, only appeal to your sense of psychological realism to get you to admit intellectually what in practice you *do* acknowledge, namely, that happiness is good and that pointless suffering is bad. If you *will* acknowledge this, I can show, as I have, that man can attain happiness even in a world without God.

Suppose some Dostoyevskian "underground man" does not care a fig about happiness. Suppose he does not even care about the sufferings of others. How then can you show him to be wrong? But suppose a man doesn't care about God or about doing what He commands either. How can you show that such an indifference to God is wrong? If we ask such abstract questions, we can see a crucial feature about the nature of morality. Sometimes a moral agent may reach a point at which he can give no further justification for his claims but must simply, by his own deliberate decision, resolve to take a certain position. Here the claims of the existentialists have a genuine relevance. We come to recognize that nothing can in the last analysis take the place of a decision or resolution. In the end we must simply decide. This recognition may arouse our anxieties and stimulate rationalization, but the necessity of making a decision is inherent in the logic of the situation. Actually the religious moralist is in a worse position, for he not only needs to subscribe to the principle that human happiness is good and that pain and suffering have no *intrinsic* value; he must also subscribe to the *outré* claims that only in God can man find happiness and that one ought to do whatever it is that God commands. That man can find lasting happiness only if he turns humbly to his Saviour has the look of a factual statement and is a statement that most assuredly calls for some kind of rational support. It is not something we must or can simply decide about. But the assertion that one ought to do what is commanded by God, like the assertion that happiness is good, does appear *simply* to call for a decision for or against. But what it is that one is deciding for when one "decides for God or for Christ" is so obscure as to be scarcely intelligible. Furthermore, the man who subscribes to that religious principle must subscribe to the secular claim as well. But why subscribe to this obscure second principle when there is no evidence at all for the claim that man can find happiness only in God?

Morality is not science. Moral claims *direct* our actions; they tell us how we *ought* to act; they do not simply *describe* what we seek or explain our preferential behavior. A secular morality need not view morality as a science or as an activity that is simply descriptive or explanatory. It can and should remain a normative activity. Secular morality starts with the assumption that happiness and self-awareness are fundamental human goods and that pain and suffering are never desirable in themselves. It may finally be impossible to prove that this is so, but if people will be honest with themselves they will see that in their behavior they clearly show that they subscribe to such a principle, and a philosopher can demonstrate that criticisms of such moral principles rest on confusions. Finally, I have tried to show that a man with secular knowledge alone can find clear and permanent sources of happiness such that whoever will avail himself of these sources of happiness can, if he is fortunate, lead a happy and purposeful life.

IV

The dialectic of our problem has not ended. The religious moralist might acknowledge that human happiness is indeed plainly a good thing while contending that secular morality, where it is consistent and reflective, will inevitably lead to some variety of egoism. An individual who recognized the value of happiness and self-consciousness might, if he were free of religious restraints, ask himself why he should be concerned with the happiness and self-awareness of *others*, except where their happiness and self-awareness would contribute to his own good. We must face the fact that sometimes, as the world goes, people's interests clash. Sometimes the common good is served only at the expense of some individual's interest. An individual must therefore, in such a circumstance, sacrifice what will make him happy for the common good. Morality requires this sacrifice of us, *when it is necessary* for the common good; morality, any morality, exists in part at least to adjudicate between the conflicting interests and demands of people. It is plainly evident that everyone cannot be happy all the time and that sometimes one person's happiness or the happiness of a group is at the expense of another person's happiness. Morality requires that we attempt to distribute happiness as evenly as possible. We must be fair: each person is to count for one and none is to count for more than one. Whether we like a person or not, whether he is useful to his society or not, his interests, and what will make him happy, must also be considered in any final decision as to what ought to be done. The requirements of justice make it necessary that each person be given equal consideration. I cannot justify my neglect of another person in some matter of morality simply on the grounds that I do not like him, that he is *not* a member of my set, or that he is *not* a productive member of society. The religious apologist will argue that behind these requirements of justice as fairness there lurks the ancient religious principle that men are creatures of God, each with an infinite worth, and thus men are never to be treated only as means but as persons deserving of respect in their own right. They have an infinite worth simply as persons.

My religious critic, following out the dialectic of the problem, should query: why should you respect someone, why should you treat all people equally, if doing this is not in your interest or not in the interests of your group? No purely secular justification can be given for so behaving. My critic now serves his *coup de grâce*: the secularist, as well as the "knight of faith," acknowledges that the principle of respect for persons is a precious one—a principle that he is unequivocally committed to, but the religious man alone can *justify* adherence to this principle. The secularist is surreptitiously drawing on Christian inspiration when he insists that all men should be considered equal and that people's rights must be respected. For a secular morality to say all it wants and needs to say, it must, at this crucial point, be parasitical upon a God-centered morality. Without such a dependence on religion, secular morality collapses into egoism.

It may well be the case that, as a historical fact, our moral concern for persons came from our religious conceptions, but it is a well known principle of logic that the validity of a belief is independent of its origin. What the religious moralist must do is to show that only on religious grounds could such a principle of respect for persons be justifiably asserted. But he has not shown that this is so; and there are good reasons for thinking that it is not so. Even if the secularist must simply subscribe to the Kantian principle, "Treat every man as an end and never as a means only," as he must subscribe to the claim, "Happiness is good," it does not follow that he is on worse ground than the religious moralist, for the religious moralist too, as we have seen, must simply subscribe to his ultimate moral principle, "Always do what God wills." *In a way*, the religious moralist's position here is simpler than the secularist's, for he needs only the fundamental moral principle that he ought to do what God wills. The secularist appears to need at least two fundamental principles. But in another and more important way the religious moralist's position is more complex, for he must subscribe to the extraordinarily obscure notion that man is a creature of God and as such has infinite worth. The Kantian principle may in the last analysis simply require subscription, but it is not inherently mysterious. To accept it does not require a crucifixion of the intellect. And if we are prepared simply to commit ourselves to one principle, why not to two principles, neither of which involves any appeal to conceptions whose very intelligibility is seriously in question?

The above argument is enough to destroy the believer's case here. But need we even make those concessions? I do not think so. There is a purely secular rationale for treating people fairly, for regarding them as persons. Let me show how this is so. We have no evidence that men ever lived in a pre-social state of nature. Man, as we know him, is an animal with a culture; he is part of a community, and the very *concept* of community implies binding principles and regulations—duties, obligations and rights. Yet, by an exercise in imagination, we could conceive, in broad outline at any rate, what it would be like to live in such a pre-social state. In such a state no one would have any laws or principles to direct his behaviour. In that sense man would be completely free. But such a life, as Hobbes graphically depicted, would be a clash of rival egoisms. Life in that state of nature would, in his celebrated phrase, "be nasty, brutish and short." Now if men were in such a state and if they were perfectly rational egoists, what kind of community life would they choose, given the fact that they were, very roughly speaking, nearly equal in strength and ability? (That in communities as we find them men are not so nearly equal in power is beside the point, for our *hypothetical* situation.) Given that they all start from scratch and have roughly equal abilities, it seems to me that it would be most reasonable, even for rational egoists, to band together into a community where each man's interests were given equal consideration, where each person was treated as deserving of respect. Each rational egoist would want others to treat him with respect, for his very happiness is contingent upon that; and he would recognize, if he were rational, that he could attain the fullest cooperation of others only if other rational egoists knew or had good grounds for believing that their interests and their persons would also be respected. Such cooperation is essential for each egoist if all are to have the type of community life which would give them the best chance of satisfying their own interests to the fullest degree. Thus, even if men were thorough egoists, we would still have rational grounds for subscribing to a principle of respect for persons. That men are not thoroughly rational, do not live in a state of nature, and are not thorough egoists, does not gainsay the fact that we have rational grounds for regarding social life, organized in accordance with such a principle, as being objectively better than a social life which ignored this principle. The point here is that even rational egoists could see that this is the best possible social organization where men are nearly equal in ability.

Yet what about the world we live in—a world in which, given certain extant social relationships, men are not equal or even nearly equal in power and opportunity? What reason is there for an egoist who is powerfully placed to respect the rights of others, when they cannot hurt him? We can say that his position, no matter how strong, might change and he might be in a position where he would need his rights protected, but this is surely not a strong enough reason for respecting those rights. To be moral involves respecting those rights, but our rational egoist may not propose to be moral. In considering such questions we reach a point in reasoning at which we must simply *decide* what sort of person we shall strive to become. But, as I have said, the religious moralist reaches the same point. He too must make a decision of principle, but the principle he adopts is a fundamentally incoherent one. He not only must decide, but his decision must involve the acceptance of an absurdity.

It is sometimes argued by religious apologists that only if there is a God who can punish men will we be assured that naturally selfish men will be fair and considerate of others. Without this punitive sanction or threat men would go wild. Men will respect the rights of others only if they fear a wrathful and angry God. Yet it hardly seems to be the case that Christians, with their fear of hell, have been any better at respecting the rights of others than non-Christians. A study of the Middle Ages or the conquest of the non-Christian world makes this plain enough. And even if it were true (as it is not) that Christians were better in this respect than non-Christians, it would not show that they had a superior moral reason for their behavior, for in so acting and in so reasoning, they are not giving a morally relevant reason at all but are simply acting out of fear for their own hides. Yet Christian morality supposedly takes us beyond the clash of the rival egoisms of secular life.

In short, Christian ethics has not been able to give us a sounder ground for respecting persons than we have with a purely secular morality. The Kantian principle of respect for persons is actually bound up in the very idea of morality, either secular or religious, and there are good reasons, of a perfectly mundane sort, why we should have the institution of morality as we now have it, namely, that our individual welfare is dependent on having a device which equitably resolves social and individual conflicts. Morality has an objective rationale in complete independence of religion. Even if God is dead, it doesn't really matter.

It is in just this last thrust, it might be objected, that you reveal your true colors and show your own inability to face a patent social reality. At this point the heart of your rationalism is very irrational. For millions of people "the death of God" means very much. It really does matter. In your somewhat technical sense, the concept of God may be chaotic or unintelligible, but this concept, embedded in our languages—embedded in "the stream of life"—has an enormous social significance for many people. Jews and Christians, if they take their religion to heart, could not but feel a great rift in their lives with the loss of God, for they have indeed organized a good bit of their lives around their religion. Their very life-ideals have grown out of these, if you will, myth-eaten concepts. What should have been said is that if "God is dead" it matters a lot, but we should stand up like men and face this loss and learn to live in the Post-Christian era. As Nietzsche so well knew, to do this involves a basic reorientation of one's life and not just an intellectual dissent to a few statements of doctrine.

There is truth in this and a kind of "empiricism about man" that philosophers are prone to neglect. Of course it does matter when one recognizes that one's religion is illusory. For a devout Jew or Christian to give up his God most certainly is important and does take him into the abyss of a spiritual crisis. But in saying that it doesn't *really* matter I was implying what I have argued for in this essay, namely, that if a believer loses his God but can keep his nerve, think the matter over, and thoroughly take it to heart, life can still be meaningful and morality yet have an objective rationale. Surely, for good psychological reasons, the believer is prone to doubt this argument, but if he will only "hold on to his brains" and keep his courage, he will come to see that it is so. In this crucial sense it remains true that if "God is dead" it doesn't really matter.

29 The Emotive Theory of Ethics*

A. J. AYER

Alfred J. Ayer (1910–) is a graduate of Oxford and presently is Wykham Professor of Logic at Oxford University. Introduced to the philosophical movement known as logical positivism at the University of Vienna, Ayer has become known as one of the principal spokesmen for this position. His most controversial book, *Language, Truth and Logic*, is a strong statement of the positivist position. He is also the author of *The Foundations of Empirical Knowledge*, *The Problem of Knowledge*, and *The Concept of a Person and Other Essays*.

It is our business to give an account of "judgements of value" which is both satisfactory in itself and consistent with our general empiricist principles. We shall set outselves to show that in so far as statements of value are significant, they are ordinary "scientific" statements; and that in so far as they are not scientific, they are not in the literal sense significant, but are simply expressions of emotion which can be neither true nor false. In maintaining this view, we may confine ourselves for the present to the case of ethical statements. What is said about them will be found to apply *mutatis mutandis*, to the case of æsthetic statements also.

The ordinary system of ethics, as elaborated in the works of ethical philosophers, is very far from being a homogeneous whole. Not only is it apt to contain pieces of metaphysics, and analyses of non-ethical concepts: its actual ethical contents are themselves of very different kinds. We may divide them, indeed, into four main classes. There are, first of all, propositions which express definitions of ethical terms, or judgements about the legitimacy or possibility of certain definitions. Secondly, there are propositions describing the phenomena of moral experience, and their causes. Thirdly, there are exhortations to moral virtue. And, lastly, there are actual ethical judgements. It is unfortunately the case that the distinction between these four classes, plain as it is, is commonly ignored by ethical philosophers; with the result that it is often very difficult to tell from their works what it is that they are seeking to discover or prove.

In fact, it is easy to see that only the first of our four classes, namely that

* From *Language, Truth and Logic* by A. J. Ayer, Dover Publications, Inc. New York, 1936. Reprinted through the permission of the publisher.

which comprises the propositions relating to the definitions of ethical terms, can be said to constitute ethical philosophy. The propositions which describe the phenomena of moral experience, and their causes, must be assigned to the science of psychology, or sociology. The exhortations to moral virtue are not propositions at all, but ejaculations or commands which are designed to provoke the reader to action of a certain sort. Accordingly, they do not belong to any branch of philosophy or science. As for the expressions of ethical judgements, we have not yet determined how they should be classified. But inasmuch as they are certainly neither definitions nor comments upon definitions, nor quotations, we may say decisively that they do not belong to ethical philosophy. A strictly philosophical treatise on ethics should therefore make no ethical pronouncements. But it should, by giving an analysis of ethical terms, show what is the category to which all such pronouncements belong. And this is what we are now about to do.

A question which is often discussed by ethical philosophers is whether it is possible to find definitions which would reduce all ethical terms to one or two fundamental terms. But this question, though it undeniably belongs to ethical philosophy, is not relevant to our present enquiry. We are not now concerned to discover which term, within the sphere of ethical terms, is to be taken as fundamental; whether, for example, "good" can be defined in terms of "right" or "right" in terms of "good," or both in terms of "value." What we are interested in is the possibility of reducing the whole sphere of ethical terms to non-ethical terms. We are enquiring whether statements of ethical value can be translated into statements of empirical fact.

That they can be so translated is the contention of those ethical philosophers who are commonly called subjectivists, and of those who are known as utilitarians. For the utilitarian defines the rightness of actions, and the goodness of ends, in terms of the pleasure, or happiness, or satisfaction, to which they give rise; the subjectivist, in terms of the feelings of approval which a certain person, or group of people, has towards them. Each of these types of definition makes moral judgements into a sub-class of psychological or sociological judgements; and for this reason they are very attractive to us. For, if either was correct, it would follow that ethical assertions were not generically different from the factual assertions which are ordinarily contrasted with them; and the account which we have already given of empirical hypotheses would apply to them also.

Nevertheless we shall not adopt either a subjectivist or a utilitarian analysis of ethical terms. We reject the subjectivist view that to call an action right, or a thing good, is to say that it is generally approved of, because it is not self-contradictory to assert that some actions which are generally approved of are not right, or that some things which are generally approved of are not good. And we reject the alternative subjectivist view that a man who asserts that a certain action is right, or that a certain thing is good, is saying that he himself approves of it, on the ground that a man who confessed that he sometimes approved of what was bad or wrong would not be contradicting himself. And a similar argument is fatal to utilitarianism. We cannot agree that to call an action right is to say that of all the actions possible in the circumstances it would cause, or be likely to cause, the greatest happiness, or the greatest balance of pleasure over pain, or the greatest balance of satisfied over unsatisfied desire, because we find that it is not self-contradictory to say that it is sometimes wrong to perform the action which would actually or probably cause the greatest happiness, or the greatest balance of pleasure over pain, or of satisfied over unsatisfied desire. And since it is not self-contradictory to say that some pleasant things are not good, or that some bad things are desired, it cannot be the case that the sentence "x is good" is equivalent to "x is pleasant," or to "x is desired." And to every other variant of utilitarianism with which I am acquainted the same objection can be made. And therefore we should, I think, conclude that the validity of ethical judgements is not determined by the felicific tendencies of actions, any more than by the nature of people's feelings; but that it must be regarded as "absolute" or "intrinsic," and not empirically calculable.

If we say this, we are not, of course, denying that it is possible to invent a language in which all ethical symbols are definable in non-ethical terms, or even that it is desirable to invent such a language and adopt it in place of our own; what we are denying is that the suggested reduction of ethical to non-ethical statements is consistent with the conventions of our actual language. That is, we reject utilitarianism and subjectivism, not as proposals to replace our existing ethical notions by new ones, but as analyses of our existing ethical notions. Our contention is simply that, in our language, sentences which contain normative ethical symbols are not equivalent to sentences which express psychological propositions, or indeed empirical propositions of any kind.

It is advisable here to make it plain that it is only normative ethical symbols, and not descriptive ethical symbols, that are held by us to be indefinable in factual terms. There is a danger of confusing these two types of symbols, because they are commonly constituted by signs of the same sensible form. Thus a complex sign of the form "x is wrong" may constitute a sentence which expresses a moral judgement concerning a certain type of conduct, or it may constitute a sentence which states that a certain type of conduct is repugnant to the moral sense of a particular society. In the latter case, the symbol "wrong" is a descriptive ethical symbol, and the sentence in which it occurs expresses an ordinary sociological proposition; in the former case, the symbol "wrong" is a normative ethical symbol, and the sentence in which it occurs does not, we maintain, express an empirical proposition at all. It is only with normative ethics that we are at present concerned; so that whenever ethical symbols are used in the course of this argument without qualification, they are always to be interpreted as symbols of the normative type.

In admitting that normative ethical concepts are irreducible to empirical concepts, we seem to be leaving the way clear for the "absolutist" view of ethics—that is, the view that statements of value are not controlled by observation, as ordinary empirical propositions are, but only by a mysterious "intellectual intuition." A feature of this theory, which is seldom recognized by its advocates, is that it makes statements of value unverifiable. For it is notorious that what seems intuitively certain to one person may seem doubtful, or even false, to another. So that unless it is possible to provide some criterion by which one may decide between conflicting intuitions, a mere appeal to intuition is worthless as a test of a proposition's validity. But in the case of moral judgements, no such criterion can be given. Some moralists claim to settle the matter by saying that they "know" that their own moral judgements are correct. But such an assertion is of purely psychologocal interest, and has not the slightest tendency to prove the validity of any moral judgement. For dissentient moralists may equally well "know" that their ethical views are correct. And, as far as subjective certainty goes, there will be nothing to choose between them. When such differences of opinion arise in connection with an ordinary empirical proposition, one may attempt to resolve them by referring to, or actually carrying out, some relevant empirical test. But with regard to ethical statements, there is, on the "absolutist" or "intuitionist" theory, no relevant empirical test. We are therefore justified in saying that on this theory ethical statements are held to be unverifiable. They are, of course, also held to be genuine synthetic propositions.

Considering the use which we have made of the principle that a synthetic proposition is significant only if it is empirically verifiable, it is clear that the acceptance of an "absolutist" theory of ethics would undermine the whole of our main argument. And as we have already rejected the "naturalistic" theories which are commonly supposed to provide the only alternative to "absolutism" in ethics, we seem to have reached a difficult position. We shall meet the difficulty by showing that the correct treatment of ethical statements is afforded by a third theory, which is wholly compatible with our radical empiricism.

We begin by admitting that the fundamental ethical concepts are unanalysable, inasmuch as there is no criterion by which one can test the validity of the judgements in which they occur. So far we are in agreement with the absolutists. But, unlike the absolutists, we are able to give an explanation of this fact about ethical concepts. We say that the reason why they are unanalysable is that they are mere pseudo-concepts. The presence of an ethical symbol in a proposition adds nothing to its factual content. Thus if I say to someone, "You acted wrongly in stealing that money," I am not stating anything more than if I had simply said, "You stole that money." In adding that this action is wrong I am not making any further statement about it. I am simply evincing my moral disapproval of it. It is as if I had said, "You stole that money," in a peculiar tone of horror, or written it with the addition of some special exclamation marks. The tone, or the exclamation marks, adds nothing to the literal meaning of the sentence. It merely serves to show that the expression of it is attended by certain feelings in the speaker.

If now I generalise my previous statement and say, "Stealing money is wrong," I produce a sentence which has no factual meaning—that is, expresses no proposition which can be either true or false. It is as if I had written "Stealing money!!"—where the shape and thickness of the exclamation marks show, by a suitable convention, that a special sort of moral disapproval is the feeling which is being expressed. It is clear that there is nothing said here which can be true or false. Another man may disagree with me about the wrongness of stealing, in the sense that he may not have the same feelings about stealing as I have, and he may quarrel with me on account of my moral sentiments. But he cannot, strictly speaking, contradict me. For in saying that a certain type of action is right or wrong, I am not making any factual statement, not even a statement about my own state of mind. I am merely expressing certain moral sentiments. And the man who is ostensibly contradicting me is merely expressing his moral sentiments. So that there is plainly no sense in asking which of us is in the right. For neither of us is asserting a genuine proposition.

What we have just been saying about the symbol "wrong" applies to all normative ethical symbols. Sometimes they occur in sentences which record ordinary empirical facts besides expressing ethical feeling about those facts: sometimes they occur in sentences which simply express ethical feeling about a certain type of action, or situation, without making any statement of fact. But in every case in which one would commonly be said to be making an ethical judgement, the function of the relevant ethical word is purely "emotive." It is used to express feeling about certain objects, but not to make any assertion about them.

It is worth mentioning that ethical terms do not serve only to express feeling. They are calculated also to arouse feeling, and so to stimulate action. Indeed some of them are used in such a way as to give the sentences in which they occur the effect of commands. Thus the sentence "It is your duty to tell the truth" may be regarded both as the expression of a certain sort of ethical feeling about truthfulness and as the expression of the command "Tell the truth." The sentence "You ought to tell the truth" also involves the command "Tell the truth," but here the tone of the command is less emphatic. In the sentence "It is good to tell the truth" the command has become little more than a suggestion. And thus the "meaning" of the word "good," in its ethical usage, is differentiated from that of the word "duty" or the word "ought." In fact we may define the meaning of the various ethical words in terms both of the different feelings they are ordinarily taken to express, and also the different responses which they are calculated to provoke.

We can now see why it is impossible to find a criterion for determining the validity of ethical judgements. It is not because they have an "absolute" validity which is mysteriously independent of ordinary sense-experience, but because they have no objective validity whatsoever. If a sentence makes no statement at all, there is obviously no sense in asking whether what it says is true or false. And we have seen that sentences which simply express moral judgements do not say anything. They are pure expressions of feeling and as such do not come under the category of truth and falsehood. They are unverifiable for the same reason as a cry of pain or a word of command is unverifiable—because they do not express genuine propositions.

Thus, although our theory of ethics might fairly be said to be radically subjectivist, it differs in a very important respect from the orthodox subjectivist theory. For the orthodox subjectivist does not deny, as we do, that the sentences of a moralizer express genuine propositions. All he denies is that they express propositions of a unique non-empirical character. His own view is that they express propositions about the speaker's feelings. If this were so, ethical judgements clearly would be capable of being true or false. They would be true if the speaker had the relevant feelings, and false if he had not. And this is a matter which is, in principle, empirically verifiable. Furthermore they could be significantly contradicted. For if I say, "Tolerance is a virtue," and someone answers, "You don't approve of it," he would, on the ordinary subjectivist theory, be contradicting me. On our theory, he would not be contradicting me, because, in saying that tolerance was a virtue, I should not be making any statement about my own feelings or about anything else. I should simply be evincing my feelings, which is not at all the same thing as saying that I have them.

The distinction between the expression of feeling and the assertion of feeling is complicated by the fact that the assertion that one has a certain feeling often accompanies the expression of that feeling, and is then, indeed, a factor in the expression of that feeling. Thus I may simultaneously express boredom and say that I am bored, and in that case my utterance of the words, "I am bored," is one of the circumstances which make it true to say that I am expressing or evincing boredom. But I can express boredom without actually saying that I am bored. I can express it by my tone and gestures, while making a statement about something wholly unconnected with it, or by an ejaculation, or without uttering any words at all. So that even if the assertion that one has a certain feeling always involves the expression of that feeling, the expression of a feeling assuredly does not always involve the assertion that one has it. And this is the important point to grasp in considering the distinction between our theory and the ordinary subjectivist theory. For whereas the subjectivist holds that ethical statements actually assert the existence of certain feelings, we hold that ethical statements are expressions and excitants of feeling which do not necessarily involve any assertions.

We have already remarked that the main objection to the ordinary subjectivist theory is that the validity of ethical judgements is not determined by the nature of their author's feelings. And this is an objection which our theory escapes. For it does not imply that the existence of any feelings is a necessary and sufficient condition of the validity of an ethical judgement. It implies, on the contrary, that ethical judgements have no validity.

There is, however, a celebrated argument against subjectivist theories which our theory does not escape. It has been pointed out by Moore that if ethical statements were simply statements about the speaker's feelings, it would be impossible to argue about questions of value.[1] To take a typical example: if a man said that thrift was a virtue, and another replied that it was a vice, they would not, on this theory, be disputing with one another. One would be saying that he approved of thrift, and the other that *he* didn't; and there is no reason why both these statements should not be true. Now Moore held it to be obvious that we do dispute about questions of value, and accordingly concluded that the particular form of subjectivism which he was discussing was false.

It is plain that the conclusion that it is impossible to dispute about questions of value follows from our theory also. For as we hold that such sentences as "Thrift is a virtue" and "Thrift is a vice" do not express propositions at all, we clearly cannot hold that they express incompatible propositions. We must therefore admit that if Moore's argument really refutes the ordinary subjectivist theory, it also refutes ours. But, in fact, we deny that it does refute even the ordinary subjectivist theory. For we hold that one really never does dispute about questions of value.

This may seem, at first sight, to be a very paradoxical assertion. For we certainly do engage in disputes which are ordinarily regarded as disputes about questions of value. But, in all such cases, we find, if we consider the matter closely, that the dispute is not really about a question of value, but about a question of fact. When someone disagrees with us about the moral value of a certain action or type of action, we do admittedly resort to argument in order to win him over to our way of thinking. But we do not attempt to show by our arguments that he has the "wrong" ethical feeling towards a situation whose nature he has correctly apprehended. What we attempt to show is that he is mistaken about the facts of the case. We argue that he has misconceived the agent's motive: or that he has misjudged the effects of the action, or its probable effects in view of the agent's knowledge; or that he has failed to take into account the special circumstances in which the agent was placed. Or else we employ more general arguments about the effects which actions of a certain type tend to produce, or the qualities which are usually manifested in their performance. We do this in the hope that we have only to get our opponent to agree with us about the nature of the empirical facts for him to adopt the same moral attitude towards them as we do. And as the people with whom we argue have gen-

---

[1] cf. *Philosophical Studies*, "The Nature of Moral Philosophy."

erally received the same moral education as ourselves, and live in the same social order, our expectation is usually justified. But if our opponent happens to have undergone a different process of moral "conditioning" from ourselves, so that, even when he acknowledges all the facts, he still disagrees with us about the moral value of the actions under discussion, then we abandon the attempt to convince him by argument. We say that it is impossible to argue with him because he has a distorted or undeveloped moral sense; which signifies merely that he employs a different set of values from our own. We feel that our own system of values is superior, and therefore speak in such derogatory terms of his. But we cannot bring forward any arguments to show that our system is superior. For our judgement that it is so is itself a judgement of value, and accordingly outside the scope of argument. It is because argument fails us when we come to deal with pure questions of value, as distinct from questions of fact, that we finally resort to mere abuse.

Chapter Four

THE PROBLEM OF POLITICAL NORMS

A SAMPLE ISSUE IN POLITICAL PHILOSOPHY

Suppose that you have tried to be a law-abiding person all your life.
You respect the law and recognize the value of a society ruled by law.
Suppose further, however, that as you grow older, you come to feel that
there are many bad, unjust laws—laws, for instance, that discriminate
against people on irrelevant grounds. Suppose moreover that as a result of
these laws, you find that you cannot be admitted to your state university,
that certain working opportunities afforded to others of your same
abilities are not available to you, that the voting rights supposedly
guaranteed to all are denied to you, and that the legal protection afforded
others is denied to you. You come to feel very strongly about these laws
and unjust circumstances and decide that something must be done to
alter them, for others as well as yourself. So you begin to try to change
these conditions by calling the injustices to the attention of others.
Then you protest to the authorities. You use every means within the legal
order, but little or nothing happens. The power structure in society
permits the same injustices to continue. Frustration or cynicism may set
in and you may simply say to yourself: Well, this is the way the world
is. I'll adapt and get along by hook or crook. If you feel as strongly
about these injustices in society as some do, however, you may decide to
resist and change certain laws not only by using every legal means but
also by refusing to obey the unjust laws (or even violating them), by
demonstrating in organized protests against these conditions in order to

bring pressure to bear on an otherwise unmoved power structure or society.

The above describes the state of affairs and the reactions to it of many black citizens in the United States. Similar unjust conditions and laws have existed in many countries over the years. The Jews certainly felt that many of the laws of Hitler's Third Reich were unjust. Individuals in this country felt the same way about some of the British laws prior to 1776. Today many black South Africans feel similarly about some of the laws there. In each of these cases, there was protest against the injustice of the laws and efforts to change them—but with little success. The problem of the dissenters in these cases is this: Is civil disobedience, even open rebellion, ever justified? If so, under what conditions?

At least some dissenters have sought to answer this question rationally, in the manner of a political philosopher. They have tried to think unemotionally and disinterestedly about it. They have not let the slogans or existing prejudices of the time determine their thinking. They have tried to get the facts clear. Most importantly, they have thought about the aims and purposes of political society and the rights and duties of men. They have offered reasoned arguments for such aims, principles, rights, and duties and then utilized them as normative premises from which they have deduced conclusions about the problem of civil disobedience.

Suppose that in the face of the conditions described, you decide on civil disobedience. What would be your reasons? Would you argue that there is a standard of justice provided by nature or by God that constitutes a test of the justice of human laws and that only laws that conform to this standard are truly laws and merit obedience? If so, what is this standard? How is it known? Suppose that there is a disagreement over the standard. Is there an independent test or method whereby this can be resolved? Are there some injustices that do not justify civil disobedience? What is the line of demarcation? Suppose that your opponent argues that civil disobedience is never justified, that it destroys the fabric of society and results in worse consequences than the unjust state of affairs. Would you disagree with the empirical aspect of his claim? Suppose that the bad consequences could be clearly predicted. Would you argue that justice must prevail no matter what the cost? Such questions indicate the complexity and multiplicity of issues involved in the attempt to answer rationally a single normative political issue. (See the selections on civil disobedience in this chapter.)

WHY HAVE POLITICAL PHILOSOPHY?

Political philosophy operates on the assumption that political decisions (such as refusing to obey the laws) and political institutions (forms of government) stand in need of justification, that both the general principles of such institutions and the policies and actions which reflect those principles must be rationally justified. (See the selections on purposes of political institutions in this chapter.) Why this demand for rational justification? It is simple enough to reply that man is a being who makes such demands. We require reasons for decisions and actions. But perhaps more to the point is the fact that the policies and actions of political institutions condition each of us and, to a large extent, make us what we are. They have far-reaching consequences for human happiness and misery. Often these policies and actions conflict with what we as individuals *want* to do or think we *ought* to do. Political institutions sometimes embody incompatible principles and policies and often conflict with the political institutions of other countries. Such conflict situations force the evaluation of political principles and institutions.

As David Hume argued in the eighteenth century, the fact that the needs and purposes of men conflict constitutes the raison d'être for moral philosophy and the concern for justice. He asks us to imagine a world in which there is no such conflict, one in which all desires and needs can be satisfied. In such a world, there would be no demand for principles of justice or their justification.[1] Sir Isaiah Berlin argues the same point with regard to political philosophy.[2] He asks: In what kind of world is political philosophy possible? He answers: "Only in a world where ends collide," a world in which there is conflict over political goals and purposes. In a world without such conflict, a world in which there is one agreed-upon goal, all conflict would fall in the area of the means to that goal. Such conflicts over means can be handled by the empirical sciences. Although Berlin admits that this oversimplifies the means-ends relationship, his point is plain. There would be no need and no demand for the moral evaluation or justification of political principles if we all agreed on political ends or goals. Our political world clearly is not of this conflict-free type. Nor is our moral world the type Hume asks us to imagine. Thus there is need for both moral and political philosophy.

POLITICAL PHILOSOPHY AS NORMATIVE

Political conflict situations may arise on a variety of levels, ranging from the most general normative principles (Should life, liberty, and the pursuit of happiness constitute our political goals?) to the more specific (Should federal voting registrars be placed in Mississippi?). Let us examine a middle-range issue—the policy of the selective service system in the United States. Is it *fair* that college students be given the opportunity to defer military service and possibly avoid the draft entirely? In terms of the utilization of human resources, it may be *better* for the country for students to complete their educations. But the question here is the fairness or justice of the policy. The two norms operating here seem to be: What is fair to the individual? and What is best for the country? Are they the true bases of military draft policy? Suppose the norms conflict? Which should take precedence?

The primary task of political philosophy is to seek rational answers to questions about political ends and means. Integral with this is the formulation and defense of a set of political norms, which are themselves used as the criteria for evaluating the use and abuse of political power. In the past,

[1] David Hume, *An Enquiry Concerning the Principles of Morals*, 1777.
[2] Sir Isaiah Berlin, "Does Political Theory Still Exist?," in Peter Laslett and W. G. Runciman (eds.), *Philosophy, Politics and Society* (Fairlawn, N.J.: Oxford University Press, 1964).

various political philosophers have set forth alternative normative principles and systems of justification. They have argued for these principles and systems in differing ways. The student of political philosophy must examine and evaluate these various principles and systems—not just to know what influential philosophers have said but to be able to take a broader, more rational approach to political problems, conflicts, and goals.

POLITICAL PHILOSOPHY AS ANALYTIC AND CONCEPTUAL

In the effort to formulate a set of normative political principles and to understand and explain the political order, ordinary human beings have developed and used concepts that are logically related to one another, such as justice, equality, freedom, law, and rights. Political philosophers have closely scrutinized these moral and political concepts, offering analyses of their meaning, logical functions, and relationships. Thus Plato tells us that justice refers to a universal; and Locke, the eighteenth-century British philosopher, remarks that obligation is a mixed mode and has no archetype in nature. Aristotle states that ethics and politics deal with variables and are to be considered sciences only in some sense of that term; and Bentham, the philosopher who initiated utilitarianism, argues that the notion of natural rights is simple nonsense. These claims are not themselves moral or political statements but statements about moral and political statements. They presumably inform us about the meaning, type, or status of the claim being made and the kind of evidence or method of verification appropriate to it. They thereby give accounts of the nature and limits of moral and political justification, that is, the role and limitation of reason in these enterprises. The same sort of analysis takes place when a contemporary philosopher such as Professor Margaret MacDonald claims that the term natural rights is a "hybrid concept," or when S. I. Benn and R. S. Peters remark that man has no essence, or when H. L. A. Hart points out that the equal right of all men to be free is logically presupposed by all talk about "general" or "special" rights.[3] These are all efforts at becoming conceptually clear about the meaning and function of certain key concepts and beliefs in political philosophy.

This analytic, conceptual activity of classical and contemporary philosophers is not ivory-tower stuff. It bears directly on the man on the street, for it is a response to puzzles about concepts which have a direct relationship to conduct. When Plato argues in the *Euthyphro* that justice does not mean something commanded by the Gods, his analysis occurs in a context in which that appeal is utilized by Euthyphro to charge his father with murder. When Jeremy Bentham claims that the notion of natural rights is nonsense, his assertion occurs in a context in which he expresses the fear that this appeal will excite and keep up a spirit of resistance to all laws. When Friedrich Engels, coauthor of *The Communist Manifesto*, denies that the idea of

---

[3] Margaret MacDonald, "Human Rights," *Proceedings of the Aristotelian Society*, 1947–1948; S. I. Benn and R. S. Peters, *The Principles of Political Thought*, (New York: Collier Books, The Macmillan Company, 1964); H. L. A. Hart, "Are There Any Natural Rghts?," *Philosophical Review*, vol. 64 (1955).

equality is an eternal truth and asserts that any demand for equality which goes beyond the proletarian demand for the abolition of classes is absurd, he does so in a context in which he is concerned to extend equality to the social and economic sphere. When Thomas Hobbes, the seventeenth-century British philosopher, utilizes the notion of a social contract, at least part of his concern is to voice a new conception of governmental authority, government by consent, and hence a way of asserting the demand for individual liberty.

The effort in all of these cases is that of getting a conceptual grasp of man's moral and political life. Acceptance of a given concept or set of concepts amounts to a way of looking at moral and political life, hopefully an illuminating way. Different philosophers, focusing on diverse parts of our experience or on different data, have offered varying concepts and contrasting frameworks of explanation. But theories are formulated for people who *live* and *act*; therefore, this conceptual activity always was and still continues to be concerned with practical human conduct.

THE EMPIRICAL COMPONENT OF POLITICAL PHILOSOPHY

A third type of activity carried on by the classical political philosopher has been directly empirical. He has accumulated data and set forth empirical hypotheses which are used as premises in arguing for certain political norms or institutions. Accordingly, Hobbes cites empirical data for his thesis of psychological egoism—the view that the motivation of every man is self-interest. Then he uses this thesis as a key premise in arriving at some of his political norms. Sometimes it is difficult to tell whether a given claim is set forth as empirical or not. Both Rousseau and Hobbes speak of the "state of nature," a condition prior to the social contract, and it seems at times that they are describing a historical state of affairs that actually existed. But it may well be that they (at least Hobbes) are not setting this forth as an empirical, historical claim but as a formulation of what *would* be the case if no social contract, no political institutions, existed. Marx and Engels set forth a theory of history which, on occasion at least, *appears* to be empirically grounded and which functions as a basic premise in developing political standards. It is the task of the political philosopher as an analyst to introduce conceptual clarity by asking whether a given assertion by a political philosopher is empirical, normative, a priori, or metaphysical.

Many empirical theses upon examination turn out to be false or at least inadequately substantiated; and some political theorists distort facts by paying exclusive attention to some details and not to others. Their normative concern to change what they take to be evil and to reorient the purposes of society leads them to give inaccurate pictures of existing societies and political institutions. That we obtain the truth about these matters is crucially important, for if we are ignorant of certain facts or misinformed about them, or if we choose to ignore them, then our normative suggestions will be irrational. In part at least, this careful attention to facts is what distinguishes the political philosopher from the utopian dreamer or the ideologue.

It is true, of course, that most of the empirical work done inadequately by the classical political philosophers is now being done by the new sciences of man—psychology, sociology, and political science. Data from these sciences undoubtedly introduce greater rationality into political decisions or decisions of public policy. If, for example, the pschologists and sociologists are correct that capital punishment does not act as a deterrent to crime, doesn't this affect one's reflection on the rationality of laws of capital punishment? Or suppose that data from these sciences show that certain men although legally regarded as sane can not control their actions. Would it be wise for society to treat them as criminals? Suppose that social scientists are able to isolate and specify the principal causes of conflict situations in labor-management relations or, say, between nations. Would not such data be crucial in the formulation of public policy on labor-management relations or in the creation of policies of one government toward another? Clearly such kinds of data are very important in arriving at rational public policy decisions or rational rules of political institutions. The advance of empirical knowledge in many areas frequently necessitates an alteration of our normative judgments.

But even though such knowledge is necessary for an adequate political philosophy, it is by no means sufficient. In itself it provides us with no political norms or directions for behavior. It provides us with no guidelines for resolving political conflicts. Some fundamental standards or goals of political institutions must be introduced that in conjunction with these facts enable us to arrive at normative conclusions.

Thus political philosophy can not be purely empirical. Nor can it be purely analytical or conceptual. It must also be normative. Bereft of its concern for principles, it can no longer perform its principal function—the rational justification of the aims and purposes of political society and the provision of guidelines for the reflective resolution of political conflicts. The empirical and conceptual elements are necessary but, in the last analysis, subsidiary to this primary task.

THE PRINCIPAL QUESTIONS OF POLITICAL PHILOSOPHY

What then are the principal questions that the political theorist must try disinterestedly to answer? Essentially they are three: Why should men live in society and have government at all? What should be the aims of political society? What form of government is the best instrument for realizing these purposes? These general questions involve a number of subsidiary questions: Where should the locus of political power reside? Should there be limits to government authority? If so, what are they? Are civil disobedience and revolution ever justified? If so, under what conditions? What is meant by justice in society? How can it be realized? Are there any inalienable rights? What is the basis of political obligation?

These questions are for the most part normative; and classical political theorists have offered different and opposing answers to them. Their answers are rooted in different moral, metaphysical, theological, and scientific beliefs. Beliefs of these different types are combined in various ways by classical political philosophers as they offer both explanation and justification of political principles. To understand and to appraise these various political philosophers and the reasoned arguments and modes of justification that each offers requires that one understand and appraise the various components constituting the essential parts of the models. It may be argued that Aristotle's political philosophy can not be understood or judged without understanding and assessing his moral theory, metaphysics, epistemology, and beliefs about facts in the world. The same holds true for Aquinas, Hobbes, and the others.

It is apparent, then, that political philosophy is a complex and difficult task. There are always new empirical data and new conceptual ways of looking at man's moral and political life, and there are constantly changing conditions of human existence. Each of the classical political philosophers has had something significant to contribute in their answers to the normative questions of political philosophy and to our understanding of political reality. But each may be inadequate in certain respects. It is the business of the political philosopher and the student of political philosophy to sort out these inadequacies, whether they be empirical, conceptual, or normative, and subsequently formulate reasoned answers to the key questions of political philosophy.

SELECTED BIBLIOGRAPHY

Barry, Brian. *Political Argument.* New York, 1965.

Benn, S. I., and Peters, R. S. *Social Principles and the Democratic State.* London, 1959.

Berlin, I. *Two Concepts of Liberty.* Fair Lawn, N.J., 1958.

Blackstone, W. T. *The Concept of Equality.* Minneapolis, 1969.

Carritt, E. F. *Ethical and Political Thinking.* Oxford, 1947.

Cohen, M. R. *Law and the Social Order.* New York, 1933.

Hart, H. L. A. *Law, Liberty and Morality.* New York, 1963.

Hobhouse, L. T. *Metaphysical Theory of the State.* London, 1918.

Hook, Sidney. *From Hegel to Marx.* Ann Arbor, Mich., 1962.

Kant, Immanuel. *Philosophy of Law.* Edinburgh, 1887.

Laslett, P. (ed.). *Philosophy, Politics and Society.* 1st ser. New York, 1956.

Laslett, P., and W. G. Runciman (eds.). *Philosophy, Politics and Society.* 2d ser. Oxford, 1964.

Mabbott, J. D. *The State and the Citizen.* London, 1948.

Machiavelli, Nicolo. *The Prince* (1513). New York, 1939.

Olafson, Frederick (ed.). *Justice and Social Policy.* Englewood Cliffs, N.J., 1961.

Olafson, Frederick. *Society, Law and Morality.* Englewood Cliffs, N.J., 1961.

Popper, Carl. *The Open Society and its Enemies.* London, 1950.

Sabine, George H. *A History of Political Theory.* New York, 1937.

Strauss, Leo. *Natural Right and History.* Chicago, 1953.

Tawney, R. H. *Equality.* London, 1931.

————. *The Acquisitive Society.* London, 1921.

Weldon, T. D. *The Vocabulary of Politics.* Baltimore, Md., 1953.

Venable, Vernon. *Human Nature: The Marxist View.* New York, 1946.

THE PURPOSES
OF POLITICAL SOCIETY

30 The Nature of the State[*]

THOMAS HOBBES

Thomas Hobbes (1588–1679) was an English philosopher whose greatest impact has been in the area of political philosophy. Best known for his *Leviathan*, Hobbes also authored *Elements of Law, De Corpore, De Homine*, and *De Cive*. These books constitute part of his ambitious effort to write philosophical treatises on physical nature, human nature, and society.

OF THE NATURAL CONDITION OF MANKIND AS CONCERNING THEIR FELICITY, AND MISERY

Nature hath made men so equal, in the faculties of the body, and mind; as that though there be found one man sometimes manifestly stronger in body, or of quicker mind than another; yet when all is reckoned together, the difference between man, and man, is not so considerable, as that one man can thereupon claim to himself any benefit, to which another may not pretend, as well as he. For as to the strength of body, the weakest has strength enough to kill the strongest, either by secret machination, or by confederacy with others, that are in the same danger with himself.

And as to the faculties of the mind, setting aside the arts grounded upon words, and especially that skill of proceeding upon general, and infallible rules, called science; which very few have, and but in few things; as being not a native faculty, born with us; nor attained, as prudence, while we look after somewhat else, I find yet a greater equality amongst men, than that of strength. For prudence, is but experience; which equal time, equally bestows on all men, in those things they equally apply themselves unto. That which may perhaps make such equality incredible, is but a vain conceit of one's

* From Thomas Hobbes, *Leviathan*, Molesworth Edition, 1841.

own wisdom, which almost all men think they have in a greater degree, than the vulgar; that is, than all men but themselves, and a few others, whom by fame, or for concurring with themselves, they approve. For such is the nature of men, that howsoever they may acknowledge many others to be more witty, or more eloquent, or more learned; yet they will hardly believe there be many so wise as themselves; for they see their own wit at hand, and other men's at a distance. But this proveth rather that men are in that point equal, than unequal. For there is not ordinarily a greater sign of the equal distribution of any thing, than that every man is contented with his share.

From this equality of ability, ariseth equality of hope in the attaining of our ends. And therefore if any two men desire the same thing, which nevertheless they cannot both enjoy, they become enemies; and in the way to their end, which is principally their own conservation, and sometimes their delectation only, endeavour to destroy, or subdue one another. And from hence it comes to pass, that where an invader hath no more to fear, than another man's single power; if one plant, sow, build, or possess a convenient seat, others may probably be expected to come prepared with forces united, to dispossess, and deprive him, not only of the fruit of his labour, but also of his life, or liberty. And the invader again is in the like danger of another.

And from this diffidence of one another, there is no way for any man to secure himself, so reasonable, as anticipation; that is, by force, or wiles, to master the persons of all men he can, so long, till he see no other power great enough to endanger him: and this is no more than his own conservation requireth, and is generally allowed. Also because there be some, that taking pleasure in contemplating their own power in the acts of conquest, which they pursue farther than their security requires; if others, that otherwise would be glad to be at ease within modest bounds, should not by invasion increase their power, they would not be able, long time, by standing only on their defence, to subsist. And by consequence, such augmentation of dominion over men being necessary to a man's conservation, it ought to be allowed him.

Again, men have no pleasure, but on the contrary a great deal of grief, in keeping company, where there is no power able to over-awe them all. For every man looketh that his companion should value him, at the same rate he sets upon himself: and upon all signs of contempt, or undervaluing, naturally endeavours, as far as he dares, (which amongst them that have no common power to keep them in quiet, is far enough to make them destroy each other), to extort a greater value from his contemners, by damage; and from others, by the example.

So that in the nature of man, we find three principal causes of quarrel. First, competition; secondly, diffidence; thirdly, glory.

The first, maketh men invade for gain; the second, for safety; and the third, for reputation. The first use violence, to make themselves masters of other men's persons, wives, children, and cattle; the second, to defend them; the third, for trifles, as a word, a smile, a different opinion, and any other sign of undervalue, either direct in their persons, or by reflection in their kindred, their friends, their nation, their profession, or their name.

Hereby it is manifest, that during the time men live without a common power to keep them all in awe, they are in that condition which is called war; and such a war, as is of every man, against every man. For WAR, consisteth not in battle only, or the act of fighting; but in a tract of time, wherein the will to contend by battle is sufficiently known: and therefore the notion of *time*, is to be considered in the nature of war; as it is in the nature of weather. For as the nature of foul weather, lieth not in a shower or two of rain; but in an inclination thereto of many days together: so the nature of war, consisteth not in actual fighting; but in the known disposition thereto, during all the time there is no assurance to the contrary. All other time is PEACE.

Whatsoever therefore is consequent to a time of war, where every man is enemy to every man; the same is consequent to the time, wherein men live without other security, than what their own strength, and their own invention shall furnish them withal. In such condition, there is no place for industry; because the fruit thereof is uncertain: and consequently no culture of the earth; no navigation, nor use of the commodities that may be imported by sea; no commodious building; no instruments of moving, and removing, such things as require much force; no knowledge of the face of the earth; no account of time; no arts; no letters; no society; and which is worst of all, continual fear, and danger of violent death; and the life of man, solitary, poor, nasty, brutish, and short.

It may seem strange to some man, that has not well weighed these things; that nature should thus dissociate, and render men apt to invade, and destroy one another; and he may therefore, not trusting to this inference, made from the passions, desire perhaps to have the same confirmed by experience. Let him therefore consider with himself, when taking a journey, he arms himself, and seeks to go well accompanied; when going to sleep, he locks his doors; when even in his house he locks his chests; and this when he knows there be laws, and public officers, armed, to revenge all injuries shall be done him; what opinion he has of his fellow-subjects, when he rides armed; of his fellow citizens, when he locks his doors; and of his children, and servants, when he locks his chests. Does he not there as much accuse mankind by his actions, as I do by my words? But neither of us accuse man's nature in it. The desires, and other passions of man, are in themselves no sin. No more are the actions, that proceed from those passions, till they know a law that forbids them: which till laws be made they cannot know: nor can any law be made, till they have agreed upon the person that shall make it.

It may peradventure be thought, there was never such a time, nor condition of war as this; and I believe it was never generally so, over all the world: but there are many places, where they live so now. For the savage people in many places of America, except the government of small families, the concord whereof dependeth on natural lust, have no government at all; and live at this day in that brutish manner, as I said before. Howsoever, it may be perceived what manner of life there would be, where there were no common power to fear, by the manner of life, which men that have formerly lived under a peaceful government, use to degenerate into, in a civil war.

But though there had never been any time, wherein particular men were in a condition of war one against another; yet in all times, kings, and persons of sovereign authority, because of their independency, are in continual jealousies, and in the state and posture of gladiators; having their weapons pointing, and their eyes fixed on one another; that is, their forts, garrisons, and guns upon the frontiers of their kingdoms; and continual spies upon their neighbours; which is a posture of war. But because they uphold thereby, the industry of their subjects; there does not follow from it, that misery, which accompanies the liberty of particular men.

To this war of every man, against every man, this also is consequent; that nothing can be unjust. The notions of right and wrong, justice and injustice have there no place. Where there is no common power, there is no law: where no law, no injustice. Force, and fraud, are in war the two cardinal virtues. Justice, and injustice are none of the faculties neither of the body, nor mind. If they were, they might be in a man that were alone in the world, as well as his senses, and passions. They are qualities, that relate to men in society, not in solitude. It is consequent also to the same condition, that there be no propriety, no dominion, no *mine* and *thine* distinct; but only that to be every man's, that he can get; and for so long, as he can keep it. And thus much for the ill condition, which man by mere nature is actually placed in; though with a possibility to come out of it, consisting partly in the passions, partly in his reason.

The passions that incline men to peace, are fear of death; desire of such things as are necessary to commodious living; and a hope by their industry to obtain them. And reason suggesteth convenient articles of peace, upon which men may be drawn to agreement. These articles, are they, which otherwise are called the Laws of Nature: whereof I shall speak more particularly, in the two following chapters.

OF THE FIRST AND SECOND NATURAL LAWS, AND OF CONTRACTS

The right of nature, which writers commonly call *jus naturale*, is the liberty each man hath, to use his own power, as he will himself, for the preservation of his own nature; that is to say, of his own life; and consequently, of doing any thing, which in his own judgment, and reason, he shall conceive to be the aptest means thereunto.

By LIBERTY, is understood, according to the proper signification of the word, the absence of external impediments: which impediments, may oft take away part of a man's power to do what he would; but cannot hinder him from using the power left him, according as his judgment, and reason shall dictate to him.

A LAW OF NATURE, *lex naturalis*, is a precept or general rule, found out by reason, by which a man is forbidden to do that, which is destructive of his life, or taketh away the means of preserving the same; and to omit that, by which he thinketh it may be best preserved. For though they that speak of this subject, use to confound *jus*, and *lex*, *right* and *law*: yet they ought to be distinguished; because RIGHT, consisteth in liberty to do, or to forbear; whereas LAW, determineth, and bindeth to one of them: so that law, and right, differ as much, as obligation, and liberty; which in one and the same matter are inconsistent.

And because the condition of man, as hath been declared in the precedent chapter, is a condition of war of every one against every one: in which case every one is governed by his own reason; and there is nothing he can make use of, that may not be a help unto him, in preserving his life against his enemies; it followeth, that in such a condition, every man has a right to every thing; even to one another's body. And therefore, as long as this natural right of every man to every thing endureth, there can be no security to any man, how strong or wise soever he be, of living out the time, which nature ordinarily alloweth men to live. And consequently it is a precept, or general rule of reason, *that every man, ought to endeavour peace, as far as he has hope of obtaining it; and when he cannot obtain it, that he may seek, and use, all helps, and advantages of war.* The first branch of which rule, containeth the first, and fundamental law of nature; which is, *to seek peace, and follow it.* The second, the sum of the right of nature; which is, *by all means we can, to defend ourselves.*

From this fundamental law of nature, by which men are commanded to endeavour peace, is derived this second law; *that a man be willing, when others are so too, as far-forth, as for peace, and defence of himself he shall think it necessary, to lay down this right to all things; and be contented with so much liberty against other men, as he would allow other men against himself.* For as long as every man holdeth this right, of doing any thing he liketh; so long are all men in the condition of war. But if other men will not lay down their right, as well as he; then there is no reason for any one, to divest himself of his: for that were to expose himself to prey, which no man is bound to, rather than to dispose himself to peace. This is that law of the Gospel; *whatsoever you require that others should do to you, that do ye to them.* And that law of all men, *quod tibi fieri non vis, alterine feceris.*

To *lay down* a man's *right* to any thing, is to *divest* himself of the *liberty*, of hindering another of the benefit of his own right to the same. For he that renounceth, or passeth away his right, giveth not to any other man a right which he had not before; because there is nothing to which every man had not right by nature: but only standeth out of his way, that he may enjoy his own original right, without hindrance from him; not without hindrance from another. So that the effect which redoundeth to one man, by another man's defect of right, is but so much diminution of impediments to the use of his own right original.

Right is laid aside, either by simply renouncing it; or by transferring it to another. By *simply* RENOUNCING; when he cares not to whom the benefit thereof redoundeth. By TRANSFERRING; when he intendeth the benefit thereof to some certain person, or persons. And when a man hath in either manner abandoned, or granted away his right; then is he said to be OBLIGED, or BOUND, not to hinder those, to whom such right is granted, or abandoned, from the benefit of it: and that he *ought*, and it is his DUTY, not to make void that voluntary act of his own: and that such hindrance is INJUSTICE, and INJURY, as being *sine jure*; the right being before renounced, or transferred. So that *injury*, or *injustice*, in the controversies of the world, is somewhat like to that, which in the disputations of scholars is called *absurdity*. For as it is there called an absurdity, to contradict what one maintained in the beginning: so in the world, it is called injustice, and injury, voluntarily to undo that, which from the beginning he had voluntarily done. The way by which a man either simply renounceth, or transferreth his right, is a declaration, or signification, by some voluntary and sufficient sign, or signs, that he doth so renounce, or transfer; or hath so renounced, or transferred the same, to him that accepteth it. And these signs are either words only, or actions only; or, as it happeneth most often, both words, and actions. And the same are the BONDS, by which men are bound, and obliged: bonds, that have their strength, not from their own nature, for nothing is more easily broken than a man's word, but from fear of some evil consequence upon the rupture.

Whensoever a man transferreth his right, or renounceth it; it is either in consideration of some right reciprocally transferred to himself; or for some other good he hopeth for thereby. For it is a voluntary act: and of the voluntary acts of every man, the object is some *good to himself*. And therefore there be some rights, which no man can be understood by any words, or other signs, to have abandoned, or transferred. As first a man cannot lay down the right of resisting them, that assault him by force, to take away his life; because he cannot be understood to aim thereby, at any good to himself. The same may be said of wounds, and chains, and imprisonment; both because there is no benefit consequent to such patience; as there is to the patience of suffering another to be wounded, or imprisoned: as also because a man cannot tell, when he seeth men proceed against him by violence, whether they intend his death or not. And lastly the motive, and end for which this renouncing, and transferring of right is introduced, is nothing else but the security of a man's person, in his life, and in the means of so preserving life, as not to be weary of it. And therefore if a man by words, or other signs, seem to despoil himself of the end, for which those signs were intended; he is not to be understood as if he meant it, or that it was his will; but that he was ignorant of how such words and actions were to be interpreted. . . .

If a covenant be made, wherein neither of the parties perform presently, but trust one another; in the condition of mere nature, which is a condition of war of every man against every man, upon any reasonable suspicion, it is void: but if there be a common power set over them both, with right and force sufficient to compel performance, it is not void. For he that performeth first, has no assurance the other will perform after; because the bonds of words are too weak to bridle men's ambition, avarice, anger, and other passions, without the fear of some coercive power; which in the condition of mere nature, where all men are equal, and judges of the justness of their own fears, cannot possibly be supposed. And therefore he which performeth first, does but betray himself to his enemy; contrary to the right, he can never abandon, of defending his life, and means of living. . . .

OF OTHER LAWS OF NATURE

From that law of nature, by which we are obliged to transfer to another, such rights, as being retained, hinder the peace of mankind, there followeth a third; which is this, *that men perform their covenants made*: without which, covenants are in vain, and but empty words; and the right of all men to all things remaining, we are still in the condition of war.

And in this law of nature, consisteth the fountain and original of JUSTICE. For where no covenant hath preceded, there hath no right been transferred, and every man has right to every thing; and consequently, no action can be unjust. But when a covenant is made, then to break it is *unjust*: and the definition of INJUSTICE, is no other than *the not performance of covenant*. And whatsoever is not unjust, is *just*.

But because covenants of mutual trust, where there is a fear of not performance on either part, as hath been said in the former chapter, are invalid; though the original of justice be the making of covenants; yet injustice actually there can be none, till the cause of such fear be taken away; which while men are in the natural condition of war, cannot be done. Therefore before the names of just, and unjust can have place, there must be some coercive power, to compel men equally to the performance of their covenants, by the terror of some punishment, greater than the benefit they expect by the breach of their covenant; and to make good that propriety, which by mutual contract men acquire, in recompense of the universal right they abandon: and such power there is none before the erection of a commonwealth. And this is also to be gathered out of the ordinary definition of justice in the Schools: for they say, that *justice is the constant will of giving to every man his own*. And therefore where there is no *own*, that is no propriety, there is no injustice; and where there is no coercive power erected, that is, where there is no commonwealth, there is no propriety; all men having right to all things: therefore where there is no commonwealth, there nothing is unjust. So that the nature of justice, consisteth in keeping of valid covenants: but the validity of covenants begins not but with the constitution of a civil power, sufficient to compel men to keep them: and then it is also that propriety begins. . . .

These are the laws of nature, dictating peace, for a means of the conservation of men in multitudes; and which only concern the doctrine of civil society. There be other things tending to the destruction of particular men; as drunkenness, and all other parts of intemperance; which may therefore also be reckoned amongst those things which the law of nature hath forbidden; but are not necessary to be mentioned, nor are pertinent enough to this place.

And though this may seem too subtle a deduction of the laws of nature, to be taken notice of by all men; whereof the most part are too busy in getting food, and the rest too negligent to understand; yet to leave all men inexcusable, they have been contracted into one easy sum, intelligible even to the meanest capacity; and that is, *Do not that to another, which thou wouldest not have done to thyself*; which sheweth him, that he has no more to do in learning the laws of nature, but, when weighing the actions of other men with his own, they seem too heavy, to put them into the other part of the balance, and his own into their place, that his own passions, and self-love, may add nothing to the weight; and then there is none of these laws of nature that will not appear unto him very reasonable.

The laws of nature oblige *in foro interno*; that is to say, they bind to a desire they should take place: but *in foro externo*; that is, to the putting them in act, not always. For he that should be modest, and tractable, and perform all he promises, in such time, and place, where no man else should do so, should but make himself a prey to others, and procure his own certain ruin, contrary to the ground of all laws of nature, which tend to nature's preservation. And again, he that having sufficient security, that others shall observe the same laws towards him, observes them not himself, seeketh not peace, but war; and consequently the destruction of his nature by violence.

And whatsoever laws bind *in foro interno*, may be broken, not only by a fact contrary to the law, but also by a fact according to it, in case a man think it contrary. For though his action in this case, be according to the law; yet his purpose was against the law; which, where the obligation is *in foro interno*, is a breach.

The laws of nature are immutable and eternal; for injustice, ingratitude, arrogance, pride, iniquity, acception of persons, and the rest, can never be made lawful. For it can never be that war shall preserve life, and peace destroy it.

The same laws, because they oblige only to a desire, and endeavour, I mean an unfeigned and constant endeavour, are easy to be observed. For in that they require nothing but endeavour, he that endeavoureth their performance, fulfilleth them; and he that fulfilleth the law, is just.

And the science of them, is the true and only moral philosophy. For moral philosophy is nothing else but the science of what is *good*, and *evil*, in the conversation, and society of mankind. *Good*, and *evil*, are names that signify our appetites, and aversions; which in different tempers, customs, and doctrines of men, are different: and divers men, differ not only in their judgment, on the senses of what is pleasant, and unpleasant to the taste, smell, hearing, touch, and sight; but also of what is conformable, or disagreeable to reason, in the actions of common life. Nay, the same man, in divers times, differs from himself; and one time praiseth, that is, calleth good, what another time he dispraiseth, and calleth evil: from whence arise disputes, controversies, and at last war. And therefore so long as a man is in the condition of mere nature, which is a condition of war, as private appetite is the measure of good, and evil: and consequently all men agree on this, that peace is good, and therefore also the way, or means of peace, which, as I have shewed before, are *justice, gratitude, modesty, equity, mercy*, and the rest of the laws of nature, are good; that is to say; *moral virtues*; and their contrary *vices*, evil. Now the science of virtue and vice, is moral philosophy; and therefore the true doctrine of the laws of nature, is the true moral philosophy. But the writers of moral philosophy, though they acknowledge the same virtues and vices; yet not seeing wherein consisted their goodness; nor that they come to be praised, as the means of peaceable, sociable, and comfortable living, place them in a mediocrity of passions: as if not the cause, but the degree of daring, made fortitude; or not the cause, but the quantity of a gift, made liberality.

These dictates of reason, men used to call by the name of laws, but improperly: for they are but conclusions, or theorems concerning what conduceth to the conservation and defence of themselves; whereas law, properly, is the word of him, that by right hath command over others. But yet if we consider the same theorems, as delivered in the word of God, that by right commandeth all things; then are they properly called laws. . . .

The only way to erect such a common power, as may be able to defend them from the invasion of foreigners, and the injuries of one another, and thereby to secure them in such sort, as that by their own industry, and by the fruits of the earth, they may nourish themselves and live contentedly; is, to confer all their power and strength upon one man, or upon one assembly of men, that may reduce all their wills, by plurality of voices, unto one will: which is as much as to say, to appoint one man, or assembly of men, to bear their person; and every one to own, and acknowledge himself to be author of whatsover he that so beareth their person, shall act, or cause to be acted, in those things which concern the common peace and safety; and therein to submit their wills, every one to his will, and their judgments, to his judgment. This is more than consent, or concord; it is a real unity of them all, in one and the same person, made by covenant of every man with every man, in such manner, as if every man should say to every man, *I authorize and give up my right of governing myself, to this man, or to this assembly of men, on this condition, that thou give up thy right to him, and authorize all his actions in like manner.* This done, the multitude so united in one person, is called a COMMONWEALTH, in Latin CIVITAS. This is the generation of that great LEVIATHAN, or rather, to speak more reverently, of that *mortal god,* to which we owe under the *immortal God,* our peace and defence. For by this authority, given him by every particular man in the commonwealth, he hath the use of so much power and strength conferred on him, that by terror thereof, he is enabled to perform the wills of them all, to peace at home, and mutual aid against their enemies abroad. And in him consisteth the essence of the commonwealth; which, to define it, is *one person, of whose acts a great multitude, by mutual covenants one with another, have made themselves every one the author, to the end he may use the strength and means of them all, as he shall think expedient, for their peace and common defence.*

And he that carrieth this person, is called SOVEREIGN, and said to have *sovereign power;* and every one besides, his SUBJECT.

31 The State of Nature and the Ends of Political Society*

JOHN LOCKE

John Locke (1632–1706) authored his *Treatises on Government* in 1685 and had a tremendous influence on the founding fathers of the American Republic. His *Essay Concerning Human Understanding* (1690) has had great impact in epistemology and philosophy of language.

OF THE STATE OF NATURE

To understand political power right and derive it from its original, we must consider what state all men are naturally in, and that is a state of perfect freedom to order their actions and dispose of their possessions and persons as they think fit, within the bounds of the law of nature, without asking leave or depending upon the will of any other man.

A state also of equality, wherein all the power and jurisdiction is reciprocal, no one having more than another; there being nothing more evident than that creatures of the same species and rank, promiscuously born to all the same advantages of nature and the use of the same faculties, should also be equal one amongst another without subordination or subjection; unless the lord and master of them all should, by any manifest declaration of his will, set one above another, and confer on him by an evident and clear appointment an undoubted right to dominion and sovereignty.

This equality of men by nature the judicious Hooker looks upon as so evident in itself and beyond all question that he makes it the foundation of that obligation to mutual love amongst men on which he builds the duties we owe one another, and from whence he derives the great maxims of justice and charity. His words are:

> The like natural inducement hath brought men to know that it is no less their duty to love others than themselves; for seeing those things which are equal must needs all have one measure; if I cannot but wish to receive good, even as much at every man's hands as any man can wish unto his own soul,

* From John Locke, *Second Treatise on Civil Government*, first published in 1689.

how should I look to have any part of my desire herein satisfied unless myself be careful to satisfy the like desire, which is undoubtedly in other men, being of one and the same nature? To have anything offered them repugnant to this desire must needs in all respects grieve them as much as me; so that, if I do harm, I must look to suffer, there being no reason that others should show greater measure of love to me than they have by me showed unto them; my desire therefore to be loved of my equals in nature, as much as possibly may be, imposeth upon me a natural duty of bearing to them-ward fully the like affection; from which relation of equality between ourselves and them that are as ourselves, what several rules and canons natural reason hath drawn, for direction of life, no man is ignorant. (*Eccl. Pol.* lib. i.).

But though this be a state of liberty, yet it is not a state of license; though man in that state have an uncontrollable liberty to dispose of his person or possessions, yet he has not liberty to destroy himself, or so much as any creature in his possession, but where some nobler use than its bare preservation calls for it. The state of nature has a law of nature to govern it, which obliges every one; and reason, which is that law, teaches all mankind who will but consult it that, being all equal and independent, no one ought to harm another in his life, health, liberty, or possessions; for men being all the workmanship of one omnipotent and infinitely wise Maker—all the servants of one sovereign master, sent into the world by his order, and about his business—they are his property whose workmanship they are, made to last during his, not one another's, pleasure; and being furnished with like faculties, sharing all in one community of nature, there cannot be supposed any such subordination among us that may authorize us to destroy another, as if we were made for one another's uses as the inferior ranks of creatures are for ours. Every one, as he is bound to preserve himself and not to quit his station wilfully, so by the like reason, when his own preservation comes not in competition, ought he, as much as he can, to preserve the rest of mankind, and may not, unless it be to do justice to an offender, take away or impair the life, or what tends to the preservation of the life, the liberty, health, limb, or goods of another.

And that all men may be restrained from invading others' rights and from doing hurt to one another, and the law of nature be observed, which wills the peace and preservation of all mankind, the execution of the law of nature is, in that state, put into every man's hands, whereby everyone has a right to punish the transgressors of that law to such a degree as may hinder its violation; for the law of nature would, as all other laws that concern men in this world, be in vain if there were nobody that in that state of nature had a power to execute that law and thereby preserve the innocent and restrain offenders. And if anyone in the state of nature may punish another for any evil he has done, everyone may do so; for in that state of perfect equality, where naturally there is no superiority or jurisdiction of one over another, what any may do in prosecution of that law, everyone must needs have a right to do.

And thus in the state of nature one man comes by a power over another; but yet no absolute or arbitrary power to use a criminal, when he has got him in his hands, according to the passionate heats or boundless extravagance of his own will; but only to retribute to him, so far as calm reason and conscience dictate, what is proportionate to his transgression, which is so much as may serve for reparation and restraint; for these two are the only reasons why one man may lawfully do harm to another, which is that we call punishment. In transgressing the law of nature, the offender declares himself to live by another rule than that of reason and common equity, which is that measure God has set to the actions of men for their mutual security; and so he becomes dangerous to mankind, the tie which is to secure them from injury and violence being slighted and broken by him. Which being a trespass against the whole species and the peace and safety of it provided for by the law of nature, every man upon this score, by the right he has to preserve mankind in general, may restrain, or, where it is necessary, destroy things noxious to them, and so may bring such evil on any one who has transgressed that law, as may make him repent the doing of it and thereby deter him, and by his example others, from doing the like mischief. And in this case, and upon this ground, *every man has a right to punish the offender and be executioner of the law of nature.*

I doubt not but this will seem a very strange doctrine to some men; but before they condemn it, I desire them to resolve me by what right any prince or state can put to death or punish any alien for any crime he commits in their country. It is certain their laws, by virtue of any sanction they receive from the promulgated will of the legislative, reach not a stranger; they speak not to him, nor, if they did, is he bound to hearken to them. The legislative authority, by which they are in force over the subjects of that commonwealth, has no power over him. Those who have the supreme power of making laws in England, France, or Holland, are to an Indian but like the rest of the world—men without authority; and therefore, if by the law of nature every man has not a power to punish offenses against it as he soberly judges the case to require, I see not how the magistrates of any community can punish an alien of another country, since, in reference to him, they can have no more power than what every man naturally may have over another.

Besides the crime which consists in violating the law and varying from the right rule of reason, whereby a man so far becomes degenerate and declares himself to quit the principles of human nature and to be a noxious creature, there is commonly injury done to some person or other, and some other man receives damage by his transgression; in which case he who has received any damage has, besides the right of punishment common to him with other men, a particular right to seek reparation from him that has done it; and any other person, who finds it just, may also join with him that is injured and assist him in recovering from the offender so much as may make satisfaction for the harm he has suffered.

From these two distinct rights—the one of punishing the crime for restraint and preventing the like offense, which right of punishing is in everybody; the other of taking reparation, which belongs only to the injured party—comes it to pass that the magistrate, who by being magistrate has the common right of punishing put into his hands, can often, where the public good demands not the execution of the law, remit the punishment of criminal offenses by his own authority, but yet cannot remit the satisfaction due to any private man for the damage he has received. That he who has suffered the damage has a right to demand in his own name, and he alone can remit; the damnified person has this power of appropriating to himself the goods or service of the offender by right of self-preservation, as every man has a power to punish the crime to prevent its being committed again, by the right he has of preserving all mankind and doing all reasonable things he can in order to that end; and thus it is that every man, in the state of nature, has a power to kill a murderer, both to deter others from doing the like injury, which no reparation can compensate, by the example of the punishment that attends it from everybody, and also to secure men from the attempts of a criminal who, having renounced reason—the common rule and measure God has given to mankind—has, by the unjust violence and slaughter he has committed upon one, declared war against all mankind, and therefore may be destroyed as a lion or a tiger, one of those wild savage beasts with whom men can have no society nor security. And upon this is grounded that great law of nature, "Whoso sheddeth man's blood, by man shall his blood be shed." And Cain was so fully convinced that every one had a right to destroy such a criminal that, after the murder of his brother, he cries out, "Every one that findeth me, shall slay me"; so plain was it written in the hearts of mankind.

By the same reason may a man in the state of nature punish the lesser breaches of that law. It will perhaps be demanded: with death? I answer: Each transgression may be punished to that degree and with so much severity as will suffice to make it an ill bargain to the offender, give him cause to repent, and terrify others from doing the like. Every offense that can be committed in the state of nature may in the state of nature be also punished equally, and as far forth as it may in a commonwealth; for though it would be beside my present purpose to enter here into the particulars of the law of nature, or its measures of punishment, yet it is certain there is such a law, and that, too, as intelligible and plain to a rational creature and a studier of that law as the positive laws of commonwealths, nay, possibly plainer, as much as reason is easier to be understood than the fancies and intricate contrivances of men, following contrary and hidden interests put into words; for so truly are a great part of the municipal laws of countries, which are only so far right as they are founded on the law of nature, by which they are to be regulated and interpreted.

To this strange doctrine—viz., that in the state of nature every one has the executive power of the law of nature—I doubt not but it will be objected that it is unreasonable for men to be judges in their own cases, that self-love will make men partial to themselves and their friends, and, on the other side, that ill-nature, passion, and revenge will carry them too far in punishing others, and hence nothing but confusion and disorder will follow; and that therefore God has certainly appointed government to restrain the partiality and violence of men. I easily grant that civil government is the proper remedy for the inconveniences of the state of nature, which must certainly be great where men may be judges in their own case; since it is easy to be imagined that he who was so unjust as to do his brother an injury will scarce be so just as to condemn himself for it; but I shall desire those who make this objection to remember that absolute monarchs are but men, and if government is to be the remedy of those evils which necessarily follow from men's being judges in their own cases, and the state of nature is therefore not to be endured, I desire to know what kind of government that is, and how much better it is than the state of nature, where one man commanding a multitude has the liberty to be judge in his own case, and may do to all his subjects whatever he pleases, without the least liberty to any one to question or control those who execute his pleasure, and in whatsoever he does, whether led by reason, mistake, or passion, must be submitted to? Much better it is in the state of nature, wherein men are not bound to submit to the unjust will of another; and if he that judges, judges amiss in his own or any other case, he is answerable for it to the rest of mankind.

It is often asked as a mighty objection, "Where are or ever were there any men in such a state of nature?" To which it may suffice as an answer at present that since all princes and rulers of independent governments all through the world are in a state of nature, it is plain the world never was, nor ever will be, without numbers of men in that state. I have named all governors of independent communities, whether they are, or are not, in league with others; for it is not every compact that puts an end to the state of nature between men, but only this one of agreeing together mutually to enter into one community and make one body politic; other promises and compacts men may make one with another and yet still be in the state of nature. The promises and bargains for truck, etc., between the two men in the desert island, mentioned by Garcilasso de la Vega, in his history of Peru, or between a Swiss and an Indian in the woods of America, are binding to them, though they are perfectly in a state of nature in reference to one another; for truth and keeping of faith belongs to men as men, and not as members of society.

OF THE STATE OF WAR

The state of war is a state of enmity and destruction; and, therefore, declaring by word or action, not a passionate and hasty but a sedate, settled design upon another man's life, puts him in a state of war with him against whom he has declared such an intention, and so has exposed his life to the other's power to be taken away by him or anyone that joins with him in his defense and espouses his quarrel; it being reasonable and just I should have a right to destroy that which threatens me with destruction; for, by the fundamental law of nature, man being to be preserved as much as possible when all cannot be preserved, the safety of the innocent is to be preferred; and one may destroy a man who makes war upon him, or has discovered an enmity to his being, for the same reason that he may kill a wolf or a lion, because such men are not under the ties of the common law of reason, have no other rule but that of force and violence, and so may be treated as beasts of prey, those dangerous and noxious creatures that will be sure to destroy him whenever he falls into their power.

And hence it is that he who attempts to get another man into his absolute power does thereby put himself into a state of war with him, it being to be understood as a declaration of a design upon his life; for I have reason to conclude that he who would get me into his power without my consent would use me as he pleased when he got me there, and destroy me, too, when he had a fancy to it; for nobody can desire to have me in his absolute power unless it be to compel me by force to that which is against the right of my freedom, i.e., make me a slave. To be free from such force is the only security of my preservation; and reason bids me look on him as an enemy to my preservation who would take away that freedom which is the fence to it; so that he who makes an attempt to enslave me thereby puts himself into a state of war with me. He that, in the state of nature, would take away the freedom that belongs to any one in that state must necessarily be supposed to have a design to take away everything else, that freedom being the foundation of all the rest; as he that, in the state of society, would take away the freedom belonging to those of that society or commonwealth must be supposed to design to take away from them everything else, and so be looked on as in a state of war.

This makes it lawful for a man to kill a thief who has not in the least hurt him, nor declared any design upon his life any farther than, by the use of force, so to get him in his power as to take away his money, or what he pleases, from him; because using force where he has no right to get me into his power, let his pretense be what it will, I have no reason to suppose that he who would take away my liberty would not, when he had me in his power, take away everything else. And therefore it is lawful for me to treat him as one who has put himself into a state of war with me, i. e., kill him if I can; for to that hazard does he justly expose himself whoever introduces a state of war and is aggressor in it.

And here we have the plain difference between the state of nature and the state of war which, however some men have confounded, are as far distant as a state of peace, good-will, mutual assistance, and preservation, and a state of enmity, malice, violence, and mutual destruction are one from another.

Men living together according to reason, without a common superior on earth with authority to judge between them, is properly the state of nature. But force, or a declared design of force, upon the person of another, where there is no common superior on earth to appeal to for relief, is the state of war; and it is the want of such an appeal [that] gives a man the right of war even against an aggressor, though he be in society and a fellow subject. Thus a thief, whom I cannot harm but by appeal to the law for having stolen all that I am worth, I may kill when he sets on me to rob me but of my horse or coat; because the law, which was made for my preservation, where it cannot interpose to secure my life from present force, which, if lost, is capable of no reparation, permits me my own defense and the right of war, a liberty to kill the aggressor, because the aggressor allows not time to appeal to our common judge, nor the decision of the law, for remedy in a case where the mischief may be irreparable. Want of a common judge with authority puts all men in a state of nature; force without right upon a man's person makes a state of war both where there is and is not a common judge.

But when the actual force is over, the state of war ceases between those that are in society and are equally on both sides subjected to the fair determination of the law, because then there lies open the remedy of appeal for the past injury and to prevent future harm. But where no such appeal is, as in the state of nature, for want of positive laws and judges with authority to appeal to, the state of war once begun continues with a right to the innocent party to destroy the other whenever he can, until the aggressor offers peace and desires reconciliation on such terms as may repair any wrongs he has already done and secure the innocent for the future; nay, where an appeal to the law and constituted judges lies open, but the remedy is denied by a manifest perverting of justice and a barefaced wrestling of the laws to protect or indemnify the violence or injuries of some men, or party of men, there it is hard to imagine anything but a state of war; for wherever violence is used and injury done, though by hands appointed to administer justice, it is still violence and injury, however colored with the name, pretenses, or forms of law, the end whereof being to protect and redress the innocent by an unbiased application of it to all who are under it; wherever that is not bona fide done, war is made upon the sufferers, who having no appeal on earth to right them, they are left to the only remedy in such cases—an appeal to heaven. . . .

OF POLITICAL OR CIVIL SOCIETY

Man, being born, as has been proved, with a title to perfect freedom and uncontrolled enjoyment of all the rights and privileges of the law of nature equally with any other man or number of men in the world, has by nature a power not only to preserve his property—that is, his life, liberty, and estate

—against the injuries and attempts of other men, but to judge of and punish the breaches of that law in others as he is persuaded the offense deserves, even with death itself in crimes where the heinousness of the fact in his opinion requires it. But because no political society can be, nor subsist, without having in itself the power to preserve the property and, in order thereunto, punish the offenses of all those of that society, there and there only is political society where every one of the members has quitted his natural power, resigned it up into the hands of the community in all cases that exclude him not from appealing for protection to the law established by it. And thus all private judgment of every particular member being excluded, the community comes to be umpire by settled standing rules, indifferent and the same to all parties, and by men having authority from the community for the execution of those rules decides all the differences that may happen between any members of that society concerning any matter of right, and punishes those offenses which any member has committed against the society with such penalties as the law has established; whereby it is easy to discern who are, and who are not, in political society together. Those who are united into one body and have a common established law and judicature to appeal to, with authority to decide controversies between them and punish offenders, are in civil society one with another; but those who have no such common appeal, I mean on earth, are still in the state of nature, each being, where there is no other, judge for himself and executioner, which is, as I have before shown it, the perfect state of nature.

And thus the commonwealth comes by a power to set down what punishment shall belong to the several transgressions which they think worthy of it committed amongst the members of that society—which is the power of making laws—as well as it has the power to punish any injury done unto any of its members by any one that is not of it—which is the power of war and peace—and all this for the preservation of the property of all the members of that society as far as is possible. But though every man who has entered into civil society and is become a member of any commonwealth has thereby quitted his power to punish offenses against the law of nature in prosecution of his own private judgment, yet, with the judgment of offenses which he has given up to the legislative in all cases where he can appeal to the magistrate, he has given a right to the commonwealth to employ his force for the execution of the judgments of the commonwealth, whenever he shall be called to it; which, indeed, are his own judgments, they being made by himself or his representative. And herein we have the original of the legislative and executive power of civil society, which is to judge by standing laws how far offenses are to be punished when committed within the commonwealth, and also to determine, by occasional judgments founded on the present circumstances of the fact, how far injuries from without are to be vindicated; and in both these to employ all the force of all the members when there shall be need.

Whenever, therefore, any number of men are so united into one society as to quit every one his executive power of the law of nature and to resign it to the public, there and there only is a political or civil society. And this is done wherever any number of men, in the state of nature, enter into society to make one people, one body politic, under one supreme government, or else when any one joins himself to, and incorporates with, any government already made; for hereby he authorizes the society or, which is all one, the legislative thereof to make laws for him as the public good of the society shall require, to the execution whereof his own assistance, as to his own decrees, is due. And this puts men out of a state of nature into that of a commonwealth by setting up a judge on earth, with authority to determine all the controversies and redress the injuries that may happen to any member of the commonwealth; which judge is the legislative, or magistrates appointed by it. And wherever there are any number of men, however associated, that have no such decisive power to appeal to, there they are still in the state of nature.

Hence it is evident that absolute monarchy, which by some men is counted the only government in the world, is indeed inconsistent with civil society, and so can be no form of civil government at all; for the end of civil society being to avoid and remedy these inconveniences of the state of nature which necessarily follow from every man being judge in his own case, by setting up a known authority to which everyone of that society may appeal upon any injury received or controversy that may arise, and which everyone of the society ought to obey. Wherever any persons are who have not such an authority to appeal to for the decision of any difference between them, there those persons are still in the state of nature; and so is every absolute prince, in respect of those who are under his dominion.

For he being supposed to have all, both legislative and executive, power in himself alone, there is no judge to be found, no appeal lies open to any one who may fairly and indifferently and with authority decide, and from whose decision relief and redress may be expected of any injury or inconvenience that may be suffered from the prince or by his order; so that such a man, however entitled, 'czar,' or 'grand seignior,' or how you please, is as much in the state of nature with all under his dominion as he is with the rest of mankind; for wherever any two men are who have no standing rule and common judge to appeal to on earth for the determination of controversies of right betwixt them, there they are still in the state of nature, and under all the inconveniences of it, with only this woeful difference to the subject, or rather slave, of an absolute prince: that, whereas in the ordinary state of nature he has a liberty to judge of his right and, according to the best of his power to maintain it; now, whenever his property is invaded by the will and order of his monarch, he has not only no appeal as those in society ought to have but, as if he were degraded from the common state of rational creatures, is denied a liberty to judge of or to defend his right; and so is exposed to all the misery and inconveniences that a man can fear from one who, being in the unrestrained state of nature, is yet corrupted with flattery and armed with power.

For he that thinks absolute power purifies men's blood and corrects the baseness of human nature need read but the history of this or any other age to be convinced of the contrary. He that would have been so insolent and injurious in the woods of America would not probably be much better in a throne, where perhaps learning and religion shall be found out to justify all that he shall do to his subject, and the sword presently silence all those that dare question it; for what the protection of absolute monarchy is, what kind of fathers of their countries it makes princes to be, and to what a degree of happiness and security it carries civil society, where this sort of government is grown to perfection, he that will look into the late relation of Ceylon may easily see.

In absolute monarchies, indeed, as well as other governments of the world, the subjects have an appeal to the law and judges to decide any controversies and restrain any violence that may happen betwixt the subjects themselves, one amongst another. This everyone thinks necessary, and believes he deserves to be thought a declared enemy to society and mankind who should go about to take it away. But whether this be from a true love of mankind and society, and such a charity as we all owe one to another, there is reason to doubt; for this is no more than what every man who loves his own power, profit, or greatness may and naturally must do—keep those animals from hurting or destroying one another who labor and drudge only for his pleasure and advantage; and so are taken care of, not out of any love the master has for them, but love of himself and the profit they bring him; for if it be asked, what security, what fence is there, in such a state, against the violence and oppression of this absolute ruler, the very question can scarce be borne. They are ready to tell you that it deserves death only to ask after safety. Betwixt subject and subject, they will grant, there must be measures, laws, and judges, for their mutual peace and security; but as for the ruler, he ought to be absolute and is above all such circumstances; because he has power to do more hurt and wrong, it is right when he does it. To ask how you may be guarded from harm or injury on that side where the strongest hand is to do it, is presently the voice of faction and rebellion, as if when men, quitting the state of nature, entered into society, they agreed that all of them but one should be under the restraint of laws, but that he should still retain all the liberty of the state of nature, increased with power and made licentious by impunity. This is to think that men are so foolish that they take care to avoid what mischiefs may be done them by polecats or foxes, but are content, nay, think it safety, to be devoured by lions.

But whatever flatterers may talk to amuse people's understandings, it hinders not men from feeling; and when they perceive that any man, in what station soever, is out of the bounds of the civil society which they are of, and that they have no appeal on earth against any harm they may receive from him, they are apt to think themselves in the state of nature in respect of him whom they find to be so, and to take care, as soon as they can, to have that safety and security in civil society for which it was instituted, and for which only they entered into it. And therefore, though perhaps at first (as shall be shown more at large hereafter in the following part of this discourse), some one good and excellent man, having got a pre-eminence amongst the rest, had this deference paid to his goodness and virtue as to a kind of natural authority, that the chief rule, with arbitration of their differences, by a tacit consent devolved into his hands, without any other caution but the assurance they had of his uprightness and wisdom; yet when time, giving authority and (as some men would persuade us) sacredness to customs which the negligent and unforeseeing innocence of the first ages began, had brought in successors of another stamp, the people, finding their properties not secure under the government as then it was—whereas government has no other end but the preservation of property—could never be safe nor at rest nor think themselves in civil society till the legislature was placed in collective bodies of men, call them 'senate,' 'parliament,' or what you please. By which means every single person became subject, equally with other the meanest men, to those laws which he himself, as part of the legislative, had established; nor could any one, by his own authority, avoid the force of the law when once made, nor by any pretense of superiority plead exemption, thereby to license his own or the miscarriages of any of his dependents. No man in civil society can be exempted from the laws of it; for if any man may do what he thinks fit, and there be no appeal on earth for redress or security against any harm he shall do, I ask whether he be not perfectly still in the state of nature, and so can be no part or member of that civil society; unless any one will say the state of nature and civil society are one and the same thing, which I have never yet found any one so great a patron of anarchy as to affirm.

OF THE BEGINNING OF POLITICAL SOCIETIES

Men being, as has been said, by nature all free, equal, and independent, no one can be put out of this estate and subjected to the political power of another without his own consent. The only way whereby any one divests himself of his natural liberty and puts on the bonds of civil society is by agreeing with other men to join and unite into a community for their comfortable, safe, and peaceable living one amongst another, in a secure enjoyment of their properties and a greater security against any that are not of it. This any number of men may do, because it injures not the freedom of the rest; they are left as they were in the liberty of the state of nature. When any number of men have so consented to make one community or government, they are thereby presently incorporated and make one body politic wherein the majority have a right to act and conclude the rest.

For when any number of men have, by the consent of every individual, made a community, they have thereby made that community one body, with a power to act as one body, which is only by the will and determination of the majority; for that which acts any community being only the consent of the individuals of it, and it being necessary to that which is one body to move one way, it is necessary the body should move that way whither the greater force carries it, which is the consent of the majority; or else it is impossible it should act or continue one body, one community, which the consent of every individual that united into it agreed that it should; and so every one is bound by that consent to be concluded by the majority. And therefore we see that in assemblies impowered to act by positive laws, where no number is set by that positive law which impowers them, the act of the majority passes for the act of the whole and, of course, determines, as having by the law of nature and reason the power of the whole.

And thus every man, by consenting with others to make one body politic under one government, puts himself under an obligation to every one of that society to submit to the determination of the majority and to be concluded by it; or else this original compact, whereby he with others incorporates into one society, would signify nothing, and be no compact, if he be left free and under no other ties than he was in before in the state of nature. For what appearance would there be of any compact? What new engagement if he were no further tied by any decrees of the society than he himself thought fit and did actually consent to? This would be still as great a liberty as he himself had before his compact, or any one else in the state of nature has who may submit himself and consent to any acts of it if he thinks fit.

For if the consent of the majority shall not in reason be received as the act of the whole and conclude every individual, nothing but the consent of every individual can make anything to be the act of the whole; but such a consent is next to impossible ever to be had if we consider the infirmities of health and avocations of business which in a number, though much less than that of a commonwealth, will necessarily keep many away from the public assembly. To which, if we add the variety of opinions and contrariety of interests which unavoidably happen in all collections of men, the coming into society upon such terms would be only like Cato's coming into the theatre only to go out again. Such a constitution as this would make the mighty leviathan of a shorter duration than the feeblest creatures, and not let it outlast the day it was born in; which cannot be supposed till we can think that rational creatures should desire and constitute societies only to be dissolved; for where the majority cannot conclude the rest, there they cannot act as one body, and consequently will be immediately dissolved again.

Whosoever, therefore, out of a state of nature unite into a community must be understood to give up all the power necessary to the ends for which they unite into society to the majority of the community, unless they expressly agreed in any number greater than the majority. And this is done by barely agreeing to unite into one political society, which is all the compact that is, or needs be, between the individuals that enter into or make up a commonwealth. And thus that which begins and actually constitutes any political society is nothing but the consent of any number of freemen capable of a majority to unite and incorporate into such a society. And this is that, and that only, which did or could give beginning to any lawful government in the world.

Every man being, as has been shown, naturally free, and nothing being able to put him into subjection to any earthly power but only his own consent, it is to be considered what shall be understood to be a sufficient declaration of a man's consent to make him subject to the laws of any government. There is a common distinction of an express and a tacit consent which will concern our present case. Nobody doubts but an express consent of any man entering into any society makes him a perfect member of that society, a subject of that government. The difficulty is, what ought to be looked upon as a tacit consent, and how far it binds—i. e., how far any one shall be looked upon to have consented and thereby submitted to any government, where he has made no expressions of it at all. And to this I say that every man that has any possessions or enjoyment of any part of the dominions of any government does thereby give his tacit consent and is as far forth obliged to obedience to the laws of that government, during such enjoyment, as anyone under it; whether this his possession be of land to him and his heirs for ever, or a lodging only for a week, or whether it be barely traveling freely on the highway; and, in effect, it reaches as far as the very being of anyone within the territories of that government.

To understand this better, it is fit to consider that every man, when he at first incorporates himself into any commonwealth, he, by his uniting himself thereunto, annexes also, and submits to the community, those possessions which he has or shall acquire that do not already belong to any other government; for it would be a direct contradiction for any one to enter into society with others for the securing and regulating of property, and yet to suppose his land, whose property is to be regulated by the laws of the society, should be exempt from the jurisdiction of that government to which he himself, the proprietor of the land, is a subject. By the same act, therefore, whereby any one unites his person, which was before free, to any commonwealth, by the same he unites his possessions which were before free to it also; and they become, both of them, person and possession, subject to the government and dominion of that commonwealth as long as it has a being. Whoever, therefore, from thenceforth by inheritance, purchase, permission, or otherwise, enjoys any part of the land so annexed to, and under the government of that commonwealth, must take it with the condition it is under—that is, of submitting to the government of the commonwealth under whose jurisdiction it is as far forth as any subject of it.

But since the government has a direct jurisdiction only over the land, and reaches the possessor of it—before he has actually incorporated himself in the society—only as he dwells upon and enjoys that, the obligation anyone is under by virtue of such enjoyment, to submit to the government, begins and ends with the enjoyment; so that whenever the owner, who has given nothing but such a tacit consent to the government, will, by donation, sale, or otherwise, quit the said possession, he is at liberty to go and incorporate himself into any other commonwealth, or to agree with others to begin a new one *in vacuis locis*, in any part of the world they can find free and unpossessed. Whereas he that has once, by actual agreement and any express declaration, given his consent to be of any commonwealth is perpetually and indispensably obliged to be and remain unalterably a subject to it, and can never be again in the liberty of the state of nature, unless by any calamity the government he was under comes to be dissolved, or else, by some public act, cuts him off from being any longer a member of it.

But submitting to the laws of any country, living quietly and enjoying privileges and protection under them, makes not a man a member of that society; this is only a local protection and homage due to and from all those who, not being in a state of war, come within the territories belonging to any government, to all parts whereof the force of its laws extends. But this no more makes a man a member of that society, a perpetual subject of that commonwealth, than it would make a man a subject to another in whose family he found it convenient to abide for some time, though, while he continued in it, he were obliged to comply with the laws and submit to the government he found there. And thus we see that foreigners, by living all their lives under another government and enjoying the privileges and protection of it, though they are bound, even in conscience, to submit to its administration as far forth as any denizen, yet do not thereby come to be subjects or members of that commonwealth. Nothing can make any man so but his actually entering into it by positive engagement and express promise and compact. That is that which I think concerning the beginning of political societies and that consent which makes any one a member of any commonwealth.

OF THE ENDS OF POLITICAL SOCIETY AND GOVERNMENT

If man in the state of nature be so free, as has been said, if he be absolute lord of his own person and possessions, equal to the greatest, and subject to nobody, why will he part with his freedom, why will he give up his empire and subject himself to the dominion and control of any other power? To which it is obvious to answer that though in the state of nature he has such a right, yet the enjoyment of it is very uncertain and constantly exposed to the invasion of others; for all being kings as much as he, every man his equal, and the greater part no strict observers of equity and justice, the enjoyment of the property he has in this state is very unsafe, very unsecure. This makes him willing to quit a condition which, however free, is full of fears and continual dangers; and it is not without reason that he seeks out and is willing to join in society with others who are already united, or have a mind to unite, for the mutual preservation of their lives, liberties, and estates, which I call by the general name 'property.'

The great and chief end, therefore, of men's uniting into commonwealths and putting themselves under government is the preservation of their property. To which in the state of nature there are many things wanting:

First, there wants an established, settled, known law, received and allowed by common consent to be the standard of right and wrong and the common measure to decide all controversies between them; for though the law of nature be plain and intelligible to all rational creatures, yet men, being biased by their interest as well as ignorant for want of studying it, are not apt to allow of it as a law binding to them in the application of it to their particular cases.

Secondly, in the state of nature there wants a known and indifferent judge with authority to determine all differences according to the established law; for every one in that state being both judge and executioner of the law of nature, men being partial to themselves, passion and revenge is very apt to carry them too far and with too much heat in their own cases, as well as negligence and unconcernedness to make them too remiss in other men's.

Thirdly, in the state of nature there often wants power to back and support the sentence when right, and to give it due execution. They who by any injustice offend will seldom fail, where they are able, by force, to make good their injustice; such resistance many times makes the punishment dangerous and frequently destructiive to those who attempt it.

Thus mankind, notwithstanding all the privileges of the state of nature, being but in an ill condition while they remain in it, are quickly driven into society. Hence it comes to pass that we seldom find any number of men live any time together in this state. The inconveniences that they are therein exposed to by the irregular and uncertain exercise of the power every man has of punishing the transgressions of others make them take sanctuary under the established laws of government and therein seek the preservation of their property. It is this makes them so willingly give up every one his single power of punishing, to be exercised by such alone as shall be appointed to it amongst them; and by such rules as the community, or those authorized by them to that purpose, shall agree on. And in this we have the original right of both the legislative and executive power, as well as of the governments and societies themselves.

For in the state of nature, to omit the liberty he has of innocent delights, a man has two powers:

The first is to do whatsoever he thinks fit for the preservation of himself and others within the permission of the law of nature, by which law, common to them all, he and all the rest of mankind are one community, make up one society, distinct from all other creatures. And, were it not for the corruption and viciousness of degenerate men, there would be no need of any other, no necessity that men should separate from this great and natural community and by positive agreements combine into smaller and divided associations.

The other power a man has in the state of nature is the power to punish the crimes committed against that law. Both these he gives up when he joins in a private, if I may so call it, or particular politic society and incorporates into any commonwealth separate from the rest of mankind.

The first power, viz., of doing whatsoever he thought fit for the preservation of himself and rest of mankind, he gives up to be regulated by laws made by the society, so far forth as the preservation of himself and the rest of that society shall require; which laws of the society in many things confine the liberty he had by the law of nature.

Secondly, the power of punishing he wholly gives up, and engages his natural force—which he might before employ in the execution of the law of nature by his own single authority, as he thought fit—to assist the executive power of the society, as the law thereof shall require; for being now in a new state, wherein he is to enjoy many conveniences from the labor, assistance, and society of others in the same community as well as protection from its whole strength, he is to part also with as much of his natural liberty, in providing for himself, as the good, prosperity, and safety of the society shall require, which is not only necessary, but just, since the other members of the society do the like.

But though men when they enter into society give up the equality, liberty, and executive power they had in the state of nature into the hands of the society, to be so far disposed of by the legislative as the good of the society shall require, yet it being only with an intention in every one the better to preserve himself, his liberty and property—for no rational creature can be supposed to change his condition with an intention to be worse—the power of the society, or legislative constituted by them, can never be supposed to extend farther than the common good, but is obliged to secure every one's property by providing against those three defects above-mentioned that made the state of nature so unsafe and uneasy. And so whoever has the legislative or supreme power of any commonwealth is bound to govern by established standing laws, promulgated and known to the people, and not by extemporary decrees; by indifferent and upright judges who are to decide controversies by those laws; and to employ the force of the community at home only in the execution of such laws, or abroad to prevent or redress foreign injuries, and secure the community from inroads and invasion. And all this to be directed to no other end but the peace, safety, and public good of the people.

32 Communism and the Materialistic Conception of History*

FRIEDRICH ENGELS

Friedrich Engels (1820–1895) coauthored the *Communist Manifesto* with Karl Marx in 1847. Active in the English working-class movement and an agitator for revolutionary reform, Engels helped to found the First International. His influential writings also include his *Anti-Dühring*; *The Origin of the Family, Property and the State*; and *Feuerbach and the End of German Classical Philosophy*.

The materialist conception of history starts from the principle that production, and next to production the exchange of its products, is the basis of every social system; that in every society arising in history the allotment of products, and with it the division of society into classes or ranks, depends upon what is produced, how it is produced, and how when produced it is exchanged. Accordingly the ultimate causes of all social changes and political revolutions are not to be looked for in the heads of men, in their growing insight into eternal truth and justice, but in changes of the methods of production and exchange; they are to be looked for not in the *philosophy*, but in the *economy* of the epoch in question. The awakening perception that existing social arrangements are unreasonable and unjust, that reason has become nonsense and goodness a scourge, is only a symptom of the fact that in the methods of production and forms of exchange alterations have silently gone on, to which the social system fitted for earlier economic conditions no longer corresponds. That amounts to saying that the means for removing the evils revealed must itself, more or less developed, be present in the altered conditions of production. This means is not something to be invented out of the head, but something to be discovered by means of the head in the material facts of production lying before us.

How does modern Socialism accord with this conception?

The present social system has been, as is now pretty generally conceded, created by the now dominant class, the bourgeoisie. The method of pro-

---

* From Friedrich Engels, *Anti-Dühring: Herr Eugen Dühring's Revolution in Science*, trans. R. C. K. Ensor (1878).

duction proper to the bourgeoisie, designated, since Marx, as the capitalistic method of production, was incompatible with the local and fixed privileges and the reciprocal personal ties of the feudal system; the bourgeoisie shattered the feudal system and erected on its ruins the bourgeois conception of society, the empire of free competition, of free locomotion, of equal rights for the possessors of commodities, and of all the other bourgeois fine things. The capitalistic method of production could now unfold itself freely. The productive forces elaborated under the direction of the bourgeoisie developed, after steam and the new machinery had transformed the old manufacture into the great industry, with hitherto unheard-of rapidity on a hitherto unheard-of scale. But as in its time manufacture and the handicraft developed under its influence came into conflict with the feudal fetters of the guilds, so the great industry in its fuller development comes into conflict with the limitations in which the capitalistic method of production has confined it. The new productive forces have already quite outgrown the bourgeois form of their utilization; and this conflict between productive forces and methods of production is not a conflict which has originated in the heads of men, like the conflict between human original sin and divine righteousness, but it exists in facts, is objective, outside of us, independent of the will or the course even of those human beings who have brought it about. Modern Socialism is nothing more than the mirroring in thought of this conflict in fact, its ideal reflection in the heads of the class, primarily, which directly suffers by it, the working-class.

In what does this conflict consist?

Before capitalistic production—that is, in the Middle Ages—there everywhere existed petty industry, on the basis of the workers owning privately their means of production: the agriculture of the small free or subject peasants, the handicraft of the towns. The means of work—land, agricultural implements, workshop, manual tools—were means of work for the individual, only calculated for individual use, so necessarily upon a small, pigmy, restricted scale. But for that very reason they belonged as a rule to the producer himself. To concentrate these fragmentary, cramped means of production, to expand them, to transform them into the powerfully operative lever of the production of to-day, was just the rôle in history of the capitalistic method of production and its agent, the bourgeoisie. How it carried this out historically after the fifteenth century in the three stages of simple co-operation, manufacture, and the great industry, Marx has depicted expressly in the fourth section of *Capital*. But the bourgeoisie, as is there proved, could not change those limited means of production into mighty productive forces, without changing them from means of production of the individual into *social* means of production only to be utilized by a *collectivity* of men. In place of the spinning-wheel, the hand-loom, and the smith's hammer, came the spinning-mule, the power-loom, and the steam-hammer; in place of the individual workshop, the factory enabling hundreds and thousands to work together. And along with the means of production, production itself changed from a series of individual performances into a series of social acts, and the products from products of individuals into social products. The yarn, the cloth, the hardware, which now came from the factory, were the common product of many workers, through whose hands they had to go in order before they were ready. No individual can say of them: "I made that; that is *my* product."

Where, however, the natural division of labour within society is the basic form of production, it stamps on the products the form of *commodities*, whose reciprocal exchange, purchase and sale, puts the individual producers in a position to satisfy their manifold needs. And in the Middle Ages this was the case. The peasant, *e.g.*, sold farm-produce to the handicraftsman, and bought from him in return the products of handicraft. Upon this society of individual producers, producers of commodities, intruded the new method of production. In the midst of the natural undesigned division of labour prevailing all through society, it set up the designed division of labour as organized in the individual factory; by the side of individual production appeared social production. The products of both were sold on the same market, therefore at prices at least approximately equal. But the designed organization was more powerful than the natural division of labour; the factories with their social labour got out their products more cheaply than the small individual producers. Individual production failed in one sphere after another; social production revolutionized the entire former method of production. But this its revolutionary character was so little recognized, that on the contrary it was introduced as a means for augmenting and advancing the production of commodities. It arose in immediate connection with definite machinery, already discovered for the production and exchange of commodities: merchant's capital, handicraft, wage-labour. While it appeared itself as a new form of the production of commodities, the forms of appropriation in force for the production of commodities remained also in full force for it.

In the production of commodities, as developed in the Middle Ages, there could arise no question as to whose should be the product of labour. As a rule, the individual producer had made it out of raw material belonging to him, and often produced by him, with his own instruments of work, and his own manual labour or that of his family. There was absolutely no need for him first to appropriate it; it belonged to him entirely of itself. A man's ownership of the product rested, therefore, on his own work. Even where outside assistance was used, this as a rule remained secondary, and commonly involved some other benefit beside wages; the guild apprentice and companion worked less for the money and the wage than for their own training to be masters. Then came the concentration of the means of production in great workshops and factories, and its alteration into a really social means of production. But the social means of production and products were treated as though they were still, as they had been, the means of production, and products, of individuals. As the possessor of the means of production had hitherto appropriated the product, because it as a rule was his own product and the labour of outside assistants was the exception, so now the possessor of the means of production continued to appropriate the product, although it was no longer his product, but exclusively the product of outside labour. Thus the products now made socially were not appropriated by those who had really set the means of production in motion and really made the products, but by the *capitalists*. Production, and the means of it, have really become social. But they are subject to a form of appropriation, which presupposes the private production of individuals, in which everyone possesses and brings to market his own product. The method of production is subject to this form of appropriation, although it does away with what this form presupposes.[1] In this contradiction, which lends to the new method of production its capitalistic character, the whole discord of the present lies already in germ. The more the new method of production came to dominate all important fields of production and all important countries, the more glaringly came perforce to light the *incompatibility of social production and capitalistic appropriation*.

The first capitalists found, as we said, the form of wage-labour already to hand. But wage-labour as an exception, a side occupation, a supplement, a transitional stage. The country labourer, who from time to time went to earn day-wages, had his few acres of his own land, from which alone he could if necessary live. The guild ordinances provided that the companion of to-day should pass on to be the master of to-morrow. But as soon as the means of production were changed and became social, and were concentrated into the hands of capitalists, this was altered. The means of production, as well as the product, of the small individual producer became more and more valueless; nothing was left for him but to go to the capitalist for wages. Wage-labour, previously an exception and a supplement, became the rule and the fundamental form of all production; formerly a side occupation, it became now the exclusive activity of the worker. The temporary wage-worker turned into the lifelong wage-worker. The multitude of lifelong wage-workers was, besides, colossally increased through the simultaneous collapse of the feudal system, dissolution of the retinues of the feudal lords, dismissal of peasants from their court posts, etc. The cleavage was complete between the means of production concentrated in the hands of the capitalists

---

[1] It need not here be explained, that although the *form* of appropriation remains the same, its *character* is no less revolutionized by the process described above than is production. If I appropriate my own product, or if I appropriate some one else's, those are naturally two very different sorts of appropriation. Note too, that wage-labour, in which the whole capitalistic method of production is contained in germ, is very old; in an individualized and scattered form it subsisted for centuries beside slavery. But the germ could not develop into the capitalistic method of production, until the historical conditions for it had come about.

on the one side, and the producers reduced to possessing nothing but their labour power on the other. The contradiction between social production and capitalistic appropriation appeared as *an opposition between proletariate and bourgeoisie.*

We saw that the capitalistic method of production intruded itself upon a society of individual producers producing commodities, the means of whose social connection was the exchange of their products. But every society resting on production of commodities has the peculiarity, that in it the producers have lost the control over their own social relations. Every one produces for himself with his means of production, whatever it may be, and for his individual exchange requirements. No one knows how much of his article comes to the market, or how much of it is needed; no one knows whether his individual product meets a real need, whether he will be able to balance his expenses, or to sell it at all. There is a prevailing anarchy of social production. But production of commodities, like every other form of production, has its peculiar, inherent laws, inseparable from it; and these laws are fixed, in spite of the anarchy, in it and through it. They appear in the single persistent form of social connection, in exchange, and they assert themselves against the individual producers as the coercive laws of competition. They are therefore at the outset unknown to these producers themselves, and have first to be gradually discovered by them through long experience. They are fixed not by the producers nor in the producers' interest, but as the blindly-operative natural laws of their form of production. The product governs the producer.

In mediæval society, that is, in the first centuries, production was essentially directed to producers' uses. It in the main satisfied only the needs of the producer and his family. Where, as in the country, there existed relations of personal dependence, it contributed also to satisfy the needs of the feudal lord. In this case no exchange took place, and the products did not acquire the character of commodities from it either. The peasant's family produced nearly everything that it needed, furniture and clothing no less than food. Only when it went so far as to produce a surplus over and above its own requirements and the tribute in kind due to the feudal lord, did it also produce commodities; this surplus, thrown into the social exchange, exposed for sale, became a commodity. The town handicraftsmen had of course from the beginning to produce for exchange. But they, too, worked principally to satisfy their own requirements; they had gardens and small fields; they sent their cattle into the common forest, which at the same time supplied them with timber and firewood; the women spun flax, wool, etc. Production for the purpose of exchange, production of commodities, was only beginning. Hence a restricted exchange, a restricted market, a stable method of production, local exclusiveness against outsiders, local unity within: the manor in the country, the guild in the town.

But with the extension of production, and in particular with the rise of the capitalistic method of production, the hitherto dormant laws of the production of commodities became more openly and powerfully realized. The old associations were relaxed, the old exclusive limits broken through, the producers converted more and more into independent, isolated producers of commodities. The anarchy of social production became apparent, and was more and more accentuated. But the main instrument, by which the capitalists' method of production enhanced this anarchy in social production, was the exact opposite of anarchy: the increasing organization of production on social lines in every separate producing establishment. With this instrument it put an end to the old peaceful stability. Where it was introduced into a branch of industry, it suffered no older industrial methods to remain beside it. Where it took hold of handicraft, it annihilated the old handicraft. The field of labour became a battle-field. The great geographical discoveries, and the colonizations which followed them, multiplied many times over the area of the market, and emphasized the change from handicraft to manufacture. Not only did the struggle break out between the separate local producers; the local struggles grew on their side to national ones, the commercial wars of the seventeenth and eighteenth centuries. Finally, the great industry and the establishment of the world-market made the struggle universal and at the same time gave it an unheard-of severity. Between single capitalists as between whole industries, and whole countries, the favour of natural or artificial conditions of production decided the question of existence. The weaker was mercilessly eliminated. It is Darwin's struggle for individual existence, transferred with heightened ferocity from nature to society. The natural standpoint of the beast appears as the summit of human development. The contradiction between social production and capitalistic appropriation, reproduces itself as an opposition between the organization of production in the individual factory and the anarchy of production in the entire society.

In these two manifestations of the contradiction imminent in it by reason of its origin, the capitalistic method of production moves, describing without any way out that vicious circle, which already Fourier discovered it in. What Fourier, of course, could not see in his time, is that this circle gradually contracts, that the movement rather describes a spiral, and must reach its end, like the movement of the planets, by a collision with the centre. It is the driving force of the social anarchy of production, which converts the great majority of human beings more and more into proletarians, and again it is the masses of proletarians which finally will put a stop to the anarchy of production. It is the driving force of the social anarchy of production, which converts the infinite perfectibility of the machines of the great industry into an imperative command that every individual industrial capitalist shall perfect his machinery more and more, on pain of ruin. But to perfect machinery means to render superfluous human labour. If the introduction and increase of machinery means the crushing out of millions of manual workers by a few machine-workers, the improvement of machinery means the crushing out of more and more of the machine-workers themselves; and, in the last instance, the production of a number of available wage-workers exceeding the average demand of capital for employees,—a regular reserve-army of industry, as I called it as far back as 1845,—available for the times when industry is working at high pressure, thrown on the pavement by the collapse which necessarily follows, at all times a lead weight tied round the feet of the working-class in its struggle for existence against capital, a regulator for depressing the wage of labour to the low level set by the capitalist demand. So it comes about that machinery, as Marx puts it, is the most powerful weapon of capital against the working-class, that the means of work is continually dashing the means of subsistence out of the worker's hand, that the worker's own product turns into a tool for the worker's enslavement. Thus it happens that the economising of the means of work leads to most reckless squandering of labour-force and robbery of what the labour-function should normally start from; that machinery, the strongest instrument for shortening work-time, is transformed into the surest instrument for converting the whole lifetime of the worker and his family into available work-time for capital to profit by; that the overemployment of one man comes to imply the unemployment of another, and that the great industry, which hunts the whole world over for fresh consumers, limits the consumption of the masses at home to a starvation minimum, and undermines thereby its own domestic market. "The law which keeps the relative surplus population or reserve army of industry, continually balancing the extent and energy of the accumulation of capital, rivets the worker more firmly to capital than Hephaestus' wedges riveted Prometheus to the rocks. It causes an accumulation of misery corresponding to the accumulation of capital. The accumulation of wealth at the one pole is therefore at the same time an accumulation of misery, hard work, slavery, ignorance, brutalization, and moral degradation at the opposite pole, *i.e.* on the side of the class, which produces its own product in the form of capital."[2] And to expect any other division of the products from the capitalistic method of production, is like wanting the electrodes of a battery, while remaining connected with it, to leave water undecomposed, instead of developing oxygen at the positive pole and hydrogen at the negative.

We saw that the maximised capacity for improvement of modern machinery turns, through the anarchy of production in society, into an imperative command that the individual industrial capitalist shall continually improve his machinery, continually raise its productive power. Into a similar imperative command turns the mere *de facto* possibility of his extending his sphere of production. The enormous power of expansion of the great industry, compared to which that of gases is simply child's play,

[2] Marx, *Capital.*

now manifests itself to us as a qualitative and quantitative *demand for expansion*, which laughs at every opposing check. Such a check is formed by the consumption, the outlet, the markets, for the products of the great industry. But the capacity of expansion of markets, extensive and intensive alike, is governed immediately by quite other laws, with a far less energetic operation. The expansion of markets cannot keep pace with the expansion of production. The clash becomes inevitable, and as it can give rise to no solution as long as it does not explode the capitalistic method of production itself, it becomes periodic. Capitalistic production gives rise to a new "vicious circle."

In fact, since 1825, when the first general crisis broke out, the whole industrial and commercial world, the production and exchange of all the civilized nations and their more or less barbarous dependencies, gets out of joint just about once every ten years. Transport comes to a standstill, the markets are glutted, products lie unremoved, as abundant as they are impossible to get rid of, ready money goes out of sight, credit disappears, factories are idle, the working masses lack the means of subsistence because they have produced too much of it, bankruptcy follows bankruptcy, and bankrupt after bankrupt is sold up. The standstill lasts for years, productive forces as well as products are squandered and destroyed wholesale, till the accumulated masses of commodities are finally disposed of more or less below value, and production and exchange gradually resume their course. After a while the pace becomes marked; it falls into a trot; the trot of industry passes into a gallop, and this again increases to the unbridled career of a complete industrial, commercial, banking, and speculative steeple-chase, so at last to attain once more the breakneck leap into the grave of the crisis. And so all over again and again. Since 1825 we have now experienced this five times, and at the present moment (1877) are experiencing it for the sixth. And the character of these crises is so sharply marked out that Fourier named them all when he named the first one: "*crise pléthorique*"— crisis from over-supply.[3]

In the crises the contradiction between social production and capitalistic appropriation breaks out violently. The circulation of commodities is for the moment annihilated; the medium of circulation, money, becomes a hindrance to circulation; all the laws of the production and circulation of commodities are turned upside down. The economic clashing has reached its maximum; the method of production is in revolt against the method of exchange, the productive forces are in revolt against the method of production, out of which they have grown.

The fact that the social organization of production inside the factory

---

[3] This theory, and its premiss that the workers only get a small fraction of the value of their work, was advanced also by the theoretic Socialist Rodbertus. Unchecked capitalism, in this view, minimizes the purchasing-power of the majority, while maximizing their producing-power; hence the crises.

has developed itself to the point at which it is incompatible with the anarchy of production existing beside and beyond it in society; this fact is made obvious to the capitalists themselves, by the powerful concentration of capitals, which, during crises, is achieved by means of the ruin of many great, and still more small, capitalists. The whole mechanism of the capitalistic method of production gives out under the pressure of the productive forces which it has itself created. It can no longer convert all these masses of the means of production into capital; they lie fallow, and for that very reason, the reserve army of industry must lie fallow also. Means of production, means of subsistence, available workers, all elements of production and of the general wealth, are present in superfluity. But "superfluity is the source of want and need" (Fourier), because it is just it which impedes the conversion of the means of production and subsistence into capital. For in capitalist society the means of production cannot come into action, unless they have previously been converted into capital, into means for the exploitation of human labour-force. Between them and the workers stands, like a spectre, the necessity for them and the means of subsistence to take the character of capital. It alone prevents the harmonious working of the material and personal factors in production; it alone forbids the means of production to function, and the workers to work and live. On the one hand, therefore, the capitalistic method of production becomes convinced of its own incapacity to control further these productive forces. On the other, these productive forces themselves bring increasing pressure to bear for the removal of the contradiction, for their release from their character as capital, for actual recognition of their character as social productive forces.

It is this opposition of the powerfully growing productive forces to their character as capital, this increasing pressure for the recognition of their social character, which compels the capitalist class itself more and more, so far as this is at all possible inside the capitalistic conditions, to treat them as social productive forces. Both the high-pressure periods of industry, with their limitless inflation of credit, and the crisis itself by the collapse of great capitalist firms, lead to that form of the socialization of larger quantities of the means of production, which confronts us in the different sorts of joint-stock companies. Many of these means of production and traffic are from the first so colossal, that, like the railways, they exclude every other form of capitalist exploitation. At a certain stage of development, this form also ceases to suffice; the official representative of capitalist society, the State, must take over their management. This need for conversion into State property appears first in the case of the great traffic concerns: the post, telegraphs, and railways.

If the crisis revealed the inability of the bourgeoisie to control further the modern productive forces, the conversion of the great producing and traffic concerns into joint-stock companies and State property shows that the bourgeoisie can be dispensed with for that purpose. Every social function of capitalists is now discharged by salaried servants. The capitalist has no social activity left, except to pocket incomes, to cut off coupons, and to gamble on the Stock Exchange, where the different capitalists relieve each other of their capital. If the capitalistic method of production at first crushed out the workers, so now it crushes out the capitalists, and rejects them, just like the workers, into the surplus population, though not immediately into the reserve-army of industry.

But neither the conversion into joint-stock companies, nor that into State property, takes away the character of capital from the productive forces. In the case of joint-stock companies this is palpable. And the modern State, again, is only the organization, which bourgeois society gives itself in order to uphold the universal outward conditions of the capitalistic method of production against the encroachments, not only of the workers, but of individual capitalists. The modern State, as indeed its form shows, is an essentially capitalist machine, a State of the capitalists, the ideal of capitalist aggregate. The more productive forces it takes over into its ownership, the more does it become a real capitalist aggregate, the more does it exploit its citizens. The workers remain wage-workers, proletarians. The relationship of capital is not removed; rather it culminates. But at the culmination comes transformation. State-ownership of productive forces is not the solution of the conflict; but it contains in itself the formal means of the solution, the handle to it.

This solution can only be found in the actual recognition of the social nature of the modern productive forces, so that the methods of production, appropriation, and exchange shall be harmonized with the social character of the means of production. This can only take place, if society, openly and without beating round the bush, seizes hold of the productive forces, which have outgrown every management but its own. Thereby the social character of the means of production and products,—which to-day turns against the producers themselves, breaks down periodically the methods of production and exchange, and only accomplishes itself in violence and destruction, as a blindly working natural law,—will be brought to its full effect by the producers acting with their eyes open, and will transform itself from a cause of disturbance and periodical collapse into the most powerful lever of production itself.

The forces operative in society operate just like natural forces—blindly, violently, destructively, so long as we do not recognize them and reckon with them. But when once we have recognized them and grasped their activity, their direction, and their workings, it only depends upon ourselves to subject them more and more to our will and to attain our objects by their means. And this holds particularly true of the powerful productive forces of to-day. So long as we obstinately refuse to understand their nature and their character—and to thwart this understanding the whole capitalistic method of production and its defenders strive,—so long do these forces work themselves out in spite of us, against us, so long do they dominate us, as we have in detail described. But once they are apprehended in their nature, they can, in the hands of the associated producers, be converted from demonic masters into willing servants. It is the difference between the destructive force of electricity in the lightning of the storm, and the fettered electricity of the telegraph and the arclight; the difference between a fiery conflagration, and fire working in the service of man. With this treatment of the modern productive forces in accordance with their ultimately recognized nature, the social anarchy of production is replaced by a socially designed regulation of production according to the acquirements of the collectivity and of every individual; the capitalistic method of appropriation, in which the product enslaves first the producer and afterwards the appropriator too, is replaced by that method of appropriating the products which is founded in the very nature of the modern means of production: on the one hand, direct social appropriation as a means for the maintenance and extension of production; on the other hand, direct individual appropriation as a means of subsistence and enjoyment.

While the capitalistic method of production more and more converts the great majority of the population into proletarians, it is creating the power which is compelled, on pain of perishing, to achieve this revolution. While it more and more forces the great socialized means of production to be converted into State property, it is itself pointing the path for this revolution's achievement. *The proletariate seizes the power of the State, and converts the means of production into State property at once.* But it thereby abolishes itself as a proletariate, abolishes all class distinctions and class antagonisms, and abolishes the State as State. Society, hitherto, stirred by class antagonisms, needed the State, *i.e.* an organization of the exploiting class in each period to maintain their external conditions of production, and especially, therefore, to hold down by force the exploited classes in the conditions of oppression afforded by the existing methods of production (slavery, serfdom or bondage, and wage-labour). The State was the official representative of the whole of society, its embodiment in a visible corporation; but it was this only in so far as it was the State of that class which itself for its period represented the whole of society—in antiquity the State of the slave-holding burgesses, in the Middle Ages that of the feudal nobility, in our time that of the bourgeoisie. When at last it really becomes representative of the whole of society, it renders itself superfluous. As soon as there is no longer a class in society to be held in subjection, as soon as, along with the class-domination and the struggle for individual existence based on the anarchy of production hitherto, the resultant clashings and excesses disappear —there is no longer anything to be repressed, which might necessitate a special repressive force, a State. The first act in which the State really appears as representative of the whole of society—the appropriation of the means of production in the name of society—is at the same time its last independent act as a State. The interference of a State authority in social relations grows superfluous in one sphere after another, and then of its own accord becomes dormant. For government of persons is substituted control of things and management of the processes of production. The State is not "abolished," it dies out. In this context should be considered the phrase "free popular State," both in its temporary rightness for purposes of agitation, and in its ultimate scientific inadequacy; so, too, should the demand of the so-called Anarchists, that the State should be abolished in twenty-four hours.

The appropriation of all the means of production by society has, ever since the appearance in history of the capitalistic method of production, hovered often more or less hazily as the future ideal before the eyes of individuals and of whole sects. But it could not become possible, could not be historically necessary, until the material conditions were present for it to be carried out. Neither it nor any other social advance becomes realizable through the acquired perception that the existence of classes is contrary to justice, equality, etc.; nor through mere willingness to abolish these classes, but through certain new economic conditions. The splitting of society into an exploiting and an exploited, a ruling and a subject class, was the necessary result of the former slight development of production. As long as the aggregate labour of society gives a yield only slightly in excess of what was needed for the bare existence of everybody, as long, therefore, as labour claims all, or nearly all, the time of the great majority of the members of society, so long does society necessarily divide itself into classes. Beside this great majority, which drudges exclusively at labour, is formed a class freed from directly productive work, which looks after the common concerns of society—management of labour, State affairs, justice, science, the arts, etc. The law of the division of labour, therefore, is what lies at the base of the division of classes. But that does not prevent this division of classes from having been established through violence and robbery, guile and fraud, nor the ruling class from having, when once in the saddle, secured their domination at the expense of the working class, and transformed the management of society into an exploitation of the masses.

But if on this view the division into classes has a certain historical justification, it has only for a given period of time, for given social conditions. It was based on the insufficiency of production; it will be swept away by the full unfolding of the modern productive forces. And, in fact, the abolition of classes in society presupposes a degree of historical development, at which the existence, not merely of this or that particular ruling class, but of a ruling class at all, and therefore of the class-distinction itself, has become an obsolete anachronism. It presupposes, therefore, a high degree of the development of production, at which for a special class in society to appropriate the means of production and products, and with them political supremacy and the monopoly of education and intellectual management, is not only superfluous, but economically, politically, and intellectually a hindrance to development. This point is now reached. While the bourgeoisie itself is hardly unaware any longer of its political and intellectual bankruptcy, its economic bankruptcy is repeated regularly every ten years. In every crisis society is suffocated under the weight of its own productive forces and products, which it cannot utilize; and stands helpless before the absurd contradiction, that the producers have nothing to consume because there is a dearth of consumers. The expansive power of the means of production is bursting the bonds which the capitalistic method of production puts upon it. Its emancipation from these bonds is the sole condition to be fulfilled for an uninterrupted, ever rapidly advancing development of productive forces, and with it a practically unlimited increase of production itself. Nor is that all. Social appropriation of the means of production removes not only the present artificial check on production, but also the positive squandering and spoiling of productive forces and products, which at present is the inevitable accompaniment of production and culminates in the crises. Moreover, it sets free for the community a mass of the means of production and products, by doing away with the imbecile expenditure upon luxuries which the now ruling classes and their political representatives practise. The possibility of securing for all members of society, by means of social production, an existence, which not only is in a material sense perfectly adequate and daily growing wealthier, but also guarantees to them the perfectly free training and exercise of their physical and mental faculties—this possibility was never ours until now, but ours it now is.

When society takes possession of the means of production, there is no more production of commodities, and therefore no more subjection of the producer to the product. The anarchy inside social production is replaced by systematic conscious organization. The struggle for individual existence ceases. In a certain sense this marks the final separation of man from the animal kingdom, and his passage from animal conditions of existence to really human ones. The circle of conditions of life environing men, which hitherto dominated them, now passes under their domination and control; they now for the first time become real, conscious masters of nature, because, and in that, they are masters of their own association. The laws of their own social action, which previously withstood them as external overmastering laws of nature, are now applied, and so mastered, by men, with full practical knowledge. The peculiar association of men, which hitherto confronted them as something doled out by nature and history, now becomes their own free act. The objective eternal powers, which controlled history, come under the control of men themselves. Henceforth for the first time men will make their own history quite consciously; henceforth the social causes which they set in motion will predominantly and in a steadily increasing measure have the results which they wish them to have. Mankind leap from the realm of necessity into the realm of freedom.

To perform this act of world-emancipation is the mission in history of the modern proletariate. To investigate its historical conditions, and so its very nature, and to make the class which is called upon to act—the oppressed class of to-day—aware of the conditions and the nature of its own action, is the object of the theoretic expression of the proletarian movement—scientific Socialism.

RIGHTS, JUSTICE,
AND FREEDOM

33 Critique of the Doctrine of
Inalienable, Natural Rights*

JEREMY BENTHAM

Jeremy Bentham (1740–1832) is generally viewed as the father of the utilitarian theory of ethics. Concerned with reform of both the penal and the civil law in England, Bentham wrote prolifically in the area of ethics and jurisprudence. His best known work is the *Introduction to the Principles of Morals and Legislation* (1789). He established the influential *Westminster Review* and assisted in founding University College, London.

PRELIMINARY OBSERVATIONS

The Declaration of Rights—I mean the paper published under that name by the French National Assembly in 1791—assumes for its subject-matter a field of disquisition as unbounded in point of extent as it is important in its nature. But the more ample the extent given to any proposition or string of propositions, the more difficult it is to keep the import of it confined without deviation, within the bounds of truth and reason. If in the smallest corners of the field it ranges over, it fail of coinciding with the line of rigid rectitude, no sooner is the aberration pointed out, than (inasmuch as there is no medium between truth and falsehood) its pretensions to the appellation of a truism are gone, and whoever looks upon it must recognise it to be false and erroneous,—and if, as here, political conduct be the theme, so far as the error extends and fails of being detected, pernicious.

In a work of such extreme importance with a view to practice, and which throughout keeps practice so closely and immediately and professedly in

---

* From Jeremy Bentham, *Anarchical Fallacies*, vol. 2 of Bowring (ed.), *Works*, 1843.

view, a single error may be attended with the most fatal consequences. The more extensive the propositions, the more consummate will be the knowledge, the more exquisite the skill, indispensably requisite to confine them in all points within the pale of truth. The most consummate ability in the whole nation could not have been too much for the task—one may venture to say, it would not have been equal to it. But that, in the sanctioning of each proposition, the most consummate ability should happen to be vested in the heads of the sorry majority in whose hands the plenitude of power happened on that same occasion to be vested, is an event against which the chances are almost as infinity to one.

Here, then, is a radical and all-pervading error—the attempting to give to a work on such a subject the sanction of government; especially of such a government—a government composed of members so numerous, so unequal in talent, as well as discordant in inclinations and affections. Had it been the work of a single hand, and that a private one, and in that character given to the world, every good effect would have been produced by it that could be produced by it when published as the work of government, without any of the bad effects which in case of the smallest error must result from it when given as the work of government.

The revolution, which threw the government into the hands of the penners and adopters of this declaration, having been the effect of insurrection, the grand object evidently is to justify the cause. But by justifying it, they invite it: in justifying past insurrection, they plant and cultivate a propensity to perpetual insurrection in time future; they sow the seeds of anarchy broadcast: in justifying the demolition of existing authorities, they undermine all future ones, their own consequently in the number. Shallow and reckless vanity!—They imitate in their conduct the author of that fabled law, according to which the assassination of the prince upon the throne gave to the assassin a title to succeed him. *"People, behold your rights! If a single article of them be violated, insurrection is not your right only, but the most sacred of your duties."* Such is the constant language, for such is the professed object of this source and model of all laws—this self-consecrated oracle of all nations. . . .

The great enemies of public peace are the selfish and dissocial passions:— necessary as they are—the one to the very existence of each individual, the other to his security. On the part of these affections, a deficiency in point of strength is never to be apprehended: all that is to be apprehended in respect of them, is to be apprehended on the side of their excess. Society is held together only by the sacrifices that men can be induced to make of the gratifications they demand: to obtain these sacrifices is the great difficulty, the great task of government. What has been the object, the perpetual and palpable object, of this declaration of pretended rights? To add as much force as possible to these passions, already but too strong,—to burst the cords that hold them in,—to say to the selfish passions, there—everywhere—is your prey!—to the angry passions, there—everywhere—is your enemy.

Such is the morality of this celebrated manifesto, rendered famous by the same qualities that gave celebrity to the incendiary of the Ephesian temple.

The logic of it is of a piece with its morality:—a perpetual vein of non-sense, flowing from a perpetual abuse of words,—words having a variety of meanings, where words with single meanings were equally at hand—the same words used in a variety of meanings in the same page,—words used in meanings not their own, where proper words were equally at hand,—words and propositions of the most unbounded signification, turned loose without any of those exceptions or modifications which are so necessary on every occasion to reduce their import within the compass, not only of right reason, but even of the design in hand, of whatever nature it may be;—the same inaccuracy, the same inattention in the penning of this cluster of truths on which the fate of nations was to hang, as if it had been an oriental tale, or an allegory for a magazine:—stale epigrams, instead of necessary distinctions, —figurative expressions preferred to simple ones,—sentimental conceits, as trite as they are unmeaning, preferred to apt and precise expressions,— frippery ornament preferred to the majestic simplicity of good sound sense, —and the acts of the senate loaded and disfigured by the tinsel of the play-house. . . .

Article II

The end in view of every political association is the preservation of the natural and imprescriptible rights of man. These rights are liberty, property, security, and resistance to oppression.

Sentence 1. The end in view of every political association, is the preserva-tion of the natural and imprescriptible rights of man.

More confusion—more nonsense,—and the nonsense, as usual, dangerous nonsense. The words can scarcely be said to have a meaning: but if they have, or rather if they had a meaning, these would be the propositions either asserted or implied:—

1. That there are such things as rights anterior to the establishment of governments: for natural, as applied to rights, if it mean anything, is meant to stand in opposition to *legal*—to such rights as are acknowledged to owe their existence to government, and are consequently posterior in their date to the establishment of government.

2. That these rights *can not* be abrogated by government: for *can not* is implied in the form of the word imprescriptible, and the sense it wears when so applied, is the cut-throat sense above explained.

3. That the governments that exist derive their origin from formal associations, or what are now called *conventions*: associations entered into by a partnership contract, with all the members for partners,—entered into at a day prefixed, for a predetermined purpose, the formation of a new govern-ment where there was none before (for as to formal meetings holden under

the controul of an existing government, they are evidently out of question here) in which it seems again to be implied in the way of inference, though a necessary and an unavoidable inference, that all governments (that is, self-called governments, knots of persons exercising the powers of government) that have had any other origin than an association of the above description, are illegal, that is, no governments at all; resistance to them, and subversion of them, lawful and commendable; and so on.

Such are the notions implied in this first part of the article. How stands the truth of things? That there are no such things as natural rights—no such things as rights anterior to the establishment of government—no such things as natural rights opposed to, in contradistinction to, legal: that the expression is merely figurative; that when used, in the moment you attempt to give it a literal meaning it leads to error, and to that sort of error that leads to mischief—to the extremity of mischief.

We know what it is for men to live without government—and living without government, to live without rights: we know what it is for men to live without government, for we see instances of such a way of life—we see it in many savage nations, or rather races of mankind; for instance, among the savages of New South Wales, whose way of living is so well known to us: no habit of obedience, and thence no government—no government, and thence no laws—no laws, and thence no such things as rights—no security—no property:—liberty, as against regular controul, the controul of laws and government—perfect; but as against all irregular controul, the mandates of stronger individuals, none. In this state, at a time earlier than the commencement of history—in this same state, judging from analogy, we, the inhabitants of the part of the globe we call Europe, were;—no government, consequently no rights: no rights, consequently no property—no legal security—no legal liberty: security not more than belongs to beasts—forecast and sense of insecurity keener—consequently in point of happiness below the level of the brutal race.

In proportion to the want of happiness resulting from the want of rights, a reason exists for wishing that there were such things as rights. But reasons for wishing there were such things as rights, are not rights;—a reason for wishing that a certain right were established, is not that right—want is not supply—hunger is not bread.

That which has no existence cannot be destroyed—that which cannot be destroyed cannot require anything to preserve it from destruction. *Natural rights* is simple nonsense: natural and imprescriptible rights, rhetorical nonsense,—nonsense upon stilts. But this rhetorical nonsense ends in the old strain of mischievous nonsense: for immediately a list of these pretended natural rights is given, and those are so expressed as to present to view legal rights. And of these rights, whatever they are, there is not, it seems, any one of which any government *can*, upon any occasion whatever, abrogate the smallest particle.

So much for terrorist language. What is the language of reason and plain sense upon the same subject? That in proportion as it is *right or proper, i.e.* advantageous to the society in question, that this or that right—a right to this or that effect—should be established and maintained, in that same proportion it is *wrong* that it should be abrogated: but that as there is no *right*, which ought not to be maintained so long as it is upon the whole advantageous to the society that it should be maintained, so there is no right which, when the abolition of it is advantageous to society, should not be abolished. To know whether it would be more for the advantage of society that this or that right should be maintained or abolished, the time at which the question about maintaining or abolishing is proposed, must be given, and the circumstances under which it is proposed to maintain or abolish it; the right itself must be specifically described, not jumbled with an undistinguishable heap of others, under any such vague general terms as property, liberty, and the like.

One thing, in the midst of all this confusion, is but too plain. They know not of what they are talking under the name of natural rights, and yet they would have them imprescriptible—proof against all the power of the laws—pregnant with occasions summoning the members of the community to rise up in resistance against the laws. What, then, was their object in declaring the existence of imprescriptible rights, and without specifying a single one by any such mark as it could be known by? This and no other—to excite and keep up a spirit of resistance to all laws—a spirit of insurrection against all governments—against the governments of all other nations instantly,—against the government of their own nation—against the government they themselves were pretending to establish—even that, as soon as their own reign should be at an end. In us is the perfection of virtue and wisdom: in all mankind besides, the extremity of wickedness and folly. Our will shall consequently reign without controul, and for ever: reign now we are living—reign after we are dead.

All nations—all future ages—shall be, for they are predestined to be, our slaves.

Future governments will not have honesty enough to be trusted with the determination of what rights shall be maintained, what abrogated—what laws kept in force, what repealed. Future subjects (I should say future citizens, for French government does not admit of subjects) will not have wit enough to be trusted with the choice whether to submit to the determination of the government of their time, or to resist it. Governments, citizens—all to the end of time—all must be kept in chains.

Such are their maxims—such their premises—for it is by such premises only that the doctrine of imprescriptible rights and unrepealable laws can be supported.

What is the real source of these imprescriptible rights—these unrepealable laws? Power turned blind by looking from its own height: self-conceit and tyranny exalted into insanity. No man was to have any other man for a servant, yet all men were forever to be their slaves. Making laws with imposture in their mouths, under pretence of declaring them—giving for laws anything that came uppermost, and these unrepealable ones, on pretence of finding them ready made. Made by what? Not by a God—they allow of none; but by their goddess, Nature.

The origination of governments from a contract is a pure fiction, or in other words, a falsehood. It never has been known to be true in any instance; the allegation of it does mischief, by involving the subject in error and confusion, and is neither necessary nor useful to any good purpose.

All governments that we have any account of have been gradually established by habit, after having been formed by force; unless in the instance of governments formed by individuals who have been emancipated, or have emancipated themselves, from governments already formed, the governments under which they were born—a rare case, and from which nothing follows with regard to the rest. What signifies it how governments are formed? Is it the less proper—the less conducive to the happiness of society—that the happiness of society should be the one object kept in view by the members of the government in all their measures? Is it the less the interest of men to be happy—less to be wished that they may be so—less the moral duty of their governors to make them so, as far as they can, at Mogadore than at Philadelphia?

Whence is it, but from government, that contracts derive their binding force? Contracts came from government, not government from contracts. It is from the habit of enforcing contracts, and seeing them enforced, that governments are chiefly indebted for whatever disposition they have to observe them.

Sentence 2. These rights [these imprescriptible as well as natural rights,] are liberty, property, security, and resistance to oppression.

Observe the extent of these pretended rights, each of them belonging to every man, and all of them without bounds. Unbounded liberty; that is, amongst other things, the liberty of doing or not doing on every occasion whatever each man pleases:—Unbounded property; that is, the right of doing with everything around him (with every *thing* at least, if not with every person,) whatsoever he pleases; communicating that right to anybody, and withholding it from anybody:—Unbounded security; that is, security for such his liberty, for such his property, and for his person, against every defalcation that can be called for on any account in respect of any of them: —Unbounded resistance to oppression; that is, unbounded exercise of the faculty of guarding himself against whatever unpleasant circumstance may present itself to his imagination or his passions under that name. Nature, say some of the interpreters of the pretended law of nature—nature gave to each man a right to everything; which is, in effect, but another way of saying —nature has given no such right to anybody; for in regard to most rights, it is as true that what is every man's right is no man's right, as that what is every man's business is no man's business. Nature gave—gave to every man a right to everything:—be it so—true; and hence the necessity of human government and human laws, to give to every man his own right, without which no right whatsoever would amount to anything. Nature gave every man a right to everything before the existence of laws, and in default of laws. This nominal universality and real nonentity of right, set up provisionally by nature in default of laws, the French oracle lays hold of, and perpetuates it under the law and in spite of laws. These anarchical rights which nature had set out with, democratic art attempts to rivet down, and declares indefeasible.

Unbounded liberty—I must still say unbounded liberty;—for though the next article but one returns to the charge, and gives such a definition of liberty as seems intended to set bounds to it, yet in effect the limitation amounts to nothing; and when, as here, no warning is given of any exception in the texture of the general rule, every exception which turns up is, not a confirmation but a contradiction of the rule:—liberty, without any pre-announced or intelligible bounds; and as to the other rights, they remain unbounded to the end: rights of man composed of a system of contradictions and impossibilities.

In vain would it be said, that though no bounds are here assigned to any of these rights, yet it is to be understood as taken for granted, and tacitly admitted and assumed, that they are to have bounds; viz. such bounds as it is understood will be set them by the laws. Vain, I say, would be this apology; for the supposition would be contradictory to the express declaration of the article itself, and would defeat the very object which the whole declaration has in view. It would be self-contradictory, because these rights are, in the same breath in which their existence is declared, declared to be imprescriptible; and imprescriptible, or as we in England should say, indefeasible, means nothing unless it exclude the interference of the laws.

It would be not only inconsistent with itself, but inconsistent with the declared and sole object of the declaration, if it did not exclude the interference of the laws. It is against the laws themselves, and the laws only, that this declaration is levelled. It is for the hands of the legislator and all legislators, and none but legislators, that the shackles it provides are intended,—it is against the apprehended encroachments of legislators that the rights in question, the liberty and property, and so forth, are intended to be made secure,—it is to such encroachments, and damages, and dangers, that whatever security it professes to give has respect. Precious security for unbounded rights against legislators, if the extent of those rights in every direction were purposely left to depend upon the will and pleasure of those very legislators!

Nonsensical or nugatory, and in both cases mischievous: such is the alternative.

So much for all these pretended indefeasible rights in the lump: their inconsistency with each other, as well as the inconsistency of them in the character of indefeasible rights with the existence of government and all peaceable society, will appear still more plainly when we examine them one by one.

1. *Liberty*, then, is imprescriptible—incapable of being taken away—out of the power of any government ever to take away: liberty,—that is, every branch of liberty—every individual exercise of liberty; for no line is drawn—no distinction—no exception made. What these instructors as well as governors of mankind appear not to know, is, that all rights are made at the expense of liberty—all laws by which rights are created or confirmed. No right without a correspondent obligation. Liberty, as against the coercion of the law, may, it is true, be given by the simple removal of the obligation by which that coercion was applied—by the simple repeal of the coercing law. But as against the coercion applicable by individual to individual, no liberty can be given to one man but in proportion as it is taken from another. All coercive laws, therefore (that is, all laws but constitutional laws, and laws repealing or modifying coercive laws,) and in particular all laws creative of liberty, are, as far as they go, abrogative of liberty. Not here and there a law only—not this or that possible law, but almost all laws, are therefore repugnant to these natural and imprescriptible rights: consequently null and void, calling for resistance and insurrection, and so on, as before.

Laws creative of rights of property are also struck at by the same anathema. How is property given? By restraining liberty; that is, by taking it away so far as is necessary for the purpose. How is your house made yours? By debarring every one else from the liberty of entering it without your leave.

2. *Property.* Property stands second on the list,—proprietary rights are in the number of the natural and imprescriptible rights of man—of the rights which a man is not indebted for to the laws, and which cannot be taken from him by the laws. Men—that is, every man (for a general expression given without exception is an universal one) has a right to property, to proprietary rights, *a right which* cannot be taken away from him by the laws. To proprietary rights. Good: but in relation to what subject? for as to proprietary rights—without a subject to which they are referable—without a subject in or in relation to which they can be exercised—they will hardly be of much value, they will hardly be worth taking care of, with so much solemnity. In vain would all the laws in the world have ascertained that I have a right to something. If this be all they have done for me—if there be no specific subject in relation to which my proprietary rights are established, I must either take what I want without right, or starve. As there is no such subject specified with relation to each man, or to any man (indeed how could there be?) the necessary inference (taking the passage literally) is, that every man has all manner of proprietary rights with relation to every subject of property with-

out exception: in a word, that every man has a right to every thing. Unfortunately, in most matters of property, what is every man's right is no man's right; so that the effect of this part of the oracle, if observed, would be, not to establish property, but to extinguish it—to render it impossible ever to be revived: and this is one of the rights declared to be imprescriptible.

It will probably be acknowledged, that according to this construction, the clause in question is equally ruinous and absurd:—and hence the inference may be, that this was not the construction—this was not the meaning in view. But by the same rule, every possible construction which the words employed can admit of, might be proved not to have been the meaning in view: nor is this clause a whit more absurd or ruinous than all that goes before it, and a great deal of what comes after it. And, in short, if this be not the meaning of it, what is? Give it a sense—give it any sense whatever,—it is mischievous: —to save it from that imputation, there is but one course to take, which is to acknowledge it to be nonsense.

Thus much would be clear, if anything were clear in it, that according to this clause, whatever proprietary rights, whatever property a man once has, no matter how, being imprescriptible, can never be taken away from him by any law: or of what use or meaning is the clause? So that the moment it is acknowledged in relation to any article, that such article is my property, no matter how or when it became so, that moment it is acknowledged that it can never be taken away from me: therefore, for example, all laws and all judgments, whereby anything is taken away from me without my free consent —all taxes, for example, and all fines—are void, and, as such call for resistance and insurrection, and so forth, as before.

3. *Security*. Security stands the third on the list of these natural and imprescriptible rights which laws did not give, and which laws are not in any degree to be suffered to take away. Under the head of security, liberty might have been included, so likewise property: since security for liberty, or the enjoyment of liberty, may be spoken of as a branch of security:—security for property, or the enjoyment of proprietary rights, as another. Security for person is the branch that seems here to have been understood:—security for each man's person, as against all those hurtful or disagreeable impressions (exclusive of those which consist in the mere disturbance of the enjoyment of liberty,) by which a man is affected in his person; loss of life—loss of limbs—loss of the use of limbs—wounds, bruises, and the like. All laws are null and void, then, which on any account or in any manner seek to expose the person of any man to any risk—which appoint capital or other corporal punishment—which expose a man to personal hazard in the service of the military power against foreign enemies, or in that of the judicial power against delinquents:—all laws which, to preserve the country from pestilence, authorize the immediate execution of a suspected person, in the event of his transgressing certain bounds.

4. *Resistance to oppression.* Fourth and last in the list of natural and imprescriptible rights, resistance to oppression—meaning, I suppose, the right to resist oppression. What is oppression? Power misapplied to the prejudice of some individual. What is it that a man has in view when he speaks of oppression? Some exertion of power which he looks upon as misapplied to the prejudice of some individual—to the producing on the part of such individual some suffering, to which (whether as forbidden by the laws or otherwise) we conceive he ought not to have been subjected. But against everything that can come under the name of oppression, provision has been already made, in the manner we have seen, by the recognition of the three preceding rights; since no oppression can fall upon a man which is not an infringement of his rights in relation to liberty, rights in relation to property, or rights in relation to security, as above described. Where, then, is the difference?—to what purpose this fourth clause after the three first? To this purpose: the mischief they seek to prevent, the rights they seek to establish, are the same; the difference lies in the nature of the remedy endeavoured to be applied. To prevent the mischief in question, the endeavour of the three former clauses is, to tie the hand of the legislator and his subordinates, by the fear of nullity, and the remote apprehension of general resistance and insurrection. The aim of this fourth clause is to raise the hand of the individual concerned to prevent the apprehended infraction of his rights at the moment when he looks upon it as about to take place.

Whenever you are about to be oppressed, you have a right to resist oppression: whenever you conceive yourself to be oppressed, conceive yourself to have a right to make resistance, and act accordingly. In proportion as a law of any kind—any act of power, supreme or subordinate, legislative, administrative, or judicial, is unpleasant to a man, especially if, in consideration of such its unpleasantness, his opinion is, that such act of power ought not to have been exercised, he of course looks upon it as oppression: as often as anything of this sort happens to a man—as often as anything happens to a man to inflame his passions,—this article, for fear his passions should not be sufficiently inflamed of themselves, sets itself to work to blow the flame, and urges him to resistance. Submit not to any decree or other act of power, of the justice of which you are not yourself perfectly convinced. If a constable call upon you to serve in the militia, shoot the constable and not the enemy;—if the commander of a press-gang trouble you, push him into the sea—if a bailiff, throw him out of the window. If a judge sentence you to be imprisoned or put to death, have a dagger ready, and take a stroke first at the judge.

34 What Is Justice?*

JOHN STUART MILL

John Stuart Mill (1806–1873) was influenced by the radical reform ideas of Jeremy Bentham and his own father, James Mill, and made important contributions to the utilitarian theory of ethics. Mill also made important philosophical contributions in the area of logic, philosophy of science, and philosophy of religion. His best-known books are *The System of Logic, On Liberty, Utilitarianism,* and *Three Essays on Religion.*

In all ages of speculation, one of the strongest obstacles to the reception of the doctrine that Utility or Happiness is the criterion of right and wrong, has been drawn from the idea of Justice. The powerful sentiment, and apparently clear perception, which that word recalls with a rapidity and certainty resembling an instinct, have seemed to the majority of thinkers to point to an inherent quality in things; to show that the Just must have an existence in Nature as something absolute—generically distinct from every variety of the Expedient, and, in idea, opposed to it, though (as is commonly acknowledged) never, in the long run, disjoined from it in fact.

In the case of this, as of our other moral sentiments, there is no necessary connexion between the question of its origin, and that of its binding force. That a feeling is bestowed on us by Nature, does not necessarily legitimate all its promptings. The feeling of justice might be a peculiar instinct, and might yet require, like our other instincts, to be controlled and enlightened by a higher reason. If we have intellectual instincts, leading us to judge in a particular way, as well as animal instincts that prompt us to act in a particular way, there is no necessity that the former should be more infallible in their sphere than the latter in theirs; it may as well happen that wrong judgments are occasionally suggested by those, as wrong actions by these. But though it is one thing to believe that we have natural feelings of justice, and another to acknowledge them as an ultimate criterion of conduct, these two opinions are very closely connected in point of fact. Mankind are always predisposed to believe that any subjective feeling, not otherwise accounted for, is a revelation of some objective reality. Our present object is to determine whether the reality, to which the feeling of justice corresponds, is one which needs any such special revelation; whether the justice or injustice of an

* From John Stuart Mill, *Utilitarianism,* first published in 1863.

action is a thing intrinsically peculiar, and distinct from all its other qualities, or only a combination of certain of those qualities, presented under a peculiar aspect. For the purpose of this inquiry, it is practically important to consider whether the feeling itself, of justice and injustice, is *sui generis* like our sensations of colour and taste, or a derivative feeling, formed by a combination of others. And this it is the more essential to examine, as people are in general willing enough to allow, that objectively the dictates of justice coincide with a part of the field of General Expediency; but inasmuch as the subjective mental feeling of Justice is different from that which commonly attaches to simple expediency, and, except in extreme cases of the latter, is far more imperative in its demands, people find it difficult to see, in Justice, only a particular kind of branch of general utility, and think that its superior binding force requires a totally different origin.

To throw light upon this question, it is necessary to attempt to ascertain what is the distinguishing character of justice, or of injustice: what is the quality, or whether there is any quality, attributed in common to all modes of conduct designated as unjust (for justice, like many other moral attributes, is best defined by its opposite), and distinguishing them from such modes of conduct as are disapproved, but without having that particular epithet of disapprobation applied to them. If, in everything which men are accustomed to characterize as just or unjust, some one common attribute or collection of attributes is always present, we may judge whether this particular attribute or combination of attributes would be capable of gathering round it a sentiment of that peculiar character and intensity by virtue of the general laws of our emotional constitution, or whether the sentiment is inexplicable, and requires to be regarded as a special provision of Nature. If we find the former to be the case, we shall, in resolving this question, have resolved also the main problem: if the latter, we shall have to seek for some other mode of investigating it.

To find the common attributes of a variety of objects, it is necessary to begin by surveying the objects themselves in the concrete. Let us therefore advert successively to the various modes of action, and arrangements of human affairs, which are classed by universal or widely spread opinion, as Just or as Unjust. The things well known to excite the sentiments associated with those names, are of a very multifarious character. I shall pass them rapidly in review, without studying any particular arrangement.

In the first place, it is mostly considered unjust to deprive any one of his personal liberty, his property, or any other thing which belongs to him by law. Here, therefore, is one instance of the application of the terms just and unjust in a perfectly definite sense, namely, that it is just to respect, unjust to violate, the *legal rights* of any one. But this judgment admits of several exceptions, arising from the other forms in which the notions of justice and injustice present themselves. For example, the person who suffers the deprivation may (as the phrase is) have *forfeited* the rights which he is so deprived of: a case to which we shall return presently. But also,

Secondly; the legal rights of which he is deprived, may be rights which *ought* not to have belonged to him; in other words, the law which confers on him these rights, may be a bad law. When it is so, or when (which is the same thing for our purpose) it is supposed to be so, opinions will differ as to the justice or injustice of infringing it. Some maintain that no law, however bad, ought to be disobeyed by an individual citizen; that his opposition to it, if shown at all, should only be shown in endeavouring to get it altered by competent authority. This opinion (which condemns many of the most illustrious benefactors of mankind, and would often protect pernicious institutions against the only weapons which, in the state of things existing at the time, have any chance of succeeding against them) is defended, by those who hold it, on grounds of expediency; principally on that of the importance, to the common interest of mankind, of maintaining inviolate the sentiment of submission to law. Other persons, again, hold the directly contrary opinion, that any law, judged to be bad, may blamelessly be disobeyed, even though it be not judged to be unjust, but only inexpedient; while others would confine the licence of disobedience to the case of unjust laws; but again, some say, that all laws which are inexpedient are unjust; since every law imposes some restriction on the natural liberty of mankind, which restriction is an injustice, unless legitimated by tending to their good. Among these diversities of opinion, it seems to be universally admitted that there may be unjust laws, and that law, consequently, is not the ultimate criterion of justice, but may give to one person a benefit, or impose on another an evil, which justice condemns. When, however, a law is thought to be unjust, it seems always to be regarded as being so in the same ways in which a breach of law is unjust, namely, by infringing somebody's right; which, as it cannot in this case be a legal right, receives a different appellation, and is called a moral right. We may say, therefore, that a second case of injustice consists in taking or withholding from any person that to which he has a *moral right*.

Thirdly, it is universally considered just that each person should obtain that (whether good or evil) which he *deserves*; and unjust that he should obtain a good, or be made to undergo an evil, which he does not deserve. This is, perhaps, the clearest and most emphatic form in which the idea of justice is conceived by the general mind. As it involves the notion of desert, the question arises, what constitutes desert? Speaking in a general way, a person is understood to deserve good if he does right, evil if he does wrong; and in a more particular sense, to deserve good from those to whom he does or has done good, and evil from those to whom he does or has done evil. The precept of returning good for evil has never been regarded as a case of the fulfilment of justice, but as one in which the claims of justice are waived, in obedience to other considerations.

Fourthly, it is confessedly unjust to *break faith* with any one: to violate an engagement, either express or implied, or disappoint expectations raised by our own conduct, at least if we have raised those expectations knowingly and voluntarily. Like the other obligations of justice already spoken of, this one is not regarded as absolute, but as capable of being overruled by a stronger obligation of justice on the other side; or by such conduct on the part of the person concerned as is deemed to absolve us from our obligation to him, and to constitute a *forfeiture* of the benefit which he has been led to expect.

Fifthly, it is, by universal admission, inconsistent with justice to be *partial*; to show favour or preference to one person over another, in matters to which favour and preference do not properly apply. Impartiality, however, does not seem to be regarded as a duty in itself, but rather as instrumental to some other duty; for it is admitted that favour and preference are not always censurable, and indeed the cases in which they are condemned are rather the exception than the rule. A person would be more likely to be blamed than applauded for giving his family or friends no superiority in good offices over strangers, when he could do so without violating any other duty; and no one thinks it unjust to seek one person in preference to another as a friend, connexion, or companion. Impartiality where rights are concerned is of course obligatory, but this is involved in the more general obligation of giving to every one his right. A tribunal, for example, must be impartial, because it is bound to award, without regard to any other consideration, a disputed object to the one of two parties who has the right to it. There are other cases in which impartiality means, being solely influenced by desert; as with those who, in the capacity of judges, preceptors, or parents, administer reward and punishment as such. There are cases, again, in which it means, being solely influenced by consideration for the public interest; as in making a selection among candidates for a Government employment. Impartiality, in short, as an obligation of justice, may be said to mean, being exclusively influenced by the considerations which it is supposed ought to influence the particular case in hand; and resisting the solicitation of any motives which prompt to conduct different from what those considerations would dictate.

Nearly allied to the idea of impartiality, is that of *equality*; which often enters as a component part both into the conception of justice and into the practice of it, and, in the eyes of many persons, constitutes its essence. But in this, still more than in any other case, the notion of justice varies in different persons, and always conforms in its variations to their notion of utility. Each person maintains that equality is the dictate of justice, except where he thinks that expediency requires inequality. The justice of giving equal protection to the right of all, is maintained by those who support the most outrageous inequality in the rights themselves. Even in slave countries it is theoretically admitted that the rights of the slave, such as they are, ought to be as sacred as those of the master; and that a tribunal which fails to enforce them with equal strictness is wanting in justice; while, at the same time, institutions which leave to the slave scarcely any rights to enforce, are not deemed unjust, because they are not deemed inexpedient. Those who think that utility requires distinctions of rank, do not consider it unjust that riches and social privileges should be unequally dispensed; but those who think this inequality inexpedient, think it unjust also. Whoever thinks that government is necessary, sees no injustice in as much inequality as is constituted by giving to the magistrate powers not granted to other people. Even among those who hold levelling doctrines, there are as many questions of justice as there are differences of opinion about expediency. Some Communists consider it unjust that the produce of the labour of the community should be shared on any other principle than that of exact equality; others think it just that those should receive most whose needs are greatest; while others hold that those who work harder, or who produce more, or whose services are more valuable to the community, may justly claim a larger quota in the division of the produce. And the sense of natural justice may be plausibly appealed to in behalf of every one of these opinions.

Among so many diverse applications of the term Justice, which yet is not regarded as ambiguous, it is a matter of some difficulty to seize the mental link which holds them together, and on which the moral sentiment adhering to the term essentially depends. . . .

In our survey of the various popular acceptations of justice, the term appeared generally to involve the idea of a personal right—a claim on the part of one or more individuals, like that which the law gives when it confers a proprietary or other legal right. Whether the injustice consists in depriving a person of a possession, or in breaking faith with him, or in treating him worse than he deserves, or worse than other people who have no greater claims, in each case the supposition implies two things—a wrong done, and some assignable person who is wronged. Injustice may also be done by treating a person better than others; but the wrong in this case is to his competitors, who are also assignable persons. It seems to me that this feature in the case—a right in some person, correlative to the moral obligation—constitutes the specific difference between justice, and generosity or beneficence. Justice implies something which it is not only right to do, and wrong not to do, but which some individual person can claim from us as his moral right. No one has a moral right to our generosity or beneficence, because we are not morally bound to practise those virtues towards any given individual. And it will be found, with respect to this as with respect to every correct definition, that the instances which seem to conflict with it are those which most confirm it. For if a moralist attempts, as some have done, to make out that mankind generally, though not any given individual, have a right to all the good we can do to them, he at once, by that thesis, includes generosity and beneficence within the category of justice. He is obliged to say, that our utmost exertions are *due* to our fellow creatures, thus assimilating them to a debt; or that nothing less can be a sufficient *return* for what society does for us, thus classing the case as one of gratitude; both of which are acknowledged cases of justice. Wherever there is a right the case is one of justice, and not of the virtue of beneficence: and whoever does not place the distinction between justice and morality in general where we have now placed it, will be found to make no distinction between them at all, but to merge all morality in justice. . . .

The idea of justice supposes two things; a rule of conduct, and a sentiment which sanctions the rule. The first must be supposed common to all mankind, and intended for their good. The other (the sentiment) is a desire that punishment may be suffered by those who infringe the rule. There is involved, in addition, the conception of some definite person who suffers by the infringement; whose rights (to use the expression appropriated to the case) are violated by it. And the sentiment of justice appears to me to be, the animal desire to repel or retaliate a hurt or damage to oneself, or to those with whom one sympathises, widened so as to include all persons, by the human capacity of enlarged sympathy, and the human conception of intelligent self-interest. From the latter elements, the feeling derives its morality; from the former, its peculiar impressiveness, and energy of self-assertion. . . .

To have a right, then, is, I conceive, to have something which society ought to defend me in the possession of. If the objector goes on to ask why it ought, I can give him no other reason than general utility . . .

If the preceding analysis, or something resembling it, be not the correct account of the notion of justice; if justice be totally independent of utility, and be a standard *per se*, which the mind can recognise by simple introspection of itself; it is hard to understand why that internal oracle is so ambiguous, and why so many things appear either just or unjust, according to the light in which they are regarded.

We are continually informed that Utility is an uncertain standard, which every different person interprets differently, and that there is no safety but in the immutable, ineffaceable, and unmistakeable dictates of Justice, which carry their evidence in themselves, and are independent of the fluctuations of opinion. One would suppose from this that on questions of justice there could be no controversy; that if we take that for our rule, its application to any given case could leave us in as little doubt as a mathematical demonstration. So far is this from being the fact, that there is as much difference of opinion, and as fierce discussion, about what is just, as about what is useful to society. Not only have different nations and individuals different notions of justice, but, in the mind of one and the same individual, justice is not some one rule, principle, or maxim, but many, which do not always coincide in their dictates, and in choosing between which, he is guided either by some extraneous standard, or by his own personal predilections. . . .

Is, then, the difference between the Just and the Expedient a merely imaginary distinction? Have mankind been under a delusion in thinking that justice is a more sacred thing than policy, and that the latter ought only to be listened to after the former has been satisfied? By no means. The exposition we have given of the nature and origin of the sentiment, recognises a real distinction; and no one of those who profess the most sublime contempt for the consequences of actions as an element in their morality, attaches more importance to the distinction than I do. While I dispute the pretensions of any theory which sets up an imaginary standard of justice not grounded on utility, I account the justice which is grounded on utility to be the chief part, and incomparably the most sacred and binding part, of all morality. Justice is a name for certain classes of moral rules, which concern the essentials of human well-being more nearly, and are therefore of more absolute obligation, than any other rules for the guidance of life; and the notion which we have found to be of the essence of the idea of justice, that of a right residing in an individual, implies and testifies to this more binding obligation. . . .

But this great moral duty rests upon a still deeper foundation, being a direct emanation from the first principle of morals, and not a mere logical corollary from secondary or derivative doctrines. It is involved in the very meaning of Utility, or the Greatest-Happiness Principle. That principle is a mere form of words without rational signification, unless one person's happiness, supposed equal in degree (with the proper allowance made for kind), is counted for exactly as much as another's. Those conditions being supplied, Bentham's dictum, 'everybody to count for one, nobody for more than one,' might be written under the principle of utility as an explanatory commentary. The equal claim of everybody to happiness in the estimation of the moralist and the legislator, involves an equal claim to all the means of happiness, except in so far as the inevitable conditions of human life, and the general interest, in which that of every individual is included, sets limits to the maxim; and those limits ought to be strictly construed. As every other maxim of justice, so this, is by no means applied or held applicable universally; on the contrary, as I have already remarked, it bends to every person's ideas of social expediency. But in whatever case it is deemed applicable at all, it is held to be the dictate of justice. All persons are deemed to have a *right* to equality of treatment, except when some recognised social expediency requires the reverse. And hence all social inequalities which have ceased to be considered expedient, assume the character not of simple inexpediency, but of injustice, and appear so tyrannical, that people are apt to wonder how they ever could have been tolerated; forgetful that they themselves perhaps tolerate other inequalities under an equally mistaken notion of expediency, the correction of which would make that which they approve seem quite as monstrous as what they have at last learnt to condemn. The entire history of social improvement has been a series of transitions, by which one custom or institution after another, from being a supposed primary necessity of social existence, has passed into the rank of an universally stigmatised injustice and tyranny. So it has been with the distinctions of slaves and freemen, nobles and serfs, patricians and plebeians; and so it will be, and in part already is, with the aristocracies of colour, race, and sex.

35 *What Are the Limits of Freedom?**

JOHN STUART MILL

John Stuart Mill (1806–1873) was influenced by the radical reform ideas of Jeremy Bentham and his own father, James Mill, and made important contributions to the utilitarian theory of ethics. Mill also made important philosophical contributions in the area of logic, philosophy of science, and philosophy of religion. His best-known books are *The System of Logic, On Liberty, Utilitarianism,* and *Three Essays on Religion.*

The subject of this Essay is not the so-called Liberty of the Will . . . but Civil, or Social Liberty: the nature and limits of the power which can be legitimately exercised by society over the individual. A question seldom stated, and hardly ever discussed, in general terms, but which profoundly influences the practical controversies of the age by its latent presence, and is likely soon to make itself recognized as the vital question of the future. It is so far from being new, that, in a certain sense, it has divided mankind, almost from the remotest ages; but in the stage of progress into which the more civilized portions of the species have now entered, it presents itself under new conditions, and requires a different and more fundamental treatment.

The struggle between Liberty and Authority is the most conspicuous feature in the portions of history with which we are earliest familiar, particularly in that of Greece, Rome, and England. But in old times this contest was between subjects, or some classes of subjects, and the Government. By liberty, was meant protection against the tyranny of the political rulers. The rulers were conceived (except in some of the popular governments of Greece) as in a necessarily antagonistic position to the people whom they ruled. They consisted of a governing One, or a governing tribe or caste, who derived their authority from inheritance or conquest, who, at all events, did not hold it at the pleasure of the governed, and whose supremacy men did not venture, perhaps did not desire, to contest, whatever precautions might be taken against its oppressive exercise. Their power was regarded as necessary, but also as highly dangerous; as a weapon which they would

---

* From John Stuart Mill, *On Liberty,* first published in 1859.

attempt to use against their subjects, no less than against external enemies. To prevent the weaker members of the community from being preyed upon by innumerable vultures, it was needful that there should be an animal of prey stronger than the rest, commissioned to keep them down. But as the king of the vultures would be no less bent upon preying on the flock than any of the minor harpies, it was indispensable to be in a perpetual attitude of defense against his beak and claws. The aim, therefore, of patriots was to set limits to the power which the ruler should be suffered to exercise over the community; and this limitation was what they meant by liberty. It was attempted in two ways. First, by obtaining a recognition of certain immunities, called political liberties or rights, which it was to be regarded as a breach of duty in the ruler to infringe, and which, if he did infringe, specific resistance, or general rebellion, was held to be justifiable. A second, and generally a later expedient, was the establishment of constitutional checks, by which the consent of the community, or of a body of some sort, supposed to represent its interests, was made a necessary condition to some of the more important acts of the governing power. To the first of these modes of limitation, the ruling power, in most European countries, was compelled, more or less, to submit. It was not so with the second; and, to attain this, or when already in some degree possessed, to attain it more completely, became everywhere the principal object of the lovers of liberty. And so long as mankind were content to combat one enemy by another, and to be ruled by a master, on condition of being guaranteed more or less efficaciously against his tyranny, they did not carry their aspirations beyond this point.

A time, however, came, in the progress of human affairs, when men ceased to think it a necessity of nature that their governors should be an independent power, opposed in interest to themselves. It appeared to them much better that the various magistrates of the State should be their tenants or delegates, revocable at their pleasure. In that way alone, it seemed, could they have complete security that the powers of government would never be abused to their disadvantage. By degrees this new demand for elective and temporary rulers became the prominent object of the exertions of the popular party, wherever any such party existed; and superseded, to a considerable extent, the previous efforts to limit the power of rulers. As the struggle proceeded for making the ruling power emanate from the periodical choice of the ruled, some persons began to think that too much importance had been attached to the limitation of the power itself. *That* (it might seem) was a resource against rulers whose interests were habitually opposed to those of the people. What was now wanted was, that the rulers should be identified with the people; that their interest and will should be the interest and will of the nation. The nation did not need to be protected against its own will. There was no fear of its tyrannizing over itself. Let the rulers be effectually responsible to it, promptly removable by it, and it could afford to trust them with power of which it could itself dictate the use to be made.

But, in political and philosophical theories, as well as in persons, success discloses faults and infirmities which failure might have concealed from observation. The notion, that the people have no need to limit their power over themselves, might seem axiomatic, when popular government was a thing only dreamed about, or read of as having existed at some distant period of the past. Neither was that notion necessarily disturbed by such temporary aberrations as those of the French Revolution, the worst of which were the work of an usurping few, and which, in any case, belonged, not to the permanent working of popular institutions, but to a sudden and convulsive outbreak against monarchical and aristocratic despotism. In time, however, a democratic republic came to occupy a large portion of the earth's surface, and made itself felt as one of the most powerful members of the community of nations; and elective and responsible government became subject to the observations and criticisms which wait upon a great existing fact. It was now perceived that such phrases as "self-government," and "the power of the people over themselves," do not express the true state of the case. The "people" who exercise the power are not always the same people with those over whom it is exercised; and the "self-government" spoken of is not the government of each by himself, but of each by all the rest. The will of the people, moreover, practically means the will of the most numerous or the most active *part* of the people; the majority, or those who succeed in making themselves accepted as the majority; the people, consequently, *may* desire to oppress a part of their number; and precautions are as much needed against this as against any other abuse of power. The limitation, therefore, of the power of government over individuals loses none of its importance when the holders of power are regularly accountable to the community, that is, to the strongest party therein. This view of things, recommending itself equally to the intelligence of thinkers and to the inclination of those important classes in European society to whose real or supposed interests democracy is adverse, has had no difficulty in establishing itself; and in political speculations "the tyranny of the majority" is now generally included among the evils against which society requires to be on its guard.

Like other tyrannies, the tyranny of the majority was at first, and is still vulgarly, held in dread, chiefly as operating through the acts of the public authorities. But reflecting persons perceived that when society is itself the tyrant—society collectively, over the separate individuals who compose it—its means of tyrannizing are not restricted to the acts which it may do by the hands of its political functionaries. Society can and does execute its own mandates: and if it issues wrong mandates instead of right, or any mandates at all in things with which it ought not to meddle, it practices a social tyranny more formidable than many kinds of political oppression, since, though not usually upheld by such extreme penalties, it leaves fewer means of escape, penetrating much more deeply into the details of life, and enslaving the soul itself. Protection, therefore, against the tyranny of the magistrate is not enough: there needs protection also against the tyranny of the prevailing opinion and feeling; against the tendency of society to impose, by other means than civil penalties, its own ideas and practices as rules of conduct on those who dissent from them; to fetter the development, and, if possible, prevent the formation, of any individuality not in harmony with its ways, and compel all characters to fashion themselves upon the model of its own. There is a limit to the legitimate interference of collective opinion with individual independence: and to find that limit, and maintain it against encroachment, is as indispensable to a good condition of human affairs, as protection against political despotism.

But though this proposition is not likely to be contested in general terms, the practical question, where to place the limit—how to make the fitting adjustment between individual independence and social control—is a subject on which nearly everything remains to be done. All that makes existence valuable to any one, depends on the enforcement of restraints upon the actions of other people. Some rules of conduct, therefore, must be imposed, by law in the first place, and by opinion on many things which are not fit subjects for the operation of law. What these rules should be, is the principal question in human affairs. . . .

There is, in fact, no recognized principle by which the propriety or impropriety of government interference is customarily tested. People decide according to their personal preferences. Some, whenever they see any good to be done, or evil to be remedied, would willingly instigate the government to undertake the business; while others prefer to bear almost any amount of social evil, rather than add one to the departments of human interests amenable to governmental control. And men range themselves on one or the other side in any particular case, according to this general direction of their sentiments; or according to the degree of interest which they feel in the particular thing which it is proposed that the government should do, or according to the belief they entertain that the government would, or would not, do it in the manner they prefer; but very rarely on account of any opinion to which they consistently adhere, as to what things are fit to be done by a government. And it seems to me that in consequence of their absence of rule or principle, one side is at present as often wrong as the other; the interference of government is, with about equal frequency, improperly invoked and improperly condemned.

The object of this Essay is to assert one very simple principle, as entitled to govern absolutely the dealings of society with the individual in the way of compulsion and control, whether the means used by physical force in the form of legal penalties, or the moral coercion of public opinion. That principle is, that the sole end for which mankind are warranted, individually or collectively, in interfering with the liberty of action of any of their number, is self-protection. That the only purpose for which power can be rightfully exercised over any member of a civilized community, against his will, is to prevent harm to others. His own good, either physical or moral, is not a sufficient warrant. He cannot rightfully be compelled to do or forbear because it will be better for him to do so, because it will make him happier, because, in the opinions of others, to do so would be wise, or even right. These are good reasons for remonstrating with him, or reasoning with him, or persuading him, or entreating him, but not for compelling him, or visiting him with any evil in case he do otherwise. To justify that, the conduct from which it is desired to deter him, must be calculated to produce evil to some one else. The only part of the conduct of any one, for which he is amenable to society, is that which concerns others. In the part which merely concerns himself, his independence is, of right, absolute. Over himself, over his own body and mind, the individual is sovereign.

It is, perhaps, hardly necessary to say that this doctrine is meant to apply only to human beings in the maturity of their faculties. We are not speaking of children, or of young persons below the age which the law may fix as that of manhood or womanhood. Those who are still in a state to require being taken care of by others, must be protected against their own actions as well as against external injury. For the same reason, we may leave out of consideration those backward states of society in which the race itself may be considered as in its non-age. The early difficulties in the way of spontaneous progress are so great, that there is seldom any choice of means for overcoming them; and a ruler full of the spirit of improvement is warranted in the use of any expedients that will attain an end, perhaps otherwise unattainable. Despotism is a legitimate mode of government in dealing with barbarians, provided the end be their improvement, and the means justified by actually effecting that end. Liberty, as a principle, has no application to any state of things anterior to the time when mankind have become capable of being improved by free and equal discussion. Until then, there is nothing for them but implicit obedience to an Akbar or a Charlemagne, if they are so fortunate as to find one. But as soon as mankind have attained the capacity of being guided to their own improvement by conviction or persuasion (a period long since reached in all nations with whom we need here concern ourselves), compulsion, either in the direct form or in that of pains and penalties for non-compliance, is no longer admissible as a means to their own good, and justifiable only for the security of others.

It is proper to state that I forgo any advantage which could be derived to my argument from the idea of abstract right, as a thing independent of utility. I regard utility as the ultimate appeal on all ethical questions; but it must be utility in the largest sense, grounded on the permanent interests of man as a progressive being. Those interests, I contend, authorize the subjection of individual spontaneity to external control, only in respect to those actions of each, which concern the interest of other people. If any one does an act hurtful to others, there is a prima facie case for punishing him, by law, or, where legal penalties are not safely applicable, by general disapprobation. There are also many positive acts for the benefit of others, which he may rightfully be compelled to perform; such as, to give evidence in a court of justice; to bear his fair share in the common defense, or in any other joint work necessary to the interest of the society of which he enjoys the protection; and to perform certain acts of individual beneficence, such as saving a fellow creature's life, or interposing to protect the defenseless against ill-usage, things which whenever it is obviously a man's duty to do, he may rightfully be made responsible to society for not doing.

But there is a sphere of action in which society, as distinguished from the individual, has, if any, only an indirect interest; comprehending all that portion of a person's life and conduct which affects only himself, or if it also affects others, only with their free, voluntary, and undeceived consent and participation. When I say only himself, I mean directly, and in the first instance: for whatever affects himself, may affect others through himself; and the objection which may be grounded on this contingency will receive consideration in the sequel. This, then, is the appropriate region of human liberty. It comprises, first, the inward domain of consciousness; demanding liberty of conscience, in the most comprehensive sense; liberty of thought and feeling; absolute freedom of opinion and sentiment on all subjects, practical or speculative, scientific, moral, or theological. The liberty of expressing and publishing opinions may seem to fall under a different principle, since it belongs to that part of the conduct of an individual which concerns other people; but, being almost of as much importance as the liberty of thought itself, and resting in great part on the same reasons, is practically inseparable from it. Secondly, the principle requires liberty of tastes and pursuits; of framing the plan of our life to suit our own character; of doing as we like, subject to such consequences as may follow: without impediment from our fellow creatures, so long as what we do does not harm them, even though they should think our conduct foolish, perverse, or wrong. Thirdly, from this liberty of each individual, follows the liberty, within the same limits, of combination among individuals; freedom to unite, for any purpose not involving harm to others: the persons combining being supposed to be of full age, and not forced or deceived.

No society in which these liberties are not, on the whole, respected, is free, whatever may be its form of government; and none is completely free in which they do not exist absolute and unqualified. The only freedom which deserves the name, is that of pursuing our own good in our own way, so long as we do not attempt to deprive others of theirs, or impede their efforts to obtain it. Each is the proper guardian of his own health, whether bodily, or mental and spiritual. Mankind are greater gainers by suffering each other to live as seems good to themselves, than by compelling each to live as seems good to the rest.

OF THE LIBERTY OF THOUGHT AND DISCUSSION

The time, it is to be hoped, is gone by, when any defense would be necessary of the "liberty of the press" as one of the securities against corrupt or tyrannical government. No argument, we may suppose, can now be needed, against permitting a legislature or an executive, not identified in interest with the people, to prescribe opinions to them, and determine what doctrines or what arguments they shall be allowed to hear. Let us suppose, therefore, that the government is entirely at one with the people, and never thinks of exerting any power of coercion unless in agreement with what it conceives to be their voice. But I deny the right of the people to exercise such coercion, either by themselves or by their government. The power itself is illegitimate. The best government has no more title to it than the worst. It is as noxious, or more noxious, when exerted in accordance with public opinion, than when in opposition to it. If all mankind minus one, were of one opinion, and only one person were of the contrary opinion, mankind would be no more justified in silencing that one person, than he, if he had the power, would be justified in silencing mankind. Were an opinion a personal possession of no value except to the owner; if to be obstructed in the enjoyment of it were simply a private injury, it would make some difference whether the injury was inflicted only on a few persons or on many. But the peculiar evil of silencing the expression of an opinion is, that it is robbing the human race; posterity as well as the existing generation; those who dissent from the opinion, still more than those who hold it. If the opinion is right, they are deprived of the opportunity of exchanging error for truth: if wrong, they lose, what is almost as great a benefit, the clearer perception and livelier impression of truth, produced by its collision with error.

It is necessary to consider separately these two hypotheses, each of which has a distinct branch of the argument corresponding to it. We can never be sure that the opinion we are endeavoring to stifle is a false opinion; and if we were sure, stifling it would be an evil still.

First: the opinion which it is attempted to suppress by authority may possibly be true. Those who desire to suppress it, of course deny its truth; but they are not infallible. They have no authority to decide the question for all mankind, and exclude every other person from the means of judging. To refuse a hearing to an opinion, because they are sure that it is false, is to assume that *their* certainty is the same thing as *absolute* certainty. All silencing of discussion is an assumption of infallibility. Its condemnation may be allowed to rest on this common argument, not the worse for being common.

Unfortunately for the good sense of mankind, the fact of their fallibility is far from carrying the weight in their practical judgment, which is always allowed to it in theory; for while every one well knows himself to be fallible, few think it necessary to take any precautions against their own fallibility, or admit the supposition that any opinion, of which they feel very certain, may be one of the examples of the error to which they acknowledge themselves to be liable. Absolute princes, or others who are accustomed to unlimited deference, usually feel this complete confidence in their own opinions on nearly all subjects. People more happily situated, who sometimes hear their opinions disputed, and are not wholly unused to be set right when they are wrong, place the same unbounded reliance only on such of their opinions as are shared by all who surround them, or to whom they habitually defer: for in proportion to a man's want of confidence in his own solitary judgment, does he usually repose, with implicit trust, on the infallibility of "the world" in general. And the world, to each individual, means the part of it with which he comes in contact; his party, his sect, his church, his class of society: the man may be called, by comparison, almost liberal and large-minded to whom it means anything so comprehensive as his own country or his own age. Nor is his faith in this collective authority at all shaken by his being aware that other ages, countries, sects, churches, classes, and parties have thought, and even now think, the exact reverse. He devolves upon his own world the responsibility of being in the right against the dissentient worlds of other people; and it never troubles him that mere accident has decided which of these numerous worlds is the object of his reliance, and that the same causes which make him a Churchman in London, would have made him a Buddhist or a Confucian in Pekin. Yet it is as evident in itself, as any amount of argument can make it, that ages are no more infallible than individuals; every age having held many opinions which subsequent ages have deemed not only false but absurd; and it is as certain that many opinions, now general, will be ejected by future ages, as it is that many, once general, are rejected by the present.

The objection likely to be made to this argument would probably take some such form as the following. There is no greater assumption of infallibility in forbidding the propagation of error, than in any other thing which is done by public authority on its own judgment and responsibility. Judgment is given to men that they may use it. Because it may be used erroneously, are men to be told that they ought not to use it at all? To prohibit what they think pernicious, is not claiming exemption from error, but fulfilling the duty incumbent on them, although fallible, of acting on their conscientious conviction. If we were never to act on our opinions, because those opinions may be wrong, we should leave all our interests uncared for, and all our duties unperformed. An objection which applies to all conduct, can be valid objection to any conduct in particular. It is the duty of governments, and of individuals, to form the truest opinions they can; to form them carefully, and never impose them upon others unless they are quite sure of being right. But when they are sure (sure reasoners may say), it is not conscientiousness but cowardice to shrink from acting on their opinions, and allow doctrines which they honestly think dangerous to the welfare of mankind, either in this life or in another, to be scattered abroad without restraint, because other people, in less enlightened times, have persecuted opinions now believed to be true. Let us take care, it may be said, not to make the same mistake: but governments and nations have made mistakes in other things, which are not denied to be fit subjects for the exercise of authority: they have laid on bad taxes, made unjust wars. Ought we therefore to lay on no taxes, and, under whatever provocation, make no wars? Men, and governments, must act to the best of their ability. There is no such thing as absolute certainty, but there is assurance sufficient for the purposes of human life. We may, and must, assume our opinion to be true for the guidance of our own conduct: and it is assuming no more when we forbid bad men to pervert society by the propagation of opinions which we regard as false and pernicious.

I answer, that it is assuming very much more. There is the greatest difference between presuming an opinion to be true, because, with every opportunity for contesting it, it has not been refuted, and assuming its truth for the purpose of not permitting its refutation. Complete liberty of contradicting and disproving our opinion, is the very condition which justifies us in assuming its truth for purposes of action; and on no other terms can a being with human faculties have any rational assurance of being right.

The beliefs which we have most warrant for, have no safeguard to rest on, but a standing invitation to the whole world to prove them unfounded. If the challenge is not accepted, or is accepted and the attempt fails, we are far enough from certainty still; but we have done the best that the existing state of human reason admits of; we have neglected nothing that could give the truth a chance of reaching us: if the lists are kept open, we may hope that if there be a better truth, it will be found when the human mind is capable of receiving it; and in the meantime we may rely on having attained such approach to truth, as is possible in our own day. This is the amount of certainty attainable by a fallible being, and this the sole way of attaining it.

In order more fully to illustrate the mischief of denying a hearing to opinions because we, in our own judgment, have condemned them, it will be desirable to fix down the discussion to a concrete case; and I choose, by preference, the cases which are least favorable to me—in which the argument against freedom of opinion, both on the score of truth and on that of utility, is considered the strongest. Let the opinions impugned be the belief in a God and in a future state, or any of the commonly received doctrines of morality. To fight the battle on such ground, gives a great advantage to an unfair antagonist; since he will be sure to say (and many who have no desire to be unfair will say it internally), Are these the doctrines which you do not deem sufficiently certain to be taken under the protection of law? Is the belief in a God one of the opinions, to feel sure of which, you hold to be assuming infallibility? But I must be permitted to observe, that it is not the feeling sure of a doctrine (be it what it may) which I call an assumption of infallibility. It is the undertaking to decide that question *for others*, without allowing them to hear what can be said on the contrary side. And I denounce and reprobate this pretension not the less, if put forth on the side of my most solemn convictions. However positive any one's persuasion may be, not only of the falsity but of the pernicious consequences—not only of the pernicious consequences, but (to adopt expressions which I altogether condemn) the immorality and impiety of an opinion; yet if, in pursuance of that private judgment, though backed by the public judgment of his country or his contemporaries, he prevents the opinion from being heard in its defense, he assumes infallibility. And so far from the assumption being less objectionable or less dangerous because the opinion is called immoral or impious, this is the case of all others in which it is most fatal. These are exactly the occasions on which the men of one generation commit those dreadful mistakes, which excite the astonishment and horror of posterity. It is among such that we find the instances memorable in history, when the arm of the law has been employed to root out the best men and the noblest doctrines.

Mankind can hardly be too often reminded, that there was once a man named Socrates, between whom and the legal authorities and public opinion of his time, there took place a memorable collision. Born in an age and country abounding in individual greatness, this man has been handed down to us by those who best knew both him and the age, as the most virtuous man in it; while *we* know him as the head and prototype of all subsequent teachers of virtue, the source equally of the lofty inspiration of Plato and the judicious utilitarianism of Aristotle, "*i maëstri di color che sanno*," the two headsprings of ethical as of all other philosophy. This acknowledged master of all the eminent thinkers who have since lived—whose fame, still growing after more than two thousand years, all but outweighs the whole remainder of the names which make his native city illustrious—was put to death by his countrymen, after a judicial conviction, for impiety and immorality. Impiety, in denying the gods recognized by the State; indeed his accuser asserted (see the *Apologia*) that he believed in no gods at all. Immorality, in being, by his doctrines and instructions, a "corruptor of youth." Of these charges the tribunal, there is every ground for believing, honestly found him guilty, and condemned the man who probably of all then born had deserved best of mankind, to be put to death as a criminal.

It will be said, that we do not now put to death the introducers of new opinions: we are not like our fathers who slew the prophets, we even build sepulchres to them. It is true we no longer put heretics to death; and the amount of penal infliction which modern feeling would probably tolerate, even against the most obnoxious opinions, is not sufficient to extirpate them.

But though we do not now inflict so much evil on those who think differently from us, as it was formerly our custom to do, it may be that we do ourselves as much evil as ever by our treatment of them. Socrates was put to death, but the Socratic philosophy rose like the sun in heaven, and spread its illumination over the whole intellectual firmament. Christians were cast to the lions, but the Christian church grew up a stately and spreading tree, overtopping the older and less vigorous growths, and stifling them by its shade. Our merely social intolerance kills no one, roots out no opinions, but induces men to disguise them, or to abstain from any active effort for their diffusion. With us, heretical opinions do not perceptibly gain, or even lose, ground in each decade or generation; they never blaze out far and wide, but continue to smolder in the narrow circles of thinking and studious persons among whom they originate, without ever lighting up the general affairs of mankind with either a true or a deceptive light. And thus is kept up a state of things very satisfactory to some minds, because, without the unpleasant process of fining or imprisoning anybody, it maintains all prevailing opinions outwardly undisturbed, while it does not absolutely interdict the exercise of reason by dissentients afflicted with the malady of thought. A convenient plan for having peace in the intellectual world, and keeping all things going on therein very much as they do already. But the price paid for this sort of intellectual pacification, is the sacrifice of the entire moral courage of the human mind. A state of things in which a large portion of the most active and inquiring intellects find it advisable to keep the general principles and grounds of their convictions within their own breasts, and attempt, in what they address to the public, to fit as much as they can of their own conclusions to premises which they have internally renounced, cannot send forth the open, fearless characters, and logical, consistent intellects who once adorned the thinking world. The sort of men who can be looked for under it, are either mere conformers to commonplace, or time-servers for truth, whose arguments on all great subjects are meant for their hearers, and are not those which have convinced themselves. Those who avoid this alternative, do so by narrowing their thoughts and interest to things which can be spoken of without venturing within the region of principles, that is, to small practical matters, which would come right of themselves, if but the minds of mankind were strengthened and enlarged, and which will never be made effectually right until then: while that which would strengthen and enlarge men's minds, free and daring speculation on the highest subjects, is abandoned.

Those in whose eyes this reticence on the part of heretics is no evil, should consider in the first place, that in consequence of it there is never any fair and thorough discussion of heretical opinions; and that such of them as could not stand such a discussion, though they may be prevented from spreading, do not disappear. But it is not the minds of heretics that are deteriorated most, by the ban placed on all inquiry which does not end in the orthodox conclusions. The greatest harm done is to those who are not heretics, and whose whole mental development is cramped, and their reason cowed, by the fear of heresy. Who can compute what the world loses in the multitude of promising intellects combined with timid characters, who dare not follow out any bold, vigorous, independent train of thought, lest it should land them in something which would admit of being considered irreligious or immoral? Among them we may occasionally see some man of deep conscientiousness, and subtle and refined understanding, who spends a life in sophisticating with an intellect which he cannot silence, and exhausts the resources of ingenuity in attempting to reconcile the promptings of his conscience and reason with orthodoxy, which yet he does not, perhaps, to the end succeed in doing. No one can be a great thinker who does not recognize, that as a thinker it is his first duty to follow his intellect to whatever conclusions it may lead. Truth gains more even by the errors of one who, with due study and preparation, thinks for himself, than by the true opinions of those who only hold them because they do not suffer themselves to think. Not that it is solely, or chiefly, to form great thinkers, that freedom of thinking is required. On the contrary, it is as much and even more indispensable, to enable average human beings to attain the mental stature which they are capable of. There have been, and may again be, great individual thinkers, in a general atmosphere of mental slavery. But there never has been, nor ever will be, in that atmosphere, an intellectually active people. When any people has made a temporary approach to such a character, it has been because the dread of heterodox speculation was for a time suspended. Where there is a tacit convention that principles are not to be disputed; where the discussion of the greatest questions which can occupy humanity is considered to be closed, we cannot hope to find that generally high scale of mental activity which has made some periods of history so remarkable.

Let us now pass to the second division of the argument, and dismissing the supposition that any of the received opinions may be false, let us assume them to be true, and examine into the worth of the manner in which they are likely to be held, when their truth is not freely and openly canvassed. However unwillingly a person who has a strong opinion may admit the possibility that his opinion may be false, he ought to be moved by the consideration that however true it may be, if it is not fully, frequently, and fearlessly discussed, it will be held as a dead dogma, not a living truth.

There is a class of persons (happily not quite so numerous as formerly) who think it enough if a person assents undoubtingly to what they think true, though he has no knowledge whatever of the grounds of the opinion, and could not make a tenable defense of it against the most superficial objections. Such persons, if they can once get their creed taught from authority, naturally think that no good, and some harm, comes of its being allowed to be questioned. Where their influence prevails, they make it nearly impossible for the received opinion to be rejected wisely and considerately, though it may still be rejected rashly and ignorantly; for to shut out discussion entirely is seldom possible, and when it once gets in, beliefs not grounded on conviction are apt to give way before the slightest semblance of an argument. Waiving, however, this possibility—assuming that the true opinion abides in the mind, but abides as a prejudice, a belief independent of, and proof against, argument—this is not the way in which truth ought to be held by a rational being. This is not knowing the truth. Truth, thus held, is but one superstition the more accidentally clinging to the words which enunciate a truth.

He who knows only his own side of the case, knows little of that. His reasons may be good, and no one may have been able to refute them. But if he is equally unable to refute the reasons on the opposite side; if he does not so much as know what they are, he has no ground for preferring either opinion. The rational position for him would be suspension of judgment, and unless he contents himself with that, he is either led by authority, or adopts, like the generality of the world, the side to which he feels most inclination. Nor is it enough that he should hear the arguments of adversaries from his own teachers, presented as they state them, and accompanied by what they offer as refutations. That is not the way to do justice to the arguments, or bring them into real contact with his own mind. He must be able to hear them from persons who actually believe them; who defend them in earnest, and do their very utmost for them. He must know them in their most plausible and persuasive form; he must feel the whole force of the difficulty which the true view of the subject has to encounter and dispose of; else he will never really possess himself of the portion of truth which meets and removes that difficulty. Ninety-nine in a hundred of what are called educated men are in this condition; even of those who can argue fluently for their opinions. Their conclusion may be true, but it might be false for anything they know: they have never thrown themselves into the mental position of those who think differently from them, and considered what such persons may have to say; and consequently they do not, in any proper sense of the word, know the doctrine which they themselves profess.

But what! (it may be asked) Is the absence of unanimity an indispensable condition of true knowledge? Is it necessary that some part of mankind should persist in error, to enable any to realize the truth? Does a belief cease to be real and vital as soon as it is generally received—and is a proposition never thoroughly understood and felt unless some doubt of it remains? As soon as mankind have unanimously accepted a truth, does the truth perish within them? The highest aim and best result of improved intelligence, it has hitherto been thought, is to unite mankind more and more in the acknowledgment of all important truths: and does the intelligence only last as long as it has not achieved its object? Do the fruits of conquest perish by the very completeness of the victory?

I affirm no such thing. As mankind improve, the number of doctrines which are no longer disputed or doubted will be constantly on the increase: and the well-being of mankind may almost be measured by the number and gravity of the truths which have reached the point of being uncontested. The cessation, on one question after another, of serious controversy, is one of the necessary incidents of the consolidation of opinion; a consolidation as salutary in the case of true opinions, as it is dangerous and noxious when the opinions are erroneous. But though this gradual narrowing of the bounds of diversity of opinion is necessary in both senses of the term, being at once inevitable and indispensable, we are not therefore obliged to conclude that all its consequences must be beneficial. The loss of so important an aid to the intelligent and living apprehension of a truth, as is afforded by the necessity of explaining it to, or defending it against, opponents, though not sufficient to outweigh, is no trifling drawback from, the benefit of its universal recognition. Where this advantage can no longer be had, I confess I should like to see the teachers of mankind endeavoring to provide a substitute for it; some contrivance for making the difficulties of the question as present to the learner's consciousness, as if they were pressed upon him by a dissentient champion, eager for his conversion.

But instead of seeking contrivances for this purpose, they have lost those they formerly had. The Socratic dialectics, so magnificently exemplified in the dialogues of Plato, were a contrivance of this description. They were essentially a negative discussion of the great questions of philosophy and life, directed with consummate skill to the purpose of convincing any one who had merely adopted the commonplaces of received opinion, that he did not understand the subject—that he as yet attached no definite meaning to the doctrines he professed; in order that, becoming aware of his ignorance, he might be put in the way to attain a stable belief, resting on a clear apprehension both of the meaning of doctrines and of their evidence. It is the fashion of the present time to disparage negative logic—that which points out weaknesses in theory or errors in practice, without establishing positive truths. Such negative criticism would indeed be poor enough as an ultimate result; but as a means to attaining any positive knowledge or conviction worthy the name, it cannot be valued too highly; and until people are again systematically trained to it, there will be few great thinkers, and a low general average of intellect, in any but the mathematical and physical departments of speculation. On any other subject no one's opinions deserve the name of knowledge, except so far as he has either had forced upon him by others, or gone through of himself, the same mental process which would have been required of him in carrying on an active controversy with opponents. That, therefore, which when absent, it is so indispensable, but so difficult, to create, how worse than absurd it is to forego, when spontaneously offering itself! If there are any persons who contest a received opinion, or who will do so if law or opinion will let them, let us thank them for it, open our minds to listen to them, and rejoice that there is some one to do for us what we otherwise ought, if we have any regard for either the certainty or the vitality of our convictions, to do with much greater labor for ourselves.

We have now recognized the necessity to the mental well-being of mankind (on which all their other well-being depends) of freedom of opinion, and freedom of the expression of opinion, on four distinct grounds; which we will now briefly recapitulate.

First, if any opinion is compelled to silence, that opinion may, for aught we can certainly know, be true. To deny this is to assume our own infallibility.

Secondly, though the silenced opinion be an error, it may, and very commonly does, contain a portion of truth; and since the general or prevailing opinion on any subject is rarely or never the whole truth, it is only by the collision of adverse opinions that the remainder of the truth has any chance of being supplied.

Thirdly, even if the received opinion be not only true, but the whole truth; unless it is suffered to be, and actually is, vigorously and earnestly contested, it will, by most of those who receive it, be held in the manner of a prejudice, with little comprehension or feeling of its rational grounds. And not only this, but fourthly, the meaning of the doctrine itself will be in danger of being lost, or enfeebled, and deprived of its vital effect on the character and conduct: the dogma becoming a mere formal profession, inefficacious for good, but cumbering the ground, and preventing the growth of any real and heartfelt conviction, from reason or personal experience.

Such being the reasons which make it imperative that human beings should be free to form opinions, and to express their opinions without reserve; and such the baneful consequences to the intellectual, and through that to the moral nature of man, unless this liberty is either conceded, or asserted in spite of prohibition.

DEMOCRACY

36 Democracy and Its Justification*

SIDNEY HOOK

Sidney Hook is a prominent American philosopher who has taught at New York University for many years. He organized the Conference on Methods in Philosophy and Science and the Congress for Cultural Freedom. He is the author of many important articles in a wide range of journals and a frequent contributor to the *New York Times Magazine* and *Book Review*. His books include *Common Sense and the Fifth Amendment*; *Education for Modern Man*; *The Hero in History*; *Heresy, Yes, Conspiracy, No.*; and *Political Power and Personal Freedom*.

Any adequate description of the nature of democracy must at the very least do justice to customary usage which distinguishes between democratic and nondemocratic societies and between historic phases within any one society, regarded as more or less democratic in relation to each other. Although for propaganda purposes even totalitarian states claim to be democratic "in a higher sense," their canonic writings recognize the differences between the structure of these states and those considered democratic in a less esoteric sense. This is often betrayed in the adjectives prefixed to the latter like "so-called," "alleged," "parliamentary," or "bourgeois." Germany and Russia and Italy are not democratic states [this was written in 1941]; England and the United States are. And when historians examine the development of English and American society they unanimously acknowledge, although they evaluate the fact differently, that these societies were less democratic when property, racial, or religious qualifications were set for citizenship than they are today when these qualifications have been eliminated or reduced.

What principle is expressed in these customary distinctions? The principle may be stated in various ways, but for our purposes we may say that a democratic state is one in which the basic decisions of government rest

* From Sidney Hook, "The Philosophical Presuppositions of Democracy," *Ethics*, vol. 52 (1941–42), pp. 275–296. Reprinted by permission of the author.

upon the freely given consent of the governed. This obviously is only a beginning. For just as soon as we begin to investigate the conditions which must be present before we grant that a state lives up to this principle, we are carried beyond the sphere of political considerations into the domain of ethics. Thus, if information has been withheld or withdrawn before consent is assessed; if the opposition is muzzled or suppressed so that consent is as unanimous as a totalitarian plebiscite; or if economic sanctions are threatened against a section of the community in the event that consent takes one form or another, we declare that the "spirit" or "logic" or "rationale" of democracy is absent from its political forms. If birth does not give divine right, neither does numbers. We are all acquainted with situations in which we say that a political democracy has traduced its own ideals. Whenever we criticize existing states which conform to the political definition of democracy on the ground that they are not democratic enough; whenever we point out that Athenian democracy was limited only to free men, or that in some parts of the American South it is limited only to white men, or in some countries it is limited only to men, we are invoking a broader principle of democracy as a controlling reference in our judgments of comparison. This principle is an ethical one.

What is this principle of ethical democracy? It is a principle of equality— and equality not of status or origin but of opportunity, relevant functions, and social participation. The enormous literature and bitter controversy which center around the concept of equality indicate that it is only a little less ambiguous than the concept of democracy. It is necessary, therefore, to block it off from some current notions before developing the argument.

(*a*) The principle of equality is not a *description* of fact about men's physical or intellectual natures. It is a *prescription* or policy of treating men.

(*b*) It is not a prescription to treat men in identical ways who are unequal in their physical or intellectual nature. It is a policy of equality of concern or consideration for men whose different needs may require differential treatment.

(*c*) It is not a mechanical policy of equal opportunity for everyone at *any* time and in *all* respects. A musical genius is entitled to greater opportunities to develop his musical talents than someone who is tone deaf. It is equality of opportunity for all individuals to develop whatever personal and socially desirable talents they possess and to make whatever unique contributions their capacities permit.

(*d*) It is not a demand for absolute uniformity of living conditions or even for arithmetically equal compensation for socially useful work. It demands that, when the productive forces of a society makes possible the gratification of basic human needs (which are, of course, historical variables), no one should be deprived of necessities in order to provide others with luxuries.

(*e*) It is not a policy of restricting the freedom of being different or becoming different. It is a policy of *encouraging* the freedom to be different, restricting only that exercise of freedom which converts talents or possessions into a monopoly that frustrates the emergence of other free personalities.

(*f*) It is not a demand that all people be leaders or that none should be. It does demand that the career of leadership, like all other careers, be open to all whose natural or acquired talents qualify them; that everyone have a say in the process of selecting leaders; that the initiative of leaders operate within a framework of basic laws; and that these laws in turn ultimately rest upon the freely given consent of the persons who constitute the community.

(*g*) It does not make the assumption of sentimental humanitarianism that all men are naturally good. It does assume that men, treated as equals in a community of persons, may become better. The emphasis upon respect for the personality of all individuals, the attitude which treats the personality not as something fixed but as a growing, developing pattern, is unique to the philosophy of democracy.

What I have been trying to show is that the logic of the democrat's position compels him to go beyond the limited conception of political democracy—the equality of freedom—to a broader attitude extending to those other phases of social existence that bear upon the effective exercise of quality of freedom. This in fact has been the historical tendency observable wherever democratic principles and programs are permitted to operate. Perhaps the synoptic phrase "social equality," whose connotations encompass political, educational, and economic democracy, may be taken as the most appropriate expression of the meaning of democracy in the broadest sense.

It is clear that the principle of equality, like any principle of justice, cannot by itself determine what is specifically right or good in each concrete case. But whatever the right is discovered to be, from the point of view of democracy it is the result of an analysis which considers equally the needs of all the persons involved in the situation; and, further, whatever the good is, it becomes better to the extent that it is shared among other members of the community. It is also clear that in concrete situations there will be conflicts between various demands for equality and that in negotiating these conflicts the methods of intelligence are indispensable for a functioning democracy. If empiricism be a generic term for the philosophic attitude which submits *all* claims of fact and value to test by experience, then empiricism as a philosophy is more congenial to a democratic than to an antidemocratic community, for it brings into the open light of criticism the interests in which moral values and social institutions are rooted. Empiricism so conceived is commitment to a procedure, not to a theory of metaphysics.

In this brief account of the nature of democracy as a way of life I have not aimed at an exhaustive analysis of the *forms* in which it may be expressed but have tried to indicate the basic ideals which are involved in the customary usage of the term and in the implications of that usage.

THE JUSTIFICATION OF DEMOCRACY

We now come to the problem which is of primary concern to philosophers. What are the grounds on which we can justify our acceptance of democracy in contradistinction to other modes of social life? So far as I can see there are four generic types of justification which have been or can be offered.

The first asserts that the rational foundation of democratic belief consists in a set of supernatural religious truths in the sense that there can be no intelligent ground for choosing between democracy and other forms of society which does not logically commit us to some kind of theology.

The second asserts the same thing about metaphysics understood as a theory of "reality." Usually these two approaches go hand in hand.

The third maintains that the choice of democracy is a nonrational preference rooted in the constitution of our natures and brought to flower by nurture and education.

The fourth affirms that the belief in democracy is a hypothesis controlled by the same general pattern of inquiry which we apply to any scientific hypothesis but referring to different subject matter, i.e., our evaluations.

1. Democracy and Religion

Does democracy as a way of life rest upon belief in supernatural religious truths in the sense that, if the latter are denied, the former must necessarily be denied? It is becoming increasingly fashionable to maintain this. Were historical considerations relevant here, I think it could be conclusively established that the great institutional religions, with the possible exception of some forms of Protestantism, have tended in fact to support theocratic forms of government. . . .

But our concern is not with historical questions, fascinating as they are, but with the logic of the position. We must consequently rephrase the question to read: Does belief in democracy logically rest upon any theological propositions in the sense that the denial of the second entails the denial of the first? And for this discussion I shall take as illustratve of theological propositions the two cardinal propositions of natural theology, viz., "God exists" and "Man has an immortal soul." To assert that whoever has no grounds for affirming the existence of God and immortality has no grounds for affirming the validity of democracy is to claim that the former are at least necessary conditions of the latter. I shall argue that they constitute neither necessary nor sufficient conditions.

(a) Before examining this claim, let us note the tremendous risk it involves. Were those who advance it ever compelled to admit that these theological propositions are indemonstrable or false, they would have to surrender their belief in democracy. But this, I submit, very few of them are prepared to do. They would search for other reasons and grounds. Like those who would make the validity of moral judgments dependent upon the existence of God and immorality, the theological defenders of democracy shift from a problem in which, although difficult, it is possible to reach an agreement on the basis of some empirical evidence to one in which the nature of the terms and sphere of discourse makes such agreement much more difficult. Confirmed democrats, it seems to me, are much more convinced of the validity of the democratic ideal than they are of the theological propositions upon which it presumably depends. They would no more exonerate an atheist or agnostic who pleaded that he had no reason to believe in God and the hereafter from the obligation of accepting the democratic ideal than they would from the obligation of living honestly.

(b) Aside from the difficulties of establishing God's existence, how can we get from the fact of his existence to the desirability of the democratic way of life? None of the attributes of God, save the moral attributes, can serve as a premise justifying one way of life rather than another. And if the moral attributes of God can serve as premises, necessary or sufficient, for the democratic way of life, it is only because *we* regard them as worthy, i.e., as truly moral. Obviously any theology which makes God's power the justification or source of his goodness is worse than useless for purposes of deriving democracy. The attribution of moral qualities to God is an expression of what we think his qualities ought to be. And this is a problem of precisely the same order as we are called upon to answer when we ask for the grounds of our democratic allegiance.

(c) The situation is the same if we grant that human beings have immortal souls. In what way is this a necessary or sufficient presupposition of democracy? The brotherhood of man may be a theological fact as it is a biological fact, but what makes it wrong for Cain to kill his brother Abel and right, under certain circumstances, for us to kill Cain is a moral principle which can no more be derived from theology than from biology—unless, of course, the moral principle is one of the premises of our theological (or biological) system. In which case we are no further along than we were when we raised the question about the democratic way of life. . . .

2. Democracy and Metaphysics

The evidence seems to me to be overwhelming that there is a definite historical connection between the social movements of a period and its dominant metaphysical teachings; further, I am prepared to defend as a historically true proposition that systems of idealistic metaphysics, because of the semiofficial roles they have played in their respective cultures, have been more generally employed to bolster antidemocratic social movements than systems of empirical or materialistic metaphysics. Whether there is always an intrinsic personal or psychological relation between a philosopher's metaphysics and his ethics or politics is a more difficult question, but one which seems to me to require an answer in the negative. But more germane to our present concern is my contention that there is no necessary logical connection between a theory of being or becoming and any particular theory of ethics or politics. Stated more accurately, it seems to me demonstrable that no system of metaphysics univocally determines a system of ethics or politics. There may be certain facts about man and nature which might have a bearing upon our judgment about what social system is of the highest worth, but, as I shall argue later, these are facts concerning which the empirical sciences are qualified to report without benefit of metaphysics.

Two species of metaphysics are most often invoked in behalf of democracy. One asserts that the value of democracy or the values from which it may be derived are "grounded in reality," a phrase which is interpreted to mean that the universe "justifies" or "guarantees" both the validity and the ultimate supremacy of basic human ideals. I must confess that it is difficult for me to understand this view except as a shamefaced kind of theology. But however that may be, there is no agreed-upon denotation of *the* universe. There are many universes. Nor is there any one basic human ideal but many human ideals which are often in conflict with one another, even though they all invoke the universe as a ground of their validity and as a guaranty of their triumph. Finally, and most important, no matter what character the universe is alleged to have, no matter what the nature of the far-off event toward which it is moving, no matter who wins or loses, nothing logically compelling in the way of judgment follows unless *we* have already morally evaluated the character of events. For most metaphysicians the very word "reality" is an implicit value term. To be sure, history may be conceived as a struggle between the Prince of Darkness and the Prince of Light, but the latter is so named because he carries *our* moral flag.

The second metaphysical view to which resort is often made is at the same time a kind of rejoinder to our position. It distinguishes between a metaphysical realm of being and a metaphysical realm of values and grounds the democratic way of life in the latter. Just as the spectrum of colors is there to be beheld by all who are not color-blind and would still be there even if man's ancestors had climbed no higher than the mole in the tree of evolution, so the spectrum of values is there to be beheld by all who are not value-blind and would still be there even if human beings had never existed at all. The view that colors would still be there even if human beings had no eyes is not without its difficulties. But they do not begin to compare in difficulty with the view that values are essentially unrelated to an evaluator and his interests. Santayana has quite aptly remarked of this doctrine that there is much sense in saying that whiskey "is pervaded as it were, by an inherent intoxication, and stands dead drunk in its bottle."

The subject is vast, but it is enough to show that this view is question-begging in precisely the same way as other theological and metaphysical derivations. The existence of these absolute norms is presumably certified or authenticated at some point by an act of immediate intuition. If the testimony of the intuition is construed not merely from what individuals *say* they intuit but from the conduct that flows from their intuition—and conduct counts more in any moral scheme than mere words—then it is clear that individuals intuit or "see" *different* values. The "great" visions are not all compatible with one another in what they command, not to mention the visions which we do not call great. Which visions are the authentic ones? Prior to every conclusion that these are the objective values of all eternity, or even of all time and existence, is the assumption that *this* is the trustworthy seer. In a dispute between two men, one of whom asserts that the other is color-blind and the other that the first is "just seeing things," there are definite ways of determining who is right. In a dispute between two seers whose immediate intuitions report conflicting news about the nature and hierarchy of absolute values, there is no rational way of reaching a consensus. The true prophet cannot be distinguished from the false by invoking absolute values whose validity depends upon a prior assumption of the reliability of prophetic testimony. The complacency with which some writers have cut the Gordian knot by introducing reference to the intuitions of "the best people" or "the most cultured people" or "the saving remnant" is evidence either of parochialism or of snobbery.

The record of human error and cruelty shows what ghastly consequences often result from the conviction that one's moral insight cannot possibly be wrong and that it needs no further justification than its own incandescent purity. No more than a solipsist can make plausible on his own assumptions the existence of another solipsist, can an absolutist find a rightful place for another absolutist who disagrees with him. Absolutists face each other over an abyss which cannot be bridged even by their weapons of war.

3. Democracy and Preferences

The view that an acceptance of democracy is an expression of a preference does not carry us far until the kind of preference is indicated. A preference may express a passing whim or a deep natural bent; it may be impulsive or reflective. Preferences are rooted in our natures. Their forms, occasions, and objects are supplied by education, i.e., broadly speaking, by social habits and intelligence. But either our natures can be changed or the educators re-educated. If neither is possible, then the fact of moral choice becomes unintelligible. If we can offer no justification of a preference except that it is ours, obviously no point of intellectual or moral issue is raised; nor, a fortiori, can any be settled by the trial of arms. If we offer a justification of a preference, it will take one of the generic forms already discussed or about to be discussed.

4. Democracy as a Hypothesis

When democracy is taken strictly as a form of political government, its superiority over other forms of government can be established to the extent that it achieves more security, freedom, and co-operative diversity than any of its alternatives. If we test the workings of political democracy by Paul's scheme of virtues or by Nietzsche's, we may perhaps reach another conclusion. So long as there is no dispute about observable effects and so long as we raise no question about the moral ideals by which we evaluate these effects, we have clear sailing.

But, as has already been made plain, by democracy as a way of life we mean a way of organizing human relationships which embodies a certain complex of moral ideals. Can these ideals be treated as hypotheses? The conventional reply has always been that no moral principle can be regarded as a hypothesis, for we must already have certain knowledge of what is good before we can evaluate the consequences of acting upon it. If any position is question-begging, surely this seems to be!

Were this a symposium on value theory, I would devote all my time to developing the general theory of moral ideals as hypotheses. But here I can only barely indicate that the notion is not viciously circular. A moral ideal is a prescription to act in a certain situation or class of situations in determinate ways that will organize the human needs and wants involved so as to fulfill a set of *other* values which are *postulated* as binding in relation to the problem in hand. No more than in other cases of inquiry do we start with an empty head. The cluster of values we bring to the situation is the result of prior experience and reflection. They are not arbitrarily postulated. The consequences of acting upon the hypothesis may lead us to challenge a postulated or assumed value. This in turn can become the subject of a similar investigation. Terminal values are always related to specific contexts; there is no absolute terminal value which is either self-evident or beyond the necessity of justifying itself if its credentials are challenged. There is no vicious infinite regress involved if we take our problems concretely and one at a time. Nor is the procedure narrowly circular. For if, in a long history of raising and solving moral problems, we postulate as a value in solving a later problem a value which had itself to be certified in an earlier problem, this would testify to the presence of a fruitful set of systematically related values in the structure of our moral behavior. New values would emerge, or be discovered, in the course of our attempt to act upon our ideals and from the necessity of mediating the conflict between the postulated values as they bear on concrete human needs in specific situations.

I should like, however, to make the general position take form out of the discussion of the theme before us. That theme is: Why should we treat individuals of unequal talents and endowments as persons who are equally entitled to relevant consideration and care? Short of a treatise I can state only the reasons, without amplification of the concrete needs of the social situation which democracy seeks to meet and the institutional practices by which it must meet them.

(*a*) This method of treating human beings is more successful than any other in evoking a maximum of creative, voluntary effort from all members of the community. Properly implemented it gives all persons a stake in the community and elicits a maximum of intelligent loyalty.

(*b*) It enlarges the scope of our experience by enabling us to acquire insight into the needs, drives, and aspirations of others. Learning to understand how life is organized by other centers of experience is both a challenge and a discipline for our imagination. In aiding the growth of others, we aid our own growth.

(*c*) The willingness to understand another man's point of view without necessarily surrendering to it makes it more likely that different points of view may negotiate their differences and learn to live peacefully with one another. A democratic community cannot be free from strife in a world where inequalities will always exist, but its ethics when intelligently acted upon makes more likely the diminution of strife or its transference to socially harmless forms than is the case when its principle of equality is denied. The consequences are less toadying, less fear, and less duplicity in the equalitarian community than in the nonequalitarian society.

(*d*) In nurturing the capacities of each individual so that they may come to their greatest fulfilment, we can best share our existing stores of truth and beauty and uncover new dimensions in these realms. How can anyone dedicated to the values of science and art consistently oppose a policy which maximizes the possibility of the discovery and widest dispersion of scientific truths and artistic meanings?

(*e*) Regard for the potentialities of all individuals makes for less cruelty of man toward man especially where cruelty is the result of blindness to, or ignorance of, others' needs. A community organized along democratic lines is guilty of cruelty only at those points where it has failed to live up to its own ideals. A totalitarian community is systematically insensitive to the personal needs not only of members of the outlawed scapegoat group but of the majority of its subjects who are excluded from policy-making discussions. At best, there is no way of determining these personal needs except by the interpretation of the dictator and his experts who operate with the dogma that they know the true interests of their subjects better than the subjects themselves. At worst, the dictator assumes not only that he speaks for his subjects but that in some mystic way he feels and thinks for them too. Despite the great limitations—limitations from the point of view of their own ideals—under which the nineteenth- and twentieth-century democracies of the Western world suffered, I think it is indisputable, on the evidence, that by and large their social life, in so far as this was the consequence of policy, displayed less cruelty than the social life of any other historical period.

(ƒ) Reasonableness of conclusions, where attitudes and interests conflict, depends upon the degree of mutual consultation and free intellectual communication between the principals involved. The democratic way of life makes possible the widest forms of mutual consultation and communication. Conclusions reached by these processes have a quality that can never be found where conclusions are imposed by force or authority—even if they are our own. Let me illustrate what I mean by taking as an example the enterprise represented by this Association. Who among us, desirous as we may be of the possibility of philosophical agreement, would forego the methods of public discussion, criticism, argument, and rejoinder for a philosophical consensus imposed by a Gestapo or a G.P.U. even if by a strange quirk of affairs it was *our* philosophic position that the goon squads of orthodoxy sought to make the way of salvation? Who among us, knowing that outside the threshold of our meeting there stood an individual of strange country, color, or faith, capable of making a contribution to our deliberations, would not open the door to him? These are not rhetorical questions framed to discover philosophical fifth columnists. They are designed to show that the procedures of critical discussion and discovery, which are pre-eminently exhibited in the work of a scientific community, take for granted that national, racial, or religious origins are irrelevant to the logic of the method by which reasonable conclusions are reached. Democracy as a way of life differs from its alternatives in that it makes possible the extension of these methods of reaching reasonable conclusions from the fields of professional science and philosophy to all areas of human experience in which genuine problems arise.

There are other grounds that may be offered in justification of democracy as the most adequate social philosophy for our times. Every one of them, like the foregoing, postulates implicitly or explicitly values or desiderata. But I repeat: these postulates are ultimate only for the problem in hand. They may require justification. When we undertake such justification, we have undertaken a new inquiry into a new problem.

There are two important consequences of approaching democracy in this way. The first is that we avoid the temptation, which is rapidly gaining vogue, of making democracy absolutely valid in and for itself. There are many today who write as if they believe that democracy should prevail even though the heavens fall, and who say in so many words that "to question the validity of democracy is to disbelieve in it" and that we can meet the blind fanatical faith of fascism only with a faith in democracy which is at least just as fanatical. This temptation, it seems to me, must be avoided because, by counterposing subrational dogma to subrational dogma, it prepares the ground for an acceptance of a might-makes-right morality. Second, those who make of democracy an absolute value, which requires no justification but its inherent rightness, tend to identify this absolute democracy with whatever particular democratic status quo exists. On the other hand, the natural tendency of those who cannot distinguish between social philosophies on the ground of their inherent rightness is to test a social philosophy by the social institutions in which it is embodied. They are, therefore, more attentive to the actual workings and effects of democracy, more historical minded, and less likely to gloss over existing imperfections.

To those who say that human beings will not fight wholeheartedly except for certainties, and emphatically not for a hypothesis which is only probable, the reply must be made that this empirical position is highly dubious. Men have fought and do fight vigorously for causes on the basis of preponderant evidence. Vigorous action, indeed, is only desirable when we have first decided what is intelligent action. And intelligent action does not result when we assume that our ideas or ideals simply cannot be wrong. That both intelligence and resoluteness are compatible is clear in fields as far apart as military science and medicine. Once it is decided that the chances of one action are relatively better than another, once it is decided that an operation gives a patient a better chance of surviving than no operation, wisdom demands that the best warranted alternative be pursued with all our heart and all our soul. Let us remember that when we fight for democracy we are not fighting for an ideal which has just been proposed as a merely possible valid ideal for our times; we already have considerable evidence in its behalf, the weight of which, unfortunately too often, is properly evaluated only when democracy is lost or imperiled.

CIVIL DISOBEDIENCE

37 On Justice and the Obligation to Obey the Law*

PLATO

Plato (427–347 B.C.) was a student of Socrates and later founded the Academy, the first "university" in Europe. He has had incalculable influence on Western thought. His best-known works are the *Apology, Crito, Meno, Protagoras, Gorgias, Phaedo, Symposium, Republic, Theatetus, Sophist, Parmenides, Phaedrus, Laws, Politicus,* and *Timaeus.*

CRITO*

PERSONS OF THE DIALOGUE

Socrates   Crito

SCENE:—*The Prison of Socrates*

Socrates. Why have you come at this hour, Crito? it must be quite early?
Crito. Yes, certainly.
Soc. What is the exact time?
Cr. The dawn is breaking.
Soc. I wonder that the keeper of the prison would let you in.
Cr. He knows me, because I often come, Socrates; moreover, I have done him a kindness.
Soc. And are you only just arrived?
Cr. No, I came some time ago.
Soc. Then why did you sit and say nothing, instead of at once awakening me?
Cr. I should not have liked myself, Socrates, to be in such great trouble

---

* From *The Dialogues of Plato,* trans. B. Jowett (New York: The Macmillan Company, 1892).

and unrest as you are—indeed I should not: I have been watching with amazement your peaceful slumbers; and for that reason I did not awake you, because I wished to minimize the pain. I have always thought you to be of a happy disposition; but never did I see anything like the easy, tranquil manner in which you bear this calamity.

Soc. Why, Crito, when a man has reached my age he ought not to be repining at the approach of death.

Cr. And yet other old men find themselves in similar misfortunes, and age does not prevent them from repining.

Soc. That is true. But you have not told me why you come at this early hour.

Cr. I come to bring you a message which is sad and painful; not, as I believe, to yourself, but to all of us who are your friends, and saddest of all to me.

Soc. What? Has the ship come from Delos, on the arrival of which I am to die?

Cr. No, the ship has not actually arrived, but she will probably be here to-day, as persons who have come from Sunium tell me that they left her there; and therefore to-morrow, Socrates, will be the last day of your life.

Soc. Very well, Crito; if such is the will of God, I am willing; but my belief is that there will be a delay of a day.

Cr. Why do you think so?

Soc. I will tell you. I am to die on the day after the arrival of the ship.

Cr. Yes; that is what the authorities say.

Soc. But I do not think that the ship will be here until to-morrow; this I infer from a vision which I had last night, or rather only just now, when you fortunately allowed me to sleep.

Cr. And what was the nature of the vision?

Soc. There appeared to me the likeness of a woman, fair and comely, clothed in bright raiment, who called to me and said: O Socrates,

'The third day hence to fertile Phthia shalt thou go.'

Cr. What a singular dream, Socrates!

Soc. There can be no doubt about the meaning, Crito, I think.

Cr. Yes; the meaning is only too clear. But, oh! my beloved Socrates, let me entreat you once more to take my advice and escape. For if you die I shall not only lose a friend who can never be replaced, but there is another evil: people who do not know you and me and will believe that I might have saved you if I had been willing to give money, but that I did not care. Now, can there be a worse disgrace than this—that I should be thought to value money more than the life of a friend? For the many will not be persuaded that I wanted you to escape, and that you refused.

Soc. But why, my dear Crito, should we care about the opinion of the many? Good men, and they are the only persons who are worth considering, will think of these things truly as they occurred.

Cr. But you see, Socrates, that the opinion of the many must be regarded, for what is now happening shows that they can do the greatest evil to any one who has lost their good opinion.

Soc. I only wish it were so, Crito; and that the many could do the greatest evil; for then they would also be able to do the greatest good—and what a fine thing this would be! But in reality they can do neither; for they cannot make a man either wise or foolish; and whatever they do is the result of chance.

Cr. Well, I will not dispute with you; but please to tell me, Socrates, whether you are not acting out of regard to me and your other friends: are you not afraid that if you escape from prison we may get into trouble with the informers for having stolen you away, and lose either the whole or a great part of our property; or that even a worse evil may happen to us? Now, if you fear on our account, be at ease; for in order to save you, we ought surely to run this, or even a greater risk; be persuaded, then, and do as I say.

Soc. Yes, Crito, that is one fear which you mention, but by no means the only one.

Cr. Fear not—there are persons who are willing to get you out of prison at no great cost; and as for the informers, they are far from being exorbitant in their demands—a little money will satisfy them. My means, which are certainly ample, are at your service, and if you have a scruple about spending all mine, here are strangers who will give you the use of theirs; and one of them, Simmias the Theban, has brought a large sum of money for this very purpose; and Cebes and many others are prepared to spend their money in helping you to escape. I say, therefore, do not hesitate on our account, and do not say, as you did in the court, that you will have a difficulty in knowing what to do with yourself anywhere else. For men will love you in other places to which you may go, and not in Athens only; there are friends of mine in Thessaly, if you like to go to them, who will value and protect you, and no Thessalian will give you any trouble. Nor can I think that you are at all justified, Socrates, in betraying your own life when you might be saved; in acting thus you are playing into the hands of your enemies, who are hurrying on your destruction. And further I should say that you are deserting your own children; for you might bring them up and educate them; instead of which you go away and leave them, and they will have to take their chance; and if they do not meet with the usual fate of orphans, there will be small thanks to you. No man should bring children into the world who is unwilling to persevere to the end in their nurture and education. But you appear to be choosing the easier part, not the better and manlier, which would have been more becoming in one who professes to care for virtue in all his actions, like yourself. And indeed, I am ashamed not only of you, but of us who are your friends, when I reflect that the whole business will be attributed entirely to our want of courage. The trial need never have come on, or might have been managed differently; and this last act, or crowning folly, will seem to have occurred through our negligence and cowardice, who might have saved you, if we had been good for anything; and you might have saved yourself, for there was no difficulty at all. See now, Socrates, how sad and discreditable are the consequences, both to us and you. Make up your mind then, or rather have your mind already made up, for the time of deliberation is over, and there is only one thing to be done, which must be done this very night, and if we delay at all will be no longer practicable or possible; I beseech you therefore, Socrates, be persuaded by me, and do as I say.

Soc. Dear Crito, your zeal is invaluable, if a right one; but if wrong, the greater the zeal the greater the danger; and therefore we ought to consider whether I shall or shall not do as you say. For I am and always have been one of those natures who must be guided by reason, whatever the reason may be which upon reflection appears to me to be the best; and now that this chance has befallen me, I cannot repudiate my own words: the principles which I have hitherto honoured and revered I still honour, and unless we can at once find other and better principles, I am certain not to agree with you; no, not even if the power of the multitude could inflict many more imprisonments, confiscations, deaths, frightening us like children with hobgoblin terrors. What will be the fairest way of considering the question? Shall I return to your old argument about the opinions of men?—we were saying that some of them are to be regarded, and others not. Now were we right in maintaining this before I was condemned? And has the argument which was once good now proved to be talk for the sake of talking—mere childish nonsense? That is what I want to consider with your help, Crito:—whether, under my present circumstances, the argument appears to be in any way different or not; and is to be allowed by me or disallowed. That argument, which, as I believe, is maintained by many persons of authority, was to the effect, as I was saying, that the opinions of some men are to be regarded, and of other men not to be regarded. Now you, Crito, are not going to die to-morrow—at least, there is no human probability of this—and therefore you are disinterested and not liable to be deceived by the circumstances in which you are placed. Tell me then, whether I am right in saying that some opinions, and the opinions of some men only, are to be valued, and that other opinions, and the opinions of other men, are not to be valued. I ask you whether I was right in maintaining this?

Cr. Certainly.

Soc. The good are to be regarded, and not the bad?

Cr. Yes.

Soc. And the opinions of the wise are good, and the opinions of the unwise are evil?

Cr. Certainly.

Soc. And what was said about another matter? Is the pupil who devotes himself to the practice of gymnastics supposed to attend to the praise and blame and opinion of every man, or of one man only—his physician or trainer, whoever he may be?

Cr. Of one man only.

Soc. And he ought to fear the censure and welcome the praise of that one only, and not of the many?

Cr. Clearly so.

Soc. And he ought to act and train, and eat and drink in the way which seems good to his single master who has understanding, rather than according to the opinion of all other men put together?

Cr. True.

Soc. And if he disobeys and disregards the opinion and approval of the one, and regards the opinion of the many who have no understanding, will he not suffer evil?

Cr. Certainly he will.

Soc. And what will the evil be, whither tending and what affecting, in the disobedient person?

Cr. Clearly, affecting the body; that is what is destroyed by the evil.

Soc. Very good; and is not this true, Crito, of other things which we need not separately enumerate? In questions of just and unjust, fair and foul, good and evil, which are the subjects of our present consultation, ought we to follow the opinion of the many and to fear them; or the opinion of the one man who has understanding? ought we not to fear and reverence him more than all the rest of the world: and if we desert him shall we not destroy and injure that principle in us which may be assumed to be improved by justice and deteriorated by injustice;—there is such a principle?

Cr. Certainly there is, Socrates.

Soc. Take a parallel instance:—if, acting under the advice of those who have no understanding, we destroy that which is improved by health and is deteriorated by disease, would life be worth having? And that which has been destroyed is—the body?

Cr. Yes.

Soc. Could we live, having an evil and corrupted body?

Cr. Certainly not.

Soc. And will life be worth having, if that higher part of man be destroyed, which is improved by justice and depraved by injustice? Do we suppose that principle, whatever it may be in man, which has to do with justice and injustice, to be inferior to the body?

Cr. Certainly not.

Soc. More honourable than the body?

Cr. Far more.

Soc. Then, my friend, we must not regard what the many say of us: but what he, the one man who has understanding of just and unjust, will say, and what the truth will say. And therefore you begin in error when you advise that we should regard the opinion of the many about just and unjust, good and evil, honourable and dishonourable.—'Well,' some one will say, 'but the many can kill us.'

Cr. Yes, Socrates; that will clearly be the answer.

Soc. And it is true: but still I find with surprise that the old argument is unshaken as ever. And I should like to know whether I may say the same of another proposition—that not life, but a good life, is to be chiefly valued?

Cr. Yes, that also remains unshaken.

Soc. And a good life is equivalent to a just and honourable one—that holds also?

Cr. Yes, it does.

Soc. From these premises I proceed to argue the question whether I ought or ought not to try and escape without the consent of the Athenians: and if I am clearly right in escaping, then I will make the attempt; but if not, I will abstain. The other considerations which you mention, of money and loss of character and the duty of educating one's children, are, I fear, only the doctrines of the multitude, who would be as ready to restore people to life, if they were able, as they are to put them to death—and with as little reason. But now, since the argument has thus far prevailed, the only question which remains to be considered is, whether we shall do rightly either in escaping or in suffering others to aid in our escape and paying them in money and thanks, or whether in reality we shall not do rightly; and if the latter, then death or any other calamity which may ensue on my remaining here must not be allowed to enter into the calculation.

Cr. I think that you are right, Socrates; how then shall we proceed?

Soc. Let us consider the matter together, and do you either refute me if you can, and I will be convinced; or else cease, my dear friend, from repeating to me that I ought to escape against the wishes of the Athenians: for I highly value your attempts to persuade me to do so, but I may not be persuaded against my own better judgment. And now please to consider my first position, and try how you can best answer me.

Cr. I will.

Soc. Are we to say that we are never intentionally to do wrong, or that in one way we ought and in another we ought not to do wrong, or is doing wrong always evil and dishonourable, as I was just now saying, and as has been already acknowledged by us? Are all our former admissions which were made within a few days to be thrown away? And have we, at our age, been earnestly discoursing with one another all our life long only to discover that we are no better than children? Or, in spite of the opinion of the many, and in spite of consequences whether better or worse, shall we insist on the truth of what was then said, that injustice is always an evil and dishonour to him who acts unjustly? Shall we say so or not?

Cr. Yes.

Soc. Then we must do no wrong?

Cr. Certainly not.

Soc. Nor when injured in return, as the many imagine; for we must injure no one at all?

Cr. Clearly not.

Soc. Again, Crito, may we do evil?

Cr. Surely not, Socrates.

Soc. And what of doing evil in return for evil, which is the morality of the many—is that just or not?

Cr. Not just.

Soc. For doing evil to another is the same as injuring him?

Cr. Very true.

Soc. Then we ought not to retaliate or render evil for evil to any one, whatever evil we may have suffered from him. But I would have you consider, Crito, whether you really mean what you are saying. For this opinion has never been held, and never will be held, by any considerable number of persons; and those who are agreed and those who are not agreed upon this point have no common ground, and can only despise one another when they see how widely they differ. Tell me, then, whether you agree with and assent to my first principle, that neither injury nor retaliation nor warding off evil by evil is ever right. And shall that be the premiss of our argument? Or do you decline and dissent from this? For so I have ever thought, and continue to think; but, if you are of another opinion, let me hear what you have to say. If, however, you remain of the same mind as formerly, I will proceed to the next step.

Cr. You may proceed, for I have not changed my mind.

Soc. Then I will go on to the next point, which may be put in the form of a question:—Ought a man to do what he admits to be right, or ought he to betray the right?

Cr. He ought to do what he thinks right.

Soc. But if this is true, what is the application? In leaving the prison against the will of the Athenians, do I wrong any? or rather do I not wrong those whom I ought least to wrong? Do I not desert the principles which were acknowledged by us to be just—what do you say?

Cr. I cannot tell, Socrates; for I do not know.

Soc. Then consider the matter in this way:—Imagine that I am about to play truant (you may call the proceeding by any name which you like), and the laws and the government come and interrogate me: 'Tell us, Socrates,' they say; 'what are you about? are you not going by an act of yours to overturn us—the laws, and the whole state, as far as in you lies? Do you imagine that a state can subsist and not be overthrown, in which the decisions of law have no power, but are set aside and trampled upon by individuals?' What will be our answer, Crito, to these and the like words? Any one, and especially a rhetorician, will have a good deal to say on behalf of the law which requires a sentence to be carried out. He will argue that this law should not be set aside; and shall we reply, 'Yes; but the state has injured us and given an unjust sentence.' Suppose I say that?

Cr. Very good, Socrates.

Soc. 'And was that our agreement with you?' the law would answer; 'or were you to abide by the sentence of the state?' And if I were to express my astonishment at their words, the law would probably add: 'Answer, Socrates, instead of opening your eyes—you are in the habit of asking and answering questions. Tell us,—What complaint have you to make against us which justifies you in attempting to destroy us and the state? In the first place did we not bring you into existence? Your father married your mother by our aid and begat you. Say whether you have any objection to urge against those of us who regulate marriage?' None, I should reply. 'Or against those of us who after birth regulate the nurture and education of children, in which you also were trained? Were not the laws, which have the charge of education, right in commanding your father to train you in music and gymnastic?' Right, I should reply. 'Well then, since you were brought into the world and nurtured and educated by us, can you deny in the first place that you are our child and slave, as your fathers were before you? And if this is true you are not on equal terms with us; nor can you think that you have a right to do to us what we are doing to you. Would you have any right to strike or revile or do any other evil to your father or your master, if you had one, because you have been struck or reviled by him, or received some other evil at his hands?—you would not say this? And because we think right to destroy you, do you think that you have any right to destroy us in return, and your country as far as in you lies? Will you, O professor of true virtue, pretend that you are justified in this? Has a philosopher like you failed to discover that our country is more to be valued and higher and holier far than mother or father or any ancestor, and more to be regarded in the eyes of the gods and of men of understanding? also to be soothed, and gently and reverently entreated when angry, even more than a father, and either to be persuaded, or if not persuaded, to be obeyed? And when we are punished by her, whether with imprisonment or stripes, the punishment is to be endured in silence; and if she leads us to wounds or death in battle, thither we follow as is right; neither may any one yield or retreat or leave his rank, but whether in battle or in a court of law, or in any other place, he must do what his city and his country order him; or he must change their view of what is just: and if he may do no violence to his father or mother, much less may he do violence to his country.' What answer shall we make to this, Crito? Do the laws speak truly, or do they not?

Cr. I think that they do.

Soc. Then the laws will say, 'Consider, Socrates, if we are speaking truly that in your present attempt you are going to do us an injury. For, having brought you into the world, and nurtured and educated you, and given you and every other citizen a share in every good which we had to give, we further proclaim to any Athenian by the liberty which we allow him, that if he does not like us when he has become of age and has seen the ways of the city, and made our acquaintance, he may go where he pleases and take his goods with him. None of us laws will forbid him or interfere with him. Any one who does not like us and the city, and who wants to emigrate to a colony or to any other city, may go where he likes, retaining his property. But he who has experience of the manner in which we order justice and administer the state, and still remains, has entered into an implied contract that he will do as we command him. And he who disobeys us is, as we maintain, thrice wrong; first, because in disobeying us he is disobeying his parents; secondly, because we are the authors of his education; thirdly, because he has made an agreement with us that he will duly obey our commands; and he neither obeys them nor convinces us that our commands are unjust; and we do not rudely impose them, but give him the alternative of obeying or convincing us;—that is what we offer, and he does neither.

'These are the sort of accusations to which, as we were saying, you, Socrates, will be exposed if you accomplish your intentions; you, above all other Athenians.' Suppose now I ask, why I rather than anybody else? they will justly retort upon me that I above all other men have acknowledged the agreement. 'There is clear proof,' they will say, 'Socrates, that we and the city were not displeasing to you. Of all Athenians you have been the most constant resident in the city, which, as you never leave, you may be supposed to love. For you never went out of the city either to see the games, except once when you went to the Isthmus, or to any other place unless when you were on military service; nor did you travel as other men do. Nor had you any curiosity to know other states or their laws: your affections did not go beyond us and our state; we were your special favourites, and you acquiesced in our government of you; and here in this city you begat your children, which is a proof of your satisfaction. Moreover, you might in the course of the trial, if you had liked, have fixed the penalty at banishment; the state which refuses to let you go now would have let you go then. But you pretended that you preferred death to exile, and that you were not unwilling to die. And now you have forgotten these fine sentiments, and pay no respect to us the laws, of whom you are the destroyer; and are doing what only a miserable slave would do, running away and turning your back upon the compacts and agreements which you made as a citizen. And first of all answer this very question: Are we right in saying that you agreed to be governed according to us in deed, and not in word only? Is that true or not?' How shall we answer, Crito? Must we not assent?

Cr. We cannot help it, Socrates.

Soc. Then will they not say: 'You, Socrates, are breaking the covenants and agreements which you made with us at your leisure, not in any haste or under any compulsion or deception, but after you have had seventy years to think of them, during which time you were at liberty to leave the city, if we were not to your mind, or if our covenants appeared to you to be unfair. You had your choice, and might have gone either to Lacedaemon or Crete, both which states are often praised by you for their good government, or to some other Hellenic or foreign state. Whereas you, above all other Athenians, seemed to be so fond of the state, or, in other words, of us her laws (and who would care about a state which has no laws?), that you never stirred out of her; the halt, the blind, the maimed were not more stationary in her than you were. And now you run away and forsake your agreements. Not so, Socrates, if you will take our advice; do not make yourself ridiculous by escaping out of the city.

'For just consider, if you transgress and err in this sort of way, what good will you do either to yourself or to your friends? That your friends will be driven into exile and deprived of citizenship, or will lose their property, is tolerably certain; and you yourself, if you fly to one of the neighbouring cities, as, for example, Thebes or Megara, both of which are well governed, will come to them as an enemy, Socrates, and their government will be against you, and all patriotic citizens will cast an evil eye upon you as a subverter of the laws, and you will confirm in the minds of the judges the justice of their own condemnation of you. For he who is a corrupter of the laws is more than likely to be a corrupter of the young and foolish portion of mankind. Will you then flee from well-ordered cities and virtuous men? and is existence worth having on these terms? Or will you go to them without shame, and talk to them, Socrates? And what will you say to them? What you say here about virtue and justice and institutions and laws being the best things among men? Would that be decent of you? Surely not. But if you go away from well-governed states to Crito's friends in Thessaly, where there is great disorder and licence, they will be charmed to hear the tale of your escape from prison, set off with ludicrous particulars of the manner in which you were wrapped in a goatskin or some other disguise, and metamorphosed as the manner is of runaways; but will there be no one to remind you that in your old age you were not ashamed to violate the most sacred laws from a miserable desire of a little more life? Perhaps not, if you keep them in a good temper; but if they are out of temper you will hear many degrading things; you will live, but how?—as the flatterer of all men, and the servant of all men; and doing what?—eating and drinking in Thessaly, having gone abroad in order that you may get a dinner. And where will be your fine sentiments about justice and virtue? Say that you wish to live for the sake of your children—you want to bring them up and educate them—will you take them into Thessaly and deprive them of Athenian citizenship? Is this the benefit which you will confer upon them? Or are you under the impression that they will be better cared for and educated here if you are still alive, although absent from them; for your friends will take care of them? Do you fancy that if you are an inhabitant of Thessaly they will take care of them, and if you are an inhabitant of the other world that they will not take care of them? Nay; but if they who call themselves friends are good for anything, they will—to be sure they will.

'Listen, then, Socrates, to us who have brought you up. Think not of life and children first, and of justice afterwards, but of justice first, that you may be justified before the princes of the world below. For neither will you nor any that belong to you be happier or holier or juster in this life, or happier in another, if you do as Crito bids. Now you depart in innocence, a sufferer and not a doer of evil; a victim, not of the laws but of men. But if you go forth, returning evil for evil, and injury for injury, breaking the covenants and agreements which you have made with us, and wronging those whom you ought least of all to wrong, that is to say, yourself, your friends, your country, and us, we shall be angry with you while you live, and our brethren, the laws in the world below, will receive you as an enemy; for they will know that you have done your best to destroy us. Listen, then, to us and not to Crito.'

This, dear Crito, is the voice which I seem to hear murmuring in my ears, like the sound of the flute in the ears of the mystic; that voice, I say, is humming in my ears, and prevents me from hearing any other. And I know that anything more which you may say will be vain. Yet speak, if you have anything to say.

Cr. I have nothing to say, Socrates.

Soc. Leave me then, Crito, to fulfil the will of God, and to follow whither he leads.

38 Social Protest and Civil Disobedience*

SIDNEY HOOK

Sidney Hook is a prominent American philosopher who has taught at New York University for many years. He organized the Conference on Methods in Philosophy and Science and the Congress for Cultural Freedom. He is the author of many important articles in a wide range of journals and a frequent contributor to the *New York Times Magazine* and *Book Review*. His books include *Common Sense and the Fifth Amendment; Education for Modern Man; The Hero in History; Heresy, Yes, Conspiracy, No;* and *Political Power and Personal Freedom.*

In times of moral crisis what has been accepted as commonplace truth sometimes appears questionable and problematic. We have all been nurtured in the humanistic belief that in a democracy, citizens are free to disagree with a law but that so long as it remains in force, they have a *prima facie* obligation to obey it. The belief is justified on the ground that this procedure enables us to escape the twin evils of tyranny and anarchy. Tyranny is avoided by virtue of the freedom and power of dissent to win the uncoerced consent of the community. Anarchy is avoided by reliance on due process, the recognition that there is a right way to correct a wrong, and a wrong way to secure a right. To the extent that anything is demonstrable in human affairs, we have held that democracy as a political system is not viable if members systematically refused to obey laws whose wisdom or morality they dispute.

Nonetheless, during the past decade of tension and turmoil in American life there has developed a mass phenomenon of civil disobedience even among those who profess devotion to democratic ideals and institutions. This phenomenon has assumed a character similar to a tidal wave which has not yet reached its crest. It has swept from the field of race relations to the campuses of some universities, subtly altering the connotation of the term "academic." It is being systematically developed as an instrument of influencing foreign policy. It is leaving its mark on popular culture. I am told it is not only a theme of comic books but that children in our more sophisticated families

* This article was published originally as "Social Protest and Civil Obedience" in *The Humanist*, XXVII, Nos. 5–6 (1967), 157–59, 192–93. Reprinted by permission of Professor Hook.

no longer resort to tantrums in defying parental discipline—they go limp!

More seriously, in the wake of civil disobedience there has occasionally developed *uncivil* disobedience, sometimes as a natural psychological development, and often because of the failure of law enforcement agencies especially in the South to respect and defend legitimate expressions of social protest. The line between civil and uncivil disobedience is not only an uncertain and wavering one in practice, it has become so in theory. A recent prophet of the philosophy of the absurd in recommending civil disobedience as a form of creative disorder in a democracy cited Shay's Rebellion as an illustration. This Rebellion was uncivil to the point of bloodshed. Indeed, some of the techniques of protesting American involvement in Vietnam have departed so far from traditional ways of civil disobedience as to make it likely that they are inspired by the same confusion between civil and uncivil disobedience.

All this has made focal the perennial problems of the nature and limits of the citizen's obligation to obey the law, of the relation between the authority of conscience and the authority of the state, of the rights and duties of a democratic moral man in an immoral democratic society. The classical writings on these questions have acquired a burning relevance to the political condition of man today. I propose briefly to clarify some of these problems.

To begin with I wish to stress the point that there is no problem concerning "social protest" as such in a democracy. Our Bill of Rights was adopted not only to make protest possible but to encourage it. The political logic, the very ethos of any democracy that professes to rest, no matter how indirectly, upon freely given consent *requires* that social protest be permitted—and not only permitted but *protected* from interference by those opposed to the protest, which means protected by agencies of law enforcement.

Not social protest but *illegal* social protest constitutes our problem. It raises the question: "When, if ever, is illegal protest justified in a democratic society?" It is of the first importance to bear in mind that we are raising the question as principled democrats and humanists in a democratic society. To urge that illegal social protests, motivated by exalted ideals are sanctified in a democratic society by precedents like the Boston Tea Party, is a lapse into political illiteracy. Such actions occurred in societies in which those affected by unjust laws had no power peacefully to change them.

Further, many actions dubbed civilly disobedient by local authorities, strictly speaking, are not such at all. An action launched in violation of a local law or ordinance, and undertaken to test it, on the ground that the law itself violates state or federal law, or launched in violation of a state law in the sincerely held belief that the state law outrages the Constitution, the supreme law of the land, is not civilly disobedient. In large measure the original sympathy with which the original sit-ins were received, especially the Freedom Rides, marches, and demonstrations that flouted local Southern laws, was due to the conviction that they were constitutionally justified, in accordance with the heritage of freedom, enshrined in the Amendments, and enjoyed in other regions of the country. Practically everything the marchers did was sanctioned by the phrase of the First Amendment which upholds "the right of the people peaceably to assemble and to petition the Government for a redress of grievances." Actions of this kind may be wise or unwise, timely or untimely, but they are not civilly disobedient.

They become civilly disobedient when they are in deliberate violation of laws that have been sustained by the highest legislative and judicial bodies of the nation, e.g., income tax laws, conscription laws, laws forbidding segregation in education, and discrimination in public accommodations and employment. Another class of examples consists of illegal social protest against local and state laws that clearly do not conflict with Federal Law.

Once we grasp the proper issue, the question is asked with deceptive clarity: "Are we under an obligation in a democratic community always to obey an unjust law?" To this question Abraham Lincoln is supposed to have made the classic answer in an eloquent address on "The Perpetuation of Our Political Institution," calling for absolute and religious obedience until the unjust law is repealed.

I said that this question is asked with deceptive clarity because Lincoln, judging by his other writings and the pragmatic cast of his basic philosophy, could never have subscribed to this absolutism or meant what he seemed literally to have said. Not only are we under no moral obligation *always* to obey unjust laws, we are under no moral obligation *always* to obey a just law. One can put it more strongly: sometimes it may be necessary in the interests of the greater good to violate a just or sensible law. A man who refused to violate a sensible traffic law if it were necessary to do so to avoid a probably fatal accident would be a moral idiot. There are other values in the world besides legality or even justice, and sometimes they may be of overriding concern and weight. Everyone can imagine some situation in which the violation of some existing law is the lesser moral evil, but this does not invalidate recognition of our obligation to obey just laws.

There is a difference between disobeying a law which one approves of in general but whose application in a specific case seems wrong, and disobeying a law in protest against the injustice of the law itself. In the latter case the disobedience is open and public; in the former, not. But if the grounds of disobedience in both cases are moral considerations, there is only a difference in degree between them. The rejection, therefore, of legal absolutism or the fetishism of legality—that one is never justified in violating any law in any circumstances—is a matter of common sense.

The implications drawn from this moral commonplace by some ritualistic liberals are clearly absurd. For they have substituted for the absolutism of law something very close to the absolutism of individual conscience. Properly rejecting the view that the law, no matter how unjust, must be obeyed in all circumstances, they have taken the view that the law is to be obeyed only when the individual deems it just or when it does not outrage his conscience. Fantastic comparisons are made between those who do not act on the dictates of their conscience and those who accepted and obeyed Hitler's laws. These comparisons completely disregard the systems of law involved, the presence of alternatives of action, the differences in the behavior commanded, in degrees of complicity of guilt, in the moral costs and personal consequences of compliance and other relevant matters.

It is commendable to recognize the primacy of morality to law but unless we recognize the centrality of intelligence to morality, we stumble with blind self-righteousness into moral disaster. Because, Kant to the contrary notwithstanding, it is not wrong sometimes to lie to save a human life; because it is not wrong sometimes to kill in defense to save many from being killed, it does not follow that the moral principles: "Do not lie!" "Do not kill!" are invalid. When more than one valid principle bears on a problem of moral experience, the very fact of their conflict means that not all of them can hold unqualifiedly. One of them must be denied. The point is that such negation or violation entails upon us the obligation of justifying it, and moral justification is a matter of reasons not of conscience. The burden of proof rests on the person violating the rules. Normally, we don't have to justify telling the truth. We do have to justify *not* telling the truth. Similarly, with respect to the moral obligation of a democrat who breaches his political obligation to obey the laws of a democratic community, the resort to conscience is not enough. There must always be reasonable justification.

This is all the more true because just as we can, if challenged, give powerful reasons for the moral principle of truth-telling, so we can offer logically coercive grounds for the obligation of a democrat to obey the laws of a democracy. The grounds are many and they can be amplified beyond the passing mention we give here. It is a matter of fairness, of social utility, of peace, or ordered progress, of redeeming an implicit commitment.

There is one point, however, which has a particular relevance to the claims of those who counterpose to legal absolutism the absolutism of conscience. There is the empirically observable tendency for public disobedience to law to spread from those who occupy high moral ground to those who dwell on low ground, with consequent growth of disorder and insecurity.

Conscience by itself is not the measure of high or low moral ground. This is the work of reason. Where it functions properly the democratic process permits this resort to reason. If the man of conscience loses in the court of reason, why should he assume that the decision or the law is mistaken rather than the deliverances of his conscience?

The voice of conscience may sound loud and clear. But it may conflict at times not only with the law but with another man's conscience. Every conscientious objector to a law knows that at least one man's conscience is wrong, *viz.*, the conscience of the man who asserts that *his* conscience tells him that he must not tolerate conscientious objectors. From this if he is reasonable he should conclude that when he hears the voice of conscience, he is hearing not the voice of God, but the voice of a finite, limited man in this time and in this place, and that conscience is neither a special nor an infallible organ of apprehending moral truth, that conscience without conscientiousness, conscience which does not cap the process of critical reflective morality, is likely to be prejudice masquerading as a First Principle or a Mandate from Heaven.

The mark of an enlightened democracy is, as far as is possible with its security, to respect the religious commitment of a citizen who believes, on grounds of conscience or any other ground, that his relation to God involves duties superior to those arising from any human relation. It, therefore, exempts him from his duty as a citizen to protect his country. However, the mark of the genuine conscientious objector in a democracy is to respect the democratic process. He does not use his exemption as a political weapon to coerce where he has failed to convince or persuade. Having failed to influence national policy by rational means within the law, in the political processes open to him in a free society, he cannot justifiably try to defeat that policy by resorting to obstructive techniques outside the law and still remain a democrat.

It is one thing on grounds of conscience or religion to plead exemption from the duty of serving one's country when drafted. It is quite another to adopt harassing techniques to prevent others from volunteering or responding to the call of duty. It is one thing to oppose American involvement in Vietnam by teach-ins, petitions, electoral activity. It is quite another to attempt to stop troop trains: to take possession of the premises of draft boards where policies are not made; to urge recruits to sabotage their assignments and feign illness to win discharge. The first class of actions fall within the sphere of legitimate social protest; the second class are implicitly insurrectionary since it is directed against the authority of a democratic government which it seeks to overthrow not by argument and discussion but by resistance—albeit passive resistance.

Nonetheless, since we have rejected legal absolutism we must face the possibility that in protest on ethical grounds individuals may refuse to obey some law which they regard as uncommonly immoral or uncommonly foolish. If they profess to be democrats, their behavior must scrupulously respect the following conditions:

First, it must be nonviolent—peaceful not only in form but in actuality. After all, the protesters are seeking to dramatize a great evil that the community allegedly has been unable to overcome because of complacency or moral weakness. Therefore, they must avoid the guilt of imposing hardship or harm on others who in the nature of the case can hardly be responsible for the situation under protest. Passive resistance should not be utilized merely as a safer or more effective strategy than active resistance of imposing their wills on others.

Secondly, resort to civil disobedience is never morally legitimate where other methods of remedying the evil complained of are available. Existing grievance procedures should be used. No grievance procedures were available to the southern Negroes. The Courts often shared the prejudices of the community and offered no relief, not even minimal protection. But such procedures *are* available in the areas of industry and education. For example, where charges against students are being heard such procedures may result in the dismissal of the charges not the students. Or the faculty on appeal may decide to suspend the rules rather than the students. To jump the gun to civil disobedience in bypassing these procedures is tell-tale evidence that those who are calling the shots are after other game than preserving the rights of students.

Thirdly, those who resort to civil disobedience are duty bound to accept the legal sanctions and punishments imposed by the laws. Attempts to evade and escape them not only involve a betrayal of the community, but erode the moral foundations of civil disobedience itself. Socrates' argument in the *Crito* is valid only on democratic premises. The rationale of the protesters is the hope that the pain and hurt and indignity they voluntarily accept will stir their fellow citizens to compassion, open their minds to second thoughts, and move them to undertake the necessary healing action. When, however, we observe the heroics of defiance being followed by the dialectics of legal evasion, we question the sincerity of the action.

Fourth, civil disobedience is unjustified if a major moral issue is not clearly at stake. Differences about negotiable details that can easily be settled with a little patience should not be fanned into a blaze of illegal opposition.

Fifth, where intelligent men of good will and character differ on large and complex moral issues, discussion and agitation are more appropriate than civilly disobedient action. Those who feel strongly about animal rights and regard the consumption of animal flesh as foods as morally evil would have a just cause for civil disobedience if *their* freedom to obtain other food was threatened. They would have no moral right to resort to similar action to prevent their fellow citizens from consuming meat. Similarly with fluoridation.

Sixth, where civil disobedience is undertaken, there must be some rhyme and reason in the time, place, and targets selected. If one is convinced, as I am not, that the Board of Education of New York City is remiss in its policy of desegregation, what is the point of dumping garbage on bridges to produce traffic jams that seriously discomfort commuters who have not the remotest connection with educational policies in New York. Such action can only obstruct the progress of desegregation in the communities of Long Island. Gandhi, who inspired the civil disobedience movement in the twentieth century, was a better tactician than many who invoke his name but ignore his teachings. When he organized his campaign of civil disobedience against the Salt Tax, he marched with his followers to the sea to make salt. He did not hold up food trains or tie up traffic.

Finally there is such a thing as historical timing. Democrats who resort to civil disobedience must ask themselves whether the cumulative consequences of their action may in the existing climate of opinion undermine the peace and order on which the effective exercise of other human rights depend. This is a cost which one may be willing to pay but which must be taken into the reckoning.

These observations in the eyes of some defenders of the philosophy of civil disobedience are far from persuasive. They regard them as evading the political realities. The political realities, it is asserted, do not provide meaningful channels for the legitimate expression of dissent. The "Establishment" is too powerful or indifferent to be moved. Administrations are voted into office that are not bound by their election pledges. The right to form minority parties is hampered by unconstitutional voting laws. What does even "the right of the people to present petitions for the redress of grievances" amount to if it does not carry with it the right to have those petitions paid attention to, at least to have them read, if not acted upon?

No, the opposing argument runs on. Genuine progress does not come by enactment of laws, by appeals to the good will or conscience of one's fellow citizens, but only by obstructions which interfere with the functioning of the system itself, by actions whose nuisance value is so high that the Establishment finds it easier to be decent and yield to demands than to be obdurate and oppose them. The time comes, as one student leader of the civilly disobedient Berkeley students advised, "when it is necessary for you to throw your bodies upon the wheels and gears and levers and bring the machine to a grinding halt." When one objects that such obstruction, as a principle of political action, is almost sure to produce chaos, and that it is unnecessary and undesirable in a democracy, the retort is made: "Amen, if only this were a democracy, how glad we would be to stop!"

It is characteristic of those who argue this way to define the presence or absence of the democratic process by whether or not *they* get their political way, and not by the presence or absence of democratic institutional processes. The rules of the game exist to enable them to win and if they lose that's sufficient proof the game is rigged and dishonest. The sincerity with which the position is held is no evidence whatsoever of its coherence. The right to petition does not carry with it the right to be heard, if that means influence on those to whom it is addressed. What would they do if they received incompatible petitions from two different and hostile groups of petitioning citizens? The right of petition gives one a chance to persuade, and the persuasion must rest on the power of words, on the effective appeal to emotion, sympathy, reason, and logic. Petitions are weapons of criticism, and their failure does not justify appeal to other kinds of weapons.

It is quite true that some local election laws do hamper minority groups in the organization of political parties; but there is always the right of appeal to the Courts. Even if this fails there is a possibility of influencing other political parties. It is difficult but so long as one is free to publish and speak, it can be done. If a group is unsuccessful in moving a majority by the weapons of criticism, in a democracy it may resort to peaceful measures of obstruction, provided it is willing to accept punishment for its obstructionist behavior. But these objections are usually a preface to some form of elitism or moral snobbery which is incompatible with the very grounds given in defending the right of civil disobedience on the part of democrats in a democracy.

All of the seven considerations listed above are cautionary, not categorical. We have ruled out only two positions—blind obedience to any and all laws in a democracy, and unreflective violation of laws at the behest of individual consciences. Between these two obviously unacceptable extremes, there is a spectrum of views which shade into each other. Intelligent persons can differ on their application to specific situations. These differences will reflect different assessments of the historical mood of a culture, of the proper timing of protest and acquiescence, and of what the most desirable emphasis and direction of our teaching should be in order to extend "the blessing of liberty" as we preserve "domestic tranquility."

Without essaying the role of a prophet, here is my reading of the needs of the present. It seems to me that the Civil Rights Acts of 1964 and the Voting Acts of 1965 mark a watershed in the history of social and civil protest in the U.S. Upon their enforcement a great many things we hold dear depend, especially those causes in behalf of which in the last decade so many movements of social protest were launched. We must recall that it was the emasculation of the 15th Amendment in the South which kept the Southern Negro in a state of virtual peonage. The prospect of enforcement of the new civil rights legislation is a function of many factors—most notably the law-abiding behavior of the hitherto recalcitrant elements in the southern white communities. Their *uncivil*, violent disobedience has proved unavailing. We need not fear this so much as that they will adopt the strategies and techniques of the civil disobedience itself in their opposition to long-delayed and decent legislation to make the ideals of American democracy a greater reality.

On the other hand, I think the movement of civil disobedience, as distinct from legal protest, in regions of the country in which Negroes have made slow but substantial advances are not likely to make new gains commensurate with the risks. Those risks are that what is begun as civil disobedience will be perverted by extremists into uncivil disobedience, and alienate large numbers who have firmly supported the cause of freedom.

One of the unintended consequences of the two World Wars is that in many ways they strengthened the position of the Negroes and all other minorities in American political life. We do not need another, a third World War, to continue the process of liberation. We can do it in peace—without war and without civil war. The Civil Rights and Voting Acts of 1964 and 1965 are far in advance of the actual situation in the country where discrimination is so rife. Our present task is to bring home and reinforce popular consciousness of the fact that those who violate their provisions are violating the highest law of the land, and that their actions are outside the law. Therefore, our goal must *now* be to build up and strengthen a mood of respect for the law, for civil obedience to laws, even by those who deem them unwise or who opposed them in the past. Our hope is that those who abide by the law may learn not only to tolerate them but, in time, as their fruits develop, to accept them. To have the positive law on the side of right and justice is to have a powerful weapon that makes for voluntary compliance—but only if the *reasonableness* of the *prima facie* obligation to obey the law is recognized.

To one observer at least, that reasonableness is being more and more disregarded in this country. The current mood is one of growing indifference to and disregard of even the reasonable legalities. The headlines from New York to California tell the story. I am not referring to the crime rate which has made frightening strides, nor to the fact that some of our metropolitan centers have become dangerous jungles. I refer to a growing mood toward law generally, something comparable to the attitude toward the Volstead Act during the Prohibition era. The mood is more diffuse today. To be law-abiding in some circles is to be "a square."

In part, the community itself has been responsible for the emergence of this mood. This is especially true in those states which have failed to abolish the *unreasonable* legalities, particularly in the fields of marriage, divorce, birth control, sex behavior, therapeutic abortion, voluntary euthanasia, and other intrusions of the right of privacy. The failure to repeal foolish laws, which makes morally upright individuals legal offenders, tends to generate skepticism and indifference toward observing the reasonable legalities.

This mood must change if the promise of recent civil rights legislation is to be realized. Respect for law today can give momentum to the liberal upswing of the political and social pendulum in American life. In a democracy we cannot make an absolute of obedience to law or to anything else except "the moral obligation to be intelligent," but more than ever we must stress that dissent and opposition—the oxygen of free society—be combined with civic obedience, and that on moral grounds it express itself as legal dissent and legal opposition.

39 Letter from Birmingham City Jail*

MARTIN LUTHER KING, JR.

Martin Luther King, Jr., (1929–1968) was a well-known leader in the civil rights movement in the United States. Winner of the Nobel Peace Prize in 1964, King's principal books are *Stride Toward Freedom, Strength to Love,* and *Why We Can't Wait.*

My dear Fellow Clergymen,

While confined here in the Birmingham City Jail, I came across your recent statement calling our present activities "unwise and untimely." Seldom, if ever, do I pause to answer criticism of my work and ideas. If I sought to answer all of the criticisms that cross my desk, my secretaries would be engaged in little else in the course of the day and I would have no time for constructive work. But since I feel that you are men of genuine goodwill and your criticisms are sincerely set forth, I would like to answer your statement in what I hope will be patient and reasonable terms.

I think I should give the reason for my being in Birmingham, since you have been influenced by the argument of "outsiders coming in." I have the honor of serving as president of the Southern Christian Leadership Conference, an organization operating in every Southern state with headquarters in Atlanta, Georgia. We have some eighty-five affiliate organizations all across the South—one being the Alabama Christian Movement for Human Rights. Whenever necessary and possible we share staff, educational, and financial resources with our affiliates. Several months ago our local affiliate here in Birmingham invited us to be on call to engage in a nonviolent direct, action program if such were deemed necessary. We readily consented and when the hour came we lived up to our promises. So I am here, along with several members of my staff, because we were invited here. I am here because I have basic organizational ties here. Beyond this, I am in Birmingham because injustice is here. Just as the eighth century prophets left their little villages and carried their "thus saith the Lord" far beyond the boundaries of their home town, and just as the Apostle Paul left his little village of Tarsus and carried the gospel of Jesus Christ to practically every hamlet and city of the

* Martin Luther King, Jr., *Letter from Birmingham City Jail.* Reprinted by permission of the American Friends Service Committee, Philadelphia, Pennsylvania.

Graeco-Roman world, I too am compelled to carry the gospel of freedom beyond my particular home town. Like Paul, I must constantly respond to the Macedonian call for aid.

Moreover, I am cognizant of the interrelatedness of all communities and states. I cannot sit idly by in Atlanta and not be concerned about what happens in Birmingham. Injustice anywhere is a threat to justice everywhere. We are caught in an inescapable network of mutuality tied in a single garment of destiny. Whatever affects one directly affects all indirectly. Never again can we afford to live with the narrow, provincial "outside agitator" idea. Anyone who lives inside the United States can never be considered an outsider anywhere in this country.

You deplore the demonstrations that are presently taking place in Birmingham. But I am sorry that your statement did not express a similar concern for the conditions that brought the demonstrations into being. I am sure that each of you would want to go beyond the superficial social analyst who looks merely at effects, and does not grapple with underlying causes. I would not hesitate to say that it is unfortunate that so-called demonstrations are taking place in Birmingham at this time, but I would say in more emphatic terms that it is even more unfortunate that the white power structure of this city left the Negro community with no other alternative.

In any nonviolent campaign there are four basic steps: (1) collection of the facts to determine whether injustices are alive; (2) negotiation; (3) self-purification; and (4) direct action. We have gone through all of these steps in Birmingham. There can be no gainsaying of the fact that racial injustice engulfs this community. Birmingham is probably the most thoroughly segregated city in the United States. Its ugly record of police brutality is known in every section of this country. Its unjust treatment of Negroes in the courts is a notorious reality. There have been more unsolved bombings of Negro homes and churches in Birmingham than any city in this nation. These are the hard, brutal, and unbelievable facts. On the basis of these conditions Negro leaders sought to negotiate with the city fathers. But the political leaders consistently refused to engage in good faith negotiation.

Then came the opportunity last September to talk with some of the leaders of the economic community. In these negotiating sessions certain promises were made by the merchants—such as the promise to remove the humiliating racial signs from the stores. On the basis of these promises Rev. Shuttlesworth and the leaders of the Alabama Christian Movement for Human Rights agreed to call a moratorium on any type of demonstrations. As the weeks and months unfolded we realized that we were the victims of a broken promise. The signs remained. As in so many experiences of the past we were confronted with blasted hopes, and the dark shadow of a deep disappointment settled upon us. So we had no alternative except that of preparing for direct action, whereby we would present our very bodies as a means of laying our case before the conscience of the local and national community. We were not unmindful of the difficulties involved. So we decided to go through a process of self-purification. We started having workshops on nonviolence and repeatedly asked ourselves the questions, "Are you able to accept blows without retaliating?" Are you able to endure the ordeals of jail?"

We decided to set our direct action program around the Easter season, realizing that with the exception of Christmas, this was the largest shopping period of the year. Knowing that a strong economic withdrawal program would be the byproduct of direct action, we felt that this was the best time to bring pressure on the merchants for the needed changes. Then it occurred to us that the March election was ahead, and so we speedily decided to postpone action until after election day. When we discovered that Mr. Connor was in the run-off, we decided again to postpone action so that the demonstrations could not be used to cloud the issues. At this time we agreed to begin our nonviolent witness the day after the run-off.

This reveals that we did not move irresponsibly into direct action. We too wanted to see Mr. Connor defeated; so we went through postponement after postponement to aid in this community need. After this we felt that direct action could be delayed no longer.

You may well ask, "Why direct action? Why sit-ins, marches, etc.? Isn't negotiation a better path?" You are exactly right in your call for negotiation. Indeed, this is the purpose of direct action. Nonviolent direct action seeks to create such a crisis and establish such creative tension that a community that has constantly refused to negotiate is forced to confront the issue. It seeks so to dramatize the issue that it can no longer be ignored. I just referred to the creation of tension as a part of the work of the nonviolent resister. This may sound rather shocking. But I must confess that I am not afraid of the word tension. I have earnestly worked and preached against violent tension, and there is a type of constructive nonviolent tension that is necessary for growth. Just as Socrates felt that it was necessary to create a tension in the mind so that individuals could rise from the bondage of myths and half-truths to the unfettered realm of creative analysis and objective appraisal, we must see the need of having nonviolent gadflies to create the kind of tension in society that will help men rise from the dark depths of prejudice and racism to the majestic heights of understanding and brotherhood. So the purpose of the direct action is to create a situation so crisis-packed that it will inevitably open the door to negotiation. We, therefore, concur with you in your call for negotiation. Too long has our beloved Southland been bogged down in the tragic attempt to live in monologue rather than dialogue.

One of the basic points in your statement is that our acts are untimely. Some have asked, "Why didn't you give the new administration time to act?" The only answer that I can give to this inquiry is that the new administration must be prodded about as much as the outgoing one before it acts. We will be sadly mistaken if we feel that the election of Mr. Boutwell will bring the millennium to Birmingham. While Mr. Boutwell is much more articulate and gentle than Mr. Connor, they are both segregationists dedicated to the task of maintaining the status quo. The hope I see in Mr. Boutwell is that he will be reasonable enough to see the futility of massive resistance to desegregation. But he will not see this without pressure from the devotees of civil rights. My friends, I must say to you that we have not made a single gain in civil rights without determined legal and nonviolent pressure. History is the long and tragic story of the fact that privileged groups seldom give up their privileges voluntarily. Individuals may see the moral light and voluntarily give up their unjust posture; but as Reinhold Niebuhr has reminded us, groups are more immoral than individuals.

We know through painful experience that freedom is never voluntarily given by the oppressor; it must be demanded by the oppressed. Frankly I have never yet engaged in a direct action movement that was "well timed," according to the timetable of those who have not suffered unduly from the disease of segregation. For years now I have heard the word "Wait!" It rings in the ear of every Negro with a piercing familiarity. This "wait" has almost always meant "never." It has been a tranquilizing thalidomide, relieving the emotional stress for a moment, only to give birth to an ill-formed infant of frustration. We must come to see with the distinguished jurist of yesterday that "justice too long delayed is justice denied." We have waited for more than three hundred and forty years for our constitutional and God-given rights. The nations of Asia and Africa are moving with jet-like speed toward the goal of political independence, and we still creep at horse and buggy pace toward the gaining of a cup of coffee at a lunch counter.

I guess it is easy for those who have never felt the stinging darts of segregation to say wait. But when you have seen vicious mobs lynch your mothers and fathers at will and drown your sisters and brothers at whim; when you have seen hate filled policeman curse, kick, brutalize, and even kill your black brothers and sisters with impunity; when you see the vast majority of your twenty million Negro bothers smothering in an air-tight cage of poverty in the midst of an affluent society; when you suddenly find your tongue twisted and your speech stammering as you seek to explain to your six-year-old daughter why she can't go to the public amusement park that has just been advertised on television, and see tears welling up in her little eyes when she is told that Funtown is closed to colored children, and see the depressing clouds of inferiority begin to form in her little mental sky, and see her begin to distort her little personality by unconsciously developing a bitterness toward white people; when you have to concoct an answer for a five-year-old son asking in agonizing pathos: "Daddy, why do white people treat colored people so mean?"; when you take a cross country drive and find it necessary to sleep night after night in the uncomfortable corners of your automobile because no motel will accept you; when you are humiliated day in and day out by nagging signs reading "white" men and "colored"; when your first name becomes "nigger" and your middle name becomes "boy" (however old you are) and your last name becomes "John," and when your wife and mother are never given the respected title "Mrs."; when you are harried by day and haunted by night by the fact that you are a Negro, living constantly at tip-toe stance never quite knowing what to expect next, and plagued with inner fears and outer resentments; when you are forever fighting a degenerating sense of "nobodiness";—then you will understand why we find it difficult to wait. There comes a time when the cup of endurance runs over, and men are no longer willing to be plunged into an abyss of injustice where they experience the bleakness of corroding despair. I hope, sirs, you can understand our legitimate and unavoidable impatience.

You express a great deal of anxiety over our willingness to break laws. This is certainly a legitimate concern. Since we so diligently urge people to obey the Supreme Court's decision of 1954 outlawing segregation in the public schools, it is rather strange and paradoxical to find us consciously breaking laws. One may well ask, "How can you advocate breaking some laws and obeying others?" The answer is found in the fact that there are two types of laws; There are *just* laws and there are *unjust* laws. I would be the first to advocate obeying just laws. One has not only a legal but moral responsibility to obey just laws. Conversely, one has a moral responsibility to disobey unjust laws. I would agree with Saint Augustine that "An unjust law is no law at all."

Now what is the difference between the two? How does one determine when a law is just or unjust? A just law is a man-made code that squares with the moral law or the law of God. An unjust law is a code that is out of harmony with the moral law. To put it in the terms of Saint Thomas Aquinas, an unjust law is a human law that is not rooted in eternal and natural law. Any law that uplifts human personality is just. Any law that degrades human personality is unjust. All segregation statutes are unjust because segregation distorts the soul and damages the personality. It gives the segregator a false sense of superiority and the segregated a false sense of inferiority. To use the words of Martin Buber, the great Jewish philosopher, segregation substitutes an "I-it" relationship for the "I-thou" relationship, and ends up relegating persons to the status of things. So segregation is not only politically, economically, and sociologically unsound, but it is morally wrong and sinful. Paul Tillich has said that sin is separation. Isn't segregation an existential expression of man's tragic separation, an expression of his awful estrangement, his terrible sinfulness? So I can urge men to obey the 1954 decision of the Supreme Court because it is morally right, and I can urge them to disobey segregation ordinances because they are morally wrong.

Let us turn to a more concrete example of just and unjust laws. An unjust law is a code that a majority inflicts on a minority that is not binding on itself. This is *difference* made legal. On the other hand a just law is a code that a majority compels a minority to follow that it is willing to follow itself. This is *sameness* made legal.

Let me give another explanation. An unjust law is a code inflicted upon a minority which that minority had no part in enacting or creating because they did not have the unhampered right to vote. Who can say the legislature of Alabama which set up the segregation laws was democratically elected? Throughout the state of Alabama all types of conniving methods are used to prevent Negrose from becoming registered voters and there are some counties without a single Negro registered to vote despite the fact that the Negro constitutes a majority of the population. Can any law set up in such a state be considered democratically structured?

These are just a few examples of unjust and just laws. There are some instances when a law is just on its face but unjust in its application. For instance, I was arrested Friday on a charge of parading without a permit. Now there is nothing wrong with an ordinance which requires a permit for a parade, but when the ordinance is used to preserve segregation and to deny citizens the First Amendment privilege of peaceful assembly and peaceful protest, then it becomes unjust.

I hope you can see the distinction I am trying to point out. In no sense do I advocate evading or defying the law as the rabid segregationist would do. This would lead to anarchy. One who breaks an unjust law must do it *openly*, *lovingly* (not hatefully as the white mothers did in New Orleans when they were seen on television screaming "nigger, nigger, nigger") and with a willingness to accept the penalty. I submit that an individual who breaks a law that conscience tells him is unjust, and willingly accepts the penalty by staying in jail to arouse the conscience of the community over its injustice, is in reality expressing the very highest respect for law.

Of course there is nothing new about this kind of civil disobedience. It was seen sublimely in the refusal of Shadrach, Meshach, and Abednego to obey the laws of Nebuchadnezzar because a higher moral law was involved. It was practiced superbly by the early Christians who were willing to face hungry lions and the excruciating pain of chopping blocks, before submitting to certain unjust laws of the Roman Empire. To a degree academic freedom is a reality today because Socrates practiced civil disobedience.

We can never forget that everything Hitler did in Germany was "legal" and everything the Hungarian freedom fighters did in Hungary was "illegal." It was "illegal" to aid and comfort a Jew in Hitler's Germany. But I am sure that, if I had lived in Germany during that time, I would have aided and comforted my Jewish brothers even though it was illegal. If I lived in a communist country today where certain principles dear to the Christian faith are suppressed, I believe I would openly advocate disobeying these anti-religious laws.

I must make two honest confessions to you, my Christian and Jewish brothers. First I must confess that over the last few years I have been gravely disappointed with the white moderate. I have almost reached the regrettable conclusion that the Negroes' great stumbling block in the stride toward freedom is not the White Citizens' "Counciler" or the Ku Klux Klanner, but the white moderate who is more devoted to "order" than to justice; who prefers a negative peace which is the absence of tension to a positive peace which is the presence of justice; who constantly says "I agree with you in the goal you seek, but I can't agree with your methods of direct action"; who paternalistically feels that he can set the time-table for another man's freedom; who lives by the myth of time and who constantly advises the Negro to wait until a "more convenient season." Shallow understanding from people of good will is more frustrating than absolute misunderstanding from people of ill will. Lukewarm acceptance is much more bewildering than outright rejection.

I had hoped that the white moderate would understand that law and order exist for the purpose of establishing justice, and that when they fail to do this they become the dangerously structured dams that block the flow of social progress. I had hoped that the white moderate would understand that the present tension in the South is merely a necessary phase of the transition from an obnoxious negative peace, where the Negro passively accepted his unjust plight, to a substance-filled positive peace, where all men will respect the dignity and worth of human personality. Actually, we who engage in non-violent direct action are not the creators of tension. We merely bring to the surface the hidden tension that is already alive. We bring it out in the open where it can be seen and dealt with. Like a boil that can never be cured as long as it is covered up but must be opened with all its pusflowing ugliness to the natural medicines of air and light, injustice must likewise be exposed, with all of the tension its exposing creates, to the light of human conscience and the air of national opinion before it can be cured.

In your statement you asserted that our actions, even though peaceful, must be condemned because they precipitate violence. But can this assertion be logically made? Isn't this like condemning the robbed man because his possession of money precipitated the evil act of robbery? Isn't this like condemning Socrates because his unswerving commitment to truth and his philosophical delvings precipitated the misguided popular mind to make him drink the hemlock? Isn't this like condemning Jesus because His unique God consciousness and never-ceasing devotion to His will precipitated the evil act of crucifixion? We must come to see, as federal courts have consistently affirmed, that it is immoral to urge an individual to withdraw his efforts to gain his basic constitutional rights because the quest precipitates violence. Society must protect the robbed and punish the robber.

I had also hoped that the white moderate would reject the myth of time. I received a letter this morning from a white brother in Texas which said: "All Christians know that the colored people will receive equal rights eventually, but is it possible that you are in too great of a religious hurry? It has taken Christianity almost 2000 years to accomplish what it has. The teachings of Christ take time to come to earth." All that is said here grows out of a tragic misconception of time. It is the strangely irrational notion that there is something in the very flow of time that will inevitably cure all ills. Actually time is neutral. It can be used either destructively or constructively. I am coming to feel that the people of ill will have used time much more effectively than the people of good will. We will have to repent in this generation not merely for the vitriolic words and actions of the bad people, but for the appalling silence of the good people. We must come to see that human progress never rolls in on wheels of inevitability. It comes through the tireless efforts and persistent work of men willing to be co-workers with God, and without this hard work time itself becomes an ally of the forces of social stagnation.

We must use time creatively, and forever realize that the time is always ripe to do right. Now is the time to make real the promise of democracy, and transform our pending national elegy into a creative psalm of brotherhood. Now is the time to lift our national policy from the quicksand of racial injustice to the solid rock of human dignity.

You spoke of our activity in Birmingham as extreme. At first I was rather disappointed that fellow clergymen would see my nonviolent efforts as those of the extremist. I started thinking about the fact that I stand in the middle of two opposing forces in the Negro community. One is a force of complacency made up of Negroes who, as a result of long years of oppression, have been so completely drained of self-respect and a sense of "somebodiness" that they have adjusted to segregation, and of a few Negroes in the middle class who, because of a degree of academic and economic security, and because at points they profit by segregation, have unconsciously become insensitive to the problems of the masses. The other force is one of bitterness and hatred and comes perilously close to advocating violence. It is expressed in the various black nationalist groups that are springing up over the nation, the largest and best known being Elijah Muhammad's Muslim movement. This movement is nourished by the contemporary frustration over the continued existence of racial discrimination. It is made up of people who have lost faith in America, who have absolutely repudiated Christianity, and who have concluded that the white man is an incurable "devil." I have tried to stand between these two forces saying that we need not follow the "do-nothingism" of the complacent or the hatred and despair of the black nationalist. There is the more excellent way of love and nonviolent protest. I'm grateful to God that, through the Negro church, the dimension of nonviolence entered our struggle. If this philosophy had not emerged I am convinced that by now many streets of the South would be flowing with floods of blood. And I am further convinced that if our white brothers dismiss us as "rabble rousers" and "outside agitators"—those of us who are working through the channels of nonviolent direct action—and refuse to support our nonviolent efforts, millions of Negroes, out of frustration and despair, will seek solace and security in black nationalist ideologies, a development that will lead inevitably to a frightening racial nightmare.

Oppressed people cannot remain oppressed forever. The urge for freedom will eventually come. This is what has happened to the American Negro. Something within has reminded him of his birthright of freedom; something without has reminded him that he can gain it. Consciously and unconsciously, he has been swept in by what the Germans call the *Zeitgeist*, and with his black brothers of Africa, and his brown and yellow brothers of Asia, South America, and the Caribbean, he is moving with a sense of cosmic urgency toward the promised land of racial justice. Recognizing this vital urge that has engulfed the Negro community, one should readily understand public demonstrations. The Negro has many pent-up resentments and latent frustrations. He has to get them out. So let him march sometime; let him have his prayer pilgrimages to the city hall; understand why he must have sit-ins and freedom rides. If his repressed emotions do not come out in these nonviolent ways, they will come out in ominous expressions of violence. This is not a threat; it is a fact of history. So I have not said to my people, "Get rid of your discontent." But I have tried to say that this normal and healthy discontent can be channeled through the creative outlet of nonviolent direct action. Now this approach is being dismissed as extremist. I must admit that I was initially disappointed in being so categorized.

But as I continued to think about the matter I gradually gained a bit of satisfaction from being considered an extremist. Was not Jesus an extremist in love? "Love your enemies, bless them that curse you, pray for them that despitefully use you." Was not Amos an extremist for justice—"Let justice roll down like waters and righteousness like a mighty stream." Was not Paul an extremist for the gospel of Jesus Christ—"I bear in my body the marks of the Lord Jesus." Was not Martin Luther an extremist—"Here I stand; I can do none other so help me God." Was not John Bunyan an extremist— "I will stay in jail to the end of my days before I make a butchery of my conscience." Was not Abraham Lincoln an extremist—"This nation cannot survive half slave and half free." Was not Thomas Jefferson an extremist —"We hold these truths to be self evident that all men are created equal." So the question is not whether we will be extremist but what kind of extremist will we be. Will we be extremists for hate or will we be extremists for love? Will we be extremists for the preservation of injustice—or will we be extremists for the cause of justice? In that dramatic scene on Calvary's hill three men were crucified. We must never forget that all three were crucified for the same crime—the crime of extremism. Two were extremists for immorality, and thus fell below their environment. The other, Jesus Christ, was an extremist for love, truth, and goodness, and thereby rose above His environment. So, after all, maybe the South, the nation, and the world are in dire need of creative extremists.

I had hoped that the white moderate would see this. Maybe I was too optimistic. Maybe I expected too much. I guess I should have realized that few members of a race that has oppressed another race can understand or appreciate the deep groans and passionate yearnings of those that have been oppressed, and still fewer have the vision to see that injustice must be rooted out by strong, persistent, and determined action. I am thankful, however, that some of our white brothers have grasped the meaning of this social revolution and committed themselves to it. They are still all too small in quantity, but they are big in quality. Some like Ralph McGill, Lillian Smith, Harry Golden, and James Dabbs have written about our struggle in eloquent, prophetic, and understanding terms. Others have marched with us down nameless streets of the South. They have languished in filthy, roach-infested jails, suffering the abuse and brutality of angry policemen who see them as "dirty nigger lovers." They, unlike so many of their moderate brothers and sisters, have recognized the urgency of the moment and sensed the need for powerful "action" antidotes to combat the disease of segregation.

Let me rush on to mention my other disappointment. I have been so greatly disappointed with the white Church and its leadership. Of course there are some notable exceptions. I am not unmindful of the fact that each of you has taken some significant stands on this issue. I commend you, Rev. Stallings, for your Christian stand on this past Sunday, in welcoming Negroes to your worship service on a non-segregated basis. I commend the Catholic leaders of this state for integrating Springhill College several years ago.

But despite these notable exceptions I must honestly reiterate that I have been disappointed with the Church. I do not say that as one of those negative critics who can always find something wrong with the Church. I say it as a minister of the gospel, who loves the Church; who was nurtured in its bosom; who has been sustained by its spiritual blessings and who will remain true to it as long as the cord of life shall lengthen.

I had the strange feeling when I was suddenly catapulted into the leadership of the bus protest in Montgomery several years ago that we would have the support of the white Church. I felt that the white ministers, priests, and rabbis of the South would be some of our strongest allies. Instead, some have been outright opponents, refusing to understand the freedom movement and misrepresenting its leaders; all too many others have been more cautious than courageous and have remained silent behind the anesthetizing security of stained glass windows.

In spite of my shattered dreams of the past, I came to Birmingham with the hope that the white religious leadership of this community would see the justice of our cause and, with deep moral concern, serve as the channel through which our just grievances could get to the power structure. I had hoped that each of you would understand. But again I have been disappointed.

I have heard numerous religious leaders of the South call upon their worshippers to comply with a desegregation decision because it is the law, but I have longed to hear white ministers say follow this decree because integration is morally right and the Negro is your brother. In the midst of blatant injustices inflicted upon the Negro, I have watched white churches stand on the sideline and merely mouth pious irrelevancies and sanctimonious trivialities. In the midst of a mighty struggle to rid our nation of racial and economic injustice, I have heard so many ministers say, "Those are social issues with which the Gospel has no real concern," and I have watched so many churches commit themselves to a completely other-worldly religion which made a strange distinction between body and soul, the sacred and the secular.

So here we are moving toward the exit of the twentieth century with a religious community largely adjusted to the status quo, standing as a tail light behind other community agencies rather than a headlight leading men to higher levels of justice.

I have travelled the length and breadth of Alabama, Mississippi, and all the other Southern states. On sweltering summer days and crisp autumn mornings I have looked at her beautiful churches with their spires pointing heavenward. I have beheld the impressive outlay of her massive religious education buildings. Over and over again I have found myself asking: "Who worships here? Who is their God? Where were their voices when the lips of Governor Barnett dripped with words of interposition and nullification? Where were they when Governor Wallace gave the clarion call for defiance and hatred? Where were their voices of support when tired, bruised, and weary Negro men and women decided to rise from the dark dungeons of complacency to the bright hills of creative protest?"

Yes, these questions are still in my mind. In deep disappointment, I have wept over the laxity of the Church. But be assured that my tears have been tears of love. There can be no deep disappointment where there is not deep love. Yes, I love the Church; I love her sacred walls. How could I do otherwise? I am in the rather unique position of being the son, the grandson, and the great grandson of preachers. Yes, I see the Church as the body of Christ. But, oh! How we have blemished and scarred that body through social neglect and fear of being nonconformist.

There was a time when the Church was very powerful. It was during that period when the early Christians rejoiced when they were deemed worthy to suffer for what they believed. In those days the Church was not merely a thermometer that recorded the ideas and principles of popular opinion; it was a thermostat that transformed the mores of society. Wherever the early Christians entered a town the power structure got disturbed and immediately sought to convict them for being "disturbers of the peace" and "outside agitators." But they went on with the conviction that they were a "colony of heaven" and had to obey God rather than man. They were small in number but big in commitment. They were too God-intoxicated to be "astronomically intimidated." They brought an end to such ancient evils as infanticide and gladiatorial contest.

Things are different now. The contemporary Church is so often a weak, ineffectual voice with an uncertain sound. It is so often the arch-supporter of the status quo. Far from being disturbed by the presence of the Church, the power structure of the average community is consoled by the Church's silent and often vocal sanction of things as they are.

But the judgment of God is upon the Church as never before. If the Church of today does not recapture the sacrificial spirit of the early Church, it will lose its authentic ring, forfeit the loyalty of millions, and be dismissed as an irrelevant social club with no meaning for the twentieth century. I am meeting young people every day whose disappointment with the Church has risen to outright disgust.

Maybe again I have been too optimistic. Is organized religion too inextricably bound to the status quo to save our nation and the world? Maybe I must turn my faith to the inner spiritual Church, the church within the Church, as the true *ecclesia* and the hope of the world. But again I am thankful to God that some noble souls from the ranks of organized religion have broken loose from the paralyzing chains of conformity and joined us as active partners in the struggle for freedom. They have left their secure congregations and walked the streets of Albany, Georgia, with us. They have gone through the highways of the South on torturous rides for freedom. Yes, they have gone to jail with us. Some have been kicked out of their churches and lost the support of their bishops and fellow ministers. But they have gone with the faith that right defeated is stronger than evil triumphant. These men have been the leaven in the lump of the race. Their witness has been the spiritual salt that has preserved the true meaning of the Gospel in these troubled times. They have carved a tunnel of hope through the dark mountain of disappointment.

I hope the Church as a whole will meet the challenge of this decisive hour. But even if the Church does not come to the aid of justice, I have no despair about the future. I have no fear about the outcome of our struggle in Birmingham, even if our motives are presently misunderstood. We will reach the goal of freedom in Birmingham and all over the nation, because the goal of America is freedom. Abused and scorned though we may be, our destiny is tied up with the destiny of America. Before the pilgrims landed at Plymouth, we were here. Before the pen of Jefferson etched across the pages of history the majestic words of the Declaration of Independence, we were here. For more than two centuries our foreparents labored in this country without wages; they made cotton "king"; and they built the homes of their masters in the midst of brutal injustice and shameful humiliation—and yet out of a bottomless vitality they continued to thrive and develop. If the inexpressible cruelties of slavery could not stop us, the opposition we now face will surely fail. We will win our freedom because the sacred heritage of our nation and the eternal will of God are embodied in our echoing demands.

I must close now. But before closing I am impelled to mention one other point in your statement that troubled me profoundly. You warmly commended the Birmingham police force for keeping "order" and "preventing violence." I don't believe you would have so warmly commended the police force if you had seen its angry violent dogs literally biting six unarmed, non-violent Negroes. I don't believe you would so quickly commend the police-men if you would observe their ugly and inhuman treatment of Negroes here in the city jail; if you would watch them push and curse old Negro women and young Negro girls; if you would see them slap and kick old Negro men and young Negro boys; if you will observe them, as they did on two occasions, refuse to give us food because we wanted to sing our grace together. I'm sorry that I can't join you in your praise for the police department.

It is true that they have been rather disciplined in their public handling of the demonstrators. In this sense they have been rather publicly "non-violent." But for what purpose? To preserve the evil system of segregation. Over the last few years I have consistently preached that nonviolence de-mands that the means we use must be as pure as the ends we seek. So I have tried to make it clear that it is wrong to use immoral means to attain moral ends. But now I must affirm that it is just as wrong, or even more so, to use moral means to preserve immoral ends. Maybe Mr. Connor and his police-men have been rather publicly nonviolent, as Chief Pritchett was in Albany, Georgia, but they have used the moral means of nonviolence to maintain the immoral end of flagrant racial injustice. T. S. Eliot has said that there is no greater treason than to do the right deed for the wrong reason.

I wish you had commended the Negro sit-inners and demonstrators of Birmingham for their sublime courage, their willingness to suffer, and their amazing discipline in the midst of the most inhuman provocation. One day the South will recognize its real heroes. They will be the James Merediths, courageously and with a majestic sense of purpose, facing jeering and hostile mobs and the agonizing loneliness that characterizes the life of the pioneer. They will be old, oppressed, battered Negro women, symbolized in a seventy-two year old woman of Montgomery, Alabama, who rose up with a sense of dignity and with her people decided not to ride the segregated buses, and responded to one who inquired about her tiredness with ungrammatical pro-fundity: "My feets is tired, but my soul is rested." They will be young high school and college students, young ministers of the gospel and a host of the elders, courageously and nonviolently sitting in at lunch counters and will-ingly going to jail for conscience sake. One day the South will know that when these disinherited children of God sat down at lunch counters they were in reality standing up for the best in the American dream and the most sacred values in our Judeo-Christian heritage, and thus carrying our whole nation back to great wells of democracy which were dug deep by the found-ing fathers in the formulation of the Constitution and the Declaration of Independence.

Never before have I written a letter this long (or should I say a book?). I'm afraid that it is much too long to take your precious time. I can assure you that it would have been much shorter if I had been writing from a com-

Chapter Five

THE PROBLEM OF FREE WILL, DETERMINISM, AND RESPONSIBILITY

Most of us operate on the assumption that we can and do freely choose among alternative courses of action in the situations that confront us every day. It is our choice that we go to class rather than stay in bed, attend a football game rather than study, shop for groceries rather than get a haircut, or read philosophy rather than bacteriology. We assume that we freely choose to keep a promise or break it, to register for the military draft or resist it, to act selfishly or for the common good. The possibilities seem open, and it is up to the individual to choose among those possibilities, we believe. And we do in fact praise or blame persons for what they do and hold them responsible for their actions on the assumption that their actions are the result of their choices. The criminal is condemned and punished for his act because we believe that he could have acted otherwise.

On the other hand, we also believe that things do not just pop into existence without a cause, for where there is an effect, there is a cause of that effect. We believe that there are laws that govern relationships among phenomena and that the phenomena *must* act in accordance with the laws. Many scientists maintain that this is an assumption of the scientific method and that their principal task is the discovery of the laws that govern and determine events. (Other scientists and philosophers of science, however, deny this, maintaining that science can proceed on the basis of laws of probability.) Thus, when the scientist observes a phenomenon like cancer, he assumes not that it just popped into existence, but that it was caused by something, that if we can isolate the cause and understand the laws governing the relationship, we might be able to control the effect. On this assumption, we initiate drives for funds to support cancer research.

Some scientists extend this assumption to human behavior. Just as a phenomenon such as cancer operates according to general although undiscovered laws, so also human behavior conforms to laws and is determined by antecedent causes. Presumably if one has adequate knowledge of a person's background, his motives and desires, one can predict with complete certainty what that person will do in any given context. This kind of prediction may be more complex, but it is no different in principle from the prediction that a tree will fall when cut.

The philosophical problem of free will and determinism and the related problem of whether one is justified in holding persons responsible for their actions result from our apparent desire to hold these *apparently* contradictory beliefs at the same time—that persons can freely choose to do one thing rather than another and that every effect is determined by antecedent causes. It seems clear that if *everything* that happens is determined to occur because of antecedent causes, then all human action is determined. Free will and free choice are impossible. On the other hand, if persons can freely choose one course of action rather than another, then not every event is completely determined, and the deterministic hypothesis is false.

Can these two apparently contradictory beliefs be reconciled? If William James is correct, the issue cannot be rationally resolved. It must be resolved on pragmatic grounds, that is, by asking what advantages or disadvantages for human life accrue from believing or not believing determinism or indeterminism. (See the selection by James in this chapter.) But before these questions can be answered, we must make clear the meaning and implications of these two beliefs and the grounds for holding them. (The selections in this chapter are designed to do this.) Let us begin with a more precise statement of the thesis of determinism.

DETERMINISM

The determinist asserts not only that every event or effect has a cause but also that every event or effect is determined to happen in just the way it does happen by the series of antecedent causes that operate upon it. It may be that our knowledge of the causes of certain effects is limited or that we are unable to specify the causes of a given effect. This limitation of human knowledge, the determinist insists, is irrelevant to the truth of determinism, for if we had the ability to perceive antecedent causes, we would then see the multiple causal relationships of which we are now ignorant. All of nature, animate and inanimate alike, is governed completely by causal laws; and ignorance of these laws does not nullify their existence. In fact, the determinist frequently speaks of the universe as a whole as a huge machine in which all events and effects are the result of the movement of some part of the machine, which is in turn moved by another part, which is moved by still another part, and so on to infinity. Whatever happens is made to happen by the causal sequence.

This principle applies not merely to trees and rocks, the determinist insists, but also to human beings. To be sure, the human machine is far more complex than other objects in nature; and the sciences of psychology and sociology are not so well developed as are the more exact fields of physics and chemistry. Causal relationships and causal laws involving human behavior that parallel the causal laws established in the physical sciences have not been established by the social sciences. Nonetheless, it is claimed that we are moving in this direction; and in the future, the causal laws and the network of causal factors that make human beings behave one way rather than another will be known. At such a time, given these laws and given knowledge of the variables centering around any given person (knowledge of his desires and objectives, his education, his beliefs, and his environment), we will be able to predict with near certainty what that person will do in any circumstance.

Admittedly, the determinist argues, all of us feel that we make free, spontaneous choices undetermined by antecedent causes. But this feeling of freedom is the result of a lack of knowledge of the causal factors involved in our behavior. The human body, just as the sky and the sea, functions in accordance with the causal laws discovered and specified by the sciences of physics and chemistry. And the human mind, its thoughts, dispositions, and feelings, is the result of a complicated nervous system that operates according to causal laws. There is no free choice in the sense of independent, uncaused free will. Even though the laws governing human behavior are, for the most part, yet to be discovered, all of the scientific evidence, the determinist argues, still favors determinism.

What are the implications of determinism for man's moral life—for holding man morally responsible for his actions, for praising or blaming him for his actions, for punishing or rewarding him through legal and social practices and institutions? *Some* determinists argue that if determinism is true, it makes no sense to hold men morally responsible for their actions or to encourage practices of reward and punishment. For if everything a man does is determined by antecedent causes, by environmental and hereditary factors, then a man *must necessarily* do whatever he does. The so-called criminal and the so-called morally good man are both caught in the web of causal connections. The differences in their behavior is not a result of some sort of autonomous choice on the part of each but simply of a difference in the causal sequence in the past of each. Both *had* to do what they did, given their causal antecedents. Consequently, neither deserves praise or blame, punishment or reward. Of course, *if* the causal antecedents (hereditary factors, home and educational environment, psychological conditioning, and so on) of the criminal had been different, then he would have behaved in rather a different way. The determinist admits this, but the admission is completely compatible with his thesis. He still insists that there is no freedom of choice and that practices or institutions based on the assumption of freedom are not justified. Many of the court arguments of the famous lawyer Clarence Darrow, including his defense of the youthful murderers Loeb and Leopold, were based on this determinist philosophical assumption.

Other determinists do not draw such radical conclusions from the truth of their doctrine. We will turn to these alternative responses in a moment.

INDETERMINISM

What is the position of the indeterminist? How does he respond to the arguments of the determinist? For one thing, he denies what the determinist affirms. He admits that determinism may well hold for the physical-material world, but he denies that man's mental life is so determined. To be sure, he concedes that a man's character and responses are *influenced* by his biological makeup and social conditions but maintains that to be influenced is not equivalent to being determined. Human beings have free will. The future is a system not of closed causes but of open possibilities. And since man has free will, he is a morally responsible being. Accordingly, it makes sense to hold reasonable, free beings responsible for their choices and to reward or punish them through various social practices and social institutions.

Indeterminists argue for their position in several ways. A basic and common-sense argument is simply that each of us is directly aware of our being free. We experience ourselves deliberating among alternative courses of action and choosing one as opposed to another. We directly *feel* our freedom every day, for we deliberate about whether to attend or cut class, to eat lunch at noon or at one o'clock, to support or not support SDS; and we opt one way or another. The determinist insists that this feeling of freedom is illusory and owing to our ignorance of the causal process; but the indeterminist insists that it is an undeniable fact of our everyday consciousness.

Other indeterminists argue for free will on theological or metaphysical grounds. Human beings possess not merely bodies, which are subject to causal laws, but also God-given souls, which are spiritual in nature and not governed by physical laws and causes. The soul by an act of will can move the body to act; and as a result of the fact that he has a soul, man has free choice, even though his character is to some extent shaped by hereditary and environmental forces.

Furthermore, some indeterminists argue, determinism is more of an assumption than a scientifically proven thesis. Determinism has not been proven, particularly with regard to the human, or social, sciences. Even in the physical sciences, there seems to be real indeterminacy at the subatomic level of quantum mechanics. (See the selection by Ledger Wood.)

FATALISM

A third position, sometimes confused with determinism, is that of fatalism. The position of the determinist cannot be identified with that of the fatalist, for whereas both maintain that everything that happens is determined, the fatalist goes further and insists that everything is determined by nonhuman causes. The future is unaffected by human action. Whatever happens is outside of human hands. Sometimes the fatalist sees the forces that determine the future as those of nature (even astrological!), sometimes, as the workings of a god or gods or of blind force. The Greeks had a concept of *Moira* that controlled even their deities. In either case, human beings, they insist, are helpless creatures, pushed this way or that by forces totally outside their control. Whatever occurs or exists, whether it be a world war, a political utopia, a castrophe, human suffering, or the Kingdom of God—all is fated. The only proper human attitude (though it too is fated) is resignation. Concomitantly, with regard to man's practical or moral life, we can not really hold men responsible for what they do, for they *must* do whatever they do. The appropriate response to socially undesirable, immoral, or criminal action is pity, not blame.

The determinist differs from the fatalist in that he maintains that along with nonhuman causes, human action, although itself totally determined by antecedent causes, *does* affect subsequent events. What human beings do is not the result of free, uncaused choice but *is* one of the components that determine the future. Human "choice" is determined by past events, human and nonhuman, but it is efficacious in shaping the future, even though the future is determined.

Some individuals will perhaps maintain that this is a distinction without a difference. If everything is determined, if there is no free will or uncaused choice, then the future is inevitable anyway. The determinist insists, however, that we distinguish between two senses of inevitable—one in which human beings are significant causes in shaping the future and one in which they are not, that is, one in which the future is always fated by nonhuman causes. This certainly seems to be an important distinction. Since human action in part determines the future, many determinists argue that it makes sense to hold men morally responsible for their actions, to praise and blame them, and to reward and punish them. They justify this not on grounds used by the indeterminist (that is, that men have uncaused choice or free will and that the future holds more than one possibility for them) but on utilitarian or pragmatic grounds. They maintain that holding a man responsible for his acts by punishing or rewarding him introduces another causal factor into the total causal nexus that determines the future. Hence, the future, which is always *in part* determined by human causes, can be partially shaped toward a desirable state of affairs by the existence of institutions and practices that punish or reward. Indeterminists deny that this is an adequate account of responsibility and of the practices of punishment and reward.

EFFORTS AT RECONCILIATION

The determinist who argues in this way is trying to reconcile his belief in determinism with the belief in human freedom and our social practices of rewarding and punishing and praising and blaming persons for their acts. Freedom turns out to be a certain sort of determinism, that is, human causation. He argues further against indeterminism and for determinism in the following way. Not only does the practice of morality and that of holding persons responsible for their acts not require spontaneous, uncaused free choice, but on the contrary, such contracausal freedom makes the attribution of moral responsibility impossible. Why? Because if human choice is uncaused, if it occurs like a "bolt out of the blue," there is no way of connecting any act to a man's character. If such is the case, how can we hold a man responsible for an act that just freely occurs, an act causally unrelated to a man's dispositions and character? Only by so relating an act can we hold a given person responsible for it, the determinist argues, and this requires the assumption of determinism.

Other efforts to reconcile determinism and indeterminism proceed in a quite different way. Some argue that we are conceptually misled by viewing determinism as the opposite of freedom. The opposite of freedom is compulsion, not determinism. As long as one's act is not internally or externally constrained, then that act is freely done, even if it is causally determined. If someone is holding a gun in your back, threatening you with death if you do not behave in a certain way, or if someone acts in a certain way because he is a psychotic or neurotic, these acts are not free but constrained, or the result of compulsion. On the other hand, even if your attendance in class is the result of an elaborate set of antecedent causes, your attendance is a free act so long as it was not done under compulsion—so long, that is, as the professor did not hold a gun to your back or so long as you are not psychotic or neurotic about class attendance. A free act, on this view, is one in which human choice is involved—determined, to be sure, but in a noncompulsory sense. This approach suggests that the whole philosophical problem of free will and determinism is a pseudo-problem based on confusing the word "determinism" conceptually with the term "compulsion."

This attempt to reconcile freedom and determinism has not convinced everyone. Some contend that even given this distinction between determinism and compulsion, human beings cannot really be said to be free or to be held responsible for their actions if determinism is true; for our actions still proceed as a result of causes, hereditary and environmental, over which we have no control. Freedom of a contracausal kind, they argue, is required if persons are to be held responsible for their acts. This amounts to pressing for some form of indeterminism.

Let us suppose, however, that indeterminism is a necessary condition for attributing responsibility to one for his actions. Suppose further that indeterminism is true. Are these sufficient conditions for attributing responsibility? Perhaps not. Consider this parallel. Knowing the difference between right and wrong satisfies the *legal* definition of sanity. But a legally sane person may not be able to control his actions and hence may not really be responsible for his actions (even though he knows the difference between right and wrong). In a similar way, even if indeterminism is a necessary condition for attributing responsibility and is in fact true, it may not be sufficient. For even though a person may be capable of choice, he may be so totally influenced by unconscious forces that he does not really choose what he does. Thus, John Hospers insists on the additional condition that one be in rational control of his acts.[1]

---

[1] See "What Means This Freedom?," in *Determinism and Freedom in the Age of Modern Science* (New York: New York University Press, 1958).

CONCLUDING REMARKS

It is obvious from what has been said that there are many different responses to the free will–determinism–responsibility problem. Aside from the straightforward determinist, fatalist, and indeterminist positions, there are different combinations of these points of view and different points of emphasis. (Predestinarianism, we have not discussed. Some traditional Calvinists apparently hold the view that some persons are destined by God to certain ends. This may be called a theological form of fatalism, but it differs because it apparently involves purposiveness.) The authors of the selections in this chapter represent these various perspectives.

Aside from its inherent philosophical interest, the free will–determinism controversy and responses to it have had considerable effect on our social life and institutions. It is not uncommon in our courts of law to find defense lawyers basing their cases on the grounds that their client was not really responsible for his act, since he was mentally deranged and consequently acted out of compulsion. Actions for which men were held morally and legally responsible in the past are frequently not so held today—alcoholism, drug addiction, and homosexuality, for example. The term "disease" frequently replaces the term "crime" in our discourse; the word "pity" replaces "blame"; "rehabilitation" and "therapy" supplant "punishment"; "alienated" and "deprived" take the place of "irresponsible" and "guilty." One can only speculate on future changes of this sort.

There is no ready agreement on the free will–determinism controversy. Psychologists of various persuasions, particularly Neo-Freudians, strongly press the view that subconscious motivation, especially libidinal, *determines* our responses.[2] And sociologists are now getting in on the show, with statistical evidence that cultural phenomena conform to certain patterns and that human behavior is sociologically determined.

More empirical evidence of this type is both relevant and necessary for resolving the free will–determinism controversy. But empirical data alone are not adequate. We need to clarify a multitude of concepts, such as rational control, causation, responsible, spontaneous, can, free, chance, person, voluntary, necessary, must, possibility, forced, compelled, power, will, desire, influence, affect, effect, decide, and choose. And we need to clarify various physiological, psychological, and sociological theories as well as recent quantum theory, all of which bear on this controversy. This is a complex and difficult matter, involving not only the various empirical sciences themselves but also theories about the various sciences and the concepts that they invoke. The student is now invited to examine some of the solutions to this problem that philosophers have proposed.

---

[2] A recent doctoral candidate in psychology who falls into this tradition, on whose examining committee I served, told me that in the psychology lab he was a determinist but at home, an indeterminist. This is indicative of the quite common theoretical-practical tension or ambivalence over this issue.

SELECTED BIBLIOGRAPHY

Adler, M. J. *The Idea of Freedom.* 5 vols. New York, 1958.

Berlin, I. *Historical Inevitability.* Fair Lawn, N.J., 1954.

Berofsky, Bernard (ed.). *Free Will and Determinism.* New York, 1966.

Broad, C. D. *Determinism, Indeterminism, and Libertarianism.* New York, 1934.

Campbell, N. *What is Science?.* London, 1921.

Eddington, Sir Arthur. *The Nature of the Physical World.* New York, 1928.

Farrer, A. *Freedom of the Will.* New York, 1958.

Feigl, Herbert, and Brodbeck, N. (eds.). *Readings in the Philosophy of Science.* New York, 1953.

Hart, H. L. A., and Honoré, A. *Causation in the Law.* London, 1959.

Lehrer, Keith (ed.). *Freedom and Determinism.* New York, 1966.

Melden, A. I. *Free Action.* London, 1961.

Morgenbesser, Sidney, and Walsh, James (eds.). *Free Will.* Englewood Cliffs, N.J., 1962.

Morris, Herbert (ed.). *Freedom and Responsibility.* Stanford, Calif., 1961.

Nowell-Smith, P. H. *Ethics.* Baltimore, Md., 1954.

Pears, T. F. (ed). *Freedom and the Will.* London, 1963.

Sartre, Jean-Paul. *Being and Nothingness.* Translated by H. E. Barnes. New York, 1956.

Schlick, Moritz. *Problems of Ethics.* Translated by D. Rynin. Englewood Cliffs, N.J., 1939.

Taylor, Richard. *Action and Purpose.* Englewood Cliffs, N.J., 1966.

40 The Dilemma of Determinism[*]

WILLIAM JAMES

William James (1842–1910) was influential both as a psychologist and philosopher. Author of numerous articles, some of his important books include *Pragmatism: A New Name for Some Old Ways of Thinking; Principles of Psychology;* and *Varieties of Religious Experience.* He is known as a leading American exponent of pragmatism.

A common opinion prevails that the juice has ages ago been pressed out of the free-will controversy, and that no new champion can do more than warm up stale arguments which every one has heard. This is a radical mistake. I know of no subject less worn out, or in which inventive genius has a better chance of breaking open new ground,—not, perhaps, of forcing a conclusion or of coercing assent, but of deepening our sense of what the issue between the two parties really is, of what the ideas of fate and of free-will imply. . . . The arguments I am about to urge all proceed on two suppositions: first, when we make theories about the world and discuss them with one another, we do so in order to attain a conception of things which shall give us subjective satisfaction; and, second, if there be two conceptions, and the one seems to us, on the whole, more rational than the other, we are entitled to suppose that the more rational one is the truer of the two. I hope that you are all willing to make these suppositions with me; for I am afraid that if there be any of you here who are not, they will find little edification in the rest of what I have to say. I cannot stop to argue the point; but I myself believe that all the magnificent achievements of mathematical and physical science—our doctrines of evolution, of uniformity of law, and the rest—proceed from our indomitable desire to cast the world into a more rational shape in our minds than the shape into which it is thrown there by the crude order of our experience. The world has shown itself, to a great extent, plastic to this demand of ours for rationality. How much farther it will show itself plastic no one can say. Our only means of finding out is to try; and, I, for one, feel as free to try conceptions of moral as of mechanical or of logical rationality. If a certain formula for expressing the nature of the world

* An Address to the Harvard Divinity Students, published in the *Unitarian Review*, September, 1884.

violates my moral demand, I shall feel as free to throw it overboard, or at least to doubt it, as if it disappointed my demand for uniformity of sequence, for example; the one demand being, so far as I can see, quite as subjective and emotional as the other is. The principle of causality, for example,—what is it but a postulate, an empty name covering simply a demand that the sequence of events shall some day manifest a deeper kind of belonging of one thing with another than the mere arbitrary juxtaposition which now phenomenally appears? It is as much an altar to an unknown god as the one that Saint Paul found at Athens. All our scientific and philosophic ideals are altars to unknown gods. Uniformity is as much so as is free-will. If this be admitted, we can debate on even terms. But if any one pretends that while freedom and variety are, in the first instance, subjective demands, necessity and uniformity are something altogether different, I do not see how we can debate at all.

To begin, then, I must suppose you acquainted with all the usual arguments on the subject. I cannot stop to take up the old proofs from causation, from statistics, from the certainty with which we can foretell one another's conduct, from the fixity of character, and all the rest. But there are two *words* which usually encumber these classical arguments, and which we must immediately dispose of if we are to make any progress. One is the eulogistic word *freedom*, and the other is the opprobrious word *chance*. The word 'chance' I wish to keep, but I wish to get rid of the word 'freedom.' Its eulogistic associations have so far overshadowed all the rest of its meaning that both parties claim the sole right to use it, and determinists to-day insist that they alone are freedom's champions. Old-fashioned determinism was what we may call *hard* determinism. It did not shrink from such words as fatality, bondage of the will, necessitation, and the like. Nowadays, we have a *soft* determinism which abhors harsh words, and, repudiating fatality, necessity, and even predetermination, says that its real name is freedom; for freedom is only necessity understood, and bondage to the highest is identical with true freedom.

Now, all this is a quagmire of evasion under which the real issue of fact has been entirely smothered. . . . But there *is* a problem, an issue of fact and not of words, an issue of the most momentous importance, which is often decided without discussion in one sentence,—nay, in one clause of a sentence, —by those very writers who spin out whole chapters in their efforts to show what 'true' freedom is; and that is the question of determinism, about which we are to talk to-night.

Fortunately, no ambiguities hang about this word or about its opposite, indeterminism. Both designate an outward way in which things may happen, and their cold and mathematical sound has no sentimental associations that can bribe our partiality either way in advance. Now, evidence of an external kind to decide between determinism and indeterminism is, as I intimated a while back, strictly impossible to find. Let us look at the difference between them and see for ourselves. What does determinism profess?

It professes that those parts of the universe already laid down absolutely appoint and decree what the other parts shall be. The future has no ambiguous possibilities hidden in its womb: the part we call the present is compatible with only one totality. Any other future complement than the one fixed from eternity is impossible. The whole is in each and every part, and welds it with the rest into an absolute unity, an iron block, in which there can be no equivocation or shadow of turning.

> With earth's first clay they did the last man knead,
> And there of the last harvest sowed the seed.
> And the first morning of creation wrote
> What the last dawn of reckoning shall read.

Indeterminism, on the contrary, says that the parts have a certain amount of loose play on one another, so that the laying down of one of them does not necessarily determine what the others shall be. It admits that possibilities may be in excess of actualities, and that things not yet revealed to our knowledge may really in themselves be ambiguous. Of two alternative futures which we conceive, both may now be really possible; and the one become impossible only at the very moment when the other excludes it by becoming real itself. Indeterminism thus denies the world to be one unbending unit of fact. It says there is a certain ultimate pluralism in it; and, so saying, it corroborates our ordinary unsophisticated view of things. To that view, actualities seem to float in a wider sea of possibilities from out of which they are chosen; and, *somewhere*, indeterminism says, such possibilities exist, and form a path of truth.

Determinism, on the contrary, says they exist *nowhere*, and that necessity on the one hand and impossibility on the other are the sole categories of the real. Possibilities that fail to get realized are, for determinism, pure illusions: they never were possibilities at all. There is nothing inchoate, it says, about this universe of ours, all that was or is or shall be actual in it having been from eternity virtually there. The cloud of alternatives our minds escort this mass of actuality withal is a cloud of sheer deceptions, to which 'impossibilities' is the only name that rightfully belongs.

The issue, it will be seen, is a perfectly sharp one, which no eulogistic terminology can smear over or wipe out. The truth *must* lie with one side or the other, and its lying with one side makes the other false.

The question relates solely to the existence of possibilities, in the strict sense of the term, as things that may, but need not, be. Both sides admit that a volition, for instance, has occurred. The indeterminists say another volition might have occurred in its place: the determinists swear that nothing could possibly have occurred in its place. Now, can science be called in to tell us which of these two point-blank contradicters of each other is right? Science professes to draw no conclusions but such as are based on matters of fact, things that have actually happened; but how can any amount of assurance that something actually happened give us the least grain of information as to whether another thing might or might not have happened in its place? Only facts can be proved by other facts. With things that are possibilities and not facts, facts have no concern. If we have no other evidence than the evidence of existing facts, the possibility-question must remain a mystery never to be cleared up.

And the truth is that facts practically have hardly anything to do with making us either determinists or indeterminists. Sure enough, we make a flourish of quoting facts this way or that; and if we are determinists, we talk about the infallibility with which we can predict one another's conduct; while if we are indeterminists, we lay great stress on the fact that it is just because we cannot foretell one another's conduct, either in war or statecraft or in any of the great and small intrigues and businesses of men, that life is so intensely anxious and hazardous a game. But who does not see the wretched insufficiency of this so-called objective testimony on both sides? What fills up the gaps in our minds is something not objective, not external. What divides us into possibility men and anti-possibility men is different faiths or postulates,—postulates of rationality. To this man the world seems more rational with possibilities in it,—to that man more rational with possibilities excluded; and talk as we will about having to yield to evidence, what makes us monists or pluralists, determinists or indeterminists, is at bottom always some sentiment like this.

The stronghold of the deterministic sentiment is the antipathy to the idea of chance. As soon as we begin to talk indeterminism to our friends, we find a number of them shaking their heads. This notion of alternative possibility, they say, this admission that any one of several things may come to pass, is, after all, only a roundabout name for chance; and chance is something the notion of which no sane mind can for an instant tolerate in the world. What is it, they ask, but barefaced crazy unreason, the negation of intelligibility and law? And if the slightest particle of it exist anywhere, what is to prevent the whole fabric from falling together, the stars from going out, and chaos from recommencing her topsy-turvy reign?

Remarks of this sort about chance will put an end to discussion as quickly as anything one can find. I have already told you that 'chance' was a word I wished to keep and use. Let us then examine exactly what it means, and see whether it ought to be such a terrible bugbear to us. I fancy that squeezing the thistle boldly will rob it of its sting.

The sting of the word 'chance' seems to lie in the assumption that it means something positive, and that if anything happens by chance, it must needs be something of an intrinsically irrational and preposterous sort. Now, chance means nothing of the kind. It is a purely negative and relative term, giving us no information about that of which it is predicated, except that it happens to be disconnected with something else,—not controlled, secured, or necessitated by other things in advance of its own actual presence. As this point is the most subtle one of the whole lecture, and at the same time the point on which all the rest hinges, I beg you to pay particular attention to it. What I say is that it tells us nothing about what a thing may be in itself to call it 'chance.' It may be a bad thing, it may be a good thing. It may be lucidity, transparency, fitness incarnate, matching the whole system of other things, when it has once befallen, in an unimaginably perfect way. All you mean by calling it 'chance' is that this is not guaranteed, that it may also fall out otherwise.

Nevertheless, many persons talk as if the minutest dose of disconnectedness of one part with another, the smallest modicum of independence, the faintest tremor of ambiguity about the future, for example, would ruin everything, and turn this goodly universe into a sort of insane sand-heap or nulliverse, no universe at all. Since future human volitions are as a matter of fact the only ambiguous things we are tempted to believe in, let us stop for a moment to make ourselves sure whether their independent and accidental character need be fraught with such direful consequences to the universe as these.

What is meant by saying that my choice of which way to walk home after the lecture is ambiguous and matter of chance as far as the present moment is concerned? It means that both Divinity Avenue and Oxford Street are called; but that only one, and that one *either* one, shall be chosen. Now, I ask you seriously to suppose that this ambiguity of my choice is real; and then to make the impossible hypothesis that the choice is made twice over, and each time falls on a different street. In other words, imagine that I first walk through Divinity Avenue, and then imagine that the powers governing the universe annihilate ten minutes of time with all that it contained, and set me back at the door of this hall just as I was before the choice was made. Imagine then that, everything else being the same, I now make a different choice and traverse Oxford Street. You, as passive spectators, look on and see the two alternative universes,—one of them with me walking through Divinity Avenue in it, the other with the same me walking through Oxford Street. Now, if you are determinists you believe one of these universes to have been from eternity impossible: you believe it to have been impossible because of the intrinsic irrationality or accidentality somewhere involved in it. But looking outwardly at these universes, can you say which is the impossible and accidental one, and which the rational and necessary one? I doubt if the most ironclad determinist among you could have the slightest glimmer of light on this point. In other words, either universe *after the fact* and once there would, to our means of observation and understanding, appear just as rational as the other. There would be absolutely no criterion by which we might judge one necessary and the other matter of chance. Suppose now we relieve the gods of their hypothetical task and assume my choice, once made, to be made forever. I go through Divinity Avenue for good and all. If, as good determinists, you now begin to affirm, what all good determinists punctually do affirm, that in the nature of things I *couldn't* have gone through

Oxford Street,—had I done so it would have been chance, irrationality, insanity, a horrid gap in nature,—I simply call your attention to this, that your affirmation is what the Germans call a *Machtspruch*, a mere conception fulminated as a dogma and based on no insight into details. Before my choice, either street seemed as natural to you as to me. Had I happened to take Oxford Street, Divinity Avenue would have figured in your philosophy as the gap in nature; and you would have so proclaimed it with the best deterministic conscience in the world.

The more one thinks of the matter, the more one wonders that so empty and gratuitous a hubbub as this outcry against chance should have found so great an echo in the hearts of men. It is a word which tells us absolutely nothing about what chances, or about the *modus operandi* of the chancing; and the use of it as a war-cry shows only a temper of intellectual absolutism, a demand that the world shall be a solid block, subject to one control,— which temper, which demand, the world may not be bound to gratify at all. In every outwardly verifiable and practical respect, a world in which the alternatives that now actually distract *your* choice were decided by pure chance would be by *me* absolutely undistinguished from the world in which I now live. I am, therefore, entirely willing to call it, so far as your choices go, a world of chance for me. To *yourselves*, it is true, those very acts of choice, which to me are so blind, opaque, and external, are the opposites of this, for you are within them and effect them. To you they appear as decisions; and decisions, for him who makes them, are altogether peculiar psychic facts. Self-luminous and self-justifying at the living moment at which they occur, they appeal to no outside moment to put its stamp upon them or make them continuous with the rest of nature. Themselves it is rather who seem to make nature continuous; and in their strange and intense function of granting consent to one possibility and withholding it from another, to transform an equivocal and double future into an inalterable and simple past.

But with the psychology of the matter we have no concern this evening. The quarrel which determinism has with chance fortunately has nothing to do with this or that psychological detail. It is a quarrel altogether metaphysical. Determinism denies the ambiguity of future volitions, because it affirms that nothing future can be ambiguous. But we have said enough to meet the issue. Indeterminate future volitions *do* mean chance. Let us not fear to shout it from the house-tops if need be; for we now know that the idea of chance is, at bottom, exactly the same thing as the idea of gift. . . .

And this at last brings us within sight of our subject. We have seen what determinism means: we have seen that indeterminism is rightly described as meaning chance; and we have seen that chance, the very name of which we are urged to shrink from as from a metaphysical pestilence, means only negative fact that no part of the world, however big, can claim to control absolutely the destinies of the whole. But although, in discussing the word 'chance,' I may at moments have seemed to be arguing for its real existence, I have not meant to do so yet. We have not yet ascertained whether this be a world of chance or no; at most, we have agreed that it seems so. And I now repeat what I said at the outset, that, from any strict theoretical point of view, the question is insoluble. To deepen our theoretic sense of the *difference* between a world with chances in it and a deterministic world is the most I can hope to do; and this I may now at last begin upon, after all our tedious clearing of the way.

I wish first of all to show you just what the notion that this is a deterministic world implies. The implications I call your attention to are all bound up with the fact that it is a world in which we constantly have to make what I shall, with your permission, call judgments of regret. Hardly an hour passes in which we do not wish that something might be otherwise; and happy indeed are those of us whose hearts have never echoed the wish of Omar Khayam—

> That we might clasp, ere closed, the book of fate,
>   And make the writer on a fairer leaf
> Inscribe our names, or quite obliterate.
>
> Ah! Love, could you and I with fate conspire
> To mend this sorry scheme of things entire,
>   Would we not shatter it to bits, and then
> Remould it nearer to the heart's desire?

Now, it is undeniable that most of these regrets are foolish, and quite on a par in point of philosophic value with the criticisms on the universe of that friend of our infancy, the hero of the fable The Atheist and the Acorn,—

> Fool! had that bough a pumpkin bore,
> Thy whimsies would have worked no more, etc.

Even from the point of view of our own ends, we should probably make a botch of remodelling the universe. How much more then from the point of view of ends we cannot see! Wise men therefore regret as little as they can. But still some regrets are pretty obstinate and hard to stifle,—regrets for acts of wanton cruelty or treachery, for example, whether performed by others or by ourselves. Hardly any one can remain *entirely* optimistic after reading the confession of the murderer at Brockton the other day: how, to get rid of the wife whose continued existence bored him, he inveigled her into a desert spot, shot her four times, and then, as she lay on the ground and said to him, "You didn't do it on purpose, did you dear?" replied, "No, I did n't do it on purpose," as he raised a rock and smashed her skull. Such an occurrence, with the mild sentence and self-satisfaction of the prisoner, is a field for a crop of regrets, which one need not take up in detail. We feel that, although a perfect mechanical fit to the rest of the universe, it is a bad moral fit, and that something else would really have been better in its place.

But for the deterministic philosophy the murder, the sentence, and the prisoner's optimism were all necessary from eternity; and nothing else for a moment had a ghost of a chance of being put into their place. To admit such a chance, the determinists tell us, would be to make a suicide of reason; so we must steel our hearts against the thought. And here our plot thickens, for we see the first of those difficult implications of determinism and monism which it is my purpose to make you feel. If this Brockton murder was called for by the rest of the universe, if it had to come at its preappointed hour, and if nothing else would have been consistent with the sense of the whole, what are we to think of the universe? Are we stubbornly to stick to our judgment of regret, and say, though it *could n't* be, yet, it *would* have been a better universe with something different from this Brockton murder in it? That, of course, seems the natural and spontaneous thing for us to do; and yet it is nothing short of deliberately espousing a kind of pessimism. The judgment of regret calls the murder bad. Calling a thing bad means, if it mean anything at all, that the thing ought not to be, that something else ought to be in its stead. Determinism, in denying that anything else can be in its stead, virtually defines the universe as a place in which what ought to be is impossible,—in other words, as an organism whose constitution is afflicted with an incurable taint, an irremediable flaw. The pessimism of a Schopenhauer says no more than this,—that the murder is a symptom; and that it is a vicious symptom because it belongs to a vicious whole, which can express its nature no otherwise than by bringing forth just such a symptom as that at this particular spot. Regret for the murder must transform itself, if we are determinists and wise, into a larger regret. It is absurd to regret the murder alone. Other things being what they are, *it* could not be different. What we should regret is that whole frame of things of which the murder is one member. I see no escape whatever from this pessimistic conclusion, if, being determinists, our judgment of regret is to be allowed to stand at all.

The only deterministic escape from pessimism is everywhere to abandon the judgment of regret. That this can be done, history shows to be not impossible. The devil, *quoad existentiam*, may be good. That is, although he be a *principle* of evil, yet the universe, with such a principle in it, may practically be a better universe than it could have been without. On every hand, in a small way, we find that a certain amount of evil is a condition by which a higher form of good is bought. There is nothing to prevent anybody from generalizing this view, and trusting that if we could but see things in the largest of all ways, even such matters as this Brockton murder would appear to be paid for by the uses that follow in their train. An optimism *quand même*, a systematic and infatuated optimism like that ridiculed by Voltaire in his Candide, is one of the possible ideal ways in which a man may train himself to look on life. Bereft of dogmatic hardness and lit up with the expression of a tender and pathetic hope, such an optimism has been the grace of some of the most religious characters that ever lived.

> Throb thine with Nature's throbbing breast,
> And all is clear from east to west.

Even cruelty and treachery may be among the absolutely blessed fruits of time, and to quarrel with any of their details may be blasphemy. The only real blasphemy, in short, may be that pessimistic temper of the soul which lets it give way to such things as regrets, remorse, and grief.

Thus, our deterministic pessimism may become a deterministic optimism at the price of extinguishing our judgments of regret.

But does not this immediately bring us into a curious logical predicament? Our determinism leads us to call our judgments of regret wrong, because they are pessimistic in implying that what is impossible yet ought to be. But how then about the judgments of regret themselves? If they are wrong, other judgments, judgments of approval presumably, ought to be in their place. But as they are necessitated, nothing else *can* be in their place; and the universe is just what it was before,—namely, a place in which what ought to be appears impossible. We have got one foot out of the pessimistic bog, but the other one sinks all the deeper. We have rescued our actions from the bonds of evil, but our judgments are now held fast. When murders and treacheries cease to be sins, regrets are theoretic absurdities and errors. The theoretic and the active life thus play a kind of seesaw with each other on the ground of evil. The rise of either sends the other down. Murder and treachery cannot be good without regret being bad: regret cannot be good without treachery and murder being bad. Both, however, are supposed to have been foredoomed; so something must be fatally unreasonable, absurd, and wrong in the world. It must be a place of which either sin or error forms a necessary part. From this dilemma there seems at first sight no escape. Are we then so soon to fall back into the pessimism from which we thought we had emerged?

But this brings us right back, after such a long détour, to the question of indeterminism and to the conclusion of all I came here to say to-night. For the only consistent way of representing a pluralism and a world whose parts may affect one another through their conduct being either good or bad is the indeterministic way. What interest, zest, or excitement can there be in achieving the right way, unless we are enabled to feel that the wrong way is also a possible and a natural way,—nay, more a manacing and an imminent way? And what sense can there be in condemning ourselves for taking the wrong way, unless we need have done nothing of the sort, unless the right way was open to us as well? I cannot understand the willingness to act, no matter how we feel, without the belief that acts are really good and bad. I cannot understand regret without the admission of real, genuine possibilities in the world. Only *then* is it other than a mockery to feel, after we have failed to do our best, that an irreparable opportunity is gone from the universe, the loss of which it must forever after mourn.

If you insist that this is all superstition, that possibility is in the eye of science and reason impossibility, and that if I act badly it is that the universe was foredoomed to suffer this defect, you fall right back into the dilemma, the labyrinth, of pessimism and subjectivism, from out of whose toils we have just wound our way.

Now, we are of course free to fall back, if we please. For my own part, though, whatever difficulties may beset the philosophy of objective right and wrong, and the indeterminism it seems to imply, determinism, with its alternative of pessimism or romanticism, contains difficulties that are greater still. But you will remember that I expressly repudiated awhile ago the pretension to offer any arguments which could be coercive in a so-called scientific fashion in this matter. And I consequently find myself, at the end of this long talk, obliged to state my conclusions in an altogether personal way. This personal method of appeal seems to be among the very conditions of the problem; and the most any one can do is to confess as candidly as he can the grounds for the faith that is in him, and leave his example to work on others as it may.

Let me, then, without circumlocution say just this. The world is enigmatical enough in all conscience, whatever theory we may take up toward it. The indeterminism I defend, the free-will theory of popular sense based on the judgment of regret, represents that world as vulnerable, and liable to be injured by certain of its parts if they act wrong. And it represents their acting wrong as a matter of possibility or accident, neither inevitable nor yet to be infallibly warded off. In all this, it is a theory devoid either of transparency or of stability. It gives us a pluralistic, restless universe, in which no single point of view can ever take in the whole scene; and to a mind possessed of the love of unity at any cost, it will, no doubt, remain forever inaccessible. A friend with such a mind once told me that the thought of my universe made him sick, like the sight of the horrible motion of a mass of maggots in their carrion bed.

But while I freely admit that the pluralism and the restlessness are repugnant and irrational in a certain way, I find that every alternative to them is irrational in a deeper way. The indeterminism with its maggots, if you please to speak so about it, offends only the native absolutism of my intellect,—an absolutism which, after all, perhaps, deserves to be snubbed and kept in check. But the determinism with its necessary carrion, to continue the figure of speech, and with no possible maggots to eat the latter up, violates my sense of moral reality through and through. When, for example, I imagine such carrion as the Brockton murder, I cannot conceive it as an act by which the universe, as a whole, logically and necessarily expresses its nature without shrinking from complicity with such a whole. And I deliberately refuse to keep on terms of loyalty with the universe by saying blankly that the murder, since it does flow from the nature of the whole, is not carrion. There are *some* instinctive reactions which I, for one, will not tamper with. The only remaining alternative, the attitude of gnostical romanticism, wrenches my personal instincts in quite as violent a way. It falsifies the simple objectivity of their deliverance. It makes the goose-flesh the murder excites in me a sufficient reason for the perpetration of the crime.

No! better a thousand times, than such systematic corruption of our moral sanity, the plainest pessimism, so that it be straightforward; but better far than that the world of chance. Make as great an uproar about chance as you please, I know that chance means pluralism and nothing more. If some of the members of the pluralism are bad, the philosophy of pluralism, whatever broad views it may deny me, permits me, at least, to turn to the other members with a clean breast of affection and an unsophisticated moral sense. And if I still wish to think of the world as a totality, it lets me feel that a world with a *chance* in it of being altogether good, even if the chance never come to pass, is better than a world with no such chance at all. That 'chance' whose very notion I am exhorted and conjured to banish from my view of the future as the suicide of reason concerning it, that 'chance' is—what? Just this,—the chance that in moral respects the future may be other and better than the past has been. This is the only chance we have any motive for supposing to exist. Shame, rather, on its repudiation and its denial! For its presence is the vital air which lets the world live, the salt which keeps it sweet.

41 The Free-Will Controversy[*]

LEDGER WOOD

Ledger Wood (1901–   ) has taught philosophy at Princeton University since 1927. He is the author of *The Analysis of Knowledge* and *A History of Philosophy*.

Few philosophical controversies have been waged with greater acrimony than the controversy between the libertarians and the determinists; the vigour with which both sides of the question have been espoused is due not only to the metaphysical importance of the issue—which is indeed considerable—but more especially to its moral and religious implications. No other philosophical issues, with the exception of those pertaining to God and the immortality of the soul, are of greater ethical and theological moment. So thoroughly has the question been debated that further consideration of it may seem futile. Has not the evidence been so completely canvassed on both sides of the controversy that further discussion will be a fruitless reiteration of long familiar arguments? The free-will problem is considered by many contemporary thinkers an admittedly unsolved but completely outmoded problem to which they respond with impatience or complete indifference. This attitude toward the problem is quite indefensible since the question of the freedom of the will is one of those perennially significant philosophical issues which takes on new meaning in every age and is particularly significant in the context of contemporary science and philosophy. Recent psychology, in large measure through the influence of Freud, has achieved a more penetrating analysis of human motivation by bringing to the fore certain hitherto obscure factors which are operative in volition. The psychology of the subconscious by filling in apparent gaps in the psychological causation of volition has furthered the case for determinism. Furthermore, behaviouristic psychology by subjecting all human behaviour, including so-called volitional acts, to a mechanistic formula bears directly on the free-will issue and like the Freudian psychology seems to strengthen the deterministic position. Recent developments in the physical sciences are not without their significance for the free-will issue; the principle of indeterminacy in quantum mechanics has been eagerly seized upon by the libertarians in the belief that it affords a physical foundation for their position. Finally, in philosophy proper the progress of philosophical analysis and of the philosophical theory

* From Ledger Wood, "The Free-Will Controversy," *Philosophy*, vol. 16 (1941), pp. 386–397. Reprinted by permission of The Royal Institute of Philosophy and the author.

of meaning renders possible a more exact statement of the free-will issue and permits a more just appraisal of the traditional arguments on both sides of the free-will controversy than has hitherto been possible. . . .

The question of the freedom of the will, reduced to its barest essentials, is simply this: *Are all human acts of will causally produced by antecedent conditions or are at least some volitional actions exempt from causal determination?* The determinist insists that all actions, even the most carefully planned and deliberate, can be causally explained and that if we knew enough about a man's hereditary traits and the environmental influences which have moulded his character, we could predict just how he would behave under any specified set of circumstances. The free-willist or libertarian, on the other hand, asserts that there are at least some human actions of the volitional type in which the individual by the exercise of his will-power, acts independently of conditioning factors; that some, and perhaps all, volitional acts are causally indeterminate, that is to say, are not conjoined in any uniform way with antecedent conditions. The uniform antecedents of free acts are, on this view, undiscoverable for the simple reason that they do not exist. . . . The free-willist introduces an element of indeterminacy into human behaviour; he admits an effect, namely, the volitional action, without a sufficient and adequate natural cause. . . .

I propose to give a brief résumé of the free-will controversy, examining first the arguments for the freedom of the will and then stating the case for determinism. Although the position taken throughout the present paper is avowedly deterministic, the attempt will be made to state with fairness the case for and against both of the rival positions and on the basis of these arguments, to give a just appraisal of the two positions. The strength of the deterministic position will be found to lie not only in the positive evidence which may be adduced to support it, but also in its easy ability to meet the arguments advanced by the free-willists.

ARGUMENTS FOR THE FREEDOM OF THE WILL

The arguments of the free-willist are for the most part humanistic and non-scientific in character and may be conveniently considered under the following heads:

(1) the introspective or psychological argument,
(2) the moral and religious arguments,
(3) the argument from physical indeterminacy.

(1) The Introspective or Psychological Argument

Most advocates of the free-will doctrine believe that the mind is directly aware of its freedom in the very act of making a decision, and thus that freedom is an immediate datum of our introspective awareness. "I feel myself free, *therefore*, I am free," runs the simplest and perhaps the most compelling of the arguments for freedom. In the elaboration of his argument, the free-willist offers a detailed description of what, in his opinion, is introspectively observable whenever the self makes a free choice. Suppose I find myself forced to choose between conflicting and incompatible lines of action. At such a time, I stand, so to speak, at the moral cross-roads, I deliberate, and finally by some mysterious and inexplicable power of mind, I decide to go one way rather than the other. Deliberative decision, if this description is correct, is analysable into these three constituents: (*a*) the envisaging of two or more incompatible courses of action, (*b*) the review of considerations favourable and unfavourable to each of the conflicting possibilities of action, and (*c*) the choice among the alternative possibilities.

Deliberative, or so-called "moral" decisions, are fairly numerous in the lives of all of us and are made on the most trivial occasions, as well as on matters of grave import. The university undergraduate's resolution of the conflict between his desire to see the latest cinema at the local playhouse and his felt obligation to devote the evening to his studies, trivial and inconsequential as it may seem, is the *type* of all moral decisions and differs in no essential respect from such a momentous decision as his choice of a life career. Each of these decisions to the extent that it is truly deliberative involves (*a*) the imaginative contemplation of alternative actions, (*b*) the weighing of considerations *for* and *against* the several alternatives involving, perhaps, an appeal to ideals and values approved by the moral agent, and finally (*c*) the choice between the several possibilities of action. At the moment of making the actual decision, the mind experiences a *feeling* of self-assertion and independence of determining influences both external and internal. The libertarian rests his case for free-will on the authenticity of his subjective feeling of freedom.

The phenomenon of decision after deliberation is an indubitable *fact* which determinist and free-willist alike must acknowledge, but the real issue is whether this fact warrants the *construction* which the free-willist puts upon it. The determinist, replying to the introspective argument, urges that the *feeling* of freedom is nothing but a sense of relief following upon earlier tension and indecision. After conflict and uncertainty, the pent-up energies of the mind—or rather of the underlying neutral processes—are released and this process is accompanied by an inner sense of power. Thus the feeling of freedom or of voluntary control over one's actions is a mere subjective illusion which cannot be considered evidence for psychological indeterminacy.

Besides the direct appeal to the sense of freedom, there is a psychological argument which *infers* freedom from the mind's ability to resolve an equilibrium of opposing motives. The allegedly "prerogative" or "critical" instance of free-will, is that in which the will makes a choice between two or more actions which are equally attractive, or equally objectionable. If, after a careful weighing of all the considerations *for* and *against* each of the alternative actions, the mind finds the rival claimants exactly equal, a decision is possible, argues the libertarian, only by a free act of will. We weigh the motives against one another, find the scale balanced, and then, in the words of William James, . . . "we feel, in deciding, as if we ourselves by our wilful act inclined the beam." This argument from the equilibrium of motives is indeed plausible, but the determinist has a ready reply. *If* the motives really had been exactly equal and opposite, then the mind would have remained indefinitely in a state of suspended judgment and consequent inaction or would, in Hamlet fashion, have oscillated between the two incompatibles, never able to yield to one or to the other. The analogy of the balanced scale would lead one to expect the will under these circumstances to do just this. Indeed, there are undoubtedly some pathological minds which are in a perpetual tug-of-war between conflicting tendencies of action and whose wills, as a consequence, are completely paralysed. But in normal minds the "Motives" on the one side or the other become momentarily stronger because of some new external factor injected into the situation or because of the inner reorganization of forces and then action immediately ensues. Often the decision is determined by accidental and contingent circumstances—a literal flip of the coin—or perhaps one allows one's action to be decided by a chance idea or impulse, that is to say, by a "mental flip of the coin." In any case the fact that a decision is actually made testifies to the eventual inequality of the opposing forces. Under no circumstances is it necessary to resort to a mysterious, inner force of will to "incline the beam" one way rather than the other.

Still another introspective fact cited by the libertarian in support of his doctrine is that the moral agent is in retrospect convinced that he might, *if he had chosen*, have followed a course of action different from that which he actually pursued. The belief that there are genuine alternatives of action and that the choice between them is indeterminate is usually stronger in prospect and in retrospect than at the time of actual decision. The alternatives exist in prospect as imaginatively envisaged possibilities of action and in retrospect as the memory of the state of affairs before the agent had, so to speak, "made up his mind." Especially in retrospect does the agent recall his earlier decision with remorse and repentance, dwelling sorrowfully upon rejected possibilities of action which now loom up as opportunities missed. How frequently one hears the lament: "I regret that decision; I should, and I could, have acted otherwise." Now the contemplation of supposed alternatives of action along with the sentiment of regret produces the illusion of indeterminate choice between alternatives, but a careful analysis of the import of the retrospective judgment, "I could have acted otherwise than I did," will, I believe, disclose it to be an empirically meaningless statement. If I decided in favour of this alternative, rather than that, it can only mean that the circumstances being what they were, and I in the frame of mind I was at the time, no other eventuation was really possible. My statement that I could have acted differently expresses only my memory of an earlier state of suspense, indecision, and uncertainty, intensified by my present remorse and the firm determination that if, in the future, I am faced with a similar choice, I shall profit by my earlier mistake. There is, however, in the deliberative situation no evidence of genuine alternatives of action, or the indeterminacy of my choice between them.

(2) *The Moral Arguments*

The moral argument assumes a variety of forms, but they all agree in their attempt to infer volitional freedom of the moral agent from some feature of the moral situation. The most characteristic feature of moral action is that it seems to be directed toward the realization of an ideal or the fulfilment of an obligation. But, argues the free-willest, it is of the very nature of an ideal or an obligation that it shall be *freely* embraced; the acceptance or rejection of a moral ideal and the acknowledgement of an obligation as binding can only be accounted for on the assumption of the agent's free choice. The very existence of moral ideals, norms, or standards which, though *coercive* are not *compulsive*, testifies to the freedom of the agent who acknowledges them. Thus did Kant in his famous formula: "I ought, therefore I can" directly infer the agent's freedom from his recognition of moral obligation.

The moral argument is so loose in its logic that, unable to put one's finger on its fallacy, one is tempted to resort to the logicians' "catch-all," and call it a *non sequitur*. A moral agent's adoption of a moral ideal or recognition of a moral obligation simply does *not* imply that he possesses a free-will in the sense of psychological indeterminacy. An adequate critique of the moral argument would require a detailed psychological account of the genesis of moral ideals and duties without recourse to freedom of the libertarian sort and I am convinced that such an account is forthcoming. The emergence of ideals in the mind of an individual moral agent along with the feeling that such ideals are coercive is largely non-volitional and even when it rises to the volitional level and represents a choice between competing ideas, there is even then no reason for abandoning psychological determinism. The moral argument for freedom is found, on close examination, to be the psychological argument in disguise and like it, is introspectively false; there is no indication of volitional freedom either in the original adoption of moral standards nor in subsequent moral decisions in accordance with those standards once they have been embraced.

The moral argument for freedom has sometimes been stated from the point of view not of the moral agent but of the moral critic who passes judgment on the action of another or even upon his own actions. A judgment of praise or blame, of approval or condemnation, so the argument runs, imputes freedom to the agent whose action is judged. When I praise your unselfish and benevolent acts, I imply that you could, if you had chosen, have been cruel and selfish instead. Condemnation of another's conduct seems even more surely to suggest that he acted willingly, or rather "wilfully." Otherwise, would it not be in order to pity rather than condemn the wrong-doer? Should we not say with condescension, "Poor misguided fool, he can't help what he does, he is simply that kind of man"? Instead, we reprove his action and by so doing implicitly acknowledge that he is a free moral agent. A novel variant of this argument is contained in William James's essay "The Dilemma of Determinism." The determinist, so James argues, finds himself in a curious logical predicament whenever he utters a judgment of regret. If I, a determinist, pass an adverse judgment on my own or another's actions, I thereby acknowledge that they ought not to have been, that others ought to have been performed in their place. But how can I meaningfully make such a statement if these particular actions, and no others, were possible? "What sense can there be in condemning ourselves for taking the wrong way, unless the right way was open to us as well?" James advanced the moral argument, not as an absolute *proof* of freedom (he admits that it is not intellectually coercive), but rather as a belief to be *freely* embraced. As a pragmatically effective, moral fiction, freedom has much to be said in its favour: the belief in freedom no doubt fosters moral earnestness, whereas the belief in determinism may, at least in certain persons, induce moral lassitude. Most defenders of the free-will doctrine do not, however, share James's cautious restraint; they advance the moral argument as a conclusive proof of an indeterminate free-will. . . .

The determinist finds no difficulty in assimilating to his deterministic scheme the facts of moral approval and disapproval. Moral valuation is not the detached and disinterested judgement of a moral critic, but is an instrumentality for the social propagation of norms of conduct. Morality is essentially a social phenomenon; society has gradually evolved its patterns of social behaviour which it imposes upon its individual members by means of various sanctions including the favourable or adverse judgments which members of society pass upon one another. Judgments of moral valuation rest upon the socially constituted norms of action and are the media through which these norms are communicated from individual to individual. I reprove your unsocial or antisocial behaviour in the belief that my adverse judgment may influence you to desist therefrom. When I pass a moral judgment on another, far from implying his free-will, I tacitly assume that my judgment of him, in so far as he takes cognizance of it, operates as a determining influence on his conduct. Thus moral criticism when interpreted naturalistically harmonizes with the theory of moral determinism.

Another moral argument, closely paralleling the argument from obligation, stresses the concept of moral responsibility. The free-willist considers freedom a *sine qua non* of responsibility; his argument runs: "Without freedom, there can be no responsibility, but there *must* be responsibility, hence man is free." . . . The concept of moral responsibility no doubt admits of precise empirical definition and exemplification; there is a real distinction between responsible and irresponsible actions. But when responsibility is analysed in this empirical and positivistic fashion, it will be found in no wise to imply volitional freedom. A careful analysis of responsible actions will show them to be if anything no more indeterminate than non-responsible and irresponsible actions. And this brings us to the second criticism of the argument from responsibility: *viz.*, the failure to establish the alleged implication of the concept of freedom by the concept of responsibility. The concepts of freedom and responsibility are by no means indissolubly connected; on the contrary, the freedom of indeterminacy, far from guaranteeing responsibility, would, if it existed, actually be prejudicial to it. If freedom is the complete divorce of the will from antecedent conditions, including my moral character, I cannot then be held accountable for my actions. A will which descends upon me like "a bolt from the blue" is not *my* will and it is manifestly unfair to take me to task for its caprices. . . .

(3) *The Argument from Physical Indeterminacy*

Free-willists have recently derived not a little encouragement from the advent of the principle of physical indeterminacy which even if it does not suffice to demonstrate freedom of the will, at least seems to remove a serious obstacle to its acceptance. If there is a real indeterminacy at the subatomic level of quantum mechanics, this affords at least the *possibility* of the physiological and ultimately of the psychological indeterminacy which constitutes the freedom of the will. Recent quantum theory seems on the surface to afford a physical basis for a volitional indeterminacy much as the swerve of the atoms invoked by the ancient Epicureans seemed to justify their free-will doctrine. But the contemporary argument is defective and in very much the same respects as its historic prototype.

Against the modern version of the indeterminacy argument, it may be urged in the first place that the physical theory of indeterminacy merely expresses an observational difficulty encountered in the attempt to determine both the position and the velocity of an electron and that consequently it posits a methodological and not the physical or ontological indeterminacy which is requisite for the purposes of the free-will doctrine. But secondly, even supposing that the indeterminacy principle is physical and not merely methodological, it has not been shown that this subatomic indeterminacy manifests itself in the behaviour of ordinary mass-objects and in particular that it is exemplified in just those neural processes which are supposedly the basis of the act of free-will. The psychophysical correlation of a neural indeterminacy with its psychological counterpart, could be effected only by the introspective observation of the volitional indeterminacy along with the underlying physical indeterminacy, and thus the evidence of introspection is an essential link in the argument from physical indeterminacy. The physical theory of indeterminacy is at the present time far from demonstrating the existence of or giving a complete picture of the *modus operandi* of a free-will and thus the freedom of indeterminacy remains, even on the background of physical indeterminacy, a mere speculative possibility.

THE CASE FOR DETERMINISM

Whereas the evidence for the free-will doctrine is largely humanistic and moralistic, the case for determinism is an appeal to scientific evidence; the determinist finds that the sciences of *physiology, psychology,* and *sociology* afford evidence that human behaviour is no exception to the casual uniformity of nature.

(1) Physiological Evidence

The more we know about the physiological and neural processes which go on inside the human organism, even when it reacts to the most complicated of stimuli, the more evident it becomes that there is no break in the continuous chain of causation. Physiology gives us a reasonably clear picture of the mechanism of human behaviour. The behaviourists, the most recent recruits to the cause of determinism, have with infinite patience applied the objective method of the physiologists to human conduct; they have described in the minutest detail the mechanism of reflexes and the manner of their conditioning. There seems to remain no missing link in the causal chain from stimulus to ultimate response—even when that response is long "delayed." Delayed responses are mediated by very complex neural processes which on their subjective side are called conflict, indecision, and deliberation, but they are no exception to the behaviouristic formula.

(2) Psychological Evidence

While the deterministic thesis receives its most obvious support from physiology and behaviouristic psychology, introspective psychology makes its contribution also. An unbiased introspective examination of volition supports the theory of psychological determinism. The more carefully I scrutinize my decisions, the more clearly do I discern the motives which determine them. If one's powers of introspection were sufficiently developed, one could presumably after any decision discover the exact psychological influences which rendered that particular decision inevitable. Doubtless for a complete explanation of certain decisions it is necessary in addition to the conscious antecedents of the volitional act to recover the more recondite sub-conscious and unconscious influences; the extensive researches of the Freudians into the submerged factors in human motivation provide the explanation of otherwise inexplicable mental acts and therefore tend to supply the missing links in the chain of psychic causation. Indeed, the existence of consciously inexplicable conscious events was one of the most compelling reasons for the original positing of an unconscious or subconscious mind. It remains true, however, that a fairly complete account of the psychological causation of volitional decisions is possible even without recourse to an unconscious mind.

Perhaps the best classical statement of the case for psychological determinism was given by David Hume. Hume, whose introspective subtlety has rarely been surpassed, commits himself unequivocally to psychological determinism in his assertion that "There is a great uniformity among the actions of men. . . . *The same motives always produce the same actions.*" Every historian, as Hume points out, appeals to this principle in judging the accuracy of historical documents; he asks himself whether the reported actions conform to what is known of human nature. And we might add, the same criterion is appealed to even in the evaluation of works of fiction. The novelist or the playwright gives a portrayal of his characters; he places them in definite situations, and then describes how they act. If his account of their behaviour under these precisely defined circumstances violates any of the recognized laws of human motivation, his literary and dramatic artistry is to that extent defective. Thus the principle of psychological determinism serves as a recognized canon on historical, literary, and dramatic criticism, and while this does not "prove" the correctness of psychological determinism, it does afford confirmation of it from an unsuspected quarter.

(3) Sociological Evidence

The social sciences yield abundant evidence for a deterministic view of human behaviour. The fact that the conduct of large aggregates of individuals is expressible in terms of statistical law, although it is by no means a conclusive proof of individual determinism, certainly points in that direction. I may not be able to predict how you as an individual will behave in any specified circumstances, but I can formulate a statistical law applicable to a large group of individuals of which you are a member. It is difficult to reconcile the possibility of the laws of groups or mass action with individual free-will.

The conclusion reached as a result of the survey of the arguments on both sides of the free-will controversy is that the strength of the deterministic position lies not only in the overwhelming array of psychological, physiological, and sociological evidence for the uniformity of human behaviour, but also in its ability to meet the psychological, moral, and religious "proofs" of free-will. Accordingly, we seem fully justified in concluding that a capricious free-will, that is to say, a will capable of acting independently of antecedent conditions, psychological or physiological, is a philosophical absurdity.

42 A Defense of Determinism[*]

BARON D. HOLBACH

Baron D. Holbach (1723–1789) was a forceful advocate of atheism, determinism, and materialism. His principal works are *Christianisme DéVoilé* and *The System of Nature*.

Man's life is a line that nature commands him to describe upon the surface of the earth, without his ever being able to swerve from it, even for an instant. He is born without his own consent; his organization does in nowise depend upon himself; his ideas come to him involuntarily; his habits are in the power of those who cause him to contract them; he is unceasingly modified by causes, whether visible or concealed, over which he has no control, which necessarily regulate his mode of existence, give the hue to his way of thinking, and determine his manner of acting. He is good or bad, happy or miserable, wise or foolish, reasonable or irrational, without his will being for anything in these various states. Nevertheless, in spite of the shackles by which he is bound, it is pretended he is a free agent, or that independent of the causes by which he is moved, he determines his own will, and regulates his own condition.

However slender the foundation of this opinion, of which everything ought to point out to him the error, it is current at this day and passes for an incontestable truth with a great number of people, otherwise extremely enlightened; it is the basis of religion, which, supposing relations between man and the unknown being she has placed above nature, has been incapable of imagining how man could merit reward or deserve punishment from this being, if he was not a free agent. Society has been believed interested in this system; because an idea has gone abroad, that if all the actions of man were to be contemplated as necessary, the right of punishing those who injure their associates would no longer exist. At length human vanity accommodated itself to a hypothesis which, unquestionably, appears to distinguish man from all other physical beings, by assigning to him the special privilege of a total independence of all other causes, but of which a very little reflection would have shown him the impossibility. . . .

The will, as we have elsewhere said, is a modification of the brain, by which it is disposed to action, or prepared to give play to the organs. This will is necessarily determined by the qualities, good or bad, agreeable or

* From Baron D. Holbach, *System of Nature*, first published in 1770, trans. H. D. Robinson.

painful, of the object or the motive that acts upon his senses, or of which the idea remains with him, and is resuscitated by his memory. In consequence, he acts necessarily, his action is the result of the impulse he receives either from the motive, from the object, or from the idea which has modified his brain, or disposed his will. When he does not act according to this impulse, it is because there comes some new cause, some new motive, some new idea, which modifies his brain in a different manner, gives him a new impulse, determines his will in another way, by which the action of the former impulse is suspended: thus, the sight of an agreeable object, or its idea, determines his will to set him in action to procure it; but if a new object or a new idea more powerfully attracts him, it gives a new directoin to his will, annihilates the effect of the former, and prevents the action by which it was to be procured. This is the mode in which reflection, experience, reason, necessarily arrests or suspends the action of man's will: without this he would of necessity have followed the anterior impulse which carried him towards a then desirable object. In all this he always acts according to necessary laws from which he has no means of emancipating himself.

If when tormented with violent thirst, he figures to himself in idea, or really perceives a fountain, whose limpid streams might cool his feverish want, is he sufficient master of himself to desire or not to desire the object competent to satisfy so lively a want? It will no doubt be conceded, that it is impossible he should not be desirous to satisfy it; but it will be said—if at this moment it is announced to him that the water he so ardently desires is poisoned, he will, notwithstanding his vehement thirst, abstain from drinking it: and it has, therefore, been falsely concluded that he is a free agent. The fact, however, is, that the motive in either case is exactly the same: his own conservation. The same necessity that determined him to drink before he knew the water was deleterious upon this new discovery equally determined him not to drink; the desire of conserving himself either annihilates or suspends the former impulse; the second motive becomes stronger than the preceding, that is, the fear of death, or the desire of preserving himself, necessarily prevails over the painful sensation caused by his eagerness to drink: but, it will be said, if the thirst is very parching, an inconsiderate man without regarding the danger will risk swallowing the water. Nothing is gained by this remark: in this case, the anterior impulse only regains the ascendency; he is persuaded that life may possibly be longer preserved, or that he shall derive a greater good by drinking the poisoned water than by enduring the torment, which, to his mind, threatens instant dissolution: thus the first becomes the strongest and necessarily urges him on to action. Nevertheless, in either case, whether he partakes of the water, or whether he does not, the two actions will be equally necessary; they will be the effect of that motive which finds itself most puissant; which consequently acts in the most coercive manner upon his will.

This example will serve to explain the whole phenomena of the human will. This will, or rather the brain, finds itself in the same situation as a bowl, which, although it has received an impulse that drives it forward in a straight line, is deranged in its course whenever a force superior to the first obliges it to change its direction. The man who drinks the poisoned water appears a madman; but the actions of fools are as necessary as those of the most prudent individuals. The motives that determine the voluptuary and the debauchee to risk their health, are as powerful, and their actions are as necessary, as those which decide the wise man to manage his. But, it will be insisted, the debauchee may be prevailed on to change his conduct: this does not imply that he is a free agent; but that motives may be found sufficiently powerful to annihilate the effect of those that previously acted upon him; then these new motives determine his will to the new mode of conduct he may adopt as necessarily as the former did to the old mode. . . .

It has been believed that man was a free agent, because it has been imagined that his soul could at will recall ideas which sometimes suffice to check his most unruly desires. Thus, the idea of a remote evil, frequently prevents him from enjoying a present and actual good: thus remembrance, which is an almost insensible or slight modification of his brain, annihilates, at each instant, the real objects that act upon his will. But he is not master of recalling to himself his ideas at pleasure; their association is independent of him; they are arranged in his brain in despite of him and without his own knowledge, where they have made an impression more or less profound; his memory itself depends upon his organization; its fidelity depends upon the habitual or momentary state in which he finds himself; when his will is vigorously determined to some object or idea that excites a very lively passion in him, those objects or ideas that would be able to arrest his action, no longer present themselves to his mind; in those moments his eyes are shut to the dangers that menace him; of which the idea ought to make him forbear; he marches forwards headlong towards the object by whose image he is hurried on; reflection cannot operate upon him in any way; he sees nothing but the object of his desires; the salutary ideas which might be able to arrest his progress disappear, or else display themselves either too faintly or too late to prevent his acting. Such is the case with all those who, blinded by some strong passion, are not in a condition to recall to themselves those motives, of which the idea alone, in cooler moments, would be sufficient to deter them from proceeding; the disorder in which they are, prevents their judging soundly; renders them incapable of foreseeing the consequences of their actions; precludes them from applying to their experience; from making use of their reason; natural operations which suppose a justness in the manner of associating their ideas, but to which their brain is then not more competent, in consequence of the momentary delirium it suffers, than their hand is to write whilst they are taking violent exercise.

Man's mode of thinking is necessarily determined by his manner of being; it must therefore depend on his natural organization, and the modification his system receives independently of his will. From this, we are obliged to conclude, that his thoughts, his reflections, his manner of viewing things, of feeling, of judging, of combining ideas, is neither voluntary nor free. In a word, that his soul is neither mistress of the motion excited in it, nor of representing to itself, when wanted, those images or ideas that are capable of counterbalancing the impulse it receives. This is the reason, why man, when in a passion, ceases to reason; at that moment reason is as impossible to be heard, as it is during an ecstacy, or in a fit of drunkenness. The wicked are never more than men who are either drunk or mad; if they reason, it is not until tranquillity is re-established in their machine; then, and not till then, the tardy ideas that present themselves to their mind enable them to see the consequence of their actions, and give birth to ideas that bring on them that trouble, which is designated *shame, regret, remorse.*

The errours of philosophers on the free agency of man, have arisen from their regarding his will as the *primum mobile,* the original motive of his actions; for want of recurring back, they have not perceived the multiplied, the complicated causes which, independently of him, give motion to the will itself; or which dispose and modify his brain, whilst he himself is purely passive in the motion he receives. Is he the master of desiring or not desiring an object that appears desirable to him? Without doubt it will be answered, no: but he is the master of resisting his desire, if he reflects on the consequences. But, I ask, is he capable of reflecting on these consequences, when his soul is hurried along by a very lively passion, which entirely depends upon his natural organization, and the causes by which he is modified? Is it in his power to add to these consequences all the weight necessary to counterbalance his desire? Is he the master of preventing the qualities which render an object desirable from residing in it? I shall be told: he ought to have learned to resist his passions; to contract a habit of putting a curb on his desires. I agree to it without any difficulty. But in reply, I again ask, is his nature susceptible of this modification? Does his boiling blood, his unruly imagination, the igneous fluid that circulates in his veins, permit him to make, enable him to apply true experience in the moment when it is wanted? And even when his temperament has capacitated him, has his education, the examples set before him, the ideas with which he has been inspired in early life, been suitable to make him contract this habit of repressing his desires? Have not all these things rather contributed to induce him to seek with avidity, to make him actually desire those objects which you say he ought to resist.

The *ambitious man* cries out: you will have me resist my passion; but have they not unceasingly repeated to me that rank, honours, power, are the most desirable advantages in life? Have I not seen my fellow citizens envy them, the nobles of my country sacrifice every thing to obtain them? In the society in which I live, am I not obliged to feel, that if I am deprived of these advantages, I must expect to languish in contempt; to cringe under the rod of oppression?

The *miser* says: you forbid me to love money, to seek after the means of acquiring it: alas! does not every thing tell me that, in this world, money is the greatest blessing; that it is amply sufficient to render me happy? In the country I inhabit, do I not see all my fellow citizens covetous of riches? but do I not also witness that they are little scrupulous in the means of obtaining wealth? As soon as they are enriched by the means which you censure, are they not cherished, considered and respected? By what authority, then, do you defend me from amassing treasure? What right have you to prevent my using means, which, although you call them sordid and criminal, I see approved by the sovereign? Will you have me renounce my happiness?

The *voluptuary* argues: you pretend that I should resist my desires; but was I the maker of my own temperament, which unceasingly invites me to pleasure? You call my pleasures disgraceful; but in the country in which I live, do I not witness the most dissipated men enjoying the most distinguished rank? Do I not behold that no one is ashamed of adultery but the husband it has outraged? Do not I see men making trophies of their debaucheries, boasting of their libertinism, rewarded with applause?

The *choleric man* vociferates: you advise me to put a curb on my passions, and to resist the desire of avenging myself: but can I conquer my nature? Can I alter the received opinions of the world? Shall I not be forever disgraced, infallibly dishonoured in society, if I do not wash out in the blood of my fellow creatures the injuries I have received?

The *zealous enthusiast* exclaims: you recommend me mildness; you advise me to be tolerant; to be indulgent to the opinions of my fellow men; but is not my temperament violent? Do I not ardently love my God? Do they not assure me, that zeal is pleasing to him; that sanguinary inhuman persecutors have been his friends? As I wish to render myself acceptable in his sight, I therefore adopt the same means.

In short, the actions of man are never free; they are always the necessary consequence of his temperament, of the received ideas, and of the notions, either true or false, which he has formed to himself of happiness; of his opinions, strengthened by example, by education, and by daily experience. So many crimes are witnessed on the earth only because every thing conspires to render man vicious and criminal; the religion he has adopted, his government, his education, the examples set before him, irresistibly drive him on to evil: under these circumstances, morality preaches virtue to him in vain. In those societies where vice is esteemed, where crime is crowned, where venality is constantly recompensed, where the most dreadful disorders are punished only in those who are too weak to enjoy the privilege of commiting them with impunity, the practice of virtue is considered nothing more than a painful sacrifice of happiness. Such societies chastise, in the lower orders, those excesses which they respect in the higher ranks; and frequently have the injustice to condemn those in the penalty of death, whom public prejudices, maintained by constant example, have rendered criminal.

Man, then, is not a free agent in any one instant of his life; he is necessarily guided in each step by those advantages, whether real or fictitious, that he attaches to the objects by which his passions are roused: these passions themselves are necessary in a being who unceasingly tends towards his own happiness; their energy is necessary, since that depends on his temperament; his temperament is necessary, because it depends on the physical elements which enter into his composition; the modification of this temperament is necessary, as it is the infallible and inevitable consequence of the impulse he receives from the incessant action of moral and physical beings.

43 God's Omniscience and Man's Free Will*

ST. AUGUSTINE

St. Augustine (354–430), a native of North Africa, became Bishop of Hippo in 395. Influential as a Christian philosopher and theologian, his writings include *On Free Will*, *Confessions*, *On The Trinity*, and *The City of God*.

The manner in which Cicero addresses himself to the task of refuting the Stoics, shows that he did not think he could effect anything against them in argument unless he had first demolished divination.[1] And this he attempts to accomplish by denying that there is any knowledge of future things, and maintains with all his might that there is no such knowledge either in God or man, and that there is no prediction of events. Thus he both denies the foreknowledge of God, and attempts by vain arguments, and by opposing to himself certain oracles very easy to be refuted, to overthrow all prophecy, even such as is clearer than the light (though even these oracles are not refuted by him).

But, in refuting these conjectures of the mathematicians, his argument is triumphant, because truly these are such as destroy and refute themselves. Nevertheless, they are far more tolerable who assert the fatal influence of the stars than they who deny the foreknowledge of future events. For, to confess that God exists, and at the same time to deny that He has foreknowledge of future things, is the most manifest folly. This Cicero himself saw, and therefore attempted to assert the doctrine embodied in the words of Scripture, "The fool hath said in his heart, There is no God."[2] That, however, he did not do in his own person, for he saw how odious and offensive such an opinion would be; and, therefore in his book on the nature of the gods,[3] he makes Cotta dispute concerning this against the Stoics, and preferred to give his own opinion in favour of Lucilius Balbus, to whom he assigned the defense of the Stoical position, rather than in favour of Cotta, who maintained that no divinity exists. However, in his book on divination, he in his

* From St. Augustine, "The Freedom of the Will," *The City of God*, trans. and ed. Marcus Dods (London: Edinburgh House, 1892), Book V, pp. 164–169.
[1] *De Divinat*. ii.
[2] Ps. xiv. 1.
[3] Bk. iii.

own person most openly opposes the doctrine of the prescience of future things. But all this he seems to do in order that he may not grant the doctrine of fate, and by so doing destroy free will. For he thinks that, the knowledge of future things being once conceded, fate follows as so necessary a consequence that it cannot be denied.

But, let these perplexing debatings and disputations of the philosophers go on as they may, we, in order that we may confess the most high and true God Himself, do confess His will, supreme power, and prescience. Neither let us be afraid lest, after all, we do not do by will that which we do by will, because He, whose foreknowledge is infallible, foreknew that we would do it. It was this which Cicero was afraid of, and therefore opposed foreknowledge. The Stoics also maintained that all things do not come to pass by necessity, although they contended that all things happen according to destiny. What is it, then, that Cicero feared in the prescience of future things? Doubtless it was this,—that if all future things have been foreknown, they will happen in the order in which they have been foreknown; and if they come to pass in this order, there is a certain order of things foreknown by God; and if a certain order of things, then a certain order of causes, for nothing can happen which is not preceded by some efficient cause. But if there is a certain order of causes according to which everything happens which does happen, then by fate, says he, all things happen which do happen. But if this be so, then is there nothing in our own power, and there is no such thing as freedom of will; and if we grant that, says he, the whole economy of human life is subverted. In vain are laws enacted. In vain are reproaches, praises, chidings, exhortations had recourse to; and there is no justice whatever in the appointment of rewards for the good, and punishments for the wicked. And that consequences so disgraceful, and absurd, and pernicious to humanity may not follow, Cicero chooses to reject the foreknowledge of future things, and shuts up the religious mind to this alternative, to make choice between two things, either that something is in our own power, or that there is foreknowledge,—both of which cannot be true; but if the one is affirmed, the other is thereby denied. He therefore, like a truly great and wise man, and one who consulted very much and very skilfully for the good of humanity, of those two choose the freedom of the will, to confirm which he denied the foreknowledge of future things; and thus, wishing to make men free, he makes them sacrilegious. But the religious mind chooses both, confesses both, and maintains both by the faith of piety. But how so? says Cicero; for the knowledge of future things being granted, there follows a chain of consequences which ends in this, that there can be nothing depending on our own free wills. And further, if there is anything depending on our wills, we must go backwards by the same steps of reasoning till we arrive at the conclusion that there is no foreknowledge of future things. For we go backwards through all the steps in the following order:—If there is free will, all things do not happen according to fate; if all things do happen according to fate, there is not a certain order of causes; and if there is not a certain order of causes, neither is there a certain order of things foreknown by God,—for things cannot come to pass except they are preceded by efficient causes,—but, if there is no fixed and certain order of causes foreknown by God, all things cannot be said to happen according as He foreknew that they would happen. And further, if it is not true that all things happen just as they have been foreknown by Him, there is not, says he, in God any foreknowledge of future events.

Now, against the sacrilegious and impious darings of reason, we assert both that God knows all things before they come to pass, and that we do by our free will whatsoever we know and feel to be done by us only because we will it. But that all things come to pass by fate, we do not say; nay we affirm that nothing comes to pass by fate; for we demonstrate that the name of fate, as it is wont to be used by those who speak of fate, meaning thereby the position of the stars at the time of each one's conception or birth, is an unmeaning word, for astrology itself is a delusion. But an order of causes in which the highest efficiency is attributed to the will of God, we neither deny nor do we designate it by the name of fate, unless, perhaps, we may understand fate to mean that which is spoken, deriving it from *fari*, to speak; for we cannot deny that it is written in the sacred Scriptures, "God hath spoken once; these two things have I heard, that power belongeth unto God. Also unto Thee, O God, belongeth mercy: for Thou wilt render unto every man according to his works."[4] Now the expression. "Once hath He spoken," is to be understood as meaning "immovably," that is, unchangeably hath He spoken, inasmuch as He knows unchangeably all things which shall be, and all things which He will do. We might, then, use the word fate in the sense it bears when derived from *fari*, to speak, had it not already come to be understood in another sense, into which I am unwilling that the hearts of men should unconsciously slide. But it does not follow that, though there is for God a certain order of all causes, there must therefore be nothing depending on the free exercise of our own wills, for our wills themselves are included in that order of causes which is certain to God, and is embraced by His foreknowledge, for human wills are also causes of human actions; and He who foreknew all the causes of things would certainly among those causes not have been ignorant of our wills. For even that very concession which Cicero himself makes is enough to refute him in this argument. For what does it help him to say that nothing takes place without a cause, but that every cause is not fatal, there being a fortuitous cause, a natural cause, and a voluntary cause? It is sufficient that he confesses that whatever happens must be preceded by a cause. For we say that those causes which are called fortuitous are not a mere name for the absence of causes, but are only latent, and we attribute them either to the will of the true God, or to that of spirits

[4] Ps. lxii. 11, 12.

of some kind or other. And as to natural causes, we by no means separate them from the will of Him who is the author and framer of all nature. But now as to voluntary causes. They are referable either to God, or to angels, or to men, or to animals of whatever description, if indeed those instinctive movements of animals devoid of reason, by which, in accordance with their own nature, they seek or shun various things, are to be called wills. And when I speak of the wills of angels, I mean either the wills of good angels, whom we call the angels of God, or of the wicked angels, whom we call the angels of the devil, or demons. Also by the wills of men I mean the wills either of the good or of the wicked. And from this we conclude that there are no efficient causes of all things which come to pass unless voluntary causes, that is, such as belong to that nature which is the spirit of life. For the air or wind is called spirit, but, inasmuch as it is a body, it is not the spirit of life. The spirit of life, therefore, which quickens all things, and is the creator of every body, and of every created spirit, is God Himself, the uncreated spirit. In His supreme will resides the power which acts on the wills of all created spirits, helping the good, judging the evil, controlling all, granting power to some, not granting it to others. For, as He is the creator of all natures, so also is He the bestower of all powers, not of all wills; for wicked wills are not from Him, being contrary to nature, which is from Him. As to bodies, they are more subject to wills: some to our wills, by which I mean the wills of all living mortal creatures, but more to the wills of men than of beasts. But all of them are most of all subject to the will of God, to whom all wills also are subject, since they have no power except what He has bestowed upon them. The cause of things, therefore, which makes but is not made, is God; but all other causes both make and are made. Such are all created spirits, and especially the rational. Material causes, therefore, which may rather be said to be made than to make, are not to be reckoned among efficient causes, because they can only do what the wills of spirits do by them. How, then, does an order of causes which is certain to the foreknowledge of God necessitate that there should be nothing which is dependent on our wills, when our wills themselves have a very important place in the order of causes? Cicero, then, contends with those who call this order of causes fatal, or rather designate this order itself by the name of fate; to which we have an abhorrence, especially on account of the word, which men have become accustomed to understand as meaning what is not true. But, whereas he denies that the order of all causes is most certain, and perfectly clear to the prescience of God, we detest his opinion more than the Stoics do. For he either denies that God exists,—which, indeed, in an assumed personage, he has laboured to do, in his book *De Natura Deorum*,—or if he confesses that He exists, but denies that He is prescient of future things, what is that but just "the fool saying in his heart there is no God"? For one who is not prescient of all future things is not God. Wherefore our wills also have just so much power as God willed and foreknew that they should have; and therefore whatever power they have, they have it within most certain limits; and whatever they are to do, they are most assuredly to do, for He whose fore-knowledge is infallible foreknew that they would have the power to do it, and would do it. Wherefore, if I should choose to apply the name of fate to anything at all, I should rather say that fate belongs to the weaker of two parties, will to the stronger, who has the other in his power, than that the freedom of our will is excluded by that order of causes, which, by an unusual application of the word peculiar to themselves, the Stoics call *Fate*.

Wherefore, neither is that necessity to be feared, for dread of which the Stoics laboured to make such distinctions among the causes of things as should enable them to rescue certain things from the dominion of necessity, and to subject others to it. Among those things which they wished not to be subject to necessity they placed our wills, knowing that they would not be free if subjected to necessity. For if that is to be called *our necessity* which is not in our power, but even though we be unwilling, effects what it can effect,—as, for instance, the necessity of death,—it is manifest that our wills by which we live uprightly or wickedly are not under such a necessity; for we do many things which, if we were not willing, we should certainly not do. This is primarily true of the act of willing itself,—for if we will, it *is*; if we will not, it *is* not,—for we should not will if we were unwilling. But if we define necessity to be that according to which we say that it is necessary that anything be of such or such a nature, or be done in such and such a manner, I know not why we should have any dread of that necessity taking away the freedom of our will. For we do not put the life of God or the foreknowledge of God under necessity if we should say that it is necessary that God should live for ever, and foreknow all things; as neither is His power diminished when we say that He cannot die or fall into error,—for this is in such a way impossible to Him, that if it were possible for Him, He would be of less power. But assuredly He is rightly called omnipotent on account of His doing what He wills, not on account of His suffering what He wills not; for if that should befall Him, He would by no means be omnipotent. Where-fore, He cannot do some things for the very reason that He is omnipotent. So also, when we say that it is necessary that, when we will, we will by free choice, in so saying we both affirm what is true beyond doubt, and do not still subject our wills thereby to a necessity which destroys liberty. Our wills, therefore, *exists* as *wills*, and do themselves whatever we do by willing, and which would not be done if we were unwilling. But when any one suffers anything, being unwilling, by the will of another, even in that case will retains its essential validity,—we do not mean the will of the party who inflicts the suffering, for we resolve it into the power of God. For if a will should simply exist, but not be able to do what it wills, it would be over-borne by a more powerful will. Nor would this be the case unless there had existed will, and that not the will of the other party, but the will of him who willed, but was not able to accomplish what he willed. Therefore,

44 Free Will
As Involving Determinism*

PHILIPPA FOOT

Philippa Foot is professor of philosophy at Summerville College, Oxford University. She is the editor of *The Theory of Ethics.*

The idea that free will can be reconciled with the strictest determinism is now very widely accepted. To say that a man acted freely is, it is often suggested, to say that he was not constrained, or that he could have done otherwise if he had chosen, or something else of that kind; and since these things could be true even if his action was determined it seems that there could be room for free will even within a universe completely subject to causal laws. Hume put forward a view of this kind in contrasting the "liberty of spontaneity . . . which is oppos'd to violence" with the nonexistent "liberty of indifference . . . which means a negation of necessity and causes."[1] A. J. Ayer, in his essay "Freedom and Necessity"[2] was summing up such a position when he said, "from the fact that my action is causally determined . . . it does not necessarily follow that I am not free"[3] and "it is not when my action has any cause at all, but only when it has a special sort of cause, that it is reckoned not to be free."[4]

I am not here concerned with the merits of this view but only with a theory which appears more or less incidentally in the writings of those who defend it. This is the argument that so far from being incompatible with determinism, free will actually requires it. It appears briefly in Hume's *Treatise* and was set out in full in an article by R. E. Hobart.[5] P. H. Nowell-Smith was expressing a similar view when he said of the idea that determinism is opposed to free will that "the clearest proof that it is mistaken or at least muddled lies in showing that I could not be free to choose what I do *unless* determinism is correct. . . . Freedom, so far from being incompatible

* From Philippa Foot, "Free Will as Involving Determinism," *The Philosophical Review,* vol. 66 (1957). Reprinted by permission of the author and *The Philosophical Review.*
[1] *Treatise,* bk. II, pt. III, sec. 2.
[2] *Polemic,* no. 5 (1946); reprinted in his *Philosophical Essays* (London, 1954).
[3] *Philosophical Essays,* p. 278.
[4] *Ibid.,* p. 281.
[5] "Freewill as Involving Determinism," *Mind,* XLIII (1934), 1–27.

with causality implies it."[6] Ayer has taken up a similar position, arguing that the absence of causal laws governing action "does not give the moralist what he wants. For he is anxious to show that men are capable of acting freely in order to infer that they can be morally responsible for what they do. But if it is a matter of pure chance that a man should act in one way rather than another, he may be free but he can hardly be responsible."[7]

This argument is not essential to the main thesis of those who use it; their own account of free will in such terms as the absence of *constraining* causes might be correct even though there were no inconsistencies in the suggestion put forward by their libertarian opponents. But if valid the argument would be a strong argument, disposing of the position of anyone who argued both that free will required the absence of determining causes and that free will was a possibility. That the argument is not valid, and indeed that it is singularly implausible, I shall now try to show. It is, I think, surprising that it should have survived so long; this is perhaps because it has not had to bear much weight. In any case the weapons which can be used against it are ones which are in general use elsewhere.

In discussing determinism and free will it is important to be clear about the sense which is given in this context to words such as "determined" and "caused." Russell gave this account:

> The law of universal causation . . . may be enunciated as follows: There are such invariable relations between different events at the same or different times that, given the state of the whole universe throughout any finite time, however short, every previous and subsequent event can theoretically be determined as a function of the given events during that time.[8]

This seems to be the kind of determinism which worries the defender of free will, for if human action is subject to a universal law of causation of this type, there will be for any action a set of sufficient conditions which can be traced back to factors outside the control of the agent.

We cannot of course take it for granted that whenever the word "determined" or the word "cause" is used this is what is implied, and what is intended may be in no way relevant to the question of free will. For instance, an action said to be determined by the desires of the man who does it is not necessarily an action for which there is supposed to be a sufficient condition. In saying that it is determined by his desires we may mean merely that he is doing something that he wants to do, or that he is doing it for the sake of something else that he wants. There is nothing in this to suggest determinism in Russell's sense. On the whole it is wise to be suspicious of expressions such as "determined by desire" unless these have been given a clear sense,

---

[6] "Freewill and Moral Responsibility," *Mind*, LVII (1948), 46.
[7] *Philosophical Essays*, p. 275.
[8] "On the Notion of Cause," in *Our Knowledge of the External World* (London, 1914), p. 221.

and this is particularly true of the phrase "determined by the agent's character." Philosophers often talk about actions being determined by a man's character, but it is not certain that anyone else does, or that the words are given any definite sense. One might suppose that an action was so determined if it was *in* character, for instance the generous action of a generous man; but if this is so we will not have the kind of determinism traditionally supposed to raise difficulties for a doctrine of free will. For nothing has been said to suggest that where the character trait can be predicated the action will invariably follow; it has not been supposed that a man who can truly be said to be generous never acts ungenerously even under given conditions.

Keeping the relevant sense of "determinism" in mind, we may now start to discuss the view that free will requires determinism. The first version which I shall consider is that put forward by Hobart, who suggests that an action which is not determined cannot properly be called an *action* at all, being something that happened to the agent rather than something he *did*. Hobart says, "*In proportion* as it [the action] is undetermined, it is just as if his legs should suddenly spring up and carry him off where he did not prefer to go." To see how odd this suggestion is we have only to ask when we would say that a man's legs were carrying him where he did not prefer to go. One can imagine the scene: he is sitting quietly in his chair and has said that he is going to go on reading his book; suddenly he cries, "Good heavens, I can't control my legs!" and as he moves across the room, he hangs on to the furniture or asks someone else to hold him. Here indeed his legs are carrying him where he does not want to go, but what has this to do with indeterminism, and what has the ordinary case, where he walks across the room, to do with determinism? Perhaps Hobart thinks that when a man does something meaning to do it, he does what he wants to do, and so his action is determined by his desire. But to do something meaning to do it is to do it in a certain way, not to do it as the result of the operation of a causal law. When one means to do something, one does not call out for help in preventing the movement of one's limbs; on the contrary, one is likely to stop other people from interfering, saying, "I want to do this." It is by such factors that walking across the room is distinguished from being carried off by one's legs. It is to be explained in terms of the things said and done by the agent, not in terms of some force, "the desire," present before the action was done and still less in terms of some law telling us that whenever this "desire" is found it will be followed by the action. The indeterminist has no difficulty in distinguishing an action from something that happens to the agent; he can say exactly the same as anyone else.

Nowell-Smith seems to be thinking along somewhat the same lines as Hobart when he attacks C. A. Campbell for saying that free will requires indeterminism:

The essence of Campbell's account is that the action should not be predictable from a knowledge of the agent's character. But, if this is so, can what he does be called his action at all? Is it not rather a *lusus naturae*, an Act of God or a miracle? If a hardened criminal, bent on robbing the poor-box, suddenly and *inexplicably* fails to do so, we should not say that he *chose* to resist or deserves *credit* for resisting the temptation; we should say, if we were religious, that he was the recipient of a sudden outpouring of Divine Grace or, if we were irreligious, that his "action" was due to chance, which is another way of saying that it was inexplicable. In either case we should refuse to use the active voice.[9]

It is hard to see why a man who does something inexplicably does not really *do* it. Let us suppose that the hardened criminal's action really is inexplicable; we can only say, "He just turned away," and not why he did so; this does not mean that he did it by accident, or unintentionally, or not of his own free will, and I see no reason for refusing to use the active voice. In any case, to explain an action is not necessarily to show that it could have been predicted from some fact about the agent's character—that he is weak, greedy, sentimental, and so forth. We may if we like say that an action is never *fully* explained unless it has been shown to be covered by a law which connects it to such a character trait; but then it becomes even more implausible to say that an action must be explicable if we are to admit it as something genuinely *done*. In the ordinary sense we explain the criminal's action if we say, for instance, that a particular thought came into his mind; we do not also have to find a law about the way such thoughts do come into the minds of such men.

A rather different version of this argument runs as follows. We hold responsible only a man who is a rational agent; if someone were always to do things out of the blue, without having any reason to do them, we should be inclined to count him as a lunatic, one who could not be held responsible for his actions, so that even if he *did* things he would do things for which he could not be held responsible. And is it not through being determined by motives that actions are those of a rational agent whom we can praise or blame?

It certainly would be odd to suppose that free will required the absence of motives for action. We do not of course expect that everything that the rational man does should be done with a motive; if he gets up and walks about the room he need not be doing so in order to take exercise; it is quite usual for people to do this kind of thing without any particular purpose in view, and no one is counted irrational for doing so. And yet we do expect a man to have a motive for a great number of the things that he does, and we would count anyone who constantly performed troublesome actions without a motive as irrational. So it looks as if a moral agent is a man whose actions are in general determined, if determinism is involved in "having a motive" for what he does.

[9] *Ethics* (London, 1954), pp. 281–282.

What does it mean to say that someone had a motive for doing what he did? Often this particular expression means that he did it with a particular intention, so we should first say something about intentions and the sense in which they can be said to determine action. We say that a man had a certain intention in acting when he aimed at a certain thing, and "his motive for such and such" often means "his aim in doing such and such," for instance, "His motive for going to the station was to take a train to London." But where motives are intentions it is clear that they cannot be determining causes; for intending to do x and being ready to take the steps thought necessary to do x are connected not empirically but analytically. A man cannot be said to have an intention unless he is reconciled to what he believes to be the intermediate steps. We cannot speak as if the intention were something which could be determined first, and "being ready to take the necessary steps" were a second stage following on the first.

It might be objected that this does not cover the case of "doing y because one wants x" where "wanting x" does not imply trying to get x. In one sense of "want" it is possible to say, "He wants x" without knowing whether he is prepared to take steps to get it. (One might, for instance, want to go to London but not be prepared to spend the money to get there.) So that *wanting* seems here to be a separate condition, which might in certain cases be connected by an empirical law to the adoption of particular courses of action. Certainly wanting is not an event, but one gets rid of wanting as a determining factor too easily if one merely says that desires are not causes because they are not occurrences.

We say "He wants" in this sense where he would adopt certain policies *if* there were no reasons for not doing so. We can say, "He wants to get to London," even when he is not prepared to take the necessary steps to get to London, provided he can say, "Trains are too expensive," or "Hitchhiking is too uncomfortable." If we offered him a spare railway ticket or otherwise disposed of his reasons against going, and he still did not go, we would have to say, "He didn't really want to go after all." So wanting in this sense is being prepared to act under certain conditions, though not being prepared to act under the given conditions. It is a description which could be applied to a man before we knew whether he was ready to act in a given situation, and it seems that there might then be a causal relation between the wanting and the acting where the latter took place. This is quite true; there could be a law to the effect that when the description "He wants x" applied at t_1, the description "He is taking the necessary steps to get x" applied at t_2. It would be possible to say this without making a mistake about what it is to *want* and inventing a hidden condition of body or mind. One could say, "Wanting in this sense just is being prepared to act under some conditions," and still maintain that there could be an empirical law connecting wanting with acting under a particular set of conditions. The mistake lies not in the idea that such laws are *possible* but in the thought that there is a reference to them in the statement that a man did one thing because he wanted something else.

So far we have been dealing only with cases in which a question about a motive was answered by specifying something aimed at or wanted. Now we should turn to the cases in which the motive is said to be kindness, vanity, ambition, meanness, jealousy, and so on, to see whether determinism is involved.

It is easy to show that a motive is not a cause in Russell's sense, for it is clearly not an antecedent cause. Professor Gilbert Ryle has pointed out that a man who acts out of vanity is not a man who had a feeling of vanity immediately before he acted, and if it is objected that the vanity which preceded the action need not have manifested itself in a feeling, one may ask what else *would* count as the vanity which was causing him to act. A man's motives are not given by what was happening to him immediately before he started to act. Nor do we discover some independent condition contemporaneous with the action and a law linking the two, for again there is nothing which would count as vanity except the tendency to do this kind of thing.

So much is implied in what Ryle says about acting out of vanity, but his own account of what it is to do so still uses something which is objectionably like a causal model. The analogy which he thinks apt is that between saying a man acted out of vanity and saying a piece of glass broke because it was brittle: "To explain an act as done from a certain motive is not analogous to saying that the glass broke because a stone hit it, but to the quite different type of statement that the glass broke, when the stone hit it, because the glass was brittle."[10] The positive part of this statement seems to me mistaken. Acting out of vanity is not so closely connected with being vain as Ryle must suppose it to be. Let us suppose that his account of what it is to be vain is entirely correct; to say that a man is vain is to say that he tends to behave in certain ways, to feel aggrieved in particular situations, and so on.[11] It does not follow that ascribing vanity as a motive for an action is bringing this action under the "lawlike" proposition that the agent is a man who tends to do these things. For it makes sense to say that a man acts out of vanity on a particular occasion although he is not in general vain, or even vain about this kind of thing. It cannot therefore be true that when we speak of an agent's motive for a particular action we are explaining it in terms of his character, as Ryle suggests; we are not saying "he *would* do that." It is of course possible to give a motive *and* to say that the agent has the character trait concerned, but the latter cannot be included in an account of what it is to assign a motive to a particular action.

The explanation of why Ryle says what he does seems to lie in the fact

---

[10] *Concept of Mind* (London, 1949), pp. 86–87.
[11] *Ibid.*, p. 86.

that he has taken a false example of explaining an action by giving a motive. He considers as his example the explanation, "He boasted because he is vain," which is not in fact an explanation of the right type; considered as a statement assigning a motive to a particular action it would be uninformative, for except in very special cases *boasting is* acting out of vanity. It is not surprising that this particular sentence has a different function—that of relating this act of vanity to the character trait. What Ryle says about the example is correct, but it is not an example of the kind of thing he is trying to describe.

It might seem as if we could reformulate the theory to meet the objection about the man who acts out of vanity on one occasion by saying that a man's acting out of vanity is like glass breaking because of a brittleness which could be temporary. "He acted out of vanity" would then be explained as meaning that at that particular time he tended to react in the ways described by Ryle. (If he finds a chance of securing the admiration and envy of others, he does whatever he thinks will produce this admiration and envy.) This is wrong because, whereas glass which is even temporarily brittle has all the reactions which go by this name, a man who is temporarily acting out of vanity is not liable to do other things of this kind. To find concepts which this model would fit one must turn to such descriptions as "a boastful mood," "a savage frame of mind," or "a fit of bad temper."

Assigning a motive to an action is not bringing it under any law; it is rather saying something about the kind of action it was, the direction in which it was tending, or what it was done *as*. A possible comparison would be with the explanation of a movement in a dance which consisted in saying what was being danced. Often in diagnosing motives we should look to purposes—to what the action was done for. This we should discover if we found out what the agent was prepared to go without and what he insisted on having; the fact that visitors are made to admire a garden even in the rain is strong evidence that they were invited out of vanity rather than kindness. In other cases finding the motive will be better described as finding what was being done—finding, for instance, that someone was *taking revenge*. We should take it that a man's motive was revenge if we discovered that he was intentionally harming someone and that his doing so was conditional on his believing that that person had injured him. In the same way we should take it that someone was acting out of gratitude if he (1) intended to confer a benefit and (2) saw this as called for by a past kindness. The fact that it is only the character of the particular action which is involved shows how far we are from anything which could involve motives as determining causes.

We have now considered two suggestions: (1) that an undetermined action would not be one which could properly be attributed to an agent as something that he *did* and (2) that an undetermined action would not be the action of a *rational* agent. A third version, the one put forward by Hume, suggests that an undetermined action would be one for which it would be impossible to praise or blame, punish or reward a man, because it would be connected with nothing permanent in his nature.

> 'Tis only [Hume says] upon the principles of necessity, that a person acquires any merit or demerit from his actions. . . . Actions are by their very nature temporary and perishing; and where they proceed not from some cause in the characters and disposition of the person, who perform'd them, they infix not themselves upon him, and can neither redound to his honour, if good, nor infamy, if evil. The action in itself may be blameable. . . . But the person is not responsible for it; and as it proceeded from nothing in him, that is durable and constant, and leaves nothing of that nature behind it, 'tis impossible he can, upon its account, become the object of punishment or vengeance.[12]

Hume is surely wrong in saying that we could not praise or blame, punish or reward, a person in whose character there was nothing "permanent or durable." As he was the first to point out, we do not need any *unchanging* element in order to say that a person is the same person throughout a period of time, and our concept of merit is framed to fit our concept of personal identity. We honor people as well as nations for what they have done in the past and do not consider what has been done merely as an indication of what may be expected in the future. Moreover, it is perfectly rational to punish people for what they have done, even if there is no reason to think that they would be likely to do it again. The argument that it will be a different *me* who will be beaten tomorrow carries no weight, for "different" or not the back which will be beaten is the one about which I am concerned today. So we have no reason to invent something durable and constant underlying the actions which we punish or reward. And it is not in fact our practice to pick out for praise or blame only those actions for which something of the kind can be found. It would be possible, of course, that we should do this, punishing the cruel action of the cruel man but not that of one usually kind. But even in such a situation there would be no argument against the man who said that moral responsibility depended upon indeterminism; for a motive is not a determining cause, nor is an habitual motive. If we say that a man constantly acts out of cruelty, we no more say that his actions are determined than if we say that he acts out of cruelty on a particular occasion. There could of course be a law to the effect that no one who has been cruel for thirty years can turn to kindness after that, and this would throw responsibility back from the later to the earlier acts. But it is clear that this is a special assumption in no way involved in the statement that cruelty is a "durable and constant" element in someone's character.

I have already mentioned Ayer's argument that moral responsibility cannot be defended on the basis of indeterminism and will now consider his version in detail. Ayer says that the absence of a cause will not give the moralist what he wants, because "if it is a matter of pure chance that a man

---

[12] *Treatise*, bk. II, pt. III, sec. 2.

should act in one way rather than another, he may be free but he can hardly be responsible."[13] To the suggestion that "my actions are the result of my own free choice," Ayer will reply with a question about how I came to make my choice:

> Either it is an accident that I choose to act as I do or it is not. If it is an accident, then it is merely a matter of chance that I did not choose otherwise; and if it is merely a matter of chance that I did not choose otherwise, it is surely irrational to hold me morally responsible for choosing as I did. But if it is not an accident that I chose to do one thing rather than another, then presumably there is some causal explanation of my choice: and in that case we are led back to determinism.[14]

The "presumably" seems to be the weak link in the argument, which assumes a straightforward opposition between causality and chance that does not in general exist. It is not at all clear that when actions or choices are called "chance" or "accidental" this has anything to do with the absence of causes, and if it has not we will not be saying that they are in the ordinary sense a matter of chance if we say that they are undetermined.

When should we say that it was a matter of chance that a man did what he did? A typical example would be the case in which a man killed someone with a bullet which glanced off some object in a totally unforeseeable way; here he could disclaim responsibility for the act. But in this instance, and that of something done "by accident," we are dealing with what is done unintentionally, and this is not the case which Ayer has in mind. We may turn, as he does, to the actions which could be said to have been "chosen" and ask how the words "chance" and "accident" apply to choices. Ayer says, "Either it is an accident that I choose to act as I do, or it is not." The notion of choosing by accident to do something is on the face of it puzzling; for usually choosing to do something is opposed to doing it by accident. What does it mean to say that the choice itself was accidental? The only application I can think of for the words "I chose by accident" is in a case such as the following. I choose a firm with which to have dealings without meaning to pick on one run by an international crook. I can now rebut the charge of *choosing a firm run by an international crook* by saying that I chose it by accident. I cannot be held responsible for this but only for any carelessness which may have been involved. But this is because the relevant action—the one with which I am being charged—was unintentional; it is for this reason and not because my action was uncaused that I can rebut the charge. Nothing is said about my action being uncaused, and if it were, this could not be argued on my behalf; the absence of causes would not give me the same right to make the excuse.

Nor does it make any difference if we substitute "chance" for "accident."

If I say that it was a matter of chance that I chose to do something, I rebut the suggestion that I chose it for this reason or for that, and this can be a plea against an accusation which has to do with my reasons. But I do not imply that there was no reason for my doing what I did, and I say nothing whatsoever about my choice being undetermined. If we use "chance" and "accident" as Ayer wants to use them, to signify the absence of causes, we shall have moved over to a totally different sense of the words, and "I chose it by chance" can no longer be used to disclaim responsibility.

45 Determinism, Crime and Punishment*

CLARENCE DARROW

Clarence Darrow (1857–1938) was a famous lawyer who defended the biology teacher John T. Scopes in the famous "monkey trial" in Tennessee. A strong believer in determinism, Darrow argued that human beings are not morally responsible for their actions. He is the author of *Crime, Its Cause and Treatment; Infidels and Heretics;* and *Resist Not Evil.*

That man is the product of heredity and environment and that he acts as his machine responds to outside stimuli and nothing else, seem amply proven by the evolution and history of man. But, quite aside from this, logic and philosophy must lead to the same conclusions. This is not a universe where acts result from chance. Law is everywhere supreme. Every process of nature and life is a continuous sequence of cause and effect. No intelligent person would ever think of an effect in the physical world which did not follow a cause or causes. It has taken man a long time to find this out. The recurrence of the seasons, the seed-time and harvest, the common phenomena of Nature, were once supposed to be outside the realm of cause and effect and due to the whim of some powerful being. But the laws of matter are now coming to be understood. Chance, accident and whim have been banished from the physical world. The acts of men alone are supposed to be outside the realm of law. There is a cause for the eternal revolution of the earth around the sun, for the succession of seed-time and harvest, for growth and decay; but not for the thoughts and actions of man.

All the teaching of the world is based on the theory that there is no free will. Why else should children be trained with so much care? Why should they be taught what is right and what is wrong? Why should so much pains be taken in forming habits? To what effect is the storing of knowledge in the brain of the child, except that it may be taught to avoid the wrong and to do the right? Man's every action is caused by motive. Whether his action is wise or unwise, the motive was at least strong enough to move him. If two or more motives pulled in opposite directions, he could not have acted from the weakest but must have obeyed the strongest. The same motives applied to some other machine might have produced an opposite result, but to his particular structure it was all-controlling. How any special motive will affect any special machine must depend upon the relative strength of the motive and make of the machine. It is for this reason that intelligent people have always taken so much pains to fortify the machine, so that it would respond to what they believed was right. To say that one could ever act from the weakest motive would bring chaos and chance into a world of method and order. Even punishment could have no possible effect to deter the criminal after release, or to influence others by the example of the punishment. As well might the kernel of corn refuse to grow upward to the sunlight, and grow downward instead.

Before any progress can be made in dealing with crime the world must fully realize that crime is only a part of conduct; that each act, criminal or otherwise, follows a cause; that given the same conditions the same result will follow forever and ever; that all punishment for the purpose of causing suffering, or growing out of hatred, is cruel and anti-social; that however much society may feel the need of confining the criminal, it must first of all understand that the act had an all-sufficient cause for which the individual was in no way responsible, and must find the cause of his conduct, and, so far as possible, remove the cause.

46 Freedom, Psychoanalysis and Moral Responsibility*

JOHN HOSPERS

John Hospers (1918–   ) has taught philosophy at Brooklyn College, Columbia University, The University of Minnesota, and is presently director of the School of Philosophy at the University of Southern California. The author of many philosophical articles, Hospers' principal books include *Introduction to Philosophical Analysis, Human Conduct, Meaning and Truth in the Arts,* and *Readings in Ethical Theory* (with W. Sellars).

As a preparation for developing my own views on the subject, I want to mention a factor that I think is of enormous importance and relevance: namely, unconscious motivation. There are many actions—not those of an insane person (however the term "insane" be defined), nor of a person ignorant of the effects of his action, nor ignorant of some relevant fact about the situation, nor in any obvious way mentally deranged—for which human beings in general and the courts in particular are inclined to hold the doer responsible, and for which, I would say, he should not be held responsible. The deed may be planned, it may be carried out in cold calculation, it may spring from the agent's character and be continuous with the rest of his behavior, and it may be perfectly true that he could have done differently *if* he had wanted to; nonetheless his behavior was brought about by unconscious conflicts developed in infancy, over which he had no control and of which (without training in psychiatry) he does not even have knowledge. He may even *think* he knows why he acted as he did, he may *think* he has conscious control over his actions, he may even *think* he is fully responsible for them; but he is not. Psychiatric casebooks provide hundreds of examples. The law and common sense, though puzzled sometimes by such cases, are gradually becoming aware that they exist; but at this early stage countless tragic blunders still occur because neither the law nor the public in general is aware of the genesis of criminal actions. The mother blames her daughter for choosing the wrong men as candidates for husbands; but though the daughter thinks she is choosing freely and spends

* Reprinted by permission of New York University Press, from *Determinism and Freedom in the Age of Modern Science,* edited by Sidney Hook. © by New York University. (Title by editor).

a considerable amount of time "deciding" among them, the identification with her sick father, resulting from Oedipal fantasies in early childhood, prevents her from caring for any but sick men, twenty or thirty years older than herself. Blaming her is beside the point; she cannot help it, and she cannot change it. Countless criminal acts are thought out in great detail; yet the participants are (without their own knowledge) acting out fantasies, fears, and defenses from early childhood, over whose coming and going they have no conscious control.

Now, I am not saying that none of these persons should be in jails or asylums. Often society must be protected against them. Nor am I saying that people should cease the practices of blaming and praising, punishing and rewarding; in general these devices are justified by the results—although very often they have practically no effect; the deeds are done from inner compulsion, which is not lessened when the threat of punishment is great. I am only saying that frequently persons we think responsible are not properly to be called so; we mistakenly think them responsible because we assume they are like those in whom no unconscious drive (toward this type of behavior) is present, and that their behavior can be changed by reasoning, exhorting, or threatening.

I

I have said that these persons are not responsible. But what is the criterion for responsibility? Under precisely what conditions is a person to be held morally responsible for an action? Disregarding here those conditions that have to do with a person's *ignorance* of the situation or the effects of his action, let us concentrate on those having to do with his "inner state." There are several criteria that might be suggested:

1. The first idea that comes to mind is that responsibility is determined by the presence or absence of *premeditation*—the opposite of "premeditated" being, presumably, "unthinking" or "impulsive." But this will not do—both because some acts are not premeditated but responsible, and because some are premeditated and not responsible.

Many acts we call responsible can be as unthinking or impulsive as you please. If you rush across the street to help the victim of an automobile collision, you are (at least so we would ordinarily say) acting responsibly, but you did not do so out of premeditation; you saw the accident, you didn't think, you rushed to the scene without hesitation. It was like a reflex action. But you acted responsibly: unlike the knee jerk, the act was the result of past training and past thought about situations of this kind; that is why you ran to help instead of ignoring the incident or running away. When something done originally from conviction or training becomes habitual, it becomes *like* a reflex action. As Aristotle said, virtue should become second nature through habit: a virtuous act should be performed *as if* by instinct; this, far from detracting from its moral worth, testifies to one's mastery of the desired type of behavior; one does not have to make a moral effort each time it is repeated.

There are also premeditated acts for which, I would say, the person is not responsible. Premeditation, especially when it is so exaggerated as to issue in no action at all, can be the result of neurotic disturbance or what we sometimes call an emotional "block," which the person inherits from long-past situations. In Hamlet's revenge on his uncle (I use this example because it is familiar to all of us), there was no lack, but rather a surfeit, of pre-meditation; his actions were so exquisitely premeditated as to make Freud and Dr. Ernest Jones look more closely to find out what lay behind them. The very premeditation camouflaged unconscious motives of which Hamlet him-self was not aware. I think this is an important point, since it seems that the courts often assume that premeditation is a criterion of responsibility. If failure to kill his uncle had been considered a crime, every court in the land would have convicted Hamlet. Again: a woman's decision to stay with her husband in spite of endless "mental cruelty" is, if she is the victim of an unconscious masochistic "will to punishment," one for which she is not responsible; she is the victim and not the agent, no matter how profound her conviction that she is the agent; she is caught in a masochistic web (of complicated genesis) dating back to babyhood, perhaps a repetition of a comparable situation involving her own parents, a repetition-compulsion that, as Freud said, goes "beyond the pleasure principle." Again: a criminal whose crime was carefully planned step by step is usually considered responsible, but as we shall see in later examples, the overwhelming impulse toward it, stemming from an unusually humiliating ego defeat in early childhood, was as compulsive as any can be.

2. Shall we say, then, that a person is not responsible for his act unless he can *defend it with reasons?* I am afraid that this criterion is no better than the previous one. First, intellectuals are usually better at giving reasons than nonintellectuals, and according to this criterion would be more respon-sible than persons acting from moral conviction not implemented by reason-ing; yet it is very doubtful whether we should want to say that the latter are the more responsible. Second, the giving of reasons itself may be suspect. The reasons may be rationalizations camouflaging unconscious motives of which the agent knows nothing. Hamlet gave many reasons for not doing what he felt it was his duty to do: the time was not right, his uncle's soul might go to heaven, etc. His various "reasons" contradicted one another, and if an overpowering compulsion had not been present, the highly intellectual Hamlet would not have been taken in for a moment by these rationalizations. The real reason, the Oedipal conflict that made his uncle's crime the accom-plishment of his own deepest desire, binding their fates into one and paralyzing him into inaction, was unconscious and of course unknown to him. One's intelligence and reasoning power do not enable one to escape from unconsciously motivated behavior; it only gives one greater facility in

rationalizing that behavior; one's intelligence is simply used in the interests of the neurosis—it is pressed into service to justify with reasons what one does quite independently of the reasons.

If these two criteria are inadequate, let us seek others.

3. Shall we say that a person is responsible for his action unless it is the *result of unconscious* forces of which he knows nothing? Many psychoanalysts would probably accept this criterion. If it is not largely reflected in the language of responsibility as ordinarily used, this may be due to ignorance of fact: most people do not know that there are such things as unconscious motives and unconscious conflicts causing human beings to act. But it may be that if they did, perhaps they would refrain from holding persons responsible for certain actions.

I do not wish here to quarrel with this criterion of responsibility. I only want to point out the fact that if this criterion is employed a far greater number of actions will be excluded from the domain of responsibility than we might at first suppose. Whether we are neat or untidy, whether we are selfish or unselfish, whether we provoke scenes or avoid them, even whether we can exert our powers of will to change our behavior—all these may, and often do, have their source in our unconscious life.

4. Shall we say that a person is responsible for his act unless it is *compelled?* Here we are reminded of Aristotle's assertion (*Nicomachean Ethics,* Book III) that a person is responsible for his act except for reasons of either ignorance or compulsion. Ignorance is not part of our problem here (unless it is unconsciously induced ignorance of facts previously remembered and selectively forgotten—in which case the forgetting is again compulsive), but compulsion is. How will compulsion do as a criterion? The difficulty is to state just what it means. When we say an act is compelled in a psychological sense, our language is metaphorical—which is not to say that there is no point in it or that, properly interpreted, it is not true. Our actions are compelled in a literal sense if someone has us in chains or is controlling our bodily movements. When we say that the storm compelled us to jettison the cargo of the ship (Aristotle's example), we have a less literal sense of compulsion, for at least it is open to us to go down with the ship. When psychoanalysts say that a man was compelled by unconscious conflicts to wash his hands constantly, this is also not a literal use of "compel"; for nobody forced his hands under the tap. Still, it is a typical example of what psychologists call *compulsive* behavior: it has unconscious causes inaccessible to introspection, and moreover nothing can change it—it is as inevitable for him to do it as it would be if someone were forcing his hands under the tap. In this it is exactly like the action of a powerful external force; it is just as little within one's conscious control.

In its area of application this interpretation of responsibility comes to much the same as the previous one. And this area is very great indeed. For if we cannot be held responsible for the infantile situations (in which we were after all passive victims), then neither, it would seem, can we be held responsible for compulsive actions occurring in adulthood that are inevitable consequences of those infantile situations. And, psychiatrists and psycho-analysts tell us, actions fulfilling this description are characteristic of all people some of the time and some people most of the time. Their occur-rence, once the infantile events have taken place, is inevitable, just as the explosion is inevitable once the fuse has been lighted; there is simply more "delayed action" in the psychological explosions than there is in the physical ones.

(I have not used the word "inevitable" here to mean "causally deter-mined," for according to such a definition every event would be inevitable if one accepted the causal principle in some form or other; and probably nobody except certain philosophers uses "inevitable" in this sense. Rather, I use "inevitable" in its ordinary sense of "cannot be avoided." To the extent, therefore, that adult neurotic manifestations *can* be avoided, once the in-fantile patterns have become set, the assertion that they are inevitable is not true.)

5. There is still another criterion, which I prefer to the previous ones, by which a man's responsibility for an act can be measured: the degree to which that act can (or could have been) *changed by the use of reasons*. Suppose that the man who washes his hands constantly does so, he says, for hygienic reasons, believing that if he doesn't do so he will be poisoned by germs. We now convince him, on the best medical authority, that his belief is ground-less. Now, the test of his responsibility is whether the changed belief will result in changed behavior. If it does not, as with the compulsive hand washer, he is not acting responsibly, but if it does, he is. It is not the *use* of reasons, but their *efficacy in changing behavior*, that is being made the criterion of responsibility. And clearly in neurotic cases no such change occurs; in fact, this is often made the defining characteristic of neurotic behavior: it is un-changeable by any rational considerations.

II

I have suggested these criteria to distinguish actions for which we can call the agent responsible from those for which we cannot. Even persons with extensive knowledge of psychiatry do not, I think, use any one of these criteria to the exclusion of the others; a conjunction of two or more may be used at once. But however they may be combined or selected in actual application, I believe we can make the distinction along some such lines as we have suggested.

But is there not still another possible meaning of "responsibility" that we have not yet mentioned? Even after we have made all the above distinctions, there remains a question in our minds whether we are, in the final analysis, *responsible for any of our actions at all*. The issue may be put this way: How can anyone be responsible for his actions, since they grow out of his character, which is shaped and molded and made what it is by influences—some hereditary, but most of them stemming from early parental environment—that were not of his own making or choosing? This question, I believe, still troubles many people who would agree to all the distinctions we have just made but still have the feeling that "this isn't all." They have the uneasy suspicion that there is a more ultimate sense, a "deeper" sense, in which we are *not* responsible for our actions, since we are not responsible for the character out of which those actions spring. This, of course, is the sense Professor Edwards was describing.

Let us take as an example a criminal who, let us say, strangled several persons and is himself now condemned to die in the electric chair. Jury and public alike hold him fully responsible (at least they utter the words "he is responsible"), for the murders were planned down to the minutest detail, and the defendant tells the jury exactly how he planned them. But now we find out how it all came about; we learn of parents who rejected him from babyhood, of the childhood spent in one foster home after another, where it was always plain to him that he was not wanted; of the constantly frustrated early desire for affection, the hard shell of nonchalance and bitterness that he assumed to cover the painful and humiliating fact of being unwanted, and his subsequent attempts to heal these wounds to his shattered ego through defensive aggression.

> The criminal is the most passive person in this world, helpless as a baby in his motorically inexpressible fury. Not only does he try to wreak revenge on the mother of the earliest period of his babyhood; his criminality is based on the inner feeling of being incapable of making the mother even feel that the child seeks revenge on her. The situation is that of a dwarf trying to annoy a giant who superciliously refuses to see these attempts. . . . Because of his inner feeling of being a dwarf, the criminotic uses, so to speak, dynamite. Of that the giant must take cognizance. True, the "revenge" harms the avenger. He may be legally executed. However, the primary inner aim of forcing the giant to acknowledge the dwarf's fury is fulfilled.[1]

The poor victim is not conscious of the inner forces that exact from him this ghastly toll; he battles, he schemes, he revels in pseudo-aggression, he is miserable, but he does not know what works within him to produce these catastrophic acts of crime. His aggressive actions are the wriggling of a worm on a fisherman's hook. And if this is so, it seems difficult to say any longer, "He is responsible." Rather, we shall put him behind bars for the protection of society, but we shall no longer flatter our feeling of moral superiority by calling him personally responsible for what he did.

Let us suppose it were established that a man commits murder only if, sometime during the previous week, he has eaten a certain combination of foods—say, tuna fish salad at a meal also including peas, mushroom soup,

---

[1] Edmund Bergler, *The Basic Neurosis* (New York: Grune and Stratton, 1949), p. 305.

and blueberry pie. What if we were to track down the factors common to all murders committed in this country during the last twenty years and found this factor present in all of them, and only in them? The example is of course empirically absurd; but may it not be that there is *some* combination of factors that regularly leads to homicide, factors such as are described in general terms in the above quotation? (Indeed the situation in the quotation is less fortunate than in our hypothetical example, for it is easy to avoid certain foods once we have been warned about them, but the situation of the infant is thrust on him; something has already happened to him once and for all, before he knows it has happened.) When such specific factors are discovered, won't they make it clear that it is foolish and pointless, as well as immoral, to hold human beings responsible for crimes? Or, if one prefers biological to psychological factors, suppose a neurologist is called in to testify at a murder trial and produces X-ray pictures of the brain of the criminal; anyone can see, he argues, that the *cella turcica* was already calcified at the age of nineteen; it should be a flexible bone, growing, enabling the gland to grow.[2] All the defendant's disorders might have resulted from this early calcification. Now, this particular explanation may be empirically false; but who can say that no such factors, far more complex, to be sure, exist?

When we know such things as these, we no longer feel so much tempted to say that the criminal is responsible for his crime; and we tend also (do we not?) to excuse him—not legally (we still confine him to prison) but morally; we no longer call him a monster or hold him personally responsible for what he did. Morever, we do this in general, not merely in the case of crime: "You must excuse Grandmother for being irritable; she's really quite ill and is suffering some pain all the time." Or: "The dog always bites children after she's had a litter of pups; you can't blame her for it: she's not feeling well, and besides she naturally wants to defend them." Or: "She's nervous and jumpy, but do excuse her: she has a severe glandular disturbance."

Let us note that the more *thoroughly* and *in detail* we know the causal factors leading a person to behave as he does, the more we tend to exempt him from responsibility. When we know nothing of the man except what we see him do, we say he is an ungrateful cad who expects much of other people and does nothing in return, and we are usually indignant. When we learn that his parents were the same way and, having no guilt feelings about this mode of behavior themselves, brought him up to be greedy and avaricious, we see that we could hardly expect him to have developed moral feelings in this direction. When we learn, in addition, that he is not aware of being ungrateful or selfish, but unconsciously represses the memory of events unfavorable to himself, we feel that the situation is unfortunate but "not really his fault." When we know that this behavior of his, which makes others angry, occurs more constantly when he feels tense or insecure, and that he

---

[2] Meyer Levin, *Compulsion* (New York: Simon and Schuster, 1956), p. 403.

now feels tense and insecure, and that relief from pressure will diminish it, then we tend to "feel sorry for the poor guy" and say he's more to be pitied than censured. We no longer want to say that he is personally responsible; we might rather blame nature or his parents for having given him an unfortunate constitution or temperament.

> In recent years a new form of punishment has been imposed on middle-aged and elderly parents. Their children, now in their twenties, thirties or even forties, present them with a modern grievance: "My analysis proves that *you* are responsible for my neurosis." Overawed by these authoritative statements, the poor tired parents fall easy victims to the newest variations on the scape-goat theory.
>
> In my opinion, this senseless cruelty—which disinters educational sins which had been burned for decades, and uses them as the basis for accusations which the victims cannot answer—is unjustified. Yes "the truth loves to be centrally located" (Melville), and few parents—since they are human—have been perfect. But granting their mistakes, they acted as *their* neurotic difficulties forced them to act. To turn the tables and declare the children not guilty because of the *impersonal* nature of their own neuroses, while at the same time the parents are *personally* blamed, is worse than illogical; it is profoundly unjust.[3]

And so, it would now appear, neither of the parties is responsible: "they acted as their neurotic difficulties forced them to act." The patients are not responsible for their neurotic manifestations, but then neither are the parents responsible for theirs; and so, of course, for their parents in turn, and theirs before them. It is the twentieth-century version of the family curse, the curse on the House of Atreus.

"But," a critic complains, "it's immoral to exonerate people indiscriminately in this way. I might have thought it fit to excuse somebody because he was born on the other side of the tracks, if I didn't know so many bank presidents who were also born on the other side of the tracks." Now, I submit that the most immoral thing in this situation is the critic's caricature of the conditions of the excuse. Nobody is excused merely because he was born on the other side of the tracks. But if he was born on the other side of the tracks *and* was a highly narcissistic infant to begin with *and* was repudiated or neglected by his parents *and* . . . (here we list a finite number of conditions), and if this complex of factors is *regularly* followed by certain behavior traits in adulthood, and moreover *unavoidably* so—that is, they occur no matter what he or anyone else tries to do—then we excuse him morally and say he is not responsible for his deed. If he is not responsible for A, a series of events occurring in his babyhood, then neither is he responsible for B, a series of things he does in adulthood, provided that B inevitably—that is, unavoidably—follows upon the occurrence of A. And according to psychiatrists and psychoanalysts, this often happens.

---

[3] Edmund Bergler, *The Superego* (New York: Grune and Stratton, 1952), p. 320.

But one may still object that so far we have talked only about neurotic behavior. Isn't nonneurotic or normal or not unconsciously motivated (or whatever you want to call it) behavior still within the area of responsibility? There are reasons for answering "No" even here, for the normal person no more than the neurotic one has caused his own character, which makes him what he is. Granted that neurotics are not responsible for their behavior (that part of it which we call neurotic) because it stems from undigested infantile conflicts that they had no part in bringing about, and that are external to them just as surely as if their behavior had been forced on them by a malevolent deity (which is indeed one theory on the subject); but the so-called normal person is equally the product of causes in which his volition took no part. And if, unlike the neurotic's, his behavior is changeable by rational considerations, and if he has the will power to overcome the effects of an unfortunate early environment, this again is no credit to him; he is just lucky. If energy is available to him in a form in which it can be mobilized for constructive purposes, this is no credit to him, for this too is part of his psychic legacy. Those of us who can discipline ourselves and develop habits of concentration of purpose tend to blame those who cannot, and call them lazy and weak-willed; but what we fail to see is that they literally *cannot* do what we expect; if their psyches were structured like ours, they could, but as they are burdened with a tyrannical super-ego (to use psychoanalytic jargon for the moment), and a weak defenseless ego whose energies are constantly consumed in fighting endless charges of the superego, they simply cannot do it, and it is irrational to expect it of them. We cannot with justification blame them for their inability, any more than we can congratulate ourselves for our ability. This lesson is hard to learn, for we constantly and naïvely assume that other people are constructed as we ourselves are.

For example: A child raised under slum conditions, whose parents are socially ambitious and envy families with money, but who nevertheless squander the little they have on drink, may simply be unable in later life to mobilize a drive sufficient to overcome these early conditions. Common sense would expect that he would develop the virtue of thrift; he would make quite sure that he would never again endure the grinding poverty he had experienced as a child. But in fact it is not so: the exact conditions are too complex to be specified in detail here, but when certain conditions are fulfilled (concerning the subject's early life), he will always thereafter be a spendthrift, and no rational considerations will be able to change this. He will listen to the rational considerations and see the force of these, but they will not be able to change him, even if he tries; he cannot change his wasteful habits any more than he can lift the Empire State Building with his bare hands. We moralize and plead with him to be thrifty, but we do not see how strong, how utterly overpowering, and how constantly with him, is the opposite drive, which is so easily manageable with us. But he is possessed by the all-consuming, all-encompassing urge to make the world see that he belongs, that he has arrived, that he is just as well off as anyone else, that the awful humiliations were not real, that they never actually occurred, for isn't he now able to spend and spend? The humiliation must be blotted out; and conspicuous, fleshy, expensive, and wasteful buying will do this; it shows the world what the world must know! True, it is only for the moment; true, it is in the end self-defeating, for wasteful consumption is the best way to bring poverty back again; but the person with an overpowering drive to mend a lesion to his narcissism cannot resist the avalanche of that drive with his puny rational consideration. A man with his back against the wall and a gun at his throat doesn't think of what may happen ten years hence. (Consciously, of course, he knows nothing of this drive; all that appears to consciousness is its shattering effects; he knows only that he must keep on spending—not why—and that he is unable to resist.) He hasn't in him the psychic capacity, the energy to stem the tide of a drive that at that moment is all-powerful. We, seated comfortably away from this flood, sit in judgment on him and blame him and exhort him and criticize him; but he, carried along by the flood, cannot do otherwise than he does. He may fight with all the strength of which he is capable, but it is not enough. And we, who are rational enough at least to exonerate a man in a situation of "overpowering impulse" when we recognize it to be one, do not even recognize this as an example of it; and so, in addition to being swept away in the flood that childhood conditions rendered inevitable, he must also endure our lectures, our criticisms, and our moral excoriation.

But, one will say, he could have overcome his spendthrift tendencies; some people do. Quite true: some people do. They are lucky. They have it in them to overcome early deficiencies by exerting great effort, and they are capable of exerting the effort. Some of us, luckier still, can overcome them with but little effort; and a few, the luckiest, haven't the deficiencies to overcome. It's all a matter of luck. The least lucky are those who can't overcome them, even with great effort, and those who haven't the ability to exert the effort.

But, one persists, it isn't a matter simply of luck; it *is* a matter of effort. Very well then, it's a matter of effort; without exerting the effort you may not overcome the deficiency. But whether or not you are the kind of person who has it in him to exert the effort is a matter of luck.

All this is well known to psychoanalysts. They can predict, from minimal cues that most of us don't notice, whether a person is going to turn out to be lucky or not. "The analyst," they say, "must be able to use the residue of the patient's unconscious guilt so as to remove the symptom or character trait that creates the guilt. The guilt must not only be present, but *available* for use, *mobilizable*. If it is used up (absorbed) in criminal activity, or in an excessive amount of self-damaging tendencies, then it cannot be used for therapeutic purposes, and the prognosis is negative." Not all philosophers will relish the analyst's way of putting the matter, but at least as a physician he can soon detect whether the patient is lucky or unlucky—and he knows that whichever it is, it *isn't the patient's fault*. The patient's conscious volition cannot remedy the deficiency. Even whether he will co-operate with the analyst is really out of the patient's hands: if he continually projects the denying-mother fantasy on the analyst and unconsciously identifies him always with the cruel, harsh forbidder of the nursery, thus frustrating any attempt at impersonal observation, the sessions are useless; yet if it happens that way, he can't help that either. That fatal projection is not under his control; whether it occurs or not depends on how his unconscious identifications have developed since his infancy. He can try, yes—but the ability to try enough for the therapy to have effect is also beyond his control; the capacity to try more than just so much is either there or it isn't—and either way "it's in the lap of the gods."

The position, then, is this: if we *can* overcome the effects of early environment, the ability to do so is itself a product of the early environment. We did not give ourselves this ability; and if we lack it we cannot be blamed for not having it. Sometimes, to be sure, moral exhortation brings out an ability that is there but not being used, and in this lies its *occasional* utility; but very often its use is pointless, because the ability is not there. The only thing that can overcome a desire, as Spinoza said, is a stronger contrary desire; and many times there simply is no wherewithal for producing a stronger contrary desire. Those of us who do have the wherewithal are lucky.

There is one possible practical advantage in remembering this. It may prevent us (unless we are compulsive blamers) from indulging in righteous indignation and committing the sin of spiritual pride, thanking God that we are not as this publican here. And it will protect from our useless moralizings those who are least equipped by nature for enduring them. As with responsibility, so with deserts. Someone commits a crime and is punished by the state; "he deserved it," we say self-righteously—as if we were moral and he immoral, when in fact we are lucky and he is unlucky—forgetting that there, but for the grace of God and a fortunate early environment, go we. Or, as Clarence Darrow said in his speech for the defense in the Loeb-Leopold case:

> I do not believe that people are in jail because they deserve to be. . . . I know what causes the emotional life. . . . I know it is practically left out of some. Without it they cannot act with the rest. They cannot feel the moral shocks which safeguard others. Is [this man] to blame that his machine is imperfect? Who is to blame? I do not know. I have never in my life been interested so much in fixing blame as I have in relieving people from blame. I am not wise enough to fix it.[4]

[4] Levin, *op. cit.*, pp. 439–40, 469.

Chapter Six

THE PROBLEM
OF THE NATURE OF MAN:
MIND-BODY AND IMMORTALITY

The question "What is the nature of man?" is as old as man himself.
It arises quite naturally in a number of contexts when man reflects upon
himself. When a friend dies, one wonders if the *person* he loved and
knew so well is nothing but the inert body on the bed. Was his *personality*
nothing more than certain dispositions to act, set in motion by a
complicated nervous system? Or is there some part of a person—a mind
or soul—that survives death? When we are told that many persons who
had inadequate diets as babies are mentally retarded today as a result of
them, we wonder whether the physical components of man's nature
completely determine the mental. But we also observe that some persons
with strong "wills" and character seem able to overcome bodily ills,
whereas persons with little hope, desire, or will power do not. We
sometimes speak of this as "mind over matter."

Philosophers have given opposing answers to this question. Some
maintain that a man is nothing but his body; others, that he is much more.
He is also a mind or a soul. Plato in his *Phaedo* speaks of man's soul as
a simple, indestructible substance that survives death. Some Christian
and Hindu theologians and philosophers also affirm that man is immortal.
(Others go further, maintaining that even man's body is resurrected
after death.) Some, such as the Buddhists, deny a soul and yet believe
in reincarnation. But if man is more than his body, what is this "more"
and how is it related to man's body? Let us briefly characterize the
principal responses that have been proposed by philosophers across the
years.

DUALISTIC INTERACTIONISM

Dualistic interactionists maintain that man is comprised of two basically different substances, mind and body, and that these two substances interact. Man's actions are the result of a two-way causal street, the mind influencing the body and the body influencing the mind. This concept of the mind-body relationship seems to be the common-sense view. In our ordinary language, we do distinguish between physical and mental phenomena. Physical phenomena, such as chairs, tables, houses, bodies, and roads, are identified as occupying space and as being publicly observable. Mental phenomena—such as beliefs, thoughts, dreams, sensations, and feelings—do not occupy space in the same sense, nor are they publicly observable. We regard such phenomena as private, as "inner." To be sure, someone may *infer* what another's thoughts or feelings are from his behavior. If I strike a person with a club, one may properly infer that I am angry. If I smile, you may properly infer that I am pleased. But my anger and my pleasure are private experiences to which no one else has direct access.

The dualistic interactionist maintains that there are such fundamental differences between physical and mental substances, but he still insists that the two are somehow causally related. For it is plain that one's visual sensations depend on the state of one's eyes and of light waves; and one's ability to think quickly and perceptively is drastically impaired if one is physically tired, or very hungry, or under the influence of drugs. Poor health is sometimes caused by worry; and one's ability to resist disease, some argue, is partially dependent on one's psychological outlook. For a more dramatic example, we may point out that patients are sometimes anesthetized by hypnotism. On the other hand, our mental states affect our bodies: our bodies sometimes quiver when we are afraid; we oftentimes stutter when we are tense, blush when we are embarrassed, cry when we are unhappy, weep when in pain, and so on.

But how are we to think of this two-way causation? Descartes, the seventeenth century philosopher who is the example par excellence of a dualistic interactionist, was himself quite puzzled about how the mental and physical components of human nature were related. The essence of mind was seen as consciousness—nonphysical and nonspatial (which, he held, was able to exist without body). The essence of body was viewed as spatial and physical. How could a physical, spatial substance causally affect something totally unlike it, a nonphysical, nonspatial substance? How could thought, mind, or will—something which has no extension and does not occupy space—cause a material substance to move? It seemed inconceivable. Descartes finally responded to the question, apparently in desperation, by locating the seat of the mind-body interaction in the "pineal gland" at the base of the brain (a gland no one has ever been able to find). It was there that unextended mind and extended matter mysteriously met.

Of course, one does not have to accept Descartes' pineal gland solution or, for that matter, his account of mind and matter as substance in order to accept interactionism. Contemporary philosophers who are dualistic inter-actionists reject most of Descartes' account. But interactionists who reject Descartes' position must provide an alternative account of the mind-body relationship.

PARALLELISM

A number of different theories representing deviations from Descartes' position emerged after him. The philosopher Leibniz (1646–1716) set forth a view generally known as "parallelism," which denies that there are any causal relationships between mental states and bodies and between bodies and mental states. How does Leibniz explain the apparent effect of body on mind and vice versa? He maintains that there are universal correlations between mental and physical events. For example, visual perception or sensation is universally correlated with sense-organ stimulation. These correlations are not accidental, but neither are they causally related. They are the result of what Leibniz calls "preestablished harmony." God, the creator, devised the world so that mental and physical events, although unrelated causally, perfectly agree and are in accord with one another. Mind and body are to be seen as two separate clocks that function in unison as a result of God's harmonious plan. They only appear to be causally related.

Malebranche (1638–1715) adopted a position now known as "occasional-ism." He makes God much more active in the mind-body relation. On *each* occasion in which there is a correlation between a mental and physical event, God intervenes, producing the correlation. It is not simply the result of pre-established harmony. God is daily involved in the affairs of men by guaranteeing the interaction of mind and body through his will.

THE IDENTITY OR DOUBLE-ASPECT THEORY

Some philosophers (and psychologists) have explained the correlation between mental and physical events without invoking either interactionism or parallelism with preestablished harmony. Spinoza (1632–1677) held that physical and mental events are in the last analysis just two aspects of the same underlying reality. They are the same thing seen from different perspectives. Subjectively experienced, substance is seen as mind, thought, or idea. Objectively, or from the "outside," it is seen as body. This seems to be a rejection of dualism, of parallelism (if parallelism is defined as a two-substance doctrine), and of interactionism. For Spinoza, this one basic substance is God; but one can hold an identity, or double-aspect, theory without such a belief in God.

Some theorists have pressed the double-aspect view all the way to "pan-psychism," the thesis that not merely human beings but all animals—indeed every entity in the universe—has a mental as well as a physical aspect. Grains of sand and trees are not purely physical but have an "inner" aspect that is akin to (but not the same as) human consciousness. However, only the higher animals in nature, especially man, have a high level of consciousness and of self-reflection.

The identity, or double-aspect, theory does have the advantage of not having to explain mind-body interaction, for there are not two substances to interact. But interactionists find this theory unconvincing. Their response is simply that there are fundamental differences between mind and matter. Furthermore, to postulate an unknown, underlying substance of which mental and physical events are simply aspects does not explain anything. Nor is the implication of panpsychism considered to be a warranted belief. It may be true that the causal relationship between mind and matter is not adequately explained, the interactionist states, but that there is such a causal relationship is a fact.

EPIPHENOMENALISM

Philosophers dissatisfied with dualistic interactionism, parallelism, and the identity, or double-aspect, theory offer other explanations of the mind-body relation. One of these is epiphenomenalism, a theory proposed by Thomas Huxley that mental phenomena are caused by physical or brain processes but themselves are not causal agents. They do not affect the physical world but merely exist as a "shadow," or "by-product," of physical events, which are the only efficacious causes.

The epiphenomenalist seems to hold a materialist view of the world, for he insists that mind and consciousness exist only because body and brain exist. Mind is not an independent substance and cannot exist on its own. When one's body and brain decay, one's mental life totally ceases. Nothing remains. However, although mind or consciousness cannot exist without body or matter, and matter is the fundamental substance in this sense, the epiphenomenalist does not reduce mind to matter. Mind is different from matter or body, but it is a mere epiphenomenon.

In spite of this disclaimer of materialism, or of the reduction of mind to matter, some critics of epiphenomenalism maintain that this position is a thinly disguised materialism. If mind exists only because body exists, if the mind dies when the body and brain dies, if only physical and not mental events are causal agents and all behavior can be explained on a mechanistic model, is not this really straightforward materialism? Even if the answer to this question is no, critics of epiphenomenalism insist that this theory is inadequate. For it denies a blatant truth, namely, that man's mental life, his thoughts, ideas, and consciousness cause tremendous changes in his life and in the physical world. If we are to take epiphenomenalism seriously, we must suppose that everything that has happened in human and natural history would have happened just as it did even if no mind, thought, or consciousness (mere epiphenomena, or by-products, of matter) existed. But, the critics argue, this is completely *absurd*.

Thus, although epiphenomenalism escapes the difficulties of the interactionists, opponents of the doctrine argue that it does this at the cost of denying the most obvious facts of our experience and leaves unexplained the peculiar mode of causation by which body or brain processes produce or cause mental or conscious epiphenomena.

MATERIALISM

If epiphenomenalism is not a purely materialistic account of mind, what constitutes such an account? I suppose it would be a theory that maintained not only that body or matter is the only substance but that mind does not even have the shadow, or by-product, kind of existence claimed by the epiphenomenalist. Mind is nothing but body or matter, consciousness is nothing but brain processes or behavior, and all mental predicates are translatable into purely physical ones. Sensations and thoughts may seem to be substantially different from skin and brains, but they are not; they are only bodily processes.

Several developments are responsible for the purely materialistic theory of mind. For several centuries scientists have theorized about the possibility of a unified science. From Descartes to the present day the possibility of a mathematical-mechanical explanation of all phenomena via certain basic physical laws and principles has held great attraction. As the particular sciences have developed, this notion of a unified physical explanation of all phenomena, including the mental, has become more pervasive. For example, some (*not* all) behaviorists in psychology identify all mental states and processes with behavioral dispositions or occurrences. Man is simply a physical body; and to say that he is thinking, feeling, sensing, and so on, is just to say that some physical operation, dispositional (a *tendency* to act in a certain way), or occurrent (an actual act or process) exists. It may seem queer to substitute "I can't make up my mind" with "I can't make up my brain," but some argue that once one understands that the former sentence merely refers to a state of the brain or nervous system, then the apparent conceptual oddity is laid to rest. Some behaviorists would deny that these two sentences are logically identical. Even though mental predicates such as thought, feeling, and sensation are not identical in meaning or synonymous with terms that designate physical states or processes, the *referential* meaning of these predicates, they declare, seems to be reducible simply to a physical referent. The selections by Skinner and Ryle in this chapter represent a form of behaviorism.

Advances in physiology have contributed to this materialist model of mind. We now know much more about the brain and the nervous system than ever before. Through careful observation and experimentation, we now know generally which parts of the brain control various functions of human consciousness—emotion, memory, and so on. Such experimentation lends credence to the view that a direct and constant correlation exists between various brain processes and various states of consciousness. Some infer from such correlations that the various states of consciousness are *nothing but* those brain processes (although this does not necessarily follow from the fact that such correlations exist). Furthermore, the recent development of computers and computer science seems to support a materialist-mechanical concept of mind. Computers, as complex engineering achievements, take in data or stimuli and put out answers or responses. In this sense they are like the human mind. If computers can be explained on a purely physical model, can not the human mind?

The materialist account of mind has also received great support from the near-universal adoption of the scientific method, and especially the criterion of intersubjective testability. Scientists who try to formulate a psychology based on *introspection*, that is, the observation and reporting of mental states and events by the private owners of those states, are now few in number. This method, it is argued, precludes by definition any "reliable" (intersubjective) test of such introspective reports. The verifiability criterion of meaning (see Chapter Seven) further enforces the behaviorist account of mind, for if the meaning of a statement is the empirical evidence that supports it, and if the only evidence for mental-state claims is some kind of human behavior, then it follows that the meaning of such claims is that behavior.

There are difficulties with the behaviorist and physiological accounts of mind. Physiology and psychology are still very young sciences. Not all of the data are in. Only some correlations of brain processes and mental states have been shown by physiologists, and behaviorists in psychology have not been able to offer viable dispositional analyses of some mental phenomena— images, for example. Still, this analysis of mind and mental predicates is very prominent today. Many think it is the most promising account or explanation. Dualistic interactionism, however, is by no means a dead alternative. Contemporary interactionists continue to stress what they take to be directly and empirically known—that mental states are different from body states. Although they agree that they cannot specify how mind and body interact, they insist that interaction is the best explanation.

IMMORTALITY

The issue of the immortality of the soul is obviously connected with the mind-body problem. If either the position of the epiphenomenalist or that of the strict materialist is correct, then nothing survives the death of the body, for body is all that exists. The matter or energy previously constituting one's body will show up in some other material form. It may well "push up daisies," as the saying goes. But no mind or soul constitutive of one's person or personality can possibly survive. On the other hand, if dualistic interactionism is correct, then at least the possibility of the mind or soul surviving bodily death exists. Descartes maintained not only that this is possible but that it is true.

Of course, everything depends on one's conception of immortality. Some Christians have believed in the resurrection of the physical body at some future time, a view which is consistent with a strict materialism. But generally where the belief in immortality is found among Christians today, what is seen as surviving death or as being resurrected is the soul, or *disembodied*, existence. St. Paul changed his mind on this, going from a bodily view to a spiritual view. Others, in particular some Hindus, conceive of immortality in two ways. As believers in reincarnation, they hold that after the death of the body, one's self or soul is reborn in a new body. This is personal immortality. But after a series of reincarnations, one escapes the Karmic "wheel". and loses self in Brahman-Atman. That is, one's soul reidentifies with a general spiritual substance that continues to exist, but one's personal characteristics are totally lost. Humanists reject both the immortality of the soul and the resurrection of the body and conceive of immortality only as the continuing social impact or memory of a person.

The conceptual and evidential problems confronting the belief in immortality obviously, depend on exactly how the belief is formulated. Faith or authority is frequently the basic ground offered for personal immortality, but there are rational defenses of this belief—as in Plato and Kant. The selections in this chapter will acquaint the student with various philosophical responses to this question and to the mind-body problem.

SELECTED BIBLIOGRAPHY

Anderson, A. D. (ed.). *Minds and Machines*. Englewood Cliffs, N.J., 1964.

Broad, C. D. *The Mind and Its Place in Nature*. London, 1925.

Chappell, Vere (ed.). *Philosophy of Mind*. Englewood Cliffs, N.J., 1962.

Ducasse, C. F. *Nature, Mind, and Death*. La Salle, Ill., 1951.

Fiegl, Herbert, and Scriven, M. (eds.). *Minnesota Studies in Philosophy of Science*, vol. 2. Minneapolis, 1962.

Flew, Antony. *A New Approach to Psychical Research*. London, 1953.

————. *Body, Mind, and Death*. New York, 1964.

Gustafson, Donald. *Essays in Philosophical Psychology*. New York, 1964.

Hampshire, Stuart. *Philosophy of Mind*. New York, 1966.

Hook, Sidney (ed.). *Dimensions of Mind*. New York, 1960.

Hull, C. L. *Principles of Behavior*. New York, 1943.

Laird, John. *Our Minds and Their Bodies*. London, 1925.

Lange, F. A. *History of Materialism*. London, 1925.

Pratt, J. B. *Matter and Spirit*. New York, 1926.

Princle-Pattison, A. *The Idea of Immortality*. Fair Lawn, N.J., 1922.

Russell, Bertrand. *Why I Am Not a Christian and Other Essays*. London, 1957.

Skinner, B. F. *Science and Human Behavior*. New York, 1953.

Smart, J. J. C. *Philosophy and Scientific Realism*. London, 1963.

Smythies, J. R. (ed.). *Brain and Mind*. New York, 1965.

Van Peursen, C. A. *Body, Soul, Spirit.* London, 1966.

Vesey, G. N. A. (ed.). *Body and Mind.* London, 1964.

————. *The Embodied Mind.* London, 1965.

Watson, J. B. *Psychology from the Standpoint of a Behaviorist.* Philadelphia, 1919.

White, Allen R. *The Philosophy of Mind.* New York, 1967.

Wisdom, John. *Problems of Mind and Matter.* Cambridge, 1934.

47 The Two-Substance Theory of Man*

RENÉ DESCARTES

René Descartes (1596–1650) is often considered the founder of modern philosophy. Recognized as the inventor of analytic geometry and as an important contributor to theoretical physics, Descartes' major philosophical works are *Discourse on Method*, *Meditations on First Philosophy*, and *Principles of Philosophy*.

But now that I begin to know myself better, and to discover more clearly the author of my being, I do not, indeed, think that I ought rashly to admit all which the senses seem to teach, nor, on the other hand, is it my conviction that I ought to doubt in general of their teachings.

And, firstly, because I know that all which I clearly and distinctly conceive can be produced by God exactly as I conceive it, it is sufficient that I am able clearly and distinctly to conceive one thing apart from another, in order to be certain that the one is different from the other, seeing they may at least be made to exist separately, by the omnipotence of God; and it matters not by what power this separation is made, in order to be compelled to judge them different; and, therefore, merely because I know with certitude that I exist, and because, in the meantime, I do not observe that aught necessarily belongs to my nature or essence beyond my being a thinking thing, I rightly conclude that my essence consists only in my being a thinking thing, [or a substance whose whole essence or nature is merely thinking]. And although I may, or rather, as I will shortly say, although I certainly do possess a body with which I am very closely conjoined; nevertheless, because, on the one hand, I have a clear and distinct idea of myself, in as far as I am only a thinking and unextended thing, and as, on the other hand, I possess a distinct idea of body, in as far as it is only an extended and unthinking thing, it is certain that I, [that is, my mind, by which I am what I am], is entirely and truly distinct from my body, and may exist without it.

Moreover, I find in myself diverse faculties of thinking that have each their special mode: for example, I find I possess the faculties of imagining and perceiving, without which I can indeed clearly and distinctly conceive

* From *Meditations and Selections from the Principles of Philosophy* by René Descartes, translated by John Veitch, Open Court Publishing Co., LaSalle, Illinois, 1952. Reprinted by permission.

myself as entire, but I cannot reciprocally conceive them without conceiving myself, that is to say, without an intelligent substance in which they reside, for [in the notion we have of them, or to use the terms of the schools] in their formal concept, they comprise some sort of intellection; whence I perceive that they are distinct from myself as modes are from things. I remark likewise certain other faculties, as the power of changing place, of assuming diverse figures, and the like, that cannot be conceived and cannot therefore exist, any more than the preceding, apart from a substance in which they inhere. It is very evident, however, that these faculties, if they really exist, must belong to some corporeal or extended substance, since in their clear and distinct concept there is contained some sort of extension, but no intellection at all. Farther, I cannot doubt but that there is in me a certain passive faculty of perception, that is, of receiving and taking knowledge of the ideas of sensible things; but this would be useless to me, if there did not also exist in me, or in some other thing, another active faculty capable of forming and producing those ideas. But this active faculty cannot be in me [in as far as I am but a thinking thing], seeing that it does not presuppose thought, and also that those ideas are frequently produced in my mind without my contributing to it in any way, and even frequently contrary to my will. This faculty must therefore exist in some substance different from me, in which all the objective reality of the ideas that are produced by this faculty, is contained formally or eminently, as I before remarked; and this substance is either a body, that is to say, a corporeal nature in which is contained formally [and in effect] all that is objectively [and by representation] in those ideas; or it is God himself, or some other creature, of a rank superior to body, in which the same is contained eminently. But as God is no deceiver, it is manifest that he does not of himself and immediately communicate those ideas to me, nor even by the intervention of any creature in which their objective reality is not formally, but only eminently, contained. For as he has given me no faculty whereby I can discover this to be the case, but, on the contrary, a very strong inclination to believe that those ideas arise from corporeal objects, I do not see how he could be vindicated from the charge of deceit, if in truth they proceeded from any other source, or were produced by other causes than corporeal things: and accordingly it must be concluded, that corporeal objects exist. Nevertheless they are not perhaps exactly such as we perceive by the senses, for their comprehension by the senses is, in many instances, very obscure and confused; but it is at least necessary to admit that all which I clearly and distinctly conceive as in them, that is, generally speaking, all that is comprehended in the object of speculative geometry, really exists external to me.

But with respect to other things which are either only particular, as for example, that the sun is of such a size and figure, etc., or are conceived with less clearness and distinctness, as light, sound, pain, and the like, although they are highly dubious and uncertain, nevertheless on the ground alone that

God is no deceiver, and that consequently he has permitted no falsity in my opinions which he has not likewise given me a faculty of correcting, I think I may with safety conclude that I possess in myself the means of arriving at the truth. And, in the first place, it cannot be doubted that in each of the dictates of nature there is some truth: for by nature, considered in general, I now understand nothing more than God himself, or the order and disposition established by God in created things; and by my nature in particular I understand the assemblage of all that God has given me.

But there is nothing which that nature teaches me more expressly [or more sensibly] than that I have a body which is ill affected when I feel pain, and stands in need of food and drink when I experience the sensations of hunger and thirst, etc. And therefore I ought not to doubt but that there is some truth in these informations.

Nature likewise teaches me by these sensations of pain, hunger, thirst, etc., that I am not only lodged in my body as a pilot in a vessel, but that I am besides so intimately conjoined, and as it were intermixed with it, that my mind and body compose a certain unity. For if this were not the case, I should not feel pain when my body is hurt, seeing I am merely a thinking thing, but should perceive the wound by the understanding alone, just as a pilot perceives by sight when any part of his vessel is damaged; and when my body has need of food or drink, I should have a clear knowledge of this, and not be made aware of it by the confused sensations of hunger and thirst: for, in truth, all these sensations of hunger, thirst, pain, etc., are nothing more than certain confused modes of thinking, arising from the union and apparent fusion of mind and body.

Besides this, nature teaches me that my own body is surrounded by many other bodies, some of which I have to seek after, and others to shun. And indeed, as I perceive different sorts of colours, sounds, odours, tastes, heat, hardness, etc., I safely conclude that there are in the bodies from which the diverse perceptions of the senses proceed, certain varieties corresponding to them, although, perhaps, not in reality like them; and since, among these diverse perceptions of the senses, some are agreeable, and others disagreeable, there can be no doubt that my body, or rather my entire self, in as far as I am composed of body and mind, may be variously affected, both beneficially and hurtfully, by surrounding bodies.

But there are many other beliefs which, though seemingly the teaching of nature, are not in reality so, but which obtained a place in my mind through a habit of judging inconsiderately of things. It may thus easily happen that such judgments shall contain error: thus, for example, the opinion I have that all space in which there is nothing to affect [or make an impression on] my senses is void; that in a hot body there is something in every respect similar to the idea of heat in my mind; that in a white or green body there is the same whiteness or greenness which I perceive; that in a bitter or sweet body there is the same taste, and so in other instances; that the stars, towers, and all distant bodies, are of the same size and figure as they appear to our eyes, etc. But that I may avoid everything like indistinctness of conception, I must accurately define what I properly understand by being taught by nature. For nature is here taken in a narrower sense than when it signifies the sum of all the things which God has given me; seeing that in that meaning the notion comprehends much that belongs only to the mind [to which I am not here to be understood as referring when I use the term nature]; as, for example, the notion I have of the truth, that what is done cannot be undone, and all the other truths I discern by the natural light [without the aid of the body]; and seeing that it comprehends likewise much besides that belongs only to body, and is not here any more contained under the name nature, as the quality of heaviness, and the like, of which I do not speak,—the term being reserved exclusively to designate the things which God has given to me as a being composed of mind and body. But nature, taking the term in the sense explained, teaches me to shun what causes in me the sensation of pain, and to pursue what affords me the sensation of pleasure, and other things of this sort; but I do not discover that it teaches me, in addition to this, from these diverse perceptions of the senses, to draw any conclusions respecting external objects without a previous [careful and mature] consideration of them by the mind; for it is, as appears to me, the office of the mind alone, and not of the composite whole of mind and body, to discern the truth in those matters. Thus, although the impression a star makes on my eye is not larger than that from the flame of a candle, I do not, nevertheless, experience any real or positive impulse determining me to believe that the star is not greater than the flame; the true account of the matter being merely that I have so judged from my youth without any rational ground. And, though on approaching the fire I feel heat, and even pain on approaching it too closely, I have, however, from this no ground for holding that something resembling the heat I feel is in the fire, any more than that there is something similar to the pain; all that I have ground for believing is, that there is something in it, whatever it may be, which excites in me those sensations of heat or pain. So also, although there are spaces in which I find nothing to excite and affect my senses, I must not therefore conclude that those spaces contain in them no body; for I see that in this, as in many other similar matters, I have been accustomed to pervert the order of nature, because these perceptions of the senses, although given me by nature merely to signify to my mind what things are beneficial and hurtful to the composite whole of which it is a part, and being sufficiently clear and distinct for that purpose, are nevertheless used by me as infallible rules by which to determine immediately the essence of the bodies that exist out of me, of which they can of course afford me only the most obscure and confused knowledge.

But I have already sufficiently considered how it happens that, notwithstanding the supreme goodness of God, there is falsity in my judgments. A difficulty, however, here presents itself, respecting the things which I am taught by nature must be pursued or avoided, and also respecting the internal sensations in which I seem to have occasionally detected error, [and thus to be directly deceived by nature]: thus, for example, I may be so deceived by the agreeable taste of some viand with which poison has been mixed, as to be induced to take the poison. In this case, however, nature may be excused, for it simply leads me to desire the viand for its agreeable taste, and not the poison, which is unknown to it; and thus we can infer nothing from this circumstance beyond that our nature is not omniscient; at which there is assuredly no ground for surprise, since, man being of a finite nature, his knowledge must likewise be of limited perfection. But we also not unfrequently err in that to which we are directly impelled by nature, as is the case with invalids who desire drink or food that would be hurtful to them. It will here, perhaps, be alleged that the reason why such persons are deceived is that their nature is corrupted; but this leaves the difficulty untouched, for a sick man is not less really the creature of God than a man who is in full health; and therefore it is as repugnant to the goodness of God that the nature of the former should be deceitful as it is for that of the latter to be so. And, as a clock, composed of wheels and counter weights, observes not the less accurately all the laws of nature when it is ill made, and points out the hours incorrectly, than when it satisfies the desire of the maker in every respect; so likewise if the body of man be considered as a kind of machine, so made up and composed of bones, nerves, muscles, veins, blood, and skin, that although there were in it no mind, it would still exhibit the same motions which it at present manifests involuntarily, and therefore without the aid of the mind, [and simply by the dispositions of its organs], I easily discern that it would also be as natural for such a body, supposing it dropsical, for example, to experience the parchedness of the throat that is usually accompanied in the mind by the sensation of thirst, and to be disposed by this parchedness to move its nerves and its other parts in the way required for drinking, and thus increase its malady and do itself harm, as it is natural for it, when it is not indisposed to be stimulated to drink for its good by a similar cause; and although looking to the use for which a clock was destined by its maker, I may say that it is deflected from its proper nature when it incorrectly indicates the hours, and on the same principle, considering the machine of the human body as having been formed by God for the sake of the motions which it usually manifests, although I may likewise have ground for thinking that it does not follow the order of its nature when the throat is parched and drink does not tend to its preservation, nevertheless I yet plainly discern that this latter acceptation of the term nature is very different from the other; for this is nothing more than a certain denomination, depending entirely on my thought, and hence called extrinsic, by which I compare a sick man and an imperfectly constructed clock with the idea I have of a man in good health and a well made clock; while by the other acceptation of nature is understood

48 Materialism and the Nature of Man[*]

BARON D. HOLBACH

Baron D. Holbach (1723–1789) was a forceful advocate of atheism, determinism, and materialism. His principal works are *Christianisme DéVoilé* and *The System of Nature*.

Man's . . . . life itself is nothing more than a long series, a succession of necessary and connected motion, which operates perpetual and continual changes in his machine; which has for its principle either causes contained within himself—such as blood, nerves, fibres, flesh, bones, in short, the matter, as well solid as fluid, of which his whole, or his body, is composed; or those exterior causes, which by acting upon him, modify him diversely.

The beings of the human species, as well as all other beings, are susceptible of two sorts of motion: the one, that of the mass, by which an entire body, or some of its parts, are visibly transferred from one place to another; the other, internal and concealed, of some of which man is sensible, while some takes place without his knowledge, and is not even to be guessed at, but by the effect it outwardly produces. In a machine so extremely complex as man, formed by the combination of such a multiplicity of matter, so diversified in its properties, so different in its proportions, so varied in its modes of action, the motion necessarily becomes of the most complicated kind; its dullness, as well as its rapidity, frequently escapes the observation of those themselves, in whom it takes place.

Let us not then be surprised, if when man would account to himself for his existence, for his manner of acting, finding so many obstacles to encounter, —he invented such strange hypotheses to explain the concealed spring of his machine—if when this motion appeared to him to be different from that of other bodies, he conceived an idea that he moved and acted in a manner altogether distinct from the other beings in nature. He clearly perceived that his body, as well as different parts of it, did act; but frequently he was unable to discover what brought them into action—from whence he received the impulse; he then conjectured he contained within himself a moving principle, distinguished from his machine, which secretly gave an impulse to the springs which set this machine in motion; that moved him by its own natural energy;

[*] From Baron D. Holbach, *A System of Nature*, first published 1770.

that consequently he acted according to laws totally distinct from those which regulated the motion of other beings: he was conscious of certain internal motion, which he could not help feeling; but how could he conceive, that this invisible motion was so frequently competent to produce such striking effects? How could he comprehend, that a fugitive idea, an imperceptible act of thought, was so frequently capacitated to bring his whole being into trouble and confusion? He fell into the belief, that he perceived within himself a substance distinguished from that self, endowed with a secret force, in which he supposed existed qualities distinctly differing from those, of either the visible causes that acted on his organs, or those organs themselves. He did not sufficiently understand, that the primitive causes which make a stone fall, or his arm move, are perhaps as difficult of comprehension, as arduous to be explained, as those internal impulses, of which his thought or his will are the effects. Thus, for want of meditating nature—of considering her under her true point of view—of remarking the conformity—of noticing the simultaneity, the unity of the motion of this fancied motive-power with that of his body—of his material organs—he conjectured he was not only a distinct being, but that he was set apart, with different energies, from all the other beings in nature; that he was of a more simple essence, having nothing in common with any thing by which he was surrounded; nothing that connected him with all that he beheld.

It is from thence has successively sprung his notions of *spirituality, immateriality, immortality*; in short, all those vague unmeaning words, he has invented by degrees, in order to subtilize and designate the attributes of the unknown power, which he believes he contains within himself, which he conjectures to be the concealed principle of all his visible actions: when man once imbibes an idea that he cannot comprehend, he meditates upon it until he has given it a complete personification: Thus he saw, or fancied he saw, the igneous matter pervade every thing; he conjectured that it was the only principle of life and activity, he proceeded to embody it, he gave it his own form, called it Jupiter, and ended by worshipping this image of his own creation, as the power from whom he derived every good he experienced, every evil he sustained. To crown the bold conjectures, he ventured to make of this internal motive-power, he supposed, that different from all other beings, even from the body that served to envelop it, it was not bound to undergo dissolution; that such was its perfect simplicity, that it could not be decomposed, nor even change its form; in short, that it was by its essence, exempted from those revolutions, to which he saw the body subjected, as well as all the compound beings with which nature is filled.

Thus man in his own ideas, became double; he looked upon himself, as a whole, composed by the inconceivable assemblage, of two different, two distinct natures; which have no point of analogy between themselves: he distinguished two substances in himself, one evidently submitted to the influence of gross beings, composed of coarse inert matter: this he called *body*:

—the other, which he supposed to be simple, of a purer essence, was contemplated as acting from itself; giving motion to the body, with which it found itself so miraculously united: this he called *soul* or *spirit*: the functions of the one, he denominated *physical corporeal, material*; the functions of the other he styled *spiritual, intellectual*. Man, considered relatively to the first, was termed the *physical man*; viewed with relation to the last, he was designated the *moral man*.

These distinctions, although adopted by the greater number of the philosophers of the present day, are, nevertheless, only founded on gratuitous suppositions. Man has always believed, he remedied his ignorance of things, by invented words, to which he could never attach any true sense or meaning. He imagined he understood matter, its properties, its faculties, its resources, its different combinations, because he had a superficial glimpse of some of its qualities: he has, however, in reality, done nothing more than obscure the faint ideas he has been capacitated to form of this matter, by associating it with a substance much less intelligible than itself. It is thus, speculative man, in forming words, in multiplying beings, has only plunged himself into greater difficulties than those he endeavoured to avoid; and thereby placed obstacles to the progress of his knowledge: whenever he has been deficient of facts he has had recourse to conjecture, which he quickly changed into fancied realities. Thus, his imagination, no longer guided by experience, hurried on by his new ideas, was lost, without hope of return, in the labyrinth of an ideal, of an intellectual world, to which he had himself given birth; it was next to impossible to withdraw him from this delusion, to place him in the right road, of which nothing but experience can furnish him the clew. Nature points out to man, that in himself, as well as in all those objects which act upon him, there is never more than matter endowed with various properties, diversely modified; that acts, by reason of these properties: that man is an organized whole, composed of a variety of matter: that like all the other productions of nature, he follows general and known laws, as well as those laws or modes of action, which are peculiar to himself and unknown.

Thus, when it shall be inquired, what is man?

We say he is a material being organized after a peculiar manner; conformed to a certain mode of thinking, of feeling, capable of modification in certain modes peculiar to himself; to his organization, to that particular combination of matter which is found assembled in him.

49 Descartes' Myth[*]

GILBERT RYLE

Gilbert Ryle (1900–) is Waynfleet Professor of Metaphysical Philosophy at Oxford University. Known as a leader in the British school of analytic philosophy, Ryle is best known for his book *The Concept of Mind*. He succeeded G. E. Moore as editor of the philosophical journal *Mind*.

(1) THE OFFICIAL DOCTRINE

There is a doctrine about the nature and place of minds which is so prevalent among theorists and even among laymen that it deserves to be described as the official theory. Most philosophers, psychologists and religious teachers subscribe, with minor reservations, to its main articles and, although they admit certain theoretical difficulties in it, they tend to assume that these can be overcome without serious modifications being made to the architecture of the theory. It will be argued here that the central principles of the doctrine are unsound and conflict with the whole body of what we know about minds when we are not speculating about them.

The official doctrine, which hails chiefly from Descartes, is something like this. With the doubtful exceptions of idiots and infants in arms every human being has both a body and a mind. Some would prefer to say that every human being is both a body and a mind. His body and his mind are ordinarily harnessed together, but after the death of the body his mind may continue to exist and function.

Human bodies are in space and are subject to the mechanical laws which govern all other bodies in space. Bodily processes and states can be inspected by external observers. So a man's bodily life is as much a public affair as are the lives of animals and reptiles and even as the careers of trees, crystals and planets.

But minds are not in space, nor are their operations subject to mechanical laws. The workings of one mind are not witnessable by other observers; its career is private. Only I can take direct cognisance of the states and processes of my own mind. A person therefore lives through two collateral histories, one consisting of what happens in and to his body, the other consisting of

* Reprinted from *The Concept of Mind*, London, 1949, pp. 11–24, with permission of the author and the publishers Hutchinson Publishing Group, Ltd., London, and Barnes & Noble, Inc., New York.

what happens in and to his mind. The first is public, the second private. The events in the first history are events in the physical world, those in the second are events in the mental world.

It has been disputed whether a person does or can directly monitor all or only some of the episodes of his own private history; but, according to the official doctrine, of at least some of these episodes he has direct and unchallengeable cognisance. In consciousness, self-consciousness and introspection he is directly and authentically apprised of the present states and operations of his mind. He may have great or small uncertainties about concurrent and adjacent episodes in the physical world, but he can have none about at least part of what is momentarily occupying his mind.

It is customary to express this bifurcation of his two lives and of his two worlds by saying that the things and events which belong to the physical world, including his own body, are external, while the workings of his own mind are internal. This antithesis of outer and inner is of course meant to be construed as a metaphor, since minds, not being in space, could not be described as being spatially inside anything else, or as having things going on spatially inside themselves. But relapses from this good intention are common and theorists are found speculating how stimuli, the physical sources of which are yards or miles outside a person's skin, can generate mental responses inside his skull, or how decisions framed inside his cranium can set going movements of his extremities.

Even when 'inner' and 'outer' are construed as metaphors, the problem how a person's mind and body influence one another is notoriously charged with theoretical difficulties. What the mind wills, the legs, arms and the tongue execute; what affects the ear and the eye has something to do with what the mind perceives; grimaces and smiles betray the mind's moods and bodily castigations lead, it is hoped, to moral improvement. But the actual transactions between the episodes of the private history and those of the public history remain mysterious, since by definition they can belong to neither series. They could not be reported among the happenings described in a person's autobiography of his inner life, but nor could they be reported among those described in some one else's biography of that person's overt career. They can be inspected neither by introspection nor by laboratory experiment. They are theoretical shuttlecocks which are forever being bandied from the physiologist back to the psychologist and from the psychologist back to the physiologist.

Underlying this partly metaphorical representation of the bifurcation of a person's two lives there is a seemingly more profound and philosophical assumption. It is assumed that there are two different kinds of existence or status. What exists or happens may have the status of physical existence, or it may have the status of mental existence. Somewhat as the faces of coins are either heads or tails, or somewhat as living creatures are either male or female, so, it is supposed, some existing is physical existing, other existing is mental existing. It is a necessary feature of what has physical existence that it is in space and time; it is a necessary feature of what has mental existence that it is in time but not in space. What has physical existence is composed of matter, or else is a function of matter; what has mental existence consists of consciousness, or else is a function of consciousness.

There is thus a polar opposition between mind and matter, an opposition which is often brought out as follows. Material objects are situated in a common field, known as 'space,' and what happens to one body in one part of space is mechanically connected with what happens to other bodies in other parts of space. But mental happenings occur in insulated fields, known as 'minds,' and there is, apart maybe from telepathy, no direct causal connection between what happens in one mind and what happens in another. Only through the medium of the public physical world can the mind of one person make a difference to the mind of another. The mind is its own place and in his inner life each of us lives the life of a ghostly Robinson Crusoe. People can see, hear and jolt one another's bodies, but they are irremediably blind and deaf to the workings of one another's minds and inoperative upon them.

What sort of knowledge can be secured of the workings of a mind? On the one side, according to the official theory, a person has direct knowledge of the best imaginable kind of the workings of his own mind. Mental states and processes are (or are normally) conscious states and processes, and the consciousness which irradiates them can engender no illusions and leaves the door open for no doubts. A person's present thinkings, feelings and willings, his perceivings, rememberings and imaginings are intrinsically 'phosphorescent'; their existence and their nature are inevitably betrayed to their owner. The inner life is a stream of consciousness of such a sort that it would be absurd to suggest that the mind whose life is that stream might be unaware of what is passing down it.

True, the evidence adduced recently by Freud seems to show that there exist channels tributary to this stream, which run hidden from their owner. People are actuated by impulses the existence of which they vigorously disavow; some of their thoughts differ from the thoughts which they acknowledge; and some of the actions which they think they will to perform they do not really will. They are thoroughly gulled by some of their own hypocrisies and they successfully ignore facts about their mental lives which on the official theory ought to be patent to them. Holders of the official theory tend, however, to maintain that anyhow in normal circumstances a person must be directly and authentically seized of the present state and workings of his own mind.

Besides being currently supplied with these alleged immediate data of consciousness, a person is also generally supposed to be able to exercise from time to time a special kind of perception, namely inner perception, or introspection. He can take a (non-optical) 'look' at what is passing in his mind.

Not only can he view and scrutinize a flower through his sense of sight and listen to and discriminate the notes of a bell through his sense of hearing; he can also reflectively or introspectively watch, without any bodily organ of sense, the current episodes of his inner life. This self-observation is also commonly supposed to be immune from illusion, confusion or doubt. A mind's reports of its own affairs have a certainty superior to the best that is possessed by its reports of matters in the physical world. Sense-perceptions can, but consciousness and introspection cannot, be mistaken or confused.

On the other side, one person has no direct access of any sort to the events of the inner life of another. He cannot do better than make problematic inferences from the observed behaviour of the other person's body to the states of mind which, by analogy from his own conduct, he supposes to be signalised by that behaviour. Direct access to the workings of a mind is the privilege of that mind itself; in default of such privileged access, the workings of one mind are inevitably occult to everyone else. For the supposed arguments from bodily movements similar to their own to mental workings similar to their own would lack any possibility of observational corroboration. Not unnaturally, therefore, an adherent of the official theory finds it difficult to resist this consequence of his premises, that he has no good reason to believe that there do exist minds other than his own. Even if he prefers to believe that to other human bodies there are harnessed minds not unlike his own, he cannot claim to be able to discover their individual characteristics, or the particular things that they undergo and do. Absolute solitude is on this showing the ineluctable destiny of the soul. Only our bodies can meet.

As a necessary corollary of this general scheme there is implicitly prescribed a special way of construing our ordinary concepts of mental powers and operations. The verbs, nouns and adjectives, with which in ordinary life we describe the wits, characters and higher-grade performances of the people with whom we have do, are required to be construed as signifying special episodes in their secret histories, or else as signifying tendencies for such episodes to occur. When someone is described as knowing, believing or guessing something, as hoping, dreading, intending or shirking something, as designing this or being amused at that, these verbs are supposed to denote the occurrence of specific modifications in his (to us) occult stream of consciousness. Only his own privileged access to this stream in direct awareness and introspection could provide authentic testimony that these mental-conduct verbs were correctly or incorrectly applied. The onlooker, be he teacher, critic, biographer or friend, can never assure himself that his comments have any vestige of truth. Yet it was just because we do in fact all know how to make such comments, make them with general correctness and correct them when they turn out to be confused or mistaken, that philosophers found it necessary to construct their theories of the nature and place of minds. Finding mental-conduct concepts being regularly and effectively used, they properly sought to fix their logical geography. But the logical geography officially recommended would entail that there could be no regular or effective use of these mental-conduct concepts in our descriptions of, and prescriptions for, other people's minds.

(2) THE ABSURDITY OF THE OFFICIAL DOCTRINE

Such in outline is the official theory. I shall often speak of it, with deliberate abusiveness, as 'the dogma of the Ghost in the Machine.' I hope to prove that it is entirely false, and false not in detail but in principle. It is not merely an assemblage of particular mistakes. It is one big mistake and a mistake of a special kind. It is, namely, a category-mistake. It represents the facts of mental life as if they belonged to one logical type or category (or range of types or categories), when they actually belong to another. The dogma is therefore a philosopher's myth. In attempting to explode the myth I shall probably be taken to be denying well-known facts about the mental life of human beings, and my plea that I aim at doing nothing more than rectify the logic of mental-conduct concepts will probably be disallowed as mere subterfuge.

I must first indicate what is meant by the phrase 'Category-mistake.' This I do in a series of illustrations.

A foreigner visiting Oxford or Cambridge for the first time is shown a number of colleges, libraries, playing fields, museums, scientific departments and administrative offices. He then asks 'But where is the university? I have seen where the members of the Colleges live, where the Registrar works, where the scientists experiment and the rest. But I have not yet seen the University in which reside and work the members of your University.' It has then to be explained to him that the University is not another collateral institution, some ulterior counterpart to the colleges, laboratories and offices which he has seen. The University is just the way in which all that he has already seen is organized. When they are seen and when their co-ordination is understood, the University has been seen. His mistake lay in his innocent assumption that it was correct to speak of Christ Church, the Bodleian Library, the Ashmolean Museum *and* the University, to speak, that is, as if 'the University' stood for an extra member of the class of which these other units are members. He was mistakenly allocating the University to the same category as that to which the other institutions belong.

The same mistake would be made by a child witnessing the march-past of a division, who, having had pointed out to him such and such battalions, batteries, squadrons, etc., asked when the division was going to appear. He would be supposing that a division was a counterpart to the units already seen, partly similar to them and partly unlike them. He would be shown his mistake by being told that in watching the battalions, batteries and squadrons marching past he had been watching the division marching past. The march-past was not a parade of battalions, batteries, squadrons *and* a division; it was a parade of the battalions, batteries and squadrons *of* a division.

One more illustration. A foreigner watching his first game of cricket learns what are the functions of the bowlers, the batsmen, the fielders, the umpires and the scorers. He then says 'But there is no one left on the field to contribute the famous element of team-spirit. I see who does the bowling, the batting and the wicket-keeping; but I do not see whose role it is to exercise *esprit de corps*.' Once more, it would have to be explained that he was looking for the wrong type of thing. Team-spirit is not another cricketing-operation supplementary to all of the other special tasks. It is, roughly, the keenness with which each of the special tasks is performed, and performing a task keenly is not performing two tasks. Certainly exhibiting team-spirit is not the same thing as bowling or catching, but nor is it a third thing such that we can say that the bowler first bowls *and* then exhibits team-spirit or that a fielder is at a given moment *either* catching *or* displaying *esprit de corps*.

These illustrations of category-mistakes have a common feature which must be noticed. The mistakes were made by people who did not know how to wield the concepts *University, division* and *team-spirit*. Their puzzles arose from inability to use certain items in the English vocabulary.

The theoretically interesting category-mistakes are those made by people who are perfectly competent to apply concepts, at least in the situations with which they are familiar, but are still liable in their abstract thinking to allocate those concepts to logical types to which they do not belong. An instance of a mistake of this sort would be the following story. A student of politics has learned the main differences between the British, the French and the American Constitutions, and has learned also the differences and connections between the Cabinet, Parliament, the various Ministries, the Judicature and the Church of England. But he still becomes embarrassed when asked questions about the connections between the Church of England, the Home Office and the British Constitution. For while the Church and the Home Office are institutions, the British Constitution is not another institution in the same sense of that noun. So inter-institutional relations which can be asserted or denied to hold between the Church and the Home Office cannot be asserted or denied to hold between either of them and the British Constitution. 'The British Constitution' is not a term of the same logical type as 'the Home Office' and 'the Church of England.' In a partially similar way, John Doe may be a relative, a friend, an enemy or a stranger to Richard Roe; but he cannot be any of these things to the Average Taxpayer. He knows how to talk sense in certain sorts of discussions about the Average Taxpayer, but he is baffled to say why he could not come across him in the street as he can come across Richard Roe.

It is pertinent to our main subject to notice that, so long as the student of politics continues to think of the British Constitution as a counterpart to the other institutions, he will tend to describe it as a mysteriously occult institution; and so long as John Doe continues to think of the Average Tax-payer as a fellow-citizen, he will tend to think of him as an elusive insubstantial man, a ghost who is everywhere yet nowhere.

My destructive purpose is to show that a family of radical category-mistakes is the source of the double-life theory. The representation of a person as a ghost mysteriously ensconced in a machine derives from this argument. Because, as is true, a person's thinking, feeling and purposive doing cannot be described solely in the idioms of physics, chemistry and physiology, therefore they must be described in counterpart idioms. As the human body is a complex organised unit, so the human mind must be another complex organised unit, though one made of a different sort of stuff and with a different sort of structure. Or, again, as the human body, like any other parcel of matter, is a field of causes and effects, so the mind must be another field of causes and effects, though not (Heaven be praised) mechanical causes and effects.

(3) THE ORIGIN OF THE CATEGORY-MISTAKE

One of the chief intellectual origins of what I have yet to prove to be the Cartesian category-mistake seems to be this. When Galileo showed that his methods of scientific discovery were competent to provide a mechanical theory which should cover every occupant of space, Descartes found in himself two conflicting motives. As a man of scientific genius he could not but endorse the claims of mechanics, yet as a religious and moral man he could not accept, as Hobbes accepted, the discouraging rider to those claims, namely that human nature differs only in degree of complexity from clockwork. The mental could not be just a variety of the mechanical.

He and subsequent philosophers naturally but erroneously availed themselves of the following escape-route. Since mental-conduct words are not to be construed as signifying the occurrence of mechanical processes, they must be construed as signifying the occurrence of non-mechanical processes; since mechanical laws explain movements in space as the effects of other movements in space, other laws must explain some of the non-spatial workings of minds as the effects of other non-spatial workings of minds. The difference between the human behaviours which we describe as intelligent and those which we describe as unintelligent must be a difference in their causation; so, while some movements of human tongues and limbs are the effects of mechanical causes, others must be the effects of non-mechanical causes, i.e. some issue from movements of particles of matter, others from workings of the mind.

The differences between the physical and the mental were thus represented as differences inside the common framework of the categories of 'thing,' 'stuff,' 'attribute,' 'state,' 'process,' 'change,' 'cause' and 'effect.' Minds are things, but different sorts of things from bodies; mental processes are causes and effects, but different sorts of causes and effects from bodily movements. And so on. Somewhat as the foreigner expected the University to be an extra edifice, rather like a college but also considerably different, so the repudiators of mechanism represented minds as extra centres of causal processes, rather like machines but also considerably different from them. Their theory was a para-mechanical hypothesis.

That this assumption was at the heart of the doctrine is shown by the fact that there was from the beginning felt to be a major theoretical difficulty in explaining how minds can influence and be influenced by bodies. How can a mental process, such as willing, cause spatial movements like the movements of the tongue? How can a physical change in the optic nerve have among its effects a mind's perception of a flash of light? This notorious crux by itself shows the logical mould into which Descartes pressed his theory of the mind. It was the self-same mould into which he and Galileo set their mechanics. Still unwittingly adhering to the grammar of mechanics, he tried to avert disaster by describing minds in what was merely an obverse vocabulary. The workings of minds had to be described by the mere negatives of the specific descriptions given to bodies; they are not in space, they are not motions, they are not modifications of matter, they are not accessible to public observation. Minds are not bits of clockwork, they are just bits of not-clockwork.

As thus represented, minds are not merely ghosts harnessed to machines, they are themselves just spectral machines. Though the human body is an engine, it it not quite an ordinary engine, since some of its workings are governed by another engine inside it—this interior governor-engine being one of a very special sort. It is invisible, inaudible and it has no size or weight. It cannot be taken to bits and the laws it obeys are not those known to ordinary engineers. Nothing is known of how it governs the bodily engine.

A second major crux points the same moral. Since, according to the doctrine, minds belong to the same category as bodies and since bodies are rigidly governed by mechanical laws, it seemed to many theorists to follow that minds must be similarly governed by rigid non-mechanical laws. The physical world is a deterministic system, so the mental world must be a deterministic system. Bodies cannot help the modifications that they undergo, so minds cannot help pursuing the careers fixed for them. *Responsibility, choice, merit* and *demerit* are therefore inapplicable concepts—unless the compromise solution is adopted of saying that the laws governing mental processes, unlike those governing physical processes, have the congenial attribute of being only rather rigid. The problem of the Freedom of the Will was the problem how to reconcile the hypothesis that minds are to be described in terms drawn from the categories of mechanics with the knowledge that higher-grade human conduct is not of a piece with the behaviour of machines.

It is an historical curiosity that it was not noticed that the entire argument was broken-backed. Theorists correctly assumed that any sane man could already recognise the differences between, say, rational and non-rational utterances or between purposive and automatic behaviour. Else there would have been nothing requiring to be salved from mechanism. Yet the explanation given presupposed that one person could in principle never recognise the difference between the rational and the irrational utterances issuing from other human bodies, since he could never get access to the postulated immaterial causes of some of their utterances. Save for the doubtful exception of himself, he could never tell the difference between a man and a Robot. It would have to be conceded, for example, that, for all that we can tell, the inner lives of persons who are classed as idiots or lunatics are as rational as those of anyone else. Perhaps only their overt behaviour is disappointing; that is to say, perhaps 'idiots' are not really idiotic, or 'lunatics' lunatic. Perhaps, too, some of those who are classed as sane are really idiots. According to the theory, external observers could never know how the overt behaviour of others is correlated with their mental powers and processes and so they could never know or even plausibly conjecture whether their applications of mental conduct concepts to these other people were correct or incorrect. It would then be hazardous or impossible for a man to claim sanity or logical consistency even for himself, since he would be debarred from comparing his own performances with those of others. In short, our characterisations of persons and their performances as intelligent, prudent and virtuous or as stupid, hypocritical and cowardly could never have been made, so the problem of providing a special causal hypothesis to serve as the basis of such diagnoses would never have arisen. The question, 'How do persons differ from machines?' arose just because everyone already knew how to apply mental-conduct concepts before the new causal hypothesis was introduced. This causal hypothesis could not therefore be the source of the criteria used in those applications. Nor, of course, has the causal hypothesis in any degree improved our handling of those criteria. We still distinguish good from bad arithmetic, politic from impolitic conduct and fertile from infertile imaginations in the ways in which Descartes himself distinguished them before and after he speculated how the applicability of these criteria was compatible with the principle of mechanical causation.

He had mistaken the logic of his problem. Instead of asking by what criteria intelligent behaviour is actually distinguished from non-intelligent behaviour, he asked 'Given that the principle of mechanical causation does not tell us the difference, what other causal principle will tell it us?' He realised that the problem was not one of mechanics and assumed that it must therefore be one of some counterpart to mechanics. Not unnaturally psychology is often cast for just this role.

When two terms belong to the same category, it is proper to construct conjunctive propositions embodying them. Thus a purchaser may say that he bought a left-hand glove and a right-hand glove, but not that he bought a left-hand glove, a right-hand glove and a pair of gloves. 'She came home in a flood of tears and a sedan-chair' is a well-known joke based on the absurdity of conjoining terms of different types. It would have been equally ridiculous to construct the disjunction 'She came home either in a flood or tears or else in a sedan-chair.' Now the dogma of the Ghost in the Machine does just this. It maintains that there exist both bodies and minds; that there occur physical processes and mental processes; that there are mechanical causes of corporeal movements and mental causes of corporeal movements. I shall argue that these and other analogous conjunctions are absurd; but, it must be noticed, the argument will not show that either of the illegitimately conjoined propositions is absurd in itself. I am not, for example, denying that there occur mental processes. Doing long division is a mental process and so is making a joke. But I am saying that the phrase 'there occur mental processes' does not mean the same sort of thing as 'there occur physical processes,' and, therefore, that it makes no sense to conjoin or disjoin the two.

If my argument is successful, there will follow some interesting consequences. First, the hallowed contrast between Mind and Matter will be dissipated, but dissipated not by either of the equally hallowed absorptions of Mind by Matter or of Matter by Mind, but in quite a different way. For the seeming contrast of the two will be shown to be as illegitimate as would be the contrast of 'she came home in a flood of tears' and 'she came home in a sedan-chair.' The belief that there is a polar opposition between Mind and Matter is the belief that they are terms of the same logical type.

It will also follow that both Idealism and Materialism are answers to an improper question. The 'reduction' of the material world to mental states and processes, as well as the 'reduction' of mental states and processes to physical states and processes, presuppose the legitimacy of the disjunction 'Either there exist minds or there exist bodies (but not both).' It would be like saying, 'Either she bought a left-hand and a right-hand glove or she bought a pair of gloves (but not both).'

It is perfectly proper to say, in one logical tone of voice, that there exist minds and to say, in another logical tone of voice, that there exist bodies. But these expressions do not indicate two different species of existence, for 'existence' is not a generic word like 'coloured' or 'sexed.' They indicate two different senses of 'exist,' somewhat as 'rising' has different senses in 'the tide is rising,' 'hopes are rising,' and 'the average age of death is rising.' A man would be thought to be making a poor joke who said that three things are now rising, namely the tide, hopes and the average age of death. It would be just as good or bad a joke to say that there exist prime numbers and Wednesdays and public opinions and navies; or that there exist both minds and bodies. In the succeeding chapters I try to prove that the official theory does rest on a batch of category-mistakes by showing that logically absurd corollaries follow from it. The exhibition of these absurdities will have the constructive effect of bringing out part of the correct logic of mental-conduct concepts.

(4) HISTORICAL NOTE

It would not be true to say that the official theory derives solely from Descartes' theories, or even from a more widespread anxiety about the implications of seventeenth century mechanism. Scholastic and Reformation theology had schooled the intellects of the scientists as well as of the laymen, philosophers and clerics of that age. Stoic-Augustinian theories of the will were embedded in the Calvinist doctrines of sin and grace; Platonic and Aristotelian theories of the intellect shaped the orthodox doctrines of the immortality of the soul. Descartes was reformulating already prevalent theological doctrines of the soul in the new syntax of Galileo. The theologian's privacy of conscience became the philosopher's privacy of consciousness, and what had been the bogy of Predestination reappeared as the bogy of Determinism.

It would also not be true to say that the two-worlds myth did no theoretical good. Myths often do a lot of theoretical good, while they are still new. One benefit bestowed by the para-mechanical myth was that it partly superannuated the then prevalent para-political myth. Minds and their Faculties had previously been described by analogies with political superiors and political subordinates. The idioms used were those of ruling, obeying, collaborating and rebelling. They survived and still survive in many ethical and some epistemological discussions. As, in physics, the new myth of occult Forces was a scientific improvement on the old myth of Final Causes, so, in anthropological and psychological theory, the new myth of hidden operations, impulses and agencies was an improvement on the old myth of dictations, deferences and disobediences.

50 Could Mental States Be Brain Processes?[*]

JEROME SHAFFER

Jerome Shaffer (1929–   ) has taught philosophy at Swarthmore College and is presently on the faculty of the University of Connecticut. He is the author of a number of journal articles on the relation of mind and body.

In recent discussions of the relation between mental states and brain processes, a view that has received much support is the Identity theory. Its adherents[1] allow that expressions that refer to mental states differ in their meaning from expressions that refer to brain processes, but they claim that the actual existents picked out by the former expressions turn out, as a matter of empirical fact, to be identical with those picked out by the latter expressions. I wish to examine this theory. For convenience, I shall refer to mental states, e.g., feeling pain, having an after-image, thinking about a problem, considering some proposition, etc., as *C-states*, and I shall refer to whatever brain process may be going on at the same time that some mental state is occurring as a *B-process*. My main contentions will be (1) that C-states cannot be identical with B-processes because they do not occur in the same place, (2) that there is nothing to stop us from making the Identity theory correct by adopting a convention for locating C-states, and (3) that the question whether it would be useful to adopt such a convention depends upon empirical facts which are at present unknown.

I

Before pointing out why the Identity theory is incorrect, I wish to defend it against some standard objections. These objections arise from the failure to see that it is *de facto* identity, not identity of meaning, that is intended. Descartes, for example, concluded that the mental and the physical could

[*] From *The Journal of Philosophy*, vol. 58 (1961). Reprinted by permission of the author.
[1] Cf. U. T. Place, "Is Consciousness a Brain Process?" *British Journal of Psychology*, 47 (1956); Herbert Feigl, "The 'Mental' and the 'Physical,' " in H. Feigl, G. Maxwell, and M. Scriven, eds., *Concepts, Theories, and the Mind-Body Problem* (Minneapolis: Univ. of Minn. Press, 1958); J. J. C. Smart, "Sensations and Brain Processes," *The Philosophical Review*, 68 (1959); Hilary Putnam, "Minds and Machines," in Sidney Hook, ed., *Dimensions of Mind* (New York, 1960).

not be identical, had to be separate and distinct substances, because of such facts as these: (1) that the concept of the mental is a quite different concept from the concept of the physical, (2) that someone might be sure of the existence of his mental process while raising doubts about the existence of his body, and (3) that God could make the mind exist in separation from the body. But none of these facts supports Descartes's conclusion that mental things cannot be identical with physical things. They show only, what is admitted by Identity theorists, that we cannot know *a priori* that the mental and physical are identical. Compare the case of the expressions, "human being" and "featherless biped." The same facts hold, namely (1) that the concept of a human being is a quite different concept from the concept of a featherless biped, (2) that someone might be sure of the existence of human beings while raising doubts about the existence of featherless bipeds, and (3) that God could have made human beings exist as separate things from featherless bipeds. Yet none of these considerations rules out the possibility that, as a matter of pure empirical fact, human beings turn out to be identical with featherless bipeds, in the sense that the two classes are co-extentional, such that anything which is a member of the one class turns out to be a member of the other, also. The same goes for C-states and B-processes. Identity theorists claim only that anything which is a C-state turns out, in fact, to be a B-process also. To put the thesis in Cartesian language, it is claimed that there is only one set of substances, physical substances, and this one set has some members that can be referred to by both physical and mental expressions. None of Descartes's considerations rules out this possibility.

Nor is it a legitimate objection to the Identity theory that where one expression is used we cannot always substitute the other and preserve the truth-value. For it is a necessary consequence of the fact that C-state expressions and B-process expressions differ in meaning that in at least two familiar cases what we can assert about the one we may not be able to assert about the other. First there is the case of the so-called verbs of intentionality: it may be true that a particular C-state is remembered or expected, for example, but false that a particular B-process is remembered or expected. Secondly there is the case of modal statements: it is true that C-states are necessarily C-states but false that B-processes are necessarily C-states. Thus that two things are *de facto* identical does not imply that any truth about the one will be a truth about the other.

II

Are C-states in fact identical with B-processes? There are a number of criteria that must be met if we wish to show that they are. For one thing, we must show that the two exist during the same time interval, for if there were some time in which one existed but the other did not, that would settle conclusively that they were not identical. For example, if we had reason to think that the object referred to by the expression "the Evening Star" did not exist in the morning, then we would have reason to think that the Evening Star was not identical with the Morning Star. This coexistence requirement seems to be met in the case of C-states and their correlated B-processes. If future discoveries in neurology and psychology were to lead us to think that they occurred at somewhat different times, then we could certainly rule out the Identity theory.

A further condition to be met for identifying C-states with B-processes is that, at any given time, both must be located in the same place. If it can be shown that one is not found in the place where the other is found, then it has been shown that they are not identical. It would be just like showing that the object referred to by the expression, "the Evening Star," was not, in the morning, in the place where the object referred to by the expression, "the Morning Star," was located; that would show they were not identical.

Is the spatial requirement met by C-states and B-processes? Do they occur in the same place? No. B-processes are, in a perfectly clear sense, located where the brain is, in a particular region of physical space. But it is not true that C-states occur in the brain, or inside the body at all, for that matter. To be sure, I may have a pain in my leg or in my head; we do locate sensations in the body. But that is not to say that we give location to the *state of consciousness* that I have when I am having a sensation. The pain is in my leg, but it is not the case that my state of being-aware-of-a-pain-in-my-leg is also in my leg. Neither is it in my head. In the case of thoughts, there is no temptation to give them location, nor to give location to the mental state of being aware of a thought. In fact, it makes no sense at all to talk about C-states as being located somewhere in the body. We would not understand someone who pointed to a place in his body and claimed that it was there that his entertaining of a thought or having of an after-image was located. It would make no more sense than to claim that his entertaining of a thought was cubical or a micrometer in diameter.

The fact that it makes no sense to speak of C-states occurring in a volume occupied by a brain means that the Identity theory cannot be correct. For it is a necessary condition for saying that something is identical with some particular physical object, state, or process that the thing be located in the place where the particular physical object, state, or process is. If it is not there, it cannot be identical with what is there. Here we have something that distinguishes the mind-body case from such examples of identity as men with featherless bipeds, Morning Star with Evening Star, water with H_2O, lightning with electrical discharge, etc. To consider another example, it has been discovered that light rays are electromagnetic radiations of certain wavelengths. The Identity theorist would claim that "*every* argument for *or against* identification would apply equally in the mind-body case and in the light-electromagnetism case."[2] But this is incorrect. There are ways of locating rays

[2] Putnam, *op. cit.*, p. 171.

of light and ways of locating electromagnetic radiations, and it turns out that wherever one is located the other is also. But this cannot be said in the mind-body case.

To do justice to the Identity theory, however, we cannot let the matter rest here. For it is not entirely correct to say that C-states are not located in the brain. That would give the false impression that they were not in the brain because they were somewhere else. Furthermore, how would one show that they were not in the brain? Do we even understand the claim that they are not in the brain? If it makes no sense to speak of C-states as in the brain, then it makes no sense to speak of them as not in the brain either. The fact of the matter is that we have no rules in our language either for asserting that C-states have a particular location or for denying that they have a particular location. So we have here a case in which it is senseless to apply the criterion of same location. But the Identity theory still will not do, because if it is senseless to apply one of the criteria for identity then it is also senseless to claim that there is identity.

III

At this point the Identity theorist may make the following suggestion:

> We may easily adopt a convention (which is not a change in our present rules for the use of experience words but an addition to them) whereby it would make sense to talk of an experience in terms appropriate to physical process.[3]

A convention we might adopt would be something like this: for any C-state, if it has a corresponding B-process, it will be said to be located in that place where its corresponding B-process is located. Given this convention, it then becomes a matter for empirical investigation whether any C-state has location in space and where that location, if any, is. The outcome of such an investigation could be settled, at least in principle, with as much exactness as we like.

If we were to adopt such a convention, we should run into the following difficulty, raised by Richard B. Brandt:

> Even if one does decide to locate them in the brain, it is possible to hold that the brain-volume contains *both* physical events *and* these other events, and to deny that they are one and the same thing.[4]

Brandt does not give examples, but it is easy to do so. Suppose we set up a magnetic field and then put a physical object into it. Then one and the same volume would contain two different things, a physical object and a magnetic field. Why should we say there are two things there, rather than one, a physical object with a particular magnetic property or in a particular

---

[3] Smart, *op. cit.*, p. 152.
[4] Richard B. Brandt, "Doubts about the Identity Theory," in *Dimensions of Mind*, p. 66.

magnetic state? Here we need a further necessary condition for identity, in addition to being in the same place at the same time. The presence of the one must be an (empirically) necessary condition for the presence of the other. In the case of the physical object and the magnetic field it is clear that neither one is an empirically necessary condition for the other; take away one and the other would still remain. In the case of C-states and B-processes we have assumed that investigations will show that you cannot have one without the other. If that turns out to be the case, then the third necessary condition of identity will have been met.

The three conditions for identity so far discussed are jointly sufficient. If all three are met, then B-processes and C-states are identical; if it is likely that all three are met, then it is likely that B-processes and C-states are identical. There is no room for any alternative. If B-processes and C-states did not exist at the same time or did not exist at the same place, then a case could be made for saying that they were functionally dependent but different. But if we assume that it will turn out to be the case that they must exist in the same place at the same time, we should be unreasonable to hold out for some other theory—a Causal theory, a Parallelist theory, or the like.

The crucial question, then, is whether we are free simply to adopt a convention for locating C-states in space. Compare the case of adopting a convention for locating fictional characters in space. Suppose we said that since it makes no sense at present to ask where, for example, Snow White is in physical space right now, we shall adopt a convention for assigning location. For any fictional character, it will be correct to say that it is, was, and always will be located in the place where its creator was when he first thought of the character. We could now point to a place and say, "There is where the fictional character, Snow White, is." But it is obvious that this could not be a way of locating an object, but only an elliptical way of saying that this is where his creator was. The reason that this could not be a convention for locating fictional objects in space does not depend upon the particular convention we might choose. Any convention of this sort would be absurd because there is no room in the concept of fictional characters for such a convention. This is because it is self-contradictory to speak of a nonexistent thing like a fictional character as having some actual location in physical space. The very meaning of "fictional character" depends upon the contrast with things that actually do have spatial location. Hence we are not free, in this case, simply to adopt a convention for locating, which we can add to our present rules governing expressions that refer to fictional characters.

In the case of C-states it seems to me that room does exist for the adoption of such a convention. There is nothing in the way we teach the use of C-state expressions that rules out their having spatial location, no direct contrast with things that actually do have spatial location. So we can adopt an additional rule that would allow us to locate C-states in space. This is, of course, to change the meanings of expressions that refer to C-states, to change our concept of C-states. It is a change that is consistent with our present rules and that allows us to keep the rest of the concept intact, but it is still a change in the concept. There is, however, no change in the extension of the terms; everything that is a C-state as it is ordinarily conceived will also be a C-state as the concept has been modified, and vice versa. The only difference is that it will now make sense to ask about the physical location of C-states.

Given this modified concept of C-states, the criteria for *de facto* identity of C-states and B-processes have been met. Those things and just those things referred to by C-state expressions will be referred to by B-process expressions. It would be as unreasonable to hold that the world contains C-states in addition to B-processes as it would be to hold that the world contains featherless bipeds in addition to human beings (assuming the two classes are coextensive) or water in addition to H_2O. Of course it is logically possible that there be disembodied C-states, with no corresponding B-processes. That is to say, an Identity theory that uses the modified concept of C-states is a genuine empirical hypothesis, like the hypotheses that human beings are featherless bipeds and that water is H_2O.

In this section I wish to discuss the objection that nothing at all would be gained by so altering our concept of C-states that the identity would hold. This objection is referred to by Smart as "the strongest with which I have to deal" (p. 150) and "the one I am least confident of having satisfactorily met" (p. 148, footnote). The objection may be put in the following way. For it to be a factual discovery that C-states and B-processes are identical, each must have some feature peculiar to itself by which it may be identified as a C-state or as a B-process; but then are we not at least committed to "the existence of irreducibly psychic *properties*" (p. 148)?

In trying to deal with this objection, Smart thinks he must show that psychic properties must be *defined* in terms of physical properties. He attempts to define C-states in the following way. He maintains that when a person reports the occurrence of a C-state, say the having of a yellowish-orange after-image:

> . . . he is saying something like this: *"There is something going on which is like what is going on when* I have my eyes open, am awake, and there is an orange illuminated in good light in front of me, that is, when I really see an orange" (p. 149).

Thus Smart attempts to represent the special features of first-person present-tense reports as nothing but rather indefinite assertions which, if made definite (although the speaker may not know enough physiology to make them definite himself), would turn out to be ordinary assertions about B-processes.

The difficulty with such a definition is that it leaves no room for the fact that we are sometimes justified in the reports we make about our own C-states although we have no information at all about B-processes, not even indefinite information. How could one report even the minimal something going on unless one noticed something? And since it obviously is the case that we can notice something even when we notice nothing in our nervous system, it obviously is the case that some other feature must be noticed which entitles us to say that something similar is going on.

In general, it is hopeless to expect to be able to *define* psychic properties in terms of physical properties, and still holds, as Identity theorists do, that it is a factual discovery that C-states and B-processes are identical. Unless there are special features that allow us independently to identify C-states, we can never be in a position to discover their *de facto* identity with B-processes.

I see no reason why the Identity theorist should be disconcerted by admitting that psychic properties are different from physical properties. For to say that psychic properties are different from physical properties is simply a way of saying that mentalistic expressions have different meanings and different conditions for ascription from physicalistic expressions. It is a fact about the world that both sets of expressions have application (how could that be denied?), but this is a fact from which the Identity theory begins, not a fact that destroys it. Furthermore, that psychic and physical properties are different does not in any way imply that they are "irreducibly" different. To take a classic case, the property of having a certain temperature must be different from the property of having a certain mean kinetic energy, or else it could never have been discovered that they were related in particular ways, ways which we indicate when we say that temperature has been reduced to mean kinetic energy. In general, for one property to be reducible to another, they must be different; something cannot be reducible to itself.

But still one might ask what is to be gained by altering our concept of C-states so as to be able to assert their *de facto* identity with B-processes? It does seem to me that one now does have a simpler conceptual scheme. The traditional Dualistic theories admitted two distinct classes of entities and events, physical entities and physical events on the one hand and mental entities and events on the other. On the Identity theory there is only one set of entities and events, the physical, and it is just these entities and events which turn out to be what is referred to when people use mentalistic expressions. This is analogous to the discovery that water and steam are not different substances but the same substance in different states. It is perfectly true that not all physical processes will be identical with C-states, only neural processes of a particular sort. And that subset of physical processes will have special features, those which are the logically necessary features of C-states. For example, (1) there will be one and only one person in the world who would know of the existence of a particular C-state even if he lacked any of the grounds that anyone else might have for knowing of the existence of that state, and (2) the one and only privileged person could not fail to know of its existence, if it occurred at all. These are features of C-states and, if

C-states turn out to be identical with B-processes, then they will be features of B-processes. Thus the simplification presented by the Identity theory has its price. One class of physical events will have the familiar and undeniable features of C-states. These features may be, in some sense, reducible to physicalistic features, but they are not thereby eliminated from the scheme of things. Only extra entities are eliminated.

The question whether the conceptual revision proposed by Identity theorists should be accepted or not cannot be determined solely by philosophers. It is in part an empirical question, to be judged in terms of future discoveries in neurology and psychology. Take the similar case of water and H_2O. Imagine the debates that must have raged when it was discovered that water could be replaced by definite proportions of hydrogen and oxygen. Were the water, on the one hand, and the two gases, on the other, merely successive states of some further, underlying thing (cf. Double Aspect theory)? Did the one produce the other (cf. Interaction theories)? Was the one a mere shadowy appearance of the other (cf. Epiphenomenalism)? Was there mere correlation of the one disappearing as the other appeared (cf. Parallelism)? Or was the water identical with the combination of the two? The adoption of new uses for such terms as "element," "compound," and "analysis" did not amount merely to trivial solution that simply begged the question in favor of the claim of identity. For it was an empirical discovery that certain substances are "compounds" of specific "elements," the discovery that a particular set of terms can be used to represent and describe these substances in such a way as to tie together a large range of phenomena, yield predictions, and furnish explanations. From a knowledge of the chemical constituents and their proportions we can predict and explain many features of the compound—mass, density, spectral patterns, radioactive properties, and frequently much of its physical and chemical behavior. It is such fruits as these that make plausible the identification of substances with the chemical combination of their constituents.

In the case of the Identity theory, the linguistic innovation consists in modifying our concept of C-states by giving criteria for the spatial location of C-states. Only future discoveries in neurophysiology can tell us how fruitful this innovation might be. If, for example, we never get beyond the point of having gross, brute correlations between C-states and B-processes, then I can see no advantages in the claim that they are identical. But suppose we can, some day, discover certain physical features which distinguish the physical processes that are identical with C-states from those which are not; suppose we can break down B-processes into structures that correspond to the internal structures of C-states; suppose that detailed theories could be worked out for showing that, given the particular neural variables, we get one C-state rather than another and we can infer new C-states from novel configurations of B-processes. If these developments occur, then, as in the example from chemistry, it would be unreasonable to hold out against the Identity theory. For we would have not merely gross correlations of C-states and B-processes but precisely the detailed kind of point-for-point correlations that entitles us in other cases to say that one property, state, or thing has been reduced to another. The value of thinking of C-states in this new way, as having location in the brain, would have been shown by empirical discoveries. But this is not to say that it would have been an empirical discovery that C-states were located in the brain.

If we were to accept the Identity theory with its new concept of C-states, the question would still remain of what the exact relation is between C-states and B-processes. One possibility, although not the only one, is that of a macro-micro relation. Even here there are alternatives. One would be that C-states were composed of neural components, analogous to the physicist's particles or the chemist's elements. If it seems strange to think that C-states might be made up of physical components, remember that even the claim that water is "composed" of hydrogen and oxygen or of a swarm of subatomic particles requires new concepts of composition and components. A different macro-micro relation might be used, such that C-states consisted of B-processes without being composed of them; such would be the case if a field theory of neural behavior were adopted. This would be analogous to the claim that a ray of light consists of wave-motion, that a bolt of lightning consists of an electrical discharge. A half-way house, here, might be a claim analogous to the claim that temperature consists of the mean kinetic energy of the molecules. I suspect that none of these details could be settled until we had a good deal more information about the brain.

If someone were to insist on knowing what the relation is between B-processes and C-states as we conceive them now (in contrast to how we might, some day, more usefully conceive them), then part of the answer is that they are not identical, since the spatial criterion is not met. Another part of the answer is that, if present information is a reliable guide, they occur simultaneously and are conjoined in a regular, law-like way. Another part of the answer consists in seeing in detail how this case is like and unlike other cases, e.g., two independent mechanisms, two objects interacting in the same system, a process and its by-products, looking at something from inside of it and from the outside, etc. I doubt if more than this can be done.

51 The Problem of Consciousness —A Debate*

BRAND BLANSHARD and B. F. SKINNER

Brand Blanshard (1892–) is an influential and distinguished American philosopher. He has taught philosophy at Yale University for many years and is now professor emeritus. Perhaps his best-known work is his two-volume *The Nature of Thought* in which he defends the coherence theory of truth and supports an idealistic metaphysic. His recent works include *Reason and Analysis* and *Reason and Goodness*.

B. F. Skinner (1904–) is professor of psychology at Harvard University. He is known as one of the foremost exponents and theoreticians of behaviorism in the United States and his novel *Walden Two* portrays a community that is run on the principles of behavioristic psychology. He applies his behavioristic theory to the full scope of human experience in his books *Science and Human Behavior* and *Cumulative Record*.

OPENING REMARKS BY PROFESSOR BLANSHARD

Behaviorism is the view that mind can be adequately studied through the behavior of the body. Sometimes it is offered as a method only, implying nothing as to whether a distinct realm of consciousness exists. But it clearly cannot stop there. If there are in fact conscious events distinct from bodily events, a method that disregards them and confines itself to the body cannot be adequate to the study of mind. If behaviorism is to be adequate as a method, it must also be sound as a philosophy; it will give us an adequate science of mind only if mental behavior *is* bodily behavior. And this bold conclusion is one that both Watson and Professor Skinner have had the courage to draw.

What is the difference between the older and the newer behaviorism? It is not a difference in philosophy; it is a difference in policy over what it is in behavior that may be most profitably studied. Watson held that the events to be studied under such heads as sensation, perception, and imagination were

* Reprinted from *Philosophy and Phenomenological Research*, vol. 27 (1966–67), by permission of the authors and *Philosophy and Phenomenological Research*.

events within the body, and particularly in the nervous system; he held what Lovejoy called a hypodermic theory of consciousness. Professor Skinner's approach is different. Without denying that events in the nervous system do largely determine behavior, he is not much interested in them, for he holds that they are all themselves conditioned by stimuli from the outside. The best course for the psychologist, therefore, is to bypass these minute and often conjectural nervous changes and to correlate observable stimuli directly with observable bodily responses. This is the new program for psychology, which is offered with the promise that if it could be carried through, it would explain every kind of human behavior.

The layman will at once have a question. Is he to understand that conscious motives, feelings and ideas have no part in determining conduct or therefore in explaining it? To this question Professor Skinner's answer is essentially the same as Watson's: ideas, motives, feelings in the traditional sense are not, even in principle, observable events, and science can take no account of them. Does this mean that they may be real events, though beyond scientific range? No. There are no events that, if factual at all, are beyond the interest of science. Are we then to dismiss distinctively conscious events altogether? Watson said Yes, on the ground that he could find no such events in his testtubes. Professor Skinner would put it less crudely, but I think his conclusion is in substance the same. He says that to resort to "nonphysical events" is to offer a "fictional explanation" (Skinner, 1953, references at end); the belief in a mind or consciousness irreducible to any form of bodily change seems to him an anachronism, a last lingering survival of primitive animism (Skinner, 1953).

I believe this view to be radically mistaken. I shall urge three points against it: (1) that there *is* such a thing as consciousness, irreducible to physical change; (2) that its denial, instead of according with modern science, is in conflict with it; and (3) that to reject the efficacy of consciousness makes nonsense of practical life (Blanshard, 1939).

First, then, there *is* such a thing as consciousness, distinct from bodily change. For a philosopher to be called upon to prove this is a strange sort of challenge. Modern philosophy began with what I think is the valid insight that consciousness is the most certain thing in the world. Descartes showed that you can doubt with some plausibility the existence of rocks and rivers; you can doubt the existence, at least when unobserved, of your own hands and feet. But you cannot coherently doubt that you are conscious, for to doubt it *is* to be conscious; you establish the fact of consciousness in the very act of doubting it. The behaviorist may reply that by "doubting" Descartes must have meant some physical response, and in taking it for a form of consciousness he was merely deluded. But this will not do either, for a delusion is clearly a fact of consciousness; matter in motion cannot be deluded.

But the behaviorist has persuaded himself that matter in motion is all there is. And if you talk about sensing or perceiving or thinking, he is commonly prepared to tell you *what* movements of matter you ought to mean by these words. For Watson, a toothache was a change in a dental nerve. What is a toothache for Professor Skinner? He says that when a person reports "my tooth aches," he is making a verbal response to an event within his body. What sort of event? Though Professor Skinner adheres to his policy of saying little about such events, this much seems to be clear: the event is a physical event, a movement of matter, since it can be investigated by science, and this is the only kind of event that science recognizes. On the point of greatest interest, Professor Skinner's behaviorism is thus at one with Watson's.

And its major difficulties are the same. The most obvious one is that the experience of pain, for example, is self-evidently *not* the same thing as a physical movement of any kind. That their identification is a confusion can be shown in various ways. First their properties are different. If a pain were any kind of physical motion, we could ask what its direction and velocity were, whereas it makes no sense to talk of the direction or velocity of a toothache. On the other hand, we speak of the pain as dull or excruciating, while a dull or excruciating motion is meaningless again.

Secondly, no behaviorist behaves as if his theory were true. For example, he has occasionally, like the rest of us, had to visit his dentist. The dentist says, "Mr. B., this may be pretty painful; shall I use a little cocaine?" "Yes, by all means," says Mr. B. He clearly wants to avert something; *what?* On his theory, it is a particular physical event, about whose nature he is not very clear. But why should he select this event for his aversion? There is nothing in it as a physical change to make it more objectionable than a million others. What makes it objectionable is plainly just one thing: it happens to carry with it, no one knows why, an excruciating pain, which is as different from the physical change that conditions it as are any two things in the world. If the behaviorist admits that it is this he is trying to avert, he has broken out of his behaviorism; if he denies it, his own conduct refutes him.

Thirdly, he continually deserts his program in his experimental practice. He agrees that, as a psychologist, he is concerned with such events as feeling rage or sorrow, as seeing colors and hearing sounds. What he insists on is that these names be now given not to conscious experiences, which cannot be scientifically studied, but to physical responses that can. But *what* responses are these old names now to mean? It would be ridiculous to give the name "rage" to the limp and drooping behavior of sorrow; one must give it to the kind of behavior that we know as the normal expression of rage. But what that implies is that even in assigning the new terms, we must fall back on the old meanings. "Rage" is now to mean the kind of behavior that we can link uniquely to the *emotion* of rage. We must resort to the conscious state as our only reliable index to the behavior that is supposed to supplant it. Perhaps the oddest achievement of this kind is the Watsonian physiological psychology. Watson would identify seeing blue with the response of the optic nerve to a definite kind of stimulation, namely that of light waves about seven microns long, and seeing red with the response to waves about four microns long. But how did he know which of these minutely different responses to call "seeing blue" and which "seeing red"? It was by starting with the conscious sensation and then looking for its nervous correlate—which meant, of course, that at every step of his experimental inquiry he assumed the very difference between sensation and nervous event which it was his main purpose to deny.

Behaviorists, old and new, have been forced into inconsistency in another way. They are concerned to explain why some responses are acquired and others stamped out. A child, if it tastes sugar, will take it readily in the future, and if given quinine will in the future avoid it. Why? Common sense and traditional psychology answer, Because it finds one pleasant and the other disagreeable. The behaviorist must profess not to know the meaning of such words. " 'Pleasant' or 'satisfying'," writes Professor Skinner, "apparently do not refer to physical properties of reinforcing events, since the physical sciences use neither these terms nor any equivalents" (Skinner, 1953). The business of science is simply to report that the sugar response is "reinforced" and the quinine response "extinguished." But *why* should sugar reinforce a response and quinine inhibit it? There is nothing in the physical properties of either, taken alone, that throws the least light on this. Hence even behaviorists as skilful as Professor Skinner in excluding reference to conscious experience find themselves willy-nilly using terms that mean such experience—or else mean nothing at all. Professor Skinner writes, for example, "though we have been reinforced with an excellent meal in a new restaurant, a bad meal may reduce our patronage to zero"; and on the next page, that in extinguishing a response, "the currently preferred technique is punishment" (Skinner, 1953). Now do such terms as "excellent," "bad," and "punishment" refer to pleasure and pain or not? If not, they are wholly irrelevant in explaining why one response is maintained and another dropped. If they do help in explaining this, as Professor Skinner here implies that they do, it is because they are drawing their force from an interpretation that behaviorism denies them.

Why should behaviorists reject this interpretation? They answer, as we have seen, that it is because it is vetoed by science, and they want above all things to be scientific. "The methods of science," writes Professor Skinner, "have been enormously successful wherever they have been tried. Let us then apply them to human affairs." What Professor Skinner seems here to be saying is that he is moved by the desire to explain things scientifically, though he cannot mean by this what most people mean. The behaviorists of the sixties, like the positivists of the thirties, dismiss as meaningless all references that go beyond physical things and events, entities that at least in principle can be publicly observed. If there was anything purely psychical about us, like old-fashioned desires and sensations, no one else could ever hope to observe them, or therefore meaningfully speak of them.

This curious "physicalism" of the early positivists has now been abandoned by the positivists themselves; Ayer, Feigl, Hempel and Carnap have all renounced it. Behaviorists apparently still cling to it. They still think it demanded by science, though in fact it is deeply at odds with science. That is my second thesis. It will be enough to support it with a single instance.

Consider the behaviorist treatment of images. Watson took the heroic course of denying that there were such things, thereby, as someone remarked, exalting a personal defect into an ontological principle. I shall not pause to argue whether images exist; I shall assume that they do. No one among us who is a fair visualizer will have any trouble in summoning up, for example, the face of Einstein, with its cloud of white hair, its moustache and wrinkles, and its sad, dark eyes. What is the behaviorist to do with such images? He cannot say that when we talk of them, we mean only certain motions among the particles in the brain, for we know too well that we do not. Nor can he say, with common sense and traditional psychology, that they exist in the realm of consciousness, for now there is no such realm. Professor Skinner struggles manfully with the problem, admitting that "perhaps the most difficult problem in the analysis of behavior is raised by responses beginning 'I see . . .', 'I hear . . .', and so on, *when customary stimuli are lacking*" (Skinner, 1953). He recognizes that such reports may be true; he has read the famous chapter of Galton in which a portrait painter is described whose imagery was so vivid that he could paint from it after his sitter was gone. Professor Skinner's explanation of such performances is that seeing is a response which may be conditioned to occur in the absence of its normal stimulus, like the salivating of Pavlov's dog. This is no doubt true, but it leaves the critical question untouched. What is the status of the imaginary or hallucinatory object that the subject admittedly "sees"? It is in the physical world for on the behaviorist account, there is nowhere else for it to be. But it is not in the subject's head, for no surgeon, nor the subject himself with the help of mirrors, will ever find it there. And of course it is not in consciousness; Professor Skinner avoids using the word "imagine" and insists on using "see", even in cases of hallucination. Now if the object thus admittedly seen is not in consciousness and not in the head, where is it? One can only conclude that it is out there in nature. But if this conclusion is offered as consistent with modern physics, it is not hard to predict the comment of the physicist. It would certainly be eloquent, but it might not be quotable.

Images have always offered special difficulty for the behaviorists, and I do not want to exploit that difficulty unduly. So perhaps I should add that precisely the same difficulty is occasioned by ordinary perception. Professor Skinner uses the example of seeing a rainbow in the sky. What is it that we are here responding to? He does not, as Watson did, develop the fact of light waves impinging on nerve ends. He holds, and rightly, that these are not what we see; what we are seeing is the reds, greens and yellows of the bow in the sky. But then these reds, greens and yellows are not really there at all. Would any responsible physicist admit for a moment that they are? He would admit, of course, that the vibrations are there, but that is a quite different matter. The whole modern tradition of physics from Newton down has relegated the reds, greens, and yellows to sensations, sense-data in our minds, caused indeed by outer vibrations, but utterly different from them. Bertrand Russell did attempt fifty years ago to work out a philosophy of science that would place even colors, tastes, and smells out there in nature, but in his last important book in philosophy (Russell, 1948), he comes full circle. He holds that *everything* we directly perceive exists in consciousness, and that the entire world of physical science is a speculative construction built on that foundation. And about the secondary qualities such as colors, sounds and smells, physics would surely agree with him. Regarding these qualities, Professor Skinner seems to me caught in a dilemma. If he puts them in physical nature, he is at odds with science. If he puts them in consciousness, he abandons behaviorism. And I doubt if he can find an ontological purgatory between these two.

My third thesis is that behaviorism leaves a vacuum at the heart of our moral and practical life. It makes us out to be hollow men in a wasteland. It tells us that we are machines—enormously complicated machines, but in the end nothing more. Let us assume for the moment that this is true, and ask what would be the value of a world in which only such machines existed and that unscientific embarrassment, consciousness, did not exist. The answer I suggest is simple: it would have no value at all. Consciousness, however frail and evanescent, is the seat of all goods and evils, of all values of all kinds, and they would go out with it like a candle.

Run down the list of things which, in the opinion of major thinkers, make life worth living. What are they? They are such things as pleasure or happiness, wisdom or understanding, friendship, the sense of beauty, the sense of duty. All of them, you will note, are forms of consciousness. The wisdom prized by Spinoza was not that of a computer, even the giant one pictured by the *New Yorker* which, to the dismay of its mechanics, is issuing from its depths a slip reading "Cogito ergo sum." What Spinoza meant was conscious insight, the *experience* of understanding. The pleasure stressed by Bentham and Mill, the friendship prized by Epicurus, the beauty prized by Schopenhauer, were the *experience* of these things; and when Kant put good will at the top of them, he meant the *conscious* recognition and choice of duty. These men would all have been bewildered by the suggestion that the goods they spoke of lay in the play of nerves or limbs; they would have said that if by some miracle an unconscious robot were to duplicate the story of St. Francis or Casanova, there would be no good or evil about it. With that judgment I agree. In an account of human conduct that confines itself to physical change, everything of intrinsic value has been left out.

Nor is that all. The behaviorist is committed to ignoring not only the goods that give life value, but also the motives that make men seek them.[1]

---

[1] The criticism has been developed in three recent books, Joseph Wood Krutch's *The Measure of Man*, Floyd W. Matson's *The Broken Image*, and Jacques Barzun's *Science the Glorious Entertainment*.

For him the only causes of human behavior lie in its physical conditions. Professor Skinner points out and deplores that it is a "common practice to explain behavior in terms of an inner agent which lacks physical dimensions and is called 'mental' or 'psychic'"; he gives as an instance of this mistake the remark about a lecturer that "what he says is often disorganized because his *ideas* are confused" (Skinner, 1953). There can be "no violation," he says "of the fundamental principle of science which rules out 'final causes'" (Skinner, 1953). Conscious purposes and intentions, even if they existed, could not affect bodily behavior; "since mental or psychic events are asserted to lack the dimensions of physical science, we have an additional reason for rejecting them" (Skinner, 1953).

Put abstractly in this way, the doctrine seems not implausible. But consider what it means in the concrete. Here are a few of the things that strictly and literally follow: Your conscious interest or desire to hear a discussion of behaviorism today had no part in making you come here. St. Francis's love for his fellows, if that means a feeling as distinct from physical conditions, had no influence on how he treated them. Hitler's hatred of the Jews contributed nothing toward his orders to have them exterminated. No gourmet has ever chosen one item on a menu rather than another because of his desire for a pleasanter food. Newton's theoretical interest had no part in keeping him at his desk, nor did his ideas of gravitation ever affect in the slightest what he said or put down on paper. No one has ever done anything because he saw it to be his duty, or even because he mistakenly thought it to be his duty. The novelists, dramatists, and historians of the world have been governed by a unanimous illusion. They have represented Othello as moved to action by feelings of jealousy, and Romeo by his love of Juliet, and Silas Marner by his love of money, and Napoleon by his love of power, and Churchill by his love of England. A psychologist with full understanding would have freed himself from such delusions. He would see that all these "mental states" are equally irrelevant in explaining how people behave.

Of course this disparity between the judgment of the world and that of the behaviorist does not *prove* the behaviorist wrong. But it does show who must assume the burden of proof. And if one asks which is the more probable: that every major moralist, historian, and man of letters has been talking nonsense about human life, or that a set of brilliant young psychologists should have been carried away by excess of zeal, one cannot hesitate long.

REFERENCES

1. Skinner, B. F., *Science and Human Behavior* (Macmillan , 1953), pp. 278, 29, 81, 70, 71, 265–6, 30, 31.
2. Russell, Bertrand, *Human Knowledge, Its Scope, and Limits* (London: Allen and Unwin), 1948.

3. Blanshard, Brand, *The Nature of Thought* (London: Allen and Unwin; N.Y.: Humanities Press, 1939); Chapter IX is an examination of the older behaviorism.

REPLY BY PROFESSOR SKINNER

Professor Blanshard correctly paraphrases the behavioristic principle that ideas, motives, and feelings have no part in determining conduct and therefore no part in explaining it, but he is wrong in saying that it is because these things are not observable. No major behaviorist has ever argued that science must limit itself to public events. The physicalism of the logical positivist has never been good behaviorism, as I pointed out twenty years ago (Skinner, 1945).[2] In an adequate science of behavior nothing that determines conduct can be overlooked no matter how difficult of access it may be. To make inferences about private events is not to abandon or destroy an "objective" position. As a behaviorist, however, I question the nature of such events and their role in the prediction and control of behavior.

I do not expect to find answers in any "hypodermic" theory of consciousness. It is the introspective psychologist who would escape from dualism through physiology. The organism is not empty, and it is important to study what goes on inside it, but most physiologists are looking for the wrong things. No matter how much they may improve their techniques, they will never find sensations, thoughts, or acts of will. On that point Professor Blanshard and I agree, but I do not agree that mental events are thereby shown to be irreducible to physical change.

Behaviorism begins with the assumption that the world is made of only one kind of stuff—dealt with most successfully by physics but well enough for most purposes by common sense. Organisms are part of that world, and their processes are therefore physical processes. In studying behavior, especially the behavior of men, we exhibit further instances of the thing we are studying. In thus behaving about behaving we may raise some tricky problems, but they have their counterparts in "thinking about thinking."

A special problem arises from the inescapable fact that a small part of the universe is enclosed within the skin of each of us. It is not different in kind from the rest of the universe, but because our contact with it is intimate and in some ways exclusive, it receives special consideration. It is said to be known in a special way, to contain the immediately given, to be the first thing a man knows and according to some the only thing he can really know. Philosophers, following Descartes, begin with it in their analysis of mind. Almost everyone seems to begin with it in explaining his own behavior. There is, however, another possible starting point—the behavior of what

[2] Skinner, B. F., "The Operational Analysis of Psychological Terms," *Psychology Review*, 1945.

Max Meyer used to call the Other-One. As a scientific analysis grows more effective, we no longer explain that behavior in terms of inner events. The world within the skin of the Other-One loses its preferred status. But what about the so-called introspective evidence?

Let us consider a few examples. The so-called *conative* aspects of consciousness have to do with the initiation and direction of action. A man is said to act when he wills to do so and to act in a given way to fulfill a purpose. A competing, external explanation is suggested by the concept of the stimulus. In determining which response will occur and when, a stimulus usurps some conative functions. But a great deal of behavior is not simply elicited by stimuli. It is true that stimulus-response theorists still try to leave the initiation and selection of behavior to a "total stimulating situation," but we often know that such a situation has acted as a stimulus only after the fact. In the concept of operant behavior, not to be confused with stimulus-response theories, the stimulus is merely the occasion for action. The initiation and selection of a response are matters concerning its probability, and probability of response is determined by other variables—in particular, by the contingencies of reinforcement. I have suggested that operant reinforcement is simply a more effective formulation of purpose (Skinner, 1963).[3] To the extent that an analysis of contingencies of reinforcement permits us to predict and control when and how a man will act, we have nothing to gain by speaking of a purposive act of will.

So-called *cognitive* functions of consciousness are also displaced by an adequate analysis of the Other-One. A hungry pigeon will repeatedly peck a colored disk if reinforced with food when it does so, but it adds nothing to say that it pecks because it knows that it will get food. Similarly, if it has been reinforced for pecking a red disk, it will also peck a yellow one, though not so rapidly, but it adds nothing to say that it has seen some similarity in the two disks and has mentally generalized from one to the other. Observable contingencies of reinforcement also account for discrimination, abstraction, and concept formation, as well as for other kinds of changes in behavior said to show cognitive processes. To the extent that they do so adequately, no explanatory role survives to be played by mental processes as such.

But the question is, do we not *see* conative and cognitive activities? Before answering it, we should ask what it means to see anything. Here the mentalist has almost succeeded in sealing off a behavioristic analysis. It has long been supposed that sensing or perceiving is something man does to the environment; we are only beginning to discover what the environment does to man. The modern concept of stimulus control reverses the very direction of action and, for that and other reasons, is not readily seen to be equivalent to "direct experience." A convenient account of stimulus control has been written by Herbert Terrace (1965).[4]

[3] Skinner, B. F., "Operant Behavior," *American Psychologist*, 1963.
[4] Terrace, Herbert, "Stimulus Control" to appear in W. K. Honig, ed., *Behavior: Areas of Research and Application*.

Instead of asking our subject to describe "what he sees," using his everyday vocabulary supplemented by a few technical terms, we can bring his behavior under the control of explicit stimuli. The subject can be an animal as well as a man. A nonverbal psychophysics, with either animals or men, is proving to be much more feasible than early critics of behaviorism foresaw. The mentalist will say that we are still getting our subject to tell us what he sees—even when he is an animal. But nothing comparable to experience enters into the formulation, although the same contingencies of reinforcement account for the same behavior, including behavior said to report the content of consciousness.

If the mentalist insists that we have still left out "seeing" itself, we must ask him what he means. What has been left out? What *is* seeing? What does a perceiver do—either to, or about, or in response to the world he perceives? "To experience" often seems to mean simply "to be in contact with." We know the world in the social sense of having been introduced to it. Knowledge is a form of "acquaintance" (the word comes from the same root as cognition). But the action is often more positive. The perceiver apprehends the world almost as one apprehends a criminal. He makes it his own almost as if he were ingesting it, as one ingests the body of a god in the rites of Mithra. He knows the world almost in the biblical sense of possessing it sexually.

Contact and possession are important elements in the concept of experience because they are related to the physical privacy of the world within one's skin. They have led to the view that the world *beyond* one's skin can be known only from copies. When the copies are discovered to be bad, it is concluded that the world can never be known as it really is. Richard Held has described the search for copies of reality and for an explanation of their shortcomings in his paper *Object and Effigy* (1965).[5] Physiologists and neurologists have tried to support the notion of inner copies by tracing the stimulus into the nervous system, where it can be more intimately possessed, but their facts seem to show that the organism begins at once to analyze stimuli and to respond to them in ways which cannot be regarded as the construction of effigies. The behaviorist has no interest in experience as contact or possession, and he quite sensibly leaves the environment where it is. And even if private copies of it existed in the external world, they would not answer the question we are asking. Put the thing you see wherever you like—at the surface of the organism, in the heart of the nervous system, or in the mind—what does it mean to say that you see it?

The behaviorist must give his own answer, and like everyone else he finds it difficult. The study of operant behavior suggests that we look to the contingencies of reinforcement. How are responses brought under stimulus control? What responses are involved? A pigeon may learn to discriminate between colors in pecking at disks for food, but surely there is nothing about

---

[5] Held, Richard, "Object and Effigy" in Gyorgy Kepes, ed., *Structure in Art and in Science*, Braziller, N.Y., 1965.

seeing color which involves pecking disks. Usually, however, an enormous number of responses come under the same kind of stimulus control, and it is possible that seeing color is something common to them. Precurrent responses of observing or attending to stimuli may be important. In verbal behavior certain generalized contingencies maximize control by stimuli and minimize control by other variables, producing the kind of response I have called a tact—and may be especially relevant. Naming a color is no closer to seeing a color than pecking a colored key, but the psychophysicist usually accepts it as an equivalent activity. A similar analysis of contingencies may eventually explain why a subject responds to one feature of a stimulus rather than to another or sees one thing as if it were something else.

All these issues, together with their uncertainties, arise when we are said to see our acts of will, our thoughts, our sensations, our images. Things of this sort *should* be seen with special clarity. They are inside our bodies; we are in contact with them; we possess them; there is no need for copies. But the fact is, they are not seen clearly at all. Two people rarely agree about them, and for good reason. A private event may be close to the perceiver, but it is remote from the environment which teaches him to perceive. We learn to tell the difference between colors when people reinforce our behavior appropriately while manipulating colored objects. We cannot learn the difference between a resolution and a wish, or between guessing and believing, in the same way. Certain techniques permit the verbal environment to circumvent the fact of privacy, but only to a limited extent (Skinner, 1945; 1957).[6] In particular, we describe our past and present behavior, even when it is not visible to others, and we appear to describe our future behavior when we announce an intention. We often do so simply because we are in a favorable position to observe the variables of which our behavior is a function, and many of these are public, but whether public or private, all the events described are physical.

Professor Blanshard must deny this. "The experience of pain . . .," he says, "is self-evidently not the same thing as a physical movement of any kind." His example is as nearly self-evident as possible, but I am afraid it does not quite make the grade. Painful stimuli, being inside the body, are both particularly strong and hard to observe in other ways, and they do not need to be copied. The experience of an external object would serve Professor Blanshard less well as an example. The expression "physical movement," taken from a contemporary analysis of matter, also contributes to the plausibility, for a *motion* is not likely to be dull or excruciating. But *things* are. Indeed, these two adjectives are applied to pain just because they apply to the things which cause pain. A dull pain is the kind of pain caused by a dull object, as a sharp pain is caused by a sharp object. The term "excruciating" is taken from the practice of crucifixion.

[6] Skinner, B. F., *Verbal Behavior*, Appleton-Century-Crofts, 1957.

Ideas, motives, and feelings are more important to Professor Blanshard's argument than pain, and they are by no means so self-evidently perceived. The processes or states which such terms describe acquire control very slowly. Only a long and complicated history of reinforcement leads one to speak of sensations, images, and thoughts. Such a history is characteristic only of certain cultures. Our own culture shows wide variations—it produces the thoroughgoing extravert on the one hand and the introspective psychologist and philosopher on the other. Some sort of history or reinforcement is essential. Descartes could not begin, as he thought he could, by saying "Cogito ergo sum." He had to begin as a baby—a baby whose subsequent verbal environment eventually generated in him (though not, I am sure, in millions of his contemporaries) certain subtle responses, one of which was "cogito." It is a loose term, not because the events it is said to describe are necessarily vague, but because they are almost inaccessible to the verbal community which builds all descriptive verbal repertoires.

Professor Blanshard seizes upon my admission that the problem of images is difficult. It is difficult for the mentalist too. What do you see when what you see is not really there—as in a memory, a fantasy, or a dream? But first, what do you see when what you see *is* there? Someone shows you a picture of a group of scientists, among them Einstein. He asks, "Is Einstein there?" and you say, "Yes," as you have been taught to do in thousands of comparable cases. But suppose he asks, "Do you *see* Einstein?" and you say, "Yes." What have you reported? Did you, in response to his question, simply look at Einstein a second time? If so, how do you distinguish between "seeing Einstein" and "seeing that you are seeing Einstein"?

A possibility which needs to be considered is that in reporting that you see Einstein, you are reporting a *response* rather than a *stimulus*. No matter how obscure its dimensions, the behavior called seeing must be involved, and you must be reporting *it*, rather than the presence of the thing seen, when you report that you see something. *You may be reporting the same thing when you report that you see something which "isn't really there"— when you are merely "imagining how Einstein looked."* Seeing something in memory is not necessarily seeing a copy. The whole concept of "stored data structures"—supported without warrant by the analogy of the computer may be quite wrong. What is stored may be responses—in this case the responses involved in seeing. *When I recall how something looked, I may simply be recalling how I once looked at something.* There was no copy inside me when I first looked at it, and there is none now. I am simply doing again what I once did when I looked at something, and I can tell you that I am doing so.

In another criticism of behaviorism, Professor Blanshard[7] has written,

---

[7] Blandshard, Brand, "Critical Reflections on Behaviorism," *Proceedings of the American Philosophical Society*, 1965.

"The bats' heads taken by the toper to be emerging from the wallpaper are clearly not physical objects—what in the world would physics do ,with them? They are not processes in the nervous system; they are not muscular responses; and it is absurd to turn one's back on them and insist that they are nothing at all." But why is it absurd? We have no more reason to assume the existence of imaginary or hallucinatory objects than of memories as sense data. The toper is quite literally "seeing things." His behavior would be most readily evoked by actual bats' heads emerging from wall-paper, but it can occur, especially after toping, in the absence of any such stimuli. Physiologists may someday find the precursors or mediators of that behavior, but they will never find anything that looks like a bat, for there is nothing of that sort inside the skin *at any time*—whether external stimuli are present or not.

The same explanation may hold for seeing something which does not closely correspond with an external stimulus. Under certain conditions, analyzed in the study of perception, the response of seeing a straight line may be evoked by a curved line. We do not need to say that the straight line is in "the world as it appears to be" and the curved line in "the world as it really is." There is no world as it "appears to be"; there are simply various ways of seeing the world as it is—in this case, a way of seeing a straight line in response to a curved line as a stimulus.

Professor Blanshard feels that I am forced into another absurd position in having to assert that "Hitler's hatred of the Jews contributed nothing toward his orders to have them exterminated" and that Newton's ideas of gravitation never "affected in the slightest degree what he said or put down on paper." But again, why are these statements absurd? If we are to speak of Hitler's hatred, it is necessarily as an inference from a long series of verbal and nonverbal actions. Hitler himself undoubtedly had other information, for he must have observed small-scale actions of the same sort not seen by anyone else, as well as responses of his autonomic nervous system. But no one part of the complex was the cause of any other part—unless, indeed, follow-ing William James, we could say that the action caused the feelings. A much more reasonable view is that the whole pattern was caused by environmental events in Hitler's personal history. It is too late to discover enough of these to make a convincing case (only historians and psychoanalysts explain indi-vidual behavior that way), but it is important to emphasize that the real causes lay in the environment, because if we want to do anything about genocide, it is to the environment we must turn. We cannot make men stop killing each other by changing their feelings. Whatever UNESCO may say to the contrary, wars do not begin in the minds of men. The situation is much more hopeful. To prevent war we must change the environment. In doing so we may well reduce the so-called mental tensions which accompany, and are erroneously said to foster, war-like acts.

And so with Newton. We infer his ideas from the things he said and wrote. Newton himself knew about things he almost said and wrote, as well as things he said or wrote, and revoked, but the ideas he did not quite express were not the causes of the ideas he expressed (in behavioristic terms, his covert responses were not the causes of his overt). The point is important if we are to induce young people to have ideas. For more than two thousand years teachers have been trying to stimulate minds, exercise rational powers, and implant or tease out ideas, and they have very little to show for it. A much more promising program is to construct an educational environment, verbal and nonverbal, in which certain kinds of verbal responses, some of them original, will be emitted. We are closer to such an environment than most educators know.

Did Shakespeare actually represent Othello as moved to action by feelings of jealousy? We should quite justly complain that he had not motivated his character if he had done so. He paints a detailed picture of jealous behavior ending in the smothering of the innocent Desdemona. Most of that behavior, as one should expect in a play, is verbal. Othello tells us about his actions, past, present, and future, and his emotional states. Some of this is public and some private, but no one part is the cause of any other part. If he had had time, he might have described the wound he inflicts upon himself, but the felt pain was no more responsible for his death than his feelings of jealousy were responsible for his jealous acts. A common cause was involved in each case. We must turn to the machinations of "honest Iago" to understand Othello's behavior, and it is a standard criticism of the play that Iago's motives are *not* clear. Certainly it will not do for Professor Blanshard to tell us that he was moved to action by his "villainy."

I am surprised that Professor Blanshard cites the contrary judgment of the world. Philosophers seldom enjoy the support of that judgment, and it seems dangerous to value it too highly. When physicists began to assert that fantastic amounts of energy could be extracted from a lump of mud, I doubt that they were much disturbed by the fact that "every major moralist, historian, and man of letters" would have called it nonsense. Against the judgment of the world, the behaviorist may set the opportunity to discover comparable sources of energy making it possible at long last to deal effectively with human behavior. I continue to argue the behavioristic position because I believe it has vast implications. Current education supplies a useful example. Powerful techniques of teaching, derived from an experimental analysis of behavior, are being widely opposed in the name of traditional philosophies of education—philosophies which are avowedly mentalistic and which receive substantial support from mentalistic, particularly cognitive, psychologists. Those who subscribe to them have no really effective new techniques to offer, but their discussions of education are warmly received because they frequently allude to the mysteries of mind. Millions of school children are being sacrificed on the altar of cognitive theory. Men have suffered long enough from that strange quirk in their behavior which keeps them from applying the methods of natural science to their own lives.

CONCLUDING REMARKS BY PROFESSOR BLANSHARD

In my opening paper, I made three criticisms of Professor Skinner's behaviorism. Has he answered them?

The first point was that a conscious event such as a toothache is not the same as a physical event—that is, a motion of particles—because its properties are self-evidently different. A motion has velocity, but not a pain; a pain may be dull or excruciating, while it is meaningless to say this of a motion. Professor Skinner replies that though a motion cannot be dull or excruciating, a physical object can be, and "these two adjectives are applied to pain just because they apply to the things which cause pain. A dull pain is the kind of pain caused by a dull object, as a sharp pain is caused by a sharp object." On this there are three comments to be made.

First, it seems to be untrue. Dull toothaches or headaches are not normally caused by dull objects, or sharp ones by sharp objects. Secondly, granting that a pain may be caused by a physical thing, that does not show that the pain itself is a physical thing; cause and effect are not necessarily alike. Thirdly, even if the term "dull" is ascribable to a physical thing as well as to a pain, it is ascribed in a wholly different sense. The dullness or sharpness of a thing is a matter of its shape; that of a pain is not, for a pain has no shape. This reply can be extended to other cases. The fact that we describe mental events in terms of metaphors drawn from the physical is no evidence that the mental *is* physical and that we are not using metaphors at all.

In maintaining that there are distinct conscious events, I pointed out, further, that philosophers from Descartes to Russell have found their own consciousness the most certain thing in the world. I am still not clear how Professor Skinner would answer them. He seems to take several lines. One is that they would not have had this certainty if their psychology had been of the right kind and had based itself on the behavior of the Other-One. This of course is true, for we never observe the consciousness of other persons, but only their bodily behavior, and hence if we were confined to this sort of psychology, all talk of consciousness would be ruled out from the beginning. But the question is whether this sort of psychology does not itself leave something out. We all talk with confidence about our own desires and purposes, and the burden of proof is clearly on anyone who would ignore them.

So Professor Skinner offers a second line of reply: we do not need them in explaining behavior. The purpose by which we explain a given action has, if it exists at all, certain conditions of a physical kind. Why not, then, bypass the purpose and connect our behavior directly with these prior conditions? If *a* causes *b*, and *b* causes *c*, then *a* causes *c*, and if we can link these two directly, we shall not need to introduce anything inner or mental whatever. The chief novelty of Professor Skinner's behaviorism lies, I suppose, in this attempt to bypass inner events, whether mental or physical, by correlating their causes directly with their effects and ignoring these events themselves. But surely you do not abolish the intermediate link in the chain by ignoring it. Every chug of the engine in your car has prior causes which are therefore the remoter causes of the car's running, but that does not mean that the engine can be eliminated. Even if you did succeed in linking event 3 with event 1 in your explanation without mentioning 2, that does not prove that there is no 2.

Furthermore, we have the most impressive positive evidence that 2 does exist, the evidence of direct awareness. I am aware that I am now thinking about behaviorism with the purpose of criticizing it. Here we meet with Professor Skinner's third line of reply: he questions this awareness. He says that we never see these inner processes. I agree, for I hold that they are not, like physical processes, the sort of events that can be seen. I can say this, but I am puzzled as to how Professor Skinner can say it. On his theory these processes are as truly physical events in space as the rolling of billaird balls, and such events *can* normally be seen. It is one of the paradoxes about behaviorists that they first tell us that pains and thoughts are just physical movements in space, and then when we draw the conclusion that we should be able to see them like other such movements, they draw back in dismay. Surely they should either give up the theory that these processes are physical movements—that is, give up behaviorism—or else go courageously forward to the view that we may hope, with a new electronic microscope, to see someone's toothache or concept of liberty lurking or scurrying about in his head. This the behaviorist feels, with the rest of us, to be absurd. On his premises, I do not see why.

Still, consistently or not, Professor Skinner does deny that pains and thoughts can be seen, and, on that ground apparently, questions whether there really are such things. But surely seeing is not the only kind of awareness. We may be vividly aware not only of shapes and sizes, but also of our activity of thinking, of our being hot, of being in doubt what should be done about Viet Nam, of the last time we saw Paris, of the funniness of a joke, or of 2-and-2's making 4. I should not for a moment deny that there are difficulties in analyzing these kinds of awareness. I should only maintain that no argument by which people have sought to analyze them away is half so certain as their own disclosures to us. If any behavioristic or Christian Scientist tells me that my consciousness of an intense pain is an illusion, I can only say, No, thank you; if that is science, I prefer to stay with common sense or (heaven help me) philosophy.

The second thesis of my paper was that behaviorism, for all its desire to be scientific, is really in conflict with science. Only physical things and events exist, says Professor Skinner. Images, hallucinations and sensations of blue, if anything at all, must therefore be physical things or events. But no physicist would accept this. No natural scientist would introduce the bats' heads seen by the toper, or our images of Einstein, or the hues we see in the rainbow, into physical space. The behaviorist is here ranging himself not against philosophy only, which he would do with equanimity, but against physics also, which he respects. What is Professor Skinner's reply?

I have had some difficulty in following it, but apparently it is this. The image of Einstein is not an object seen or imagined at all, and hence the problem of finding a place for it does not arise. At some time in the past we have seen Einstein in person or in a picture, and when we now have an image of him, we are repeating the response or activity of seeing. "No matter how obscure its dimensions, the behavior called seeing must be involved, and you may be reporting *it* rather than the presence of the thing seen when you report that you see something." That is, the seeing occurs, but without an object. To have an image is to engage in an activity of seeing into which the alleged object is telescoped or dissolved. And this activity of seeing is of course bodily activity.

What is most striking about this theory, to my mind, is its appeal from experienced fact to a materialist metaphysics; it could hardly have been suggested by the facts themselves. I report that I have an image of Einstein, so clear that I can see the fluffy hair and some of the wrinkles; I am told that in fact I am seeing nothing at all. I report that in my own experience seeing is always a seeing of something or other, that to see and yet see nothing is impossible. I am told that the impossible is perfectly possible, and this must be regarded as a case of it. I report that in my own experience there is a sharp difference between the object of a response and the response itself; I am told that here the object has been absorbed in the response in a way to which nothing in the facts seems to correspond. I report that in my own experience there is a difference between contemplating and acting, that I can envisage a face or a scene without doing anything about it. I am told that there is no such distinction, that contemplating *is* behaving. I report that seeing Einstein in imagination, even if it is in a sense behaving, seems at the farthest possible remove from the making of a bodily adjustment. I am assured that my having an image *is* a bodily adjustment and nothing more.

Now I believe in philosophy, but in a philosophy that starts from facts as given, not as moulded to suit the interest of a materialist or any other metaphysics. The behaviorist is committed to an antecedent philosophical theory which requires him to regard images, like everything else, as physical. But he meets with so stout a resistance from the physicist that he feels compelled to change his tactics and to say that the image is not a physical thing; it is really the physical activity of seeing. But this does not remove the difficulty; it doubles it; for now in addition to calling an image physical, he is trying to dissolve an object into the process of responding to it. It cannot be done. If my image of Einstein is not a physical thing, neither is it a physical process.

My third thesis was that in denying consciousness, behaviorism makes us robots or hollow men, since consciousness is the seat of all values and all motives. Regarding values, Professor Skinner says nothing, and I remain in the dark as to how values of any kind can exist in a world of matter in motion. Regarding motives, however, he is gratefully clear. He accepts my reading of behaviorism as implying that Hitler's hatred had nothing causally to do with his acts of genocide, and adds that mental tensions are "erroneously said to foster war-like acts." Newton's "ideas" made no difference to what he wrote, and Othello's feelings of jealousy were no more responsible for his jealous acts than his feelings of pain were responsible for his death. To the comment that here he would have against him "every major moralist, historian, and man of letters" Professor Skinner replies that these men would also have opposed modern science when it said you could extract vast energy from a lump of mud.

Now I do not think they would; humanists are more likely to be helplessly credulous when scientists speak in their own field. But even if they did, the testimony of humanists when in turn they speak in their own field can hardly thus be brushed aside. They feel threatened by a rising wave of computerized philistinism, which seems bent on liquidating the world they live in. They are coming to learn with bewilderment that the new science of mind rules out as an antiquated delusion the entire realm of mind once occupied by the humanities. It says that in the traditional humanistic sense the poetry of Keats, the thought of Kant, the music of Mozart, the morality of Schweitzer, the religion of Tillich, even the scientific reflection of Newton and Darwin, literally never existed at all, and that there was really nothing about these men except their bodily complexity to distinguish them from an IBM computer. And the theory not only destroys the humanities in principle; it makes education in them or any other field pointless, for there is nothing about a complex robot to make it more worth being than a simple robot. "We cannot make men stop killing each other," says Professor Skinner, "by changing their feelings." Why educate their feelings at all, one wonders, if not even the hatred of a Hitler or the jealousy of an Othello can make the slightest difference in what they do? It seems equally pointless to educate men to reflect, for the foresight of the consequences of their conduct can never affect that conduct. Indeed it is hard to see why, in a behaviorist world, any consequences should be better than any others. Why should I not impose suffering on others if it is only a mentalistic unreality? Fortunately Professor Skinner is so unreasonable a behaviorist as to be a very kindly and considerate man.

He has quoted a name we both revere, and may I do so too in closing? William James, our greatest psychologist, was a man who believed in science thoroughly, but also believed in the existence, the importance, and the efficacy of consciousness. He concluded his Lowell Lectures with this sentence: "I, for one, as a scientist and practical man alike, deny utterly that science

52 Of Personal Identity*

DAVID HUME

David Hume (1711–1776) has had a tremendous influence on the developments of modern philosophy. Along with John Locke and Bishop Berkeley, he began the philosophical tradition known as empiricism. His principal philosophical works are A Treatise of Human Nature, Inquiry Concerning the Human Understanding, and Dialogues Concerning Natural Religion.

There are some philosophers who imagine we are every moment intimately conscious of what we call our *self*; that we feel its existence and its continuance in existence; and are certain, beyond the evidence of a demonstration, both of its perfect identity and simplicity. The strongest sensation, the most violent passion, say they, instead of distracting us from this view, only fix it the more intensely, and make us consider their influence on *self* either by their pain or pleasure. To attempt a further proof of this were to weaken its evidence; since no proof can be derived from any fact of which we are so intimately conscious; nor is there anything of which we can be certain if we doubt of this.

Unluckily all these positive assertions are contrary to that very experience which is pleaded for them; nor have we any idea of *self*, after the manner it is here explained. For, from what impression could this idea be derived? This question it is impossible to answer without a manifest contradiction and absurdity; and yet it is a question which must necessarily be answered, if we would have the idea of self pass for clear and intelligible. It must be some one impression that gives rise to every real idea. But self or person is not any one impression, but that to which our several impressions and ideas are supposed to have a reference. If any impression gives rise to the idea of self, that impression must continue invariably the same, through the whole course of our lives; since self is supposed to exist after that manner. But there is no impression constant and invariable. Pain and pleasure, grief and joy, passions and sensations succeed each other, and never all exist at the same time. It cannot therefore be from any of these impressions, or from any other, that the idea of self is derived; and consequently there is no such idea.

But further, what must become of all our particular perceptions upon this hypothesis? All these are different, and distinguishable, and separable from

* From David Hume, A Treatise of Human Nature, first published in 1739.

each other, and may be separately considered, and may exist separately, and have no need of anything to support their existence. After what manner therefore do they belong to self, and how are they connected with it? For my part, when I enter most intimately into what I call *myself*, I always stumble on some particular perception or other, of heat or cold, light or shade, love or hatred, pain or pleasure. I never can catch *myself* at any time without a perception, and never can observe anything but the perception. When my perceptions are removed for any time, as by sound sleep, so long am I insensible of *myself*, and may truly be said not to exist. And were all my perceptions removed by death, and could I neither think, nor feel, nor see, nor love, nor hate, after the dissolution of my body, I should be entirely annihilated, nor do I conceive what is further requisite to make me a perfect nonentity. If any one, upon serious and unprejudiced reflection, thinks he has a different notion of *himself*, I must confess I can reason no longer with him. All I can allow him is, that he may be in the right as well as I, and that we are essentially different in this particular. He may, perhaps, perceive something simple and continued, which he calls *himself*; though I am certain there is no such principle in me.

But setting aside some metaphysicians of this kind, I may venture to affirm of the rest of mankind, that they are nothing but a bundle or collection of different perceptions, which succeed each other with an inconceivable rapidity, and are in a perpetual flux and movement. Our eyes cannot turn in their sockets without varying our perceptions. Our thought is still more variable than our sight; and all our other senses and faculties contribute to this change; nor is there any single power of the soul, which remains unalterably the same, perhaps for one moment. The mind is a kind of theater, where several perceptions successively make their appearance; pass, repass, glide away, and mingle in an infinite variety of postures and situations. There is properly no *simplicity* in it at one time, nor *identity* in different, whatever natural propension we may have to imagine that simplicity and identity. The comparison of the theater must not mislead us. They are the successive perceptions only, that constitute the mind; nor have we the most distant notion of the place where these scenes are represented, or of the materials of which it is composed.

What then gives us so great a propension to ascribe an identity to these successive perceptions, and to suppose ourselves possessed of an invariable and uninterrupted existence through the whole course of our lives? In order to answer this question we must distinguish betwixt personal identity, as it regards our thought or imagination, and as it regards our passions or the concern we take in ourselves. The first is our present subject; and to explain it perfectly we must take the matter pretty deep, and account for that identity, which we attribute to plants and animals; there being a great analogy betwixt it and the identity of a self or person.

We have a distinct idea of an object that remains invariable and uninterrupted through a supposed variation of time; and this idea we call that of *identity* or *sameness*. We have also a distinct idea of several different objects existing in succession, and connected together by a close relation; and this to an accurate view affords as perfect a notion of *diversity* as if there was no manner of relation among the objects. But though these two ideas of identity, and a succession of related objects, be in themselves perfectly distinct, and even contrary, yet it is certain that, in our common way of thinking, they are generally confounded with each other. That action of the imagination, by which we consider the uninterrupted and invariable object, and that by which we reflect on the succession of related objects, are almost the same to the feeling, nor is there much more effort of thought required in the latter case than in the former. The relation facilitates the transition of the mind from one object to another, and renders its passage as smooth as if it contemplated one continued object. This resemblance is the cause of the confusion and mistake, and makes us substitute the notion of identity, instead of that of related objects. However at one instant we may consider the related succession as variable or interrupted, we are sure the next to ascribe to it a perfect identity, and regard it as invariable and uninterrupted. Our propensity to this mistake is so great from the resemblance above mentioned, that we fall into it before we are aware; and though we incessantly correct ourselves by reflection, and return to a more accurate method of thinking, yet we cannot long sustain our philosophy, or take off this bias from the imagination. Our last resource is to yield to it, and boldly assert that these different related objects are in effect the same, however interrupted and variable. In order to justify to ourselves this absurdity, we often feign some new and unintelligible principle, that connects the objects together, and prevents their interruption or variation. Thus we feign the continued existence of the perceptions of our senses, to remove the interruption; and run into the notion of a *soul*, and *self*, and *substance*, to disguise the variation. But, we may further observe, that where we do not give rise to such a fiction, our propension to confound identity with relation is so great, that we are apt to imagine something unknown and mysterious, connecting the parts, beside their relation; and this I take to be the case with regard to the identity we ascribe to plants and vegetables. And even when this does not take place, we still feel a propensity to confound these ideas, though we are not able fully to satisfy ourselves in that particular, nor find anything invariable and uninterrupted to justify our notion of identity.

Thus the controversy concerning identity is not merely a dispute of words. For when we attribute identity, in an improper sense, to variable or interrupted objects, our mistake is not confined to the expression, but is commonly attended with a fiction, either of something invariable and uninterrupted, or of something mysterious and inexplicable, or at least with a propensity to such fictions. What will suffice to prove this hypothesis to the satisfaction of every fair inquirer, is to show, from daily experience and observation, that the objects which are variable or interrupted, and yet are supposed to continue the same, are such only as consist of a succession of parts, connected together by resemblance, contiguity, or causation. For as such a succession answers evidently to our notion of diversity, it can only be by mistake we ascribe to it an identity; and as the relation of parts, which leads us into this mistake, is really nothing but a quality, which produces an association of ideas, and an easy transition of the imagination from one to another, it can only be from the resemblance, which this act of the mind bears to that by which we contemplate one continued object, that the error arises. Our chief business, then, must be to prove, that all objects, to which we ascribe identity, without observing their invariableness and uninterruptedness, are such as consist of a succession of related objects.

In order to this, suppose any mass of matter, of which the parts are contiguous and connected, to be placed before us; it is plain we must attribute a perfect identity to this mass, provided all the parts continue uninterruptedly and invariably the same, whatever motion or change of place we may observe either in the whole or in any of the parts. But supposing some very *small* or *inconsiderable* part to be added to the mass, or subtracted from it; though this absolutely destroys the identity of the whole, strictly speaking, yet as we seldom think so accurately, we scruple not to pronounce a mass of matter the same, where we find so trivial an alteration. The passage of the thought from the object before the change to the object after it, is so smooth and easy, that we scarce perceive the transition, and are apt to imagine, that it is nothing but a continued survey of the same object.

There is a very remarkable circumstance that attends this experiment; which is, that though the change of any considerable part in a mass of matter destroys the identity of the whole, yet we must measure the greatness of the part, not absolutely, but by its *proportion* to the whole. The addition or diminution of a mountain would not be sufficient to produce a diversity in a planet; though the change of a very few inches would be able to destroy the identity of some bodies. It will be impossible to account for this, but by reflecting that objects operate upon the mind, and break or interrupt the continuity of its actions, not according to their real greatness, but according to their proportion to each other; and therefore, since this interruption makes an object cease to appear the same, it must be the uninterrupted progress of the thought which constitutes the imperfect identity.

This may be confirmed by another phenomenon. A change in any considerable part of a body destroys its identity; but it is remarkable, that where the change is produced *gradually* and *insensibly*, we are less apt to ascribe to it the same effect. The reason can plainly be no other, than that the mind, in following the successive changes of the body, feels an easy passage from the surveying its condition in one moment, to the viewing of it in another, and in no particular time perceives any interruption in its actions. From which continued perception, it ascribes a continued existence and identity to the object.

But whatever precaution we may use in introducing the changes gradually, and making them proportionable to the whole, it is certain, that where the changes are at last observed to become considerable, we make a scruple of ascribing identity to such different objects. There is, however, another artifice, by which we may induce the imagination to advance a step further; and that is, by producing a reference of the parts to each other, and a combination to some *common end* or purpose. A ship, of which a considerable part has been changed by frequent reparations, is still considered as the same; nor does the difference of the materials hinder us from ascribing an identity to it. The common end, in which the parts conspire, is the same under all their variations, and affords an easy transition of the imagination from one situation of the body to another.

But this is still more remarkable, when we add a *sympathy* of parts to their *common end*, and suppose that they bear to each other the reciprocal relation of cause and effect in all their actions and operations. This is the case with all animals and vegetables; where not only the several parts have a reference to some general purpose, but also a mutual dependence on, and connection with, each other. The effect of so strong a relation is, that though every one must allow, that in a very few years both vegetables and animals endure a *total* change, yet we still attribute identity to them, while their form, size, and substance, are entirely altered. An oak that grows from a small plant to a large tree is still the same oak, though there be not one particle of matter or figure of its parts the same. An infant becomes a man, and is sometimes fat, sometimes lean, without any change in his identity.

We may also consider the two following phenomena, which are remarkable in their kind. The first is, that though we commonly be able to distinguish pretty exactly betwixt numerical and specific identity, yet it sometimes happens that we confound them, and in our thinking and reasoning employ the one for the other. Thus, a man who hears a noise that is frequently interrupted and renewed, says it is still the same noise, though it is evident the sounds have only a specific identity or resemblance, and there is nothing numerically the same but the cause which produced them. In like manner it may be said, without breach of the propriety of language, that such a church, which was formerly of brick, fell to ruin, and that the parish rebuilt the same church of freestone, and according to modern architecture. Here neither the form nor materials are the same, nor is there anything common to the two objects but their relation to the inhabitants of the parish; and yet this alone is sufficient to make us denominate them the same. But we must observe, that in these cases the first object is in a manner annihilated before the second comes into existence; by which means, we are never presented, in any one point of time, with the idea of difference and multiplicity; and for that reason are less scrupulous in calling them the same.

Secondly, we may remark, that though, in a succession of related objects, it be in a manner requisite that the change of parts be not sudden nor entire, in order to preserve the identity, yet where the objects are in their nature changeable and inconstant, we admit of a more sudden transition than would otherwise be consistent with that relation. Thus, as the nature of a river consists in the motion and change of parts, though in less than four-and-twenty hours these be totally altered, this hinders not the river from continuing the same during several ages. What is natural and essential to anything is, in a manner, expected; and what is expected makes less impression, and appears of less moment than what is unusual and extraordinary. A considerable change of the former kind seems really less to the imagination than the most trivial alteration of the latter; and by breaking less the continuity of the thought, has less influence in destroying the identity.

We now proceed to explain the nature of *personal identity*, which has become so great a question in philosophy, especially of late years, in England, where all the abstruser sciences are studied with a peculiar ardor and application. And here it is evident the same method of reasoning must be continued which has so successfully explained the identity of plants, and animals, and ships, and houses, and of all compounded and changeable productions either of art or nature. The identity which we ascribe to the mind of man is only a fictitious one, and of a like kind with that which we ascribe to vegetable and animal bodies. It cannot therefore have a different origin, but must proceed from a like operation of the imagination upon like objects.

But lest this argument should not convince the reader, though in my opinion perfectly decisive, let him weigh the following reasoning, which is still closer and more immediate. It is evident that the identity which we attribute to the human mind, however perfect we may imagine it to be, is not able to run the several different perceptions into one, and make them lose their characters of distinction and difference, which are essential to them. It is still true that every distinct perception which enters into the composition of the mind, is a distinct existence, and is different, and distinguishable, and separable from every other perception, either contemporary or successive. But as, notwithstanding this distinction and separability, we suppose the whole train of perceptions to be united by identity, a question naturally arises concerning this relation of identity, whether it be something that really binds our several perceptions together, or only associates their ideas in the imagination; that is, in other words, whether, in pronouncing concerning the identity of a person, we observe some real bond among his perceptions, or only feel one among the ideas we form of them. This question we might easily decide, if we would recollect what has been already proved at large, that the understanding never observes any real connection among objects, and that even the union of cause and effect, when strictly examined, resolves itself into a customary association of ideas. For from thence it evidently follows, that identity is nothing really belonging to these different perceptions, and uniting them altogether, but is merely a quality which we attribute to them, because of the union of their ideas in the imagination when we reflect upon them. Now, the only qualities which can give ideas a union in the imagination, are these three relations above mentioned. These are the uniting principles in the ideal world, and without them every distinct object is separable by the mind, and may be separately considered, and appears not to have any more connection with any other object than if disjoined by the greatest difference and remoteness. It is therefore on some of these three relations of resemblance, contiguity, and causation, that identity depends; and as the very essence of these relations consists in their producing an easy transition of ideas, it follows that our notions of personal identity proceed entirely from the smooth and uninterrupted progress of the thought along a train of connected ideas, according to the principles above explained.

The only question, therefore, which remains is, by what relations this uninterrupted progress of our thought is produced, when we consider existence of a mind or thinking person. And here it is evident we must confine ourselves to resemblance and causation, and must drop contiguity, which has little or no influence in the present case.

To begin with *resemblance*; suppose we could see clearly into the breast of another; and observe that succession of perceptions which constitutes his mind or thinking principle, and suppose that he always preserves the memory of a considerable part of past perceptions, it is evident that nothing could more contribute to the bestowing a relation on this succession amidst all its variations. For what is the memory but a faculty, by which we raise up the images of past perceptions? And as an image necessarily resembles its object, must not the frequent placing of these resembling perceptions in the chain of thought, convey the imagination more easily from one link to another, and make the whole seem like the continuance of one object? In this particular, then, the memory not only discovers the identity, but also contributes to its production, by producing the relation of resemblance among the perceptions. The case is the same, whether we consider ourselves or others.

As to *causation*; we may observe that the true idea of the human mind, is to consider it as a system of different perceptions or different existences, which are linked together by the relation of cause and effect, and mutually produce, destroy, influence, and modify each other. Our impressions give rise to their correspondent ideas; and these ideas, in their turn, produce other impressions. One thought chases another, and draws after it a third, by which it is expelled in its turn. In this respect, I cannot compare the soul more properly to anything than to a republic or commonwealth, in which the several members are united by the reciprocal ties of government and subordination, and give rise to other persons who propagate the same republic in the incessant changes of its parts. And as the same individual republic may not only change its members, but also its laws and constitutions; in like manner the same person may vary his character and disposition, as well as his impressions and ideas, without losing his identity. Whatever changes he endures, his several parts are still connected by the relation of causation. And in this view our identity with regard to the passions serves to corroborate that with regard to the imagination, by the making our distant perceptions influence each other, and by giving us a present concern for our past or future pains or pleasures.

As memory alone acquaints us with the continuance and extent of this succession of perceptions, it is to be considered, upon that account chiefly, as the source of personal identity. Had we no memory, we never should have any notion of causation, nor consequently of that chain of causes and effects, which constitute our self or person. But having once acquired this notion of causation from the memory, we can extend the same chain of causes, and consequently the identity of our persons beyond our memory, and can comprehend times, and circumstances, and actions, which we have entirely forgot, but suppose in general to have existed. For how few of our past actions are there, of which we have any memory? Who can tell me, for instance, what were his thoughts and actions on the first of January 1715, the eleventh of March 1719, and the third of August 1733? Or will he affirm, because he has entirely forgot the incidents of these days, that the present self is not the same person with the self of that time; and by that means overturn all the most established notions of personal identity? In this view, therefore, memory does not so much *produce* as *discover* personal identity, by showing us the relation of cause and effect among our different perceptions. It will be incumbent on those who affirm that memory produces entirely our personal identity, to give a reason why we can thus extend our identity beyond our memory.

The whole of this doctrine leads us to a conclusion, which is of great importance in the present affair, viz. that all the nice and subtile questions concerning personal identity can never possibly be decided, and are to be regarded rather as grammatical than as philosophical difficulties. Identity depends on the relations of ideas; and these relations produce identity, by means of that easy transition they occasion. But as the relations, and the easiness of the transition may diminish by insensible degrees, we have no just standard by which we can decide any dispute concerning the time when they acquire or lose a title to the name of identity. All the disputes concerning the identity of connected objects are merely verbal, except so far as the relation of parts gives rise to some fiction or imaginary principle of union, as we have already observed.

What I have said concerning the first origin and uncertainty of our notion of identity, as applied to the human mind, may be extended with little or no variation to that of *simplicity*. An object, whose different coexistent parts are bound together by a close relation, operates upon the imagination after much the same manner as one perfectly simple and indivisible, and requires not a much greater stretch of thought in order to its conception. From this similarity of operation we attribute a simplicity to it, and feign a principle of union as the support of this simplicity, and the center of all the different parts and qualities of the object.

. . . Upon a more strict review of the section concerning *personal identity*, I find myself involved in such a labyrinth that, I must confess, I neither know how to correct my former opinions, nor how to render them consistent. If this be not a good *general* reason for scepticism, it is at least a sufficient one (if I were not already abundantly supplied) for me to entertain a diffidence and modesty in all my decisions. I shall propose the arguments on both sides, beginning with those that induced me to deny the strict and proper identity and simplicity of a self or thinking being.

When we talk of *self* or *subsistence*, we must have an idea annexed to these terms, otherwise they are altogether unintelligible. Every idea is derived from preceding impressions; and we have no impression of self or substance, as something simple and individual. We have, therefore, no idea of them in that sense.

Whatever is distinct is distinguishable, and whatever is distinguishable is separable by the thought or imagination. All perceptions are distinct. They are, therefore, distinguishable, and separable, and may be conceived as separately existent, and may exist separately, without any contradiction or absurdity.

When I view this table and that chimney, nothing is present to me but particular perceptions, which are of a like nature with all the other perceptions. This is the doctrine of philosophers. But this table, which is present to me, and that chimney, may, and do exist separately. This is the doctrine of the vulgar, and implies no contradiction. There is no contradiction, therefore, in extending the same doctrine to all the perceptions.

In general, the following reasoning seems satisfactory. All ideas are borrowed from preceding perceptions. Our ideas of objects, therefore, are derived from that source. Consequently no proposition can be intelligible or consistent with regard to objects, which is not so with regard to perceptions. But it is intelligible and consistent to say that objects exist distinct and independent, without any common *simple* substance or subject of inhesion. This proposition, therefore, can never be absurd with regard to perceptions.

When I turn my reflection on *myself*, I never can perceive this *self* without some one or more perceptions; nor can I ever perceive anything but the perceptions. It is the composition of these, therefore, which forms the self.

We can conceive a thinking being to have either many or few perceptions. Suppose the mind to be reduced even below the life of an oyster. Suppose it to have only one perception, as of thirst or hunger. Consider it in that situation. Do you conceive anything but merely that perception? Have you any notion of *self* or *substance*? If not, the addition of other perceptions can never give you that notion.

The annihilation which some people suppose to follow upon death, and which entirely destroys this self, is nothing but an extinction of all particular perceptions; love and hatred, pain and pleasure, thought and sensation. These, therefore, must be the same with self, since the one cannot survive the other.

Is *self* the same with *substance*? If it be, how can that question have place, concerning the substance of self, under a change of substance? If they be distinct, what is the difference betwixt them? For my part, I have a notion of neither, when conceived distinct from particular perceptions.

Philosophers begin to be reconciled to the principle, *that we have no idea of external substance, distinct from the ideas of particular qualities.* This must pave the way for a like principle with regard to the mind, *that we have no notion of it, distinct from the particular perception.*

So far I seem to be attended with sufficient evidence. But having thus loosened all our particular perceptions, when I proceed to explain the principle of connection, which binds them together, and makes us attribute to them a real simplicity and identity, I am sensible that my account is very defective, and that nothing but the seeming evidence of the precedent reasonings could have induced me to receive it. If perceptions are distinct existences, they form a whole only by being connected together. But no connections among distinct existences are ever discoverable by human understanding. We only *feel* a connection or determination of the thought to pass from one object to another. It follows, therefore, that the thought alone feels personal identity, when reflecting on the train of past perceptions that compose a mind, the ideas of them are felt to be connected together, and naturally introduce each other. However extraordinary this conclusion may seem, it need not surprise us. Most philosophers seem inclined to think, that personal identity *arises* from consciousness, and consciousness is nothing but a reflected thought or perception. The present philosophy, therefore, has so far a promising aspect. But all my hopes vanish when I come to explain the principles that unite our successive perceptions in our thought or consciousness. I cannot discover any theory which gives me satisfaction on this head.

In short, there are two principles which I cannot render consistent, nor is it in my power to renounce either of them, viz. *that all our distinct perceptions are distinct existences,* and *that the mind never perceives any real connection among distinct existences.* Did our perceptions either inhere in something simple and individual, or did the mind perceive some real connection among them, there would be no difficulty in the case. For my part, I must plead the privilege of a sceptic, and confess that this difficulty is too hard for my understanding. I pretend not, however, to pronounce it absolutely insuperable. Others, perhaps, or myself, upon more mature reflections, may discover some hypothesis that will reconcile those contradictions.

53 Is Life After Death Possible?*

C. J. DUCASSE

Curt J. Ducasse (1881–1969) was born in France and taught philosophy at Brown University for many years. Although very critical
of religious beliefs, Ducasse considered that evidence from para-
psychology supported the belief in survival after death. Included
among his books are *Nature, Mind and Death; A Philosophical Scrutiny of Religion;* and *A Critical Examination of the Belief in a Life
After Death.*

The question whether human personality survives death is sometimes asserted
to be one upon which reflection is futile. Only empirical evidence, it is
said, can be relevant, since the question is purely one of fact.

But no question is purely one of fact until it is clearly understood; and
this one is, on the contrary, ambiguous and replete with tacit assumptions.
Until the ambiguities have been removed and the assumptions critically
examined, we do not really know just what it is we want to know when we
ask whether a life after death is possible. Nor, therefore, can we tell until
then what bearing on this question various facts empirically known to us
may have.

To clarify its meaning is chiefly what I now propose to attempt. I shall
ask first why a future life is so generally desired and believed in. Then I
shall state, as convincingly as I can in the time available, the arguments
commonly advanced to prove that such a life is impossible. After that, I
shall consider the logic of these arguments, and show that they quite fail
to establish the impossibility. Next, the tacit but arbitrary assumption, which
makes them nevertheless appear convincing, will be pointed out. And
finally, I shall consider briefly a number of specific forms which a life after
death might take, if there is one.

Let us turn to the first of these tasks.

* From the Forster Lecture delivered at the University of California at Berkeley in
May, 1947. Reprinted with the kind permission of Mrs. Mable Ducasse.

WHY MAN DESIRES LIFE AFTER DEATH

To begin with, let us note that each of us here has been alive and conscious at all times in the past which he can remember. It is true that sometimes our bodies are in deep sleep, or made inert by anesthetics or injuries. But even at such times we do not experience unconsciousness in ourselves, for to experience it would mean being conscious of being unconscious, and this is a contradiction. The only experience of unconsciousness in ourselves we ever have is, not experience of total unconsciousness, but of unconsciousness *of this or that*; as when we report: "I am not conscious of any pain," or "of any bell-sound," or "of any difference between those two colors," etc. Nor do we ever experience unconsciousness in another person, but only the fact that, sometimes, some or all of the ordinary activities of his body cease to occur. That consciousness itself is extinguished at such times is thus only a hypothesis which we construct to account for certain changes in the behavior of another person's body or to explain in him or in ourselves the eventual lack of memories relating to the given period.

Being alive and conscious is thus, with all men, a lifelong experience and habit; and conscious life is therefore something they naturally—even if tacitly—expect to continue. As J. B. Pratt has pointed out, the child takes the continuity of life for granted. It is the fact of death that has to be taught him. But when he has learned it, and the idea of a future life is then put explicitly before his mind, it seems to him the most natural thing in the world.[1]

The witnessing of death, however, is a rare experience for most of us, and, because it breaks so sharply into our habits, it forces on us the question whether the mind, which until then was manifested by the body now dead, continues somehow to live on, or, on the contrary, has become totally extinct. This question is commonly phrased as concerning "the immortality of the soul," and immortality, strictly speaking, means survival forever. But assurance of survival for some considerable period—say a thousand, or even a hundred, years—would probably have almost as much present psychological value as would assurance of survival strictly forever. Most men would be troubled very little by the idea of extinction at so distant a time—even less troubled than is now a healthy and happy youth by the idea that he will die in fifty or sixty years. Therefore, it is survival for some time, rather than survival specifically forever, that I shall alone consider.

The craving for continued existence is very widespread. Even persons who believe that death means complete extinction of the individual's consciousness often find comfort in various substitute conceptions of survival. They may, for instance, dwell on the continuity of the individual's germ

<hr>

[1] J. B. Pratt, *The Religious Consciousness*, p. 225.

plasm in his descendants. Or they find solace in the thought that, the past being indestructible, their individual life remains eternally an intrinsic part of the history of the world. Also—and more satisfying to one's craving for personal importance—there is the fact that since the acts of one's life have effects, and these in turn further effects, and so on, therefore what one has done goes on forever influencing remotely, and sometimes greatly, the course of future events.

Gratifying to one's vanity, too, is the prospect that, if the achievements of one's life have been great or even only conspicuous, or one's benefactions or evil deeds have been notable, one's name may not only be remembered by acquaintances and relatives for a little while, but may live on in recorded history. But evidently survival in any of these senses is but a consolation prize—but a thin substitute for the continuation of conscious individual life, which may not be a fact, but which most men crave nonetheless.

The roots of this craving are certain desires which death appears to frustrate. For some, the chief of these is for reunion with persons dearly loved. For others, whose lives have been wretched, it is the desire for another chance at the happiness they have missed. For others yet, it is desire for further opportunity to grow in ability, knowledge or character. Often, there is also the desire, already mentioned, to go on counting for something in the affairs of men. And again, a future life for oneself and others is often desired in order that the redressing of the many injustices of this life shall be possible. But it goes without saying that, although desires such as these are often sufficient to cause belief in a future life, they constitute no evidence at all that it is a fact.

In this connection, it may be well to point out that, although both the belief in survival and the belief in the existence of a god or gods are found in most religions, nevertheless there is no necessary connection between the two beliefs. No contradiction would be involved in supposing either that there is a God but no life after death or that there is a life after death but no God. The belief that there is a life after death may be tied to a religion, but it is no more intrinsically religious than would be a belief that there is life on the planet Mars. The after-death world, if it exists, is just another region or dimension of the universe.

But although belief in survival of death is natural and easy and has always been held in one form or another by a large majority of mankind, critical reflection quickly brings forth a number of apparently strong reasons to regard that belief as quite illusory. Let us now review them.

THE ARGUMENTS AGAINST SURVIVAL

There are, first of all, a number of facts which definitely suggest that both the existence and the nature of consciousness wholly depend on the presence of a functioning nervous system. It is pointed out, for example, that wherever consciousness is observed, it is found associated with a living and functioning body. Further, when the body dies, or the head is struck a heavy blow, or some anesthetic is administered, the familiar outward evidences of consciousness terminate, permanently or temporarily. Again, we know well that drugs of various kinds—alcohol, caffein, opium, heroin, and many others—cause specific changes at the time in the nature of a person's mental states. Also, by stimulating in appropriate ways the body's sense organs, corresponding states of consciousness—namely, the various kinds of sensations—can be caused at will. On the other hand, cutting a sensory nerve immediately eliminates a whole range of sensations.

Again, the contents of consciousness, the mental powers, or even the personality, are modified in characteristic ways when certain regions of the brain are destroyed by disease or injury or are disconnected from the rest by such an operation as prefrontal lobotomy. And that the nervous system is the indispensable basis of mind is further suggested by the fact that, in the evolutionary scale, the degree of intelligence of various species of animals keeps pace closely with the degree of development of their brain.

That continued existence of mind after death is impossible has been argued also on the basis of theoretical considerations. It has been contended, for instance, that what we call states of consciousness—or more particularly, ideas, sensations, volitions, feelings, and the like—are really nothing but the minute physical or chemical events which take place in the tissues of the brain. For, it is urged, it would be absurd to suppose that an idea or a volition, if it is not itself a material thing or process, could cause material effects such as contractions of muscles.

Moreover, it is maintained that the possibility of causation of a material event by an immaterial, mental cause is ruled out a priori by the principle of the conservation of energy; for such causation would mean that an additional quantity of energy suddenly pops into the nervous system out of nowhere.

Another conception of consciousness, which is more often met with today than the one just mentioned, but which also implies that consciousness cannot survive death, is that "consciousness" is only the name we give to certain types of behavior, which differentiate the higher animals from all other things in nature. According to this view, to say, for example, that an animal is conscious of a difference between two stimuli means nothing more than that it responds to each by different behavior. That is, the difference of *behavior* is what consciousness of difference between the stimuli *consists in*; and is not, as is commonly assumed, only the behavioral *sign* of something mental and not public, called "consciousness that the stimuli are different."

Or again, consciousness, of the typically human sort called thought, is identified with the typically human sort of behavior called speech; and this, again not in the sense that speech *expresses* or *manifests* something different from itself, called "thought," but in the sense that speech—whether uttered or only whispered—*is* thought itself. And obviously, if thought, or any mental activity, is thus but some mode of behavior of the living body, the mind cannot possibly survive death.

Still another difficulty confronting the hypothesis of survival becomes evident when one imagines in some detail what survival would have to include in order to satisfy the desires which cause man to crave it. It would, of course, have to include persistence not alone of consciousness, but also of personality; that is, of the individual's character, acquired knowledge, cultural skills and interests, memories, and awareness of personal identity. But even this would not be enough, for what man desires is not bare survival, but to go on living in some objective way. And this means to go on meeting new situations and, by exerting himself to deal with them, to broaden and deepen his experience and develop his latent capacities.

But it is hard to imagine this possible without a body and an environment for it, upon which to act and from which to receive impressions. And, if a body and an environment were supposed, but not material and corruptible ones, then it is paradoxical to think that, under such radically different conditions, a given personality could persist.[2]

To take a crude but telling analogy, it is past belief that, if the body of any one of us were suddenly changed into that of a shark or an octopus, and placed in the ocean, his personality could, for more than a very short time, if at all, survive intact so radical a change of environment and of bodily form.

THE ARGUMENTS EXAMINED

Such, in brief, are the chief reasons commonly advanced for holding that survival is impossible. Scrutiny of them, however, will, I think, reveal that they are not as strong as they first seem and far from strong enough to show that there can be no life after death.

Let us consider first the assertion that "thought," or "consciousness," is but another name for subvocal speech, or for some other form of behavior, or for molecular processes in the tissues of the brain. As Paulsen and others have pointed out,[3] no evidence ever is or can be offered to support that assertion, because it is in fact but a disguised proposal to make the words "thought," "feeling," "sensation," "desire," and so on, denote facts quite different from those which these words are commonly employed to denote.

---

[2] Cf. Gardner Murphy, "Difficulties Confronting the Survival Hypothesis," *Journal of the American Society for Psychical Research* for April, 1945, p. 72; Corliss Lamont, "The Illusion of Immortality" (New York, 1935), pp. 26ff.

[3] F. Paulsen, "Introduction to Philosophy" (trans. by F. Thilly, 2d ed.), pp. 82–83.

To say that those words are but other names for certain chemical or behavioral events is as grossly arbitrary as it would be to say that "wood" is but another name for glass, or "potato" but another name for cabbage. What thought, desire, sensation, and other mental states are like, each of us can observe directly by introspection; and what introspection reveals is that they do not in the least resemble muscular contraction, or glandular secretion, or any other known bodily events. No tampering with language can alter the observable fact that thinking is one thing and muttering quite another; that the feeling called anger has no resemblance to the bodily behavior which usually goes with it; or that an act of will is not in the least like anything we find when we open the skull and examine the brain. Certain mental events are doubtless connected in some way with certain bodily events, but they are not those bodily events themselves. The connection is not identity.

This being clear, let us next consider the arguments offered to show that mental processes, although not identical with bodily processes, nevertheless depend on them. We are told, for instance, that some head injuries, or anesthetics, totally extinguish consciousness for the time being. As already pointed out, however, the strict fact is only that the usual bodily signs of consciousness are then absent. But they are also absent when a person is asleep; and yet, at the same time, dreams, which are states of consciousness, may be occurring.

It is true that when the person concerned awakens, he often remembers his dreams, whereas the person that has been anesthetized or injured has usually no memories relating to the period of apparent blankness. But this could mean that his consciousness was, for the first time, dissociated from its ordinary channels of manifestation, as was reported of the co-conscious personalities of some of the patients of Dr. Morton Prince.[4] Moreover, it sometimes occurs that a person who has been in an accident reports lack of memories not only for the period during which his body was unresponsive but also for a period of several hours *before* the accident, during which he had given to his associates all the ordinary external signs of being conscious as usual.

But, more generally, if absence of memories relating to a given period proved unconsciousness for that period, this would force us to conclude that we were unconscious during the first few years of our lives, and indeed have been so most of the time since; for the fact is that we have no memories whatever of most of our days. That we were alive and conscious on any long past specific date is, with only a few exceptions, not something we actually remember, but only something which we infer must be true.

---

[4] "My Life as a Dissociated Personality" (edited by Morton Prince; Boston: Badger).

EVIDENCE FROM PSYCHICAL RESEARCH

Another argument advanced against survival was, it will be remembered, that death must extinguish the mind, since all manifestations of it then cease. But to assert that they invariably then cease is to ignore altogether the considerable amount of evidence to the contrary, gathered over many years and carefully checked by the Society for Psychical Research. This evidence, which is of a variety of kinds, has been reviewed by Professor Gardner Murphy in an article published in the Journal of the Society.[5] He mentions first the numerous well-authenticated cases of apparition of a dead person to others as yet unaware that he had died or even been ill or in danger. The more strongly evidential cases of apparition are those in which the apparition conveys to the person who sees it specific facts until then secret. An example would be that of the apparition of a girl to her brother nine years after her death, with a conspicuous scratch on her cheek. Their mother then revealed to him that she herself had made that scratch accidentally while preparing her daughters body for burial, but that she had then at once covered it with powder and never mentioned it to anyone.

Another famous case is that of a father whose apparition some time after death revealed to one of his sons the existence and location of an unsuspected second will, benefiting him, which was then found as indicated. Still another case would be the report by General Barter, then a subaltern in the British Army in India, of the apparition to him of a lieutenant he had not seen for two or three years. The lieutenant's apparition was riding a brown pony with black mane and tail. He was much stouter than at their last meeting, and, whereas formerly clean-shaven, he now wore a peculiar beard in the form of a fringe encircling his face. On inquiry the next day from a person who had known the lieutenant at the time he died, it turned out that he had indeed become very bloated before his death; that he had grown just such a beard while on the sick list; and that he had some time before bought and eventually ridden to death a pony of that very description.

Other striking instances are those of an apparition seen simultaneously by several persons. It is on record that an apparition of a child was perceived first by a dog, that the animal's rushing at it, loudly barking, interrupted the conversation of the seven persons present in the room, thus drawing their attention to the apparition, and that the latter then moved through the room for some fifteen seconds, followed by the barking dog.[6]

[5] "An Outline of Survival Evidence," *Journal of the American Society for Psychical Research*, January, 1945.

[6] The documents obtained by the Society for Psychical Research concerning this case, that of the lieutenant's apparition, and that of the girl with the scratch, are reproduced in Sir Ernest Bennett's "Apparitions and Haunted Houses" (London: Faber and Faber, 1945), pp. 334–337, 28–35, and 145–150 respectively.

Another type of empirical evidence of survival consists of communications, purporting to come from the dead, made through the persons commonly called sensitives, mediums, or automatists. Some of the most remarkable of these communications were given by the celebrated American medium, Mrs. Piper, who for many years was studied by the Society for Psychical Research, London, with the most elaborate precautions against all possibility of fraud. Twice, particularly, the evidences of identity supplied by the dead persons who purportedly were thus communicating with the living were of the very kinds, and of the same precision and detail, which would ordinarily satisfy a living person of the identity of another living person with whom he was not able to communicate directly, but only through an intermediary, or by letter or telephone.[7]

Again, sometimes the same mark of identity of a dead person, or the same message from him, or complementary parts of one message, are obtained independently from two mediums in different parts of the world.

Of course, when facts of these kinds are recounted, as I have just done, only in abstract summary, they make little if any impression upon us. And the very word "medium" at once brings to our minds the innumerable instances of demonstrated fraud perpetrated by charlatans to extract money from the credulous bereaved. But the modes of trickery and sources of error, which immediately suggest themselves to us as easy, natural explanations of the seemingly extraordinary facts, suggest themselves just as quickly to the members of the research committees of the Society for Psychical Research. Usually, these men have had a good deal more experience than the rest of us with the tricks of conjurers and fraudulent mediums, and take against them precautions far more strict and ingenious than would occur to the average sceptic.[8]

But when, instead of stopping at summaries, one takes the trouble to study the detailed, original reports, it then becomes evident that they cannot all be just laughed off; for to accept the hypothesis of fraud or malobservation would often require more credulity than to accept the facts reported.

To *explain* those facts, however, is quite another thing. Only two hypotheses at all adequate to do so have yet been advanced. One is that the communications really come, as they purport to do, from persons who have died and have survived death. The other is the hypothesis of telepathy—that is, the supposition, itself startling enough, that the medium is able to gather information directly from the minds of others, and that this is the

---

[7] A summary of some of the most evidential facts may be found in the book by M. Sage, entitled "Mrs. Piper and the Society for Psychical Research" (New York: Scott-Thaw Co., 1904); others of them are related in some detail in Sir Oliver Lodge's "The Survival of Man," Sec. IV (New York: Moffat, Yard and Co., 1909) and in A. M. Robbins' "Both Sides of the Veil," Part II (Boston: Sherman, French, and Co., 1909). The fullest account is in the *Proceedings of the Society for Psychical Research*.

[8] Cf. H. Carrington, "The Physical Phenomena of Spiritualism, Fraudulent and Genuine" (Boston: Small, Maynard & Co., 1908).

true source of the information communicated. To account for all the facts, however, this hypothesis has to be stretched very far, for some of them require us to suppose that the medium can tap the minds even of persons far away and quite unknown to him, and can tap even the subconscious part of their minds.

Diverse highly ingenious attempts have been made to devise conditions that would rule out telepathy as a possible explanation of the communications received; but some of the most critical and best-documented investigators still hold that it has not yet been absolutely excluded. Hence, although some of the facts recorded by psychical research constitute, prima facie, strong empirical evidence of survival, they cannot be said to establish it beyond question. But they do show that we need to revise rather radically in some respects our ordinary ideas of what is and is not possible in nature.

CAN MENTAL STATES CAUSE BODILY EVENTS?

Let us now turn to another of the arguments against survival. That states of consciousness entirely depend on bodily processes, and therefore cannot continue when the latter have ceased, is proved, it is argued, by the fact that various states of consciousness—in particular, the several kinds of sensations—can be caused at will by appropriately stimulating the body.

Now, it is very true that sensations and some other mental states can be so caused; but we have just as good and abundant evidence that mental states can cause various bodily events. John Laird mentions, among others, the fact that merely willing to raise one's arm normally suffices to cause it to rise; that a hungry person's mouth is caused to water by the idea of food; that feelings of rage, fear or excitement cause digestion to stop; that anxiety causes changes in the quantity and quality of the milk of a nursing mother; that certain thoughts cause tears, pallor, blushing or fainting; and so on.[9] The evidence we have that the relation is one of cause and effect is exactly the same here as where bodily processes cause mental states.

It is said, of course, that to suppose something non-physical, such as thought, to be capable of causing motion of a physical object, such as the body, is absurd. But I submit that if the heterogeneity of mind and matter makes this absurd, then it makes equally absurd the causation of mental states by stimulation of the body. Yet no absurdity is commonly found in the assertion that cutting the skin causes a feeling of pain, or that alcohol, caffein, bromides, and other drugs, cause characteristic states of consciousness. As David Hume made clear long ago, no kind of causal connection is intrinsically absurd. Anything might cause anything; and only observation can tell us what in fact can cause what.

[9] John Laird, "Our Minds and Their Bodies" (London, 1925), pp. 16–19.

Somewhat similar remarks would apply to the allegation that the principle of the conservation of energy precludes the possibility of causation of a physical event by a mental event. For if it does, then it equally precludes causation in the converse direction, and this, of course, would leave us totally at a loss to explain the occurrence of sensations. But, as Keeton and others have pointed out,[10] that energy is conserved is not something observation has revealed or could reveal, but only a postulate—a defining postulate for the notion of an "isolated physical system."

That is, conservation of energy is something one has to have if, but only if, one insists on conceiving the physical world as wholly self-contained, independent, isolated. And just because the metaphysics which the natural sciences tacitly assume does insist on so conceiving the physical world, this metaphysics compels them to save conservation by postulations *ad hoc* whenever dissipation of energy is what observation reveals. It postulates, for instance, that something else, which appears at such times but was not until then regarded as energy, is energy too, but it is then said, "in a different form."

Furthermore, as Broad has emphasized, all that the principle of conservation requires is that when a quantity Q of energy disappears at one place in the physical world an equal quantity of it should appear at some other place there. And the supposition that, in some cases, what causes it to disappear here and appear there is some mental event, such perhaps as a volition, does not violate at all the supposition that energy is conserved.[11]

A word, next, on the parallelism between the degree of development of the nervous system of various animals and the degree of their intelligence. This is alleged to prove that the latter is the product of the former. But the facts lend themselves equally well to the supposition that, on the contrary, an obscurely felt need for greater intelligence in the circumstances the animal faced was what brought about the variations which eventually resulted in a more adequate nervous organization.

In the development of the individual, at all events, it seems clear that the specific, highly complex nerve connections which become established in the brain and cerebellum of, for instance, a skilled pianist are the results of his will over many years to acquire the skill.

We must not forget in this context that there is a converse, equally consistent with the facts, for the theory, called epiphenomenalism, that mental states are related to the brain much as the halo is to the saint, that is, as effects but never themselves as causes. The converse theory, which might be called hypophenomenalism, and which is pretty well that of Schopenhauer, is that the instruments which the various mechanisms of the body constitute are the objective products of obscure cravings for the corresponding powers;

[10] M. T. Keeton, "Some Ambiguities in the Theory of the Conservation of Energy," *Philosophy of Science*, Vol. 8, No. 3, July 1941.
[11] C. D. Broad, "The Mind and Its Place in Nature," pp. 103 ff.

and, in particular, that the organization of the nervous system is the effect and material isomorph of the variety of mental functions exercised at a given level of animal or human existence.

THE INITIAL ASSUMPTION BEHIND THE ARGUMENTS AGAINST SURVIVAL

We have now scrutinized all but the last of the reasons mentioned earlier for rejecting the possibility of survival, and we have found them all logically weak. Before examining the one which remains, it will be useful for us to pause a moment and inquire why so many of the persons who advance those reasons nevertheless think them convincing.

It is, I believe, because these persons approach the question of survival with a certain unconscious metaphysical bias. It derives from a particular initial assumption which they tacitly make. It is that *to be real is to be material.* And to be material, of course, is to be some process or part of the perceptually public world, that is, of the world we all perceive by means of our so-called five senses.

Now the assumption that to be real is to be material is a useful and appropriate one for the purpose of investigating the material world and of operating upon it; and this purpose is a legitimate and frequent one. But those persons, and most of us, do not realize that the validity of that assumption is strictly relative to that specific purpose. Hence they, and most of us, continue making the assumption, and it continues to rule judgment, even when, as now, the purpose in view is a different one, for which the assumption is no longer useful or even congruous.

The point is all-important here and therefore worth stressing. Its essence is that the conception of the nature of reality that proposes to define the real as the material is not the expression of an observable fact to which everyone would have to bow, but is the expression only of a certain direction of interest on the part of the persons who so define reality—of interest, namely, which they have chosen to center wholly in the material, perceptually public world. This specialized interest is of course as legitimate as any other, but it automatically ignores all the facts, commonly called facts of mind, which only introspection reveals. And that specialized interest is what alone compels persons in its grip to employ the word "mind" to denote, instead of what it commonly does denote, something else altogether, namely, the public behavior of bodies that have minds.

Only so long as one's judgment is swayed unawares by that special interest do the logically weak arguments against the possibility of survival, which we have examined, seem strong.

It is possible, however, and just as legitimate, as well as more conducive to a fair view of our question, to center one's interest at the start on the facts of mind as introspectively observable, ranking them as most real in the sense that they are the facts the intrinsic nature of which we most directly experience, the facts which we most certainly know to exist; and moreover, that they are the facts without the experiencing of which we should not know any other facts whatever—such, for instance, as those of the material world.

The sort of perspective one gets from this point of view is what I propose now to sketch briefly. For one thing, the material world is then seen to be but one among other objects of our consciousness. Moreover, one becomes aware of the crucially important fact that it is an object postulated rather than strictly given. What this means may be made clearer by an example. Suppose that, perhaps in a restaurant we visit for the first time, an entire wall is occupied by a large mirror and we look into it without realizing that it is a mirror. We then perceive, in the part of space beyond it, various material objects, notwithstanding that in fact they have no existence there at all. A certain set of the vivid color images which we call visual sensations was all that was strictly given to us, and these we construed, automatically and instantaneously, but nonetheless erroneously, as signs or appearances of the existence of certain material objects at a certain place.

Again, and similarly, we perceive in our dreams various objects which at the time we take as physical but which eventually we come to believe were not so. And this eventual conclusion, let it be noted, is forced upon us not because we then detect that something, called "physical substance," was lacking in those objects, but only because we notice, as we did not at the time, that their behavior was erratic—incoherent with their ordinary one. That is, their appearance was a *mere* appearance, deceptive in the sense that it did not then predict truly, as ordinarily it does, their later appearances. This, it is important to notice, is the *only* way in which we ever discover that an object we perceive was not really physical, or was not the particular sort of physical object we judged it to be.

These two examples illustrate the fact that our perception of physical objects is sometimes erroneous. But the essential point is that, even when it is veridical instead of erroneous, *all* that is literally and directly given to our minds is still only *some set of sensations*. These, on a given occasion, may be only color sensations; but they often include also tactual sensations, sounds, odors, and so on. It is especially interesting, however, to remark here in passing that, with respect to almost all the many thousands of persons and other "physical" objects we have perceived in a life time, *vivid color images* were the only data our perceiving strictly had to go by; so that, if the truth should happen to have been that those objects, like ghosts or images in a mirror, were actually intangible—that is, were *only* color images— we should never have discovered that this was the fact. For all we *directly* know, it *may* have been the fact!

To perceive a physical object, then, instead of merely experiencing passively certain sensations (something which perhaps hardly ever occurs, is always to *interpret*, that is to *construe*, given sensations as signs of, and appearances to us of, a postulated something other than themselves, which we believe is causing them in us and is capable of causing in us others of specific kinds. We believe this because we believe that our sensations too must have some cause, and we find none for them among our other mental states.

Such a postulated extramental something we call "a physical object." We say that we observe physical objects, and this is true. But it is important for the present purpose to be clear that we "observe" them never in any more direct or literal manner than is constituted by the process of interpretive postulation just described—never, for example, in the wholly direct and literal manner in which we are able to observe our sensations themselves and our other mental states. . . .

54 The Illusion of Immortality*

CORLISS LAMONT

Corliss Lamont is well known as a spokesman for the philosophy of humanism. He has taught at Columbia, Cornell, Harvard, and the New School for Social Research. He is the author of a number of books including *Humanism as a Philosophy* and *The Illusion of Immortality*.

For Humanism, as for most philosophies, the most important and far-reaching problem connected with the nature and destiny of man is what sort of relationship exists between the physical body and the personality, which includes the mind in its every aspect. Is the relation between body and personality so close and fundamental that they constitute an indissoluble unity (the monistic theory); or is it so loose and unessential that the personality can be considered a separable and independent entity which is able in the final analysis to function without the body (the dualistic theory)? Are men, in short, fundamentally a one-ness or a two-ness? Is the human self built and nurtured and maintained only on the basis of living flesh and blood or can it somehow continue its existence, like the captain of a ship that is sunk, after the dissolution of its life partnership with the bodily organism?

Involved in this issue to a considerable extent are problems of knowledge, of ethics, of education and of individual freedom. Most directly involved of all for philosophy and religion is the question of death and of personal immortality. If the dualistic theory or psychology is true, as the traditional religions of the world hold, then a future life is probable or at least possible. If, on the other hand, the monistic theory or psychology is true, as Naturalism, Materialism and Humanism claim, then there is no possibility that the human consciousness, with its memory and awareness of self-identity intact, can survive the shock and disintegration of death. According to this view, the body and personality live together; they grow together; and they die together.

The issue of mortality versus immortality is crucial in the argument of

* From Corliss Lamont, *The Philosophy of Humanism*, (New York: Frederick Ungar Publishing Co., 1965).

Humanism against supernaturalism. For if men realize that their careers are limited to this world, that this earthly existence is all that they will ever have, then they are already more than half-way on the path toward becoming functioning Humanists, no matter what their general attitude toward the universe and no matter what they think about a Deity. In my opinion the history of philosophy and religion demonstrates that in the West, at least, the idea of immortality has on the whole played a more important part than the idea of God. William James asserts unqualifiedly that "the popular touchstone for all philosophies is the question, 'What is their bearing on a future life?'" If this is true, then James is also correct in observing that for most men God has been primarily the guarantor of survival beyond the grave.

Christianity in particular, with its central emphasis on the resurrection and eternal life, came into being first and foremost as a death-conquering religion. And in modern times the priority of immortality in the Christian faith has become ever more insistent, with the very existence of God being more and more frequently deduced from the alleged perseverance of the human personality after death. A brilliant student of religious psychology, Professor James B. Pratt, penetrates to the heart of the situation when he writes: "As the belief in miracles and special answers to prayer and in the interference of the supernatural within the natural has gradually disappeared, almost the only *pragmatic* value of the supernatural left to religion is the belief in a personal future life."

Fraught with the greatest significance, then, is the Humanist position affirming the truth of the monistic or naturalistic psychology, with its sweeping implications regarding the idea of immortality. And I believe that the facts of science offer overwhelming evidence in support of the Humanist thesis of the inseparable coexistence of body and personality.

To begin with, biology has conclusively shown that man and all other forms of life were the result, not of a supernatural act of creation by God, but of an infinitely long process of evolution stretching over at least three or four hundred million years. In that gradual evolutionary advance which started with the lowly amoeba and those even simpler things marking the transition from inanimate matter to life, body was prior and basic. With its increasing complexity, there came about an accompanying development and integration of animal behavior and control, culminating in the species man and in the phenomenon called mind. Mind, in short, appeared at the present apex of the evolutionary process and not at the beginning.

The human body itself is an organism of the most prodigious intricacy, its multitudinous parts adjusted to one another to the last degree of nicety and its billions upon billions of cells normally working together in all but perfect harmony. Specifically it is the relatively greater complexity of the brain in man, and particularly of the cerebral cortex, that has bestowed on him the incomparable power of thought and raised him so immeasurably above all other creatures of the earth. We can be certain that if ever a species more advanced than ourselves emerges upon this planet, it will possess a brain, and therefore a mind, more highly developed than that of contemporary man.

Just as in the evolution of species, mind and personality appear when bodily organization has reached a certain stage, so it is in the history of every normal human being, from conception to the prime of life. Neither the embryo nor the newborn infant possess the distinguishing features of mind, though their potentialities for eventual mental development are of course already present. The laws of heredity, with the hundreds of thousands of genes from each parent determining the inherent mental and physical characteristics of each individual, show in the first instance the intimate correlation between the physical organism and the self. The laws of sex, with their ever-powerful influence on behavior, character and aptitude, tell the same story. It is obvious that the fundamental differences between the male and female personalities depend primarily upon different bodily organization. Always the general rule is that the kind of personality one has is conditioned to a decisive degree by the kind of body one has and by the more fundamental changes that take place in that body.

Any father or mother who carefully watches the growth of a child from birth through adolescence to maturity can make a thousand and one commonplace observations that convincingly testify to the progressive unity of body and mind. This correlation of the physical and the psychic continues through adulthood and old age to the last hour of breath. In the words of Lucretius two thousand years ago: "We feel that the understanding is begotten along with the body and grows together with it, and along with it comes to old age. For as children totter with feeble and tender body, so a weak judgment of mind goes with it. Then when their years are ripe and their strength hardened, greater is their sense and increased their force of mind. Afterward, when now the body is shattered by the stern strength of time, and the frame has sunk with its force dulled, then the reason is maimed, the tongue raves, the mind stumbles, all things give way and fail at once."

Of course Lucretius's statement requires qualification. Men can grow very old and remain quite alert and clear in their minds until the very end. However, some slowing down in the mental processes does take place in practically all persons during advanced years; and definite personality changes usually occur beyond middle age if only for the reason that the human organism then no longer possesses the same physical strength and recuperative powers as in the days of youth. Thus as a rule athletic champions do not come from the older generation.

The very process of dying throws additional light on the relation between body and personality. As at the beginning of an individual's life, during gestation and infancy, the body is controlling, so, too, at the end of life. Just as no personality can enter this world until some body issues, as it were, a passport, so no personality can depart this life until the body gives the word by ceasing all vital functions. Men can be recalled from what is almost equivalent to a state of death, as when they are revived from drowning, suffocation or electric shock, through various types of artificial respiration or of drastic therapy directly involving the heart. The clear implication of these different medical techniques is that personalities, or *souls* in the older phraseology, are very intimately bound up with their this-earthly bodies and that in such situations as I have indicated they come and go according to the expert manipulation of these bodies.

Psychology and its associated sciences give the most conclusive proof of all in support of the oneness of body and personality. Our conscious experience depends on the nervous system with its numberless circuits running through the brain, the spinal cord, the sense organs, and indeed all parts of the body. Our thinking processes are centered in the outer layer of the brain, the cerebral cortex, which consists of well over nine billion nerve cells or neurones. The total number of distinct and different connections, both actual and possible, in this organ is simply staggering and for practical purposes approaches infinity. Along the neuronic pathways of the cortex are laid down those enduring memory patterns which are so absolutely essential for the operation of the mind and the survival of which, in great measure, is a necessity for personal immortality. It is beyond all comprehension how they could possibly outlast the dissolution of the living brain in which they originated and had their being.

Analysis of different types of mental states, including outright abnormality or insanity, strengthens these conclusions. A severe blow on the head, a fracture of the skull, destruction of the brain tissue by disease, lack of thyroid secretion, diminution of the blood supply to the brain, alteration of its quality or rate of circulation through the use of alcohol or drugs—all of these things impair more or less seriously normal intellectual activity. Backing up this evidence of the close inter-relation between the brain and thought is the scientific correlation of functions such as seeing, hearing and speech coordination with identifiable sections of the cerebral cortex.

Everyday experience and observation reinforce these more technical considerations. Everyone knows what happens when you drink too much, but we turn again to Lucretius for the perfect description: "When the stinging strength of wine has entered into a man, and its heat has spread abroad throughout his veins, why is it that there follows a heaviness in the limbs, his legs are entangled as he staggers, his tongue is sluggish, and his mind heavy, his eyes swim, shouting, sobbing, quarreling grows apace, and then all the other signs of this sort that go along with them; why does this come to pass, except that the mastering might of the wine is wont to confound the soul even within the body? But whenever things can be so confounded and entangled, they testify that, if a cause a whit stronger shall have made its way within, they must needs perish, robbed of any further life."

The common processes of sleep and fatigue well illustrate some of the points I have been making. As the body grows tired, the mind grows tired with it. Though it is possible to fight off sleep for no little time, the natural thing is for the whole man as a unit to want and take repose. During slumber a person remains unconscious, except in the sense of occasionally having dreams. Were it not for the substantial and efficacious connecting links that memory provides between the successive days of our lives, we should arise each morning with no consciousness of the past and without the awareness of continuing self-identity so essential to human selfhood. And surely it is legitimate to infer that if a person temporarily loses consciousness in sleep for a third or fourth of every twenty-four hour day, he may at death lose that consciousness permanently.

If one sleeps poorly or perhaps not at all for even a single night, the deleterious effects on the mind and especially on its ability to concentrate become quickly apparent. Bad digestion is likewise only too well-known an enemy of clear and unimpeded thinking; and in fact any sort of ill health may impair intellectual efficiency to some extent or other. Not everything, however, that goes on in the body at large has immediately important consequences for the brain and its powers of thought. This is why people may have serious, long-drawn-out and often fatal diseases, such as cancer or tuberculosis, without their mental faculties being substantially impaired. Cases of this kind show that while the human organism is a closely integrated system, some parts of it in some ways are relatively independent of other parts.

It is so evident, however, that digestion and respiration are functions, primarily, of the stomach and the lungs that it would at once seem absurd to imagine them as operating without these organs. But since the complete functional dependence of personality and mind on the body and brain is less generally known and accepted, it does not offhand appear so unreasonable to talk of them as if they existed minus their indispensable physical base. Actually it makes no more sense to postulate a special brain-soul in order to account for the activities of the mind than to postulate a special stomach-soul in order to explain the functioning of the stomach or a special lung-soul to explain the phenomenon of breathing. And in this whole discussion it would be most helpful for us to remember that mind is not a separate agent or thing-itself, but is a particular type of doing, of activity, on the part of a human being. Thought always signifies thinking; reason is always reasoning.

Certain eminent twentieth-century philosophers, such as the late Henri Bergson, have persisted in adhering to the dualistic psychology; but their theory of a separable and independent soul involves them in a number of unresolvable dilemmas. It is, for example, impossible either to understand how an immaterial soul can act upon and control a material body or to distinguish between those human characteristics which belong to the immortal soul and to the mortal this-earthly organism. The hypothesis that the brain-body acts as a transmissive apparatus through which the soul manifests itself, as a light shines through a colored glass, also breaks down at numerous points.

The dualistic position becomes especially vulnerable when we bring into play the scientific law of parsimony, which requires that any scientific explanation be based on the fewest possible assumptions that succeed in accounting for all the facts. The dualist assumption of a supernatural soul violates this law because of being unnecessary and superfluous for explaining the emotional profundities and the intellectual powers of men. It is as much out of place as the old-time attribution of invisible little devils or demons to account for insanity and hysteria. The amazing complexity and resources of the human body as a whole, evolved from the lower forms of life through veritable aeons of time, and the infinite intricacy of the brain and its cerebral cortex are fully competent to sustain the multifarious activities and achievements of human personalities.

Science not only refutes the dualistic psychology, but also casts a good deal of light on why this theory is so frequently advanced. For scientific analysis does make a number of valid distinctions in describing the human organism. Breathing, after all, is not the same as digesting; nor does one eat ideas. Furthermore, there are certain natural divisions within the human brain itself. On the one hand we have the cerebral cortex, the thin, outer, upper layer of gray matter that carries on a man's conscious thinking and coordinating. On the other hand we have the thalamus, the cerebellum and the brain-stem which together constitute the lower half of the brain, which function to a large extent as the seat of the emotions, and which govern automatic processes like respiration and the circulation of the blood.

This lower half of the brain developed first in evolution and is often in conflict with the upper half known as the cerebrum. Modern psychologists and psychoanalysts attribute many of the neuroses so characteristic of civilized life to discoordination between the two main parts of the brain; to the subconscious or unconscious working at cross-purposes with the conscious. This wholly *natural* dualism within the brain that I have been discussing is the basis for numerous arguments claiming a *supernatural* dualism, in which the functioning of the cortex is explained in terms of a super-physical soul. The point to keep in mind is that whatever distinctions we make within the human brain or body, they are always distinctions within the same natural body; and that whatever distinctions we draw between man and other things, animate or inanimate, they are always distinctions within the same realm of Nature.

Curiously enough, various forms of supernatural religion render striking support to the thesis of unity between body and personality implied by modern science. The religions of ancient times found it most difficult to imagine a substantial and happy hereafter for human beings who had been deprived of their natural bodies by death. So it was that the ancient Greeks had an extremely gloomy conception of the after-existence as a dark, cheerless under-world where the sickly phantoms of the departed flitted about forlorn and futile, with faint voices and nerveless limbs. It is no wonder that on one occasion the shade of Achilles, as recounted in Homer's *Odyssey*, told Ulysses: "Better to be the hireling of a stranger, and serve a man of mean estate whose living is but small, than to be ruler over all these dead and gone." Plato, it will be recalled, suggested that this and similar passages be deleted from the poets, lest such ideas of the beyond make the warriors of the ideal state less enthusiastic about sacrificing their lives in war.

The ancient Egyptians thought that a desirable immortality was possible, but that it was inseparably connected with the practice of mummification and the proper preservation of the natural body. To this fact the great pyramids of Egypt, built primarily to shelter permanently the bodies of the kings and their families, bear imposing witness. Members of the nobility and of the wealthy class set aside enormous fortunes for the expert embalming and lasting care of their dead bodies, some of which are on display as mummies in museums to this day. The immense amount of time, energy and thought that the Egyptians devoted to mummification and supplementary ceremonies is evidence that they could not conceive of a worthwhile immortality without the cooperation of the old, this-earthly body. And I could cite many beliefs and practices akin to those of the Egyptians among a number of other peoples with a developed civilization, as well as among tribes still on a primitive level. Some such tribes, for example, have followed a religious custom of killing off old people before they reach the age of decrepitude, on the supposition that only if their bodies are in fairly good condition at the time of death will their souls be able to lead a satisfactory after-life.

The dominant views of the Old Testament Hebrews either conceived of death as the annihilation of the personality or held that the enfeebled spirits of the dead went to a sad and somber place called Sheol, quite similar to the Hades of the Greeks. In relation to this particular religious background, as described in the Bible, the resurrection idea of the New Testament Christians came as a brilliant solution. For it promised that the old this-earthly bodies would rise triumphant from the tomb, and enabled the faithful to envisage a splendid immortality in which their souls would be united with their former bodies become glorified and incorruptible. Despite a number of embarrassing questions posed by the world's stubborn refusal to come to an end, as expected by the early Christians, the resurrection dogma is still accepted by hundreds of millions of regular Catholics, Protestant Fundamentalists, Greek Orthodox Christians, Hebrew traditionalists and faithful Mohammedans.

No religious doctrine has ever more dramatically reinforced the idea of a close and indissoluble union between body and personality than that of the Christian resurrection. The mainstream of Christian thought has insisted from the earliest days that it will be a resurrection of the flesh, the identical body of this world without a hair or a fingernail missing. The seriousness with which the Catholic Church believes in a literal resurrection is seen in its constant and deep-seated antagonism to the cremation of the dead, a practice which psychologically, at any rate, tends to weaken faith in the resurrection of the corpse. During the development of medicine as a science many churchmen opposed surgery and dissection on the ground that these techniques would mutilate the body and therefore interfere with a perfect resurrection.

The more modernistic and sophisticated of the Protestants, however, influenced by the rise of science and the displacement of miracle by law, found themselves compelled to give up the notion of a literal resurrection. But they filled the well-recognized need of the immortal personality for a bodily partner by inventing spiritual, celestial, etheric, astral, and other extraordinary kinds of supernatural bodies. In so doing they assumed basically the same position—and for the same reason—taken by certain characteristically modern sects such as the Spiritualists, the Swedenborgians and the Theosophists. Indeed, there can be no doubt that the believers in immortality, of every age and culture, bestow on the surviving personality, either explicitly or by implication, a very real body. There can be no question, either, that this constitutes a sort of backhanded recognition of the monistic principle that the human personality and the human body are fundamental and inseparable accompaniments of each other.

To summarize, my brief survey of scientific facts concerning the body-mind problem, buttressed by the reactions of simple common sense and the insistence of supernatural religion upon the need of some kind of future-life body, builds up a most compelling verdict in support of the unbreakable unity of the body and personality, including the mind and consciousness. Testifying always and everywhere to the union, one and inseparable, between body and personality, the monistic or naturalistic psychology stands today as one of the greatest achievements in the history of science. That psychology, while not yet able to describe in exact detail all the intricate workings of the body-personality, does on the whole provide a satisfactory account of the complex human organism.

The monistic relation, then, between body and personality has the standing of a proven psychological law and makes untenable any theory of a worth-while personal survival after death. Even if there existed a wise and good God who had guided the evolution of life upon this earth, he would presumably continue to follow the natural laws that he had himself established. And he could bring about immortality for men only by violating the monistic principle that he had used in the development and construction of human beings; only by becoming a miracle-worker and preternatural magician in the old style. Hence only by believing in miracles can one give credence to the idea of personal immortality; and whoever believes in miracles can literally believe in any fantasy whatsoever.

55 The Christian Hope of Immortality*

A. E. TAYLOR

Alfred E. Taylor (1869–1945) was professor of moral philosophy at Edinburgh University for many years. His volume *Plato: The Man and His Work* is well known. His books also include *The Christian Hope of Immortality*, *Does God Exist?*, and *The Faith of a Moralist*.

Let us begin our examination, then, by setting down briefly some of the leading characteristics that seemed to us to distinguish an "immortality" such as it is reasonable at least to hope for from one which would be a mere arbitrary fancy without any rational justification.

(1) It is the attainment of a completed rational self-hood, or personality, conscious of itself and in harmonious possession both of all its own internal resources and of its "environment". Since it is only in and through intercourse with one another that personality is developed and maintained in us, such a life can only be that of a *society* of persons of one heart and mind from which the veil of mystery now making each of us so much a riddle to the rest, and the self-centred "private interest" which sets barriers to community of will, purpose, and sympathy have been eliminated.

(2) It is a life communicated to those who share in it, in the first instance, from the supreme personality presupposed by the very existence of the world and of ourselves. At that fountain our personality is fed; if we enter into and share the life of one another, in the way proper to moral persons, it is because we are all admitted to be sharers in His life. The "brotherhood of all men", so often dreamed of and longed for, is only possible in so far as all men recognize themselves as "sons of God".

(3) It is no privilege reserved to an *élite* of the richly dowered and gifted, but a heritage open to all mankind, high and low, learned and unlearned, refined or homely, bond or free, in virtue of their common endowment with the capacity for personality.

(4) But, though it is thus, in the end, an inheritance and a gift, it is a gift which has to be appropriated by genuine effort on our own part. We can render ourselves increasingly fit for it by steady and strenuous endeavour, or we can fail more and more to appropriate it by our own carelessness and

* From A. E. Taylor, *The Christian Hope of Immortality* (London: Geoffrey Bles Ltd., 1938). Reprinted by permission.

596

sloth. Even in what we now see of human life, we are familiar enough with the fact that as a man uses or abuses his opportunities, he tends to grow more and more into true personality or to degenerate from it. It is possible to "save one's soul", but equally possible to lose it; eternal life can be won, but it can also be thrown away. And thus, in the end, we must expect it to be with each of us strictly "according to his works", good or evil, though we must never allow ourselves to forget that it is only the supreme Wisdom which knows the full good and evil of any man's "work" as it truly is; the account is not to be rendered to me, and my judgment of the quality of any man's work, and particularly perhaps of that of my own, must always be uncertain. To judge you or myself with the judgment of God, I should need first to see myself or you with the "all-seeing" eyes of the reader of all hearts, and that vision is not vouchsafed to us in our earthly pilgrimage.

(It should hardly be necessary, though to obviate a certain kind of criticism it may be judicious to say that in speaking of the Christian representation of the life to come, our attention will be confined to the few and reticent statements definitely made in the New Testament. We are not in the least concerned with the sometimes rather grotesque pictorial imagery of certain types of popular hymn or sermon. Such utterances are no part of the authoritative teaching of the Christian Church; their language, as everyone understands, is purely metaphorical, and the metaphors employed, being so largely borrowed from Old Testament poetry, are often not those which would spontaneously commend themselves to a modern European imagination, not to add that many of them have the further glaring fault of improperly transferring to the eternal life of "blessed spirits" in Heaven language used in the Apocalypse expressly of the "new Jerusalem" of an earthly "millennium". The golden streets, gates of pearl and foundations of precious stones, for example, all belong to the seer's imaginative description of the renovated terrestrial city; they have nothing to do with "Heaven" and "eternity".)

If we turn, then, to the four points we have just specified and take them in order, we shall, I believe, find that on each and all of them the teaching of Christianity exhibits a complete agreement with what we have called our natural and reasonable anticipations, but at the same times does more than merely repeat those anticipations; it adds something of its own, strictly in conformity with the "natural light", but yet not discoverable apart from an actual historical disclosure, first through the "prophets", and finally through the teaching, and even more, the life, death, and resurrection of our Lord Jesus Christ. Christianity—that is, if it is what it professes to be—is really a *revelation*, a disclosure of God's purposes for us, made from the side of God Himself, and, at the same time, the God to whom it bears witness is no other than the God to whom the careful and unbiased use of our own intelligence has been directing us. It is certainly a faith, but no less certainly, rightly apprehended a reasonable faith.

As to the first of our four points, we may note that the one thing definitely said about the hope held out to the Christian in the New Testament is that it is a being fully alive and fully conscious of the whole truth about our Maker, ourselves, and the world. Thus in the fourth Gospel the Evangelist's leading thought is that the divine Christ who, in the fullness of time has appeared among men, is Himself an eternal living personality, and has come into our midst in order to impart such personality to us. He was "in the beginning with God" and "was God". All creation was made "through Him", and, the writer goes on to explain—if we follow what seems the most probable punctuation—"that which was made was life in Him, and the life was the *light* of men". The life, that is, which is eternally inherent in the Christ is no blind "life force"; it is an intelligent personality, like that we find in a most imperfect measure in ourselves at our best, and aspire to possess in a fuller manner. So in the great prayer of Chapter xvii. our Lord describes the eternal life, which it is His mission to bestow on those who believe, as consisting in knowledge of "the only true God and Jesus Christ whom He has sent". What this implies is expressed in so many words in the First Epistle of John, where, amid all the reserve with which the writer confesses that we know and can know little or nothing, at present, of what eternal life is ("it doth not yet appear what we shall be"), he also insists that at least we shall be "like Him", because "we shall see Him as He is". That is, the knowledge of God as He is will transform us, as we attain to it, into God's likeness, since our personality inevitably shapes itself on the model of that which supplies the food of its habitual contemplation and meditation.

St. Paul again strikes the same note both in his reserves and in his certainties. He, too, will commit himself to no rash theosophic dreams of the future which lies before him; as he tells his Corinthian converts "what God has prepared for them that love Him" is something which "has not entered into man's heart", something transcending all our imaginative speculation; here on earth the best of us only see the reality dimly, through a mirror, so to say, and "in a riddle"; it is elsewhere, "yonder" as the Neo-Platonist philosophers were fond of saying, that it will be for us to see it as it is, and without the distortions which arise from the interposition of the "mirror", to "know even as we are known". Here our most certain knowledge is beset all around with a penumbra of obscurity and darkness; as the old proverb says, as soon as we pursue any of our inquiries more than a very little way, we come upon the inexplicable, *omnia abeunt in mysterium*; "yonder" there will be no unintelligibilities left, our vision will have the limpid transparency of God's, and our wills will be in perfect harmony with themselves and one another because our vision is clear. We shall be what we are here at best seeking to become, persons in full and conscious possession of our own personality.

The tradition of the great Christian divines has always been true to the lines thus laid down in the New Testament. The Greek Fathers did not shrink from translating the Johannine language about likeness to God as the result of "seeing Him as He is", into the formula that the process of attaining eternal life is one of *theosis* (*deification*), becoming ourselves divine, and the formula was retained by the Western Church, though with a preference for replacing the word *deification*, which might be misunderstood as though it were meant to efface the impassable gulf between the Creator and His creatures, by the less dangerous term, *deiformity*. If even that word sounds too presumptuous to certain modern ears we may gloss it by saying that in view of the thorough-going rationalism of medieval Christian thought, to achieve deiformity means neither more nor less than what we have ourselves spoken of as the attainment of an assured and conscious complete personality. When the great men of the Middle Ages spoke of human life as a pilgrimage of the soul to God, they did not mean, as an Indian Yogi might, that the goal of the pilgrim's journey is to lose himself in the impersonal. "The dewdrops slip into the boundless sea" may be a pretty phrase, but to the Christian ear it is charged with deadly heresy; the goal, as Christians have seen it, is not to lose one's personal self, but to find it for the first time and to find it beyond all possibility of loss. Certainly, according to the Gospels, the man who is set on keeping a dwarfish and misgrown self with its trivial lusts and limited and conflicting loves, will in the end lose himself, but he who is ready to set this more than half unreal self on the hazard will end by finding himself "unto life eternal", he will find the personality which God meant to be his, and he is the only man who will do so.

As to our second point, it would be wasting words to take up unnecessary space in dwelling on the fact that eternal life is always represented in the New Testament as a *gift* from God. It is enough for us to remember that St. Paul lays special stress on the contrast between the death which is the *wage* of sin and the eternal life which is not a wage but a free gift of God, and that the same thought reappears in the fourth Gospel when we find Christ saying that He grants it to His disciples to have life in themselves, as the Father has granted it to Him to have life in Himself. It is more to our purpose to note that the gift is not represented in the New Testament as bestowed on men by the fact of their creation. Men are not thought of as already sons of God and heirs of eternal life in virtue of their birth into the world as men; that is a modern "humanitarian" remodelling of the thought; according to the New Testament, men acquire sonship to God and the inheritance of eternal life by being "adopted" into the Christian fellowship; they are adopted, not natural sons of the Father in Heaven. This is why the first step on the way to eternal life can be called by St. Paul being a *"new* creation", and in the fourth Gospel being "born *again*", and why in the Epistle of St. Peter God is said to have "begotten us again unto a lively hope *by the resurrection of Jesus Christ*". Those who are still outside the Christian fellowship are said, on the contrary, to be without hope in the world, and are spoken of not as sons of God, but as "children of wrath". The Christian conception is that eternal life is a gift which Christ is empowered to confer on His followers, and only on them, though sight is never lost of the fact that any man is potentially a son of God, since any man may be re-born into the Christian fellowship.

This is not to say that the New Testament writers teach the doctrine of the "natural mortality of the soul". As their constant references to judgment to come show, they accept as something familiar to themselves and their readers the belief that we all survive what we call the death of the body. It is possible, no doubt, by a suitable exegesis to read into their writings a doctrine of "conditional immortality", if that phrase is taken to mean that the final doom of the man who distinctly rejects Christ and His gift is complete dissolution of personality, but we cannot force on them the thought this dissolution is effected at the death of the present body. That, they assume, we shall all survive. But such mere survival, even if indefinitely prolonged, is not what they mean by "incorruptibility" or eternal life. They keep those names for the new quality of life enjoyed by the man who is "with the Lord" and "sees Him as He is." This is a point which is unfortunately obscured when Christian thinkers set themselves, as they have often done in the past, to try to demonstrate the immortality of the soul by reasoning based simply on a theory of *its* nature, without any reference to God, except perhaps as the Creator of the soul and of everything else. It is therefore, perhaps, from the Christian point of view a gain that arguments of this kind have fallen under suspicion, even excessive suspicion, ever since Kant's vigorous onslaught on them in the *Critique of Pure Reason*. An "immortality" which could be demonstrated without any reference to God would be only an indefinite survival which might conceivably prove to be the fact in a world where there was no God at all; this is not the "better life" that any religiously minded man, least of all a Christian, is particularly interested in.

It should be hardly necessary to remark, again, that there is a complete absence from the New Testament of any trace of the insidious tendency to regard God's gift of a full and completed personality as restricted to some little aristocracy of the intellectually highly endowed. "Heaven", as Christianity conceives it, is not reserved for "superior persons"; it is full of "common people". This is, indeed, a direct consequence of the way in which, in the New Testament, the "promises" are regularly made not to the isolated individual, but to the whole society of the "re-born". They are promises to a "you", not to a "thou". We can, of course, understand how, in the necessary reaction of modern times against the coarsening and hardening of the original thought of the Gospel into the notion of a "salvation" to be mechanically earned by membership of a particular visible organization, men's minds should have been driven in the opposite direction, to the point of regarding "religion" as a purely private affair between the individual soul and its God.

But neither this extreme "protestantism" (which, of course, was never contemplated by the original Protestants) nor its opposite, an extreme "institu-
tionalism" has any true warrant in the New Testament. According to the
New Testament, "salvation" certainly depends on a *personal* relation
between God and the individual soul; if a man has not in him "the spirit of
Christ", he is none of Christ's, no matter what he may seem to be from his
superficial inclusion in any visible organization. But the personal relation is
not a *private* one. It carries with it, and should normally show itself by, a
relation of the most intimate kind to all the other persons who together
constitute "the body of Christ". Hence the inseparability of the love of God,
which is the first commandment of the New Law from the love of one's neighbour, which is the second, and the apostle's insistence that absence of the
love of the brethren may be taken as proof of the absence of love of God.
This is, in fact, a consequence of the very nature of personality itself. Personality can only develop in an atmosphere of reciprocal intimate and loving
fellowship between persons; the closer and more intimate this fellowship,
the more real the personality attained by those who share in it; a narrow and
"self-centred" person (even when, as may be often the case, his isolation is
rather his misfortune than his fault) is not fully a person. St. Paul's way of
putting this is to say that in virtue of the fact that each of us is a "member"
of the body of Christ, we are also "members of one another". Disease or
weakness of one limb or organ of a living body inevitably has its effect on
the health and strength of the whole, and the reason for the closeness of this
connection between the different organs is precisely that all are related as
"organs" to the life of the single self, which *is* not any of the "organs" but
finds its expression through them all.

It is not meant that there is no distinction between the magnitude of the
tasks executed by different organs; the very perfection of organization
demands that there should be distinction and discrimination. But all alike,
conspicuous or inconspicuous, primary or secondary, have their own special
communication to make to the single life of the whole, and all are alike alive
with its life. So in the Christian fellowship, not all who belong to it are
apostles, or teachers, or share in the gifts of wisdom and knowledge to the
same degree, but all are alike alive with the distinctive Christian life, all
have in principle been "re-born into eternity". In the community of the
re-born there are no barriers of race, or colour, or class, and the degree to
which any man has attained possession of *his* true personality is not to be
measured by the place he holds in any scale drawn up with a view to mundane standards. A simple uninstructed man may rank much higher in the
scale of genuine personality than a great scholar or man of science; an
indigent negro than a "cultivated English gentleman". Those of us whose
work in the world is discharged in one of the so-called "learned professions",
perhaps, need particularly to be ·warned that whenever we yield to the
temptation to confuse spiritual worth with intellectual attainments, or deli-

cate taste, or "culture", as the word is commonly understood, we are deserting the Christian standard.

Finally, though the eternal life spoken of in the New Testament is, in its
origin, a free gift bestowed by God, it is one which has to be appropriated
by the recipient and the appropriation involves a lifetime of work and care.
The gift may always be thrown away by our own wilfulness or carelessness,
and none of us is secure gaainst these faults. Hence the need that "he who
seems to stand" should take unremitting care "lest he fall". No New Testament writer is more emphatic in his declarations that eternal life is not a
"wage" or "salary" for services rendered but a gift than St. Paul, but it is he
also who most expressly enjoins his converts to "work out their own salvation" in "fear and trembling", and openly envisages the possibility that, even
in himself, negligence might end in "becoming a castaway". The High
Calvinists of a bygone age were accustomed to find the warrant for their
assertion "once in grace, always in grace" in certain passages of the Epistle
to the Romans; yet it is clear that the author of the epistle would never have
ventured to say of himself what some of his exponents have said, that he
knew himself to be now and for ever finally "in grace".

If it is a paradox to say that something which is a free gift of God may
also be forfeited unless we strive towards it diligently and unremittingly, it
is a paradox which runs through the whole New Testament. No honest
exegesis can get rid of the patent fact that, when all is said, the New
Testament doctrine of man's destiny is no mere message of comfort for the
indolent; there is a side to it which is distinctly disquieting. Eternal life can
be won, and won by him who will, but it can also be thrown away, and
apparently—though the New Testament, intelligently read, is not very
explicit in this—finally thrown away. That any man has actually made such a
final "great refusal" is, perhaps, more than the New Testament ever says, but
at least, for each of us, there is the possibility of making it. It is emphatically *not* the Christian doctrine that the persistent "waster" has only to pass
through the portals of death to find himself in a world which automatically
"makes this world right". And this also is as it should be if what is at stake is
personality itself. Personality cannot be thrust upon us from without; it has
to be asserted by each of us for himself by resolute concentration of thought
and will, and if a man "lets himself drift", he rapidly sinks to a more
impersonal level. If I choose, I can degrade myself into something like a
mere self of momentary impulses and feelings, and we all find that we are
too apt to act thus, especially as age steals over us. We have no reason to
suppose that it can be otherwise in the hereafter.

If what we have so far said is true, then, we may fairly claim for the
Christian hope that, when rightly understood, it is no fantastic dream, pleasing but baseless; in substance it accords with anticipations which are independently inevitable in all of us, just because we are reasonable creatures
in a universe where reason is at home. But Christianity also gives a new and

determinate character to these anticipations, which would otherwise remain vague and uncertain, and because it does this, we rightly receive it as a "revelation". It is wholly misleading to speak of Christianity, in the fashion of the eighteenth-century latitudinarians, as "the religion of nature republished", with the implication that it contains only what might have been, and presumably was, equally well known to the reflective and devout of all ages, and that the mission of our Lord was no more than to remind the thoughtless of what they had allowed themselves to forget. Christ, according to the New Testament, did not come into the world simply to help men to "brush up" their "natural religion" as middle-aged men may "brush up" the French and Latin they learned in their schooldays. He came primarily not to *teach* us something in the short course of His earthly life, but to *do* something for us which no mere teacher could do; so far as He came to teach, it was to teach us something we did not know before, and without Him could not know at all.

What the New Testament adds to the statement that eternal life is the gift of God is, in the first place, that the gift has been bestowed on us specifically through Christ, and that Christ is no mere envoy through whom a far-away God has conveyed a message to us, but one who is Himself both a man of our own flesh and blood and also divine, "one with the Father". (The New Testament writers do not, of course, use the technical terminology which was subsequently developed for the express purpose of putting an end to discussions about their meaning, but it is recognized to-day by scholars of all shades of personal opinion that the New Testament everywhere presents Christ as a divine being who may rightly receive the adoration due to God, and whose acts are rightly described as acts of God. It is just the impossibility of reducing the Lord Jesus of "primitive Christianity" to purely human dimensions which leads ingenious but ill-balanced writers in our own times to make attempts, discountenanced by all serious historians, Christian or non-Christian, to get rid altogether of the historical Jesus Christ and to reduce Him to a "myth". Preposterous[1] as the device is, it is prompted by the sound perception that the Christ of our earliest documents is *already* presented as a divine being.)

Now here is, as has been said—for example, by Dr. E. R. Bevan—the

---

[1] How preposterous is shown, for example, by the theory of some literary men that the Jesus of the Gospels is identical with the Joshua of the Old Testament. We are thus to assume (1) that Joshua was an old and forgotten Hebrew divinity, and (2) that at the Christian era there was, for some unknown reason, a revival of the cult of this obsolete god. But there is not one scrap of evidence that Joshua was ever regarded by any Israelite as being a deity. His story, as we have it in the Old Testament, is simply that of a successful leader of Hebrew tribes in their first penetration into the country of the Canaanites, and there is no reason to think that anyone had ever supposed him to be anything else. We do not even hear that the Israelites made a colossal statue of him and hammered nails into it for luck. The Germans did this sort of thing for Hindenburg some twenty years ago, but a man who should assert that Hindenburg was a resurrected Wotan would only make himself ridiculous.

characteristically new note of the New Testament as compared with the Old. Ezekiel, in particular, had said long before that God would once more gather together his people, now scattered in bondage, as a shepherd might go out into the wilderness and collect his strayed flock. But to the Jewish reader this had apparently meant only that God would raise up in the future some wonderful human leader who would gather together again the "dispersion" of Israel. It would be, after all, only this wonderful man who could actually go out into the desert to reassemble the "sheep"; God would only be concerned in the business as the far-off being who had sent him on his costly and perilous errand, as a monarch may sit comfortably at home in his palace and send out devoted servants on a distant enterprise; the undertaking would be God's only on the principle that *qui facit per alium facit per se*. The courage and devotion would really be those of the envoy, and, to the strictly logical mind, they would be proof of *his* goodness, but no proof of the goodness of the sovereign to whom they cost nothing. Christianity, on the other hand, declared that it was actual fact that the divine shepherd had Himself come into the wilderness after the strayed sheep and had faced all its hardships and privations in His own person. The historical events were thus witnesses to the self-forgetting love, not of a great teacher or prophet, but of the very Lord of creation Himself. "So God loved the world" thus came to have a depth of meaning for Christians which it had never had for an Israelite, and the new significance of the thought gave a new meaning to the Christian life as a response to this love; it was possible henceforth for life to be inspired by a supreme, grateful love, not simply to a great human benefactor, but to the Maker of "all things visible and invisible."

The result is a changed attitude to the whole drama of human life and death. Even in a world morally indifferent—as the world depicted in Shakespeare's greatest tragedies sometimes looks to be—to good and bad; even in a world definitely and positively evil, we could still feel love and devotion to a human benefactor who had at least protected us, to the best of his power, against "fortune's spite"; some of us might steel ourselves, when he fell, to fall not utterly unmanned by his side. But in an evil world we should certainly know, and in an indifferent world we should have overpowering reasons for believing that our hero and we were at best falling together in a forlorn hope. The order of things would be against us, and our highest courage would be the courage of despair dying "game to the last". Now despair can for a time nerve to a vigorous achievement, but as a permanent attitude it is not invigorating but enervating. At least, it must be so with us, who are not wolves or weasels but men, reasonable animals. If we are once firmly convinced that the order of things is irrevocably against our ideals, we cannot avoid the paralyzing suspicion that these ideals, however much we cherish them, are futile and arbitrary, and we shall come to ask ourselves doubtingly whether they are, after all, worth the blood and tears they cost, whether mankind had not better do without them.

This is why, for my own part, I doubt very much whether a virile human morality can flourish apart from some conviction about the universal world-order which, thought out, proves to imply belief in God and His goodness. One may say, no doubt, that "value" and "existence" have nothing to do with one another, but belong to wholly different worlds of thought; one may say "What we need as inspiration to action is not belief in the *existence* of any thing or any person, but belief in the *worth* of courage and love", and the like. But divorced from belief in the overpowering actuality of the "love whose smile kindles the universe", your declaration "I believe in love" only means "I personally choose to regard love as supremely good"; and if your only reason for your profession is a *hoc volo, sic jubeo,* why should you not change your choice? *Le peu de chose que sont les hommes!* and if *l'amour* is, to put it brutally, only an episode in the career of these little creatures, *le peu de chose qu'est l'amour.*[2] It is, you will say, what I care most about. But it is not what all men, perhaps not what many men, care most about, and it may be that to-morrow, or next year, I shall have changed my scale of "values"; if these values are no more than creations of my personal will, there is nothing sacred about them, they arise and perish as my fancy flickers, like the "fancy values of commerce. There can, indeed, be no worth except in relation to some will which finds satisfaction in it, but the will to which genuine and abiding worth has this relation cannot be merely your mutable willing or mine; it can only be a "living will that shall endure when all that seems shall suffer shock". To the good man love is sacred and duty is sacred, but neither could be so if they were more expressions of his own will as this individual man; the good man is not an idolator of himself and his private will. And if I, or all mankind, were to-morrow to turn against the old sanctities and tread love and duty under our feet, they would lose nothing of their sacredness; it would not really be they, but our own wills, which would be profaned.

Now if the central doctrine of the Christian is true, then we have such a certainty as the world cannot otherwise afford that love and duty are indeed sacred. For then it is a fact that the Master of all things has not merely told us to be loving and dutiful and will hold us to account if we fail; He has Himself, in the person of the historical Lord Jesus, entered into the life of humanity, has Himself led the life of selfless love and duty to the bitter end, and triumphed over all the obstacles that beset it; we, who have still the obstacles and hindrances to conflict with, have received from him not merely the inspiration of His teaching and example, but the certainty that the values which are sustained by the eternal "living will" are precisely those which were affirmed in practice by the Lord Jesus and are dearest to

[2] Rupert Brooke wrote of the First World War as a welcome recall from "all the little emptiness of love." Presumably the kind of "love" he had in his mind was none of the loftiest, but if the noblest love we know is, after all, *only* the "idiosyncrasy" of a particular species of animal, is it not all, in the end, "little" and "empty"?

our own hearts—love, dutifulness, humility, courage, patience. We know, then, that, however appearances may be against them, these values can "never fail"; they are the foundation-stones on which the frame of things is built. This is why an apostle can speak of the faith of the Christian fellowship as one which conquers the world. It is not merely that, to quote Blake, "a strong persuasion that a thing is so makes it so"; for you cannot make falsehood into truth by the violence of your "persuasion" of the falsehood. The "world-conquering" quality of the Christian faith, if it is not an illusion, depends, first and foremost, on the nature of the person towards whom it is directed. It can conquer the world because, if it is true at all, it is a confidence based on a real disclosure of the character of the unseen source of the world. If the mind of God has been truly disclosed by the life, death, and triumph of Jesus, then it is certain that God's world is not really either indifferent or hostile to our highest human aspirations, and for the true "members of Christ's body" eternal life ceases to be only what Plato had called it, a "great hope", and becomes a fact. It is the confidence in the fact which accounts for the strange "joy" so characteristic of the obscure, toil-worn, despised and persecuted first Christians in the midst of a world full of pleasures, refined or sordid, but, as students of the period have so often noted, as deficient in joy as it was avid of pleasure.

These considerations also explain what might otherwise seem a singular fact about the history of Christian theology. When the Church set itself to codify and formulate its convictions it was not content with the emphatic assertion of the divinity of its founder; it insisted no less emphatically on his genuine and complete humanity. If it was declared deadly heresy to pronounce him in any way "inferior to the Father as touching this divinity", it was an equal heresy to abate anything from his humanity. You were not to withhold from him any jot of the worship due to the supreme Creator; equally you were not to exempt him from anything incidental to full human normality—hunger, thirst, weariness, pain, temptation. He was to be thought of neither as a deity of second rank, nor as a "superman". This, more than anything else, was what perplexed and shocked the ordinary outsider. He would not have found it incredible that a god, at any rate a minor god should show himself in the visible form of a man. But that a god should feel genuine want or pain, should shed tears at the grave of a friend, should be insulted, beaten, crucified, and should feel the pain and shame of such things was a veritable scandal. Yet obviously if the life of Christ is to be evidence that *our* highest human values are also the eternal and absolute values, it is precisely this union in one historical person of Deity and complete humanity which must be maintained. To whittle away either the divinity or the humanity—to be either "Liberal Protestant" or Docetist—is to surrender the very "ground of all our hopes".

56 Can a Man Witness His Own Funeral?*

ANTONY G. N. FLEW

Antony Flew (1923–   ) is professor of philosophy at the University of Keele, Staffordshire, England. He is coeditor (with Alastair MacIntyre) of *New Essays in Philosophical Theology*, editor of *Logic and Language* (first and second series), *Hume's Philosophy of Belief*, and *God and Philosophy*.

I

"Whether we are to live in a future state, as it is the most important question which can possibly be asked, so it is the most intelligible one which can be expressed in language" (Bishop Butler in the dissertation *Of Personal Identity*).

The purposes of this paper are, *first*, to try to begin to raise what Butler called "strange perplexities"[1] about the meaningfulness of this question and, *second*, to attempt to dispose of the counter-thesis, maintained by Schlick, that it must be significant because the possibility being discussed is not merely conceivable but also imaginable. These are very strictly limited objectives. We shall not, and shall not pretend to, do more than attack these two of the vast complex of problems, both logical and empirical, compendiously described as the questions of Survival and Immortality.

II

Now suppose someone offers the gambit "We all of us survive death" or "We all of us live forever." Might we not reply "Whatever in the world do you mean? For, in the ordinary senses of the words you use, the former sentence is self-contradictory and the latter denies one of the most securely established of all empirical generalisations; for it is the contrary of that traditional darling of the logicians 'All men are mortal'." As the objections to the two sentences are different, let us deal with each of them separately.

"We all of us survive death" is self-contradictory because we use the words "death" and "survival" and their derivatives in such a way that the

---

* From Antony G. N. Flew, "Can a Man Witness His Own Funeral?," *The Hibbert Journal*, 1956. Reprinted by permission of the author.
[1] *Loc. cit.*: also in Ch. I of the *Analogy of Religion* he writes of "strange difficulties."

classification of the crew of a torpedoed ship into "Dead" and "Survivors" is both exclusive and exhaustive. Every member of the crew must (logical "must") have either died or survived: and no member of the crew could (logical "could") have both died and survived. It is easy to overlook that "We all of us survive death" is self-contradictory because we all habitually and wisely give all utterances the benefit of the doubt. Generously assuming that other people usually have something intelligible to express even when they speak or write in unusual or incorrect ways, we attempt to attach sense even to expressions which are strictly self-contradictory. This tendency is frequently exploited by advertisers. Posters advertising the film *Bachelor Husband* catch the eye precisely because the expression "bachelor husband" is self-contradictory, and therefore paradoxical. We tend to puzzle over the title, to ponder—doubtless to the advertiser's eventual profit—over the non-linguistic improprieties suggested by this linguistically improper expression. If we see the headline "We survived death!" we do not just exclaim (in the tone of voice of rigid logical schoolmasters) "Nonsense: you either survive or you die!", but, curiosity aroused, we read on to learn how the death was only 'death' (in inverted commas), that the people in question had only pretended, been reported, appeared, to die; but had not of course in fact died. Sometimes, for instance, people show all the usual 'symptoms' of death, all the usually reliable signs that they will not walk, or talk, or joke again, but then, surprisingly, recover and do walk and talk and joke once more. This happened quite often in World War II: Russian doctors in particular reported many cases of patients who showed the usual indications of death— the heart not beating and so forth—but were brought back to life by shock treatments, blood transfusions, and suchlike. These patients thus survived 'death' (in inverted commas). The doctors then adapted their language—or at least the language of *Soviet War News* (London) was adapted—to meet the new situation: "We cannot survive death" was retained as the expression of a necessary truth; and the expression "clinical death" was introduced as a more precise and less awkward substitute for "death" (in inverted commas) to refer to the condition of the patients who showed all the usual 'symptoms' but who nevertheless might or might not survive to tell the tale. "We survive death" thus was, and remains, self-contradictory. The paradox use of "survives death" in advertising and headlines, and the inverted-comma use of 'death' in which people can be said to return from the "dead" (in inverted commas), do not in the least weigh against this contention. They positively reinforce it: it is precisely because "He survived death" is self-contradictory that it is a good headline; it is precisely because "to survive death" is self-contradictory that the doctors put the word "death" between warning inverted commas when first they had to report that a patient survived 'death,' and later introduced the new expression "clinical death" to replace the makeshift 'death' (in inverted commas) when similar cases occurred repeatedly.

"We all of us live forever" is, on the other hand, not self-contradictory but just as a matter of fact false, being as it is the flat contrary of the massively confirmed generalisation "All men are mortal." (Though if you choose to use the latter expression to express not a factual generalisation but an artificial truth of logic, making it true by definition that all *men* are mortal, thus incurring the probably unwelcome consequence that on this definition neither the prophet Elijah[2] nor—on the Roman view[3]—the Virgin Mary can count as human beings; then, of course, "we all of us [men] live forever" will on your definition become self-contradictory, and not merely false as a matter of manifest empirical fact.) But, like "We all of us survive death," "We all of us live forever" has what we might call 'headline value.' Both are 'shockers' and thus catch the eye and arouse curiosity. They make us wonder what the writer is up to, what is the story which he is going to tell under these arresting headlines. For surely he cannot really be intending to say something so obviously nonsensical or so notoriously false as what at first glance he seems to be saying.

Now many stories have been and still more could be told under these headlines. People have claimed that "We all of us live forever, *because* the evil (and sometimes even the good) that men do lives after them." People have argued that "We survive death, *because* our descendants will live on after we are dead." And in the variety and irrelevance of their supporting reasons they have revealed the variety and irrelevance of the theses which they have been concerned to maintain when they used these and similar paradoxical expressions. The only use with which we are concerned here— and certainly the only use which would justify Butler's claim that here was "the most important question which can possibly be asked"—is that in which they are intended to support or express what Wisdom has called "the logically unique expectation,"[4] the expectation that we shall see and feel, or at any rate and more non-committally, that we shall 'have experiences' after we are dead. Therefore we shall take it that the person who has said "We all of us survive death" or "We all of us live forever" was making a move intended to justify such expectations.

And against this move the simple-minded counter-move is to attempt a sort of philosophical fools' mate. Clearly this expectation cannot (logical "cannot") be well grounded unless we are going to exist after our deaths.[5] But we have been insisting that it is not merely false but actually self-

[2] See II Kings, ii. 11.
[3] See *Munificentissimus Deus* of 1. xi. 50.
[4] In 'Gods' *PAS* 44/5, reprinted in *Logic and Language* I (Ed. A. G. N. Flew: Blackwell, 1951).
[5] Lucretius exploited this point: Debet enim, misere si forte aegreque futurum est, Ipse quoque esse in eo tum tempore, cui male possit Accidere. [For if there is going to be misery and pain in the future then the person it's going to happen to has got to exist at that time.] *De Rerum Natura*, Book III, 861–3.

contradictory to say that we survive death. So we cannot (logical "cannot") exist after our deaths. Therefore these logically unique expectations cannot be well founded. Indeed the suggestion on which they are based, the assumption which they presuppose (viz. that "We survive death") is self-contradictory and therefore senseless.

III

Well, of course there are several possible defences against this sort of attack; and the possible variations on these defences are innumerable. The traditional one depends on the distinction between body and mind, or body and soul (what Professor Ryle, unaccountably ignoring Plato, insists on calling the *Cartesian* Myth; a notion which—far from being a philosopher's fancy—is incapsulated in the idiom of innumerable languages and is a widespread, though not universal, element in folklore and religion). The first stage is to maintain that people consist of two elements, one, the body, visible, tangible and corporeal, the other, the mind or soul, invisible, intangible and incorporeal. The second stage is to maintain that we are our souls or minds. This stage is indispensable: unless we are our souls the survival of our souls will not be our survival; and the news that our souls were to be preserved after we died would be of no more importance or concern to us than the news that any other parts of us—our appendices, say—were to be preserved. Granted these two presuppositions (and "presuppositions" is surely the *mot juste*: for they are rarely either distinguished from one another or argued for[6]) it is then significant and even plausible to say that we (our incorporeal souls, that is) survive death (which is "the mere death of the body"). The desire to allow doctrines of personal immortality to be significant and plausible is one of the main drives behind dualist conceptions, and one perhaps insufficiently stressed by Professor Ryle in *The Concept of Mind*.[7] But this is a vast and another subject; here we propose to concentrate exclusively on one more modern defence, that which claims that "I shall survive my death" cannot be self-contradictory and therefore senseless, because it refers to a possibility which is not merely conceivable but imaginable.[8]

This argument was used by Moritz Schlick.[9] "I take it for granted

---

[6] But there are arguments to be found: e.g., in Plato's *Alcibiades* I§§ 128 ff., Descartes' *Meditation* II, and Butler's *Analogy*, Ch. I.

[7] There are some, but surprisingly few, references: cf. pp. 11, 23, 26 and 186. As I have twice mentioned Professor Ryle only to disagree, I should like to add here that I owe him an enormous debt.

[8] For a clear and very relevant elucidation of the senses of "imagine" and an examination of the relation and lack of relation between the ability to form mental pictures and the deciding of questions of significance and non-significance see Annis Flew 'Images, Supposing, and Imagining' in *Philosophy*, 1953.

[9] *Philosophical Review*, July, 1936, p. 356. Reprinted in Feigl and Sellars' *Readings in Philosophical Analysis*, pp. 159–60.

that . . . we are concerned with the question of survival after 'death'."—
[His inverted commas. These surely tacitly concede the claim that "to survive death" is a self-contradictory expression: compare the similar tacit
admission made in the tombstone insistence "Not dead but sleeping". A.F.]
I think we may agree with Professor Lewis when he says about this hypothesis: "Our understanding of what would verify it has no lack of clarity. In
fact I can easily imagine, e.g. witnessing the funeral of my own body and
continuing to exist without a body, for nothing is easier than to describe a
world which differs from our ordinary world only in the complete absence
of all data which I would call parts of my own body. We must conclude that
immortality, in the sense defined, should not be regarded as a metaphysical
'problem', but is an empirical hypothesis, because it possesses logical verifiability. It could be verified by following the prescription 'Wait until you die!'."
A briefer and more puckish version of the same argument can be found in
John Wisdom's unending saga *Other Minds*. "I know indeed what it would
be like to witness my own funeral—the men in tall silk hats, the flowers, and
the face beneath the glass-topped coffin"[10] and it is also deployed by Dr.
Casimir Lewy in his 'Is the Notion of Disembodied Existence Self-contradictory?'[11]

So far as I know this argument has never been challenged: presumably
partly because we can most of us imagine (image) a scene such as Wisdom
describes; and partly because no one wants to arrogate to himself the right
to decide what Wisdom or Schlick or anyone other than he himself can or
cannot imagine (image). But the argument can and should be challenged:
and it can be done without arbitrarily prescribing any limit to Wisdom's
obviously very considerable imaginative powers. For there is all the difference in the world between: imagining what it would be like to witness my
own funeral (which requires only a minor effort); and imagining what it
would be like to witness me witnessing *my own* funeral (which is logically
impossible. Or at least, less dogmatically, is very far from being a logically
straightforward matter). If it really is I who witness it then it is not my
funeral but only 'my funeral' (in inverted commas): and if it really is my
funeral then I cannot be a witness, for I shall be dead and in the coffin.

Of course I can imagine many situations which might be described as my
watching 'my own funeral' (in inverted commas): I can remember Harry
Lime in the film *The Third Man* watching 'his own funeral,' and of course
I can imagine being in the same situation as Harry Lime; but it was not
really Harry Lime's own funeral, and what I can imagine would not really

[10] *Mind*, 1942, p. 2 and *Other Minds* (Blackwell, 1952), p. 36. Perhaps this is not
Wisdom's own view but only that of one of his characters. In any case I should like
to stress how much delight and illumination this series of articles has given me.
[11] *PAS*, 1942–3, pp. 64–5: this is a non-linguistic aberration from the method of the
rest of this strenuous paper; a paper of which I hope shortly to publish a detailed
criticism.

be mine. Again I can imagine my own funeral—I shall not try to better Wisdom's whimsical description of such a scene—but now what I am imagining is not *my* witnessing *my own* funeral but merely my own funeral. (Parenthetically, it should be pointed out that Wisdom is far too good a writer to have committed himself to the former—and improper—description of his imaginings (imagings). What he wrote was "I know indeed what it would be like to witness my own funeral." Unfortunately, this will not, under examination, support his thesis: which requires that he should be able to imagine his surviving his own death and his witnessing his own funeral: which seems to be impossible, since the latter supposition, like the former, is apparently self-contradictory).

But surely this is merely slick? Surely I can perfectly well imagine my own funeral, really my own funeral with my body in the coffin and not a substitute corpse or a weight of bricks; with me there watching it all, but invisible, intangible, a disembodied spirit? Well, yes, this seems all right: until someone asks the awkward question "Just how does all this differ from your imagining your own funeral without your being there at all (except as the corpse in the coffin)?"[12]

Certainly Schlick could imagine, as he claimed, "the funeral of his own body": though it is perhaps a pity that he should describe what he imagined in this way and not, more naturally, as "his own funeral." But then he goes on to talk of imagining his "continuing to exist without a body": which he tries to justify by claiming that "nothing is easier than to describe a world which differs from our ordinary world only in the complete absence of all data which I would call parts of my own body." But the fact that we can all of us describe, or even imagine, a world which would differ from our ordinary world only in the complete absence of all data describable as parts of our respective bodies has not, by itself, the slightest tendency to show that anyone could imagine or describe a world in which, after his funeral, he continued to exist without a body. By itself it merely shows that we can each imagine what the world would be like if he were obliterated from it entirely, and no trace of his corpse remained. Schlick has misdescribed what he could imagine. Misled by the fact that a man can easily imagine what his funeral will be like, and hence what it would be like to watch it, it is tempt-

---

[12] Here we might compare Wisdom on "picture preferences" in 'Other Minds' in *Mind*, 1940 and in *Other Minds*, Ch. I; which will suggest how much, how very much, difference there may be even when "there is no *factual* difference." Utterances of a belief in the immortality of the soul usually form part of a whole attitude to the world (cf. σῶμα σῆμα—"the body is a prison"). But though this paper does not even begin to come to grips with this sort of complex of belief and attitude of which utterances about the immortality of the soul form a part, it is worth pointing out that, rightly or wrongly, most people who have held such faiths have believed that 'the logically unique expectation' was in fact justified: and would be no longer able or willing (psychologically) to maintain their faiths if convinced that it was not. See my 'Theology and Falsification' and 'Death' in *University* (Blackwell's, 1950 and 1952), Vol. I, No. 3 and Vol. II, No. 2; reprinted in *Essays in Philosophical Theology* (S.C.M. Press, 1955: edited by A. MacIntyre and A. G. N. Flew).

ing to insist that he can imagine what it would be like *for him* to watch *his own* funeral. Schlick is thus able to "conclude that immortality, in the sense defined . . . is an empirical hypothesis. . . . It could be verified by following the prescription 'Wait until you die!' " But he has not defined a sense of "immortality" at all: apparently he has merely misdescribed some rather humdrum exercises of his imagination in an extremely exciting and misleading way. He has failed to say anything to prevent his opponent from objecting to his conclusion: "But, on the contrary, nothing whatever could be verified (by me) by (my) following the prescription 'Wait until you die!': (for me my) death is so final that it is logically impossible (for me) to survive it to verify any hypotheses at all."

IV

We have now fulfilled the two strictly limited purposes of this paper. But perhaps it is worth while to add comments on three other possible objections to the attempted philosophical fools' mate; emphasising that nothing we have said or shall say must be interpreted to mean that we ourselves consider it to be decisive. *First* it may be said that this is all too cut and dried, the logic of our ordinary language is not as sharp, clear, and uncomplicated as has been made out. This is true and important. To take only one example: any adequate treatment of the logic of survival and immortality (the enquiry initiated by Plato's *Phaedo*) would demand the use of the distinction between death and dissolution; just as any full discussion of the logic of metempsychosis and pre-existence (the enquiry initiated by Plato's *Meno*) would have to take account of the parallel distinction between birth and conception. But for our first purpose, the raising of "strange perplexities," soft shading and rich detail is confusing, while for the second, dealing with one counter-move crudely made, it is unnecessary.

Second, it may be suggested that, although Schlick and Wisdom as a matter of fact only succeeded in imagining their own funerals and the world going on without them (and then misdescribed and/or mistook the significance of what they did imagine), it would nevertheless be quite possible to imagine all sorts of bizarre phenomena which we should feel inclined to describe as "the activities of disembodied people" or even as "evidence of survival." This again is true and important. Anyone who has read at all widely in the literature of psychical research must often have felt inclined to apply such expressions to phenomena, or putative phenomena, recorded in that literature.[13] But it is all too easy to misinterpret what we shall be doing if we do allow ourselves to describe such *outré* phenomena in these paradoxical ways. In fact we shall be attaching sense to an expression—"disembodied

---

[13] Compare for instance Kenneth Richmond's compendium *Evidence of Identity* (Bell, 1939) or the classic *Phantasms of the Living* by Gurney, Myers and Podmore (Abridged, Kegan Paul, 1918). I have discussed briefly the relations between our present problems and such phenomena in my *A New Approach to Psychical Research* (C. A. Watts, 1953), Ch. VII.

person"—for which previously no sense had been provided: either directly as an idiomatic expression; or indirectly through the uses given to its constituent words. We are thereby introducing a new sense of the word "person."[14] Yet it may appear to us and to others as if we have discovered a new sort of person, or a new state in which a person can be. Whereas a disembodied person is no more a special sort of person than is an imaginary person: and (except in the Services—which have their peculiar sense of the word "disembodied") disembodiment is no more a possible state of a person than is non-existence.

Now it is perfectly possible to specify a sense for the expression "disembodied person": just as it is possible to attach sense to any expression, even one which on present usage would be self-contradictory. The difficulty is to attach a sense to it so that some expression incorporating it will, if true, provide a ground for the logically unique expectation. In their present use person words have logical liaisons of the very greatest importance: personal identity is the necessary condition of both accountability and expectation; which is only to say that it is unjust to reward or punish someone for something unless (as a minimum condition) he is the same person who did the deed; and also that it is absurd to expect experiences for Flew in 1984 unless (as a minimum condition) there is going to be a person in existence in 1984 who will be the same person as I. The difficulty, not necessarily insuperable, is to change the use of person words so radically that it becomes significant to talk of people surviving dissolution, without changing it to such an extent that these vital logical liaisons are lost.

The *third* obvious criticism returns us to the traditional foundation for what we might call a "logic of immortality." The objection might be made that it has been assumed throughout that people are merely bodies, that people are bodies and nothing more. Even though we have excluded discussion of the traditional dualisms from this paper, this criticism has to be met. It is met by pointing out that no one has either argued or assumed anything of the sort. What has been done is merely to take for granted the ordinary meaning and use of person words, and to use them—we hope—in the conventional and proper way: a very different matter. People are what you meet. Person words refer to men and women like you and me and the other fellow. They are taught by pointing at people: indeed how else could they or should they be taught? They do not refer to anything invisible and elusive, to any mysterious incorporeal substances. Even children can be taught them, can and do know what is meant by "Father," "I," "man," "person," or "butcher." But that is not to say that they refer merely or at all to bodies. "Person" is no synonym for "body": though "body" is used peculiarly in the

---

[14] "I am not at all clear what I ought to mean by this disembodied existence, merely because I could mean so many things by it."—J. N. Findlay in *P.A.S.*, 1949–50, p. 61.

Services as a slightly pejorative substitute for "person," the degrading point of the substitution would be lost if the words were really synonymous; there is a difference, a difference of life and death, between "We brought a person down from the foot of the Z'mutt ridge" and "We brought a body down from the foot of the Z'mutt ridge."[15] Person words do not mean either bodies or souls nor yet any combination of the two: "I" is no synonym for "my body" nor yet for "my mind" or "my soul" nor yet for any combination of these (as anyone who tries a few substitutions must soon discover). If we are indeed compound of two such disparate elements, that is a contingent fact about people and not part of what is meant by "person" and other person words.[16] To suggest that it has been assumed that people are merely bodies is surely to reveal that you yourself assume that everyone must be a dualist— or at least a dualist with one component missing—a sort of one-legged dualist. And this is a mistake. But though this third criticism is mistaken, it does go straight to the heart of the matter. For the whole position does depend on the fact that people are what you meet: we do not just meet the sinewy containers in which other people are kept; they do not just encounter the fleshy houses which we ourselves inhabit.[17] The whole position depends on the obvious, crucial, but constantly neglected fact that person words mean what they do mean. This paper has consisted in insistent and obstinate underlining of this fact; and in pointing out two implications of it, important but limited in scope: that Butler was wrong to deny that there were logical difficulties about the notion of a future life; and that Schlick's short way with these difficulties will not do. Perhaps attention to it can transform discussion of the problems of Survival and Immortality in a way very similar to that in which Moore's insistence that we do know that some material things exist has transformed discussions of Idealism and of the problems of Epistemology.[18] As Berkeley, with his usual insight, remarked, "the grand mistake is that we know not what we mean by 'we', 'selves' or 'mind', etc."[19]

---

[15] Consider this item from the London *Times* of 3/1/51: *Climber Killed by an Avalanche.* "Five mountaineers were trapped by an avalanche yesterday. . . . Two escaped. Two others were extricated by an R.A.F. Mountain Rescue squad. . . . Mr. N. Ryder . . . was buried under several feet of snow, and another rescue party located his body early this morning."

[16] I have written more about this in "Locke and the Problem of Personal Identity" in *Philosophy*, Jan., 1951.

[17] Contrast Bishop Butler: "It is as easy to conceive—that we may exist out of bodies as in them, that we might have animated bodies of any other organs and senses wholly different from those now given us, and that we may hereafter animate these same or new bodies variously modified and organised—as to conceive how we can animate such bodies as our present" (*Analogy*, Ch. I). This assumption that people are not what we meet but are elusive entities which mysteriously 'animate' human bodies (and possibly non-human bodies or even no bodies at all) is fundamental and crucial to his argument.

[18] Compare papers by Ambrose, Wisdom, Malcolm, Mace and others in *The Philosophy of G. E. Moore.* (Edited Paul A. Schilpp.)

[19] Albeit with a different intent. *Philosophical Commentaries* (Ed. A. A. Luce), p. 301.

Chapter
Seven

THE PROBLEM
OF KNOWLEDGE

Most of us in the course of our lives encounter numerous situations
that leave us in doubt about what to believe. Our doubts or queries center
around claims of various kinds: Will the stockmarket rise or fall? Does
the smoking of cigarettes cause cancer? Is there a God or gods? *Should*
Red China be admitted to the United Nations? Should I keep or break
my promise? Is Picasso a better artist than Raphael? Is ether necessary
for the transmission of light? These doubts involve beliefs about nearly
every aspect of man's experience—scientific, moral, political, religious
and aesthetic.

Seldom do any of us attempt systematically to doubt or question *all*
our beliefs in the manner of the philosopher Rene Descartes. (See
selection in this chapter.) Nor do we deny the possibility of knowledge,
as does the extreme skeptic. Rather, our questions arise in specific
contexts and are quite particular in nature. When they arise, we want to
find out if a given belief about them is true or false, whether we are
justified in believing something on the basis of the evidence, or whether
any belief can properly be labeled knowledge. To be sure, concern
with the problem of knowledge may be purely theoretical. But it is
generally the result of practical questions about what to believe or not to
believe or what to do and not to do. That is, the principal reason for
distinguishing the true from the false and knowledge from opinion is to

enable us to decide what we *ought* to believe. (See the selection by   James Oliver.)

These terms—belief, true, false, justified belief, unwarranted belief, knowledge, opinion, and the like—are generally known as epistemological terms or concepts. Concern with the meaning and the proper application of these terms to beliefs, statements, and theories is the beginning of epistemology. The term "epistemology" comes from the Greek word *episteme* which means "knowledge." Epistemology means "theory of knowledge" and it is concerned with the nature and foundations of knowledge. In a sense it is the attempt to obtain knowledge or enlightenment about the very possibility of knowledge itself—*any* kind of knowledge.

The basic tasks of epistemology include analyzing key epistemic concepts, providing criteria for the proper application of these concepts to beliefs and statements, and justifying these criteria. Criteria for terms such as true, false, and knowledge function as standards in the evaluation of various statements, claims, or beliefs; and the central objective of epistemology is the providing of these norms. The distinctions and norms that epistemology provides, if they are to fulfill their purpose, must assist us in deciding which epistemic attitude to adopt toward beliefs and purported knowledge claims of various kinds.

In evaluating knowledge claims, most human beings do not adopt the attitudes of complete certainty or complete disbelief (although perhaps a rationalist such as Descartes would want to restrict us to these two extremes) but have a scale of epistemic attitudes, including complete certainty, high probability, mere probability, improbability, possibility, dubitability, and so on. The formulation of such a scale of degrees of belief and a classification of all of the various kinds of statements or assertions seems essential in fulfilling the normative function of epistemology. Of course, there are disagreements among epistemologists. They are both conceptual and normative. Epistemologists disagree in their classification of statements—on the kinds of statements that "exist"—and on the recommended norms or rules for the resolution of epistemic doubt.

Given the centrality of epistemology to the entire enterprise of philosophy, it is obvious that the questions which it raises will be wide-ranging. The distinctions it formulates will be multiple and intricate, and the entailments and impact upon man's beliefs (and perhaps his practices) will be far-reaching indeed. Two examples will suffice to illustrate this point. Recall the discussion of the emotive theory of ethics in Chapter Three, "The Problem of Moral Norms." It was there seen that the noncognitive account of moral judgments together with the conclusion that there is no objective validity in ethics were views at least in part rooted in the acceptance of a certain epistemology—the application of certain epistemological considerations to the domain of moral discourse. And in Chapter Two, "The Problem of the Existence of God," we saw that religious skepticism and atheism were sometimes based on the use of certain epistemological rules or norms in evaluating evidence for God's existence. These norms involve criteria that fall roughly into three areas: (1) criteria of meaning, (2) criteria of truth, and (3) criteria of knowledge. Let us briefly characterize these three areas.

CRITERIA OF MEANING

Language is an instrument used for a variety of purposes, one of which is the communication of ideas and knowledge. Most of us in most situations have little difficulty communicating with one another. But language is an intricate and complex instrument. Its signs or symbols can easily be misused, combined in incoherent ways, improperly extended in this direction or that—with the result being not communication but confusion.

Epistemologists attempt at least to minimize the confusion and maximize communication and understanding by distinguishing the various uses or functions of signs or symbols. Their concern with language, however, is restricted; they do *not* try to do the work of the anthropological linguist or the grammarian—although they find the uses and language constructions uncovered by these professionals helpful. Rather, they distinguish types of language uses and functions and linguistic or grammatical constructions in order to be able to distinguish and identify statements and claims which are significant in a *cognitive* sense (that is, statements to which we can properly apply the predicates true or false) as opposed to those which are not. The meaning criteria or rules specified by the epistemologist as a result of his analysis he then uses as norms or tests for ascertaining the intelligibility and cognitive status of any purported knowledge claim.

For example, suppose that someone says to you, "Blue is rounder than green," and intends this as a literally true statement. Does it conceptually make sense? Agreed, as a metaphor or nonliteral statement, it may have value. But is it significant as a literal truth claim? Are colors the sorts of things that can be properly said to be round, square, or triangular? Or suppose that while reading a book you run across this string of words: Green undergirth not outerspace the. Probably you would say to yourself: What a ridiculous misprint. But suppose that the author insists that this is exactly what he intends to say and further that it is literally true. Does it make any literal sense? Is it an intelligible statement?

The answer to these questions is obviously in the negative, for the arrangements of the words do not conform to the rules implicit in our language for the intelligible formulation of statements. The rules of formation that specify the ways in which linguistic signs can be properly connected with one another are generally known as rules of "syntax." But there are two other kinds of rules with which the epistemologist is concerned: rules of "pragmatics," which center around the appeal and expressive functions of language and the general relation of language to behavior; and rules of "semantics," which center around the referential or designative function of concepts and the notion of truth. Although pragmatic functions and rules of language are important in understanding much of our language, the epistemologist concentrates more directly on semantic functions and rules; for when concepts and statements are used as signs of designation and as truth claims or claims about reality, the issue of cognitive assessment directly arises.

Some epistemologists argue that cognitive statements or truth claims are of two types: (1) analytic statements, or those which are true or false simply as a result of the meanings of concepts, of the formal or logical relationships of concepts within our language, and of the rules of logical derivation or transformation (and whose denials are seen as logically self-contradictory); and (2) synthetic statements, or those which are true or false as a result of their accurately representing or characterizing some facts or states of affairs about the world (and whose denials are not logically self-contradictory). Synthetic truths are generally characterized as contingent truths, because they can be falsified by empirical facts; whereas analytic truths are characterized as necessary, because their being true or false is not contingent upon the existence of any empirical state of affairs but only on the meanings of concepts and the rules of our language. Statements such as "all unmarried men are bachelors," "all equiangular triangles are equilateral," and "2 + 2 = 4" are instances of analytic truths. In such truths, concepts are explained, or "unpacked." Statements such as "Mother is in the kitchen," "cigarette smoking causes cancer," and "enrollment at the University of Georgia is 18,000" are instances of synthetic truth claims. In these cases, new information is added to a concept. Some philosophers have characterized this difference between analytic and synthetic statements in this way: Whatever we can know *independently* of sense experience or empirical channels is an *a priori* truth, whereas all knowledge that requires empirical evidence for verification is *a posteriori*. They go on to characterize all a priori truth as analytic and all a posteriori truth as synthetic.

It goes without saying that this assimilation of all cognitive meaning or all truth claims to analytic and synthetic statements (or analytic a priori and synthetic a posteriori) is highly controversial, and the adequacy of the analytic-synthetic classification is challenged by some philosophers. Immanual Kant, for example, maintained that *not all* necessary truth is analytic and that there are some logically necessary truths which are synthetic, that is, which are *about* the world and not about our language. His precursor, Gottfried Leibniz, went much further, maintaining that *all* synthetic truths are necessary. The opinion that some truths are contingent Leibniz attributes to the limitations of the human mind in perceiving connections. Some current philosophers argue that there are bona fide knowledge claims (value judgments, for example) that are *neither* analytic nor synthetic; and recently W. V. O. Quine, after a careful scrutiny of the notion of analytic, concluded that the term cannot be defined in general terms.

Similar objections have been urged against various attempts to formulate a criterion for synthetic truth claims. Such criteria are generally set forth as definitions of "empirical significance." For example, the logical positivist Moritz Schlick argued that the meaning of a proposition is the method of its verification, that we cannot know the meaning of a statement unless we are able to indicate precisely the circumstances under which it would be true (or false), and further, that genuine empirical statements must be capable of conclusive verification.[1] A goal of Schlick and the logical positivists was the clarification of language and the recognition of sense and non-sense in lan-

[1] Moritz Schlick, "The Future of Philosophy," *College of The Pacific Publications in Philosophy*, I, 1932.

guage uses. The verifiability criterion was set forth as a tool for accomplishing this. They thought that much theology and metaphysics—indeed even some so-called sciences—were literally non-sense. However, it was not long before it was seen that this strong verification test, known as the verifiability criterion of meaning, had insuperable difficulties confronting it. Not only did it rule out as empirically meaningful much metaphysical and theological discourse; it also ruled out as senseless much of science, for scientific laws or statements of universal form cannot be conclusively verified. It was a case of throwing out the baby with the bath water.

Recognizing the self-stultifying nature of the conclusive verification test, other philosophers sympathetic to the general aim of clarifying purported knowledge claims substituted "confirmability," or "verifiability in principle," for conclusive verification.[2] This substitution required only that some conceivable facts or state of affairs be relevant to the establishment of the truth or falsity of a statement, not that the statement be completely verified or actually verified at all. For example, the statement that there is uranium on Mars, although neither conclusively verifiable nor practically verifiable (given our existing technology), is verifiable in principle and hence empirically significant. Under the earlier test, it had to be characterized as empirically meaningless. Carl Hempel has since qualified the verification test even further.[3] But some contemporary philosophers deny even the possibility of an adequate test or general criterion of empirical significance.

CRITERIA OF TRUTH

The issue of whether a statement is meaningful or not, in particular, of whether it has cognitive meaning, is one which perhaps must be settled prior to that of whether it is true. But the nature or definition of truth has proven to be just as philosophically puzzling as that of meaning. The ancient philosopher Protagoras said that "man is the measure of all things." Does this mean that truth is totally relative to each person and to the way he perceives the world? In ethics, this doctrine has been interpreted as entailing that right conduct is contingent upon the preferences, the whim or caprice, of each person and that there are no objective moral standards. Does it mean in epistemology that no truth claims have objective status, that the truth of a statement is not dependent upon facts or states of affairs in the world but only on one's personal feelings? Few have held this doctrine; and if they did, they would not try to persuade anyone to hold it. It is an extreme and self-stultifying view. Most philosophers as well as scientists, theologians, and untutored laymen have concerned themselves with the nature of truth

[2] See, for example, Rudolf Carnap, "Testability and Meaning," *Philosophy of Science*, vols. 3 and 4 (1936, 1937); A. J. Ayer, *Language, Truth and Logic*, (London: Victor Gallancz, Ltd., 1946); Hans Reichenbach, *Experience and Prediction*, (Chicago: Univ. of Chicago Press, 1938); and Karl Popper, *The Logic of Scientific Discovery*, (London: Hutchinson, 1959).

[3] Carl Hempel, "The Concept of Cognitive Significance," *Proceedings of the American Academy of Arts and Sciences*, vol. 80 (1951).

because they recognize that human beings frequently err in their judgments and that we need criteria for identifying errors so that errors or mistaken judgments can be minimized and truth found. The world can be very hard on human beings who make erroneous judgments about it. We generally recognize, therefore, that truth is not dependent simply on personal feeling or whim.

However, there has been, and continues to be, considerable disagreement over the definition or nature of truth, and several different analyses or theories of truth have been proposed. Some philosophers subscribe to the "correspondence" theory of truth, which maintains that truth is a relation of correspondence between a belief or statement and some fact or facts about the world. Thus, my belief that I am thirty-seven years old is true if in fact I am thirty-seven years old. It is false if I am less than thirty-seven. However commonsensical this account appears, it has frequently been rejected. Critics ask what is to be meant by "belief" or "statement." Do these terms refer to mental states? If so, in what sense do mental states correspond to reality? Surely making a true judgment about reality is not having a mental picture of reality, for we make such judgments without having such mental pictures. If not, what does correspondence mean?

Given the difficulties in specifying the meaning of correspondence, some philosophers (see the selection by Blanshard) advanced the "coherence" theory of truth. This view holds that truth is a relationship not between statements and reality but between statements about reality and other statements about reality. A belief or statement was seen as true if it cohered with other beliefs or statements accepted, or if it fit into a coherent *system* of beliefs, as related to evidence. But difficulties were immediately raised about this theory. Suppose that a belief coheres with some beliefs but not with others. Does this mean that it is true to some extent and false to some extent? Is truth a matter of degrees? Furthermore, is it not possible for a belief to cohere with a set, or system, of beliefs in the sense of being logically consistent with them and yet the belief and other beliefs in the system be false? If so, the coherence theory must be inadequate, it was argued.

Subsequently, some philosophers adopted what came to be known as the "pragmatic" theory of truth. This theory defined a true belief as one that "works." It works if it enables one to cope with one's environment or adjust to the world or if it results in some type of practical "success in inquiry." Surely, however, a belief can perform these functions even if it is false. For example, one might believe that God exists. This belief may give one great satisfaction and security and yet no God actually exist. Although the American philosophers William James and John Dewey are sometimes interpreted as holding this narrow form of the pragmatic theory, one finds emphasis on the correspondence criterion in the thought of both men.

More recently, some philosophers, notably P. F. Strawson, have argued that "true" should not be seen as a *predicate* applied to beliefs or statements but as an endorsement of a belief or statement.[4] True does not designate a property but functions as a sign of assent or endorsement.

[4] P. F. Strawson, "Truth," *Analysis*, vol. 9 (1949).

Fortunately, resolution of the issue of the meaning or nature of truth is not necessary in order to have criteria for the identification of true propositions. Not having a definitive answer to the question, therefore, does not interfere with the ongoing activities of the scientist, lawyer, economist, or even philosopher.

CRITERIA OF KNOWLEDGE

Truth is obviously related to knowledge. But in what way? It seems to reflect a truth about our language that we cannot properly say that a belief constitutes knowledge unless it is true. That is, the notion of false knowledge is contradictory. However, is this condition sufficient for knowledge? Could a belief be true and yet *not* be knowledge? Surely this is the case, for there may be any number of truths toward which no one has ever adopted an attitude of belief. Thus, not only the truth of a statement but also the adoption of an epistemic attitude toward that statement seems to be required. (Some insist that this attitude be one of certainty.) But the very notion of knowledge does seem to require a knowing subject.

Now are these two conditions—a believing subject and a true belief—sufficient for knowledge? Most philosophers deny this. A further condition is generally required, namely, that one have sound evidence for his belief or that one's belief be properly supported by evidence. (Some philosophers have insisted that the evidence be conclusive.) This additional requirement seems to be supported by our language about "know": We do not say that someone knows x even if he believes x and x is true, unless that person has evidence that justifies his believing x. Thus, even if I believe that smoking cigarettes causes cancer and it is true that cigarettes cause cancer, this belief still does not constitute knowledge unless I have strong supporting evidence that cancer is caused by smoking. Without such evidence, one is not justified in believing this claim, even if it is in fact true. Furthermore, it follows that one is justified in believing what is false if that false belief is supported by strong evidence. It would be irrational not to believe it, even though such justified belief could never be said to be knowledge.

When are we justified in believing a statement? When is a belief properly supported and hence rational? The extreme sceptic denies that we are justified in believing anything. Such sceptics are rare indeed; for if they consistently held to their doctrine, they probably would not live very long, because the adoption of attitudes of belief and disbelief are necessary for survival. But a highly specific answer to these questions seems neither possible nor appropriate, for what constitutes evidence or rational support depends on the kind of statement or belief in question. "I see a blue sky," "cigarette smoking causes cancer," "$e = m/c^2$," "democracy is better than totalitarianism," "$2 + 2 = 4$"—all these statements are of different kinds. Hence criteria for justified belief for each of these claims will probably vary.

Some philosophers argue that there are essentially only two kinds of knowledge claims, formal and factual. Formal knowledge is all analytic. It provides no information about the world and is the result of the relationships between signs or meanings and rules of inference or proof rules. A formal knowledge claim is justified if it follows or is logically deducible from certain premises in accordance with the accepted rules of inference. This is what is meant by a valid deductive argument—one in which the conclusion is "contained" in the premises. An invalid deductive argument is one in which the conclusion drawn extends beyond that which is contained in or implied by the premises. This kind of knowledge is exemplified in logic, mathematics, and geometry. No empirical evidence can falsify such knowledge claims (although, of course, one must have experience in order to know the postulates and rules of inference of logic, geometry, and mathematics).

On the other hand, criteria for a justified factual knowledge claim are quite different. Such a knowledge claim is warranted, when it is warranted, not because of the logical relationship that it has with other statements but because it accurately describes or explains facts about the world. The testing procedure for factual claims are numerous and various, depending on the subject matter of the claim and the kind of evidence relevant to it. Data from direct and indirect observation, from testimony, from memory, statistical data, and the like are different kinds of relevant evidence for factual beliefs. Multiple factors increase or decrease the reliability of evidence of each kind. When the evidence is reliable and when it supports a given belief, with little or no disconfirming evidence, we are justified in accepting that belief as knowledge. This is generally called a valid inductive inference.

In the case of most factual claims, perhaps with the exception of claims about one's immediate, transitory experience, it is at least possible that future experience will disconfirm them. What seemed to be a highly probable belief on the basis of existing evidence may turn out to be probably false, given additional future data. Hence, a belief which at one time was a justified knowledge claim may not be so at another time. Rationality requires that one change one's mind on the matter, and further that one entertain different degrees of belief, depending upon the degree of probability of the claim under consideration.

As already indicated in our discussion of the analytic-synthetic distinction, some philosophers deny the sharp distinction between formal and factual knowledge. Some formal knowledge, they argue, though *necessarily* true, given the semantic and syntactical rules of our language, is nonetheless about the world. This means that synthetic necessary truth is possible and hence so is a knowledge state that accompanies it. Furthermore, some maintain that normative knowledge claims in such areas as ethics and politics are neither formal nor factual but unique or *sui generis.* An adequate epistemology, it is argued, must include all types and kinds of knowledge. Of course, cases must be made out that there is such knowledge, and these issues are highly controversial in contemporary epistemology.

From what has been said, it is plain that epistemology is fundamental to the entire enterprise of philosophy, for it provides us with criteria and norms for evaluating knowledge claims. Some philosophers have entertained the hope that epistemology can show that we can know truths about the world that are necessary and synthetic, which hold for all possible experience and are not merely contingently true. With such knowledge, perhaps we could possess an objective, universal, unshakable foundation for morality, political norms, theology, and so on (parallel to the Cartesian geometrical model of absolutely certain knowledge). Even if this Cartesian model of certainty is not possible (though perhaps some modified form of it is), the value of epistemology remains, for clarification and enlightened assessment of knowledge claims—no matter what degree of certainty can be attained—is surely a desideratum of all rational beings.

SELECTED BIBLIOGRAPHY

KNOWLEDGE

Ackermann, Robert. *Theories of Knowledge: A Critical Introduction.* New York, 1965.

Ayer, A. J. *The Foundations of Empirical Knowledge.* New York, 1940.

———. *The Problem of Knowledge.* Harmondsworth, England, 1956.

Broad, C. D. *Scientific Thought.* London, 1927.

Chisholm, Roderick M. *Perceiving: A Philosophical Study.* Ithaca, N.Y., 1957.

———. *Theory of Knowledge.* Englewood Cliffs, N.J., 1966.

Griffiths, A. Phillips (ed.). *Knowledge and Belief.* London, 1967.

Hill, Thomas E. *Contemporary Theories of Knowledge.* New York, 1961.

Lean, Martin. *Sense-Perception and Matter.* London, 1953.

Lewis, C. I. *An Analysis of Knowledge and Valuation.* La Salle, Ill., 1947.

———. *Mind and the World Order.* New York, 1929.

Lovejoy, A. O. *The Revolt Against Dualism.* La Salle, Ill., 1930.

Malcolm, Norman. *Knowledge and Certainty.* Englewood Cliffs, N.J., 1963.

Merleau-Ponty, M. *Phenomenology of Perception.* London, 1962.

Moore, G. E. *Some Main Problems of Philosophy.* London, 1953.

Nagel, Ernest, and Brandt, Richard B. *Meaning and Knowledge: Systematic Readings in Epistemology.* New York, 1956.

Prichard, H. A. *Knowledge and Perception.* Oxford, 1950.

Russell, Bertrand. *Our Knowledge of the External World.* Norton, N.Y., 1929.

Walsh, W. H. *Reason and Experience.* Oxford, 1947.

TRUTH

Black, Max. "The Semantic Definition of Truth," *Language and Philosophy*, Ithaca, N.Y., 1949.

Dummet, Michael. "Truth," *Proceedings of the Aristotelian Society*, vol. 59 (1958–1959).

Joachim, H. H. *The Nature of Truth.* Oxford, 1906.

Pitcher, George (ed.). *Truth.* Englewood Cliffs, N.J., 1964.

Russell, Bertrand. *Philosophical Essays.* New York, 1966. Chapters 5, 6, and 7.

Strawson, P. F. "Truth," *Proceedings of the Aristotelian Society*, suppl. vol. 24 (1950).

Woozley, A. D. *Theory of Knowledge.* New York, 1966. Chapters 6 and 7.

INDUCTION

Barker, Stephen F. *Induction and Hypothesis.* Ithaca, N.Y., 1957. Chapters 8 and 9.

Braithwaite, R. B. *Scientific Explanation.* Cambridge, 1953. Chapter 8.

Katz, Jerrold J. *The Problem of Induction and Its Solution.* Chicago, 1962.

Keynes, J. M. *A Treatise on Probability.* London, 1921. Part 3.

Kneale, W. *Probability and Induction.* Oxford, 1949.

Madden, Edward H. (ed.). *The Structure of Scientific Thought.* Boston, 1960. Part 6.

Russell, Bertrand. *Human Knowledge: Its Scope and Limits.* New York, 1948. Part 5.

Salmon, Wesley C. *The Foundations of Scientific Inference.* Pittsburgh, 1967.

CONCEPTIONS
OF KNOWLEDGE

57 *The Divided Line and the Allegory of the Cave**

PLATO

Plato (427–347 B.C.) was a student of Socrates and later founded the Academy, the first "university" in Europe. He has had incalculable influence on Western thought. His best known works are the *Apology, Crito, Meno, Protagoras, Gorgias, Phaedo, Symposium, Republic, Theatetus, Sophist, Parmenides, Phaedrus, Laws, Politicus,* and *Timaeus.*

FOUR STAGES OF COGNITION. THE LINE

Chapter XIX contrasted the realm of sensible appearances and shifting beliefs with the realm of eternal and unchanging Forms, dominated (as we now know) by the Good. The philosopher was he whose affections were set on knowledge of that real world. The Guardians' primary education in literature and art was mainly confined to the world of appearance and belief, though it culminated in the perception of 'images' of the moral ideals, the beauty of which would excite love for the individual person in whose soul they dwelt (402, p. 91). The higher intellectual training now to be described is to detach the mind from appearances and individuals and to carry it across the boundary between the two worlds and all the way beyond to the vision of the Good. It thus corresponds to the 'greater mysteries' of which Diotima speaks in the Symposium *(210), where Eros, detached from its individual object, advances to the vision of Beauty itself (the Good considered as the object of desire). The next chapter will give an allegorical picture of this progress.*

* From *The Republic of Plato,* trans. F. M. Cornford (New York: Oxford University Press, 1945). Reprinted by permission.

The allegory is here prefaced by a diagram. A line is divided into two parts, whose inequality symbolizes that the visible world has a lower degree of reality and truth than the intelligible. Each part is then subdivided in the same proportion as the whole line, (thus $A + B : C + D = A : B = C : D$). The four sections correspond to four states of mind or modes of cognition, each clearer and more certain than the one below.

The lower part $(A + B)$ is at first called 'the Visible,' but elsewhere the field of doxa *in the wide sense explained above (p. 181); and so it includes the 'many conventional notions of the multitude' about morality (479 D, p. 188). It is the physical and moral world as apprehended by those 'lovers of appearance' who do not recognize the absolute ideals which Plato calls real* (p. 189).

	Objects		States of Mind
	The Good		
			Intelligence (*noesis*) or
	Forms	D	Knowledge
Intelligible World			(*episteme*)
	Mathematical objects	C	Thinking (*dianoia*)
	Visible Things	B	Belief (*pistis*)
World of Appearances			
	Images	A	Imagining (*eikasia*)

(A) *The lowest form of cognition is called* eikasia. *The word defies translation, being one of those current terms to which Plato gives a peculiar sense, to be inferred from the context. It is etymologically connected with* eikon = *image, likeness, and with* eikos = *likely, and it can mean either likeness (representation) or likening (comparison) or estimation of likelihood (conjecture). Perhaps 'imagining' is the least unsatisfactory rendering. It seems to be the wholly unenlightened state of mind which takes sensible appearances and current moral notions at their face value—the condition of the unreleased prisoners in the Cave allegory below, who see only images of images.*

(B) *The higher section stands for common-sense belief* (pistis) *in the reality of the visible and tangible things commonly called substantial. In the moral sphere it would include 'correct beliefs without knowledge'* (506 C,

p. 216), *such as the young Guardians were taught to hold. True beliefs are sufficient guides for action, but are insecure until based on knowledge of the reasons for them* (Meno 97).

Higher education is to effect an escape from the prison of appearances by training the intellect, first in mathematics, and then in moral philosophy. (C) *The lower section of the intelligible contains the subject-matter of the mathematical sciences* (511 B, p. 225). *Two characteristics of mathematical procedure are mentioned:* (a) *the use of visible diagrams and models as imperfect illustrations of the objects and truths of pure thought. Here is a sort of bridge carrying the mind across from the visible thing to the intelligible reality, which it must learn to distinguish.* (b) *Each branch of mathematics starts from unquestioned assumptions* (*postulates, axioms, definitions*) *and reasons from them deductively. The premises may be true and the conclusions may follow, but the whole structure hangs in the air until the assumptions themselves shall have been shown to depend on an unconditional principle.* (*This may be conjectured to be Unity itself, an aspect of the Good.*) *Meanwhile the state of mind is* dianoia, *the ordinary word for 'thought' or 'thinking,' here implying a degree of understanding which falls short of perfect knowledge* (533 D, p. 254). *Dianoia suggests discursive thinking or reasoning from premiss to conclusion, whereas* noesis *is constantly compared to the immediate act of vision and suggests rather the direct intuition or apprehension of its object.*

(D) *The higher method is called Dialectic, a word which since Hegel has acquired misleading associations. In the* Republic *it simply means the technique of philosophic conversation* (*dialogue*) *carried on by question and answer and seeking to render, or to receive from a respondent, an 'account'* (logos) *of some Form, usually a moral Form such as Justice in this dialogue. At this stage visible illustrations are no longer available, and the movement at first is not downward, deducing conclusions from premisses, but upward, examining the premisses themselves and seeking the ultimate principle on which they all depend. It is suggested that, if the mind could ever rise to grasp the supreme Form, it might then descend by a deduction confirming the whole structure of moral and mathematical knowledge. The state of mind is called intelligence or rational intuition* (noesis) *and knowledge* (episteme, 533 E, p. 254) *in the full sense. The procedure of Dialectic will be further described in Chapter XXVII.*

CONCEIVE, then, that there are these two powers I speak of, the Good reigning over the domain of all that is intelligible, the Sun over the visible world —or the heaven as I might call it; only you would think I was showing off my skill in etymology. At any rate you have these two orders of things clearly before your mind: the visible and the intelligible?

I have.

Now take a line divided into two unequal parts, one to represent the visible order, the other the intelligible; and divide each part again in the same proportion, symbolizing degrees of comparative clearness or obscurity. Then (A) one of the two sections in the visible world will stand for images. By images I mean first shadows, and then reflections in water or in close-grained, polished surfaces, and everything of that kind, if you understand.

Yes, I understand.

Let the second section (B) stand for the actual things of which the first are likenesses, the living creatures about us and all the works of nature of human hands.

So be it.

Will you also take the proportion in which the visible world has been divided as corresponding to degrees of reality and truth, so that the likeness shall stand to the original in the same ratio as the sphere of appearances and belief to the sphere of knowledge?

Certainly.

Now consider how we are to divide the part which stands for the intelligible world. There are two sections. In the first (C) the mind uses as images those actual things which themselves had images in the visible world; and it is compelled to pursue its inquiry by starting from assumptions and travelling, not up to a principle, but down to a conclusion. In the second (D) the mind moves in the other direction, from an assumption up towards a principle which is not hypothetical; and it makes no use of the images employed in the other section, but only of Forms, and conducts its inquiry solely by their means.

I don't quite understand what you mean.

Then we will try again; what I have just said will help you to understand. (C) You know, of course, how students of subjects like geometry and arithmetic begin by postulating odd and even numbers, or the various figures and the three kinds of angle, and other such data in each subject. These data they take as known; and, having adopted them as assumptions, they do not feel called upon to give any account of them to themselves or to anyone else, but treat them as self-evident. Then, starting from these assumptions, they go on until they arrive, by a series of consistent steps, at all the conclusions they set out to investigate.

Yes, I know that.

You also know how they make use of visible figures and discourse about them, though what they really have in mind is the originals of which these figures are images: they are not reasoning, for instance, about this particular square and diagonal which they have drawn, but about *the* Square and *the* Diagonal; and so in all cases. The diagrams they draw and the models they make are actual things, which may have their shadows or images in water; but now they serve in their turn as images, while the student is seeking to behold those realities which only thought can apprehend.

True.

This, then, is the class of things that I spoke of as intelligible, but with two qualifications: first, that the mind, in studying them, is compelled to employ assumptions, and, because it cannot rise above these, does not travel upwards to a first principle; and second, that it uses as images those actual things which have images of their own in the section below them and which, in comparison with those shadows and reflections, are reputed to be more palpable and valued accordingly.

I understand: you mean the subject-matter of geometry and of the kindred arts.

(D) Then by the second section of the intelligible world you may understand me to mean all that unaided reasoning apprehends by the power of dialectic, when it treats its assumptions, not as first principles, but as *hypotheses* in the literal sense, things 'laid down' like a flight of steps up which it may mount all the way to something that is not hypothetical, the first principle of all; and having grasped this, may turn back and, holding on to the consequences which depend upon it, descend at last to a conclusion, never making use of any sensible object, but only of Forms, moving through Forms from one to another, and ending with Forms.

I understand, he said, though not perfectly; for the procedure you describe sounds like an enormous undertaking. But I see that you mean to distinguish the field of intelligible reality studied by dialectic as having a greater certainty and truth than the subject-matter of the 'arts,' as they are called, which treat their assumptions as first principles. The students of these arts are, it is true, compelled to exercise thought in contemplating objects which the senses cannot perceive; but because they start from assumptions without going back to a first principle, you do not regard them as gaining true understanding about those objects, although the objects themselves, when connected with a first principle, are intelligible. And I think you would call the state of mind of the students of geometry and other such arts, not intelligence, but thinking, as being something between intelligence and mere acceptance of appearances.

You have understood me quite well enough, I replied. And now you may take, as corresponding to the four sections, these four states of mind: *intelligence* for the highest, *thinking* for the second, *belief* for the third, and for the last *imagining*. These you may arrange as the terms in a proportion, assigning to each a degree of clearness and certainty corresponding to the measure in which their objects possess truth and reality.

I understand and agree with you. I will arrange them as you say.

THE ALLEGORY OF THE CAVE

The progress of the mind from the lowest state of unenlightenment to knowledge of the Good is now illustrated by the famous parable comparing the world of appearance to an underground Cave. In Empedocles' religious poem the powers which conduct the soul to its incarnation say, 'We have come under this cavern's roof.' The image was probably taken from mysteries held in caves or dark chambers representing the underworld, through which the candidates for initiation were led to the revelation of sacred objects in a blaze of light. The idea that the body is a prison-house, to which the soul is condemned for past misdeeds, is attributed by Plato to the Orphics.

One moral of the allegory is drawn from the distress caused by a too sudden passage from darkness to light. The earlier warning against plunging untrained minds into the discussion of moral problems (498 A, p. 206), as the Sophists and Socrates himself had done, is reinforced by the picture of the dazed prisoner dragged out into the sunlight. Plato's ten years' course of pure mathematics is to habituate the intellect to abstract reasoning before moral ideas are called in question (537 E, ff., p. 259).

NEXT, said I, here is a parable to illustrate the degrees in which our nature may be enlightened or unenlightened. Imagine the condition of men living in a sort of cavernous chamber underground, with an entrance open to the light and a long passage all down the cave. Here they have been from child-hood, chained by the leg and also by the neck, so that they cannot move and can see only what is in front of them, because the chains will not let them turn their heads. At some distance higher up is the light of a fire burning behind them; and between the prisoners and the fire is a track with a parapet built along it, like the screen at a puppet-show, which hides the performers while they show their puppets over the top.

I see, said he.

Now behind this parapet imagine persons carrying along various artifi-cial objects, including figures of men and animals in wood or stone or other materials, which project above the parapet. Naturally, some of these persons will be talking, others silent.

It is a strange picture, he said, and a strange sort of prisoners.

Like ourselves, I replied; for in the first place prisoners so confined would have seen nothing of themselves or of one another, except the shadows thrown by the fire-light on the wall of the Cave facing them, would they?

Not if all their lives they had been prevented from moving their heads.

And they would have seen as little of the objects carried past.

Of course.

Now, if they could talk to one another, would they not suppose that their words referred only to those passing shadows which they saw?

Necessarily.

And suppose their prison had an echo from the wall facing them? When one of the people crossing behind them spoke, they could only suppose that the sound came from the shadow passing before their eyes.

No doubt.

In every way, then, such prisoners would recognize as reality nothing but the shadows of those artificial objects.

Inevitably.

Now consider what would happen if their release from the chains and the healing of their unwisdom should come about in this way. Suppose one of them set free and forced suddenly to stand up, turn his head, and walk with eyes lifted to the light; all these movements would be painful, and he would be too dazzled to make out the objects whose shadows he had been used to see. What do you think he would say, if someone told him that what he had formerly seen was meaningless illusion, but now, being somewhat nearer to reality and turned towards more real objects, he was getting a truer view? Suppose further that he were shown the various objects being carried by and were made to say, in reply to questions, what each of them was. Would he not be perplexed and believe the objects now shown him to be not so real as what he formerly saw?

Yes, not nearly so real.

And if he were forced to look at the fire-light itself, would not his eyes ache, so that he would try to escape and turn back to the things which he could see distinctly, convinced that they really were clearer than these other objects now being shown to him?

Yes.

And suppose someone were to drag him away forcibly up the steep and rugged ascent and not let him go until he had hauled him out into the sunlight, would he not suffer pain and vexation at such treatment, and, when he had come out into the light, find his eyes so full of its radiance that he could not see a single one of the things that he was now told were real?

Certainly he would not see them all at once.

He would need, then, to grow accustomed before he could see things in that upper world. At first it would be easiest to make out shadows, and then the images of men and things reflected in water, and later on the things themselves. After that, it would be easier to watch the heavenly bodies and the sky itself by night, looking at the light of the moon and stars rather than the Sun and the Sun's light in the day-time.

Yes, surely.

Last of all, he would be able to look at the Sun and contemplate its nature, not as it appears when reflected in water or any alien medium, but as it is in itself in its own domain.

No doubt.

And now he would begin to draw the conclusion that it is the Sun that produces the seasons and the course of the year and controls everything in the visible world, and moreover is in a way the cause of all that he and his companions used to see.

Clearly he would come at last to that conclusion.

Then if he called to mind his fellow prisoners and what passed for wisdom in his former dwelling-place, he would surely think himself happy in the change and be sorry for them. They may have had a practice of honouring and commending one another, with prizes for the man who had the keenest eye for the passing shadows and the best memory for the order in which they followed or accompanied one another, so that he could make a good guess as to which was going to come next. Would our released prisoner be likely to covet those prizes or to envy the men exalted to honour and power in the Cave? Would he not feel like Homer's Achilles, that he would far sooner 'be on earth as a hired servant in the house of a landless man' or endure anything rather than go back to his old beliefs and live in the old way?

Yes, he would prefer any fate to such a life.

Now imagine what would happen if he went down again to take his former seat in the Cave. Coming suddenly out of the sunlight, his eyes would be filled with darkness. He might be required once more to deliver his opinion on those shadows, in competition with the prisoners who had never been released, while his eyesight was still dim and unsteady; and it might take some time to become used to the darkness. They would laugh at him and say that he had gone up only to come back with his sight ruined; it was worth no one's while even to attempt the ascent. If they could lay hands on the man who was trying to set them free and lead them up, they would kill him.

Yes, they would.

Every feature in this parable, my dear Glaucon, is meant to fit our earlier analysis. The prison dwelling corresponds to the region revealed to us through the sense of sight, and the fire-light within it to the power of the Sun. The ascent to see the things in the upper world you may take as standing for the upward journey of the soul into the region of the intelligible; then you will be in possession of what I surmise, since that is what you wish to be told. Heaven knows whether it is true; but this, at any rate, is how it appears to me. In the world of knowledge, the last thing to be perceived and only with great difficulty is the essential Form of Goodness. Once it is perceived, the conclusion must follow that, for all things, this is the cause of whatever is right and good; in the visible world it gives birth to light and to the lord of light, while it is itself sovereign in the intelligible world and the parent of intelligence and truth. Without having had a vision of this Form no one can act with wisdom, either in his own life or in matters of state.

So far as I can understand, I share your belief.

58 Science and the Idols of Men[*]

FRANCIS BACON

Francis Bacon (1561–1629) was not only an important philosopher but also an influential political figure in England. Sometimes referred to as the founding father of modern science, Bacon is famous for his contributions to the development of the empirical method. His best known work is the *Novum Organum*.

NOVUM ORGANUM

xxxviii

The idols and false notions which are now in possession of the human understanding, and have taken deep root therein, not only so beset men's minds that truth can hardly find entrance, but even after entrance obtain, they will again in the very insaturation of the sciences meet and trouble us, unless men being forewarned of the danger fortify themselves as far as may be against their assaults.

xxxix

There are four classes of idols which beset men's minds. To these for distinction's sake I have assigned names,—calling the first class *Idols of the Tribe*; the second, *Idols of the Cave*; the third, *Idols of the Market-place*; the fourth, *Idols of the Theater*.

xl

The formation of ideas and axioms by true induction is no doubt the proper remedy to be applied for the keeping off and clearing away of idols. To point them out, however, is of great use, for the doctrine of idols is to the interpretation of nature what the doctrine of the refutation of sophisms is to common logic.

xli

The Idols of the Tribe have their foundation in human nature itself, and in the tribe or race of men. For it is a false assertion that the sense of man

[*] From Francis Bacon, *Novum Organum*.

is the measure of things. On the contrary, all perceptions, as well of the sense as of the mind, are according to the measure of the individual and not according to the measure of the universe. And the human understanding is like a false mirror, which, receiving rays irregularly, distorts and discolors the nature of things by mingling its own nature with it.

xlii

The Idols of the Cave are the idols of the individual man. For everyone (besides the errors common to human nature in general) has a cave or den of his own, which refracts and discolors the light of nature; owing either to his own proper and peculiar nature or to his education and conversation with others; or to the reading of books, and the authority of those whom he esteems and admires; or to the differences of impressions, accordingly as they take place in a mind preoccupied and predisposed or in a mind indifferent and settled; or the like. So that the spirit of man (according as it is meted out to different individuals) is in fact a thing variable and full of perturbation, and governed as it were by chance. Whence it was well observed by Heraclitus that men look for sciences in their own lesser worlds, and not in the greater or common world.

xliii

There are also idols formed by the intercourse and association of men with each other, which I call Idols of the Market-place, on account of the commerce and consort of men there. For it is by discourse that men associate; and words are imposed according to the apprehension of the vulgar. And therefore the ill and unfit choice of words wonderfully obstructs the understanding. Nor do the definitions or explanations wherewith in some things learned men are wont to guard and defend themselves, by any means set the matter right. But words plainly force and overrule the understanding, and throw all into confusion, and lead men away into numberless empty controversies and idle fancies.

xliv

Lastly, there are idols which have immigrated into men's minds from the various dogmas of philosophies, and also from wrong laws of demonstration. These I call Idols of the Theater; because in my judgment all the received systems are but so many stage-plays, representing worlds of their own creations after an unreal and scenic fashion. Nor is it only of the systems now in vogue, or only of the ancient sects and philosophies, that I speak: for many more plays of the same kind may yet be composed and in like artificial manner set forth; seeing that errors the most widely different have nevertheless causes for the most part alike. Neither again do I mean this only of entire systems, but also of many principles and axioms in science, which by tradition, credulity, and negligence have come to be received.

But of these several kinds of idols I must speak more largely and exactly, that the understanding may be duly cautioned.

xlv

The human understanding is of its own nature prone to suppose the existence of more order and regularity in the world than it finds. And though there be many things in nature which are singular and unmatched, yet it devises for them parallels and conjugates and relatives which do not exist. Hence the fiction that all celestial bodies move in perfect circles; spirals and dragons being (except in name) utterly rejected. Hence too the element of fire with its orb is brought in, to make up the square with the other three which the sense perceives. Hence also the ratio of density of the so-called elements is arbitrarily fixed at ten to one. And so on of other dreams. And these fancies affect not dogmas only, but simple notions also.

xlvi

The human understanding when it has once adopted an opinion (either as being the received opinion or as being agreeable to itself) draws all things else to support and agree with it. And though there be a greater number and weight of instances to be found on the other side, yet these it either neglects and despises, or else by some distinction sets aside and rejects; in order that by this great and pernicious predetermination the authority of its former conclusions may remain inviolate. And therefore it was a good answer that was made by one who when they showed him hanging in a temple a picture of those who had paid their vows as having escaped shipwreck, and would have him say whether he did not now acknowledge the power of the gods,— "Aye," asked he again, "but where are they painted that were drowned after their vows?" And such is the way of all superstition, whether in astrology, dreams, omens, divine judgments, or the like; wherein men, having a delight in such vanities, mark the events where they are fulfilled, but where they fail, though this happen much oftener, neglect and pass them by. But with far more subtlety does this mischief insinuate itself into philosophy and the sciences; in which the first conclusion colors and brings into conformity with itself all that come after, though far sounder and better. Besides, independently of that delight and vanity which I have described, it is the peculiar and perpetual error of the human intellect to be more moved and excited by affirmatives than by negatives; whereas it ought properly to hold itself indifferently disposed towards both alike. Indeed in the establishment of any true axiom, the negative instance is the more forcible of the two.

xlvii

The human understanding is moved by those things most which strike and enter the mind simultaneously and suddenly, and so fill the imagination; and then it feigns and supposes all other things to be somehow, though it cannot see how, similar to those few things by which it is surrounded. But for that going to and fro to remote and heterogeneous instances, by which axioms are tried as in the fire, the intellect is altogether slow and unfit, unless it be forced thereto by severe laws and overruling authority.

xlviii

The human understanding is unquiet; it cannot stop or rest, and still presses onward, but in vain. Therefore it is that we cannot conceive of any end or limit to the world; but always as of necessity it occurs to us that there is something beyond. Neither again can it be conceived how eternity has flowed down to the present day: for that distinction which is commonly received of infinity in time past and in time to come can by no means hold; for it would thence follow that one infinity is greater than another, and that infinity is wasting away and tending to become finite. The like subtlety arises touching the infinite divisibility of lines, from the same inability of thought to stop. But this inability interferes more mischievously in the discovery of causes: for although the most general principles in nature ought to be held merely positive, as they are discovered, and cannot with truth be referred to a cause; nevertheless the human understanding being unable to rest still seeks something prior in the order of nature. And then it is that in struggling towards that which is further off it falls back upon that which is more nigh at hand,—namely, on final causes; which have relation clearly to the nature of man rather than to the nature of the universe, and from this source have strangely defiled philosophy. But he is no less an unskilled and shallow philosopher who seeks causes of that which is most general, than he who in things subordinate and subaltern omits to do so.

xlix

The human understanding is no dry light, but receives an infusion from the will and affections; whence proceed sciences which may be called "sciences as one would." For what a man had rather were true he more readily believes. Therefore he rejects difficult things from impatience of research; sober things, because they narrow hope; the deeper things of nature, from superstition; the light of experience, from arrogance and pride, lest his mind should seem to be occupied with things mean and transitory; things not commonly believed, out of deference to the opinion of the vulgar. Numberless in short are the ways, and sometimes inperceptible, in which the affections color and infect the understanding.

l

But by far the greatest hindrance and aberration of the human understanding proceeds from the dullness, incompetency, and deceptions of the senses; in that things which strike the sense outweigh things which do not immediately strike it, though they be more important. Hence it is that speculation commonly ceases where sight ceases, insomuch that of things invisible there is little or no observation. Hence all the working of the spirits inclosed in tangible bodies lies hid and unobserved of men. So also all the more subtle changes of form in the parts of coarser substances (which they commonly call alteration, though it is in truth local motion through exceedingly small spaces) is in like manner unobserved. And yet unless these two things just mentioned be searched out and brought to light, nothing great can be achieved in nature, as far as the production of works is concerned. So again the essential nature of our common air, and of all bodies less dense than air (which are very many), is almost unknown. For the sense by itself is a thing infirm and erring; neither can instruments for enlarging or sharpening the senses do much: but all the truer kind of interpretation of nature is effected by instances and experiments fit and apposite; wherein the sense decides touching the experiment only, and the experiment touching the point in nature and the thing itself.

li

The human understanding is of its own nature prone to abstractions and gives a substance and reality to things which are fleeting. But to resolve nature into abstractions is less to our purpose than to dissect her into parts; as did the school of Democritus, which went further into nature than the rest. Matter rather than forms should be the object of our attention, its configurations and changes of configuration, and simple action, and law of action or motion; for forms are figments of the human mind, unless you will call those laws of action forms.

lii

Such then are the idols which I call *Idols of the Tribe*; and which take their rise either from the homogeneity of the substance of the human spirit, or from its preoccupation, or from its narrowness, or from its restless motion, or from an infusion of the affections, or from the incompetency of the senses, or from the mode of impression.

liii

The *Idols of the Cave* take their rise in the peculiar constitution, mental or bodily, of each individual; and also in education, habit, and accident. Of this kind there is a great number and variety; but I will instance those the pointing out of which contains the most important caution, and which have most effect in disturbing the clearness of the understanding.

liv

Men become attached to certain particular sciences and speculations, either because they fancy themselves the authors and inventors thereof, or because they have bestowed the greatest pains upon them and become most habituated to them. But men of this kind, if they betake themselves to philosophy and contemplations of a general character, distort and color them in obedience to their former fancies; a thing especially to be noticed in Aristotle, who made his natural philosophy a mere bondservant to his logic, thereby rendering it contentious and well nigh useless. The race of chemists again out of a few experiments of the furnace have built up a fantastic philosophy, framed with reference to a few things; and Gilbert also, after he had employed himself most laboriously in the study and observation of the lodestone, proceeded at once to construct an entire system in accordance with his favorite subject.

lv

There is one principal and as it were radical distinction between different minds, in respect of philosophy and the sciences; which is this: that some minds are stronger and apter to mark the differences of things, others to mark their resemblances. The steady and acute mind can fix its contemplations and dwell and fasten on the subtlest distinctions; the lofty and discursive mind recognizes and puts together the finest and most general resemblances. Both kinds however easily err in excess, by catching the one at gradations, the other at shadows.

lvi

There are found some minds given to an extreme admiration of antiquity, others to an extreme love and appetite for novelty; but few so duly tempered that they can hold the mean, neither carping at what has been well laid down by the ancients, nor despising what is well introduced by the moderns. This however turns to the great injury of the sciences and philosophy: since these affectations of antiquity and novelty are the humors of partisans rather than judgments; and truth is to be sought for not in the felicity of any age, which is an unstable thing, but in the light of nature and experience, which is eternal. These factions therefore must be abjured, and care must be taken that the intellect be not hurried by them into assent.

lvii

Contemplations of nature and of bodies in their simple form break up and distract the understanding, while contemplations of nature and bodies in their composition and configuration overpower and dissolve the understanding: a distinction well seen in the school of Leucippus and Democritus as compared with the other philosophies. For that school is so busied with the particles that it hardly attends to the structure; while the others are so lost in admiration of the structure that they do not penetrate to the simplicity of nature. These kinds of contemplation should therefore be alternated and taken by turns; that so the understanding may be rendered at once penetrating and comprehensive, and the inconveniences above mentioned, with the idols which proceed from them, may be avoided.

lviii

Let such then be our provision and contemplative prudence for keeping off and dislodging the Idols of the Cave, which grow for the most part either out of the predominance of a favorite subject, or out of an excessive tendency to compare or to distinguish, or out of partiality for particular ages, or out of the largeness or minuteness of the objects contemplated. And generally let every student of nature take this as a rule,—that whatever his mind seizes and dwells upon with peculiar satisfaction is to be held in suspicion, and that so much the more care is to be taken in dealing with such questions to keep the understanding even and clear.

lix

But the *Idols of the Market-place* are the most troublesome of all: idols which have crept into the understanding through the alliances of words and names. For men believe that their reason governs words; but it is also true that words react on the understanding; and this it is that has rendered philosophy and the sciences sophistical and inactive. Now words, being commonly framed and applied according to the capacity of the vulgar, follow those lines of division which are most obvious to the vulgar understanding. And whenever an understanding of greater acuteness or a more diligent observation would alter those lines to suit the true divisions of nature, words stand in the way and resist the change. Whence it comes to pass that the high and formal discussions of learned men end oftentimes in disputes about words and names; with which (according to the use and wisdom of the mathematicians) it would be more prudent to begin, and so by means of definitions reduce them to order. Yet even definitions cannot cure this evil in dealing with natural and material things; since the definitions themselves consist of words, and those words beget others: so that it is necessary to recur to individual instances, and those in due series and order; as I shall say presently when I come to the method and scheme for the formation of notions and axioms.

lx

The idols imposed by words on the understanding are of two kinds. They are either names of things which do not exist (for as there are things left unnamed through lack of observation, so likewise are there names which result from fantastic suppositions and to which nothing in reality corresponds), or they are names of things which exist, but yet confused and ill-defined, and hastily and irregularly derived from realities. Of the former kind are Fortune, the Prime Mover, Planetary Orbits, Elements of Fire, and like fictions which owe their origin to false and idle theories. And this class of idols is more easily expelled, because to get rid of them it is only necessary that all theories should be steadily rejected and dismissed as obsolete.

But the other class, which springs out of a faulty and unskillful abstraction, is intricate and deeply rooted. Let us take for example such a word as *humid*, and see how far the several things which the word is used to signify agree with each other; and we shall find the word *humid* to be nothing else than a mark loosely and confusedly applied to denote a variety of actions which will not bear to be reduced to any constant meaning. For it both signifies that which easily spreads itself round any other body; and that which in itself is indeterminate and cannot solidize; and that which readily yields in every direction; and that which easily divides and scatters itself; and that which easily unites and collects itself; and that which readily flows and is put in motion; and that which readily clings to another body and wets it; and that which is easily reduced to a liquid, or being solid easily melts. Accordingly when you come to apply the word,—if you take it in one sense, flame is humid; if in another, air is not humid; if in another, fine dust is humid; if in another, glass is humid. So that it is easy to see that the notion is taken by abstraction only from water and common and ordinary liquids, without any due verification.

There are however in words certain degrees of distortion and error. One of the least faulty kinds is that of names of substances, especially of lowest species and well-deduced (for the notion of *chalk* and of *mud* is good, of *earth* bad); a more faulty kind is that of actions, as *to generate, to corrupt, to alter*; the most faulty is of qualities (except such as are the immediate objects of the sense) as *heavy, light, rare, dense*, and the like. Yet in all these cases some notions are of necessity a little better than others, in proportion to the greater variety of subjects that fall within the range of the human sense.

lxi

But the *Idols of the Theater* are not innate, nor do they steal into the understanding secretly, but are plainly impressed and received into the mind from the play-books of philosophical system and the perverted rules of demonstration. To attempt refutations in this case would be merely inconsistent with what I have already said: for since we agree neither upon principles nor upon demonstrations there is no place for argument. And this is so far well, inasmuch as it leaves the honor of the ancients untouched. For they are no wise disparaged—the question between them and me being only as to the way. For as the saying is, the lame man who keeps the right road outstrips the runner who takes a wrong one. Nay it is obvious that when a man runs the wrong way, the more active and swift he is the further he will go astray.

But the course I propose for the discovery of sciences is such as leaves but little to the acuteness and strength of wits, but places all wits and understandings nearly on a level. For as in the drawing of a straight line or a perfect circle, much depends on the steadiness and practice of the hand, if it be done by aim of hand only, but if with the aid of rule or compass, little or nothing; so is it exactly with my plan. But though particular confutations would be of no avail, yet touching the sects and general divisions of such systems I must say something; something also touching the external signs which show that they are unsound; and finally something touching the causes of such great infelicity and of such lasting and general agreement in error; that so the access to truth may be made less difficult, and the human understanding may the more willingly submit to its purgation and dismiss its idols.

lxii

Idols of the Theater, or of Systems, are many, and there can be and perhaps will be yet many more. For were it not that now for many ages men's minds have been busied with religion and theology; and were it not that civil governments, especially monarchies, have been averse to such novelties, even in matters speculative; so that men labor therein to the peril and harming of their fortunes,—not only unrewarded, but exposed also to contempt and envy: doubtless there would have arisen many other philosophical sects like to those which in great variety flourished once among the Greeks. For as on the phenomena of the heavens many hypotheses may be constructed, so likewise (and more also) many various dogmas may be set up and established on the phenomena of philosophy. And in the plays of this philosophical theater you may observe the same thing which is found in the theater of the poets, that stories invented for the stage are more compact and elegant, and more as one would wish them to be, than true stories out of history.

In general however there is taken for the material of philosophy either a great deal out of a few things, or a very little out of many things; so that on both sides philosophy is based on too narrow a foundation of experiment and natural history, and decides on the authority of too few cases. For the rational school of philosophers snatches from experience a variety of common instances, neither duly ascertained nor diligently examined and weighed, and leaves all the rest to meditation and agitation of wit.

There is also another class of philosophers, who having bestowed much diligent and careful labor on a few experiments, have thence made bold to educe and construct systems; wresting all other facts in a strange fashion to conformity therewith.

And there is yet a third class, consisting of those who out of faith and veneration mix their philosophy with theology and traditions; among whom the variety of some has gone so far aside as to seek the origin of science among spirits and genii. So that this parent stock of errors—this false philosophy—is of three kinds; the *sophistical*, the *empirical*, and the *superstitious*.

lxiii

The most conspicuous example of the first class was Aristotle, who corrupted natural philosophy by his logic: fashioning the world out of categories; assigning to the human soul, the noblest of substances, a genus from words of the second intention; doing the business of density and rarity (which is to make bodies of greater or less dimensions, that is, occupy greater or less spaces), by the frigid distinction of act and power; asserting that single bodies have each a single and proper motion, and that if they participate in any other, then this results from an external cause; and imposing countless other arbitrary restrictions on the nature of things: being always more solicitous to provide an answer to the question and affirm something positive in words, than about the inner truth of things; a failing best shown when his philosophy is compared with other systems of note among the Greeks. For the *homœomera* of Anaxagoras; the atoms of Leucippus and Democritus; the Heaven and Earth of Parmenides; the Strife of Friendship of Empedocles; Heraclitus's doctrine how bodies are resolved into the indifferent nature of fire, and remolded into solids; have all of them some taste of the natural philosopher—some savor of the nature of things, and experience, and bodies; whereas in the physics of Aristotle you hear hardly anything but the words of logic; which in his metaphysics also, under a more imposing name and more forsooth as a realist than a nominalist, he has handled over again. Nor let any weight be given to the fact that in his books on animals, and his *Problems,* and other of his treatises, there is frequent dealing with experiments. For he had come to his conclusion before: he did not consult experience, as he should have done, in order to the framing of his decisions and axioms; but having first determined the question according to his will, he then resorts to experience, and bending her into conformity with his placets leads her about like a captive in a procession: so that even on this count he is more guilty than his modern followers, the schoolmen, who have abandoned experience altogether.

lxiv

But the empirical school of philosophy gives birth to dogmas more deformed and monstrous than the sophistical or rational school. For it has its foundations not in the light of common notions (which, though it be a faint and superficial light, is yet in a manner universal, and has reference to many things) but in the narrowness and darkness of a few experiments. To those therefore who are daily busied with these experiments, and have infected their imagination with them, such a philosophy seems probable and all but certain; to all men else incredible and vain. Of this there is a notable instance in the alchemists and their dogmas; though it is hardly to be found elsewhere in these times, except perhaps in the philosophy of Gilbert. Nevertheless with regard to philosophies of this kind there is one caution not to be omitted; for I foresee that if ever men are roused by my admonitions to betake themselves seriously to experiment and bid farewell to sophistical doctrines, then indeed through the premature hurry of the understanding to leap or fly to universals and principles of things, great danger may be apprehended from philosophies of this kind; against which evil we ought even now to prepare.

lxv

But the corruption of philosophy by superstition and an admixture of theology is far more widely spread, and does the greatest harm, whether to entire systems or to their parts. For the human understanding is obnoxious to the influence of the imagination no less than to the influence of common notions. For the contentious and sophistical kind of philosophy ensnares the understanding; but this kind, being fanciful and tumid and half poetical, misleads it more by flattery. For there is in man an ambition of the understanding, no less than of the will, especially in high and lofty spirits.

Of this kind we have among the Greeks a striking example in Pythagoras, though he united with it a coarser and more cumbrous superstition; another in Plato and his school, more dangerous and subtle. It shows itself likewise in parts of other philosophies, in the introduction of abstract forms and final causes and first causes, with the omission in most cases of causes intermediate, and the like. Upon this point the greatest caution should be used. For nothing is so mischievous as the apotheosis of error; and it is a very plague of the understanding for vanity to become the object of veneration. Yet in this vanity some of the moderns have with extreme levity indulged so far as to attempt to found a system of natural philosophy on the first chapters of Genesis, on the book of Job, and other parts of the sacred writings; seeking for the dead among the living: which also makes the inhibition and repression of it the more important, because from this unwholesome mixture of things human and divine there arises not only a fantastic philosophy but also an heretical religion. Very meet it is therefore that we be sober-minded, and give to faith that only which is faith's.

59 Scepticism and Certainty*

RENÉ DESCARTES

René Descartes (1596–1650) is often considered the founder of modern philosophy. Recognized as the inventor of analytic geometry and as an important contributor to theoretical physics, Descartes' major philosophical works are *Discourse on Method, Meditations on First Philosophy,* and *Principles of Philosophy.*

MEDITATION I

Of the Things of Which We May Doubt

Several years have now elapsed since I first became aware that I had accepted, even from my youth, many false opinions for true, and that consequently what I afterwards based on such principles was highly doubtful; and from that time I was convinced of the necessity of undertaking once in my life to rid myself of all the opinions I had adopted, and of commencing anew the work of building from the foundation, if I desired to establish a firm and abiding superstructure in the sciences. But as this enterprise appeared to me to be one of great magnitude, I waited until I had attained an age so mature as to leave me no hope that at any stage of life more advanced I should be better able to execute my design. On this account, I have delayed so long that I should henceforth consider I was doing wrong were I still to consume in deliberation any of the time that now remains for action. To-day, then, since I have opportunely freed my mind from all cares, [and am happily disturbed by no passions], and since I am in the secure possession of leisure in a peaceable retirement, I will at length apply myself earnestly and freely to the general overthrow of all my former opinions. But, to this end, it will not be necessary for me to show that the whole of these are false—a point, perhaps, which I shall never reach; but as even now my reason convinces me that I ought not the less carefully to withhold belief from what is not entirely certain and indubitable, than from what is manifestly false, it will be sufficient to justify the rejection of the whole if I shall find in each some ground for doubt. Nor for this purpose will it be necessary even to deal with each belief individually, which would be truly an endless

---

* From *Meditations and Selections from the Principles of Philosophy* by René Descartes, translated by John Veitch, Open Court Publishing Co., LaSalle, Illinois, 1952. Reprinted by permission.

labour; but, as the removal from below of the foundation necessarily involves the downfall of the whole edifice, I will at once approach the criticism of the principles on which all my former beliefs rested.

All that I have, up to this moment, accepted as possessed of the highest truth and certainty, I received either from or through the senses. I observed, however, that these sometimes misled us; and it is the part of prudence not to place absolute confidence in that by which we have even once been deceived.

But it may be said, perhaps, that, although the senses occasionally mislead us respecting minute objects, and such as are so far removed from us as to be beyond the reach of close observation, there are yet many other of their informations (presentations), of the truth of which it is manifestly impossible to doubt; as for example, that I am in this place, seated by the fire, clothed in a winter dressing-gown, that I hold in my hands this piece of paper, with other intimations of the same nature. But how could I deny that I possess these hands and this body, and withal escape being classed with persons in a state of insanity, whose brains are so disordered and clouded by dark bilious vapours as to cause them pertinaciously to assert that they are monarchs when they are in the greatest poverty; or clothed [in gold] and purple when destitute of any covering; or that their head is made of clay, their body of glass, or that they are gourds? I should certainly be not less insane than they, were I to regulate my procedure according to examples so extravagant.

Though this be true, I must nevertheless here consider that I am a man, and that, consequently, I am in the habit of sleeping, and representing to myself in dreams those same things, or even sometimes others less probable, which the insane think are presented to them in their waking moments. How often have I dreamt that I was in these familiar circumstances,—that I was dressed, and occupied this place by the fire, when I was lying undressed in bed? At the present moment, however, I certainly look upon this paper with eyes wide awake; the head which I now move is not asleep; I extend this hand consciously and with express purpose, and I perceive it; the occurrences in sleep are not so distinct as all this. But I cannot forget that, at other times, I have been deceived in sleep by similar illusions; and, attentively considering those cases, I perceive so clearly that there exist no certain marks by which the state of waking can ever be distinguished from sleep, that I feel greatly astonished; and in amazement I almost persuade myself that I am now dreaming.

Let us suppose, then, that we are dreaming, and that all these particulars —namely, the opening of the eyes, the motion of the head, the forth-putting of the hands—are merely illusions; and even that we really possess neither an entire body nor hands such as we see. Nevertheless, it must be admitted at least that the objects which appear to us in sleep are, as it were, painted representations which could not have been formed unless in the likeness of realities; and, therefore, that those general objects, at all events,—namely, eyes, a head, hands, and an entire body—are not simply imaginary, but really existent. For, in truth, painters themselves, even when they study to represent sirens and satyrs by forms the most fantastic and extraordinary, cannot bestow upon them natures absolutely new, but can only make a certain medley of the members of different animals; or if they chance to imagine something so novel that nothing at all similar has ever been seen before, and such as is, therefore, purely fictitious and absolutely false, it is at least certain that the colours of which this is composed are real.

And on the same principle, although these general objects, viz. [a body], eyes, a head, hands, and the like, be imaginary, we are nevertheless absolutely necessitated to admit the reality at least of some other objects still more simple and universal than these, of which, just as of certain real colours, all those images of things, whether true and real, or false and fantastic, that are found in our consciousness (*cogitatio*), are formed.

To this class of objects seem to belong corporeal nature in general and its extension; the figure of extended things, their quantity or magnitude, and their number, as also the place in, and the time during, which they exist, and other things of the same sort. We will not, therefore, perhaps reason illegitimately if we conclude from this that Physics, Astronomy, Medicine, and all the other sciences that have for their end the consideration of composite objects, are indeed of a doubtful character; but that Arithmetic, Geometry, and the other sciences of the same class, which regard merely the simplest and most general objects, and scarcely inquire whether or not these are really existent, contain somewhat that is certain and indubitable: for whether I am awake or dreaming, it remains true that two and three make five, and that a square has but four sides; nor does it seem possible that truths so apparent can ever fall under a suspicion of falsity [or incertitude].

Nevertheless, the belief that there is a God who is all-powerful, and who created me, such as I am, has, for a long time, obtained steady possession of my mind. How, then, do I know that he has not arranged that there should be neither earth, nor sky, nor any extended thing, nor figure, nor magnitude, nor place, providing at the same time, however, for [the rise in me of the perceptions of all these objects, and] the persuasion that these do not exist otherwise than as I perceive them? And further, as I sometimes think that others are in error respecting matters of which they believe themselves to possess a perfect knowledge, how do I know that I am not also deceived each time I add together two and three, or number the sides of a square, or form some judgment still more simple, if more simple indeed can be imagined? But perhaps Deity has not been willing that I should be thus deceived, for He is said to be supremely good. If, however, it were repugnant to the goodness of Deity to have created me subject to constant deception, it would seem likewise to be contrary to his goodness to allow me to be occasionally deceived; and yet it is clear that this is permitted. Some, indeed, might perhaps be found who would be disposed rather to deny the existence of a Being so powerful than to believe that there is nothing certain. But let us for the present refrain from opposing this opinion, and grant that all which is here said of a Deity is fabulous: nevertheless in whatever way it be supposed that I reached the state in which I exist, whether by fate, or chance, or by an endless series of antecedents and consequents, or by any other means, it is clear (since to be deceived and to err is a certain defect) that the probability of my being so imperfect as to be the constant victim of deception, will be increased exactly in proportion as the power possessed by the cause, to which they assign my origin, is lessened. To these reasonings I have assuredly nothing to reply, but am constrained at last to avow that there is nothing of all that I formerly believed to be true of which it is impossible to doubt, and that not through thoughtlessness or levity, but from cogent and maturely considered reasons; so that henceforward, if I desire to discover anything certain, I ought not the less carefully to refrain from assenting to those same opinions than to what might be shown to be manifestly false.

But it is not sufficient to have made these observations; care must be taken likewise to keep them in remembrance. For those old and customary opinions perpetually recur—long and familiar usage giving them the right of occupying my mind, even almost against my will, and subduing my belief; nor will I lose the habit of deferring to them and confiding in them so long as I shall consider them to be what in truth they are, viz., opinions to some extent doubtful, as I have already shown, but still highly probable, and such as it is much more reasonable to believe than deny. It is for this reason I am persuaded that I shall not be doing wrong, if, taking an opposite judgment of deliberate design, I become my own deceiver, by supposing, for a time, that all those opinions are entirely false and imaginary, until at length, having thus balanced my old by my new prejudices, my judgment shall no longer be turned aside by perverted usage from the path that may conduct to the perception of truth. For I am assured that, meanwhile, there will arise neither peril nor error from this course, and that I cannot for the present yield too much to distrust, since the end I now seek is not action but knowledge.

I will suppose, then, not that Deity, who is sovereignly good and the fountain of truth, but that some malignant demon, who is at once exceedingly potent and deceitful, has employed all his artifice to deceive me; I will suppose that the sky, the air, the earth, colours, figures, sounds, and all external things, are nothing better than the illusions of dreams, by means of which this being has laid snares for my credulity; I will consider myself as without hands, eyes, flesh, blood, or any of the senses, and as falsely believing that I am possessed of these; I will continue resolutely fixed in this belief, and if indeed by this means it be not in my power to arrive at the knowledge of truth, I shall at least do what is in my power, viz., [suspend my judgment], and guard with settled purpose against giving my assent to what is false, and being imposed upon by this deceiver, whatever be his power and artifice.

But this undertaking is arduous, and a certain indolence insensibly leads me back to my ordinary course of life; and just as the captive, who, perchance, was enjoying in his dreams an imaginary liberty, when he begins to suspect that it is but a vision, dreads awakening, and conspires with the agreeable illusions that the deception may be prolonged; so I, of my own accord, fall back into the train of my former beliefs, and fear to arouse myself from my slumber, lest the time of laborious wakefulness that would succeed this quiet rest, in place of bringing any light of day, should prove inadequate to dispel the darkness that will arise from the difficulties that have now been raised.

MEDITATION II

Of the Nature of the Human Mind; And That It Is More Easily Known than the Body

The Meditation of yesterday has filled my mind with so many doubts, that it is no longer in my power to forget them. Nor do I see, meanwhile, any principle on which they can be resolved; and, just as if I had fallen all of a sudden into very deep water, I am so greatly disconcerted as to be unable either to plant my feet firmly on the bottom or sustain myself by swimming on the surface. I will, nevertheless, make an effort, and try anew the same path on which I had entered yesterday, that is, proceed by casting aside all that admits of the slightest doubt, not less than if I had discovered it to be absolutely false; and I will continue always in this track until I shall find something that is certain, or at least, if I can do nothing more, until I shall know with certainty that there is nothing certain. Archimedes, that he might transport the entire globe from the place it occupied to another, demanded only a point that was firm and immoveable; so also, I shall be entitled to entertain the highest expectations, if I am fortunate enough to discover only one thing that is certain and indubitable.

I suppose, accordingly, that all the things which I see are false (fictitious); I believe that none of those objects which my fallacious memory represents ever existed; I suppose that I possess no senses; I believe that body, figure, extension, motion, and place are merely fictions of my mind. What is there, then, that can be esteemed true? Perhaps this only, that there is absolutely nothing certain.

But how do I know that there is not something different altogether from the objects I have now enumerated, of which it is impossible to entertain the slightest doubt? Is there not a God, or some being, by whatever name I may designate him, who causes these thoughts to arise in my mind? But why suppose such a being, for it may be I myself am capable of producing them? Am I, then, at least not something? But I before denied that I possessed senses or a body; I hesitate, however, for what follows from that? Am I so dependent on the body and the senses that without these I cannot exist? But I had the persuasion that there was absolutely nothing in the world, that there was no sky and no earth, neither minds nor bodies; was I not, therefore, at the same time, persuaded that I did not exist? Far from it; I assuredly existed, since I was persuaded. But there is I know not what being, who is possessed at once of the highest power and the deepest cunning, who is constantly employing all his ingenuity in deceiving me. Doubtless, then, I exist, since I am deceived; and, let him deceive me as he may, he can never bring it about that I am nothing, so long as I shall be conscious that I am something. So that it must, in fine, be maintained, all things being maturely and carefully considered, that this proposition (*pronunciatum*) I am, I exist, is necessarily true each time it is expressed by me, or conceived in my mind.

But I do not yet know with sufficient clearness what I am, though assured that I am; and hence, in the next place, I must take care, lest perchance I inconsiderately substitute some other object in room of what is properly myself, and thus wander from truth, even in that knowledge (cognition) which I hold to be of all others the most certain and evident. For this reason, I will now consider anew what I formerly believed myself to be, before I entered on the present train of thought; and of my previous opinion I will retrench all that can in the least be invalidated by the grounds of doubt I have adduced, in order that there may at length remain nothing but what is certain and indubitable. What then did I formerly think I was? Undoubtedly I judged that I was a man. But what is a man? Shall I say a rational animal? Assuredly not; for it would be necessary forthwith to inquire into what is meant by animal, and what by rational, and thus, from a single question, I should insensibly glide into others, and these more difficult than the first; nor do I now possess enough of leisure to warrant me in wasting my time amid subtleties of this sort. I prefer here to attend to the thoughts that sprung up of themselves in my mind, and were inspired by my own nature alone, when I applied myself to the consideration of what I was. In the first place, then, I thought that I possessed a countenance, hands, arms, and all the fabric of members that appears in a corpse, and which I called by the name of body. It further occurred to me that I was nourished, that I walked, perceived, and thought, and all those actions I referred to the soul; but what the soul itself was I either did not stay to consider, or, if I did, I imagined that it was something extremely rare and subtile, like wind, or flame, or ether, spread through my grosser parts. As regarded the body, I did not even doubt of its nature, but thought I distinctly knew it, and if I had wished to describe it according to the notions I then entertained, I should have explained myself in this manner: By body I understand all that can be terminated by a certain figure; that can be comprised in a certain place, and so fill a certain space as therefrom to exclude every other body; that can be perceived either by touch, sight, hearing, taste, or smell; that can be moved in different ways, not indeed of itself, but by something foreign to it by which it is touched [and from which it receives the impression]; for the power of self-motion, as likewise that of perceiving and thinking, I held as by no means pertaining to the nature of body; on the contrary, I was somewhat astonished to find such faculties existing in some bodies.

But [as to myself, what can I now say that I am], since I suppose there exists an extremely powerful, and, if I may so speak, malignant being, whose whole endeavours are directed towards deceiving me? Can I affirm that I possess any one of all those attributes of which I have lately spoken as belonging to the nature of body? After attentively considering them in my own mind, I find none of them that can properly be said to belong to myself. To recount them were idle and tedious. Let us pass, then, to the attributes of the soul. The first mentioned were the powers of nutrition and walking; but, if it be true that I have no body, it is true likewise that I am capable neither of walking nor of being nourished. Perception is another attribute of the soul; but perception too is impossible without the body: besides, I have frequently, during sleep, believed that I perceived objects which I afterwards observed I did not in reality perceive. Thinking is another attribute of the soul; and here I discover what properly belongs to myself. This alone is inseparable from me. I am—I exist: this is certain; but how often? As often as I think; for perhaps it would even happen, if I should wholly cease to think, that I should at the same time altogether cease to be. I now admit nothing that is not necessarily true: I am therefore, precisely speaking, only a thinking thing, that is, a mind (*mens sive animus*), understanding, or reason,—terms whose signification was before unknown to me. I am, however, a real thing, and really existent; but what thing? The answer was, a thinking thing. The question now arises, am I aught besides? I will stimulate my imagination with a view to discover whether I am not still something more than a thinking being. Now it is plain I am not the assemblage of members called the human body; I am not a thin and penetrating air diffused through all these members, or wind, or flame, or vapour, or breath, or any of all the things I can imagine; for I supposed that all these were not, and, without changing the supposition, I find that I still feel assured of my existence.

But it is true, perhaps, that those very things which I suppose to be non-existent, because they are unknown to me, are not in truth different from myself whom I know. This is a point I cannot determine, and do not now enter into any dispute regarding it. I can only judge of things that are known to me: I am conscious that I exist, and I who know that I exist inquire into what I am. It is, however, perfectly certain that the knowledge of my existence, thus precisely taken, is not dependent on things, the existence of which is as yet unknown to me: and consequently it is not dependent on any of the things I can feign in imagination. Moreover, the phrase itself, I frame an image (*effingo*), reminds me of my error; for I should in truth frame one if I were to imagine myself to be anything, since to imagine is nothing more than to contemplate the figure or image of a corporeal thing; but I already know that I exist, and that it is possible at the same time that all those images, and in general all that relates to the nature of body, are merely dreams [or chimeras]. From this I discover that it is not more reasonable to say, I will excite my imagination that I may know more distinctly what I am, than to express myself as follows: I am now awake, and perceive something real; but because my perception is not sufficiently clear, I will of express purpose go to sleep that my dreams may represent to me the object of my perception with more truth and clearness. And, therefore, I know that nothing of all that I can embrace in imagination belongs to the knowledge which I have of myself, and that there is need to recall with the utmost care the mind from this mode of thinking, that it may be able to know its own nature with perfect distinctness.

But what, then, am I? A thinking thing, it has been said. But what is a thinking thing? It is a thing that doubts, understands, [conceives], affirms, denies, wills, refuses, that images also, and perceives. Assuredly it is not little, if all these properties belong to my nature. But why should they not belong to it? Am I not that very being who now doubts of almost everything; who, for all that, understands and conceives certain things; who affirms one alone as true, and denies the others; who desires to know more of them, and does not wish to be deceived; who imagines many things, sometimes even despite his will; and is likewise percipient of many, as if through the medium of the senses. Is there nothing of all this as true as that I am, even although I should be always dreaming, and although he who gave me being employed all his ingenuity to deceive me? Is there also any one of these attributes that can be properly distinguished from my thought, or that can be said to be separate from myself? For it is of itself so evident that it is I who doubt, I who understand, and I who desire, that it is here unnecessary to add anything by way of rendering it more clear. And I am as certainly the same being who imagines; for, although it may be (as I before supposed) that nothing I imagine is true, still the power of imagination does not cease really to exist in me and to form part of my thought. In fine, I am the same being who perceives, that is, who apprehends certain objects as by the organs of sense, since, in truth, I see light, hear a noise, and feel heat. But it will be said that these presentations are false, and that I am dreaming. Let it be so. At all events it is certain that I seem to see light, hear a noise, and feel heat; this cannot be false, and this is what in me is properly called perceiving (*sentire*), which is nothing else than thinking. From this I begin to know what I am with somewhat greater clearness and distinctness than heretofore.

But, nevertheless, it still seems to me, and I cannot help believing, that corporeal things, whose images are formed by thought, [which fall under the senses], and are examined by the same, are known with much greater distinctness than that I know not what part of myself which is not imaginable; although, in truth, it may seem strange to say that I know and comprehend with greater distinctness things whose existence appears to me doubtful, that are unknown, and do not belong to me, than others of whose reality I am persuaded, that are known to me, and appertain to my proper nature; in a word, than myself. But I see clearly what is the state of the case. My mind is apt to wander, and will not yet submit to be restrained within the limits of truth. Let us therefore leave the mind to itself once more, and, according to it every kind of liberty, [permit it to consider the objects that appear to it from without], in order that, having afterwards withdrawn it from these gently and opportunely, [and fixed it on the consideration of its being and the properties it finds in itself], it may then be the more easily controlled.

Let us now accordingly consider the objects that are commonly thought to be [the most easily, and likewise] the most distinctly known, viz., the bodies we touch and see; not, indeed, bodies in general, for these general notions are usually somewhat more confused, but one body in particular. Take, for example, this piece of wax; it is quite fresh, having been but recently taken from the bee-hive; it has not yet lost the sweetness of the honey it contained; it still retains somewhat of the odour of the flowers from which it was gathered; its colour, figure, size, are apparent (to the sight); it is hard, cold, easily handled; and sounds when struck upon with the finger. In fine, all that contributes to make a body as distinctly known as possible, is found in the one before us. But, while I am speaking, let it be placed near the fire—what remained of the taste exhales, the smell evaporates, the colour changes, its figure is destroyed, its size increases, it becomes liquid, it grows hot, it can hardly be handled, and, although struck upon, it emits no sound. Does the same wax still remain after this change? It must be admitted that it does remain; no one doubts it, or judges otherwise. What, then, was it I knew with so much distinctness in the piece of wax? Assuredly, it could be nothing of all that I observed by means of the senses, since all the things that fell under taste, smell, sight, touch, and hearing are changed, and yet the same wax remains. It was perhaps what I now think, viz., that this wax was neither the sweetness of honey, the pleasant odour of flowers, the whiteness, the figure, nor the sound, but only a body that a little before appeared to me conspicuous under these forms, and which is now perceived under others. But, to speak precisely, what is it that I imagine when I think of it in this way? Let it be attentively considered, and, retrenching all that does not belong to the wax, let us see what remains. There certainly remains nothing, except something extended, flexible, and movable. But what is meant by flexible and movable? Is it not that I imagine that the piece of wax, being round, is capable of becoming square, or of passing from a square into a triangular figure? Assuredly such is not the case, because I conceive that it admits of an infinity of similar changes; and I am, moreover, unable to compass this infinity by imagination, and consequently this conception which I have of the wax is not the product of the faculty of imagination. But what now is this extension? Is it not also unknown? for it becomes greater when the wax is melted, greater when it is boiled, and greater still when the heat increases; and I should not conceive [clearly and] according to truth, the wax as it is, if I did not suppose that the piece we are considering admitted even of a wider variety of extension than I ever imagined. I must, therefore, admit that I cannot even comprehend by imagination what the piece of wax is, and that it is the mind alone (*mens*, Lat., *entendement*, F.) which perceives it. I speak of one piece in particular; for, as to wax in general, this is still more evident. But what is the piece of wax that can be perceived only by the [understanding or] mind? It is certainly the same which I see, touch, imagine; and, in fine, it is the same which, from the beginning, I believed it to be. But (and this it is of moment to observe) the perception of it is neither an act of sight, of touch, nor of imagination, and never was either of these, though it might formerly seem so, but is simply an intuition (*inspectio*) of the mind, which may be imperfect and confused, as it formerly was, or very clear and distinct, as it is at present, according as the attention is more or less directed to the elements which it contains, and of which it is composed.

But, meanwhile, I feel greatly astonished when I observe [the weakness of my mind, and] its proneness to error. For although, without at all giving expression to what I think, I consider all this in my own mind, words yet occasionally impede my progress, and I am almost led into error by the terms of ordinary language. We say, for example, that we see the same wax when it is before us, and not that we judge it to be the same from its retaining the same colour and figure: whence I should forthwith be disposed to conclude that the wax is known by the act of sight, and not by the intuition of the mind alone, were it not for the analogous instance of human beings passing on in the street below, as observed from a window. In this case I do not fail to say that I see the men themselves, just as I say that I see the wax; and yet what do I see from the window beyond hats and cloaks that might cover artificial machines, whose motions might be determined by springs? But I judge that there are human beings from these appearances, and thus I comprehend, by the faculty of judgment alone which is in the mind, what I believed I saw with my eyes.

The man who makes it his aim to rise to knowledge superior to the common, ought to be ashamed to seek occasions of doubting from the vulgar forms of speech: instead, therefore, of doing this, I shall proceed with the matter in hand, and inquire whether I had a clearer and more perfect perception of the piece of wax when I first saw it, and when I thought I knew it by means of the external sense itself, or, at all events, by the common sense (*sensus communis*), as it is called, that is, by the imaginative faculty; or whether I rather apprehend it more clearly at present, after having examined with greater care, both what it is, and in what way it can be known. It would certainly be ridiculous to entertain any doubt on this point. For what, in that first perception, was there distinct? What did I perceive which any animal might not have perceived? But when I distinguish the wax from its exterior forms, and when, as if I had stripped it of its vestments, I consider it quite naked, it is certain, although some error may still be found in my judgment, that I cannot, nevertheless, thus apprehend it without possessing a human mind.

But, finally, what shall I say of the mind itself, that is, of myself? for as yet I do not admit that I am anything but mind. What, then! I who seem to possess so distinct an apprehension of the piece of wax,—do I not know myself, both with greater truth and certitude, and also much more distinctly and clearly? For if I judge that the wax exists because I see it, it assuredly follows, much more evidently, that I myself am or exist, for the same reason: for it is possible that what I see may not in truth be wax, and that I do not even possess eyes with which to see anything; but it cannot be that when I see, or, which comes to the same thing, when I think I see, I myself who think am nothing. So likewise, if I judge that the wax exists because I touch it, it will still also follow that I am; and if I determine that my imagination, or any other cause, whatever it be, persuades me of the existence of the wax, I will still draw the same conclusion. And what is here remarked of the piece of wax, is applicable to all the other things that are external to me. And further, if the [notion or] perception of wax appeared to me more precise and distinct, after that not only sight and touch, but many other causes besides, rendered it manifest to my apprehension, with how much greater distinctness must I now know myself, since all the reasons that contribute to the knowledge of the nature of wax, or of any body whatever, manifest still better the nature of my mind? And there are besides so many other things in the mind itself that contribute to the illustration of its nature, that those dependent on the body, to which I have here referred, scarcely merit to be taken into account.

But, in conclusion, I find I have insensibly reverted to the point I desired; for, since it is now manifest to me that bodies themselves are not properly perceived by the senses nor by the faculty of imagination, but by the intellect alone; and since they are not perceived because they are seen and touched, but only because they are understood [or rightly comprehended by thought], I readily discover that there is nothing more easily or clearly apprehended than my own mind. But because it is difficult to rid one's self so promptly of an opinion to which one has been long accustomed, it will be desirable to tarry for some time at this stage, that, by long continued meditation, I may more deeply impress upon my memory this new knowledge.

THEORIES OF TRUTH

60 The Coherence Theory of Truth*

BRAND BLANSHARD

Brand Blanshard (1892–   ) is an influential and distinguished American philosopher. He has taught philosophy at Yale University for many years and is now professor emeritus. Perhaps his best-known work is his two-volume *The Nature of Thought* in which he defends the coherence theory of truth and supports an idealistic metaphysic. His recent works include *Reason and Analysis* and *Reason and Goodness*.

The view that truth *is* coherence rests on a theory of the relation of thought to reality, and since this is the central problem of the theory of knowledge, to begin one's discussion by assuming the answer to it or by trying to make one out of whole cloth would be somewhat ridiculous. But as this was our main problem in the long discussions of Book II, we may be pardoned here for brevity. First we shall state in *résumé* the relation of thought to reality that we were there driven to accept, and sketch the theory of truth implicit in it. . . .

To think is to seek understanding. And to seek understanding is an activity of mind that is marked off from all other activities by a highly distinctive aim. This aim is to achieve systematic vision, so to apprehend what is now unknown to us as to relate it, and relate it necessarily, to what we know already. We think to solve problems; and our method of solving problems is to build a bridge of intelligent relation from the continent of our knowledge to the island we wish to include in it. Sometimes this bridge is causal, as when we try to explain a disease; sometimes teleological, as when we try to fathom the move of an opponent over the chess board; sometimes geometrical, as in Euclid. But it is always systematic; thought in its very nature

* From Brand Blanshard, *The Nature of Thought*, (London: George Allen & Unwin, Ltd., 1939). Reprinted by permission of Humanities Press, Inc.

is the attempt to bring something unknown or imperfectly known into a sub-system of knowledge, and thus also into that larger system that forms the world of accepted beliefs. That is what explanation is. *Why* is it that thought desires this ordered vision? Why should such a vision give satisfaction when it comes? To these questions there is no answer, and if there were, it would be an answer only because it had succeeded in supplying the characteristic satisfaction to this unique desire.

But may it not be that what satisfies thought fails to conform to the real world? Where is the guarantee that when I have brought my ideas into the form my ideal requires, they should be *true*? Here we come round again to the tortured problem of Book II. In our long struggle with the relation of thought to reality we saw that if thought and things are conceived as related only externally, then knowledge is luck; there is no necessity whatever that what satisfies intelligence should coincide with what really is. It may do so, or it may not; on the principle that there are many misses to one bull's-eye, it more probably does not. But if we get rid of the misleading analogies through which this relation has been conceived, of copy and original, stimulus and organism, lantern and screen, and go to thought itself with the question what reference to an object means, we get a different and more hopeful answer. To think of a thing is to get that thing itself in some degree within the mind. To think of a colour or an emotion is to have that within us which if it *were developed and completed*, would identify itself with the object. In short, if we accept its own report, thought is related to reality as the partial to the perfect fulfilment of a purpose. The more adequate its grasp the more nearly does it approximate, the more fully does it realize in itself, the nature and relations of its objects.

We may look at the growth of knowledge, individual or social, either as an attempt by our own minds to return to union with things as they are in their ordered wholeness, or the affirmation through our minds of the ordered whole itself. And if we take this view, our notion of truth is marked out for us. Truth is the approximation of thought to reality. It is thought on its way home. Its measure is the distance thought has travelled, under guidance of its inner compass, toward that intelligible system which unites its ultimate object with its ultimate end. Hence at any given time the degree of truth in our experience as a whole is the degree of system it has achieved. The degree of truth of a particular proposition is to be judged in the first instance by its coherence with experience as a whole, ultimately by its coherence with that further whole, all-comprehensive and fully articulated, in which thought can come to rest.

But it is time we defined more explicitly what coherence means. To be sure, no fully satisfactory definition can be given; and as Dr. Ewing says, 'it is wrong to tie down the advocates of the coherence theory to a precise definition. What they are doing is to describe an ideal that has never yet been completely clarified but is none the less immanent in all our thinking.'

Certainly this ideal goes far beyond mere consistency. Fully coherent knowledge would be knowledge in which every judgement entailed, and was entailed by, the rest of the system. Probably we never find in fact a system where there is so much of interdependence. What it means may be clearer if we take a number of familiar systems and arrange them in a series tending to such coherence as a limit. At the bottom would be a junk-heap, where we could know every item but one and still be without any clue as to what that remaining item was. Above this would come a stone-pile, for here you could at least infer that what you would find next would be a stone. A machine would be higher again, since from the remaining parts one could deduce not only the general character of a missing part, but also its special form and function. This is a high degree of coherence, but it is very far short of the highest. You could remove the engine from a motor-car while leaving the other parts intact, and replace it with any one of thousands of other engines, but the thought of such an interchange among human heads or hearts shows at once that the interdependence in a machine is far below that of the body. Do we find then in organic bodies the highest conceivable coherence? Clearly not. Though a human hand, as Aristotle said, would hardly be a hand when detached from the body, still it would be something definite enough; and we can conceive systems in which even this something would be gone. Abstract a number from the number series and it would be a mere unrecognizable x; similarly, the very thought of a straight line involves the thought of the Euclidean space in which it falls. It is perhaps in such systems as Euclidean geometry that we get the most perfect examples of coherence that have been constructed. If any proposition were lacking, it could be supplied from the rest; if any were altered, the repercussions would be felt through the length and breadth of the system. Yet even such a system as this falls short of ideal system. Its postulates are unproved; they are independent of each other, in the sense that none of them could be derived from any other or even from all the others together; its clear necessity is bought by an abstractness so extreme as to have left out nearly everything that belongs to the character of actual things. A completely satisfactory system would have none of these defects. No proposition would be arbitrary, every proposition would be entailed by the others jointly and even singly, no proposition would stand outside the system. The integration would be so complete that no part could be seen for what it was without seeing its relation to the whole, and the whole itself could be understood only through the contribution of every part.

It may be granted at once that in common life we are satisfied with far less than this. We accept the demonstrations of the geometer as complete, and do not think of reproaching him because he begins with postulates and leaves us at the end with a system that is a skeleton at the best. In physics, in biology, above all in the social sciences, we are satisfied with less still. We test judgements by the amount of coherence which in that particular subject-matter it seems reasonable to expect. We apply, perhaps unconsciously, the advice of Aristotle, and refrain from asking demonstration in the physical sciences, while in mathematics we refuse to accept less. And such facts may be thought to show that we make no actual use of the ideal standard just described. But however much this standard may be relaxed within the limits of a particular science, its influence is evident in the grading of the sciences generally. It is precisely in those sciences that approach most nearly to system as here defined that we achieve the greatest certainty, and precisely in those that are most remote from such system that our doubt is greatest whether we have achieved scientific truth at all. Our immediate exactions shift with the subject-matter; our ultimate standard is unvarying.

Now if we accept coherence as the test of truth, does that commit us to any conclusions about the *nature* of truth or reality? I think it does, though more clearly about reality than about truth. It is past belief that the fidelity of our thought to reality should be rightly measured by coherence if reality itself were not coherent. To say that the nature of things may be *in*coherent, but we shall approach the truth about it precisely so far as our thoughts become coherent, sounds very much like nonsense. And providing we retained coherence as the test, it would still be nonsense even if truth were conceived as correspondence. On this supposition we should have truth when, our thought having achieved coherence, the correspondence was complete between that thought and its object. But complete correspondence between a coherent thought and an incoherent object seems meaningless. It is hard to see, then, how anyone could consistently take coherence as the test of truth unless he took it also as a character of reality.

Does acceptance of coherence as a test commit us not only to a view about the structure of reality but also to a view about the nature of truth? This is a more difficult question. As we saw at the beginning of the chapter, there have been some highly reputable philosophers who have held that the answer to 'What is the test of truth?' is 'Coherence', while the answer to 'What is the nature or meaning of truth?' is 'Correspondence'. These questions are plainly distinct. Nor does there seem to be any direct path from the acceptance of coherence as the test of truth to its acceptance as the nature of truth. Nevertheless there is an indirect path. If we accept coherence as our test, we must use it everywhere. We must therefore use it to test the suggestion that truth *is* other than coherence. But if we do, we shall find that we must reject the suggestion as leading to *in*coherence. Coherence is a pertinacious concept and, like the well-known camel, if one lets it get its nose under the edge of the tent, it will shortly walk off with the whole.

Suppose that, accepting coherance as the test, one rejects it as the nature of truth in favour of some alternative; and let us assume, for example, that this alternative is correspondence. This, we have said, is incoherent; why? Because if one holds that truth is correspondence, one cannot intelligibly hold either that it is tested by coherence or that there is any dependable test at all. Consider the first point. Suppose that we construe experience into the most coherent picture possible, remembering that among the elements included will be such secondary qualities as colours, odours, and sounds. Would the mere fact that such elements as these are coherently arranged prove that anything precisely corresponding to them exists 'out there'? I cannot see that it would, even if we knew that the two arrangements had closely corresponding patterns. If on one side you have a series of elements a, b, c . . . , and on the other a series of elements a, β, γ . . . , arranged in patterns that correspond, you have no proof as yet that the *natures* of these elements correspond. It is therefore impossible to argue from a high degree of coherence within experience to its correspondence in the same degree with anything outside. And this difficulty is typical. If you place the nature of truth in one sort of character and its test in something quite different, you are pretty certain, sooner or later, to find the two falling apart. In the end, the only test of truth that is not misleading is the special nature or character that is itself constitutive of truth.

Feeling that this is so, the adherents of correspondence sometimes insist that correspondence shall be its own test. But then the second difficulty arises. If truth does consist in correspondence, no test can be sufficient. For in order to know that experience corresponds to fact, we must be able to get at that fact, unadulterated with idea, and compare the two sides with each other. And we have seen in the last chapter that such fact is not accessible. When we try to lay hold of it, what we find in our hands is a judgement which is obviously not itself the indubitable fact we are seeking, and which must be checked by some fact beyond it. To this process there is no end. And even if we did get at the fact directly, rather than through the veil of our ideas, that would be no less fatal to correspondence. This direct seizure of fact presumably gives us truth, but since that truth no longer consists in correspondence of idea with fact, the main theory has been abandoned. In short, if we can know fact only through the medium of our own ideas, the original forever eludes us; if we can get at the facts directly, we have knowledge whose truth is not correspondence. The theory is forced to choose between scepticism and self-contradiction.

Thus the attempt to combine coherence as the test of truth with correspondence as the nature of truth will not pass muster by its own test. The result is *incoherence*. We believe that an application of the test to other theories of truth would lead to a like result. The argument is: assume coherence as the test, and you will be driven by the incoherence of your alternatives to the conclusion that it is also the nature of truth. . . .

Coherence means more than consistency. It means not only that the various constituents entering into the system of truth are compatible with each other, but also that they necessitate each other. The system assumed is a system ideally perfect, for nothing less than this would satisfy intelligence as stable beyond rectification. In such a system there would be no loose ends. Difference anywhere would be reflected in difference everywhere.

Now it has been held that this ideal is merely a cloud-castle, that it can never be made to embrace the facts of our actual disorderly world. There are many who would freely admit that nothing exists or occurs out of relation to *some* other things, but would regard the view that everything is related by necessity to *everything* else as demonstrably false. If the fact is that Bishop Stubbs died in his bed, this surely might be false without everything else being false that is now accepted as true.

Now it is obvious that we cannot show *in detail* that a difference anywhere in the system of truth must be reflected everywhere; we do not know enough, nor is it likely we ever shall. But we can do something else that is as near to this as can be reasonably asked. We can show that in the system of truth, *so far as reflected in our knowledge*, such interconnection holds, and that the denial of an apparently isolated judgement does in fact have implications for every other. The argument is as follows: When I say that Bishop Stubbs died in his bed, or indeed when I say anything, I always do so on evidence. This evidence may be hard or easy to bring to light, but it is there invariably; I never simply discharge judgements into the air with no ground or warrant at all. And by the rules of hypothetical argument, to admit the falsity of a judgement is to throw doubt upon its ground. Indeed it is to do more. It is to throw doubt, if I am consistent, upon *all* evidence of this kind and degree. Now the evidence on which it is believed that Bishop Stubbs died a natural death is of the kind and degree that would be accepted without hesitation by any historian or scientist. It is the sort of evidence on which science and history generally rest. Hence if I deny this proposition, and thus call in question the value of this sort of evidence, I must in consistency call in question most science and history also. And that would shatter my world of knowledge. Thus the truth about Bishop Stubbs is anything but isolated. However unimportant practically, it is so entangled with my system of beliefs that its denial would send repercussions throughout the whole.

To some this reply may seem an *ignoratio elenchi*. It is one thing, they may say, to show that the abandonment of a *belief* would logically compel the abandonment of other beliefs; it is another thing to show that in the real world about which these beliefs are held, a change in one fact or event would necessitate that all others be different. Suppose I climb the hill behind my farm house in Vermont and look across at Mount Washington. I am wearing a felt hat at the time. Is it sensible or quite sane to argue that if I had worn a straw hat instead, that fact would have made a difference to Mount Washington?

I not only believe it would, but that the argument for this conclusion is strong almost to demonstration. In outline it is as follows: my putting on this particular hat had causes, which lay in part in the workings of my brain; these workings also had causes, which lay in part in the workings of other bodily organs; these in turn depended upon countless physical factors in the way of food, air, light, and temperature, every one of which had its own conditions. It is plain that before we took many steps in this retreat, we should find ourselves involved in millions of conditions, and that if we were able *per impossibile* to traverse all the diverging branches, there would probably be no region of the universe that would remain unpenetrated. Now if we reject, as I suppose we must, the plurality of causes, and hold that the causal relation is reciprocating, then a denial of the causal consequent will require a denial of its antecedent. A different event, then, from that on which these various lines converge would require differences throughout the range of the countless conditions themselves. Very well; let us assume such a different event to have occurred—my wearing a straw hat instead of a felt one—and having ascended the causal lines, let us now descend them. If the antecedents of the present event were scattered throughout the universe, and we suppose them altered throughout, is there any reason whatever to suppose that the present state of the world would be as we find it? The answer is obvious. The world would not only be different, but so extensively different that we could point neither to Mount Washington nor to anything else and say that it would be exempt from change.

61 The Correspondence Theory of Truth*

BERTRAND RUSSELL

Bertrand Russell (1872–1969) was perhaps the most influential and controversial philosopher of the twentieth century. He taught and lectured at universities around the world and wrote on nearly every philosophical topic. Perhaps his most famous philosophical work is *Principia Mathematica* (with Alfred North Whitehead), a study of the foundations of mathematics.

Thus coherence as the definition of truth fails because there is no proof that there can be only one coherent system.

The other objection to this definition of truth is that it assumes the meaning of 'coherence' known, whereas, in fact, 'coherence' presupposes the truth of the laws of logic. Two propositions are coherent when both may be true, and are incoherent when one at least must be false. Now in order to know whether two propositions can both be true, we must know such truths as the law of contradiction. For example, the two propositions, 'this tree is a beech' and 'this tree is not a beech,' are not coherent, because of the law of contradiction. But if the law of contradiction itself were subjected to the test of coherence, we should find that, if we choose to suppose it false, nothing will any longer be incoherent with anything else. Thus the laws of logic supply the skeleton or framework within which the test of coherence applies, and they themselves cannot be established by this test.

For the above two reasons, coherence cannot be accepted as giving the *meaning* of truth, though it is often a most important *test* of truth after a certain amount of truth has become known.

Hence we are driven back to *correspondence with fact* as constituting the nature of truth. It remains to define precisely what we mean by 'fact,' and what is the nature of the correspondence which must subsist between belief and fact, in order that belief may be true.

In accordance with our three requisites, we have to seek a theory of truth which (1) allows truth to have an opposite, namely falsehood, (2) makes truth a property of beliefs, but (3) makes it a property wholly dependent upon the relation of the beliefs to outside things. . . .

* From Bertrand Russell, *The Problem of Philosophy*, 1912, by permission of the Clarendon Press, Oxford.

Thus a belief is *true* when it *corresponds* to a certain associated complex, and *false* when it does not. Assuming, for the sake of definiteness, that the objects of the belief are two terms and a relation, the terms being put in a certain order by the 'sense' of the believing, then if the two terms in that order are united by the relation into a complex, the belief is true; if not, it is false. This constitutes the definition of truth and falsehood that we were in search of. Judging or believing is a certain complex unity of which a mind is a constituent; if the remaining constituents, taken in the order which they have in the belief, form a complex unity, then the belief is true; if not, it is false.

Thus although truth and falsehood are properties of beliefs, yet they are in a sense extrinsic properties, for the condition of the truth of a belief is something not involving beliefs, or (in general) any mind at all, but only the *objects* of the belief. A mind, which believes, believes truly when there is a *corresponding* complex not involving the mind, but only its objects. This correspondence ensures truth, and its absence entails falsehood. Hence we account simultaneously for the two facts that beliefs (*a*) depend on minds for their *existence*, (*b*) do not depend on minds for their *truth*.

We may restate our theory as follows: If we take such a belief as 'Othello believes that Desdemona loves Cassio,' we will call Desdemona and Cassio the *object-terms*, and loving the *object-relation*. If there is a complex unity 'Desdemona's love for Cassio,' consisting of the object-terms related by the object-relation in the same order as they have in the belief, then this complex unity is called the *fact corresponding to the belief*. Thus a belief is true when there is a corresponding fact, and is false when there is no corresponding fact.

It will be seen that minds do not *create* truth or falsehood. They create beliefs, but when once the beliefs are created, the mind cannot make them true or false, except in the special case where they concern future things which are within the power of the person believing, such as catching trains. What makes a belief true is a *fact*, and this fact does not (except in exceptional cases) in any way involve the mind of the person who has the belief.

62 The Pragmatic Theory of Truth*

WILLIAM JAMES

William James (1842–1910) was influential both as a psychologist and philosopher. Author of numerous articles, some of his important books include *Pragmatism: A New Name for Some Old Ways of Thinking; Principles of Psychology;* and *Varieties of Religious Experience.* He is known as a leading American exponent of pragmatism.

Truth, as any dictionary will tell you, is a property of certain of our ideas. It means their 'agreement,' as falsity means their disagreement, with 'reality.' Pragmatists and intellectualists both accept this definition as a matter of course. They begin to quarrel only after the question is raised as to what may precisely be meant by the term 'agreement,' and what by the term 'reality,' when reality is taken as something for our ideas to agree with.

In answering these questions the pragmatists are more analytic and painstaking, the intellectualists more offhand and irreflective. The popular notion is that a true idea must copy its reality. Like other popular views, this one follows the analogy of the most usual experience. Our true ideas of sensible things do indeed copy them. Shut your eyes and think of yonder clock on the wall, and you get just such a true picture or copy of its dial. But your idea of its 'works' (unless you are a clockmaker) is much less of a copy, yet it passes muster, for it in no way clashes with the reality. Even though it should shrink to the mere word 'works,' that word still serves you truly; and when you speak of the 'time-keeping function' of the clock, or of its spring's 'elasticity,' it is hard to see exactly what your ideas can copy.

You perceive that there is a problem here. Where our ideas cannot copy definitely their object, what does agreement with that object mean? Some idealists seem to say that they are true whenever they are what God means that we ought to think about that object. Others hold the copy-view all through, and speak as if our ideas possessed truth just in proportion as they approach to being copies of the Absolute's eternal way of thinking.

These views, you see, invite pragmatistic discussion. But the great assumption of the intellectualists is that truth means essentially an inert static rela-

* From William James, *Pragmatism: A New Name For Some Old Ways of Thinking* (London: Longmans, Green & Co., Ltd., 1907).

tion. When you've got your true idea of anything, there's an end of the matter. You're in possession; you *know*; you have fulfilled your thinking destiny. You are where you ought to be mentally; you have obeyed your categorical imperative; and nothing more need follow on that climax of your rational destiny. Epistemologically you are in stable equilibrium.

Pragmatism, on the other hand, asks its usual question. "Grant an idea or belief to be true," it says, "what concrete difference will its being true make in any one's actual life? How will the truth be realized? What experiences will be different from those which would obtain if the belief were false? What, in short, is the truth's cash-value in experiential terms?"

The moment pragmatism asks this question, it sees the answer: *True ideas are those that we can assimilate, validate, corroborate and verify. False ideas are those that we can not.* That is the practical difference it makes to us to have true ideas; that, therefore, is the meaning of truth, for it is all that truth is known-as.

This thesis is what I have to defend. The truth of an idea is not a stagnant property inherent in it. Truth *happens* to an idea. It *becomes* true, is *made* true by events. Its verity *is* in fact an event, a process: the process namely of its verifying itself, its veri-*fication*. Its validity is the process of its valid-*ation*.

But what do the words verification and validation themselves pragmatically mean? They again signify certain practical consequences of the verified and validated idea. It is hard to find any one phrase that characterizes these consequences better than the ordinary agreement-formula—just such consequences being what we have in mind whenever we say that our ideas 'agree' with reality. They lead us, namely, through the acts and other ideas which they instigate, into or up to, or towards, other parts of experience with which we feel all the while—such feeling being among our potentialities—that the original ideas remain in agreement. The connexions and transitions come to us from point to point as being progressive, harmonious, satisfactory. This function of agreeable leading is what we mean by an idea's verification. Such an account is vague and it sounds at first quite trivial, but it has results which it will take the rest of my hour to explain.

Let me begin by reminding you of the fact that the possession of true thoughts means everywhere the possession of invaluable instruments of action; and that our duty to gain truth, so far from being a blank command from out of the blue, or a 'stunt' self-imposed by our intellect, can account for itself by excellent practical reasons.

The importance to human life of having true beliefs about matters of fact is a thing too notorious. We live in a world of realities that can be infinitely useful or infinitely harmful. Ideas that tell us which of them to expect count as the true ideas in all this primary sphere of verification, and the pursuit of such ideas is a primary human duty. The possession of truth, so far from being here an end in itself, is only a preliminary means towards other vital satisfactions. If I am lost in the woods and starved, and find what looks like a cow-path, it is of the utmost importance that I should think of a human habitation at the end of it, for if I do so and follow it, I save myself. The true thought is useful here because the house which is its object is useful. The practical value of true ideas is thus primarily derived from the practical importance of their objects to us. Their objects are, indeed, not important at all times. I may on another occasion have no use for the house; and then my idea of it, however verifiable, will be practically irrelevant, and had better remain latent. Yet since almost any object may some day become temporarily important, the advantage of having a general stock of *extra* truths, of ideas that shall be true of merely possible situations, is obvious. We store such extra truths away in our memories, and with the overflow we fill our books of reference. Whenever such an extra truth becomes practically relevant to one of our emergencies, it passes from cold-storage to do work in the world and our belief in it grows active. You can say of it then either that 'it is useful because it is true' or that 'it is true because it is useful.' Both these phrases mean exactly the same thing, namely that here is an idea that gets fulfilled and can be verified. True is the name for whatever idea starts the verification-process, useful is the name for its completed function in experience. True ideas would never have been singled out as such, would never have acquired a class-name, least of all a name suggesting value, unless they had been useful from the outset in this way.

From this simple cue pragmatism gets her general notion of truth as something essentially bound up with the way in which one moment in our experience may lead us towards other moments which it will be worth while to have been led to. Primarily, and on the common-sense level, the truth of a state of mind means this function of *a leading that is worth while*. When a moment in our experience, of any kind whatever, inspires us with a thought that is true, that means that sooner or later we dip by that thought's guidance into the particulars of experience again and make advantageous connexion with them. This is a vague enough statement, but I beg you to retain it, for it is essential.

Our experience meanwhile is all shot through with regularities. One bit of it can warn us to get ready for another bit, can 'intend' or be 'significant of' that remoter object. The object's advent is the significance's verification. Truth, in these cases, meaning nothing but eventual verification, is manifestly incompatible with waywardness on our part. Woe to him whose beliefs play fast and loose with the order which realities follow in his experience; they will lead him nowhere or else make false connexions.

By 'realities' or 'objects' here, we mean either things of common sense, sensibly present, or else common-sense relations, such as dates, places, distances, kinds, activities. Following our mental image of a house along the cow-path, we actually come to see the house; we get the image's full verification. *Such simply and fully verified leadings are certainly the originals and prototypes of the truth-process.* Experience offers indeed other forms of truth-process, but they are all conceivable as being primary verifications arrested, multiplied or substituted one for another.

Take, for instance, yonder object on the wall. You and I consider it to be a 'clock,' altho no one of us has seen the hidden works that make it one. We let our notion pass for true without attempting to verify. If truths mean verification-process essentially, ought we then to call such unverified truths as this abortive? No, for they form the overwhelmingly large number of the truths we live by. Indirect as well as direct verifications pass muster. Where circumstantial evidence is sufficient, we can go without eye-witnessing. Just as we here assume Japan to exist without ever having been there, because it *works* to do so, everything we know conspiring with the belief, and nothing interfering, so we assume that thing to be a clock. We *use* it as a clock, regulating the length of our lecture by it. The verification of the assumption here means its leading to no frustration or contradiction. Verifi*ability* of wheels and weights and pendulum is as good as verification. For one truth-process completed there are a million in our lives that function in this state of nascency. They turn us *towards* direct verification; lead us into the *surroundings* of the objects they envisage; and then, if everything runs harmoniously, we are so sure that verification is possible that we omit it, and are usually justified by all that happens.

Truth lives, in fact, for the most part on a credit system. Our thoughts and beliefs 'pass,' so long as nothing challenges them, just as bank-notes pass so long as nobody refuses them. But this all points to direct face-to-face verifications somewhere, without which the fabric of truth collapses like a financial system with no cash-basis whatever. You accept my verification of one thing, I yours of another. We trade on each other's truth. But beliefs verified concretely by *somebody* are the posts of the whole superstructure. . . .

So far, intellectualists can raise no protest. They can only say that we have barely touched the skin of the matter.

Realities, mean, then, either concrete facts, or abstract kinds of things and relations perceived intuitively between them. They furthermore and thirdly mean, as things that new ideas of ours must no less take account of, the whole body of other truths already in our possession. But what now does 'agreement' with such threefold realities mean?—to use again the definition that is current.

Here it is that pragmatism and intellectualism begin to part company. Primarily, no doubt, to agree means to copy, but we saw that the mere word 'clock' would do instead of a mental picture of its works, and that of many realities our ideas can only be symbols and not copies. 'Past time,' 'power,' 'spontaneity,'—how can our mind copy such realities?

To 'agree' in the widest sense with a reality *can only mean to be guided either straight up to it or into its surroundings, or to be put into such working touch with it as to handle either it or something connected with it better than if we disagreed.* Better either intellectually or practically! And often agreement will only mean the negative fact that nothing contradictory from the quarter of that reality comes to interfere with the way in which our ideas guide us elsewhere. To copy a reality is, indeed, one very important way of agreeing with it, but it is far from being essential. The essential thing is the process of being guided. Any idea that helps us to *deal*, whether practically or intellectually, with either the reality or its belongings, that doesn't entangle our progress in frustrations, that *fits*, in fact, and adapts our life to the reality's whole setting, will agree sufficiently to meet the requirement. It will hold true of that reality. . . .

Agreement thus turns out to be essentially an affair of leading—leading that is useful because it is into quarters that contain objects that are important. True ideas lead us into useful verbal and conceptual quarters as well as directly up to useful sensible termini. They lead to consistency, stability and flowing human intercourse. They lead away from eccentricity and isolation, from foiled and barren thinking. The untrammelled flowing of the leading-process, its general freedom from clash and contradiction, passes for its indirect verification; but all roads lead to Rome, and in the end and eventually, all true processes must lead to the face of directly verifying sensible experiences *somewhere*, which somebody's ideas have copied.

Such is the large loose way in which the pragmatist interprets the word agreement. He treats it altogether practically. He lets it cover any process of conduction from a present idea to a future terminus, provided only it run prosperously. It is only thus that 'scientific' ideas, flying as they do beyond common sense, can be said to agree with their realities. It is, as I have already said, *as if* reality were made of ether, atoms or electrons, but we must n't think so literally. The term 'energy' does n't even pretend to stand for anything 'objective.' It is only a way of measuring the surface of phenomena so as to string their changes on a simple formula.

Yet in the choice of these man-made formulas we can not be capricious with impunity any more than we can be capricious on the common-sense practical level. We must find a theory that will *work*; and that means something extremely difficult; for our theory must mediate between all previous truths and certain new experiences. It must derange common sense and previous belief as little as possible, and it must lead to some sensible terminus or other that can be verified exactly. To 'work' means both these things; and the squeeze is so tight that there is little loose play for any hypothesis. Our theories are wedged and controlled as nothing else is. Yet sometimes alternative theoretic formulas are equally compatible with all the truths we know, and then we choose between them for subjective reasons. We choose the kind of theory to which we are already partial; we follow 'elegance' or 'economy.' Clerk-Maxwell somewhere says it would be 'poor scientific taste' to choose the more complicated of two equally well-evidenced conceptions; and you will all agree with him. Truth in science is what gives us the maximum possible sum of satisfactions, taste included, but consistency both with previous truth and with novel fact is always the most imperious claimant. . . .

'The true,' to put it very briefly, is only the expedient in the way of our thinking, just as 'the right' is only the expedient in the way of our behaving. Expedient in almost any fashion; and expedient in the long run and on the whole of course; for what meets expediently all the experience in sight won't necessarily meet all farther experiences equally satisfactorily. Experience, as we know, has ways of *boiling over*, and making us correct our present formulas.

The 'absolutely' true, meaning what no farther experience will ever alter, is that ideal vanishing-point towards which we imagine that all our temporary truths will some day converge. It runs on all fours with the perfectly wise man, and with the absolutely complete experience; and, if these ideals are ever realized, they will all be realized together. Meanwhile we have to live to-day by what truth we can get to-day, and be ready to-morrow to call it falsehood. Ptolemaic astronomy, euclidean space, aristotelian logic, scholastic metaphysics, were expedient for centuries, but human experience has boiled over those limits, and we now call these things only relatively true, or true within those borders of experience. 'Absolutely' they are false; for we know that those limits were casual, and might have been transcended by past theorists just as they are by present thinkers. . . .

The most fateful point of difference between being a rationalist and being a pragmatist is now fully in sight. Experience is in mutation, and our psychological ascertainments of truth are in mutation—so much rationalism will allow; but never that either reality itself or truth itself is mutable. Reality stands complete and ready-made from all eternity, rationalism insists, and the agreement of our ideas with it is that unique unanalyzable virtue in them of which she has already told us. As that intrinsic excellence, their truth has nothing to do with our experiences. It adds nothing to the content of experience. It makes no difference to reality itself; it is supervenient, inert, static, a reflexion merely. It doesn't *exist*, it *holds* or *obtains*, it belongs to another dimension from that of either facts or fact-relations, belongs, in short, to the epistemological dimension—and with that big word rationalism closes the discussion.

Thus, just as pragmatism faces forward to the future, so does rationalism here again face backward to a past eternity. True to her inveterate habit, rationalism reverts to 'principles,' and thinks that when an abstraction once is named, we own an oracular solution. . . .

INDUCTION

63 Scepticism and Induction*

DAVID HUME

David Hume (1711–1776) has had a tremendous influence on the developments of modern philosophy. Along with John Locke and Bishop Berkeley, he began the philosophical tradition known as empiricism. His principal philosophical works are A *Treatise of Human Nature, Inquiry Concerning the Human Understanding,* and *Dialogues Concerning Natural Religion.*

All the objects of human reason or inquiry may naturally be divided into two kinds, to wit, *Relations of Ideas,* and *Matters of Fact.* Of the first kind are the sciences of Geometry, Algebra, and Arithmetic; and in short, every affirmation which is either intuitively or demonstratively certain. *That the square of the hypothenuse is equal to the square of the two sides,* is a proposition which expresses a relation between these figures. *That three times five is equal to the half of thirty,* expresses a relation between these numbers. Propositions of this kind are discoverable by the mere operation of thought, without dependence on what is anywhere existent in the universe. Though there never were a circle or triangle in nature, the truths demonstrated by Euclid would forever retain their certainty and evidence.

Matters of fact, which are the second objects of human reason, are not ascertained in the same manner; nor is our evidence of their truth, however great, of a like nature with the foregoing. The contrary of every matter of fact is still possible; because it can never imply a contradiction, and is conceived by the mind with the same facility and distinctness, as if ever so conformable to reality. *That the sun will not rise tomorrow* is no less intelligible a proposition, and implies no more contradiction than the affirmation, *that it will rise.* We should in vain, therefore, attempt to demonstrate its falsehood. Were it demonstratively false, it would imply a contradiction, and could never be distinctly conceived by the mind.

* From David Hume, An *Enquiry Concerning Human Understanding,* first published in 1748.

It may, therefore, be a subject worthy of curiosity, to inquire what is the nature of that evidence which assures us of any real existence and matter of fact, beyond the present testimony of our senses, or the records of our memory. This part of philosophy, it is observable, has been little cultivated, either by the ancients or moderns; and therefore our doubts and errors, in the prosecution of so important an inquiry, may be the more excusable; while we march through such difficult paths without any guide or direction. They may even prove useful, by exciting curiosity, and destroying that implicit faith and security, which is the bane of all reasoning and free inquiry. The discovery of defects in the common philosophy, if any such there be, will not, I presume, be a discouragement, but rather an incitement, as is usual, to attempt something more full and satisfactory than has yet been proposed to the public.

All reasonings concerning matter of fact seem to be founded on the relation of *Cause and Effect*. By means of that relation alone we can go beyond the evidence of our memory and senses. If you were to ask a man, why he believes any matter of fact, which is absent; for instance, that his friend is in the country, or in France; he would give you a reason; and this reason would be some other fact; as a letter received from him, or the knowledge of his former resolutions and promises. A man finding a watch or any other machine in a desert island, would conclude that there had once been men in that island. All our reasonings concerning fact are of the same nature. And here it is constantly supposed that there is a connection between the present fact and that which is inferred from it. Were there nothing to bind them together, the inference would be entirely precarious. The hearing of an articulate voice and rational discourse in the dark assures us of the presence of some person: Why? because these are the effects of the human make and fabric, and closely connected with it. If we anatomize all the other reasonings of this nature, we shall find that they are founded on the relation of cause and effect, and that this relation is either near or remote, direct or collateral. Heat and light are collateral effects of fire, and the one effect may justly be inferred from the other.

If we would satisfy ourselves, therefore, concerning the nature of that evidence, which assures us of matters of fact, we must inquire how we arrive at the knowledge of cause and effect.

I shall venture to affirm, as a general proposition, which admits of no exception, that the knowledge of this relation is not, in any instance, attained by reasonings *a priori*; but arises entirely from experience, when we find that any particular objects are constantly conjoined with each other. Let an object be presented to a man of ever so strong natural reason and abilities; if that object be entirely new to him, he will not be able, by the most accurate examination of its sensible qualities, to discover any of its causes or effects. Adam, though his rational faculties be supposed, at the very first, entirely perfect, could not have inferred from the fluidity and transparency of water that it would suffocate him, or from the light and warmth of fire that it would consume him. No object ever discovers, by the qualities which appear to the senses, either the causes which produced it, or the effects which will arise from it; nor can our reason, unassisted by experience, ever draw any inference concerning real existence and matter of fact.

This proposition, *that causes and effects are discoverable, not by reason but by experience,* will readily be admitted with regard to such objects, as we remember to have once been altogether unknown to us; since we must be conscious of the utter inability, which we then lay under, of foretelling what would arise from them. Present two smooth pieces of marble to a man who has no tincture of natural philosophy; he will never discover that they will adhere together in such a manner as to require great force to separate them in a direct line, while they make so small a resistance to a lateral pressure. Such events, as bear little analogy to the common course of nature, are also readily confessed to be known only by experience; nor does any man imagine that the explosion of gunpowder, or the attraction of a loadstone, could ever be discovered by arguments *a priori.* In like manner, when an effect is supposed to depend upon an intricate machinery or secret structure of parts, we make no difficulty in attributing all our knowledge of it to experience. Who will assert that he can give the ultimate reason, why milk or bread is proper nourishment for a man, not for a lion or a tiger?

But the same truth may not appear, at first sight, to have the same evidence with regard to events, which have become familiar to us from our first appearance in the world, which bear a close analogy to the whole course of nature, and which are supposed to depend on the simple qualities of objects, without any secret structure of parts. We are apt to imagine that we could discover these effects by the mere operation of our reason, without experience. We fancy, that were we brought on a sudden into this world, we could at first have inferred that one Billiard-ball would communicate motion to another upon impulse; and that we needed not to have waited for the event, in order to pronounce with certainty concerning it. Such is the influence of custom, that, where it is strongest, it not only covers our natural ignorance, but even conceals itself, and seems not to take place, merely because it is found in the highest degree.

But to convince us that all the laws of nature, and all the operations of bodies without exception, are known only by experience, the following reflections may, perhaps, suffice. Were any object presented to us, and were we required to pronounce concerning the effect, which will result from it, without consulting past observation; after what manner, I beseech you, must the mind proceed in this operation? It must invent or imagine some event, which it ascribes to the object as its effect; and it is plain that this invention must be entirely arbitrary. The mind can never possibly find the effect in the supposed cause, by the most accurate scrutiny and examination. For the effect is totally different from the cause, and consequently can never be discovered in it. Motion in the second Billiard-ball is a quite distinct event from motion in the first; nor is there anything in the one to suggest the smallest hint of the other. A stone or piece of metal raised into the air, and left without any support, immediately falls: but to consider the matter *a priori*, is there anything we discover in this situation which can beget the idea of a downward, rather than an upward, or any other motion, in the stone or metal?

And as the first imagination or invention of a particular effect, in all natural operations, is arbitrary, where we consult not experience; so must we also esteem the supposed tie or connection between the cause and effect, which binds them together, and renders it impossible that any other effect could result from the operation of that cause. When I see, for instance, a Billiard-ball moving in a straight line towards another; even suppose motion in the second ball should by accident be suggested to me, as the result of their contact or impulse; may I not conceive, that a hundred different events might as well follow from that cause? May not both these balls remain at absolute rest? May not the first ball return in a straight line, or leap off from the second in any line or direction? All these suppositions are consistent and conceivable. Why then should we give the preference to one, which is no more consistent or conceivable than the rest? All our reasonings *a priori* will never be able to show us any foundation for this preference.

In a word, then, every effect is a distinct event from its cause. It could not, therefore, be discovered in the cause, and the first invention or conception of it, *a priori*, must be entirely arbitrary. And even after it is suggested, the conjunction of it with the cause must appear equally arbitrary; since there are always many other effects, which, to reason, must seem fully as consistent and natural. In vain, therefore, should we pretend to determine any single event, or infer any cause or effect, without the assistance of observation and experience.

Hence we may discover the reason why no philosopher, who is rational and modest, has ever pretended to assign the ultimate cause of any natural operation, or to show distinctly the action of that power, which produces any single effect in the universe. It is confessed, that the utmost effort of human reason is to reduce the principles, productive of natural phenomena, to a greater simplicity, and to resolve the many particular effects into a few general causes, by means of reasonings from analogy, experience, and observation. But as to the causes of these general causes, we should in vain attempt their discovery; nor shall we ever be able to satisfy ourselves, by any particular explication of them. These ultimate springs and principles are totally shut up from human curiosity and inquiry. Elasticity, gravity, cohesion of parts, communication of motion by impulse; these are probably the ultimate causes and principles which we shall ever discover in nature; and we may esteem ourselves sufficiently happy, if, by accurate inquiry and reasoning, we can trace up the particular phenomena to, or near to, these general principles. The most perfect philosophy of the natural kind only staves off our ignorance a little longer: as perhaps the most perfect philosophy of the moral or meta-physical kind serves only to discover larger portions of it. Thus the observation of human blindness and weakness is the result of all philosophy, and meets us at every turn, in spite of our endeavors to elude or avoid it.

II

But we have not yet attained any tolerable satisfaction with regard to the question first proposed. Each solution still gives rise to a new question as difficult as the foregoing, and leads us on to farther inquiries. When it is asked, *What is the nature of all our reasonings concerning matter of fact?* the proper answer seems to be, that they are founded on the relation of cause and effect. When again it is asked, *What is the foundation of all our reasonings and conclusions concerning that relation?* it may be replied in one word, Experience. But if we still carry on our sifting humor, and ask, *What is the foundation of all conclusions from experience?* this implies a new question, which may be of more difficult solution and explication. Philosophers, that give themselves airs of superior wisdom and sufficiency, have a hard task when they encounter persons of inquisitive dispositions, who push them from every corner to which they retreat, and who are sure at last to bring them to some dangerous dilemma. The best expedient to prevent this confusion, is to be modest in our pretensions; and even to discover the difficulty ourselves before it is objected to us. By this means, we may make a kind of merit of our very ignorance.

I shall content myself, in this section, with an easy task, and shall pretend only to give a negative answer to the question here proposed. I say then, that, even after we have experience of the operations of cause and effect, our conclusions from that experience are not founded on reasoning, or any process of the understanding. This answer we must endeavor both to explain and to defend.

It must certainly be allowed, that nature has kept us at a great distance from all her secrets, and has afforded us only the knowledge of a few superficial qualities of objects; while she conceals from us those powers and principles on which the influence of those objects entirely depends. Our senses inform us of the color, weight, and consistence of bread; but neither sense nor reason can ever inform us of those qualities which fit it for the nourishment and support of a human body. Sight or feeling conveys an idea of the actual motion of bodies; but as to that wonderful force or power, which would carry on a moving body forever in a continued change of place, and which bodies never lose but by communicating it to others; of this we cannot form the most distant conception. But notwithstanding this ignorance of natural powers[1] and principles, we always presume, when we see like sensible qual-

---

[1] The word, Power, is here used in a loose and popular sense. The more accurate explication of it would give additional evidence to this argument.

ities, that they have like secret powers, and expect that effects, similar to those which we have experienced, will follow from them. If a body of like color and consistence with that bread, which we have formerly eat, be presented to us, we make no scruple of repeating the experiment, and foresee, with certainty, like nourishment and support. Now this is a process of the mind or thought, of which I would willingly know the foundation. It is allowed on all hands that there is no known connection between the sensible qualities and the secret powers; and consequently, that the mind is not led to form such a conclusion concerning their constant and regular conjunction, by anything which it knows of their nature. As to past *Experience*, it can be allowed to give *direct* and *certain* information of those precise objects only, and that precise period of time, which fell under its cognizance: but why this experience should be extended to future times, and to other objects, which for aught we know, may be only in appearance similar; this is the main question on which I would insist. The bread, which I formerly eat, nourished me; that is, a body of such sensible qualities was, at that time, endued with such secret powers: but does it follow, that other bread must also nourish me at another time, and that like sensible qualities must always be attended with like secret powers? The consequence seems nowise necessary. At least, it must be acknowledged that there is here a consequence drawn by the mind; that there is a certain step taken; a process of thought, and an inference, which wants to be explained. These two propositions are far from being the same, *I have found that such an object has always been attended with such an effect*, and *I foresee, that other objects, which are, in appearance, similar, will be attended with similar effects*. I shall allow, if you please, that the one proposition may justly be inferred from the other: I know, in fact, that it always is inferred. But if you insist that the inference is made by a chain of reasoning, I desire you to produce that reasoning. The connection between these propositions is not intuitive. There is required a medium, which may enable the mind to draw such an inference, if indeed it be drawn by reasoning and argument. What that medium is, I must confess, passes my comprehension; and it is incumbent on those to produce it, who assert that it really exists, and is the origin of all our conclusions concerning matter of fact.

This negative argument must certainly, in process of time, become altogether convincing, if many penetrating and able philosophers shall turn their inquiries this way and no one be ever able to discover any connecting proposition or intermediate step, which supports the understanding in this conclusion. But as the question is yet new, every reader may not trust so far to his own penetration, as to conclude, because an argument escapes his inquiry, that therefore it does not really exist. For this reason it may be requisite to venture upon a more difficult task; and enumerating all the branches of human knowledge, endeavor to show that none of them can afford such an argument.

All reasonings may be divided into two kinds, namely, demonstrative reasoning, or that concerning relations of ideas, and moral reasoning, or that concerning matter of fact and existence. That there are no demonstrative arguments in the case seems evident; since it implies no contradiction that the course of nature may change, and that an object, seemingly like those which we have experienced, may be attended with different or contrary effects. May I not clearly and distinctly conceive that a body, falling from the clouds, and which, in all other respects, resembles snow, has yet the taste of salt or feeling of fire? Is there any more intelligible proposition than to affirm, that all the trees will flourish in December and January, and decay in May and June? Now whatever is intelligible, and can be distinctly conceived, implies no contradiction, and can never be proved false by any demonstrative argument or abstract reasoning a priori.

If we be, therefore, engaged by arguments to put trust in past experience, and make it the standard of our future judgment, these arguments must be probable only, or such as regard matter of fact and real existence, according to the division above mentioned. But that there is no argument of this kind, must appear, if our explication of that species of reasoning be admitted as solid and satisfactory. We have said that all arguments concerning existence are founded on the relation of cause and effect; that our knowledge of that relation is derived entirely from experience; and that all our experimental conclusions proceed upon the supposition that the future will be conformable to the past. To endeavor, therefore, the proof of this last supposition by probable arguments, or arguments regarding existence, must be evidently going in a circle, and taking that for granted, which is the very point in question.

In reality, all arguments from experience are founded on the similarity which we discover among natural objects, and by which we are induced to expect effects similar to those which we have found to follow from such objects. And though none but a fool or madman will ever pretend to dispute the authority of experience, or to reject that great guide of human life, it may surely be allowed a philosopher to have so much curiosity at least as to examine the principle of human nature, which gives this mighty authority to experience, and makes us draw advantage from that similarity which nature has placed among different objects. From causes which appear *similar* we expect similar effects. This is the sum of all our experimental conclusions. Now it seems evident that, if this conclusion were formed by reason, it would be as perfect at first, and upon one instance, as after ever so long a course of experience. But the case is far otherwise. Nothing so like as eggs; yet no one, on account of this appearing similarity, expects the same taste and relish in all of them. It is only after a long course of uniform experiments in any kind, that we attain a firm reliance and security with regard to a particular event. Now where is that process of reasoning which, from one instance, draws a conclusion, so different from that which it infers from a hundred instances that are nowise different from that single one? This question I propose as much for the sake of information, as with an intention of raising difficulties. I cannot find, I cannot imagine any such reasoning. But I keep my mind still open to instruction, if any one will vouchsafe to bestow it on me.

Should it be said that, from a number of uniform experiments, we *infer* a connection between the sensible qualities and the secret powers; this, I must confess, seems the same difficulty, couched in different terms. The question still recurs, on what process of argument this *inference* is founded? Where is the medium, the interposing ideas, which join propositions so very wide of each other? Is it confessed that the color, consistence, and other sensible qualities of bread appear not, of themselves, to have any connection with the secret powers of nourishment and support. For otherwise we could infer these secret powers from the first appearance of these sensible qualities, without the aid of experience; contrary to the sentiment of all philosophers, and contrary to plain matter of fact. Here, then, is our natural state of ignorance with regard to the powers and influence of all objects. How is this remedied by experience? It only shows us a number of uniform effects, resulting from certain objects, and teaches us that those particular objects, at that particular time, were endowed with such powers and forces. When a new object, endowed with similar sensible qualities, is produced, we expect similar powers and forces, and look for a like effect. From a body of like color and consistence with bread we expect like nourishment and support. But this surely is a step or progress of the mind, which wants to be explained. When a man says, *I have found, in all past instances, such sensible qualities conjoined with such secret powers*: And when he says, *Similar sensible qualities will always be conjoined with similar secret powers*, he is not guilty of a tautology, nor are these propositions in any respect the same. You say that the one proposition is an inference from the other. But you must confess that the inference is not intuitive; neither is it demonstrative: Of what nature is it, then? To say it is experimental, is begging the question. For all inferences from experiences suppose, as their foundation, that the future will resemble the past, and that similar powers will be conjoined with similar sensible qualities. If there be any suspicion that the course of nature may change, and that the past may be no rule for the future, all experience becomes useless, and can give rise to no inference or conclusion. It is impossible, therefore, that any arguments from experience can prove this resemblance of the past to the future; since all these arguments are founded on the supposition of that resemblance. Let the course of things be allowed hitherto ever so regular; that alone, without some new argument or inference, proves not that, for the future, it will continue so. In vain do you pretend to have learned the nature of bodies from your past experience. Their secret nature, and consequently all their effects and influence, may change, without any change in their sensible qualities. This happens sometimes, and with regard to some objects: Why may it not happen always, and with regard to all objects? What logic, what process of argument secures you against this supposition? My practice, you say, refutes my doubts. But you mistake the purport of my question. As an agent, I am quite satisfied in the point; but as a philosopher, who has some share of curiosity, I will not say skepticism, I want to learn the foundation of this inference. No reading, no inquiry has yet been able to remove my difficulty, or give me satisfaction in a matter of such importance. Can I do better than propose the difficulty to the public, even though, perhaps, I have small hopes of obtaining a solution? We shall at least, by this means, be sensible of our ignorance, if we do not augment our knowledge.

I must confess that a man is guilty of unpardonable arrogance who concludes, because an argument has escaped his own investigation, that therefore it does not really exist. I must also confess that, though all the learned, for several ages, should have employed themselves in fruitless search upon any subject, it may still, perhaps, be rash to conclude positively that the subject must, therefore, pass all human comprehension. Even though we examine all the sources of our knowledge, and conclude them unfit for such a subject, there may still remain a suspicion, that the enumeration is not complete, or the examination not accurate. But with regard to the present subject, there are some considerations which seem to remove all this accusation of arrogance or suspicion of mistake.

It is certain that the most ignorant and stupid peasants—nay infants, nay even brute beasts—improve by experience, and learn the qualities of natural objects, by observing the effects which result from them. When a child has felt the sensation of pain from touching the flame of a candle, he will be careful not to put his hand near any candle; but will expect a similar effect from a cause which is similar in its sensible qualities and appearance. If you assert, therefore, that the understanding of the child is led into this conclusion by any process of argument or ratiocination, I may just require you to produce that argument; nor have you any pretence to refuse so equitable a demand. You cannot say that the argument is abstruse, and may possibly escape your inquiry; since you confess that it is obvious to the capacity of a mere infant. If you hesitate, therefore, a moment, or if, after reflection, you produce any intricate or profound argument, you, in a manner, give up the question, and confess that it is not reasoning which engages us to suppose the past resembling the future, and to expect similar effects from causes which are, to appearance, similar. This is the proposition which I intended to enforce in the present section. If I be right, I pretend not to have made any mighty discovery. And if I be wrong, I must acknowledge myself to be indeed a very backward scholar; since I cannot now discover an argument which, it seems, was perfectly familiar to me long before I was out of my cradle.

METAPHYSICAL KNOWLEDGE

64 Is Metaphysical Knowledge Possible?*

IMMANUEL KANT

Immanuel Kant (1726–1806) is one of the most influential philosophers in the history of thought. He formulated his rationalistic system of thought in his *Critique of Pure Reason* (1781). Other of his influential philosophical treatises include the *Prolegomena to all Future Metaphysics, The Critique of Practical Reason, The Foundations of the Metaphysics of Morals, Religion within the Limits of Pure Reason,* and *The Critique of Judgment.*

. . . My object is to persuade all those who think Metaphysics worth studying, that it is absolutely necessary to pause a moment, and, neglecting all that has been done, to propose first the preliminary question, 'Whether such a thing as metaphysics be at all possible?'

If it be a science, how comes it that it cannot, like other sciences, obtain universal and permanent recognition? If not, how can it maintain its pretensions, and keep the human mind in suspense with hopes, never ceasing, yet never fulfilled? Whether then we demonstrate our knowledge or our ignorance in this field, we must come once for all to a definite conclusion respecting the nature of this so-called science, which cannot possibly remain on its present footing. It seems almost ridiculous, while every other science is continually advancing, that in this, which pretends to be Wisdom incarnate, for whose oracle every one inquires, we should constantly move round the same spot, without gaining a single step. And so its followers having melted away, we do not find men confident of their ability to shine in other sciences venturing their reputation here, where everybody, however ignorant in other matters, may deliver a final verdict, as in this domain there is as yet no standard weight and measure to distinguish sound knowledge from shallow talk.

* From Immanuel Kant, *Prolegomena to any Future Metaphysics,* ed. and trans. Paul Carus (La Salle, Ill.: The Open Court Publishing Company, 1902).

After all it is nothing extraordinary in the elaboration of a science, when men begin to wonder how far it has advanced, that the question should at last occur, whether and how such a science is possible? Human reason so delights in constructions, that it has several times built up a tower, and then razed it to examine the nature of the foundation. It is never too late to become wise; but if the change comes late, there is always more difficulty in starting a reform.

The question whether a science be possible, presupposes a doubt as to its actuality. But such a doubt offends the men whose whole possessions consist of this supposed jewel; hence he who raises the doubt must expect opposition from all sides. Some, in the proud consciousness of their possessions, which are ancient, and therefore considered legitimate, will take their metaphysical compendia in their hands, and look down on him with contempt; others, who never see anything except it be identical with what they have seen before, will not understand him, and everything will remain for a time, as if nothing had happened to excite the concern, or the hope, for an impending change.

Nevertheless, I venture to predict that the independent reader of these Prolegomena will not only doubt his previous science, but ultimately be fully persuaded, that it cannot exist unless the demands here stated on which its possibility depends, be satisfied; and, as this has never been done, that there is, as yet, no such thing as Metaphysics. But as it can never cease to be in demand,[1]—since the interests of common sense are intimately interwoven with it, he must confess that a radical reform, or rather a new birth of the science after an original plan, are unavoidable, however men may struggle against it for a while.

Since the Essays of Locke and Leibnitz, or rather since the origin of metaphysics so far as we know its history, nothing has ever happened which was more decisive to its fate than the attack made upon it by David Hume. He threw no light on this species of knowledge, but he certainly struck a spark from which light might have been obtained, had it caught some inflammable substance and had its smouldering fire been carefully nursed and developed.

Hume started from a single but important concept in Metaphysics, viz., that of Cause and Effect (including its derivatives force and action, etc.). He challenges reason, which pretends to have given birth to this idea from herself, to answer him by what right she thinks anything to be so constituted, that if that thing be posited, something else also must necessarily be posited; for this is the meaning of the concept of cause. He demonstrated irrefutably

---

[1] Says Horace:

"Rusticus expectat, dum defluat amnis, at ille
Labitur et labetur in omne volubilis aevum;"

"A rustic fellow waiteth on the shore
For the river to flow away,
But the river flows, and flows on as before,
And it flows forever and aye."

that it was perfectly impossible for reason to think *a priori* and by means of concepts a combination involving necessity. We cannot at all see why, in consequence of the existence of one thing, another must necessarily exist, or how the concept of such a combination can arise *a priori*. Hence he inferred, that reason was altogether deluded with reference to this concept, which she erroneously considered as one of her children, whereas in reality it was nothing but a bastard of imagination, impregnated by experience, which subsumed certain representations under the Law of Association, and mistook the subjective necessity of habit for an objective necessity arising from insight. Hence he inferred that reason had no power to think such combinations, even generally, because her concepts would then be purely fictitious, and all her pretended *a priori* cognitions nothing but common experiences marked with a false stamp. In plain language there is not, and cannot be, any such thing as metaphysics at all.[2]

However hasty and mistaken Hume's conclusion may appear, it was at least founded upon investigation, and this investigation deserved the concentrated attention of the brighter spirits of his day as well as determined efforts on their part to discover, if possible, a happier solution of the problem in the sense proposed by him, all of which would have speedily resulted in a complete reform of the science.

But Hume suffered the usual misfortune of metaphysicians, of not being understood. It is positively painful to see how utterly his opponents, Reid, Oswald, Beattie, and lastly Priestly, missed the point of the problem; for while they were ever taking for granted that which he doubted, and demonstrating with zeal and often with impudence that which he never thought of doubting, they so misconstrued his valuable suggestion that everything remained in its old condition, as if nothing had happened.

The question was not whether the concept of cause was right, useful, and even indispensable for our knowledge of nature, for this Hume had never doubted; but whether that concept could be thought by reason *a priori*, and consequently whether it possessed an inner truth, independent of all experience, implying a wider application than merely to the objects of experience. This was Hume's problem. It was a question concerning the *origin*, not concerning the *indispensable need* of the concept. Were the former decided, the conditions of the use and the sphere of its valid application would have been determined as a matter of course.

But to satisfy the conditions of the problem, the opponents of the great

---

[2] Nevertheless Hume called this very destructive science metaphysics and attached to it great value. Metaphysics and morals [he declares in the fourth part of his Essays] are the most important branches of science; mathematics and physics are not nearly so important. But the acute man merely regarded the negative use arising from the moderation of extravagant claims of speculative reason, and the complete settlement of the many endless and troublesome controversies that mislead mankind. He overlooked the positive injury which results, if reason be deprived of its most important prospects, which can alone supply to the will the highest aim for all its endeavor.

thinker should have penetrated very deeply into the nature of reason, so far as it is concerned with pure thinking,—a task which did not suit them. They found a more convenient method of being defiant without any insight, viz., the appeal to *common sense*. It is indeed a great gift of God, to possess right, or (as they now call it) plain common sense. But this common sense must be shown practically, by well-considered and reasonable thoughts and words, not by appealing to it as an oracle, when no rational justification can be advanced. To appeal to common sense, when insight and science fail, and no sooner—this is one of the subtle discoveries of modern times, by means of which the most superficial ranter can safely enter the lists with the most thorough thinker, and hold his own. But as long as a particle of insight remains, no one would think of having recourse to this subterfuge. For what is it but an appeal to the opinion of the multitude, of whose applause the philosopher is ashamed, while the popular charlatan glories and confides in it? I should think that Hume might fairly have laid as much claim to common sense as Beattie, and in addition to a critical reason (such as the latter did not possess), which keeps common sense in check and prevents it from speculating, or, if speculations are under discussion, restrains the desire to decide because it cannot satisfy itself concerning its own arguments. By this means alone can common sense remain sound. Chisels and hammers may suffice to work a piece of wood, but for steel-engraving we require an engraver's needle. Thus common sense and speculative understanding are each serviceable in their own way, the former in judgments which apply immediately to experience, the latter when we judge universally from mere concepts, as in metaphysics, where sound common sense, so called in spite of the inapplicability of the word, has no right to judge at all.

I openly confess, the suggestion of David Hume was the very thing, which many years ago first interrupted my dogmatic slumber, and gave my investigations in the field of speculative philosophy quite a new direction. I was far from following him in the conclusions at which he arrived by regarding, not the whole of his problem, but a part, which by itself can give us no information. If we start from a well-founded, but undeveloped, thought, which another has bequeathed to us, we may well hope by continued reflection to advance farther than the acute man, to whom we owe the first spark of light.

I therefore first tried whether Hume's objection could not be put into a general form, and soon found that the concept of the connexion of cause and effect was by no means the only idea by which the understanding thinks the connexion of things *a priori*, but rather that metaphysics consists altogether of such connexions. I sought to ascertain their number, and when I had satisfactorily succeeded in this by starting from a single principle, I proceeded to the deduction of these concepts, which I was now certain were not deduced from experience, as Hume had apprehended, but sprang from the pure understanding. This deduction (which seemed impossible to my acute predecessor, which had never even occurred to any one else, though no one had hesitated to use the concepts without investigating the basis of their objective validity) was the most difficult task ever undertaken in the service of metaphysics; and the worst was that metaphysics, such as it then existed, could not assist me in the least, because this deduction alone can render metaphysics possible. But as soon as I had succeeded in solving Hume's problem not merely in a particular case, but with respect to the whole faculty of pure reason, I could proceed safely, though slowly, to determine the whole sphere of pure reason completely and from general principles, in its circumference as well as in its contents. This was required for metaphysics in order to construct its system according to a reliable method.

PREAMBLE ON THE PECULIARITIES OF ALL METAPHYSICAL COGNITION

1. Of the Sources of Metaphysics

If it becomes desirable to formulate any cognition as science, it will be necessary first to determine accurately those peculiar features which no other science has in common with it, constituting its characteristics; otherwise the boundaries of all sciences become confused, and none of them can be treated thoroughly according to its nature.

The characteristics of a science may consist of a simple difference of object, or of the sources of cognition, or of the kind of cognition, or perhaps of all three conjointly. On this, therefore, depends the idea of a possible science and its territory.

First, as concerns the sources of metaphysical cognition, its very concept implies that they cannot be empirical. Its principles (including not only its maxims but its basic notions) must never be derived from experience. It must not be physical but metaphysical knowledge, viz., knowledge lying beyond experience. It can therefore have for its basis neither external experience, which is the source of physics proper, nor internal, which is the basis of empirical psychology. It is therefore *a priori* knowledge, coming from pure Understanding and pure Reason.

But so far Metaphysics would not be distinguishable from pure Mathematics; it must therefore be called pure philosophical cognition; and for the meaning of this term I refer to the *Critique of the Pure Reason* (II. "Method of Transcendentalism," Chap. I., Sec. i), where the distinction between these two employments of the reason is sufficiently explained. So far concerning the sources of metaphysical cognition.

2. Concerning the Kind of Cognition Which Can Alone Be Called Metaphysical

a. Of the Distinction between Analytical and Synthetical Judgments in General.—The peculiarity of its sources demands that metaphysical cognition must consist of nothing but *a priori* judgments. But whatever be their origin, or their logical form, there is a distinction in judgments, as to their content, according to which they are either merely explicative, adding nothing to the content of the cognition, or expansive, increasing the given cognition: the former may be called analytical, the latter synthetical, judgments.

Analytical judgments express nothing in the predicate but what has been already actually thought in the concept of the subject, though not so distinctly or with the same (full) consciousness. When I say: All bodies are extended, I have not amplified in the least my concept of body, but have only analysed it, as extension was really thought to belong to that concept before the judgment was made, though it was not expressed; this judgment is therefore analytical. On the contrary, this judgment: All bodies have weight, contains in its predicate something not actually thought in the general concept of the body; it amplifies my knowledge by adding something to my concept, and must therefore be called synthetical.

b. *The Common Principle of all Analytical Judgments is the Law of Contradiction.*—All analytical judgments depend wholly on the law of Contradiction, and are in their nature *a priori* cognitions, whether the concepts that supply them with matter be empirical or not. For the predicate of an affirmative analytical judgment is already contained in the concept of the subject, of which it cannot be denied without contradiction. In the same way its opposite is necessarily denied of the subject in an analytical, but negative, judgment, by the same law of contradiction. Such is the nature of the judgments: all bodies are extended, and no bodies are unextended (i.e., simple).

For this reason all analytical judgments are *a priori* even when the concepts are empirical, as, for example, Gold is a yellow metal; for to know this I require no experience beyond my concept of gold as a yellow metal: it is, in fact, the very concept, and I need only analyse it, without looking beyond it elsewhere.

c. *Synthetical Judgments require a different Principle from the Law of Contradiction.*—There are synthetical *a posteriori* judgments of empirical origin; but there are also others which are proved to be certain *a priori*, and which spring from pure Understanding and Reason. Yet they both agree in this, that they cannot possibly spring from the principle of analysis, viz., the law of contradiction, alone; they require a quite different principle, though, from whatever they may be deduced, they must be subject to the law of contradiction, which must never be violated, even though everything cannot be deduced from it. I shall first classify synthetical judgments.

1. *Empirical Judgments* are always synthetical.   For it would be absurd to base an analytical judgment on experience, as our concept suffices for the purpose without requiring any testimony from experience. That body is extended, is a judgment established *a priori*, and not an empirical judgment. For before appealing to experience, we already have all the conditions of the judgment in the concept, from which we have but to elicit the predicate according to the law of contradiction, and thereby to become conscious of the necessity of the judgment, which experience could not even teach us.

2. *Mathematical Judgments* are all synthetical. This fact seems hitherto to have altogether escaped the observation of those who have analysed human reason; it even seems directly opposed to all their conjectures, though incontestably certain, and most important in its consequences. For as it was found that the conclusions of mathematicians all proceed according to the law of contradiction (as is demanded by all apodeictic certainty), men persuaded themselves that the fundamental principles were known from the same law. This was a great mistake, for a synthetical proposition can indeed be comprehended according to the law of contradiction, but only by presupposing another synthetical proposition from which it follows, but never in itself.

First of all, we must observe that all proper mathematical judgments are *a priori*, and not empirical, because they carry with them necessity, which cannot be obtained from experience. But if this be not conceded to me, very good; I shall confine my assertion to *pure Mathematics*, the very notion of which implies that it contains pure *a priori* and not empirical cognitions.

It might at first be thought that the proposition $7 + 5 = 12$ is a mere analytical judgment, following from the concept of the sum of seven and five, according to the law of contradiction. But on closer examination it appears that the concept of the sum of $7 + 5$ contains merely their union in a single number, without its being at all thought what the particular number is that unites them. The concept of twelve is by no means thought by merely thinking of the combination of seven and five; and analyse this possible sum as we may, we shall not discover twelve in the concept. We must go beyond these concepts, by calling to our aid some concrete image (*Anschauung*), i.e., either our five fingers, or five points (as Segner has it in his Arithmetic), and we must add successively the units of the five, given in some concrete image (*Anschauung*), to the concept of seven. Hence our concept is really amplified by the proposition $7 + 5 = 12$, and we add to the first a second, not thought in it. Arithmetical judgments are therefore synthetical, and the more plainly according as we take larger numbers; for in such cases it is clear that, however closely we analyse our concepts without calling visual images (*Anschauung*) to our aid, we can never find the sum by such mere dissection.

All principles of geometry are no less analytical. That a straight line is the shortest path between two points, is a synthetical proposition. For my concept of straight contains nothing of quantity, but only a quality. The attribute of shortness is therefore altogether additional, and cannot be obtained by any analysis of the concept. Here, too, visualisation (*Anschauung*) must come to aid us. It alone makes the synthesis possible.

Some other principles, assumed by geometers, are indeed actually analytical, and depend on the law of contradiction; but they only serve, as identical propositions, as a method of concatenation, and not as principles, e.g., $a = a$, the whole is equal to itself, or $a + b > a$, the whole is greater than its part. And yet even these, though they are recognised as valid from mere concepts, are only admitted in mathematics, because they can be represented in some visual form (*Anschauung*). What usually makes us believe that the predicate of such apodeictic judgments is already contained in our concept, and that the judgment is therefore analytical, is the duplicity of the expression, requesting us to think a certain predicate as of necessity implied in the thought of a given concept, which necessity attaches to the concept. But the question is not what we are requested to join in thought *to* the given concept, but what we actually think together with and in it, though obscurely; and so it appears that the predicate belongs to these concepts necessarily indeed, yet not directly but indirectly by an added visualisation (*Anschauung*).

3. A Remark on the General Division of Judgments into Analytical and Synthetical

This division is indispensable, as concerns the Critique of human understanding, and therefore deserves to be called classical, though otherwise it is of little use, but this is the reason why dogmatic philosophers, who always seek the sources of metaphysical judgments in Metaphysics itself, and not apart from it, in the pure laws of reason generally, altogether neglected this apparently obvious distinction. Thus the celebrated Wolf, and his acute follower Baumgarten, came to seek the proof of the principle of Sufficient Reason, which is clearly synthetical, in the principle of Contradiction. In Locke's Essay, however, I find an indication of my division. For in the fourth book (chap. iii. § 9, seq.), having discussed the various connexions of representations in judgments, and their sources, one of which he makes "identity and contradiction" (analytical judgments), and another the coexistence of representations in a subject, he confesses (§ 10) that our *a priori* knowledge of the latter is very narrow, and almost nothing. But in his remarks on this species of cognition, there is so little of what is definite, and reduced to rules, that we cannot wonder if no one, not even Hume, was led to make investigations concerning this sort of judgments. For such general and yet definite principles are not easily learned from other men, who have had them obscurely in their minds. We must hit on them first by our own reflexion, then we find them elsewhere, where we could not possibly have found them at first, because the authors themselves did not know that such an idea lay at the basis of their observations. Men who never think independently have nevertheless the acuteness to discover everything, after it has been once shown them, in what was said long since, though no one ever saw it there before.

4. The General Question of the Prolegomena.—Is Metaphysics at All Possible?

Were a metaphysics, which could maintain its place as a science, really in existence; could we say, here is metaphysics, learn it, and it will convince you irresistibly and irrevocably of its truth: this question would be useless, and there would only remain that other question (which would rather be a test of our acuteness, than a proof of the existence of the thing itself), "How is the science possible, and how does reason come to attain it?" But human reason has not been so fortunate in this case. There is no single book to which you can point as you do to Euclid, and say: This is Metaphysics; here you may find the noblest objects of this science, the knowledge of a highest Being, and of a future existence, proved from principles of pure reason. We can be shown indeed many judgments, demonstrably certain, and never questioned; but these are all analytical, and rather concern the materials and the scaffolding for Metaphysics, than the extension of knowledge, which is our proper object in studying it (§ 2). Even supposing you produce synthetical judgments (such as the law of Sufficient Reason, which you have never proved, as you ought to, from pure reason *a priori*, though we gladly concede its truth), you lapse when they come to be employed for your principal object, into such doubtful assertions, that in all ages one Metaphysics has contradicted another, either in its assertions, or their proofs, and thus has itself destroyed its own claim to lasting assent. Nay, the very attempts to set up such a science are the main cause of the early appearance of scepticism, a mental attitude in which reason treats itself with such violence that it could never have arisen save from complete despair of ever satisfying our most important aspirations. For long before men began to inquire into nature methodically, they consulted abstract reason, which had to some extent been exercised by means of ordinary experience; for reason is ever present, while laws of nature must usually be discovered with labor. So Metaphysics floated to the surface, like foam, which dissolved the moment it was scooped off. But immediately there appeared a new supply on the surface, to be ever eagerly gathered up by some, while others, instead of seeking in the depths the cause of the phenomenon, thought they showed their wisdom by ridiculing the idle labor of their neighbors.

The essential and distinguishing feature of pure mathematical cognition among all other *a priori* cognitions is, that it cannot at all proceed from concepts, but only by means of the construction of concepts (see Critique II., Method of Transcendentalism, chap. I., sect. 1). As therefore in its judgments it must proceed beyond the concept to that which its corresponding visualisation (*Anschauung*) contains, these judgments neither can, nor ought to, arise analytically, by dissecting the concept, but are all synthetical.

I cannot refrain from pointing out the disadvantage resulting to philosophy from the neglect of this easy and apparently insignificant observation. Hume being prompted (a task worthy of a philosopher) to cast his eye over the whole field of *a priori* cognitions in which human understanding claims such mighty possessions, heedlessly severed from it a whole, and indeed its most valuable, province, viz., pure mathematics; for he thought its nature, or, so to speak, the state-constitution of this empire, depended on totally different principles, namely, on the law of contradiction alone; and although he did not divide judgments in this manner formally and universally as I have done here, what he said was equivalent to this: that mathematics contains only analytical, but metaphysics synthetical, *a priori* judgments. In this, however, he was greatly mistaken, and the mistake had a decidedly injurious effect upon his whole conception. But for this, he would have extended his question concerning the origin of our synthetical judgments far beyond the metaphysical concept of Causality, and included in it the possibility of mathematics *a priori* also, for this latter he must have assumed to be equally synthetical. And then he could not have based his metaphysical judgments on mere experience without subjecting the axioms of mathematics equally to experience, a thing which he was far too acute to do. The good company into which metaphysics would thus have been brought, would have saved it from the danger of a contemptuous ill-treatment, for the thrust intended for it must have reached mathematics, which was not and could not have been Hume's intention. Thus that acute man would have been led into considerations which must needs be similar to those that now occupy us, but which would have gained inestimably by his inimitably elegant style.

Metaphysical judgments, properly so called, are all synthetical. We must distinguish judgments pertaining to metaphysics from metaphysical judgments properly so called. Many of the former are analytical, but they only afford the means for metaphysical judgments, which are the whole end of the science, and which are always synthetical. For if there be concepts pertaining to metaphysics (as, for example, that of substance), the judgments springing from simple analysis of them also pertain to metaphysics, as, for example, substance is that which only exists as subject; and by means of several such analytical judgments, we seek to approach the definition of the concept. But as the analysis of a pure concept of the understanding pertaining to metaphysics, does not proceed in any different manner from the dissection of any other, even empirical, concepts, not pertaining to metaphysics (such as: air is an elastic fluid, the elasticity of which is not destroyed by any known degree of cold), it follows that the concept indeed, but not the analytical judgment, is properly metaphysical. This science has something peculiar in the production of its *a priori* cognitions, which must therefore be distinguished from the features it has in common with other rational knowledge. Thus the judgment, that all the substance in things is permanent, is a synthetical and properly metaphysical judgment.

If the *a priori* principles, which constitute the materials of metaphysics, have first been collected according to fixed principles, then their analysis will be of great value; it might be taught as a particular part (as a *philosophia definitiva*), containing nothing but analytical judgments pertaining to metaphysics, and could be treated separately from the synthetical which constitute metaphysics proper. For indeed these analyses are not elsewhere of much value, except in metaphysics, i.e., as regards the synthetical judgments, which are to be generated by these previously analysed concepts.

The conclusion drawn in this section then, is that metaphysics is properly concerned with synthetical propositions *a priori*, and these alone constitute its end, for which it indeed requires various dissections of its concepts, viz., of its analytical judgments, but wherein the procedure is not different from that in every other kind of knowledge, in which we merely seek to render our concepts distinct by analysis. But the generation of *a priori* cognition by concrete images as well as by concepts, in fine of synthetical propositions *a priori* in philosophical cognition, constitutes the essential subject of Metaphysics.

Weary therefore as well of dogmatism, which teaches us nothing, as of scepticism, which does not even promise us anything, not even the quiet state of a contented ignorance; disquieted by the importance of knowledge so much needed; and lastly, rendered suspicious by long experience of all knowledge which we believe we possess, or which offers itself, under the title of pure reason: there remains but one critical question on the answer to which our future procedure depends, viz., *Is Metaphysics at all possible?* But this question must be answered not by sceptical objections to the asseverations of some actual system of metaphysics (for we do not as yet admit such a thing to exist), but from the conception, as yet only problematical, of a science of this sort.

In the *Critique of Pure Reason* I have treated this question synthetically, by making inquiries into pure reason itself, and endeavoring in this source to determine the elements as well as the laws of its pure use according to principles. The task is difficult, and requires a resolute reader to penetrate by degrees into a system, based on no data except reason itself, and which therefore seeks, without resting upon any fact, to unfold knowledge from its original germs. *Prolegomena*, however, are designed for preparatory exercises; they are intended rather to point out what we have to do in order if possible to actualise a science, than to propound it. They must therefore rest upon something already known as trustworthy, from which we can set out with confidence, and ascend to sources as yet unknown, the discovery of which will not only explain to us what we knew, but exhibit a sphere of many cognitions which all spring from the same sources. The method of *Prolegomena*, especially of those designed as a preparation for future metaphysics, is consequently analytical.

But it happens fortunately, that though we cannot assume metaphysics to be an actual science, we can say with confidence that certain pure *a priori* synthetical cognitions, pure Mathematics and pure Physics are actual and given; for both contain propositions, which are thoroughly recognised as apodeictically certain, partly by mere reason, partly by general consent arising from experience, and yet as independent of experience. We have therefore some at least uncontested synthetical knowledge *a priori*, and need not ask *whether* it be possible, for it is actual, but *how* it is possible, in order that we may deduce from the principle which makes the given cognitions possible the possibility of all the rest.

5. The General Problem: How Is Cognition from Pure Reason Possible?

We have above learned the significant distinction between analytical and synthetical judgments. The possibility of analytical propositions was easily comprehended, being entirely founded on the law of Contradiction. The possibility of synthetical *a posteriori* judgments, of those which are gathered from experience, also requires no particular explanation; for experience is nothing but a continual synthesis of perceptions. There remain therefore only synthetical propositions *a priori*; of which the possibility must be sought or investigated, because they must depend upon other principles than the law of contradiction.

But here we need not first establish the possibility of such propositions so as to ask whether they are possible. For there are enough of them which indeed are of undoubted certainty, and as our present method is analytical, we shall start from the fact, that such synthetical but purely rational cognition actually exists; but we must now inquire into the reason of this possibility, and ask, *how* such cognition is possible, in order that we may from the principles of its possibility be enabled to determine the conditions of its use, its sphere and its limits. The proper problem upon which all depends, when expressed with scholastic precision, is therefore:

How are Synthetic Propositions a priori possible?

For the sake of popularity I have above expressed this problem somewhat differently, as an inquiry into purely rational cognition, which I could do for once without detriment to the desired comprehension, because, as we have only to do here with metaphysics and its sources, the reader will, I hope, after the foregoing remarks, keep in mind that when we speak of purely rational cognition, we do not mean analytical, but synthetical cognition.[3]

Metaphysics stands or falls with the solution of this problem: its very existence depends upon it. Let any one make metaphysical assertions with ever so much plausibility, let him overwhelm us with conclusions, if he has not previously proved able to answer this question satisfactorily, I have a right to say: this is all vain baseless philosophy and false wisdom. You speak through pure reason, and claim, as it were to create cognitions *a priori* by not only dissecting given concepts, but also by asserting connexions which

---

[3] It is unavoidable that as knowledge advances, certain expressions which have become classical, after having been used since the infancy of science, will be found inadequate and unsuitable, and a newer and more appropriate application of the terms will give rise to confusion. [This is the case with the term "analytical."] The analytical method, so far as it is opposed to the synthetical, is very different from that which constitutes the essence of analytical propositions: it signifies only that we start from what is sought, as if it were given, and ascend to the only conditions under which it is possible. In this method we often use nothing but synthetical propositions, as in mathematical analysis, and it were better to term it the regressive method, in contradistinction to the synthetic or progressive. A principal part of Logic too is distinguished by the name of Analytics, which here signifies the logic of truth in contrast to Dialectics, without considering whether the cognitions belonging to it are analytical or synthetical.

do not rest upon the law of contradiction, and which you believe you conceive quite independently of all experience; how do you arrive at this, and how will you justify your pretensions? An appeal to the consent of the common sense of mankind cannot be allowed; for that is a witness whose authority depends merely upon rumor. Says Horace:

"Quodcunque ostendis mihi sic, incredulus odi."
"To all that which thou provest me thus, I refuse to give credence."

The answer to this question, though indispensable, is difficult; and though the principal reason that it was not made long ago is, that the possibility of the question never occurred to anybody, there is yet another reason, which is this that a satisfactory answer to this one question requires a much more persistent, profound, and painstaking reflexion, than the most diffuse work on Metaphysics, which on its first appearance promised immortality to its author. And every intelligent reader, when he carefully reflects what this problem requires, must at first be struck with its difficulty, and would regard it as insoluble and even impossible, did there not actually exist pure synthetical cognitions *a priori*. This actually happened to David Hume, though he did not conceive the question in its entire universality as is done here, and as must be done, should the answer be decisive for all Metaphysics. For how is it possible, says that acute man, that when a concept is given me, I can go beyond it and connect with it another, which is not contained in it, in such a manner as if the latter necessarily belonged to the former? Nothing but experience can furnish us with such connexions (thus he concluded from the difficulty which he took to be an impossibility), and all that vaunted necessity, or, what is the same thing, all cognition assumed to be *a priori*, is nothing but a long habit of accepting something as true, and hence of mistaking subjective necessity for objective.

Should my reader complain of the difficulty and the trouble which I occasion him in the solution of this problem, he is at liberty to solve it himself in an easier way. Perhaps he will then feel under obligation to the person who has undertaken for him a labor of so profound research, and will rather be surprised at the facility with which, considering the nature of the subject, the solution has been attained. Yet it has cost years of work to solve the problem in its whole universality (using the term in the mathematical sense, viz., for that which is sufficient for all cases), and finally to exhibit it in the analytical form, as the reader finds it here.

All metaphysicians are therefore solemnly and legally suspended from their occupations till they shall have answered in a satisfactory manner the question, "How are synthetic cognitions *a priori* possible?" For the answer contains the only credentials which they must show when they have anything to offer in the name of pure reason. But if they do not possess these credentials, they can expect nothing else of reasonable people, who have been deceived so often, than to be dismissed without further ado.

If they on the other hand desire to carry on their business, not as a science, but as an art of wholesome oratory suited to the common sense of man, they cannot in justice be prevented. They will then speak the modest language of a rational belief, they will grant that they are not allowed even to conjecture, far less to know, anything which lies beyond the bounds of all possible experience, but only to assume (not for speculative use, which they must abandon, but for practical purposes only) the existence of something that is possible and even indispensable for the guidance of the understanding and of the will in life. In this manner alone can they be called useful and wise men, and the more so as they renounce the title of metaphysicians; for the latter profess to be speculative philosophers, and since, when judgments *a priori* are under discussion, poor probabilities cannot be admitted (for what is declared to be known *a priori* is thereby announced as necessary), such men cannot be permitted to play with conjectures, but their assertions must be either science, or are worth nothing at all.

65 Metaphysical Knowledge
Is Impossible*

A. J. AYER

Alfred J. Ayer (1910–) is a graduate of Oxford and presently is
Wykham Professor of Logic at Oxford University. Introduced to the
philosophical movement known as logical positivism at the University
of Vienna, Ayer has become known as one of the principal spokesmen
for this position. His most controversial book, *Language, Truth and
Logic*, is a strong statement of the positivist position. He is also the
author of *The Foundations of Empirical Knowledge*, *The Problem of
Knowledge*, and *The Concept of a Person and Other Essays*.

The traditional disputes of philosophers are, for the most part, as unwarranted as they are unfruitful. The surest way to end them is to establish
beyond question what should be the purpose and method of a philosophical
enquiry. And this is by no means so difficult a task as the history of philosophy would lead one to suppose. For if there are any questions which science
leaves it to philosophy to answer, a straightforward process of elimination
must lead to their discovery.

We may begin by criticising the metaphysical thesis that philosophy
affords us knowledge of a reality transcending the world of science and
common sense. Later on, when we come to define metaphysics and account
for its existence, we shall find that it is possible to be a metaphysician without
believing in a transcendent reality; for we shall see that many metaphysical
utterances are due to the commission of logical errors, rather than to a conscious desire on the part of their authors to go beyond the limits of experience. But it is convenient for us to take the case of those who believe that it
is possible to have knowledge of a transcendent reality as a starting-point for
our discussion. The arguments which we use to refute them will subsequently
be found to apply to the whole of metaphysics.

One way of attacking a metaphysician who claimed to have knowledge of
a reality which transcended the phenomenal world would be to enquire from
what premises his propositions were deduced. Must he not begin, as other
men do, with the evidence of his senses? And if so, what valid process of

* From *Language, Truth and Logic* by A. J. Ayer, Dover Publications, Inc. New York,
1936. Reprinted through the permission of the publisher.

reasoning can possibly lead him to the conception of a transcendent reality? Surely from empirical premises nothing whatsoever concerning the properties, or even the existence, of anything super-empirical can legitimately be inferred. But this objection would be met by a denial on the part of the metaphysician that his assertions were ultimately based on the evidence of his senses. He would say that he was endowed with a faculty of intellectual intuition which enabled him to know facts that could not be known through sense-experience. And even if it could be shown that he was relying on empirical premises, and that his venture into a non-empirical world was therefore logically unjustified, it would not follow that the assertions which he made concerning this non-empirical world could not be true. For the fact that a conclusion does not follow from its putative premise is not sufficient to show that it is false. Consequently one cannot overthrow a system of transcendent metaphysics merely by criticising the way in which it comes into being. What is required is rather a criticism of the nature of the actual statements which comprise it. And this is the line of argument which we shall, in fact, pursue. For we shall maintain that no statement which refers to a "reality" transcending the limits of all possible sense-experience can possibly have any literal significance; from which it must follow that the labours of those who have striven to describe such a reality have all been devoted to the production of nonsense.

It may be suggested that this is a proposition which has already been proved by Kant. But although Kant also condemned transcendent metaphysics, he did so on different grounds. For he said that the human understanding was so constituted that it lost itself in contradictions when it ventured out beyond the limits of possible experience and attempted to deal with things in themselves. And thus he made the impossibility of a transcendent metaphysic not, as we do, a matter of logic, but a matter of fact. He asserted, not that our minds could not conceivably have had the power of penetrating beyond the phenomenal world, but merely that they were in fact devoid of it. And this leads the critic to ask how, if it is possible to know only what lies within the bounds of sense-experience, the author can be justified in asserting that real things do exist beyond, and how he can tell what are the boundaries beyond which the human understanding may not venture, unless he succeeds in passing them himself. As Wittgenstein says, "in order to draw a limit to thinking, we should have to think both sides of this limit,"[1] a truth to which Bradley gives a special twist in maintaining that the man who is ready to prove that metaphysics is impossible is a brother metaphysician with a rival theory of his own.[2]

Whatever force these objections may have against the Kantian doctrine,

---

[1] *Tractatus Logico-Philosophicus*, Preface.
[2] Bradley, *Appearance and Reality*, 2nd ed., p. 1.

they have none whatsoever against the thesis that I am about to set forth. It cannot here be said that the author is himself overstepping the barrier he maintains to be impassable. For the fruitlessness of attempting to transcend the limits of possible sense-experience will be deduced, not from a psychological hypothesis concerning the actual constitution of the human mind, but from the rule which determines the literal significance of language. Our charge against the metaphysician is not that he attempts to employ the understanding in a field where it cannot profitably venture, but that he produces sentences which fail to conform to the conditions under which alone a sentence can be literally significant. Nor are we ourselves obliged to talk nonsense in order to show that all sentences of a certain type are necessarily devoid of literal significance. We need only formulate the criterion which enables us to test whether a sentence expresses a genuine proposition about a matter of fact, and then point out that the sentences under consideration fail to satisfy it. And this we shall now proceed to do. We shall first of all formulate the criterion in somewhat vague terms, and then give the explanations which are necessary to render it precise.

The criterion which we use to test the genuineness of apparent statements of fact is the criterion of verifiability. We say that a sentence is factually significant to any given person, if, and only if, he knows how to verify the proposition which it purports to express—that is, if he knows what observations would lead him, under certain conditions, to accept the proposition as being true, or reject it as being false. If, on the other hand, the putative proposition is of such a character that the assumption of its truth, or falsehood, is consistent with any assumption whatsoever concerning the nature of his future experience, then, as far as he is concerned, it is, if not a tautology, a mere pseudo-proposition. The sentence expressing it may be emotionally significant to him; but it is not literally significant. And with regard to questions the procedure is the same. We enquire in every case what observations would lead us to answer the question, one way or the other; and, if none can be discovered, we must conclude that the sentence under consideration does not, as far as we are concerned, express a genuine question, however strongly its grammatical appearance may suggest that it does.

As the adoption of this procedure is an essential factor in the argument of this book, it needs to be examined in detail.

In the first place, it is necessary to draw a distinction between practical verifiability, and verifiability in principle. Plainly we all understand, in many cases believe, propositions which we have not in fact taken steps to verify. Many of these are propositions which we could verify if we took enough trouble. But there remain a number of significant propositions, concerning matters of fact, which we could not verify even if we chose; simply because we lack the practical means of placing ourselves in the situation where the relevant observations could be made. A simple and familiar example of such a proposition is the proposition that there are mountains on the farther side of the moon.[3] No rocket has yet been invented which would enable me to go and look at the farther side of the moon, so that I am unable to decide the matter by actual observation. But I do know what observations would decide it for me, if, as is theoretically conceivable, I were once in a position to make them. And therefore I say that the proposition is verifiable in principle, if not in practice, and is accordingly significant. On the other hand, such a metaphysical pseudo-proposition as "the Absolute enters into, but is itself incapable of, evolution and progress,"[4] is not even in principle verifiable. For one cannot conceive of an observation which would enable one to determine whether the Absolute did, or did not, enter into evolution and progress. Of course it is possible that the author of such a remark is using English words in a way in which they are not commonly used by English-speaking people, and that he does, in fact, intend to assert something which could be empirically verified. But until he makes us understand how the proposition that he wishes to express would be verified, he fails to communicate anything to us. And if he admits, as I think the author of the remark in question would have admitted, that his words were not intended to express either a tautology or a proposition which was capable, at least in principle, of being verified, then it follows that he has made an utterance which has no literal significance even for himself.

A further distinction which we must make is the distinction between the "strong" and the "weak" sense of the term "verifiable." A proposition is said to be verifiable, in the strong sense of the term, if, and only if, its truth could be conclusively established in experience. But it is verifiable, in the weak sense, if it is possible for experience to render it probable. In which sense are we using the term when we say that a putative proposition is genuine only if it is verifiable?

It seems to me that if we adopt conclusive verifiability as our criterion of significance, as some positivists have proposed,[5] our argument will prove too much. Consider, for example, the case of general propositions of law—such propositions, namely, as "arsenic is poisonous"; "all men are mortal"; "a body tends to expand when it is heated." It is of the very nature of these propositions that their truth cannot be established with certainty by any finite series of observations. But if it is recognised that such general propositions of law are designed to cover an infinite number of cases, then it must be admitted that they cannot, even in principle, be verified conclusively. And

---

[3] This example has been used by Professor Schlick to illustrate the same point.
[4] A remark taken at random from *Appearance and Reality*, by F. H. Bradley.
[5] e.g. M. Schlick, "Positivismus und Realismus," *Erkenntnis*, Vol. I, 1930. F. Waismann, "Logische Analyse des Warscheinlichkeitsbegriffs," *Erkenntnis*, Vol. I, 1930.

then, if we adopt conclusive verifiability as our criterion of significance, we are logically obliged to treat these general propositions of law in the same fashion as we treat the statements of the metaphysician.

In face of this difficulty, some positivists[6] have adopted the heroic course of saying that these general propositions are indeed pieces of nonsense, albeit an essentially important type of nonsense. But here the introduction of the term "important" is simply an attempt to hedge. It serves only to mark the authors' recognition that their view is somewhat too paradoxical, without in any way removing the paradox. Besides, the difficulty is not confined to the case of general propositions of law, though it is there revealed most plainly. It is hardly less obvious in the case of propositions about the remote past. For it must surely be admitted that, however strong the evidence in favour of historical statements may be, their truth can never become more than highly probable. And to maintain that they also constituted an important, or unimportant, type of nonsense would be unplausible, to say the very least. Indeed, it will be our contention that no proposition, other than a tautology, can possibly be anything more than a probable hypothesis. And if this is correct, the principle that a sentence can be factually significant only if it expresses what is conclusively verifiable is self-stultifying as a criterion of significance. For it leads to the conclusion that it is impossible to make a significant statement of fact at all.

Nor can we accept the suggestion that a sentence should be allowed to be factually significant if, and only if, it expresses something which is definitely confutable by experience.[7] Those who adopt this course assume that, although no finite series of observations is ever sufficient to establish the truth of a hypothesis beyond all possibility of doubt, there are crucial cases in which a single observation, or series of observations, can definitely confute it. But, as we shall show later on, this assumption is false. A hypothesis cannot be conclusively confuted any more than it can be conclusively verified. For when we take the occurrence of certain observations as proof that a given hypothesis is false, we presuppose the existence of certain conditions. And though, in any given case, it may be extremely improbable that this assumption is false, it is not logically impossible. We shall see that there need be no self-contradiction in holding that some of the relevant circumstances are other than we have taken them to be, and consequently that the hypothesis has not really broken down. And if it is not the case that any hypothesis can be definitely confuted, we cannot hold that the genuineness of a proposition depends on the possibility of its definite confutation.

Accordingly, we fall back on the weaker sense of verification. We say that the question that must be asked about any putative statement of fact is not,

---

[6] e.g. M. Schlick, "Die Kausalität in der gegenwärtigen Physik," *Naturwissenschaft*, Vol. 19, 1931.

[7] This has been proposed by Karl Popper in his *Logik der Forschung*.

Would any observations make its truth or falsehood logically certain? but simply, Would any observations be relevant to the determination of its truth or falsehood? And it is only if a negative answer is given to this second question that we conclude that the statement under consideration is nonsensical.

A RESTATEMENT OF THE PROBLEM

66 *The Problem of Epistemology**

JAMES W. OLIVER

James W. Oliver (1912–   ) has taught at the Universities of Florida and Southern California. Presently professor of philosophy and chairman of the department of philosophy at the University of South Carolina, he is the author of several articles in philosophical journals and books.

My purpose is to propose that a question which I shall state be taken as the central problem of epistemology. The term 'epistemology' may then be defined so that all and only those discussions which are pertinent to this question will be regarded as epistemological. But I should think it hardly worthwhile to provide an additional and peculiar entry for dictionaries. A more important aim is to encourage philosophers to concentrate on the heart of the matter and to avoid extraneous issues which continue to fill the journals with elaborately profitless discussions.

First I shall state, and comment on, the question which is properly the central problem of epistemology. Then I shall criticize some of the problems which have often been regarded as belonging to this branch of philosophy. Finally I shall answer one possible objection to the position outlined here.

But first I wish to make two comments of what follows. The first is that I am aware that there are unsolved problems connected with what is said below. Thus one needs an account better than any now available as to what a clear literal statement in a natural language is. It may, however, give direction to work on the solution of this problem if it is understood that a purpose for which the solution is wanted is to have something as a basis for discussions in epistemology.

* From *The Journal of Philosophy*, vol. 57, no. 9, (1960). Reprinted by permission of the author and the *Journal of Philosophy*.

The second comment is that, of all the sentences in the following paragraphs, a number are either normative principles or evaluations. I regard these as involving an element of personal opinion, and as views to be held somewhat tentatively. It would, however, be superfluous to begin all of them with such phrases as 'I think that' or 'In my opinion,' but the absence of such phrases should not suggest the absence of a tentative attitude on the writer's part. I see no reason to avoid using such sentences in philosophical writing; on the contrary, an argument could be offered that philosophical writing must contain them, whatever they may lack in the way of finality.

What is to be taken as the fundamental problem of epistemology is concerned with attitudes of belief toward statements; the crucial question—in a preliminary formulation—is 'What statements should an individual believe?' As one makes a quick survey of the history of philosophy and asks what is the point of philosophical discussions of truth, perception, reason, intuition, etc., it seems apparent that the question of belief here formulated has rarely, if ever, been explicitly raised, and yet, a vague awareness that this is the fundamental question seems to have guided, sporadically and inefficiently, discussions in theory of knowledge from Plato down to the present day. Why should one be interested in distinguishing what is true from what is false except as a means of deciding what ought to be believed?

Though it will be desirable to refine the first formulation of the question, it may be emphasized at the start that the problem to be taken as the central one in epistemology is a normative question; anything that would constitute an answer at all will contain the word 'should' or an alternative normative expression. Also, the problem as stated is one in pragmatics. It is concerned with the attitudes of interpreters of a language toward *some* of the sentences in that language. Furthermore, it is intended that this question have the maximum possible neutrality among philosophical systems. I am here attempting to give an issue greater clarity and precision; it is beyond my purpose to offer a solution, even partial, and it would also be inappropriate to formulate the issue so that some one solution is favored. In particular, the formulation gives an advantage to neither empiricism nor rationalism.

The formulation given makes statements the subject matter of epistemology. The term 'statement' is used here in the sense in which it appears in Quine's *Methods of Logic*: statements are sentences in a natural language; each of them is either true or false; not all sentences in a natural language such as English are statements, and, in particular, neither evaluations nor normative principles are statements.

A common alternative to the present view regards propositions as the subject matter of epistemology. Although the notion of proposition has never, to my knowledge, been explicated with anything like the clarity which characterizes the term 'statement', it appears from most accounts that there is a one-to-one correspondence between propositions and the sentences which, as it is usually put, express them. Furthermore, for most assertions *about* statements there seem to be analogous assertions *about* propositions and vice versa. It might appear, then, that taking propositions as the subject matter of epistemology in accordance with a long tradition would be equally as good as the position taken in this paper. There are, however, advantages in formulating the problem in terms of statements. Foremost among these advantages is the possibility of utilizing, wherever appropriate, contemporary researches in logic and semiotic. Also, speaking of statements rather than of propositions seems to make easier the avoidance of confusions of philosophy with psychology. It is preferable, then, to say that our problem is about statements.

As a first step in refining the formulation of the question account should be taken of the obvious point that there are some sentences which are not within the scope of epistemology at all. Whitman says of grass, "it is the handkerchief of the Lord"; the hymnal says "God is love"; and Croce maintains that "art is vision or intuition." These are, apparently, statements, but there is a good reason why an epistemologist should say neither that such sentences ought to be believed nor that they ought not to be believed. The quotation from Whitman is clearly a metaphor; perhaps 'God is love' is also a metaphor, but this is not clear; and the sentence from Croce, even when examined in its context, is not clear enough to permit profitable discussion of its acceptability for belief. Many sentences in ordinary language are, of course, not to be taken literally. Sometimes a literal interpretation of them may be possible; but this sort of "interpretation" is not without its problems, and the epistemologist should be concerned only with the literal result of the process, whatever it may be, and not with the metaphor itself. And while it may be difficult to establish a useful criterion of clarity, surely it should be required that there be some clear meaning for a statement before the question of believing it is considered at all. Hence it is desirable to say that it is only clear literal statements which are to be the concern of the epistemologist, and the problem may be reformulated at this point as 'What clear literal statements should an individual believe?'

A second consideration will result in a further modification of the question. Although Descartes, and the rationalists generally, have advocated views involving only two attitudes of belief—those of complete certainty and complete disbelief—other philosophers—for example, Locke—have noted that people can and do take toward statements a wide range of attitudes or degrees of belief, including the two which interested Descartes, and also including an attitude of no opinion. There is a problem, subordinate to the central one of epistemology, of providing a useful scale of degrees of belief; in general it should try to provide as many degrees as any epistemologist would want, though anyone may use only so many as he finds convenient.

Historically, of course, epistemologists have been interested in different degrees of belief in order to associate them with different kinds of statements, and some comprehensive classification of statements is needed. There is, however, no place in the literature in which one can find a sufficiently complete classification to permit separation, relation, and adequate discussion of all issues of concern to epistemologists. There are, whether completely satisfactory or not, classifications among analytic, synthetic, and self-contradictory statements; among universal, existential, and singular statements; and among statements in various levels of language. Further distinctions have been made among statements purporting to refer to phenomena, those purporting to refer to physical objects, those purporting to refer to abstract entities, and those purporting to refer to supernatural beings, and, since statements saying what is remembered and those which are predictions may be affected by different epistemological considerations, some classification involving a temporal basis seems called for. A comprehensive cross-classification of statements that will permit one to take into account all the relevant factors discussed in the history of epistemology is a problem preliminary to the solution of the central problem of epistemology. To avoid confusing the normative issue with the selection of a classification, it will, most likely, be desirable to use no normative or evaluative expressions in setting up the kinds of statements for which normative principles are wanted.

What has just been said about degrees of belief and kinds of statements leads to the following modified formulation of the problem:

> What degrees of belief should an individual accord to clear literal statements of various kinds?

Further refinement of the problem is desirable, but we leave our own peculiar view at this point with the observation that the answer to this question will be a set of sentences all of which will be rules or criteria, none of which will be a statement, all of which will be metalinguistic. A simple example might be:

> If 'p' is equivalent to 'q', an individual should accord to 'p' and 'q' the same degree of belief.

Turning now from the special view which I have been advocating, I shall criticize some of the generally recognized problems of epistemology. I take these problems from the excellent article by Ledger Wood in Runes' *Dictionary of Philosophy*. It will be argued, for each of the eight problems mentioned by Professor Wood, either that it is better regarded as not epistemological at all, or that it cannot be profitably discussed until after we have obtained a solution of the proposed central problem of epistemology, or that, when clarified, it is a part of, or identical with, this problem.

The first problem referred to by Professor Wood is "that of the very *possibility of knowledge.* Is genuine knowledge at all attainable?" As formulated, the problem appears to be just as factual in character as the question 'Is salt soluble?' But the formulation only conceals the fundamental question; "use of the term "knowledge' here without a definition makes it appear possible to discuss a factual question, whereas this cannot be done until the normative question stated in the first part of this paper is answered. For what can knowledge be but sound belief? And how can a belief be said to be sound except by reference to a set of rules? Max Black has pointed out that a justification of something requires showing it to be consistent with, or deducible from, a standard. And Carnap has argued that a "question of right or wrong must always refer to a system of rules." Just so, the soundness of belief in a statement is a question of conformity with rules for belief. The term 'knowledge', therefore, has no clear meaning until some answer to the fundamental problem of epistemology has been furnished. The question of whether genuine knowledge is possible is not to be discussed until after a set of rules for belief has been provided. And one may doubt that anything worth talking about in this connection will remain after such a set of rules has been provided.

A second problem is that of determining the limits of knowledge. Again, this appears to be a factual question; again, the question has the misleading appearance of being factual only so long as the term 'knowledge' is not recognized as involving a reference to normative principles; again, the question presupposes an answer to the central problem of epistemology; and again, once the central problem is solved nothing of importance remains to be discussed in connection with the limits of knowledge. For providing a set of rules for belief is also determining what the limits of knowledge are.

The third problem mentioned by Professor Wood is that of "*the origin of knowledge. By what faculty or faculties of mind is knowledge attainable?*" One can repeat here the objection to the occurrence of the unanalyzed term 'knowledge'; one can also object to the notion of faculties; but the most important reason for rejecting this question is that discussions of it always or almost always turn out to be inept psychology, or distressing confusions of psychological issues with other questions. My complaint is, of course, an old one; to cite one example, 1937 is the date of the English translation of Carnap's *Logical Syntax of Language*, in which epistemology is criticized as an "inextricable tangle of problems," in which psychological and logical problems are confused. Even when the question being discussed is rather clearly one in psychology—such as Russell's discussion of the origin of the idea corresponding to expressions of negation—all we have is incompetent psychology. The elimination of confusions of philosophical with psychological issues, and the avoidance of unsound work in psychology under the guise of philosophy are two of the purposes of th: foregoing normative, metalinguistic formulation of the central problem of epistemology. The question of the origin of knowledge is best regarded as not epistemological at all.

A fourth problem of epistemology is the methodological problem. Though this is not clear, the question presumably has to do with the procedures which *should* be used in the acquisition and elaboration of knowledge. If this *is* the question, it would seem that the principal purpose to be served by advocating deductive, inductive, or other methods is in connection with the problem of the degrees of belief to be accorded to statements arrived at deductively, inductively, or otherwise. Thus, what we have called the central problem of epistemology is comprehensive enough to include the methodological problem, insofar as this problem goes beyond semiotic.

Professor Wood lists as a fifth question that of the *a priori*. "The problem," he says, "is that of isolating the *a priori* or non-empirical elements in knowledge and accounting for them in terms of human reason." Here again, the term 'knowledge' needs definition, and psychological issues should be avoided. But more important is the need to clarify the term '*a priori*'; is this to be taken as a normative or descriptive expression? Are the assertions that there are or are not synthetic *a priori* statements to be regarded as the matters of fact that they appear to be? Defining '*a priori*' as 'that which can be known by reason alone' (*Webster's International*) or "knowledge independent of experience" (Hofstadter's "Basic Philosophy Data Guide") makes use of expressions which, as we have previously seen, conceal the normative problem, and the normative character of the term '*a priori*' is thereby also concealed. A less misleading formulation of the problem of the synthetic *a priori* is: 'Should any synthetic statements be believed regardless of empirical evidence or its absence?' More generally, if the term '*a priori*' is used as a normative expression, the problem of the *a priori* becomes a part of our central problem. An answer to the fundamental problem of epistemology will be, at the same time, an answer to the problem of the *a priori*.

The sixth of Professor Wood's questions in epistemology need not detain us long. This is the "problem of differentiating *the principal kinds of knowledge*." From what has been said previously, it seems clear that, when clarified, this problem becomes part of that proposed in the first part of this paper.

The seventh type of inquiry has to do with "*the structure of the knowledge-situation.* . . . [It attempts] to determine . . . the constitutents of the knowledge situation in their relation to one another." The relations among the elements of perception and the relations of the subjective and objective components of the knowledge situation are examples of these inquiries. It is preferable, however, to reject this problem as having no place in epistemology. One readily understands why philosophers have discussed them, but the discussions are either psychological or metaphysical. If psychological, our earlier comments apply; if metaphysical, we should discard them from epistemology, for establishing our criteria for sound statements should precede our assertions of any clear literal statements that there may be in metaphysics.

Professor Wood says, "*The problem of truth* is perhaps the culmination of epistemological inquiry—in any case it is the problem which brings the inquiry to the threshold of metaphysics." It may have brought many philosophers there, but fortunately we may back off without entering. It is, of course, a commonplace that many different questions have become entangled in discussions of truth, and that the first project in unraveling the issues is the problem of defining the predicate 'is true.' Beyond this the intelligible question is: 'What ought to be believed?', or, more precisely, the central problem of epistemology.

Thus, taking the question formulated in the first part of this paper as the central problem to which epistemologists should direct their attention helps to clarify some traditional issues, and assists in separating epistemological inquiries from those in other fields such as psychology and ontology.

Now let us consider an objection to the view we have been urging. We have steadily insisted on the normative character of epistemology, but there are, of course, many who reject any discussion of normative questions. The verifiability theory of meaning, or, as it is more modestly named by its ablest advocates, the empiricist criterion of meaning, condemns as meaningless any answer to our problem. The logical empiricist will graciously allow that rules for belief may be "rich" in their "non-cognitive import by virtue of their emotive appeal or the moral inspiration they offer." The epistemologist in our sense, then, speaks poetry without realizing it or else he is a preacher without a pulpit.

This is not the place to express one's sympathy with the purposes which it was hoped the empiricist criterion of meaning would serve, nor to analyze the proposal at length. It is sufficient here to note that this criterion either does or does not define the term 'meaningful' or the term 'cognitively meaningful'. If the criterion defines one of these expressions, then it is trivial. If it does not, then it is not clear. For surely if there is one thing that *is* clear, after all the recent discussions of meaning and meaningfulness, it is that these conceptions are not clear, except where some special usage is explicitly indicated. If, then, the criterion is analytic, it is trivial; if it is synthetic, it is obscure.

But, whether the criterion is acceptable or not, it has probably been the center of so much controversy because discussions advocating the criterion have maintained that normative principles are not verifiable and have strongly suggested that they should be discarded as nonsense. We admit, without arguing for these views, that normative principles are different from statements, that only statements can be confirmed, and that no normative principle is either true or false. But from none of these admissions does it follow that discussions in which rules or normative principles are affirmed should be abandoned. Indeed, if they should be, then we cannot say so.

The methods of confirmation and of choice among alternative hypotheses used by scientists or proposed by philosophers of science are, most likely, not to be carried over without modification as a methodology for normative principles. But surely reasons can be given for advocating one set of epistemological rules rather than some alternative. The patterns of inference involved may need further study, but the unsuitability of scientific method should not lead to the conclusion that no method will be suitable.

In conclusion I restate my proposal for the central problem of epistemology: 'What degrees of belief should an individual accord to statements of various kinds?' I have suggested that work in the field will be improved if philosophers concentrate on this question. I also believe that this is one of the great problems which confront all reflective human beings; just as a review of his beliefs led Descartes to doubt and to a need for normative principles governing belief, so a similar review can lead others to a similar need. Perhaps a concentration on their problem will lead to an increased interest in philosophy on the part of educated laymen.

Chapter Eight

THE PROBLEM OF LANGUAGE, MEANING, AND REALITY

THE IMPORTANT ROLE OF LANGUAGE

Language plays an enormous role in the lives of human beings. Indeed, some would say that we would not be human without it. The ability to conceptualize and to obtain and transmit knowledge sets man off from other animals, and this would not be possible without language. But inherent in the tools and abilities that make us human are pitfalls and dangers that can make us fools. One of these pitfalls is the tendency to objectify or personify words or abstractions. Some philosophers, in fact, believe that the source of all philosophical puzzles or problems is this tendency to be misled by language, to let the "surface grammar" of language mislead us into thinking that concepts or words, which in fact refer to psychological states or perform some other function, designate entities or properties in the world. We saw in Chapter Two that Feuerbach holds that the concept "God" is simply a human "projection" on the universe. In Chapter Three we saw that some philosophers argue that the moral concepts "good," "right," and, we might add, "justice" designate not objective standards or values but merely individual or cultural preferences or, perhaps, only the feelings of the person using the concept. In Chapter Four we saw that political philosophers radically disagree on the meaning of terms, such as natural rights, inalienable rights, and political freedom. We saw the radical disagreement over the meaning of freedom, choice, and responsibility in Chapter Five. The concepts of mind, body, soul, and person were seen in Chapter Six to be just as problematic, as were the concepts of truth and knowledge in Chapter Seven.

In all these cases the problem was: What is the meaning or proper analysis of a given word or concept? We have seen that it is no easy matter to answer this question. We have also seen that a great deal hangs on whatever answer or analysis is accepted, for man's theoretical and practical life is in part determined by the answer implicitly or explicitly accepted. Huxley (in this chapter) cites the example of the famous scientist Clerk Maxwell as one who is led into a scientific absurdity (the denial that any process can modify the internal structure of individual atoms) in part by objectifying and personalizing the concepts "science" and "nature." Other examples of the practical import of the acceptance or rejection of some given analysis of the meaning of terms were cited in the chapters on the existence of God, on moral norms, and on political norms. Huxley stresses the negative practical effect of linguistic error even further in claiming that "most of the crimes and lunacies committed in the name of religion, in the name of patriotism, in the name of political and economic ideologies" are, in large part, the result of objectifying psychological states and projecting them into the external world.

THREE THEORIES OF LANGUAGE AND MEANING

How do we discover the meaning of a word or concept? How can we avoid being misled by language? These questions (along with the intrinsic interest of the question) have led philosophers to ask for "the meaning of meaning" and to attempt to formulate a general account of what it means for words to have meaning. Various theories have been formulated, but it is not possible to go into all of them here. However, several of the principal theories are represented in this chapter: (1) that of John Locke, the seventeenth-century British philosopher, (2) that of the logical positivist (summarized and evaluated by B. L. Clarke), and (3) that of the informal language analyst, sometimes called the "ordinary-use" approach (represented in the selection by Gilbert Ryle).

(1) Locke devotes Book III of his *Essay Concerning Human Understanding* (1690) to the problem of language and meaning. He argues that the meaning of a word is the idea(s) that the word stands for. Ideas are the private possessions of each person, and hence the meanings of words vary somewhat from one person to the next. Locke's theory accounts well for the variability in the meaning of words, although it is questionable whether or not it accounts for the identity of the meaning of words among users of a language. How can we communicate if words mean or designate the private ideas of individuals? Other problems in Locke's account are his lack of clarity about the meaning of the term "idea" and the fact that he leaves out of account many words that seem not to refer to ideas at all. Still, his theory is important as an early philosophical treatment of language and meaning. John Stuart Mill (*System of Logic*, 1843) accepts much of Locke's position but goes well beyond it. Mill's theory is discussed by Ryle in this chapter.

(2) The principal components of the logical positivist's position are the verifiability criterion of meaning and the classification of all cognitive state-

ments into the analytic or synthetic mold. These components were discussed in Chapter Seven in connection with the theory of knowledge, and we saw the results of the application of positivism to moral and religious discourse in Chapters Two and Three. However, a detailed account of the positivistic theory of meaning and its historical origin and evolution was not presented. B. L. Clarke presents one in this chapter. Clarke also gives an account of the very ambitious project of the logical positivists, that of attempting to bring all of the empirical sciences into a unified science, an overall scientific description of the world, and indicates the reasons for the failure of this project. An adequate philosophical account of meaning, he argues, must include a tripartite division and treatment of the rules of descriptive language —those of syntax, semantics, and pragmatics. Contemporary philosophers who fall into the general tradition of positivism recognize this. (A fine statement of these distinctions is found in Charles Morris, *Signs, Language, and Behavior*, 1946.) Rules of syntax are those which govern the relationships between the symbols themselves without any reference to the symbol user or to what the symbols stand for. These rules specify how sentences should be properly formed and the logical rules of inference. Semantical rules, on the other hand, specify the relationships between symbols and their referents and include the rules for determining the truth or falsity of sentences. Pragmatic rules specify the relationships between the symbols and the symbol users. Recognition of these different kinds of symbol relationships and their rules is of immense value in the analysis of meaning. In fact, Clarke shows how these distinctions may be instrumental in resolving philosophical disputes of long standing, in particular those between empiricists and rationalists.

Logical positivism, he concludes, attempted to fuse some of the components of traditional empiricism and some of traditional rationalism. It failed, but it demonstrated that neither position by itself is tenable. Clarke suggests the reasons why this is so and concludes that ironically logical positivism, which originated as an effort to eliminate metaphysics as nonsense, has really brought philosophy back to the metaphysical task and has provided some invaluable tools for getting on with that task.

(3) The answer of the informal-language, or ordinary-use, theorist to the problem of language and meaning is based in part on a rejection both of the Locke-Mill type of position (in which the meaning of a word is the object it stands for and the meaning of a sentence is that set of things which the words in the sentence stand for) and of the positivist's position (in which the cognitive meaning of all sentences was identified with their method of verification or their tautological status). Meaning is not mere naming. Most words are not nouns. There are many other parts of speech and language uses other than naming. The positivist's classification of all cognitive meaning as analytic or empirically verifiable statements is seen as both problematic (the analytic-synthetic distinction itself is questioned) and philosophically inadequate (it too glibly rules out the rationality of all normative discourse).

The father of the informal-use approach was Ludwig Wittgenstein who in his *Philosophical Investigations* reversed the position held earlier in his *Tractatus*, in which he was entrenched in the denotationist (meaning is the object denoted by a word) and positivist camp. His famous statement "Don't ask for the meaning, ask for the use" stimulated a position in which meaning is identified with use, in which the multiple uses and functions ("language games") of language are stressed, and in which various language uses are not ruled out as senseless simply because they do not fit some preconceived model for meaning. To know the meaning of an expression requires knowing the uses to which it can be put or the rules of its use. Gilbert Ryle, whose essay in this chapter represents this tradition, concludes that "the notion of denotation, so far from providing the final explanation of the notion of meaning, turns out itself to be just one special branch or twig on the tree of signification."

LANGUAGE AND REALITY

The informal-language analysts properly emphasize that language is a multifaceted instrument that is constantly changing. (This emphasis is not new. Socrates and Bacon, for example, pointed to the same facts about language.) But, for the most part, they do not adequately stress an important issue emphasized by some linguists (Benjamin Whorf,[1] for example) and philosophers, namely, the effect of the vocabulary and syntax of various languages in channeling human thought by classifying and conceptualizing experience in certain ways. It goes without saying that this is a two-way street: we change our language as a result of experience. But we do frequently overlook the tremendous role that the acceptance and use of a given language have on our views of the world, in spite of the fact that linguists and philosophers have frequently pointed to the impact of syntax and vocabularly on philosophical world views such as aristotelianism, in which the substance-attribute syntax played a central role in the organization of experience and in the formulation of a logic and a metaphysic. Friedrich Waismann (in this chapter) does not seem to go too far in saying that "a whole world picture is wedded to the use of the transitive verb and the actor-action scheme that goes with it—that if we spoke a different language we would perceive a different world." There is, for example, considerable evidence that Greenlanders see the world in a quite different way than do we who use the English language.

What is the philosophical import of these views? There are several. One is that the philosophers who appeal to the ordinary use of language as a standard for resolving philosophical controversies may be offering us a limited tool or method. Natural languages vary greatly from one culture to another. If the appeal to ordinary use amounts to the appeal to the use of certain concepts within a conventional language in a given culture, it surely will not take us very far in the resolution of philosophical problems. Quite the con-

[1] See *Language, Thought, and Reality* (Cambridge, Mass.: M.I.T. Press, 1962).

trary, it commits us to a very narrow horizon—indeed, to a kind of cultural relativism (or perhaps game theory) in philosophy.

One does get the impression from certain contemporary linguistic philosophers that they are unaware that natural languages vary greatly and are in a constant state of flux and change. To the extent that these philosophers insist on conformity to ordinary use in the narrow sense, it may well lead to quelling independent inquiry and originality, and to what Waismann calls a "sort of philistinism which insists on the observance of the cliché," the result being a "harakiri of living thoughts." As noted, similar difficulties confront philosophers who insist upon a language in which there is a one-to-one correspondence between word and referent. This theory imposes unnecessary strictures on human thought and communication and renders certain types of human communication impossible. There is an important sense in which language must be flexible and adaptable to new situations if it is to cope with human experience and with life. There is, in fact, a frequent need to break the bond of conventional usage in order to characterize a new experience, a new theory, or a new way of seeing things. Waismann may well be correct in his claim that if Einstein "had been brought up as a pupil of G. E. Moore, imbued with a belief in the infallibility of the ordinary modes of expression, he could never have made his discovery, clogged as he would have been by the dead weight of usage."[2]

However, ordinary-use philosophers do not always, and certainly need not, restrict themselves to the study of one language and to the logical functions of certain concepts within a given language. Moreover, they do distinguish between use and usage, that is, between the logical function of concepts and their dictionary and philological function. It may well be the case, and in fact there is evidence to this effect, that certain concepts such as "good" in English, *bon* in French, or *gut* in German, fulfill roughly the same logical functions in these different languages and that, to this extent, the functions are international phenomena, not simply reflections of the peculiar syntax and vocabulary of a conventional language. Furthermore, awareness of the functions of concepts of this type can be extremely valuable in the resolution of philosophical problems and complexities. It may well be the case, then, that the methods of some ordinary-language philosophers have suffered from excessive provincialism in the past, but this is not a built-in obstacle to a linguistic approach to philosophical problems.

Linguistic philosophy need not be either provincial or confining. Nor need it bemoan the fact that language is flexible and that certain conventional uses are frequently violated in the effort to conceptualize anew. It can welcome new conceptual uses of terms, but always with the assumption that we must examine the functions of the uses and of the more conventional uses of concepts with a view toward avoiding confusion and discovering the categorical features of reality implicitly presupposed in such uses. Linguistic

[2] Moore in his essay "A Defense of Common Sense," in J. H. Muirhead, (ed.) *Contemporary British Philosophy*, 2d ser. (London: The Macmillan Co., 1925) and his book *Some Main Problems of Philosophy* (London: George Allen & Unwin, Ltd., 1953), is often interpreted as holding that the appeal to the correct use of ordinary language is all that is required to resolve philosophical problems.

philosophers who are aware of both the existence and the need for flexibility and the creative use of language are also aware not only of the fact that the surface grammar of language can lead one into certain philosophical puzzles but also of the fact that the uncritical use of the vocabulary and syntax of a given language can unwittingly impose upon one's thought, to some extent at least, certain categories or interpretations of the world. They consequently insist that philosophy must be distrustful of language or at least extremely observant of the conventional forms, vocabulary, and syntax of language.

A second important philosophical issue raised by the fact that the syntax and vocabulary of various natural languages imposes on human thought different forms or ways of perceiving the world is this: Which conceptual scheme or set of categories is correct or the most adequate? What constitutes a test of adequacy? If Everett Hall is correct, we are to some extent in a "categoriocentric predicament," for we cannot talk about the world without already imposing some conceptual scheme upon it[3] (as Kant also argued). A straightforward correspondence test is not possible. Hubert Alexander argues similarly, stressing that there is no way of totally stepping outside our cultural shoes and conceptual schemes and comparing them with an unstructured or unconceptualized reality.[4] True, some conceptual schemes, especially those in the realm of mechanical technology, have paid off better than others. For this reason, Alexander argues, the scientific method and the conceptual schemes employed with it are preferable. But no one culture or language or set of categories encapsulates reality or has a monopoly on truth about reality. In fact, he argues, science—its method and categories—has a "limited scope of application" (a point made in another way in the selection by H. J. Paton).

Does this mean that there can be no test of adequacy, that we cannot change or improve our conceptual scheme at all? No. If Quine is correct "it is meaningless . . . to inquire into the absolute correctness of a conceptual scheme as a mirror of reality. Our standard for achieving basic changes of conceptual scheme must be, not a realistic standard of correspondence to reality, but a pragmatic standard." Correspondence as a test is out, Quine argues, but "we can change it bit by bit, plank by plank, though meanwhile there is nothing to carry us along but the evolving conceptual scheme itself. The philosopher's task was well compared by Neurath to that of a mariner who must rebuild his ship on the open sea."[5] A negative test is offered by Alexander, who says that we should avoid conceptual schemes which defeat "ordinary thought and normal human understanding." Hall appeals to the "grammar of common sense united with the structure of our national experience" as a test, although he admits that neither the grammar nor the structure speak with one voice and are "not certainly true." Whatever the problems with these appeals, and they are certainly vague, these thinkers try to avoid

---

[3] *Philosophical Systems, A Categorical Analysis* (Chicago: University of Chicago Press, 1960).
[4] "Communication, Technology and Culture," in *The Philosophy Forum*, vol. 7 (1968); and *Language and Thinking* (Princeton, N.J.: Princeton University Press, 1967).
[5] W. V. O. Quine, "Identity, Ostension, and Hypothesis," *From a Logical Point of View* (New York: Harper and Row, 1963), p. 79.

both linguistic provincialism and circularity. Hall obviously thinks that Gilbert Ryle too easily accuses other philosophers of "category-mistakes,"[6] noting that Ryle "fails to see that such mistakes are mistakes only to or for one in a certain categorical framework. . . ."[7]

SCIENCE, RELIGION, AND REALITY

The preceding remarks lead one quite naturally to a consideration of the comparative adequacy of the language and concepts of science and the language and concepts of religion, an issue that was to some extent treated in Chapter Two. If science and religion are seen as competing explanations of man and the world, then there is a necessary conflict between these two points of view, for they frequently say quite different things. H. J. Paton (in this chapter) argues that *properly seen* these two points of view do *not* compete and do not conflict. The intellectual climate of our contemporary world, he suggests, is not favorable to religion. This is partly the result of the extension of scientific knowledge and the accompanying assumption that science alone can provide knowledge. Paton denies this assumption. To be sure, religious believers are themselves at fault in not acknowledging and accepting the conclusions of science. They are often excessively dogmatic and inflexible in both belief and practice. They themselves frequently view religion as competing with science in explaining the world and as providing a kind of superscientific knowledge. In all this, Paton argues, they are wrong. But such faults do not disprove the value and import of religion.

If Paton is correct, both the scientific and religious points of view, taken as separate and exclusive perspectives, are inadequate. The language and concepts of science explain much, but science is still a limited and partial point of view. It can provide no practical guide to life; and with its insistence that all knowledge must be objective and intersubjectively testable, it arbitrarily rules out the possibility of suprasensible reality and knowledge of "reality as it is in itself." Paton recognizes the obscurities and difficulties of this type of knowledge. But he insists that just as the religious believer "should live in the open-air world of science with all its chill, and not in the opium den of religious hallucination," so also the scientist should recognize the partial and limited perspective of science. Religion gives meaning and significance to man's life, and science alone cannot do this.

Kurt Baier (in this chapter) disagrees sharply with Paton. Not only are the religious (Christian) explanations of the universe and the facts in it false or absurd (Paton himself accepts this to some extent) but religion is unnecessary; for science is in principle capable of providing complete explanations of every entity and occurrence in the universe. It can do this without robbing our lives of meaning and significance. In fact, the (frequent) Christian evaluation of earthly life as worthless; its insistence that without an afterlife, life is meaningless; its picturing of man as a divine artifact or robot; its

---

[6] See Ryle's *The Concept of Mind* (London: Hutchinson & Co. (Publishers), Ltd., 1949), p. 28, for his use of the notion of a category mistake. In this volume, see Chapter Six.

[7] Hall, *op. cit.*, p. 28.

emphasis upon original sin, the total depravity of man, and the wrath of God at Judgment Day—all of these, Baier insists, are negative contributions to the meaning and significance of man's life.

The main thrust of Baier's argument, however, is not so much that the language and concepts of science are all that we need and that religion therefore is unnecessary but that the argument of the religious believer that life has no meaning unless one accepts the religious (Christian) explanation of man and the world is not only false but is based on a *conceptual* confusion. The conceptual confusion is clarified, he contends, by distinguishing between (1) the meaning or purpose *of* life and (2) the meaning and purpose *in* life. Acceptance of the scientific world picture entails a denial of 1, that all of life has a single purpose or meaning in which God, the Creator, "erects the stage and writes, in outline, the plot." But such acceptance in no way entails the denial of 2, that the lives of human beings have meaning, purpose, and significance. In fact, there is almost an infinite number of ways in which our lives can have meaning and significance in sense 2. Rejection of meaning in sense 1 does not entail rejection of meaning in sense 2; those who think it does are guilty of conceptual confusion.

Baier's essay is an example of the application of conceptual analysis to what many take to be the central problem of philosophy. It is appropriate that this volume, which began with a consideration of the question "What is the meaning of life?" (see the selection by Rogers in Chapter One) ends with a treatment of this question. In fact, all the essays in this chapter have important things to say about the issue discussed in Chapter One—the nature and objectives of philosophy.

SELECTED BIBLIOGRAPHY

Alston, William P. *The Philosophy of Language.* Englewood Cliffs, N.J., 1964.

Austin, J. L. *How to Do Things With Words.* London, 1962.

Ayer, A. J. (ed.). *Logical Positivism.* New York, 1959.

Blanshard, Brand. *Reason and Analysis.* La Salle, Ill., 1962.

————. *The Nature of Thought.* New York, 1940.

Caton, Charles E. (ed.). *Philosophy and Ordinary Language.* Urbana, Ill., 1963.

Chappell, V. C. (ed.). *Ordinary Language.* Englewood Cliffs, N.J., 1964.

Chomsky, Noam. *Syntactic Structures.* The Hague, 1957.

Feigl, Herbert, and Sellars, Wilfred (eds.). *Readings in Philosophical Analysis.* New York, 1949. Parts 1 and 2.

Fodor, J. A., and Katz, J. J. *The Structure of Language.* Englewood Cliffs, N.J., 1965.

Henle, Paul (ed.). *Language, Thought and Culture.* Ann Arbor, 1958.

Lewis, C. I. *Analysis of Knowledge and Valuation.* La Salle, Ill., 1946. Chapters 3, 4, and 6.

Lewis, H. D. (ed.). *Clarity is Not Enough: Essays in Criticism of Linguistic Philosophy.* New York, 1963.

Linsky, L. (ed). *Semantics and the Philosophy of Language.* Urbana, Ill., 1952.

Ogden, C. K., and Richards, I. A. *The Meaning of Meaning.* New York, 1938.

Quine, W. V. *Word and Object.* New York, 1960.

Roty, Richard (ed.). *The Linguistic Turn.* Chicago, 1967.

Russell, Bertrand. *The Problems of Philosophy.* London, 1912. Chapter 12.

Skinner, B. F. *Verbal Behavior.* New York, 1957.

Tarski, S. "The Semantic Conception of Truth," *Philosophy and Phenomenological Research*, vol. 4, (1944).

Urmson, J. O. *Philosophical Analysis: Its Development Between the Two World Wars.* Oxford, 1956.

Waismann, F. *The Principles of Linguistic Philosophy.* London, 1965.

Wittgenstein, Ludwig. *Philosophical Investigations.* Translated by G. E. M. Anscombe. New York, 1953.

————. *The Blue and Brown Books.* Oxford, 1958. Pages 1 to 44.

————. *Tractatus Logico-Philosophicus.* Translated by D. F. Pears and B. F. McGuinness. London, 1961.

Ziff, Paul. *Semantic Analysis.* Ithaca, N.Y., 1960.

67 Words and Their Meanings[*]

ALDOUS HUXLEY

Aldous Huxley (1894–) is a well-known author and essayist. A prolific writer, he is perhaps best known for his novels Point Counterpoint and Brave New World.

Words and their meanings—this is the subject I have chosen. Some of you, no doubt, will wonder at my choice; for the subject will strike you as odd and unimportant, even rather silly. This is quite understandable. For a long time past, thinking men have tended to adopt a somewhat patronizing attitude towards the words they use in communicating with their fellows and formulating their own ideas. "What do you read, my lord?" Polonius asked. And with all the method that was in his madness Hamlet scornfully replied, "Words, words, words." That was at the beginning of the seventeenth century; and from that day to this the people who think themselves realists have gone on talking about words in the same contemptuous strain.

There was a reason for this behaviour—or at least an excuse. Before the development of experimental science, words were too often regarded as having magical significance and power. With the rise of science a reaction set in, and for the last three centuries words have been unduly neglected as things having only the slightest importance. A great deal of attention has been paid, it is true, to the technical languages in which men of science do their specialized thinking, particularly, of course, to mathematics. But the colloquial usages of everyday speech, the literary and philosophical dialects in which men do their thinking about the problems of morals, politics, religion and psychology—these have been strangely neglected. We talk about 'mere matters of words' in a tone which implies that we regard words as things beneath the notice of a serious-minded person.

This is a most unfortunate attitude. For the fact is that words play an enormous part in our lives and are therefore deserving of the closest study. The old idea that words possess magical powers is false; but its falsity is the distortion of a very important truth. Words *do* have a magical effect—but not in the way that the magicians supposed, and not on the objects they were trying to influence. Words are magical in the way they affect the minds of those who use them. "A mere matter of words," we say contemptuously,

* From Aldous Huxley, *Words and Their Meanings* (Los Angeles, Ward Richie Press, 1940). Reprinted by permission of the publishers.

forgetting that words have power to mould men's thinking, to canalize their feeling, to direct their willing and acting. Conduct and character are largely determined by the nature of the words we currently use to discuss ourselves and the world around us. The magician is a man who observes that words have an almost miraculous effect on human behaviour and who thinks that they must therefore be able to exercise an equal power over inanimate nature. This tendency to objectify psychological states and to project them, thus objectified, into the external world is deeply rooted in the human mind. Men have made this mistake in the past, men are making it now; and the results are invariably deplorable. We owe to it not only the tragic fooleries of black magic, but also (and this is even more disastrous) most of the crimes and lunacies committed in the name of religion, in the name of patriotism, in the name of political and economic ideologies. In the age-long process by which men have consistently stultified all their finest aspirations, words have played a major part. It was, I believe, the realization of this fact that prompted the founders of the two great world religions to insist upon the importance of words. In the Christian gospels the reference to this matter is contained in one of those brief and enigmatic sayings which, like so many of the *logia*, unfortunately lend themselves to a great variety of interpretations. "But I say unto you, that every idle word that men shall speak, they shall give account thereof in the day of judgment. For by thy words thou shalt be justified, and by thy words thou shalt be condemned." It is possible to interpret this utterance in terms of a merely magical theory of the significance of language. It is equally possible to put another construction on the saying and to suppose that what Jesus was referring to was what may be called the psychological magic of words, their power to affect the thinking, feeling and behaviour of those who use them. That it was the intention of the Buddha to warn men against such psychological magic the surviving documents leave us in no doubt whatever. 'Right speech' is one of the branches of the Buddhist's Eightfold Path; and the importance of restraint in the use of words for intellectual purposes is constantly stressed in all those passages in the Pali Scriptures, where Gotama warns his followers against entangling themselves in the chains of metaphysical argument.

It is time now to consider a little more closely the mechanism by which words are able to exercise their psychological magic upon the minds of men and women. Human beings are the inhabitants, not of one universe, but of many universes. They are able to move at will from the world, say, of atomic physics to the world of art, from the universe of discourse called 'chemistry' to the universe of discourse called 'ethics'. Between these various universes philosophy and science have not as yet succeeded in constructing any bridges. How, for example, is an electron, or a chemical molecule, or even a living cell related to the G Minor quintet of Mozart or the mystical theology of St. John of the Cross? Frankly, we don't know. We have no idea how thought and feeling are related to physical events in a living brain and only the very vaguest notions about the way in which a brain is related to the charges of electrical energy which appear to be its ultimate components. So far as we are concerned, the only connection between these various universes consists in the fact that we are able to talk about all of them and in some of them to have direct intuitions and sensuous experiences. The various universes we inhabit all belong to *us*; that is the only thing that unites them. Logical and scientific bridges are non-existent; when we want to pass from one to another, we have to jump.

Now, all these various universes in which we live are members of one or other of two super-universes; the universe of direct experience and the universe of words. When I look at this paper in my hand I have a direct sensuous experience. If I choose to, I can keep my mouth shut and say nothing about this experience. Alternatively, I may open my mouth and, making use of a certain system of signs, called the English language, I may impart the information that my experience consisted of whiteness mitigated by rows of black marks which I recognize as belonging to the alphabetical system by means of which spoken language can be rendered in terms of a visible equivalent.

To discuss the formal mechanism by which the world of immediate human experience is related to the various languages of mankind is a task which, even if I had the time, I should be quite incompetent to perform. And fortunately it is not necessary for our present purposes that it should be performed. It is enough, in this context, to point out that, between the world of immediate experience and the world of language, between things and words, between events and speech, certain relations have in fact been established; and that these relations are governed by rules that are in part purely arbitrary, in part dictated by the nature of our common experiences. The form of the rules varies from language to language. We are not, however, concerned with these variations. For our present purposes, the significant fact is that all human societies use some kind of language and have done so from the remotest antiquity.

Human behaviour as we know it, became possible only with the establishment of relatively stable systems of relationships between things and events on the one hand and words on the other. In societies where no such relationship has been established, that is to say, where there is no language, behaviour is nonhuman. Necessarily so; for language makes it possible for men to build up the social heritage of accumulated skill, knowledge and wisdom, thanks to which it is possible for us to profit by the experiences of past generations, as though they were our own. There may be geniuses among the gorillas; but since gorillas have no conceptual language, the thoughts and achievements of these geniuses cannot be recorded and so are lost to simian posterity. In those limited fields of activity where some form of progress is possible, words permit of progress being made.

Nor is this all. The existence of language permits human beings to behave with a degree of purposefulness, perseverance and consistency unknown among the other mammals and comparable only to the purpose-fulness, perseverance and consistency of insects acting under the compulsive force of instinct. Every instant in the life, say, of a cat or a monkey tends to be irrelevant to every other instant. Such creatures are the victims of their moods. Each impulse as it makes itself felt carries the animal away completely. Thus, the urge to fight will suddenly be interrupted by the urge to eat; the all-absorbing passion of love will be displaced in the twinkling of an eye by a no less absorbing passion to search for fleas. The consistency of human behaviour, such as it is, is due entirely to the fact that men have formulated their desires, and subsequently rationalized them, in terms of words. The verbal formulation of a desire will cause a man to go on pressing forward towards his goal, even when the desire itself lies dormant. Similarly, the rationalization of his desire in terms of some theological or philosophical system will convince him that he does well to persevere in this way. It is thanks to words and to words alone that, as the poet says:

> Tasks in hours of insight willed
> May be in hours of gloom fulfilled.

And let us remember incidentally that by no means all of our tasks are willed in hours of insight. Some are willed in hours of imbecility, some in hours of calculating self-interest, some under the stress of violent emotion, some in mere stupidity and intellectual confusion. If it were not for the descriptive and justificatory words with which we bind our days together, we should live like the animals in a series of discrete and separate spurts of impulse. From the psychological point of view, a theology or a philosophy may be defined as a device for permitting men to perform in cold blood and continuously actions which, otherwise, they could accomplish only by fits and starts and when the impulse was strong and hot within them. It is worth remarking, in this context, that no animals ever make war. They get into individual squabbles over food and sex; but they do not organize themselves in bands for the purpose of exterminating members of their own species in the name of some sacred cause. The emphasis here must be placed on the word 'name.' For, of course, animals have no lack of sacred causes. What could be more sacred to a tiger than fresh meat or tigresses? What is lacking in the animal's world is the verbal machinery for describing and justifying these sacred causes. Without words, perseverance and consistency of behaviour are, as we have seen, impossible. And without perseverance in slaughter and consistency in hatred there can be no war.

For evil, then, as well as for good, words make us the human beings we actually are. Deprived of language we should be as dogs or monkeys. Possessing language, we are men and women able to persevere in crime no less than in heroic virtue, capable of intellectual achievements beyond the scope of any animal, but at the same time capable of systematic silliness and stupidity such as no dumb beast could ever dream of.

It is time now that I gave a few typical instances of the way in which words have power to modify men's thought, feeling and conduct. But before doing so, I must make a few more remarks of a general nature. For our present purposes, words may be divided into three main classes. The first class consists of words which designate definite and easily recognizable objects or qualities. Table, for example, is an easily recognizable object and brown an easily recognizable quality. Such words are unambiguous. No serious doubts as to their meaning exist. The second class contains words which designate entities and qualities less definite and less easily recognizable. Some of these are highly abstract words, generalizing certain features of many highly complex situations. Such words as 'justice,' 'science,' 'society,' are examples. In the same class we must place the numerous words which designate psychological states—words such as 'beauty,' 'goodness,' 'spirit,' 'personality.' I have already mentioned the apparently irresistible human tendency to objectify psychological states and project them, on the wings of their verbal vehicle, into the outer world. Words like those I have just mentioned are typical vehicles of objectification. They are the cause of endless intellectual confusion, endless emotional distress, endless misdirections of voluntary effort.

Our third class contains words which are supposed to refer to objects in the outer world or to psychological states, but which in fact, since observation fails to reveal the existence of such objects or states, refer only to figments of the imagination. Examples of such words are the 'dragon' of the Chinese and the 'death instinct' of Freudian psychologists.

The most effective, the most psychologically magical words are found in the second category. This is only to be expected. Words of the second class are more ambiguous than any others and can therefore be used in an almost indefinite number of contexts. A recent American study has shown that the word 'nature' has been used by the philosophers of the West in no less than thirty-nine distinct senses. The same philosopher will give it, all unconsciously of course, three or four different meanings in as many paragraphs. Given such ambiguity, any thesis can be defended, any course of action morally justified, by an appeal to nature.

Ambiguity is not the only characteristic which makes these words peculiarly effective in determining conduct. Those which stand for generalizations and those which designate psychological states lend themselves, as we have already seen, to objectification. They take verbal wings and fly from the realm of abstraction into the realm of the concrete, from the realm of psychology into the external universe.

The objectification and even the personification of abstractions is something with which every political speech and newspaper article has made us familiar. Nations are spoken of as though they were persons having thoughts, feelings, a will and even a sex, which, for some curious reason, is always female. This female, personal nation produces certain psychological effects on those who hear it (or rather her) being talked about—effects incomparably more violent than those that would be produced if politicians were to speak about nations as what in fact they are: organized communities inhabiting a certain geographical area and possessing the means to wage war. This last point is crucially important. California is an organized community; but since it does not possess an army and navy, it cannot qualify for a place in the League of Nations.

Another familiar entity in political speeches is the pseudo-person called 'Society.' Society has a will, thoughts and feelings, but, unlike the Nation, no sex. The most cursory observation suffices to show that there is no such thing as Society with a large S. There are only very large numbers of individual societies, organized in different ways for different purposes. The issue is greatly complicated by the fact that the people who talk about this nonexistent Society with a big S, tend to do so in terms of biological analogies which are, in many cases, wholly inapplicable. For example, the so-called philosophical historians insist on talking of a society as though it were an organism. In some aspects, perhaps, a society does resemble an organism. In others, however, it certainly does not. Organisms grow old and die and their component cells break down into inanimate substances. This does not happen to a society, though many historians and publicists loosely talk as though it did. The individuals who compose what is called a decadent or collapsed society do not break down into carbon and water. They remain alive; but the cells of a dead organism are dead and have ceased to be cells and become something else. If we want to talk about the decline and fall of societies in terms of scientific analogies, we had better choose our analogy from physics rather than biology. A given quantity of water, for example, will show least energy, more energy, most energy according to its temperature. It has most energy in the form of super-heated steam, least in the form of ice. Similarly, a given society will exhibit much energy or little energy according to the way in which its individual members live their lives. The society of Roman Italy, for example, did not die; it passed from a high state of energy to a lower state of energy. It is for historians to determine the physiological, psychological, economic and religious conditions accompanying respectively a high and a low degree of social energy.

The tendency to objectify and personify abstractions is found not only among politicians and newspaper men, but also among those who belong to the, intellectually speaking, more respectable classes of the community. By way of example, I shall quote a paragraph from the address delivered by Clerk Maxwell to the British Association in 1873. Clerk Maxwell was one of the most brilliantly original workers in the whole history of physics. He was also what many scientists, alas, are not—a highly cultivated man capable of using his intelligence in fields outside his particular specialty. Here is what he could say before a learned society, when at the height of his powers.

"No theory of evolution," he wrote, "can be formed to account for the similarity of molecules." (Throughout this passage, Maxwell is using the

word 'molecule' in the sense in which we should now use the word 'atom'.)
"For evolution necessarily implies continuous change, and the molecule is
incapable of growth or decay, of generation or destruction. None of the
processes of Nature, from the time when Nature began, have produced the
slightest difference in the properties of any molecule. We are therefore
unable to ascribe either the existence of the molecules or the identity of
their properties to any of the causes which we call natural. Thus we have
been led along a strictly scientific path very near to the point at which
Science must stop. . . . In tracing back the history of matter Science is
arrested when she assures herself, on the one hand that the molecule has
been made and, on the other, that it has not been made by any of the
processes which we call natural."

The most interesting point that emerges from these lines is the fact
that, like the Nation, but unlike Society, Science has a sex and is a female.
Having recorded this item in our text books of natural history, we can go on
to study the way in which even a mind of the calibre of Clerk Maxwell's can
be led into absurdity by neglecting to analyze the words which it uses to
express itself. The word 'science' is current in our everyday vocabulary. It
can be spelt with a capital S. Therefore it can be thought of as a person; for
the names of persons are always spelt with capital letters. A person who is
called Science must, *ex hypothesi*, be infallible. This being so, she can
pronounce without risk of contradiction, that "none of the processes of
Nature, since the time when Nature bagan," (Nature is also spelt with a capital letter and is of course also a female) "have produced the slightest difference in the properties of any molecule." Twenty-three years after the date of
Maxwell's speech, Becquerel observed the radioactivity of uranium. Two
years after that Mme. Curie discovered radium. At the turn of the new
century Rutherford and Soddy demonstrated the fact that the radium atom
was in a process of rapid disintegration and was itself derived from uranium
whose atoms were disintegrating at a much slower rate.

This cautionary story shows how fatally easy it is for even the greatest
men of science to take the particular ignorance of their own time and place,
and raise it to the level of a universal truth of nature. Such errors are
particularly easy when words are used in the entirely illegitimate way in
which Maxwell employed the word 'Science.' What Maxwell should have said
was something like this, "Most Western scientists in the year 1873 believe
that no process has ever modified the internal structure of individual atoms.
If this is so (and of course the beliefs of 1873 may have to be modified at
any moment in the light of new discoveries), then perhaps it may be
legitimate to draw certain inferences of a theological nature regarding the
creation of matter."

How was it possible, we may ask ourselves, that a man of Clerk Maxwell's
prodigious intellectual powers, should have committed a blunder so mon-
strously ridiculous, so obvious, when attention is called to it, to people of

even the most ordinary mental capacities? The question demands a double answer—the first on the purely intellectual level, the second in terms of feeling and will. Let us deal with these in order. Maxwell made his mistake, first of all, out of a genuine intellectual confusion. He had accepted the English language without question or analysis, as a fish accepts the water it lives in. This may seem curious in the light of the fact that he had certainly not accepted the technical language of mathematics without question or analysis. We must remember, however, that non-technical language is picked up in infancy, by imitation, by trial and error, much as the arts of walking and rudimentary cleanliness are acquired. Technical languages are learned at a later period in life, are applied only in special situations where analysis is regarded as creditable and the ordinary habits of daily living are in abeyance. Children and young people must be deliberately taught to analyze the non-technical language of daily life. With very few exceptions, they will never undertake the task of their own initiative. In this respect, Maxwell was not exceptional. He turned his intensely original and powerful mind on to the problems of physics and mathematics, but never on those of everyday, untechnical language. This he took as he found it. And as he found in it such words as 'Science' with a capital S and a female sex, he made use of them. The results, as we have seen, were disastrous.

The second reason for Maxwell's error was evidently of an emotional and voluntary nature. He had been piously brought up in the Protestant tradition. He was also, as the few letters to his wife which have been printed seem to indicate, a practising mystic. In announcing that 'Science' with the capital S and the female sex had proved that atoms had not evolved, but had been created and kept unchangingly themselves by non-natural forces, he had a specifically religious purpose in view. He wanted to show that the existence of a demiurge after the pattern of Jehovah, could be demonstrated scientifically. And he wanted also, I suspect, to prove to himself that the psychological states into which he entered during his moments of mystical experience could be objectified and personified in the form of the Hebraic deity, in whose existence he had been taught to believe during childhood.

This brings us to the threshold of a subject, profoundly interesting indeed, but so vast that I must not even attempt to discuss it here; the subject of God and of the relations subsisting between that word and the external world of things and events, between that word and the inner world of psychological states. Shelley has sketched the nature of the problem in a few memorable sentences. "The thoughts which the word, 'God,' suggests to the human mind are suceptible of as many varieties as human minds themselves. The Stoic, the Platonist and the Epicurean, the Polytheist, the Dualist and the Trinitarian, differ infinitely in their conceptions of its meaning. . . . And not only has every sect distinct conceptions of the application of this name, but scarcely two individuals of the same sect, who exercise in any degree the freedom of their judgment, or yield themselves with any candour of feeling to the influencings of the visible world, find perfect coincidence of opinion to exist between them." Such, I repeat, is the problem. No complete solution of it is possible. But it can at least be very considerably clarified by anyone who is prepared to approach it armed with equipment suitable to deal with it. What is the nature of this suitable equipment? I would assign the first place to an adequate vocabulary. Students of religion have need of a language sufficiently copious and sufficiently analytical to make it possible for them to distinguish between the various types of religious experience, to recognize the difference between things and words, and to realize when they are objectifying psychological states and projecting them into the outside world. Lacking such a language they will find that even a wide knowledge in the fields of theology, of comparative religion and of human behavior will be of little use to them. It will be of little use for the simple reason that such knowledge has been recorded, up to the present time, in words that lend themselves to the maximum amount of intellectual confusion and the minimum of clarity and distinctness.

Words and their meanings—the subject is an enormous one. "Had we but world enough and time" as the poet says, we could continue our discussion of it almost indefinitely. But unfortunately, or perhaps fortunately, world and time are lacking, and I must draw to a close. I have been able in this place to let fall only a few casual and unsystematic remarks about those particular aspects of the science of signs which Charles Morris has called the semantic and pragmatic dimensions of general semiosis. I hope, however, that I have said enough to arouse an interest in the subject, to evoke in your minds a sense of its profound importance and a realization of the need to incorporate it systematically into the educational curriculum.

Any education that aims at completeness must be at once theoretical and practical, intellectual and moral. Education in the proper use of words is complete in the sense that it is not merely intellectual and theoretical. Those who teach, teach not only the science of signs, but also a universally useful art and a most important moral discipline. The proper use of language is an important moral discipline, for the good reason that, in this field as in all others, most mistakes have a voluntary origin. We commit intellectual blunders because it suits our interests to do so, or because our blunders are of such a nature that we get pleasure or excitement from committing them. I have pointed out that one of the reasons for Maxwell's really monstrous misuse of language must be sought in that great man's desire to reconcile his scientific ideas with the habits of religious belief he had contracted in childhood. There was a genuine confusion of thought; but a not entirely creditable wish was very definitely the father of this confusion. And the same is true, of course, about those who for propagandist purposes, personify such abstractions as 'Society' or 'the Nation.' A wish is father to their mistaken thought—the wish to influence their hearers to act in the way they would like them to act. Similarly, a wish is the father of the mistaken thought of those who allow themselves to be influenced by such preposterous abuses of language—the wish to be excited, to 'get a kick,' as the phrase goes. Objectified in the form of a person, the idea of a nation can arouse much stronger feelings than it can evoke when it is spoken of in more sober and accurate language. The poor fools who, as we like to think, are helplessly led astray by such machiavellian demogogues as Hitler and Mussolini are led astray because they get a lot of emotional fun out of being bamboozled in this way. We shall find, upon analysis, that very many of the intellectual errors committed by us in our use of words have a similar emotional or voluntary origin. To learn to use words correctly is to learn, among other things, the art of foregoing immediate excitements and immediate personal triumphs. Much self control and great disinterestedness are needed by those who would realize the ideal of never misusing language. Moreover, a man who habitually speaks and writes correctly is one who has cured himself, not merely of conscious and deliberate lying, but also (and the task is much more difficult and at least as important) of unconscious mendacity.

When Gotama insisted on Right Speech, when Jesus stressed the significance of every idle word, they were not lecturing on the theory of semiosis; they were inculcating the practice of the highest virtues. Words and the meanings of words are not matters merely for the academic amusement of linguists and logisticians, or for the aesthetic delight of poets; they are matters of the profoundest ethical significance to every human being.

68 Of the Signification of Words*

JOHN LOCKE

John Locke (1632–1706) authored his *Treatises on Government* in 1685 and had a tremendous influence on the founding fathers of the American Republic. His *Essay Concerning Human Understanding* (1690) has had great impact in epistemology and philosophy of language.

1. Man, though he have great variety of thoughts, and such from which others as well as himself might receive profit and delight; yet they are all within his own breast, invisible and hidden from others, nor can of themselves be made to appear. The comfort and advantage of society not being to be had without communication of thoughts, it was necessary that man should find out some external sensible signs, whereof those invisible ideas, which his thoughts are made up of, might be made known to others. For this purpose nothing was so fit, either for plenty or quickness, as those articulate sounds, which with so much ease and variety he found himself able to make. Thus we may conceive how *words*, which were by nature so well adapted to that purpose, came to be made use of by men as the signs of their ideas; not by any natural connexion that there is between particular articulate sounds and certain ideas, for then there would be but one language amongst all men; but by a voluntary imposition, whereby such a word is made arbitrarily the mark of such an idea. The use, then, of words, is to be sensible marks of ideas; and the ideas they stand for are their proper and immediate signification.

2. The use men have of these marks being either to record their own thoughts, for the assistance of their own memory; or, as it were, to bring out their ideas, and lay them before the view of others: words, in their primary or immediate signification, stand for nothing but *the ideas in the mind of him that uses them,* how imperfectly soever or carelessly those ideas are collected from the things which they are supposed to represent. When a man speaks to another, it is that he may be understood: and the end of speech is, that those sounds, as marks, may make known his ideas to the hearer. That then which words are the marks of are the ideas of the speaker:

---

* From John Locke *An Essay Concerning Human Understanding*, first published in 1690, Book III, Chapter 2.

nor can any one apply them as marks, immediately, to anything else but the ideas that he himself hath: for this would be to make them signs of his own conceptions, and yet apply them to other ideas; which would be to make them signs and not signs of his ideas at the same time; and so in effect to have no signification at all. Words being voluntary signs, they cannot be voluntary signs imposed by him on things he knows not. That would be to make them signs of nothing, sounds without signification. A man cannot make his words the signs either of qualities in things, or of conceptions in the mind of another, whereof he has none in his own. Till he has some ideas of his own, he cannot suppose them to correspond with the conceptions of another man; nor can he use any signs for them: for thus they would be the signs of he knows not what, which is in truth to be the signs of nothing. But when he represents to himself other men's ideas by some of his own, if he consent to give them the same names that other men do, it is still to his own ideas; to ideas that he has, and not to ideas that he has not.

3. This is so necessary in the use of language, that in this respect the knowing and the ignorant, the learned and the unlearned, use the words they speak (with any meaning) all alike. They, in every man's mouth, stand for the ideas he has, and which he would express by them. A child having taken notice of nothing in the metal he hears called *gold*, but the bright shining yellow colour, he applies the word gold only to his own idea of that colour, and nothing else; and therefore calls the same colour in a peacock's tail gold. Another that hath better observed, adds to shining yellow great weight: and then the sound gold, when he uses it, stands for a complex idea of a shining yellow and a very weighty substance. Another adds to those qualities fusibility: and then the word gold signifies to him a body, bright, yellow, fusible, and very heavy. Another adds malleability. Each of these uses equally the word gold, when they have occasion to express the idea which they have applied it to: but it is evident that each can apply it only to his own idea; nor can he make it stand as a sign of such a complex idea as he has not.

4. But though words, as they are used by men, can properly and immediately signify nothing but the ideas that are in the mind of the speaker; yet they in their thoughts give them a secret reference to two other things.

First, *They suppose their words to be marks of the ideas in the minds also of other men, with whom they communicate*: for else they should talk in vain, and could not be understood, if the sounds they applied to one idea were such as by the hearer were applied to another, which is to speak two languages. But in this men stand not usually to examine, whether the idea they, and those they discourse with have in their minds be the same: but think it enough that they use the word, as they imagine, in the common acceptation of that language; in which they suppose that the idea they make it a sign of is precisely the same to which the understanding men of that country apply that name.

5. Secondly, Because men would not be thought to talk barely of their

own imagination, but of things as really they are; therefore they often suppose the *words to stand also for the reality of things*. But this relating more particularly to substances and their names, as perhaps the former does to simple ideas and modes, we shall speak of these two different ways of applying words more at large, when we come to treat of the names of mixed modes and substances in particular: though give me leave here to say, that it is a perverting the use of words, and brings unavoidable obscurity and confusion into their signification, whenever we make them stand for anything but those ideas we have in our own minds.

6. Concerning words, also, it is further to be considered:

First, That they being immediately the signs of men's ideas, and by that means the instruments whereby men communicate their conceptions, and express to one another those thoughts and imaginations they have within their own breasts; there comes, by constant use, to be such a connexion between certain sounds and the ideas they stand for, that the names heard, almost as readily excite certain ideas as if the objects themselves, which are apt to produce them, did actually affect the senses. Which is manifestly so in all obvious sensible qualities, and in all substances that frequently and familiarly occur to us.

7. Secondly, That though the proper and immediate signification of words are ideas in the mind of the speaker, yet, because by familiar use from our cradles, we come to learn certain articulate sounds very perfectly, and have them readily on our tongues, and always at hand in our memories, but yet are not always careful to examine or settle their significations perfectly; it often happens that men, even when they would apply themselves to an attentive consideration, do set their thoughts more on words than things. Nay, because words are many of them learned before the ideas are known for which they stand: therefore some, not only children but men, speak several words no otherwise than parrots do, only because they have learned them, and have been accustomed to those sounds. But so far as words are of use and signification, so far is there a constant connexion between the sound and the idea, and a designation that the one stands for the other; without which application of them, they are nothing but so much insignificant noise.

8. Words, by long and familiar use, as has been said, come to excite in men certain ideas so constantly and readily, that they are apt to suppose a natural connexion between them. But that they signify only men's peculiar ideas, and that *by a perfect arbitrary imposition*, is evident, in that they often fail to excite in others (even that use the same language) the same ideas we take them to be signs of: and every man has so inviolable a liberty to make words stand for what ideas he pleases, that no one hath the power to make others have the same ideas in their minds that he has, when they use the same words that he does. And therefore the great Augustus himself, in the possession of that power which ruled the world, acknowledged he could not make a new Latin word: which was as much as to say, that he could not

arbitrarily appoint what idea any sound should be a sign of, in the mouths and common language of his subjects. It is true, common use, by a tacit consent, appropriates certain sounds to certain ideas in all languages, which so far limits the signification of that sound, that unless a man applies it to the same idea, he does not speak properly: and let me add, that unless a man's words excite the same ideas in the hearer which he makes them stand for in speaking, he does not speak intelligibly. But whatever be the consequence of any man's using of words differently, either from their general meaning, or the particular sense of the person to whom he addresses them; this is certain, their signification, in his use of them, is limited to his ideas, and they can be signs of nothing else.

69 The Contribution of Logical Positivism*

BOWMAN L. CLARKE

Bowman L. Clarke (1927–) is professor of philosophy at the University of Georgia. He is the author of a number of articles in the area of philosophy of religion and of *Language and Natural Theology*.

Toward the latter part of 1930, a new journal appeared on the philosophical scene. The introductory article was entitled: "The Turning Point in Philosophy". The turning point, according to the author, was to be the end of centuries of what he called "the fruitless conflict" of philosophic systems. He was quite optimistic: "We are already at the present", he wrote, "in possession óf methods which make every such conflict in principle unnecessary."[1] What was to bring about this turning point? It was the realization that philosophy was not a system of cognitions, but "a system of acts". Philosophy was to be viewed as an activity, a method of logical analysis, through which the meaning of statements was revealed or determined. To quote the article: "By means of philosophy statements are explained, by means of science they are verified". Science "is concerned with the truth of statements"; philosophy "with what they actually mean."[2] The article closes with this prediction:

> Certainly there will still be many a rear-guard action. Certainly many will for centuries continue to wander further along the traditional paths. Philosophical writers will long continue to discuss the old pseudo-questions. But in the end they will no longer be listened to; they will come to resemble actors who continue to play for some time before noticing that the audience has slowly departed.[3]

The name of the new journal was *Erkenntnis*; the author of the article was Moritz Schlick; and this was the official introduction of logical positivism to the philosophic world.

---

* From Bowman L. Clarke, *Methodos*, vol. 15 (1963). Reprinted with permission of the author and *Methodos*.
[1] Reprinted in *Logical Positivism*, ed. A. J. Ayer (Glencoe, Illinois, Free Press, 1959), p. 54.
[2] *Ibid.*, p. 56.
[3] *Ibid.*, p. 59.

The nucleus from which logical positivism, or logical empiricism developed was the well-known Vienna Circle. This Circle evolved in 1923 out of a seminar led by Schlick at the University of Vienna. It quickly grew to include many of the most brilliant minds in Vienna, representing a variety of disciplines, physics, psychology, sociology, history, mathematics, and philosophy. The most decisive period, according to Herbert Feigl, one of the original members of the seminar, came in 1926 when Rudolph Carnap joined the faculty in Vienna and the Circle began a study of Ludwig Wittgenstein's *Tractatus Logico-Philosophicus*. The influence of these two men was formative. Under their influence the thinking of the group became crystallized, and by 1929 they were able to issue a joint manifesto entitled, "A Scientific World View: The Vienna Circle". Joergensen summarizes the basic aim, as set forth in the manifesto, in this way: "To further and propagate a scientific world view" by

> . . . the use of the logical method of analysis, worked out by Peano, Frege, Whitehead and Russell, which serves to eliminate metaphysical problems and assertions as meaningless as well as to clarify the meanings of concepts and sentences of empirical science by showing their immediately observable content.[4]

This particular quote is significant for it gives, in a summary fashion, three of the tenets which are most commonly used to characterize logical positivism: a scientific world view through the unification of the empirical sciences, the elimination of traditional metaphysics, and a theory of meaning based on observation, or what has more commonly been formulated as the verifiability criterion of meaning. In fact the general reading public is prone to identify logical positivism with the verifiability criterion of *Language, Truth and Logic*. What has been even more unfortunate is the popular identification of the verifiability criterion, and consequently logical positivism, with Ayer's emotive theory of ethical statements, the position that moral judgments are "pure expressions of feeling" and cannot be said to be either true or false.[5] As a result, logical positivism has often been condemned, like Socrates, as a corrupter of the morals of the youth.

The more scientifically minded, however, have naturally been attracted to logical positivism's attempt to unify the various empirical sciences into an overall scientific description of the world. Consequently, they have viewed logical positivism primarily as philosophy's long-over-due attempt to come of age and to develop a truly scientific philosophy. It is seen as the triumph of Auguste Comte. On the other hand, those who see something in the scientific method which they would consider as alien to man's true nature, tend to view such a scientific world view as demonic, as destructive of that which is truly human in man. The logical positivist, consequently, is characterized as

---

4 "The Development of Logical Positivism," *International Encyclopedia of Unified Science*, Vol. II (Chicago, University of Chicago Press, 1951), p. 4.
5 *Language, Truth and Logic* (New York, Dover Publications, n.d.), p. 108.

a successor of Thomas Gradgrind in Dickens' *Hard Times*: "A man of facts and calculations . . . With a rule and a pair of scales, and the multiplication table always in his pocket, . . . ready to weigh and measure any parcel of human nature, and tell you exactly what it comes to."[6]

And then there have been those who, for one reason or another, have always been suspicious of the value of the traditional metaphysical speculations of philosophy. These, consequently, have been tempted to view logical positivism primarily as an attempt to eliminate metaphysics and to find in the movement a way to rid philosophy of this dreaded disease. On the other hand, those who feel at home in the speculations of traditional philosophy are most likely to characterize the movement as subversive and to view it as a traitor within the very ranks of philosophy itself.

But whatever a person's reaction to these three tenets may be, either pro or con, if he uses them to characterize logical positivism and evaluates the movement in terms of them, the score will not look good. For on all three accounts the movement could easily be judged as something of a failure. The attempt to formulate a criterion of meaning solely in terms of verifiability has been altered, revised, or outright rejected, by nearly every member of the Circle. Likewise, the original project for the unification of all the sciences now appears to have been a far too ambitious, if not impossible, task. For example, the *Journal of Unified Science* was discontinued shortly after it was begun, and the present *International Encyclopedia of Unified Science* seems to bear little resemblance to the original vision of the Vienna Circle. As for the elimination of metaphysics, by 1954 one of the original members of the group had published a book entitled, of all things, *The Metaphysics of Logical Positivism*,[7] in which he argued that logical positivism does not eliminate traditional metaphysics, rather it is a means of clarifying the disputes and aids in their solution. And when Carnap's article, "The Elimination of Metaphysics," originally published in 1932, was republished in 1957, he felt compelled to add the following footnote on his use of the term "metaphysics" in that article. He writes: "This term used in this paper . . . includes systems like those of Fichte, Schelling, Hegel, Bergson, Heidegger. But it does not include endeavours toward a synthesis and generalization of the results of the various sciences".[8]

What then are we to say of logical positivism's contribution to philosophy? I do not think that the genius of logical positivism lies in these three tenets which are so commonly used to characterize the movement. Rather I think it is to be found in what Schlick referred to in his introductory article as the insight that philosophy was not a system of cognitions, but a system of acts and what the manifesto called the "logical method of analysis, worked out by Peano, Frege, Whitehead and Russell". The verifiability

[6] (New York, The New American Library of World Literature, 1961), p. 12.
[7] Gustav Bergmann, *The Metaphysics of Logical Positivism* (New York, Longmans, Green, 1954).
[8] Reprinted in *Logical Positivism*, ed. A. J. Ayer, p. 80.

criterion of meaning, the idea of a scientific world view, and the distaste for metaphysics are all rooted in the old positivism of Comte and in traditional empiricism. But the genius of logical positivism was an attempt to wed these old ideas to a new conception of philosophy and a new method of logical analysis. This wedding is exemplified in the very names logical positivism and logical empiricism. But these new ideas have different roots. According to Schlick, "Leibniz saw their beginning, Bertrand Russell and Gottlob Frege opened up important stretches . . ., but Ludwig Wittgenstein is his *Tractatus* is the first to have pushed forward to the decisive turning point".[9]

In order to clarify this new conception of philosophy and its logical method of analysis, first, I want to examine Wittgenstein's *Tractatus* in order to determine the kind of analysis which he is doing. Secondly, I want to trace the development of some of these ideas in the work of Rudolph Carnap, and then I hope to be able to show the applicability of these ideas to some traditional philosophical problems.

It is generally agreed that the *Tractatus* is anything but easy to read. It is an unusual combination of logical precision and ineffable mysticism, of clear insight and inexcuseable ambiguity. Here, however, we shall not be concerned with the details of the book, only with the main outline and the type of investigation which Wittgenstein is inaugurating. This, I think, is relatively clear. The work consists of seven cryptic aphorisms with a series of equally cryptic comments, all arranged and numbered in an elaborate system. The seven aphorisms are:

(1) The world is everything that is the case.
(2) What is the case, the fact, is the existence of atomic facts.
(3) The logical picture of the fact is the thought.
(4) The thought is the significant proposition.
(5) Propositions are truth-functions of elementary propositions.
(6) The general form of truth-function is: $(p. Z, N(Z))$. This is the general form of proposition.
(7) Whereof one cannot speak, thereof one must be silent.[10]

I want to raise the question: What is the problem with which Wittgenstein is concerned in these seven aphorisms? The order of the seven aphorisms gives the impression that he is beginning with the ontological question, What is there? But this is not the case; his starting point is not a directly intuited ontology, but a theory of meaning. As Russell puts it, he is attempting to answer the question, "What relation must one fact (such as a sentence) have to another to be capable of being a symbol for that other?".[11] In other words, Wittgenstein is attempting to answer the question: What is the logical structure of descriptive language? Or, in more modern terms: What

[9] *Ibid.*, p. 54.
[10] All quotes from the *Tractatus Logico-Philosophicus* are from the G. K. Ogden edition (London, Routledge and Kegan Paul, Ltd., 1955).
[11] *Ibid.*, p. 8.

are the rules which govern the descriptive use of language? With all due respect to Wittgenstein's elaborately worked out order, the problem can, I think, be seen more clearly if we take the aphorisms in their reverse order.

Aphorism 7 is stated more fully in the "Preface": "Its whole meaning," he writes of the book, "can be summed up somewhat as follows: What can be said at all can be said clearly; and whereof one cannot speak, thereof he must be silent."[12] The other six aphorisms and their comments are designed to show what is involved in speaking clearly, that is, in making clear and precise true and false assertions about the world. Since it is by means of propositions that we make true and false assertions, it is the structure of propositions and their relation to the world that Wittgenstein proposes to analyze. And in order to understand what is involved in Wittgenstein's analysis, I think Schlick is quite right, we must go back to Leibniz to see "the beginning."

In the seventeenth century Leibniz conceived of a technique which he called the Combinatorial Art and which he hoped would reform all science. It consisted of a universal scientific language and a calculus of reasoning for the manipulation of the language. This conception of a universal language was based on the belief that all scientific predicates could be analyzed into a few primitive undefined predicates in terms of which all the other more complex conceptions of science could be defined. The calculus of reasoning, which was to be the structure of the language, consisted in the formulation of the rules of logic in a mathematical calculus. The purpose of this project was to provide a common language for all the sciences and to facilitate the process of logical deduction by substituting symbols for the words of ordinary language. This was to be the solution for all philosophical problems and an end to all disputes. With the gentility of a seventeenth century gentleman, Leibniz explains: "If controversies were to arise, there would be no more need of disputation between two philosophers than between two accountants. For it would suffice to take their pens in their hands, to sit down to their desks, and to say to each other, 'Let us calculate'."[13] Leibniz conceived of this idea when he was only twenty and although he spent the rest of his life trying to work it out, he had very little success.

It was, in fact, two centuries later that George Boole, an English mathematician, became the first to successfully reduce a part of logic to a complete and workable calculus. This work, along with the logical studies of Peirce and Schroeder, the axiomatic studies of arithmetic by Peano and the logical analyses of Frege, culminated in 1910–1913 in the publication by A. N. Whitehead and Bertrand Russell of the three volume classic in symbolic logic, *Principia Mathematica*. Thus a calculus of reasoning, which Leibniz

---

[12] *Ibid.*, p. 27.
[13] Quoted in Bertrand Russell, *Mysticism and Logic* (Garden City, Doubleday and Co., Inc., 1957), p. 75.

had envisioned two hundred and fifty years earlier, became an accomplished fact. *Principia Mathematica* did not give Leibniz his primitive predicates in terms of which all the concepts of science could be defined, but it did give the logical structure of the propositions of any scientific theory plus the primitive concepts in terms of which virtually all the concepts of classical mathematics could be defined.

Although Wittgenstein rejected the development of mathematics in *Principia Mathematica*, it is the logical structure and the analysis of propositions developed there which lie behind Aphorisms 5 and 6 in the *Tractatus*. He took over from *Principia Mathematica* the division of propositions into atomic and molecular, and the thesis that molecular propositions are constructed from atomic propositions by the application of truth functional connectives. In 1913 H. M. Sheffer discovered that all the connectives could be defined in terms of only one connective, 'not both p and 'q' where 'p' and 'q' here stand for any propositions. It is this connective which Wittgenstein used to characterize what he calls the general truth function in Aphorism 6. All possible combinations of true and false propositions could be gotten by the successive application of this general truth function to atomic propositions, including, Wittgenstein maintained, universal and existential propositions. Thus this general truth function is the general form of propositions, or the logical structure of propositions. And since the truth or falsity of all molecular propositions is determined by the truth or falsity of the atomic components, we have Aphorism 5: "The proposition is a truth function of elementary (or atomic) propositions".

Aphorisms 3 and 4 concern the relationship between propositions and what the propositions are about. The significant proposition, that is, the meaningful proposition is a thought, and a thought is a logical picture of a fact. But in order for the proposition to be a logical picture of a fact, it must have something in common with that fact. What the picture must have in common with that which it pictures is the logical form of representation. A photograph, for example, is a picture of a landscape because it has in common with the landscape a certain structure. A map is a picture of a particular area by virtue of having a structure in common with the area; it preserves, for example, the relationship between nations, mountains, rivers, seas, etc. Likewise, if we are to make true and false statements about the world, language must have in common with the world its logical structure; that is, the logical structure of propositions. To quote Wittgenstein: "To give the essence of propositions means to give the essence of all description, therefore the essence of the world." (5.4711)

Since a proposition pictures a fact, an elementary, or atomic proposition, pictures an atomic fact. And since all other propositions are but possible combinations of atomic facts, all possible facts are but combinations of atomic facts. Consequently, we have aphorisms 1 and 2. The world is everything that is the case, and what is the case is the existence of atomic facts. The world, then, is that which is pictured by all true atomic propositions.

In analyzing the structure of propositions, Wittgenstein found that a certain set of propositions will always be false regardless of the truth or falsity of the atomic propositions which compose it. For example, "socrates is mortal and it is not the case that Socrates is mortal," is false regardless of the atomic facts. These he called contradictions and they picture no logically possible fact. Then there are those propositions which could be either true or false depending upon the truth or falsity of the components. These propositions are empirical propositions and picture logically possible facts and form the domain of the empirical sciences. It is the task of science, not philosophy, to determine their truth or falsity. But there is a third set of propositions: those propositions which are always true regardless of the truth or falsity of their atomic components. Take, for example, the proposition "Socrates is mortal or it is not the case that Socrates is mortal." This proposition is true independently of the atomic facts; it is logically true. Such propositions Wittgenstein labeled tautologies. Since they are true independently of the atomic facts, they assert nothing about the state of atomic facts, and consequently, concludes Wittgenstein, they say nothing whatsoever about the world; that is, the world defined as atomic facts.

Although logically true propositions *say* nothing about the world, they do *show* something. They show the logical structure of the world. He writes: "The logical propositions describe the scaffolding of the world, or rather they present it." (6.124) But this logical structure itself cannot be talked about. "Propositions can represent the whole of reality, but they cannot represent what they must have in common with reality . . . the logical form". (4.12) The reason for this is obvious. Propositions, as Wittgenstein has defined them, are things which are either true or false. A statement, however, which tells you about the structure of true and false propositions cannot be either true or false, for such statements would themselves presuppose that very structure. Consequently, we use the structure of propositions to assert things about the world, but we cannot assert anything about the structure itself. This structure, according to Wittgenstein, is "the inexpressible. This shows itself; it is the mystical." (6.522)

Such a position raises two obvious questions: First, if the task of philosophy is to analyze the structure of propositions and, yet, one cannot assert anything about the structure of propositions, where does that leave philosophy? "The object of philosophy," writes Wittgenstein, "is the logical clarification of thought. Philosophy is not a theory but an activity . . . The result of philosophy is not a number of "philosophical propositions," but to make propositions clear." (4.112) The second obvious question which comes to mind is this: Is it not strange that Wittgenstein writes a book in which he certainly appears to talk about propositions and yet maintains that one cannot talk about propositions? Here again he has an answer. He simply says that his book is senseless. He concludes the *Tractatus* with this comment:

My propositions are elucidatory in this way: he who understands me finally recognizes them as senseless, when he has climbed out through them, on them, over them. (He must so to speak throw away the ladder, after he has climbed up on it.)

He must surmount these propositions; then he sees the world rightly. (6.54)

Whereof one cannot speak, thereof one must be silent.

This strange and mystical paradox inspired Julian Bell to write a poem on Wittgenstein in which he complains:

> he talks nonsense, numberous statements makes,
> Forever his own vow of silence breaks.
>
> . . . .
>
> A mystic in the end, confessed and plain,
> The ancient enemy returned again.[14]

The members of the Vienna Circle, it appears, were not any happier with Wittgenstein's resort to nonsense and his mystical turn at the end of the *Tractatus* than was Julian Bell. Carnap's development of Wittgenstein's conception of logical analysis can, I think, be viewed partially as an attempt to get around this problem. His first step was to take seriously a thesis advanced in the *Tractatus*, the thesis that all logically true propositions could be recognized by the form of the proposition alone. For example, Wittgenstein writes: "It is the characteristic mark of logical propositions that one can perceive in the symbol alone that they are true; and this fact contains in itself the whole philosophy of logic." (6.113) Thus, it seems that the rules of logic could be formulated without any reference whatsoever to what the symbols stand for. This, however, would mean that all the statements which refer to the relationship between statements and the world must be translated into rules which refer only to the symbols themselves. If this could be done, then the statements which Wittgenstein makes about this relationship could be eliminated, and with them a large part of the so-called "nonsense" of the *Tractatus*. This would mean that logic would be strictly formal, or as Alexander Maslow characterizes it: "Logic deals with rules and not with the reality to which the symbols may happen to refer."[15]

Carnap attempts to do this by translating statements in what he calls the material mode of speech—that is, statements which appear to talk about things—into statements in a formal mode which make no reference "either to the meaning of the symbols (for example, the words) or the sense of the expressions (for example, the sentence), but simply and solely to the kinds and orders of the symbols from which the expressions are constructed."[16]

---

[14] "Epistle on the Subject of the Ethical and Aesthetic Beliefs of Herr Ludwig Wittgenstein" quoted in J. A. Passmore, *A Hundred Years of Philosophy* (London, Duckworth, 1957), p. 384.

[15] *A Study in Wittgenstein's "Tractatus"* (Berkeley, University of California Press, 1961), p. 53.

[16] *The Logical Syntax of Language*, trans. Amethe Smeaton (London, Routledge and Kegan Paul, Ltd., 1949), p. 1.

For example, one of Wittgenstein's comments in the *Tractatus* is: "The world is the totality of facts, not of things." (1.1) When this is translated into the formal mode by Carnap, it becomes "Science is a system of sentences, not of names".[17] Thus all reference to the world, facts, things is eliminated in the formal mode. Another sentence from the *Tractatus*, "If I know an object, then I also know all the possibilities of its occurrence in (atomic) facts" (2.0123) becomes when translated into the formal mode, "if the genus of a symbol is given then all the possibilities of its occurrence in sentences are also given."[18] Even such sentences as "The moon is a thing, five is not a thing, but a number" become when translated " 'Moon' is a thing-word; 'five' is not a thing-word, but a number-word".[19]

The second step toward an elimination of the so-called nonsense of the *Tractatus* was to demonstrate that all the formal rules which governed the symbols of a language could be stated in the language itself. This would amount to a disproof of Wittgenstein's contention that the logical structure of a language could not be expressed in the language itself. Taking advantage of certain metamathematical studies of Hilbert and Goedel, Carnap was able to demonstrate this is his *Logical Syntax of Language*, which he published in 1934. In this way the formal rules of a language become meaningful.

In this work Carnap also repudiated another, at least apparent, thesis of the *Tractatus*, the thesis that there is only one descriptive language. In the *Logical Syntax of Language*, Carnap demonstrated that there are alternate sets of formal rules for descriptive language, consequently, which set one chooses becomes mere convention. There he proposes his "Principle of Tolerance": "Everyone is at liberty to build up his own logic, i.e., his own form of language, as he wishes. All that is required of him is that, if he wishes to discuss it, he must state his methods clearly, and give syntactical rules instead of philosophical arguments".[20]

Thus in the *Logical Syntax of Language*, the senseless statements and the mysticism of the *Tractatus* completely vanish. Philosophy is defined as the study of the formal properties of the languages of the empirical sciences. Logically true statements are true solely on the basis of the arbitrary, or conventional, rules which govern the kind and order of the symbols used in the statements made in the empirical sciences. This position could justifiably be called the classical position of logical positivism on logic and language. It is the work that lies behind, for example, much of Ayer's *Language Truth and Logic*,[21] and the position which is frequently identified with logical positivism.

Only five years later, however, when Carnap published his *Foundations*

---

[17] *Ibid.*, p. 303.
[18] *Ibid.*, p. 303.
[19] *Ibid.*, p. 297.
[20] *Ibid.*, p. 52.
[21] In the "Preface," for example, Ayer in stating his indebtedness to the Vienna Circle, writes, "I owe most to Rudolph Carnap." (p. 32).

of Logic and Mathematics (1939)[22] he had abandoned these three major theses. In all three cases he reverted to a position which is somewhat closer to the *Tractatus*. For he came to see that it was impossible to express all of what he took to be the logical properties of a language in strictly formal rules, ignoring the relationship between the symbols and what the symbols stand for. And largely under the influence of Tarski, Carnap in his later writings has developed a theory of logic which takes the semantic relationship, the relationship between the symbol and what the symbol stands for not only as necessary, but as basic. In his *Introduction to Semantics*, for example, he writes:

> . . . the use of this method for the construction of a theory of truth by Tarski and its use in the present book for the construction of a theory of logical deduction and a theory of interpretation of formal systems seems to justify the expectation that semantics will not only be of accidental help to pure logic but will supply the basis for it.[23]

This apparent reversal by Carnap is significant and the reasons for it are very important. He repudiated the thesis that the logical properties of a language could be fully expressed in formal, or purely syntactical, rules for several reasons. For one thing, Carnap recognized that semantical rules were, in fact, implicit in the logical analysis which he and his contemporaries were doing. "Some essential features," he writes, "in the contemporary work of logicians are guided by instinct and common sense, although they could be guided by explicit rules. These rules, however, would be not syntactical but semantical."[24] When one reads, for example, the attempt in *The Logical Syntax of Language* to construct a purely syntactical set of rules, he cannot help but feeling that it is a *tour de force*. To translate, for example, a statement such as 'The moon is a thing; five is not a thing, but a number' into the statement " 'Moon' is a thing-word; 'five' is not a thing-word, but a number-word", is not to eliminate semantics, it is merely to disguise the relation between the symbol and what it stands for.

Another reason for the rejection of the purely formalistic programs proposed in *The Logical Syntax of Language* is the fact that certain logical problems cannot be treated in a purely syntactical system. In the *Formalization of Logic*, Carnap points to the fact that the question as to whether or not a proposed calculus formalizes a given theory adequately and completely cannot be treated in pure syntax; "it is a matter of the relations between a calculus and an interpreted system, and hence requires semantics in addition to syntax."[25] But an even more important problem, perhaps, is the problem of the distinction between logically true statements, which are dependent

---

[22] In *International Encyclopedia of Unified Science*, Vol. I.
[23] (Cambridge, Harvard University Press, 1942), p. viii.
[24] *Ibid.*, p. xi.
[25] (Cambridge, Harvard University Press, 1943), p. vii.

solely upon the semantical rules for the determination of their truth value, and factually true statements, which in addition, are dependent upon the contingent facts for the determination of their truth value. The distinction here is a distinction which, Carnap writes, "is indispensable for the logical analysis of science."[26]

This rejection of the formalistic thesis forced Carnap to abandon his other two theses. All the rules which Carnap now considered as logical rules could no longer be formulated in the language itself. But this was unimportant since rules are not taken as asserting true and false statements. Likewise he was forced to abandon his thesis that the logical rules of a language were merely arbitrary, or conventional. For when one considers the subject matter of a language, he finds that the logical rules which govern the language can no longer be strictly arbitrary. The subject matter imposes certain restrictions.[27] These developments have subsequently led Carnap to divide the logical analysis of the rules of descriptive language into three different aspects: the rules of syntax, the rules of semantics, and the rules of pragmatics. The most obvious thing about a descriptive language is that it is a group of symbols which stand *for* something *for* somebody. Thus one may study a language purely from the perspective of the rules which govern the relationship between the symbols themselves without any reference to what they stand for or the user of the symbols. These rules are the syntactical rules and they govern the proper formation of sentences and the logical rules of inference. On the other hand, one might study a language from the perspective of the rules which govern the relationships between the symbols and what they stand for. These are the semantical rules and they include rules for the interpretation of the symbols and rules for the determination of the truth or falsity of the sentences, including both logical and factual sentences. Thirdly, one can study a language from the perspective of the rules which govern and express the relationships between the symbols and the users of the symbols. These rules are called pragmatic rules and they govern such relationships as 'believes', 'verifies', or 'knows.' For example, 'I believe the statement, "Socrates is mortal," be true' expresses a relationship between me and the statement 'Socrates is mortal.'

If one maintains that the type of logical analysis which we have traced through Wittgenstein and Carnap is a major contribution to philosophy, then he should be able to show how these distinctions clarify and aid in the solution of some of the traditional problems in philosophy. In order to illustrate how this analysis of descriptive language can be fruitful, let us take an actual seventeenth century dispute between Hobbes and Descartes. In Hobbe's Fourth Objection to Descartes' *Meditations*, he makes the following proposal:

---

[26] *Introduction to Semantics*, p. viii.
[27] See *Foundations of Logic and Mathematics*, pp. 26 ff.

. . . what shall we say, if reasoning chance to be nothing more than the uniting and stringing together of names or designations by word is? It will be a consequence of this that reason gives us no conclusion about the nature of things, but only about the terms that designate them, whether, indeed, or not there is a convention (arbitrarily made about their meanings) according to which we join these names together.[28]

Descartes replies to this by saying,

. . . in reasoning we unite not names but the things signified by the names; and I marvel that the opposite can occur to anyone . . . For, if he admits that words signify anything, why will he not allow our reasonings to refer to this something that is signified, rather than to words alone?[29]

Descartes may have marveled that the opposite could occur to anyone, but it has certainly occurred to many since Descartes. For this is not only a major dispute between Hobbes and Descartes, it is one of the major points which has split philosophy into empiricists and rationalists. And after 300 years of philosophical debate, I know of no one who has phrased this difference as clearly as Descartes and Hobbes. For if Descartes is right, then logically true statements tell us something about the nature of things and we know these statements to be true independently of confirmation by contingent fact. On the other hand, if Hobbes is right, the logically true statements tell us nothing about the nature of things, but merely something about our arbitrary and conventional use of words or symbols. As a result, we must depend upon our observation of contingent facts for the confirmation of any statement concerning the nature of things.

Now how can logical analysis help in clarifying this dispute and propose a method for its solution? If we interpret Hobbes as saying that the rules of logic which govern our descriptive use of language can be formulated without any reference to what the symbols stand for, then the answer of logical analysis is, "try and see if they can". If they can, then perhaps "reasoning is nothing more than the uniting and stringing together of names" and logically true statements assert nothing about "the nature of things". And this is precisely what Carnap attempted to do in the *Logical Syntax of Language* and found to be inadequate. Consequently, it would seem that we are forced to conclude with Descartes that in reasoning we "unite not names but the things signified by the names," and that logically true statements assert something about the nature of things, not symbols.

However, before we let Descartes and traditional rationalism run off with the prize, let us look at another dispute between Hobbes and Descartes. In Objection XIII, Hobbes raises an objection which calls into question Des-

---

[28] *The Complete Works of Descartes*, trans. Elizabeth S. Haldane and G. R. T. Ross (Cambridge, Cambridge University Press, 1955), reprinted in Walter Kaufmann, *Philosophic Classics*, Vol. II (Englewood Cliffs, Prentice-Hall, Inc., 1961), p. 80.
[29] *Ibid.*, p. 81.

cartes' famous method of doubt, and with it his entire rationalistic method. Descartes began the *Meditations* with a process of doubting in order to discover at least one thing that was "certain and indubitable" which was to serve as the foundation of "a firm and abiding superstructure in the sciences".[30] As an analogy, he refers to Archimedes' boast that he could move the entire globe from the place it occupied to another if he had one point which was firm and immovable. This hope seems to be the backbone of the rationalist's method. Guided by the deductive structure of Euclidian geometry, they seek a certain and indubitable point, or axioms, from which to logically deduce necessarily true statements. Hobbes' objection to this is quite simple: the inability to doubt a statement "may be the cause that makes a man obstinately defend or hold some opinion, it is not the cause of his knowing it to be true".[31] Therefore, according to Hobbes, Descartes has no indubitable starting point which is therefore necessarily true, for his inability to doubt has nothing to do with the truth or falsity of any statement.

Now what would our method of logical analysis have to say of this controversy? In the first place it would point out that the relationship of doubting is a pragmatic relationship. Descartes' inability to doubt a statement is a relationship between Descartes and the statement, not between the statement and a state-of-affairs. And we must remember that Descartes has already defined truth semantically. Consequently, neither his doubt nor his certainty has anything to do with the truth or falsity of any statement. In this case Hobbes is right. Descartes' certainty may be "the cause of his obstinately defending or holding some opinion", but it has nothing to do with its truth or falsity. One may ask, what happens, then, to the axioms in a deductive system if they are not self-evident or indubitable starting points? If there is one thing which the contemporary analysis of deductive systems in both logic and mathematics has made clear, it is that axioms have no self-evidently preferable status over the theorems which are deduced from them. In fact, which statements are taken as axioms and which are taken as theorems is purely a practical consideration to aid in the mechanical procedure of deduction. Just as Archimedes could find no firm and immovable point with which to move the entire globe, there is no indubitable, and therefore necessarily true, starting point in any deductive system.

In the beginning of this paper, I maintained that the genius of logical positivism lay in its attempt to wed traditional empiricism and positivism to a conception of logical analysis which was rooted in Leibniz's rationalistic preoccupation with deductive systems. And I would like to propose that the result of this wedding has been a demonstration that neither position, traditional empiricism nor rationalism, is tenable. Traditional empiricism is

---

[30] "Meditation I," *Ibid.*, p. 33.
[31] *Ibid.*, p. 88.

untenable because every descriptive language involves logically true statements which assert something about the nature of things. But traditional
rationalism is, likewise, untenable because there is no privileged and
indubitable starting point from which one can deduce logically true propositions about the nature of things. For logically true propositions depend upon
the syntactical and semantical rules of a language, and these in turn depend
upon the subject matter.

Let me illustrate with Wittgenstein's analogy of a ladder. The syntactical
and semantical rules of a descriptive language, as he suggested, are like a
ladder which one uses in order to see clearly. The logically true statements
of a language are those statements whose truth value can be determined
solely on the basis of the rules themselves. If there are alternate ladders,
then which ladder one uses depends upon what it is one wishes to see, that
is, the subject matter. Not to recognize this is to put oneself in the quandary
of Alice, who when she meets the Cheshire Cat, asks: "Would you tell me,
please, which way I ought to go?". The cat's reply is quite sound: "That
depends a good deal on where you want to get to". So it is with the rules of
a descriptive language; they are neither arbitrary nor conventional, as the
empiricist seems to suggest, nor are they in some sense self-evident and
absolute as the rationalist seems to suggest. Neither of these formulations of
the problem are adequate, rather, as the Cheshire Cat might say, the rules
"depend a good deal on what it is you want to talk about".

Along with this somewhat negative contribution of the method of logical
analysis, there is a more positive one. It is the suggestion that the major aim
of philosophy is the logical analysis of descriptive language used in the
empirical sciences. It is not the aim of such a task to confirm nor to refute,
to add to nor to take from the empirical statements of the sciences; its sole
aim, as Wittgenstein suggested, is to see the world clearly and consistently.
Such an endeavor is not new to philosophy. It bears a distinct resemblance
to what Plato called the dialectic, what Aristotle called the search for the
first principles of the sciences, and what Whitehead has called "the endeavor
to frame a coherent, logical, necessary system of general ideas in terms of
which every element of our experience can be interpreted."[32] For this reason Stuart Hampshire justifiably calls the *Tractatus* an "attempt at a metaphysical system"[33] and places it in the "tradition of philosophical writings
which effectively begins with Aristotle and passes through Aquinas and
others in the Middle Ages, come to life again in Descartes, Spinoza and
Leibniz, suffers an enormous change in Kant, and continues in this century
in the early work of Russell."[34]

After thirty years, when one looks back at the optimism expressed in

[32] *Process and Reality* (New York, The Humanities Press, 1955), p. 4.
[33] "Metaphysical Systems," *The Nature of Metaphysics*, ed. D. F. Pears (London, Macmillan and Co., Ltd., 1957), p. 26.
[34] *Ibid.*, p. 29.

Schlick's introductory article, "The Turning Point in Philosophy", his optimism certainly appears excessive. Philosophic conflict has not vanished. Nevertheless it has been the contribution of logical positivism to recall philosophy to one of its major tasks and to give philosophy more effective tools for accomplishing this task in the twentieth century. The aim and the method of logical analysis which was suggested in the *Tractatus* and formed the inspiration for Vienna Circle and which has been developed by Carnap could result in the determination of those logically true statements which would form the necessary framework for empirical science. This necessary framework would be the metaphysics suggested by Carnap in the footnote to his article entitled "The Elimination of Metaphysics"—that is, a metaphysics based on "a synthesis and generalization of the results of the various sciences". The determination of this necessary framework is a task which was denied by traditional empiricism and distorted in traditional rationalism. It may be the irony of philosophy in the twentieth century that the movement which began as an attempt to eliminate metaphysics has, perhaps, called philosophy back to this traditional task and suggested the tools with which to accomplish it.

70 The Theory of Meaning*

GILBERT RYLE

Gilbert Ryle (1900–   ) is Waynfleet Professor of Metaphysical Philosophy at Oxford University. Known as a leader in the British school of
analytic philosophy, Ryle is best known for his book *The Concept
of Mind*. He succeeded G. E. Moore as editor of the philosophical
journal *Mind*.

We can all use the notion of *meaning*. From the moment we begin to learn
to translate English into French and French into English, we realize that one
expression does or does not mean the same as another. But we use the notion
of meaning even earlier than that. When we read or hear something in our
own language which we do not understand, we wonder what it means and
ask to have its meaning explained to us. The ideas of understanding, misunderstanding and failing to understand what is said already contain the
notion of expressions having and lacking specifiable meanings.

It is, however, one thing to ask, as a child might ask, What, if anything,
is meant by 'vitamin', or 'abracadabra' or '$(a = b)^2 + a^2 + b^2 + 2ab$'?
It is quite another sort of thing to ask What are meanings? It is, in the same
way, one thing to ask, as a child might ask, What can I buy for this shilling?,
and quite another sort of thing to ask What is purchasing-power? or What
are exchange-values?

Now answers to this highly abstract question, What are meanings? have,
in recent decades, bulked large in philosophical and logical discussions.
Preoccupation with the theory of meaning could be described as the occupa-
tional disease of twentieth-century Anglo-Saxon and Austrian philosophy.
We need not worry whether or not it is a disease. But it might be useful to
survey the motives and the major results of this preoccupation.

Incidentally it is worth noticing that many of these issues were explicitly
canvassed—and some of them conclusively settled—in certain of Plato's later
Dialogues, and in the logical and other works of Aristotle. Some of them,
again, were dominant issues in the late Middle Ages and later still with
Hobbes; and some of them, thickly or thinly veiled in the psychological
terminology of 'ideas', stirred uneasily inside British epistemology between

* From *British Philosophy in the Mid-Century*, ed. C. A. Mace (New York: The Macmillan Company, 1957). © George Allen and Unwin, Ltd., London. Reprinted by
permission of the publisher.

Locke and John Stuart Mill. But I shall not, save for one or two back-references, discuss the early history of these issues.

The shopkeeper, the customer, the banker and the merchant are ordinarily under no intellectual pressure to answer or even ask the abstract questions What is purchasing-power? and What are exchange-values? They are interested in the prices of things, but not yet in the abstract question What is the real nature of that which is common to two articles of the same price? Similarly, the child who tries to follow a conversation on an unfamiliar topic, and the translator who tries to render Thucydides into English are interested in what certain expressions mean. But they are not necessarily interested in the abstract questions What is it for an expression to have a meaning? or What is the nature and status of that which an expression and its translation or paraphrase are both the vehicles? From what sort of interests, then, do we come to ask this sort of question? Doubtless there are many answers. I shall concentrate on two of them which I shall call 'the Theory of Logic' and 'the Theory of Philosophy'. I shall spend a good long time on the first; not so long on the second.

THE THEORY OF LOGIC

The logician, in studying the rules of inference has to talk of the components of arguments, namely their premisses and conclusions and to talk of them in perfectly general terms. Even when he adduces concrete premisses and conclusions, he does so only to illustrate the generalities which are his proper concern. In the same way, he has to discuss the types of separable components or the types of distinguishable features of these premiss-types and conclusion-types, since it is sometimes on such components or features of premisses and conclusions that the inferences from and to them pivot.

Now the same argument may be expressed in English or in French or in any other language; and if it is expressed in English, there may still be hosts of different ways of wording it. What the logician is exploring is intended to be indifferent to these differences of wording. He is concerned with what is said by a premiss-sentence or a conclusion-sentence, not with how it is worded.

So, if not in the prosecution of his inquiry, at least in his explanations of what he is doing, he has to declare that his subject-matter consist not of the sentences and their ingredient words in which arguments are expressed, but of the propositions or judgments and their constituent terms, ideas or concepts of which the sentences and words are the vehicles. Sometimes he may say that his subject matter consists of sentence-meanings and their constituent word-meanings or phrase-meanings, though this idiom is interestingly repellent. Why it is repellent we shall, I hope, see later on. So in giving this sort of explanation of his business, he is talking *about* meanings, where in the prosecution of that business he is just operating *upon* them.

For our purposes it is near enough true to say that the first influential discussion of the notion of meaning given by a modern logician was that with which John Stuart Mill opens his *System of Logic* (1843). He acknowledges debts both to Hobbes and to the Schoolmen, but we need not trace these borrowings in detail.

Mill's contributions to Formal or Symbolic Logic were negligible. It was not he but his exact contemporaries, Boole and de Morgan, and his immediate successors, Jevons, Venn, Carroll, McColl and Peirce who, in the English-speaking world, paved the way for Russell. On the other hand, it is difficult to exaggerate the influence which he exercised, for good and for ill, upon British and Continental philosophers; and we must include among these philosophers the Symbolic Logicians as well, in so far as they have philosophized about their technical business. In particular, Mill's theory of meaning set the questions, and in large measure, determined their answers for thinkers as different as Brentano, in Austria; Meinong and Husserl, who were pupils of Brentano; Bradley, Jevons, Venn, Frege, James, Peirce, Moore and Russell. This extraordinary achievement was due chiefly to the fact that Mill was original in producing a doctrine of meaning at all. The doctrine that he produced was immediately influential, partly because a doctrine was needed and partly because its inconsistencies were transparent. Nearly all of the thinkers whom I have listed were in vehement opposition to certain parts of Mill's doctrine, and it was the other parts of it from which they often drew their most effective weapons.

Mill, following Hobbes's lead, starts off his account of the notion of meaning by considering single words. As we have to learn the alphabet before we can begin to spell, so it seemed natural to suppose that the meanings of sentences are compounds of the components, which are the meanings of their ingredient words. Word-meanings are atoms, sentence-meanings are molecules. I say that it seemed natural, but I hope soon to satisfy you that it was a tragically false start. Next Mill, again following Hobbes's lead, takes it for granted that all words, or nearly all words, are names, and this, at first, sounds very tempting. We know what it is for 'Fido' to be the name of a particular dog, and for 'London' to be the name of a particular town. There, in front of us, is the dog or the town which has the name, so here, one feels, there is no mystery. We have just the familiar relation between a thing and its name. The assimilation of all or most other single words to names gives us, accordingly, a cosy feeling. We fancy that we know where we are. The dog in front of us is what the word 'Fido' stands for, the town we visited yesterday is what the word 'London' stands for. So the classification of all or most single words as names makes us feel that what a word means is in all cases some manageable thing that that word is the name of. Meanings, at least word-meanings, are nothing abstruse or remote, they are, *prima facie*, ordinary things and happenings like dogs and towns and battles.

Mill goes further. Sometimes the grammatical subject of a sentence is not a single word but a many-worded phrase, like 'the present Prime Minister' or 'the first man to stand on the summit of Mt. Everest'. Mill has no qualms in classifying complex expressions like these also as names, what he calls 'many-worded names'. There do not exist proper names for everything we want to talk about; and sometimes we want to talk about something or somebody whose proper name, though it exists, is unknown to us. So descriptive phrases are coined by us to do duty for proper names. But they are still, according to Mill, names, though the tempting and in fact prevailing interpretation of this assertion differs importantly from what Mill usually wanted to convey. For, when Mill calls a word or phrase a 'name', he is using 'name' not, or not always, quite in the ordinary way. Sometimes he says that for an expression to be a name it must be able to be used as the subject or the predicate of a subject-predicate sentence—which lets in, e.g. adjectives as names. Sometimes his requirements are more stringent. A name is an expression which can be the subject of a subject-predicate sentence—which leaves only nouns, pronouns and substantival phrases. 'Name', for him, does not mean merely 'proper name'. He often resisted temptations to which he subjected his successors.

Before going any further, I want to make you at least suspect that this initially congenial equation of words and descriptive phrases with names is from the outset a monstrous howler—if, like some of Mill's successors, though unlike Mill himself, we do systematically construe 'name' on the model of 'proper name'. The assumption of the truth of this equation has been responsible for a large number of radical absurdities in philosophy in general and the philosophy of logic in particular. It was a fetter round the ankles of Meinong, from which he never freed himself. It was a fetter round the ankles of Frege, Moore and Russell, who all, sooner or later, saw that without some big emendations, the assumption led inevitably to fatal impasses. It was, as he himself says in his new book, a fetter round the ankles of Wittgenstein in the *Tractatus*, though in that same book he had found not only the need but the way to cut himself partially loose from it.

I am still not quite sure why it seems so natural to assume that all words are names, and even that every possible grammatical subject of a sentence, one-worded or many-worded, stands to something as the proper name 'Fido' stands to the dog Fido, and, what is a further point, that the thing it stands for is what the expression means. Even Plato had had to fight his way out of the same assumption. But he at least had a special excuse. The Greek language had only the one word ὄνομα where we have the three words 'word', 'name' and 'noun'. It was hard in Greek even to say that the Greek counterpart to our verb 'is' was a word but not a noun. Greek provided Plato with no label for verbs, or for adverbs, conjunctions etc. That 'is' is a word, but is not a name or even a noun was a tricky thing to say in Greek where ὄνομα did duty both for our word 'word', for our word 'name' and, eventually, for our word 'noun'. But even without this excuse people still find it natural to assimilate all words to names, and the meanings of words to the bearers of those alleged names. Yet the assumption is easy to demolish.

First, if every single word were a name, then a sentence composed of five words, say 'three is a prime number' would be a list of the five objects named by those five words. But a list, like 'Plato, Aristotle, Aquinas, Locke, Berkeley' is not a sentence. It says nothing, true or false. A sentence, on the contrary, may say something—some one thing—which is true or false. So the words combined into a sentence at least do something jointly which is different from their severally naming the several things that they name if they do name any things. What a sentence means is not decomposable into the set of things which the words in it stand for, if they do stand for things. So the notion of *having meaning* is at least partly different from the notion of *standing for*.

More than this. I can use the two descriptive phrases 'the Morning Star' and 'the Evening Star', as different ways of referring to Venus. But it is quite clear that the two phrases are different in meaning. It would be incorrect to translate into French the phrase 'the Morning Star' by 'l'Étoile du Soir'. But if the two phrases have different meanings, then Venus, the planet which we describe by these two different descriptions, cannot be what these descriptive phrases mean. For she, Venus, is one and the same, but what the two phrases signify are different. As we shall see in a moment Mill candidly acknowledges this point and makes an important allowance for it.

Moreover it is easy to coin descriptive phrases to which nothing at all answers. The phrase 'the third man to stand on the top of Mt. Everest' cannot, at present, be used to refer to anybody. There exists as yet no one whom it fits and perhaps there never will. Yet it is certainly a significant phrase, and could be translated into French or German. We know, we have to know, what it means when we say that it fits no living mountaineer. It means *something*, but it does not designate *somebody*. What it means cannot, therefore, be equated with a particular mountaineer. Nor can the meaning conveyed by the phrase 'the first person to stand on the top of Mr. Everest' be equated with Hillary, though, we gather, it fits him and does not fit anyone else. We can understand the question, and even entertain Nepalese doubts about the answer to the question 'Is Hillary the first person to conquer Mt. Everest?' where we could not understand the question 'Is Hillary Hillary?'

We could reach the same conclusion even more directly. If Hillary was, *per impossibile*, identified with what is meant by the phrase 'the first man to stand on the top of Mt. Everest', it would follow that the meaning of at least one phrase was born in New Zealand, has breathed through an oxygen-mask and has been decorated by Her Majesty. But this is patent nonsense. Meanings of phrases are not New Zealand citizens; what is expressed by a particular English phrase, as well as by any paraphrase or translation of it, is not something with lungs, a surname, long legs and a sunburnt face. People are born and die and sometimes wear boots; meanings are not born and do not die and they never wear boots—or go barefoot either. The Queen does not decorate meanings. The phrase 'the first man to stand on the top of Mt. Everest' will not lose its meaning when Hillary dies. Nor was it meaningless before he reached the summit.

Finally, we should notice that most words are not nouns; they are, e.g. adverbs, or verbs, or adjectives or prepositions or conjunctions or pronouns. But to classify as a name a word which is not even a noun strikes one as intolerable the moment one considers the point. How could 'ran' or 'often' or 'and' or 'pretty' be the name of anything? It could not even be the grammatical subject of a sentence. I may ask what a certain economic condition, moral quality or day of the week is called and get the answer 'inflation', 'punctiliousness' or 'Saturday'. We do use the word 'name' for what something is called, whether it be what a person or river is called, or what a species, a quality, an action or a condition is called. But the answer to the question 'What is it called?' must be a noun or have the grammar of a noun. No such question could be answered by giving the tense of a verb, an adverb, a conjunction or an adjective.

Mill himself allowed that some words like 'is', 'often', 'not', 'of', and 'the' are not names, even in his hospitable use of 'name'. They cannot by themselves function as the grammatical subjects of sentences. Their function, as he erroneously described it, is to subserve, in one way or another, the construction of many-worded names. They do not name extra things but are ancillaries to the multi-verbal naming of things. Yet they certainly have meanings. 'And' and 'or' have different meanings, and 'or' and the Latin 'aut' have the same meaning. Mill realized that it is not always the case that for a word to mean something, it must denote somebody or some thing. But most of his successors did not notice how important this point was.

Even more to Mill's credit was the fact that he noticed and did partial justice to the point, which I made a little while back, that two different descriptive phrases may both fit the same thing or person, so that the thing or person which they both fit or which, in his unhappy parlance, they both name is not to be equated with either (or of course both) of the significations of the two descriptions. The two phrases 'the previous Prime Minister' and 'the father of Randolph Churchill' both fit Sir Winston Churchill, and fit only him; but they do not have the same meaning. A French translation of the one would not be a translation of the other. One might know or believe that the one description fitted Sir Winston Churchill while still questioning whether the other did so too. From just knowing that Sir Winston was Prime Minister one could not infer that Randolph Churchill is his son, or *vice versa*. Either might have been true without the other being true. The two phrases cannot, therefore, carry the same information.

Mill, in effect, met this point with his famous theory of denotation and connotation. Most words and descriptive phrases, according to him, do two things at once. They *denote* the things or persons that they are, as he unhappily puts it, all the names of. But they also *connote* or signify the simple or complex attributes by possessing which the thing or person denoted is fitted by the description. Mill's word 'connote' was a very unhappily chosen word and has misled not only Mill's successors but Mill himself. His word 'denote' was used by him in a far from uniform way, which left him uncommitted to consequences from which some of his successors, who used it less equivocally, could not extricate themselves. For Mill, proper names denote their bearers, but predicate-expressions also denote what they are truly predicable of. Fido is denoted by 'Fido' and by 'dog' and by 'four-legged'.

So to ask for the function of an expression is, on Mill's showing, to ask a double question. It is to ask Which person or persons, thing or things the expression denotes? in one or other of Mill's uses of this verb—Sir Winston Churchill, perhaps—; but it is also to ask What are the properties or characteristics by which the thing or person is described?—say that of having begotten Randolph Churchill. As a thing or person can be described in various ways, the various descriptions given will differ in connotation, while still being identical in denotation. They characterize in different ways, even though their denotation is identical. They carry different bits of information or misinformation about the same thing, person or event.

Mill himself virtually says that according to our ordinary natural notion of meaning, it would not be proper to say that, e.g. Sir Winston Churchill is the meaning of a word or phrase. We ordinarily understand by 'meaning' not the thing denoted but only what is connoted. That is, Mill virtually reaches the correct conclusions that the meaning of an expression is never the thing or person referred to by means of it; and that descriptive phrases and, with one exception, single words are never names, in the sense of 'proper names'. The exception is just those relatively few words which really are proper names, i.e. words like 'Fido', and 'London', the words which do not appear in dictionaries.

Mill got a further important point right about these genuine proper names. He said that while most words and descriptive phrases both denote or name and connote, proper names only denote and do not connote. A dog may be called 'Fido', but the word 'Fido' conveys no information or misinformation about the dog's qualities, career or whereabouts, etc. There is, to enlarge this point, no question of the word 'Fido' being paraphrased, or correctly or incorrectly translated into French. Dictionaries do not tell us what proper names mean—for the simple reason that they do not mean anything. The word 'Fido' names or denotes a particular dog, since it is what he is called. But there is no room for anyone who hears the word 'Fido' to understand it or misunderstand it or fail to understand it. There is nothing for which he can require an elucidation or a definition. From the information that Sir Winston Churchill was Prime Minister, a number of consequences follow, such as that he was the leader of the majority party in Parliament. But from the fact that yonder dog is Fido, no other truth about him follows at all. No information is provided for anything to follow from. Using a proper name is not committing oneself to any further assertions whatsoever. Proper names are appellations and not descriptions; and descriptions are descriptions and not appellations. Sir Winston Churchill *is* the father of Randolph Churchill. He is not *called* and was not christened 'the father of Randolph Churchill'. He is called 'Winston Churchill'. The Lady Mayoress of Liverpool can give the name *Mauretania* to a ship which thenceforward has that name. But if she called Sir Winston Churchill 'the father of Sir Herbert Morrison' this would be a funny sort of christening, but it would not make it true that Morrison is the son of Sir Winston Churchill. Descriptions carry truths or falsehoods and are not just arbitrary bestowals. Proper names are arbitrary bestowals, and convey nothing true and nothing false, for they convey nothing at all.

Chinese astronomers give the planets, stars and constellations names quite different from those we give. But it does not follow that a single proposition of Western astronomy is rejected by them, or that a single astronomical position rejected by us is accepted by them. Stellar nomenclature carries with it no astronomical truths or falsehoods. Calling a star by a certain name is not saying anything about it, and saying something true or false about a star is not naming it. Saying is not naming and naming is not saying.

This brings out a most important fact. Considering the meaning (or Mill's 'connotation') of an expression is considering what can be said with it, i.e. said truly or said falsely, as well as asked, commanded, advised or any other sort of saying. In this, which is the normal sense of 'meaning', the meaning of a sub-expression like a word or phrase, is a functional factor of a range of possible assertions, questions, commands and the rest. It is tributary to sayings. It is a distinguishable common locus of a range of possible tellings, askings, advisings, etc. This precisely inverts the natural assumption with which, as I said earlier, Mill and most of us start, the assumption namely that the meanings of words and phrases can be learned, discussed and classified before consideration begins of entire sayings, such as sentences. Word-meanings do not stand to sentence-meanings as atoms to molecules or as letters of the alphabet to the spellings of words, but more nearly as the tennis-racket stands to the strokes which are or may be made with it. This point, which Mill's successors and predecessors half-recognized to hold for such little words as 'if', 'or', 'all', 'the' and 'not', holds good for all significant words alike. Their significances are their rôles inside actual and possible sayings. Mill's two-way doctrine, that nearly all words and phrases both denote, or are names, and connote, i.e. have significance, was therefore, in effect, though unwittingly, a coalition between an atomistic and a functionalist view of words. By the irony of fate, it was his atomistic view which was, in most quarters, accepted as gospel truth for the next fifty or seventy years. Indeed, it was more than accepted, it was accepted without the important safeguard which Mill himself provided when he said that the thing or person denoted by a name was not to be identified with what that name meant. Mill said that to mean is to connote. His successors said that to mean is to denote, or, more rarely, both to denote and to connote. Frege was for a long time alone in seeing the crucial importance of Mill's argument that two or more descriptive phrases with different senses may apply to the same planet or person. This person or planet is not, therefore, what those phrases mean. Their different senses are not their common denotation. Russell early realized the point which Mill did not very explicitly make, though Plato had made it, that a sentence is not a list. It says one thing; it is not just an inventory of a lot of things. But only much later, if at all, did Russell see the full implications of this.

I surmise that the reason why Mill's doctrine of denotation, without its safeguards, caught on, while his truths about connotation failed to do so, were two. First, the word 'connote' naturally suggests what we express by 'imply', which is not what is wanted. What the phrase 'the previous Prime Minister of the United Kingdom' signifies is not to be equated with any or all of the consequences which can be inferred from the statement that Churchill is the previous Prime Minister. Deducing is not translating. But more important was the fact that Mill himself rapidly diluted his doctrine of connotation with such a mass of irrelevant and false sensationalist and associationist psychology, that his successors felt forced to ignore the doctrine in order to keep clear of its accretions.

Let me briefly mention some of the consequences which successors of Mill actually drew from the view, which was not Mill's, that to mean is to denote, in the toughest sense, namely that all significant expressions are proper names, and what they are the names of are what the expressions signify.

First, it is obvious that the vast majority of words are unlike the words 'Fido' and 'London' in this respect, namely, that they are general. 'Fido' stands for a particular dog, but the noun 'dog' covers this dog Fido, and all other dogs past, present and future, dogs in novels, dogs in dog breeders' plans for the future, and so on indefinitely. So the word 'dog', if assumed to denote in the way in which 'Fido' denotes Fido, must denote something which we do not hear barking, namely either the set or class of all actual and imaginable dogs, or the set of canine properties which they all share. Either would be a very out-of-the-way sort of entity. Next, most words are not even nouns, but adjectives, verbs, prepositions, conjunctions and so on. If these are assumed to denote in the way in which 'Fido' denotes Fido, we shall have a still larger and queerer set of nominees or *denotata* on our

hands, namely nominees whose names could not even function as the grammatical subjects of sentences. (Incidentally it is not true even that all
ordinary general nouns can function by themselves as subjects of sentences.
I can talk about *this* dog, or *a* dog, or *the* dog which . . .; or about *dogs, all*
dogs, or *most* dogs, and so on. But I cannot make the singular noun 'dog' by
itself the grammatical subject of a sentence, save inside quotes, though I can
do this with nouns like 'grass', 'hydrogen' and 'Man'.) Finally, since complexes of words, like descriptive and other phrases, and entire clauses and
sentences have unitary meanings, then these too will have to be construed as
denoting complex entities of very surprising sorts. Now Meinong in Austria
and Frege in Germany, as well as Moore and Russell in this country, in
their early days, accepted some or most of these consequences. Consistently
with the assumed equation of signifying with naming, they maintained the
objective existence or being of all sorts of abstract and fictional *entia rationis*.

Whenever we construct a sentence, in which we can distinguish a grammatical subject and a verb, the grammatical subject, be it a single word or a
more or less complex phrase, must be significant if the sentence is to say
something true or false. But if this nominative word or phrase is significant,
it must, according to the assumption, denote something which is there to be
named. So not only Fido and London, but also centaurs, round squares, the
present King of France, the class of albino Cypriots, the first moment of
time, and the non-existence of a first moment of time must all be credited
with some sort of reality. They must *be*, else we could not say true or false
things of them. We could not truly say that round squares do not exist,
unless in some sense of 'exist' there exist round squares for us, in another
sense, to deny existence of. Sentences can begin with abstract nouns like
'equality' or 'justice' or 'murder' so all Plato's Forms or Universals must be
accepted as entities. Sentences can contain mentions of creatures of fiction,
like centaurs and Mr. Pickwick, so all conceivable creatures of fiction
must be genuine entities too. Next, we can say that propositions are true or
false, or that they entail or are incompatible with other propositions, so any
significant 'that'-clause, like 'that three is a prime number' or 'that four is a
prime number', must also denote existent or subsistent objects. It was accordingly, for a time, supposed that if I know or believe that three is a prime
number, my knowing or believing this is a special relation holding between
me on the one hand and the truth or fact, on the other, denoted by the
sentence 'three is a prime number'. If I weave or follow a romance, my
imagining centaurs or Mr. Pickwick is a special relation holding between me
and these centaurs or that portly old gentleman. I could not imagine him
unless he had enough being to stand as the correlate-term in this postulated
relation of being imagined by me.

Lastly, to consider briefly what turned out, unexpectedly, to be a crucial
case, there must exist or subsist classes, namely appropriate *denotata* for
such collectively employed plural descriptive phrases as 'the elephants in

Burma' or 'the men in the moon'. It is just of such classes or sets that we say that they number 3000, say, in the one case, and 0 in the other. For the results of counting to be true or false, there must be entities submitting to numerical predicates; and for the propositions of arithmetic to be true or false there must exist or subsist an infinite range of such classes.

At the very beginning of this century Russell was detecting some local unplausibilities in the full-fledged doctrine that to every significant grammatical subject there must correspond an appropriate *denotatum* in the way in which Fido answers to the name 'Fido'. The true proposition 'round squares do not exist' surely cannot require us to assert that there really do subsist round squares. The proposition that it is false that four is a prime number is a true one, but its truth surely cannot force us to fill the Universe up with an endless population of objectively existing falsehoods.

But it was classes that first engendered not mere unplausibilities but seemingly disastrous logical contradictions—not merely peripheral logical contradictions but contradictions at the heart of the very principles on which Russell and Frege had taken mathematics to depend. We can collect into classes not only ordinary objects like playing-cards and bachelors, but also such things as classes themselves. I can ask how many shoes there are in a room and also how many pairs of shoes, and a pair of shoes is already a class. So now suppose I construct a class of all the classes that are not, as anyhow most classes are not, members of themselves. Will this class be one of its own members or not? If it embraces itself, this disqualifies it from being one of the things it is characterized as embracing; if it is not one of the things it embraces, this is just what qualifies it to be one among its own members.

So simple logic itself forbids certain ostensibly denoting expressions to denote. It is at least unplausible to say that there exist objects denoted by the phrase 'round squares'; there is self-contradiction in saying that there exists a class which is a member of itself on condition that it is not, and *vice versa*.

Russell had already found himself forced to say of some expressions which had previously been supposed to name or denote, that they had to be given exceptional treatment. They were not names but what he called 'incomplete symbols', expressions, that is, which have no meaning, in the sense of denotation, by themselves; their business was to be auxiliary to expressions which do, as a whole, denote. (This was what Mill had said of the syncategorematic words.) The very treatment which had since the Middle Ages been given to such little words as 'and', 'not', 'the', 'some' and 'is' was now given to some other kinds of expressions as well. In effect, though not explicitly, Russell was saying that, e.g. descriptive phrases were as syncategorematic as 'not', 'and' and 'is' had always been allowed to be. Here Russell was on the brink of allowing that the meanings or significations of many kinds of expressions are matters not of *naming* things. But he was, I think, still held up by the idea that saying is itself just another variety of naming, i.e. naming a complex or an 'objective' or a proposition or a fact—some sort of postulated *Fido rationis*.

He took a new and most important further step to cope with the paradoxes, like that of the class of classes that are not members of themselves. For he now wielded a distinction, which Mill had seen but left inert, the distinction between sentences which are either true or false on the one hand, and on the other hand sentences which, though proper in vocabulary and syntax, are none the less nonsensical, meaningless or absurd; and therefore neither true nor false. To assert them and to deny them are to assert and deny nothing. For reasons of a sort which are the proper concern of logic, certain sorts of concatenations of words and phrases into sentences produce things which cannot be significantly said. For example, the very question Is the class of all classes which are not members of themselves a member of itself or not? has no answer. Russell's famous 'Theory of Types' was an attempt to formulate the reasons of logic which make it an improper question. We need not consider whether he was successful. What matters for us, and what made the big difference to subsequent philosophy, is the fact that at long last the notion of meaning was realized to be, at least in certain crucial contexts, the obverse of the notion of the nonsensical—what can be said, truly or falsely, is at last contrasted with what cannot be significantly said. The notion of meaning had been, at long last, partly detached from the notion of naming and reattached to the notion of saying. It was recognized to belong to, or even to constitute the domain which had always been the province of logic; and as it is at least part of the official business of logic to establish and codify rules, the notion of meaning came now to be seen as somehow compact of rules. To know what an expression means involves knowing what can (logically) be said with it and what cannot (logically) be said with it. It involves knowing a set of bans, fiats and obligations, or, in a word, it is to know the rules of the employment of that expression.

It was, however, not Russell but Wittgenstein who first generalized or half-generalized this crucial point. In the *Tractatus Logico-Philosophicus*, which could be described as the first book to be written on the philosophy of logic, Wittgenstein still had one foot in the denotationist camp, but his other foot was already free. He saw and said, not only what had been said before, that the little words, the so-called logical constants, 'not', 'is', 'and' and the rest do not stand for objects, but also, what Plato had also said before, that sentences are not names. Saying is not naming. He realized, as Frege had done, that logicians' questions are not questions about the properties or relations of the *denotata*, if any, of the expressions which enter into the sentences whose logic is under examination. He saw, too, that all the words and phrases that can enter into sentences are governed by the rules of what he called, slightly metaphorically, 'logical syntax' or 'logical grammar'. These rules are what are broken by such concatenations of words and phrases as result in nonsense. Logic is or includes the study of these rules. Husserl had at the beginning of the century employed much the same notion of 'logical grammar.'

It was only later still that Wittgenstein consciously and deliberately withdrew his remaining foot from the denotationist camp. When he said 'Don't ask for the meaning, ask for the use', he was imparting a lesson which he had had to teach to himself after he had finished with the *Tractatus*. The use of an expression, or the concept it expresses, is the rôle it is employed to perform, not any thing or person or event for which it might be supposed to stand. Nor is the purchasing power of a coin to be equated with this book or that car-ride which might be bought with it. The purchasing power of a coin has not got pages or a terminus. Even more instructive is the analogy which Wittgenstein now came to draw between significant expressions and the pieces with which are played games like chess. The significance of an expression and the powers or functions in chess of a pawn, a knight or the queen have much in common. To know what the knight can and cannot do, one must know the rules of chess, as well as be familiar with various kinds of chess-situations which may arise. What the knight may do cannot be read out of the material or shape of the piece of ivory or boxwood or tin of which this knight may be made. Similarly to know what an expression means is to know how it may and may not be employed, and the rules governing its employment can be the same for expressions of very different physical compositions. The word 'horse' is not a bit like the word 'cheval'; but the way of wielding them is the same. They have the same rôle, the same sense. Each is a translation of the other. Certainly the rules of the uses of expressions are unlike the rules of games in some important respects. We can be taught the rules of chess up to a point before we begin to play. There are manuals of chess, where there are not manuals of significance. The rules of chess, again, are completely definite and inelastic. Questions of whether a rule has been broken or not are decidable without debate. Moreover we opt to play chess and can stop when we like, where we do not opt to talk and think and cannot opt to break off. Chess is a diversion. Speech and thought are not only diversions. But still the partial assimilation of the meanings of expressions to the powers or the values of the pieces with which a game is played is enormously revealing. There is no temptation to suppose that a knight is proxy for anything, or that learning what a knight may or may not do is learning that it is a deputy for some ulterior entity. We could not learn to play the knight correctly without having learned to play the other pieces, nor can we learn to play a word by itself, but only in combination with other words and phrases.

Besides this, there is a further point which the assimilation brings out. There are six different kinds of chess-pieces, with their six different kinds of rôles in the game. We can imagine more complex games involving twenty or two hundred kinds of pieces. So it is with languages. In contrast with the denotationist assumption that almost all words, all phrases and even all sentences are alike in having the one rôle of naming, the assimilation of language to chess reminds us of what we knew *ambulando* all along, the fact that there are indefinitely many kinds of words, kinds of phrases, and kinds of sentences—that there is an indefinitely large variety of kinds of rôles performed by the expressions we use in saying things. Adjectives do not do what adverbs do, nor do all adjectives do the same sort of thing as one another. Some nouns are proper names, but most are not. The sorts of things that we do with sentences are different from the sorts of things that we do with most single words—and some sorts of things that we can significantly do with some sorts of sentences, we cannot significantly do with others. And so on.

There is not one basic mould such as the 'Fido'-Fido mould, into which all significant expressions are to be forced. On the contrary, there is an endless variety of categories of sense or meaning. Even the *prima facie* simple notion of naming or denoting itself turns out on examination to be full of internal variegations. Pronouns are used to denote people and things, but not in the way in which proper names do so. No one is *called* 'he' or 'she'. 'Saturday' is a proper name, but not in the same way as 'Fido' is a proper name—and neither is used in the way in which the fictional proper name 'Mr. Pickwick' is used. The notion of denotation, so far from providing the final explanation of the notion of meaning, turns out itself to be just one special branch or twig on the tree of signification. Expressions do not mean because they denote things; some expressions denote things, in one or another of several different manners, because they are significant. Meanings are not things, not even very queer things. Learning the meaning of an expression is more like learning a piece of drill than like coming across a previously unencountered object. It is learning to operate correctly with an expression and with any other expression equivalent to it.

THE THEORY OF PHILOSOPHY

I now want to trace, rather more cursorily, the other main motive from which thinkers have posed the abstract question What are meanings? or What is it for an expression to have a certain sense?

Until fairly recently philosophers have not often stepped back from their easels to consider what philosophy is, or how doing philosophy differs from doing science, or doing theology, or doing mathematics. Kant was the first modern thinker to see or try to answer this question—and a very good beginning of an answer he gave; but I shall not expound his answer here.

This question did not begin seriously to worry the general run of philosophers until maybe sixty years ago. It began to become obsessive only after the publication of the *Tractatus*. Why did the philosophy of philosophy start so late, and how did it come to start when and as it did?

It is often not realized that the words 'philosophy' and 'philosopher' and their equivalents in French and German had for a long time much less specific meanings than they now possess. During the seventeenth, the eighteenth and most of the nineteenth centuries a 'philosopher' was almost any sort of a *savant*. Astronomers, chemists and botanists were called 'philosophers' just as much as were Locke, Berkeley or Hume. Descartes's philosophy covered his contributions to optics just as much as his contributions to epistemology. In English there existed for a long time no special word for the people we now call 'scientists'. This noun was deliberately coined only in 1840, and even then it took some time to catch on. His contemporaries could not call Newton a 'scientist', since there was no such word. When a distinction had to be made, it was made by distinguishing 'natural philosophy' from 'moral' and 'metaphysical philosophy'. As late as 1887, Conan Doyle, within two or three pages of one story, describes Sherlock Holmes as being totally ignorant of philosophy, as we use the word now, and yet as having his room full of philosophical, i.e. scientific, instruments, like test-tubes, retorts and balances. A not very ancient Oxford Chair of Physics still retains its old label, the Chair of Experimental Philosophy.

Different from this quite important piece of etymological history is the fact that both in Scotland and in England there existed from perhaps the time of Hartley to that of Sidgwick and Bradley a strong tendency to suppose that the distinction between natural philosophy, i.e. physical and biological science on the one hand and metaphysical and moral philosophy, perhaps including logic, on the other, was that the latter were concerned with internal, mental phenomena, where the former were concerned with external, physical phenomena. Much of what we now label 'philosophy', *sans phrase*, was for a long time and by many thinkers confidently, but quite wrongly equated with what we now call 'psychology'. John Stuart Mill sometimes, but not always, uses even the grand word 'metaphysics' for the empirical study of the workings of men's minds. Protests were made against this equation particularly on behalf of philosophical theology, but for a long time the anti-theologians had it their own way. A philosopher, *sans phrase*, was a Mental and Moral Scientist—a scientist who was exempted from working in the laboratory or the observatory only because his specimens were collected at home by introspection. Even Mansel, himself a philosophical theologian with a good Kantian equipment, maintained that the science of mental phenomena, what we call 'psychology', was the real basis of even ontological or theological speculations.

So not only did the wide coverage of the word 'philosophy' encourage people not to look for any important differences between what scientists, as we now call them, do and what philosophers, as we now call them, do; but even when such differences were looked for, they were apt to be found in the differences between the investigation of physical phenomena by the laboratory scientist and the investigation of psychological phenomena by the introspecting psychologist.

As I see it, three influences were chiefly responsible for the collapse of the assumption that doing philosophy, in our sense, is of a piece with doing natural science or at least of a piece with doing mental science or psychology.

First, champions of mathematics like Frege, Husserl and Russell had to save mathematics from the combined empiricism and psychologism of the school of John Stuart Mill. Mathematical truths are not mere psychological generalizations; equations are not mere records of deeply rutted associations of ideas; the objects of geometry are not of the stuff of which mental images are made. Pure mathematics is a non-inductive and a non-introspective science. Its proofs are rigorous, its terms are exact, and its theorems are universal and not merely highly general truths. The proofs and the theorems of Formal or Symbolic Logic share these dignities with the proofs and theorems of mathematics. So, as logic was certainly a part of philosophy, not all of philosophy could be ranked as 'mental science'. There must, then, be a field or realm besides those of the material and the mental; and at least part of philosophy is concerned with this third realm, the realm of non-material and also non-mental 'logical objects'—such objects as concepts, truths, falsehoods, classes, numbers and implications.

Next, armchair mental science or introspective psychology itself began to yield ground to experimental, laboratory psychology. Psychologists like James began to put themselves to school under the physiologists and the statisticians. Scientific psychology began first to rival and then to oust both *a priori* and introspective psychology, and the tacit claim of epistemologists, moral philosophers and logicians to be mental scientists had to be surrendered to those who used the methods and the tools of the reputable sciences. So the question raised its head What then were the objects of the inquiries of epistemologists, moral philosophers and logicians, if they were not, as had been supposed, psychological states and processes? It is only in our own days that, anyhow in most British Universities, psychologists have established a Faculty of their own separate from the Faculty of Philosophy.

Thirdly, Brentano, reinforcing from medieval sources a point made and swiftly forgotten by Mill, maintained as an *a priori* principle of psychology itself, that it is of the essence of mental states and processes that they are *of* objects or contents. Somewhat as in grammar a transitive verb requires an accusative, so in the field of ideas, thoughts and feelings, acts of consciousness are directed upon their own metaphorical accusatives. To see is to see something, to regret is to regret something, to conclude or suppose is to conclude or suppose that something is the case. Imagining is one thing, the thing imagined, a centaur, say, is another. The centaur has the body of a horse and does not exist. An act of imagining a centaur does exist and does not have the body of a horse. Your act of supposing that Napoleon defeated Wellington is different from my act of supposing it; but what we suppose is the same and is what is expressed by our common expression 'that Napoleon defeated Wellington'. What is true of mental acts is, in general, false of their accusatives or 'intentional objects', and *vice versa.*

Brentano's two pupils, Meinong and Husserl, happened, for different reasons, to be especially, though not exclusively, interested in applying this principle of intentionality or transitivity to the intellectual, as distinct from the sensitive, volitional or affective acts of consciousness. They set out, that is, to rectify the Locke-Hume-Mill accounts of abstraction, conception, memory, judgment, supposal, inference and the rest, by distinguishing in each case, the various private, momentary and repeatable acts of conceiving, remembering, judging, supposing and inferring from their public, non-momentary accusatives, namely, the concepts, the propositions and the implications which constituted their objective correlates. Where Frege attacked psychologistic accounts of thinking from the outside, they attacked them from the inside. Where Frege argued, for instance, that numbers have nothing psychological or, of course, physical about them, Husserl and Meinong argued that for the mental processes of counting and calculating to be what they are, they must have accusatives or objects numerically and qualitatively other than those processes themselves. Frege said that Mill's account of mathematical entities was false because psychological; Husserl and Meinong, in effect, said that the psychology itself was false because non-'intentional' psychology. The upshot, however, was much the same. With different axes to grind, all three came to what I may crudely dub 'Platonistic' conclusions. All three maintained the doctrine of a third realm of non-physical, non-psychological entities, in which realm dwelled such things as concepts, numbers, classes and propositions.

Husserl and Meinong were both ready to lump together all these accusatives of thinking alike under the comprehensive title of Meanings (*Bedeutungen*), since what I think is what is conveyed by the words, phrases or sentences in which I express what I think. The 'accusatives' of my ideas and my judgings are the meanings of my words and my sentences. It easily followed from this that both Husserl and Meinong, proud of their newly segregated third realm, found that it was this realm which provided a desiderated subject-matter peculiar to logic and philosophy and necessarily ignored by the natural sciences, physical and psychological. Mental acts and states are the subject-matter of psychology. Physical objects and events are the subject-matter of the physical and biological sciences. It is left to philosophy to be the science of this third domain which consists largely, though not entirely, of thought-objects or Meanings—the novel and impressive entities which had been newly isolated for separate investigation by the application of Brentano's principle of intentionality to the specifically intellectual or cognitive acts of consciousness.

Thus, by the first decade of this century it was dawning upon philosophers and logicians that their business was not that of one science among others, e.g. that of psychology; and even that it was not an inductive, experimental or observational business of any sort. It was intimately concerned with, among other things, the fundamental concepts and principles of mathematics; and it seemed to have to do with a special domain which was not bespoken by any other discipline, namely the so-called third realm of logical objects or Meanings. At the same time, and in some degree affected by these influences, Moore consistently and Russell spasmodically were prosecuting their obviously philosophical and logical inquiries with a special *modus operandi*. They, and not they alone, were deliberately and explicitly trying to give analyses of concepts and propositions—asking What does it really mean to say, for example, that this is good? or that that is true? or that centaurs do not exist? or that I see an inkpot? or What are the differences between the distinguishable senses of the verb 'to know' and the verb 'to be'? Moore's regular practice and Russell's frequent practice seemed to exemplify beautifully what, for example, Husserl and Meinong had declared in general terms to be the peculiar business of philosophy and logic, namely to explore the third realm of Meanings. Thus philosophy had acquired a right to live its own life, neither as a discredited pretender to the status of the science of mind, nor yet as a superannuated handmaiden of *démodé* theology. It was responsible for a special field of facts, facts of impressively Platonized kinds.

Before the first world war discussions of the status and rôle of philosophy *vis-à-vis* the mathematical and empirical sciences were generally cursory and incidental to discussions of other matters. Wittgenstein's *Tractatus* was a complete treatise dedicated to fixing the position mainly of Formal Logic but also, as a necessary corollary, the position of general philosophy. It was this book which made dominant issues of the theory of logic and the theory of philosophy. In Vienna some of its teachings were applied polemically, namely to demolishing the pretensions of philosophy to be the science of transcendent realities. In England, on the whole, others of its teachings were applied more constructively, namely to stating the positive functions which philosophical propositions perform, and scientific propositions do not perform. In England, on the whole, interest was concentrated on Wittgenstein's description of philosophy as an activity of clarifying or elucidating the meanings of the expressions used, e.g. by scientists; that is, on the medicinal virtues of his account of the nonsensical. In Vienna, on the whole, interest was concentrated on the lethal potentialities of Wittgenstein's account of nonsense. In both places, it was realized that the criteria between the significant and the nonsensical needed to be systematically surveyed, and that it was for the philosopher and not the scientist to survey them.

At this point, the collapse of the denotationist theory of meaning began to influence the theory of philosophy as the science of Platonized Meanings. If the meaning of an expression is not an entity denoted by it, but a style of operation performed with it, not a nominee but a rôle, then it is not only repellent but positively misleading to speak as if there existed a Third Realm whose denizens are Meanings. We can distinguish this knight, as a piece of ivory, from the part it or any proxy for it may play in a game of chess; but the part it may play is not an extra entity, made of some mysterious non-ivory. There is not one box housing the ivory chessmen and another queerer box housing their functions in chess games. Similarly we can distinguish an expression as a set of syllables from its employment. But its use or sense is not an additional substance or subject of predication. It is not a non-physical, non-mental object—but not because it is either a physical or a mental object, but because it is not an object. As it is not an object, it is not a denizen of a Platonic realm of objects. To say, therefore, that philosophy is the science of Meanings, though not altogether wrong, is liable to mislead in the same way as it might mislead to say that economics is the science of exchange-values. This, too, is true enough, but to word this truth in this way is liable to make people suppose that the Universe houses, under different roofs, commodities and coins here and exchange-values over there.

Hence, following Wittgenstein's lead, it has become customary to say, instead, that philosophical problems are linguistic problems—only linguistic problems quite unlike any of the problems of philology, grammar, phonetics, rhetoric, prosody, etc., since they are problems about the logic of the functionings of expressions. Such problems are so widely different from, e.g. philological problems, that speaking of them as linguistic problems is, at the moment, as Wittgenstein foresaw, misleading people as far in one direction, as speaking of them as problems about Meanings or Concepts or Propositions had been misleading in the other direction. The difficulty is to steer between the Scylla of a Platonistic and the Charybdis of a lexicographical account of the business of philosophy and logic.

There has been and perhaps still is something of a vogue for saying that doing philosophy consists in analysing meanings, or analysing the employments of expressions. Indeed, from Transatlantic journals I gather that at this very moment British philosophy is dominated by some people called 'linguistic analysts'. The word 'analysis' has, indeed, a good laboratory or Scotland Yard ring about it; it contrasts well with such expressions as 'speculation', 'hypothesis', 'system-building' and even 'preaching' and 'writing poetry'. On the other hand it is a hopelessly misleading word in some important respects. It falsely suggests, for one thing, that any sort of careful elucidation of any sorts of complex or subtle ideas will be a piece of philosophizing; as if the judge, in explaining to the members of the jury the differences between manslaughter and murder, was helping them out of a philosophical quandary. But, even worse, it suggests that philosophical problems are like the chemist's or the detective's problems in this respect, namely that they can and should be tackled piecemeal. Finish problem A this morning, file the answer, and go on to problem B this afternoon. This suggestion does violence to the vital fact that philosophical problems inevitably interlock in all sorts of ways. It would be patently absurd to tell someone to finish the problem of the nature of truth this morning, file the answer and go on this afternoon to solve the problem of the relations between naming and saying, holding over until tomorrow problems about

appeared to the Romans who had in their language no word for grey, brown, nor any *generic* word for blue (though they had a number of words to denote particular shades of this colour.) How curiously different, it would seem, must human action appear when seen through the filter of Eskimo language where, owing to the lack of transitive verbs, it is likely to be perceived as a sort of happening without an active element in it. (In Greenlandic one cannot say 'I kill him', 'I shoot the arrow', but only 'He dies to me', 'The arrow is flying away from me', just as 'I hear' is expressed by 'me-sound-is'). Eskimo philosophers, if there were any, would be likely to say that what we call action is "really" a pattern, or gestalt, of succeeding impressions. Just as Greenlandic assimilates action to impression—which strikes us as strange—so our language tends to bias us in just the opposite way: it makes us assimilate perception to action. We say not only 'I cut the tree', but also 'I see the tree': the use of the same construction makes it appear as if the 'I' was the *subject* form which issued the seeing, and as if the seeing was a sort of action directed at the tree; nor are we any better off if we use the passive voice 'The tree is seen by me'—for now it almost looks as if something *happened* to the tree, as if it had to undergo or suffer my seeing it. Following the clues of speech, we are led to interpret the world of experience one-sidedly, just as "owing to the common philosophy of grammar", as Nietzsche put it, i.e. "owing to the unconscious domination and guidance of similar grammatical functions the way seems barred against certain other possibilities of world-interpretation". In other words, every language contains, deep-sunken in it, certain moulds, designs, forms to apprehend phenomena, human action, etc., It is hardly going too far to say that a whole world picture is wedded to the use of the transitive verb and the actor-action scheme that goes with it—that if we spoke a different language we would perceive a different world. By growing up in a certain language, by thinking in its semantic and syntactical grooves, we acquire a certain more or less uniform outlook on the world—an outlook we are scarcely aware of until (say) by coming across a language of a totally different structure we are shocked into seeing the oddity of the obvious, or what seemed to be obvious. Finally, I want to say that philosophy *begins* with distrusting language—that medium that pervades, and warps, our very thought. But this is perhaps too strong an expression. I do not mean to say that language *falsifies* experience, twists it into something else; the point is that it supplies us with certain categorial forms without which the formation of a coherent system of experience, a world picture, would be impossible. In this sense, language shapes and fashions the frame in which experience is set, and different languages achieve this in different ways. A philosopher, more than others, should be sensitive to this sort of influence, alive to the dangers that lie dormant in the forms of expression—the very thing, that is, which, so misguidedly, has been raised to the standard in philosophical controversy.

When I spoke of the change of language I was not thinking of those cases which delight the heart of a philologist—umlaut, ablaut, and the like. Nor was I referring to changes in meaning and vocabulary—what was originally stupid, wanton, Latin *nescius*, becomes 'nice'; a horse that is well-fed and grows a smooth, shiny coat is 'glad'—*glatt* in German; what is now silly was formerly 'sely' corresponding to German *selig*—happy, blessed; for while such changes are instructive in many ways, they are hardly such as to deserve the philosopher's attention. Neither was I thinking of those more subtle changes in the *valeurs* of a word which—as in the case of 'romantic',—are significant of a change in the tone of thought of a whole period—of a half-conscious awakening of new ways of feeling and responses to nature, so elusive and yet, to the historian, so important. What I had in mind were cases which are best illustrated by a few examples.

Nothing is so opposed as day and night; yet there is a sense, as when we speak of a 'three days' journey', in which 'day' includes night. 'Man' is used in contrast to woman, but occasionally as a term including woman; and a similar shift of sense is perceptible in 'he' and 'she'—as an arguer, also woman is 'he'. We say of a child that he is two years 'old', not two years 'young', just as we inquire 'How *long* (not how *short*) will you stay?' or 'How *far* (not how *near*) is it from here to the station'? The word 'quality', while for the most part used indifferently, is sometimes uttered in a peculiar tone—as when we say 'He has quality'. White and black are commonly contrasted with colours in the strict and proper sense ('illustrations in colour' *versus* 'illustrations in black and white'), yet in certain contexts we are inclined to reckon them amongst the colours; as when we say 'Look round you—everything you see has some colour or other', thinking, perhaps, that even air and vapour, or glass and water are possessed by some very pale, some very pearly tone. Thus 'colour' tends to absorb into its meaning all shades, even black and white, the otherwise 'colourless' hues. But these are instances betraying a deeper drift. In the ordinary sense, motion is opposed to rest, speed to slowness, size to littleness, numerous to a few, depth to shallowness, strength to weakness, value to worthlessness, just as far is opposed to near, hot to cold, dry to wet, dark to bright, heavy to light, and true to false. And this was, roughly, the way in which Greek philosophers regarded such contrasts. 'Up' for them was simply 'not-down', 'soft' 'not-hard', 'dry' 'not wet', and so on.[2] The fact that two polar terms were in use may have played a role in underpinning the belief that things which are hot and cold, or hard and soft, etc., are different, not in degree, but in kind—a fateful belief, for on it hinged their understanding—no, their lack of understanding of change. They signally failed to penetrate it. The Greeks never mastered the problem of motion—which is but the simplest case—they never evolved a science of dynamics, which is surprising enough in view of their

[2] See e.g. A. P. Rossiter, *The Growth of Science*, 1939.

genius for mathematics. They give the impression that they somehow got started on the wrong track—for them heavenly and terrestrial motion were entirely different, the one governed by law, eternal and unchanging, the other lawless, corrupt, confused; if faced with a change, such as a thing getting heated, they thought that one quality must be destroyed to let the opposite quality take its place. Thus they were, perhaps as a consequence of their quaint ideas, mightily impeded in coming to grips with the problem of change.

In science a language has come into use in which those contrasted terms are looked upon as degrees of one and the same quality—darkness as light intensity of illumination, slowness as the lower range of speed, rest as the limiting case of motion; there is a scale only of hardness, not of softness, only a physical theory of heat, not a theory of coldness; what we measure is the strength of a rope, a current, etc., not its weakness, what we count is number, not fewness; the air has a degree of moisture, not of dryness; and everything has weight and mass, even an electron. Again, we speak of health irrespective of whether it is good or bad health, and of the value of things which are of no value. Under the influence of such examples, it would seem, a term like 'truth-value' has been coined to cover both truth and falsity of a statement, just as 'verification' is, prevalently, used to include falsification. 'Distance', 'width', 'wealth', 'intelligence' are further nouns which had the same career; though the same is not so true of the adjectives—'distant', 'wealthy', 'intelligent' are not yet relativized, any more than 'hard', 'hot', 'speedy', 'weighty' are, or 'healthy', 'valuable' and 'worthy'; on the contrary, they retain the original sense. Adjectives, it would appear, have a much tougher life than nouns, and not only in English. But that only in passing.

Here we see a whole array of terms shifting in a parallel way, and in a way which is of far-reaching consequence: for the construction of modern science is bound up with it and would not have been possible without it. The change-over from the static view—where the adjective is seen as the expression of a permanent quality—to a dynamical which apprehends quality as a variable degree within a certain scale made possible 'functional thinking' (I use the word as mathematicians do), the kind of thinking that can cope with change and the conceptual difficulties it presents. What happened was obviously this: one term of a pair of contraries had a tendency to swallow up the other and stand for the whole range of variation. Whether this tendency can be traced to the rationalising influence of science, or whether it is prior to science and has itself given an impetus to that revolution of thought is a question still undecided.[3] It is in this context, perhaps, not without significance that Latin and Greek were lacking in all the finer means to express continuous change and functional dependence: in

[3] My attention has been drawn to this aspect of the matter by my former pupil J. L. Hevesi.

Latin, for instance, there are no *general* terms to express the relation "the more—the less"; the phrases used for "the more—the more" are confined to simple *proportionality*, the analogue to *statics*.[4] Nor has any classical language an equivalent for 'to become' (*devenir* in French, *devenire* in medieval Latin) so essential to our way of describing a change in quality, for neither *fieri* nor γίγνεσθαι can be used in the same way to express the idea of *continuous* change. There are no uses of intransitive verbs such as 'to soften', (*rubesco* is inceptive), etc.

The new idiom, which sprang up first in the vernacular about the 14th century, has not entirely displaced the older one (as can still be seen from the adjectives cited above). Both exist side by side. Though the use of 'moisture' for dry as well as wet (as in meteorology), or of 'truth-value' in logic still has the ring of jargon, in other instances the new idiom has become completely naturalised—as with 'distance' for near and far, 'age' for young and old, 'size' for big and small, 'density' for thick and thin. Yet even so, we can use any such term in two distinct ways—we may ask '*Is* he old?' or '*How* old is he?'; and so in the other cases.

At the time of Nicole Oresme, Bishop of Lisieux, when a new way of looking at change was growing up, and with it a new way of speaking of qualities, this must have been felt as a shocking departure from the ordinary use, supported and sanctioned as it was by old tradition. How the cloisters of the schoolmen must have resounded with 'intensio et remissio formarum' —the disputes as to whether a quality might have degrees and, in changing, could yet remain the same, or whether this was patent nonsense. One may imagine the indignant outcries of the purists of the time, their loathing of what must have appeared to them as "new-fangled ways of speaking" and as a "complete perversion" of grammar. The latter, more even than the vocabulary, embodies a good deal of the conservatism of mankind, and progress had often to be made in the teeth of the enormous resistance offered by its structure to ways of thinking which do not, or not smoothly, fit its grooves. (See what has been said in the foregoing on Greek language and absence of dynamics.) Grammar draws a *cordon sanitaire* against any rebellious ideas that dare to crop up.

The importance of functional correlation can, moreover, be seen in a different domain: in perspective, and the enthusiasm with which it was universally greeted when it was discovered—another coincidence?—at the very time when new aspects of thought and feeling were just about to take shape: Duccio's Maesta and Giotto's wall paintings in the Capella degli Scrovegni in Padua both belong to the early 14th century. The "strange fascination which perspective had for the Renaissance mind cannot be accounted for exclusively by a craving for verisimilitude", as Panofsky[5]

---

[4] Cf. Ettmayer, *Analytische Syntax der Franzoischen Sprache*, vol. ii, 1936, p. 935 ff.
[5] E. Panofsky, Albrecht Dürer, 1945, vol. i, p. 260.

observes. A sensibility to functional relation is apparent in this, and the interest in perspective—so alien to the Greeks—is almost symbolic of the time. A reflex of it can still be caught from the writings of Leonardo da Vinci and Dürer. As perspective rests essentially on a clear understanding of the way in which two variables, the apparent size of an object and its distance from the beholder, are connected, Leonardo saw in painting a 'science'. He certainly must have been struck by the affinity between this 'science' and the philosophical speculations on dynamics of the schoolmen of which he was fully aware (he even employed their ideas in his theory of painting).

If those pedantic schoolmen and masters had had their way, there would to-day be no science and no dynamics; but, for consolation, 'correct' grammar. To look at any departure from the norm as a crime is nothing but a blind prejudice; and a fateful one at that as it tends to drain the life-blood of any independent inquiry. Language is an instrument that must, as occasion requires, be bent to one's purpose. To stick to language as it is can only lead to a sort of Philistinism which insists on the observance of the *cliché* and will end up with a harakiri of living thought. Indeed, the guardian of language who jealously watches over its 'correctness' is in the long run bound to turn into a reactionary who looks askance at any innovation. Correctness is a useful, but a negative virtue. Follow those prophets, and you will soon find yourself imprisoned in a language cage, clean, disinfected, and unpleasant like a sanatorium room.

Understandably enough, there is an instinctive prejudice against neologisms, in part springing from a wholesome fear that novelty of speech may screen poverty of thought. We all dislike new words. And yet there is another and perfectly proper urge to give expression to meanings so far unexpressed, or, in the present language, indeed inexpressible. When Freud, for instance, says *der Patient erinnert den Vorfall* he is using the verb *erinnern* in a novel manner; in the ordinary way, the verb is used reflexively, *sich an etwas erinnern*. Why has Freud (who wrote a very good style) diverged at this point? There is a queer way in which a neurotic person who is under treatment may suddenly remember long-forgotten scenes of his early life which, as Freud puts it, have been 'repressed' and are now being re-lived. What has been inaccessible to the patient, however hard he may have tried, breaks, in a violent storm of emotion, through to consciousness In order to set apart this kind of remembrance from the ordinary one where we remember at will, Freud uses the verb transitively, in a way no one has done before; and with this syntactical innovation goes a semantic change. By this use Freud has enriched the German language. Such stray deviations, hit upon in a lucky hour and accepted by custom, these little, yet expressive departures from the beaten track, have not only a vividness, a sparkle of their own, but they sharpen the tools of thought and keep language from going blunt. So why cavil at them?

What those sticklers for correctness prefer not to see is that we are living in a *changing world*, and that language is always lagging behind these changes. To cite only one sort of examples out of a great many parallel ones —in psychological experiments one constantly comes across situations which call for new ways of describing. If Maxwell disks, for instance, are rotated one sees, so long as the movement is slow, several colour sectors, and when the disk is spinning rapidly, a uniform colour, the result of fusion, but in between there is a certain point where a flicker is seen. There are cases in which the colour itself is seen flickering, and others, as when the disk is watched through a small screen-hole, which are more aptly described by saying that there is a flickering *across* the disk or *before* it in space, or again that the disk's surface is seen *behind* the flicker. These modes of expression, though perfectly natural and instantly understood by every one, yet digress from the norm. For 'before' and 'behind', while clearly denoting spatial relations, are used in such a way that it makes no longer sense to ask, 'Exactly how many millimeters before the disk is the flickering?' Here we have a sense of 'before' which admits of no distance. To cite a few similar cases—if we look at a metal its colour seems to lie *behind* its surface, just as its glitter appears *in front of*, or *superimposed* on it; the glow of a piece of red-hot iron is seen not simply as colour that lies on its surface but as *extending back* into the object. Again, it has been said that, when a person is speaking with someone in complete darkness, the voice of the other sounds distinctly *behind* the darkness, not *in* the darkness. In some cases an object is seen as 'desurfaced', with a filmy, fluffy sort of outline, a bit unreal perhaps. Queer idioms which say what cannot quite be said by anything else: but condemn them on account of that? Notice with what unerring instinct language contrives to say, at the cost of a slight departure, what would be unsayable if we moved along the rigid grooves of speech. Indeed, how should one describe such phenomena if not by breaking away from the *clichés*? Is there anything objectionable in that? If so, language could never keep pace with life. Yet new situations, unforeseen, arise, and with them the need of describing them; it can only be met by adjusting language—either by coining new words, or, as the word-creating faculty is scanty, by pressing old ones into new services, in this way cutting through the dead mass of convention. It is precisely because speech runs so much in ready-made moulds that an occasional anomaly, a happy flouting of the laws of grammar, an uncommon phrasing, arouses our attention and lends lustre to the point we want to bring out. It is in this way, by *transgressing*, that language manages to achieve what it is meant to achieve, and that it grows. Why, then, the squeamishness?

Not only should the scientist be free to deviate from common language, where the need arises, but he is bound to do so if he is to convey a new insight not in conformity with the ideas dominant of the time, with ideas, moreover, precipitated in language. The classical example of this is Einstein. When he was groping his way, there was, in his own words, 'a feeling of direction', of going towards something he didn't quite know—which centred more and more on a suspicion that all was not well with the idea of simultaneity. He could at first not say what was wrong with it, and yet felt that here, if anywhere, was the key to all the dark puzzles that troubled the physicists at that time. Had he been brought up as a pupil of G. E. Moore, imbued with a belief in the infallibility of the ordinary modes of expression, he could never have made his discovery, clogged as he would have been by the dead weight of usage. As it was, he paid no respect to common sense, let alone the common speech. He insisted on asking himself, Do I *really* understand what I mean when I say that two events are simultaneous? Once the question was brought into sharp focus, he came to see, gradually perhaps and to his surprise, that there was a gap in his understanding. For the sense in which we speak of two events happening at the same time, when they are in the same place, or nearby, cannot be applied to events in distant places. It would be *blind*, he felt, to apply the familiar meaning of 'simultaneous' to these other cases—it would only land us in perplexities beyond resolve. Einstein saw that the term 'simultaneous' had first to be *defined* for the case of distant events, and defined in such a way that the definition supplies us with a method to decide experimetally whether or not two events are simultaneous. This 'seeing' of a crucial point in the meaning of 'simultaneous' has *absolutely nothing* to do with the way the word is actually used in language. It is as well to remind you that in 1905, when Einstein's first essay appeared, there was only *one* use, not two uses of 'simultaneous', and that it would be absurd to pretend that, when Einstein found a difference in meaning, he was making a *linguistic* discovery. (A side-light on how wrong the philosophical equation meaning = use is). On the contrary, anyone who had taken ordinary language, or common sense, for his guide, and had been asked whether he understood what 'simultaneous' meant, would have replied with a decided yes—no matter whether he could, or could not, specify a method for finding out. He would have said that the meaning of the word is clear in itself and needs no further explanation. In fact, no one before Einstein, whether a plain man, a scientist, or a philosopher, doubted for a minute that the concept was clear to him, so clear that he need not trouble. That's precisely what made people slur over the decisive point. Einstein *saw*: that is how he freed himself from the thought-habits imposed on us by speech, radically so. By following the lead of language, or of the common sense philosophers one would have barred oneself from the spark to insight which was to be the dawn of a new era in physics.

These facts speak for themselves. That science cannot live under the tutelage of any ideas on 'correctness', will perhaps be conceded. But this is true not only of science. Poetry is forever groping along the borders of the unspeakable, wresting new land from the vast void of the unexpressed. It is its mission to break through the wall of conventional views that encloses us, to startle us into seeing the world through fresh eyes. This is what all the great poets from Dante to Baudelaire have performed, and that is their glory. However, it is a large subject, too large to be treated here. I shall pick out only one tiny point, and one, moreover, that concerns prose—Flaubert's style which, in Proust's phrase, has 'renewed our vision of things'. In a work of fiction, nature is usually treated as background to men; against this background stand out the main characters of the story, the way they act, think, speak, feel and behave. The contrast between the uniformity of nature and the uniqueness of the human world is, in French, expressed by the use of two tenses—the imperfect for things and processes, and the perfect for men and actions. But with Flaubert, what men do is, in essence, always the same—it is like the succession of rain and sunshine, spring and summer, the ripening of the corn, and the phases of the moon. There is something dull and repetitive about them which pervades them with a sort of dispassionate sadness. There is a passage in *Madame Bovary* where Flaubert speaks of "the eternal monotony of passion which has ever the same forms and the same language". A revealing passage; for what he has tried to do and has done is to bring about something like a shift in our way of seeing people and things; and this he achieves, simply, by his relentless use of the imperfect, assimilating, in language, his apprehension of men to that of things, (remember Greenlandic!) Everything, including human action, is resolved into a perpetual and monotonous flux, revealing the melancholy essence of human existence. Describing people in the forms appropriate to things produces a peculiar effect indeed—"what, up to the time of Flaubert, had been merely action, has become impression", as Proust puts its. As we read over the pages of his novels, we are made to feel in what people say that they would always say precisely the same thing, that their whole life can be poured into a phrase as into a little vial. And when the perfect is used—on rare occasions only as when the narrative changes direction—it is again with a queer effect: it gives to a thing (when it occupies the place of a subject) a character of activity, it is as if a furtive ray of sunlight was falling on it, imparting to it, for a fleeting instant, a life of its own: change suddenly turns into action. And from this arises that unique Flaubertian vision of things which, like any artist's vision, can only be communicated through his style. Besides the tenses, the conjunction 'and' is used in an entirely new way. It hardly ever binds phrase to phrase, but has a more musical function —to mark a pause in the beat of the rhythm, to indicate that the moving wave we have been following has spent itself, and that another is about to build itself up. To this must be added a novel use of the present participles, of adverbs, and of certain pronouns and prepositions—grammatical peculiarities which all contribute to give shape to a world picture in which life is seen as a smooth change of one state passing into another without the persons taking any active part in the action—a picture that reminds one of some huge escalator which goes on and on, never stopping, never breaking its monotony. But where an 'action' does intervene in the flow of events, its protagonists are, in general, *things*, acting on a plane of non-human drama. What a vision! And yet a vision attained by distorting syntax. This, I think, should be enough to instil a drop of scepticism into the belief that all is well with ordinary language; it makes one wonder whether there is not, after all, a hard atom of truth in the view that ordinary speech is only good for saying things that are no longer worth saying.

By giving so copious examples my aim was to drive home the point defended here—that the ideal of correctness is a deadening one, that it is in vain to set up a language police to stem living developments. (I have always suspected that correctness is the last refuge of those who have nothing to say).

Poets and literary critics feel, today perhaps more keenly than ever before, that there is something disquieting about language. If I correctly read the signs, there is a susceptibility to the perils of words, a growing one, and a suspicion that language comes between us and the things we want to say. "In speaking one always says more than one intends to" observes Sartre; and T. S. Eliot, having noticed the vanity of words to express what is unique in experience, says "The particular has no language". Philosophers, on the other hand, are on the whole more likely to be found in the opposite camp —'debunking' all this talk as "pseudo-complaints which masquerade as genuine".[6] I think that this is a mistaken attitude for a number of reasons, and this is perhaps the place to set out some of them.

First, to talk of *the* ordinary use of language is, as I have already hinted in a previous article, unrealistic. Though I would not go so far as Ezra Pound in saying that our whole speech is "churning and chugging" today, the fact remains that language is in a state of flux. But, it will be said, that is the concern of the historian of language, not of the philosopher. All the philosopher needs to know is the *stock*-use of a word or phrase, as it is employed at present, in contrast with its non-stock uses.[7] This answer is unsatisfactory. Though it would be silly to pretend that one did not know the stock-use of 'cat' or 'shut the door', there are other cases where one would feel less sure. Is a 'taste of onions' the stock-use and a 'taste for history' derived, secondary, figurative? (But it is not *felt* as a metaphor!) Is only a 'brilliant sunshine' standard-use and a 'brilliant style' non-standard? Is 'day' as opposed to night, or as including night the norm? What about speaking of a 'wild laughter', a 'brooding silence', or saying that a 'recollection of this experience moved in his eyes'? It is easy to see that the 'stock-use' shifts with the context, and shifts in time. What was stock-use may become obsolescent and fall into the limbo of silence, just as new uses may spring up and may, in their turn, become standard language; but where is

---

[6] Alice Ambrose, 'The Problems of Linguistic Inadequacy;' *Philosophical Analysis*, ed. Max Black, Cornell University Press, 1950.
[7] I am indebted here to Prof. G. Ryle for letting me read an article of his in which such distinctions are discussed.

one to draw the line? It is well to remember that almost all expressions which refer to the mental are derived from others whose primary sense was sensuous and that this is a process which goes on to the present day; just as a good many words, under the influence of science, philosophy, or something still more elusive, have only in fairly recent times undergone a change in meaning—e.g. 'organic', 'nervous', 'unconscious', 'original', 'creative', 'objective', 'curiosity', 'to entail', etc. There is continuous change and continuous creation in language. Finally, there is such a thing as ambiguity which—except in exceptional cases—mars any attempt to single out one use as the stock one. Exactly how many standard-uses has 'nature'? What about 'in', 'on', 'about' etc.? "The English prepositions", says Empson, "from being used in so many ways and in combination with so many verbs, have acquired not so much a number of meanings as a body of meaning continuous in several dimensions.[8]" If so, or if the uses shade off into one another imperceptibly, how can one peel off and throw away all the non-stock uses and retain the stock ones? Yes, this view *is* unrealistic.

Next, and this raises a bigger issue, even if there was such a thing as a stock-use, it need not matter much to the philosopher. I mean, he need not be *bound* to this use; I should even go further and say that, sooner or later, he is bound to commit the crime and depart from it—that is, if he has something new to say. In this respect, his position is not altogether different from that of the poet or the scientist, and for similar reasons. He, too, may have come to see something which, in the ordinary way, cannot quite be said. I shall argue later that this is a characteristic feature of some philosophising. To mention here just one small point, the English language has been enriched by many words coined by philosophers who were sensitive to gaps in our vocabulary. 'Optimism', for instance, is due to Leibniz, and was borrowed from him by Voltaire. 'Impression' in its modern sense was introduced by Hume, 'intuition' by De Quincey, 'intuitionism' by Sidgwick, 'intuitionist' by H. Spencer. 'Scientist' is an invention of Whewell, 'aesthetic' one of Baumgarten, and so on. That even the laws of grammar can be flouted with salubrious effect can be seen from Lichtenberg's remark that one should say 'It thinks in me'.

My third point is that certain features of one's own language are noticed and appreciated in their full significance only when it is compared with other languages—with German (verbal way of expressing colour), Greenlandic (dominance of the impression verb), Latin (absence of words for blue, grey, and brown), etc. Is, then, the philosopher to go to the Eskimos to learn his trade? Not exactly; yet the mere *awareness* of other possibilities is, philosophically, of the utmost importance: it makes us see in a flash other ways of world-interpretation of which we are unaware, and thus drives home what is conventional in our outlook. The technique of the ordinary-use

---

[8] Seven Types of Ambiguity, p. 5.

philosophers has suffered from the fact that they restricted themselves to the study of one language to the exclusion of any other—with the result that they became blind to those ubiquitous features of their own language on which their whole mode of thinking, indeed their world picture, depends.

Connected with this is another large point—the misleadingness of our speech-forms. That language, "the embodied and articulated Spirit of the Race", as Coleridge put it, is in many ways inadequate can, I take it, by no one be doubted. In particular, it is the syntax and the field of analogies embedded in language which, unperceived, hold our thought in thrall, or push it along perilous lines. We shall soon have occasion to substantiate this point.

But there are still more reasons for guarding against this official doctrine. The one is that its champions pay heed only to the actual use of language not to its gaps revealing as they are. Suppose, for instance, that I say 'I ought to do so-and-so'; when I say that it is obvious that the I is here only a pseudo-subject from which the ought seems to proceed, whereas in fact it is more a *point d'appui* to which it is directed. We regard a rule of ethics, politeness, etc., as something outside ourselves which applies to us as objects. We are rather in a passive (obedient) frame of mind, and what is active is, at most, the consent we give to that duty. 'I am under an obligation,' 'it is my duty' and therefore phrases which are more appropriate. That 'ought' does not refer to an occult activity betrays itself in a number of features; thus we do not say 'I will ought', 'I choose (decide) to ought', any more than we say 'I ought to ought', or 'I am resolved upon oughting'. There is no such thing as a 'will to ought'. The complete absence of these idioms *is* revealing. That philosophers have concentrated on the use, and neglected the non-use of expressions is a further weakness of their technique. . . .

72 The Modern Predicament*

H. J. PATON

H. J. Paton is emeritus professor of moral philosophy at the University of Oxford. His works include *The Good Will, Kant's Metaphysics of Experience, The Categorical Imperative,* and *The Modern Predicament.*

1. THE MODERN PREDICAMENT

The modern predicament, if I may try to sum up this long discussion, is that man seems to be faced with an unbridgeable gulf between science and religion or—it might be better to say—between knowledge and faith. This is a permanent human predicament as well as a modern one, but at the present time it is particularly cruel. Religion was born and bred in a world different from ours—a tiny, comfortable world, full of signs and wonders and divine interventions, where it was easy for man to consider himself the end for which all things were made. That ancient world has been nibbled away by science, and the question arises whether against a new and scientific background religion in any form will find it possible to survive.

The present situation is not to be taken too crudely. Scientific discoveries cannot be said to contradict the doctrines of theology except when theologians are rash enough to make pseudo-scientific assertions about events in the world of nature. Within science itself the problems of religion—like those of morality and art—simply do not arise: they are merely irrelevant. The conflict, so far as there is one, is not between abstractions like science and theology nor even between two different sets of men. It is a conflict of different attitudes in the soul of each individual man. This struggle is not to be easily described, yet it is very real and very obvious to many at the present time. Catherine Carswell, for example, the Scottish writer, speaks of herself as "religious of heart, but profoundly sceptical in mind." A divorce between mind and heart is bound to be unhealthy.

For those who are wholly satisfied with the findings of science there is no theoretical predicament; and if they are practising scientists, their minds may be more than fully occupied at their own job. But is there perhaps a practical predicament? If we suppose that moral judgements, because they are not scientific, must be based on sheer emotion, it may be hard to keep our faith in goodness and in the duty of respecting other men even to our own loss. If, on the other hand, like the Marxists, we are confused enough to extract moral judgements from supposedly scientific ones, we may find a faith for which we are willing to live and die, but one which makes us indifferent to justice and mercy and even to truth—a process in which science suffers as well as religion. From this last desperate error the English are usually saved by their distrust of philosophy and their love of fair play—perhaps even by a sense of humour. But there are among intellectuals many who speak of our sick society, and who feel themselves lost as individuals because they are without faith in the value of human living.

The divorce between mind and heart is far more dangerous to religion than to science; for it is directly opposed to that very wholeness at which religion aims. The religious man cannot afford to sweep aside science as the scientist can sweep aside religion. Whether he likes it or not, scientific knowledge must now provide the bony structure of the world in which he has to live and act; and it is foolish of him to shudder as if science were the skeleton of the feast of life. At every feast we are all skeletons underneath; but without our bony structure we should be too flabby to be interesting. Although we may prefer to look at the human body as artists rather than as anatomists, we shall do this all the better if we are anatomists as well.

2. POINTS OF VIEW

The relation between art and anatomy already shows that it may be legitimate to look at the same thing from different points of view. Is it possible that this may afford a clue to the more complicated relations between science and religion? The question has forced itself upon us during the whole course of our enquiry, and perhaps we should try to bring together in short compass some of the answers that have suggested themselves. Readers who dislike jejune repetitions may go straight on to 6.

There are different points of view even within science itself. The physicist, the chemist, the biologist, and the psychologist—each has his own special point of view, his particular assumptions, his appropriate methods; and consequently he finds different things, or at least different laws, in the world he studies. But each, as a scientist, assumes that these different laws are compatible with one another and can be combined in one whole. This assumption is not itself a scientific discovery but a kind of faith; and if we ask how the combination can be effected, we are already asking a philosophical question. If we are empirical philosophers, we should not assume *a priori* that all scientific laws can be reduced to the laws of physics.

If there is uncertainty about the way in which the points of view appropriate to different sciences can be combined in one whole, there is greater uncertainty about the way in which the scientific point of view is to be combined with points of view appropriate to the artist, the good man, and the saint. The danger is that each type of man, when he tries to consider this problem philosophically, will assume that his own point of view is the only possible one. This is legitimate and necessary as long as he is conducting his own business. When carried into philosophy it substitutes inertia for insight.

Philosophy too, as it actually exists, has always its own point of view, and every philosopher suffers from a kind of narrowness more obvious to other people than to himself—perhaps even painfully obvious. Yet it is the aim of philosophy, or at least of one powerful tradition in philosophy, to enter into different points of view, to formulate their assumptions, to examine the world as seen from each of them, and to fit the different vistas as far as possible into one coherent whole. This is why the problems we have been considering are philosophical problems—not scientific ones. It is also why the task of philosophy is almost beyond human strength.

The prestige of science is now so great that some philosophers are tempted to concern themselves exclusively with the scientific point of view and even to adopt it as their own. In so doing they have contributed much to the study of scientific method and scientific language—including the method and language of mathematics and mathematical logic—and also to the theory of knowledge. But there has been a danger of neglecting other problems or treating them superficially or even distorting them by the application of inappropriate standards borrowed from elsewhere. A narrowness not unnatural in the excitement of new discoveries may also react unfavourably on theories about science itself. There are signs that this narrowness is gradually being overcome.

All this is a matter of controversy, but one thing is beyond dispute. A philosophy that restricts itself to a scientific point of view can have no use for religion.

3. THE SCIENTIFIC POINT OF VIEW

Within its own limits science is, and must be, supreme: it can be contradicted only by better science; and there is no observable part of reality or of human life that can claim immunity from its investigations. Nevertheless the scientific point of view is, like others, still partial and limited.

First of all, science is concerned only with certain aspects of reality, however hard they may be to describe. Fifty years ago we might have said that it was concerned only with quantity and measurement, but to-day we are sometimes told that it is turning instead to concepts of shape and structure and is becoming more geometrical, like the early science of the Greeks.

What remains clear is that it has, and can have, no concern with judgements of value or with judgements of what ought to be: it can treat these only as emotive utterances or psychological events.

In the second place, it is occupied only with the relation of part to part within the whole of reality: it does not pretend to make judgements about reality as a whole. Scientists may assume for their own purposes that reality as a whole consists only of more and more of the sort of thing that they investigate; but if they assert this explicitly, they are making, not a scientific, but a metaphysical statement, and one open to question, as all metaphysical statements are.

It is often held that the scientist makes assumptions only about his own methods and not about the reality he proposes to investigate. This is one reason why we have to say that explicit assumptions about reality are metaphysical, not scientific; and it is right to insist that if the scientist makes any such assumptions, they are only provisional. Nevertheless it seems clear that any suppositions about a method of investigation must take for granted certain characteristics in the objects to be investigated—for example, that they conform to law.

What is not so commonly recognized is that to adopt a method of investigation is also to make assumptions about the character of the investigator. These assumptions are so different from suppositions about the character of the objects investigated that they may never come officially within the purview of the investigator himself. Science seeks to be objective—to concern itself solely with objects and to eliminate all merely personal points of view. Yet to adopt such an aim is itself to take up a point of view—a point of view from which things can be seen objectively and impersonally. However much we may attribute this to the method rather than to the individual, it raises questions about how such an objective point of view is possible for imperfect human beings. This is a question for philosophy, not for science, but it is one we cannot afford to neglect.

Similarly, a scientist may take it for granted that his objects are in some sense determined, and of this assumption he may be fully aware. But he also takes it for granted that he himself is free—free to think in accordance with rational principles and so to distinguish between truth and error. Of this assumption he need hardly be aware at all—it is certainly no object of his science—but it should not be ignored by philosophers. Hence it is philosophically false—though it may be scientifically true—to say that there is no freedom in his world. And although truth is not one of the objects he investigates, it is always truth that he is seeking. Hence it is philosophically false—though it may be scientifically true—to say that there is no truth in his world. The contradiction arises only because the word "world" is being used in two senses; but the point is that the world of science is one from which something is being systematically left out.

4. A CRITICAL PHILOSOPHY

A critical philosophy cannot afford to leave out what is properly ignored by science: it must take into account, not only the world as known to the scientist, but also the scientist as claiming to know the world. Nor is there any reason why it should confine itself to scientists and neglect all other forms of human experience. It has to recognize that human activity is not confined to science and that all men in all their activities are subjects as well as objects.

Unless we screw ourselves religiously to the scientific point of view and regard all deviations as temptations of the devil, we may reasonably ask ourselves what kind of world we should know if our scientific investigations were as successful as possible. Although this is rank heresy to-day, I have maintained that even then our world of objects would be incomplete: it would leave out too much. If we take the relativity of science seriously, we have to say that we can have knowledge only of reality as it must appear to finite minds like our own, and not of reality as it is in itself. We should still be haunted with the thought of something beyond, possibly of something not contingent, but unconditioned and absolute—not intelligible merely in relation to something else, but intelligible in itself. Such a thought is admittedly obscure and may even contain contradictions. Whether rightly or wrongly, I have insisted that it can give us no knowledge of ultimate reality: it can certainly never be confirmed by any conceivable development of scientific observations. Nevertheless we are at least entitled to regard our between-world, as I have called it, as leaving a blank—perhaps even a God-shaped blank—beyond itself.

This view I take to be more than confirmed if we consider human knowledge, not as a series of subsistent propositions nor as a succession of events looked at from outside, but as it can be analysed from within. It is not enough to say, as some do, that the world we know must be relative to our sense-organs and to a brain which does not merely receive impressions but is always itself continually active. This is indeed a puzzle, but it appears to assume that the brain itself is a kind of absolute, whereas it can on this hypothesis only be part of the relative world we know. The real crux is that we seem to start from given impressions which, apart from our own activity, are indeterminate and constantly changing (so far as the indeterminate can change); and on this precarious basis we have to construct, in accordance with spontaneous principles of thought and imagination, an ordered world which is always a perspective viewed from a particular, and changing, point in time and space. To suppose that this world of ours is reality as it is in itself, or is all the world there is, may appear on reflexion to be useful and necessary for practical purposes and yet to be theoretically indefensible.

Farther than this it seems impossible to go in a philosophical theory based only on the character of our knowledge; but on such suppositions we can at least admit that points of view other than the scientific may be possible and legitimate. Of these the moral point of view is the most fundamental for our purposes so far as it recognizes the possibility of obeying an absolute moral law and fulfilling an unconditioned duty; for moral action so understood seems to give a concrete meaning to terms which might otherwise be supposed to be unintelligible. In spite of admitted difficulties I have maintained that the moral point of view is as rational and as legitimate as that of science itself. Its assumption of freedom and value is closely akin to a very similar assumption made by the scientific thinker (and perhaps also in some ways by the artist). In all such assumptions man is committed to the view that the world of objects known to science is not all the world there is.

We trespass upon more difficult ground if we seek to pass from this to theological beliefs. The passage is certainly a natural one, and it has been held to be logically necessary; but perhaps it requires what may be called a rational leap of faith more like our assurance that physical objects and other minds exist than like any scientific theory of logical proof, and yet different from all of these. I must here describe it without qualifications.

A good man—if this term may be applied to a man who is trying to do his duty—must assume that his duty can be done; and, at least if he has a religious bent, he will find himself acting as if the laws of duty were the commands of God—as if God existed and man were immortal. He will find himself thinking of God, not merely as unconditioned and self-sufficient, but as all-wise and all-holy. To think thus is to conceive God under the analogy of a perfect human being, and not merely as the supreme reality. By the aid of such concepts man is able, however confusedly, to think about God, and to act as if the God-shaped blank in reality as he knows it (and perhaps also in his own life) were filled by God himself. Such a practical belief can never become knowledge, and if he fails to recognize this, he will have to meet overwhelming theoretical difficulties; but considered as a living faith it will be confirmed, or perhaps we should rather say aroused and strengthened, by his experience of what he takes to be divine grace.

Such processes of thought, here summarily outlined, may reflect on an abstract level some deeper and more obscure religious experience. They will not prove either God's existence or His goodness; but they may provide some assurance that religious belief is not unreasonable and is not to be disproved by any extension of scientific knowledge.

To the saint and the sceptic alike this may seem a lame conclusion to draw from a halting argument; but both may be asked to remember that theology is not a substitute for religion. Religion is simple, while theology is complicated; religion is a rich experience, and theology—especially natural theology—only abstract thinking. It is not the business of a natural theologian to persuade the sceptic or to edify the saint. What should be clear to them both is that in the modern world religion is desperately in need of some philosophic defence if it is to survive without taking refuge in absurdity; and if the saints are dissatisfied with the line of defence suggested here, it is high time they should find a better.

As for those who hold that the world as revealed to science is all the world there is and that anything else is frills and furbelows, they are unanswerable—like Karl Barth—so long as they stick to their own point of view. But the question is whether we should stick to one point of view.

5. PSYCHOLOGY

There are many who suppose that we must look to psychology for the explanation of religious experience—and even of such philosophical considerations as I have put forward on its behalf. One word must be added about this if we are to avoid the charge of ignoring the obvious answer to all our questions.

It is certainly right and proper that psychology should concern itself with the whole of human experience, and it would be absurd to claim any exemption for religion. As a science psychology indeed is only in its infancy; it has as yet not attained to one consistent point of view; it suffers too often from a jargon which is lacking in precision; and it appears to hesitate between admitting and excluding judgements of value. Broadly speaking, it has had greater success in dealing with the more elementary mental activities than with the more developed, and with the abnormal rather than with the normal. A behaviouristic approach to religion must be superficial; and although some thinkers not unsympathetic to religion are inclined to look to psycho-analysis for help, this type of enquiry is more likely to illuminate religious aberrations than religious sanity, or even to treat all religion as an aberration. However it may explain, or explain away, his experience, the religious man will still insist that the same experience may be understood differently from different points of view, and even that psychology can touch only on its accidental concomitants and outer fringes—not on its inner core of rationality.

The plain fact is that an appeal to psychology is merely another example of the assumption that the scientific point of view is completely adequate by itself and that all other points of view can be ignored. This is the assumption that is being questioned.

On this topic it is desirable to avoid dogmatism, for as psychology develops, it may have to adopt a point of view and a method peculiar to itself— all I say must be taken as provisional. But—subject to this qualification—it would seem that so far as psychology is a science, it must take the view of a detached spectator; it must regard mental events as a causal succession; it must refrain from all judgements of value and ignore the function of rational principles; it must look on the individual as one object among others, and consider his experience, not as it appears to the individual himself, but as it appears to the psychologist, who sees it from outside and seeks to determine its place in nature.

The legitimacy and value of all this is not to be questioned; but it leaves too much out, and it can be no substitute for an attempt, however imperfect, to analyse experience from the subject's own point of view. Such an analysis is not an attempt to trace causal connexions between successive mental events or even to follow the growth of a mind from infancy to maturity. It is rather an endeavour to formulate the principles without which there could be no rational experience at all—no science, no psychology, and, if we suppose religion to be rational, no religion.

Analysis of this kind is not easy. It means that we have to abandon our ordinary habit of looking at objects without reflecting on their relation to subjects. If the effort is made, all our thinking will undergo a complete revolution, and we shall see everything (including religion) in a different light.

6. THE SCIENTIFIC ATTITUDE OF LIFE

Perhaps in conclusion we may be allowed to leave these dusty regions and survey again the human situation with its practical difficulties and varying responses. What is to be said about the scientific and religious attitudes to life?

The scientific attitude, while wholly beneficent in its own realm, must here be taken as one which looks to science for all practical guidance and refuses to have any truck with religion or metaphysics. This is perhaps the dominant mood of the present age.

If man were a purely intellectual being, there would be much to recommend this view. Those who adopt it have ample warrant for preferring the solid certainty of science to the misty speculation of theology, especially where these seem to conflict; and they may be well advised to devote themselves to urgent scientific work instead of wasting their time on insoluble problems. Even as regards the practical business of life, they are seeking to act in the world with the most accurate knowledge that is available to man. If the world as known to science is a less agreeable world than we might wish, this—they may hold—is no reason for indulging in vague yearnings and rosy dreams. If men want poetry, let them take it as poetry, and not as philosophy or science. It is more manly to face the world in all its harshness and not delude ourselves and others with false hopes. We must free ourselves from the foolish superstitions by which religion has been riddled and progress impeded. An honest man should live in the open-air world of science with all its chill, and not in the opium den of religious hallucinations. Even in the hour of danger or death he should fall back on natural human courage; for he certainly has nothing more.

This view—although, like any other, it may be held in a superficial way —is at least a manly and honest one: intellectual honesty, as well as moral toleration, has been greatly fostered by the development of scientific method. On the intellectual side the most it can be charged with is a lack of philosophical curiosity—an unwillingness to explore first principles and to look beyond the solution of particular problems; but, so far as theory is concerned, there may be more important things to do, and the unwillingness may rest on the considered conviction that there are no first principles to explore.

The fundamental difficulty here is that although we are provided with much, we do not seem to be offered any philosophy of life.

This contention should not be exaggerated. Every way of life has in it a kind of unreflective philosophy; and although, as I have insisted, we cannot extract principles of action (other than technical ones) from what scientists discover, perhaps we can from what they do.

The detachment and impersonality of science—the willingness to consider evidence from every source and to set aside all prejudice and self-interest—is closely akin to the detachment and impersonality necessary to moral judgment: this is one ground for the claim that it is legitimate to speak of practical, as well as of theoretical, reason. To see our situation and ourselves objectively is the first condition of spiritual health and good action: even without judgements of value it may offer a substitute for that self-examination which, although practised at times in an unbalanced way, is necessary to a religious life. And since scientists are also men, they do in fact make judgements of value about their own activity: they recognize their duty as scientists, and devotion to truth is sometimes taken as an absolute duty and even as a kind of religion.

Attitudes and judgements of this kind are not objects or discoveries of science, and they are as much in need of philosophical criticism as any other moral attitudes and moral judgements. Some scientists, for example, being rightly exercised at their part in the creation of the hydrogen bomb, insist that they have an absolute duty to publish the truth, since they alone know it. If they mean that they should make the public aware of its devastating effects, this can probably be better done by trained journalists. If they mean that the physical theory behind its construction should be made more widely known, this task, although laudable enough, can affect only the few who have the necessary training and intelligence to understand them. If they mean that they should impart technical secrets to an unscrupulous enemy of their country and of human freedom, they are merely showing that a scientific education does not always equip men for making political and moral judgements.

Whatever the scientific attitude may take for granted without reflexion, it can, by its very nature, give no account of any objective standards by which we may guide our lives. The artist need not be greatly perturbed if he is told in consequence that one man's taste is as good as another's: in practice he knows very well that this is nonsense, that aesthetic judgements are not dependent on scientific measurements, and that a good scientist may be an arrant philistine. In any case the artist can live happily with his dreams. The man of action is not in the same comfortable position: it is a serious matter, both for the individual and for society, if men are to be told that there can be no objective moral principles because these are not the same as scientific generalizations. Science provides man with a most potent instrument, but it can provide no directions for its use. This is like putting a hydrogen bomb in the hands of a child.

So far as this is true, the scientific attitude, in the sense here employed, leaves men in a practical predicament, if not in a theoretical one; for vast ranges of human life are abandoned to mere impulse or emotion, and we are left to struggle blindly for we know not what. It is not surprising if this should produce our modern discontent and even despair.

Within its own sphere science is the most astounding achievement of modern man. Any philosopher who seeks to condemn it, or even to correct it, merely makes himself a laughing-stock. Yet science by itself cannot satisfy the whole of man's needs: for purposes of action he requires at least a system of moral beliefs. In an age of criticism such a system is unable to stand unless it is supported by a rational ethics, which cannot conceivably be merely an inductive science. Whether wisely or unwisely, I have maintained that moral action and ethical beliefs bring men at least to the threshold of religion, and that rational ethics has to face the problems of theology. If we act consistently on the assumption that science is to be a substitute for all our other ways of thinking, there is a danger of falling, not merely into philosophical error, but into practical disaster. Such consistency is not likely to be found in human action; but if it were, man would tend to become an ill-balanced, divided, dissatisfied, and possibly heartless creature, incapable of spiritual wholeness and spiritual health. He might even end in self-destruction.

7. THE RELIGIOUS ATTITUDE TO LIFE

The religious attitude leads to a different predicament—to one which in its origin is mainly theoretical.

The climate of the modern world is unfavourable to religion, partly because the habits and attitudes of scientific investigation are different from the habits and attitudes of religious life, but mainly because so many of us assume, consciously or unconsciously, that science is the only source of knowledge and rational belief. This assumption, in spite of its psychological influence, is, I have maintained, a philosophical error and not a scientific truth. Nevertheless it has to be admitted that religious faith cannot pretend to be knowledge, and that theology does not provide us either with scientific knowledge or with a super-scientific knowledge such as has been ascribed in the past to metaphysics. The utmost we can claim is that our moral judgements may reasonably be regarded as providing knowledge and rational beliefs of a non-scientific kind; and that moral and speculative philosophy together may be able to supply a defence of religious faith and a protection against religious aberrations. Yet even if this be granted—and many philosophers would reject it—there remains a wide-spread impression that religion, as we know it, is opposed, not only to a scientific attitude which claims too much, but to science itself. If this belief is to be dispelled, it can only be by a supreme effort of religious thinking; for the belief has its roots in a theological obscurantism which has ignored or controverted or even persecuted scientific discovery. This may be the main source, although not the only one, of modern indifference.

Religious leaders are already conscious of living in what they call a pagan world: they regard themselves as missionaries to the heathen and are seeking to recover territory which they once held, even if with light forces, and have now lost. For this purpose they have their own well-tried methods of prayer and meditation and religious rites, as well as of preaching and teaching; and the best of them know that success will come, if it comes at all, only from a wholehearted devotion—from scrupulous toleration and kindness, from a continual battle for justice, from genuine love of others and complete forgetfulness of self. Some of them may believe that man cannot seek for God, or that seeking he will not find, but can only await the divine condescension. Yet even this waiting is a kind of seeking—a turning away from too much absorption in the goods of this world, a retiral into the self and a readiness to receive what may be given. In these matters it is to be presumed that religious men know their own business: they are in no need of advice or criticism, but only of God's grace.

When all this is said, it may still be true that in its present predicament religion is in dire need of an intellectual reformation. The great teachers of religion have always had to get rid of the useless lumber which accumulates in its progress—the rigid dogmatism, the narrow legalism, the mechanical rites, the silly superstitions which may become a substitute for religious life. But in our times there is a special need for intellectual honesty, or intellectual scrupulousness. These words have to be used in no crude sense: they must not be taken to suggest that religious men, or religious leaders, are guilty of rank dishonesty or wilful unscrupulousness—that in short they are conscious hypocrites. This would be far from the truth and would merely be insulting. Yet the fact remains that many men to-day are encouraged to regard religion as a cheat because they suspect their preceptors of failing to face the results of scientific discovery and Biblical criticism, of imposing moral rules based on chance texts accepted blindly without regard to their setting, and even of not telling the whole truth as they see it. Religious teachers must be humble enough to face intellectual difficulties and to admit how little they can know; and in their arguments they must not give the impression that they accept the conclusions first and select or twist the premises to fit them. The tasks that lie before theology are not for every one—there are many who, however transparently sincere, are lacking in the necessary intellectual equipment. These tasks are being tackled by the courageous few against inertia and opposition within the Church itself; but the world is not convinced of their success.

The work of intellectual reformation is bound to be a thankless one. It may have to lay its hands on the dearest idols of the past—to break with much that is embedded, not only in the language of theology, but in the traditional language of religion itself. Criticism is not a religious exercise, even though it may be carried on in a religious spirit; and it may seem to empty religion and so to weaken its appeal. Yet religion, which has always to struggle against spurious sentiment and twisted morality, must to-day free itself also from the primitive science and false history it has taken over from an earlier age. In the ancient and mediaeval worlds, where there was no vast gulf between the religious and the secular views, it was easier to adjust them to one another than it is under present conditions. Good men who reject theological dogmatism may still attach themselves to religious institutions in which they find the elements of grace; but until theology can be adapted to its modern scientific background and so can recover its ancient integrity, not only will the indifferent masses remain indifferent, but many men and women who either are, or long to be, religious in heart will continue to live their lives outside the Churches, especially if these treat honest attempts at criticism—not to mention one another—with hostility or intolerance. Simone Weil, for example, who combined a deeply religious spirit with a passion for intellectual integrity, found herself in many ways—in spite of her wider sympathies and her queer ideas of history—astonishingly close to the doctrines and rites of the Roman Catholic Church; and yet felt herself obliged to remain outside—perhaps most of all because of the two little words *"anathema sit."*

A revival of religion will never come by mere thinking, not even by religious thinking; but without a supreme effort of thought which will satisfy the mind as well as the heart, religion will not easily recover its former influence or restore to men the spiritual wholeness which many of them prize but seek in vain.

8. FAITH AND KNOWLEDGE

What I have said is unlikely to please either the sceptics or the orthodox, especially if they expect more from natural theology than it can give. Both may regard the whole discussion as an attempt to defend the pale relics of an earlier and more full-blooded doctrine, which to the first is sheer superstition and to the second is true religion. If a complaint about lack of intellectual honesty is to be bandied about, they may perhaps even unite to bring this charge against a plea for seeking to combine the religious and scientific points of view.

Such a plea, it may be said, is only an effort to revive a double standard of truth or—in the blunter language of today—to defend the dishonest practice of double-talk or double-thinking. I have suggested that a binocular rather than a monocular vision may give us the most satisfactory view of reality—perhaps a stereoscopic view. When one eye becomes much weaker than the other, there is a tendency for the weaker eye not to be used at all; and something like this seems to be happening to modern man. His scientific eye is, so to speak, ousting his religious eye, while in the old days it was the other way about. If it is retorted that such contentions can lead only to a spiritual intoxication in which men are reduced to seeing double, I must reply that they are seeing double now and are in need of an operation to adjust the focus of their eyes to one another.

These metaphors take us nowhere. Whatever my errors in detail, the theoretical question is this: If, as I think, it is the business of philosophy to look at the world from different points of view and try to see how far these views can be consistently combined, can this be done in the case of religion and science? An honest attempt at an answer, however imperfect, may at least help others to see what the problem is. But the question of religion, like that of morality, is not one of theory: it is a question of the life a man is going to lead. This is a matter for personal decision and personal commitment in a world of which we can know only the surface appearance, although there is no need to surround this with an atmosphere of portentousness and despair. For the religious man the decision may come only by the grace of God, but even so it should not be taken blindly in the dark. The leap of faith—or the leap of doubt—should be made in the light of all that each man can know, not merely of science, but of action and of art and of religion itself.

The predicament caused by the gulf between faith and knowledge is acute in the modern world, but it is also very old. Perhaps I cannot do better than conclude with some words which in the *Phaedo* Plato puts into the mouth of Simmias:

"I think, Socrates, as perhaps you do yourself, that about such matters it is either impossible or supremely difficult to acquire clear knowledge in our present life. Yet it is cowardly not to test in every way what we are told about them, or to give up before we are worn out without studying them from every point of view. For we ought to do one of the following things: either we should learn the truth about them from others; or we should find it out for ourselves; or, if this is impossible, we should take what is at least the best human account of them, the one hardest to disprove, and sailing on it, as on a raft, we should voyage through life in the face of risks—unless one might be able on some stouter vessel, some divine account, to make the journey with more assurance and with fewer perils."

73 The Meaning of Life*

KURT BAIER

Kurt Baier (1917–) is professor of philosophy at the University of Pittsburgh. He is the author of a number of important articles in ethics and of *The Moral Point of View* (1958).

Tolstoy, in his autobiographical work, "A Confession", reports how, when he was fifty and at the height of his literary success, he came to be obsessed by the fear that life was meaningless.

> At first I experienced moments of perplexity and arrest of life, as though I did not know what to do or how to live; and I felt lost and became dejected. But this passed, and I went on living as before. Then these moments of perplexity began to recur oftener and oftener, and always in the same form. They were always expressed by the questions: What is it for? What does it lead to? At first it seemed to me that these were aimless and irrelevant questions. I thought that it was all well known, and that if I should ever wish to deal with the solution it would not cost me much effort; just at present I had no time for it, but when I wanted to, I should be able to find the answer. The questions however began to repeat themselves frequently, and to demand replies more and more insistently; and like drops of ink always falling on one place they ran together into one black blot.[1]

A Christian living in the Middle Ages would not have felt any serious doubts about Tolstoy's questions. To him it would have seemed quite certain that life had a meaning and quite clear what it was. The medieval Christian world picture assigned to man a highly significant, indeed the central part in the grand scheme of things. The universe was made for the express purpose of providing a stage on which to enact a drama starring Man in the title role.

To be exact, the world was created by God in the year 4004 B.C. Man was the last and the crown of this creation, made in the likeness of God, placed in the Garden of Eden on earth, the fixed centre of the universe, round which revolved the nine heavens of the sun, the moon, the planets

* From Inaugural Lecture at Canberra University College, 1957, *The Meaning of Life*, pp. 3–4, 18–29. Reprinted by kind permission of the author and the Academic Registrar, The School of General Studies, The Australian National University.
[1] Count Leo Tolstoy, "A Confession," reprinted in *A Confession, The Gospel in Brief, and What I Believe*, No. 229, The World's Classics (London: Geoffrey Cumberlege, 1940).

and the fixed stars, producing as they revolved in their orbits the heavenly harmony of the spheres. And this gigantic universe was created for the enjoyment of man, who was originally put in control of it. Pain and death were unknown in paradise. But this state of bliss was not to last. Adam and Eve ate of the forbidden tree of knowledge, and life on this earth turned into a death-march through a vale of tears. Then, with the birth of Jesus, new hope came into the world. After He had died on the cross, it became at least possible to wash away with the purifying water of baptism some of the effects of Original Sin and to achieve salvation. That is to say, on condition of obedience to the law of God, man could now enter heaven and regain the state of everlasting, deathless bliss, from which he had been excluded because of the sin of Adam and Eve.

To the medieval Christian the meaning of human life was therefore perfectly clear. The stretch on earth is only a short interlude, a temporary incarceration of the soul in the prison of the body, a brief trial and test, fated to end in death, the release from pain and suffering. What really matters, is the life after the death of the body. One's existence acquires meaning not by gaining what this life can offer but by saving one's immortal soul from death and eternal torture, by gaining eternal life and everlasting bliss.

The scientific world picture which has found ever more general acceptance from the beginning of the modern era onwards is in profound conflict with all this. At first, the Christian conception of the world was discovered to be erroneous in various important details. The Copernican theory showed up the earth as merely one of several planets revolving round the sun, and the sun itself was later seen to be merely one of many fixed stars each of which is itself the nucleus of a solar system similar to our own. Man, instead of occupying the centre of creation, proved to be merely the inhabitant of a celestial body no different from millions of others. Furthermore, geological investigations revealed that the universe was not created a few thousand years ago, but was probably millions of years old.

Disagreements over details of the world picture, however, are only superficial aspects of a much deeper conflict. The appropriateness of the whole Christian outlook is at issue. For Christianity, the world must be regarded as the "creation" of a kind of Superman, a person possessing all the human excellences to an infinite degree and none of the human weaknesses, Who has made man in His image, a feeble, mortal, foolish copy of Himself. In creating the universe, God acts as a sort of playwright-cum-legislator-cum-judge-cum-executioner. In the capacity of playwright, He creates the historical world process, including man. He erects the stage and writes, in outline, the plot. He creates the *dramatis personae* and watches over them with the eye partly of a father, partly of the law. While on stage, the actors are free to extemporise, but if they infringe the divine commandments, they are later dealt with by their creator in His capacity of judge and executioner.

Within such a framework, the Christian attitudes towards the world are natural and sound: it is natural and sound to think that all is arranged for the best even if appearances belie it; to resign oneself cheerfully to one's lot; to be filled with awe and veneration in regard to anything and everything that happens; to want to fall on one's knees and worship and praise the Lord. These are wholly fitting attitudes within the framework of the world view just outlined. And this world view must have seemed wholly sound and acceptable because it offered the best explanation which was then available of all the observed phenomena of nature.

As the natural sciences developed, however, more and more things in the universe came to be explained without the assumption of a supernatural creator. Science, moreover, could explain them better, that is, more accurately and more reliably. The Christian hypothesis of a supernatural maker, whatever other needs it was capable of satisfying, was at any rate no longer indispensable for the purpose of explaining the existence or occurrence of anything. In fact, scientific explanations do not seem to leave any room for this hypothesis. The scientific approach demands that we look for a natural explanation of anything and everything. The scientific way of looking at and explaining things has yielded an immensely greater measure of understanding of, and control over, the universe than any other way. And when one looks at the world in this scientific way, there seems to be no room for a personal relationship between human beings and a supernatural perfect being ruling and guiding men. Hence many scientists and educated men have come to feel that the Christian attitudes towards the world and human existence are inappropriate. They have become convinced that the universe and human existence in it are without a purpose and therefore devoid of meaning.[2]

THE PURPOSE OF MAN'S EXISTENCE

Our conclusion in the previous section [omitted here, ed.] has been that science is in principle able to give complete and real explanations of every occurrence and thing in the universe. This has two important corollaries: (i) Acceptance of the scientific world picture cannot be *one's reason* for the belief that the universe is unintelligible and therefore meaningless, though coming to accept it, after having been taught the Christian world picture, may well have been, in the case of many individuals, *the only or the main cause* of their belief that the universe and human existence are meaningless. (ii) It is not in accordance with reason to reject this pessimistic belief on the grounds that scientific explanations are only provisional and incomplete and must be supplemented by religious ones.

---

[2] See e.g. Edwyn Bevan, *Christianity*, pp. 211–227. See also H. J. Paton, *The Modern Predicament* (London: George Allen and Unwin Ltd., 1955), pp. 103–116, 374.

In fact, it might be argued that the more clearly we understand the explanations given by science, the more we are driven to the conclusion that human life has no purpose and therefore no meaning. The science of astronomy teaches us that our earth was not specially created about 6,000 years ago, but evolved out of hot nebulae which previously had whirled aimlessly through space for countless ages. As they cooled, the sun and the planets formed. On one of these planets at a certain time the circumstances were propitious and life developed. But conditions will not remain favourable to life. When our solar system grows old, the sun will cool, our planet will be covered with ice, and all living creatures will eventually perish. Another theory has it that the sun will explode and that the heat generated will be so great that all organic life on earth will be destroyed. That is the comparatively short history and prospect of life on earth. Altogether it amounts to very little when compared with the endless history of the inanimate universe.

Biology teaches us that the species man was not specially created but is merely, in a long chain of evolutionary changes of forms of life, the last link, made in the likeness not of God but of nothing so much as an ape. The rest of the universe, whether animate or inanimate, instead of serving the ends of man, is at best indifferent, at worst savagely hostile. Evolution to whose operation the emergence of man is due is a ceaseless battle among members of different species, one species being gobbled up by another, only the fittest surviving. Far from being the gentlest and most highly moral, man is simply the creature best fitted to survive, the most efficient if not the most rapacious and insatiable killer. And in this unplanned, fortuitous, monstrous, savage world man is madly trying to snatch a few brief moments of joy, in the short intervals during which he is free from pain, sickness, persecution, war or famine until, finally, his life is snuffed out in death. Science has helped us to know and understand this world, but what purpose or meaning can it find in it?

Complaints such as these do not mean quite the same to everybody, but one thing, I think, they mean to most people: science shows life to be meaningless, because life is without purpose. The medieval world picture provided life with a purpose, hence medieval Christians could believe that life had a meaning. The scientific account of the world takes away life's purpose and with it its meaning.

There are, however, two quite different senses of "purpose". Which one is meant? Has science deprived human life of purpose in both senses? And if not, is it a harmless sense, in which human existence has been robbed of purpose? Could human existence still have meaning if it did not have a purpose in that sense?

What are the two senses? In the first and basic sense, purpose is normally attributed only to persons or their behaviour as in "Did you have a purpose in leaving the ignition on?" In the second sense, purpose is normally attributed only to things, as in "What is the purpose of that gadget you installed in the workshop?" The two uses are intimately connected. We cannot attribute a purpose to a thing without implying that someone did something, in the doing of which he had some purpose, namely, to bring about the thing with the purpose. Of course, *his* purpose is not identical with *its* purpose. In hiring labourers and engineers and buying materials and a site for a factory and the like, the entrepreneur's purpose, let us say, is to manufacture cars, but the purpose of cars is to serve as a means of transportation.

There are many things that a man may do, such as buying and selling, hiring, labourers, ploughing, felling trees, and the like, which it is foolish, pointless, silly, perhaps crazy, to do if one has no purpose in doing them. A man who does these things without a purpose is engaging in inane, futile pursuits. Lives crammed full with such activities devoid of purpose are pointless, futile, worthless. Such lives may indeed be dismissed as meaningless. But it should also be perfectly clear that acceptance of the scientific world picture does not force us to regard our lives as being without a purpose in this sense. Science has not only not robbed us of any purpose which we had before, but it has furnished us with enormously greater power to achieve these purposes. Instead of praying for rain or a good harvest or offspring, we now use ice pellets, artificial manure, or artificial insemination.

By contrast, having or not having a purpose, in the other sense, is value neutral. We do not think more or less highly of a thing for having or not having a purpose. "Having a purpose", in this sense, confers no kudos, "being purposeless" carries no stigma. A row of trees growing near a farm may or may not have a purpose: it may or may not be a windbreak, may or may not have been planted or deliberately left standing there in order to prevent the wind from sweeping across the fields. We do not in any way disparage the trees if we say they have no purpose, but have just grown that way. They are as beautiful, made of as good wood, as valuable, as if they had a purpose. And, of course, they break the wind just as well. The same is true of living creatures. We do not disparage a dog when we say that it has no purpose, is not a sheep dog or a watch dog or a rabbiting dog, but just a dog that hangs around the house and is fed by us.

Man is in a different category, however. To attribute to a human being a purpose in that sense is not neutral, let alone complimentary: it is offensive. It is degrading for a man to be regarded as merely serving a purpose. If, at a garden party, I ask a man in livery, "What is your purpose?" I am insulting him. I might as well have asked, "What are you *for*?" Such questions reduce him to the level of a gadget, a domestic animal, or perhaps a slave. I imply that *we* allot to *him* the tasks, the goals, the aims which he is to pursue; that *his* wishes and desires and aspirations and purposes are to count for little or nothing. We are treating him, in Kant's phrase, merely as a means to our ends, not as an end in himself.

The Christian and the scientific world pictures do indeed differ fundamentally on this point. The latter robs man of a purpose in this sense. It sees him as a being with no purpose allotted to him by anyone but himself. It robs him of any goal, purpose, or destiny appointed for him by any outside agency. The Christian world picture, on the other hand, sees man as a creature, a divine artefact, something halfway between a robot (manufactured) and an animal (alive), a homunculus, or perhaps Frankenstein, made in God's laboratory, with a purpose or task assigned him by his Maker.

However, lack of purpose in this sense does not in any way detract from the meaningfulness of life. I suspect that many who reject the scientific outlook because it involves the loss of purpose of life, and therefore meaning, are guilty of a confusion between the two senses of "purpose" just distinguished. They confusedly think that if the scientific world picture is true, then their lives must be futile because that picture implies that man has no purpose given him from without. But this is muddled thinking, for, as has already been shown, pointlessness is implied only by purposelessness in the other sense, which is not at all implied by the scientific picture of the world. These people mistakenly conclude that there can be no purpose *in* life because there is no purpose *of* life; that *men* cannot themselves adopt and achieve purposes because *man*, unlike a robot or a watchdog, is not a creature with a purpose.[3]

However, not all people taking this view are guilty of the above confusion. Some really hanker after a purpose of life in this sense. To some people the greatest attraction of the medieval world picture is the belief in an omnipotent, omniscient, and all-good Father, the view of themselves as His children who worship Him, of their proper attitude to what befalls them as submission, humility, resignation in His will, and what is often described as the "creaturely feeling".[4] All these are attitudes and feelings appropriate to a being that stands to another in the same sort of relation, though of course on a higher plane, in which a helpless child stands to his progenitor. Many regard the scientific picture of the world as cold, unsympathetic, unhomely, frightening, because it does not provide for any appropriate object of this creaturely attitude. There is nothing and no one in the world, as science depicts it, in which we can have faith or trust, on whose guidance we can rely, to whom we can turn for consolation, whom we can worship or submit to—except other human beings. This may be felt as a keen disappointment, because it shows that the meaning of life cannot lie in submission to His will, in acceptance of whatever may come, and in worship.

---

[3] See e.g. "Is Life Worth Living?" B.B.C. Talk by the Rev. John Sutherland Bonnell in *Asking Them Questions*, Third Series, ed. by R. S. Wright (London: Geoffrey Cumberlege, 1950).

[4] See e.g. Rudolf Otto, *The Idea of the Holy*, pp. 9–11. See also C. A. Campbell, *On Selfhood and Godhood* (London: George Allen & Unwin Ltd., 1957) p. 246, and H. J. Paton, *The Modern Predicament*, pp. 69–71.

But it does not imply that life can have *no* meaning. It merely implies that it must have a different meaning from that which it was thought to have. Just as it is a great shock for a child to find that he must stand on his own feet, that his father and mother no longer provide for him, so a person who has lost his faith in God must reconcile himself to the idea that he has to stand on his own feet, alone in the world except for whatever friends he may succeed in making.

But is not this to miss the point of the Christian teaching? Surely, Christianity can tell us the meaning of life because it tells us the grand and noble end for which God has created the universe and man. No human life, however pointless it may seem, is meaningless because in being part of God's plan, every life is assured of significance.

This point is well taken. It brings to light a distinction of some importance: we call a person's life meaningful not only if it is worthwhile, but also if he has helped in the realization of some plan or purpose transcending his own concerns. A person who knows he must soon die a painful death, can give significance to the remainder of his doomed life by, say, allowing certain experiments to be performed on him which will be useful in the fight against cancer. In a similar way, only on a much more elevated plane, every man, however humble or plagued by suffering, is guaranteed significance by the knowledge that he is participating in God's purpose.

What, then, on the Christian view, is the grand and noble end for which God has created the world and man in it? We can immediately dismiss that still popular opinion that the smallness of our intellect prevents us from stating meaningfully God's design in all its imposing grandeur.[5] This view cannot possibly be a satisfactory answer to our question about the purpose of life. It is, rather, a confession of the impossibility of giving one. If anyone thinks that this "answer" can remove the sting from the impression of meaninglessness and insignificance in our lives, he cannot have been stung very hard.

If, then, we turn to those who are willing to state God's purpose in so many words, we encounter two insuperable difficulties. The first is to find a

---

[5] For a discussion of this issue, see the eigtheenth century controversy between Deists and Theists, for instance, in Sir Leslie Stephen's *History of English Thought in the Eighteenth Century* (London: Smith, Elder & Co., 1902) pp. 112–119 and pp. 134–163. See also the attacks by Toland and Tindal on "the mysterious" in *Christianity not Mysterious* and *Christianity as Old as the Creation, or the Gospel a Republication of the Religion of Nature*, resp., parts of which are reprinted in Henry Bettenson's *Doctrines of the Christian Church*, pp. 426–431. For modern views maintaining that mysteriousness is an essential element in religion, see Rudolf Otto, *The Idea of the Holy*, esp. pp. 25–40, and most recently M. B. Foster, *Mystery and Philosophy* (London: S.C.M. Press, 1957) esp. Chs. IV. and VI. For the view that statements about God must be nonsensical or absurd, see e.g. H. J. Paton, op. cit. pp. 119–120, 367–369. See also "Theology and Falsification" in *New Essays in Philosophical Theology*, ed. by A. Flew and A. MacIntyre (London: S.C.M. Press, 1955) pp. 96–131; also N. Mc-Pherson, "Religion as the Inexpressible," ibid., esp. pp. 137–143.

purpose grand and noble enough to explain and justify the great amount of undeserved suffering in this world. We are inevitably filled by a sense of bathos when we read statements such as this: ". . . history is the scene of a divine purpose, in which the whole of history is included, and Jesus of Nazareth is the centre of that purpose, both as revelation and as achievement, as the fulfilment of all that was past, and the promise of all that was to come . . . If God is God, and if He made all these things, why did He do it? . . . God created a universe, bounded by the categories of time, space, matter, and causality, because He desired to enjoy for ever the society of a fellowship of finite and redeemed spirits which have made to His love the response of free and voluntary love and service."[6] Surely this cannot be right? Could a God be called omniscient, omnipotent, *and* all-good who, for the sake of satisfying his desire to be loved and served, imposes (or has to impose) on his creatures the amount of undeserved suffering we find in the world?

There is, however, a much more serious difficulty still: God's purpose in making the universe must be stated in terms of a dramatic story many of whose key incidents symbolize religious conceptions and practices which we no longer find morally acceptable: the imposition of a taboo on the fruits of a certain tree, the sin and guilt incurred by Adam and Eve by violating the taboo, the wrath of God,[7] the curse of Adam and Eve and all their progeny, the expulsion from Paradise, the Atonement by Christ's bloody sacrifice on the cross which makes available by way of the sacraments God's Grace by which alone men can be saved (thereby, incidentally, establishing the valuable power of priests to forgive sins and thus alone make possible a man's entry to heaven,[8]) Judgment Day on which the sheep are separated from the goats and the latter condemned to eternal torment in hellfire.

Obviously it is much more difficult to formulate a purpose for creating the universe and man that will justify the enormous amount of undeserved suffering which we find around us, if that story has to be fitted in as well. For now we have to explain not only why an omnipotent, omniscient, and all-good God should create such a universe and such a man, but also why, foreseeing every move of the feeble, weak-willed, ignorant, and covetous creature to be created, He should nevertheless have created him and, having done so, should be incensed and outraged by man's sin, and why He should deem it necessary to sacrifice His own son on the cross to atone for this sin

---

[6] Stephen Neill, *Christian Faith To-day* (London: Penguin Books, 1955) pp. 240–241.
[7] It is difficult to feel the magnitude of this first sin unless one takes seriously the words "Behold, the man has eaten of the fruit of the tree of knowledge of good and evil, and is become as one of us; and now, may he not put forth his hand, and take also of the tree of life, and eat, and live forever?" Genesis iii, 22.
[8] See in this connection the pastoral letter of 2nd February, 1905, by Johannes Katsch-taler, Prince Bishop of Salzburg on the honour due to priests, contained in *Quellen zur Geschichte des Papsttums*, by Mirbt, pp. 497–9, translated and reprinted in *The Protestant Tradition*, by J. S. Whale (Cambridge: University Press, 1955) pp. 259–262.

which was, after all, only a disobedience of one of his commands, and why this atonement and consequent redemption could not have been followed by man's return to Paradise—particularly of those innocent children who had not yet sinned—and why, on Judgment Day, this merciful God should condemn some to eternal torment.[9] It is not surprising that in the face of these and other difficulties, we find, again and again, a return to the first view: that God's purpose cannot meaningfully be stated.

It will perhaps be objected that no Christian to-day believes in the dramatic history of the world as I have presented it. But this is not so. It is the official doctrine of the Roman Catholic, the Greek Orthodox, and a large section of the Anglican Church.[10] Nor does Protestantism substantially alter this picture. In fact, by insisting on "Justification by Faith Alone" and by rejecting the ritualistic, magical character of the medieval Catholic interpretation of certain elements in the Christian religion, such as indulgences, the sacraments, and prayer, while at the same time insisting on the necessity of grace, Protestantism undermined the moral element in medieval Christianity expressed in the Catholics' emphasis on personal merit.[11] Protestantism, by harking back to St. Augustine, who clearly realized the incompatibility of grace and personal merit,[12] opened the way for Calvin's doctrine of Predestination (the intellectual parent of that form of rigid determinism which is usually blamed on science) and Salvation or Condemnation from all eternity.[13] Since Roman Catholics, Lutherans, Calvinists, Presbyterians and Baptists officially subscribe to the views just outlined, one can justifiably claim that the overwhelming majority of professing Christians hold or ought to hold them.

It might still be objected that the best and most modern views are wholly different. I have not the necessary knowledge to pronounce on the accuracy of this claim. It may well be true that the best and most modern views are such as Professor Braithwaite's who maintains that Christianity is, roughly speaking, "morality plus stories", where the stories are intended merely to make the strict moral teaching both more easily understandable and more palatable.[14] Or it may be that one or the other of the modern

---

[9] How impossible it is to make sense of this story has been demonstrated beyond any doubt by Tolstoy in his famous "Conclusion of A Criticism of Dogmatic Theology," reprinted in *A Confession, The Gospel in Brief, and What I Believe.*
[10] See "The Nicene Creed," "The Tridentine Profession of Faith," "The Syllabus of Errors," reprinted in *Documents of the Christian Church,* pp. 34, 373 and 380 resp.
[11] See e.g. J. S. Whale, *The Protestant Tradition,* Ch. IV., esp. pp. 48–56.
[12] See ibid., pp. 61 ff.
[13] See "The Confession of Augsburg" esp. Articles II., IV., XVIII., XIX., XX.; "Christianae Religionis Institutio," "The Westminster Confession of Faith," esp. Articles III., VI., IX., X., XI., XVI., XVII.; "The Baptist Confession of Faith," esp. Articles III., XXI., XXIII., reprinted in *Documents of the Christian Church,* pp. 294 ff., 298 ff., 344 ff., 349 ff.
[14] See e.g. his *An Empiricist's View of the Nature of Religious Belief* (Eddington Memorial Lecture).

views on the nature and importance of the dramatic story told in the sacred Scriptures is the best. My reply is that, even if it is true, it does not prove what I wish to disprove, that one can extract a sensible answer to our question, "What is the meaning of life?" from the kind of story subscribed to by the overwhelming majority of Christians, who would, moreover, reject any such modernist interpretation at least as indignantly as the scientific account. Moreover, though such views can perhaps avoid some of the worst absurdities of the traditional story, they are hardly in a much better position to state the purpose for which God has created the universe and man in it, because they cannot overcome the difficulty of finding a purpose grand and noble enough to justify the enormous amount of undeserved suffering in the world.

Let us, however, for argument's sake, waive all these objections. There remains one fundamental hurdle which no form of Christianity can overcome: the fact that it demands of man a morally repugnant attitude towards the universe. It is now very widely held[15] that the basic element of the Christian religion is an attitude of worship towards a being supremely worthy of being worshipped and that it is religious feelings and experiences which apprise their owner of such a being and which inspire in him the knowledge or the feeling of complete dependence, awe, worship, mystery, and self-abasement. There is, in other words, a bi-polarity (the famous "I-Thou relationship") in which the object, "the wholly-other", is exalted whereas the subject is abased to the limit. Rudolf Otto has called this the "creature-feeling"[16] and he quotes as an expression of it, Abraham's words when venturing to plead for the men of Sodom: "Behold now, I have taken upon me to speak unto the Lord, which am but dust and ashes". (Gen. XVIII.27). Christianity thus demands of men an attitude inconsistent with one of the presuppositions of morality: that man is not wholly dependent on something else, that man has free will, that man is in principle capable of responsibility. We have seen that the concept of grace is the Christian attempt to reconcile the claim of total dependence and the claim of individual responsibility (partial independence), and it is obvious that such attempts must fail. We may dismiss certain doctrines, such as the doctrine of original sin or the doctrine of eternal hellfire or the doctrine that there can be no salvation outside the Church as extravagant and peripheral, but we cannot reject the doctrine of total dependence without rejecting the characteristically Christian attitude as such.

---

[15] See e.g. the two series of Gifford Lectures most recently published: *The Modern Predicament* by H. J. Paton (London: George Allen & Unwin Ltd., 1955) pp. 69 ff., and *On Selfhool and Godhood* by C. A. Campbell (London: George Allen & Unwin Ltd., 1957) pp. 231–250.
[16] Rudolf Otto, *The Idea of the Holy*, p. 9.

THE MEANING OF LIFE

Perhaps some of you will have felt that I have been shirking the real problem. To many people the crux of the matter seems as follows. How can there be any meaning in our life if it ends in death? What meaning can there be in it that our inevitable death does not destroy? How can our existence be meaningful if there is no after-life in which perfect justice is meted out? How can life have any meaning if all it holds out to us are a few miserable earthly pleasures and even these to be enjoyed only rarely and for such a piteously short time?

I believe this is the point which exercises most people deeply. Kirilov, in Dostoevsky's novel, *The Possessed*, claims, just before committing suicide, that as soon as we realize that there is no God, we cannot live any longer, we must put an end to our lives. One of the reasons which he gives is that when we discover that there is no paradise, we have nothing to live for.

". . . there was a day on earth, and in the middle of the earth were three crosses. One on the cross had such faith that He said to another, 'To-day thou shalt be with me in paradise'. The day came to an end, both died, and they went, but they found neither paradise nor resurrection. The saying did not come true. Listen: that man was the highest of all on earth . . . There has never been any one like Him before or since, and never will be . . . And if that is so, if the laws of Nature did not spare even *Him*, and made even Him live in the midst of lies and die for a lie, then the whole planet is a lie and is based on a lie and a stupid mockery. So the very laws of the planet are a lie and a farce of the devil. What, then, is there to live for?"[17] And Tolstoy, too, was nearly driven to suicide when he came to doubt the existence of God and an after-life.[18] And this is true of many.

What, then, is it that inclines us to think that if life is to have a meaning, there would have to be an after-life? It is this. The Christian world view contains the following three propositions. The first is that since the Fall, God's curse of Adam and Eve, and the expulsion from Paradise, life on earth for mankind has not been worth while, but a vale of tears, one long chain of misery, suffering, unhappiness, and injustice. The second is that a perfect after-life is awaiting us after the death of the body. The third is that we can enter this perfect life only on certain conditions, among which is also the condition of enduring our earthly existence to its bitter end. In this way, our earthly existence which, in itself, would not (at least for many people if not all) be worth living, acquires meaning and significance: only if we endure it, can we gain admission to the realm of the blessed.

17 Fyodor Dostoyevsky, *The Devils* (London: The Penguin Classics, 1953) pp. 613–614.
18 Leo Tolstoy, *A Confession, The Gospel in Brief, and What I Believe*, The World's Classics, p. 24.

It might be doubted whether this view is still held to-day. However, there can be no doubt that even to-day we all imbibe a good deal of this view with our earliest education. In sermons, the contrast between the perfect life of the blessed and our life of sorrow and drudgery is frequently driven home and we hear it again and again that Christianity has a message of hope and consolation for all those "who are weary and heavy laden".[19]

It is not surprising, then, that when the implications of the scientific world picture begin to sink in, when we come to have doubts about the existence of God and another life, we are bitterly disappointed. For if there is no afterlife, then all we are left is our earthly life which we have come to regard as a necessary evil, the painful fee of admission to the land of eternal bliss. But if there is no eternal bliss to come and if this hell on earth is all, why hang on till the horrible end?

Our disappointment therefore arises out of these two propositions, that the earthy life is not worth living, and that there is another perfect life of eternal happiness and joy which we may enter upon if we satisfy certain conditions. We can regard our lives as meaningful, if we believe both. We cannot regard them as meaningful if we believe merely the first and not the second. It seems to me inevitable that people who are taught something of the history of science, will have serious doubts about the second. If they cannot overcome these, as many will be unable to do, then they must either accept the sad view that their life is meaningless or they must abandon the first proposition: that this earthly life is not worth living. They must find the meaning of their life in this earthly existence. But is this possible?

A moment's examination will show us that the Christian evaluation of our earthly life as worthless, which we accept in our moments of pessimism and dissatisfaction, is not one that we normally accept. Consider only the question of murder and suicide. On the Christian view, other things being equal, the most kindly thing to do would be for every one of us to kill as many of our friends and dear ones as still have the misfortune to be alive, and then to commit suicide without delay, for every moment spent in this life is wasted. On the Christian view, God has not made it that easy for us. He has forbidden us to hasten others or ourselves into the next life. Our bodies are his private property and must be allowed to wear themselves out in the way decided by Him, however painful and horrible that may be. We are, as it were, driving a burning car. There is only one way out, to jump clear and let it hurtle to destruction. But the owner of the car has forbidden it on pain of eternal tortures worse than burning. And so we do better to burn to death inside.

On this view, murder is a less serious wrong than suicide. For murder can always be confessed and repented and therefore forgiven, suicide cannot—unless we allow the ingenious way out chosen by the heroine of Graham

[19] See for instance J. S. Whale, *Christian Doctrine*, pp. 171, 176–178, &c. See also Stephen Neill, *Christian Faith To-day*, p. 241.

Greene's play, The Living Room, who swallows a slow but deadly poison and, while awaiting its taking effect, repents having taken it. Murder, on the other hand, is not so serious because, in the first place, it need not rob the victim of anything but the last lap of his march in the vale of tears, and, in the second place, it can always be forgiven. Hamlet, it will be remembered, refrains from killing his uncle during the latter's prayers because, as a true Christian, he believes that killing his uncle at that point, when the latter has purified his soul by repentance, would merely by doing him a good turn, for murder at such a time would simply despatch him to undeserved and everlasting happiness.

These views strike us as odd, to say the least. They are the logical consequence of the official medieval evaluation of this our earthly existence. If this life is not worth living, then taking it is not robbing the person concerned of much. The only thing wrong with it is the damage to God's property, which is the same both in the case of murder and suicide. We do not take this view at all. Our view, on the contrary, is that murder is the most serious wrong because it consists in taking away from some one else against his will his most precious possession, his life. For this reason, when a person suffering from an incurable disease asks to be killed, the mercy killing of such a person is regarded as a much less serious crime than murder because, in such a case, the killer is not robbing the other of a good against his will. Suicide is not regarded as a real crime at all, for we take the view that a person can do with his own possessions what he likes.

However, from the fact that these are our normal opinions, we can infer nothing about their truth. After all, we could easily be mistaken. Whether life is or is not worthwhile, is a value judgment. Perhaps all this is merely a matter of opinion or taste. Perhaps no objective answer can be given. Fortunately, we need not enter deeply into these difficult and controversial questions. It is quite easy to show that the medieval evaluation of earthly life is based on a misguided procedure.

Let us remind ourselves briefly of how we arrive at our value judgments. When we determine the merits of students, meals, tennis players, bulls, or bathing belles, we do so on the basis of some criteria and some standard or norm. Criteria and standards notoriously vary from field to field and even from case to case. But that does not mean that we have no idea about what are the appropriate criteria or standards to use. It would not be fitting to apply the criteria for judging bulls to the judgment of students or bathing belles. They score on quite different points. And even where the same criteria are appropriate as in the judgment of students enrolled in different schools and universities, the standards will vary from one institution to another. Pupils who would only just pass in one, would perhaps obtain honours in another. The higher the standard applied, the lower the marks, that is, the merit conceded to the candidate.

The same procedure is applicable also in the evaluation of a life. We examine it on the basis of certain criteria and standards. The medieval Christian view uses the criteria of the ordinary man: a life is judged by what the person concerned can get out of it: the balance of happiness over unhappiness, pleasure over pain, bliss over suffering. Our earthly life is judged not worthwhile because it contains much unhappiness, pain, and suffering, little happiness, pleasure, and bliss. The next life is judged worth while because it provides eternal bliss and no suffering.

Armed with these criteria, we can compare the life of this man and that, and judge which is more worth while, which has a greater balance of bliss over suffering. But criteria alone enable us merely to make comparative judgments of value, not absolute ones. We can say which is more and which is less worth while, but we cannot say which is worth while and which is not. In order to determine the latter, we must introduce a standard. But what standard ought we to choose?

Ordinarily, the standard we employ is the average of the kind. We call a man and a tree tall if they are well above the average of their kind. We do not say that Jones is a short man because he is shorter than a tree. We do not judge a boy a bad student because his answer to a question in the Leaving Examination is much worse than that given in reply to the same question by a young man sitting for his finals for the Bachelor's degree.

The same principles must apply to judging lives. When we ask whether a given life was or was not worth while, then we must take into consideration the range of worthwhileness which ordinary lives normally cover. Our end poles of the scale must be the best possible and the worst possible life that one finds. A good and worthwhile life is one that is well above average. A bad one is one well below.

The Christian evaluation of earthly lives is misguided because it adopts a quite unjustifiably high standard. Christianity singles out the major shortcomings of our earthly existence: there is not enough happiness; there is too much suffering; the good and bad points are quite unequally and unfairly distributed; the underprivileged and underendowed do not get adequate compensation; it lasts only a short time. It then quite accurately depicts the perfect or ideal life as that which does not have any of these shortcomings. Its next step is to promise the believer that he will be able to enjoy this perfect life later on. And then it adopts as its standard of judgment the perfect life, dismissing as inadequate anything that falls short of it. Having dismissed earthly life as miserable, it further damns it by characterizing most of the pleasures of which earthly existence allows as bestial, gross, vile, and sinful, or alternatively as not really pleasurable.

This procedure is as illegitimate as if I were to refuse to call anything tall unless it is infinitely tall, or anything beautiful unless it is perfectly flawless, or any one strong unless he is omnipotent. Even if it were true that there is available to us an after-life which is flawless and perfect, it would still not be legitimate to judge earthly lives by this standard. We do not fail every candidate who is not an Einstein. And if we do not believe in an after-life, we must of course use ordinary earthly standards.

I have so far only spoken of the worthwhileness, only of what a person can get out of a life. There are other kinds of appraisal. Clearly, we evaluate people's lives not merely from the point of view of what they yield to the persons that lead them, but also from that of other men on whom these lives have impinged. We judge a life more significant if the person has contributed to the happiness of others, whether directly by what he did for others, or by the plans, discoveries, inventions, and work he performed. Many lives that hold little in the way of pleasure or happiness for its owner are highly significant and valuable, deserve admiration and respect on account of the contributions made.

It is now quite clear that death is simply irrelevant. If life can be worthwhile at all, then it can be so even though it be short. And if it is not worthwhile at all, then an eternity of it is simply a nightmare. It may be sad that we have to leave this beautiful world, but it is so only if and because it is beautiful. And it is no less beautiful for coming to an end. I rather suspect that an eternity of it might make us less appreciative, and in the end it would be tedious.

It will perhaps be objected now that I have not really demonstrated that life has a meaning, but merely that it can be worthwhile or have value. It must be admitted that there is a perfectly natural interpretation of the question, "What is the meaning of life?" on which my view actually proves that life has no meaning. I mean the interpretation discussed in section 2 of this lecture [omitted here, ed.], where I attempted to show that, if we accept the explanations of natural science, we cannot believe that living organisms have appeared on earth in accordance with the deliberate plan of some intelligent being. Hence, on this view, life cannot be said to have a purpose, in the sense in which man-made things have a purpose. Hence it cannot be said to have a meaning or significance in that sense.

However, this conclusion is innocuous. People are disconcerted by the thought that *life as such* has no meaning in that sense only because they very naturally think it entails that no individual life can have meaning either. They naturally assume that *this* life or *that* can have meaning only if *life as such* has meaning. But it should by now be clear that your life and mine may or may not have meaning (in one sense) even if life as such has none (in the other). Of course, it follows from this that your life may have meaning while mine has not. The Christian view guarantees a meaning (in one sense) to every life, the scientific view does not (in any sense). By relating the question of the meaningfulness of life to the particular circumstances of an individual's existence, the scientific view leaves it an open question whether an individual's life has meaning or not. It is, however, clear that the latter is the important sense of "having a meaning". Christians, too, must feel that their life is wasted and meaningless if they have not achieved salvation. To know that even such lost lives have a meaning in another sense is no consolation to them. What matters is not that life should have a guaranteed meaning, whatever happens here or here-after, but that, by luck (Grace) or the right temperament and attitude (Faith) or a judicious life (Works) a person should make the most of his life.

"But here lies the rub," it will be said. "Surely, it makes all the difference whether there is an after-life. This is where morality comes in." It would be a mistake to believe that. Morality is not the meting out of punishment and reward. To be moral is to refrain from doing to others what, if they followed reason, they would not do to themselves, and to do for others what, if they followed reason, they would want to have done. It is, roughly speaking, to recognize that others, too, have a right to a worthwhile life. Being moral does not make one's own life worthwhile, it helps others to make theirs so.

CONCLUSION

I have tried to establish three points: (i) that scientific explanations render their explicanda as intelligible as pre-scientific explanations; they differ from the latter only in that, having testable implications and being more precisely formulated, their truth or falsity can be determined with a high degree of probability; (ii) that science does not rob human life of purpose, in the only sense that matters, but, on the contrary, renders many more of our purposes capable of realization; (iii) that common sense, the Christian world view, and the scientific approach agree on the criteria but differ on the standard to be employed in the evaluation of human lives; judging human lives by the standards of perfection, as Christians do, is unjustified; if we abandon this excessively high standard and replace it by an everyday one, we have no longer any reason for dismissing earthly existence as not worthwhile.

On the basis of these three points I have attempted to explain why so many people come to the conclusion that human existence is meaningless and to show that this conclusion is false. In my opinion, this pessimism rests on a combination of two beliefs, both partly true and partly false: the belief that the meaningfulness of life depends on the satisfaction of at least three conditions, and the belief that this universe satisfies none of them. The conditions are, first, that the universe is intelligible, second, that life has a purpose, and third, that all men's hopes and desires can ultimately be satisfied. It seemed to medieval Christians and it seems to many Christians to-day that Christianity offers a picture of the world which can meet these conditions. To many Christians and non-Christians alike it seems that the scientific world picture is incompatible with that of Christianity, therefore with the view that these three conditions are met, therefore with the view that life has a meaning. Hence they feel that they are confronted by the dilemma of accepting either a world picture incompatible with the discoveries of science or the view that life is meaningless.

I have attempted to show that the dilemma is unreal because life can be meaningful even if not all of these conditions are met. My main conclusion, therefore, is that acceptance of the scientific world picture provides no reason for saying that life is meaningless, but on the contrary every reason for saying that there are many lives which are meaningful and significant. My subsidiary conclusion is that one of the reasons frequently offered for retaining the Christian world picture, namely, that its acceptance gives us a guarantee of a meaning for human existence, is unsound. We can see that our lives can have a meaning even if we abandon it and adopt the scientific world picture instead. I have, moreover, mentioned several reasons for rejecting the Christian world picture: (i) the biblical explanations of the details of our universe are often simply false; (ii) the so-called explanations of the whole universe are incomprehensible or absurd; (iii) Christianity's low evaluation of earthly existence (which is the main cause of the belief in the meaninglessness of life) rests on the use of an unjustifiably high standard of judgment.

Index